Voter Registration Application

Before completing this form, review the General, Application, and Sta[te specific instructions.]

Are you a citizen of the United States of America?	☐ Yes	☐ No	This space for o[ffice use only] D1033724
Will you be 18 years old on or before election day?	☐ Yes	☐ No	

If you checked "No" in response to either of these questions, do not complete form.
(Please see state-specific instructions for rules regarding eligibility to register prior to age 18.)

1	(Circle one) Mr. Mrs. Miss Ms.	Last Name	First Name	Middle Name(s)	(Circle one) Jr Sr II III IV

2	Home Address	Apt. or Lot #	City/Town	State	Zip Code
3	Address Where You Get Your Mail If Different From Above		City/Town	State	Zip Code

4	Date of Birth / / Month Day Year	5	Telephone Number (optional)	6	ID Number - (See Item 6 in the instructions for your state)
7	Choice of Party (see item 7 in the instructions for your State)	8	Race or Ethnic Group (see item 8 in the instructions for your State)		

9

I have reviewed my state's instructions and I swear/affirm that:

- I am a United States citizen
- I meet the eligibility requirements of my state and subscribe to any oath required.
- The information I have provided is true to the best of my knowledge under penalty of perjury. If I have provided false information, I may be fined, imprisoned, or (if not a U.S. citizen) deported from or refused entry to the United States.

Please sign full name (or put mark) ▲

Date: / / Month Day Year

If you are registering to vote for the first time: please refer to the application instructions for information on submitting copies of valid identification documents with this form.

Please fill out the sections below if they apply to you.

If this application is for a **change of name,** what was your name before you changed it?

A	Mr. Mrs. Miss Ms.	Last Name	First Name	Middle Name(s)	(Circle one) Jr Sr II III IV

If you were **registered before but this is the first time you are registering from the address in Box 2**, what was your address where you were registered before?

B	Street (or route and box number)	Apt. or Lot #	City/Town/County	State	Zip Code

If you live in a rural area but do not have a street number, or if you have no address, please show on the map where you live.

C

- Write in the names of the crossroads (or streets) nearest to where you live.
- Draw an **X** to show where you live.
- Use a dot to show any schools, churches, stores, or other landmarks near where you live, and write the name of the landmark.

Example

Route #2

● Grocery Store

Woodchuck Road

Public School ●

X

NORTH ↑

If the applicant is unable to sign, who helped the applicant fill out this application? Give name, address and phone number (phone number optional).

D

Mail this application to the address provided for your State.

Revised 10/29/2003

UNDERSTANDING AMERICAN POLITICS AND GOVERNMENT

MyPoliSciLab®

2012 ELECTION EDITION

John J.
COLEMAN
University of Wisconsin—Madison

Kenneth M.
GOLDSTEIN
University of Wisconsin—Madison

William G.
HOWELL
University of Chicago

PEARSON

Boston Columbus Indianapolis New York San Francisco
Upper Saddle River Amsterdam Cape Town Dubai London Madrid Milan
Munich Paris Montréal Toronto Delhi Mexico City São Paulo Sydney
Hong Kong Seoul Singapore Taipei Tokyo

Editorial Director: Craig Campanella
Editor-in-Chief: Dickson Musslewhite
Senior Acquisitions Editor: Vikram Mukhija
Assistant Editor: Beverly Fong
Editorial Assistant: Emily Sauerhoff
Editorial Assistant: Isabel Schwab
Director of Development: Sharon Geary
Associate Development Editor: Corey Kahn
Director of Marketing: Brandy Dawson
Executive Manrketing Manager: Wendy Gordon
Marketing Coordinator: Theresa Graziano
Marketing Assistant: Zakiyyah Wiley
Senior Managing Editor: Ann Marie McCarthy
Procurement Specialist: Mary Ann Gloriande
Project Manager: Carol O'Rourke
Creative Director: Blair Brown
Art Director: John Christiana, Kathryn Foot
Director of Digital Media: Brian Hyland
Senior Digital Media Editor: Paul DeLuca
Digital Media Editor: Alison Lorber
Multimedia Production Manager: Michael Granger
Media Project Manager: Joseph Selby
Full Service Project Management and Composition: PreMediaGlobal
Full Service Project Manager: Joyce Franzen/Katy Gabel
Printer and Binder: Courier, Kendalville
Cover Printer: Lehigh-Phoenix Color/Hagerstown

Credits and acknowledgments borrowed from other sources and reproduced, with permission, in this textbook appear on pages 679–682.

Library of Congress Cataloging-in-Publication Data on file.

10 9 8 7 6 5 4 3 2 1

Student Edition:
ISBN-13: 978-0-205-87520-7
ISBN-10: 0-205-87520-3
A la Carte Edition:
ISBN-13: 978-0-205-86286-3
ISBN-10: 0-205-86286-1

BRIEF CONTENTS

On MyPoliSciLab

- The Declaration of Independence
- The Constitution of the United States
- Federalist No. 10
- Federalist No. 15
- Federalist No. 51
- Federalist No. 78
- Anti-Federalist No. 17
- *Marbury* v. *Madison*
- *McCulloch* v. *Maryland*
- *Brown* v. *Board of Education*
- The Gettysburg Address
- Washington's Farewell Address

***The icons listed here and throughout this book lead to learning resources on MyPoliSciLab.**

CONTENTS

***The icons listed here and throughout this book lead to learning resources on MyPoliSciLab.**

On MyPoliSciLab

- The Declaration of Independence
- The Constitution of the United States
- Federalist No. 10
- Federalist No. 15
- Federalist No. 51
- Federalist No. 78
- Anti-Federalist No. 17
- *Marbury* v. *Madison*
- *McCulloch* v. *Maryland*
- *Brown* v. *Board of Education*
- The Gettysburg Address
- Washington's Farewell Address

TO THE STUDENT

- Does it matter who wins the next election for president?
- Can I expect our elected officials to address the challenges on which my future depends?
- Does my vote even count?

To answer these questions, you need two things: substantive knowledge about politics and tools for how to think about politics. This book helps you understand the government as it actually operates and assess the many claims and counter-claims that are made about it. The political air is thick with facts and fictions, with cable television, talk news, and the blogosphere dishing up a nearly constant deluge of partisan posturing and half-baked arguments. You can cut through the noise and elucidate the extraordinary ways in which politics actually does shape our lives.

To do this, we do not want you to think like a liberal or conservative; we want you to think like a political scientist—a student of politics. Politics and government need not be distant and mysterious quantities, as so many Americans view them. Indeed, opportunities abound for you to participate in and shape our politics. For some, it may involve the simple act of voting. Others of you may decide to work for a candidate or political party in a campaign, join an advocacy group of some kind, engage in traditional or social media, and follow the news closely. And all of us, whether over the dinner table or among friends, at one time or another join in deliberations about our government and policy.

And just as you engage politics, so does politics engage you. In material ways, it intrudes upon your daily lives, influencing what career or job path you take, what club or social circle you join, what news source you select. It shapes the conversations you have, the industries you work in, the opportunities you face, the values you will hold dear. Understanding politics is not an idle past time. It is absolutely central to navigating contemporary life in America.

By giving you the substantive knowledge about how our politics and government are organized and the tools needed to critically evaluate political arguments, we hope to help you become a more informed individual, a more effective agent of social change, and a more empowered citizen.

Meet Your Authors

 **Watch** on **MyPoliSciLab**

JOHN J. COLEMAN is Professor and Chair of the Political Science Department at the University of Wisconsin, Madison; he is the Lyons Family Faculty Fellow and has received a Chancellor's Distinguished Teaching Award. John's current research examines the effect of various campaign finance rules and regulations on electoral and policy outcomes in the states.

KENNETH M. GOLDSTEIN is Professor of Political Science at the University of Wisconsin, Madison where he won the Kellet Award for his career research accomplishments and the Chancellor's Distinguished Teaching Award. He is also president of Kantar Media's Campaign Media Analysis Group as well as a consultant for the ABC News elections unit and a member of their election night decision team.

WILLIAM G. HOWELL is the Sydney Stein Professor in American Politics at the University of Chicago. He has written widely on separation of powers issues and American political institutions, especially the presidency. Will's recent research examines the relationships between war and presidential power.

TO THE INSTRUCTOR

- How did Mitt Romney's experience as governor of Massachusetts affect his chances of winning the Republican nomination for president? To what degree did economic conditions affect Barack Obama's reelection chances?
- Have the federal government's economic policies helped, hindered, or had no effect on the country's economic situation?
- Did the House Republicans or the Senate Democrats and a Democratic president throw Washington, D.C. into gridlock?
- Have the mobilization efforts of outside groups—so-called "Super PACs"—helped or hurt our democracy?

These political puzzles are among the dozens asked during the 2012 election and since the publication of the prior edition of this book. Despite the certainty of the answers offered by journalists, pundits, and other talking heads, we have seen that the answers and predictions about U.S. politics often were very, very wrong.

Why? Because many of us—not just talking heads—often attempt to explain events in our political world by oversimplifying and making causal connections where none are warranted. Our explanations flow from our own political viewpoints or the need to explain something quickly. Although such answers make for good television debates and effective headlines, they fail to give us the understanding of the political world that we need to make informed decisions and demand real accountability from our political leaders.

As political scientists, we see the world differently. We believe that simple answers often belie complex realities, and that sorting out fact from fiction can be a challenge. We gather and analyze evidence. We evaluate research and interpret arguments. We use the tools of our discipline to go beyond knee-jerk or partisan answers in a quest to explain and provide real understanding of politics and government.

The tools of political science are not just for political scientists, however. Our goal in writing *Understanding American Politics and Government*, as in our own teaching, is to give students these same critical thinking tools so they are empowered to make sense of the political world themselves; and, moreover, to identify and sort through the copious causal arguments that pervade not just the news, but also students' everyday lives. Although we expose students to cutting edge research in political science, our intention is not to transform them into members of our own professional tribe. Rather, it is to simultaneously deepen students' substantive knowledge of American politics while instilling in them the skills and interest needed to spot, dissect, and gauge causal arguments in domains of public life. At a time when the political parties are more polarized than ever, when the media is partitioned into narrow bands of like-minded citizens, and when political campaigns are chocker block full of accusations and negativity, *Understanding American Politics and Government* cuts through the noise and offers students the tools and knowledge they need to solve enduring political puzzles.

New to This Edition

Unresolved Debate

In Times of War or Emergency, Does the Constitution Limit the President's Commander in Chief Authority?

In 2011, President Barack Obama involved the United States in military hostilities in Libya, and in 2012 he authorized drone strikes to target and kill terrorists overseas. Critics of the program argued it violated constitutional checks and balances and civil liberties, charging that the program proceeded with little congressional oversight of the deployment of the drones or of the specific individuals targeted for death, including some Americans living overseas. Supporters responded that the president's constitutional war powers give presidents wide latitude to use the available technology at hand to conduct war and that the drones had a number of tactical advantages and produced less incidental loss of life. MQ-1 Predators, such as the one pictured here, were used heavily in Afghanistan, Pakistan, Yemen, Somalia, and northern Iraq.

YES

Louis Fisher, a political scientist who served at the Library of Congress, argues that the Framers were determined that the president would be the Commander in Chief of the armed forces, but Congress would have the power to declare war and to make laws regulating, arming, and funding the military. The Framers viewed a president with complete discretion over the military to be inconsistent with the idea of a republic. To make his case, Fisher argues the following:

- The original understanding of the Constitution was that the president's powers in times of emergency are subject to limitations;
- Historically, presidents accepted these limitations and the nation successfully survived many security challenges. Only in recent administrations have presidents argued for their ability to act without congressional authorization;
- The claim that there are no limits on presidential power in times of war or emergency renders the Constitution meaningless precisely at the times its constraints are most needed. The Constitution is not an invitation to dictatorship.

NO

John Yoo, a legal scholar at the University of California, Berkeley, who was also a lawyer in the administration of President George W. Bush, argues that there can be no limits on the "inherent executive power" of the president in matters involving national security. When the country's security is threatened, a president is authorized to do what he thinks necessary to defend it, and these may involve new techniques over time unforeseen by the Framers. To make his case, Yoo argues that:

- When the Constitution was being written, it was a common perspective, that the sovereign had unlimited power to defend the state, so the president's authority in this area is independent of the Constitution;
- Provisions of the Constitution giving power over war and related matters to Congress should be interpreted flexibly so that the president can respond effectively to new challenges unforeseen by the Framers;
- Ultimately, accepting any constitutional limitation on the powers of the president in this crucial area could leave the nation defenseless against its enemies. The Constitution is not a "suicide pact."

CONTRIBUTING TO THE DEBATE

The basic disagreements expressed by Fisher and Yoo over the proper way to interpret the Constitution are unlikely to be resolved definitively. Nonetheless, the debate can be advanced through careful analysis that recognizes and specifies the advantages and risks that come with either of these competing perspectives.

WHAT DO YOU THINK?

1. Should we think about presidential war powers differently from way we think about other constitutional questions concerning government power? Why or why not?
2. Should we rely on the Framers' original understanding to answer some questions, but the conditions of modern life to answer others? Why or why not?

80

Politics in America never stands still, but the last two years have been particularly eventful. Since the publication of the prior edition of this book and after a long campaign, voters returned Barack Obama to the White House in the 2012 presidential election while returning a Democratic majority to the U.S. Senate and a Republican majority to the U.S. House of Representatives. Before that, the Supreme Court acted on major cases in health care reform and immigration, among others; there were two years of divided government in which the President and Congress struggled to avoid careening off a fiscal cliff; anti-terror strategies took a new turn as **Osama Bin Laden was killed by Navy SEALS** and the United States significantly stepped up its use of unmanned drones to attack terrorist targets; and governments across the Middle East fell during the Arab Spring with unexpected and unpredictable consequences for the United States and its allies. Economic troubles in Europe deepened and the American economy failed to pick up steam. **Same sex marriage** made major legal advances in some states and in some federal court decisions, while remaining deeply controversial among many Americans.

Our experience as teachers has shown us that the best way to explain theory and fundamentals is to illustrate them with relevant and recent examples for students. Accordingly, we discuss all these events and controversies—and more—in this new edition, using them as examples for many of the lessons and analytical tools in the book. Many chapters have new opening stories and new "How Do We Know?" features that examine ongoing subjects of political science research on topics that range from the effectiveness of international sanctions to the qualities that make a successful leader.

The updates in this volume go further still. Throughout this book, chapters have been revised with new political puzzles and the latest political science research on topics that range from campaigns and elections to interest group mobilization to the design and operations of the various branches of government.

The fundamental and most up-to-date lessons that political scientists have discovered about how American politics works can shed light upon and solve some of the puzzles that the events of the last four years have presented. And, where political science cannot provide the answers or where there is debate in the field, we point that out as well. Specifically, we have added a completely new feature in each chapter—**Unresolved Debates**. Each of these looks at a major question in American politics and outlines, in easily understood terms, the divergent views of different sets of scholars. Each of these debates is structured as a Yes/No question with the positions of scholars positioned on each side.

Over 30% of the photos in this edition are new. They capture major events from the last few years, of course, but to illustrate politics' relevancy, they show political actors and processes as well as people affected by politics, creating a visual narrative that enhances rather than repeats the text. Also, all of the figures and tables reflect the latest available data.

Finally, to create a tighter pedagogical connection between this book and MyPoliSciLab, we integrated several new features that move students from the book to online active learning opportunities. (NB: The icons listed throughout the book lead to learning resources on MyPoliSciLab.)

- A new design simplifies the presentation of content to facilitate print *and* digital reading experiences. It also focuses reading by turning our book's **learning objectives** into a clear learning path backed by personalized study plans on MyPoliSciLab.

- **Videos** now support the narrative in each chapter. We—the authors—frame each chapter topic, and interviews with political scientists and everyday citizens look at interesting aspects of each topic. The videos are listed at each chapter's start and can be watched on MyPoliSciLab.
- **Infographics** demonstrate how political scientists use data to answer questions like "How Long Did it Take to Ratify the Constitution?" or "What Influences a President's Public Approval?" On MyPoliSciLab, students can use interactive data to further investigate the same question.
- In every chapter, **On MyPoliSciLab** helps students review what they just read. In addition to a chapter summary, key term list, short quiz, and further reading list, there are reminders to use the chapter audio, practice tests, and flashcards on MyPoliSciLab.

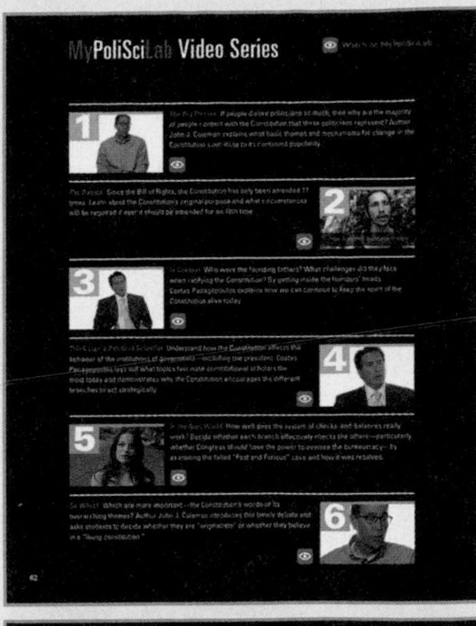

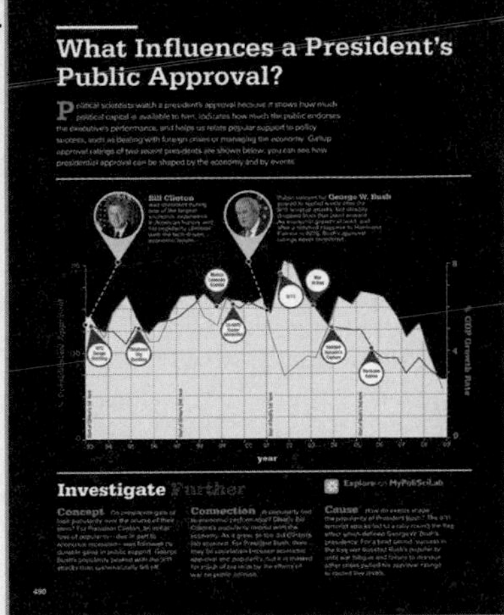

Features

From the very first chapter, the book trains students to distinguish between the concepts of *correlation* and *causation* as they examine political phenomena, helping them become better critical thinkers and more thoughtful citizens as they are confronted with political puzzles.

This book begins by introducing students to the broad cultural, constitutional, and historical origins of U.S. politics. It then exposes students to the ways in which changing conceptions of civil liberties and civil rights animate our politics. After surveying the ways in which average citizens, interest groups, political parties, and the media behave in American politics, the textbook then walks through the major institutions—Congress, the presidency, the judiciary, and bureaucracy—that constitute our system of separated and federated powers. It concludes with coverage of economic, social, and foreign policy.

Each chapter opens with a vignette designed to grab students' attention and draw them into the chapter's subject matter. Students are further assisted through learning objectives that are tied to each major section of a chapter. In addition, the book features headline style headings that provide students with a key point to be taken from the following section of the chapter.

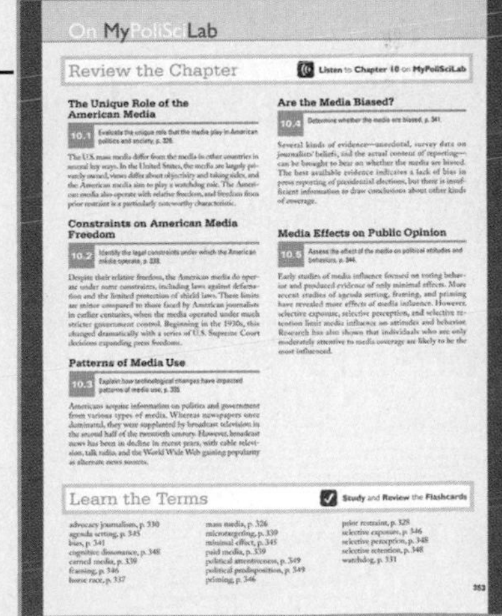

Throughout each chapter, the text raises and discusses various causal questions concerning how government and politics work. These discussions are woven directly into the text to emphasize that these questions are not distinct from learning the substance of American politics but *are* the substance. In addition, the **How Do We Know?** (and the new Unresolved Debates) features in every chapter pose provocative political questions and then demonstrate the techniques political scientists use to answer them. Complete with data related to the puzzle, this feature goes beyond the in-text discussions of causal questions and political puzzles by providing more detail and background on the question and by getting students involved in its investigation.

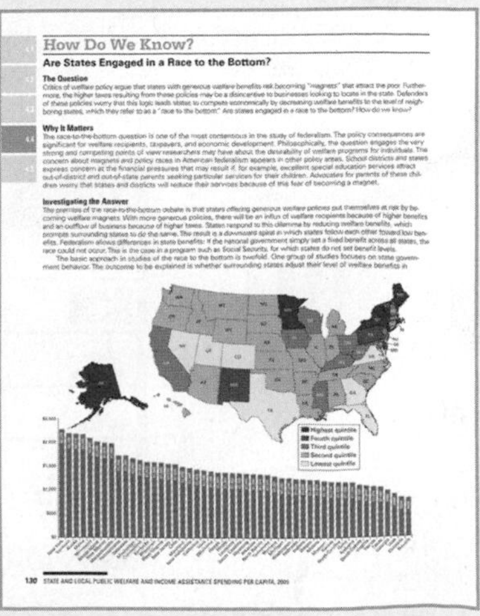

Every chapter includes a marginal glossary to support students' understanding of new and important concepts at first encounter. For easy reference, key terms from the **marginal glossary** are repeated at the end of each chapter and in the end-of-book glossary.

Through these features, the book repeatedly emphasizes to students the need to think critically and analytically about American politics. Puzzles, questions, and debates are featured prominently along with discussion of the foundations and building blocks of American government and politics. The book is tightly integrated around these concerns—every feature in each chapter underscores this focus. This discussion of what scholars know, what we do not know, and how we try to find answers, is set within a context that includes historical development, current events analysis, political culture, and comparative examples. The book aims to convey to students the excitement of analyzing politics that motivates political scientists and to develop the confidence they need to participate effectively in the political system.

MyPoliSciLab

MYPOLISCILAB is an online homework, tutorial, and assessment product that improves results by helping students better master concepts and by providing educators a dynamic set of tools for gauging individual and class performance. Its immersive experiences truly engage students in learning, helping them to understand course material and improve their performance. And MyPoliSciLab comes from Pearson—your partner in providing the best digital learning experiences.

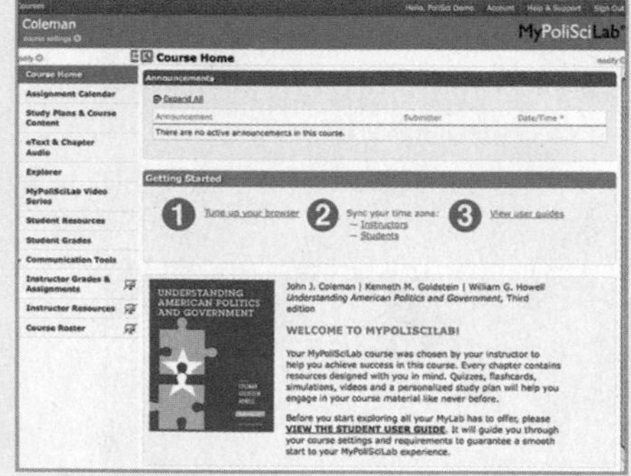

PERSONALIZE LEARNING. Reach every student at each stage of learning, engage them in active rather than passive learning, and measure that learning. Refined after a decade of real-world use, **MyPoliSciLab** is compatible with major learning management systems like Blackboard and can be customized to support each individual student's and educator's success. You can fully control what your students' course looks like; homework, applications, and more can easily be turned on or off. You can also add your own original material.

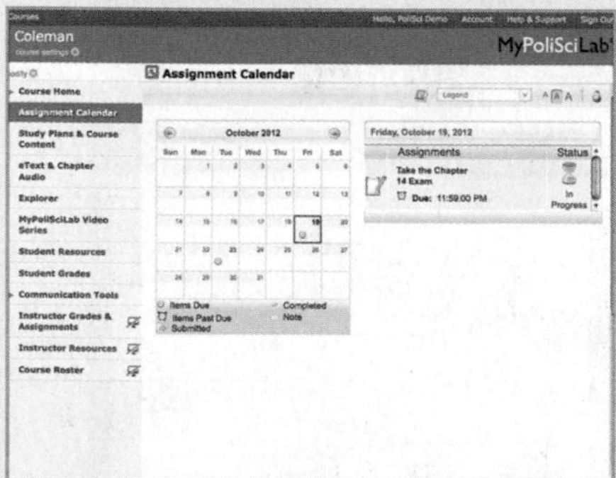

- The intuitive assignment **calendar** lets instructors drag and drop assignments to the desired date and gives students a useful course organizer.
- Automatically graded assessment flows into the **gradebook**, which can be used in MyPoliSciLab or exported.

EMPHASIZE OUTCOMES. Keep students focused on what they need to master course concepts.

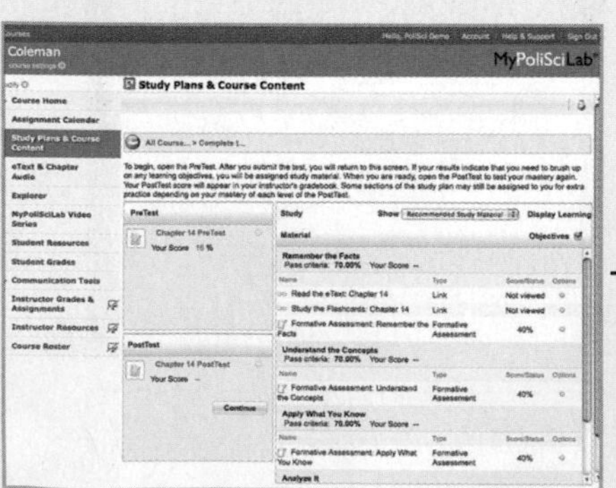

- **Practice tests** help students achieve this book's learning objectives by creating personalized study plans. Based on a pre-test diagnostic, the study plan suggests reading and multimedia for practice and moves students from comprehension to critical thinking.
- Students can study key terms and concepts with their own personal set of **flashcards**.

ENGAGE STUDENTS. Students—each one is different. Reach *all* of them with the new **MyPoliSciLab Video Series**, which features this book's authors and top scholars discussing the big ideas in each chapter and applying them to enduring political issues. Each chapter is supported by six videos that help students work through the material and retain its key lessons.

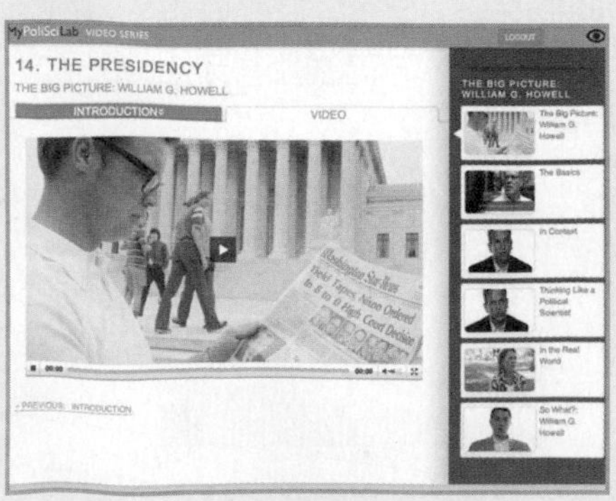

- ***The Big Picture.*** Understand how the topic fits into the American political system.
- ***The Basics.*** Review the topic's core learning objectives.
- ***In Context.*** Examine the historical background of the topic.
- ***Thinking Like a Political Scientist.*** Solve a political puzzle related to the topic.

- ***In the Real World.*** Consider different perspectives on a key issue in American politics.
- ***So What?*** Connect the topic to what is at stake for American democracy.

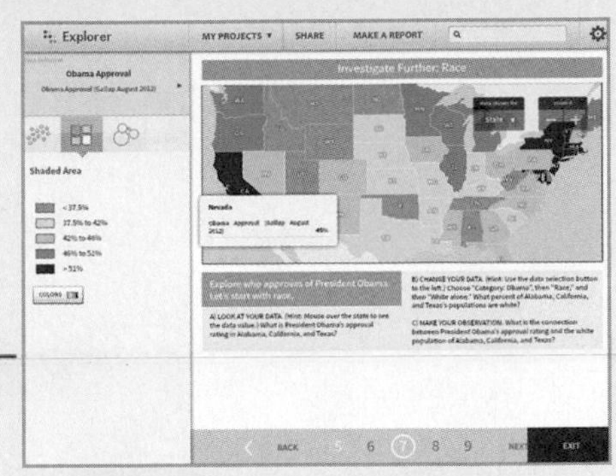

IMPROVE CRITICAL THINKING. Improve critical thinking. Students get a lot of information about politics; your challenge as an instructor is to turn them into critical consumers of that information. **Explorer** is a hands-on way to develop quantitative literacy and to move students beyond punditry and opinion. In the book, infographics introduce key questions about politics. On MyPoliSciLab, guided exercises ask students to read the data related to the questions and then find connections among the data to answer the questions. Explorer includes data from the United States Census, General Social Survey, Statistical Abstract of the United States, Gallup, American National Election Studies, and Election Data Services with more data being regularly added.

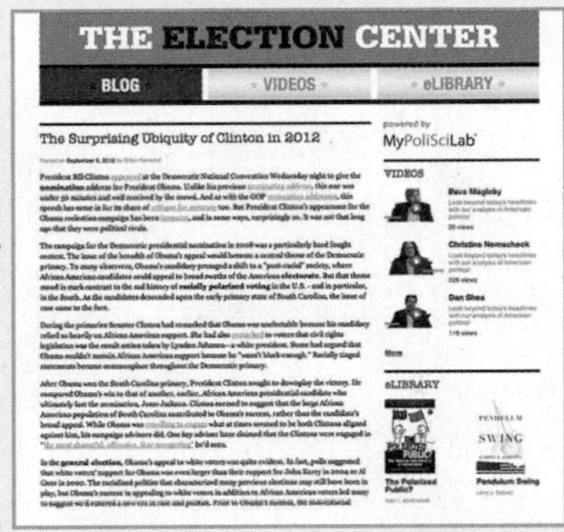

ANALYZE CURRENT EVENTS. Prepare students for a lifetime of following political news. Coverage of the campaigns, issues, and outcomes of the 2012 elections and more keeps politics relevant and models how to analyze developments in the American political system.

- Get up-to-the-minute analysis by top scholars on MyPoliSciLab's **blogs**, take the weekly quiz, and register to vote.
- Or reflect on a theoretical case with the **simulations** in MyPoliSciLab. Easy to assign and complete in a week, each simulation is a game-like opportunity to play the role of a political actor and apply course concepts to make realistic political decisions.

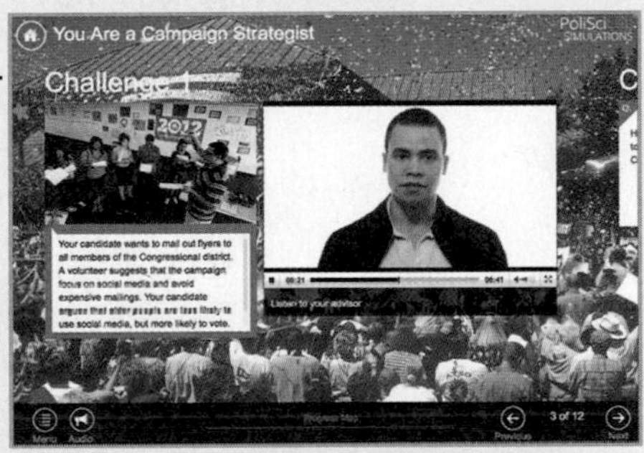

THE PEARSON ETEXT offers a full digital version of the print book and is readable on Apple iPad and Android tablets with the Pearson eText app. Like the printed text, students can highlight relevant passages and add notes. The Pearson eText also includes **primary sources** like the Declaration of Independence, Constitution of the United States, selected Federalist Papers, key Supreme Court decisions, Lincoln's Gettysburg Address, and Washington's Farewell Address.

CHAPTER AUDIO lets students listen to the full text of this book.

Visit **WWW.MYPOLISCILAB.COM** to test drive MyPoliSciLab, set up a class test of MyPoliSciLab, and read about the efficacy of Pearson's MyLabs. You can also learn more from your local Pearson representative; find them at **www.pearsonhighered.com/replocator.**

Supplements

Make more time for your students with instructor resources that offer effective learning assessments and classroom engagement. Pearson's partnership with educators does not end with the delivery of course materials; Pearson is there with you on the first day of class and beyond. A dedicated team of local Pearson representatives will work with you to not only choose course materials but also integrate them into your class and assess their effectiveness. Our goal is your goal—to improve instruction with each semester.

Pearson is pleased to offer the following resources to qualified adopters of *Understanding American Politics and Government*. Several of these supplements are available to instantly download on the Instructor Resource Center (IRC); please visit the IRC at **www.pearsonhighered.com/irc** to register for access.

TEST BANK. Evaluate learning at every level. Reviewed for clarity and accuracy, the Test Bank measures this book's learning objectives with multiple-choice, true/false, fill-in-the-blank, short answer, and essay questions. You can easily customize the assessment to work in any major learning management system and to match what is covered in your course. Word, BlackBoard, and WebCT versions are available on the IRC and Respondus versions are available upon request from **www.respondus.com.**

PEARSON MYTEST. This powerful assessment generation program includes all of the questions in the Test Bank. Quizzes and exams can be easily authored and saved online and then printed for classroom use, giving you ultimate flexibility to manage assessments anytime and anywhere. To learn more, visit **www.pearsonhighered.com/mytest.**

INSTRUCTOR'S MANUAL. Create a comprehensive roadmap for teaching classroom, online, or hybrid courses. Designed for new and experienced instructors, the Instructor's Manual includes a sample syllabus, lecture and discussion suggestions, activities for in or out of class, essays on teaching American Government, and suggestions for using MyPoliSciLab. Available on the IRC.

INSTRUCTOR'S ETEXT. The instructor's eText offers links to relevant instructor's resources and student activities in MyPoliSciLab. You can access these resources by simply clicking on an icon at the start of each chapter. Available on MyPoliSciLab.

POWERPOINT PRESENTATION WITH CLASSROOM RESPONSE SYSTEM (CRS). Make lectures more enriching for students. The PowerPoint Presentation includes a full lecture script, discussion questions, photos and figures from the book, and links to MyPoliSciLab multimedia. With integrated clicker questions, get immediate feedback on what your students are learning during a lecture. Available on the IRC.

CLASS PREPARATION. Add multimedia, figures, photos, and lots more from any of our political science books to your lectures. Available on MyPoliSciLab.

ALTERNATE EDITIONS. Don't teach policy? Removing this book's policy chapters is easy with Pearson Custom Library. To learn more, visit **www.pearsoncustomlibrary.com.**

TEXAS, CALIFORNIA, AND GEORGIA GOVERNMENT. Need coverage of your state's government? Add chapters from our bestselling Texas, California, and Georgia government books with Pearson Custom Library. To learn more, visit **www.pearsoncustomlibrary.com.**

Acknowledgments

Understanding American Politics and Government is the result of an extensive development process that included the input of instructors and students through reviews, focus groups, and class tests. We are grateful to all of them for their assistance.

We would also like to thank David Brent, Hannah Cook, Colleen Dolan, Paul Manna, Howard Schweber, and Patricia Strach for their help with this edition. The book also benefitted from the assessment of experts who provided thoughts on suggested readings and important unresolved debates in the study of American government and politics.

We are also grateful to the first-rate team at Pearson that it was our distinct pleasure to work with once again. Authors could not ask for a more talented or more supportive group. This book is better because of their dedication, energy, and creative thinking.

Listen to Chapter I on MyPoliSciLab

1 Thinking About American Politics

As the days ticked off before the 2012 election, the nation was divided not only between those who favored President Obama and those who favored Governor Romney, but between those who predicted an Obama victory and those who predicted a Romney victory. That the two groups were composed of the same people was not surprising. Each side accepted evidence that favored their candidate while dismissing those data which did not.

All too often, those who participate only occasionally in politics confidently predict an outcome, or declare a conclusion, or derive great meaning from anecdotal evidence. They do so because politics is seen as open to amateurs and volunteers, and welcoming to non-scientific approaches and interpretations. It is. But politics still is an outcome of specific and meaningful strategies, actions and principles. Those who run campaigns successfully do so precisely because they recognize that not all campaigns are equal—some are run effectively and some are not. They recognize that no two elections are the same—some benefit from underlying economic conditions, while others are hampered by them. They recognize that no single poll is reliable, but that a collection of polls tell a meaningful picture about the state of a race.

The goal of this book is to challenge the way you think about politics and democracy. It's not cynical, conspiratorial and corrupt, as many believe. It is actually a simple outgrowth of our society, with all its relative strengths and weaknesses. And because it basically represents how we think, organize, give voice to our views and relate to one another, it follows certain core principles and patterns that can be anticipated.

1.1 Explain the purposes of government and why it is necessary, p. 5.

1.2 Compare and contrast the U.S. government with other democratic systems, and identify core values and beliefs within American political culture, p. 11.

1.3 Assess the challenges that researchers face when studying causal relationships within politics, p. 15.

OBAMA WINS Although the margin was narrow in many states, as the polls predicted, President Obama was re-elected. This ran counter to some punditry and perhaps some wishful thinking by many who speculated that this was an election in which the social science evidence would be wrong.

The Big Picture Wondering if you should have signed up for a different social science class? Author Kenneth M. Goldstein gives three reasons for why you made the right decision enrolling in this American Government course.

The Basics What function does government serve? In this video, you will analyze this question and explore the core values that shape our political system and how the growing diversity of our population is changing—and reaffirming—the definition of what it means to be American.

In Context Where did the basic principles of American government come from? Boston University political scientist Neta C. Crawford uncovers the Greek, Roman, and Iroquois roots of our political system. She also traces the expansion of the concept of accountability since the birth of the nation.

Think Like a Political Scientist Find out how and why research on American politics has shifted. Boston University political scientist Neta C. Crawford discusses how scholars who once focused on voters and institutions are now looking at deliberation as the primary indicator of the health of a democratic system.

In the Real World What is the government's function in everyday life? Real people share their opinions on how involved the federal government should be in education by evaluating the effectiveness of the No Child Left Behind Act, which encourages standardized testing.

So What? What do the Super Bowl and the Supreme Court's ruling on health care have in common? Author Kenneth M. Goldstein compares political junkies to sports fanatics, and he describes the tools both need in order to develop informed opinions.

The Purpose of Government

1.1 Explain the purposes of government and why it is necessary.

Government, broadly defined, consists of those publicly funded institutions that create and enforce rules for a specific territory and people. In this text, we focus almost exclusively on the workings of the federal government based in Washington, D.C., even though U.S. citizens are also subject to the authority of many other forms of government. These include state and county governments, city and town councils, local school boards, and special entities that cross the boundaries of local governments such as water, tourism, and transportation authorities. Although each of these governments is distinctive, all serve the same fundamental purpose: to create and administer public policies for a particular territory and the people within it. All may have direct relevance to you and your family as they determine everything from the amount of local taxes you pay, to the quality of your schools, to the size of your community's police force.

government
the institutions that have the authority and capacity to create and enforce public policies (rules) for a specific territory and people.

Government is a Social Contract

Government is different from other institutions in society because it alone has a broad right to use force. To put the matter bluntly, government can make citizens do things they otherwise might not want to do (such as pay taxes, educate their children, carry car insurance, and pay for lost library books). If citizens refuse to do these things, or insist on doing things that are prohibited by law, government can take action against them—imposing financial or other penalties, including extreme ones, such as life imprisonment or, in some states, death.

No other institution or segment of society has such wide-ranging authority or ability to enforce its rules. Even corporations and wealthy individuals, no matter how powerful, ultimately must depend on the court system—that is, the laws established by the government—to get others to do anything.

Why do people willingly grant government this monopoly on force and compulsion? Because, as people often say about getting older, it beats the alternative. The alternative to a government monopoly on force is a collection of individuals with each trying to impose his or her will on someone else. Imagine, for example, that you and your neighbor enter into a dispute over where your property ends and hers begins. Without government processes, rules, and authorities to mediate the dispute, you would be left to resolve it on your own. If you could not do so on peaceful, mutually agreeable terms, one or both of you might seek to enforce your will through force. If the government did not maintain a monopoly over the right to use such force, there would be no limit to the use of force to resolve any dispute, no matter how small.

Here's another example: Imagine your neighbor was hungry, but you had an abundant food supply. If you did not wish to share, your neighbor might attempt to steal some of your food to feed his family. Without government, the only way to stop this would be to take matters into your own hands. You would have to forcibly prevent your neighbor from stealing, and maybe leave him with a lump on his head as a token of your displeasure. He, of course, would try to resist all of this, perhaps leaving you with a lump on your head. Now imagine these scenarios multiplied tens of thousands of times per day, as men and women pursued their own self-interest without any restrictions, regulations, or protection provided by a governing authority.

Few would choose to live this way. That is why Thomas Hobbes, a political thinker who lived during the English Civil War in the 1600s, predicted in *Leviathan*, his famous treatise on government, that a society without government would soon devolve into "a war of all against all" and result in a world in which life was "solitary, poor, nasty, brutish, and short."[1]

Explore on MyPoliSciLab

How Do You Measure Freedom?

We use two indicators to measure freedom in any given country: the right to free speech and the right to privacy. History has shown us that defense of these rights becomes even more important in the face of a foreign threat. Below, we look at data that shows how committed Americans are to two ideals of freedom.

Free Speech Strengthens in the United States

Between 1980 and 2010, more Americans support free speech for more groups. The exceptions are racists and radical Muslims.

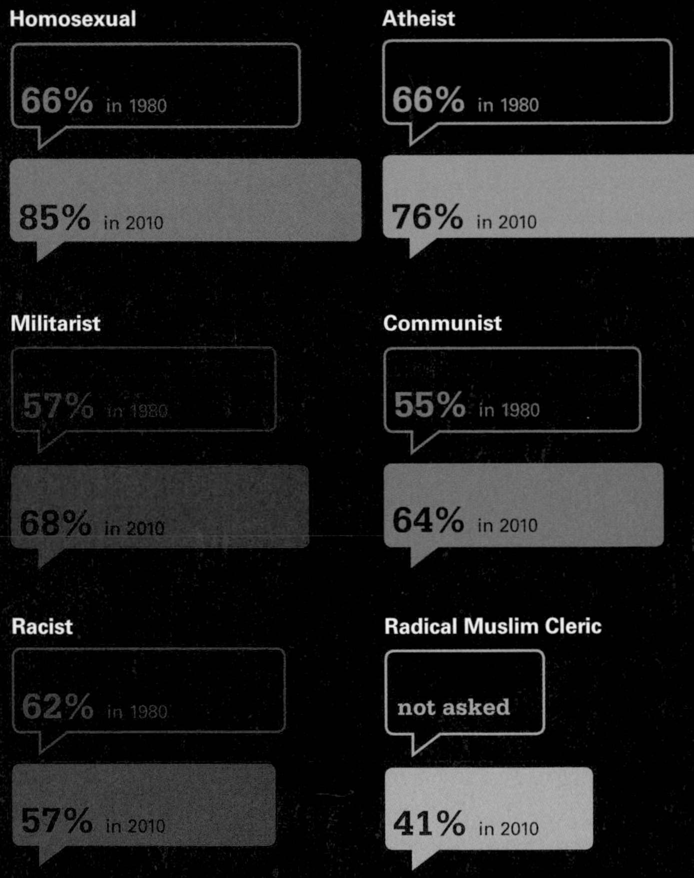

SOURCE: Data from General Social Survey, 1980, 2006, and 2010

Right to Privacy Weakens in the United States

If the government suspects that a terrorist act is about to happen, do you think the authorities should have the right to ...

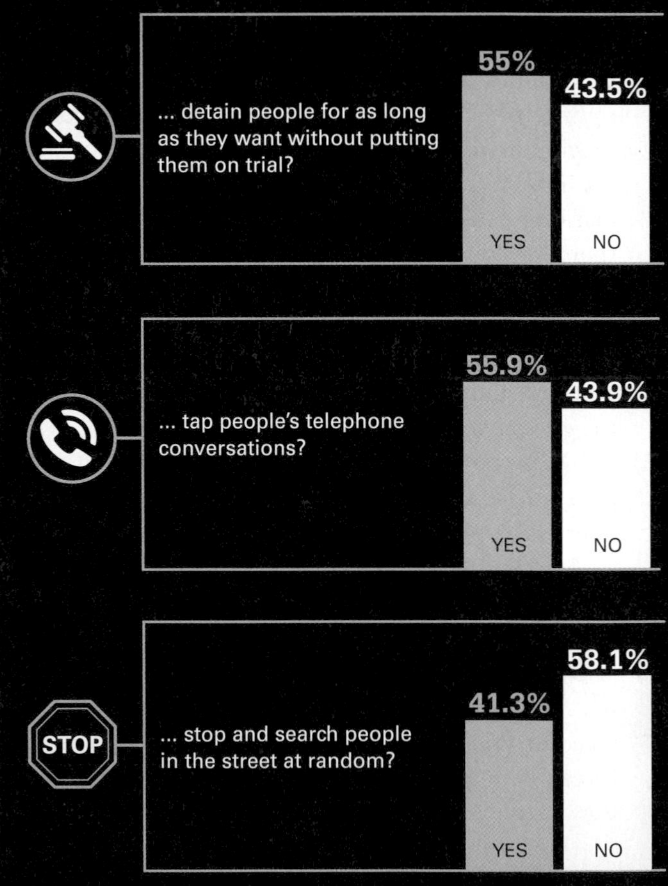

Investigate Further

Concept How does support for free speech and individual privacy measure freedom? Protecting free speech ensures that all ideas can be expressed and debated, even if they are unpopular. Likewise, protecting the privacy rights of everyone, even those who appear to be threatening, ensures equal treatment for all.

Connection How has Americans' support for free speech changed between 1980 and 2010? Overall, Americans are more tolerant of speech from "controversial" groups. More Americans support free speech for people who were previously marginalized, particularly atheists and homosexuals. Fewer are willing to tolerate racist speech.

Cause How did the threat of terrorism change freedom in America? Most Americans will still not tolerate random public frisks of people who might not be suspects. But after 9/11, Americans don't support speech by radical Muslim clerics and they are willing to detain potential terrorists indefinitely and wire-tap suspects' phones.

Governments exist because individuals generally do not wish to live in such a world. Accordingly, they enter into a **social contract** with one another to create, and give authority to, a governing body with a legal monopoly on power or force. In such a social contract, individuals give up any claim to use force to get what they want. They yield the absolute right to do whatever they want to the instruments of the government—laws, courts, police, and prisons, for example. In exchange, individuals receive basic government protections that enable them to enjoy life and liberty and pursue happiness without constant fear of outside interference.

In the United States, the social contract is the Constitution. Enlightenment thinkers such as Hobbes, as well as English philosopher John Locke and Genevan philosopher Jean-Jacques Rousseau, popularized the idea that a written document like the Constitution is a manifestation of a social contract.[2] As a written document, the Constitution has an added advantage of permanence—it can be changed only by the consent of the governed. Locke's ideas had significant influence on the Framers of the U.S. Constitution. Writing in seventeenth-century Britain, Locke laid a logical foundation for the creation of government and civil society. Locke sought to protect individual property, by which he meant each individual's "life, liberty, and estate." For Locke, the existence of government was premised on the existence of these basic rights.

Locke shared Hobbes's concern that in the absence of government, individual property would be continually threatened. Individuals, then, logically surrendered some rights to a government to gain protection for their property. The justification for government lay in its primary function to protect individual property, not as some kind of force for a larger social good or virtue.

According to Locke, the government receives its authority from the people. It is decidedly not the case that government grants rights. Rather, the people decide—through their contract with one another—which rights and authorities they will give to government and which they will retain for themselves. Moreover, if the government breaks its side of the contract and engages in tyranny, the people retain the right to revolt. For Locke, the right to rebellion and revolution constituted the ultimate check on government tyranny.

Because in a democracy governmental authority rests on an agreement among the governed, the people can also modify that authority. In the United States, for example, the people can alter government's authority by changing or amending the Constitution, or they can revoke the authority of government altogether. This is one check against the possibility of government overstepping its bounds under the terms of the Constitution, or any social contract.

Our Constitution has defined the relationship between the people and their leaders in the United States for more than two hundred years. The Constitution structures the institutions and the political decisions and debates that happen today.

The rights and freedoms granted by our Constitution stand in stark contrast to conditions in nations ruled by authoritarian systems with no social contracts. The North Korean government is an extreme example of an **authoritarian system**. The country's centralized government controls most aspects of the lives of its citizens—where they work, whether they receive an education, whether they can travel outside of the country, and whether what they say constitutes a crime deserving of imprisonment. With restrictions on freedom of speech, press, assembly, and privacy, and even access to the Internet and cell phones, the North Korean leadership not only has an absolute monopoly over force, it also has an absolute monopoly over most of the choices made by its citizens—including the choice of government leaders.

Such authoritarian systems are rare, but many governments employ some of the core elements of authoritarianism, whereas others have become more authoritarian over time. For example, although Venezuela has a constitution and its leader is chosen through an election process, in 1998, citizens elected Hugo Chavez as president. Since that time, Chavez has consolidated power, pressed forward with a plan to serve beyond a constitutionally limited two terms, and changed the legislature from a two-party to a one-party system. The legislature, filled with Chavez's supporters, then gave

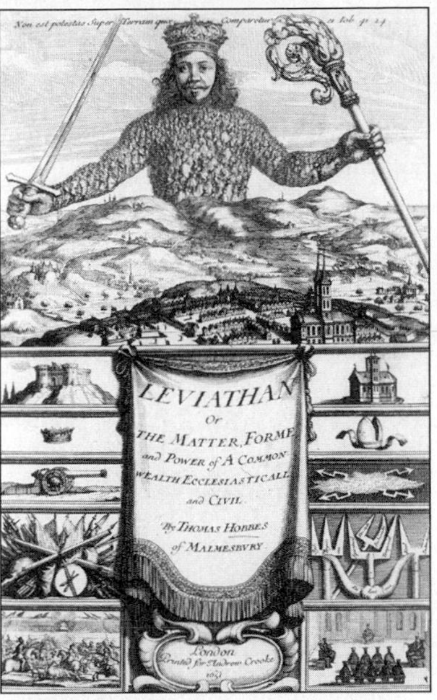

A WAR OF ALL AGAINST ALL

Thomas Hobbes's *Leviathan* popularized the idea of a social contract that people enter into with one another to create and give authority to government.

social contract
an agreement among members of a society to form and recognize the authority of a centralized government that is empowered to make and enforce laws governing the members of that society.

authoritarian (or totalitarian) system
a political system in which one person or group has absolute control over the apparatus of government, and in which popular input in government is minimal or nonexistent.

public goods
goods (and services) that are enjoyed by all citizens and unlikely to be provided by any organization other than government.

him the power to create laws unilaterally. There are also significant questions as to whether elections in Venezuela are free from government intimidation.[3] Venezuela may not stand at the same extreme end of the authoritarianism spectrum as North Korea, but in the past two decades, it has moved significantly from a society governed by a durable social contract to one governed by the will and power of a single individual. The absence of a respected social contract is one of the hallmarks of a society lacking in fundamental freedoms, just as Locke and Hobbes described four centuries ago.

Throughout this book, we will make comparisons between American politics and government and the corresponding processes and institutions in other countries. These sorts of comparisons help clarify the unique features of American government.

□ Government Provides Public Goods and Services

Government not only serves to protect us from threat. It also provides citizens with public goods. **Public goods** are products or services that all citizens enjoy that cannot easily be provided by anyone other than government. Nongovernmental institutions generally cannot, or will not, provide public goods because

- it would be too difficult for them to marshal sufficient resources to provide the good; and
- it is difficult, if not impossible, to exclude those who do not pay from receiving the good.

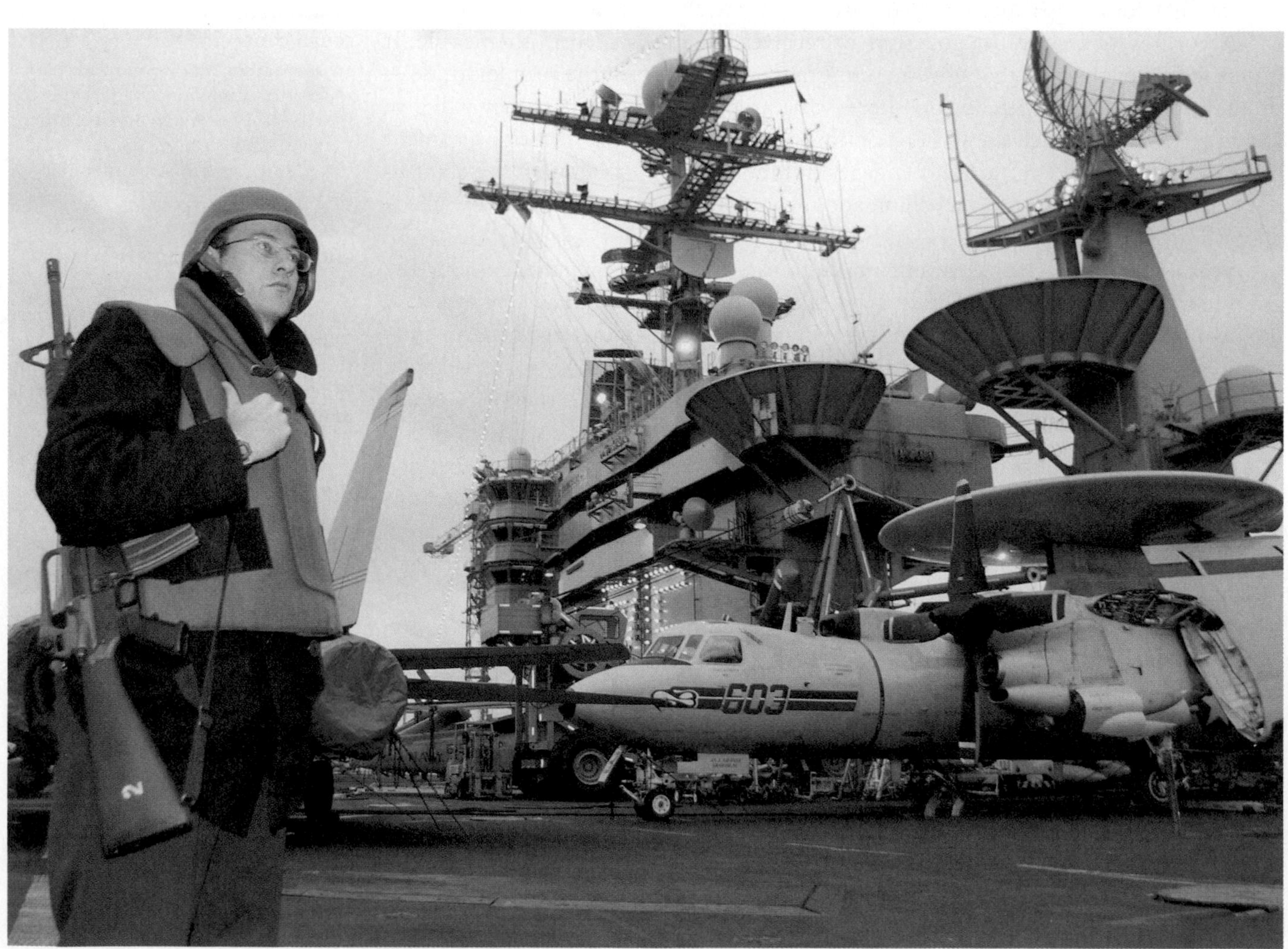

BILLIONS OF DOLLARS IN MILITARY HARDWARE

The funding of the military is a classic example of a public good. Everyone shares in the benefits of advanced national defense. No single citizen could fund it, and those who might choose to not contribute cannot be excluded from its benefits.

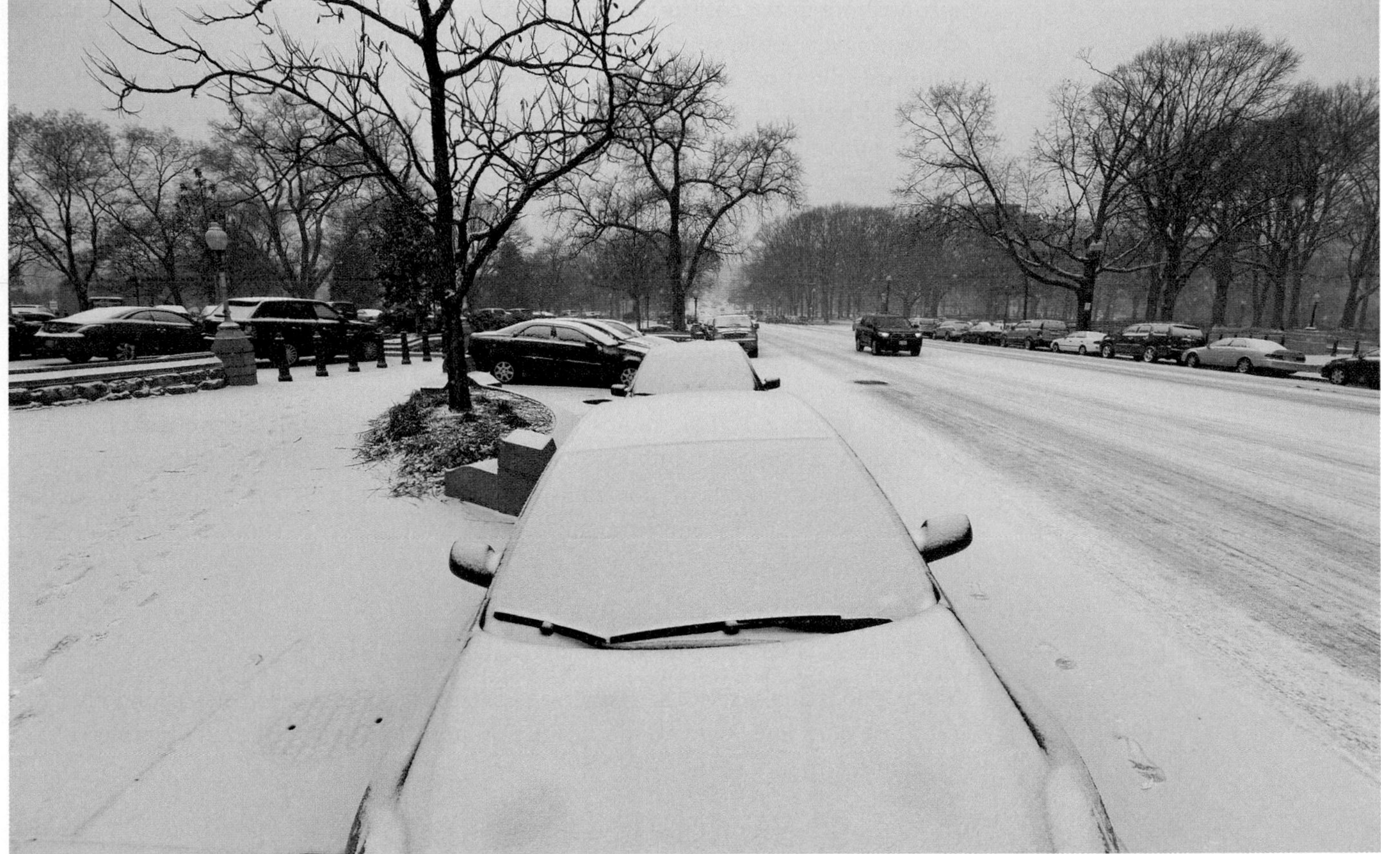

WHO'S GOING TO CLEAR THE ROAD?

Although it is certainly in every motorist's best interest to have the road cleared of snow, there is no incentive for any car owner to clear the road on his or her own. This is one public good that government can provide to all residents.

The best example of a public good is national defense. The United States currently spends more than $400 billion per year on various elements of its national defense. This kind of investment, year in and year out, is simply beyond the reach of any private-sector institution.

It is also difficult to exclude citizens from the benefits of national defense, even if they do not pay for it. Imagine that a private company provided U.S. national defense, and individual consumers could choose to pay to be defended. Now imagine that only half of the homeowners in a particular state decided to pay for this service. If a missile headed toward this state, there would be no way for the defense company to protect only those homeowners who had paid for its services. Instead, the company would have to defend all of the state's residents, regardless of who had paid.

This scenario is problematic in two respects. First, the company is providing a service—some people are paying for the service and some are not, but all receive the same benefit. Why would the company want to stay in this business? Second, this is not fair to the homeowners who paid for the service. Why should they continue to pay if others are receiving the service for free? Either the company will get out of the business or homeowners will just stop paying for the defense service. Either way, national defense will not likely be provided.

Government provides other public goods. For example, governments generally take responsibility for clearing public roads following a snowstorm. If some citizens get together and pay for a private company to clear the road instead, everyone who drives or walks on that road will benefit from the service even if they have not paid for it; this is unfair to those who have paid.

Government overcomes this problem of "free-riders" (those who reap benefits without paying for them) by providing the service itself and then compelling everyone

politics
individual and collective efforts to influence the workings of government.

to contribute to the cost by paying taxes. For example, some consider access to public schools to be a public good, even though others do not because of the wide availability of private education. Fire protection is a public good that most people are thankful not to need. Public buses; subsidized mass transit; and national, state, and local parks are seen as public goods, to be supported by everyone, even if they are enjoyed by only a percentage of the population. In each case, the government assumes a responsibility to provide the public with something it might not have access to otherwise.

In addition to providing these public goods, keeping order, and protecting individual rights, the government has taken onto itself other responsibilities. In the United States, one of the federal government's largest areas of responsibility is providing retirement security for workers and their families through the Social Security system. Although the Constitution does not require this service, and many citizens prepare for their own retirement though individual savings, this is a public service that has come to be seen as a significant public responsibility, akin to a public good. The definition of what constitutes a public responsibility or public good is a significant source for debate about the proper role of government.

□ Politics Is About Influencing Decisions

Which goods and services are public and how they are provided can vary significantly, and those questions depend significantly on **politics**. Engaging in politics means trying to influence

- who will lead government,
- how government will operate and make decisions,
- what the nature and substance of government decisions will be, and
- how government will enforce its decisions.

Politics may mean working to elect a particular person as mayor, state senator, judge, or president. It may mean collecting signatures to put on the ballot a requirement that raising taxes requires more than a majority vote in the state legislature. It may mean attending a town hall meeting to voice concerns about changes to the boundaries that determine neighborhood schools or proposed restrictions that would close an open-air farmer's market. Politics may mean forming a group to demonstrate against the death penalty outside of a prison. It may also mean participating in an organized effort for a higher minimum wage, increased student loan programs, or the end of a war. In whatever form it takes, politics involves the difficult work of sorting out interests among various citizens at the local and national levels.

Politics is often referred to in a negative manner: "It was all about politics," or so and so "was just playing politics." But there is nothing inherently negative in the definition of politics. Certainly, politics can seem distasteful. Even so, efforts to influence the workings of government can be rooted in noble purposes and deeply affect people's lives. The use of politics to achieve certain benefits for a segment of the population can seem selfish; in another light, however, it can also be the very purpose of a representative democracy and well-functioning government.

Although we might cringe at times at the way politics is conducted—petty partisanship, shrill language, naked appeals to selfish interests, broken promises, and so on—it is surely better than the alternative. Without politics, many differences would be settled violently, outside the relatively peaceful processes of government. Americans experienced that most clearly in the Civil War, when differences over slavery were settled on the battlefield and at the cost of hundreds of thousands of lives.

Not surprisingly, politics often occurs around issues that divide the nation. Issues of shared consensus provoke little need for political debate, but certain contentious issues appear to crop up in American political life with great regularity, although in different forms. For example, Americans regularly debate the appropriate governmental oversight of the content of media. Although the nation has long respected the

MAKING YOUR VOICE HEARD
Attending town hall meetings is one of the many ways you can influence policy and politics.

freedom of speech, those using public airwaves are subject to restrictions over content. Should government police speech? Some would say that individual businesses and consumers could deal appropriately with this matter. Others say that government should have the right to require that the content of movies, music, and video games meets basic decency standards at the very least. At the core of the debate is a disagreement over the role of the government—should it be active and expansive or inert and reluctant?

One of President Barack Obama's biggest initiatives during his first two years in office was the establishment of a requirement for every citizen to carry health insurance—and a proposal that the government help those who could not afford it otherwise. This was a debate as much about the role of the government as it was about the problem of expensive health insurance. On one side were those resistant to an increase in government involvement in health care, broadly defined. On the other side were those who viewed health care as a public good worthy of government support and active involvement. Both sides came to the specific debate over health care with a strong sense of the proper role of government.

Clearly, then, politics "starts" even before a specific policy idea makes it to the governmental agenda. As this book will frequently note, much Much of the substance of politics is devoted to complex questions about which issues belong on that agenda in the first place.

Contexts for Studying American Government and Politics

1.2 Compare and contrast the U.S. government with other democratic systems, and identify core values and beliefs within American political culture.

Understanding American politics and government requires an understanding of the unique features and beliefs of the American system. It also requires the ability to differentiate America's values and beliefs from those of other governmental systems around the world.

1.1

1.2

1.3

democracy

a form of government in which the people rule; this can take place directly, through participation by the people in actual lawmaking, or indirectly, through free elections in which the people choose representatives to make laws on their behalf.

autocracy

a form of government in which a single person rules with effectively unlimited power.

direct democracy

a form of democracy in which the people themselves make the laws and set the policies adopted by the government.

representative democracy

a form of democracy in which the people, through free elections, select representatives to make laws on their behalf and set policies adopted by the government.

constitutional democracy

a form of democracy in which there is a foundational document (such as the U.S. Constitution) that describes the structure, powers, and limits of government.

Representation and Rights are Central to American Government

Democracy, a word derived from ancient Greek, means "rule by the many" (in contrast to its opposite, **autocracy**, which means "rule by a single person," such as a king or an emperor). The defining principle in a democracy is that government is based on the consent of the governed. In other words, democratic government operates at the pleasure or will of the people.

Democracy in its purest form is known as **direct democracy**. In a direct democracy, the people vote directly on laws. Many U.S. states, such as California, have a form of direct democracy in which citizens can both initiate and vote on ballot measures to change state law. (Examples are the initiatives in a number of states to amend state constitutions to limit property tax increases or to ban same-sex marriage.)

The U.S. government, however, has no such mechanism. It is organized entirely as a **representative democracy**, in which people vote for their leaders through elections. Those leaders, not the people themselves, make the laws. Whether direct or representative, democracy implies more than just providing avenues for individuals to influence government. American democracy, for example, is also characterized by the following principles:

- **Political equality.** All adult Americans (with a few exceptions) have the right to vote, and each American's vote counts equally. Furthermore, all adult Americans have an equal right to participate in politics at every level.
- **Plurality rule and minority rights.** *Plurality rule* means that whoever or whatever gets the most votes wins, and in American politics, the will of the plurality of people usually prevails. Whoever gets the most votes wins elective office; bills pass with a plurality vote in the legislature; Supreme Court decisions must command a plurality in order to have the force of law. In any of these settings, however, the dominant status of pluralities cannot trample the rights of those in the minority. Specific minority rights are guaranteed in state and federal laws, in state and federal constitutions, in state and federal court decisions, and in the operating rules at various levels of government. Thus, even if one group could muster a winning margin for the proposition that a smaller group be denied the right to vote, state and federal constitutions would prevent this from happening.
- **Equality before the law.** With only a few exceptions, every American has the same legal rights and obligations as do all other Americans. Every American is subject to the same laws as everyone else, and every American must be treated the same by government. The American government is not permitted to discriminate arbitrarily among groups or individuals. Of course, in reality, this is a principle or goal that has not been fully realized in American democracy. Certain individuals or groups can have advantages over their fellow citizens (such instances of unequal power will be identified throughout this text).

America is a **constitutional democracy**. The U.S. Constitution holds, defines, and constrains government's exercise of power. It expressly identifies, for example, the responsibilities of each branch of government, with the goal of making sure the president, Congress, and the courts maintain significant restraints on the other branches. The Constitution also makes clear, through the Bill of Rights, that the government must do certain things and may not do certain things. For example, it must ensure that criminal defendants receive a speedy and fair trial, and it must not limit freedom of speech, religion, or assembly.

As we will discuss in the chapter dealing with political culture, the The healthy functioning of a democratic government depends greatly on people's attitudes toward their government, their role as citizens in a democracy, and their support for the freedoms that government is supposed to protect. As the legendary U.S. Circuit Court Judge Learned Hand (1872–1971) reminds us,

> Liberty lies in the hearts of men and women; when it dies there, no constitution, no law, no court can save it; no constitution, no law, no court can even do much to help it. While it lies there it needs no constitution, no law, no court to save it.[4]

Hand describes the responsibility of the citizenry: to be the best and ultimate guardian of their own rights and freedoms. As long as Americans believe in the democratic system and are willing to engage in it, there can be no serious threat to liberty or democratic stability. If Americans lose faith in the system, fail to hold it accountable, or abandon the democratic values that support it, the very concepts of self-rule and liberty may be at risk.

America does not Provide the Only Model for Politics or Democracy

America is one among a number of the world's democracies. It shares some common features with all of them, such as a commitment to majority rule through elections. It also differs from them in many respects. The U.S. Constitution, for example, is rightly seen as a limiting document, one intended by the founders as a defense against the possibility of governmental tyranny. Not all democracies set such limits on themselves.

For example, when Israel became a state, its major political interests were unable to agree on a constitution. In place of a single constitutional document, therefore, Israel has a series of "basic laws" and court decisions that have accumulated over the years. These define the contours of government responsibility. Similarly, the United Kingdom has no single, limiting document like the U.S. Constitution. Instead, it has an evolving set of laws, judicial decisions, customs, and practices that are the rough equivalent of American constitutional law.

American democracy also differs from others in that its federal system is responsible for the affairs of the nation as a whole, and 50 separate state governments have responsibility for affairs within state borders. Thus, as we will discuss in the federalism chapter, much of the federal governing apparatus—a president, a Congress, and federal courts—is duplicated at the state level, with governors, state legislatures, and state courts.

Although democracy in the United States depends on this particular federalist structure, other countries organize their democracies differently. For example, France, Japan, and Uruguay have only one layer of decision-making authority—at the national level. In these countries, there are no equivalents to American governors or state legislatures. Canada, Germany, and India, though, are more like the United States and are organized as federal systems, with a national government and regional governments.

Finally, the United States differs from most other democracies in being a presidential system rather than a parliamentary one. In a **presidential system**, the voters select their chief executive and their legislators separately. In 2012, for example, a voter living in Massachusetts could have "split the ticket," casting one vote for Democrat Barack Obama for president and a separate vote for Republican Scott Brown for senator.

In a **parliamentary system**, this kind of split-ticket voting in which one votes for one party for president and another for Congress would be impossible. In fact, in the United Kingdom, voters do not cast a ballot for the chief executive at all. Instead, they vote for representatives to the national legislative assembly, the House of Commons. From among their ranks, the members of that body then choose the chief executive, the prime minister.

Unique Values and Attitudes Define Politics in America

American politics and government are continually shaped by the uniquely American political culture. **Political culture** refers to the orientation of citizens toward the

presidential system
a political system in which the head of the executive branch is selected by some form of popular vote and serves a fixed term of office; the United States has a presidential system.

parliamentary system
a political system in which the head of the executive branch is selected by members of the legislature rather than by popular vote.

political culture
the values and beliefs of citizens toward the political system and toward themselves as actors in it.

political system and toward themselves as actors in it—the basic values, beliefs, attitudes, predispositions, and expectations that citizens bring to political life.

The United States has a dominant political culture, sometimes referred to as the American creed. The main ideas and values that make up the creed are individualism, democracy, equality, and liberty, as well as respect for private property and religion. Most Americans strongly embrace these concepts in the abstract, and often in specific cases as well. However, these values can clash. For example, does equality dictate that the incomes of everyone in America should be equal? Not necessarily. When Americans express their belief in the value of equality, they generally mean equality of opportunity—all people having an equal chance to rise as high as their talents will carry them. This is not the same, however, as everyone enjoying equal outcomes. That is an idea that most Americans do not embrace.

American political culture gives a sense of what is politically possible in the United States: what the American people demand, expect, and will tolerate from government; which public policy undertakings are likely to be viewed favorably and which negatively; which political messages are consistent winners and losers with American voters; and which social, political, and demographic trends are likely to put pressure on government.

The American political culture is not a perfectly harmonious set of beliefs. When it comes to specific cases, some values and ideas in the culture clash, and others give way to more practical considerations. Although it the culture establishes some clear boundaries for American political discourse and governmental action, those boundaries are fairly expansive. We will explain the American political culture in comparative and historical contexts and periodically invoke American political culture throughout the text, as we believe that viewing American political culture in comparative and historical contexts is a useful lens through which you can view U.S. politics and government.

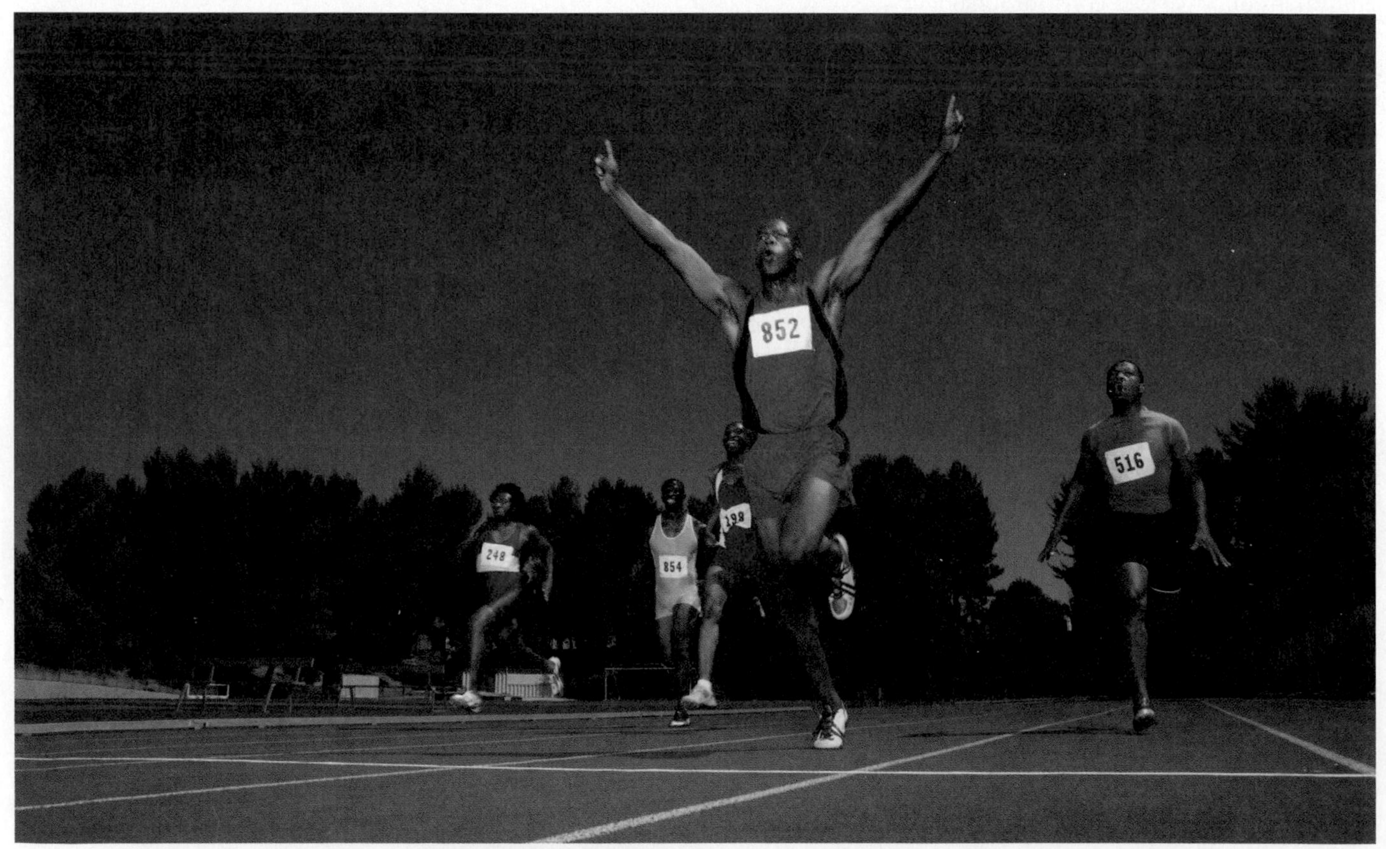

EQUAL AT THE STARTING LINE, BUT A WINNER EMERGES

Most Americans hold that citizens should have equal opportunities, but—like runners in a race—they understand that our society, economy, and politics will generate both winners and losers. Are there any areas in which you think there should be an equal outcome?

Thinking About Politics

1.3 Assess the challenges that researchers face when studying causal relationships within politics.

In addition to understanding American politics and government in light of comparative and cultural contexts, this text seeks to help you begin to think logically and carefully about important causal questions related to American government. **Causal questions** concern "what causes what." Such questions address the roots or origins of particular events or behaviors. They attempt to explain which factor or factors made a particular outcome occur. You deal with causal questions every day: Did I get a "C" on that exam because I didn't study hard enough or because I didn't study the right material? Which major gives me the best chance of getting into law school—political science or economics? Which will improve my job prospects more—taking extra classes during the summer or working in an unpaid internship? In all of these cases, you are trying to understand how to achieve an actual or potential outcome—getting a "C," getting into law school, getting a good job. In this sense, you are always asking and trying to answer causal questions.

causal question
a question regarding the factors responsible for a particular outcome.

Explore on MyPoliSciLab
Simulation: You Are a Candidate for Congress

Answering causal questions in the realm of politics and government is what political science and this text are all about. The question of Sarah Palin and her impact on the outcome of the 2008 election is a particular causal question. However, before you address this sort of question and identify the factors that determine different sorts of political behaviors or outcomes, you should first be able to describe and understand the basic characteristics and organization of American government and society. Furthermore, questions regarding a specific politician's impact on the outcome of a presidential election can lead to larger questions about who and what forces influence election outcomes, policy decisions, and governing more generally. Which factors combine for a successful campaign? How can politicians and groups influence voters? Who decides what goes on the policy agenda? How do politicians of different parties and ideologies govern together?

Public officials, political activists, journalists, and pundits often have simple answers to such questions. Simple answers are not necessarily wrong, but they often ignore important causal elements. Sometimes the political issues of the day are rooted in deep and profound disagreements. Sorting out the issues and understanding them in the hurly-burly of political debate can be difficult, however, and can make citizens wary about getting involved in political arguments or political activity. Although you do not need to run for office or get involved in every political campaign, knowing the fundamentals of your political system and the fundamentals of good thinking allows you to keep your leaders—not to mention your friends and family—accountable. How health care will be funded, what sorts of taxes you will pay, and the shape of your retirement are all major issues that will surely be debated in the coming years. One day, you may even need to decide whether you or your children will fight in a future war.

This text provides you with the tools to see through simplistic answers that often get put forward in political debates, on cable talk shows, and during dinner-table conversations and to help you become a more informed and active citizen. The text will talk a lot about power and how it is wielded. We want to give you the confidence to take part in politics and influence America's democracy. Throughout this text, you will encounter political scientists' answers to important questions in American politics in each of these areas. As you study each topic, pay close attention to the different ways researchers gather and analyze evidence as they try to understand politics and political decisions.

Whatever the topic, we encourage you to take a critical view of how these arguments are framed and made. This will not only enable you to make sense of class material but will also give you the confidence to evaluate research and make arguments in other settings—academic, political, professional, or even social. By a critical view, we don't simply mean questioning or criticizing what you read. Rather, when you use critical thinking, you also allow the views of others to affect how you think about an issue. You consider how a fresh point of fact can disprove something you have long believed. You take into account how others can look at the same information and come to completely different conclusions. You learn to see how political debates can be rooted in issues that appear to be far from relevant to the ones being discussed. In short, critical thinking is what happens when you consider new facts, challenge old assumptions, determine the consequences and implications of an idea, understand context, evaluate arguments, and sharpen your views.

We will discuss a variety of topics that require critical thinking and analysis. Examples of these topics and questions include the following:

- Which factors influence the outcome of presidential elections?
- Why do some people become Democrats, others Republicans, and others independents?
- Why does the United States have low rates of voter turnout compared with other countries?
- Do the major media in this country give preferential treatment to one political party over the other?
- Why are members of Congress reelected at such high rates?
- Why do views of the president fluctuate so much over the course of a term in office?

All of these questions have outcomes that political scientists try to explain: party attachments, voter turnout, media bias, congressional election outcomes, and presidential approval. In addressing these questions and explaining these outcomes, the first step for researchers is to identify which factors could influence or cause change in the specific outcome they are studying. If the president's approval rating is the outcome to be studied, one of the explanatory causes would be the state of the national economy. This is just another way of saying that the performance of the U.S. economy is one factor that affects presidential job approval.

☐ Simple Solutions to Political Questions are Rare

Most good studies associate more than one causal or explanatory factor with each outcome. Political scientists tend to believe, for example, that although the state of the economy has an important influence on presidential approval, it is not the only relevant factor. The percentage of the electorate that has an attachment to the political party of the president (Republican or Democrat) is another factor that influences presidential approval. Another would be whether the nation is at war or at peace or whether the president is perceived as responding well to a natural disaster or major geopolitical crisis.

Whereas political scientists see a world in which more than one factor contributes to an outcome, journalists and politicians often focus on one major cause, even claiming it is the sole cause of an event or outcome. If the economy is bad, it is because taxes are too high. If a candidate loses an election, it is because he or she ran a poor campaign. If the president suffers a legislative defeat, it is because the media covered his proposal in negative ways. If a political protest evolves into a riot, it is because the police failed to keep order. Simple answers make the journalist's job and the politician's job much easier.

Often these single-cause explanations flow from a particular viewpoint or partisan posture, or—in today's world—the need to explain something in a quick sound bite. Generally, they do not represent good theory or good social science research, or even the whole story. Political scientists see the world as complex, with most conditions having not just one but a variety of causes. One of our goals in this text is to help you get beyond the shouting matches on television news shows and give you the tools to make, interpret, and evaluate arguments on your own—and thus to be an informed and critical citizen who can question the black-and-white world of sound bites and television talk shows and see the issues in more realistic and more complex terms.

correlation
a relationship between factors such that change in one is accompanied by change in the other.

causation
a relationship between variables such that change in the value of one is directly responsible for change in the value of the other.

spurious relationship
a relationship between variables that reflects correlation but not causation.

Correlation does not Equal Causation

Analysts face challenges when they conduct research on politics. One challenge occurs with such frequency that it needs special attention as you learn about others' research and come up with your own conclusions: Correlation is not the same as causation. Here is an example of this challenge: It is a fact that the more firefighters who respond to a fire, the worse the damage and the injuries from that fire. Why is that? Do more firefighters get in one another's way and cause injuries? Not likely. A more likely explanation is that more dangerous fires simply require additional firefighters. And so although these two factors occur together, they do not necessarily cause one another. In other words, the two factors are **correlated**, but correlation does not always mean **causation**.

Political scientists call this example a **spurious relationship**. The more serious the fire, the more likely it is that damage and injuries will occur. The same factor that influences the number of firefighters that are sent also influences the amount of damages and injuries that result.

Figure 1.1 illustrates a relationship that is correlated but not causal. A third factor influences both of the other two outcomes. In this case, the seriousness of the fire influences both the number of firefighters who are called to the fire and the amount of damage from the fire.

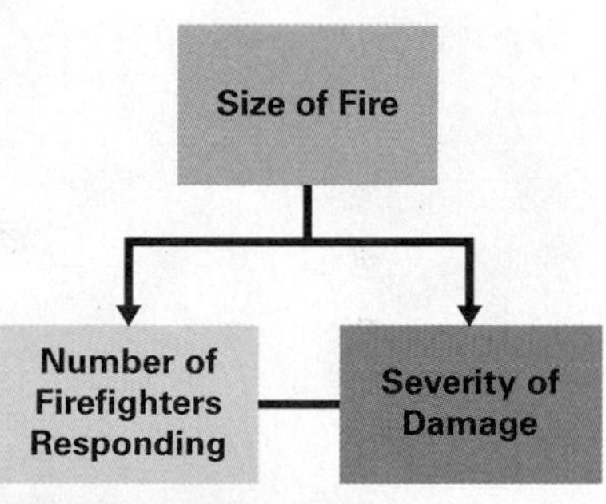

FIGURE 1.1 CORRELATION DOES NOT EQUAL CAUSATION.
When you hear people make causal arguments, make sure there is not some other factor at work. A small fire will probably cause less damage and injuries, but not just because there are fewer firefighters.

Another way of thinking about this concept is to take the classic political science example of the "Golden Arches Theory of Conflict Prevention" first presented in 1996 by American journalist and commentator Thomas Friedman. The idea behind this theory, also known as the McDonald's theory, is that two countries that both have a McDonald's restaurant would never go to war with each other. Friedman argues that countries that can support a McDonald's franchise are sufficiently wealthy and developed and have a middle class filled with people who "don't like to fight wars; they like to wait in line for burgers."[5] Therefore, according to Friedman, who admitted that no one should take the theory at face value, the relationship between the people and the McDonald's franchises causes the outcome—no war.

Logically, just because two countries have a McDonald's franchise and have not gone to war with each other does not mean that having a McDonald's franchise actually prevents conflict. The two factors may be correlated, but one does not cause the other. In fact, in 2008, Russia and the country of Georgia, both of which are home to a Golden Arches, actually did go to war. Clearly, this correlation did not equal causation.

Let's consider another example: the relationship between incarcerating criminals and a drop in violent crime rates. Since 1990, we have put more criminals in jail, and we have also seen a historic drop in crime rates—from 758 victims for every 100,000 people in 1991 to 429 victims in 2009.[6] Some critics of sentencing laws, which often force judges to keep convicts in jail longer than they might otherwise demand, say that these laws are unnecessary because crime rates have fallen so precipitously. Others say just the opposite—the increases in the prison population are helping reduce crime in our communities. So many explanations for the drop in crime are possible that, in the end, both sides of this debate may be disappointed.

Now, consider another political example in which the question of causation is immediate. Do politicians change their votes in response to campaign donations? This is no small issue: If citizens views votes as essentially for sale, they will become increasingly cynical about the democratic process and about the virtue of their elected representatives in general. But it is not so easy to tell whether this is so. Congressional studies do show that politicians tend to vote in ways consistent with the preferences of the interest groups that contribute to their campaigns. Politicians who receive funds from the National Rifle Association (NRA), for example, reliably vote against gun control legislation and any other measures that they view as an infringement on the Second Amendment to the Constitution, which deals with the rights of citizens to bear arms.

PREVENTING CONFLICT BY WAY OF McDONALD'S?

Just because two pieces of information are correlated does not mean that they are causal. There are more fundamental reasons why Russia and the United States are not at war other than the fact that you can get a Big Mac in Moscow.

You could conclude from this example that the NRA is buying votes—that the correlation between its campaign contributions and the votes of members of Congress is actually evidence of causation. This is precisely the sort of case, however, in which one must exercise caution. Causation may be working in reverse here. Perhaps the NRA supports those candidates who vote in favor of its issue positions. Rather than the NRA buying votes with its contributions, maybe members of Congress are attracting NRA contributions with their votes.

How do you sort through such issues? First, for a particular factor or change in situation to cause a change in an outcome, the factor or situation must precede the outcome. World War II could not have caused World War I. If you want to assert a causal relationship between two factors, be sure any change in the value of the one precedes a change in the value of the other. Second, try to rule out the possibility of outside factors that may be responsible for the movement or change. For example, a researcher in France found a strong, positive correlation between young men who play sports and those who took part in riots in the suburbs of France's biggest cities. The argument was that playing sports made young men more aggressive and prone to violence. Still, this finding seems surprising since conventional wisdom and the rationale behind the funding of many sports programs are that they instill discipline and keep kids off the streets—helping to decrease crime. The positive correlation between playing sports and violent behavior could be driven by a third factor. We know that those without jobs are more likely to engage in crime. Perhaps those without jobs also have more time to play sports (see Figure 1.2).

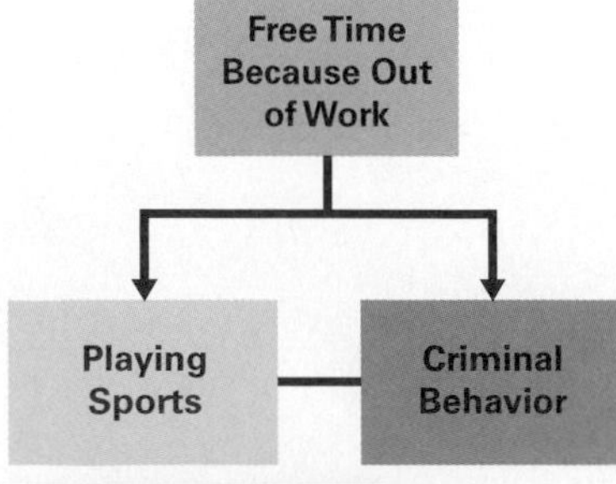

FIGURE 1.2 CORRELATION DOES NOT EQUAL CAUSATION.

Here's another example of correlation not corresponding to causality. Having free time may lead to both criminal behavior and lots of time playing sports.

These examples reinforce an earlier point: The world is complex, and any observed effect rarely has a single cause. We should always be careful, therefore, to consider all variables that might be driving a relationship we have observed.

1.1

1.2

1.3

How Do We Know?

How Do We Know that We Are Right?

How do political scientists arrive at answers that they can be confident are better than simple, single-cause answers? What techniques do they use and what techniques can you use to be a more informed citizen and make better arguments? The explanations in this text are based on the findings of the most recent research in our field. But instead of just presenting you with the results of that research and expecting you to accept it, we want to help you understand how such research is done and how you can employ good research and good thinking both in and out of the classroom. First of all, it's interesting stuff, but more importantly, it will help you see beyond the simplistic explanations about government and politics that you see and hear in the media. Therefore, each chapter contains a feature called "How Do We Know?"

The "How Do We Know?" features begin with an important research question, puzzle, or serious methodological challenge relevant to the material in the chapter and to being a good citizen. For example, when we study political participation, we will examine how we know how to calculate voter turnout. When we study elections, we will examine the challenges involved in determining the effect of campaign spending on election outcomes. We describe each question, puzzle, or challenge in some detail and tell you why political scientists consider it important. We then explain how scholars have tried to answer the question, solve the puzzle, or meet the challenge using the methods and principles discussed in this chapter. Through the "How Do We Know?" features, we hope you will see how political scientists approach their work, and that you will begin to use some of those methods as you observe the activities of American government and the coverage of those events in the media.

Unresolved Debate

Some Political Debates Remain Unresolved

We also want you to see how many of the concepts we discuss in the book have tangible, real-world consequences. We study politics and tackle causal questions because we find issues revolving around elections, presidential power, congressional decisions, and public policy debates to be interesting and important. We, therefore, asked political science scholars and experts to identify what they believe are the biggest causal debates in the field. Then we used their responses to develop a feature on "Unresolved Debates" that examines competing sides of real-world political issues based on real scholarship (rather than simply our opinions). As an example, the chapter on the presidency features a debate over whether presidents' public appeals work as a political strategy.

We enjoy following current politics and political battles. Today, however, lots of partisan bickering and hyperbolic media coverage of politics can turn people off and make them cynical about their government. Pundits and politicians make causal claims at every turn, and it can be difficult—even intimidating—to wade into these arguments and participate in politics. Despite this, for American democracy to survive and thrive, students must engage in politics and in political arguments. We believe that providing you with the tools to explore answers to political questions and make political arguments can make you more confident and give you the skills to be more thoughtful, critical, and empowered citizens.

On MyPoliSciLab

Review the Chapter

Listen to **Chapter 1** on **MyPoliSciLab**

The Purpose of Government

1.1 Explain the purposes of government and why it is necessary, p. 5.

Government is necessary because only government has the broad right to force citizens to do things they otherwise might not do. Citizens grant government this monopoly on force and coercion in order to gain public goods such as roads, military defense, clean water, and education and to protect themselves against fellow citizens trying to enforce their wills through coercion or violence. Individuals give up any claim to use force to get what they want and, in return, get security for themselves, their families, and their property. Still, in a democracy, government receives its power from the people—citizens decide, through a social contract with their leaders, which rights and authorities they will relinquish to government and which they will retain for themselves. Politics in America is a competition about which rights and authorities are best handled by government and what government will do with its authority. America is a constitutional democracy in which the U.S. Constitution identifies the responsibilities of each branch of government: executive, legislative, and judicial. The Constitution also makes clear, through the Bill of Rights, that the government may not do certain things—abridge freedom of speech, religion, or assembly, for example—and that it must do certain things, such as ensure that criminal defendants receive a speedy and fair trial.

Contexts for Studying American Government and Politics

1.2 Compare and contrast the U.S. government with other democratic systems, and identify core values and beliefs within American political culture, p. 11.

The American model of government is one sort among many. By studying models and practices in other countries, we can learn a great deal about our own. America is a democracy, and like all democracies, it is committed to majority rule through elections. Differences in governmental structure and the core values of citizens influence the path of politics in different democracies. We can better understand the major features of American politics and the major factors that drive political decisions and outcomes by comparing our system to governmental systems in other countries. Decisions made throughout our history also influence the path of politics today. We can learn much about how American leaders and citizens behave today by looking at how they dealt with previous situations, and how our past actions affect decisions and outcomes in today's politics. American politics and government are influenced by the uniquely American dominant political culture, sometimes referred to as the American creed. The main ideas and values that make up the creed are individualism, democracy, equality, liberty, and respect for private property and religion.

Thinking About Politics

1.3 Assess the challenges that researchers face when studying causal relationships within politics, p. 15.

Political science focuses on politics and government and how government leaders and citizens behave. Political scientists typically try to determine what factor, or combination of factors, produced a particular outcome. Political scientists strive to be rigorous, thorough, and scientific researchers. To be good citizens and to understand how government and society work, students of American politics should also understand some basic rules of rigorous thinking. One important rule, often violated by politicians and pundits alike, is that correlation does not equal causation. Just because two factors may move together—for example, two countries having a McDonald's franchise and those same countries being at peace—does not mean that one is causing the other.

Learn the Terms

Study and **Review** the **Flashcards**

authoritarian (or totalitarian) system, p. 7
autocracy, p. 12
causal question, p. 15
causation, p. 17
constitutional democracy, p. 12
correlation, p. 17
democracy, p. 12
direct democracy, p. 12
government, p. 5
parliamentary system, p. 13
political culture, p. 13
politics, p. 10
presidential system, p. 13
public goods, p. 8
representative democracy, p. 12
social contract, p. 7
spurious relationship, p. 17

Test Yourself

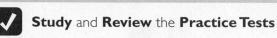

1.1 Explain the purposes of government and why it is necessary.

All of the following are true of governments EXCEPT

- **a.** Governments provide public goods.
- **b.** Governments constitute a social contract.
- **c.** Governments enable citizens to exercise unlimited freedoms.
- **d.** Governments protect citizens from threats.
- **e.** Governments hold a monopoly on force.

1.2 Compare and contrast the U.S. government with other democratic systems, and identify core values and beliefs within American political culture.

Which of the following is NOT a core principle of American democracy?

- **a.** Minority rule
- **b.** Political equality
- **c.** Minority rights
- **d.** Equality before the law
- **e.** Plurality rule

1.3 Assess the challenges that researchers face when studying causal relationships within politics.

Which of the following is true about the challenges that researchers face when studying causal relationships within politics?

- **a.** Researchers face no challenges when studying causal relationships within politics.
- **b.** Most political questions have simple solutions.
- **c.** Journalists and politicians always highlight multiple factors behind outcomes.
- **d.** Most good studies associate more than one causal or explanatory factor with each outcome.
- **e.** When two factors are correlated, it almost always means that one factor caused the other factor.

Explore Further

SUGGESTED READINGS BY TOP SCHOLARS

David Friedman. *Hidden Order: The Economics of Everyday Life.* New York: Harper Business. 1996. Argues that economics can explain everything from general wants, choices, and values to consumer preferences, street crimes, financial speculations, and political campaign spending.

John Gerring. *Social Science Methodology: A Critical Framework.* New York: Cambridge University Press. 2001. An introduction to social science methodology suggesting that task and criteria, not fixed rules of procedure, lead to methodological adequacy.

Gary King, Robert O. Keohane, and Sidney Verba. *Designing Social Inquiry: Scientific Inference in Qualitative Research.* Princeton: Princeton University Press. 1994. A unified approach to developing valid descriptive and causal inference, arguing that qualitative and quantitative researchers face similar difficulties that can be overcome in similar ways.

Steven Levitt and Stephen Dubner. *Freakonomics: A Rogue Economist Explores the Hidden Side of Everything.* New York: William Morrow, 2006. Looks at different puzzles in American society, providing a good illustration of how one social science method can help us understand vexing social issues.

Michael M. Lewis. *Moneyball: The Art of Winning an Unfair Game.* New York: Norton, 2003. Describes how Billy Bean, manager of the Oakland Athletics baseball team, took a modernized, statistics-heavy approach to running an organization and recruiting valuable players overlooked by better-resourced teams.

SUGGESTED WEBSITES

Freakonomics Blog: www.freakonomics.blogs.nytimes.com
The authors of Freakonomics continue their search for new and interesting social science puzzles.

United Kingdom Parliament: www.parliament.uk
Information on the workings of the British government as well as links to the House of Lords and House of Commons.

Constitution for Israel: www.cfisrael.org//home.html
Explains the continuous work of the Constitution, Law, and Justice Committee of the Knesset toward drafting a constitution for the state of Israel.

Robert Wood Johnson Foundation: Coverage for the Uninsured: www.rwjf.org/coverage/index.jsp
Information about various health care issues and health reform plans by a major foundation in the medical policy field.

Initiative and Referendum Institute at the University of Southern California: www.iandrinstitute.org/statewide_i&r.htm
Describes the governmental processes for placing issues on the ballot in each of the 50 states.

2

Listen to **Chapter 2** on **MyPoliSciLab**

Political Culture

RELIGION, LIBERTY, AND EQUALITY

ven as the U.S. Supreme Court heard challenges to President Barack Obama's landmark health reform law in 2012, implementation of the law had begun. The Affordable Care Act, enacted in 2010, included more than $100 billion in funding that enabled federal agencies to begin writing the rules to put the law in place gradually over several years. The act also allowed states to begin developing procedures for their new responsibilities. For example, states could begin to develop the rules for that would guide the "insurance exchanges" where individuals could compare and purchase health care plans.[1]

One provision in the law required that employer health insurance plans provide free contraceptive coverage, including the so-called "morning after" pill, for female employees. The U.S. Department of Health and Human Services (HHS) announced in August 2011 that churches, synagogues, mosques, and other houses of worship would be exempt and would not have to provide such coverage to their employees. Institutions affiliated with these religious groups, such as schools, hospitals, and food pantries, however, would not be exempt.

Religious groups, in particular the U.S. Bishops Conference of the Catholic Church, expressed concern that the exemption did not apply to religiously affiliated organizations. Catholic teaching does not include the use of artificial contraception. To the bishops, the federal policy required Catholic institutions, such as hospitals, to subsidize a practice contrary to the teachings of their faith. They began lobbying HHS to change its ruling and allow more institutions to fall under the umbrella of the church exemption. On January 20, 2012, however, HHS confirmed its original decision. Presenting the issue as one of women's access to vital health services, the agency kept the religious exemption as it had previously been defined.[2]

The response was immediate and vocal. Catholic officials, conservative commentators, and Republican politicians denounced the agency's action as an assault on religious liberty. After three

2.1 Define political culture, and explain how certain values and beliefs achieve dominance within a society, p. 25.

2.2 Illustrate how the key values and beliefs of the American creed shape politics and government today, p. 31.

2.3 Evaluate the consequences of American political culture such as limited government and a weak sense of sovereign power, p. 40.

2.4 Describe the major challenges and alternatives to the dominant political culture, p. 48.

LIBERTY AND EQUALITY Provisions in President Barack Obama's Affordable Care Act requiring coverage for contraceptive services, including some services that opponents considered equivalent to abortion, led to a dispute between the demands for religious liberty and individual equality in American politics.

The Big Picture What is the difference between public opinion and political culture? Author John J. Coleman defines both terms and explains the paradox of American political culture in which we have the same values—democracy, religious freedom, right to property—but disagree strongly on how they are interpreted.

The Basics What is political culture and how is it formed? In this video, you will hear how some people describe American political culture. In the process, you will discover what core political values Americans share, how they are formed, and what major ideologies American embrace.

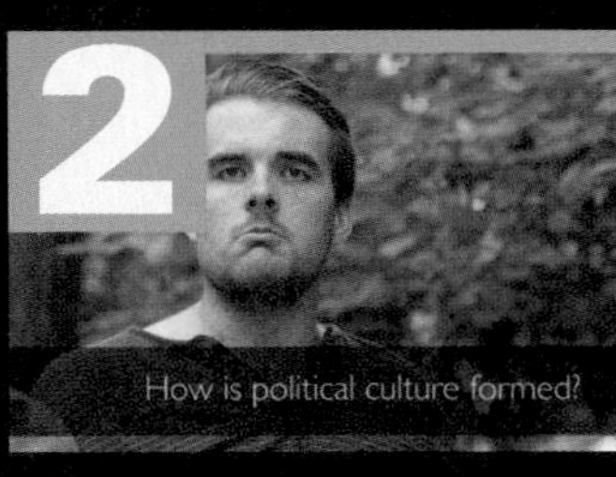
How is political culture formed?

In Context Discuss the importance of American exceptionalism in American political culture. In this video, University of Oklahoma political scientist Allyson Shortle examines the core values that make up American political culture. She also discusses how these values gave rise to the American Dream.

Think Like a Political Scientist Find out what questions political scientists are investigating in the field of political culture. Southern Methodist University political scientist James Matthew Wilson assesses the impact of globalization and the emergence of ethnic and religious subcultures in the United States.

In the Real World Should the government correct the gap between the rich and the poor in the United States? This segment examines two opposing social movements—the Occupy movement and the Tea Party movement—and it considers the differences between their expectations for government.

So What? Should the government be large or small? The Founders called this seemingly simple question "The Great Debate". Author John J. Coleman discusses how this enduring part of our national political culture interacts with our personal experience, forcing us to take sides in this key question.

weeks of outcry, the Obama administration announced a new policy that would require insurance companies, rather than the religious institutions, to cover the cost of the contraceptives. With the revised policy, a new round of criticism emerged: Under what authority could the federal government require a company to provide a service and then demand that the company not be compensated for providing the service? Critics argued that this requirement was antithetical to American beliefs in free enterprise and property rights.

As the debates over religious liberty and property rights simmered, groups supportive of the health care law and the HHS regulations moved to counter the criticisms. Democrats in the House of Representatives convened an unofficial panel to hear testimony about contraceptive coverage and the role it played in women's equality. One witness, Georgetown University Law School student Sandra Fluke, testified about the high cost of contraception as one reason the regulations mattered for women. Fluke's testimony caught the attention of radio talk show host Rush Limbaugh, who publicly disparaged her. Limbaugh's comments soon became the focus of national attention, and critics portrayed them as part of a conservative "war on women."[3]

Polls began to show that a majority of the public viewed the issue as one of women's equal access to health care coverage rather than religious liberty or a matter of private property rights. The bishops, however, were undeterred. In May 2012, the bishops announced that 43 Catholic institutions had filed lawsuits in 12 federal district courts challenging the law as a violation of religious freedom.[4]

The intense conflict over the contraceptive mandate in the Affordable Care Act reflects beliefs that are part of American political culture: the belief in religious freedom, the belief in economic liberty and private property rights, and the belief in equality. Most Americans would say they believe fervently in these values, but sometimes values are in conflict. Such conflict is difficult not only for citizens, who must sort out their views and their priorities, but also for politicians, who must determine how to act in the wake of competing views.

More so than in many other economically advanced countries, religious belief is an important part of America's self-perception.[5] But it is only one part. Despite widely held beliefs, much room still exists in American politics for deep conflict about values. For example, to what degree should a public official bring his or her religious values into decisions about public policy? The value of free speech is deeply cherished in American political culture, but what about speech that is vile and hateful toward particular groups? Individuals should be able to achieve and earn all they can, but is it nonetheless appropriate through taxation to take hard-earned resources from one group in order to improve the opportunities for another? Americans are inescapably faced with difficult choices and questions. At their deepest, these choices and questions affect Americans' self-identity and their understanding of what America is and what it means to be American.

political culture
the values and beliefs of citizens toward the political system and toward themselves as actors in it.

2.1
2.2
2.3
2.4

What Does It Mean to Be an American?

2.1 Define political culture and explain how certain values and beliefs achieve dominance within a society.

What makes Americans *American*? Given the country's remarkable diversity, it cannot be a shared ethnic heritage. Nor can it be a long, shared history—Americans arrived here in waves of immigration, so the starting point of their sense of being American varies widely. For most Americans, what defines being an American is a set of beliefs or ideals. The idea that individuals pursuing opportunity can make a better life for themselves, often referred to as the American Dream, is widely shared. This is part of American political culture. For a further discussion of the American Dream, see *Unresolved Debate: Does Belief in the American Dream Lead Americans to Oppose Government Programs?*

Culture refers to a way of thinking or mode of behavior. **Political culture** refers to the basic values, beliefs, attitudes, predispositions, and expectations of citizens

2.1

2.2

2.3

2.4

Unresolved Debate

Does Belief in the American Dream Lead Americans to Oppose Government Programs?

The idea of the American Dream is a powerful aspect of American political culture. It suggests that all individuals have the opportunity to pursue their goals and dreams and change their fortune in life. In recent years, discussion of the American Dream has often included a parallel discussion about income inequality. The degree to which American income distribution has in fact changed and the causal factors behind the change are the subject of substantial scholarly debate. Some arguments suggest that the income gap has grown, whereas others suggest that the degree of change has been overstated. An accompanying debate asks whether increased inequality is inherently a bad thing. And scholars have also asked whether belief in the American Dream weakens public support for government programs, even if Americans think inequality is growing. Does the American Dream lead Americans to oppose government programs?

THE AMERICAN DREAM

References to the American Dream, and to fears that it may be eroding, can be symbolically powerful in American politics.

YES

Political scientist Larry Bartels argues that the belief in the American Dream during a time of increasing income inequality does not lead to more support for government programs.[a] Using survey data, he argues that:

- Americans have a vague sense about growing income inequality.
- Americans do not have much knowledge about inequality in practice.
- Americans do not identify specific or new government programs as being necessary to reduce the gap in income distribution.

NO

Political scientists Benjamin Page and Lawrence Jacobs see the combination of changes in income distribution and enduring belief in the American Dream as potentially spurring support for government programs.[b] They assert, using survey data, that:

- Americans know about growing income gaps.
- Americans care about these gaps.
- Americans support government remedies to address the gaps.

CONTRIBUTING TO THE DEBATE

Identifying causal mechanisms related to political culture is difficult because culture in its most powerful form becomes such a default way of thinking that an individual may not even be aware of the specific assumptions that are guiding their thinking—rather, a belief "just is." This feature of political culture complicates the use of public opinion surveys, an important tool in social science analysis. Creative experiments with alternative question wording can help minimize this problem.

WHAT DO YOU THINK?

1. Should we expect belief in the American Dream to change as income distribution changes? Why or why not?
2. Income gaps can grow because lower income Americans see their incomes decline and higher income Americans see their income rise, or they can grow because both groups receive more income but the income growth is larger at the top. Would support for government programs or belief in the American Dream differ in these two scenarios?

[a]Benjamin I. Page and Lawrence R. Jacobs, *Class War? What Americans Really Think about Economic Inequality.* (Chicago: University of Chicago Press, 2009).
[b]Larry M. Bartels, *Unequal Democracy: The Political Economy of the New Gilded Age.* (New York: Russell Sage, 2008).

toward their political system and toward themselves as participants in it. Take, for example, the value of freedom of speech. Survey results over a long period of time suggest that freedom of speech is a bedrock value in the United States, enshrined in the Constitution, with 90 percent or more of the public agreeing with statements such as "I believe in free speech for all no matter what their views might be." When evaluating an issue concerning speech, most Americans start from the premise that free speech is important and should be encouraged and that they have a right to speak their minds. Freedom of speech is part of American political culture.

Political culture is not the same as public opinion. Public opinion focuses more on the issues of the day and is more susceptible to change, even over relatively short periods. It reveals, for example, what the public believes about a particular candidate or issue. Political culture is a broader, more permanent set of beliefs. Whether the public approves of the president's job performance is in the realm of public opinion; the idea that presidents should be guided by the will of the people is in the realm of political culture. Culture is pervasive and present in ways that you may not even be aware of, such as in the symbols used by candidates and organizations, in the language used to appeal to people, in the kinds of themes in popular culture that Americans seem to "naturally" gravitate toward, in what Americans assume to be important. Off-the-cuff comments such as "it's a free country" convey how deeply political culture influences our thinking and carry many layers of meaning for most Americans.

Political Culture Provides a Framework for Political Evaluation

Political culture does not necessarily explain how Americans will respond to every situation. For instance, we noted that more than 90 percent of Americans consistently say they believe in free speech for all, regardless of the views of the speakers. But when pushed, Americans will sometimes back away from this commitment. In surveys during World War II, for example, only 15 to 20 percent of Americans were willing to allow fascists and communists to hold meetings and express their political views.[6] Table 2.1 gives other examples of Americans' support for free speech in specific circumstances, including racist and antireligious speech. Even though support for free

TABLE 2.1 SUPPORT FOR FREE SPEECH IN SPECIFIC CIRCUMSTANCES (PERCENTAGES)

	Year of Survey			
	1977	**1988**	**1998**	**2008**
Allow book in library that				
States blacks are genetically inferior	61%	62%	63%	64%
Is against churches and religion	60	64	69	71
Advocates homosexuality	55	60	70	76
Argues against elections and for military rule	55	57	67	69
Allow someone to teach in college who				
Believes blacks are genetically inferior	41	41	47	45
Is against churches and religion	39	45	57	60
Is a homosexual man	49	57	74	79
Argues against elections and for military rule	34	37	51	51
Allow someone to make a speech in your community who				
Believes blacks are genetically inferior	59	61	63	58
Is against churches and religion	64	70	74	76
Is a homosexual man	62	70	81	82
Argues against elections and for military rule	50	56	66	65

Source: General Social Survey 2008.

2.1

2.2

2.3

2.4

American creed
the dominant political culture in the United States, marked by a set of beliefs in individualism, democracy, liberty, property, and religion, tied together by the value of equality.

speech has been increasing in recent decades, many Americans find their principles wavering in certain scenarios.

Significant inconsistencies often appear when moving from abstract beliefs to concrete decisions and issues, but abstract principles still matter. Most of you would agree with the old saying that "honesty is the best policy." You likely also believe that people should obey the law, that laws should be enforced, and that enforcement of the law should be done fairly. Yet few people think being brutally honest is right if it would needlessly hurt someone. And most of us who drive have probably found ourselves, on occasion, driving over the posted speed limit when there were no police watching (we plead guilty).

Does that inconsistency mean your general belief that honesty is the best policy is a farce? No. You start with that policy when you evaluate what to do. The belief provides a framework for decision making. The confirmation that beliefs and values matter is that even when we violate them, we feel compelled to understand and justify why we do so.

Political culture works the same way. It provides a general framework and a starting point to evaluate issues, candidates, and the actions of public officials. Politicians or political activists looking to score a victory can also exploit it. They know that these themes and beliefs resonate with the public, so they adjust their language accordingly.

The American Creed Is the Dominant Political Culture in the United States

The dominant political culture in the United States consists of beliefs in individualism, democracy, liberty, property rights, and religious freedom, all tied together by the value of equality. This set of beliefs has been labeled with many terms; we will call it the **American creed**.[7] It provides the frame of reference most Americans use to evaluate candidates and issues. For that reason, politicians make heavy use of this frame of reference to reach Americans, which then reinforces its importance. Barack Obama spoke of "the enduring power of our ideals: democracy, liberty, opportunity, and unyielding hope" on election night in 2008, and in his 2012 State of the Union Address, he noted America's support globally "for the rights and dignity of all human beings . . . [for] policies that lead to strong and stable democracies and open markets."

These beliefs are ideals, and as such they are general rather than specific. To say there is a widely shared political culture is *not* to say that Americans agree on all the specifics about politics and that there is no conflict in the United States. It is also not to say that these beliefs always describe the political reality for all groups. Even a passing glance at American political history reveals that not all groups have had full property rights or access to democratic politics. Instead, to say that there is a strong, widely held political culture is to say that most Americans start with a general set of beliefs and predispositions when they think about issues. It is to say that most Americans share a set of general presumptions about politics and that most political debate operates within those general boundaries. The debate within those boundaries, however, can be intense. Challenges to the American creed have also had a significant place in American politics, and they will be discussed later in this chapter.

In many countries, including those with far less diverse populations than the United States, competing political cultures are at the core of politics. There might be competition between a secular and religious outlook, between one language and another, or between one region of the country and others. In industrialized democracies, one of the most common splits has been between a capitalist orientation and a socialist orientation. Generally, a socialist worldview calls for a strong role for government in owning or heavily regulating significant proportions of industry and a broad range of redistributive programs to offset inequalities that result from economic competition. Socialist worldviews emphasize the importance of social class conflict, equality and fairness, and the need for government's "visible hand" to guide the economy. Capitalist worldviews, on the other hand, argue that the greatest number of individuals thrive best when ownership of industry is private with minimal limitations imposed by government. Capitalist worldviews emphasize the importance of individuals pursuing their goals, liberty and opportunity, and the need for individual decision making in the market to be the "invisible hand" that guides the economy. European countries such as Spain and France regularly pit equally competitive socialist parties against capitalist parties. These different perspectives offer fundamentally different beliefs to guide citizens and politicians.

The population of the United States gradually became more ethnically varied as waves of immigration reshaped the demographic landscape, and it is now among the most diverse of any country in history. Americans named well over one hundred ethnicities when identifying their ancestry in the 2011 American Community Survey conducted by the U.S. Census. In some parts of the country, notably California and Texas, the terms *minority* and *majority* are becoming outmoded as the non-Hispanic white majority becomes a minority of the population and current minority groups such as blacks, Hispanic whites, and Asians together become the majority, a development that is likely to be mirrored elsewhere in the United States.[8] This extraordinary diversity makes American political culture all the more interesting. We might expect that such demographic diversity would lead to sharply competing sets of basic political values and beliefs—competing political cultures—but that has not been the case.

Considering the varied backgrounds of the American population, the agreement in the United States around a set of general political beliefs is remarkable. Other conflicting beliefs, discussed at the end of this chapter, have played an important role in American politics, but there is nonetheless a widespread adherence in spirit, if not always in day-to-day politics, to the general ideals embodied in the American creed. However, that agreement has not been without significant racial, ethnic, and religious strife.

Through all the waves of immigration, charges have been made that new immigrants were too "different" to fit into American life. As the children and grandchildren of immigrants grow up within American culture, they often find themselves culturally at odds with previous generations. Efforts to "Americanize" immigrants through instruction in values, culture, language, childrearing methods, household management, and dress were explicit in past immigration waves and implicit in more recent attempts to make English the official language of the United States. One argument holds that without knowledge of the dominant language, immigrants cannot fully partake of political and economic liberty, democracy, or equality, which will set them apart from the American creed and corrode American social cohesion. Language, according to this view, acts like glue and lets Americans talk, share ideas, and debate the meaning of the American creed. Critics argue that the evidence to support this causal relationship is thin. Societies with single languages may still have high levels of conflict, whereas other societies with multiple languages may function consensually.[9] Moreover, critics point out that in the late nineteenth and early twentieth centuries, it was common in American cities for official documents to be printed in multiple languages, but immigrants nonetheless adopted American creed beliefs, which often served as their main motivation for immigrating to the United States.[10]

American Creed Beliefs Became Dominant for Several Reasons

Why one particular set of values and beliefs would become dominant in the face of such diversity is a puzzle. One explanation is that Americans hear numerous messages from politicians, economic leaders, and educators that reinforce and tout the superiority of those beliefs. Other messages that reinforce political culture come from outside politics, for example, the entertainment media. Popular culture, whether fictional or based on actual events, tends to embrace the individualistic ideals and wants of Americans, celebrating the self-reliant individual who overcomes the odds.

This explanation is helpful, but it does not tell us why Americans believe and "buy into" these repeated messages. Scholars have proposed other explanations for the

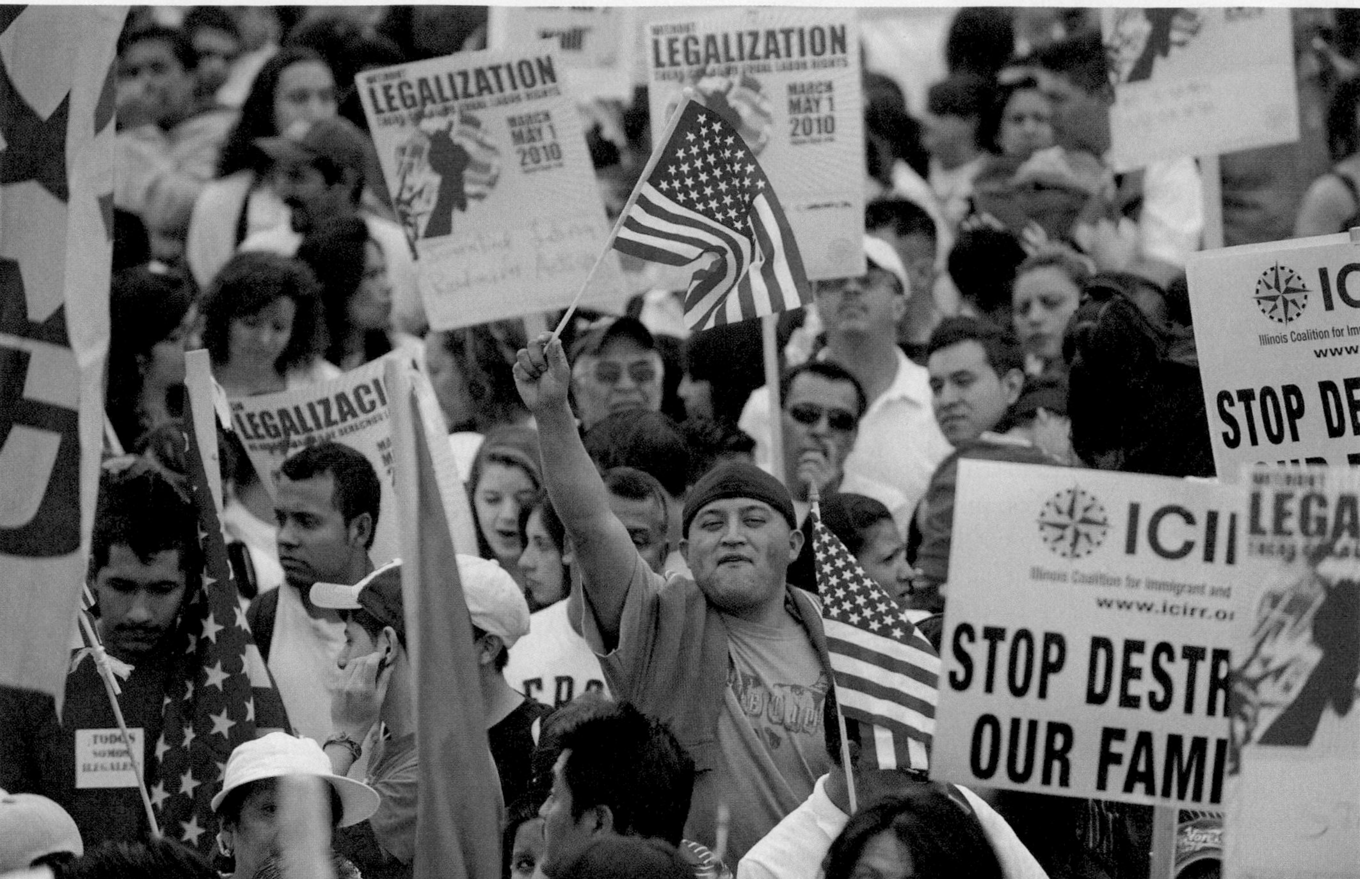

DOES IMMIGRATION THREATEN NATIONAL COHESION?

Even though they acknowledge the contributions of immigrants to society and often are children or grandchildren of immigrants themselves, many Americans worry that immigration threatens the sense of national identity conveyed by shared values. Advocates for expanded immigration stress that the historical record shows that immigrants unite around core American creed beliefs.

dominance of the American creed. Addressing the question "Why is there no socialism in the United States?" one scholar offered three reasons.[11] First, because white men were given the vote early in the country's history, the political system in the United States was relatively more open to working-class influence than in other countries. It did not take a socialist movement or party for workers to gain these rights. Second, prosperity in the United States made it difficult for competing political cultures to take firm root; the creed seemed to work. And last, in contrast to European countries, the United States did not experience the same history of strict and hierarchical class relations that might have been necessary for an alternative to the creed to take root.[12]

Other scholars have been less optimistic, arguing that government's use of repressive tactics and judicial rulings played a stronger role in thwarting opposition to the creed than these interpretations suggest. They point to examples ranging from nineteenth-century labor activists being beaten and jailed to investigations such as those launched by Senator Joseph McCarthy in the 1950s to root out suspected communists in government, entertainment, and other industries as evidence that the government has often taken action to squelch dissent against the American creed.[13] Although these efforts to thwart alternative views are certainly important parts of the American experience, in a comparative context they fall short of the widespread repression seen in some other regimes or the complete denial of rights, such as freedom of the press, found in others.

These competing explanations are insufficient on their own, but together they show the many factors at play that sustain the preeminence of the American creed. A widespread popular mind-set, based on life experience, that the creed works and produces individual opportunity is the broad foundation for the creed's success. Upon that foundation, government tactics at times have likely had chilling effects on targeted groups. Because the public is already receptive to the message, the reiteration of the culture's beliefs by politicians, media figures, and entertainers reinforces the place of these beliefs in American life and carries them to the next generation. These repeated messages discourage cracks from forming in the foundation.

In sum, it is reasonable to describe American political culture as one based in the American creed, but—as this chapter will show—consensus does not eliminate conflict. There is substantial conflict in American politics within the confines of the creed. How much weight to place on each belief and what the beliefs themselves mean are often up for debate. In addition, other competing beliefs have had important impacts on American political life. These alternative approaches have mixed and mingled with the beliefs of the creed, proving that American political culture is dynamic and changing.

equality
the value that all Americans should be treated the same under the law, be able to influence government, and have equal opportunity to succeed in life.

The Beliefs of the American Creed

2.2 Illustrate how the key values and beliefs of the American creed shape politics and government today.

A sense of **equality** and freedom underlies each of the specific beliefs of the creed—individualism, democracy, liberty, property, and religion.[14] Americans value treating every person the same under the law, being able to influence government, having an equal opportunity to succeed in life, and being free to make their own choices about their path in life. These expectations do not mean that everyone will or should have equal results, but that all people should "play by the same rules." The American experience has fallen short of these ideals many times in many places, however. We will discuss these shortfalls in this and other chapters. For now, as you read the descriptions that follow, remember that the

LOVE, WAR, AND EQUALITY

Two U.S. Navy officers embrace in December 2011, after the repeal of the "Don't Ask, Don't Tell" policy that prohibited gay and lesbian service members from disclosing their sexuality.

Explore on MyPoliSciLab

Can You Get Ahead in America?

Whether or not the American Dream is still attainable is a question that goes to the core of American national identity. In 1994 and 2010, survey researchers asked Americans "Do you think your own standard of living is better than that of your parents?" In both years, the majority believe the Dream exists, but there are distinct differences across generations caused by economic factors such as the unemployment rate.

Generational Differences

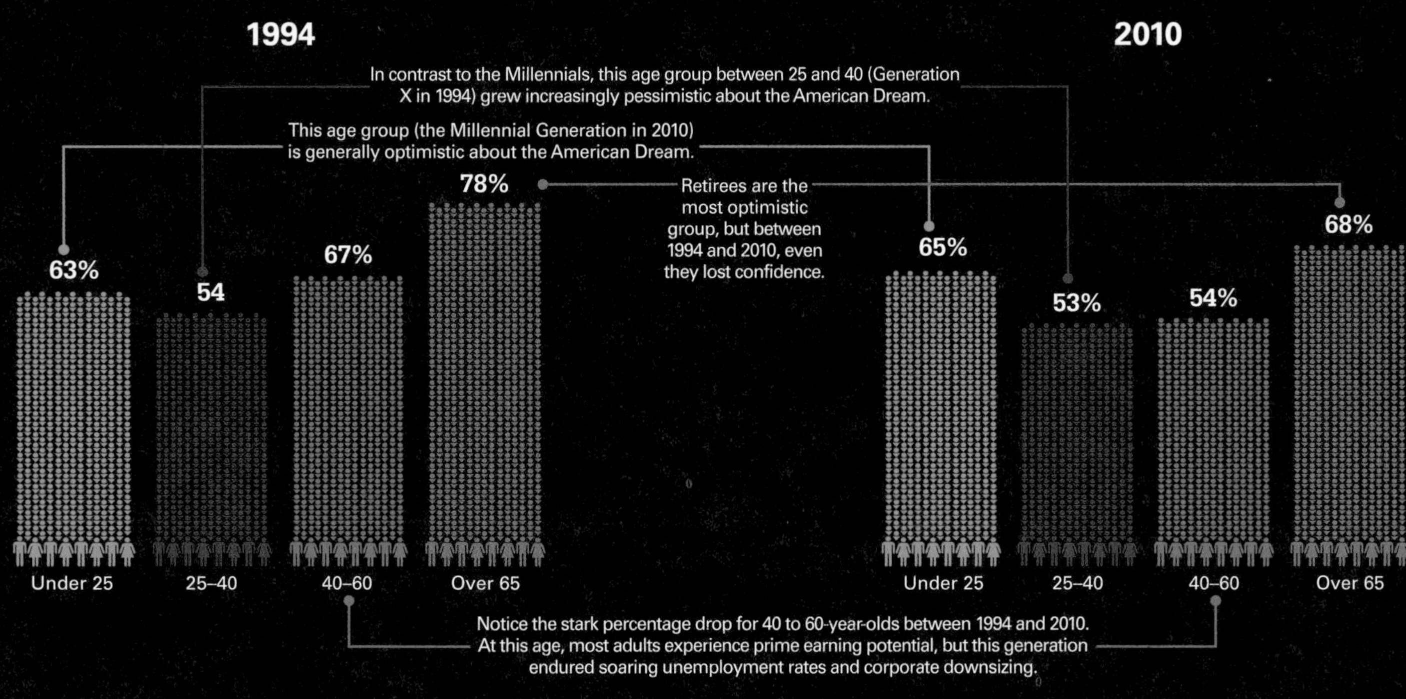

Unemployment in the United States

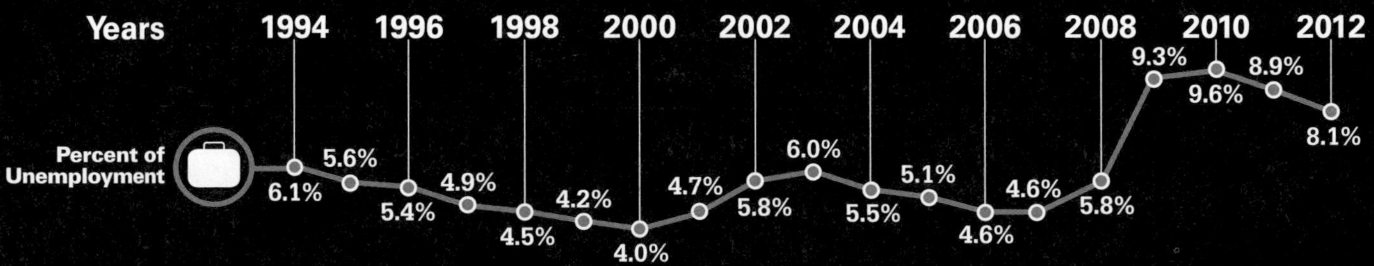

SOURCE: Data from General Social Survey, 1994 and 2010; and the U.S. Bureau of Labor Statistics.

Investigate Further

Concept What is included in the American Dream? One belief in the American Dream is that the next generation will do better than the one before it. It is measured by asking people if they think they are doing better than their parents at the same stage of life.

Connection How do the generations differ when it comes to the American Dream? Millennials face high unemployment, but they are more likely to believe in the dream than 25 to 40-year-olds in 2010. Generation X, now middle aged, was increasingly less likely to believe in the Dream from 1994 to 2010.

Cause Why is Generation X less likely to believe in the Dream? Initial and prime earning years for this age group were accompanied by recessions in 1990, 2000, and 2009, and by spikes in unemployment that affect both them and their children's generation.

emphasis here is on the general ideals to which Americans say they aspire and how those ideals affect the ways Americans think about politics and government.

individualism
a belief that all individuals should be able to succeed to the maximum extent possible given their talents and abilities, regardless of race, religion, or other group characteristics.

Individualism: People Should Choose Their Own Path Through Life

For most Americans, individuals—not groups or classes—are the fundamental political unit. Americans believe in **individualism**, meaning that all individuals should be able to succeed to the maximum extent possible given their talents and abilities. Americans' thoughts about individualism and freedom are closely connected: the leading example of what Americans mean by freedom is the ability of individuals to choose their own path in life (see Table 2.2). Americans generally believe that individuals should be treated equally, regardless of group membership or other characteristics, and be free to pursue their dreams and aspirations. Marketers recognize the power of these cultural beliefs and advertise how their products, from automobiles on the open road to the personalized music experience of an MP3 player, allow individuals to live as they please. Presidential candidates are similarly not shy about casting their biographies as triumphs of American individualism. From Ronald Reagan's rising from his modest, Midwest roots through Barack Obama's mixed-race heritage and his experience of being raised largely by a single parent and grandparents, presidential candidates hope their stories resonate with voters as examples of American opportunity and success.

Americans generally prefer that individuals have an equal chance for success rather than a guarantee of equal results. A 2012 survey found that about two-thirds of Americans disagreed with the idea that success in life is mostly determined outside an individual's control. The same proportion agreed with the idea that hard work leads to success. Ninety percent said they admired people who got rich by working hard. About 90 percent of adult Americans agreed that "our society should do what is necessary to make sure that everyone has an equal opportunity to succeed." And most Americans in an earlier survey—by a margin of three to one—placed the responsibility for failure to succeed on the individual rather than on society.[15] These views do not mean that Americans oppose government helping those in need, especially in a targeted fashion such as financial aid for college, food aid programs, and medical assistance, but they demonstrate that Americans place a strong emphasis on individual responsibility.

In preferring equality of opportunity to equality of outcome, the United States is unique. In a 2006 survey of 33 countries, the United States ranked 32nd in the percentage of respondents saying that it should be a responsibility of government to

TABLE 2.2 WHAT FREEDOM MEANS TO AMERICANS (IN PERCENTAGES)

Characteristics of Freedom	One of the Most Important Things About Freedom	Extremely Important	Very Important	Moderately, Somewhat, or Not Too Important
Having the power to choose and do what I want in life	45%	27%	22%	6%
Being able to express unpopular ideas without fearing for my safety	40	29	24	7
The right to participate in politics and elections	36	27	26	11
Having a government that doesn't spy on me or interfere in my life	30	26	32	12
Being left alone to do what I want	27	23	28	22

Note: Percentages add across each row. Survey respondents were asked for each characteristic of freedom whether it was one of the most important things about freedom; extremely important; very important; or moderately, somewhat, or not too important an aspect of freedom.

Source: General Social Survey 2000.

2.1

2.2

2.3

2.4

TABLE 2.3 PUBLIC PERCEPTIONS OF THE CAUSES OF INCOME INEQUALITY

Survey Question: Next, we'd like to know why you think it is, that in America today, some people have better jobs and higher incomes than others do. I'm going to read you some possible explanations, and I want you to tell me how important you think each is. Because . . .

	Very Important	Somewhat Important	Not Important
Some people don't get a chance to get a good education	55%	35%	9%
Some people just don't work as hard	45	42	13
Some people have more in-born ability to learn	33	43	23
Discrimination holds some people back	26	50	23
Government policies have helped high-income workers more	25	39	35
Some people just choose low-paying jobs	19	38	41
God made people different from one another	22	26	49

Note: Percentages add across rows.

Source: Data presented in Larry Bartels, *Unequal Democracy: The Political Economy of the New Gilded Age* (Princeton, NJ: Princeton University Press, 2008).

"reduce income differences between the rich and the poor."[16] Almost 95 percent of citizens in Portugal saw reducing income differences as something government definitely or probably should be involved in, as did about 85 percent in Spain and Israel and 75 to 80 percent in France, Finland, Venezuela, and Ireland. About half of Americans agreed that government should do something, but only 30 percent saw this task as something government "definitely" should be doing.[17] A different survey showed that asking about "people with high incomes and people with low incomes" rather than "the rich and the poor" resulted in only one-third of Americans stating government had a responsibility to reduce income differences.[18] Examining surveys across a broader time period produces the same result: Americans are just as likely as citizens in other countries to think that income inequality is a problem, but they are less likely than citizens of other countries to believe that government has an obligation to reduce income differences.[19] Americans are more likely to see economic inequality as something created by personal opportunities rather than by fate or the actions of others (see Table 2.3).

Democracy: Government Actions Should Reflect the Will of the People

The second belief of the American creed is that government should adhere to democratic principles. Democracy is a form of government in which the people rule. This rule can take place directly, through participation by the people in actual lawmaking, or indirectly, through free elections in which the people choose representatives to make laws. Between elections, people have indirect input in democracy through a variety of means—hearings, writing to public officials, signing petitions, and lobbying, for example, and Americans partake of these means of participation more than citizens in other countries. Because all segments of American society do not engage in voting and these other activities equally, many political observers are highly critical of the performance of American democracy compared to the ideal. To Americans, the ideal suggests four criteria in particular: the will of the people, the consent of the governed, equal opportunity to influence government, and equal treatment by the law.

THE WILL OF THE PEOPLE First, government actions should reflect the will of the people. The people's wishes are not always easy to identify, but the general principle is that they should guide government as much as possible.[20] Frequent elections enable the people to remove officials who have not lived up to this standard. The United States holds elections on a regular schedule. In many other countries, legislative elections at the national level can occur as many as five years apart and have to be "called" by government officials.

THE CONSENT OF THE GOVERNED Second, and closely related, power is granted to public officials by the consent of the governed. In this view, power that is exercised by a public official is always an extension of the public will and can potentially be reclaimed by the people. At its most extreme, the notion of consent means that citizens have a right to abolish the government altogether if they conclude that it is using power inappropriately.[21]

EQUAL OPPORTUNITY TO INFLUENCE GOVERNMENT Third, to Americans, democracy also means an equal opportunity to influence government. This includes not only the opportunity to vote, but also access to government by citizens from all walks of life. Americans are uneasy with the idea—although recognizing that it is the reality—that some individuals or groups may have "inside connections" with government officials, so that their views are more influential than those of the "average" person.[22] In 2012, 75 percent of Americans agreed that "too much power is concentrated in the hands of a few large companies," about the same percentage as during the previous 20 years.[23] Candidates and public officials go to great lengths to clobber their opponents for being cronies of "special interests."

EQUAL TREATMENT BY THE LAW Fourth, to Americans, democracy means equal treatment by the law. Laws, regulations, and penalties should be enforced regardless of the social stature of the individual. This does not mean that judges, juries, or public officials should ignore circumstances when determining penalties or benefits. Rather, it means that the same actions taken under the same set of circumstances should result in equal penalties or benefits, regardless of the social status, religion, ethnicity, race, income, or other characteristics of the individuals involved. Of course, Americans recognize and are concerned when these ideals are violated in everyday life. For example, wealthier individuals can hire more talented lawyers and thus increase the odds that a case works out to their advantage. The fact that Americans are troubled by such inequities is a sign of the potency of the idea of equal treatment.

Liberty: Government Restraint on Individual Behavior Should Be Minimal

The third belief in the American creed is liberty, which was the dominant demand of the American Revolution. Americans often define **liberty** as freedom from government restriction on the exercise of one's rights; that is, whenever possible, government should let people do as they please. Government's obligation, in this view, is not to make decisions for you about what would make your life better, but to protect your right to decide what a "better life" is and to protect your freedom to go for it.

NATURAL RIGHTS Associated with this belief is the conviction that government does not grant rights. Rather, rights are inherent, part of what makes people human: These are **natural rights**. Americans consider the rights to free speech, to associate in groups, and to hold and practice religious faith to be effectively sewn into human beings upon birth, not rights that government gives us. The Declaration of Independence provides a clear statement of this idea: "We hold these truths to be self-evident, that all men are created equal, that they are endowed by their Creator with certain unalienable rights, that among these are life, liberty, and the pursuit of happiness." Government's job is to protect these rights from being violated by other citizens and by government at other levels.[24]

GOVERNMENT'S ROLE IN SECURING LIBERTY To Americans, government secures liberty either by not restricting rights or by restricting them only when their expression has a negative impact on the rights of other individuals. The freedoms of speech and assembly are considered fundamental rights, but government commonly restricts them. Slanderous and libelous speech can lead to punishment. Marching and demonstrating without a permit can result in fines or other sanctions. When Americans believe national security is threatened, they often tolerate what would be considered unacceptable infringements on liberty at other times. Any of these limitations can be a matter of great political controversy.

liberty
the belief that government should leave people free to do as they please and exercise their natural rights to the maximum extent possible.

natural rights
rights inherent in the essence of people as human beings; government does not provide these rights but can restrict the exercise of them.

2.1

2.2

2.3

2.4

property rights
the belief that people should be able to acquire, own, and use goods and assets free from government constraints, as long as their acquisition and use does not interfere with the rights of other individuals.

Individuals in other countries view liberty in somewhat different ways from those in America. In Scandinavian countries, liberty requires being given something by government in order to thrive fully as a human being. This may mean health care, education, housing, or any number of other services. In this view, the freedom to speak or to earn a living is weak unless citizens are given the tools to use these freedoms effectively. For example, without a health care system to provide for all citizens, the promise of "life" or the "pursuit of happiness" is empty. Without high-quality education for all, "free speech" quickly becomes the province of a relatively small elite. Without both of these, one's opportunities to pursue success, whether in one's career or elsewhere, are sharply limited.

In the United States, the perspective is different. Many or even most Americans may agree that universal health care and quality education are important goals for government. However, relatively few would say that liberty is absent if government does not provide these services. Even in the major debate over health care reform in 2009 and 2010, the argument that reform was necessary to promote liberty was rarely heard. Proponents for reform made arguments on other grounds, and liberty was more often entered into the debate by those opposed to expanding the government's role in this policy area.

Property: Individuals Should Be Free to Acquire, Own, and Use Goods and Assets

Americans have long thought of property ownership as providing individuals with incentives to safeguard their own rights as well as the rights of others in the community. Through the 1830s, property ownership was a common qualification for voting. Throughout much of American history, the idea of owning a home has been considered a part of the American Dream itself, a step in life that grounded a person more deeply in his or her local community. Americans believe in extensive **property rights**—that people should be able to acquire, own, and use goods and assets free from government constraints, so long as their acquisition and use do not interfere with the rights of other individuals. Property rights are therefore twofold: freedom to acquire property and freedom to use property.

FREEDOM TO ACQUIRE PROPERTY First, people should have the right to acquire private property without limitations. This means that individuals should be paid whatever they can command in the economic marketplace for their goods or their work. With their talents or resources, individuals should be able to obtain property—money, goods, services, real estate, stocks—with minimal meddling by society or government. You may think it excessive or even be angry that a professional athlete or movie star makes $20 million a year, or that a corporate executive receives $20 million when leaving a company, but few Americans believe that this level of pay should be prohibited.[25]

FREEDOM TO USE PROPERTY Second, individuals should be free to use property with few restrictions. Some acceptable restrictions protect the property of others or protect some societal interest. Many communities prohibit the use of jet skis on lakes or at certain hours, and most have noise ordinances of some type. Another restriction is the ban on building a house on sensitive wetlands.

Exactly how property rights coexist with democracy in the confines of a single political culture is an enduring puzzle. Historically, one prominent school of thought feared that the growth of democracy would lead to property rights being tossed aside: Voters with little property would use government to take wealth from others. The Framers of the U.S. Constitution shared this fear. To them, keeping the fruits of one's labor was considered essential to preserving other freedoms—once government believed it had free access and entitlement to your property, it was a short step for it to invade other aspects of your freedom. Because democracy might pose a risk to property rights, the Framers believed a careful structure of institutions, rules, and procedures was needed to protect property from the people's "passions." Another approach saw property rights and political freedoms as mutually reinforcing.[26] The individual freedoms prized in a market economy—the ability to make choices with minimal government restrictions on one's action—will be attractive as political liberties as well.

BUILDING IN A DANGER ZONE

Property rights generally confer on individuals the right to use their property as they see fit. However, around the country, individuals build houses in zones where tornadoes, fires, landslides, floods, and hurricanes are common. How far should government go to restrict or regulate such building?

Thus, in this view, the spread of free markets and property rights will themselves generate support for the protection of property rights because of general support for the ideas of individual liberty and personal freedom from government intrusion.

Political scientists have noted a third way in which the two can fit together: Property rights, as expressed in activities such as shopping, could lead to skepticism about government, as individuals might perceive the free market as ultimately more democratic and equal than the political system. In the market, you can buy a product—like anyone else—if you can afford it: Every dollar is equal. By contrast, to many individuals, the political system might not seem nearly so open and understandable, and the process to obtain an economic benefit from the government can appear to be much more time consuming and complicated. The twin perceptions that it can be difficult to get economic gains through government and that the economic system is relatively open and accessible may reduce, though certainly not eliminate, the number of demands placed on government to take property from one group and give it to another.[27]

religious freedom
a belief that individuals should be free to choose and practice their religious faith and that government should not establish any particular religion as the official or preferred religion.

Religion: Individuals Should Be Free to Practice Their Religious Faith

Americans believe in **religious freedom**, the idea that individuals should be free to choose and practice their religious faith and that government should not establish any particular religion as the official or preferred religion.[28]

FREEDOM OF RELIGIOUS EXPRESSION Americans view the freedom to practice their religion as akin to the right to free speech. Early in the nation's history, so-called dissenting Protestants immigrated to the colonies in part as a way to practice their faith. They fled societies, England in particular, where official government religions made it difficult for individuals with other religious beliefs to practice their faith. The idea that government

2.1
2.2
2.3
2.4

FAITH AS AN AMERICAN TOUCHSTONE

References to faith appear frequently in American political culture. Presidents routinely end their speeches by saying "God Bless the United States of America," and other references abound in places such as the Pledge of Allegiance, the Declaration of Independence, and U.S. currency.

should remain neutral among religions was therefore closely linked to the idea of freedom of religious practice. Such freedom was more easily stated than accomplished, however, and religious intolerance in the colonies was common. Favoring a particular religion—and effectively discriminating against others—was also a practice of many local and state governments into the twentieth century. Anti-Catholicism, in particular, was a strong force in many areas. The twin beliefs in freedom of expression and noninterference by government, although not common at the time of the American Revolution, were enshrined in the Constitution and have grown gradually over time.

IMPORTANCE OF RELIGION IN AMERICAN POLITICAL LIFE Religious belief has been central to American political discourse. Major efforts such as the antislavery, civil rights, and anti-abortion movements relied on religious language and principles. Presidents of both parties, including Presidents George W. Bush and Barack Obama, have sprinkled religious language in their speeches and ended major addresses with the exhortation "God Bless the United States of America." Americans oppose the idea of an official religion or church, but *religiosity*, the tendency of people to have some sort of religion, pervades political culture.

Survey results provide a sense of just how important religion is to Americans today. Eighty percent of Americans in 2012 said they completely or mostly agree that they never doubt the existence of God, whereas nearly that many said that prayer is an important part of their daily life, and that everyone will have to answer to God for their sins.[29] Nearly three-quarters of Americans in 2008 said it was important for a president to have strong religious beliefs, and only about 30 percent thought politicians expressed their religious faith too much.[30]

This degree of religiosity is unusually high. Half of American Christians think of themselves as Christians primarily and Americans secondarily, but less than a quarter of Christians in Germany, Spain, Britain, and France say they think of themselves in terms of their religion first and their nationality second.[31] Moreover, the general pattern around the globe is that citizens in countries that are wealthier, more developed, and industrialized tend to place less emphasis on the importance of religious beliefs in their lives (see Figure 2.1). One possible explanation is that scientific and rationalistic reasoning move people away from faith-based beliefs. A second is that the vast

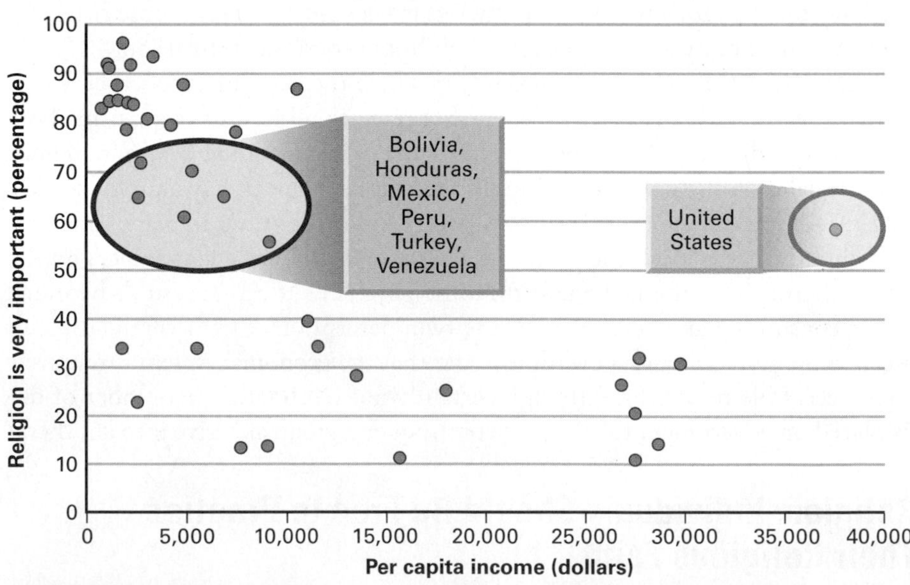

FIGURE 2.1 RELATIONSHIP BETWEEN RELIGION'S IMPORTANCE IN PEOPLE'S LIVES AND ECONOMIC DEVELOPMENT.

High percentages of Americans state that religion is a very important part of their daily lives, which is unusual for a relatively wealthy country. In the graph, 44 countries are represented by a dot. Countries with similar levels of religious belief to the United States fall within the purple oval. The United States is much wealthier than these countries.

NOTE: Survey question asked in 44 countries, 2002. "How important is religion in your life—very important, somewhat important, not too important, or not at all important?

SOURCE: Survey data: Pew Center for the People and the Press, people-press.org/reports/display.php3?ReportID=167. Income data (gross national income per capita, 2003): World Bank, http://siteresources.worldbank.org/DATASTATISTICS/Resources/GNIPC.pdf.

entertainment and leisure options of the modern world draw attention away from spiritual matters.[32] The United States, however, bucks the trend. Why? The exceptionally diverse scope of religious denominational choices in the United States may be one reason. This competitive marketplace draws attention to religion while also providing many niches that can satisfy Americans' differing spiritual needs.

The American Creed Provides a Starting Point for Most Americans to Evaluate Issues, Candidates, and Government Actions

The five beliefs of the American creed have endured even though these ideals have not always been honored in practice. For much of the nation's history, not all groups have shared equally in the promises and benefits of creedal beliefs or the overarching value of equality. During the Revolutionary era, only about 15 to 30 percent of the adult population could take full advantage of the promises of life, liberty, and the pursuit of happiness. Laws and customs made sure that women, blacks, white indentured servants, and non-propertied adult white males could not.[33]

Despite this widespread exclusion, the remarkable fact is that these groups still believed in the promise of the American creed. They did not argue that this set of beliefs should be discarded. Instead, women, white men without property, blacks, and other racial and ethnic minorities demanded to be let into the club. These groups engaged in massive social movements for individual rights, liberty, property, and participation in the democratic process, a testament to just how powerful these beliefs were to those on the outside looking in. By championing the equality promised by the American creed, these movements had a strong impact on public opinion concerning equal treatment across race, gender, and group. Figure 2.2 shows that equality as defined by the women's rights movement has gained support from the American public.

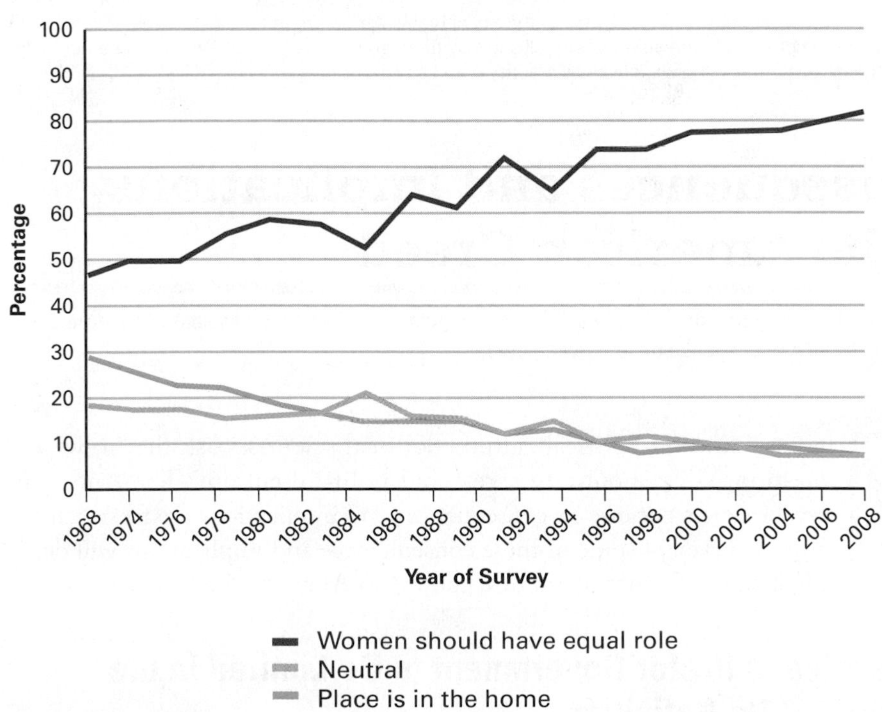

FIGURE 2.2 SUPPORT FOR WOMEN'S EQUAL ROLE, 1972–2008.

In 1972, nearly half the U.S. population held neutral views or believed women's place was in the home, but by 2008, less than one-sixth of the population held those views.

NOTE: Answers to the question: "Some people feel that women should have an equal role with men in running business, industry and government. Others feel that women's place is in the home. Where would you place yourself on this 7-point scale or haven't you thought much about this?" "Equal role" indicates respondent chose point 1, 2, or 3 on the 7-point scale; "Neutral" is point 4; "In the home" is point 5, 6, or 7. Remaining percentage had no opinion. Questions not asked in 1986, 2002, 2006.

SOURCE: The American National Election Studies (www.electionstudies.org). THE 1948–2004 ANES CUMULATIVE FILE [data set]. Stanford University and the University of Michigan [producers and distributors], 2008.

EQUAL RIGHTS

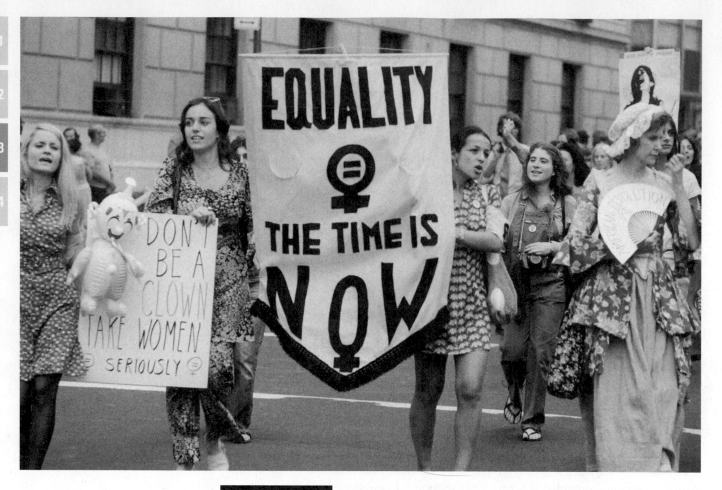

Marchers in New York supporting the addition of the Equal Rights Amendment to the U.S. Constitution. Although the attempt to ratify the amendment fell short by three states, the women's rights movement had a profound effect on American laws, business practices, and society.

Consequences and Implications of the American Creed

2.3 Evaluate the consequences of American political culture such as limited government and a weak sense of sovereign power.

limited government
the idea that the scope of government activities should be narrow and that government should act only when the need is great and other sectors of society are unable to meet the need.

When it comes to political culture, political scientists ask the "so what?" question: Why should we care about political culture? The American creed matters because its consequences and implications are far-reaching. A brief survey of some of these consequences and implications will demonstrate the important influence of political culture on American life.

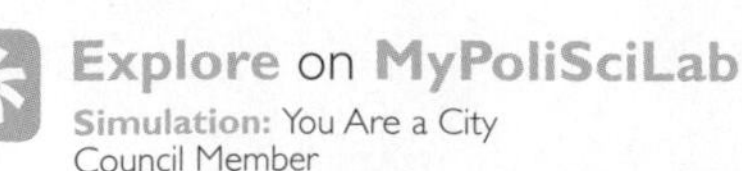

Explore on MyPoliSciLab
Simulation: You Are a City Council Member

Americans Prefer Government to Be Limited in the Scope of Its Activities

One consequence of the American creed is a preference for the idea of **limited government** rather than a large, active government. Government is seen as a last resort for solving problems. People do not need to be convinced that it is appropriate for real estate developers to build houses, for instance, but they may need to be convinced that it is appropriate for government to build housing, to subsidize mortgages for home buyers, or to pay part of the costs for certain people to rent housing. Americans tend to rely first on other arenas—family, church, the marketplace, nonprofit institutions, self-improvement—and they turn to government only when these alternatives fail or they are overwhelmed by the scope of a problem. Lawmakers in 2008 enacted a $700 billion rescue of financial institutions, largely based on concerns that no other sector of society could resolve the crisis. Using similar reasoning, President Obama argued that government had to prod major changes in health care, leading to the passage of the Affordable Care Act in March 2010. This law made the health insurance industry similar to a public utility, with limits on its profit margin and prices, rules about products it must supply, and requirements about which customers it must accept.

"Government as last resort" does not mean that Americans will not look to government to solve many problems and provide many services. They do, and the policy areas in which Americans expect government to act have grown significantly over time. Retirement payments in the form of Social Security, health insurance for the poor and seniors through Medicaid and Medicare, grants and loans for college students via federal financial aid, and money from the unemployment insurance program to assist those who lose their jobs are just a few benefits Americans today routinely expect government to provide. Moreover, government can be active while using what seem to be limited government methods. Through targeted incentives—tax credits for buying energy-efficient appliances, for example—government can create much the same impact as it could by creating a program that directly provides individuals with these appliances.[34]

Some political scientists describe American opinion as philosophically conservative but operationally liberal, meaning that Americans may genuinely believe in limited government while simultaneously supporting specific government programs.[35] Figure 2.3 shows an American public reluctant to cut federal government spending,

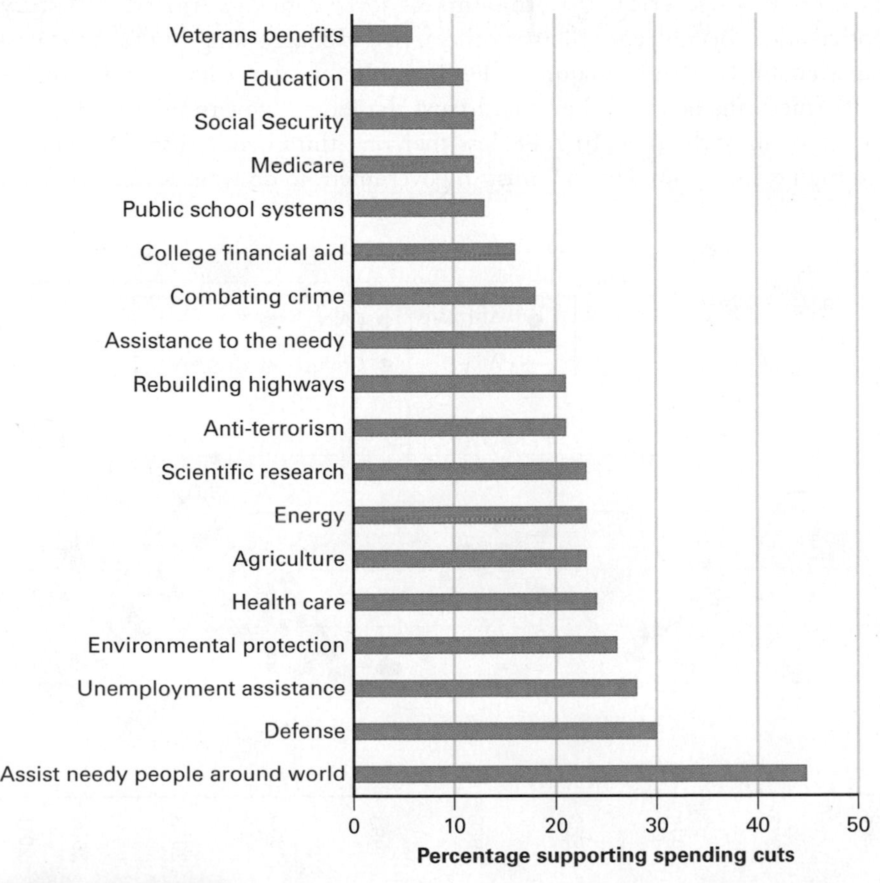

FIGURE 2.3 PUBLIC SUPPORT FOR CUTTING FEDERAL GOVERNMENT SPENDING, 2011.

Americans generally support the idea of a small, efficient government, but they find it difficult to identify areas they would like to see cut. Although 60 percent of Republicans, Democrats, and independents cited the federal budget deficit as a top national priority, there was no majority support for cutting any of the programs listed above.

SOURCE: Data from Pew Center on the People and the Press, www.people-press.org/2011/07/07/section-2-entitlements-vs-deficit-reduction/

even when it considered reducing the federal budget deficit to be a high priority. This reluctance was evident even though about two-thirds of the American public in 2011 believed that federal government programs were usually inefficient and wasteful and that the government had too much influence in their daily lives. In addition, a majority of the American public believes that government regulation of business usually does more harm than good. But when given the choice between strengthening regulations, reducing them, or keeping them the same in specific industries, 20 percent or less of the public supported reduced regulation.[36]

Dedication to the idea of limited government is stronger in the United States than in other industrialized democracies. In general, governments in these countries are larger and have more control over society and the economy than is true in the United States. One must interpret these comparisons with caution, as there are many ways to measure government's role. Nonetheless, when comparing the size of government to the size of the economy, especially when focusing on domestic rather than military spending, the United States regularly falls at the low end of the list. Government in the United States often hires private-sector firms to do a wide range of work, including counseling, job skills training, rubbish collection, and more, that in other countries might be done by government employees. Expanding government's reach through the use of private-sector firms and organizations can be less politically controversial than hiring scores of new public employees.[37]

Americans Often Do Not Trust That Government Will Do the Right Thing

A second consequence of the American creed has been a pervasive skepticism about the effectiveness of American government. At some times in American history, this skepticism has been deeper than at others. In 1958, according to the American National Election Studies, a major academic public opinion survey, about three-fourths of Americans believed they could trust the federal government to do what is right most or all of the time. In 2008, less than one-third believed so.[38] Surveys in 2011 (see Figure 2.4) showed overall trust in government to do what is right at about 20 percent.[39]

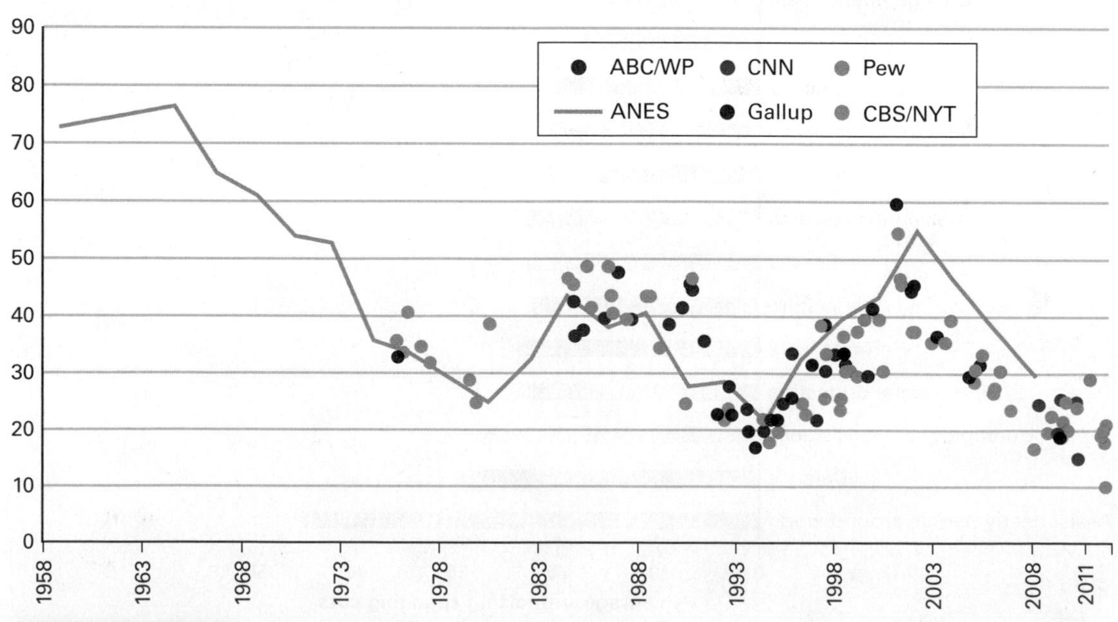

FIGURE 2.4 PERCENTAGE OF AMERICANS SAYING THEY TRUST THE FEDERAL GOVERNMENT TO DO THE RIGHT THING JUST ABOUT ALWAYS OR MOST OF THE TIME.

Americans' trust that the federal government will do the right thing has dropped from the high levels recorded 50 years ago by the American National Election Studies. Despite fluctuations and differences between partisan groups—Democrats will be more trusting when Democrats control the presidency and Congress than when Republicans do, and vice versa—the general trend is a decline in trust since the mid-1960s.

SOURCE: Data from Pew Center on the People and the Press.

What might explain this decline in trust? A succession of difficult events in American politics plays some role. The long, controversial Vietnam War in the 1960s; the political scandal known as Watergate that led to the resignation of President Richard Nixon in 1974; the protracted period of high inflation and high unemployment, known as stagflation, throughout the 1970s; escalating economic competition from other countries and the pressure this competition placed on American workers; the increasingly unpopular Iraq War that began in 2003; and the slow recovery from a deep recession in the first years of the 2010s would be on this list.

Other factors play a role as well. Political life tends to be complicated. Thus, political scientists have proposed and established some validity for a variety of additional factors:

- Trust was artificially inflated in the years after the Great Depression and World War II. After the United States overcame these calamities and stood atop the world in economics, science, and many other categories, trust in government was high. This high trust, rather than the more recent period of low trust, may be the anomaly, and trust has simply declined to more "normal" levels.
- American politics among activists, candidates, and elected officials has become more divisive, and news coverage in turn has focused disproportionately on conflict and stalemate rather than on cooperation and accomplishment.
- American economic life has become less secure, traditional moral values have been challenged, and government has been unwilling or unable to do much to reverse these trends, to the dismay of the various groups concerned about them.
- Respect has declined for all large institutions, not simply government.
- Trust has declined across advanced industrial democracies, suggesting some non-America-specific causes may play a role also.[40]

Governing within the American constitutional system has never been easy. Low levels of trust may complicate the job of political leaders.[41] On one hand, that might be a reasonable price to pay to keep government in check, consistent with American political culture. On the other hand, high levels of distrust can increase the difficulty of making necessary and tough policy decisions, thus reinforcing the skepticism about government's ability to perform effectively.

sovereign power
the individual or institution in a political system whose decisions are binding and cannot be overturned by other individuals or institutions.

There is No "Final" Authority in American Government

A third consequence of the American creed, closely related to the idea of limited government, is that there is no "final" authority or decision maker in the U.S. government, a concept referred to as sovereign power. A **sovereign power** is an individual or institution in a political system whose decisions are binding and cannot be overturned by other individuals or institutions. American government is structured so that one part of government can challenge and check other parts of government. For example, Congress can pass legislation, but the president can veto it. With enough votes, Congress can then override that veto. The Supreme Court can declare unconstitutional the actions of both Congress and the president. Congress and the states can pass constitutional amendments that will guide future Court decisions, or the president can nominate and the Senate can approve new Supreme Court justices who might render different decisions. There is no ultimate seat of power in the system at the national level.

What about the claim that the American people are sovereign? In the abstract, this is true. Sovereign power is ultimately rooted in the people: through elected officials, Americans can change the policies and personnel of government. The people reserve the ultimate right to push for a rewriting of the Constitution or to enter into a revolution. But on a practical, day-to-day level, the people have limited sovereignty. This is not an accident but an intended result of the Constitution. American government is designed to hear the voice of the people, but not to translate that voice into immediate action. When the

American people are dissatisfied, the strongest practical recourse they have is to replace members of government, but there is never a time when Americans can vote out all members of government in a single election. Members of the federal judiciary and bureaucracy, who are unelected, are never up for direct public removal. Thus, the sovereign power of the people is limited, and some parts of government are only indirectly controlled.

□ Competing Ideas Are Viewed With Suspicion

A fourth consequence of the American creed is that competing ideas are often viewed with suspicion. In general, the American people and their leaders tend to assume the superiority of the creed's values. Only rarely do U.S. policy makers, at least publicly, seriously talk about the policies and programs of other countries as examples to be followed, the assumption being that the underlying values and beliefs guiding these programs would not be relevant in the American context. For a long time in the United States, one way to discredit an idea has been to label it socialistic. Some conservative critics of President Obama aim to tie him to both of these sensitive cultural critiques, depicting him as a socialist whose policies are geared toward making the United States look more like Europe.

"UN-AMERICAN" BELIEFS Competing ideas not only challenge the American creed but also are sometimes deemed "un-American." Throughout U.S. history, ideas that have challenged the creed were often seen as infections on the body politic caused by outsiders. In few countries is a set of political beliefs so intertwined with national identity that to oppose or challenge these beliefs can sometimes be perceived as a challenge to the nation itself.

In the 1950s, the House Un-American Activities Committee investigated a large number of individuals suspected of holding or being sympathetic to "un-American" ideas, chiefly socialism and communism. At other points in American history, efforts to remove immigrants and to restrict the future flow of immigration were based on the idea that these individuals brought disruptive beliefs and values to the United States. At one time or another in American history, Catholics, Irish, Chinese, Japanese, Eastern and Southern Europeans, Jews, Muslims, and others have been deemed dangerous because of the cultural practices and beliefs they might bring into the United States.

APPEALS TO SOCIAL CLASS Attempts to appeal to Americans as members of social classes are often considered a danger to national harmony. With the exception of references to the middle class—which politicians use frequently and in very broad terms—directly appealing to class interest is often denounced. To supporters, the Occupy Wall Street movement that emerged in late 2011 told important truths about American society when it emphasized the plight of "the 99 percent" at the hands of the "1 percent." To its opponents, the movement was instead attempting to create class antagonisms in an attempt to redistribute income away from those who had earned it. When President Obama promised that he would raise taxes "on the wealthiest Americans" while leaving other "hardworking Americans" untouched, critics denounced him for advocating "class warfare" and demonizing financially successful Americans. President Obama and other Democrats asserted that, on the contrary, it was Republicans who were engaged in class politics by skewing their policies toward the interests of higher-income individuals and families. These competing views were expressed frequently during the 2012 presidential election campaign by Obama and Mitt Romney, the Republican presidential nominee. The concerns on both sides that policy is being devised to promote one class at the expense of another are often sincerely held, as are the fears that class-based politics invites disharmony and division. But the provocative charge that the rich are warring on the poor or the poor are warring on the rich can also be a strategy for halting serious discussion about a particular policy.

Other countries have been more comfortable talking about class and challenging individualistic political culture. Socialism has had a more sympathetic reception elsewhere, particularly in the form of strong labor unions and a Labour Party (Australia,

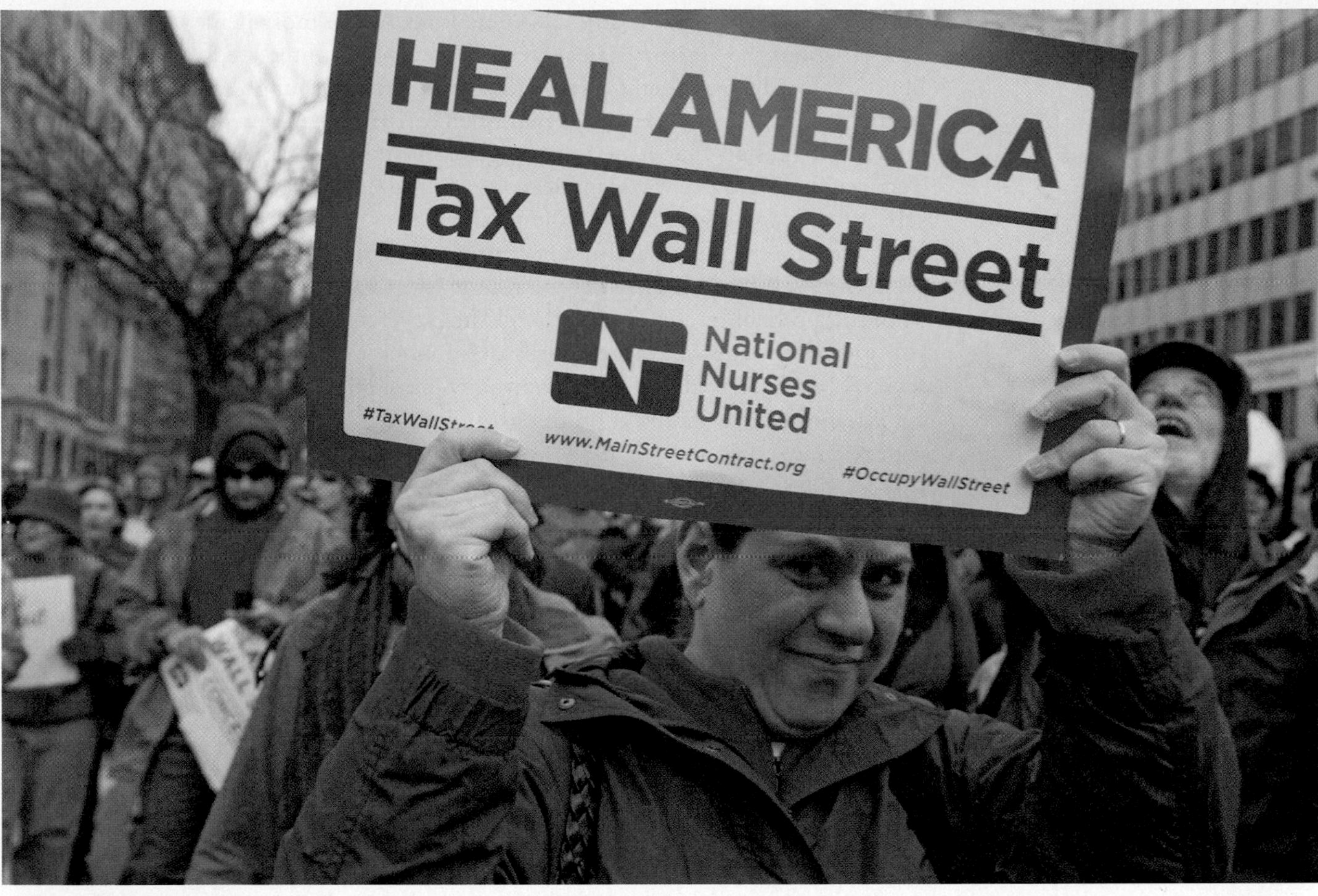

LOOKING UP

Member of National Nurses United rally in Washington, D.C. in November 2011. Depending on the listener, "Wall Street" can be a class-based reference meaning financial firms, individual financial sector employees, or affluent Americans in general.

Ireland, New Zealand, United Kingdom), Social Democratic Party or New Democrat Party (Canada, Germany, Sweden), or Socialist Party (France). Although socialist parties in the early twentieth century had some success in industrial cities in the United States, they made little impact on the national scene. One causal explanation for the success of class-based appeals in other countries may be that class-oriented political parties thrived as one option among many. The success of these class-based parties may have in turn made the publics in these countries more comfortable with class being at the center of political discussions.

It Is Difficult to Identify and Promote the Public Interest

A fifth consequence of the American creed is that it can be difficult for politicians and the public to act in the public interest or even to define it. In a nation where individualism and skepticism of government are strong, references to "the public interest" might be interpreted by the public as a rhetorical gloss employed to make what is in someone else's individual interest sound more noble. Because American political culture has such a strong emphasis on individual freedom, opportunity, and rights, can you convince people to sacrifice their self-interest for the public interest? When advocating policies, politicians and political activists continually wrestle with the tension between appealing to the interests of the community and the interests of the individual. Barack Obama in the 2008 election asked Americans to "look after not only ourselves, but each other," while his opponent John McCain implored Americans to "put country first."

Alexis de Tocqueville, a French historian and political theorist, visited the United States in the 1830s and wrote a sweeping analysis of the nature of American politics and society that is still considered one of the most perceptive studies ever written about the United States. He was particularly interested in the interplay of liberty, individualism, democracy, and equality in the young American republic. In his famous *Democracy in America*, published in 1835 when he was 30 years old, Tocqueville suggested that Americans engage in "self interest rightly understood." In Tocqueville's view, one way Americans reconciled the conflict between pursuing their self-interest and sacrificing for the public interest was by seeing how engaging in kind acts toward others and being concerned about the public interest could also serve their self-interest. In other words, the "sacrifice" could reap personal dividends. Vote for a school referendum that will "help the children" and the community, and your property value will increase because communities with good schools are attractive to homebuyers. Help others, and you will feel good about yourself. Volunteer for community service and do good things, and you will have another impressive line on your résumé.

Political Conflict Emerges from Tension Among the Creed's Beliefs and from Debate Over the Meaning of the Beliefs

An important and ironic final consequence of the widely shared American creed is that it also produces much of the political conflict in the United States. The creed creates political tension because, first, its beliefs are often in conflict with one another, and second, the meaning of the individual beliefs is open to debate.[42] Both of these sources of tension have led to significant political debate and struggle in the United States. In fact, much of the conflict between the two major political parties may be attributed to the differing emphases they place on American creed beliefs when these beliefs conflict, or to the different meaning parties may attach to a belief such as liberty. Similarly, the conflict in American politics between conservatives, who find themselves mostly in the Republican Party, and liberals, who find themselves mostly in the Democratic Party, arises from these tensions.

Liberals and Democrats, for example, have tended to argue for campaign finance laws that limit the amount of funds that individuals may donate to candidates or may spend independently to influence election outcomes. In their eyes, an unequal distribution of property (i.e., income) leads to an unequal ability to donate or spend. To ensure fair competition, liberals and Democrats argue, democracy requires limits on this spending. Conservatives and Republicans, on the other hand, argue that telling Americans what they can spend their money on is an infringement on their liberty. Money is spent to facilitate the communication of political messages, they argue, and government has no proper role limiting freedom of speech in a quest to realize its vision of the "correct" balance of speech across various groups. To liberals, the American creed, and particularly the belief in democracy, demands more stringent campaign finance restrictions. To conservatives, the American creed, and particularly the beliefs in property rights and liberty, demands that government back off when individuals wish to spend their money to promote messages with which they agree.

TENSION AMONG THE CREED'S BELIEFS Most Americans share the general ideals of the American creed, but the tension inherent in the creed leaves plenty of room for political debate, conflict, and struggle. Consider a low-income high school student. She has worked hard, is an excellent student, and has qualified for admission at a prestigious university. Her ability to maximize her potential depends on her going to college, the most prestigious one for which she is qualified. Being poor, however, she cannot afford such a university. Her situation poses a conflict between two beliefs. According to the belief in individualism, this young woman should be able to achieve all she can without any artificial barriers, certainly not the barrier of her parents' income. But does this mean that other people with more money should be required to help provide the resources to send this student to college? According to the belief in property rights, these wealthier people should be able to keep what they earn: their property is their property and that money is theirs. If they want to donate voluntarily to a scholarship fund that would help students like this, they can do that, but they should not be forced by government to give their money to someone else.

As a society, Americans have resolved this particular conflict between American creed beliefs by deemphasizing property rights to elevate individual opportunity. That is, Americans have created federal financial aid programs that take tax dollars from one set of individuals and redistribute them to another set of individuals like this student. The government takes property from one group and gives it to another. This example reinforces the point made earlier that beliefs can prevail at the abstract level but weaken in specific circumstances. Americans do believe that, on the whole, people should be able to do with their property as they wish. When this belief collides with the belief in individual opportunity, Americans, through government, have to weigh each belief and decide whether it is right to redistribute property from one group to help the individual opportunities of another group.

CULTURAL DIFFERENCES ACROSS REGIONS When the beliefs of the American creed are in conflict, no balance is inherently right or wrong. Instead, there is a balance that can gain the strongest political support nationally at a particular moment in time. But what does this national balance mean at the state or regional level? Even a quick glance at the United States shows significant variation across the states in partisan strength, public opinion, and the content of laws and policies. In addition to federal student financial aid programs, for example, most states have their own programs, ranging from modest to generous. If national political culture is important, it is puzzling to find such diversity across states. Why do states vary? Is the variation simply random, or do particular factors contribute to it? More specifically, does political culture play a systematic role in this cross-state variation?

The regional variety in laws and political behavior has led some political scientists to suggest that although a balance of creedal beliefs at the national level shapes policy, the balance among creedal beliefs also varies systematically from region to region, state to state, and even within states. Migration and immigration have contributed to this variation. Ethnic groups and nationalities have been distributed unevenly across the country, and their heavy presence in a particular state or city would encourage further immigration to that area. This was as true of European immigrants in the 1890s as it is of Asian and Latino immigrants today. Their beliefs have influenced the practice of politics where they have lived. In one part of the country, property rights might receive more emphasis. In another, it might be religious freedom. These areas would then be appealing relocation destinations for other Americans who shared those preferences. This geographical variation in political culture is one factor that helps explain differences in state laws and politics.

One famous classification of American political beliefs speaks of moralistic, traditionalistic, and individualistic subcultures that dominate or mix in different parts of the United States.[43] The moralistic subculture has been most prominent in the northern states and the Pacific Northwest, the traditionalistic in the southern states, and the individualistic through the middle tier of states and in California. The moralistic subculture views government as a positive force and tends to place heavy emphasis on the needs of the community and government's ability to satisfy those needs. A more active government is welcomed and popular participation is encouraged. A traditionalist subculture favors limited government that works to sustain the social relations and values already dominant in society and the economy. Popular participation is not strongly encouraged and historically was actively discouraged for some groups. The individualistic subculture sees politics neither as a means to transform society (as moralism does) nor as a way to preserve society (as traditionalism does), but as a mechanism through which private interests are advanced and government is expected to encourage, enable, and support private initiative. Political scientists have used these regional cultural differences as one factor among many to explain differences in voting turnout, election outcomes, and social policy across states.

COMPETING INTERPRETATIONS OF BELIEFS Political tension results not only from the conflict between beliefs, but also from different interpretations of beliefs in the American creed.[44] Americans may generally believe in democracy, or liberty, or the other beliefs of the American creed, but their understanding of what those terms mean will always be a battleground for public officials, political activists, and other citizens. For example, consider the process of redistricting, which was in the news extensively following the 2010 U.S. Census.

Redistricting refers to the drawing of boundaries around legislative districts every 10 years to make the districts within a state equal in size. What does a seemingly technical matter such as redistricting have to do with a creedal belief such as democracy? A lot, as it turns out. In 1964, the Supreme Court, in two famous decisions, concluded that democracy hinges on the principle of "one person, one vote," the idea that every citizen has one vote, each voter is equally powerful in selecting legislators, and each voter is equally represented in the legislature.[45] The Court's one person, one vote principle provides no explicit guidance about how to draw the lines that separate districts.

As discussed earlier, to Americans, democracy includes having an equal opportunity to influence the actions of government. How does that idea best translate to the drawing of district lines? Is democracy better served if lines are drawn in a way that some districts are likely to be heavily Republican and others heavily Democratic? The individuals elected to the legislature in these districts are apt to represent their constituents very well because they tend to share common viewpoints. However, competitive elections will be rare in these districts—the weaker party is unlikely to have any chance to win, so voters might not believe they have much of a choice on the ballot, which does not sound democratic. On the other hand, if the lines are drawn with an intent to spread Democratic and Republican voters about equally across the two districts, elections may be more competitive—considered by many to be a fundamental sign of a healthy democracy—but large numbers of people in the districts may realize that they share few beliefs and values with the elected officials who represent them in the legislature. They might feel unrepresented by these officials, and that hardly seems democratic either.[46] Americans believe in democracy, but examples such as this one show they can legitimately disagree on precisely what that belief requires them to do in specific cases.

Challenges to the American Creed

2.4 Describe the major challenges and alternatives to the dominant political culture.

Although the American creed has had strong allegiance, alternative beliefs have also influenced American politics. At times, people might profess the creed's beliefs while also agreeing with some of the alternatives. This combination may seem logically impossible, but individuals often put ideas together in surprising ways. Even within a society such as the United States, where one set of beliefs generally predominates, the mosaic of cultural beliefs and values can be incredibly rich and complex because of the way that American creed ideals are mixed and combined with other beliefs. American political culture is dynamic, not fixed and unchanging.

Communitarianism Emphasizes the Contributions and Interests of the Community

Whereas the American creed gives primacy to the individual in society, **communitarianism** focuses on society and the community.[47] In the communitarian view, individuals are not self-made: society makes us and we owe something to society in return. In the words of Revolutionary leader Samuel Adams, "A citizen owes everything to the Commonwealth."[48] The communitarian approach does not dispute that individuals are personally responsible and need to work hard. But it would point out that we all depend on the resources provided by others and by the community, whether education, transportation, an array of commercial and cultural choices, or the bounty of the earth and water. These resources do not determine whether we will reach our goals, but they influence our ability to reach them, and we rely on others to provide them.

Communitarianism also says that the goal of self-improvement should not focus only on the self, but on how self-improvement serves the community and society more broadly. This way of thinking suggests that it is not an inherently bad thing for an individual to make a lot of money, but it asks whether society is served in the process.

communitarianism
the view that the needs of the community are of higher priority in government than the needs of the individual, even if the result is a restriction of individual liberties.

COMMUNITARIAN BELIEFS IN AMERICAN HISTORY Communitarianism has been influential throughout American history. In the colonial and Revolutionary eras, this was the dominant mode of thought, often referred to by historians and political scientists as classical republicanism.[49] Political rhetoric of those eras placed great emphasis on having self-sacrificing virtuous people—those who would pursue the common good—as political leaders. Communitarian themes were emphasized along with individualistic ones. It was common practice for government to regulate wages, prices, and the entry of new businesses into the marketplace, all to maintain social stability and, it was believed, to produce a just society. Gradually, individualistic beliefs gained ascendancy. Communitarian ideals survived, but in a less prominent position than previously.

Periodically, these ideals flourished in the advocacy of social, political, or economic reform. Populists from 1875 through 1900 expressed deep concern about the disruption of communities by industrial capitalism and proposed many reforms to rectify the perceived exploitation of government by private interests. Communitarian ideas alone were not enough to lead to reform—political activists and politicians needed to organize people who held these views. Major reform movements such as Progressivism (1904–1918), the New Deal (1930s), and the Great Society (1960s) were successfully infused with the idea that politics or economics needed to be reformed for the greater interest of the community. It was not just liberals that made these arguments. The rise of conservative politics in the 1970s and 1980s was based in part on arguments that liberal public policy had created many special interests, from large corporations to individuals on welfare, who had grown dependent on the expansion of government to provide them with contracts, payments, and services.

Right up through today, language condemning a politics of "the powerful versus the people" can resonate with many Americans. Liberals such as TV host Rachel Maddow on MSNBC offer critiques of those she perceives as greedy corporate executives or tax-shirking millionaires and billionaires, whereas conservatives such as TV host Sean Hannity on the Fox News Channel assail the influence of what he sees as the elite liberal media and powerful interest groups such as public employee unions.

PRIVATE INTEREST AND THE PUBLIC GOOD To communitarians, the rights of individuals and the interests of the community are not necessarily in conflict. But when they are, the public good should trump private interest.[50] For example, in some

discrimination
the view that not all groups in society are deserving of equal rights and opportunities.

states and municipalities, police set up sobriety checkpoints and stop drivers at random to screen them for drunk driving. These checkpoints bypass the normal requirement that police can stop drivers only if they believe they have probable cause to investigate them. Sobriety checkpoints are surely an infringement on the privacy rights of individuals, but they have been defended as serving the community's interests. If drivers realize they might get pulled over even when they are not driving erratically, they will be more cautious about drinking and driving, thereby enhancing everyone's safety and reducing the social costs involved with car crashes, injuries, and loss of life.[51]

REFINING THE AMERICAN CREED One way to look at communitarianism is that it refines the American creed without necessarily rejecting it.[52] On their own, creedal beliefs about individualism can appear harsh, advocating a "sink or swim" society in which individuals either succeed or fail, with little compassion for those who fall behind. Communitarian ideas remove this harsh edge by supporting government programs to provide social resources and services for individuals who are struggling, if that is in the community's interest. Consider unemployment compensation. Whereas a strict application of the creed's emphasis on individual responsibility would see unemployment compensation as unnecessary—people could land new jobs by moving, accepting lower wages, or being flexible about the jobs they would take—communitarianism would view such compensation as necessary, at least for a time, to prevent the social disruption of unpaid rent and mortgages, delinquent bills, and families in disarray. Similar beliefs motivated some of the advocates for national health insurance (see *How Do We Know? Why Was the Path to Universal Health Insurance Coverage So Difficult?*).

PUBLIC SUPPORT FOR COMMUNITARIANISM Public opinion reveals the persistence of communitarian ideals today. Although Americans are not antibusiness, in 2012 about three-fifths of Americans charged that business fails to strike "a fair balance between making profits and serving the public interest." The same proportion concluded that "business corporations make too much profit."[54] The very notion of "too much profit" is telling. In the creedal beliefs of property, liberty, and individualism, the idea of "too much" profit makes no sense. If an individual or business is clever enough to make a product for which demand is high, how can we say "too much" profit is being made? Assuming you have choices, you are not forced to buy the product. If you believe the price is too high, you should not purchase it.

Whereas the creedal view holds that substantial profit indicates a good business plan, communitarianism worries that businesses may be taking advantage of customers individually and society more generally. The Occupy Wall Street movement that emerged around the country during 2011 expressed strong critiques of corporate behavior, and many Americans, such as those upset in 2012 at oil companies when gasoline prices spiked up sharply, share the communitarian belief that it is wrong for businesses to "exploit" certain situations—such as a shortage of a key resource—and increase their profit.

Discrimination Stresses That Not All Groups Deserve Equal Treatment

Another challenge to the American creed, particularly the value of equality, is **discrimination**. According to this view, society is a hierarchy in which not all groups deserve all the rights and benefits the American creed can offer—some groups are favored and others are disfavored. The most glaring example of discrimination in American history is the treatment of racial minorities, especially blacks. Those holding hierarchical ideas considered blacks inherently inferior to whites. Some of the language used to describe blacks in comparison to whites was degrading and offensive,

How Do We Know?

Why Was the Path to Universal Health Insurance Coverage So Difficult?

The Question

In nearly all industrialized countries, health care coverage for every individual is guaranteed by the national government. The government either pays for private health care services or directly provides services, or there is some combination of these two options. In the United States, non-governmental expenditures are a far larger share of the total spent on health care than is true elsewhere. In 2010, after nearly a century of attempts and after a bruising legislative battle, the United States adopted a set of reforms designed to provide nearly universal health care coverage. Why was the path to universal health insurance coverage so difficult? How do we know?

Why It Matters

Over the past decade, at any given time, nearly 45–50 million Americans, or about 16 percent of the population, had no health insurance. These figures are a matter of dispute, but they are the most widely cited ones.[53] Among the unemployed, the poor, and racial and ethnic minorities, the rate is even higher, and many Americans drop into and out of heath care coverage for short periods of time over a two- or three-year period. Whether you believe that universal health insurance is crucially important to individuals' health and life opportunities, or you believe that it will harm more than help medical care overall, the answer to the question matters. By understanding what made the adoption of national health insurance so difficult, you learn the ingredients that contributed to its success in 2010.

Investigating the Answer

For political scientists, explaining why something did not happen is similar to explaining why it did happen: A researcher needs to come up with an idea that connects the outcome to factors that might explain it. The outcome we are interested in is the absence or presence of national health insurance that covers all individuals. The possible cause we are especially interested in is political culture. The hunch is that the American creed's emphasis on individualism, liberty, and property is incompatible with the idea that health care should be considered a federal government responsibility. Individualism demands personal responsibility, and liberty means allowing choices. Moreover, in the American free enterprise economy, health insurance is a benefit offered by employers to entice prospective employees and retain their current workers. If different jobs provide different levels of benefits, workers have choices. They might trade health insurance for higher income, more flexible work schedules, or overtime opportunities.

The most straightforward way to test this idea is through examining public opinion. Depending on the survey, half to three-quarters of Americans say they favor "providing health care coverage for all," even if it means raising taxes. American political culture is rooted predominantly in the American creed, however, and we see its influence in public opinion also. In one survey, a majority said they favored national health insurance provided by government, but support dropped off if the program would limit one's choice of doctors or if there were waiting lists for nonemergency treatments or if the

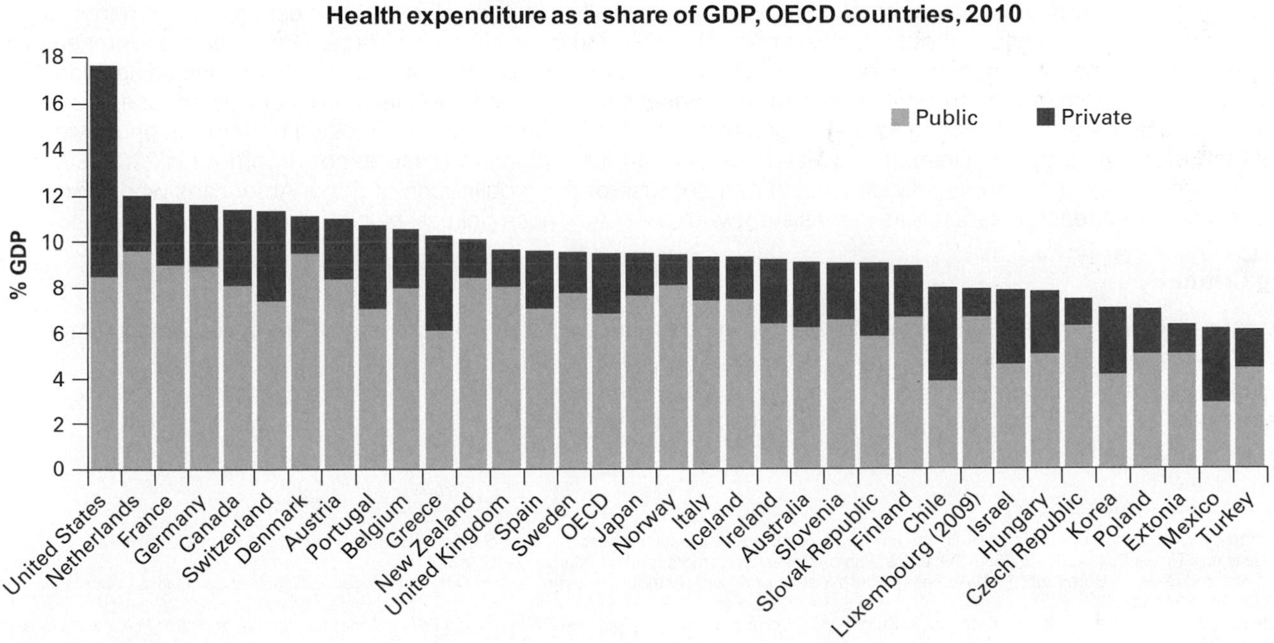

PUBLIC AND PRIVATE HEALTH CARE EXPENDITURES AS PERCENTAGE OF GROSS DOMESTIC PRODUCT.

The United States devotes a much larger share of its economy to health care expenditures than other countries and has a much larger role for the private sector. American national and state governments also spend substantial sums on health care.

SOURCE: Organization for Economic Co-operation and Development, *OECD Health Data 2009*. Updated April 2010: www.oecd.org/dataoecd/46/4/38980557.pdf

respondent personally had to pay higher taxes. Adding these new opponents to those who initially opposed a universal health insurance program would make opposition the majority view.[a] During the 2009–2010 debate, the measurement of public opinion on health reform was highly dependent on question wording and the information provided to respondents. About 90 percent of Americans in mid-2009 expressed support for "fundamental changes" in or "completely rebuilding" American health care, but when asked about their personal situation, nearly as high a percentage reported being satisfied with their health care.[b] Overall, it is fair to say that American political culture did not rule out national health insurance, but it also did not lend clear support for it if advantages of the current system might be lost.

Although the United States has not previously had universal national health insurance, it does have the Medicare and Medicaid programs, which provide insurance for the elderly and the poor, respectively. U.S. national and state governments spend huge sums on health care, even more than in many other countries. If American political culture prior to 2010 simply would not allow any form of national health insurance, the existence of these two programs and all that spending would be a real puzzle.[c]

Given the mixed public opinion results and the presence of these two partial forms of national health insurance in the United States, how might we further try to explain the long, difficult path toward universal health insurance? One possibility is to add another factor: American political institutions.[d] For something as massive as national health insurance—which entails changes throughout the health care industry—the president, Congress, different parts of the federal bureaucracy, state governments, and possibly even the Supreme Court would be involved in the policy-making process. With influence dispersed across institutions and across majority and minority parties, there are many locations in the American political process where legislation could be defeated. Add a political culture that is only partly supportive of national health insurance and the intersection of culture and institutions posed significant hurdles for national health insurance.

The political activity of "special interests" is another factor to consider.[e] Traditionally, one part of the health care industry or another was likely to oppose movements toward national health insurance because it feared bureaucratic oversight of its business practices, interference with patient care, and depression of prices and salaries that would make the industry less efficient economically and less desirable as a career. The interests opposed to national health insurance were likely to be already very well organized and persistent on the issue because they had a lot at stake financially. Those individuals or groups in favor of national health insurance, on the other hand, needed to get organized to fight this battle, frequently had many different points of view, and often did not have as intense an interest in creating national health insurance as opponents had in stopping it.[f] A battle between a movement divided across several different reform plans and groups relatively unified to protect their turf will usually be won by the latter, even if there are more people in the former.

The Bottom Line

Political culture, institutional features of American government, and the politics of special interests historically formed a thicket of obstacles to the adoption of national health insurance. So what made 2010 different from past years?

The role of culture in 2010 ultimately is best thought of as neither advancing nor defeating universal health insurance, but as shaping the construction of the program. The health care reform effort in 2009–2010 differed most from previous experiences in the institutions that became involved. Lowering some of the institutional barriers to reform were a president who made health insurance a major priority, the substantial majority of seats held by his party in the House and Senate, adroit use of legislative procedures by Democratic leaders, and a fear that failure would lead to deep discontent among their staunchest party activists and supporters. As for interests, the growing worry, even among former opponents of reform, that health care costs had become economically unsustainable for businesses, governments, and individuals, prodded a recalculation about the desirability of some kind of universal coverage. Organizations representing senior citizens, physicians, pharmaceutical companies, hospitals, businesses, labor, and many others, including even the insurance companies themselves, committed early in the process to work with, or at least not actively oppose, the reform efforts. The change of heart among former opponents was due in part to the odds looking better than on previous occasions that reform might pass. Despite this historically friendly institutional and interest environment in 2009–2010, the path to reform was still extraordinarily difficult, in part because of the mobilization of those Americans who saw government-mandated health insurance as inconsistent with basic American political beliefs.

Thinking Critically

- If you were a political strategist, how would you convince Americans that universal health care coverage guaranteed by the federal government is consistent with American political culture?
- Do any of these causal factors—culture, institutions, or interests—seem more important than the others, or does each seem about equally important in explaining the long path toward universal coverage? Explain your answer.

---

[a] See polls at http://www.pollingreport.com/health3.htm, and David W. Brady and Daniel P. Kessler, "Who Supports Health Reform?" *PS* 43, 1 (2010): 1–6.

[b] CBS News/New York Times Poll, April 22–26, 2009; CNN/Opinion Research Corporation Poll, March 12–15, 2009.

[c] See John T. Scott and Brian H. Bornstein, "What's Fair in Foul Weather and Fair? Distributive Justice across Different Allocation Contexts and Goods," *Journal of Politics* 71, 3 (2009): 831–46.

[d] See Sven Steinmo and Jon Watts, "It's the Institutions, Stupid! Why Comprehensive National Health Insurance Fails in America," *Journal of Health Politics, Policy and Law* 20, 2 (1995): 329–72.

[e] See Colin Gordon, *Dead on Arrival: The Politics of Health Care in Twentieth-Century America* (Princeton, NJ: Princeton University Press, 2003); Jacob S. Hacker, "The Historical Logic of National Health Insurance: Structure and Sequence in the Development of British, Canadian, and U.S. Medical Policy," *Studies in American Political Development* 12, 1 (1998): 57–130.

[f] M. Kate Bunford and Victor R. Fuchs, "Who Favors National Health Insurance? Who Opposes It? And Why?" talk delivered at the Center for Health Policy and Center for Primary Care and Outcomes Research, Stanford University, March 8, 2006. http://chppcor.stanford.edu/events/4436

depicting blacks as anything from children to savages. Racism was so pervasive in American history that even many of those who opposed slavery did not consider blacks fully equal and fully deserving of the same rights as whites.

Discrimination cannot be dismissed as an inconvenient blip in history, or a negative set of ideas held by relatively few people on the bottom rungs of society, or the distorted worldview of a few white supremacist organizations such as the Ku Klux Klan. Political, educational, and business leaders believed in these ideas. Across the country, businesses refused to hire minorities, paid them less when they did, and often refused to serve them as customers. Many public officials pandered to racist views held by the public. Well into the twentieth century, American public policy at the national and state levels was greatly influenced by the racist, anti-equality premises of discrimination, denying minorities equal access to the opportunities in America's society, economy, and polity. University researchers of the late nineteenth and early twentieth centuries measured the brain size of blacks and whites to demonstrate "objectively" the innate superiority of whites. The research lent an air of scientific justification to the denial of economic, social, and political rights to blacks. More broadly, eugenics, the study of the "betterment" of society by discouraging reproduction by particular "inferior" groups, was used as the basis for sterilization laws in over 30 states. The laws typically targeted groups such as the mentally disabled. Some advocates, however, called for wider use of sterilization, and the central theme of eugenics—the

SUPPLY, DEMAND, AND QUESTIONS

When gas prices escalated in recent years, many Americans were suspicious that big oil companies were "gouging" consumers with high prices. Despite the reassurances of most economists that large corporations were not manipulating the oil and gasoline markets, Americans remained skeptical as oil company profits hit all-time highs. Defenders of the industry noted that it still had a profit rate much lower than that of many other industries.

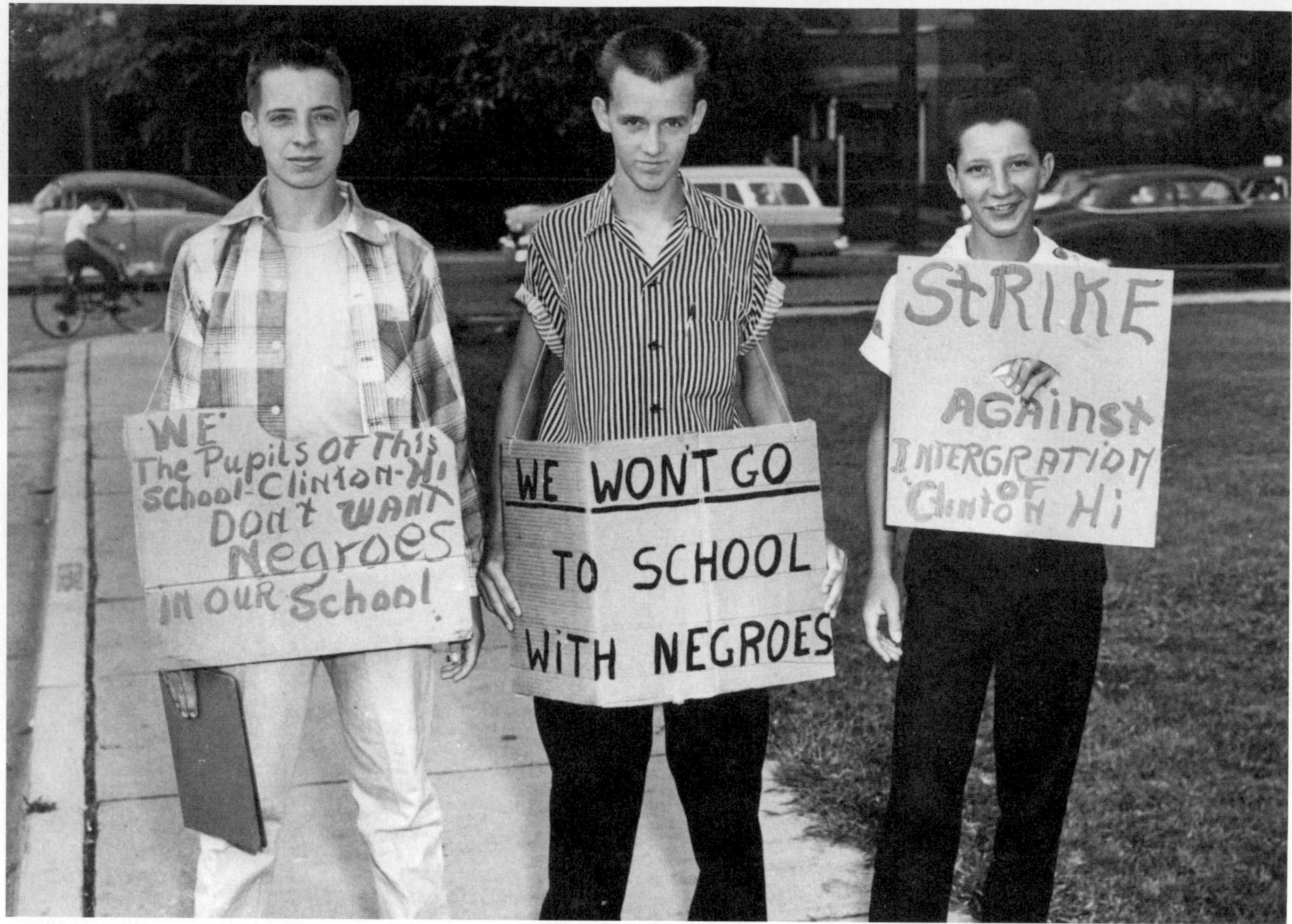

NO WELCOME MAT

Efforts to integrate the nation's schools during the civil rights movement faced strong opposition in some areas of the country.

multiculturalism
the view that group identity influences political beliefs and that because groups are naturally diverse in their beliefs, the idea of a shared or dominant political culture merely reflects the imposition of a dominant group's beliefs on subordinate groups.

need to discourage the intergenerational transmission of bad characteristics and traits—was often invoked to support laws restricting immigration and prohibiting interracial marriage.[55]

The same group inferiority and social hierarchy arguments used to limit the individual rights of blacks were also historically used against other ethnic groups, Native Americans, and women. The derogatory labels questioning the maturity, character, intelligence, and emotional stability of blacks were applied to these groups as well. Some people today argue that homosexuals face some of the same kinds of unequal treatment. Visions of the United States as a social hierarchy are still part of the mixture of American political culture, but not in the same bold, public, and widespread manner as in previous eras.[56]

Multiculturalism Questions Whether a Common American Political Culture Is Desirable

Multicultural thought began sweeping through the United States in the 1980s, particularly on college campuses and in popular culture. The defining characteristics of **multiculturalism** are a belief that American society consists of multiple cultures and a focus on group identity rather than on the individualism strongly emphasized in the American creed. Advocates of multiculturalism are skeptical about the notion of any common American political culture. If there is such a culture, it is seen as reflecting the domination of one group in society—white men of European descent in particular—over other groups. Rather than bringing people together in social cohesion, the notion of one American political culture to which most individuals

DOMINANT CULTURE OR DOMINATING CULTURE?

Some proponents of multiculturalism argue that given people's diverse experiences and worldviews, no true consensus around a single set of political beliefs and values is possible. Instead, any claim that there is a unified political culture is better seen as an attempt by a majority group to impose its set of beliefs on minority groups. Does the presence of a widely shared political culture in fact mean that the majority is dominating minority groups?

subscribe is seen as an exercise of power by dominant groups in society over weaker groups. In this view, as groups become more aware of how the dominant culture has cemented their subordinate position in society, they become more determined to protect and advocate their separate group identity and culture. They may interact with "mainstream" American society, but they also wish to preserve their distinctive language, customs, and beliefs.[57] *Identity politics* is a recently coined term used to describe such political activity.

RECOGNITION AND TOLERANCE OF DIVERSITY In its least controversial version, multiculturalism simply calls for a recognition that the United States is composed of many ethnic, racial, religious, gender, sexual preference, class, and nationality groups making distinctive contributions to American society. If one views the American creed in this way, it is possible to conceive of it as a national political culture, even while acknowledging that many aspects of culture and behavior might differ from one group to another. It is from this version of multiculturalism that frequent calls for toleration, diversity, and "embracing our differences" are heard in public discourse.

REJECTION OF A COMMON CULTURE In a more controversial version, multiculturalism means that any concept of a unified national political culture is false and is inherently an attempt by dominant groups to exert their power. Some multiculturalists contend not only that national political culture is highly diverse rather than unified, but also that individuals themselves reflect multiple cultural beliefs. Because of unique histories and life experiences, people look at the world differently. People "carry" a culture with them based on their group identity, but people usually have a collection of identities based on race, gender, ethnicity, and other characteristics, so the mix of beliefs may differ markedly from person to person.

libertarianism
a view that emphasizes the importance of individual choice and responsibility, the private sector, and the free market, in which government's primary obligations are to defend the country militarily, protect individuals from crime, and ensure that people fulfill contracts entered into freely.

CONFLICT WITH THE AMERICAN CREED This more controversial version of multiculturalism can lead to direct conflicts with beliefs in the American creed, particularly as they pertain to equality and individualism. For example, the nature of gender relations in some cultures has led to the rise of "cultural defenses" in American court cases.[58] The cases are inherently inflammatory and controversial. Some have involved men charged with kidnap and rape who defended their actions as part of a particular marriage custom in their culture, and men who explained the murder of their wives as a culturally sanctioned response to their wives' adultery or mistreatment. In other cases, mothers who killed their children have explained their actions as instigated by the shame of a husband's infidelity and as part of a cultural practice of mother–child suicide. Expert testimony about a defendant's cultural background has sometimes led to dropped or reduced charges or reduced sentences.[59]

Cases such as these raise challenging questions. Advocates of the American creed would ask whether equality is better served by emphasizing the equal and free status of each individual or by emphasizing the equal status of different cultural beliefs, which might differentiate between the rights accorded to men and women. Advocates of multiculturalism would ask whether these defenses are any different from those offered earlier in American history by individuals with a European cultural heritage. For a long time in the United States, they note, legal rights were sharply different for men and women, largely because of Western cultural understandings about gender relations.

Libertarianism Argues for a Very Limited Government Role

Libertarianism is the belief that individuals are responsible for their own lives, and society is best off with individuals as free from government restraints as possible. Government's responsibilities should be very limited, libertarians argue, and should not intrude on individual property rights or liberties. Its fundamental duties are to defend the country militarily, to protect individuals from crime, and to ensure that people fulfill contracts entered into freely. Beyond those duties, individual choice, the market, and voluntary action are what drive society, and government should not interfere. Outside these core responsibilities, each and every act of government compromises individual freedom.

In the United States, many citizens and politicians of both major political parties profess to hold some libertarian beliefs. This pick-and-choose method is usually unsatisfactory to libertarians: limited government activity and the primacy of the individual and a free market are core principles that should apply across all policy areas, and not be applied only when politically convenient. The American creed prizes individualism and limited government, but to libertarians the creed tolerates too big a role for government.

American Political Culture Is a Mosaic of Beliefs

The beliefs of the American creed have been powerful guides for public thinking about politics. As noted earlier, these beliefs are ideals that mark the starting point for most Americans when they think about political issues. Americans may be convinced to change their understanding of the meaning of these beliefs, or they may find severe tension between the beliefs and have to determine the acceptable balance between them. They may in some cases simply choose to ignore, or be persuaded to ignore, one of the beliefs that they profess to support.

For some people, American creed beliefs may be displaced by alternative sets of beliefs, such as those just discussed. More common, however, is that Americans hold many of these beliefs simultaneously and in some tension—supporting the American creed, for example, but also holding strong communitarian beliefs or even views supportive of discrimination. Perhaps some hold beliefs from all three of these streams—American creed, communitarianism, discrimination—simultaneously. Or they could embrace the joining of other beliefs such as multiculturalism or libertarianism with the American creed beliefs.

The beliefs of the American creed—democracy, individualism, liberty, property rights, religious freedom—and the value of equality are powerful touchstones in American politics that guide the way most individuals think about politics and government, but they do not preclude other beliefs and ideals holding important places in the mosaic of American political culture. Each generation works with the political culture template left by previous generations and makes its own adjustments, either minor or major, of what is permissible and impermissible, proper and improper, in American politics and government. The remarkable and dynamic mosaic of American political culture endures but also is periodically redefined and reshaped.

On MyPoliSciLab

Review the Chapter

Listen to **Chapter 2** on **MyPoliSciLab**

What Does It Mean to Be an American?

2.1 Define political culture and explain how certain values and beliefs achieve dominance within a society, p. 25.

Political culture consists of the basic values, beliefs, attitudes, predispositions, and expectations within which politics operates. It is where citizens start as they process and assess issues, causes, groups, parties, candidates, and public officials. Political culture provides a language used by politicians in speaking to the public.

The Beliefs of the American Creed

2.2 Illustrate how the key values and beliefs of the American creed shape politics and government today, p. 31.

The American creed is built around beliefs in individualism, democracy, liberty, property rights, and religion, all tied together by the value of equality. These beliefs are frequently discussed during the formation of public policy. One of the key story lines of American history is that over time, groups that had been discriminated against, such as racial minorities and women, demanded that they, too, be able to receive the benefits of the creed.

Consequences and Implications of the American Creed

2.3 Evaluate the consequences of American political culture such as limited government and a weak sense of sovereign power, p. 40.

Several consequences emerge from the creed's dominance in American political culture, including a preference for limited government, a weak sense of sovereign power, tension between private and public interests, and concern about the impact of competing beliefs. The beliefs of the creed can sometimes conflict. The belief in liberty might lead toward one policy solution, but the belief in democracy might lead toward another. Tension also arises because the beliefs themselves may be defined differently or definitions might change over time. Terms such as *democracy* and *liberty* might mean different things to different people. Tension between beliefs and over the definition of each belief creates much of the debate in American politics.

Challenges to the American Creed

2.4 Describe the major challenges and alternatives to the dominant political culture, p. 48.

Throughout American history, other views have challenged the creed. Alternative modes of thinking about political life have had important effects in the United States. Communitarianism emphasized the role of society or community rather than the centrality of the individual. Communitarianism was prominent during the colonial and Revolutionary periods and continues to influence politics. Discrimination also has had a profound influence on American politics. Justification and defense of social hierarchy and inequality, particularly those based on race and gender, have played a large role in American history. Multiculturalism questions the desirability of a consensus in political culture, arguing that any such consensus is more likely the imposition of the values and beliefs of dominant groups upon groups that are weaker. Libertarianism tolerates only the most minimal role for government, proposing instead that individuals should be given the maximum latitude to make choices and decisions free from government coercion and constraint.

Learn the Terms

Study and **Review** the **Flashcards**

American creed, p. 28
communitarianism, p. 49
discrimination, p. 50
equality, p. 31
individualism, p. 33
libertarianism, p. 56
liberty, p. 35
limited government, p. 40
multiculturalism, p. 54
natural rights, p. 35
political culture, p. 25
property rights, p. 36
religious freedom, p. 37
sovereign power, p. 43

Test Yourself

2.1 Define political culture and explain how certain values and beliefs achieve dominance within a society.

The heavy emphasis on individualism in American political culture sometimes makes it difficult to

a. be highly religious.
b. convince people that there is a "public" interest.
c. move geographically in search of better opportunities.
d. appeal to people's self interest.
e. convince people that they should be free to pursue their dreams and aspirations.

2.2 Illustrate how the key values and beliefs of the American creed shape politics and government today.

Which of the following statements is NOT a reflection of the key values and beliefs of the American creed?

a. People should choose their own path through life.
b. Individuals should be free to acquire, own, and use goods and assets.
c. Government restraint on individual behavior should be minimal.
d. Government actions should reflect the will of the people.
e. Governments should actively support all religious faiths.

2.3 Evaluate the consequences of American political culture such as limited government and a weak sense of sovereign power.

Which of the following is a consequence of the American creed?

a. Americans view competing ideas with suspicion.
b. The Supreme Court serves as the final authority in American government.
c. Americans trust government to do the right thing.
d. Americans welcome competing ideas.
e. It is easy to identify and promote the public interest.

2.4 Describe the major challenges and alternatives to the dominant political culture.

Which of the following is NOT a challenge to the American creed?

a. Communitarianism
b. Multiculturalism
c. Discrimination
d. Individualism
e. Libertarianism

Explore Further

SUGGESTED READINGS BY TOP SCHOLARS

Christopher Ellis and James A. Stimson. 2012. *Ideology in America*. New York: Cambridge University Press. Explores how Americans hold political views that are often philosophically conservative but operationally liberal, such as believing in limited government but supporting government programs, and considers how religious beliefs intersect with this seeming contradiction.

Calvin C. Jillson. 2004. *Pursuing the American Dream: Opportunity and Exclusion over Four Centuries*. Lawrence: University Press of Kansas. Provides a sweeping overview of the idea of opportunity in American thought and its institutionalization in social, economic, and political life.

Benjamin I. Page and Lawrence R. Jacobs. 2009. *Class War? What Americans Really Think About Economic Inequality*. Chicago: University of Chicago Press. Argues that Americans are more supportive of measures to address income inequality than is typically assumed.

Patricia Strach. 2007. *All in the Family: The Private Roots of American Public Policy*. Stanford, CA: Stanford University Press. Argues that to understand the full scope of American government, one must examine how government uses the family to implement many policies.

Elizabeth Theiss-Moore. 2009. *Who Counts as an American? The Boundaries of National Identity*. New York: Cambridge University Press. Discusses how Americans think about who is and who is not part of the American nation, and how these boundaries create both community and exclusionary tendencies.

SUGGESTED WEBSITES

E Pluribus Unum: The Bradley Project on America's National Identity: www.bradleyproject.org/bradleyprojectreport.html
Data and analysis exploring the idea of a shared national identity, perceived threats to that identity, and differences between demographic groups.

U.S. Religious Landscape Survey: religions.pewforum.org/
A survey of more than 35,000 adult Americans on their religious practices, beliefs, and opinions on issues.

Trends in Political Values and Core Attitudes: 1987–2009: www.people-press.org/2009/05/21/independents-take-center-stage-in-obama-era/
A survey of American attitudes across an array of fundamental beliefs as well as some specific policy areas.

Public Agenda: www.publicagenda.org/citizen
Of particular interest are the issue guides, which examine major issues and present the basic policy choices. The choices provide a good sense of different trade-offs in American creed beliefs, as well as competing beliefs such as communitarianism and libertarianism. See also the surveys of immigrants in 2002 and 2009 ("A Place to Call Home").

World's Smallest Political Quiz: www.theadvocates.org/quizp/index.html
A quiz published by the Advocates for Self-Government, a libertarian group. The quiz analyzes your answers and labels your political ideology.

Listen to Chapter 3 on MyPoliSciLab

The Constitution

LOWERING THE VOTING AGE TO 18

oung Americans between the ages of 18 and 21 did not always have the right to vote. Today they do. The uniform adoption of an 18-year-old voting age across the United States was accomplished through the ratification of the Twenty-sixth Amendment to the U.S. Constitution in 1971. A handful of states had previously lowered their voting age, at least for some elections. Most states, however, still had 21 as the legal age for voting at the beginning of the 1970s. This was consistent with the societal consensus that 21 was the age of maturity.[1]

The Vietnam War provided one key catalyst to changing thoughts about the age of maturity. Eighteen- to twenty-year-olds were dying in large numbers on the battlefield, but they did not have the right to vote for the leaders who sent them to war. Similar pressure had arisen following World War II and the Korean War, however, but amendments to change the voting age had gone nowhere. Many Americans saw young people of 18 to 20 as rebellious, uncertain, and susceptible to emotional appeals and rabble rousing rather than as sober and thoughtful citizens.

Vietnam changed everything. Unlike the previous conflicts, this one became tremendously controversial and highly unpopular among large segments of the population. It was especially unpopular among younger Americans, in part because of the military draft, and they protested in unconventional ways because they could not vote. States began to reconsider their laws, and support grew again at the national level for an amendment. In addition to the organizations that had supported the idea for decades, a number of youth organizations pressed for the 18-year-old vote, as did labor unions, some church groups, and organizations linked to the civil rights movement. The societal consensus for an 18-year-old voting age grew.

The path to an amendment accelerated in 1970, with the addition of a provision in the Senate's renewal of the Voting Rights Act (originally passed in 1965) that lowered the age for all elections

3.1 Trace the developments that led to the American Revolution and the country's first constitution, p. 63.

3.2 Outline the problems the Framers of the Constitution attempted to resolve and the solutions they devised, p. 73.

3.3 Compare and contrast the arguments of Anti-Federalists and Federalists, p. 86.

3.4 Explain the processes of constitutional change, p. 91.

FIT TO SERVE BUT NOT TO VOTE Young American soldiers of the Ninth Infantry along the South Vietnamese–Cambodian border in May 1970. The contrast between young adults ages 18–20 serving in combat but being unable to vote led to demands, as during previous wars, that the voting age be lowered. One reason the demand succeeded at this time was the controversy over the war itself. Not only were the troops unable to vote, but the young adults who marched in large numbers against and for the war were also shut out of the ballot box.

The Big Picture If people dislike politicians so much, then why are the majority of people content with the Constitution that these politicians represent? Author John J. Coleman explains what basic themes and mechanisms for change in the Constitution contribute to its continued popularity.

The Basics Since the Bill of Rights, the Constitution has only been amended 17 times. Learn about the Constitution's original purpose and what circumstances will be required if ever it should be amended for an 18th time.

How does the Constitution change?

In Context Who were the founding fathers? What challenges did they face when ratifying the Constitution? By getting inside the founders' heads, Costas Panagopoulos explains how we can continue to keep the spirit of the Constitution alive today.

Think Like a Political Scientist Understand how the Constitution affects the behavior of the institutions of government—including the president. Costas Panagopoulos lays out what topics fascinate constitutional scholars the most today and demonstrates why the Constitution encourages the different branches to act strategically.

In the Real World How well does the system of checks-and-balances really work? Decide whether each branch effectively checks the others—particularly, whether Congress should have the power to oversee the bureaucracy—by examining the failed "Fast and Furious" case and how it was resolved.

So What? Which are more important—the Constitution's words or its overarching themes? Author John J. Coleman introduces this timely debate and asks students to decide whether they are "originalists" or whether they believe in a "living constitution."

to 18. A challenge to the provision quickly reached the Supreme Court. In *Oregon v. Mitchell* (1970), a divided Court concluded that Congress could set the age for federal elections but not state elections. Therefore, the country was now faced with an 18-year-old voting age for federal elections (president, U.S. House, U.S. Senate) and whatever age each state set for its own elections.

This scenario promised a very difficult election in 1972. Many states would have to monitor different voting ages for different parts of the ballot. Even if they wanted to change their voting age to 18, in many states that change might require voter approval of a proposed state constitutional amendment at two subsequent elections. A national consensus now existed that lowering the voting age uniformly was right, whether on policy grounds or because of the difficulties facing election administration without a uniform age.

Spurred by the Court's action, Congress moved quickly. Within a month of the *Oregon v. Mitchell* decision, Randolph Jennings, who had proposed the first constitutional amendment on the issue in 1942, introduced another one to lower the voting age. The Senate approved the amendment unanimously, and the House approved the amendment with fewer than 20 dissenting votes, before it was sent to the states for ratification. The amendment needed quick passage to be in effect for 1972. A little over three months after being sent to the states, the Twenty-sixth Amendment had been ratified and added to the Constitution.

The quick response and ratification of this amendment across the states mark it as unusual. However, in terms of the importance of causal factors such as societal consensus; interest-group pressure; and politicians who believed in the proposal for reasons of good policy or electoral advantage, or both, the story of the Twenty-sixth Amendment resembles those of other successful amendments.[2]

In addition to establishing voting rights, the U.S. Constitution wrestles with many questions. What are the responsibilities of the different branches of government? How can the Constitution ensure that no one part of American government becomes too powerful or too unchecked in its exercise of power? How can it protect the liberties and rights of the people, and what are the limits to those liberties and rights? In this chapter, we explore how the Framers answered these questions as they wrote the Constitution. Based on their experience with Great Britain, as well as their experience in governing the new country after the Revolution in 1776, the Framers were deeply concerned with power—its use, abuse, extent, and proper exercise—as they designed a new system of government. Over the centuries since, public officials have worked within the Constitution's constraints but also, in turn, have sought to reshape and redefine those constraints.

From Revolution to Constitution

3.1 Trace the developments that led to the American Revolution and the country's first constitution.

omentous in its impact, the American Revolution has been difficult for historians to classify. Unlike other revolutions, it was not a revolt of one social class against another or a replacement of one economic system by another. If it was not a revolution in these ways, then what was it?

The American Revolution Changed Ideas About Governance

One answer provided by political scientists and historians is that the American Revolution was an "ideological" revolution, which is to say a revolution most notably about ideas and philosophy of governing.[3] To colonial leaders, human beings were inherently susceptible to being corrupted and to using the instruments of government power, whether legislation, rules, and regulations or criminal sanctions, to advantage themselves and harm others. Government was necessary, they believed, but government could also be used to impose its will over other individuals and groups. The victims of the abusive use of government power were individual liberty and freedom. To defend liberty and thwart excessive power required vigilance and virtue from ordinary people as well as political leaders. Voters needed to select their leaders with care and to be sure they were individuals of honesty and integrity. Leaders needed to exercise self-discipline and to use government power judiciously. Voters as well as leaders had to refrain from seeing government power as primarily a means to benefit themselves and harm others.

The colonists drew insights from their own experience and borrowed liberally from various political theorists and writers. British political theorist John Locke's ideas on limited government and social contracts were especially influential. The idea of the social contract was that the relationship between the governed and those people in power was equivalent to a business contract in which each side had obligations to fulfill or the contract would become void.[4] The governed were not bound indefinitely to corrupt or dysfunctional political institutions. From this foundation, the colonists built a new understanding of politics based on the concepts of representation, constitutional rights, and sovereignty.

During the decade prior to the colonists' formal declaration of independence, the language of democratic representation was a key rallying cry to build enthusiasm for the prospect of a separation from Great Britain. The expression "no taxation without representation" highlights one of the most famous demands from the American Revolution and has been learned by every schoolchild since then as a key to what the revolution was about. British government officials attempted to convince the colonists they were "virtually represented"—that even though the colonists did not elect members of Parliament, members of Parliament in effect represented their interests because they tended to the interests of the British Empire in general, and these two sets of interests were the same. The colonists, instead, touted the concept of direct representation: the job of the representative was to reflect faithfully the opinions of the constituents who elected him. Citizens should send representatives to the legislature with specific instructions about how to vote.

In addition, the colonists believed that constitutions should mark the boundaries of legitimate government power. People had natural, inherent rights that preceded any government action, and written constitutions were needed to protect these rights. The belief in the importance of written language to constrain the use of power and to protect liberties had a long heritage in England, dating back to the Charter of Liberties in the twelfth century, which spelled out protections for church officials among others; and the Magna Carta in the thirteenth century, which delineated some of the limits on the sovereign's authority, detailed the rights of Parliament, and specified some liberties of individuals. During the seventeenth century, England adopted other documents such as the Bill of Rights, which further protected individual rights. Although England did not have a single written constitution, it did have foundational written documents that, taken together, served a similar role.

Lastly, the colonists challenged the dominant view of sovereignty. In Britain, the idea that there could be only one final, ultimate authority—sovereignty—was undisputed. The colonists, however, argued that sovereignty could be divided. Authority could be located in different geographical locations, for example at the local and national levels, as well as in different institutions, such as the executive and legislative branches.

The combination of these beliefs generated a radical view of the people as self-governing. The concept of "the people" as a positive, active force, rather than just passive subjects of government, became a touchstone for much of the oratory of the period.[5] The people's role had been transformed from occasional watchdog to participant: the people were not only a check on government, they in effect were the government. In this new conceptual understanding of how politics should work, the active and continuous consent of the governed was necessary.[6]

The Colonists Rebelled Against Taxes Imposed Unilaterally by the British Government

The immediate impetus for the revolution was a series of economic and political events, many of which received prominent billing in the Declaration of Independence. The causal forces are difficult to disentangle. Would the events have had such resonance in the absence of new ideas about the right of the people to self-government? For decades, the colonists had been out of the practical reach of British rulers and had been allowed to operate with extensive freedom. This experience built their confidence in their ability to self-govern. So we can flip the question and ask: would those ideas about self-government have flourished as thoroughly in the absence of a set of provocative events? After all, the revolutionary leaders were not simply dreamily concocting new political ideas from the sidelines—they were practical and strategic politicians whose ideas about government were forged in the political battles within the colonies and with Britain.

The best resolution to these questions is to see the events and ideas as mutually reinforcing. When Britain began to clamp down on the colonies, the colonists believed the freedom they had already achieved was being threatened, and this threat reinforced the appeal of self-governance. To colonists, the revolution was needed to maintain their freedom, not to create it. As they saw it, a campaign was afoot to demolish American liberty. These causal factors—ideas and events—cannot be completely separated, as each furthered the other and both in turn fostered sentiment for revolution.

The two most influential economic groups of the day were New England merchants and southern planters. These two groups had long been fiercely loyal to the British government, and by controlling key positions of power in the colonies, they prevented more radical elements from pushing toward conflict with the mother country. However, they also became agitated by the changes in British policies, particularly the tax policies. Beginning in the 1650s, a sequence of actions by the British government sought to bring the colonies under control.

NAVIGATION ACTS The British government passed the Navigation Acts between 1651 and 1696. The Navigation Acts were a series of laws that set the rules for trade to and from the colonies. Economic growth in the American colonies benefited England, so although the Acts generally did not seek to depress trade, they did set rules about which products must be transported in English ships, which products had to be shipped to England prior to their final destination, which products were subject to a tax when unloaded or inspected in England, and so on.

MOLASSES AND SUGAR ACTS In 1733, the Molasses Act imposed a heavy tax on shipments of molasses from locations other than the British West Indies, which drove up the costs to producers (especially of rum) and merchants in America. The law was widely flouted through smuggling, and in 1764 the Sugar Act provided for a lower rate than the existing molasses tax but also promised much stricter enforcement and added new limits on the markets to which certain exports, such as lumber, could be sent.

CURRENCY ACT The Currency Act of 1764 established that the colonial governments could issue paper currency, but this currency could not be used as legal tender in the repayment of public or private debts (gold and silver, relatively scarce in the colonies, would need to be used instead). This act helped protect British creditors and merchants from being paid in paper currency of depreciated value.

STAMP ACT From 1754 to 1760 in North America, and from 1756 to 1763 in Europe, Britain engaged in the French and Indian War, which depleted the British treasury. In North America, the war resulted in France transferring land in what is now Canada and areas west of the British colonies to Great Britain and transferring the region known as Louisiana to Spain, while Spain transferred the region known as

Florida to Great Britain (this region would return to Spanish control at the end of the American Revolutionary War in 1783). The French and Indian War was a major, expensive conflict. Believing that many of its costs were related to maintaining the safety of the American colonists and that the colonists had experienced a free ride for some time while British citizens subsidized the colonies extensively, the British government instituted new policies designed to extract some revenue from this

TAXATION WITHOUT REPRESENTATION

Taxes are rarely popular. They are even more unpopular when people believe they have been imposed without fair representation of their point of view. One of the chief debates between the colonists and the British government was over the nature of representation. Actions such as the Stamp Act convinced Americans that they had no genuine representation in the British political system.

growing part of its empire. The Stamp Act, passed by Parliament in 1765, required all legal documents, licenses, commercial contracts, newspapers, and pamphlets to obtain a tax stamp. The colonists immediately rebelled. Stamp agents were attacked by mobs, and many had their property destroyed. Protests erupted, and several colonial assemblies passed resolutions against the act. The Stamp Act Congress, also known as the First Congress of the American Colonies, marked the first time that a number of the colonies sent representatives to a meeting to discuss a response to British actions. The Congress, representing nine colonies, signed the Declaration of Rights and Grievances at its meetings in October 1765. The Declaration, although stating the colonies' affection for the king and respect for parliamentary authority, argued that Parliament could not impose the stamp tax because the colonies were not directly represented in Parliament. In addition to the widespread discontent in the colonies, a boycott of British goods finally led Parliament to repeal the tax. But Parliament then passed the Declaratory Act on the same day of the repeal in March 1766, stating it was the right of the British government to pass laws that would be binding on the colonists. The British government wanted to send a clear message that the colonies were indeed part of the British Empire and subject to its edicts.

TOWNSHEND ACTS That message would soon be reinforced with the Townshend Acts, named after Charles Townshend, prime minister of Britain beginning in 1767, the year of the passage of the Acts. One of these acts suspended the New York legislature because that colony had not complied with a law requiring that British soldiers be quartered in (that is, reside in) housing owned by the colonists. The Revenue Act, the second of the Townshend Acts, imposed customs duties (taxes) on colonial imports of glass, lead, paint, paper, and tea. Generally, these fees were passed along to the colonists in the form of higher price tags on such products. Resistance to the Revenue Act was considerable. The British disbanded the Massachusetts Assembly in 1768 because of its unwillingness to enforce the law. Tensions rose during the next 18 months, culminating with the Boston Massacre in March 1770. British soldiers, enduring another day of taunting from a crowd gathered at the Customs House, killed five colonists. The event and the subsequent acquittals of the soldiers further agitated the colonists. Ultimately, boycotts and merchants' refusal to import goods led to the repeal of all the Townshend duties except that on tea.

TEA ACT In 1773, the British government enacted a particularly controversial new economic policy, the Tea Act. Tea was an extremely important industry in that era. Leaders of the economically advanced countries of the day believed that tea, much like high technology today or automobiles 40 years ago, stimulated the national economy. Nearly every country wanted a piece of this industry. Competition was brisk, but the profit potential was enormous. The Tea Act allowed the British-controlled East India Company to export its tea to America without paying the tea duty that had been imposed by the Townshend Acts. The Tea Act made the British tea cheaper than Dutch tea, which up to that point had dominated the American market and was sold by colonial merchants (in violation of the Navigation Acts). The East India Company used its own British agents to sell the tea or relied on merchants with political connections to colonial governors appointed by the king, thereby squeezing out many colonial merchants.

The colonists' response was the incident known as the Boston Tea Party. Inflammatory language unmistakably threatened death to anyone who assisted the East India Company in unloading its tea. In December 1773, protesters prevented the unloading of East India Company tea and threw the tea in the harbor. The British government viewed the Tea Party as an act of terrorism—random violence and property damage coupled with random threats designed to intimidate colonists and British officials alike, all to prevent a company from carrying out its legal activities. To Americans, however, the Tea Party became a symbol of reaction against powerful government, a symbol that every schoolchild for generations has learned. The Tea Party movement that emerged in 2009 is the latest in a long line of protests that use Boston Tea Party imagery to link back to this iconic event.

Declaration of Independence document announcing the intention of the colonies to separate from Great Britain based on shared grievances about the treatment of the colonists by the British government.

INTOLERABLE ACTS When the Boston Town Meeting refused Parliament's demand for compensation for the tea, the British government retaliated with what colonists referred to as the Intolerable Acts. These acts closed the port of Boston, restricted the power of the Massachusetts Assembly and local town meetings, quartered troops in private houses, and exempted British officials from trial in Massachusetts. In response, 12 of the 13 colonies banded together to establish the First Continental Congress in September and October 1774.[7]

Thomas Jefferson wrote "A Summary View of the Rights of British America" to guide the Virginia delegates who attended the Congress, and the document was later shared with delegates from the other colonies. In addition to specific complaints about the British laws discussed previously, Jefferson argued more theoretically that Parliament's governing authority did not include the colonies, that the colonists had natural rights rather than rights granted to them by the king, and that whatever loyalty the colonists offered the king was voluntary and not obligatory. Although "A Summary View" did not call for the colonies to break from Great Britain, Jefferson's strongly worded argument led some scholars to consider it his first draft of the Declaration of Independence.[8] "A Summary View" also greatly increased Jefferson's national visibility as a visionary and stirring writer. Ultimately, the Congress issued demands to the king in the form of a Declaration and Resolves. Although more mildly stated and less challenging to British authority than Jefferson's words, the Declaration and Resolves made it clear that the conflict in America was reaching a boiling point. In addition to issuing this document, the delegates at the Congress developed plans for colonial resistance to what they deemed to be an overbearing imperial government.

□ The Declaration of Independence Aimed to Build a Nation

The Continental Congress met a second time from May 1775 through December 1776 in a charged atmosphere. In April 1775, skirmishes had broken out in Lexington and Concord, Massachusetts, representing the start of the Revolutionary War. Parliament had rejected the First Continental Congress's Declaration and Resolves, which set out complaints about economic policies, lack of representation, British domination of the colonial judicial system, and disbanding of colonial legislatures. Communications within and between the colonies about the trouble with the British government were frequent and impassioned, with writers such as Thomas Paine using pamphlets and his 1776 book *Common Sense* to arouse opposition to the royal government.

Recognizing the drift of events and opinion, the Second Continental Congress began the process of building a new government by approving the issuance of currency, establishing diplomatic and trade relations with other countries, and creating an army. George Washington served as the general of the new Continental Army, and throughout the war he used a combination of troops from the Army and the state militias.

Influenced by experience, their reading of history, the lessons of the republics of antiquity in Greece and Rome, and the ideas of a range of writers, political leaders began building the intellectual framework necessary to justify revolution. On July 4, 1776, their efforts bore fruit, as the Second Continental Congress approved the **Declaration of Independence,** which was the product of a committee created by the Second Congress and largely drafted by Thomas Jefferson, borrowing many themes from his earlier "A Summary View of the Rights of British America."

The Declaration asserted that rights of life, liberty, property, and the pursuit of happiness were "unalienable," meaning they cannot be given away. Similarly, as expressed earlier by British philosopher John Locke, these rights were natural, present in people as an essential part of their being. Government did not provide these rights—the most it could do was restrict them. When it restricted them arbitrarily and unjustly, then revolution was an appropriate response. The Declaration of Independence was also an attempt to find common ground that would join the colonists

THE DECLARATION OF INDEPENDENCE

The Second Continental Congress adopted the Declaration of Independence on July 4, 1776. The Declaration sought to build a sense of national unity. Creating a nation, and the shared goals and sacrifices that go with it, was one contributing factor in the success of the Revolutionary effort.

as "Americans." Although "nation" is often used as synonymous with "country," from a political science perspective a **nation** is a distinctive concept. It refers to a shared sense of understanding among a people that they are different and separate from other peoples; that basic principles, values, and outlooks unite them; and that they have a right to self-government. The Declaration attempted to inspire that sense of nationhood.

nation
a shared sense of understanding and belonging among a people that they are different and separate from other peoples with particular characteristics and that they have a right to self-government over a defined territory.

France, Spain, and the Dutch Republic supplemented the efforts of the Americans. All of these countries were long-time opponents of the British. France challenged Britain militarily in America, and the Spanish and Dutch engaged in conflicts with Britain in Europe, stretching British military resources thin. In October 1781, American and French troops combined for a decisive victory at the Battle of Yorktown (Virginia), which led to the surrender of the British Army. The Americans and the British negotiated the terms of peace in 1782 and signed the Treaty of Paris to end the war officially in September 1783.

The Articles of Confederation Aimed to Build a Government

The next step after declaring independence was to build a set of government institutions infused by fundamental principles, rules of operation, values, and beliefs.[9] A government enhances a population's sense of nationhood. Constructing a government that can rule effectively and is consistent with a population's sense of nationhood was a significant challenge in 1776, just as it is in emerging democracies today. Rules and

3.1

3.2

3.3

3.4

Articles of Confederation
the first constitution of the United States, which based most power in the states.

procedures guide how governments operate, and rules laid down early can be difficult to change later. The stakes, therefore, are high.

The first attempt to devise governing principles and draft a national constitution was the **Articles of Confederation.** The move to draft the Articles began in June 1776 at the same time the Second Continental Congress began drafting the Declaration of Independence. John Dickinson, an attorney and politician from Pennsylvania, was appointed as the chair of the drafting committee. Dickinson was known nationally as the author of *Letters from a Farmer in Pennsylvania*, a collection of 12 essays published in 1767–1768 that challenged the Townshend Acts and specifically the authority of Parliament to levy taxes in the colonies to raise revenue for Great Britain.

After one month, the committee presented a first draft of the Articles to the Second Continental Congress. The Second Congress approved them in November 1777, and each of the 13 former colonies (now called states) had to ratify the document. Upon ratification in 1781, the Second Continental Congress became the Congress of the Confederation, more commonly called the Continental Congress, with the members of the Second Congress maintaining their seats in the new legislative body.

The Articles remained in effect until 1789 and were, in effect, the governing document of the United States during the Revolutionary War despite formal ratification not being completed until 1781.[10] The challenge facing the authors of the Articles of Confederation was to create a government that embraced the sense of nationhood expressed in the Declaration of Independence, while also recognizing that Americans primarily identified themselves by the individual states in which they lived. The Articles of Confederation reflected a deep fear of centralized political power, born out of the Americans' experience with Parliament and British monarchs and expressed in the Declaration of Independence. It also provided a leading role for the states. For both these reasons, it seemed a reasonable fit for the new country.

Under the Articles, the national government was based in Congress. Members of Congress were selected by state legislatures, paid by the states, and able to be recalled and removed from office by the states. Laws were to be implemented by the individual states. There was neither an executive branch nor a judiciary. It was difficult for Congress to pass legislation. Although state legislatures typically sent three representatives to Congress, each state cast only one vote. For a bill to pass, a simple majority of 7 of the 13 states was not enough. Instead, a supermajority—a set amount that is more than a simple majority—of 9 states had to agree. Changing the Articles required the approval of all 13 states.

PROBLEMS WITH THE ARTICLES OF CONFEDERATION QUICKLY BECAME APPARENT Difficulties with the Articles set in almost immediately, in part because Congress's powers were limited. Although this was consistent with American ideas about limited government, the government also needed to perform basic functions. Congress could declare war—but there was no standing national army. It could regulate trade with Native Americans—but it could not regulate trade between the states. It could borrow or coin money—but it could not institute taxes. Effectively, the system of government built under the Articles of Confederation made the national government almost entirely dependent on the voluntary cooperation of the states. There was little this government controlled and little it could do to force action.

Action was sometimes needed internationally, but the United States had no coherent way to deal with other countries. Economic treaties were a free-for-all, with states making their own arrangements with foreign countries. Under the Articles, Congress would have had no way to enforce international treaties even if it had been able to negotiate them. Although Congress could declare war and could name senior army officers, any military action required pulling together the disparate state militias.

Given the control of portions of North America by European countries, and the ongoing interactions with Indian tribes, a more coordinated effort with national leadership was an appealing idea to many public officials.

Action was sometimes needed internally as well. The domestic upheaval during the 1780s shook many politicians, merchants, and creditors. In a number of states, legislatures passed laws extending the terms of repayments for debts and reducing penalties for nonpayment. Others provided paper currency not backed by guaranteed conversion into specific amounts of silver or gold, asking creditors and merchants to accept potentially worthless paper in exchange for the land, services, or goods they had provided. Rhode Island's legislature went the furthest, though, first issuing paper currency for debt repayment; next mandating that creditors and merchants accept the currency or face fines; and finally when its highest court declared the mandated currency to be in violation of the state constitution, dismissing several members of the

COURTING TROUBLE

Shays's Rebellion, in which rebels in western Massachusetts took control of courthouses, as shown here, was a wake-up call to political and business leaders around the country.

3.1

3.2

3.3

3.4

Shays's Rebellion
a protest by farmers in western Massachusetts in 1786–1787 to stop foreclosures on property by state courts; it convinced many political leaders that the Articles of Confederation were insufficient to govern the United States.

court and appointing new members. To leaders in government and business, democracy had degenerated into rule by the mob, or "mobocracy." In their view, all that was wrong under the Articles was illustrated in the incident known as **Shays's Rebellion,** a protest by farmers in western Massachusetts in 1786–1787 to stop foreclosures on property by state courts.

Daniel Shays was a former army officer angered by the growing number of people being thrown off their land in western Massachusetts, in large part for an inability to pay land taxes. In previous incidents in Massachusetts and other states, citizens physically challenged government officials seeking to collect property taxes. But no one had quite seen anything like what happened in Massachusetts. To prevent further foreclosures, from August 1786 through February 1787, Shays joined and then led like-minded men numbering anywhere from the high hundreds to several thousand and bearing firearms. They assembled outside courthouses to prevent the courts from opening. Shays's supporters also attempted to raid the federal arsenal in Springfield, where weapons were stockpiled. Massachusetts officials asked the Continental Congress for assistance, but the national government was ill equipped to pull together either financial resources or military personnel, and the state itself had no permanent militia. To displace Shays and his supporters, Boston businessmen raised private money to fund the state militia. Three thousand militiamen descended on western Massachusetts to confront the rebels over a period of about six months. Massachusetts successfully put down the rebellion, but the incident sent shockwaves around the country.

The political system created by the Articles of Confederation seemed unable to manage either international or domestic affairs. As a result, the political and economic leaders concluded that the new nation's first constitution had already failed.

Frustration with the Articles of Confederation Led to the Writing of a New Constitution

The 1780s unsettled political and economic leaders, with many worrying that the people's capacity for restrained self-government had failed. Schooled in the communitarian belief that concern for the public good should outweigh personal interests, these leaders believed that people were using power to advance certain groups at the expense of others and that a critical juncture had been reached. Not everyone agreed that the experience of the 1780s was so dire, but those who did shared a sense of worry over the country's direction and concluded that change was necessary.[11]

The first attempt to repair the Articles had occurred before Shays's Rebellion. In the fall of 1786, accepting an invitation from the Virginia legislature, delegates from five states (Delaware, New Jersey, New York, Pennsylvania, and Virginia) met in Annapolis, Maryland, to discuss the problems facing the young national government. Delegates from four other states did not arrive in time for the meeting, and four other states did not respond to Virginia's invitation. With only five states present, the Annapolis Convention was not in a position to make specific proposals for changes in the Articles. Instead, the delegates approved a resolution drafted by Alexander Hamilton that called for possible revision of the Articles. Hamilton had been an assistant to George Washington in the Revolutionary War and would later play a large role in the ratification of the Constitution and as secretary of the Treasury in Washington's administration.[12] His resolution called for Congress to send delegates to Philadelphia at some future date to make the Articles more effective in managing domestic and international affairs.

Shocked by Shays's Rebellion, Congress called on each state to send delegates to Philadelphia in May 1787 to discuss revision of the articles. Every state participated except Rhode Island, which objected to the convention based on concerns that a strong national government was a threat to local self-government. Delegates met with a sense of crisis in the air: the national government appeared to be unable to handle international disputes, establish civility and cooperation between the states, or react to domestic insurrection. The delegates quickly concluded that revision of the Articles was pointless. They decided to start over and establish a new set of ground rules for an effective American government.[13] The delegates were politically experienced, with more than half having served in the Continental Congress. Eight had signed the Declaration of Independence; six had signed the Articles of Confederation. Several had served as governors of their respective states.

The efforts of the 55 delegates who met to work out the details of a new framework for American government would culminate in the Constitution, the young country's second attempt to build a government that would rule effectively and unify the new American nation. Although the delegates were still concerned about threats to personal liberty posed by the concentration of too much power in a national government, they now believed that too weak a national government was just as severe a threat. As they struggled to devise a new set of rules for the national government, the Framers would need to find a way to blend power with liberty, freedom with order, and national authority with state sovereignty.

3.1 3.2 3.3 3.4

Crafting the Constitution

3.2 Outline the problems the Framers of the Constitution attempted to resolve and the solutions they devised.

Although they may often be skeptical about the individuals in power, in general Americans are proud of the Constitution and the system of government, liberties, and responsibilities it created. Indeed, for many of us, the American form of government essentially defines democracy. People may be critical of politicians, but they believe that the constitutional system works fairly and effectively. If a system of rules is legitimate, people will agree to challenge policies and actions through constitutionally established procedures. In its protection for liberty, property rights, religion, democracy, and equality, the Constitution adheres to beliefs deeply held by most Americans across many diverse groupings, which enhances the esteem in which it is held.

For the most part, this satisfaction is reasonable. The U.S. Constitution is now the oldest national written constitution in the world, and the vast majority of countries have followed the American model of a written constitution. In the United States and other countries with written constitutions, such as Canada, Mexico, France, and Germany, the interpretation of the text might change, but "the constitution" is a well-defined, explicit document. Similarly, the means to amend it are precisely stated, normally requiring a procedure that differs from the one used to pass legislation. In contrast, Great Britain provides the primary example of a country with an unwritten constitution. The British constitution might be thought of as "an understanding" that has emerged from statutes, traditions, and historical documents.

Fashioning a constitution is an exercise in problem solving that reflects the particular circumstances present at the document's creation. This was no less true for Americans in 1787 than it was for constitution writers in West Germany after World War II or those attempting to construct a constitution in Libya in 2011. In their problem solving, the Germans prohibited political parties based on Nazism. The drafters of Libya's constitution sought ways to give different ethnic and religious groups a stake in the broader sense of nationhood, and to determine the balance between central and regional authority that would be best for governing and most practical for the political task of ratifying the constitution. Throughout the Middle East in 2011 and 2012, people who had overthrown their governments as part of the Arab Spring confronted the question of what comes next. The powers of the new governments; the relationship among the executive, legislative, and judicial branches; the rights and liberties of the people; the role of civilian, military, and religious authorities; how to keep peace between different groups in the population; whether to enshrine specific public policy in the constitution—all of these questions faced the constitution builders in places such as Libya and Egypt.

Constitutions are complex. The resolution of one problem might well create new problems and unintended consequences. The more detailed and complicated the document, the higher the risk that it might institutionalize ideas that have only passing or temporary allegiance. This criticism has been lodged against state constitutions in the United States. Too thin a framework, however, runs the risk that the document will not be taken seriously as a guide to behavior or a limit on the abuse of power. As they worked on the draft, the Framers of the new American constitution were well aware of these considerations.[14]

The results of the deliberations of the Constitution Convention can be thought about and categorized in many ways. Table 3.1 lists the seven articles of the Constitution. Rather than review the Constitution article by article, however, we will discuss the crafting of the new constitution as an exercise in problem solving. In particular, the Framers had five major objectives:

- Resolve fundamental disputes over representation in the new government.
- Encourage public input while limiting both "excessive" democracy and concentrated power.
- Protect commerce and property.
- Create legitimacy for the new system.
- Provide a coordinated approach to international relations and national defense.

TABLE 3.1 THE CONSTITUTION

Article I: The Legislative Branch
Bicameral legislature
Nature of election
Powers and duties
Article II: The Executive Branch
Nature of election
Qualifications
Powers and duties
Article III: The Judicial Branch
Nature of appointment and tenure
Creation of Supreme Court
Types of cases
Article IV: National Unity
"Full faith and credit" to acts of other states
All "privileges and immunities" to be same whether or not a state's citizen
Guarantee of republican government
Admitting new states
Article V: The Amending Process
Procedures to amend Constitution
Article VI: National Supremacy
Constitution to be "supreme law" of the land
No religious test for public office
Article VII: Ratification Process
Procedure to ratify Constitution

The Great Compromise and Three-Fifths Compromise Resolved Fundamental Splits Over Representation

Two issues facing the delegates absolutely had to be resolved if the convention were to succeed. Both involved the distribution of political power. The delegates' solutions did not guarantee success, but without them failure was assured.

More so than many of us can understand or appreciate today, the delegates were oriented toward their individual states. Political history, tradition, and loyalty, as they knew it, had much more to do with their colonies, now states, than with the American nation at large. In their view, the Union that was to be created was less a union of disparate individuals and more a union of sovereign states.

The name of the new country—the United States—is significant in that regard. Indeed, it was not until 80 years later, when Abraham Lincoln would try to rebuild the Union in the Civil War, that Americans would routinely refer to the "United States" in the singular rather than the plural—"the United States is" rather than "the United States are." We see this plural conception reflected in the references to "them" and "their" in Article III of the Constitution: "Treason against the United States, shall consist only in levying War against them, or in adhering to their Enemies."

THE LARGE STATE–SMALL STATE SPLIT Given this strong allegiance to the states, the relative influence of the various states in the new system rose immediately as a contentious issue. The first split was the division between large and small states. If the new system were to be based at least in part on a representative legislature, how would states be represented in that body? Should representation be based on a state's population or should each state have equal representation?

The battle lines were predictable. Large states gravitated around the **Virginia Plan** written by James Madison (the future U.S. president who was a frequent speaker at the convention and who played a key role in getting the Constitution approved in the Constitutional Convention) and offered by Virginia governor Edmund Randolph (later the first U.S. Attorney General and the second U.S. Secretary of State).[15]

The Virginia Plan called for state representation in the national legislature to be based on state population: the larger a state's population, the more representatives it would send to the legislature. The people would elect this so-called lower house, which, in turn, would select the members of the upper house, based on lists of candidates provided by state legislatures.

Delegates from small states saw this plan as an unacceptable push toward large-state domination of the new political system. Their response was the **New Jersey Plan,** introduced by William Paterson (the former attorney general of New Jersey, who would go on to become a U.S. senator, governor of New Jersey, and justice on the U.S. Supreme Court). Like the Virginia Plan, the New Jersey Plan addressed more than just the issue of representation, but it was on this issue that the two competing visions of the new government were especially divided.[16] The New Jersey Plan called for equal state representation in a single-house legislature. Regardless of a state's population, it would send the same number of representatives to the legislature as any other state.

With the two plans on the table, each side staked out strong stances. If the small states wanted to destroy the Union, the large-state delegates opined, then so be it. If the large states wanted to throw their power around, declared the small states, any number of foreign countries would be more than happy to create a new government with the small states. The convention and the task of writing a new constitution faced a deep fracture, but returning to what nearly all the delegates concluded was a defunct and ineffective status quo was not a reassuring prospect for either side, so each was open to compromise.

Although sometimes in politics there is an obvious compromise or consensus position when developing rules, policies, or institutions, often this position is not reached

Virginia Plan
one of the rival plans at the Constitutional Convention, it argued for a two-house legislature, with representation based on a state's population; the lower house would be elected directly by the people, and that house would then select the members of the upper house.

New Jersey Plan
one of the rival plans at the Constitutional Convention, it called for, among other things, equal representation of the states in a single-house legislature.

Great Compromise
the agreement between small states and large states that representation in the Senate would be equal for each state, as small states preferred, and representation in the House would be based on population, as large states preferred.

Three-fifths Compromise
an agreement between slave states and free states that a state's slave population would be counted at 60 percent for purposes of determining a state's representation in the House of Representatives.

until after many rounds of bargaining and negotiation. There may even be a solution no one offered at the outset. The solution to the big state–small state split came in the form of the Connecticut Plan, also known as the **Great Compromise.** Under this plan, representation in the House of Representatives would be based on population, as the large states preferred, and the people would elect the legislators. A second legislative body, the Senate, would have equal representation of all the states, as the small states preferred, and its members would be elected by the state legislatures. The idea of a bicameral, or two-house, legislature was not new: Great Britain had a House of Commons and House of Lords, and the existence of two legislative houses was the norm in the colonies and in the states.

The vote for the Great Compromise was close: five states voted in favor, four were opposed—the two largest population states (Virginia and Pennsylvania) and the two smallest states (South Carolina and Georgia)—and one state's vote was divided (Massachusetts, the third largest state) and thus did not count. Although the plan was not entirely satisfactory to either side, it did prevent either group of states from dominating the new system of government.

THE SLAVE STATE–FREE STATE SPLIT Similar calculations drove the other critical division between political leaders. This split was between states where slavery was forbidden and states where slavery was allowed, which geographically meant a split between northern and southern states, respectively. If representation in the House of Representatives were to be determined by a state's population, how would population be determined? In particular, would slaves count as part of the population? Southern states argued that slaves should count; the northern states said they should not. Delegates from northern states believed it was hypocritical for southern states to count slaves towards population while considering them to be property for all other legal purposes. Ironically, the positions of the North and South had been reversed in a 1783 debate over the Articles of Confederation. At that time, a proposed amendment would have changed the system of determining the taxes owed by each state from its land value to its population. The North argued that slaves should fully count in a state's population for tax purposes. The South argued that slaves, being property, should not count at all. Although they compromised on counting a portion of a state's slave population, the amendment to the Articles was ultimately defeated.

In the debate at the Constitutional Convention in 1787, both sides were concerned with the balance of power in the new legislature. There were more free states than slave states, so the South was disadvantaged in the Senate. And the population of the North exceeded that of the South, so the South faced the prospect of being outvoted in the House as well. Southern delegates made it clear that this was a make-or-break issue: either include slaves in the population count or the convention ends.

A resolution was reached through the **Three-fifths Compromise.** Under this plan, 60 percent of a state's slave population would be counted toward the state's overall population. Sixty percent was chosen not as a philosophical statement, but because this number would balance representation between the North and South in the House. Neither side could dominate the other.[17]

It is a popular misconception, hundreds of years after the convention, to say that the delegates ignored the issue of slavery and were uniformly uninterested in the plight of slaves. The evidence usually offered for this assertion is the lack of direct discussion of slavery in the Constitution. If the issue does not appear prominently in the Constitution, the logic goes, the cause must be lack of interest or concern about the issue.

But the critics' contention makes the analytical mistake of assuming that what we can see is a reliable indicator of what matters most to politicians. In politics, however, sometimes what is not visible is equally as important as what is visible. Rather than ignore slavery, the delegates returned frequently to the issue, which often lurked in the

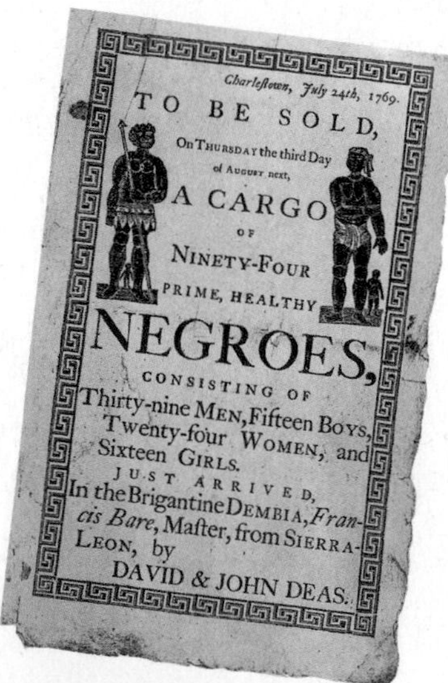

PEOPLE AS PROPERTY

Delegates from slaveholding states wanted to count slaves toward their state population, to boost their representation in the House of Representatives. Delegates from other states saw this as inconsistent with the usual treatment of slaves as property, not people. Why, they asked, should these states now benefit from treating slaves as people for the purpose of gaining more representation in the House? The Three-fifths Compromise resolved the dispute.

background of their discussions.[18] Some were ardent defenders of slavery. Others opposed the practice on economic or moral grounds. Individual states had wrestled with the issue in years prior to the convention, with 10 of the 13 states banning the importation of slaves by the time of the Constitutional Convention. Everyone recognized the explosive nature of the issue. It was ironically the importance of the issue, not the lack of interest in it, that led to its being given less visibility in the Constitution than critics today might wish.

Believing that politicians usually act strategically in important situations, political scientists would reject the analytical leap made by critics and reframe the question. If it was not due to lack of interest or concern, what would cause the Framers to avoid placing heavy emphasis on slavery in the Constitution? The answer is the immediate strategic imperative of crafting a constitution—this is the causal force contributing most heavily to slavery's lack of prominence in the Constitution. The Framers had to address the issue of slavery in a way that would not undermine their interest in producing a new document. Would a constitution have been possible if opponents of slavery were determined to use the document to eliminate it? Most of the Framers thought not, and ultimately they were more determined to write a constitution. In the twenty-first century, our moral revulsion against slavery makes it deeply disturbing to even think about this kind of trade-off, but that was the real-world situation as the Framers perceived it.[19]

Although the terms *slave* and *slavery* do not appear in the Constitution, three provisions directly concerned slavery. The first is the Three-fifths Compromise, which boosted southern representation in the House of Representatives. Second, the Constitution forbade Congress from prohibiting the importation of slaves prior to 1808. And third, any slave escaping to a free state would have to be returned to his or her master. Those who opposed slavery and saw it as a violation of the tenets of the Declaration of Independence were frustrated by these provisions, but they also realized that no new government would be formed if they pressed the issue. Their hope was that the new government would, over time, devise a way to deal with the problem of slavery. Political bargains in the first half of the nineteenth century gradually confined slavery to the southern states, but the issue remained unresolved, exploding in the calamity of the Civil War.

The Framers Wanted Public Officials to Hear the Voice of the People While Also Preventing "Excessive" Democracy

The Framers believed that the people should have a voice in government. One option would have been to allow direct rule by the people—the classic definition of democracy. The Framers had experience with that kind of government, because many municipalities in America did much of their important business in town meetings during which citizens directly voted on matters of public policy. Despite that experience, or perhaps because of it, the Framers did not believe that the people's voice should dictate the behavior of public officials. The people's input should influence the decisions of government, they concluded, but there must be a buffer between the people's demands and the government's actions. They feared that a government that was too close to the people would get swept up in the people's passions and impulsive desires. Such a government could threaten the rights of minority groups, including the minority that owned significant amounts of property.[20]

To the Framers, those were the risks of democracy. The political system needed to be structured in a way that took account of the people's views but also allowed for a cooling off of those views. At the same time, the people's voice would be impotent if government were weak. Power and authority needed to be both encouraged and restrained.

republic
a system in which people elect representatives to make policy and write laws, in contrast to direct democracy in which the people do these activities themselves.

indirect election
an election in which voters select other individuals who directly vote for candidates for a particular office; U.S. Senate and presidential elections were of this type in the Constitution, but Senate elections are now direct elections.

separation of powers
the principle that the executive, legislative, and judicial functions of government should be primarily performed by different institutions in government.

For these reasons, the Framers did not create a democracy in the technical sense, one in which the people themselves directly rule. Rather, they created a **republic,** in which the people select representatives who are entrusted to make the laws.[21] Preventing excessive democracy meant not only protecting government from the people's passions, but also protecting citizens from each other—preventing groups from using government to oppress other groups. The Framers accomplished these goals in several ways.

SELECTION OF PUBLIC OFFICIALS The Constitution provided for staggered terms of office for elected officials (Articles I and II). House members would serve two-year terms; senators would serve six-year terms, with one-third of the senators up for election in any given election year; and the president would serve a four-year term. This arrangement means that Americans can never dismiss all government officials at once because all officials are never up for election in the same year. Americans can "clean house" in government, but it is always only a partial cleaning: in any given election year, two-thirds of the senators will not be up for election, and the president will be up for election only every other election year. Regardless of the passions that may be stirring the public, it would take six years before all the elected officials in the national government could be replaced. And the public has no direct way to choose federal judges. Once nominated by the president and confirmed by the Senate, federal judges—unlike judges in many states—have lifetime tenure and do not face elections. This provision again provides a buffer between the people's voice and the government's actions.

Should the people try to change the system to make it more immediately responsive to their demands, they would have to work through the difficult process of amending the Constitution (Article V). The Framers did not want the people to be able to easily rewrite the rules. Such a process was not just for the Framers' benefit, however—it reduced the likelihood that one group would amend the Constitution in a manner to reject or restrict the rights of another group.

In the Constitution as ratified, the people directly elected only the members of the U.S. House of Representatives. The people also voted for state legislators, who then selected the state's U.S. senators, a process known as **indirect election.** Not until the passage of the Seventeenth Amendment in 1913 would the people directly elect their U.S. senators. Presidents were also elected indirectly. Voters in most states chose electors (in some states, the state legislature selected the electors), and these electors then met in their states in the Electoral College to cast ballots for president and vice president. The candidate who received a majority of the electoral vote would be the president. Even today, although ballots list the presidential candidates, voters are technically voting for a group of electors who have pledged to cast their electoral vote for the particular candidate. The logic was that the people could select the electors, but the electors, presumably individuals who were wise, knowledgeable, and distinguished, would evaluate the presidential candidates more carefully.

SEPARATION OF POWERS The Framers most famously attempted to protect against the effects of excessive democracy by balancing power. In the colonists' eyes, prior to 1763, this had been the defining achievement of British politics and a source of great pride. The colonies, too, relied on the idea of balancing power against power, with legislators checking the power of the governor, who served on behalf of Britain. The Framers drew heavily upon the ideas of political philosophers such as Charles de Montesquieu (1689–1755), a French political thinker who wrote at length about separation of powers.

Recall that in the Articles of Confederation, the legislature was the national government, albeit a weak one. By contrast, in the Constitution, the Framers provided for three independent centers of authority in a legislature, executive, and judiciary (in Articles I, II, and III, respectively). **Separation of powers** means that the major branches of government would have different primary functions and

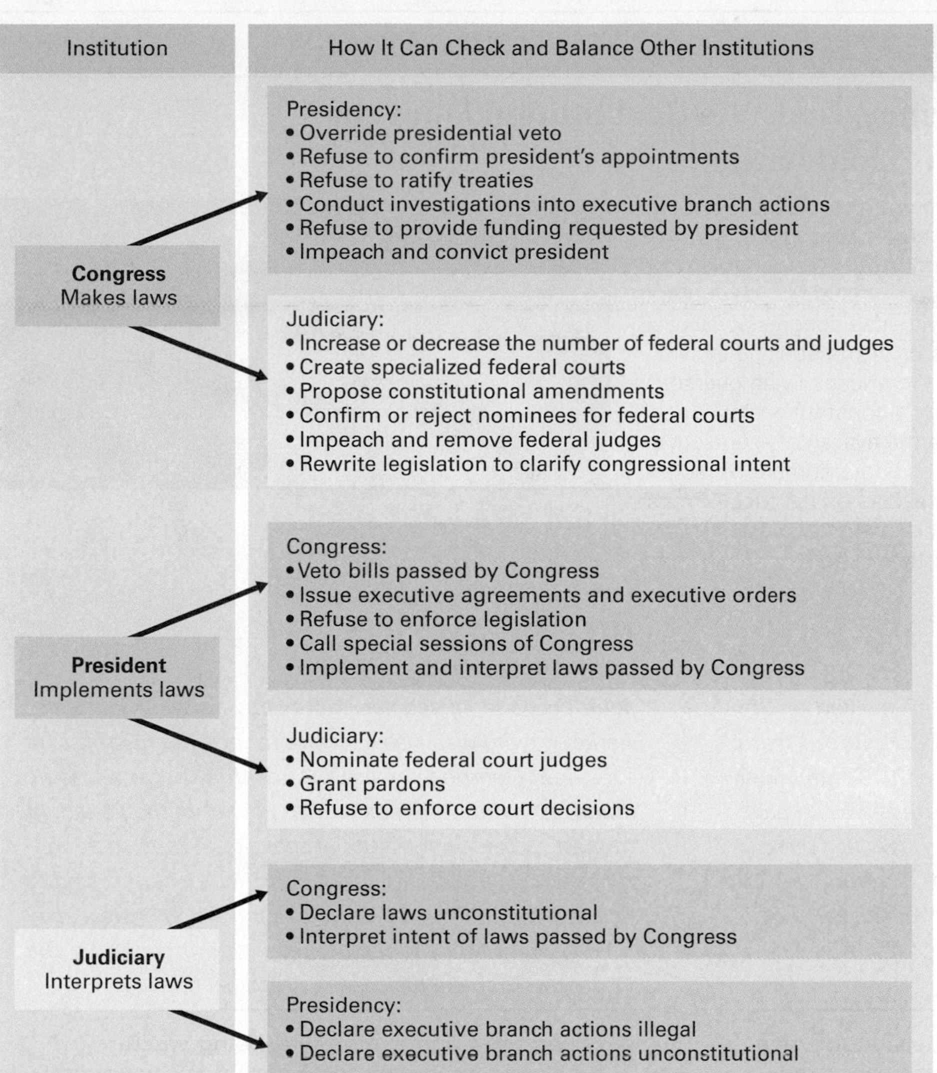

Institution
How It Can Check and Balance Other Institutions
Congress
Makes laws
Presidency:
• Override presidential veto
• Refuse to confirm president's appointments
• Refuse to ratify treaties
• Conduct investigations into executive branch actions
• Refuse to provide funding requested by president
• Impeach and convict president
Judiciary:
• Increase or decrease the number of federal courts and judges
• Create specialized federal courts
• Propose constitutional amendments
• Confirm or reject nominees for federal courts
• Impeach and remove federal judges
• Rewrite legislation to clarify congressional intent
President
Implements laws
Congress:
• Veto bills passed by Congress
• Issue executive agreements and executive orders
• Refuse to enforce legislation
• Call special sessions of Congress
• Implement and interpret laws passed by Congress
Judiciary:
• Nominate federal court judges
• Grant pardons
• Refuse to enforce court decisions
Judiciary
Interprets laws
Congress:
• Declare laws unconstitutional
• Interpret intent of laws passed by Congress
Presidency:
• Declare executive branch actions illegal
• Declare executive branch actions unconstitutional

FIGURE 3.1 SEPARATION OF POWERS AND CHECKS AND BALANCES.
With separation of powers and checks and balances, each branch of government has distinct but overlapping responsibilities.

responsibilities—the legislature would make law, the executive would implement law, and the judiciary would interpret law (see Figure 3.1). The separation would be reinforced by alternative methods of selecting the leadership of each branch—legislators were directly and indirectly elected (House and Senate, respectively), the president was indirectly elected, and judges were appointed. In practice, the division in functions has not been quite this neat and tidy, so some observers suggest that a better description of separation of powers is "separated institutions sharing powers."[22] Rather than rigid demarcation between branches, this formulation suggests that each institution trespasses somewhat on the jurisdiction of the others. For a discussion about the separation of powers and the president's role as commander in chief, see *Unresolved Debate: In Times of War or Emergency, Does the Constitution Limit the President's Commander in Chief Authority?*

checks and balances
the principle that each branch of the federal government has the means to thwart or influence actions by other branches of government.

CHECKS AND BALANCES The system of checks and balances provides the main set of mechanisms through which the branches monitor one another. **Checks and balances** means that each branch of government has a way to affect and, in some instances, to stop the actions of the others. Many of the checks and balances techniques are likely familiar; they are listed in Figure 3.1. They reinforce the idea of separated institutions sharing power. Lawmaking, for example, is not the province of Congress alone. The president has to approve any bills before they

3.1

3.2

3.3

3.4

Unresolved Debate

In Times of War or Emergency, Does the Constitution Limit the President's Commander in Chief Authority?

In 2011, President Barack Obama involved the United States in military hostilities in Libya, and in 2012 he authorized drone strikes to target and kill terrorists overseas. Critics of the program argued it violated constitutional checks and balances and civil liberties, charging that the program proceeded with little congressional oversight of the deployment of the drones or of the specific individuals targeted for death, including some Americans living overseas. Supporters responded that the president's constitutional war powers give presidents wide latitude to use the available technology at hand to conduct war and that the drones had a number of tactical advantages and produced less incidental loss of life. MQ-1 Predators, such as the one pictured here, were used heavily in Afghanistan, Pakistan, Yemen, Somalia, and northern Iraq.

YES

Louis Fisher, a political scientist who served at the Library of Congress, argues that the Framers were determined that the president would be the Commander in Chief of the armed forces, but Congress, would have the power to declare war and to make laws organizing, arming, and funding the military.[a] *The Framers viewed a president with complete discretion over the military to be inconsistent with the idea of a republic. To make his case, Fisher argues the following:*

- **The original understanding of the Constitution was that the president's powers in times of emergency are subject to limitations;**
- **Historically, presidents accepted these limitations and the nation successfully survived many security challenges. Only in recent administrations have presidents argued for their ability to act without congressional authorization;**
- **The claim that there are no limits on presidential power in times of war or emergency renders the Constitution meaningless precisely at the times its constraints are most needed. The Constitution is not an invitation to dictatorship.**

NO

John Yoo, a legal scholar at the University of California, Berkeley, who was also a lawyer in the administration of President George W. Bush, argues that there can be no limits on the "inherent executive power" of the president in matters involving national security.[b] *When the country's security is threatened, a president is authorized to do what he thinks necessary to defend it, and these may involve new techniques over time unforeseen by the Framers.*[c] *To make his case, Yoo argues that:*

- **When the Constitution was being written, it was a common perspective, that the sovereign had unlimited power to defend the state, so the president's authority in this area is independent of the Constitution;**
- **Provisions of the Constitution giving power over war and related matters to Congress should be interpreted flexibly so that the president can respond effectively to new challenges unforeseen by the Framers;**
- **Ultimately, accepting any constitutional limitation on the powers of the president in this crucial area could leave the nation defenseless against its enemies. The Constitution is not a "suicide pact."**[d]

CONTRIBUTING TO THE DEBATE

The basic disagreements expressed by Fisher and Yoo over the proper way to interpret the Constitution are unlikely to be resolved definitively. Nonetheless, the debate can be advanced through careful analysis that recognizes and specifies the advantages and risks that come with either of these competing perspectives.

WHAT DO YOU THINK?

1. Should we think about presidential war powers differently from way we think about other constitutional questions concerning government power? Why or why not?
2. Should we rely on the Framers' original understanding to answer some questions, but the conditions of modern life to answer others? Why or why not?

[a]Louis Fisher, *Presidential War Power,* 2nd ed. (Lawrence: University Press of Kansas, 2004).

[b]John Yoo, Office of Legal Counsel memorandum September 25, 2001, available at www.justice.gov/olc/warpowers925.htm.

[c]John C. Yoo, _The Powers of War and Peace: The Constitution and Foreign Affairs After 9/11 (Chicago: University of Chicago Press, 2006); John Yoo, *Crisis and Command: A History of Executive Power from George Washington to George W. Bush* (New York: Kaplan Publishing, 2010)

[d]*Terminiello v. City of Chicago.* (1949).

can become law.[23] As a result of legislative bicameralism—Congress is divided into two houses, each of which must approve the same version of a bill before it can be sent to the president for approval—Congress has internal checks and balances. In some areas, notably approval of treaties and confirmation of judges, the Framers wanted the people involved, but only through their indirectly elected representatives in the Senate. Finally, although the judiciary's power was only briefly described in the Constitution, this branch would early on, in the case of *Marbury v. Madison* (1803), assert the power of **judicial review,** meaning it would decide whether the laws and other actions of government officials were or were not constitutional. This meant the judiciary could strike down a federal or state law altogether and overturn non-legislative actions such as a policy or procedure implemented by an executive-branch agency. Thus, the judiciary has the power to determine what the text of the Constitution means. As for checks on this branch, Congress and the president can counteract the judiciary's power through constitutional amendments, new appointments to the courts, and restructuring of the courts.[24]

There were competing views early in the convention on how to check and balance power. In the Virginia Plan, the president and judiciary, to be selected by the legislature, would form a Council of Revision that could veto legislative acts. However, the legislature would have been able to override those vetoes and would also have had the authority to veto state laws. The New Jersey Plan called for a single-chamber Congress in which each state had one vote. Congress would appoint a multi-person executive, which would in turn appoint the judiciary. Both these plans gave the legislature the strongest position in American government, as Congress selected the members of the other branches. The Framers ultimately prioritized Congress—it is Article I in the Constitution and the institution with the most detailed list of responsibilities and duties—but they dispersed power and increased the independence of the other branches more than either the Virginia or New Jersey Plans.[25] The Framers wanted to make sure that any pressure from the people was heard by government, but that it was diffused across the three branches. If one branch reached too far in pushing a new policy demanded by the people, the other branches could slow it down or stop it altogether. Moreover, the Framers wanted a strong national government, but they also wanted to be sure that it would not become so powerful as to threaten liberty and property. The proposed government was designed to thwart the power-grabbing tendencies of human nature, according to James Madison. "If men were angels, no government would be necessary," he wrote, "If angels were to govern men, neither external nor internal controls on government would be necessary."[26]

The checks and balances system was one aspect of the careful balancing act between government power and personal freedom. Each seemed necessary, yet each threatened to dominate the other. The task of the Framers was to keep the two in balance. As they saw it, dispersing power this way both protected against abuse of the people by government and made it more difficult for any one part of the public to capture all of the power centers in government. Madison referred to this system, in combination with federalism (described in the next section), as a "double security" against tyrannical government.[27]

FEDERALISM Despite differences concerning the relative power and authority of the national and state governments, delegates agreed that federalism would be an underlying principle of the new system. **Federalism** is a governing arrangement that distributes power across a national government and subnational governments and guarantees the survival of these different levels of government. As noted, resolving the distribution of power between the states and the national government was a key practical concern. At the level of principle, however, federalism was a bulwark against the risk of concentrated power and excessive democracy. The states check the power of the national government, but the national government checks the power of the states.

judicial review
the power of the judiciary to interpret and overturn actions taken by the legislative and executive branches of government.

federalism
a form of government that distributes power across a national government and subnational governments and ensures the existence of the subnational governments.

FIRST AMONG EQUALS

General George Washington's reputation towered above all others of his generation. As commander in chief of the Revolutionary forces, his remarkable organizational, military, and political skills held the war effort together and led the American troops to victory. He came out of retirement to preside over the Constitutional Convention. There was no doubt among the delegates that he would be selected as the country's first president.

parliamentary system
a political system in which the head of the executive branch is selected by members of the legislature rather than by popular vote.

THE PARLIAMENTARY SYSTEM AS AN ALTERNATIVE DISTRIBUTION OF POWER The choices made by the Constitutional Convention delegates differ significantly from the choices made in later years in other parts of the world. In Europe, especially, the **parliamentary system** was the structure of choice for those building governments. In a parliamentary system, the prime minister, who serves as the chief executive, is selected from the parliament (the legislature) by other members. Although voters are usually well aware of the candidates for prime minister, they do not vote on the position nationally or directly. The prime minister then selects department heads from among his or her fellow partisans in the legislature. Typically in a parliamentary system, the legislature ultimately interprets what the constitution means (even if the constitution is unwritten, as in Great Britain). In this system, the legislature is supreme, and the notions of checks and balances and separation of powers are not particularly relevant.

Opponents of the parliamentary system charge that it puts too much power in the hands of the majority party. Unlike in the American system, control of the executive branch and the legislature cannot be split between two parties, even if that would be the voters' preference. In the view of these critics, parliamentary systems leave voters who do not support the majority party powerless. Advocates of the parliamentary system respond that it is a government that is not at cross-purposes with itself. Rather than checking and balancing power, parceling power out to different parts of government, and having branches of government intentionally frustrate each other and the majority's will, the ideal behind the parliamentary system is to gather power

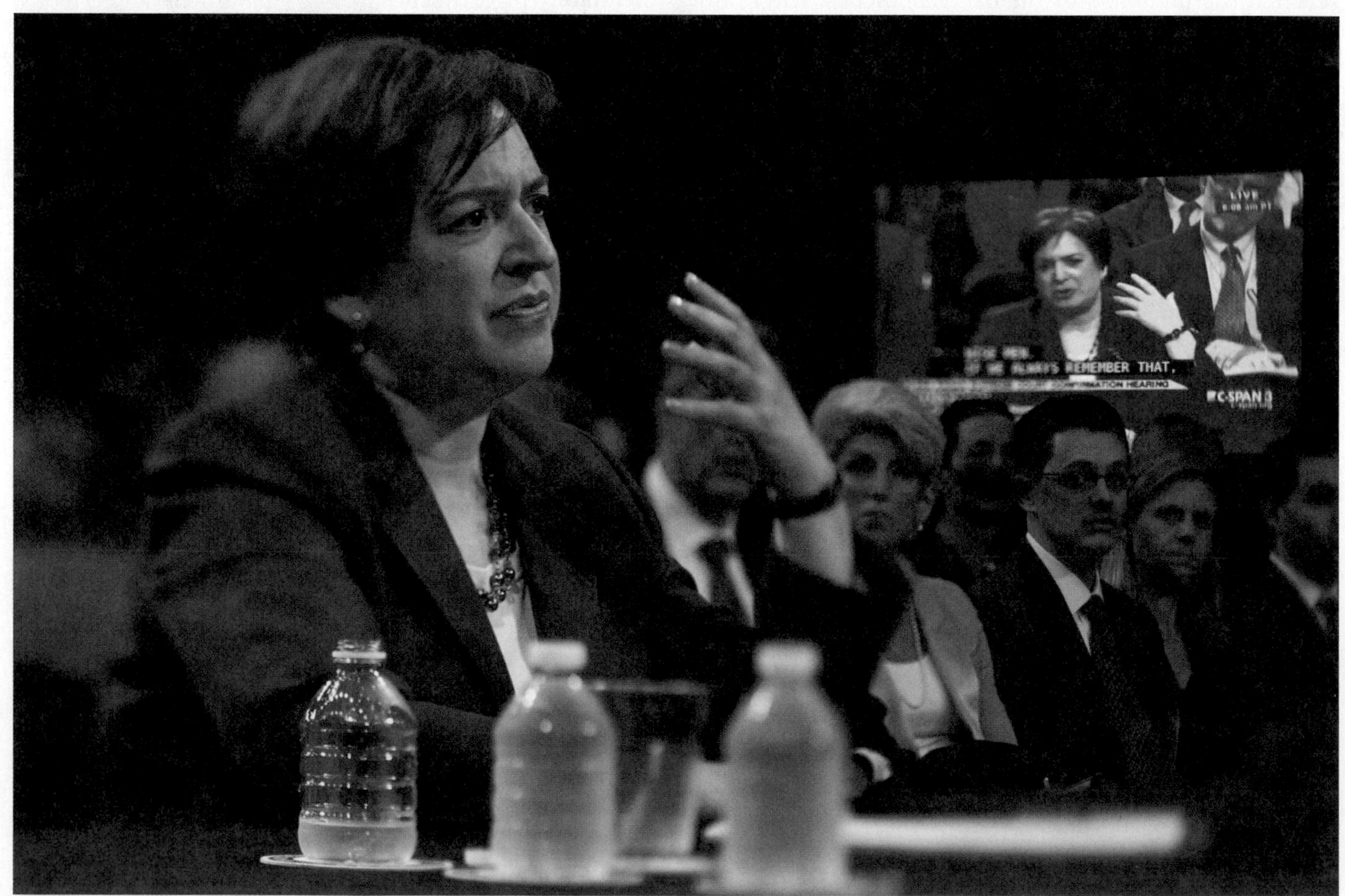

CONFIRMING A JUSTICE

Supreme Court justices are appointed and have lifetime terms, raising issues of democratic accountability. For this reason, both elected branches of government are involved in selecting Supreme Court justices. Elena Kagan, President Obama's nominee, appears here before the Senate Judiciary Committee for her confirmation hearing in 2010. What difference, if any, would it make if federal judges served fixed terms rather than lifetime tenure?

in the leading party or a coalition of parties in the legislature to enable swift action. The Framers of the American Constitution were wary of giving any entity, including the majority of the population, so much power.

The Framers Included Constitutional Provisions Designed to Protect Commerce and Property

Events in the states in the 1780s, such as Shays's Rebellion and the printing of currency of questionable worth, panicked New England merchants, southern planters, and the entire spectrum of businesspeople in between. Therefore, one chief concern of the Framers was to protect commerce and property from the designs of the national government, the state governments, and states pitted against states.

Delegates included many provisions in the Constitution to do this. First, they established that the national government would have primary regulatory control over commerce and finance. The national government would regulate commerce between the states and with other countries and be responsible for producing coinage and currency, establishing bankruptcy laws, and creating protections for copyrights and patents (Article I in the Constitution). This arrangement still allowed differences among the states—for example, states could have varying insurance or banking regulations—but it prevented states from creating alliances with each other or with another country that harmed the commercial or property interests of citizens in other states. It also prevented states from inflating their currency or devising other schemes to make it easy for their citizens to escape from debt obligations.

REGULATING SAFETY

Firefighters rescue passengers trapped in a commuter train that collided head-on with a freight train near Los Angeles, leading to 25 deaths and 95 individuals seriously or critically injured. In accidents like this one, the Office of Railroad Safety of the Federal Railroad Administration will investigate, along with local and state officials. The federal government's constitutional power to regulate interstate commerce provid the legal authority for the agency to act and to establish railroad safety regulations.

supremacy clause
a clause in the Constitution that declares that national laws and treaties have supremacy over state laws and treaties.

equal privileges and immunities clause
a clause in the Constitution stating that states are to treat their citizens and the citizens of other states equally.

full faith and credit clause
a clause in the Constitution stating that states are to honor the official acts of other states.

Second, the Constitution's **supremacy clause** declared that national laws and treaties would take precedence over state laws and treaties (Article VI). State laws could differ from a national law, but they had to be consistent with it. For example, states can enact antipollution laws more stringent but not more relaxed than those the federal government requires. Federal law can, however, preempt the states from deviating from federal standards. For example, the Federal Cigarette Labeling and Advertising Act imposes national rules on cigarette advertising and prohibits state governments from imposing additional advertising regulations.[28]

States were also to be nondiscriminatory toward each other (Article IV). Under the **equal privileges and immunities clause,** states are to treat their citizens and citizens of other states similarly. Through the **full faith and credit clause,** states are to honor the official acts of other states, such as public records and the results of judicial proceedings. However, Congress and the president will sometimes override this clause, arguing the Constitution gives them the authority to do so. Such an override happened in 1996 with the passage of the Defense of Marriage Act, which stipulated that states need not honor same-sex marriages performed in other states. Normally, the full faith and credit clause would dictate that a marriage that is legal in one state would be recognized as legal in the others, but states were given an exemption in this instance.

The Constitution included additional protections for commerce and property. Article VI stipulated that any contracts entered into before the Constitution must still be honored after the Constitution was ratified: the adoption of a new political system did not negate ongoing economic commitments. This provision was motivated chiefly by concern that debts incurred during the Revolutionary War would be paid, but it applied to debts incurred after the war as well. The national government also guaranteed each state a republican—that is, representative—form of government and pledged to protect the states against domestic violence, a reaction to Shays's Rebellion.

Lastly, the Framers provided for a president who would be a counterweight to Congress. As the Framers saw it, representatives would often allow the narrow interests of their districts to guide their decisions, whereas senators would have the somewhat broader but still biased self-interests of their states in mind. Only the president would represent the country as a whole and have an ongoing commitment to the national interest rather than to any special interest of a state or district.

The Framers Emphasized Certain Measures and Principles to Enhance the Proposed System's Legitimacy

Legitimacy is about trust. When you believe that an arrangement is legitimate, you believe it is fair and reasonable. You may not trust individual officials, but you trust the system. Americans had come to see the British government, or at least its control over the colonies, as illegitimate. The idea that the colonies were "virtually represented" but not directly represented in Parliament struck many Americans as foolish. Americans then placed their trust in the new governmental system of the Articles of Confederation, but many saw that, too, as a failure. To the Framers, establishing legitimacy for the new government was critical, and they addressed the challenge in three ways.

First, they emphasized the representativeness of the new government. In the House, Senate, and presidency, they noted, distinct parts of society were represented—parts of states, states, and the country, respectively. Direct popular election of the House of Representatives was another legitimacy-building feature. The House would be the "people's house." Its members would have shorter terms than in any other part of government, giving the people frequent input into its composition. And, because of the system of checks and balances, relatively little could be done that did not have to pass through the people's house.

Second, the Framers built the case for legitimacy around the notion that the new government would not be dominating. It would have more power than it did under the Articles, but with constraints. The checks-and-balances system would prevent government from acting recklessly. With its idea of federalism, the Constitution delegated specific powers to the federal government and left others to the states. Public officials would take the Constitution seriously—Article VI required public officials to swear to uphold the Constitution, not the wishes of a monarch, church, or select group. The Constitution, the Framers noted, was a social contract between rulers and ruled. If the rulers violated this contract, the people had a right to remove them, and if the violations were extensive, the people had a right to scrap the contract and construct a new system of government. Further, the Framers promised that a bill of rights guaranteeing personal liberties would be added to the Constitution as the first order of business after ratification.

Third, they created an enduring but flexible framework for government. They wanted the people to believe that the Constitution had roots—that its meaning and content would have some stability—but they also wanted the people to believe that the system could be changed if necessary. By providing for amendments, the Framers created a document that would be flexible. By making the amending process difficult, they created a document that would be enduring. We discuss the amendment process in detail later.

Balancing stability and flexibility was also achieved by writing a Constitution that provided a basic framework for government and politics. The Constitution lays down the essential rules of how government will work and how officials will be selected. It also indicates the responsibilities of government officials. It presents a general outline for how public policy will be made, but it contains very little actual policy.

For example, it gives Congress the power to regulate interstate commerce, declare war, and establish currency, but it does not set in stone any particular policy about how interstate commerce should take place or when declarations of war should and should not occur. Nothing in the Constitution says how much should be spent on national defense, how many roads should be built, and so on. The Framers left that kind of detail to the branches of government to work out in the form of laws. They realized that preferences about particular issues would change over time, so enshrining them in the Constitution would be problematic in two respects. If the Constitution were difficult to change, citizens would be stuck with policies they no longer agreed with. If the Constitution were easy to change, it would lose the sense that it had permanency and was above competitive politics.

The Civil War provides the most glaring exception to the rule that Americans believe their political differences can be worked out through constitutional provisions. The Constitution could not contain the depth of division between North and South. And for much of American history, the Constitution was seen as compatible with discrimination of the worst sort against racial, ethnic, and religious minorities and women. Americans today, however, are more likely to fault the people and the politicians in power during those times rather than the Constitution itself, because the Constitution also provided the means to change these patterns.[29]

The Framers Provided the Means for a Coordinated Approach to International Relations and National Defense

The foreign threats facing Americans in the 1780s were significant. Britain controlled the territory around the Great Lakes. Aside from Britain's own disagreements with the United States, the tension between Britain and France meant that Americans being caught in their crossfire was a distinct possibility. Spain controlled Florida and areas to the west. Skirmishes with Native American tribes were frequent. The Constitution provided the promise of executive and legislative leadership and coordination to respond to these challenges. The president would be the operational head of military actions and the representative of the United States to other countries. He would appoint ambassadors and negotiate treaties, but both of these would require the Senate's approval. Congress's control over military budgets and taxes and the declaration of war was intended to make foreign policy a cooperative venture. States would have to follow the national lead on military matters, including those with Native American tribes. They could not enter into treaties or alliances with other countries or tribes, arrange discriminatory tariffs, or enter into military conflict unless invaded or facing a similar immediate emergency.[30]

The Battle for Ratification

3.3 Compare and contrast the arguments of Anti-Federalists and Federalists.

Federalists
individuals who supported the proposed Constitution and favored its ratification.

Anti-Federalists
individuals opposed to the proposed Constitution, fearing it concentrated too much power in the national government.

Sending the Constitution to the states for ratification at state conventions was a risky gambit. The Framers could not look to other countries to see how a national ratification effort would fare, or what the risks and rewards were of giving the people this much influence. The experience of other countries in later years shows just how risky it was. In France, popular ratification failed in 1789, 1791, 1793, and 1830. Canadian leaders chose not to risk a popular ratification process for their constitution. Britain's unwritten constitution was similarly not subject to a ratification process. Among English-speaking countries, only Australia followed the U.S. ratification model, more than a century later.[31] In the American context, however, supporters of the Constitution believed that ratification in the states was a political necessity. It was also, they realized, an opportunity for opponents to derail the document.

Battle lines over ratification of the Constitution were drawn between the **Federalists,** who supported ratification, and the **Anti-Federalists,** who opposed it.[32] The central debate concerned not democracy, which might be the center-stage issue today, but liberty: what kind of governmental arrangement would best preserve liberty? See *How Do We Know? What Motivated the Framers of the Constitution?* for an analysis of how political scientists have examined the Framers' motivations.

Anti-Federalists Argued that the Constitution Threatened Liberty

Anti-Federalists argued that the proposed Constitution threatened the people's liberty. Distant from the people, this kind of government might begin to tax heavily, override state court decisions, have a permanent army at its disposal, or absorb functions performed by the states—fears that later history showed were not far-fetched. Legendary patriots such as Patrick Henry, a stalwart supporter of the Revolution, saw the proposed Constitution as a counterrevolution, pushing back toward more central authority, reducing democratic influence on government, and protecting the interests of political and economic leaders.

To the Anti-Federalists, a different kind of government was needed, one more along the lines of the government established by the Articles of Confederation. The loose union of states that characterized the Articles was the ideal arrangement to protect liberty—the central government's powers were so limited, it lacked the means to restrict liberty, even if public officials were so inclined.[33]

Given the public's apparent preference for a stronger national government, the Anti-Federalists offered some principles to guide its development. They argued that such a government should have many restrictions on its power. For example, they suggested reducing the range of cases the Supreme Court could hear; creating a council to review all presidential decisions; leaving military affairs to state militias; enlarging the House of Representatives, which would mean creating smaller districts so that representatives would feel more closely bound to their constituents; and adding a "bill of rights" to protect individual freedoms.

Only on this last item were the Anti-Federalists successful. Supporters of the Constitution initially argued that a bill of rights was unnecessary—unless the Constitution gave Congress the specific authority, for example, to establish an official religion, government should not be presumed to have that authority. A listing of the rights or liberties of individuals could effectively become a limitation on rights and liberties if misinterpreted as comprehensive. In the climate of the ratification debate, however, a strong symbolic statement was needed, so the proponents of ratification agreed that after the Constitution was ratified, a bill of rights would be sent to the

3.1

3.2

3.3

3.4

How Do We Know?

What Motivated the Framers of the Constitution?

The Question

The men sent to the Constitutional Convention in Philadelphia in 1787 had risen to prominence in their respective states. Overall, however, the U.S. Constitution reduced the autonomy of the states. For political scientists, this outcome raises a research puzzle. Why would ambitious, intelligent political leaders agree to a system that might reduce the power of the states in which they had been politically influential? What motivated the Framers of the Constitution? How do we know?

Why It Matters

Why should any of us care what motivated the Framers of the Constitution so long ago? The reason is simple: If Americans wish to know whether contemporary American politics and government live up to founding values, they must know why the system was designed the way it was.

Investigating the Answer

One answer, offered by economist Charles Beard early in the twentieth century, is that the Constitution reflected the economic self-interest of those drafting and voting for it.[a] Beard complained that previous accounts of the Constitution had been based on ideals and wishful thinking. He called for social scientists to conduct hardheaded, systematic analyses of the world as it was.

Assuming that political action is guided by self-interest, Beard hypothesized that delegates' financial self-interest determined how they voted on the Constitution. By analyzing the financial holdings and economic interests of the delegates, he concluded that the Framers protected their commercial interests, including currency, public securities, manufacturing, and trade and shipping. Knowing the economic interests of those who supported the document, he argued, reveals the motivations of the document's writers.[b]

Beard's critics offer a different answer to the question about the Framers' motivations, and a different approach to political investigation. They took more interest in the convention delegates' ideas and rhetoric. They saw the Framers' actions as grounded more in their practical political assessment of what was necessary to keep the country united and afloat or in their sincere interest in the political ideals they were espousing.[c] To the critics, Beard mistakenly assumed that correlation equals causation: The fact that delegates' financial self-interest and their votes in the convention were correlated did not prove that the interests caused the votes.[d] But by assuming that the ideals of those who supported the Constitution were unified and that therefore their motives were the same, Beard's critics may also have erred. For example, James Madison and Alexander Hamilton wrote the bulk of the *Federalist Papers,* but within a few years, it was clear that their political ideologies were radically different.[e] They may have both supported the Constitution, but their motivations were likely not identical.

Rather than looking at a political outcome and then assuming that the result reflects some group's motives, political scientists can look to the historical record—memoirs, journals, interviews, and other sources—to determine what drove individuals to take particular actions. In a study of the crafting of the Constitution, for example, one political scientist concluded that the final document was a defeat for some of its most ardent proponents, such as Madison.[f] Throughout the convention, Madison unsuccessfully pushed for a more powerful national government than the one created in the final document. Careful analysis of the day-by-day proceedings shows Madison to be frequently on the defensive. Rather than his rhetoric in the *Federalist Papers* being a completely clear signal of his true preferences, he shaped his argument around the Constitution that was approved by the convention.

Such analysis highlights the importance of sequence and timing in explaining political outcomes. Early decisions, even small decisions, can have tremendous impact because they begin a process that influences future decisions. Once the delegates decided on an elected presidency, for example, that decision affected their votes on other aspects of the Constitution, and rethinking that decision would have been difficult, because everything else afterward depended on it.

The Bottom Line

The Framers of the Constitution were motivated by a number of factors, including political ideals and principles, a belief that the status quo was unacceptable, concerns about what would be politically palatable to the states, and likely some political and economic self-interest as well. But to correlate the convention votes with economic self-interest and then assume that self-interest was the primary causal motivation behind the Constitution is faulty social science. In political analysis, it is important to consider multiple causal factors and to realize that the sequence and timing of decisions, as well as the rules for making decisions, affect the outcome. These factors can even lead an individual to support something he or she believes falls short. Just as Madison vigorously supported a document that did not entirely reflect his preferences, a president must sometimes sign legislation that does not precisely reflect his or her leanings.

---

[a]Charles A. Beard, *An Economic Interpretation of the Constitution of the United States* (New York: Macmillan, 1913); Jerry Fresia, *Toward an American Revolution: Exposing the Constitution and Other Illusions* (Boston: South End Press, 1988).

[b]Karen Orren and Stephen Skowronek, *The Search for American Political Development* (New York: Cambridge University Press, 2004), 53–54.

[c]John P. Roche, "The Founding Fathers: A Reform Caucus in Action," *American Political Science Review* 55, 4 (1961): 799–816; Calvin C. Jillson and Cecil L. Eubanks, "The Political Structure of Constitution Making: The Federal Convention of 1787," *American Journal of Political Science* 28, 3 (1984): 435–58.

[d]Robert E. Brown, *Charles Beard and the Constitution: A Critical Analysis of "An Economic Interpretation of the Constitution"* (Princeton, NJ: Princeton University Press, 1956).

[e]Colleen A. Sheehan, "Madison v. Hamilton: The Battle Over Republicanism and the Role of Public Opinion," *American Political Science Review* 98, 3 (2004): 405–20.

[f]David Brian Robertson, "Madison's Opponents and Constitutional Design," *American Political Science Review* 99, 2 (2005): 405–20.

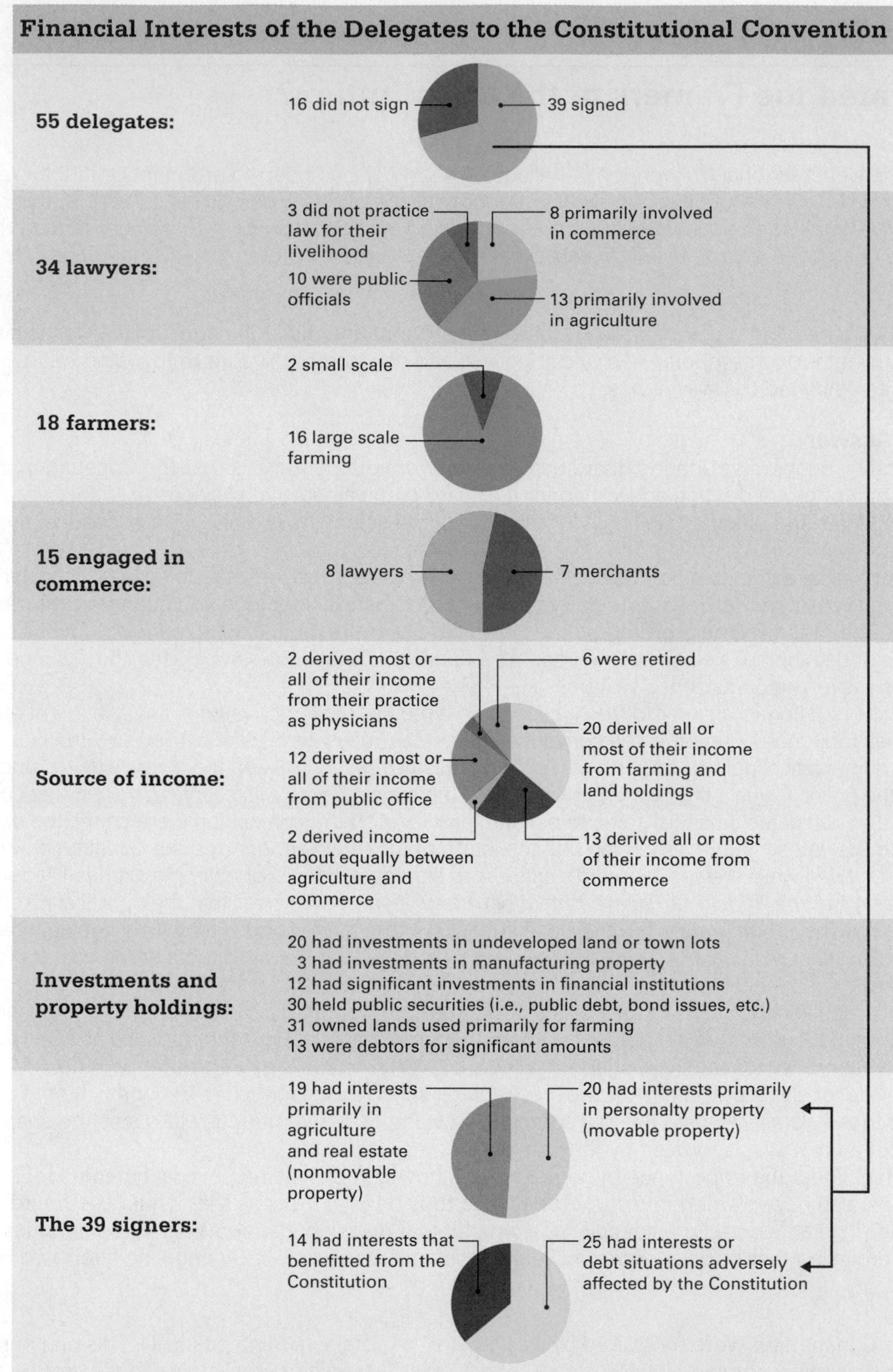
Financial Interests of the Delegates to the Constitutional Convention
55 delegates:
16 did not sign
39 signed
34 lawyers:
3 did not practice law for their livelihood
8 primarily involved in commerce
10 were public officials
13 primarily involved in agriculture
18 farmers:
2 small scale
16 large scale farming
15 engaged in commerce:
8 lawyers
7 merchants
Source of income:
2 derived most or all of their income from their practice as physicians
6 were retired
20 derived all or most of their income from farming and land holdings
12 derived most or all of their income from public office
2 derived income about equally between agriculture and commerce
13 derived all or most of their income from commerce
Investments and property holdings:
20 had investments in undeveloped land or town lots
3 had investments in manufacturing property
12 had significant investments in financial institutions
30 held public securities (i.e., public debt, bond issues, etc.)
31 owned lands used primarily for farming
13 were debtors for significant amounts
The 39 signers:
19 had interests primarily in agriculture and real estate (nonmovable property)
20 had interests primarily in personalty property (movable property)
14 had interests that benefitted from the Constitution
25 had interests or debt situations adversely affected by the Constitution

Source: Forrest McDonald, *We the People: The Economic Origins of the Constitution*, Chicago: University of Chicago Press, 1958, pp. 86–110.

FINANCIAL INTERESTS OF THE DELEGATES TO THE CONSTITUTIONAL CONVENTION

Thinking Critically

- In what ways might you imagine the American political system would be different if the delegates had decided early in their deliberations to have a president elected for a single six-year term?
- When is it acceptable or unacceptable for a representative—for example, a delegate to a convention or a legislature in a legislative body—to vote in a manner consistent with his or her economic interests?

states for their approval. As ultimately ratified by the states, the **Bill of Rights** refers to the first 10 amendments to the Constitution, which focus primarily on preserving individual freedoms.

Bill of Rights
the first 10 amendments to the U.S. Constitution, intended to protect individual liberties from federal government intrusion.

Madison Responded in the *Federalist Papers* that a Large Republic is the Best Defense for Liberty

The argument between Federalists and Anti-Federalists was fought out in speeches, handbills, and newspaper columns. The most famous of all these was a set of newspaper opinion columns penned under pseudonyms by James Madison, Alexander Hamilton, and John Jay (Secretary for Foreign Affairs under the Articles of Confederation, first Chief Justice of the U.S. Supreme Court, and a governor of New York). Collectively, these columns, which discussed the many nuances of the proposed government, would come to be called the *Federalist Papers*. They presented the theoretical basis of American government, covering such concepts as federalism, the separation of powers, and checks and balances. Although it is probably true that the columns were not widely read, those who did read them were likely to be opinion leaders—individuals who, because of their status, could shape the opinions of others.

The Anti-Federalist argument about the desirability of democracies and small republics was rejected in the most famous of the *Federalist Papers*, number 10. In *Federalist 10*, James Madison argues that liberty is actually most at risk in direct democracies and small republics. It is safest in precisely the kind of large republic being proposed in the Constitution.

Like politicians today, Madison made causal claims. The outcome to be explained was the preservation of liberty. Madison begins by stating that the most severe threat to liberty is the presence of factions. To Madison, factions are defined by having some self-interest or common passion that threatens the rights of other citizens, and they can be either a majority or minority of the population. Factions are natural, Madison argues, as people naturally cluster with like-minded individuals. Trying to prevent the emergence of factions would require authoritarian and conformist measures that would be a "cure worse than the disease." The real question, therefore, was how to control factions and their effects—especially, for Madison, their effects on property rights. Could democracy cure the effects of factions? Madison said no. In a democracy, a majority faction has no check on its behavior. It would be quite easy for a majority of the population to deny rights or otherwise oppress a minority.

The proposed republic, on the other hand, could control excessive factional influence. This is Madison's key causal link between the proposed Constitution and the protection of liberty. First, in Madison's view, having a relatively small number of representatives increases the likelihood that voters are selecting individuals of honor, merit, and virtue for public office. Second, larger, more diverse districts will send mixed policy messages to representatives, encouraging them to sift out the bad ideas and keep the good. Representatives with large districts are less likely to be "captured" by any one interest, because they will try to represent a broader cross-section of their constituency. Third, in a geographically large political system, more opposing interests will vie for attention; as interest battles interest, a majority faction is less likely to form. Madison thought it unlikely that the same dangerous idea would arise in far-flung parts of the country, and if it did, it would be difficult logistically to organize a majority faction over a large area, which again protects liberty.

The bottom line of Madison's argument is a remarkable rejection of the conventional causal wisdom of his day. Rather than holding onto communitarian hopes about civic virtue—selfless political participants concerned only for the common welfare—Madison suggests the country allow self-interest to serve public ends. Each individual's self-interest, he reasons, gives that person an incentive to ensure that other individuals do not abuse power, thus producing precisely the best outcome for society. Madison takes this argument one step further in *Federalist 51*, where he notes that governmental power would be distributed across the national and state governments and across the three major branches of government, whose officials would challenge one another and thus prevent the monopolization of power. Their self-interest would protect liberty.[34]

THE REACH OF MEDIA
With portable electronic devices, the Internet, and social media, politicians are in real-time communications with constituents. Politicians are always under the watchful eye of the public, and the public has a number of means to express their views to public officials quickly and in sizable numbers. Does contemporary communication technology negate James Madison's arguments about the advantages of a large republic?

Explore on MyPoliSciLab

How Long Did It Take to Ratify the Constitution?

Americans today overwhelmingly support the principles of the Constitution, but after the Framers adjourned on September 17, 1787, three years passed before all thirteen states approved the document. The ensuing ratification debate was an inherently political game of multiple moves, in which the Constitution was kept alive by relatively narrow majorities, particularly in two strategically located states.

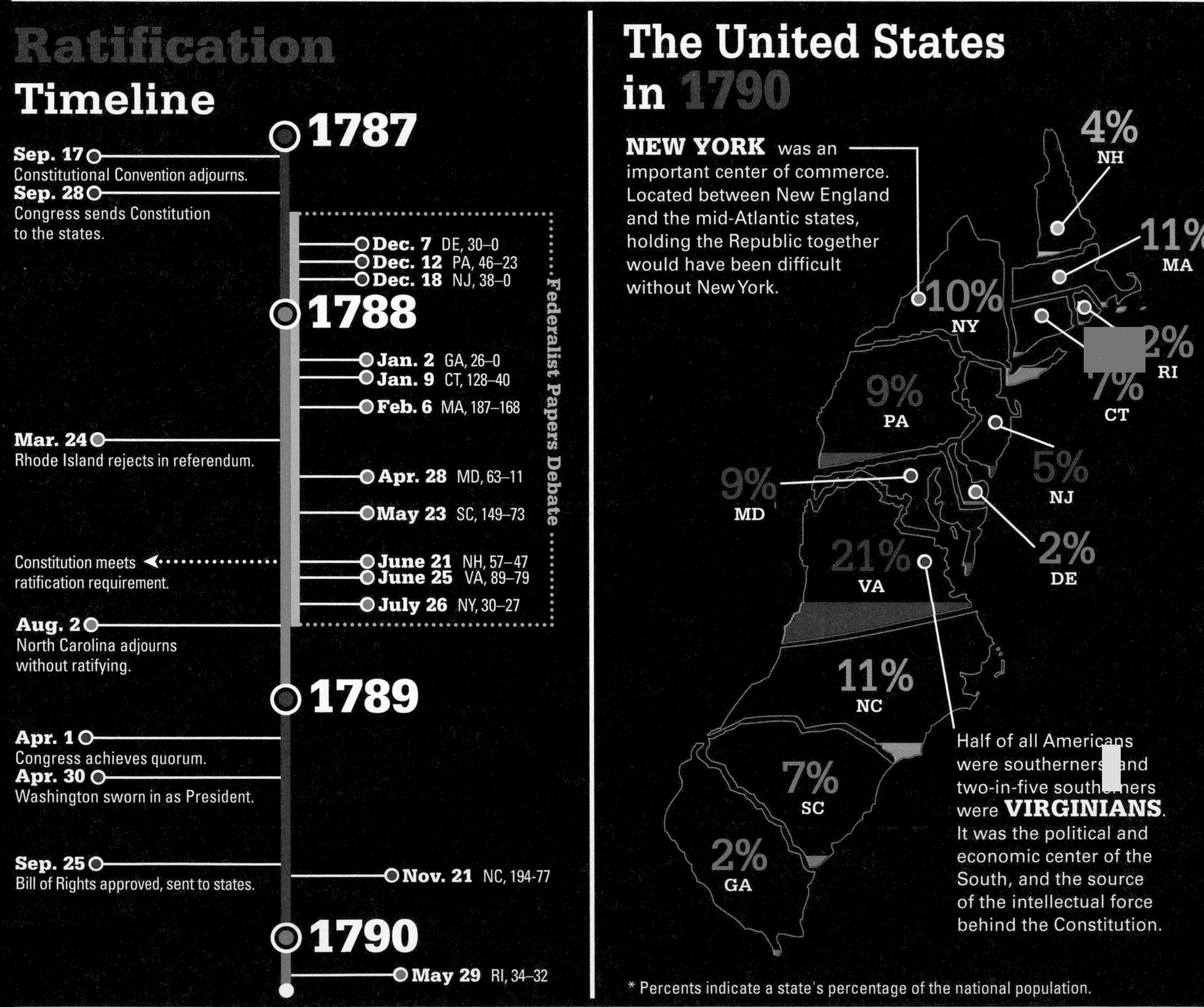

Investigate Further

Concept Why did it take three years to ratify the Constitution? The first states to ratify the Constitution did so with a strong majority of support for the document. But as those states signed on, opposition in remaining states grew, and the ratification debate intensified.

Connection Which states were most closely divided on ratification? The debate intensified in two strategic states: New York and Virginia. Ratification in those two holdout states was necessary in order to lend legitimacy to the new government.

Cause What were the issues of the debate? Written in support of the new government, *The Federalist Papers* addressed New Yorkers' concerns about federal power. For Virginians, the sticking point was a Bill of Rights, which James Madison promised to introduce in the

One of the key underlying ideas in Madison's thinking is the difficulty factions that are widely dispersed would face in discovering that they had a common interest and then mobilizing around it. Are today's high-tech communications a threat to that aspect of the Madisonian model? Individuals anywhere in the United States can communicate with others instantaneously. Congressional members can be pressured very quickly. Political figures can build followings and organizations that are truly national in scope and that can be reached, mobilized, and spurred to action with great speed. On the other hand, as Madison notes, power remains dispersed across branches and levels of government, which may not be equally responsive to public desires or may be responsive to different groups if different political parties control them. As Madison also points out, the more interests that are brought into politics, the more likely it is that other interests will seek to participate, reducing the likelihood of any interest having a monopoly on what legislators hear. These features of American politics might offset a relationship between the people and government that is today much tighter and more immediate than Madison may have wanted.

Belief that Change was Necessary Assisted the Federalists' Ratification Campaign

Citizens in the states voted for delegates to attend state ratifying conventions. Ratification was not a sure thing. The debate between the Federalists and Anti-Federalists was intense, and the opposition message voiced by the Anti-Federalists—that the Constitution went too far in the direction of a powerful national government and threatened the sovereignty of the states—was a powerful one for many Americans. Nine states needed to approve the Constitution for it to be in effect. The first state to ratify was Delaware, in December 1787. Seven months later, when New Hampshire became the ninth state to approve, the Constitution was ratified. In eight states, the Constitution received the support of at least 65 percent of the delegates. In the remaining five states, majorities were thin, with support for the Constitution running from about 51 to 55 percent. One state, North Carolina, had originally voted against the Constitution but voted to support it after it had been ratified.

In the end, the Federalists won the debate. In part, this victory appears due to the more convincing arguments of the Federalists. In part, it resulted from the absence of a comprehensive Anti-Federalist alternative. Many who voted for the Constitution might well have shared some of the Anti-Federalists' fears about a strong central government, but they also feared domestic disturbances and foreign threats. At bottom, the decision became whether to adopt the Constitution, stick with the Articles of Confederation, or start over again. Given the sense that the young country faced both foreign and domestic challenges, the appeal of continuing with the Articles or renewing the debate was limited. Change was needed, most people believed, and the Constitution provided that change. The Constitution was also politically attractive because it incorporated the beliefs of the American creed. Liberty, religious freedom, property rights, and democracy were the focus of many constitutional rules and principles. And underlying many of these constitutional principles was the belief in the notion of individual opportunity and the value of equality.

Amending the Constitution

3.4 Explain the processes of constitutional change.

The structure of the constitutional system sometimes frustrates Americans. Features usually thought of as strengths can sometimes be seen as negatives. The separation of powers and checks and balances protect liberty, but they can also slow government responses to important national problems. The American system is designed for the cautious use of power, consistent with

3.1

3.2

3.3

3.4

the American creed, but Americans often get upset when government does not act. Federalism allows for diversity and innovation, but it can frustrate those who believe that national standards in some areas are necessary. Thus, the structure of the Constitution can lead to some annoyance, but on the whole most Americans believe that the system works.

Part of the process of establishing legitimacy for the Constitution, however, was providing a procedure by which it could be revised. With the Constitution established as a broad framework for government, the Framers were free to create amending procedures that were difficult but not impossible. The underlying premise of the Constitution's amendment process is that any change in the Constitution has to have broad consensus throughout society. The consensus required is not as extensive as that in the Articles of Confederation, however, which required the congressional representatives of every state to agree to any proposed change.[35]

□ Amendments Should have Broad Societal Acceptance

The introduction of amendments is essentially a national-level process, while the ratification of amendments is a state-level process (see Figure 3.2). Moreover, supermajorities are a requirement of all four paths to amendment. Amendments will not be added to the Constitution unless they receive supermajority support at two stages—three stages, if we consider that a proposed amendment must have supermajority support separately in the House and in the Senate. (The president has no formal role in the amending process.) The premise that amendments should have broad social acceptance is therefore built into the process, and the presence or absence of such acceptance is often a chief point of debate.[36]

In the two paths used for the introduction of all amendments to date (paths A and C in Figure 3.2), it is not enough to get the support of just over half the members of Congress, a simple majority. Rather, two-thirds of the members of the House and two-thirds of the members of the Senate who are present and voting are needed to approve a proposed constitutional amendment. Echoing the Great Compromise, the process in paths A and C ensures that two-thirds of the representatives of the people—House members—must agree to the amendment, as well as two-thirds of the representatives of the states—U.S. senators.

The constitutional rules for the introduction of an amendment using paths B and D are less clear, as this method has never been used. The Constitution does not

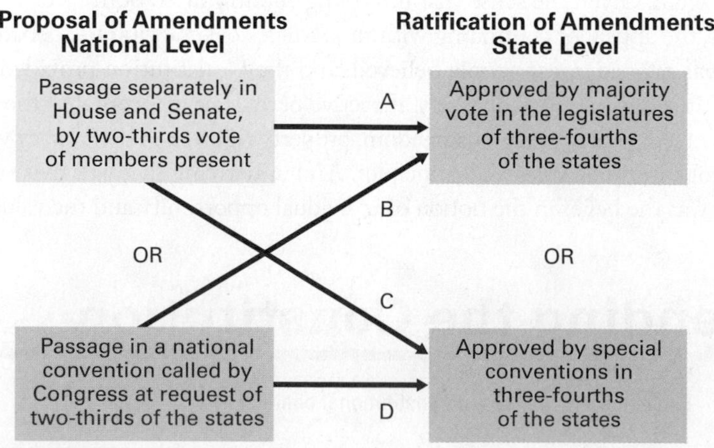

FIGURE 3.2 PATHS TO AMENDING THE CONSTITUTION

The amending process is based on supermajorities at both the proposal and ratification stages.

NOTE: Congress chooses which path is used. Path A: Used for 26 amendments. Path B: Never used. Path C: Used for one amendment (Twenty-first). Path D: Never used.

TABLE 3.2 FAILED ATTEMPTS TO AMEND THE CONSTITUTION SINCE 1980

Amendment	Year defeated
Equal Rights Amendment*	1982
No right to abortion	1983
School prayer allowable	1984
Grant District of Columbia residents full voting rights*	1985
Term limits for Congress	1995
Prohibit flag "desecration"	1995, 2006
Require supermajority to increase taxes	1996
Require balanced budget (multiple attempts)	1982–1997

*Amendment was rejected by the states. In all other cases, amendment passed one house of Congress only.
Note: Years indicate when these proposed amendments passed the second house of Congress.

indicate whether votes at a national convention would need to be supermajorities. Most likely, given that the Constitution gives Congress the power to call the convention if two-thirds of the states request it, Congress would set the rules for how the convention would be run. Some observers worry that it could become a "runaway convention," proposing amendments on any number of issues. The Constitution seems to imply that Congress could prevent this possibility by establishing ground rules for the convention.[37]

At the ratification level, we again see the Framers' desire that constitutional changes have broad societal acceptance. Three-quarters of the states, or 38 today, either in the state legislature or specially convened state conventions, are needed to ratify an approved amendment. Table 3.2 lists potential amendments since 1980 that had supermajority support in at least one house of Congress but failed in the other house or in the states. Table 3.3 lists all the proposed constitutional amendments in U.S. history that were passed by both houses of Congress but did not receive the necessary support in the states. The short length of the list in Table 3.3 may seem surprising, but it makes short sense. Members of Congress have little incentive to approve a proposed amendment that seems to lack sufficient support in the states to be ratified. On some occasions, however, initial supportive conditions can deteriorate as opponents mobilize against the proposal. For instance, when members of Congress sent the Equal Rights Amendment (ERA) to the states in the 1970s, they had good reason to believe it would be ratified. The proposed amendment stated that "Equality of rights under the law shall not be denied or abridged by the United States or by any State on account of sex." After a rapid string of state ratifications, however, the ERA proved susceptible to the arguments of opponents in some states that its implications were vague and its interpretation so uncertain that extensive litigation would be a likely result.[38] Supporters were unable to build sufficient societal consensus in the wake of these critiques. What looked like a relatively easy victory at the outset turned into defeat.

TABLE 3.3 PROPOSED AMENDMENTS REJECTED BY THE STATES

Amendment	Year approved by Congress
Regulate size of House	1789
U.S. citizens cannot accept titles of nobility	1810
Prohibit any amendments that would interfere with slavery	1861
Give Congress power to limit child labor	1926
Equal Rights Amendment	1972
Grant District of Columbia residents full voting rights	1978

Congress has the responsibility to decide which ratification path a proposed amendment will take. Congress also determines whether proposed amendments have any time limits attached to their ratification. The most recent amendment, the Twenty-seventh, was actually introduced at the same time as the Bill of Rights but did not gather enough state support to be ratified—mostly because it had been forgotten—until 1992. This amendment states that a congressional pay raise cannot take effect until after the next election. On the other hand, the ERA fell just short of receiving the support of three-fourths of the states and died with the expiration of its 10-year time limit, which Congress had already extended from the original 7 years.

Twenty-Seven Amendments Have Been Added to the Constitution

The proof that the federal amending process is difficult is in the numbers. Since 1789, more than 11,000 proposals for constitutional amendments have been introduced in Congress. Of these, only 27 have been ratified. Ten were ratified almost immediately, as part of the Bill of Rights. Since 1791, only 17 amendments have been added to the Constitution, less than one per decade on average. The country can go long periods without any amendments—more than 60 years elapsed between the Twelfth and Thirteenth Amendments, and more than 40 between the Fifteenth and Sixteenth Amendments—and then have a number of amendments ratified over a short period. Between 1961 and 1971, four amendments were added to the Constitution.[39]

As Table 3.4 shows, amendments have followed the logic of the articles of the Constitution, emphasizing the basic framework of government, the powers of government, the size of the electorate, and the relationship between people and government. The amendments have generally not dealt with matters of social or economic policy, with three exceptions: the elimination of slavery, the approval of a federal income tax, and the prohibition—and then repeal of the prohibition—of alcohol production and sales. Slavery and taxation were issues addressed in the Constitution, implicitly and explicitly, respectively, so these amendments did not address new areas. The failure of Prohibition is often considered a prime example of why specific social policy should not be included in the Constitution.[40]

The Constitution Can Be "Amended" Through Judicial Interpretation and Other Less Formal Means

Although the amending process does provide some flexibility to that enhances the legitimacy of the constitutional system, it is, as we have seen, infrequently successful, and the country can go long periods without any formal change to the Constitution. Whether the Framers expected this degree of structural stability is difficult to say. After all, they saw the Constitution amended 10 times—the Bill of Rights—within two years. By 1804, another two amendments had been ratified, so that 12 of the 27 amendments, or nearly 45 percent, had been added to the Constitution within 15 years of its adoption.

The infrequent amendment of the Constitution since then therefore presents a puzzle. The easy answer, often given, is that the Framers disdained the idea of frequent revision of the document and provided a role model of appropriate behavior for later generations. From the view of political science, however, the empirical record is difficult to match up with this answer. Yes, the Framers were concerned conceptually about overly frequent revision to the document, but they also had to deal with practical political reality. Americans are sometimes so swept up with notions of wise, philosophical Framers that they neglect how astute and capable they were as politicians. In the world of practical politics, the Framers were not adamantly

AN AMENDMENT DEFEATED

Senator Jesse Helms (R-NC) and Phyllis Schafly celebrate the defeat of the Equal Rights Amendment in 1982. Schafly, an attorney and political activist, was one of the chief organizers of the effort to block the Equal Rights Amendment by putting public pressure on state legislators to oppose the amendment. She began her efforts at a time when it appeared the ERA was virtually certain to be ratified by the 38 states needed to add it to the Constitution.

opposed to the idea of amending the document to achieve their goals. In addition to the 12 successful amendments noted earlier, they proposed two more as part of the set of Bill of Rights amendments—one, on the size of House districts, was unsuccessful, and the other, on congressional pay raises, was finally ratified as the Twenty-seventh Amendment in 1992. The bottom line is that if the Framers were setting an example for future generations to follow, it was not one of restraint in the amendment process.

If infrequent amendments cannot be attributed to the Framers as role models, what other factors might be important? One key factor noted by political scientists is that the supermajority processes involved in the proposal and ratification stages create a high barrier to adding new amendments. In addition, the formal amending process is not the only means of constitutional change: the Supreme Court's interpretation of the Constitution can change its meaning. Most likely, the causality runs both ways.

TABLE 3.4 AMENDMENTS TO THE CONSTITUTION

Amendment	Purpose	Year adopted
	Relationship of People and Government	
1st	Freedom of religion, speech, press, assembly, petition	1791
2nd	Right of people to keep arms	1791
3rd	No housing of militia without due process	1791
4th	Restrictions on search and seizure	1791
5th–8th	Rights in judicial proceedings	1791
9th–10th	Nonenumerated rights reserved to the states or people	1791
13th	Slavery prohibited	1865
14th	Civil liberties and civil rights protections extended to states	1865
	Government Structure	
12th	Changes in Electoral College process	1804
17th	Direct election of U.S. senators	1913
20th	Starting dates for terms; procedure when president-elect dies	1933
22nd	Presidents limited to two terms	1951
25th	Succession in cases of president's death or disability	1967
27th	Congressional pay raises require intervening election	1992
	Size of the Electorate	
15th	Extend voting rights to all races	1870
19th	Extend voting rights to women	1920
23rd	Extend voting rights to residents of District of Columbia	1961
24th	Eliminate payment of "poll tax" as requirement to vote	1964
26th	Extend voting rights to citizens 18 years of age and older	1971
	Powers of Government	
11th	Restricts federal courts' role in cases involving states	1795
16th	National income tax	1913
18th	Prohibition of sale, manufacture, and transportation of alcohol	1919
21st	Repeal of Eighteenth Amendment	1933

The difficulty of the formal amending process leads individuals to look to the Supreme Court for new interpretations of the Constitution, and because the Court engages in constitutional interpretation, individuals may see less need to engage in the lengthy formal amendment process.

Consider the Court's *Plessy v. Ferguson* decision of 1896. The Supreme Court declared that racial segregation was legally permissible under the Constitution. Nearly 60 years later, however, in the *Brown v. Board of Education* decision, the Court concluded precisely the opposite. The language of the Constitution had not changed in the meantime with regard to this issue, yet the Court, with different members, in a different time, read the meaning of the Constitution differently.

Think of the amending process detailed in the Constitution as producing formal amendments: they actually change the text of the document. Constitutional interpretation as performed by the courts produces what might be considered informal amendments: the constitutional text remains the same, but the meaning of that text is read differently. To some observers of American politics, this practice creates the risk of allowing judges to insert their policy preferences into the Constitution by decreeing that the Constitution requires or prohibits something that had previously been left to elected officials to decide. In this view, too much power is placed in the hands of unelected federal judges, rather than the elected officials who would have to pass constitutional amendments. On the other hand, informal amendments undeniably provide additional adaptability to the system, which was a goal of the Framers. Most likely, it would have proved impossible to pass a formal constitutional amendment between 1896 and 1954 stating that segregation was unconstitutional, but through a change in interpretation, the Constitution was, in effect, amended.

Both formal and informal amendments have been involved in what some scholars refer to as "constitutional moments"—times of great debate on the fundamental principles of American government, politics, and the Constitution.[41] The 1780s, with the creation of the Articles of Confederation and the Constitution, are often seen as one such period. The 1860s, with a new relationship between the national and state governments, as well as the social revolution brought by the end of slavery, are another. The 1930s and 1940s, with the rise of a federal government of larger and more extensive scope and power than that seen previously, are a third. Formal amendments and constitution writing dominated the first two moments, while informal amendments dominated the latter. Each significantly changed the nature of American government from what it had previously been.

On MyPoliSciLab

Review the Chapter

Listen to **Chapter 3** on **MyPoliSciLab**

From Revolution to Constitution

3.1 Trace the developments that led to the American Revolution and the country's first constitution, p. 63.

Although scholars still debate the causes and effects of the American Revolution, we can safely say that ideas about liberty and democracy were prominent rallying cries of the colonists. After a series of acts by the British government led to support for independence, the Americans turned their attention to building a structure of governance. The first attempt at a constitution, the Articles of Confederation, proved to be insufficient in building a national government with sufficient power and authority over the states.

Crafting the Constitution

3.2 Outline the problems the Framers of the Constitution attempted to resolve and the solutions they devised, p. 73.

The Framers focused on resolving five problems: overcoming fundamental disputes on representation in the new government; allowing for public input while limiting "excessive" democracy and concentrated power through election procedures, separation of powers, checks and balances, and federalism; protecting commerce and property; creating legitimacy by constructing an adaptable but stable governing framework; and providing for national defense. As they wrote a new constitution, the Framers sought to meld power and liberty, freedom and order, and national authority and state sovereignty.

The Battle for Ratification

3.3 Compare and contrast the arguments of Anti-Federalists and Federalists, p. 86.

Federalists and Anti-Federalists debated the system of government set out in the Constitution. The Federalists argued that the best protection for liberty would be a stronger national government, a large republic rather than a small democracy, and a system with some distance between the people and government power, so that any "passions" that swept through the population would not immediately find their way into law. The Anti-Federalists favored a system closer to that provided by the Articles of Confederation—a loose union of the states in which the national government was clearly subordinate. At the very least, they wanted a national government that was close to the people and had many checks on its power.

Amending the Constitution

3.4 Explain the processes of constitutional change, p. 91.

The amending process includes the introduction or proposal of an amendment, which happens at the national level, and the ratification of a proposed amendment, which happens at the state level. Through this two-level process, and through the use of supermajorities in Congress and the states, the Framers hoped to ensure that only those amendments with broad societal approval would be added to the Constitution. To date, only 27 out of more than 10,000 amendments proposed have made it through both levels of the amending process. The Constitution does not change only when the text is changed, however. When judges interpret the Constitution, they give it specific meaning. When those interpretations change, the meaning of the Constitution changes also, even though the text remains unchanged.

Learn the Terms

Study and **Review** the **Flashcards**

Anti-Federalists, p. 86
Articles of Confederation, p. 70
Bill of Rights, p. 89
checks and balances, p. 79
Declaration of Independence, p. 68
equal privileges and immunities clause, p. 84
federalism, p. 81
Federalists, p. 86
full faith and credit clause, p. 84
Great Compromise, p. 76
indirect election, p. 78
judicial review, p. 81
nation, p. 69
New Jersey Plan, p. 75
parliamentary system, p. 82
republic, p. 78
separation of powers, p. 78
Shays's Rebellion, p. 72
supremacy clause, p. 84
Three-fifths Compromise, p. 76
Virginia Plan, p. 75

Test Yourself

3.1 Trace the developments that led to the American Revolution and the country's first constitution.

Shays's Rebellion in Massachusetts raised concerns because it seemed to indicate that

a. Congress under the Articles of Confederation lacked the power to confront significant national emergencies.
b. Congress under the Articles of Confederation was too powerful.
c. the national government under the Articles of Confederation was equipped to meet only naval attacks.
d. states such as Massachusetts were distributing land for free to radical farmer advocates such as Shays.
e. individuals loyal to Great Britain were committing violent acts after the Americans had won the Revolutionary War.

3.2 Outline the problems the Framers of the Constitution attempted to resolve and the solutions they devised.

Which one of the following was NOT a goal of the Framers of the Constitution?

a. Resolve divisions among elites
b. Limit excessive democracy
c. Eliminate the Great Compromise
d. Establish legitimacy for the new government
e. Protect commerce and property

3.3 Compare and contrast the arguments of Anti-Federalists and Federalists.

The Anti-Federalists argued all of the following EXCEPT

a. The proposed Constitution threatened the people's liberty.
b. The proposed Constitution would enable individuals' self-interest to protect liberty.
c. The proposed Constitution would reduce the democratic influence on government.
d. A government more like the one established by the Articles of Confederation was needed.
e. A bill of rights was necessary to protect individual freedoms.

3.4 Explain the processes of constitutional change.

Which of the following is an informal constitutional amendment?

a. An amendment that passes by only a simple majority in the both the House and Senate
b. An amendment that is set to expire after a certain number of years
c. An amendment that recommends rather than requires government action
d. A president nominating judges who share his ideology
e. A Court opinion that interprets the Constitution's meaning in a new way

Explore Further

SUGGESTED READINGS BY TOP SCHOLARS

Richard Beeman. 2009. *Plain, Honest Men: The Making of the American Constitution*. New York: Random House. Details the day-to-day debates and decisions at the Constitutional Convention.

Mark A. Graber. 2006. *Dred Scott and the Problem of Constitutional Evil*. New York: Cambridge University Press. Provides a provocative examination, through the lens of the *Dred Scott* decision, of how constitutions, in their effort to make accommodations between rival factions, can also provide support for injustice.

Sanford Levinson. 2006. *Our Undemocratic Constitution: Where the Constitution Goes Wrong (And How We the People Can Correct It)*. New York: Oxford University Press. Argues that the Constitution thwarts the will of the people and promotes ineffective governance, and offers suggestions for reforming the document.

Pauline Maier. 2010. *Ratification: The People Debate the Constitution, 1787–1788*. New York: Simon & Schuster. The first extensive history of the ratification process in the states; covers the people involved as well as the practical and philosophical battles in each state, focusing particularly on the conflict in Pennsylvania, Massachusetts, Virginia, and New York.

Keith E. Whittington. 2007. *Political Foundations of Judicial Supremacy: The Presidency, the Supreme Court, and Constitutional Leadership in U.S. History*. Princeton, NJ: Princeton University Press. Contrary to the idea that the judiciary has claimed power rightfully belonging to the other branches, the book argues that the courts have had power pushed upon them by politicians who found judicial supremacy to serve their interests.

SUGGESTED WEBSITES

Library of Congress, Primary Documents in American History: www.memory.loc.gov/ammem/help/constRedir.html
Site with links and discussion of the key documents in American political history, including draft versions. Includes key documents that preceded and contributed to the Declaration of Independence, Articles of Confederation, and U.S. Constitution.

Congressional Research Service Annotated Constitution: www.law.cornell.edu/constitution
A helpful guide that includes commentary, background, historical developments, and relevant court cases for each article, section, and amendment of the Constitution.

Avalon Project: The U.S. Constitution: www.yale.edu/lawweb/avalon/constpap.htm
An outstanding collection of documents related to the development of the Constitution. From the Avalon Project home page, you can access document collections on many other topics in American politics and law.

Constitution Finder: http://confinder.richmond.edu
Constitutions from around the world.

Constitution of the Confederate States of America: www.civilwarhome.com/csconstitution.htm
The Confederate Constitution used the U.S. Constitution as a framework. This site shows where the two constitutions matched and where they diverged.

American Law Sources Online: www.lawsource.com/also
Provides a gateway to state constitutions and other state legal documents and information.

((**Listen** to **Chapter 4** on **MyPoliSciLab**

4

Federalism

THE STATE OF THEIR UNIONS

Among the issues that gay and lesbian advocacy groups see as fundamental to equality, the most publicly prominent has been same-sex marriage. Same-sex marriage illustrates several causal questions at the heart of federalism. How is federal policy influenced by state policy, and how is state policy influenced by federal policy? Under what conditions are federal policy makers likely to intervene to impose uniform rules and regulations across the states, and when do they prefer to have states make their own choices? How do outcomes at the federal level or in one state affect political strategy and outcomes in others?

Marriage confers favorable treatment in a range of areas—inheritance, taxation, health care, child custody, immigration, property rights, hospital visitation, and Social Security survivor benefits. More than 1,000 federal laws include reference to marital status.

Typically, marriage has been a legal status determined by state law. The issue of same-sex marriage first entered the national political conversation in the mid-1990s when it appeared the state of Hawaii might—although ultimately it did not—legalize this type of marriage. In 1996, the federal government responded with the Defense of Marriage Act (DOMA) signed by President Clinton. This act stipulates that for the purpose of federal programs and benefits such as Social Security and Medicare, marriage consists of "the legal union between one man and one woman as husband and wife." It also specifies that states need not honor same-sex marriages that are legal in another state. Article IV, Section 1, of the U.S. Constitution requires states to honor the official acts of other states as part of the "full faith and credit" clause. That section also gives Congress the power to control the "effect" of this interstate recognition. Supporters of DOMA argue that this provision gives Congress the constitutional authority to exempt states from their usual full faith and credit obligations; opponents of DOMA disagree.

4.1

Explain how the Constitution serves as a framework for federalism and why debates about the proper role of the federal and state governments remain, p. 103.

4.2

Describe how state constitutions and local government charters provide the structure and operations of state and local governments, p. 108.

4.3

Outline the principles of dual federalism and their basis in the Supreme Court's traditional understanding of interstate commerce, p. 112.

4.4

Trace the evolution from dual to cooperative federalism, and identify methods of cooperative federalism, p. 115.

4.5

Assess the extent and nature of changes in federalism since the mid-1990s, p. 132.

TOP OF THE WORLD The debate over same-sex marriage has occurred at the national and state levels. In 2011, New York State became the sixth state to allow same-sex marriage. Shawn Klein and Phil Fung were one of two same-sex couples married atop the Empire State Building in February 2012.

The Big Picture What do health care and immigration have in common? Both issues illustrate how complicated federalism can get. Using these two issues, author John J. Coleman explains how we moved from dual federalism to a more complex cooperative federalism where the line between nation and state is increasingly blurred.

The Basics Are you a states-right advocate? This video will help you understand how powers and responsibilities are divided between the national and state governments. You'll also discover how the powers of the national government have expanded and consider whether this is in the best interests of the people.

Should the national government have so much power?

In Context What is the primary mechanism for federalism in the United States? In this video, Barnard College political scientist Scott L. Minkoff explains how the national government tries to force state governments to adopt its policies and how state governments respond.

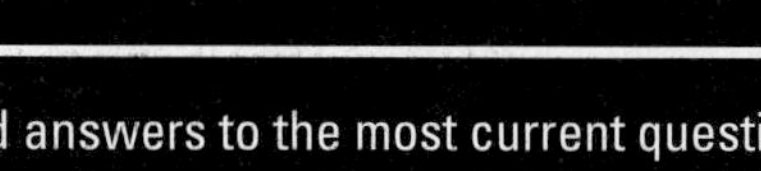

Think Like a Political Scientist Find answers to the most current questions that scholars of federalism are raising in the areas of welfare reform and state rights. Barnard College political scientist Scott L. Minkoff explores the challenges faced by state-rights advocates once they are elected to Congress.

In the Real World Should the federal government be allowed to mandate health care reform or should that power belong to the states? Hear supporters and detractors of Obamacare explain their opinions, and learn about the recent Supreme Court decision that handed this power to the federal government.

So What? Don't like Massachusetts's laws? Then move to Maryland. Most Americans value federalism because of this flexibility that it offers at the state level. However, author John J. Coleman asks students to consider the challenge of deciding what should be a national standard and what should be left up to the states.

Because marriage has traditionally been a state issue and the chances for success have been greater at that level, gay and lesbian civil rights advocates have focused most of their attention there. In 2004, the Massachusetts Supreme Judicial Court decided that banning same-sex marriage violated the state constitution's guarantee of equal protection under the law. Supreme courts in Connecticut and Iowa did likewise in 2008 and 2009, respectively. By 2012, eight states and the District of Columbia permitted same-sex marriage, and ten states allowed a "civil union" or "domestic partnership" that permits some or most of the benefits of marriage. Voters in Maine, Maryland, and Washington in 2012 became the first to vote in favor of same-sex marriage.

Although marriage has traditionally been a state issue, the U.S. Supreme Court has upheld the federal government's authority to pass laws banning certain state-approved marriage arrangements, such as polygamy. It has also struck down some state marriage restrictions. In *Loving v. Virginia* (1967), the Court declared Virginia's ban on interracial marriage to be a violation of the U.S. Constitution's promise of equal protection of the laws. In the Court's view, the law had no purpose outside of "invidious racial discrimination." Gay and lesbian civil rights activists point to the ban on same-sex marriage as presenting precisely the same discriminatory issues as *Loving*. Opponents of same-sex marriage reject this parallel, saying that banning interracial marriage was purely based on discrimination, whereas banning same-sex marriage is based on preserving the basic definition of a social institution.[1]

Accordingly, critics have led a countermovement designed to stop the legal recognition of same-sex marriages. Part of the strategy has been passage of laws and constitutional amendments in the states to prohibit same-sex marriage. These efforts have been highly successful, with 38 states limiting marriage to a man and a woman either in state law or the state constitution. Another part of the strategy was the proposal of an amendment to the U.S. Constitution to prohibit same-sex marriage. This effort has not been successful as of 2012.

Gay and lesbian rights advocates have focused their efforts largely at the state level, but in 2012 they won a major victory when a federal appeals court ruled that an amendment to the California constitution that prohibited same-sex marriage violated the U.S. Constitution. Both supporters and opponents of the appeals court decision expect that the case will ultimately arrive at the U.S. Supreme Court. Supporters of same-sex marriage have also urged that DOMA be repealed. The Department of Justice indicated in 2011 that it would no longer defend the law in federal court, believing it to be unconstitutional, but the law nonetheless remains in effect. In 2012, a federal appeals court struck down DOMA as unconstitutional, increasing the likelihood the U.S. Supreme Court will be asked to rule on the matter.

Same-sex marriage illuminates the principles and practices of federalism and the fault lines in American politics among different levels of government and among different institutions. It raises questions about where the responsibilities of the state governments end and those of the federal government begin. And it shows us how federalism has strong causal effects in American politics, with state actions leading to federal responses, federal actions leading to interest group recalculations of their best strategy to achieve their ends, and actions by governments and activists in one state prompted by developments in other states.[2] This chapter explores these principles and practices of federalism and the politics surrounding them.

The Nature of the Union

4.1 **Explain how the Constitution serves as a framework for federalism and why debates about the proper role of the federal and state governments remain.**

When the Framers crafted the Constitution and sent it to the states for ratification, Federalists and Anti-Federalists debated the nature of liberty. But, as the names of the two sides suggest, they also debated federalism, and the interaction of liberty and federalism.

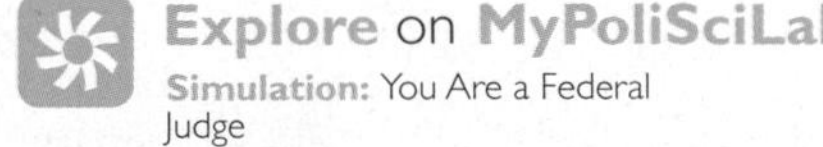

4.1

4.2

4.3

4.4

4.5

confederation
a loose grouping of independent political units, such as states or countries, whose main purpose is to govern the relationship between those units.

unitary system
a form of government in which government at the highest level has the power to create, combine, or disband lower-level governments and determine what powers will be allowed at the lower levels.

Federalists and Anti-Federalists clashed about ideas, but they also engaged in an intensely political battle. Both groups had views about public policy, and they realized some arrangements of national and state power would be more likely than others to advance these policies. This clash started a long trend of federalism being a political battleground on which politicians, judges, and activist groups jostle to advance their positions. Politicians frequently invoke federalism to justify particular policies or to argue against their opponents. Those arguments can be inconsistent, demanding more national control in one area and more state control in another. Politicians' philosophy about federalism and the Constitution can drive their actions, but politicians can also be federalism opportunists, willing to support strengthening Washington or strengthening the states depending on how the issue suits their own policy preferences, ideology, or reelection prospects. Federal judges also can be influenced by ideology or by particular outcomes they wish to see. Federalism is not a settled topic of constitutional doctrine—it is a matter of intense debate that brings together philosophy, power, politics, and policy.

Confederal and Unitary Arrangements Are Two Ways to Organize Power Between National and Subnational Governments

What was the appropriate relationship between the state governments and the national government? Federalists and Anti-Federalists believed the answer to this question had significant implications for preserving liberty, a key element of American political culture embodied in the proposed new government. However, they disagreed about what type of relationship between national and subnational governments would work best. Federalists insisted that a strong national government was essential to safeguard liberty and property rights. By contrast, Anti-Federalists maintained that a system with a distant, powerful national government would likely threaten individual liberty and the independence of the states. State governments, in the view of the Anti-Federalists, could be better monitored and controlled by the people and, thus, were less a danger to their liberty.

Anti-Federalists, therefore, preferred a **confederation,** as in the Articles of Confederation, where independent entities—states, in the American case—join together to pursue some common purposes. The joint government in a confederation tends to have limited authority over the individual member governments, and that authority must usually be explicitly granted by the members—the joint government does not itself have ongoing powers independent of the members.

Governing a confederation can be a challenge. Under the Articles of Confederation, American government was similar to the structure we see today in the United Nations (UN). UN decisions can be difficult to enforce because they depend on countries to comply voluntarily; resources can be hard to come by because members can choose to withhold their contribution to the organization; and member countries frequently compete, trying to best or disadvantage one another, especially economically. The United States under the Articles of Confederation paralleled these governing difficulties.

The Framers did not share the Anti-Federalists' enthusiasm for a confederal arrangement that made the national government dependent on the states, but neither did they construct a **unitary system** that would make the states dependent on the national government. In a unitary system, lower levels of government are subordinate to the national government and have little, if any, independent governing authority. The upper-level government is free to create, combine, or disband lower-level governments. Lower levels of government also typically have limited ability to raise funds on their own. In the United States, the District of Columbia is an example of this type of arrangement. Washington, D.C., has its own city government, but that government's independent authority is limited by Congress, which controls the city budget and can revoke laws passed by the city government.

State governments are essentially unitary systems with respect to local municipalities. Typically they allow substantial independence to the localities within their borders, but this arrangement is at the convenience of the state government. The Constitution makes no mention of cities and counties or other substate governments, nor does it guarantee their existence: their creation is up to the states. Around the world, the unitary system of government is the norm.

federalism
a form of government that distributes power across a national government and subnational governments and ensures the existence of the subnational governments.

reserved powers
Tenth Amendment guarantee to state governments of any powers other than those granted to the national government or those specifically prohibited for the states.

The Constitution Provides the Framework for Intergovernmental Relations Through Federalism

The Framers steered a middle course between a confederation and a unitary government. They were not unanimous in their vision. Some would have favored a unitary system, with power centralized at the national level. Some preferred a confederal arrangement, in which the states were supreme. Others preferred a middle-ground position between the unitary and confederal extremes, a federal system in which the national and state governments would share power (see Figure 4.1).

Federalism is a system that distributes political power across a national government and subnational governments. In the United States, these subnational governments are the states. Federalism ensures that the subnational units can make some final decisions and have their existence protected. According to the *supremacy clause* of the U.S. Constitution, when the national and state governments conflict, national laws overrule state laws. And powers delegated to the national government are not available to the states. On the other hand, the Tenth Amendment provides that powers not delegated to the national government by the Constitution and not prohibited for state governments are reserved for the states or for the people—these are known as **reserved powers.** States also are guaranteed equal voting rights in the U.S.

Confederal

Subnational governments create the national government and grant it some limited areas of responsibility. The national government relies on the subnational governments for funding and to implement decisions made by the national government. The national government typically lacks enforcement mechanisms and relies on the voluntary compliance of the subnational governments. Sovereign power (the ultimate decision maker) is at the subnational level.

Federal

Both the national government and the subnational governments have areas in which they hold primary sovereign power and have their own sources of funds and ability to implement policies. They have some areas of shared authority and may compete for control. The existence of the subnational governments is guaranteed. Sovereign power exists at both levels.

Unitary

The national government creates the subnational governments. It may grant governing authority to the subnational governments in certain policy areas, but this authority is not independent or guaranteed—it can be eliminated by the national government, as can the subnational governments themselves. Sovereign power is at the national level.

FIGURE 4.1 FLOW OF POWER IN THREE SYSTEMS OF GOVERNMENT.

The confederal, federal, and unitary systems of government provide alternative distributions of political power. The confederal system places sovereignty in the subnational governments, while the unitary system places it in the national government. The federal system is a blend, with sovereignty at both the national and subnational levels.

4.1

4.2

4.3

4.4

4.5

compact theory
a theory of the founding of the American government that argues states were sovereign units that joined together in the new national government but did not give up their status as sovereign, independent governments.

sovereignty
having the ultimate authority to make decisions within one's borders, without interference by other governments.

nullification
the theory that states have the right to nullify national laws to which they object and believe violate the U.S. Constitution.

Senate, protection against domestic insurrection and foreign invasion, and the preservation of a representative form of government. Existing states, via their representation in the U.S. Congress, have a role in the admission of new states, and existing states cannot have any of their territory shifted to a new state without their consent.

The Constitution also mandates fair play among the states with three crucial provisions that are intended to prevent states from discriminating against one another or cutting special deals that would aggravate relations with other states or potentially other countries. The *full faith and credit clause* requires states to honor the official acts of other states, such as public records and the results of judicial proceedings. The *equal privileges and immunities clause* requires states to treat their citizens and citizens of other states similarly. And the *commerce clause* places the regulation of interstate commerce and foreign economic trade in the federal government, not the individual states. The evolution of interstate commerce has played a key role in the evolution of federalism and so is discussed at length later in this chapter.

Federalism and the federal system refer to the arrangement of power distributed across the national and state levels. As a practical matter, however, in the United States the term *federal government* refers to the government created by the U.S. Constitution and ratified by the states. This term is used interchangeably with *national government.* In common usage, references to the federal government or to the national government both mean the government created by the Constitution and based in Washington, D.C.

Debate Over the Appropriate Balance of National and State Power Continues

Ratification of the Constitution did not end disputes over the nature of the new system. From the start, the question of precisely how much control the national government had over the states was a matter of contention. Advocates of a limited national role, including Thomas Jefferson, preferred a **compact theory** of federalism, which suggested the states were sovereign entities that joined together. **Sovereignty** refers to a government having the ultimate authority to make decisions about what happens within its borders, free from interference by other governments. "The United States are" represented an appealing phrase for this group. The Constitution was an instrument for these sovereign states to coordinate and pursue their interests. The states gave up some limited and specific powers, but the national government could make no other demands beyond those in the Constitution, nor could it intrude into relations between these sovereign states and their citizens. Except in ways that they explicitly consented to, the states were to be left alone.

This approach to understanding federalism was particularly prominent in the South, where it led to the doctrine of **nullification**—the idea that states could nullify national government laws with which they disagreed and which they believed violated the letter or spirit of the U.S. Constitution. Identified most strongly with Vice President John Calhoun of South Carolina (1825–1832), nullification was frequently and controversially employed in the decades prior to the Civil War, especially with regard to the slavery issue, but it had been present in political circles long before that.[3]

In later years, the compact theory would sometimes be referred to as the "states' rights" position. This became a controversial term in the 1950s and 1960s when it was most commonly invoked to thwart the push of the national government to end racial segregation, particularly in southern states. The compact view of federalism, however, should not be seen as limited to issues concerning civil rights, nor does it inherently advocate a limited, minimalist government. State governments could be quite active within the compact framework. The key concern for the politicians advocating it was less about the reach of government authority in the abstract than it was that decisions made by government be made by that government closest to home, over which they had more influence.[4]

The **nationalist theory,** more prominent in northern states, provided an alternative to the compact theory. Nationalists would be more comfortable with the phrase "the United States is." This approach stressed that the Framers intended the Constitution to be a departure from the limited government of the Articles of Confederation. The Constitution represented "the people," not the states, coming together. The preamble to the Constitution could have begun "We the people of the states"—an option the delegates considered—but it did not. The very language "We the people," according to the nationalist view, indicates that the Constitution's purpose was to provide the institutions and rules by which a nation of people, rather than a collection of states, could be governed. This did not mean abusing the states or ignoring their independence, but it did mean that at times, states would have to accept national direction and demands, especially if the national action could be portrayed as promoting the general well-being of the country.

nationalist theory
a theory of the founding of the American government that sees the Constitution more as the joining together of the people than the joining together of the states.

Alexander Hamilton, secretary of the Treasury under President Washington, strongly identified with the nationalist theory. Among executive branch officials in the early years of the republic, Hamilton had the most expansive vision for national government power, especially with regard to economic matters. He proposed that the national government establish a bank and that it invest heavily in building the roads, canals, and other infrastructure that would help unite the new country and advance economic development.

Given the unhappy experience of centralized British power during the colonial era, how could Hamilton go about creating the political coalition to support such a plan? His answer was to mastermind a deal in which the federal government assumed all the debt that state governments had incurred in fighting the Revolutionary War. To Hamilton, this plan would link wealthy individuals and institutions in financial arrangements with the national government rather than with the states, and the stability, power, and authority of the national government would become critical in their eyes. To many who subscribed to the compact theory, however, Hamilton's nationalist vision veered toward monarchy.

Across the course of American politics, debate has flourished concerning the appropriate balance of power between the national and state governments. And the debate matters in very concrete ways. Issues as diverse as slavery, punishment for violence against women, regulation of business, environmental protection, minimum wages, end-of-life decisions, and enforcement of antidiscrimination statutes, among many others are influenced heavily by interpretations of federalism. People who care about these issues need to care about federalism, because in the American political system prevailing interpretations of federalism will strongly shape what, if anything, government can or should do about these matters, and which level of government should do it.

In the case of national health care reform, a major debating point was whether the national government had the constitutional authority to do what the president and his allies in Congress proposed. It was a battle over the meaning of the Constitution, but it was also a practical political battle. To achieve his policy goals and satisfy his supporters who wanted to see some version of health care reform pass, President Obama argued for pulling major aspects of health policy away from the states and setting national rules and requirements. He ultimately settled for less of a national role than he and many of his supporters originally desired.[5] To achieve their policy objectives and satisfy their supporters, opponents of his plan argued for maintaining state control and enhancing consumer choice. Some of their favored proposals, such as allowing consumers to purchase insurance across state lines, would have required a convergence of insurance regulations across the states to work effectively.[6]

4.1

4.2

4.3

4.4

4.5

State and Local Governments

4.2 Describe how state constitutions and local government charters provide the structure and operations of state and local governments.

When the national Congress that existed under the Articles of Confederation adjourned to allow the writing of the Constitution, it passed the Northwest Ordinance of 1787, which was critical in shaping the United States and the state governments. In Article 5 of the Ordinance, Congress provided for the admission of additional states to the Union with the full status of the first 13. This provision meant that all states would have the same rights and privileges:

> **Article 5**: . . . And, whenever any of the said States shall have sixty thousand free inhabitants therein, such State shall be admitted, by its delegates, into the Congress of the United States, on an equal footing with the original States in all respects whatever, and shall be at liberty to form a permanent constitution and State government: Provided, the constitution and government so to be formed, shall be republican, and in conformity to the principles contained in these articles; and, so far as it can be consistent with the general interest of the confederacy, such admission shall be allowed at an earlier period, and when there may be a less number of free inhabitants in the State than sixty thousand.

The other major provision of Article 5 was the requirement that new states have constitutions acceptable to Congress. Thus, territories petitioning for statehood had an incentive to adopt constitutions similar to those of the states already in the Union. The five states that were carved out of the Northwest Territory—Ohio, Indiana, Illinois, Michigan, and Wisconsin—submitted constitutions almost identical to those of New York and Massachusetts, the states from which most of the initial settlers in the territory had originated. The strategy of each of the territories was to propose constitutions that members of Congress would recognize. Ohio was the first to join the Union (in 1803) and Wisconsin the last of the Northwest Territories (1848).

State Constitutions Primarily Limit the Power of Government

The first state constitutions were drafted before the passage of the U.S. Constitution. When the authors of the constitutions of the original 13 states did their work, their primary concern was to make certain that state governments did not have the power and discretion of their colonial predecessors. The American Revolution was about providing power to the governed and limiting that of the government. As new states formed, they drafted constitutions that maintained this perspective, and as new policy issues emerged over time, states amended their constitutions to address them.

EVOLUTION OF THE STATE CONSTITUTIONS From the beginning, state constitutions included clauses that limited officials from placing restrictions on an individual's speech and assembly, participating in unreasonable searches and seizures, and using cruel and inhumane punishment. New Hampshire's constitution even makes clear that citizens have a right to revolt. The major limiting clauses of the U.S. Constitution are the first 10 amendments, the Bill of Rights, which were added as a condition for ratification by the first 13 states. The states considered individual liberties and limits on government power important enough to include in the national as well as the state constitutions.

The first state constitutions designed weak government institutions.[7] Legislatures were part time and governors served only two-year terms. Governors of the new states had nothing close to the authority and discretion of colonial governors. State constitutions stipulated that these offices be primarily ceremonial and made legislatures the primary center of decision-making authority. Initially, only South Carolina, New York, and Massachusetts allowed their governors to veto legislation.

The tradition of weak state governments continued with the adoption of constitutions in the aftermath of the Civil War, as the country expanded westward.[8] Former Confederate states had to write new constitutions that did not include the right of individuals to own slaves. Individual southern states adopted and repealed as many as four different constitutions between 1865 and 1880. With white southern economic and social elites still smarting from federal government intrusions of the Reconstruction era, the end results were state constitutions severely limiting the power and role of government, allowing elites to govern informally.

When western states joined the Union, the **Progressive movement** attempted to prevent the emergence of political party "machines" by granting voters new authority over state governments. Progressives added new techniques: empowering voters with the **initiative,** which allows voters to enact new laws by putting a proposal on the ballot if enough people sign a petition, and the **recall,** which allows for the removal of elected officials through popular vote rather than impeachment. Although these mechanisms of direct democracy are most common in the constitutions of western states, nine states in other regions eventually adopted them. Initiatives are used frequently, but recalls are relatively rare. Recalls have only been attempted four times against sitting governors for example, most recently in 2012 when Wisconsin Governor Scott Walker became the first governor to win a recall election and remain in office.

With constitutional changes adopted in the 1960s and 1970s, state institutions increased in power.[9] A 1962 U.S. Supreme Court ruling mandated legislative redistricting in the states, which generally increased the power of urban areas and subsequently prompted reforms that give state governments a larger role in policy making. All governors now have veto authority and, except for New Hampshire and Vermont, now serve four-year terms. More legislatures are full time, and state courts have become more streamlined and professional. But the historic distrust of powerful government continues, and state constitutions still include many restrictions.

Progressive movement
movement advocating measures to destroy political machines and instead have direct participation by voters in the nomination of candidates and the establishment of public policy.

initiative
a process in which a proposal for legislation is placed on the ballot and voters can either enact or reject the proposal without further action by the governor or legislature.

recall
a process in which voters can petition for a vote to remove officials between elections.

OTHER ATTRIBUTES OF STATE CONSTITUTIONS State constitutions do more than protect the rights of individual citizens and establish the institutions of state governments. State constitutions also deal with the basic functions of government. Observers have often noted that state constitutions are longer than the U.S Constitution. On average, they have more than three times as many words. The federal Constitution falls short of 9,000 words; several state constitutions exceed 90,000. Why are state constitutions longer?

One reason is the extensive list of state areas of responsibility, which include any duties not granted to the national government or specifically prohibited for states. Another reason is the four dozen references to the states in the U.S. Constitution; many of these references are shorthand for areas that state constitutions would need to fill out in detail. For example, the U.S. Constitution as originally passed provided little guidance on who was qualified to vote—the state constitutions had to fill in this gap. The U.S. Constitution could be shorter because the state constitutions would contain the longer detail. A third reason for the longer state constitutions is that because state governments were seen as closer to the people, their constitutions are easier to amend than is the federal constitution. Much of the length of state constitutions results from the amendments, which often number in the hundreds. These amendments, unlike the amendments concerning process, structure, and the rights of the individual that are typical at the national level, often contain a significant amount of policy detail and prescriptions. If the amending process is not inordinately difficult, then legislators have an incentive to put policy provisions into constitutions, as they will still be harder for future legislators to change than laws would be.[10]

Almost all state constitutions include a collection of policies and details that are similar to laws and regulations. For instance, a clause in the California constitution dictates the length of a wrestling match. In some states, constitutions protect the special interests of farmers and ranchers. In others, oil and mining industry interests receive protection.[11]

Native American Tribes Intersect with State and National Authority

Long before the Founding Fathers led a revolution and crafted a constitution, Native Americans governed territory in what would come to be the United States. This history created a particularly difficult problem for governance in the United States: how would these Native American, or Indian, nations be incorporated into the American political system?

The answer was to grant tribes some degree of sovereignty within the United States and within the individual states. The tribes, in other words, are part of the American system of federalism. The Supreme Court has upheld this principle, noting that the tribes hold "attributes of sovereignty over both their members and their territory."[12] In the Constitution's commerce clause (Article I, Section 8), Indian tribes are made the equivalent of other sovereign entities: Congress is responsible "To regulate Commerce with foreign Nations, and among the several States, and with the Indian Tribes." In an executive memorandum in April 1994, President Bill Clinton reaffirmed that federal government agencies are to operate on a "government to government" basis with Indian tribes.[13]

Native Americans are citizens of their tribe, the state they live in, and the United States. They pay individual federal income tax and pay state income tax unless they

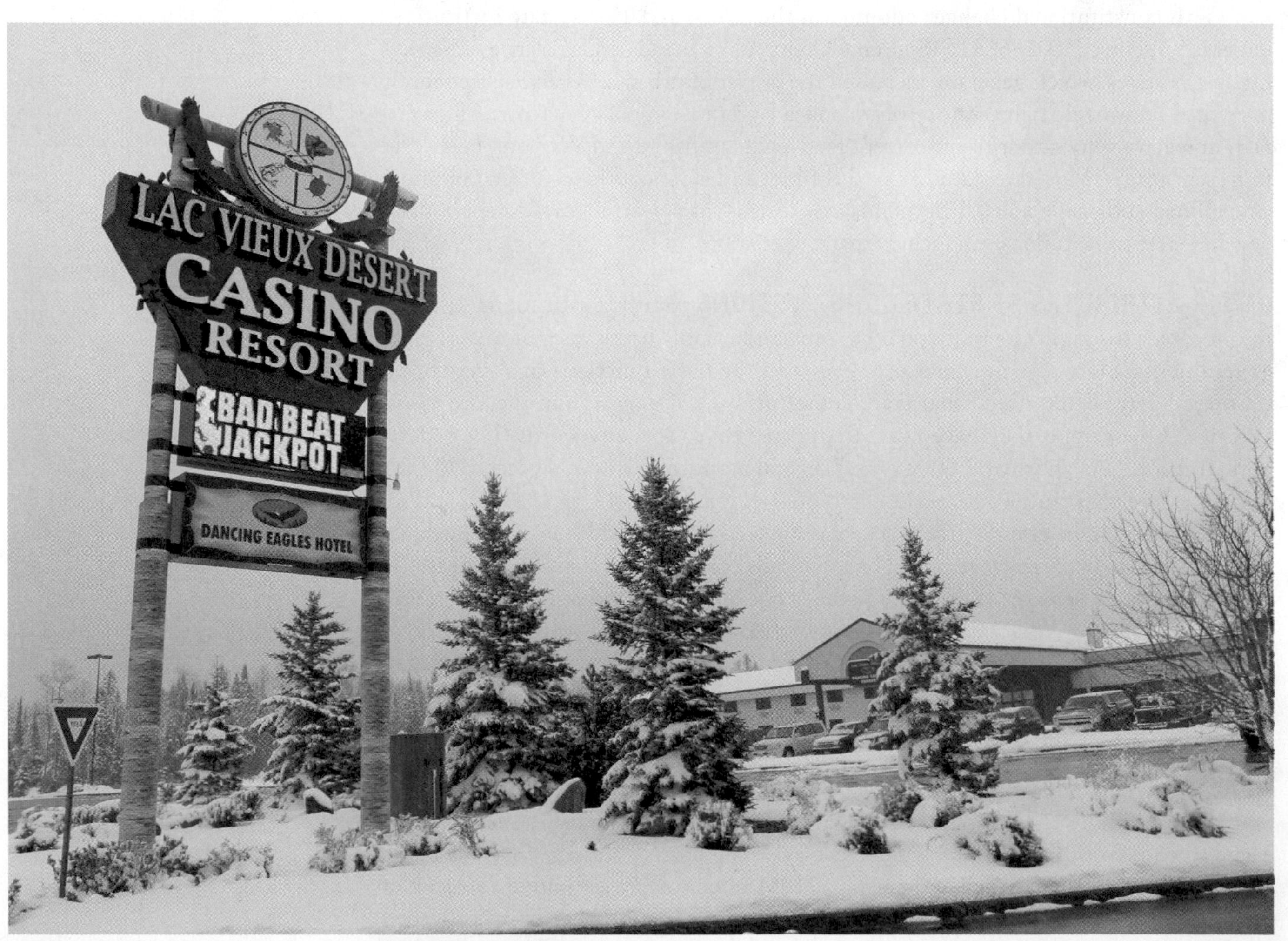

INDIAN GAMING AND FEDERALISM

Indian tribes, as a part of American federalism, often need to negotiate with the federal and state governments. Gaming is no exception. Under a federal law, the tribes enter into agreements with state governments concerning the nature of the gaming and the share of the proceeds that will go to the state. This profit sharing encourages states to sign the agreements. The most recent data indicate there are 240 tribes, including small tribes like the Lac Vieux Desert Tribe, operating nearly 450 casinos in 28 states, taking in revenue of about $27 billion.

work for the tribe and live on tribal lands. As governmental entities, the 565 federally recognized tribes do not pay taxes to other governments, just as the federal and state governments do not pay taxes to each other.[14]

Over the past two decades, gaming operations run by Native American tribes have been a flashpoint of conflict between tribes and the states. In 1996, the Seminole tribe in Florida filed suit in federal court, complaining that the state had violated the national Indian Gaming Regulatory Act by not bargaining in good faith to establish a gaming compact. In *Seminole Tribe v. Florida*, the Supreme Court rejected the tribe's case. The Court concluded in a 5–4 decision that the Eleventh Amendment gave states, as sovereign bodies, immunity from lawsuits in federal courts without their consent. Just as a sovereign body can be undermined if another entity taxes it, it can be undermined if another entity encourages lawsuits against it. In the Court's view, Congress did not have the constitutional authority to remove state immunity simply because of its interstate commerce powers to regulate the tribes and states.[15]

Although states sometimes complain that Indian sovereignty compromises their own sovereignty, they have been able to use the *Seminole* decision—itself based on state sovereignty—to wrest more profitable casino deals with the tribes in difficult budgetary times. At the same time, states without casinos or with less attractive gaming options see their citizens and other tourists pouring into neighboring states to gamble at Indian casinos, and this gives some negotiating power back to the tribes. Within states, Indian casino gambling has emerged as a political football, as governors and legislatures battle to determine who has the authority to negotiate and sign the gaming compacts.

charter
a document that, like a constitution, specifies the basic policies, procedures, and institutions of a local government.

county
a district created by state government for establishing a local government responsible for implementing a variety of state laws and for providing general governmental services.

Charters Authorize Local Governments to Make and Enforce Laws

Unlike the states and Native American tribes, local governments are not mentioned in the U.S. Constitution. Local governments are not the building blocks of states; rather, they are created by the states. State governments recognize the existence of local governments by granting them **charters,** which are similar to constitutions. Charters describe the institutions of government, the processes used to make legally binding decisions, the scope of issues and services that will be provided, and the ways in which the expenses of government will be funded.

Some local governments are created top-down. A legislature will divide the state into counties, for example, and write a charter that guides how they will operate. States use **counties** as basic administrative units for welfare and environmental programs; courts and law enforcement; registering land, births, and deaths; and for holding elections (see Table 4.1).

Local governments can also be created by a bottom-up process. When businesses and families cluster in a particular area or when a city grows in land and population, residents may petition the state legislature to be recognized as a legal entity with powers to pass and enforce laws, collect taxes and fees, and provide services. Such a petition must include either a standard charter available from the state or a charter written for that proposed government. Municipal governments, which include towns, villages,

TABLE 4.1 TYPES AND NUMBERS OF LOCAL GOVERNMENTS

Types of local governments	Number
County	3,033
Townships and towns	16,519
Municipalities	19,492
Special districts (school districts)	37,381 (13,051)

Source: U.S. Bureau of the Census, "2007 Census of Governments," http://www.census.gov//govs/cog/.

and cities, emerge from this process. States typically distinguish among these governments based on the size of the population, but they provide more authority in charters to cities than in charters for towns and villages.

Most local governments are **special districts**—that is, they focus on a particular function or service. The most common special district is a school district. Other examples are water districts, sewerage districts, park districts, and lake districts.[16] Not only are these governments restricted in what they control or provide, but they are also limited in how they may obtain revenue. Special districts often rely on a fee, such as a charge for using water, or on grants from other governments. School districts typically levy a tax on property and otherwise rely on state and national funds. Municipal and county governments also rely heavily on property taxes.

Other local governments, such as counties, towns, and cities, have a wide scope of responsibilities. Almost all states offer **home rule** charters to these jurisdictions.[17] These charters allow local governments to make and enforce public policy on any issue not under the mandate of a special district or explicitly prohibited under state law. Traditional charters itemized the kinds of policies that municipalities were authorized to develop and enforce. Home rule uses the approach that anything goes unless it is prohibited.

School districts are special districts created to divide an entire state into smaller educational units, and boundaries can be arbitrary. In some cities and towns, neighbors send their children to different schools simply because a street in the neighborhood is the boundary between two school districts. Whereas counties have a general set of responsibilities, state legislatures establish school districts to deal only with public education.

special district
local governments created for a narrowly defined purpose and with a restricted source of revenue.

home rule
a local government with authority to pass laws and provide services as long as those laws or services are not provided by a special district or otherwise prohibited under state law.

dual federalism
a form of federalism in which the national and state governments have distinct areas of authority and power, and individuals have rights as both citizens of states and citizens of the United States.

dual sovereignty
the idea that both the national and state governments have sovereignty, but over different policy areas and functions.

Dual Federalism

4.3 Outline the principles of dual federalism and their basis in the Supreme Court's traditional understanding of interstate commerce.

istinct lines separating the national and state governments are the hallmark of the system of **dual federalism,** which dominated American politics through the mid-1930s. This model of federalism embraces the ideas of dual sovereignty and dual citizenship. In dual federalism, the national government is sovereign in some areas, and the state governments are sovereign in others. The essence of dual federalism is the idea of a constitutional division of labor between the national and state governments.

Dual Sovereignty Provides Separate Areas of Authority for the National and State Governments

In dual federalism, the two levels of government have **dual sovereignty**; they are both dominant over their separate functions and areas of authority. In the nineteenth century, the federal government had control over setting tariffs on foreign goods, granting patents and copyright protection, managing the country's currency, establishing agreements with other countries, and providing defense and postal services. Some concurrent powers were shared by the two levels of government. Both could collect taxes; establish courts; create roads and other internal improvements, such as canals and opening public lands to development; and borrow and spend money. States in the nineteenth century were responsible for pretty much everything else: banking and insurance law; family and morals regulation; public health; education; criminal law; construction codes; water use; health, safety, and environmental regulations; and so on. For ambitious politicians, a career in state politics might well have been more satisfying than one in national politics, simply because of the broader range of activity afforded to state governments. Collectively, this list of duties is often referred to as the **police power** reserved to state governments by the Tenth Amendment—protection of public safety, health, welfare, and morality. This power was thought to be closer to the people if centered at the state level.

police power
the protection of public safety, health, welfare, and morality by a government.

dual citizenship
the idea that an individual is a citizen of both his or her state and the United States. Rights and responsibilities can vary from state to state and can be different on the state and national levels.

commerce clause
a provision in the U.S. Constitution that gives Congress the power to regulate commerce with other countries, among the states, and with Indian tribes.

Citizens of the United States are Also Citizens of a State

If you are a U.S. citizen, you are also a citizen of a state.[18] Under dual federalism, this is known as **dual citizenship.** As a citizen of the United States, you have the same rights as other citizens of the United States. As a citizen of your state, you will have rights and responsibilities that may be different from those of citizens of another state. For example, in many states, citizens have a constitutional guarantee of what may be referred to alternatively as a "uniform" or "equal" or "suitable" education system. This language has led to lawsuits in those states charging that this right means per pupil spending should be equal across districts within a state. In 7 states, including 4 states following the 2012 election your right to hunt or fish is constitutionally protected.[19] The ability to purchase alcohol legally, to marry, and to use a handheld cell phone while driving varies across states.[20] Responsibilities regarding jury duty, one's obligation to help strangers, and the process by which life support can be terminated also vary.

The case of *Barron v. Baltimore* (1833) illustrates the principle of dual citizenship under dual federalism. John Barron operated a commercial wharf in Baltimore. During construction projects, the city began dumping dirt and fill in the harbor. With ships facing great difficulty navigating in or out of the area near Barron's wharf, his business collapsed. Barron sued the city, arguing that the Fifth Amendment to the U.S. Constitution guarantees that citizens will be compensated when government takes their property for public purposes (known as the *takings clause*). Barron won his case, but the city appealed and won in the Maryland appeals court. Barron appealed that decision to the U.S. Supreme Court. The Court agreed that Barron was injured by Baltimore but said he was not entitled to any compensation. In the Court's view, the Fifth Amendment—indeed, the Bill of Rights as a whole—applied only to Barron as a citizen of the United States, not as a citizen of Maryland. In this case, Barron was not injured by the U.S. government—he was injured by a state government. If Maryland's constitution had a "takings" clause, then Barron would have recourse through the state's courts.

What would cause the Court to reach this conclusion? The distinction between Barron's rights as a state citizen and as a national citizen may seem odd, but it is consistent with the forces that led to the Bill of Rights. Recall that the Federalists agreed to add a Bill of Rights to respond to the charge that the Constitution did not sufficiently protect the people from the national government. Anti-Federalist agitation for the Bill of Rights was based not on the premise that the people needed to be protected from state governments—the Anti-Federalists surely would have said that citizens worried about state government power should work through the state legislature to rectify their concern—but on the premise that the national government needed to be constrained. Had it been the U.S. government rather than a state government that had taken Barron's property, he would have had a valid claim as a citizen of the United States.

Interpretation of the Commerce Clause Affects National Government Power

Interstate commerce has been a central political and legal battleground on which the meaning of federalism has been fought. Consistent with dual federalism, the Constitution marks out the regulation of interstate commerce as within the realm of federal government authority. The Constitution's **commerce clause,** in Article I, Section 8, gives Congress the power to "regulate commerce with foreign nations, and among the several states, and with the Indian tribes." Intrastate commerce was, implicitly, under the jurisdiction of the states.

Regarding interstate commerce, the Supreme Court confirmed the national government's primacy in this policy area in its decision in *Gibbons v. Ogden* (1824). The state of New York granted exclusive rights to two individuals to operate steamboats on the state's waters. This policy created problems because the water flowed into and from other states—New York required boats entering from another state to obtain a permit to navigate on New York waters. A steamboat owner whose business required him to travel between New Jersey and New York challenged this law. In its decision, the Court concluded that because of the Constitution's supremacy clause, federal law regulating coastal trade overrode New York's licensing requirement. Chief Justice John Marshall's opinion made it clear that in addition to the buying and selling of goods and services, commerce included navigation on interstate waterways and, thus, was an arena solely for federal government regulation.

Gibbons v. Ogden represented a judicial victory for national commercial authority over the states. The Sherman Anti-Trust Act of 1890 signified a legislative victory. Congress passed the law in response to the growth of huge corporations that monopolized sales in their particular industries. For many Americans, the sheer size of these corporations called into question the promises of equality and democracy in the American creed, particularly because the law treated corporations as "persons." Others saw these corporations as a threat to the property rights embodied in the creed. As monopolies, or nearly so, they could price their products excessively high to gain extra profit, or they could price excessively low to drive out any remaining competitors. In response, the antitrust act prohibited contracts, mergers, or conspiracies that restrained trade or commerce between states or with other countries.

Subsequent Court decisions refined and limited the federal government's control over interstate commerce. By 1892, the E. C. Knight Company, through stock purchases of other sugar refining companies, controlled about 98 percent of the sugar-refining business in the United States. In a blow to the federal government's regulation over interstate commerce, the Supreme Court ruled in 1895 that "commerce" did not include manufacturing and that the Sherman Act applied only to commerce, the actual sale and moving of goods across state lines, not to monopolies in manufacturing.[21] To the Court, manufacturing was a local activity that preceded commerce, regardless of the fact that E. C. Knight controlled firms in more than one state. Although the Court recognized that monopoly over manufacturing might be linked to restraint of commerce, it sought to keep the two separate in the interests of dual federalist principles. States, but not the federal government, could regulate in-state manufacturing; the federal government, but not the states, could regulate interstate commerce.[22]

The Court reiterated its interpretation of interstate commerce in other controversial cases. For example, the Keating-Owen Child Labor Act prohibited the interstate shipment of goods produced by child labor.[23] Roland Dagenhart challenged the law on behalf of his two sons, each below the age of 16. Both children worked in a cotton mill with their father in Charlotte, North Carolina. The Court ruled that the law was unconstitutional because the regulation of manufacturing, which was not part of commerce, was reserved to the states by the Tenth Amendment.[24] If states wanted to limit child labor, they could, but the federal government could not use its commerce powers to do so.

Although this judicial definition of interstate commerce placed limits on what the federal government could do, it did not leave that government powerless. In the early twentieth century, the government expanded its reach into economic matters. The Pure Food and Drug Act of 1906 gave the federal government the regulatory authority to monitor food and drug safety and, in particular, to ensure the accurate labeling of these products. Regulating misleading information was acceptable because such information could affect commercial transactions. The agency responsible for these tasks was later named the Food and Drug Administration. Prior to the 1906 law, most regulation of this type had been at the state level. The Federal Trade Commission (FTC) is another example of increased federal power under the traditional definition of commerce. Created in 1914 in the Federal Trade Commission Act, the FTC monitors false and deceptive advertising as well as corporate mergers with implications for commerce.

YOU ARE WHAT YOU EAT

As part of its authority to regulate commerce, the national government has the authority to require health and safety labeling on food and other products. The information on the label and its formatting are determined by the Food and Drug Administration.

Cooperative Federalism

4.4 Trace the evolution from dual to cooperative federalism, and identify methods of cooperative federalism.

Dual federalism's sharp line of separation between national and state responsibilities was blurred by **cooperative federalism,** which rose to prominence beginning in the 1930s. In this form of federalism, still prominent today, the national and state governments share many functions and areas of authority. For political activists frustrated by their inability to pursue their policy goals as a result of the Supreme Court's dual federalist orientation, this new form of federalism provided some hope. Cooperative federalism diminished the notion of separate spheres of state and national authority embodied in dual federalism.

cooperative federalism
a form of federalism in which the national and state governments share many functions and areas of authority.

necessary and proper clause
a provision in the U.S. Constitution that gives Congress the authority to make the laws needed to carry out the specific duties assigned to Congress by the Constitution.

enumerated powers
the specifically listed duties that the U.S. Constitution assigns to Congress.

implied powers
functions and actions that Congress could perform in order to implement and exercise its enumerated powers.

Implied Powers Increase the Scope of Permissible Federal Government Activity

Changes in constitutional interpretation were necessary to facilitate the evolution from dual federalism to cooperative federalism. One important step happened early in American history, in the case of *McCulloch v. Maryland* (1819). The Supreme Court's decision in this case expanded Congress's ability to become involved in policy areas previously considered to be the responsibility of the states. The case involved the Second Bank of the United States. The bank, chartered by Congress, had a branch in Baltimore, Maryland. Traditionally, states had chartered banks, so they eyed this new national role warily. In response, Maryland taxed the bank. The U.S. government challenged this tax and filed suit against Maryland in the Supreme Court.

The Court had to resolve two questions. Could Congress charter a national bank? The Court's answer was yes. Its justification was twofold. First, Chief Justice John Marshall, the author of the Court's decision, argued against the compact theory of the Constitution in favor of the nationalist theory. Maryland presented the argument that the states had created the federal government and owed no deference to it in banking. Marshall responded that it was not the states, but the people, who had formed the national government, and the national government, therefore, did not require the consent of the states to carry out its powers, nor was it subordinate to the states.

Second, the Court pointed to the **necessary and proper clause,** sometimes referred to as the elastic clause. Article I, Section 8, of the Constitution gives Congress the authority "to make all laws which shall be necessary and proper for carrying into execution the foregoing powers, and all other powers vested by this Constitution in the Government of the United States, or in any Department or Officer thereof." The "foregoing powers" refers to a list of duties prescribed in Article I as the responsibilities of Congress. These listed duties, specifically mentioned in the Constitution, are known as Congress's **enumerated powers.**

What the Court said in *McCulloch* is that the necessary and proper clause gave Congress **implied powers,** meaning it could make laws needed to carry out its enumerated powers. It was reasonable, in the Court's view, for a Congress given the power to pay debts, borrow money, regulate commerce, and coin money, to create a bank to facilitate the performance of these duties. The creation of the bank was an implied power that resulted from Congress's need to carry out its enumerated powers.

Having answered the first question by ruling that the bank was constitutional, the Court now had to answer the second question—whether Maryland could tax the bank. The Court's answer, in Chief Justice Marshall's opinion, was no. "The power to tax," the Court unanimously and famously stated, "involves the power to destroy." Under a federal system, a single state government has no right to destroy an entity of the national government. Maryland could not force the national government out of banking by onerous taxation.

The *McCulloch* decision opened the door for Congress to expand the reach of the national government and chip away some of the wall separating state and national government functions and responsibilities. The decision certainly broadened the scope of what could be considered legitimate federal government activity. Congress did not rush to move the national government onto the policy turf of the state governments, but the decision established the precedent that Congress potentially could do so.[25]

The Supreme Court's Redefinition of Interstate Commerce Expands Federal Government Power

If the door to cooperative federalism cracked open in 1819, it swung fully open in 1937, much to the relief of public officials looking for a more active role for the federal government, and much to the worry of those concerned about federal government power. In *National Labor Relations Board v. Jones & Laughlin Steel Corporation* (1937), the Supreme Court expanded the scope of what was meant by interstate commerce.

Jones & Laughlin had fired workers for labor union activity. The recently enacted National Labor Relations Act (1935) prohibited employers engaged in interstate commerce from taking such actions. The act declared that labor-management relations were an aspect of commerce and thus subject to federal government regulation. When challenged by the National Labor Relations Board, which was created by the 1935 law, the steel company argued that labor-management relations were not part of commerce and, therefore, were not subject to federal regulation. Traditionally, the Supreme Court interpreted interstate commerce to mean not what happened inside a factory—that was manufacturing, not commerce—but what was involved in the transfer of products from one state to another. The national government could regulate shipping rates, for example, and it could regulate the entry of firms into the business of shipping steel, but what happened inside a steel plant was not in and of itself interstate commerce. Using this definition of commerce, Jones & Laughlin argued that the National Labor Relations Act represented an invalid federal intrusion into its business practices.

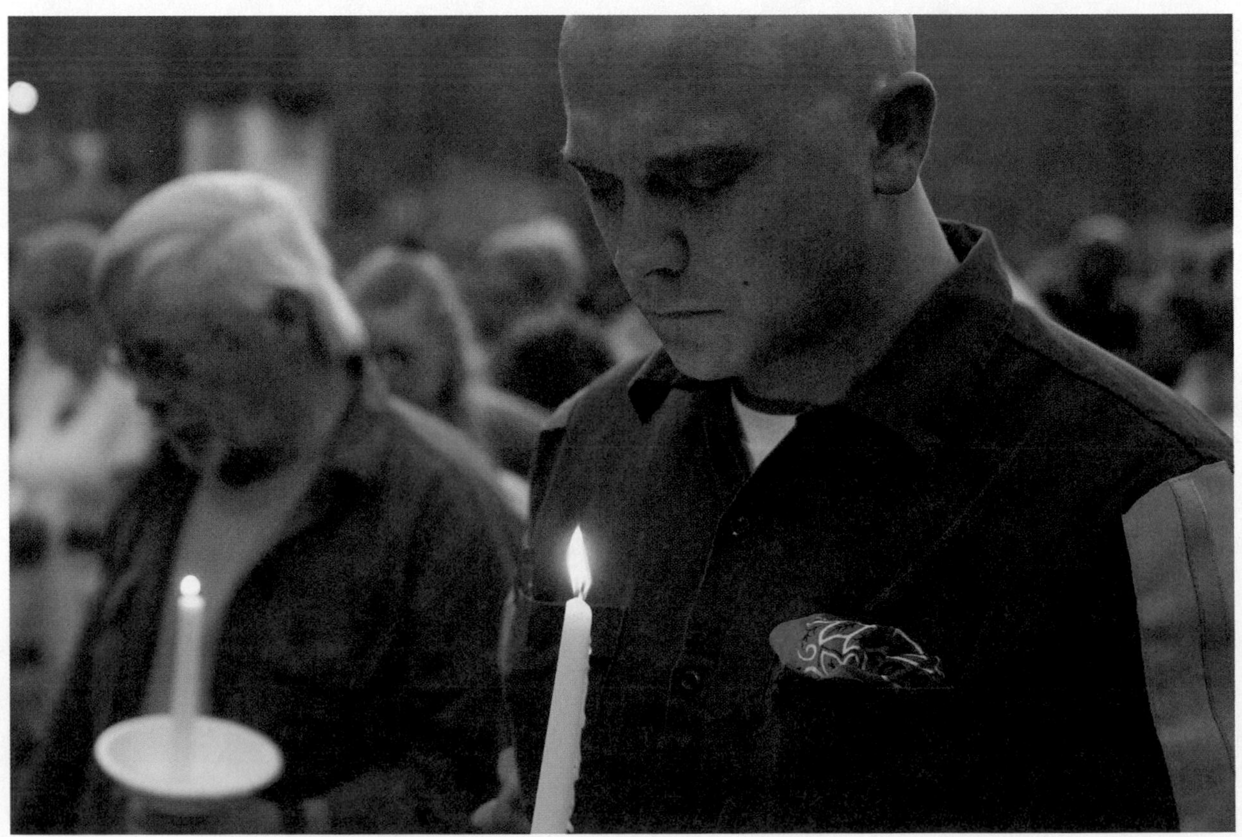

WORKPLACE SAFETY

Coal miners hold a vigil for 25 miners killed in a 2010 mine explosion in West Virginia. The Supreme Court's *Jones & Laughlin (1937)* decision redefining interstate commerce opened the door to federal regulation of local workplace safety. The Mine Safety Health Administration conducts inspections to make sure mines are in compliance with health and safety standards.

In its decision in *Jones & Laughlin*, the Supreme Court concluded that this conception was too narrow. Instead, a company that uses any interstate products in its business or sells any product interstate is part of the stream of interstate commerce, and the stream involves the company's entire operations. Poor labor-management relations can lead to industrial strife, and this strife can affect the stream of commerce. In the Court's view, the fundamental principle was that some activities may appear to be intrastate when considered alone, but if they have a close relationship to interstate commerce, then Congress must be given the authority to regulate those activities to prevent obstructions to commerce.

The *Jones & Laughlin* decision meant, in effect, that national government action on issues such as worker safety, environmental controls, health codes, work hours and conditions, and overtime pay were justified by the government's responsibility to regulate interstate commerce. The Court's decision in *Wickard v. Filburn* (1942) underlined this point. Under authority granted by the Agricultural Adjustment Act of 1938, the U.S. Department of Agriculture, in an attempt to avoid overproduction and plummeting prices, allocated about 11 acres for Roscoe Filburn to grow wheat. Filburn grew wheat on another dozen acres, and although he said this was for his local use on his farm, the Court ruled that Filburn could be ordered to stop. By growing wheat beyond his quota, Filburn was having an effect on interstate commerce by not purchasing the needed wheat from another farm. The Court ruled that any activity that has "a substantial economic effect on interstate commerce," even if products did not move across state lines, is within Congress's regulatory reach.

Everything in the stream of commerce was now ripe for federal involvement. Once solely under the purview of the states, these responsibilities would now be shared. And in accordance with the Constitution's premise of the supremacy of national laws, it would be the states that would have to conform with federal standards in these areas, not the other way around.

Although the Court cautioned that its new definition of interstate commerce must be "a matter of degree," the principle of the stream of interstate commerce provided a nearly limitless range to congressional action. Anything in the stream or any action or practice that might affect the stream was now open to national government involvement. The Court declared that it was up to Congress to decide the appropriate use of its newly expanded interstate commerce powers.[26] With the constitutional basis of cooperative federalism now firmly established and the role of Congress and the president in deciding what activities came under the interstate umbrella in place, the scope of federal government activity in society and in the economy was poised to grow accordingly. Today, debate over that growth continues.

The interpretation of the federal government's role in regulating interstate commerce has, for example, been a central point of debate since the passage of health care reform legislation in 2010. The federal requirement that individuals purchase insurance is particularly controversial. If insurers must provide coverage to individuals with preexisting health conditions, everyone, healthy or not, needs to be in the insurance market to pay for it. Obviously, insurers would be under great financial pressure if individuals who do not have insurance, and thus have not been paying for it, then contract a disease , at which point they decide to buy the insurance to pay for expensive treatment. Until health care reform, the federal government had not used an interstate commerce justification to compel someone to purchase a product under threat of penalty. To opponents of the health care reform law, forcing an individual to enter interstate commerce by buying insurance when he or she does not choose to do so is not consistent with the Framers' vision of regulating commerce between the states. Governors or attorneys general in more than 25 states cited this mandate as one way the law violates the commerce clause and filed lawsuits to block it. To supporters, this mandate is a "necessary and proper" action for Congress to take as part of its enumerated power of regulating interstate commerce. In their view, individuals' failure to buy insurance ultimately has a substantial effect on the health care market and is thus a form of economic activity. Ultimately, the Supreme Court upheld the mandate with a mixed decision in *NFIB v. Sebelius* (2012). The Court rejected the view that Congress could use its commerce clause powers to mandate that individuals enter the insurance market and purchase insurance. However, the Court also ruled that Congress was free, as part of its taxing authority, to impose a tax on individuals who did not purchase insurance, thus upholding the law's insurance requirement.

Cooperative Federalism Requires a Careful Balancing of Federal and State Interests

For the liberal reformers of the 1910s and especially the 1930s, cooperative federalism opened the doors to policy successes that were impossible as long as dual federalism held sway. Given the depths of the Great Depression, in which industrial production plummeted and nearly a quarter of the population was unemployed, these reformers saw both a policy rationale for expansive national government action and a political opportunity to move public policy in a long-term liberal direction. At the state level, public officials in many states were overwhelmed by the scope of the crisis and receptive to the idea of national assistance.

The national and state governments jointly financed and administered many of the new social programs adopted during the 1930s, including welfare, unemployment insurance, and jobs programs. This is a puzzle. Why would power-seeking national politicians, particularly Democrats who had just swept into office with huge majorities, place partial control of these programs at the state level? Why not centralize all the control in Washington, D.C.? Political scientists suggest that the national-state blend was often done for practical political reasons rather than for reasons of grand philosophy. The national government in the early 1930s was small. The New Deal, as the collection of new programs in the 1930s was known, called for a significant expansion of the role of the national government in American life. Instantly expanding federal agencies would have been difficult—so, state agencies could help in launching programs. And although the misery of the Great Depression pushed even state politicians toward supporting this new federal role, state officials were sure to be reluctant

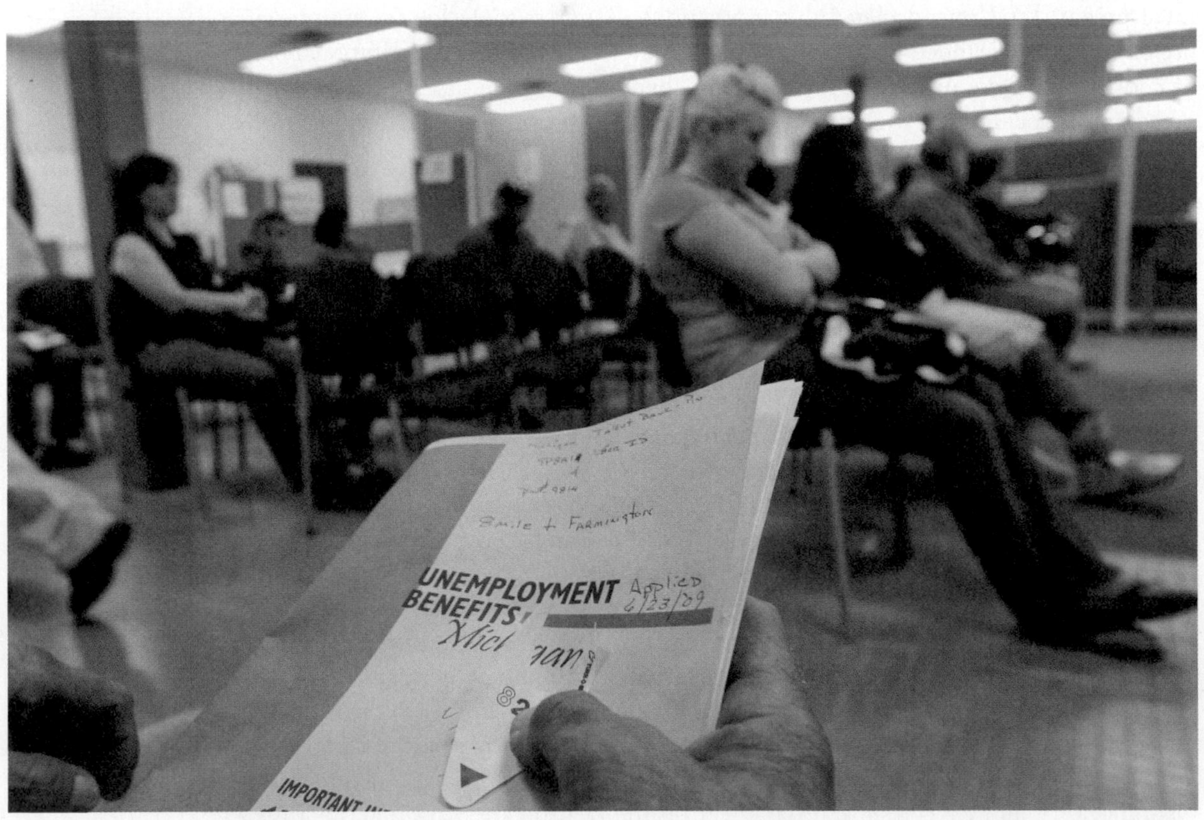

HARD TIMES IN MICHIGAN

Hoping for better times, unemployed workers wait to speak to an agent. Financing and administering unemployment compensation has been a joint federal and state effort since 1935. States are allowed flexibility in eligibility requirements and benefits.

to give up power. This was especially true in southern states where white legislators wanted to deflect national government programs that might erode the South's traditional social structure and lead to upheaval in black-white relations.[27] A joint program might have been necessary in some instances to ensure passage through Congress.

The support of state officials often hinged on whether they would have a piece of the action in administering a new program. If benefits were to be distributed to their constituents, they wanted some say in the matter and some of the political credit. In other cases, if a program seemed likely to have significant and possibly disruptive social and economic effects, state officials would want to have some flexibility in managing the program. For example, Congress crafted the national minimum wage law in such a way as to omit agricultural workers, meaning that a large proportion of blacks in southern states fell outside the law's protection.[28] This design was motivated by southern political leaders' dual goals of holding down costs in agriculture and maintaining racial order. For northern politicians, this was the price they had to pay to pass a national minimum wage law. They also recognized that southern support for a range of other New Deal policies might hinge on the negotiations over the minimum wage.

Since the 1930s, minimum wage policy has been consistently cooperative. The national government sets minimum wage standards that states have to meet. States, however, are free to exceed those wages if they so choose and may establish minimum wages for workers not covered under federal law. Figure 4.2 shows how states vary on

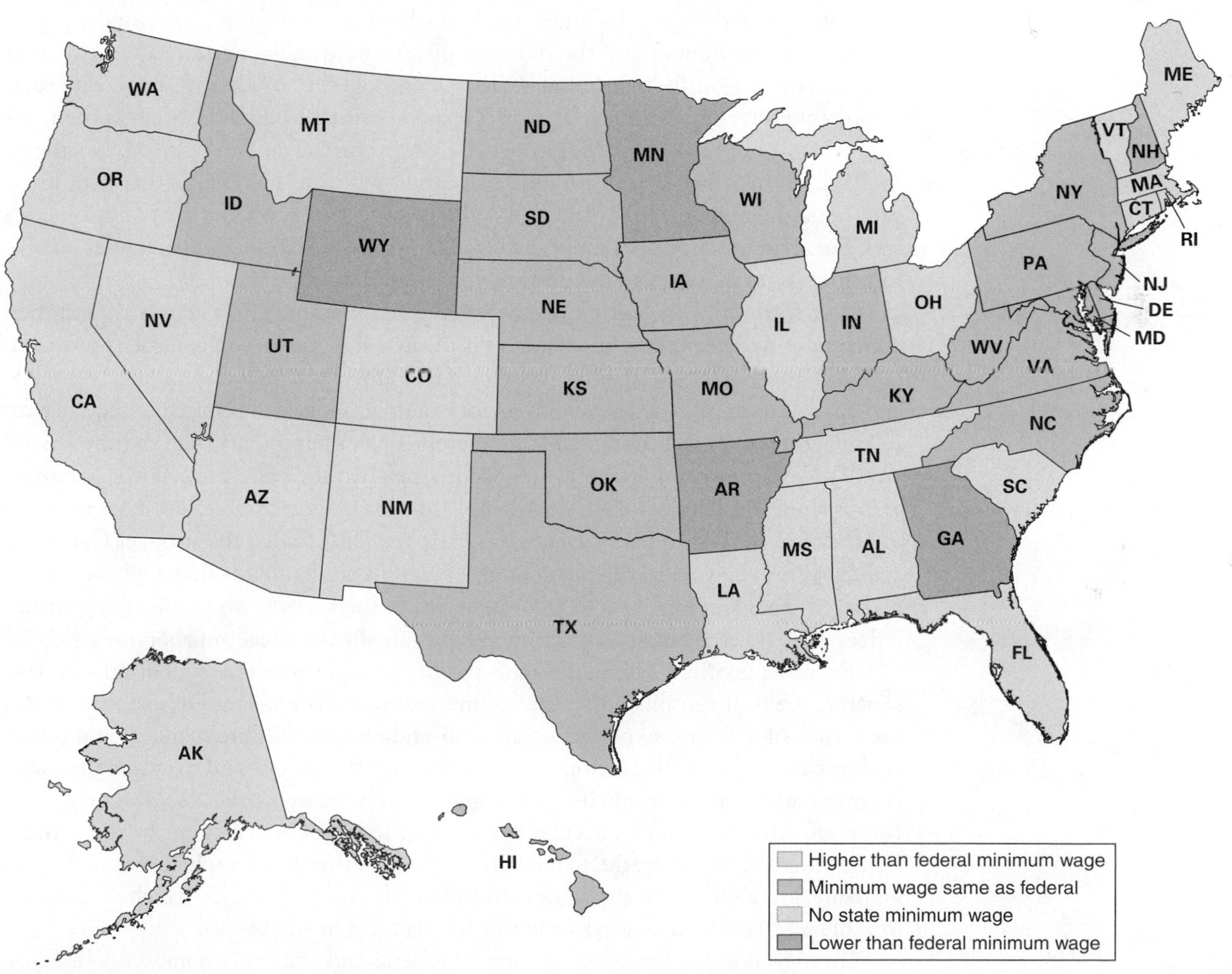

FIGURE 4.2 DIFFERENCES IN STATE MINIMUM WAGES, 2012.

State minimum wages can match or exceed the federal minimum wage. For work categories not covered by the federal law, states can set a minimum wage below the wage assigned for categories that are federally covered or can go without a minimum wage. Until the federal minimum wage was increased to $7.25 in 2009, many more states exceeded the federal wage than is true today.

Source: U.S. Department of Labor, http://www.dol.gov/esa/minwage/america.htm.

the minimum wage. Where the map indicates the state level is lower, the federal rate prevails except for workers who are not covered by the federal minimum wage law (generally workers at non-interstate businesses that gross less than $500,000).[29]

The federal government mirrored the practice used in the crafting of the minimum wage law in other contentious policy areas, such as welfare. Prior to 1996, the national government had specific programs designed to address the needs of poor families with children. The states, however, had substantial leeway in administering these programs, most notably in the benefit levels. After the passage of welfare reform legislation in 1996, state-by-state variation became even more pronounced. National law set a few guidelines for states to work within—most importantly, national laws limited the number of years an individual could receive welfare benefits, and state programs needed to focus on moving recipients from welfare to work—but the programs themselves were entirely the creation of the states. Before 1996, states administered one national program but in 50 different ways; now states administer 50 different state programs within broad national guidelines. Each of these two approaches is an example of cooperative federalism.

The Federal and State Governments Collaborate to Implement Policy in Some Issue Areas

The national-state relationship in cooperative federalism may involve collaboration, mandates, or persuasion. To understand collaboration, consider environmental policy. State governments and the national government collect and share significant amounts of data on the environment. They work together to identify and create rules to protect endangered species. They will respond jointly to disasters such as the massive oil spill in the Gulf of Mexico in 2010 and Hurricane Sandy in the Northeast in 2012. State offices often provide personnel who implement, at the state level, programs that are created at the national level, such as water and air pollution control. Sometimes these agreements and sharing of information and personnel involve multiple states in a region, in addition to the federal government.

As a form of collaboration, the national government may set standards and then allow states to exceed those standards, as is the case in air pollution control. A provision added to the Clean Air Act in 1967 allowed California to seek exemptions from federal air pollution rules. One exemption, for example, allowed California to require auto manufacturers to meet more demanding emissions requirements than did the federal law. If an exemption was granted, other states then had the option of following the federal or California standards. In the example of auto emissions, thirteen states opted to use the stronger California standards. In 2010, the EPA folded the stronger California standards into new national emissions and fuel mileage standards that apply across the country.[30] Freedom for states to tailor policy to fit their needs, while still falling within federal guidelines, increases the likelihood of mutually beneficial collaboration.[31]

Even while collaborating, the state and national governments will often still have separate areas of responsibility, the hallmark of dual federalism. For example, states are responsible for noise pollution and non-endangered wildlife management policy within their borders. The national government, on the other hand, controls the management and disposal of nuclear waste generated by national defense needs. Both of these are environmental concerns, but the two levels of government work on them independently. Similarly, the federal government sets policy on which pesticides can be made, but a state, or a city if allowed to by the state, may decide which of these allowable pesticides can be used within its borders and in what ways.

Immigration has been another area of federal and state collaboration. While the federal government has responsibility for immigration itself, states often pass laws that address issues related to immigration or that arise because of immigration. In the 15 months from January 2011 through March 2012, states introduced nearly 2,500 proposed laws and resolutions concerning immigrants and immigration, with about 400 of these laws and resolutions being enacted. Federal law is supreme, but states have enforcement roles and can make decisions about which benefits and services immigrants

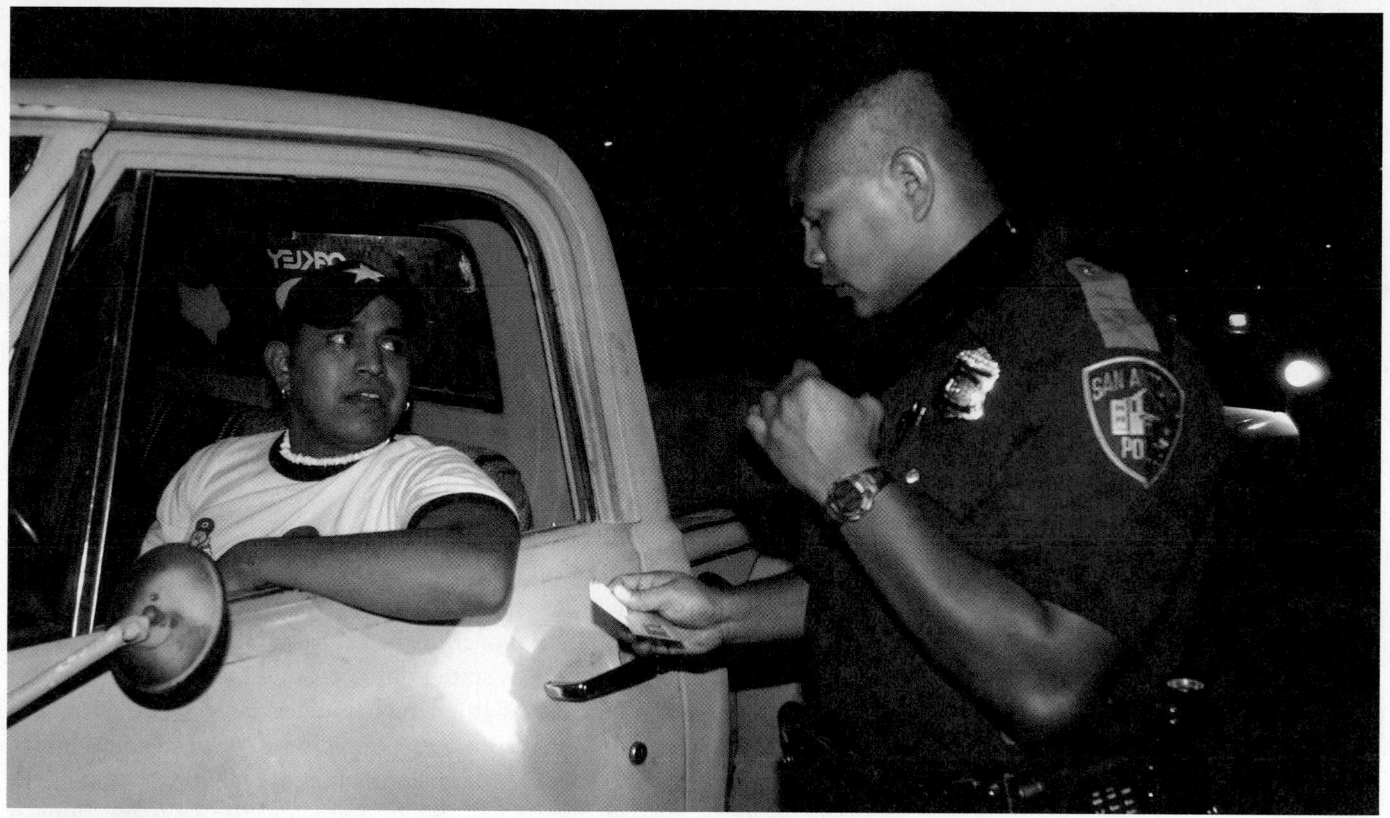

POLICE OFFICER CHECKS DRIVER'S LICENSE

Should states and cities be responsible for enforcing federal immigration laws? Some states and cities have bristled at the idea. It is illegal under federal law for states and cities to adopt formal sanctuary policies, but many, nonetheless, prohibit their employees from asking about immigration status or contacting federal officials if they discover someone is not in the United States legally. In 2010, however, Arizona passed a controversial law that supporters said enhanced the enforcement of existing federal immigration law, but opponents said the law made arbitrary harassment of Hispanics more likely.

may receive. Although laws requiring strict enforcement and verification of legal immigrant status receive the most publicity, many of the laws enacted offer benefits to immigrants. Similarly, laws are not always about illegal immigration, but about the obligations and privileges of legal immigrants as well. Issues addressed include health care benefits, driver's licenses, allowed and disallowed techniques to verify legal immigration status, sanctions on employers who hire illegal immigrants, and eligibility for in-state college tuition rates.

Regarding tuition, the U.S. Supreme Court ruled in 1982 that states could not deny any child, regardless of immigration status, access to public kindergarten through grade 12 schooling on the same terms as other children. That ruling, however, did not extend to higher education. As of 2012, a dozen states allow in-state tuition rates at public colleges and universities for students without legal immigration status. Of these twelve states, three allow students to receive state financial aid and nine do not.[32]

The state of Arizona and the federal government clashed over a law enacted in that state in 2010 that authorized police to check the residency status of individuals when they were investigating them for other behavior, such as a traffic violation. The U.S. Justice Department sued the state, arguing that Arizona had intruded on the federal government's enforcement power in immigration, and the case made its way to the U.S. Supreme Court. In *Arizona v. United States* (2012), the Court upheld the state's right to determine an individual's residency status as part of a lawful stop, while striking down three provisions of the law that the Justices determined violated national supremacy. Although states sometimes act on immigration because they have concluded the federal government will not do so—Arizona argued that the U.S. government was inadequately enforcing immigration law—collaboration has been more common than conflict, despite the headlines.

4.1

4.2

4.3

4.4

4.5

mandate
an order from the federal government that requires state governments to take a certain action.

unfunded mandate
a law requiring certain actions without appropriating the necessary funds to carry them out.

The Federal Government May Enact Policy Mandates that Require States to Take Certain Actions

Another possibility is for the national government to issue a **mandate** that orders state governments to take certain actions. Beginning in the 1960s, the volume of federal government mandates upon the states increased sharply. For example, in the area of education, states must follow the rules established by the national government in the Individuals with Disabilities Education Act. This law sets out the services that states and localities must provide to students with learning or other disabilities and provides some federal funding. Here "cooperative" federalism need not mean that there is harmony and agreement between the two levels of government. Instead, the national government may set the rules that states are required to follow, regardless of the views of the states toward these rules. Some analysts refer to this practice as "coercive federalism."[33]

Federal mandates have rankled state officials for two reasons. First, the mandates may force states to take actions they would prefer not to take or for which there is only modest support from state residents. Second, mandates impose demands on the states but often do not provide federal financial assistance to carry out the demands. States long complained that they were spending far too much to meet the policy demands and policy preferences of federal government officials and politicians, draining money from policies of more interest to state politicians and residents. The city of Danville, Virginia, complained in 1993 that federal mandates absorbed 16 percent of its local revenue, and the state of Texas estimated it would need to spend $11.4 billion in 1994–1995 to accommodate federal government mandates. When the Republican Party gained control of the U.S. House and Senate following the 1994 elections, it made elimination of **unfunded mandates**—federal requirements that states take some action, but without provision of sufficient resources to do so—a major priority.

The result, after lengthy controversy and extensive lobbying by groups such as the National Association of Counties, the National Conference of State Legislatures, and the U.S. Conference of Mayors, was the 1995 Unfunded Mandates Reform Act. The bill required congressional committees to get estimates of the cost of proposed legislation that would mandate new expenses on states, localities, or businesses. If the cost exceeded $50 million on states and localities or $100 million on the private sector, legislators could then be required to vote that the benefits of the bill exceeded the costs. These figures were adjusted for inflation, reaching $71 million and $142 million, respectively, in 2011.[34] The act did not apply to existing unfunded mandates and did not apply to mandates that protected the constitutional rights of individuals, prohibited discrimination, or were labeled emergency legislation.

Unfunded mandates seemingly declined after the act was passed. By one accounting, only five new mandates had been passed during the decade after the law's enactment, and the law had changed the way Congress interacted with the states. Between 2007 and 2011, the Congressional Budget Office identified almost 200 mandates imposed on the states but determined that only 11 of these mandates reached a dollar value that exceeded the inflation-adjusted mandate threshold.[35]

However, this correlation between the law and the drop in unfunded mandates may be misleading. Evidence on the effectiveness of the act has been mixed. Another accounting argues the law looked effective only because its exemptions allowed major new unfunded mandates that simply were not labeled as such, including education reforms in the No Child Left Behind Act, education services for disabled children, Medicaid, and a requirement after 2000 that states meet standards for voting technology.[36] The U.S. Government Accountability Office noted, in its examination of unfunded mandates, that the most common complaint it heard from academic and think tank experts, public interest advocacy organizations, businesspeople, federal agencies, and state and local government officials was that the law defined unfunded mandates too narrowly.[37] The National Conference of State Legislatures (NCSL) discontinued its Mandate Monitor in 1995 but restarted it in 2004 because of state complaints about a renewed escalation of unfunded mandates. The NCSL estimated that unfunded mandates, interpreted more broadly than the federal law, totaled approximately

$131 billion from 2004 through 2009, the most recent five-year data available.[38] These data suggest that some of the "success" of the federal law resulted from narrowly labeling what counts as an unfunded mandate, rather than from actually reducing the fiscal burdens imposed on the states.

Similarly to mandating that states take some action, the federal government can pass **preemption legislation** that declares, or mandates, certain actions off-limits for state governments. For example, federal law passed in 2005 prohibits certain kinds of liability suits from being filed against firearms manufacturers in state courts.[39] The Family Smoking Prevention and Tobacco Control Act of 2009 preempts state laws in areas such as warning labels and tobacco product standards—flavored cigarettes except for menthol, for example, are prohibited by federal law.

preemption legislation
legislation that declares, or mandates, certain actions off-limits for state governments.

fiscal federalism
a technique of persuasion in which the federal government offers resources to states that agree to take certain actions.

categorical grant
funds provided by the federal government to a state or local government for a specific, defined purpose.

The Federal Government May Use Money to Persuade States to Take Certain Actions

In addition to collaboration and mandates, cooperative federalism can work through persuasion (see Table 4.2). The national government might try to influence or persuade a state government to take some action in the area of education, the environment, or some other policy area, but not require it. Typically, this will involve providing some incentive for states to agree to take the desired action.

One of the best incentives is money. **Fiscal federalism** refers to the national government's use of its financial resources to persuade the states to take particular actions. The restrictions on the use of the money might be specific or general. With a **categorical grant,** the federal government provides money that is to be used for very specific purposes. Funds might be provided for a particular form of science instruction for children in grades 1–3 who attend schools with a large proportion of low-income students. To receive the categorical grant funds, the state or locality would have to agree to these and any other restrictions on their use. As Table 4.2 shows, the tools the federal government can employ can make it difficult for a state not to comply with federal demands. Various rules about discrimination, environmental protection, and employment and contract requirements, for example, are built into a large group of federal grants. A state not willing to accept any one of these rules will shut itself out of dozens or hundreds of programs.

TABLE 4.2 TOOLS OF FEDERAL INFLUENCE OVER STATE GOVERNMENTS

Tools	Description
Mandates	**States are required to follow federal policy orders**
Direct orders	An order is imposed by the federal government on state governments requiring that they carry out a federal policy or program
Total preemption	A state is prohibited from implementing its own program or law in a policy area
Partial preemption	A state is partially prohibited from implementing its own standards and regulations in a policy area—typically it may implement a standard higher than the federal standard but not below the federal standard
Persuasion	**States are prodded to follow federal policy preferences through financial inducements**
Conditions on grants	A state must meet conditions and requirements established by the federal government in order to receive a federal grant
Crosscutting requirements	The federal government places the same set of requirements across a large number of grant and funding programs, making it more difficult for a state to choose not to meet the requirement
Crossover sanctions	The federal government requires compliance with requirements on small grant programs in order for a state to continue to receive federal funds in larger, often unrelated, federal funding programs

SOURCE: Paul L. Posner, *The Politics of Unfunded Mandates: Whither Federalism?* Washington, DC: Georgetown University Press, 1998.

NOTE: The federal government imposes these tools directly on local governments as well. Within states, state governments use similar tools in relation to local governments.

4.1

4.2

4.3

4.4

4.5

block grant
funds provided by the federal government to a state or local government in general support of a broad government function such as education or transportation.

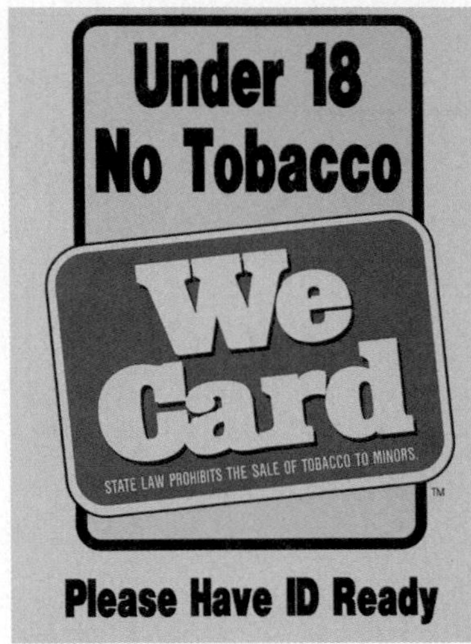

PERSUASION THROUGH FISCAL FEDERALISM

In order to receive their full share of federal substance abuse prevention and treatment block grant funds, states have to prohibit tobacco sales to minors. States that do not, or that inadequately enforce the law, can lose up to 40 percent of their block grant funds. Should the federal government put conditions on the receipt of its funds?

Categorical grants can be either formula based or competitive. Formula-based grants are, as the name suggests, based on a formula that determines the amount of funds a state will receive. Precisely what should be in the formula is the focus of intense political maneuvering. Several factors are usually included, and each will reward some states more than others.[40] A formula based on state unemployment rates may funnel more funds to state A than state B, while a formula based on the increase in the state unemployment rate over the prior 12 months might provide more funds to state B. The Individuals with Disabilities Education Act, mentioned earlier, has three formula-based programs that provide funds for the education of students who qualify for special services. Competitive grants require an application or proposal and are rated based on criteria specified by the granting agency. The highest-rated applications are then funded. Applicants typically have to meet eligibility criteria. For example, states could apply for "Race to the Top" funds from the U.S. Department of Education from 2009 to 2012 only if they agreed to allow the evaluation of teachers and principals to be linked to students' academic achievement.

Block grants, which began during the presidency of Richard Nixon (1969–1974), are more general and provide greater flexibility to the states. These grants are for broad categories of spending: transportation funds, welfare program funds, child care services, substance abuse prevention and treatment, homeland security, and so on. States are free to spend those funds more or less as they please, within those particular policy areas, and the amounts states receive are based on formulas determined by the federal government. Block grants can come with conditions, however. For example, in 1984, a new federal law required a portion of transportation block grants to be withheld from any state that did not raise its legal drinking age to 21. Similarly, states that do not comply with portions of the federal Clean Air Act will lose some of their highway funding.

Since 1987, the federal government has provided funds to state and local governments through block grants and categorical grants that comprise more than 20 percent of all state and local expenditures.[41] This proportion recently spiked because of the large infusion of federal stimulus and economic recovery funds sent to state governments beginning in 2009. The most rapidly growing area of federal aid to states and localities has been assistance for health expenses, increasing from about $44 billion in 1990 to a projected $440 billion in 2017.[42] Although the percentage of state and local budgets financed by federal aid stayed about the same over the past two decades, much more of that aid is now dedicated to medical expenses (see Figure 4.3).

Fiscal federalism is attractive to state governments. It provides states with funding to enact programs they otherwise would be unable to provide. Whenever an elected official can provide a benefit to his or her constituents but have someone else's constituents pay the cost, it is an attractive proposition.

But fiscal federalism creates problems as well. One is that these cash infusions may come with strings attached, so that the state may be creating some programs or services primarily because there is money available to do so, rather than because it is a priority of the state government or the people of the state. After September 11, 2001, the federal government sent more than $25 billion in grants to the states to enhance domestic security. States complained that the grants required them to fund what they considered unnecessary counterterrorism projects. Improvised explosive devices, or IEDs, were a problem in Baghdad, they argued, not in the streets of American cities and towns. Federal officials complained that states were diverting the funds to local purposes such as reducing gang violence. Either way, federally funded programs can mean jobs and an infusion of cash to the state economy, and those can be difficult to refuse.

Education funds provide another example. To compete for a share of $4 billion in federal education grant funds under the Race to the Top program mentioned earlier, some states began changing state law to comply with the program's criteria for funding. In some states, this new federal requirement may have allowed

Explore on MyPoliSciLab

Which States Win and Lose the Federal Aid Game?

The national government collects taxes from everyone, but it doesn't always spend money in the state where it gets it. Instead, the federal government transfers wealth from state to state. Recipient states pay less in federal taxes than they receive, while donor states pay more in taxes than they receive back. In 2007, there were 19 donor states and 31 recipient states. The political explanation for who were donor and recipient states is surprising.

Who pays? DELAWARE, MINNESOTA, NEW JERSEY, and CONNECTICUT

all paid at least $6,000 more in federal taxes per person than they received in federal aid. 15 other states were net donors.

Net Donor: Over $5,000 Per Person			
Connecticut $6,241	New Jersey $6,644	Minnesota $7,431	Delaware $12,285

Net Donor: Between $1 and $5,000 per person			
Ohio $49	North Carolina $1,108	Massachusetts $2,133	Rhode Island $2,732
Georgia $434	California $1,466	Colorado $2,176	Illinois $3,640
Washington $773	Nevada $1,616	Nebraska $2,850	New York $4,502
Wisconsin $1,000	Arkansas $1,723	Texas $2,243	

Who receives? ALASKA

took in twice the federal money in 2007 that it paid in taxes. 31 states are recipient states. Of the top six recipient states, four are southern.

Net Recipient: Over $5,000 Per Person					
Alaska -$7,448	New Mexico -$7,143	Mississippi -$6,765	Virginia -$6,239	West Virginia -$5,820	Alabama -$5,130

Net Recipient: Between $1 and $5,000 per person				
Hawaii -$4983	South Carolina -$3,756	Arizona -$1,976	Utah -$792	Pennsylvania -$385
North Dakota -$4,856	Kentucky -$3,012	Idaho -$1,281	Indiana -$723	Oklahoma -$376
South Dakota -$4,414	Maryland -$3,010	Wyoming -$1,205	Tennessee -$603	New Hampshire -$349
Maine -$4,221	Vermont -$2,854	Missouri -$1,190	Florida -$581	Michigan -$171
Montana -$4,149	Louisiana -$2,180	Iowa -$1,075	Oregon -$474	Kansas -$154

SOURCE: Data from United States Internal Revenue Service; *Statistical Abstract of the United States 2012*; and *U.S. Census of Population and Housing, 2010*.

Who are the Recipient States?

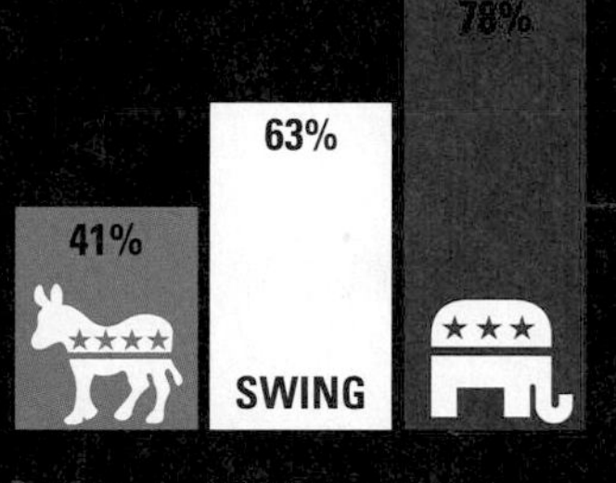

18 out of 23 Republican-voting states (78%) are recipient states compared to 8 out of the 19 Democratic-voting states (42%).

Recipient states by poverty level

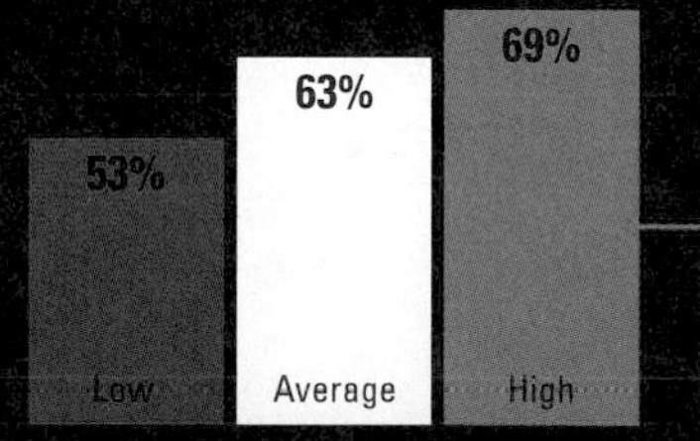

9 of 13 states with high poverty levels are recipient states (69%), while only 9 of 17 states with low poverty levels are recipient states (53%).

Investigate Further

Concept How do we determine donor and recipient states? Per person, we subtract the federal aid dollars sent to a state from the federal tax dollars paid in a state. If the result is positive, a state is a donor state, otherwise it's a recipient state.

Connection What relationship exists between partisanship and aid? Today, recipient states tend to vote Republican in national politics and donor states are more Democratic. However, many states have shifted their partisan preference over time while their donor or recipient status remained unchanged.

Cause Is there a policy explanation for which states are recipient states? The federal government fights poverty by moving money around the country. Recipient states usually have higher poverty levels and lower average incomes. Therefore, they tend to pay less federal tax than they receive per person.

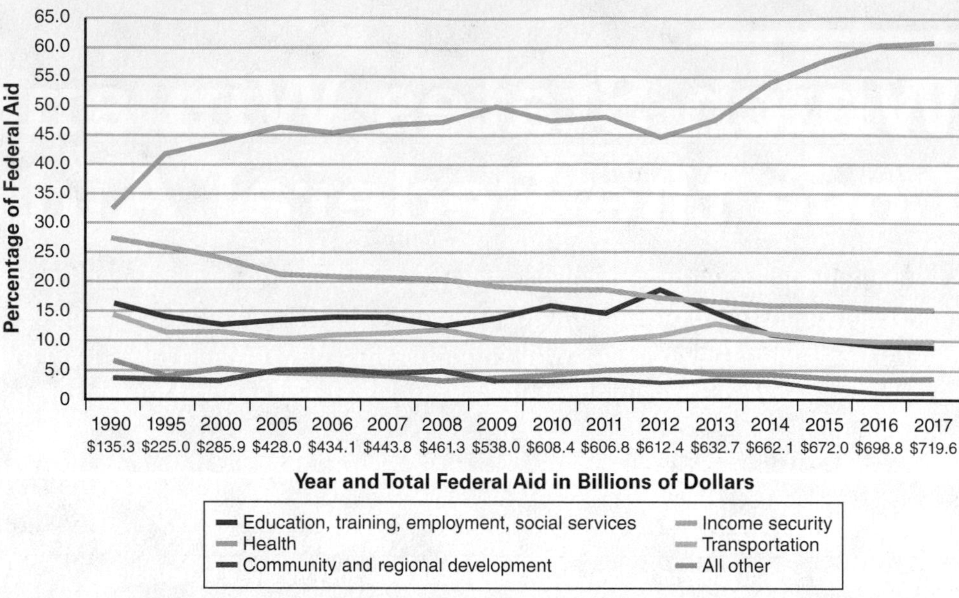

FIGURE 4.3 FEDERAL AID TO STATES AND CITIES BY FUNCTION.

Federal dollars going to the states for health and medical expenses have been an increasing share of all federal aid provided to states and cities.

Note: Data for 2012–2017 are estimates provided in the 2013 U.S. budget.

Source: Budget of the United States Government: Historical Tables Fiscal Year 2013, Table 12-2, http://www.gpoaccess.gov/usbudget/fy13/hist.html.

governors to institute changes they had long sought. In other states, changes may have been unpopular but were considered necessary to compete for the federal funds. States that already had those provisions in place were better positioned to focus on burnishing other aspects of their proposals for funding, possibly giving them a competitive edge.[43]

States have frequently complained that federal laws denying funds unless states take certain actions are coercive. Not until 2012, however, did the Supreme Court agree. The Affordable Care Act, the health care reform law of 2010, provided that states agreeing to expand their Medicaid programs would receive federal funding to cover the cost of the expansion in full for the first several years. States that did not expand Medicaid would not only lose access to these new funds, but also would be stripped of all the Medicaid funds they currently received from the federal government. In *NFIB v. Sebelius*, the Supreme Court struck down this provision of the law as unconstitutionally coercive toward the states, leaving them in a position where they had no real option but to expand their Medicaid programs. States will no doubt test other federal funding provisions in future litigation.

Another problem with fiscal federalism is that states battle one another to get a larger share of federal funds. The criteria used by federal officials to distribute aid will benefit some states more than others, so they are hotly debated (see *Unresolved Debate: Should Federal Grants Be Allocated Based on Competitions Instead of Formulas?*). In effect, states that win grant competitions such as these are being subsidized by the federal tax payments made by citizens of the losing states. State officials pay acute attention to how much their citizens pay into the federal government and how much the state receives in return (see Figure 4.4).[44]

A final problem with fiscal federalism is the difficulty of a state or city to speak with one voice. Officials at the highest levels of state and local government, such as governors or mayors, typically prefer the flexibility of block grants and lobby the federal government for more. Officials in state and city agencies, however, as well as organized interest groups, are often equally determined to obtain categorical grants that they know will be used for a defined purpose. This desire to obtain targeted funding can both arise from and perpetuate the policy silo problem. *Policy silos* refer to employees in government programs in similar areas—for example, unemployment offices

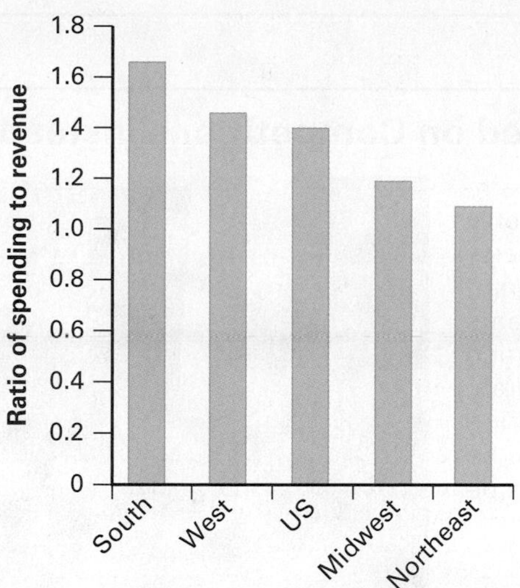

FIGURE 4.4 RATIO OF FEDERAL FUNDS RECEIVED COMPARED TO FEDERAL TAX REVENUE PAID, BY REGION, 2010.

With high federal budget deficits, all regions of the country receive more in federal spending than they pay in taxes. Nationally, for each $1.00 raised in revenue, $1.40 is spent: the national ratio of spending to revenue is 1.40. The South and West are the largest net recipients of federal spending, with ratios higher than 1.40.

Source: Consolidated Federal Funds Report for Fiscal Year 2010: http://www.census.gov/prod/2011pubs/cffr-10.pdf; and Internal Revenue Service Tax Statistics: http://www.irs.gov/taxstats/article/0,,id=206488,00.html.

and job training offices—working in isolation. Two seemingly related programs may have different funding sources, reporting requirements to Washington, and rules for distribution of funds in the states. The availability of specialized federal funds can lead employees in different parts of the same state agency to remain isolated as they seek to win these narrowly targeted funds. Success in winning funds increases their ability to continue operating in isolation.

In addition, state and city officials can have different political incentives. In particular, to the extent that federal grants go directly to cities, state political leaders will not receive political credit for new programs and spending. Moreover, the funds being received by the city might, in the view of state officials, be put to better use elsewhere. This view might be based on an assessment that competing needs in the state should have higher priority, or it might be based on a calculation that spreading resources to other constituents will be more politically beneficial for the state official, or both of these. One of the reasons federal officials sometimes wish to funnel funds directly to cities is precisely because they are concerned that states will shortchange the cities. City officials, of course, have the same incentive as state officials, hoping to receive federal funds directly so they can claim full credit for this success.

Members of Congress, even if they philosophically believe in the principle of block grants, often gravitate toward the more defined grants because they can claim more credit for obtaining them. For members of Congress few things are better than a grateful constituent who can thank them for a specific program or service that came about through the initiative of the federal government. Despite the wishes of some politicians at both the federal and state levels, categorical grants have continued to grow more rapidly than block grants.

So which are better—categorical grants or block grants? The answer will vary depending on whom you ask. Categorical grants reveal the national government's priorities, or at least the priorities of those members of Congress who voted in favor of a federal agency's budget. With block grants, the national government has money spent generally where it wants, but the states decide how they want to spend it. Thus, national lawmakers can be less sure that funds are being spent in a way they would desire. For federal lawmakers, the trade-off is between the close control of categorical grants and the potential state-level innovation and effectiveness of block grants. Within the states, political activists and government agency officials may

Unresolved Debate

Should Federal Grants Be Allocated Based on Competitions Instead of Formulas?

The vast majority of federal grants to states and local governments are now distributed based on formulas that commonly incorporate variables such as the population size or poverty level of potential recipient governments to determine grant awards. Medicaid grants and public school education grants based on Title I of the Elementary and Secondary Education Act of 1965 are two examples. Growing interest in program performance has led some people to argue that requiring states and local governments to compete for grants would be more effective than using formulas. Should federal grants be allocated based on competitions instead of formulas?

RACING TO THE TOP

President Obama and Secretary of Education Arne Duncan meet with 6th grade students in January 2010. The two men were traveling around the country to promote their Race to the Top grant program for educational innovation.

YES

In an era when fewer dollars are available to tackle pressing and difficult problems, Brian Collins and Brian Gerber note that injecting a competitive element into grant programs can help ensure that federal dollars have the greatest impact:[a]

- Competitions require potential recipients to offer specific plans for how they will use awarded funds.
- Competitions are one way to help spark innovations and creative problem solving, especially when federal grant contests allow potential recipient governments to submit joint proposals.[b]
- Formula grants with very few dollars at stake often spread funds too thinly across numerous jurisdictions and, therefore, have limited substantive impacts.

NO

Paul Manna and Laura Ryan argue that a major advantage of formula grants over competition grants is that they can better account for the administrative realities facing governments at all levels:[c]

- States or localities facing deep poverty and few administrative resources may be unable to compete for funds because of their limited capacities to assemble a compelling application.
- Grant competitions require huge federal administrative efforts to evaluate applicants' proposals.
- Federal administrators running competitions can invite criticism when they fail to allocate resources to program enforcement, which can enable grant winners to renege without penalty on the promises they made in their applications.

CONTRIBUTING TO THE DEBATE

Determining whether grant formulas or competitions are the more effective way to distribute federal funds can be difficult, in part because competitions, especially for large programs, have occurred relatively rarely. But if federal spending tightens, more programs may move to grant competitions, boosting the ability to analyze their effects.

WHAT DO YOU THINK?

1. In which policy areas do you think it would be more appropriate to allocate grants based on formulas? In which areas do you think competitions could be more helpful? Why?
2. How would a shift to more competitive grants influence the ability of politicians in Congress and the White House to appeal to their constituents?

---

[a] Brian K. Collins and Brian J. Gerber. "Redistributive Policy and Devolution: Is State Administration a Road Block (Grant) to 4-2 Equitable Access to Federal Funds?" *Journal of Public Administration Research and Theory* 16, 4 (2006): 613–32. The Race to the Top program combines competitive elements and formulas in this way.

[b] Kenneth N. Bickers and Robert M. Stein. "Interlocal Cooperation and the Distribution of Federal Grant Awards." *Journal of Politics* 66 3 (2004): 800–822.

[c] Paul Manna and Laura L. Ryan. "Competitive Grants and Educational Federalism: President Obama's Race to the Top Program in Theory and Practice," *Publius: The Journal of Federalism* 41, 3 (2011): 522–46.

prefer the specific funding that comes with categorical grants rather than having to compete for a share of a state's block grants. Because categorical grants do not allow state elected officials to steer funds toward favored groups and causes, governors and legislators might prefer the flexibility of block grants. Elected officials will rarely turn down what appears to be "free" federal money, however, whether block or categorical.[45]

☐ Federalism Can Create Both Problems and Solutions

The more general question raised by the choice between categorical grants and block grants is what type of relationship one desires between the national and state governments. For those who favor more national standards and control, the concerns with allowing the states a great degree of independence in setting policy are multiple. States may simply not have access to the same expertise available to the federal government. One state's solutions may create problems for bordering states. If states are not required to meet high national standards, there may be a "race to the bottom" in which states try to provide minimal services and cut taxes and regulation in an attempt to attract business (see *How Do We Know? Are States Engaged in a Race to the Bottom?*).

Political power is a factor as well. If particular ideas and politicians dominate national politics—whether conservative or liberal—these politicians may be tempted to use that opportunity to implement uniform conservative or liberal policies, respectively, across the country. Even ardent advocates of a strong role for the states can be attracted to the idea of writing national policies and rules that the states must follow, especially if they believe their political opponents have a foothold on state governments.

For those who favor allowing states more flexibility and leeway, the advantages are also multiple. Allowed flexibility in solving problems, the states become "laboratories of democracy," a phrase coined by Supreme Court Justice Louis Brandeis early in the twentieth century to describe an environment in which numerous policy proposals could be implemented and tested. States vary tremendously in the substance of their policies in areas such as taxation, entrepreneurship, education, welfare, consumer protection, organized labor, and health care, and in outcomes such as economic growth and income distribution.[46] As of 2012, for example, every state except Illinois allowed individuals to carry concealed handguns, but states vary in terms of whether this right applies to both residents and nonresidents, whether a permit is required, and the criteria that must be satisfied for an individual to obtain a permit.[47] States also vary in their political processes. The veto power of governors, the making of state budgets, the length of legislative sessions, voter registration laws, access of minor parties to election ballots, campaign finance laws, lobbying regulations, and many other aspects of the political process are quite different from one state to another. Political scientists consider factors such as these when trying to explain why some states adopt a particular policy while other states do not.

Those who favor more flexibility for the states and fewer national standards believe that ultimately the country as a whole gains when states can borrow those policy reforms that prove to be effective, efficient, or popular and avoid those that have not proven successful. Citizens also have the advantage of choice—they can choose where to live based on a number of factors, including the different styles and roles of government across the states.

Some examples of state innovations adopted by many states—known as policy diffusion—include reforms of welfare and worker retraining programs in social policy, raising standards and creating charter schools in education, and "three strikes" laws and minimum sentencing standards in criminal justice.[48] Policy diffusion occurs not only because public officials look across state borders and share ideas with their peers in other states, but also because those businesses, unions, and interest groups that seek to influence the legislative and regulatory process look across state lines, are often national in scope, talk to their peers in other states, and provide

How Do We Know?

Are States Engaged in a Race to the Bottom?

The Question

Critics of welfare policy argue that states with generous welfare benefits risk becoming "magnets" that attract the poor. Furthermore, the higher taxes resulting from these policies may be a disincentive to businesses looking to locate in the state. Defenders of these policies worry that this logic leads states to compete economically by decreasing welfare benefits to the level of neighboring states, which they refer to as a "race to the bottom." Are states engaged in a race to the bottom? How do we know?

Why It Matters

The race-to-the-bottom question is one of the most contentious in the study of federalism. The policy consequences are significant for welfare recipients, taxpayers, and economic development. Philosophically, the question engages the very strong and competing points of view researchers may have about the desirability of welfare programs for individuals. The concern about magnets and policy races in American federalism appears in other policy areas. School districts and states express concern at the financial pressures that may result if, for example, excellent special education services attract out-of-district and out-of-state parents seeking particular services for their children. Advocates for parents of these children worry that states and districts will reduce their services because of this fear of becoming a magnet.

Investigating the Answer

The premise of the race-to-the-bottom debate is that states offering generous welfare policies put themselves at risk by becoming welfare magnets. With more generous policies, there will be an influx of welfare recipients because of higher benefits and an outflow of business because of higher taxes. States respond to this dilemma by reducing welfare benefits, which prompts surrounding states to do the same. The result is a downward spiral in which states follow each other toward low benefits. Federalism allows differences in state benefits: If the national government simply set a fixed benefit across all states, the race could not occur. This is the case in a program such as Social Security, for which states do not set benefit levels.

The basic approach in studies of the race to the bottom is twofold. One group of studies focuses on state government behavior. The outcome to be explained is whether surrounding states adjust their level of welfare benefits in

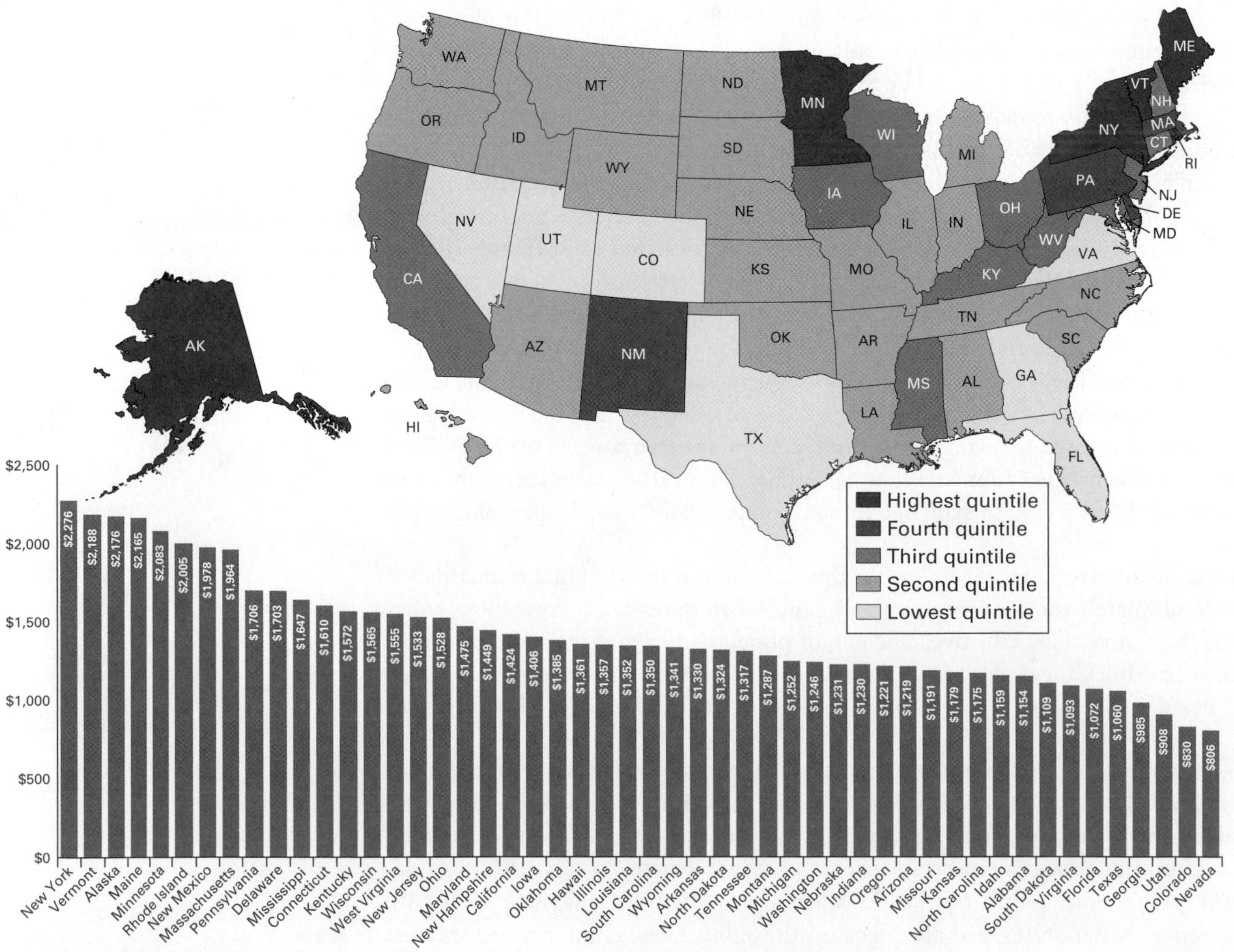

 STATE AND LOCAL PUBLIC WELFARE AND INCOME ASSISTANCE SPENDING PER CAPITA, 2009

reaction to changing levels in neighboring states. The causal relationship being tested by the researchers is whether lower benefits in one state lead to lower benefits in surrounding states. This requires tracking benefit levels over time.

These researchers may also seek to determine whether a state is a "welfare magnet" by looking at states that make benefits more generous and then seeing whether the poverty level in those states changes. The logic is that if increased benefits lure the poor, then at least initially a state's poverty rate would increase after benefits were raised because poor residents from other states will have migrated to the more generous state.

Any investigation of state government welfare benefits needs to take account of a number of factors other than the actions of other states that might affect a state's benefit levels. Wealthier states can more easily afford higher benefits per person because they have a smaller percentage of their population receiving benefits than do poorer states. States with more liberal public opinion might also be expected to have higher spending. On the other hand, states with declining wages might reduce welfare benefits to discourage workers from leaving jobs to enter the welfare system.

A second set of studies focuses on the behavior of individuals rather than state governments. These studies seek to determine why low-income individuals move from one state to another and, in particular, whether welfare benefits are part of that decision. Researchers tracking the movement of individuals from one state to another need to consider other factors that may lead individuals to move, particularly family concerns and better work opportunities in another state. The latter is particularly important. A low-income individual might move to a higher-benefit state not because of the higher benefits, but because that state is more likely to be prosperous and have more available jobs. Thus, the increased economic opportunity, not the generous welfare policy, would be the magnet. Although there would be a correlation between welfare benefits and migration, the benefits would not actually be causing the migration.

Research on the race-to-the-bottom thesis faces other complications. Most studies, for example, assume that neighboring states are the relevant set of states—these are the states that a state government is "competing with" in terms of welfare benefits and also the states from which migration is most likely. However, this assumption is not always accurate. California, for example, has more migrants from Texas, New York, Illinois, and Florida than from neighboring Oregon. Also, what if state officials set their benefits not in reaction to actual reductions in other states but in anticipation that other states will reduce their benefits? As a result, the cause of their behavior may well be behavior in other states that has not even happened yet and thus would be hard for a researcher to demonstrate. A similar problem is that states may reduce their welfare benefits to be more in line with nearby states even if individuals do not behave in the manner presumed by the welfare magnet thesis. State government officials might assume that individuals will migrate for benefits and therefore reduce their state welfare expenditures to preempt migration. In this scenario, state policy makers are influenced by the threat of movement, rather than by any demonstrated fact that individuals do move for welfare reasons. Even though most studies focus on benefit levels, states could compete in other arenas as well. They could keep benefits per recipient largely unchanged but make access to a program more difficult. Or their focus could be on changing the overall cost to taxpayers, which could entail some combination of benefit and access revisions.

The Bottom Line

Despite these research challenges, political scientists have reached some conclusions on the race-to-the-bottom theory. Overall, research has found support for the notion that states compete on benefit levels. States tend to follow one another as benefits are lowered, but they do not seem to follow one another if benefits increase. The size and the speed of the copying behavior, however, are not clear. Some studies report that states match nearly dollar for dollar what other states do, whereas in other studies, the matching is modest—state benefits are adjusted only a few cents to every dollar in a competing state.[a] Although access levels and overall cost to the state are less frequently examined, some copying behavior is evident there as well.[b]

There have been fewer studies on whether individuals move to welfare magnets, but these generally conclude that factors other than welfare benefits are more important in determining the location decisions of low-income individuals. Once cost-of-living is factored in, some studies suggest, state-to-state differences in welfare benefits are not as large as they would seem initially and, thus, are less an incentive to move from one state to another. On the other hand, for policy makers, it may not matter whether welfare benefits are the only reason an individual moves or a major reason: What might matter is simply whether welfare benefits influence location decisions to any degree.[c]

The Obama administration has urged states to think more regionally about economic development, and to see these regions as being in competition with other countries rather than with each other or with other states. Achieving such a change on any large scale would require a significant shift in the thinking of both politicians and citizens. It would also require the federal government to change its practices significantly, as much of its funding flows to states and inherently pits states in competition with one another.[d]

Thinking Critically

- Imagine a policy area in which a state might choose to provide higher benefits to encourage migration to the state. What are the key characteristics of that policy area that would make state officials decide to increase rather than decrease benefits?
- If a state were determined to spend a fixed amount on income assistance programs, would you recommend higher benefits but less access or lower benefits but more access? What do you think the strategy would be for legislators worried about the state becoming a welfare magnet?

---

[a]See Sanford F. Schram and Samuel H. Beer, eds., *Welfare Reform? A Race to the Bottom?* (Princeton, NJ: Woodrow Wilson Center Press, 1999); Joe Soss, Sanford F. Schram, Thomas P. Vartanian, and Erin O'Brien, "Welfare Policy Choices in the States: Does the Hard Line Follow the Color Line? *Focus* 23, 1 (2004): 9–15.

[b]See Schram and Beer, *Welfare Reform? A Race to the Bottom?*; Soss et al., "Welfare Policy Choices in the States."

[c]Race-to-the-bottom research and findings are discussed in William D. Berry, Richard C. Fording, and Russell L. Hanson, "Reassessing the 'Race to the Bottom' in State Welfare Policy," *Journal of Politics* 65, 2 (2003): 327–49; Michael A. Bailey, "Depressing Federalism: Re-Assessing Theory and Evidence on the 'Race to the Bottom,'" manuscript, April 2002; John Kennan and James R. Walker, "Wages, Welfare Benefits, and Migration," *Journal of Econometrics* 156, 1 (2010): 229–38.

[d]Stephen C. Fehr, "The United Regions of America," Pew Center on the States, Stateline.org, April 22, 2010, http://www.stateline.org/live/details/story?contentId=478959. See also Rebecca M. Blank, *It Takes a Nation: A New Agenda for Fighting Poverty* (Princeton, NJ: Princeton University Press, 1997).

devolution
a process in which the authority over a government program's rules and implementation is largely transferred from a higher-level government to a lower-level government.

4.1
4.2
4.3
4.4
4.5

policy makers with frameworks of legislation or regulation that can be promoted in multiple states.

Advocates of federalism note that societies with potentially deep divisions are best governed with federal arrangements. Federalism is not a cure-all, they concede. The tortured history of conflict between Catholics and Protestants in Northern Ireland provides one example; the mixed record of federalism in Africa provides another. However, countries with distinctive clusters of ethnic groups or groups that see themselves as "nations," such as the French-speaking population in Canada, might particularly benefit from this mode of government. Critics reply that although federalism might help prevent conflict, it gives rival groups competing bases of power, which may also perpetuate conflict once it emerges. Even in Canada, federalism did not discourage separatists from seeking Quebec's independence, although they have yet to succeed.[49] Political scientists' research into these questions has produced mixed results, in part because the term *federalism* embraces a vast spectrum of systems, and the term *conflict* is equally difficult to pin down. Moreover, some societies prone to conflict may choose federalism precisely for that reason; if these societies continue to be fractious, is federalism really the "cause" of that conflict? Researchers also must make judgments based on time spans.

Overall, research suggests that federalism works best in societies where the economic pie provides ample slices to share. In very poor countries, federalism may spawn, or at least not deter, violent conflict.[50] Does federalism in the United States prevent conflict? One answer might be yes, with the Civil War being the exception that proves the rule. That is, however, a very large exception.[51]

Federalism in Flux

4.5 Assess the extent and nature of changes in federalism since the mid-1990s.

Since the early 1990s, American federalism has changed. "Revolutionary" is probably too strong a term to describe the change, but certainly a significant departure from previous decades has taken place in the way elected officials and the judiciary have interpreted and implemented American federalism.

Elected Officials Have Shifted Power to the States Through Devolution and Negotiated Rule Making

Congress instigated part of the shift. After Republicans won control of the House and Senate in the 1994 congressional elections, they pushed an agenda of devolution and block grants. **Devolution** refers to the transfer of authority over program details and implementation from a higher level of government to a lower level of government. This transfer could be from federal to state, from state to local, or from federal to local, depending on the issue. In the devolution starting in the 1990s, transfer from the federal to state level was especially prominent. The federal government remained involved, but it allowed the states to use more discretion in deciding how to run programs. The most famous example is the reform of the national welfare system in 1996. The environment is another example. The federal Environmental Protection Agency has shifted authority for nearly 800 federal environmental programs to the states. State governments now run more than 80 percent of the programs related to the Clean Air Act. In other policy areas as well, block grants have been used more extensively to give states more flexibility in spending federal funds.

Another way in which Congress has shifted authority to the states is through a process known as *negotiated rule making*. In this process, Congress inserts into legislation a requirement that federal agencies negotiate with states and groups representing other relevant interests over the content of the federal regulations that will implement the law. For example, regulations regarding the transport of hazardous waste materials were developed using negotiated rulemaking. Agencies may decide voluntarily to use negotiated rule making in cases where Congress does not require it. This process does not give states or other participants veto power over agency regulations, but it ensures them a formal, ongoing role in the process of developing regulations that goes beyond the traditional comments that anyone in the public can offer on pending regulations.[52]

The Supreme Court Has Restored the Influence of Dual Federalist Principles

Even more dramatic than the changes initiated by elected officials were the changes produced by the Supreme Court. In a series of controversial decisions starting in the mid-1990s, the Court began to redraw the boundaries between federal and state responsibilities and authority. It did this by scaling back Congress's use of the interstate commerce clause to justify legislation and by reasserting dual sovereignty ideals. In these efforts, the Court majority believed it was breathing new life into the Tenth Amendment—powers not delegated to the United States are reserved for the states or the people—and the Eleventh Amendment—federal judicial power does not extend to cases of private individuals against states. Many of these decisions were decided by 5–4 Court majorities and were cheered by conservatives and Republicans while being denounced by liberals and Democrats.

REINING IN CONGRESS'S USE OF THE COMMERCE CLAUSE Following the Supreme Court's 1937 decision in *National Labor Relations Board v. Jones & Laughlin Steel Corporation* (described earlier), Congress used the Court's new interpretation of the interstate commerce clause to move the federal government into areas previously relegated to the states. Until 1995, the Supreme Court acceded to this expansion of federal power. That year, however, in *United States v. Lopez*, the Supreme Court signaled a change in direction. The Gun-Free School Zones Act of 1990 prohibited the possession of firearms within 1,000 feet of a school. Congress justified its intervention in this area by arguing that guns were an item of interstate commerce, but the Court struck down the law.[53] In the Court's view, Congress improperly involved itself in matters of local policing and used the interstate commerce clause as a thin and unconvincing rationale for its action. If states and localities wished to pass such restrictions on firearm possession, they were free to do so, but this was not a matter for federal government involvement. For the first time in nearly six decades, the Court refused to agree to Congress's use of the interstate commerce clause to expand federal power. Congress passed a revised law in 1996 that took account of the Court's decision by limiting the law to firearms that had moved through or might substantially affect interstate commerce, and by including findings to demonstrate that the possession of firearms near a school has effects on interstate commerce.

In 2000, the Court's decision in *United States v. Morrison* confirmed this new direction. In the Violence Against Women Act, part of President Clinton's 1994 package of anticrime legislation, Congress allowed women to file civil suits in federal courts against their attackers. Congress supported its action on interstate commerce grounds, noting that fear of violence suppressed women's full participation in economic life. The Court struck down this provision of the law, determining once again that Congress did not have authority over local criminal activity and that Congress's interstate commerce justification for its action was not credible. Although the Court majority agreed that the violence in the case—a rape of a college student—was reprehensible, it

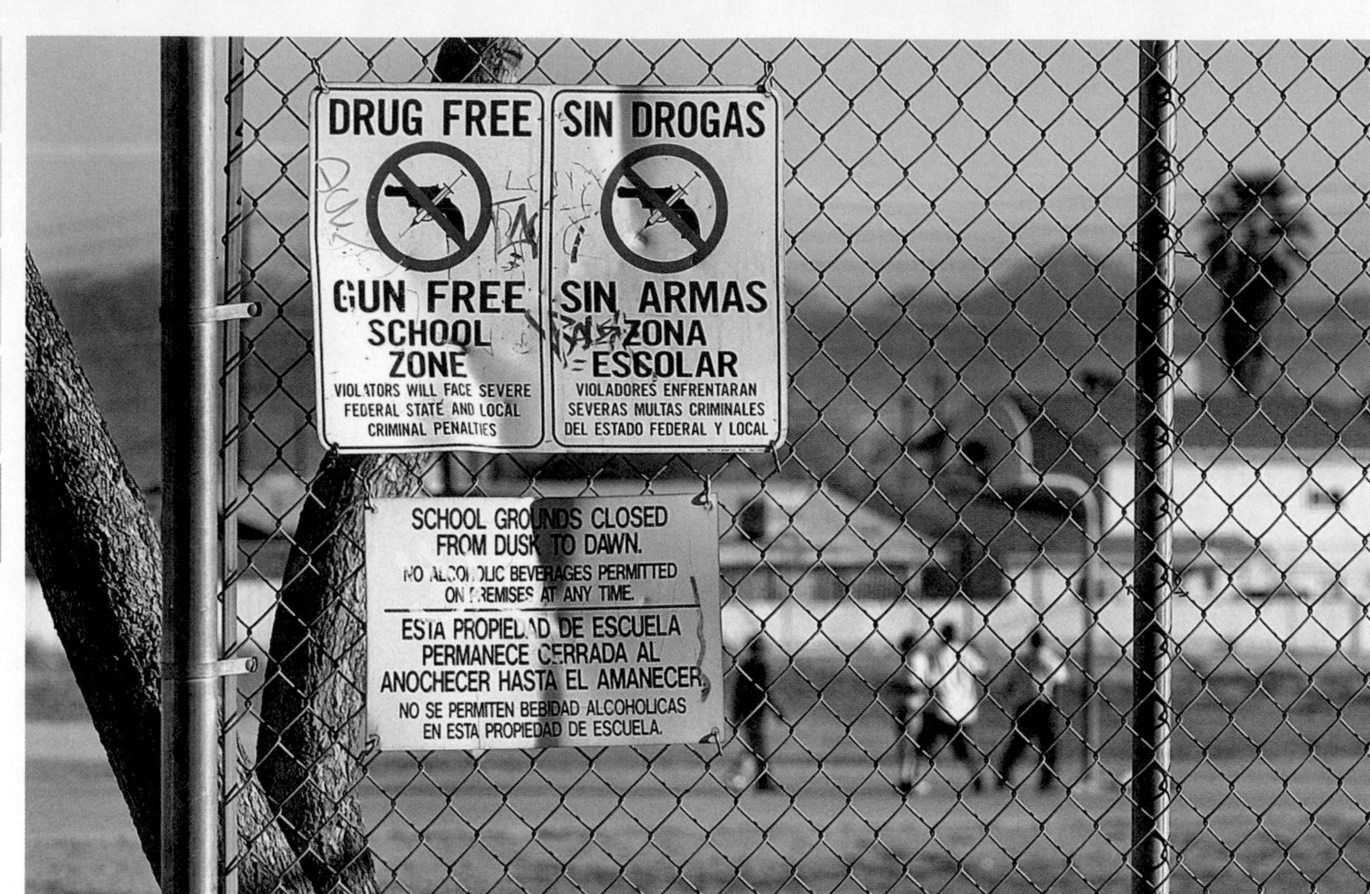

GUNS PROHIBITED NEAR SCHOOL PROPERTY

The Supreme Court went nearly 60 years after the *Jones & Laughlin* decision before objecting to Congress's use of the commerce clause to justify a law. In 1995, the Court did so, striking down the Gun-Free School Zone Act of 1990. The following year, a new version of the law was passed that in the view of Congress and the president provided a stronger justification for the law's connection to interstate commerce. The new law still stands and has not been challenged in court.

sovereign immunity
the principle that state governments cannot be sued by private parties in federal court unless they consent to the suits or Congress has constitutionally provided an exemption that allows suits to be filed.

argued that the proper remedy was to be found through the laws of Virginia, not the United States.

REASSERTING DUAL SOVEREIGNTY Another issue in the Court's new federalism offensive was whether states could be sued by private parties, such as individuals or organizations, in federal court. In a set of controversial decisions, the Court concluded that under the Eleventh Amendment, states had **sovereign immunity** against these suits—in essence, the states could not be sued in federal court unless they chose to allow themselves to be sued or Congress made a compelling case that it should be able to override this immunity.[54] The Court majority in these decisions added that even without the Eleventh Amendment, the states were sovereign entities prior to the creation of the Constitution and had not given up that status. This view reaffirms the compact theory explained earlier in this chapter.

Under this framework, the Court restricted the use of federal courts to sue states. For example, the Court ruled that public employees complaining that they had not received overtime pay required under the federal Fair Labor Standards Act could not sue the states in federal courts. States were not subject to age discrimination suits arising from the Age Discrimination in Employment Act or some suits arising from the Americans with Disabilities Act.[55] Only under certain conditions, the Court concluded in these cases, could Congress subject the states to suit by private parties in federal courts. A state, for instance, could be sued if its receipt of federal funds was conditional upon allowing this option, or if a private party was seeking only to order a state official to not take an action, rather than seeking money from the state treasury to compensate for alleged damages sustained by the private party.[56]

Other decisions reasserted principles of dual sovereignty and were designed to limit the federal government's ability to impose its will on the states. In *Printz v. United States* (1997), the Court declared that the federal government could not require state officials to perform federal functions. The issue in this case was background checks for handgun purchasers, a function that the law known as the Brady Bill had assigned temporarily to local law enforcement officials until a federal system was in place. The Court concluded that the Constitution's necessary and proper clause did not entitle Congress to compel state or local law enforcement officials to perform federal tasks without their consent. In *City of Boerne v. Flores* (1997), the Court concluded that Congress had exceeded its power in the Religious Freedom Restoration Act by attempting to impose restrictions on local zoning, health, and other regulations in order to prevent perceived threats to religious freedom. The case concerned a complaint by the archbishop in San Antonio over the city's historic preservation zoning regulations. He charged that regulations prohibiting him from expanding his church violated his religious freedom.[57] And in *Gonzales v. Oregon* (2006), the Court concluded that the federal government did not have the authority, under the Controlled Substances Act, to prohibit the use of regulated but legal drugs for physician-assisted suicide in Oregon. The Court majority reasoned that Congress had intended to prevent physicians from engaging in the sale and distribution of what the federal government considered legal drugs, not to define standards of medical practice, an arena traditionally left to state governments.

The 2012 Supreme Court hearings on the constitutionality of the Affordable Care Act also raised the question of whether the national government was being excessively dominant over the states. As noted earlier, one of the arguments made by the states that filed suit was that the Medicaid expansion provisions in the law in effect made it near impossible for states to decline the expansion, because to do so meant losing all their Medicaid funds and exposing their states to huge budgetary shortfalls. The Court agreed that these provisions were impermissibly coercive.

The cumulative effect of the Court's jurisprudence in this era was to send Congress and the president stark messages that they had to tread carefully in their attempts to intervene in states' relationships with their citizens and in other areas traditionally established as matters of state concern. It was a clear attempt to restore the influence of dual federalist principles and the ideas of the compact theory, described earlier in this chapter. The narrow 5–4 majorities on many of the decisions heightened the political tension surrounding future Supreme Court nominations. Liberals did not want to lose ground, and conservatives did not want to see their 5–4 majority flip to a 4–5 minority on federalism issues.

State Officials Have Implemented Significant New Policy and Challenged Federal Authority

As law and constitutional interpretation shifted at the federal level, policy innovation in the states expanded. In areas as diverse as the minimum wage, greenhouse gas emissions, health care coverage, civil unions and same-sex marriage, and the importation of prescription drug, state governments enacted significant legislation. In some of these areas, states acted because of their dissatisfaction with national government policies. In other areas, the federal government's involvement had waned as government officials focused their concerns elsewhere. These state laws and regulations were especially attractive to those groups that believed their chances for success at the national level had declined. With Republicans holding the majority in Congress from 1995 through 2006, and with a Republican president from 2001 through 2008, liberal activists and politicians pushed for legislation and regulation on the state level. With a turn to a Democratic Congress in 2007 and a Democratic president in 2009, conservative activists and politicians fought against federal government actions and pushed for their legislative and regulatory agenda on the state level. Each set of activists and politicians, even though preferring national policies in some issue areas, realized that those national policies were unlikely to happen. Politicians are often opportunistic about federalism and will favor whichever level of government gives them the best chance to win elections, enact policies they favor, and thwart their opponents.

States have also pushed back against federal authority in areas of traditional state dominance. One example of the pull and tug of federalism links terrorism and driver's licenses—two seemingly distinct areas of federal and state responsibility, respectively. Congress, in the REAL ID Act of 2005, sought as an antiterrorism measure to require all states to demand proof of citizenship or permanent residency before issuing driver's licenses; 10 states had no such requirements. In addition, licenses were to be standardized in certain ways across the states, such as the information stored on the machine-readable cards. State license databases would need to be linked to a national database. If a state's licenses were not consistent with the federal standard, individuals holding those licenses would not be able to use them for identification purposes with federal agencies, such as the Transportation Security Administration, which handles security at the nation's airports, or to enter federal buildings. Proponents of the law argued it would make it more difficult for terrorists to operate in the United States and more difficult for illegal immigrants to obtain legal employment. Some of the hijackers involved in the September 11, 2001, attacks had acquired driver's licenses and been able to board planes despite being in the United States illegally.

Opposition to the REAL ID Act spread through the states in early 2007. Legislators in many states objected to this federal intervention in traditional state responsibility, its perceived threats to privacy, and the cost imposed on state governments.[58] Groups from across the ideological spectrum expressed concerns about threats to privacy rights. Quickly, 25 states passed laws or resolutions objecting to the law and pledging not to implement it, and 15 passed laws prohibiting any state or local official from assisting with the law's implementation.[59] The federal government extended its deadline for implementation first to 2009, then 2011, and finally 2013. By the time of a congressional hearing in 2012, it appeared that the Department of Homeland Security's regulations for implementation had effectively watered down the law's most onerous requirements in a way that most states could be considered in compliance as long as they had made some basic changes to their driver's license process. The pushback by almost all states and the outright refusal to comply with the law by others effectively forced the federal government to retreat.[60]

☐ Has There Been a Federalism Revolution?

Given these strong moves by Congress, the president, the Supreme Court, and the states, why consider the change in federalism to be anything short of a revolution? Many media and advocacy group critics of the moves describe the changes, especially the Court's decisions, precisely that way. These conclusions, however, tend to generalize from only part of the evidence—particular laws or decisions that rankled the critics. Bringing a wider body of evidence into the analysis suggests that "revolution" is too strong a word to describe the changing balance of national and state power.

One reason is that the federal government still remains involved in those policy areas known for devolution, such as welfare. States are free to design their programs as they wish, but they are not free to eliminate those programs. In addition, the federal government's role has become more pronounced in other areas. [61] States have not been allowed to place term limits on members of Congress. In the conduct of elections, which were once considered completely the province of the states, national norms have emerged over time, including about who can vote. The National Voter Registration Act of 1993 (often referred to as the Motor Voter law) mandated that voting registration be made available at government offices such as motor vehicle bureaus. Following problems with counting votes in the 2000 presidential election, the Help America Vote Act of 2002 mandated changes in states' voting technology—eliminating punch card ballots, for example (although an effort in Congress to go one step further and require all states to accept "no excuse" absentee voting was unsuccessful in 2010).[62]

A particularly notable example of an expanded federal role has been in education, long a bastion of state and local governments. The No Child Left Behind Act championed by President George W. Bush and passed by Congress in 2002 required school districts to test each child in grades 3–8 and specified penalties for schools whose students do poorly and do not improve. President Barack Obama's Race to the Top program aimed to reward states with competitive grants for innovations in curriculum standards, student assessment, and teacher training. Both of these presidents attempted to push and influence from the national level the state and local practice of education.[63]

Another reason not to overstate the extent of the new federalism revolution is that the Supreme Court did not completely defer to the states in its decisions about sovereign immunity from lawsuits. When cases involved Fourteenth Amendment issues of equal protection, particularly in the areas of race and gender, the Court allowed states to be subject to federal authority. For example, the Court concluded that an individual could sue a state in federal court for that state's alleged gender-based discrimination in implementing the Family Medical Leave Act, and that these suits were consistent with Congress's intent when it passed the act.[64]

This idea, that Congress could respond to widespread and persistent discrimination, was also at the core of *Tennessee v. Lane* (2004). The case concerned a paraplegic who could not attend a court case because of a lack of elevators in the court building. To the Supreme Court, the fundamental importance of citizen access to the courts overrode the state's claim to immunity from a discrimination lawsuit. Congress was right to allow an exception to sovereign immunity, in the view of the 5–4 Court majority, because it had amassed evidence of recurrent, extensive violations of equal access by the states. If the Court believes a right is of special gravity, it will give Congress more leeway to force states to comply with federal rules that might otherwise be seen as exceeding federal constitutional authority.[65]

The Supreme Court also has been willing to trim state power. The Court rejected a California law that allowed Holocaust survivors to pursue insurance claims through lawsuits rather than through international diplomacy as called for by federal law. The California statute, in the Court's view, interfered with the federal government's authority over foreign policy.[66] And in *Gonzales v. Raich* (2005), the Court upheld Congress's power to prohibit the personal growing and possession of marijuana for medical use, superseding a first-in-the-nation 1996 California law that allowed such use. The federal Controlled Substances Act prohibited exemptions for the medical use of marijuana, the Court held, and the federal government could regulate those products involved in interstate commerce. Although growth for personal medicinal use might appear to be entirely local and thus not an area for federal regulation, the Court concluded that personal medicinal use nonetheless affected supply and demand and was in effect a part of the national marijuana market. Therefore, it was subject to the national government's interstate commerce power.[67]

So where does federalism stand today? Federalism continues to evolve. Today's federalism remains cooperative in many respects, including aspects of collaboration, mandates, and persuasion, but it does so within dual federalism boundaries, which have been reasserted by elected officials and by the Supreme Court's enforcement via the Tenth and Eleventh Amendments. Politicians and judges push and pull federalism in multiple directions, as they wrestle with the balance of national and state power.

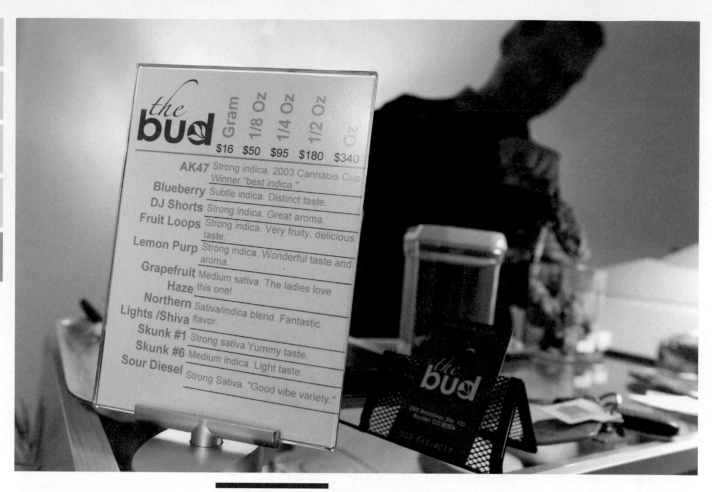

WOULD YOU LIKE SOME HIGHS WITH THAT?

In 2000, Colorado voters supported the use of marijuana for medicinal purposes. The U.S. Supreme Court in 2005, however, upheld Congress's power to prohibit the growing and possession of medical marijuana, superseding the Colorado law. Voters in Arkansas and Massachusetts approved medical marijuana in 2012, while voters in Washington and Colorado legalized pot for recreational use. How aggressive should federal government enforcement be when state laws contradict federal laws?

Although it is uncertain how President Obama's appointments to the Supreme Court will affect this blend of dual and cooperative federalism, they could possibly lead to a new direction. The president's two appointments to the Court during his first term replaced liberal justices with new justices who are also liberal, thus suggesting the Court's overall view on issues concerning the balance of national and state power would remain consistent. The key question in the president's second term is which, if any, justices will leave the Court. As the president began his second term, four of the justices were over 70 years old—two liberals (Ruth Bader Ginsburg and Stephen Breyer) and two conservatives (Anthony Kennedy and Antonin Scalia). If either of the conservative justices were to retire during President Obama's second term, the future direction of the Court's rulings on federalism issues could shift because the Court would no longer have a 5-4 conservative majority.

Review the Chapter

 **Listen** to **Chapter 4** on **MyPoliSciLab**

The Nature of the Union

4.1 Explain how the Constitution serves as a framework for federalism and why debates about the proper role of the federal and state governments remain, p. 103.

The Constitution defines the framework within which American federalism operates, identifying areas in which the national government is supreme over the states. But disputes about the role of the states in the federal system have never gone away. Differing interpretations of the formation of the United States contribute to the dispute. To some, the Union was a joining together of "the people," which weakens the primacy that states should have in federalism. To others, the Union was a joining together of the states, in which states reserved a substantial amount of the sovereignty they held prior to creating the United States.

State and Local Governments

4.2 Describe how state constitutions and local government charters provide the structure and operations of state and local governments, p. 108.

State constitutions and local government charters provide frameworks in much the same way that the U.S. Constitution guides the national government. The constitutions specify individual rights that state governments must respect and describe the basic institutions and processes for selecting officials and enacting public policies. In large part because territories that petitioned to join the Union as states had to have a constitution acceptable to Congress, states have borrowed from one another, and their constitutions are generally similar. Like the national government, states have separate legislative, judicial, and executive branches. Local governments do not inherently have a right to exist nor do they hold automatic powers. State governments use charters to authorize specific local governments and outline the extent of their power and authority, including whether or not they can levy taxes or enforce laws.

Dual Federalism

4.3 Outline the principles of dual federalism and their basis in the Supreme Court's traditional understanding of interstate commerce, p. 112.

The two major forms of federal-state relations in American history have been dual federalism and cooperative federalism. Dual federalism delineates separate and independent spheres of function and responsibility for the federal and state governments. All citizens have dual citizenship, being a citizen of both their state and the country. Prevailing Supreme Court interpretation of Congress's power to regulate interstate commerce reinforced dual federalism.

Cooperative Federalism

4.4 Trace the evolution from dual to cooperative federalism, and identify methods of cooperative federalism, p. 115.

Redefining interstate commerce played a significant role in expanding the scope of federal government responsibility and moving the country from dual to cooperative federalism. Rather than relying on strict spheres of federal and state duties, cooperative federalism allows for many areas of overlapping responsibilities for these two layers of government. Collaboration, mandates, and persuasion in the form of fiscal federalism are types of federal-state interaction in cooperative federalism. The federal government was generally the more powerful in this cooperative arrangement; thus, cooperative did not always mean harmonious. Mandates are sometimes described as coercive federalism, and fiscal federalism can apply pressure on state officials to follow federal government wishes.

Federalism in Flux

4.5 Assess the extent and nature of changes in federalism since the mid-1990s, p. 132.

Over the past two decades, the relationship between the federal and state governments has shifted. State officials became more active in policy areas where they had previously deferred to national leadership. At the national level, elected officials sought to provide states with more flexibility and responsibility over some policies. In a number of important decisions, the Supreme Court clamped down on Congress's use of the interstate commerce justification, concluded that the federal government had become improperly involved in areas of state government responsibility, and asserted the argument that the sovereignty of state governments shielded them from some federal government regulation. Not everything has moved in the direction of more state authority, however. In few policy areas has the federal government fully withdrawn, and it has inserted itself into new areas that had traditionally been the purview of the states.

Learn the Terms

block grant, p. 124
categorical grant, p. 123
charters, p. 111
commerce clause, p. 113
compact theory, p. 106
confederation, p. 104
cooperative federalism, p. 115
counties, p. 111
devolution, p. 132
dual citizenship, p. 113
dual federalism, p. 112
dual sovereignty, p. 112
enumerated powers, p. 115
federalism, p. 105
fiscal federalism, p. 123
home rule, p. 112
implied powers, p. 115
initiative, p. 109
mandate, p. 122
nationalist theory, p. 107
necessary and proper clause, p. 115
nullification, p. 106
police power, p. 113
preemption legislation, p. 123
Progressive movement, p. 109
recall, p. 109
reserved powers, p. 105
sovereign immunity, p. 134
sovereignty, p. 106
special districts, p. 112
unfunded mandate, p. 122
unitary system, p. 104

Test Yourself

4.1 Explain how the Constitution serves as a framework for federalism and why debates remain.

Which of the following represents the federalism framework established by the Constitution?

a. Powers delegated to the national government are not available to the states, but the powers not delegated to the national government (and not prohibited for state governments) are reserved for the states or for the people.
b. Powers delegated to the national government are also available to the states.
c. Powers not delegated to the national government are also not available to the states.
d. The states were designed to be subordinate to the national government and to have little, if any, independent governing authority.
e. The national government was designed to be subordinate to the state governments and to have little, if any independent governing authority.

4.2 Describe how state constitutions and local government charters provide the structure and operations of state and local governments.

Which of the following is TRUE of state and local governments?

a. Both state and local governments are mentioned explicitly in the U.S. Constitution.
b. State governments do not recognize local governments, but the national government recognizes both state and local governments.
c. Local governments are not the building blocks of states; rather, they are the creatures of states.
d. State governments are created from local governments.
e. Local governments are the building blocks of states.

4.3 Outline the principles of dual federalism and their basis in the Supreme Court's traditional understanding of interstate commerce.

Which of the following is NOT true of dual federalism?

a. The national and state levels of government have dual sovereignty.
b. Citizens of the United States are also citizens of a state.
c. Distinct lines separate the national and state governments.
d. The national government is sovereign in some areas, and the state governments are sovereign in others.
e. The national government is sovereign in all areas.

4.4 Trace the evolution from dual to cooperative federalism, and identify methods of cooperative federalism.

Which statement provides the BEST definition of cooperative federalism?

a. State governments issue mandates to request assistance from the national government.
b. National and state responsibilities overlap extensively and in many policy areas.
c. The states send representatives and senators to Washington who then cooperate in the making of legislation.
d. The state and national governments work together voluntarily and harmoniously on matters of mutual interest, with neither side issuing orders, mandates, or threats to withhold funds.
e. The state and national governments have exclusive jurisdiction over their assigned policy areas, with no overlap.

4.5 Assess the extent and nature of changes in federalism over the past two decades.

Which of the following statements BEST describes what has happened to federalism over the past two decades?

a. There has been a revolution in federalism.
b. The Supreme Court has ruled almost exclusively in favor of the states in all federalism cases.
c. The Supreme Court has ruled almost exclusively in favor of the national government in all federalism cases.
d. Federalism continues to evolve; it remains cooperative in many respects, but it does so within the boundaries of dual federalism.
e. States have refused to push back against federal authority, ceding almost all control to the national government.

Explore Further

SUGGESTED READINGS BY TOP SCHOLARS

Alison LaCroix. 2010. *The Ideological Origins of American Federalism*. Cambridge, MA: Harvard University Press. Views American federalism as not so much an adaptation to circumstances that Americans backed into, but as a major theory and ideology that held a prominent position in American political thought in the eighteenth century prior to the writing of the Constitution.

John D. Nugent. 2009. *Safeguarding Federalism: How States Protect Their Interests in National Policymaking*. Norman: University of Oklahoma Press. Argues that even though today's federalism differs from the form first established by the Framers of the Constitution, the states still have multiple methods to influence national policy and protect their interests.

David Brian Robertson. 2011. *Federalism and the Making of America*. New York: Routledge. Focuses on federalism as a political arena for conflict on major issues across American history and how preferences for national versus state authority have been held by both liberals and conservatives depending on the political circumstances of the day.

Daniel Treisman. 2007. *The Architecture of Government: Rethinking Political Decentralization*. New York: Cambridge University Press. Contends that neither theory nor evidence supports the argument that moving decision making from national level of government to lower levels produces more effective policy or more efficient governance.

Joseph Zimmerman. 2009. *Contemporary American Federalism: The Growth of National Power*, 2nd ed. Albany: State University of New York Press. A sweeping and comprehensive overview of multiple aspects of American federalism, including intergovernmental relations at the national and state levels as well as within states.

SUGGESTED WEBSITES

National Conference of State Legislatures: www.ncsl.org
Excellent resource with policy analysis, election results, and a range of other helpful data comparing states and examining federal–state issues.

Education Commission of the States: www.ecs.org
Useful site for comparing state education policies and implementation of the federal government's No Child Left Behind Act.

Statistical Abstract of the United States: www.census.gov/compendia/statab
Terrific collection of data published by the U.S. Census Bureau that includes hundreds of tables and downloadable spreadsheets, many at the state level, and data on intergovernmental finances.

Urban Institute: www.urban.org/government/federalism.cfm
Good collection of studies on a wide range of issues facing federalist systems in the United States and around the world.

Grants.gov: www.grants.gov
Easy-to-use searchable database of federal grants.

5

Listen to Chapter 5 on MyPoliSciLab

Civil Liberties

IS MONEY SPEECH?

Americans viewed well over 1 million televised ads in the 2012 presidential election.[1] But the ads were not run just by the candidates and the political parties. Other groups, organized under various parts of the tax code and election regulations—some of which require that donors be identified and some of which do not—also ran ads. The amount spent by groups such as Restore Our Future, a conservative group, and Priorities USA Action, a liberal group, totaled hundreds of millions of dollars.[2]

The role for these groups expanded in 2010 when it became possible for them to raise funds from corporations and unions. The Supreme Court had ruled in January of that year that corporations have a right to spend their funds independently to support or oppose candidates by running television ads or other forms of communication. By extension, the ruling applied to labor unions also, and to both for-profit and nonprofit corporations. The majority in the 5–4 *Citizens United v. FEC* decision argued that the First Amendment does not allow the government to choose favored and disfavored speakers through its regulations. The minority argued that the First Amendment was never intended to give corporate entities the same free speech protection as it provides to individuals. A later federal court ruling in 2010 confirmed that corporations could donate to other groups like Restore Our Future and Priorities USA Action that engage in independent campaign spending.

At issue in *Citizens United* was *Hillary Clinton: The Movie*, a critical documentary produced by Citizens United, a small nonprofit corporation funded mostly by individual contributions. At the time, Clinton was running for the Democratic Party's 2008 nomination for the presidency. The company wanted to distribute its documentary by video-on-demand services on cable television, and it also wished to air short advertisements promoting the documentary. Fearing that the Federal Election Commission (FEC) would consider the documentary and ads to be a violation of the Bipartisan Campaign Reform Act of 2002 (BCRA),

5.1 Define the civil liberties guaranteed by the Constitution, and trace the process by which they became binding on state governments, p. 146.

5.2 Analyze the different standards by which the Supreme Court has determined whether restrictions on freedom of speech are acceptable, p. 155.

5.3 Evaluate how the Supreme Court has interpreted cases regarding religion and how Congress has reacted to the Court's actions, p. 165.

5.4 Trace the expansion of the rights of the accused and their balance with the needs of police and prosecutors, p. 170.

5.5 Explain how the Ninth and Fourteenth Amendments have helped establish rights other than those specifically listed in the Constitution, p. 177.

A DISSENTING OPINION Protesters gather in Boston, Mass. on the two-year anniversary of the U.S. Supreme Court's ruling in Citizens United v. FEC. The Court's decision declared that corporate entities, whether non-profit, for-profit, or labor unions, had the right to spend independently in campaigns. Corporate entities cannot contribute directly to candidates or political parties in federal elections.

MyPoliSciLab Video Series

Watch on MyPoliSciLab

The Big Picture Does the freedom of assembly apply to groups standing in the middle of an intersection at rush hour? Does freedom of speech extend to someone shouting hateful things about America? Author John J. Coleman encourages students to consider how far these freedoms that we value should go.

The Basics What are civil liberties and where do they come from? In this video, you will learn about our First Amendment guarantees and about protections the Bill of Rights provides those accused of crimes. In the process, you'll discover how our liberties have changed over time to reflect our changing values and needs.

In Context Uncover the importance of civil liberties in a changing American society. University of Massachusetts at Boston political scientist Maurice T. Cunningham identifies the origins of our civil liberties and evaluates the clash between national security and civil liberties in a post 9/11 age.

Think Like a Political Scientist What are some of the challenges facing political scientists in regards to civil liberties? In this video, University of Massachusetts at Boston political scientist Maurice T. Cunningham raises some of the thought provoking questions regarding civil liberties that have arisen during the last decade.

In the Real World The American legal system and the American people have both struggled over whether the death penalty should be imposed in this country. In this segment, we'll hear what citizens have to say about the death penalty.

So What? Two thirds of states allow capital punishment. What do you think about that? Author John J. Coleman, explains how important it is for students to consider when it is acceptable for the government to restrict liberties, so that they can engage in national debates on issues, such as the death penalty, abortion, and free speech.

Citizens United sought an injunction against any FEC action. BCRA prohibited corporations from using their general treasury funds for independent electioneering activities—that is, any broadcast, cable, or satellite communication within 30 days of a primary election or 60 days of a general election that specifically mentions a candidate for federal office. Citizens United lost and the case moved to the Supreme Court.

The response to the Supreme Court's decision was thunderous. Critics denounced the *Citizens United* ruling as a devastating blow to democracy and fair elections: "This appalling decision . . . will further weaken the quality and fairness of our politics. The Court has given lobbyists, already much too powerful, a nuclear weapon. . . . The conservative justices savaged canons of judicial restraint they themselves have long praised."3 Critics charged that corporate speech would "drown out" speech from candidates and other sources.

Supporters cheered the decision as a stirring victory for free speech: "Hopefully, this ruling marks an end to 20 years of jurisprudence in which the Court has provided less protection to core political speech than it has to Internet pornography . . . flag burning, commercial advertising, topless dancing, and burning a cross outside an African American church."[4] Supporters claimed that the ruling would lead to more vibrant campaigns—speech begets more speech in response, and the public is ultimately the beneficiary.

Critics promised legislative responses that would require extensive disclosure and place limits on campaign involvement by some corporations. The DISCLOSE Act, the first legislative response to *Citizens United*, faltered in the summer of 2010.[5] A revised version introduced in 2012 also failed. Supporters promised to pursue vigorous legal challenges to other campaign finance laws that in their view restricted freedom of speech or circumvented the intent of the Court's ruling.

Praise for and condemnation of the Supreme Court's reasoning, and impassioned debate over what the First Amendment does and does not demand regarding free speech, were central issues in the post-decision discussion. Although the Court considered new issues in the *Citizens United* case, at its base, the Court's conclusion rested on its determination more than 30 years previously in *Buckley v. Valeo* (1978) that in the context of political campaigns, money is the equivalent of speech. That is, money spent to support a candidate or to express opinions on an issue is itself a form of speech.

In addition, the Court determined, money is a means by which speech is made possible: running advertisements, printing brochures, hiring media consultants, and so on, all require money. If money is speech, then regulating money in campaigns amounts to the regulation of speech. Given a strong pro–free speech orientation in American politics, how is such regulation to be done constitutionally?

The Court's rulings over the past three decades have stated that in the area of campaign contributions—money given to a candidate or party to be spent on a campaign or money given to a political committee that would then contribute to the candidate or party—government can limit the amount of the contributions. The Court balanced what it saw as the free speech right of the contributor with the compelling government interest in avoiding corruption or the appearance of corruption and concluded that limits on contributions were acceptable. In the area of independent expenditures—funds spent to elect or defeat candidates but that are not coordinated with any candidate's campaign—spending could not constitutionally be limited. The Court argued that because these funds are not given to a candidate's campaign or to a party for campaign purposes, but are spent independently, they do not raise the same concerns about corruption or the appearance of corruption. What *Citizens United* added to the mix was that corporations (both nonprofit and for-profit) and unions could use funds directly from their general treasuries for independent expenditures rather than separately raising funds for campaign purposes. Prior to *Citizens United,* about half the states allowed unlimited campaign spending by corporations and unions in state and local elections. In June 2012, the Supreme Court confirmed in *American Tradition Partnership v. Bullock* that the *Citizens United* ruling also applied to elections at these levels, as well as federal elections.

The debates over the propriety of the Supreme Court's decision and the soundness of its formulation that "money is speech" will continue. Constitutional guarantees such as freedom of speech, freedom of religion, and the right to assemble are general principles, but politics is also about specifics, and these specifics lead to conflict. In these conflicts, choices must be made, through law, executive actions, or court decisions, each of which

civil liberties
individual rights and freedoms that government is obliged to protect, normally by not interfering in the exercise of these rights and freedoms.

is examined in this chapter. You will see that a number of Supreme Court decisions were decided by votes of 5–4, suggesting just how deep the conflict over defining proper protections for civil liberties can be, and how a change in the members of the Court can lead to significant changes in these definitions. You will also see how Court decisions prompt legislative action, to which the Court may have to respond in the future.

In addition to conflict, another constant of civil liberties is change. What is considered appropriate at one time might not be considered so at another. This chapter emphasizes how the scope of civil liberties protections has changed across time. Historically, three paths have led to this change in scope. First, the civil liberties restrictions placed on the federal government by the U.S. Constitution were gradually applied to state governments. Second, as membership in the Supreme Court changed, interpretation of the Constitution's meaning also changed. And third, Supreme Court decisions have established individual rights that are not specifically mentioned in the Constitution.

Civil Liberties in American Politics and the Constitution

5.1 Define the civil liberties guaranteed by the Constitution and trace the process by which they became binding on state governments.

ivil liberties are another name for individual rights and freedoms. The Declaration of Independence makes eight references to a "right" or "rights." In contrast, civil rights focus on equality, another important principle in the American governmental framework, but one that is mentioned only twice. Even "the people," a staple of revolutionary thought and language, appears less frequently than rights. And this rights language is not just a thing of the past. The Democratic and Republican parties' 2012 platforms also mention rights dozens of times. The parties' references range from very general mentions of rights to more specific notions such as the right not to join a union or the right to health care.

We can safely say that very few words are more important to Americans' understanding of their political system than *rights*. Political rhetoric in America is full of references to rights, whether individual rights, such as the right to speak freely, or collective rights, such as the right of the people to assemble. American political culture, with its emphasis on individual independence, liberty, property ownership, religious freedom, and democratic government, is infused throughout with individual rights.

Civil Liberties Identify Areas Where Government Should Not Interfere

In the United States, **civil liberties** focus on individual rights that government is obliged to protect, normally by not interfering in the exercise of these rights and freedoms. When Americans talk about civil liberties, they are typically talking about places where government should not intrude: speech, the press, religious expression, organizing for political purposes, and so on.[6] American political culture, and its understanding of liberty, suggests that these rights are not *granted* to us or *given* to us by government—they are inherent in us as people. What government can do is protect or restrict the exercise of these individual rights.[7]

As a matter of definition, civil liberties are easy enough to understand. But politically, civil liberties issues often create a contest between elected officials and the judiciary to define what is and what is not consistent with the text and values of the Constitution. Causal chain reactions are common. Congress passes a law. The courts respond. Congress revisits the issue with a new law. Maybe the states pass their own versions of the federal law. The courts will often then be asked to rule again on the civil liberties issue in question.

A PRAYER IN CONGRESS FOR ACTION ON POVERTY

The House of Representatives starts each day with a prayer delivered by religious figures from various faiths. Is this an unconstitutional violation of the separation between church and state or an acknowledgment of the importance of freedom of religious practice in American civil liberties? Here, former House Speaker Nancy Pelosi (center) joins with church and faith-based organization members and with other members of the House of Representatives.

In some instances, Americans will tolerate limits on civil liberties to preserve public safety, order, or other important societal goals. For example, Americans have the right to assemble, but that does not extend into a right to assemble in the middle of a city street and stop traffic. Government has to be concerned with the conflicting rights of both the assemblers and those needing to go about their lives and go to work, school, or wherever they might need to travel. Part of civil liberties protection, therefore, is that when government restricts the exercise of rights, it does so with **due process**. The Fifth Amendment to the Constitution states that no person shall "be deprived of life, liberty, or property, without due process of law." This clause means that there must be procedural safeguards in place prior to the restriction of rights. Government officials exercising due process have to follow clear guidelines and established procedures. In the case of gathering in the street, for example, groups have to follow procedures to obtain a permit to assemble and march.

due process
procedural safeguards that government officials are obligated to follow prior to restricting rights of life, liberty, and property.

A related concept also found in the Fifth Amendment requires that government must compensate you for taking your private property for a public use ("nor shall private property be taken for public use, without just compensation"—known as the "takings clause"). As with many terms in the Constitution, *public use* can be defined broadly or narrowly. In 2005, a divided 5–4 Supreme Court in *Kelo v. City of New London* upheld New London, Connecticut's desire to take private property for economic development, which in practice meant building private office space and a conference hotel. In effect, property was transferred from one private party to another as a "public use." This high-profile decision set off a firestorm of protest that the Court was trampling on the

5.1 5.2 5.3 5.4 5.5

rights of property owners. In the wake of that highly controversial decision, many states passed laws to prohibit this kind of government action. This response by states to *Kelo* demonstrates another way in which Americans' civil liberties are protected: through state-level constitutions, bills of rights, and laws. Because Americans are dual citizens (of the states they live in as well as of the United States), they can have additional protections for their liberty in their states. Thus, a case such as the one that occurred in New London may not violate the takings clause in the U.S. Constitution, but it might be determined as violating a state's laws or the takings clause in a state's constitution.

On the whole, civil liberties protections are strong in the United States. Although Americans often think of the United States as unique in this regard, it is among the 50 countries judged in 2011 to have the strongest protection for civil liberties among all 195 independent countries by Freedom House, an international political rights and civil liberties watchdog group. Freedom House describes these countries as having freedom of expression, assembly, association, education, and religion; having an established and equitable rule of law; and enjoying free economic activity. Figure 5.1 shows the countries Freedom House considers to be free, partly free, and not free.[8]

In general, civil liberties protections are strongest in Europe and the Americas and weakest in Asia and Africa. In the Middle East, in places such as Egypt, Libya, and Tunisia, some improvements occurred in 2011 and 2012. However, in places such as Syria and Bahrain, violent crackdowns took place during that same period. These global patterns correlate roughly with the distribution of prosperity around the globe, prompting social scientists to examine whether civil liberties result from or create prosperity. Their research suggests that both processes are present: Civil liberties encourage economic growth, and economic growth encourages civil liberties.[9] The relationships are not automatic, however. Economic prosperity varies among countries with strong civil liberties protection, and countries with increasing prosperity, such as China, do not necessarily support civil liberties strongly. Overall, however, the two appear to work in tandem.

The Constitution Protects Civil Liberties

When Americans think about the constitutional protection of civil liberties, they think first of the Bill of Rights, the first 10 amendments to the Constitution. But this is only one of the Constitution's protections of liberty. To the Framers, the structural principles in the articles of the Constitution—separation of powers, checks and balances, federalism, and limited government—all worked to enhance the general protection of the people's liberty. The Framers also included specific civil liberties protections in the articles of the Constitution. For example, the Constitution declares that only courts and juries—not the legislature—can determine whether an individual is guilty of a crime. The intent is to ensure that before any rights are restricted, the proceedings that might lead to that outcome are fair, impartial, proper, and not subject to the political pressures that exist in a legislature. The Constitution also prohibits both the federal and state governments from passing a bill of attainder, which is legislation that declares a person guilty of a crime and establishes punishment, all without a trial.

The articles of the Constitution protect civil liberties in other ways. Religious tests or oaths for federal employment are prohibited. The writ of *habeas corpus*, which gives an accused individual the right to appear in court to hear the formal charges against him or her, cannot be suspended except to enhance public safety during times of rebellion or invasion. And an individual cannot be tried based on ex post facto ("after the fact") laws passed by state governments or the federal government, meaning that a person cannot be tried for an act that was not illegal at the time it was committed.

The Bill of Rights Primarily Protects Freedom of Expression and the Rights of the Accused

The Bill of Rights is at the heart of constitutional civil liberties protections. The Federalists believed that a Bill of Rights was unnecessary. In their view, the articles of the Constitution themselves contained specific guarantees of liberty; the Constitution's general structure was designed to protect liberty, and state constitutions had bills of rights. The

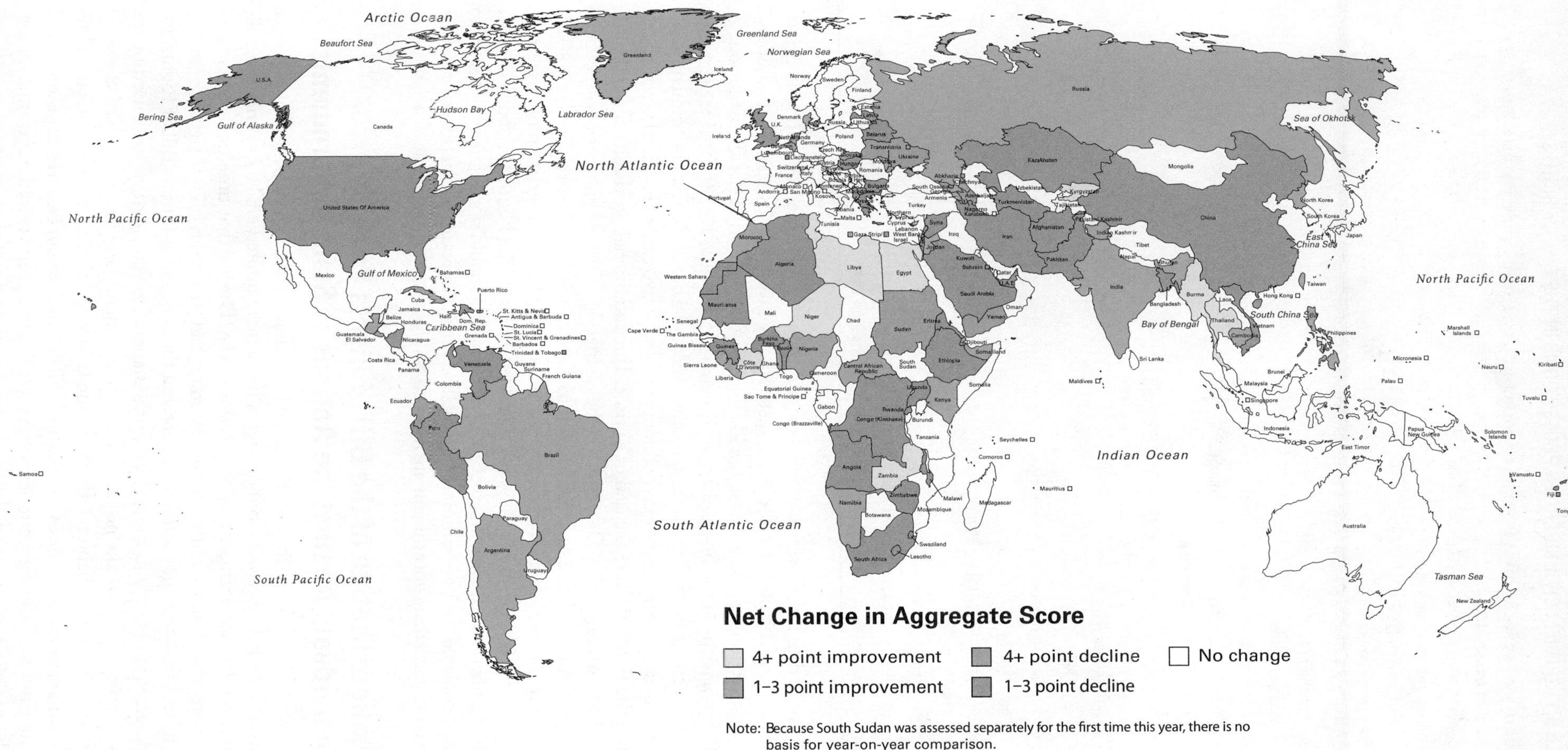

FIGURE 5.1 FREEDOM AROUND THE GLOBE, 2012.

The number of free or partly free countries has increased over the past decade, but there is still significant regional variation in the spread of political rights and civil liberties around the globe.

Source: http://www.freedomhouse.org/sites/default/files/inline_images/FIW%202012%20Booklet–Final.pdf.

TABLE 5.1 SPECIFIC CIVIL LIBERTIES PROTECTIONS IN THE BILL OF RIGHTS

Category of specific civil liberties protected (Amendment in parentheses)
Freedom of expression
Freedom to exercise religion (1st)
No establishment of religion (1st)
Freedom of speech (1st)
Freedom of assembly (1st)
Freedom to petition government (1st)
Freedom of the press (1st)
Rights of defendants
Cannot search for or seize evidence without court warrant and probable cause (4th)
Right to grand jury hearing in criminal cases (5th)
Cannot be forced to incriminate oneself (5th)
Cannot be tried for the same crime more than once (5th)
Right to jury trial in criminal and civil cases (6th and 7th)
Right to speedy trial (6th)
Right to hear charges against oneself (6th)
Right to confront witnesses and offer own witnesses (6th)
Right to legal counsel (6th)
Bail cannot be excessive and punishment cannot be cruel and unusual (8th)
Other protections
Right of people to keep and bear arms (2nd)
Cannot use citizen homes to house soldiers without due process (3rd)
Property cannot be taken for public use without fair compensation (5th)

risk of specifying rights was that government might be presumed to be free to ignore all rights not mentioned. But the Federalists quickly saw that the promise of additional specific protections would increase the likelihood of ratification of the Constitution.[10]

The provisions in the first eight amendments of the Bill of Rights provide protection against the actions of the legislative, executive, and judicial branches of government. Table 5.1 shows that the protections overwhelmingly deal with two categories: freedom of expression and the rights of those accused of a crime. Three additional provisions do not fit into the previous two categories. One of these, the quartering of troops in homes, has not been especially significant since its ratification into the Constitution, but the other two—the right to keep and bear arms and the compensation for public appropriation of property—have been the subject of extensive political and legal debate. The Ninth Amendment states that the failure to list rights in the preceding amendments should not be presumed to mean that the people do not have additional rights. The Tenth Amendment declares that powers not given to the federal government are reserved for the states or the people.[11]

Nationalization of the Bill of Rights Protected Individuals Against the Actions of State Governments

Despite its importance in the constitutional ratification debate and despite the reverence with which it is held today, the Bill of Rights had a more limited effect on American politics during the nineteenth century than it does today. During that time, government was much more active on the state level. Many states had their own bills of rights to protect their citizens from state government actions, but the U.S. Constitution's Bill of Rights was considered to apply only to the actions of the national government, as evidenced by the words "Congress shall make no law" in the First Amendment. In the case of *Barron v. Baltimore*, discussed in chapter 4, the Supreme Court declared that Barron was not entitled to compensation under the Constitution's Fifth Amendment because it was the city of Baltimore, not the federal government, that took Barron's property without compensation.

The nationalization of the Bill of Rights was the first of three paths that initiated changes in the scope of civil liberties protection. First, beginning in 1897, through the incorporation process, as explained in the following sections, the Supreme Court began to see the Bill of Rights as limiting the actions of state governments as well as the national government. This revolutionary shift opened the door for increased federal government authority.[12] Second, over time, the Supreme Court shifted its interpretation of constitutional provisions in areas such as freedom of speech, free religious practice, and the rights of the accused, leading to expansions or contractions in the range of protection. And third, the Supreme Court has declared additional liberties to be protected beyond those specifically listed in the Constitution. We discuss each of these paths in this chapter.

THE FOURTEENTH AMENDMENT AND INCORPORATION The Fourteenth Amendment has been profoundly important to American life. Ratified in July 1868 as part of the post–Civil War reconstruction of American government and society, it was the first amendment to limit state action directly, declaring that "no State shall make or enforce any law which shall abridge the privileges or immunities of citizens of the United States; nor shall any State deprive any person of life, liberty, or property, without due process of law; nor deny to any person within its jurisdiction the equal protection of the laws." If we consider the battle over state versus national power during the framing of the Constitution, and the many protections for state sovereignty in the Constitution and in law, this declaration represented a remarkable turnabout. Keep in mind that three-quarters of the states needed to ratify this amendment. In effect, they would be voting to limit their independence. Why the change? Political scientists often point to the importance of ideas, interests, and institutions in explaining political change, and all three can be brought to bear on this puzzle. Some of those legislators voting to ratify the amendment may have done so based on a sincere belief in the *idea* that the Union needed to have some consistent civil liberties standards to protect all citizens, but especially the recently emancipated slaves.

Given that the collapse of a unified nation contributed to the descent into a horrific war, it was in the *interests* of a majority of politicians and the public to support

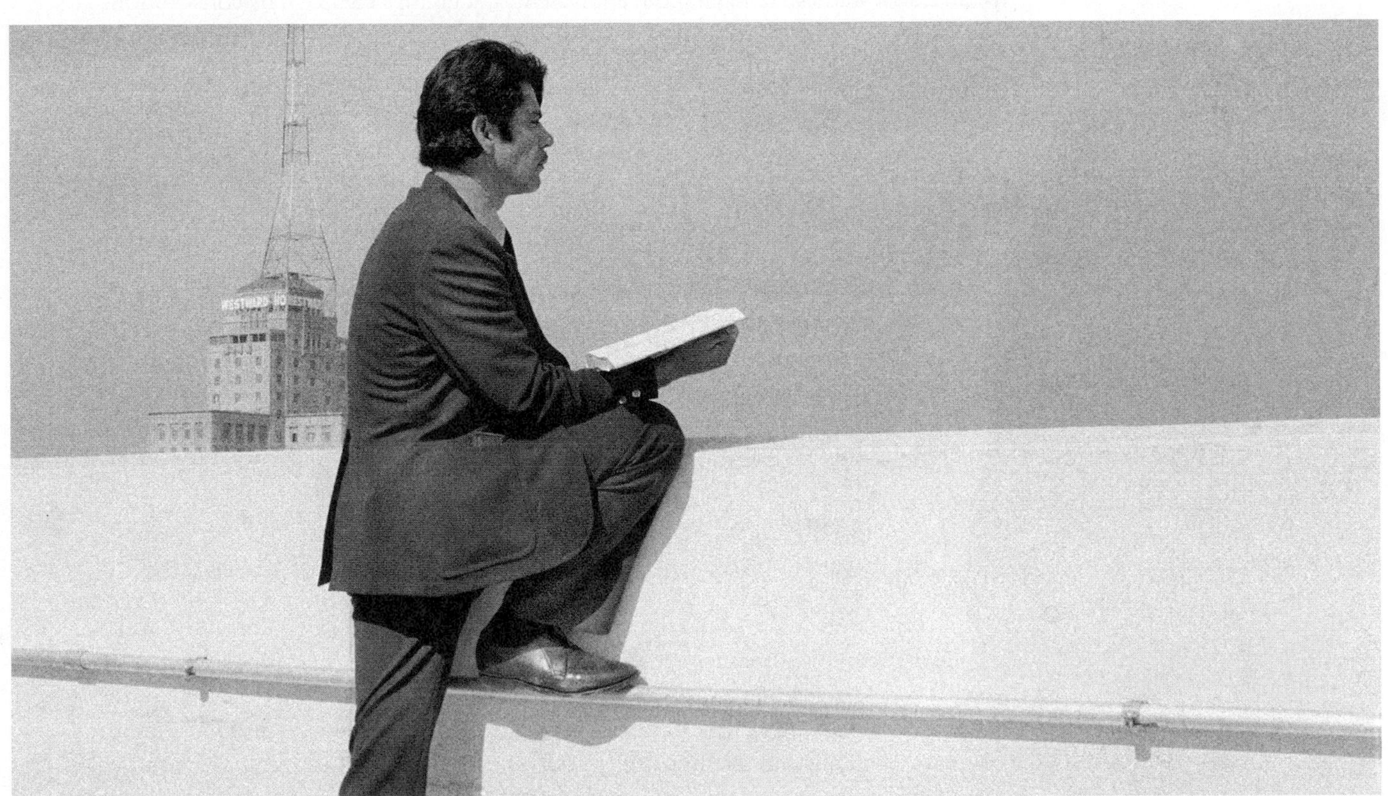

THE RIGHT NOT TO SPEAK

The Fifth Amendment protects individuals against self-incrimination. In 1966, the Supreme Court ruled that this right, construed as the right to remain silent, also protected the accused in state and local legal proceedings because of the Fourteenth Amendment's guarantee of due process. The failure of police to inform Ernesto Miranda of his rights upon arrest, including the right to remain silent, led the Court to require police to deliver the now-familiar *Miranda* warning when an individual is arrested. After Miranda's conviction was overturned, he was tried again without his confession and convicted. He is pictured here in 1973 in Phoenix.

incorporation process
the application, through the Fourteenth Amendment, of the civil liberties protections in the Bill of Rights to state governments.

selective incorporation
the process by which protections in the Bill of Rights were gradually applied to the states, as the Supreme Court issued decisions on specific aspects of the Bill of Rights.

constitutional provisions that could prevent states from straying too far from fundamental protections of life, liberty, and property. Whether ideas or interests were ultimately more important to a northern state legislator voting to ratify the amendment, an important *institutional* rule further helps explain the amendment's success—southern states were required to accept the amendment prior to being readmitted to the Union, and they were not allowed representation in Congress until they were readmitted. Even if they opposed the content of the amendment—and some southern states did initially vote against ratification—self-interest ultimately led them to ratify it.

The Supreme Court used the **incorporation process** to apply the Bill of Rights to the states, and the Fourteenth Amendment was key to this process. Stated technically, the Bill of Rights was incorporated into, or included within, the Fourteenth Amendment and through this inclusion became binding on the states. Most importantly, the "due process clause" of the Fourteenth Amendment brings protection from state government intrusions on life, liberty, and property into the U.S. Constitution.[13] But what exactly does that mean in specific practice rather than abstract words? What specifically could government do and not do? The Supreme Court began to determine the real–world meaning of the due process clause in a series of major decisions.

SELECTIVE INCORPORATION The Court began the process with a decision concerning property. In 1897, the Court decided 7–1 in *Chicago, Burlington, and Quincy Railroad v. Chicago* that in order for the Fourteenth Amendment's general protection of property to be a meaningful concept, it required compensation when property was taken for public use. The Fifth Amendment's takings clause, which states that private property cannot be taken for public use unless the property owner is compensated, was thus incorporated into the Fourteenth Amendment and, therefore, now applied to the states. This decision effectively overturned *Barron v. Baltimore* (1833) by stating that the Fifth Amendment in the U.S. Constitution now protected a property owner, who no longer had to rely on an individual's state having the equivalent of a takings clause in its constitution.

More than a quarter century would pass before the Court took another incorporation step. In 1925, the Court decided in *Gitlow v. New York* that the Fourteenth Amendment's protection of liberty must include a free speech guarantee—free speech was fundamental to the concept of liberty. The case concerned a New York law that punished speakers who promoted the overthrow of the U.S. government by force. The Court did not declare the law unconstitutional, but it did assert that state laws of this type were reviewable by the U.S. Supreme Court. The First Amendment's free speech guarantee was thus incorporated into the Fourteenth Amendment's protection for liberty, and now it, too, applied to the action of state governments.

Notice that these two cases incorporated only some of the Bill of Rights guarantees into the Fourteenth Amendment. In practice, the Supreme Court has incorporated civil liberties guarantees in bits and pieces through a process known as **selective incorporation.** The Supreme Court did not simply declare that the entire Bill of Rights applied to the states. Rather, the Court worked with the issues in the cases before it. As cases raised issues concerning particular parts of the amendments that comprise the Bill of Rights, the Court decided whether that particular right was fundamental enough to the Fourteenth Amendment's general protection of life, liberty, and property that it should now apply to the states.

Although there was no guarantee that incorporation would go beyond the First and Fifth Amendments, over time the Court declared that additional portions of the Bill of Rights also applied to state governments. Why did the Court take this stance? Four factors seem chiefly important in the spread of selective incorporation. First, dramatic events gave increased credibility and legitimacy to extending the protections of the Bill of Rights against actions by state and local governments. Abusive search and seizure cases during Prohibition; the mistreatment of blacks by southern police and court systems; and the hostility toward Jehovah's Witnesses before and during World War II because of their beliefs, including a refusal to salute the flag, were especially important. Second, the wars against fascism and communism, enemies defined in large part by their disdain for civil liberties, contributed to an environment for spreading civil liberties protections in the U.S. Constitution to the states. Third, new justices on the Court brought changing perspectives. Political scientists have shown that changes in membership in key governmental institutions can lead to dramatic changes in the constitutional interpretation of individual rights by introducing new ideas, judicial philosophies, and policy preferences into judicial and legislative debates.[14] These new justices received their legal training during a time when incorporation existed, so their training and the ideas and doctrines they became acquainted with inevitably differed from those of the justices who preceded them. A final key factor was the cumulative process of incorporation itself. As the Court incorporated each part of the Bill of Rights, the logic of future decisions leaned toward incorporating similar constitutional provisions.[15] Table 5.2 shows that selective incorporation has been a lengthy process.

THE SECOND AMENDMENT RIGHT TO KEEP AND BEAR ARMS Only recently has the Second Amendment right to keep and bear arms been seen as an individual right, and not until 2010 did the Supreme Court incorporate this right and apply it to the states.[16] Prior to the Supreme Court's recent rulings, a long-lasting disconnect existed between the public debate over the right of gun ownership and the Supreme Court's interpretation of the Second Amendment.

The Second Amendment states that "a well regulated Militia, being necessary to the security of a free State, the right of the people to keep and bear Arms, shall not be infringed." The Supreme Court traditionally considered this language to be a collective guarantee of the self-defense of the states, rather than a guarantee of individual ownership of arms. State governments called in militias to repel threats to public order. As long as the Supreme Court considered constitutionally protected gun ownership to be connected to state militias rather than individuals, it was unlikely to conclude that gun control laws violated the Second Amendment.

In 2008, in a case involving the prohibition of handgun ownership in the District of Columbia, however, the Supreme Court declared for the first time that the Second Amendment protected an individual's right to have a gun in his or her home. The decision struck down the handgun ban in Washington, D.C., and the National Rifle Association, the country's leading advocacy group for gun owners, quickly filed challenges to gun control laws in Chicago and other cities. Because the District of Columbia is a federal entity and not a state, the Court needed to decide in a subsequent case whether its decision in *District of Columbia v. Heller* should be incorporated and thus apply to the states and their cities. It did so in *McDonald v. Chicago* (2010). That decision does not end the story, however. We can expect causal reactions between judicial and legislative action. Future cases will continue to determine the scope and limits of an individual's right to possess firearms, including possession outside the home, and government's ability to regulate them. States and cities are likely to respond by passing new laws to determine exactly what the Court will and will not allow.

Nationalization Does Not Require Uniformity in States' Protection of Civil Liberties

Nationalization of civil liberties means that most of the Bill of Rights guarantees now also apply to state governments. But in some areas, the Supreme Court has allowed substantial flexibility in how states apply these protections. Federal constitutional protection has not been eliminated in these areas, but the Supreme Court allows variation in how states regulate the exercise of a right.

Consider freedom of religious practice. The freedom to practice one's religion is fundamentally the same in New Hampshire as it is in New Mexico, the same in Oregon as Ohio, the same in Tennessee as Texas. The Supreme Court considers freedom of religious practice to be a fundamental right and part of the very essence of liberty.

The Court has made it clear that other rights, although undeniably of value and importance, do not rise to the same level. With fundamental rights such as religious freedom—rights that are linked closely to human autonomy and liberty—the Supreme Court tolerates little variation from state to state. A state would need to show it had a compelling interest at stake that required a limit on the right (known as the Court taking a *strict scrutiny approach*), and that it had pursued this limitation by the narrowest means possible (known as seeking a

TABLE 5.2 SELECTIVE INCORPORATION OF THE BILL OF RIGHTS INTO THE FOURTEENTH AMENDMENT

Amendment	Issue	Year	Key Case
Amendments Fully Incorporated			
1st	Freedom of speech	1925	*Gitlow v. New York*
1st	Freedom of the press	1931	*Near v. Minnesota*
1st	Freedom of assembly	1937	*De Jonge v. Oregon*
1st	Freedom of religious exercise	1940	*Cantwell v. Connecticut*
1st	No establishment of religion	1947	*Everson v. Board of Education*
1st	Freedom of association	1958	*NAACP v. Alabama*
1st	Right to petition	1963	*NAACP v. Button*
2nd	Right to keep and bear arms	2010	*McDonald v. Chicago*
4th	No unreasonable search and seizure	1949	*Wolf v. Colorado*
4th	No search and seizure without warrant	1961	*Mapp v. Ohio*
6th	Right to counsel in capital punishment cases	1932	*Powell v. Alabama*
6th	Right to public trial	1948	*In re Oliver*
6th	Right to counsel in felony cases	1963	*Gideon v. Wainwright*
6th	Right to confront witnesses	1965	*Pointer v. Texas*
6th	Right to impartial jury	1966	*Parker v. Gladden*
6th	Right to speedy trial	1967	*Klopfer v. North Carolina*
6th	Right to compel supportive witnesses to appear in court	1967	*Washington v. Texas*
6th	Right to jury trial for serious crimes	1968	*Duncan v. Louisiana*
6th	Right to counsel for all crimes involving jail terms	1972	*Argersinger v. Hamlin*
Amendments Partially Incorporated			
5th	Compensation for public taking of private property	1897	*Chicago, Burlington, and Quincy Railroad v. Chicago*
5th	No compulsory self-incrimination	1964	*Malloy v. Hogan*
5th	No forced confession	1964	*Escobedo v. Illinois*
5th	Right to remain silent	1966	*Miranda v. Arizona*
5th	No double jeopardy	1969	*Benton v. Maryland*
5th	Right to grand jury hearing in criminal cases	Not incorp.	
8th	No cruel and unusual punishment	1962	*Robinson v. California*
8th	No excessive bail or fines	Not incorp.	
Amendments Not Incorporated			
3rd	Limits on quartering of soldiers	Not incorp.	
7th	Right to jury trial in civil cases	Not incorp.	
7th	Facts determined in jury trials not reexamined on appeal	Not incorp.	

narrowly tailored solution). With non-fundamental rights—such as the right to be compensated when harmed by the actions of a business—the Supreme Court allows states more flexibility. For example, states have a wide range of laws regarding what happens in the case of medical malpractice, including when cases must be filed, the amount that a patient can receive in economic damages to replace lost wages, and whether payments for noneconomic damages ("pain and suffering") can be made. In between these two poles are issues such as abortion. The Court considers abortion in part a fundamental right because of its privacy aspects, but the Court has allowed restrictions on abortion access, so long as those restrictions do not create an "undue burden" on a woman's right to access abortion services. In practice, this approach has allowed a wide range of policies to exist from state to state that make access more difficult in some states than in others.

As mentioned earlier, the scope and reach of civil liberties protections have changed over time in three ways: the nationalization of civil liberties protections through the incorporation of the Bill of Rights, the Supreme Court and Congress developing new interpretations of what the Constitution requires and forbids, and the discovery of new rights in the Constitution. The following sections will examine the second of these three paths by exploring the changing scope of civil liberties protections in the areas of speech, freedom of religion, and rights of the accused.

prior restraint
government intervention to prevent the publication of material it finds objectionable.

5.1
5.2
5.3
5.4
5.5

Freedom of Speech

5.2 Analyze the different standards by which the Supreme Court has determined whether restrictions on freedom of speech are acceptable.

To Americans, freedom of speech is the most prized of all the rights guaranteed by the Constitution and perhaps the most definably *American* right. The freedom to speak one's mind is a hallmark of America's political and popular culture, though as we saw in chapter 2, Americans' general support for free speech can sometimes diminish when they are faced with specific situations. Tolerance for free speech can differ depending on which group is doing the speaking (see *Unresolved Debate: Does Knowledge Increase Tolerance?*). This section examines the changing scope of the free speech guarantee of the Constitution and also considers how governments, and particularly the U.S. Supreme Court, handle particular categories of speech such as obscenity.

Explore on MyPoliSciLab
Simulation: You Are a Police Officer

Government Can Attempt to Limit Speech Before and After its Utterance

Government may limit speech in two ways. **Prior restraint** refers to action that prevents speech from being uttered. This is censorship in its truest form: preventing certain speech from being expressed by requiring some kind of permission or pre-clearance from government that the content of the speech is acceptable or by simply forbidding the speech. Most often this kind of restraint has concerned the news media. The Supreme Court today is reluctant to tolerate restraint of this type. The Court first established its position in *Near v. Minnesota* (1931), when it struck down a Minnesota law that allowed government to prevent the publication of malicious material as a violation of the First Amendment. The most famous prior restraint case is *New York Times v. United States* (1971). The U.S. government attempted to prevent the newspaper from printing the "Pentagon Papers," a history of the Vietnam War based on State Department documents that had been leaked to the *Times* and the *Washington Post* by a former State Department official. Despite the government's argument that publishing the documents threatened national security, the Court agreed with the newspaper's contention that the public had a right to the information. Federal courts only rarely agree to prior restraint.

Government may also limit speech by treating it as a crime after it has been uttered. In practice, this can have the same censoring effect as prior restraint by deterring individuals from engaging in particular types of speech. One of the most controversial examples of this type of speech restriction concerns "hate speech." Hate speech emerged as a major concern on college campuses and in society more broadly in the 1990s. More than 300 institutions of higher education adopted speech codes that punished the use of derogatory speech based on group characteristics such as race, gender, and ethnicity.[17] Some cities did

Unresolved Debate

Does Knowledge Increase Tolerance?

Education builds cognitive skills, exposes students to diverse people and views, and increases the knowledge of democratic norms and processes, all of which have been cited as links to increased political tolerance—support for protecting the civil liberties of various groups. Does knowledge increase tolerance?

TWO PERSPECTIVES ON TOLERANCE

In 2010, the issue of locating an Islamic center and mosque near the site of the September 11, 2001 terrorist attacks in New York City rubbed raw emotions on both sides. Those arguing for the mosque argued that opponents needed to avoid punishing New York's Muslims for the acts of the 9/11 terrorists. Those arguing against the mosque argued that the mosque supporters needed to be more sensitive to how the location of the mosque affected the feelings of the families of those who lost their lives on 9/11.

YES

Political scientists Michael Delli Carpini and Scott Keeter asked survey respondents to answer five civil liberties knowledge items and to identify which of three groups they liked least (communists, atheists, or the Ku Klux Klan). They were then asked if they would allow someone from this group to make a speech locally or to teach in the public schools.[a]

- Respondents with 4 or 5 knowledge items correct were more tolerant than intolerant; respondents with fewer answers correct were more intolerant than tolerant.
- Political knowledge was a significant predictor of one's tolerance even when education was also included in the analysis as a predictor.
- Knowledge specifically about civil liberties and the Supreme Court is more important for building tolerance than is general political knowledge.

NO

Political scientist Donald Green and his colleagues randomly assigned over 1000 students in 59 high schools a supplementary civil liberties curriculum taught by teachers.[b] *Green et al. created indexes of students' civil liberties knowledge and civil liberties tolerance (their views on free speech, dissent, and due process).*

- Scores on the civil liberties knowledge and civil liberties tolerance indexes were highly correlated across all students.
- As measured in pre- and post-tests, students in the enhanced curriculum classes gained significantly more knowledge about civil liberties than students in the conventional classes.
- Tolerance, however, was unaffected by exposure to the curriculum. Despite the correlation between knowledge and tolerance, gaining knowledge about civil liberties in the enhanced curriculum did not lead to more tolerance.

CONTRIBUTING TO THE DEBATE

Numerous studies have shown a correlation between education, political knowledge, and tolerance, but pinning down the causal mechanisms among these items has proven difficult. Moving the debate forward will require scholars to examine other attributes from formal education, such as building cognitive skills and experiencing diverse viewpoints, to determine whether they rather than knowledge levels specifically, might have causal linkages to tolerance .

THINKING CRITICALLY

1. Should Americans always have the same level of tolerance for the civil liberties and free expression of all groups in society? Why or why not?
2. Increasing students' knowledge about civil liberties is not controversial, but efforts to teach them what they should think about civil liberties as a means to increase tolerance might be. Should schools avoid teaching students what they should think about civil liberties?

[a] Michael X. Delli Carpini and Scott Keeter, *What Americans Know About Politics and Why It Matters* (New Haven, CT: Yale University Press, 1996).

[b] Donald P. Green et al., "Does Knowledge of Constitutional Principles Increase Support for Civil Liberties? Results from a Randomized Field Experiment," *Journal of Politics* 73, 2 (2011): 463–76.

the same. In 1992, the Court considered a case in which a cross was burned on the lawn of a black family.[18] The defendant was charged under St. Paul, Minnesota's Bias Motivated Crime Ordinance, which prohibited the display of a symbol that was known to arouse "anger, alarm or resentment in others on the basis of race, color, creed, religion or gender." The Court struck down St. Paul's law, concluding that it violated the First Amendment by criminalizing speech based on a particular viewpoint. Hate speech cannot be considered a crime simply because of its hatefulness. The speech in question in this case was symbolic speech, rather than the actual utterance or writing of words. In recent decades, the Supreme Court has tended to consider symbolic speech and actual speech to be deserving of the same protection. The Court has also been generally protective of "speech plus"—the combination of speech and some activity such as picketing or a demonstration.[19]

A decade later, the Court refined its stance in *Virginia v. Black* (2003). The case concerned a Virginia law that prohibited cross burning on someone's property, along a highway, or in any public place "with the intent of intimidating any person or group." In its decision, the Court ruled that a state could constitutionally ban cross burning because of that symbol's historical use to intimidate and terrorize targeted groups. The fact that Virginia's law automatically *assumed* that the intent of cross burning was to intimidate, however, made that aspect of the law unconstitutional. Cross burning, even though hateful, is constitutionally protected if it is not designed to be intimidating and make particular targets fear for their safety. Following these Court decisions, some colleges included the equivalent of speech codes in more general codes of conduct.[20]

In 2011, the Supreme Court ruled on hateful speech toward gays and lesbians. The small Westboro Baptist Church, headed by the Reverend Fred Phelps, had made a habit of protesting at the funerals of members of the military. Using the funerals as an opportunity to say America was being punished for its sins, church members held signs and made statements alleging God's hatred for homosexuals and taunting families by seeming to

CROSS BURNING AND FREE SPEECH

In a 2002 decision, the Supreme Court declared that cross burning, even though hateful, was constitutionally protected free speech if it was not designed to be intimidating and make particular targets fear for their safety. In those instances, it would be protected as symbolic speech representing a point of view. If intimidating and making people fear for their safety were the intent, the cross burning would not be constitutionally protected speech. Should the same symbol be treated two different ways legally?

5.1

5.2

5.3

5.4

5.5

bad tendency standard
a free speech standard that took as its starting point a presumption that government restrictions on speech were reasonable and constitutional, thus leaving the burden of proof to those who objected to the restriction.

clear and present danger standard
used in free speech cases, this standard permitted government restrictions on speech if public officials believed that allowing the speech created a risk that some prohibited action would result.

revel in the death of soldiers. Albert Snyder, father of U.S. Marine Matthew Snyder who was killed in Iraq in 2006, sued the church for defamation, invasion of privacy, and infliction of emotional distress. Although successful at a lower level court, Snyder lost his case at the Supreme Court. In *Snyder v. Phelps* (2011), the Court ruled 8–1 that the church members were within their rights to make their hateful speech. Although Westboro Baptist's contribution to public discourse might be "negligible," the Court ruled that the church was commenting on matters of general public importance in a peaceful and lawful manner. Although the church's hateful words inflicted pain, Chief Justice John Roberts ruled in his opinion that "we cannot react to that pain by punishing the speaker."

The "Bad Tendency" Standard Assumes Government Restrictions on Speech Are Necessary

Over time, the Supreme Court has generally expanded the scope of free speech rights in the United States. The strongest test for freedom of speech may be the following: Can speech that appears to be supportive of criminal actions be tolerated? The Court often faces the need to balance free speech with social order. How has the Court handled this difficult question?

Until 1919, the Supreme Court was guided by the **bad tendency standard.** Using this standard, the Court sided with government, presuming that government restrictions on speech were reasonable unless proven otherwise. If certain acts were criminal, then speech that seemed to advocate such conduct—speech that had a "bad tendency"—was itself criminal. The burden, therefore, fell on the individual to demonstrate that the government's speech restriction was in some way unreasonable or that the speech in question was not actually supportive of illegal conduct. Convictions under this standard were frequent, particularly during World War I, when speech that might hinder the war effort was deemed a crime.[21] The government was not required to show under this standard that actual criminal conduct would occur, but rather that there was a bad tendency for the speech to produce that potential outcome.

The "Clear and Present Danger" Standard Makes It More Difficult for Government to Justify Restricting Speech

The **clear and present danger standard** replaced the bad tendency standard in 1919. Charles Schenck and Elizabeth Baer mailed pamphlets to men drafted to serve in World War I, arguing that the draft was motivated by the needs of Wall Street financial interests and was illegal. They encouraged draftees to "assert your rights" and "do not submit to intimidation" but did not advocate any violent or illegal activity, suggesting instead actions such as organizing petition drives to repeal the draft. The Espionage Act of 1917 prohibited actions that would cause insubordination in the military or would hinder recruiting. Schenck and Baer were found guilty of violating the Espionage Act and were sentenced to prison.

In *Schenck v. United States* (1919), the Supreme Court upheld the convictions. Although speech is technically not action, the Court concluded that it can effectively be the same thing. If speech brings about a "clear and present danger" that prohibited actions will take place, then that speech itself can be considered a criminal act. Chief Justice Oliver Wendell Holmes, writing for the Court, noted that speech that is constitutionally protected in one circumstance might not be protected in another. Holmes famously noted that "the most stringent protection of free speech would not protect a man in falsely shouting fire in a theatre and causing a panic." In *Schenck*, the distinction between wartime and peacetime was key. Words could be prohibited under this new standard if there were a clear and present danger that would encourage the kinds of actions that government is constitutionally authorized to prevent—for example, actions that hinder the war effort. Holmes's argument paralleled public thinking, which has also varied in its support for restrictions on speech and civil liberties during times of war and peace (see *How Do We Know? Does Concern for National Security Lead to Public Support for Civil Liberties Restrictions?*). The clear and present danger standard was more demanding on government, in that

THE LIBERTY-SECURITY TRADE-OFF
After 9/11, Americans grew used to enhanced security procedures at the nation's airports. Here, a Transportation Security Administration agent screens a passenger at O'Hare Airport in Chicago.

How Do We Know?

Does Concern for National Security Lead to Public Support for Civil Liberties Restrictions?

The Question

American political culture includes a strong belief in liberty—at least in the abstract. Public opinion polls consistently show high levels of support among the American public for basic civil liberties principles. But support can plummet when individuals feel threatened by certain ideas or lifestyles or are worried about their physical security.[a] Following the terrorist attacks of September 11, 2001, Americans indicated greater support for measures that infringed on civil liberties. Does concern for national security lead to more public support of civil liberties protections? How do we know?

Why It Matters

Extensive protection for civil liberties is a central part of the American experiment in democracy. To most Americans, freedom is synonymous with civil liberties. Therefore, it is critical to understand when civil liberties can be restricted and for what reason. Civil liberties restrictions are particularly likely during wartime, but when war ends or ebbs, those restrictions are eventually repealed, overturned by the courts, or weakened substantially.[b] For this reason, many observers are concerned about current restrictions on civil liberties as the country battles terrorism. Unlike traditional war, the conclusion of this conflict—because of the very nature of terrorism—will be difficult to define.

Investigating the Answer

Americans' commitment to civil liberties appears to weaken—alarmingly—when put to the test in specific cases. Using public opinion research, one study of public attitudes after September 11, 2001, considered a number of possible factors that might explain an individual's level of support for civil liberties. The researchers found that the greater the perceived sense of threat to oneself or to the country, the more willing individuals were to sacrifice civil liberties. Trust in government played an important role also. Regardless of whether people perceived a great or modest terrorist threat, people with less trust of government were less willing to give government additional power to reduce civil liberties. People who were more trusting toward government were more willing to make the trade-off.[c] In a related issue, some scholarly experiments have found that individuals who express intolerant attitudes are more likely to act on those attitudes, and those who are more tolerant are quicker to abandon their tolerance when they confront a competing value such as security. Another study, however, found that individuals motivated by concerns of security and order become more tolerant toward groups seen as extreme when a civil liberties case for free speech is made.[d]

The USA PATRIOT Act (the Uniting and Strengthening America by Providing Appropriate Tools Required to Intercept and Obstruct Terrorism Act, more typically referred to as the Patriot Act) instituted after the 2001 terrorist attacks, enabled the government to engage in searches and investigations without the judicial approval typically required for other investigations.[e] It was the focus of sustained opposition by groups such as the American Civil Liberties Union, and a handful of states and more than 100 cities, towns, and counties voted not to cooperate with any provisions of the Patriot Act that officials believed violated civil liberties or civil rights. Over time, public support for the act diminished, even as support for some of the investigatory activities that it authorized—stronger document and physical security checks for travelers, expanded

Restrictions on Liberties that Received Passive Support

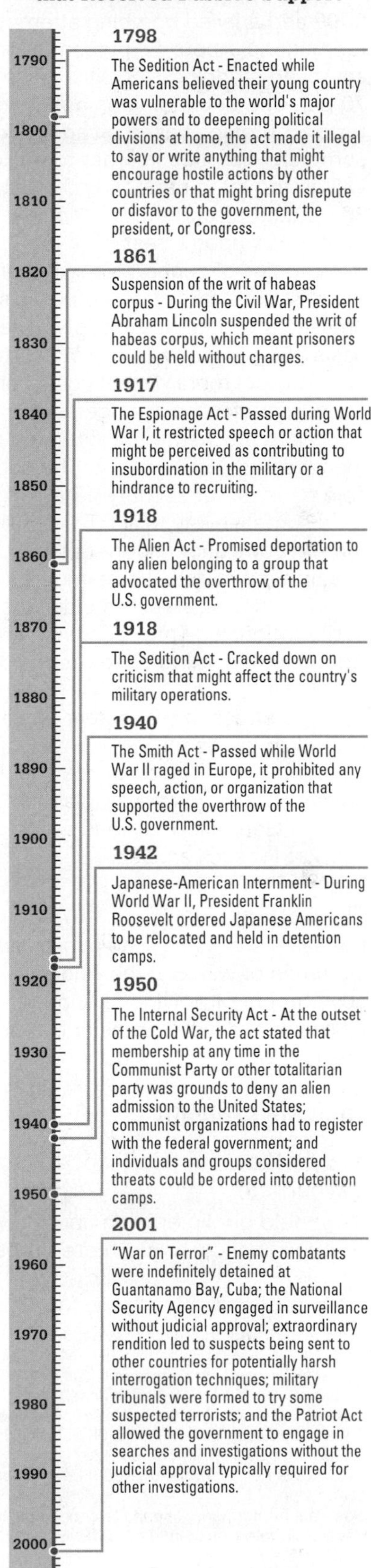

1790
1800
1810
1820
1830
1840
1850
1860
1870
1880
1890
1900
1910
1920
1930
1940
1950
1960
1970
1980
1990
2000
1798
The Sedition Act - Enacted while Americans believed their young country was vulnerable to the world's major powers and to deepening political divisions at home, the act made it illegal to say or write anything that might encourage hostile actions by other countries or that might bring disrepute or disfavor to the government, the president, or Congress.
1861
Suspension of the writ of habeas corpus - During the Civil War, President Abraham Lincoln suspended the writ of habeas corpus, which meant prisoners could be held without charges.
1917
The Espionage Act - Passed during World War I, it restricted speech or action that might be perceived as contributing to insubordination in the military or a hindrance to recruiting.
1918
The Alien Act - Promised deportation to any alien belonging to a group that advocated the overthrow of the U.S. government.
1918
The Sedition Act - Cracked down on criticism that might affect the country's military operations.
1940
The Smith Act - Passed while World War II raged in Europe, it prohibited any speech, action, or organization that supported the overthrow of the U.S. government.
1942
Japanese-American Internment - During World War II, President Franklin Roosevelt ordered Japanese Americans to be relocated and held in detention camps.
1950
The Internal Security Act - At the outset of the Cold War, the act stated that membership at any time in the Communist Party or other totalitarian party was grounds to deny an alien admission to the United States; communist organizations had to register with the federal government; and individuals and groups considered threats could be ordered into detention camps.
2001
"War on Terror" - Enemy combatants were indefinitely detained at Guantanamo Bay, Cuba; the National Security Agency engaged in surveillance without judicial approval; extraordinary rendition led to suspects being sent to other countries for potentially harsh interrogation techniques; military tribunals were formed to try some suspected terrorists; and the Patriot Act allowed the government to engage in searches and investigations without the judicial approval typically required for other investigations.

---

[a] Herbert McClosky and Alida Brill, *Dimensions of Political Tolerance: What Americans Believe About Civil Liberties* (New York: Russell Sage, 1983), 203; Herbert McClosky and John Zaller, *The American Ethos: Public Attitudes Toward Capitalism and Democracy* (Cambridge, MA: Harvard University Press, 1984), 25, 37, 38, 74, 75; Pew Center for the People and the Press surveys.

[b] See Geoffrey R. Stone, *Perilous Times: Free Speech in Wartime from the Sedition Act of 1798 to the War on Terrorism* (New York: W. W. Norton, 2004).

[c] Darren W. Davis and Brian D. Silver, "Civil Liberties vs. Security: Public Opinion in the Context of the Terrorist Attacks on America," *American Journal of Political Science* 48, 1 (2004): 28–46. See also Cindy D. Kam and Donald R. Kinder, "Terror and Ethnocentrism: Foundations of American Support for the War on Terrorism," *Journal of Politics* 69, 2 (2007): 320–38.

[d] George E. Marcus, John L. Sullivan, Elizabeth Theiss-Morse, and Sandra L. Wood, *With Malice toward Some: How People Make Civil Liberties Judgments* (New York: Cambridge University Press, 1995); Mark Peffley, Pia Knigge, and Jon Hurwitz, [first names available per style?] "A Multiple Values Model of Political Tolerance," *Political Research Quarterly* 54 (2001): 379–406; Claudia Zilli Ramirez and Maykel Verkuyten, "Values, Media Framing, and Political Tolerance for Extremist Groups," *Journal of Applied Social Psychology* 41, 7 (2011): 1583–1602.

[e] Controversial provisions of the Patriot Act can be viewed at the following websites: http://www.npr.org/news/specials/patriotact/patriotactdeal.html And http://www.aclu.org/reform-patriot-act

undercover activities to investigate suspicious groups, closer monitoring of banking and credit card transactions, expanded camera surveillance on streets and public places, and monitoring of Internet chat rooms and other forums—still retained majority support. In times of uneasiness, Americans tend to tilt the scales more toward security and somewhat away from liberty.[f] With some revisions, both President Bush and President Obama signed extensions of the Patriot Act into law.

Following some failed terrorist episodes in recent years—an unsuccessful attempted Christmas Day airline bombing in 2009 and a failed bombing attempt in New York City's Times Square in 2010—Americans were more receptive to civil liberties restrictions. About 70 percent approved the increased use of surveillance cameras in public places. The same percentage approved stripping U.S. citizenship from individuals "who support or affiliate with terrorist groups." Anywhere from 50 to 70 percent, depending on question wording and the date of the survey, supported extra scrutiny of airline passengers who fit terrorist profiles based on age, sex, and ethnicity. When asked in January 2010, "do you think that it is necessary to give up some civil liberties in order to make the country safe from terrorism, or [do you think] some of the government's proposals will go too far in restricting the public's civil liberties?" 51 percent believed it was necessary to sacrifice some liberties, while 36 percent disagreed. On the other hand, modest to strong majorities of Americans thought terror suspects should be read their rights upon arrest.[g]

Studies of support for civil liberties show that the manner in which an issue is framed—whether it is free speech or security at stake—can influence public support for civil liberties.[h] For example, in 2005, whereas only 29 percent of the public expressed a willingness to allow government to monitor telephone calls and e-mail messages of "ordinary Americans on a regular basis," 56 percent would allow such monitoring of "Americans that the government is suspicious of." Similarly, as the events of 9/11 grew more distant across time, a growing majority of Americans from 2003 through 2009 rejected the idea that it was "necessary for the average person to give up some civil liberties" to combat terrorism.[i]

What if government instituted restrictions on civil liberties with the rationale that war or other international threats demanded such action? Given the public's fears of terrorism, might people simply view these initiatives passively, as an acceptable trade-off for security? They might. Absent an intensely hostile public attitude against civil liberties restrictions, politicians have some leeway to act. The correlation between public support for civil liberties restrictions and public policy might be just that—a correlation, not necessarily a causal link from beliefs to policy. The public may not cause politicians to restrict civil liberties, but it may tolerate restrictions when they happen.[j]

The historical record indicates that the public may well be willing to sacrifice some liberty if it is given a convincing security rationale.[k] Throughout American history, particularly when the national government feared war or foreign disruption of American life, it imposed restrictions on civil liberties that usually received at least passive support from large segments of the public.

The stress of war or fear of war led Americans to distinguish between their abstract preference for civil liberties and their perceived needs for the country's safety under specific circumstances.[l] Certainly support was not unanimous, as these actions did arouse determined opposition. But overall the public tolerated restrictions that seemed to fit a particular context. If public opinion polling were available during World War I, for example, it might have shown strong support for government investigations of German Americans based on their ethnic background; asking that same question today would likely provoke very little support for such an idea.

The Bottom Line

Research shows that the public certainly is willing to veer from its general principles in support of civil liberties, especially during times of war. But the evidence suggests it is more likely that public opinion responds to restrictive actions taken by the government or provides a supportive environment for governmental actions rather than directly causing those actions. The significance of difficult times or events in prompting public support for restrictions suggests that the support is likely to fade as the precipitating concerns became a more distant memory.

Thinking Critically

- What level of detail about security threats should government officials provide to justify a restriction on civil liberties?
- Should public opinion about civil liberties always be taken into account by government officials when they are crafting public policy, or are there times when the public's view should not be relevant to policy makers?

---

[f]Harris Poll, 1,015 adults nationwide, June 7–12, 2005, and September 19–24, 2001.

[g]FOX News/Opinion Dynamics Poll, May 18–19, 2010, 900 registered voters nationwide; FOX News/Opinion Dynamics Poll, May 4–5, 2010, 900 registered voters nationwide; Ipsos/McClatchy Poll, January 7–11, 2010, 1,336 adults nationwide; *USA Today*/Gallup Poll, January 8–10, 2010, 1,023 adults nationwide; CBS News Poll, January 6–10, 2010, 1,216 adults nationwide.

[h]For example, see Thomas E. Nelson, Rosalee A. Clawson, and Zoe M. Oxley, "Media Framing of a Civil Liberties Conflict and Its Effect on Tolerance," *American Political Science Review* 91, 3 (1997): 567–83; W. Kip Viscusi and Richard J. Zeckhauser, "Sacrificing Civil Liberties to Reduce Terrorism Risks," *Journal of Risk and Uncertainty* 26, 2–3 (2003): 99–120.

[i]CBS News Poll, April 13–16, 2005; Pew Research Center survey, May 21, 2009, http://people-press.org/reports/questionnaires/517.pdf, question Q33F1, 1,492 adults nationwide.

[j]See Paul Sniderman, Joseph Fletcher, Peter H. Russell, and Philip E. Tetlock, *The Clash of Rights: Liberty, Equality, and Legitimacy in Pluralist Democracy* (New Haven, CT: Yale University Press, 1996); and Robert W. Jackman, "Political Elites, Mass Publics, and Support for Democratic Principles," *Journal of Politics* 54, 3 (1992): 753–73.

[k]George E. Marcus, John L. Sullivan, and Elizabeth Theiss-Morse, *With Malice Toward Some: How People Make Civil Liberties Judgments* (New York: Cambridge University Press, 1995); John L. Sullivan and Henriet Hendriks, "Public Support for Civil Liberties Pre- and Post-9/11," *Annual Review of Law and Social Science* 5 (2009):375–91; Jeffery J. Mondak and Jon Hurwitz, "Examining the Terror Exception: Terrorism and Commitments to Civil Liberties," *Public Opinion Quarterly* 2012 [note: does not yet have pagination info, only online so far].

[l]Researchers can infer support for these measures from public opinion surveys or, for times prior to polling, letters in newspapers, election results, and policy statements by organized groups with large memberships.

speech that had only a bad tendency to produce illegal outcomes was not sufficient for a conviction. Nonetheless, convictions for speech remained common under this standard.

gravity of the danger standard
a free speech standard in which the Supreme Court allowed restrictions on speech if the danger espoused by the speech was sufficiently evil, even if that evil was unlikely to occur.

The "Gravity of the Danger" Standard Allows Restrictions on Speech if Its Subject Matter Is Sufficiently "Evil"

Schenck guided Court decisions until the late 1960s, but through the 1950s and 1960s, clear and present danger proved less useful as a standard as every word—*clear, and, present, danger*—was up for debate and interpreted with great variation around the country.[22] The Court turned then to the **gravity of the danger standard.** Here, the Court asserted it would consider the potential "evil" advocated by someone's speech when deciding whether government could punish that speech.[23] *Dennis v. United States* (1951)—the case introducing this standard—concerned the Smith Act, which made it illegal to advocate overthrowing the U.S. government by force. Leaders of the Communist Party of America had been arrested under the Smith Act for such advocacy. Although these attempts were highly unlikely to be

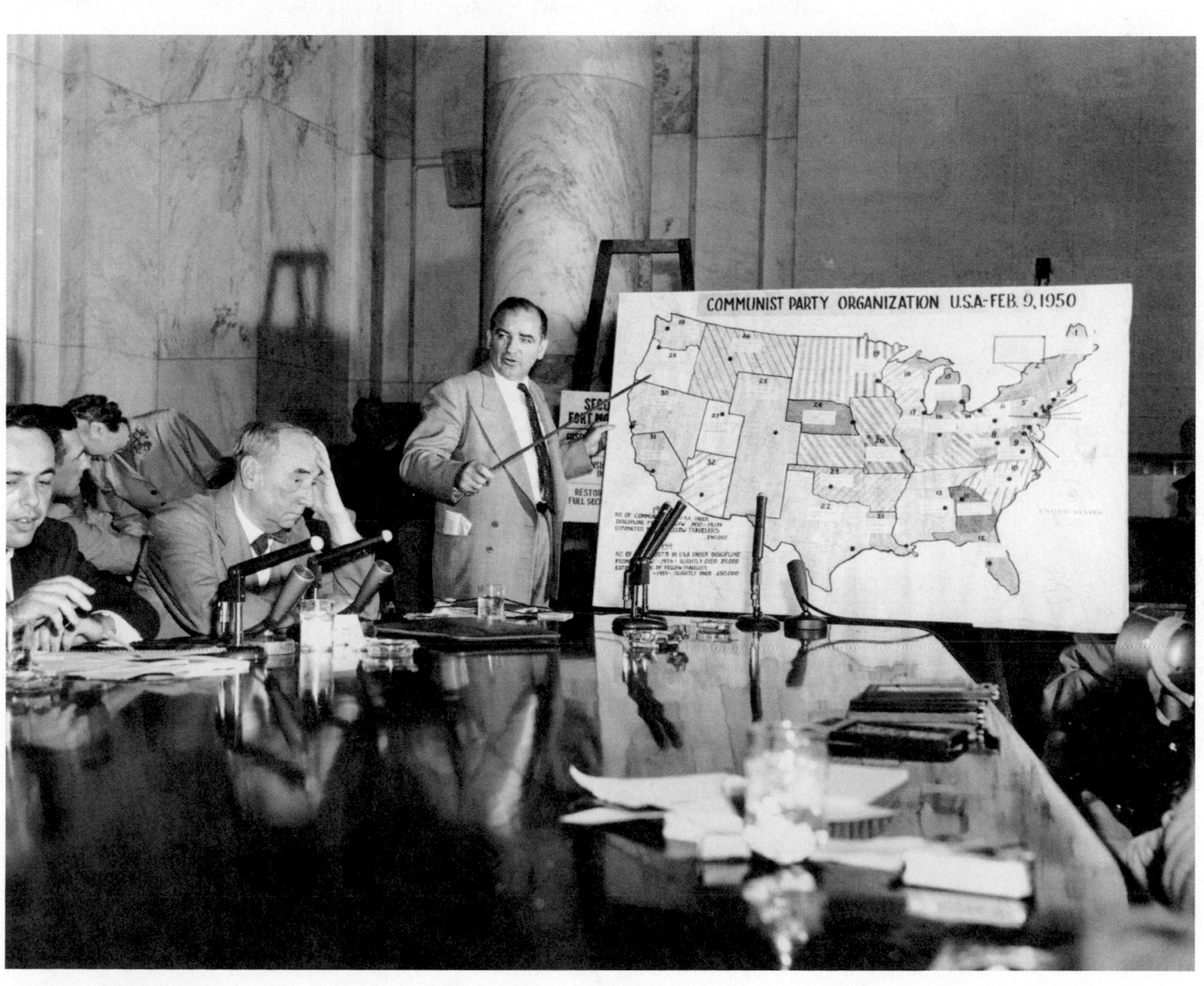

SENATOR JOSEPH MCCARTHY TESTIFIES ON COMMUNIST ACTIVITY IN THE UNITED STATES, 1950

Although his investigations raised cries of outraged opposition and complaints about their effects on individuals' livelihoods, fear of communism led many Americans to support investigations such as that by Senator McCarthy. A number of states passed restrictions or penalties on communist political activity. The federal courts frequently upheld these policies, concluding that the evil of communism was so great that it could be controlled even if its political success was highly unlikely.

5.1

5.2

5.3

5.4

5.5

preferred position
the idea, endorsed by the Supreme Court, that protections of First Amendment rights predominates over other rights.

successful, and thus the clear and present danger was low, the Court approved the convictions, using the gravity of the danger standard. If the evil of the potential outcome from speech—in this case, the overthrow of the government—was great enough, the improbability of its actually happening need not deter government from restricting it. In the Court's view, Communist Party leaders advocating the overthrow of the U.S. government was a profound evil, and, despite the fact that the Communist Party was unlikely to be successful, government could limit this advocacy without violating the First Amendment. On the other hand, something that posed a danger, but of a lesser significance, would need a higher level of probability of its happening for government to restrict it. For example, a community ordinance prohibiting individuals from distributing literature from door to door simply because homeowners might find these individuals to be a nuisance would violate the First Amendment. The probability of the evil—namely, citizens being annoyed—might be extremely high, but the gravity of that evil would be relatively trivial; therefore, the speech must be permitted.[24]

Throughout the 1950s and 1960s, the Supreme Court used the gravity of the danger standard to evaluate convictions based on individuals' membership in groups deemed dangerous by a government entity. Given the Cold War era in which the standard emerged, government actions against individuals with communist affiliations were especially likely to be upheld.[25]

The "Preferred Position" Standard Presumes the Unreasonableness of Restrictions on Speech

Change in membership on the Court in the 1960s led to the strongest support yet for the protection of free speech rights and abandonment of the gravity of the danger standard. The Court had maintained for decades that the First Amendment and its protection for freedom of speech, the press, and religion held a "preferred position" among the amendments.[26] A **preferred position** means that First Amendment freedoms should be abridged only with great reluctance, and that if these freedoms conflict with other rights, the First Amendment protections, such as free speech, should prevail. But only in the late 1960s, in *Brandenburg v. Ohio* (1969), did the Court explicitly adopt preferred position—also referred to as *absolutism*—as its primary free speech standard.

Clarence Brandenburg, a speaker at a Ku Klux Klan rally in 1964, was convicted under an Ohio law—similar to laws in many states—that made it illegal to advocate "crime, sabotage, violence, or unlawful methods of terrorism as a means of accomplishing industrial or political reform" or to assemble with those who promote criminal behavior in the pursuit of political or economic reform. The Court concluded in a unanimous decision that Ohio's law was unconstitutional. The decision established a two-part rule to determine whether speech acts could be considered criminal: First, was the speech "directed at inciting or producing imminent lawless action"? Second, was the speech "likely to incite or produce such action"? If the answer was yes to both, then government could restrict the speech. The Court concluded that the Ohio law ignored the second part of this test: The law focused on the advocacy of lawless action, but it did not address whether such advocacy would actually incite lawless action. The state of Ohio could not simply ban speech for advocating lawless acts. Given the preferred position of free speech, unless a speech was extremely likely to *produce* immediate lawless behavior, it could not be restricted or considered illegal itself.

With its strong statement in *Brandenburg*, the Court effectively reversed the burden of proof in free speech cases. Under the bad tendency standard, prior to 1919, it was up to the individual charged with a crime related to speech to prove that a governmental restriction on speech was unreasonable. Under the clear and present danger standard and the gravity of the danger standard, up through the 1960s, the Court pushed more of the burden toward government. And with the preferred position standard, which remains in effect today, the Court moved to a benchmark that assumes that government restrictions on speech are likely to be inherently unreasonable. Government now has the burden to show, through a stringent two-part test, that limiting speech is necessary and desirable.

The Supreme Court Determines Which Categories of Speech Merit Constitutional Protection and Which Do Not

The Supreme Court has determined that some categories of speech do not merit constitutional protection. These include fighting words, defamation, commercial speech, student speech by minors, and obscenity. Fighting words or inflammatory words that create an immediate threat to public safety are not constitutionally protected.[27] The person who uses such words could be validly charged with disturbing the peace. Defamation means speaking (slander) or writing (libel) a false statement that is heard or read by a third party and harms the target's reputation.[28] For public figures—public officials and others, such as celebrities who are frequently in the public's attention—defamation also requires that the person who spoke or wrote the offensive words did so knowing they were false.[29]

Commercial speech has gained growing protection from the courts, as it, like political speech, transmits information. In 2011, the Supreme Court struck down a Vermont law that prohibited pharmaceutical companies from marketing to doctors based on the doctors' histories of prescription writing. The fact that these marketing efforts might persuade doctors to prescribe the marketed drugs was not an acceptable reason for the state to prohibit the marketing, and neither was the possibility that doctors might find the marketing to be bothersome. Unlike political speech, however, the government can regulate commercial speech to be sure it is accurate and not misleading.[30]

Minors have generally not been accorded the same speech rights as adults, but that is not the same as being without rights, as the Court noted in *Tinker v. Des Moines* (1969) when it declared that "students do not shed their constitutional rights . . . at the schoolhouse gate." Striking down a federal law in 2010, the Supreme Court declined to add depictions of animal cruelty as another area of speech that did not merit First Amendment protection. Doing so would have been the first category of speech the Court added to the list of categories unprotected by the First Amendment since child pornography was added in 1982.[31]

Governments at all levels have passed numerous laws attempting to thwart the distribution of obscene materials, and challenges to these laws have generated a lengthy trail of court decisions. In *Roth v. United States* (1957), the Supreme Court defined as obscene any material whose "dominant theme" appealed to the "prurient interest" of an "average person, applying contemporary community standards." The *Roth* test proved difficult for the Court to apply in subsequent cases, and different justices interpreted its various words in different ways. Most famously, Justice Potter Stewart in a 1964 case leaned toward an interpretation that only "hard-core pornography" was not constitutionally protected speech, but even there he noted that although he could not easily define hard-core pornography, "I know it when I see it, and the motion picture involved in this case is not that."[32]

Overall, the *Roth* ruling made it easier for sexually oriented materials to be distributed than had been true previously, and *Memoirs v. Massachusetts* (1966) furthered this trend. In this case, a plurality of the Court held that unless material depicted sexual conduct in a way that was "patently offensive" and "utterly without redeeming social value," it was constitutionally protected. By the time of its decision in *Miller v. California* (1973), the Court had split into two camps, a majority of five that wanted more flexibility for governments to restrict the distribution of obscene materials, and a minority of four that was inclined to allow the distribution of these materials in most instances, so long as the recipient was not a minor. The

Court's ruling revised the definition of obscenity and, in the process, made it easier for governments to clamp down on materials deemed obscene. The ruling retained the "community standards" provision from *Roth*, the "patently offensive" provision from *Memoirs*, and added that to be obscene and not constitutionally protected (and thus subject to government restrictions) a work also must have no serious literary, artistic, political, or scientific value. These criteria increased the range of materials governments could potentially restrict—for example, it could be simpler for a government to show that material had no "serious" value as opposed to it being "utterly without redeeming social value." The ruling made regulation of adult bookstores, movie theaters, and nude dancing (as a symbolic form of speech) more likely to be upheld as constitutional.[33] State efforts to shoehorn other kinds of speech under the obscenity category have been less successful. The Court struck down a California law prohibiting the sale or rental of violent video games in *Brown v. Entertainment Merchants Association* (2011), with the lead opinion by Justice Antonin Scalia noting that the obscenity category referred to sexual conduct and not other types of potentially disagreeable or controversial speech.

Controlling the spread of obscene materials provides a test of the Supreme Court's impact on political outcomes and on society—known to political scientists as judicial impact studies. The question is twofold: Did a Court ruling prompt elected officials to take new actions? And did the ruling prompt major societal changes? The impact produces four possible outcomes that political scientists can analyze: (1) no new actions taken and no societal changes occur; (2) new actions taken but societal changes do not occur; (3) no new actions taken but societal changes occur; and (4) new actions taken and societal changes occur.

The Communications Decency Act (CDA) of 1996 prohibited making available to minors online any obscene or indecent material that shows or describes "sexual or excretory activities or organs" in a way that would be considered offensive by community standards. The act launched a causal chain reaction common in civil liberties cases. Responding to the CDA, the Supreme Court in 1997 declared the law to be an unconstitutional limit on free speech.[34] Including "indecent" materials, the Court ruled, made the law overly broad, not narrowly tailored, and intruded too far on the speech rights of adults—the Court ruling distinguished between indecency, which it deemed constitutionally protected, and obscenity, which is not. Congress responded with the Children's Online Protection Act of 1998 (COPA), which required websites to provide age-verification systems (for example, providing credit card information) to keep harmful content from minors. Dissatisfied, the Court in *Ashcroft v. American Civil Liberties Union* (2004) suspended enforcement of the act unless Congress could demonstrate that there were no other methods available to achieve its goals that would be less intrusive on personal privacy. In between COPA and *Ashcroft*, Congress passed the Children's Internet Protection Act of 2000, which required public libraries that received federal funds to install filtering software on their publicly accessible computers. The Supreme Court in 2003 upheld the law, concluding that it did not violate patrons' First Amendment rights.[35]

So what was the judicial impact of these rulings? Overall, we do see the Court prompting action by elected officials, the first test of judicial impact studies. But what about societal change, the second test? Here, the outcome is murkier. Few would declare that the spread of obscene materials on the Web has declined or that it is significantly difficult for minors to access them. In that sense, the Court did not have a societal impact. And certainly the Court is not always attempting to change society. The justices in the majority in these decisions might argue that their job is not to stop the spread of obscenity in society per se, but to make sure that government attempts to do so do not violate other individual rights. Other decisions might arguably lead more directly to societal change—the classic example is *Brown v. Board of Education* (1954), which upended laws that required racial segregation in public schools—although these decisions may be influenced by prior changes in society as well. *Brown* may have changed society, but previous changes in society might also have led the way for the Court to issue its decision in *Brown*.

The legal treatment of pornography has varied across countries. One particularly interesting case is Canada. Rather than following the U.S. model, which places individual freedom of expression at its core, Canada takes a communitarian approach. Although the 1982 Canadian Charter of Rights and Responsibilities guarantees protection of free speech, the protection is qualified by the need to promote gender equality and to consider what should be acceptable in a democratic society. In a key case, the Canadian Court rejected a challenge to Canada's criminalization of the possession and distribution of obscene materials. The Canadian Court concluded that degrading materials that place women in subordinate, servile, or humiliating positions violate principles of equal human dignity. This type of material, the Canadian Court ruled, would be prohibited not for moral reasons, but because public opinion considers it harmful to the community.[36]

establishment clause
a clause in the First Amendment that prevents government from establishing an official religion, treating one religion preferably to another, proselytizing, or promoting religion over non-religion.

free exercise clause
a clause in the First Amendment that prohibits government from interfering with individuals' practice of their religion.

Freedom of Religion

5.3 Evaluate how the Supreme Court has interpreted cases regarding religion and how Congress has reacted to the Court's actions.

As with speech, the First Amendment sets out the Constitution's basic principles regarding freedom of religion.[37] The amendment states, "Congress shall make no law respecting an establishment of religion, or prohibiting the free exercise thereof." "Respecting an establishment of religion" is referred to as the **establishment clause.** Government must not designate any official religion; appear to embrace some religions at the expense of others; become involved in religious teaching; or, as interpreted by some scholars and justices, favor religion over non-religion. "Prohibiting the free exercise thereof" is referred to as the **free exercise clause**. This clause declares that government should not interfere with the individual practice of religious beliefs. Because of incorporation, the establishment and free exercise clauses also apply to the states.

As with speech, the Supreme Court has not interpreted the seemingly unconditional text of the First Amendment to mean that there can be no restrictions on religious freedom. And regulating church–state relations also follows the example of speech in that over time, the courts have altered the scope of the right to freedom of religion. What Americans would now consider to be violations of religious freedom, such as official churches, religious oaths of office, and voting restrictions based on religious identity, were common from the colonial era through the 1960s. Evangelical Christians, members of nontraditional denominations, and individuals whose worldview was guided more by science and reason were particularly active in urging church-state separation, and the Constitution represented a victory for these groups.[38]

Even though the U.S. Constitution avoids references to specific religions, and an early treaty declared that the United States was not founded specifically upon Christianity, Supreme Court decisions sometimes referred to the United States as a Christian nation.[39] Prior to the nationalization of the Bill of Rights, officeholders in some states took religious oaths prior to holding office, and laws prohibited nonbelievers and members of specific religions, most commonly Catholics and Jews, from holding public office. In other states, attending Catholic parochial school was illegal. Government intrusion into religious practice and some forms of establishment did not simply disappear after the colonial era.

The U.S. Constitution is not alone in discussing religion. Most—other democracies around the world, whose constitutions are newer than America's, also incorporate provisions for freedom of religious expression. Some democracies, such as Denmark and Greece, have official churches but also provide for free religious expression. And some constitutions, for example those of Italy and Poland, detail the relationship between the government and the major church in the country, the Catholic Church in both instances.[40]

5.1

5.2

5.3

5.4

5.5

***Lemon* test**
a three-part establishment clause test used by the Supreme Court that states that to be constitutional, a governmental action must have a plausible nonreligious purpose; its primary or principal effect must be to neither advance nor inhibit religion; and it must not foster excessive government entanglement with religion.

Establishment Clause Cases Have Been Decided Using the *Lemon* Test

The ***Lemon* test** provides the U.S. Supreme Court's current standard on establishment clause issues. Drawn from its decision in *Lemon v. Kurtzman* (1971), the Court considered laws in Pennsylvania and Rhode Island that provided materials and financial support to teachers of nonreligious subjects in private schools, including schools affiliated with churches and other houses of worship. In this ruling, the Court used standards from previous cases and applied a three-part test to determine whether a governmental action was permissible. First, the law or action must have a plausible secular—that is, nonreligious—purpose. Second, its primary effect must not be to either advance or inhibit religion. Third, it must not foster "excessive government entanglement with religion." A law or action violating any of these three precepts would be considered unconstitutional under this test. Regarding the Pennsylvania and Rhode Island laws, the Court concluded that providing financial subsidies to private religious schools for nonreligious subject instruction excessively entangled government and religion and was therefore unconstitutional. Because these were religious schools, the Court was concerned that the need for ongoing government surveillance of church financial records involved government too intimately in church affairs.

RELAXATION OF THE *LEMON* TEST The *Lemon* test continues to guide establishment clause decisions, but the Court has relaxed its understanding of what is allowable. For example, in 1985, the Court considered New York's deployment of public school remedial education teachers to parochial schools to be in violation of the establishment clause because of excessive entanglement.[41] In *Agostini v. Felton* (1997), however, the Court directly overturned this decision and concluded that New York's program was constitutional. The Court majority did not discard the *Lemon* test but noted that its view toward "excessive entanglement" had begun to shift over the previous decade—it no longer considered the "pervasive monitoring" of teachers to be necessary to avoid excessive entanglement. If a teacher acted inappropriately, then a case could be brought in that individual instance. Moreover, the Court no longer assumed that receiving government funds necessarily reduced the independence of the religiously oriented school. In both these respects, the Court moved away from assuming that extensive interactions between church and state necessarily led to entanglements that either promoted religion or harmed it.

Another sign of the Court's more lenient view toward establishment clause cases appeared in its 2002 decision regarding educational vouchers in *Zelman v. Simmons-Harris*. Vouchers are public funds that provide parents or guardians with a stipend to use for a child's tuition at a private school. One such program provided need-based assistance to parents in the Cleveland school district. Parents could use the vouchers to enroll their children in any one of a range of private schools, but 90 percent of the funds were used to send children to religious schools. The Court, by a narrow 5–4 vote, concluded that the program was intended to increase educational opportunity and choice and did not constitute establishment of religion. The program was secular on its face, and if parents used the funds to send their children to religious schools, that was their decision, not the government's.

ISSUES TESTING THE ESTABLISHMENT CLAUSE Two important issues that test the establishment clause are school prayer and public religious displays. In a long line of cases starting with the landmark decisions in *Engel v. Vitale* (1962) and *Abington School District v. Schempp* (1963), the Court has ruled that an official prayer (*Engel*) or public school prayers or similar activities such as Bible readings constitute establishment of religion (*Abington*), if they rely on public resources or imply the sponsorship or endorsement of the school. The Court has disallowed prayer time in classrooms, classroom Bible reading exercises, prayers delivered at graduation events, and student-initiated and student-led prayers at sporting events.[42] Individual student decisions such as wearing religious symbols to public school or praying privately while in school are not considered establishment.

Evaluating a religious display in 2005, the Court concluded by a 5–4 vote that a Ten Commandments display in Austin, Texas, was constitutional because it had a valid secular purpose, was part of a large number of statues, and had been on display for more than 40 years without complaint that it was advocating a particular religion. It determined in a separate case on the same day that a courthouse display in Kentucky was unconstitutional because it had clearer religious intent, had been posted initially in courtrooms without any other historical documents, and was modified later only after complaints were lodged by the American Civil Liberties Union.[43] A unanimous 2009 Court decision, *Pleasant Grove City v. Summum,* clarified that governments are not required to accommodate every religious group wishing to add a religious symbol to a public display. The city of Pleasant Grove, Utah, had placed a privately donated monument of the Ten Commandments in Pioneer Park, where it stood with 10 nonreligious, privately donated monuments. The Summum church argued that it, too, should be able to install a similarly sized monument, but the city denied the request, stating that its policy was to accept only monuments that concerned the city's history or that came from organizations with long-standing community ties. Justice Samuel Alito, the author of the Court's ruling, drew a distinction between monuments, which take on different meanings over time because of their permanence and history and become part of a community, and nonpermanent displays that use a public forum (such as a park) for a short time. The government is allowed to engage in speech when it accepts a monument, Alito determined—when the United States received the Statue of Liberty from France, he noted, it was not obliged to also add a Statue of Autocracy. In 2011, Justice Clarence Thomas, unhappy that the Court had chosen not to accept a case concerning the private placement of crosses along highways in Utah where state police officers had died, argued that the Court's rulings on religious symbols had "rendered the constitutionality of displays of religious imagery on government property anyone's guess."[44]

The placement of religious symbols in public places has stirred controversy in other countries as well. In 1991, parents of elementary school children challenged a Bavarian law that required a crucifix to be placed in every public school. Based on Germany's constitution, the Basic Law, which declares freedom of faith to be "inviolable," the parents successfully argued that the Christian crucifix infringed on their religious freedom. In the justices' view, religious freedom demanded that government be neutral in matters of faith, especially because students were mandated to be in school.[45] In 2004, France banned students from wearing "conspicuous" religious symbols in public schools. Prohibited items include Muslim veils or headscarves, Sikh turbans, Jewish yarmulkes, and Christian crucifixes. By contrast, U.S. federal courts have made it clear that students must be allowed to wear religious symbols to school. In 2011, France went further by banning face-covering Islamic veils in all public places, because of concerns about security and the effect of the veils on French identity. During the first year, about 500 women wearing the veils were fined or received warnings. The wearing of the veils has become a controversial issue in many European countries. France was the first to institute such a ban, followed soon after by Belgium.[46]

The Balancing Standard Carves Out a Zone of Protection for Religious Free Expression

In addition to prohibiting any establishment of religion, the First Amendment also guarantees the free exercise of religion. Are restrictions on free exercise ever permissible? If so, when and why? As with establishment cases, the Court has answered these questions with standards that it then applied to subsequent cases. From 1963 through 1990, the Court relied on the **balancing test,** introduced in *Sherbert v. Verner* (1963). Adeil Sherbert, a Seventh-day Adventist, lost her job when she refused to work on Saturday, her Sabbath Day. After she was unable to find other work for the same reason, she applied to the state of South Carolina for temporary unemployment benefits.

balancing test
used by the Supreme Court in free exercise of religion cases, this two-part test first determined whether a government action or law was a burden on religious practice and, if it was, whether a compelling government interest was at stake that would make the burden constitutionally acceptable.

neutrality test
the Supreme Court's most recent approach to deciding free exercise of religion cases, this test declares that a government law or action with a neutral intent and application is constitutional, even if it burdens religion and there is no compelling government interest at stake.

The state denied her any benefits, because the state believed she could have taken a job requiring Saturday work.

The Supreme Court applied a two-part test to resolve the dispute. First, did the government law or policy impose a significant burden on religious exercise? The Court concluded in this instance that South Carolina's eligibility requirements for unemployment compensation did significantly burden Sherbert's ability to practice her faith. With that established, the Court turned to the second part of the test. Was a compelling government interest served by this burdensome law or policy? If it were, then the policy or law would be constitutional despite its interference with religious expression. Here, the Court determined that there was no compelling state interest that justified the burden on Sherbert's religious practice. On the basis of the two-part test, the Court ruled in favor of Sherbert.

The Neutrality Standard Narrows the Scope of Religious Free Expression

The two-part balancing test survived for nearly three decades before being demoted in favor of a new test.[47] The new standard made it surprisingly more difficult to carve out space for religious expression. The case establishing the new standard involved Alfred Smith and Galen Black, who participated in Native American church ceremonies that involved the ingestion of peyote, an illegal hallucinogen. Unlike many other states, Oregon law provided no exception for use of the drug for sacramental purposes. Smith and Black were fired from their jobs at a private drug rehabilitation center because their drug use was considered work-related misconduct. They were denied state unemployment benefits on those grounds.

In *Employment Division v. Smith* (1990), the Supreme Court upheld Oregon's refusal to provide unemployment benefits. In a striking shift away from the balancing test established in *Sherbert*, the decision introduced the Court's **neutrality test** for free exercise cases: a neutral law applied in a neutral way can validly impose a burden on religious practice, even if there is no compelling government interest at stake. If a law was not neutral in intent and application, the Court would employ the balancing test.

In the Court's view, the law prohibiting peyote and other drugs validly regulated an area that government is allowed to regulate, and it did so in a neutral way. Its enactment was not targeted at any one group and it was applied equally across groups. Restriction of religious expression was an "incidental effect" of the law, not an intentional goal. There is no religious exemption from the law, just as there is no religious exemption if one believes one's taxes support causes that one finds spiritually repugnant.

A notable example of the Court's application of the neutrality test concerned the issue of animal sacrifice. The city of Hialeah, Florida, passed several laws to forbid the practice of animal sacrifice or slaughter but exempted state-licensed activities from the new regulation, including slaughterhouses, food establishments, and some hog and cattle slaughter that did not occur in areas zoned for slaughterhouses. In its decision in *Church of the Lukumi Babalu Aye v. Hialeah* (1993), the Supreme Court struck down the city's ordinances as an undue burden on the religious practice of the Santeria religion, which used animal sacrifice. Had the laws been designed neutrally and applied neutrally, they could have been upheld even though burdening religion. They were not neutral, however. The Court concluded that the city could have found other ways to protect public health and prevent animal cruelty without targeting one group's religious practice.[48]

This test does not mean that a neutral law or policy cannot be challenged on other grounds. The Court in *Rosenberger v. University of Virginia* (1995) ruled that even though the University of Virginia had a neutral student organization policy that allowed funding of religious groups and thus did not violate the establishment clause, it engaged in viewpoint discrimination and violated free speech protection when it refused to fund one specific religiously oriented student newspaper based on the beliefs it expressed.

The Court's most significant recent ruling on free exercise came in 2010. A Christian group at the University of California's Hastings Law School was denied recognition as a registered student organization because it required adherence to a particular set of beliefs and behaviors for voting members and officers. This policy ran afoul of the university's nondiscrimination rule, which was based on state law. The rule required all groups that wished to receive registered student organization status to accept all those students interested in joining. The university argued that its rule was neutrally applied to all groups and that the Christian Legal Society, the student group, had abided by the rule until it became affiliated with a national organization. The Christian Legal Society challenged the university in federal court, arguing its constitutional free speech, freedom to associate with others of like-minded interests, and free exercise rights were violated. In a 5–4 decision, the Court upheld the constitutionality of the university's rule, determining that the rule was created and applied neutrally and was not targeted toward religious beliefs in general or Christian beliefs in particular.[49]

Protest Over the Court's Neutrality Standard in Free Exercise Cases Prompts Congress to Respond With Legislation

The Court's neutrality standard sparked a chain of legislative and judicial actions. Responding to a massive outcry among religious groups, Congress responded to the Court's new neutrality test by passing the Religious Freedom Restoration Act (RFRA) of 1993. Referring directly to the Court's *Smith* decision, RFRA attempted to erase the Court's use of the neutrality test by prohibiting the federal and state governments

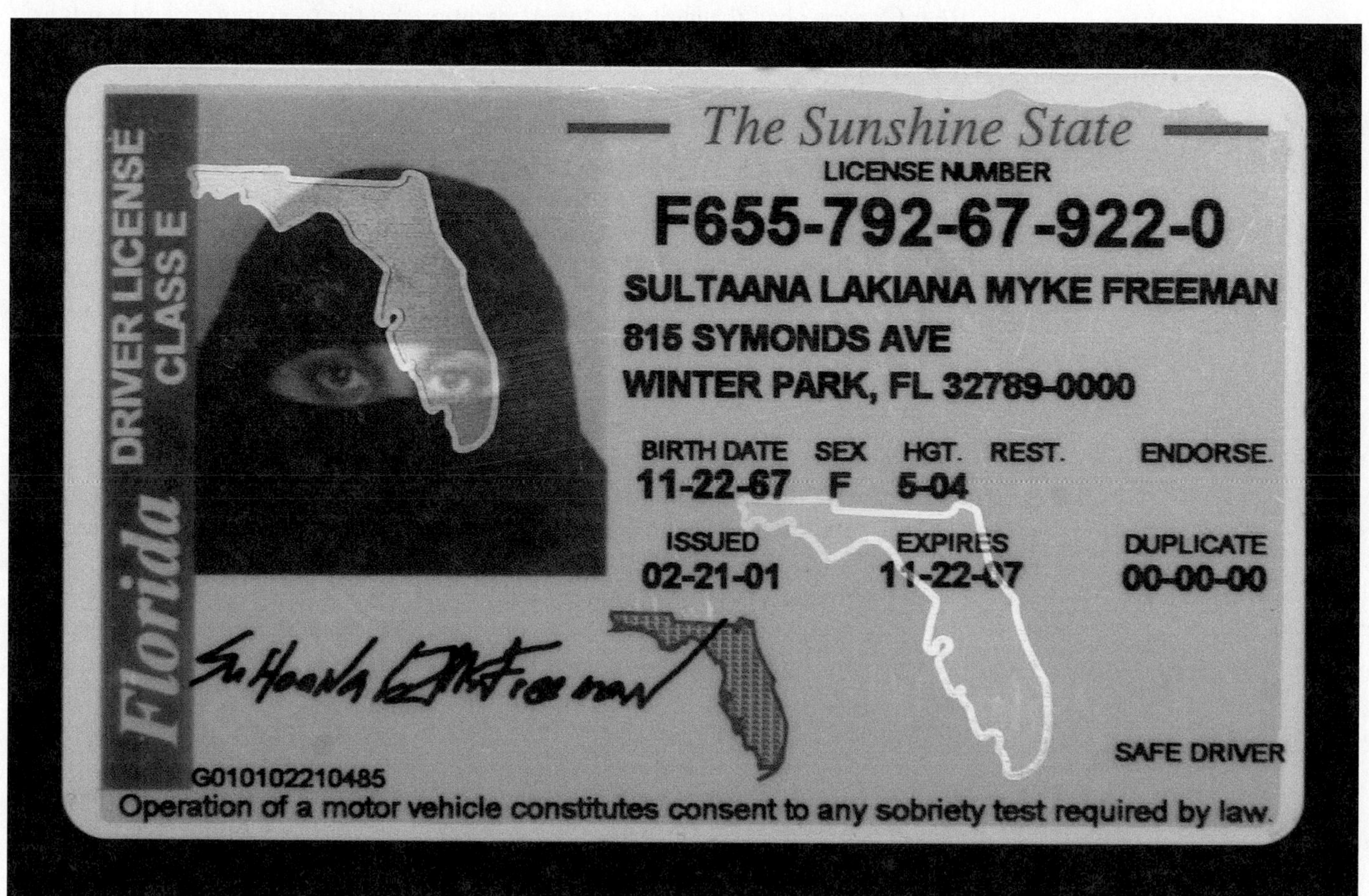

THE NEUTRALITY STANDARD IN PRACTICE

Is the requirement to remove a veil for a driver's license photo an unconstitutional burden on religious freedom? A Florida appeals court used the neutrality standard to reject Sultana Freeman's case in 2002, noting that the requirement was valid because it was created and applied in a neutral fashion.

from restricting an individual's free exercise of religion unless such restriction served a compelling government interest and was narrowly tailored to meet that interest (meaning as minimally invasive on rights as possible in its quest to advance that interest). In short, with RFRA, Congress told the Court that balancing, not neutrality, was the standard by which to judge religious practice cases. Congress passed follow-up legislation in 1994, the American Indian Religious Freedom Act Amendments, which specifically protected Native Americans' use of peyote.

In *City of Boerne v. Flores* (1997), the Supreme Court invalidated the underlying premise of RFRA and declared its applicability to the states to be unconstitutional. The case began when the Archbishop of San Antonio sued the city of Boerne, Texas, under RFRA for its denial of a building permit. The city responded that RFRA was unconstitutional and overly restrictive toward the states and the cities within them. The Court majority concluded that RFRA intruded too far into the judiciary's responsibilities in the American separation of powers system by attempting to define what a constitutional right contains, a task left to the Court. The Court also determined that the law was too extensive and invasive in its impact and so could not be imposed on state governments. RFRA could, however, apply to the federal government because Congress has the authority to set the guidelines by which federal agencies make decisions. The Court unanimously reiterated in 2006 that federal agencies needed to abide by the balancing requirements imposed by Congress in RFRA.[50]

Rather than trying to tell the Court how to interpret the Constitution and apply it to the states, supporters of RFRA passed the Religious Land Use and Institutionalized Persons Act of 2000 (RLUIPA). This time, using its power of fiscal federalism, Congress required states that chose to receive certain federal funds to use the balancing test when deciding whether and how to accommodate religion for institutionalized persons. In June 2005, the Supreme Court upheld RLUIPA unanimously, ruling that Congress had the authority to set conditions on the receipt of federal funds as it did in the.[51]

Rights of the Accused

5.4 Trace the expansion of the rights of the accused and their balance with the needs of police and prosecutors.

s with freedom of speech and freedom of religion, the scope of rights accorded to individuals accused of a crime has changed significantly over the past 50 years. Much of what Americans now take for granted as "standard operating procedure" by police and criminal prosecutors in fact marks a stark change from practice prior to the 1960s. Although acknowledging generally the need for procedural safeguards for defendants, Americans can nonetheless be frustrated when criminals go free because of what appear to be "technicalities."

The rights of the accused concern both the behavior of police and government prosecutors and the processes related to trials. Today, Americans may wonder why the system is so concerned with the rights of those accused of crimes. But it makes perfect sense that the Framers of the Constitution, especially the Anti-Federalists who demanded a Bill of Rights, were eager to protect the rights of defendants. Remember their experience with the British government. They feared a powerful government that could fabricate charges or corrupt the legal process to get the results it desired. They chose to err on the side of caution and crafted a series of safeguards that they hoped would prevent government from imprisoning the innocent, even if sometimes letting the guilty go free. Table 5.3 lists these rights, ordered from initial investigation to subsequent trial and sentencing.

One of the chief differences between how civil liberties are protected in the United States and other countries lies in the nature of each country's legal system.

TABLE 5.3 CONSTITUTIONAL RIGHTS OF THE ACCUSED FROM INVESTIGATION TO SENTENCING

(Location in Constitution in parentheses)
Investigation and arrest
• No unreasonable or unwarranted searches and seizures (4th Amendment)
• No arrest without probable cause (4th)
• No entrapment (4th)
• Must be informed of rights (to remain silent, to counsel) (5th)
• No coerced confession and no illegal interrogation (5th)
• No self-incrimination during arrest or trial (5th)
• Be informed of charges (6th)
• Prompt arraignment (6th)
• Legal counsel (6th)
• No excessive bail (8th)
• Grand jury hearing to determine if case is viable (5th)
Trial
• Trial before a judge (Article I, Section 9)
• Speedy and public trial before an impartial jury (6th)
• Trial atmosphere free from prejudice and external interference (6th)
• Evidence obtained by illegal search not admissible during trial (4th)
• Right to confront witnesses (6th)
• No double jeopardy (5th)
Sentencing
• No cruel and unusual punishment (8th)
• Opportunity to appeal verdicts (8th)

The American legal system, like that found in the United Kingdom, is adversarial. This means the two sides put together the arguments and evidence and present them before a judge or a jury. The assumption underlying this system is that the competition between the two sides will produce a just outcome. In this system, the attorneys presenting the cases dominate proceedings, the rights of the accused are given great weight, and defects in procedures such as gathering evidence and informing suspects of their rights are treated very seriously. By contrast, in an inquisitorial system like that found in many other advanced democracies, including most of Europe, the judge sits at the center. It is her or his job to direct the gathering of the evidence and conduct the inquiry that will help resolve the case. The judge can interview witnesses, communicate directly with intelligence and other investigative agencies, and detain suspects. The rights of the accused are important, but they are given less weight than in the adversarial system. Someone accused of a crime cannot, for example, refuse to testify in most inquisitorial systems.

The Supreme Court Has Established Guidelines for the Constitutional Gathering of Evidence

The job of the police and prosecutors depends fundamentally on uncovering evidence that links an individual with a crime. Thus, the gathering of evidence is absolutely critical. But, as the Framers of the Constitution feared, investigators might be overzealous in their attempts to unearth damaging information. At the extreme, investigators might even manufacture evidence in order to obtain a conviction. The protections in the Bill of Rights are designed to minimize that threat.

Central to these protections is the nature of the search-and-seizure process. The Fourth Amendment of the Constitution protects citizens against "unreasonable" searches and seizures, noting that people are to be "secure in their persons, houses, papers, and effects." The amendment mandates that prior to any search, police obtain warrants specifically indicating the place to be searched and the items to be seized. To

SEEKING EVIDENCE

Before entering property to conduct a search, police officers need to obtain a warrant that specifies the location of the search and the items or information sought in the search. Evidence seized in the absence of a judge's warrant may be deemed inadmissible in court.

obtain a warrant, police must have probable cause—that is, they must have enough information suggesting that a crime has taken place and that an individual or location is linked to the crime. Police must also obtain a warrant before engaging in wiretaps of phone and electronic communication, but for obvious reasons, these need not be shown to the target of the investigation. Originally, these provisions protected individuals from federal government action. Later, through incorporation, they became binding on the states as well.

The Fourth Amendment prohibits unreasonable searches, but it does not specify what is reasonable or what should happen if police overstep "reasonable" boundaries. For example, can police look through your trash without a warrant? They can. According to the Supreme Court, individuals cannot assume that trash placed by public streets is covered by any expectation of privacy.[52] Can you be subject to a strip search in a jail, even if you are arrested for only minor offenses? You can. In a 5–4 decision in *Florence v. Board of Chosen Freeholders of the County of Burlington* (2012), the Court ruled that these searches were a reasonable precaution in a jail setting. Can police stop you while driving even if you are not suspected of wrongdoing? They can. The Court has confirmed that police are allowed to conduct "sobriety checkpoints," in which motorists are stopped without cause in order to deter drunk driving, because the government's compelling interest in public safety outweighs the minor intrusion on personal liberty.[53] On the other hand, police cannot stop vehicles without cause or for traffic violations and search them for drugs or other contraband—with no immediate safety issue, the intrusion on liberty outweighs the government's interest in regulating the contraband.[54]

Convictions May Not Be Based on Illegally Obtained Evidence

In *Weeks v. United States* (1914), the Supreme Court prohibited federal courts from basing decisions on evidence obtained improperly—a principle known as the **exclusionary rule**. According to this rule, evidence that is gathered during an illegal search cannot be introduced in a trial, even if that evidence is absolutely necessary to obtain a conviction. In *Mapp v. Ohio* (1961), the Supreme Court applied the rule to the states also. Even after a trial, a conviction can be overturned if a defendant can convince an appeals court that the evidence used for conviction was obtained improperly and should not have been introduced at trial. No other country has any provision regarding evidence that is as extensive as the exclusionary rule.[55]

Over time, the Court has become flexible in its enforcement of the exclusionary rule. The general principle stands, but the Court has allowed for the introduction of questionably obtained evidence in specific circumstances. Generally, the Court in these cases has considered the exclusionary rule to be a deterrent to improper government behavior, rather than being a right held personally by individuals. For example, the Court has concluded that it is acceptable to introduce evidence obtained illegally if police can show that they would have eventually obtained the evidence through legal means or needed to act because the evidence was mobile—in an automobile, for example. The Court has also allowed evidence that was technically collected improperly but that police exercised "good faith" to collect properly or, most recently in a 2009 decision, was collected as a result of a simple police error. In addition, if a person agrees to a search even without a warrant, these searches are legal, so long as the individual did not feel intimidated into complying with the police request. Police do not need to obtain warrants to seize illegal goods that are in open view—firearms, for example.[56]

exclusionary rule
principle established by the Supreme Court, according to which evidence gathered illegally cannot be introduced into trial, and convictions cannot be based on this evidence.

***Miranda* warning**
ruling that requires police, when arresting suspects, to inform them of their rights, including the right to remain silent and have an attorney present during questioning.

The Constitution Protects Defendants During Investigations and Trials

Individuals accused of crimes have a number of rights during the process of investigation and litigation. These rights leave much leeway for interpretation by the courts. What is "excessive" bail? What is a "speedy" trial? What is "cruel and unusual" punishment? Questions such as these have spawned a long line of judicial clarifications of what the Constitution requires.

THE FIFTH AMENDMENT AND SELF-INCRIMINATION As any viewer of television dramas knows, police are required to read suspects their rights when placing them under arrest if they intend to interrogate them. One of these rights is the right to remain silent. The basic idea is that individuals should not be coerced or intimidated into offering a confession, that individuals must be informed that they are not required to speak to the police except to respond to basic questions of identification, that anything they say can be used against them in court, that they have a right to have an attorney present during questioning, and that an attorney will be provided if they cannot afford one. Confessions made in the absence of these conditions would be inadmissible in court. This procedure is known as the ***Miranda* warning,** based on the Court's 1966 decision in the case of *Miranda v. Arizona*. It emerged from the Fifth Amendment's guarantee that no citizen "shall be compelled in any criminal case to be a witness against himself" and the Sixth Amendment's guarantee of the right to legal counsel. Despite occasional congressional attempts to overturn it, the *Miranda* warning remains binding on police during investigations. Over time, however, the Court has made the burden on the police less restrictive—for example, unless individuals explicitly request to speak to an attorney, police need not assume that they would like to do so.[57]

Two more recent 5–4 rulings continued this trend. In *Montejo v. Louisiana* (2009), the Court ruled that police may continue questioning a suspect after the suspect has requested to consult with legal counsel. And in *Berghuis v. Thompkins* (2010), the Court ruled that a suspect must state to police that he or she is invoking the right to remain silent—not talking for an extended period does not itself invoke the right. Thus, comments a suspect makes, even after a long period of silence, would be admissible as evidence, if the suspect had not explicitly stated the right to remain silent.

The right not to incriminate oneself stretches back well before the U.S. Constitution. English courts honored this right by the seventeenth century, and the U.S. Supreme Court pointed to this English legal tradition in *Miranda*. English courts and Parliament, however, neither require English police to offer *Miranda*-like warnings nor require prosecutors to exclude evidence obtained from improper searches. As of 1995, an act of the British Parliament allows judges and prosecutors to assume the guilt of anyone who refuses to testify in his or her own defense. Other major European countries are more consistent with the American model. Germany, France, and Italy all exclude statements from trial if the police failed to inform defendants of their right to remain silent, but the time at which suspects must be informed differs. Italy's practice is closest to that of the United States, with expectations that suspects will be informed of their right to remain silent at the time of arrest.

THE SIXTH AMENDMENT AND THE RIGHT TO COUNSEL One of the rights guaranteed by the Constitution and mentioned in the *Miranda* warning is the right to have the advice of legal counsel during questioning and trial. As it selectively incorporated the Sixth Amendment, the Court broadened the range of cases that fit within the right to counsel (see the entries for the Sixth Amendment in Table 5.2). Moreover, the Court made the individual's right to counsel an obligation upon governments to *provide* counsel for defendants who could not afford an attorney. The defining case was *Gideon v. Wainwright* (1963). Clarence Earl Gideon, not entitled to public counsel under Florida law unless he faced the death penalty, defended himself at trial and was convicted and sentenced. Gideon appealed to the Supreme Court, and the Court unanimously concluded that individuals in all felony cases must be provided with legal assistance if they cannot afford their own. Lawyers in criminal cases, the Court ruled, are not a luxury but, rather, a necessity for a fair trial. The broad right to counsel established in this case extended even further in subsequent years, with defendants able to challenge convictions based on the poor quality of the publicly provided legal representation that they received.

THE EIGHTH AMENDMENT AND CRUEL AND UNUSUAL PUNISHMENT Once a defendant is found guilty, a judge or jury must declare an appropriate sentence. The Constitution forbids "cruel and unusual" punishment, and the Supreme Court has focused on the "and." A punishment can be cruel but not unusual, or unusual but not cruel. The Supreme Court is most concerned when it is both.

Capital punishment—the death penalty—is the area that most often reaches the Supreme Court for review under the Eighth Amendment's prohibition against cruel and unusual punishment. Though opponents of the practice decry it as inhumane, the Court has never declared the death penalty in general to constitute cruel and unusual punishment. It has, however, prohibited capital punishment in cases of rape, including rape of a child.[58] In addition, in recent years, the Court has decided that the death penalty constitutes cruel and unusual punishment for individuals with severe mental developmental disabilities and for minors.[59] In 2010, the Court added in a 5–4 vote that the lesser penalty of life terms without parole also constitute cruel and unusual punishment for minors when the minors are not charged with murder. And in 2012, the Court ruled, again by a 5–4 vote, that minors could not be subject to mandatory life sentences without parole in the case of murder. Judges in that situation had to be allowed the flexibility to give a minor a less harsh sentence.[60]At the time, 29 states had laws requiring mandatory life sentences without parole for murder convictions.

These decisions concerning minors and the mentally disabled were notable for the references to international trends and law in the majority's rulings. Justices

Should the Government Apply the Death Penalty?

The United States is the only advanced democracy that practices capital punishment. Proponents argue that the death penalty is a deterrent to violent crimes, but since 1992, public support for it has declined. A majority of Americans still believe the death penalty should exist, but there are racial differences among supporters.

Death Penalty Supporters by Race

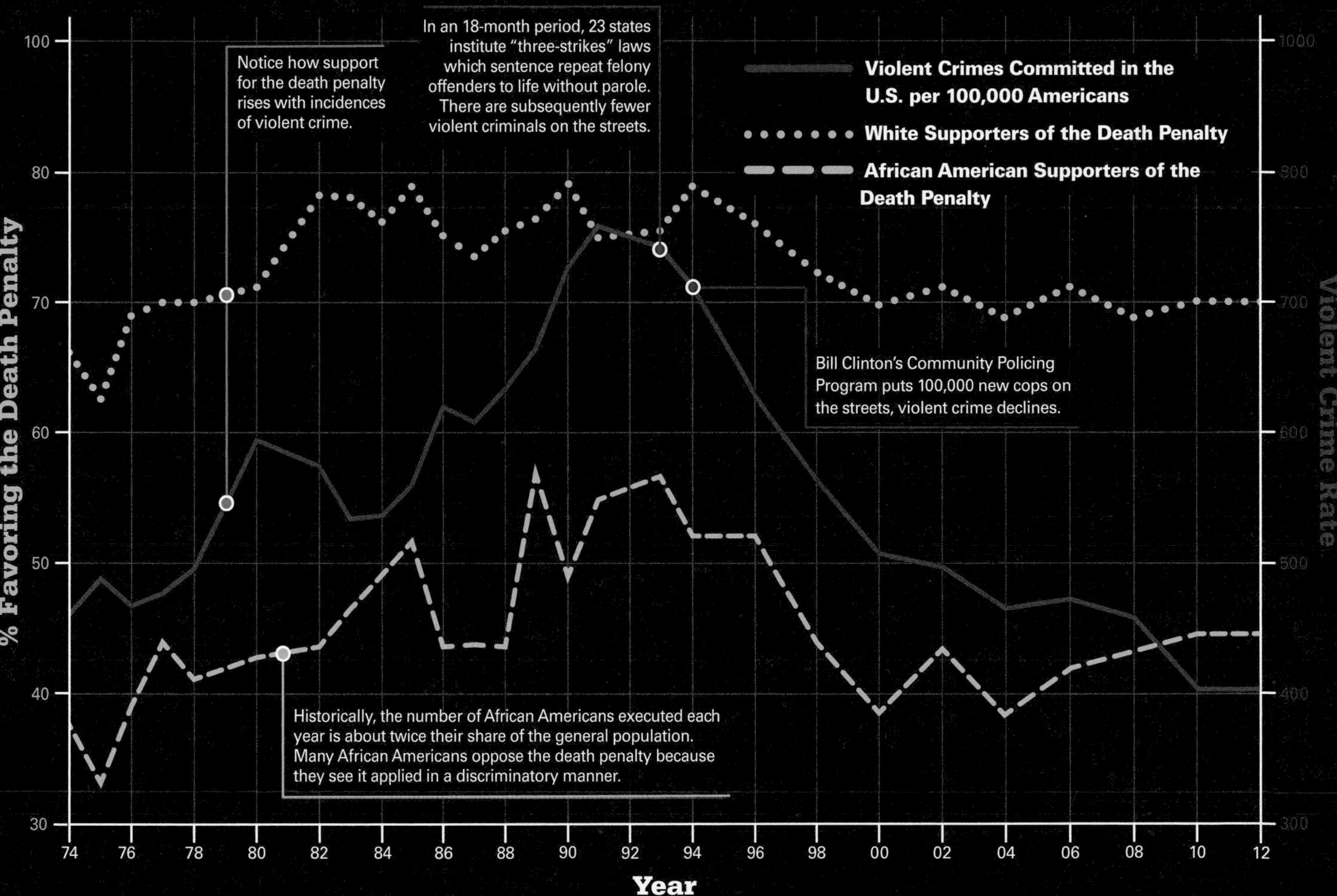

Notice how support for the death penalty rises with incidences of violent crime.
In an 18-month period, 23 states institute "three-strikes" laws which sentence repeat felony offenders to life without parole. There are subsequently fewer violent criminals on the streets.
Violent Crimes Committed in the U.S. per 100,000 Americans
White Supporters of the Death Penalty
African American Supporters of the Death Penalty
Bill Clinton's Community Policing Program puts 100,000 new cops on the streets, violent crime declines.
Historically, the number of African Americans executed each year is about twice their share of the general population. Many African Americans oppose the death penalty because they see it applied in a discriminatory manner.
% Favoring the Death Penalty
100
80
70
60
50
40
30
Violent Crime Rate
1000
800
700
600
500
400
300
74 76 78 80 82 84 86 88 90 92 94 96 98 00 02 04 06 08 10 12
Year

SOURCE: Data from General Social Survey, 1972-2010; Bureau of Justice Statistics, U.S. Department of Justice.

Investigate Further

Concept How widespread is American support for using the death penalty? A majority of Americans endorse capital punishment, but support is stronger among whites than African Americans. The racial disparities are due in part to the fact that African Americans are more likely to be on death row than Anglo whites.

Connection Is support for the death penalty related to lower crime rates? When violent crime goes up nationally, so does support for the death penalty because supporters believe it will decrease the crime rate. However, this effect is contested by death penalty opponents and those who see other explanations for less crime.

Cause Are there any competing explanations for the decline of crime, besides the death penalty? There are at least two non-death penalty related reasons for the decline of crime: increased federal spending to put more cops on the street, and states using stiffer sentencing for repeat felony offenders.

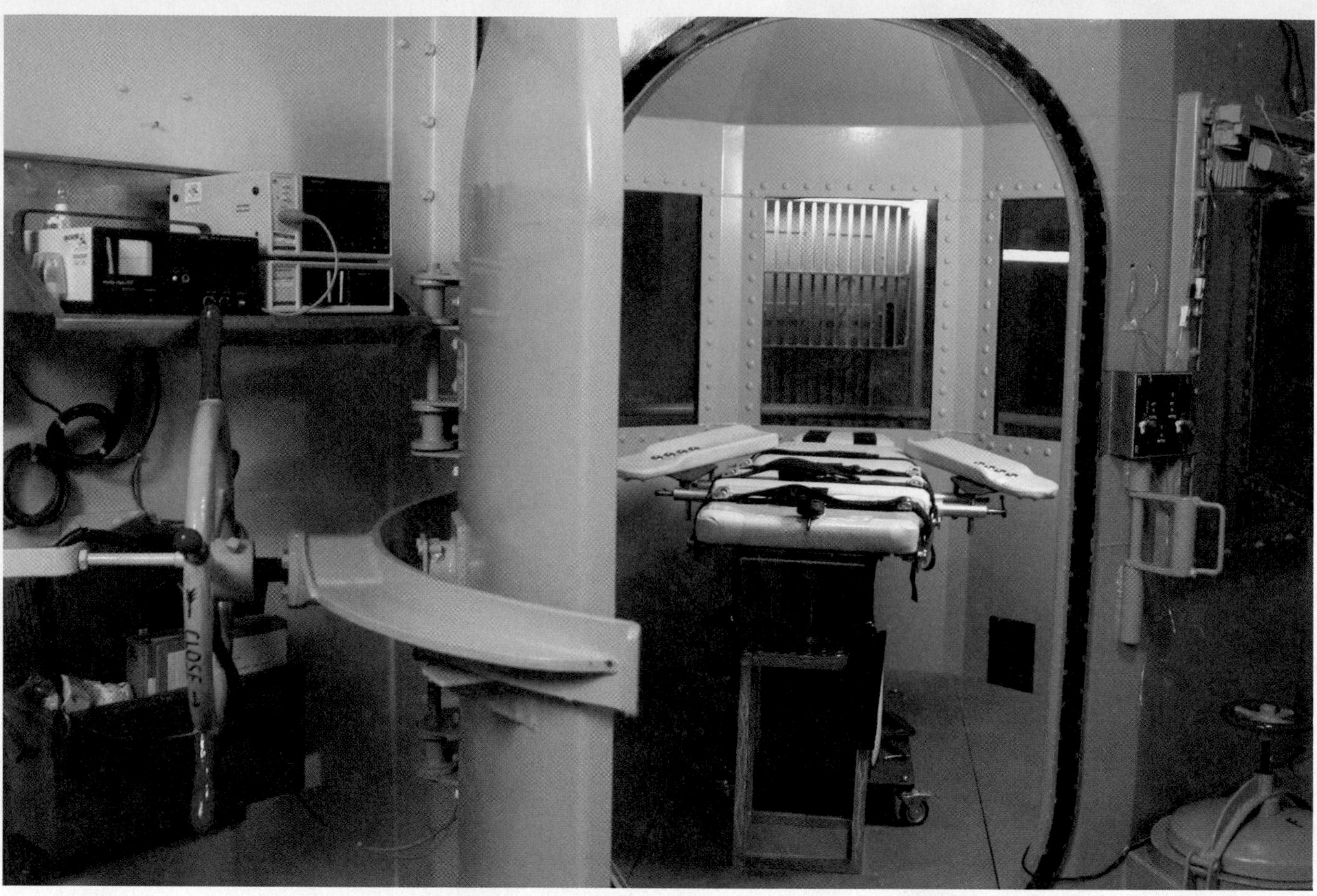

THE TECHNOLOGY OF CAPITAL PUNISHMENT

This chamber at San Quentin prison in California was used for execution by lethal injection through 2007, when it was replaced by a new facility. In 2008, the U.S. Supreme Court lifted the restriction it had placed on lethal injection executions. The Court determined that this method of execution did not constitute cruel and unusual punishment and was constitutional.

Stephen Breyer and Antonin Scalia have expressed publicly—and often in joint appearances—the two ends of the spectrum. Breyer argues that consideration of foreign trends and law is appropriate for, in this case, understanding what is currently deemed cruel and unusual punishment, whereas Scalia argues that international trends and rulings are irrelevant considerations for a court that is interpreting and applying the U.S. Constitution. It is too early to determine whether the Court is influenced by changing global opinion or whether these are merely additional facts marshaled for decisions that would have been the same even without these international references. But as more cases make these kinds of references, political scientists will be in a stronger position to sort out the influence of international court decisions, laws in other countries, and legal briefs filed by international human rights organizations versus the influence of domestic opinion, legal precedent, briefs filed by domestic groups, and the changing membership of the Court, among other possible factors.

For individuals other than minors and the mentally challenged, the Court has sought to ensure that defendants' due process rights are adhered to rigorously in capital punishment cases. Although it is uncommon, the Court will overturn death sentences if it believes a defendant received a defense so inadequate that it violates the constitutional right to counsel.[61] The Court also considers whether the method of execution is cruel and unusual. In *Baze v. Rees* (2008), the Supreme Court ended its eight-month moratorium on the death penalty when it decided that death by lethal injection—the primary method used in the 35 capital punishment states—did not constitute cruel and unusual punishment.

The current system of regulating capital punishment began with the Supreme Court's decision in *Furman v. Georgia* (1972). In that ruling, the justices struck down three death penalty sentences, concluding that the use of capital punishment was impermissibly arbitrary. The decision did not eliminate capital punishment, but it did lead to a five-year hiatus in its use. States needed to reexamine their procedures for imposing the penalty. This meant, first, being specific about which crimes might justify capital punishment, so that a jury could not impose the death penalty arbitrarily. Second, cases would have two stages, with a jury first determining guilt or innocence and then, if its verdict was guilty, determining whether the crime warranted the death penalty. Today, federal law and the law in 33 states allow the use of the death penalty under this procedure, with nearly all executions taking place at the state level.[62] Death penalty sentences totaled 78 in 2011, and the number of executions in that year was 43. These numbers continue a downward trend over the previous 10 to 15 years.[63]

Illinois abolished the death penalty in 2011, sparked in part by Northwestern University journalism and law students' investigations and the work of the university's Center for Wrongful Convictions. The center held a conference in November 1998 featuring 31 exonerated death row inmates, and in February 1999, the case of released death penalty inmate Anthony Porter received widespread attention in the state. Illinois Governor George Ryan instituted a moratorium on the death penalty in 2000, largely as a result of the number of wrongful convictions in death penalty cases—of the 289 defendants sentenced to the death penalty since 1976 in the state, 17 had been exonerated and a much larger number had been resentenced to other punishment upon appeal. In 2002, Ryan moved death row inmates to life sentences.[64] After lengthy study and controversy, the state formally eliminated the death penalty nine years later. Connecticut in 2012 was the most recent state to abolish the option of capital punishment. Later that year, California voters rejected a bid to outlaw the death penalty in that state.

The death penalty is a highly charged emotional and moral issue. To opponents, it is morally wrong, applied inconsistently across racial and ethnic groups, and no more effective than other deterrents to crime. Opponents also point to the elimination of capital punishment in many countries around the world as evidence that it is widely considered inhumane. By 2012, a total of 141 countries had either eliminated the death penalty in law or in practice, including Mexico and Canada and all the countries in Europe and South America, while 57 countries—including India, China, Japan, and the United States—allowed it.[65] To supporters, capital punishment is justified on personal responsibility grounds as an appropriately harsh response to a criminal's destruction of the liberty and life of other individuals, and on communitarian grounds as an appropriate protection of the community's safety and sense of justice, which outweigh the life and liberty interest of the convicted criminal.

Discovering New Rights That Are Protected by the Constitution

5.5 Explain how the Ninth and Fourteenth Amendments have helped establish rights other than those specifically listed in the Constitution.

The scope of civil liberties has changed with nationalization and with changing judicial interpretations of the protections included in the Constitution. However, it has also changed through a third path, the discovery of new rights that are protected by the Constitution. Lawyers and Supreme Court justices use the Ninth Amendment, which states that rights not specifically mentioned in the Constitution are reserved to the people, and the Fourteenth Amendment, particularly the due process clause, to establish additional rights.

The Right to Privacy Has Revolutionized the Law Concerning Birth Control, Abortion, and Same-Sex Relationships

Some of the most momentous civil liberties decisions of the past 50 years have been based on a right that is not even explicitly guaranteed in the Constitution, the right to privacy. Court decisions concerning birth control, abortion, and homosexual behavior have all focused on individuals' right to privacy. This right connects deeply to beliefs in individualism and liberty in American political culture. The Court used the Ninth Amendment to discover this right.[66]

BIRTH CONTROL From 1873 through 1938, the federal government criminalized the distribution of birth control material across state lines.[67] Many states, following the federal government's lead, also restricted the use of birth control within their borders. In the early 1960s, 28 states still prohibited married couples from using contraceptive devices. Challenges to such laws made only limited headway. Federal courts initially struck down state laws that were not flexible enough to allow physicians to prescribe contraceptives to protect patients' health, but the courts otherwise left the contraception bans in place.

In 1961, the Planned Parenthood League of Connecticut opened a birth control clinic in defiance of state law. The clinic provided information and instruction on contraceptive use to married couples. Ten days after opening the clinic, Estelle Griswold, the league's executive director, and Charles Lee Buxton, the medical director, were arrested and convicted for violating Connecticut's law barring the dissemination of information about birth control devices and techniques. Four years later, in *Griswold v. Connecticut* (1965), the U.S. Supreme Court overturned the convictions and declared by a 7–2 majority that there was a constitutional right to privacy for married couples, later extended to unmarried heterosexual couples.[68] The Court's majority concluded that even though the word *privacy* does not appear in the Constitution, the Ninth Amendment, combined with provisions of the First, Third, Fourth, and Fifth Amendments, implicitly suggested that the Constitution contained a right to privacy.[69] Protections in these amendments create "zones of privacy" in the Constitution. The dissenting justices in *Griswold* argued unsuccessfully that by declaring a general right to privacy beyond the specific privacy protections mentioned in the Constitution, the unelected justices of the Supreme Court were displacing the appropriate role of elected officials in the states and of the voters who elected them.

ABORTION *Roe v. Wade* (1973) demonstrated the extensive impact of the *Griswold* decision. Abortion had been illegal by law in Texas since 1854, unless medical personnel determined it was necessary to save the life of the mother. Similar laws existed in almost every state by the 1950s; most dated back to the latter half of the nineteenth century. During the 1960s, several states liberalized their abortion statutes, but a majority still had laws similar to that in Texas. Norma McCorvey—known in the legal case as "Jane Roe"—wishing to terminate her pregnancy legally, filed a challenge to Texas's law in 1970. Building from the *Griswold* decision, the suit contended that the statute violated McCorvey's right to privacy.

The Supreme Court, by a 7–2 majority, agreed. A woman's privacy right was not absolute, however. The Court determined that the right to privacy in the abortion decision could be conditional upon important government interests in health, medical standards, and protecting potential life. The privacy interest dominates at first, but as pregnancy advances, these government interests begin to balance the woman's privacy interest. Based on this framework and on what it took to be generally consensual understandings of fetal development, the Court established a trimester arrangement. During the first three months of pregnancy, women were free to obtain abortions. During the second trimester—after the first three months but before fetal viability (i.e., before the fetus could potentially live outside the mother's womb)—*Roe* allowed the state to regulate abortion in a manner consistent with its interest in protecting maternal health. During the final trimester, a state could regulate or prohibit abortion, consistent with its interest in protecting potential human life.[70]

In later years, the Court would allow states to adopt some first-trimester restrictions consistent with their interest in protecting potential life, but none that could put an undue burden on a woman's right to obtain an abortion.[71] The Court defined an undue burden as a "substantial obstacle in the path of a woman seeking an abortion before the fetus attains viability." By this standard, in *Planned Parenthood v. Casey* (1992), the Court accepted a mandatory 24-hour waiting period before an abortion procedure could be performed, requiring doctors to counsel women on alternatives to abortion (see Figure 5.2), and requiring minors to obtain consent from parents (or a judge's approval as an alternative to parental consent) as reasonable and constitutional restrictions on abortion access. Requiring a woman to notify her husband before obtaining an abortion was struck down as an undue burden. No state can deny access to abortion completely, but some have made it more difficult than others to exercise this right.

Nebraska and Oklahoma opened new fronts in the conflict over abortion in 2010. Nebraska became the first state to restrict abortions on the basis of fetal pain. The state banned most abortions 20 weeks after conception—exceptions were made for medical emergency, imminent death of the pregnant woman, and substantial and irreversible physical impairment—concluding that fetuses at that point can feel pain. Previously, and consistent with *Roe*, the state did not allow abortions after fetal viability, which

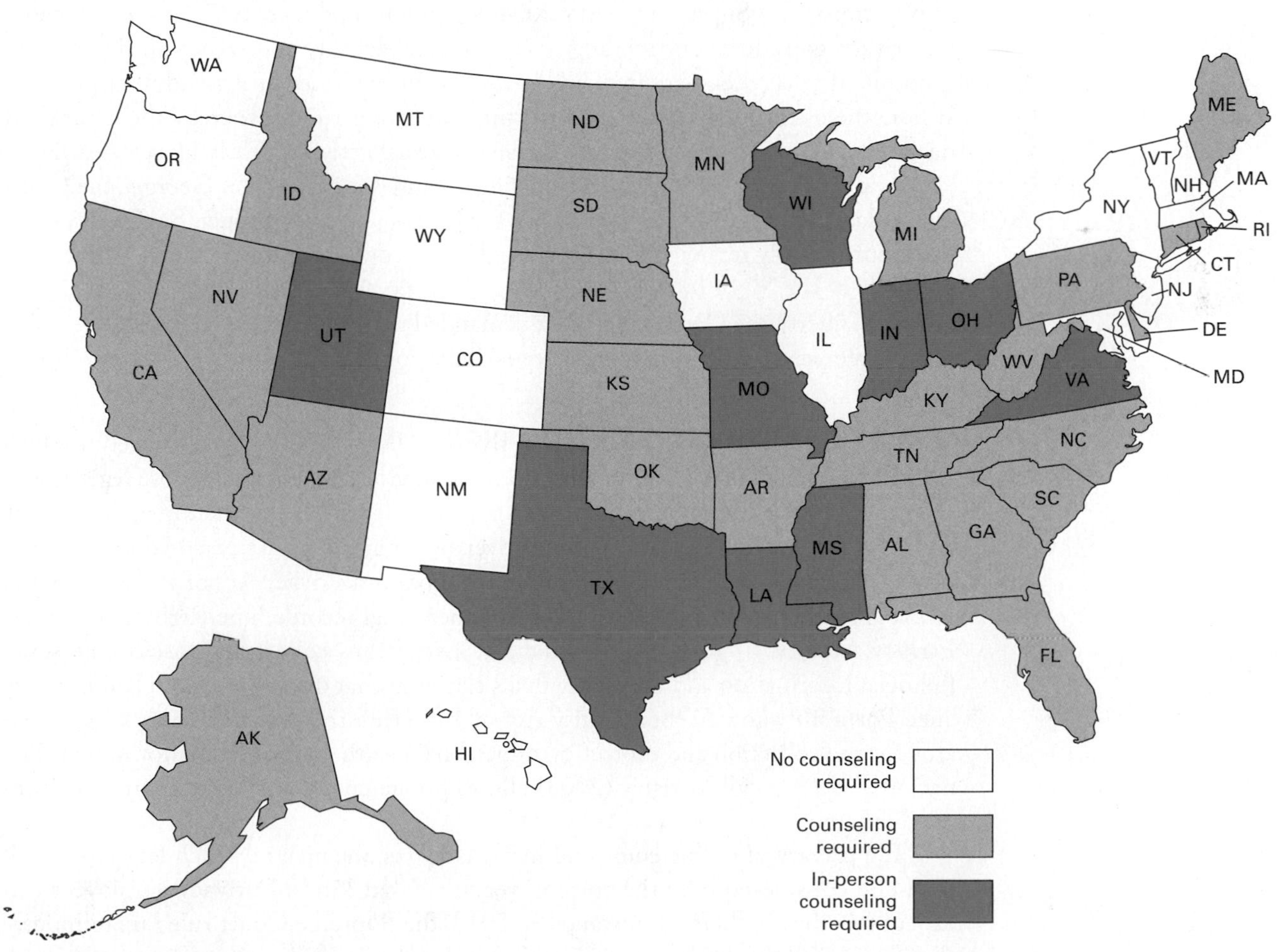

FIGURE 5.2 COUNSELING REQUIREMENTS FOR WOMEN SEEKING AN ABORTION, 2012.

The Supreme Court has declared that abortion is a protected constitutional right, meaning that states cannot prohibit it. But because access to abortion is not considered a fundamental right, significant variation in law and policy across the states is permissible, as long as states do not create an "undue burden" on access to abortion. Most states require women to obtain counseling before having an abortion, with various requirements regarding what the counseling must cover. Counseling is usually coupled with a waiting period of 24 hours prior to the abortion being performed.

Source: http://www.guttmacher.org/statecenter/spibs/spib_MWPA.pdf .

5.1

5.2

5.3

5.4

5.5

at the earliest was thought to be about 22 weeks (viability was determined on a case-by-case basis). Although the law could be challenged and end up in the U.S. Supreme Court, pro-choice advocates would have to determine if they wished to take the strategic risk that the Court might add fetal pain as another criterion that states could constitutionally use, in addition to viability, in regulating the availability of abortion. In Oklahoma, the legislature passed, over the governor's veto, a law that requires providers of abortion services to set up an ultrasound monitor so that the woman can see the fetus and to describe to her the fetus's heart, limbs, and organs. The law does not exempt victims of rape or incest. Other states require ultrasounds, but Oklahoma was the first to mandate that the woman be shown the image and be given a detailed description. The law, however, was struck down by a state judge in 2012 for violating the state's constitution. By 2012, 11 states required abortion clinics to provide women seeking abortions with information about fetal pain. Seven states required an ultrasound, with one state (Texas) requiring the provider to show and describe the image. In the other states, the provider must offer to do so.[72]

At the national level, the most significant recent restriction on abortion access came in 2003, when President George W. Bush signed into law the Partial Birth Abortion Ban Act, which prohibited one specific type of abortion procedure. The Supreme Court, by 5–4, upheld the constitutionality of the law in *Gonzales v. Carhart* (2007).

SEXUAL ACTIVITY *Griswold* and *Roe* were landmark decisions with significant social implications. The Supreme Court's 2004 decision in *Lawrence v. Texas* was not based on privacy considerations relating to homosexual activity, but rather on the broader grounds of what the guarantee of "liberty" in the Fourteenth Amendment protects. It nonetheless had the effect of overturning an earlier ruling whereby the Court had declined to extend privacy rights to same-sex sexual activity. Nearly 20 years earlier in *Bowers v. Hardwick* (1986), a case involving an anti-sodomy law in Georgia, the Court concluded that there was no right to privacy for homosexual conduct. But in *Lawrence,* the Court sharply repudiated its previous decision, declaring that by defining the issue narrowly as the "right to engage in sodomy," the previous court minimized the liberty at stake. Liberty, the Court concluded, demanded that homosexuals not lose "their dignity as free persons" because of their sexual behavior in the confines of their own home.

LEGISLATIVE PROTECTION OF THE RIGHT TO PRIVACY Privacy need not be a constitutional right for government to protect it. Government can choose legislatively or administratively to protect aspects of privacy if it wishes. For example, the Privacy Act (1974) places restrictions on how government agencies use personal information about individuals. The Family Educational Rights and Privacy Act of 1974 (known as FERPA) protects the privacy of students' educational records. The Right to Financial Privacy Act (1978) governs how financial institutions collect and disclose personal financial information and how individuals can limit that disclosure. The Health Insurance Portability and Accountability Act of 1996 (referred to as HIPAA) sets standards for the collection and protection of personal health and medical information. The national "do not call" registry (2003) allows phone customers to prohibit calls from telemarketers.

The privacy of online consumer information is one area in which legislation will likely be considered over the coming years.[73] What kind of privacy employees can expect may be another. For instance, in 2010, the Supreme Court ruled unanimously that police employees in Ontario, California, who were given pagers for their jobs, could not assume they have an expectation of privacy when sending text messages on the pagers.[74] Written city policy stated that e-mail messages were not private, and employees were told verbally that text messages were considered e-mails. A third area in which legislation is likely to emerge concerns how technology intersects with police surveillance of individuals. In *U.S. v. Jones* (2012), the Supreme Court ruled unanimously that the attachment of a GPS tracking device to a car used by a suspect constituted a search as envisioned by the Fourth Amendment and, therefore, required a warrant before it could be placed on the car. The Court's ruling was relatively narrow, however, and relied heavily on the physical placement of the GPS device on the car, which the Court considered to be a trespass onto the suspect's property. Other kinds of tracking that do not require such physical placement—for example, tracking of smartphone use—will pose new issues in future cases.

DEBATE OVER A GENERAL RIGHT TO PRIVACY The constitutional right to privacy will remain contentious because it implies a much broader scope of privacy than these legislative enactments provide, and a scope that will be determined not by elected officials but by judges. Scholars, activists, and justices who see no general right to privacy argue that the Constitution prohibits some specific violations of privacy but is silent on others. Where the Constitution is silent, they argue, it should be up to legislatures, not judges, to determine whether to extend privacy protections. And just how far does a *general* right to privacy go? Does a general right to privacy require that euthanasia be legal? Suicide? Assisted suicide? What about bigamy or polygamy? Must laws prohibiting prostitution be struck down?

The Court has ruled on each of these issues. In some cases, such as upholding state or federal laws restricting bigamy, polygamy, and prostitution, the decisions came before the privacy right was fully established, but the Court today might see a compelling government interest at stake that would justify limiting privacy. In end-of-life issues, the Court's decisions have been more recent. In *Cruzan v. Director, Missouri Department of Health* (1990), the Court declared that a patient can refuse unwanted medical treatment. If the patient is incompetent and unable to articulate his or her wishes, a state is constitutionally allowed to require that there be "clear and convincing" evidence that the patient would have refused the treatment.

If an individual has a privacy right to reject treatment, which can passively result in death, does an individual also have a specific privacy right to end his or her life deliberately? In 1997, the Court upheld the state bans on physician-assisted suicide in Washington and New York, firmly and unanimously rejecting the idea that liberty includes a right to suicide. In 2006, however, the Court let stand Oregon's law that allowed physician-assisted suicide.[75] Because the Court does not see suicide as a right but has not concluded that it is constitutionally prohibited, it appears to be allowing states latitude either to prohibit or to allow physician-assisted suicide.

To defenders of the Court's discovery of a general right to privacy, these decisions show that there need be no "slippery slope" that leads to potentially problematic social outcomes in areas such as prostitution, suicide, and marriage among multiple partners. They argue that—as with other liberties—privacy is outweighed when government can show that it has a compelling need to restrict it.

Substantive Due Process Discovers New Rights by Applying Specific Guarantees to the Fourteenth Amendment's General Guarantee of Life, Liberty, and Property

The federal courts have established that the Constitution protects many rights other than those specifically listed in the document. There is, for example, a right of association, a right against compelled association and compelled speech, a right to supervise the education of one's children, a right to an attorney's being present while one is being questioned about a crime, and a right to procreate.[76]

Where does protection for these rights come from? The answer is through the concept of substantive due process. Due process is normally thought of as procedural—did a government official follow the specified rules and accord an individual all the rights and appeals allowed before restricting some aspect of the person's life, liberty, or property? Were the rules clear so that individuals did not inadvertently fail to defend a right because the process was unclear? Were they clear enough that the individual knew the

PARENTS' RIGHTS IN EDUCATION

The Supreme Court used substantive due process to affirm key decisions in 1923 and 1925 that parents have a right to control their children's education. Home schooling is an option for parents, such as those in this Muslim family in Phoenix in 2008, who believe public schools do not meet their children's needs or that they clash with their religious or cultural values.

substantive due process
an interpretation of the due process clause in the Fourteenth Amendment that says the clause's guarantee of "life, liberty, and property" provides a means to discover new rights not mentioned elsewhere in the Constitution, and that these rights would exist at both the national and state levels of government.

consequence of taking certain actions? Procedural due process, then, is doing the "right thing" by way of process.

Substantive due process, by contrast, is doing the right thing by way of substance. It says that "life, liberty, and property," mentioned in the Fourteenth Amendment, have specific meanings that must be discovered by and protected by the courts because of their fundamental nature or their place in American tradition.[77] Substantive due process has had a large impact on civil liberties interpretation. The right to privacy was discussed earlier as an example of discovering new rights through the Ninth Amendment. It has also been considered an aspect of substantive due process by some judges, participants in legal proceedings, and political scientists.[78] Opponents of Connecticut's birth control restrictions, for example, did not claim that the state of Connecticut was violating *procedural* due process when it arrested individuals who distributed birth control materials—the state followed the law and proper procedures. The claim, instead, was that privacy to use birth control must be protected as part of the *substance* of the liberty protected by the Fourteenth Amendment's due process clause.

Since the early 1990s, , the Supreme Court has been reluctant to read new rights into the Constitution via substantive due process. For example, the Court ruled unanimously against a substantive due process claim that workers have a right to be free from "unreasonable risk of harm" or that the public has a right to safety that is violated when innocent bystanders are injured during high-speed pursuit of criminal suspects by the police.[79] The general protection of life in the Fourteenth Amendment did not require the protection of these specific rights. However, the Court has tended to uphold and sometimes expand rights established by substantive due process in previous decisions.[80]

Review the Chapter

 **Listen** to **Chapter 5** on **MyPoliSciLab**

Civil Liberties in American Politics and the Constitution

5.1 Define the civil liberties guaranteed by the Constitution, and trace the process by which they became binding on state governments, p. 146.

Civil liberties are guaranteed in the U.S. Constitution and in the Bill of Rights. Civil liberties address concerns such as speech, the practice of one's religion, and the use and ownership of property, with Americans usually believing that these are areas where government should not interfere unless there are fundamental and compelling reasons to do so. Through selective incorporation, the Bill of Rights gradually became binding upon the states.

Freedom of Speech

5.2 Analyze the different standards by which the Supreme Court has determined whether restrictions on freedom of speech are acceptable, p. 155.

Over time, the Supreme Court has adopted a series of standards that have expanded the right of free speech, even in difficult cases when the speech might lead to illegal acts. The Court's interpretation of particular categories of speech, such as obscenity, has also shifted over time. First Amendment freedoms, including freedom of speech, hold a preferred position among Americans' civil liberties.

Freedom of Religion

5.3 Evaluate how the Supreme Court has interpreted cases regarding religion and how Congress has reacted to the Court's actions, p. 165.

The Constitution's religious freedom guarantee is twofold: individuals are to be free to exercise their religion, and government is not to establish religion. Since 1990, the Court has employed a neutrality standard, which is less likely to provide legal exemptions for religious practice as long as a law is conceived and implemented neutrally. Establishment cases since the 1970s have been decided by the three-prong *Lemon* test.

Rights of the Accused

5.4 Trace the expansion of the rights of the accused and their balance with the needs of police and prosecutors, p. 170.

The Supreme Court in the 1960s added significant safeguards to protect the rights of the accused when evidence is gathered, during investigations and trials, and at the time of sentencing. Well-known features of the legal system such as the *Miranda* warning and the obligation of government to provide counsel were introduced during this era. Since the 1980s, the Supreme Court has given police more leeway in their investigations.

Discovering New Rights That Are Protected by the Constitution

5.5 Explain how the Ninth and Fourteenth Amendments have helped establish rights other than those specifically listed in the Constitution, p. 177.

The discovery of new rights that are protected by the Constitution has come about in two ways: through the Ninth Amendment and through the Fourteenth Amendment. One or the other of these means has established many significant new rights. The most far-reaching of these rights in terms of its social impact has been the right to privacy, which is the basis most notably for dramatic changes in government regulation of birth control, abortion, and sexual behavior.

Learn the Terms

 **Study** and **Review** the **Flashcards**

bad tendency standard, p. 158
balancing test, p. 167
civil liberties, p. 146
clear and present danger standard, p. 158
due process, p. 147
establishment clause, p. 165
exclusionary rule, p. 173
free exercise clause, p. 165
gravity of the danger standard, p. 161
incorporation process, p. 152
Lemon test, p. 166
Miranda warning, p. 173
neutrality test, p. 168
preferred position, p. 162
prior restraint, p. 155
selective incorporation, p. 152
substantive due process, p. 182

Test Yourself

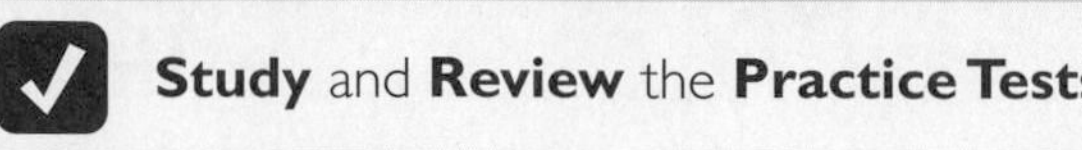

5.1 Define the civil liberties guaranteed by the Constitution, and trace the process by which they became binding on state governments.

What did the Supreme Court declare with the selective incorporation process?

a. The Constitution applied to corporations as well as persons.
b. The Bill of Rights applied to the states immediately.
c. The Bill of Rights applied to the states on a step-by-step gradual basis.
d. Corporations faced national government regulation because of changing interpretations of the commerce clause.
e. State constitutions could take precedence over the U.S. Constitution in certain instances.

5.2 Analyze the different standards by which the Supreme Court has determined whether restrictions on freedom of speech are acceptable.

What did the Supreme Court's movement away from the bad tendency standard and toward the preferred position standard represent?

a. An increased willingness to allow the national government to regulate the economy
b. An extension of the scope of the free speech provision of the Bill of Rights
c. An acknowledgment that the nationalization of the Bill of Rights directly violates the Constitution
d. An acknowledgment that in some cases affirmative action was acceptable to correct past injustices
e. A presumption that government restrictions on speech were reasonable unless proven otherwise

5.3 Evaluate how the Supreme Court has interpreted cases regarding religion and how Congress has reacted to the Court's actions.

What did the *Lemon* test do?

a. It gave the Court a method to evaluate whether the government is violating the establishment clause of the First Amendment.
b. It gave the Court a method to evaluate whether the government is violating the free exercise clause of the First Amendment.
c. It determined that certain religious freedoms would represent a "clear and present" danger to public safety.
d. It provided a four-part test to determine whether governmental action is permissible when it comes to restrictions on the free exercise of religion.
e. It established that Congress was using fiscal federalism properly in civil liberties laws.

5.4 Trace the expansion of the rights of the accused and their balance with the needs of police and prosecutors.

All of the following are rights of the accused EXCEPT

a. The right to remain silent and the right to counsel
b. Prompt arraignment
c. Trial before a judge
d. The right to refuse capital punishment
e. The opportunity to appeal a verdict

5.5 Explain how the Ninth and Fourteenth Amendments have helped establish rights other than those specifically listed in the Constitution.

What can be said about the right to privacy?

a. It has been inferred from a combination of constitutional amendments.
b. It is specifically listed in one of the first 10 amendments.
c. It was of major importance in the reinterpretation of the commerce clause.
d. It was the basis for the *Brown v. Board of Education* decision.
e. It can be inferred from the First and Second Amendments to the Constitution.

Explore Further

SUGGESTED READINGS BY TOP SCHOLARS

Steven M. Feldman. 2008. *Free Expression and Democracy in America*. Chicago: University of Chicago Press. Comprehensive and careful review of the changes in the law and politics of free speech doctrine in America since the colonial era.

Jon B. Gould. 2005. *Speak No Evil: The Triumph of Hate Speech Regulation.* Chicago: University of Chicago Press. Examines the rise of hate speech codes and other forms of hate speech regulation.

Ken I. Kersch. 2004. *Constructing Civil Liberties: Discontinuities in the Development of American Constitutional Law.* New York: Cambridge University Press. A provocative work that challenges interpretations of civil liberties jurisprudence in the 1960s as a culmination of progressive politics, arguing instead that the court decisions of that era often contrasted sharply with earlier sentiments in progressivism.

Martha Nussbaum. 2008. *Liberty of Conscience: In Defense of America's Tradition of Religious Equality.* New York: Basic

Books. An accessible and wide-ranging analysis of conflicts over religious liberty and freedom across American history.

Geoffrey R. Stone. 2004. *Perilous Times: Free Speech in Wartime from the Sedition Act of 1798 to the War on Terrorism.* New York: W. W. Norton. Focuses on six periods of war and social stress in American history and analyzes the restrictions on civil liberties in those years.

SUGGESTED WEBSITES

American Civil Liberties Union: www.aclu.org

The largest civil liberties advocacy group in the United States, active both in legislation and lawsuits. Site provides overviews of key civil liberties issues.

Institute for Justice: www.ij.org

A major civil liberties advocacy group. Their positions sometimes coincide with those of the ACLU, but the IJ is generally more aligned with conservative perspectives and the ACLU with liberal perspectives.

Electronic Frontier Foundation: www.eff.org

The leading group focused on civil liberties and free speech issues in cyberspace and digital media. Site provides issue analysis and court case updates.

First Amendment Center: www.firstamendmentcenter.org

Excellent starting point for research. "First Amendment Topics" provides gateway to description, overview, and analysis of a wide range of civil liberties issues.

Freedom House: www.freedomhouse.org

Site monitors civil liberties and democratic and economic freedom worldwide. Provides annual ranking of each country in these categories and analysis of key issues.

Oyez: www.oyez.org

Helpful and friendly site with analysis and description of U.S. Supreme Court decisions in easily understood terms. Links to audio of oral arguments and text of the Court's decision, among other features.

Listen to **Chapter 6** on **MyPoliSciLab**

6 Civil Rights

APOLOGIZING FOR THE PAST

On December 7, 1941, Japan's air force attacked the U.S. military base at Pearl Harbor, Hawaii, bringing World War II to American soil. Japanese Americans immediately found themselves the targets of suspicion and hostility, not for anything they had done, but for who they were. Two months later, in February 1942, President Franklin D. Roosevelt directed the secretary of the Department of War to move citizens supposedly vulnerable to enemy sabotage or spying (everyone knew that meant Japanese Americans) to detention centers away from military zones on the West Coast. A month later, Congress passed a law making it a crime to violate the president's directive.

The U.S. government relocated more than 120,000 Japanese Americans, and most remained in the detention centers for more than two years. They were forced to leave behind their belongings, homes, and careers. The detainees were considered un-American and were not treated equally as citizens, simply because of their ethnic identity. In 1944, the Supreme Court ruled that excluding individuals from the military zone was constitutional as an exercise of national security.[1]

The victims remained silent for decades. But in the 1970s, inspired by the successes of the black civil rights movement, the Japanese American Citizens League (JACL), an organization that lobbied on issues of interest to Japanese Americans, began to act. Under considerable pressure, President Gerald Ford issued a proclamation that rescinded President Roosevelt's order, expressing regret for this "setback to fundamental American principles." JACL passed resolutions calling for financial reimbursement for those who had been sent to the detention camps and pushed for Congress to create a federal investigatory commission, with the hope that compensation legislation would follow the commission's report.

The Commission on Wartime Relocation and Internment of Civilians began work in 1981 and issued a report in 1983 labeling the internment "a grave injustice" directly linked to racial prejudice. The commission called for a federal apology, $20,000 for each surviving detainee, and

6.1

Trace the advances and setbacks in the quest for civil rights in the nineteenth century, p. 190.

6.2

Explain the demise of the separate but equal doctrine and the creation of civil rights laws and regulations, p. 194.

6.3

Analyze the changes that led to the success and splintering of the civil rights movement, p. 205.

6.4

Describe legal and legislative actions to extend equal protection guarantees to other groups, p. 212.

SINGLED OUT With the United States at war with Japan, over 120,000 Japanese Americans were relocated to internment camps under an executive order issued by President Franklin Roosevelt. The order was justified by the president as a security necessity, but for many Americans of Japanese descent, the order stung of racial and ethnic prejudice. These unidentified children are at the Manzanar internment camp in Independence, California.

The Big Picture Should gender, ethnicity, and race be considered in college admission decisions? Author John J. Coleman looks at the progression of civil rights from Brown v. Board of Education to affirmative action today, and he explains two contemporary views of this civil rights issue.

The Basics Discover whether we have always had civil rights and whether all American citizens have them. Watch as ordinary people answer questions about where our civil rights come from and how we won them. Consider what equal treatment and protection under the law means today.

In Context Discover how civil rights issues have permeated our society since the United States was founded. In the video, University of Oklahoma political scientist Alisa H. Fryar talks about how civil rights has expanded in scope since the Civil Rights Movement of the twentieth century.

Think Like a Political Scientist Where are we headed in terms of civil rights research in the United States? University of Oklahoma political scientist Alisa H. Fryar discusses how current research on voting rights, municipal election methods, and education address civil rights issues.

In the Real World The Defense of Marriage Act declares that the federal government does not recognize same-sex marriage. Is that constitutional? Hear real people argue both sides as they discuss their beliefs about same-sex marriage, and find out how public opinion has changed dramatically over the years.

So What? Is the government obligated to do more for certain groups? Author John J. Coleman poses this and other tough questions that students need to consider when devising strategies for tackling civil rights issues, from affirmative action to same-sex marriage.

funds for research and education about the relocation of Japanese Americans. After the report was issued, the four Japanese American members of Congress introduced a bill that would implement the commission's recommendations.

Debate continued in Congress for over five years. To many members of Congress, the internment had been a reasonable response during a time of crisis. The four members of Congress who introduced the bill played a critical role in the discussions, and JACL also developed a sophisticated lobbying plan to influence Congress through letter writing and personal testimony. In August 1988, President Ronald Reagan signed the bill that provided funds for research and education, a $20,000 payment for each internee or a descendant, and a national apology for the relocation and detention of Japanese Americans.[2]

The success of the Japanese American effort stands in contrast to that of Mexican Americans. In the 1930s, an estimated 200,000 to 2 million individuals of Mexican descent—most of them legal residents or U.S. citizens, many of whom had lived their entire lives in the United States—were deported to Mexico as part of a "repatriation" program. President Herbert Hoover authorized the program, and although discontinued by President Franklin Roosevelt at the national level, many states and counties continued with their own efforts. The stated reason for the program was the Great Depression and the shortage of jobs. Public opinion, including from the organized labor movement, generally supported the deportations.[3]

Although scholars began discussing the repatriation program in the 1970s, the full scope and extent of the deportations have become clearer only over the past 20 years. Mexican American groups have been able to study the Japanese American experience as a guide to possible political action and strategy. As did the JACL, the Mexican American Legal Defense and Educational Fund (known as MALDEF) played a particularly active leadership role pushing for legislation and filing lawsuits. In 2005, then California Governor Arnold Schwarzenegger signed a bill championed by California State Senator Joseph Dunn that authorized an official apology, but he vetoed a bill that would establish a commission to consider financial reparations. Part of the act signed by Schwarzenegger called for an official memorial to the repatriation, which led to the unveiling of a monument in downtown Los Angeles in 2012. A class-action lawsuit on behalf of the surviving deportees, promoted by MALDEF, was unsuccessful.[4] Congressional efforts, cosponsored by then Representative Hilda Solis (who became Secretary of Labor in the Obama administration), to create a commission to study the deportations and consider a national apology and possible reparations were also unsuccessful.[5]

The experiences of the Japanese American internees and the Mexican American and Mexican deportees mirror the political courses of action often seen throughout the history of American civil rights activism. A group is singled out and treated differently from the rest of the population. Through shared memories, the group begins to think about its common interests. But having shared memories and interests is not enough—the group must determine how to influence the political process. Is the group unified enough to present a clear argument for its case? Should it focus on the courts, Congress, or the president? The national government or the state governments? What specific strategies and tactics might a group use to press its case? What is the right timing? Can the group draw on beliefs in the American creed to make its case, or does it need to change people's thinking? What kinds of redress, if any, could gain widespread support among government officials and the public? These are the kinds of strategic calculations and questions that groups must consider when they believe that constitutional guarantees of equal protection under the law have been violated. They are also the kinds of strategic calculations political scientists study to understand the politics of civil rights and to unlock the causal puzzle of why political involvement and action lead to successes for some groups but not for others.

This chapter reviews the major civil rights developments in the United States, looking at the substance and causes of changes in court interpretations, executive branch actions, and laws passed by Congress. The experience of black civil rights has been a thread woven through American political history and has set the model for legal and political developments for other groups, so the chapter begins with that experience and then expands to consider how other groups experienced civil rights challenges and changes in American politics.

Equality and Civil Rights

6.1 Trace the advances and setbacks in the quest for civil rights in the nineteenth century.

civil rights
guarantees of equal opportunities, privileges, and treatment under the law that allow individuals to participate fully and equally in American society.

Barack Obama, an African American of mixed racial heritage, became president of the United States in 2009 and began his second term in 2013. His victories did not end the American civil rights story, but shine a bright light on dramatic changes in American politics and society.

Understanding the significance of President Obama's accomplishment requires a close look at the politics and evolution of **civil rights** in the United States. Civil rights are the guarantees of government to provide equal opportunities, privileges, and treatment under the law for all individuals. They entail sharing in the equal rights and responsibilities of citizenship and being fully part of the American nation.

When Americans claim that civil rights have been violated, they usually mean that the government needs to defend the rights of an individual or group that has been denied some form of access or opportunity based on race, ethnicity, color, gender, religion, sexual orientation, or other group characteristic. When groups or individuals assert their civil rights, they are telling government that it needs to act on behalf of those receiving unequal treatment in society.

In American politics, discriminatory treatment toward different groups has led to angry and sometimes bloody conflict over civil rights. This experience has torn through the history of many groups. The experience of black Americans has been a particular touchstone for civil rights. Most civil rights laws and court decisions arose originally in the area of black-white relations and set the framework for the legal status of other groups. Because the black civil rights movement was also the earliest to be extensively organized, it provides a historical example that has played a key role in the evolution of American civil rights for other groups.

The Constitution Did Not Prohibit Slavery

The Framers of the Constitution faced a dilemma. After independence, several northern states prohibited slavery, while southern states retained it. Addressing slavery in any direct way during the Constitutional Convention might well have been a deal breaker, ending the possibility of crafting a constitution to unite the 13 colonies. But the issue could not be entirely avoided.

Although the word *slavery* did not appear in the original Constitution, three provisions in the document related to it. First, the Three-fifths Compromise determined that three-fifths of a state's slave population would be added to its headcount for purposes of allocating representatives in the House of Representatives. Second, the importation of slaves was to cease after 1808. Third, fugitive slaves were to be returned to their owners.[6] The net result of these provisions was the constitutional acceptance of slavery.

For 70 years following ratification of the Constitution, slavery repeatedly flared up as an issue, particularly when it came to America's westward expansion. Political leaders tried to keep the nation together through legislative compromises and to balance the power of slave states and free states.

The Supreme Court Rejects Black Citizenship in *Dred Scott v. Sandford*

One particularly dramatic development brought the issue of slavery to the Supreme Court. Dred Scott, a slave from Missouri, traveled with his owner to Illinois, a free state, and to other free territories north of the line established by the Missouri Compromise of 1820. The compromise had established in which territories and states slavery would be legal. Scott and his owner lived in these free areas for seven years, ultimately returning to Missouri, a slave state. When his owner died, Scott filed a lawsuit in Missouri, arguing that he should be considered a free man because he had been living on free soil.[7] The owner's widow opposed Scott's petition. After a series of court decisions in Scott's home state of Missouri, Scott brought the case to federal court. To file a federal lawsuit, however, Scott had to demonstrate that he was a citizen.

In one of the most notorious opinions in its history, the Supreme Court ruled in ***Dred Scott v. Sandford*** (1857) that Scott could not bring his case to federal court. To Chief Justice Roger Taney, the question was straightforward: "Can a negro, whose ancestors were imported into this country, and sold as slaves, become a member of the political community formed and brought into existence by the Constitution of the United States, and as such become entitled to all the rights, and privileges, and immunities, guaranteed by that instrument to the citizen?" Taney's answer was no: Slaves could not be citizens, and neither could the descendants of slaves, whether or not they were free. When the Constitution was written, the Court concluded, blacks were considered "subordinate and inferior" to the "dominant race." Therefore, they could not possibly be considered citizens or part of "the people" as understood by the authors of the Constitution.

Dred Scott v. Sandford
Supreme Court decision in 1857 declaring that neither slaves nor the descendants of slaves could be U.S. citizens.

equal protection clause
clause in the Fourteenth Amendment stating that states are not to deny any person equal treatment under the law.

The Civil War Amendments Bring Civil Rights Into the Constitution

The *Dred Scott* decision also declared the Missouri Compromise to be an unconstitutional use of congressional power because it deprived slaveholders of their property without due process of law. The political firestorm it triggered was one of the contributing factors to the country's move toward civil war. By mid-1865, when the Civil War drew to a close, a nation disassembled by war needed to be put back together—not on its old terms, but recast, with black Americans as citizens. From 1865 through 1877, this process, known as Reconstruction, repeated the efforts of the revolutionary and constitutional eras to build both a sense of shared nationhood and a government capable of delivering the war's hard-won gains to blacks. It was, in effect, the third time the young country would try to lay a new foundation for itself.

Following the Civil War, the Thirteenth, Fourteenth, and Fifteenth Amendments—commonly referred to as the Civil War amendments—were added to the Constitution. All concerned civil rights for blacks. Congress included a section in each amendment giving it the authority to enforce the amendment by "appropriate legislation." This was an attempt to prevent the Supreme Court from saying that Congress did not have constitutional authority to act, as the Court had ruled in the *Dred Scott* decision. For a country imbued with a political culture of limited government, the addition of that power-expanding language represented a remarkable move by Congress. The Thirteenth Amendment, ratified in December 1865, made slavery unconstitutional anywhere within the United States. The Fifteenth Amendment, ratified in March 1870, made it unconstitutional for the national government or state governments to deny an individual the right to vote based on race, color, or previous history of having been a slave or of having been descended from a slave.

The Fourteenth Amendment, ratified in July 1868, has had an extraordinary impact on American politics and life. It established that anyone born or naturalized in the United States is a citizen of the United States and also the state in which he or she lives. This edict made it clear that former slaves were fully citizens. It then declared that no state shall "deny to any person within its jurisdiction the equal protection of the laws." This **equal protection clause** would be the basis of much of the subsequent legislation and many of the court decisions concerning civil rights.

Congress Passes Civil Rights Legislation to Bring Blacks Into American Civic Life

In addition to the Civil War amendments, Reconstruction included other legislation that assisted the promotion of black civil rights. The Freedmen's Bureau, created in 1865, provided food, clothing, and fuel; established schools; supervised labor-management relations; and created a system by which blacks could become landowners. The Civil Rights Act of 1866 guaranteed blacks the same property and legal rights as whites.[8] It also provided for the punishment of those who violated an individual's rights because of race or color.[9] In response to violence and the rise of the Ku Klux Klan, a secretive group that terrorized blacks, Congress passed four "enforcement acts" in 1870 and 1871 to ensure the implementation of these legislative promises.[10] They provided protection for black voters, ensured access to office holding and jury duty for blacks, and monitored equal treatment under the law. As a result, blacks, running as Republicans, were elected to state governments and to Congress. They began attending schools and entering professions in large numbers. The final legislative action was the Civil Rights Act of 1875, which concerned the private sector. It promised blacks the "full and equal enjoyment" of hotels, transportation, and places of entertainment such as theaters.

"Equal Protection of the Laws" Does Not Prohibit Private Discrimination

The Civil Rights Act of 1875 seemed to mark the end of a decade of civil rights action that promised substantial equality and integration for blacks. But reality proved otherwise. By 1877, federal troops had been removed from the South, and the former Confederate states were essentially on their own. Southern state governments came

SOUTH CAROLINA LEGISLATURE, 1873

During Reconstruction, blacks advanced to new positions in southern society. In many states, blacks were elected to the legislature in significant numbers. The white backlash against this success would take firm root after Reconstruction's end in 1877. Blacks were routinely denied the right to vote and violently harassed when they sought to exercise this right, and black officeholding quickly disappeared.

under the control of whites who had been unhappy with the changes since 1865. And the Supreme Court interpreted civil rights laws and amendments in a narrow way that significantly hampered black equality with whites.

One major stumbling block was whether the Civil War amendments covered actions in the private sector. The Court ruled that they did not. *Strauder v. West Virginia* (1880) was the first case in which the Court was asked to apply the equal protection clause to black civil rights. The Court struck down a West Virginia law that limited jury duty to white males. The decision indicated the Court saw the Fourteenth Amendment as directly applicable to the actions of state governments, known as the doctrine of **state action.** But what about private sector discriminatory actions? In the *Civil Rights Cases* (1883), the Court consolidated five cases from California, Kansas, Missouri, New Jersey, and Tennessee, in which blacks had been denied service in private establishments—seemingly a violation of the Civil Rights Act of 1875. The Court declared the 1875 act unconstitutional because it concerned discriminatory private, as opposed to government, action.[11] The Fourteenth Amendment, in the Court's view, applied to the actions of governments: It did not apply to discriminatory private behavior between individuals.[12] This state action view of the Fourteenth Amendment has remained a binding standard for Court decisions.

state action
Supreme Court interpretation of the equal protection clause holding that the clause prohibited unfair discriminatory actions by government, not by private individuals.

The Supreme Court Declares That Segregating the Races Does Not Violate Equal Protection in *Plessy v. Ferguson*

The Court's decisions in the *Civil Rights Cases* established that government actions that discriminated against blacks violated equal protection but that private discrimination was not unconstitutional. Working within these guidelines, some state governments proved creative in their attempts to perpetuate a society in which whites

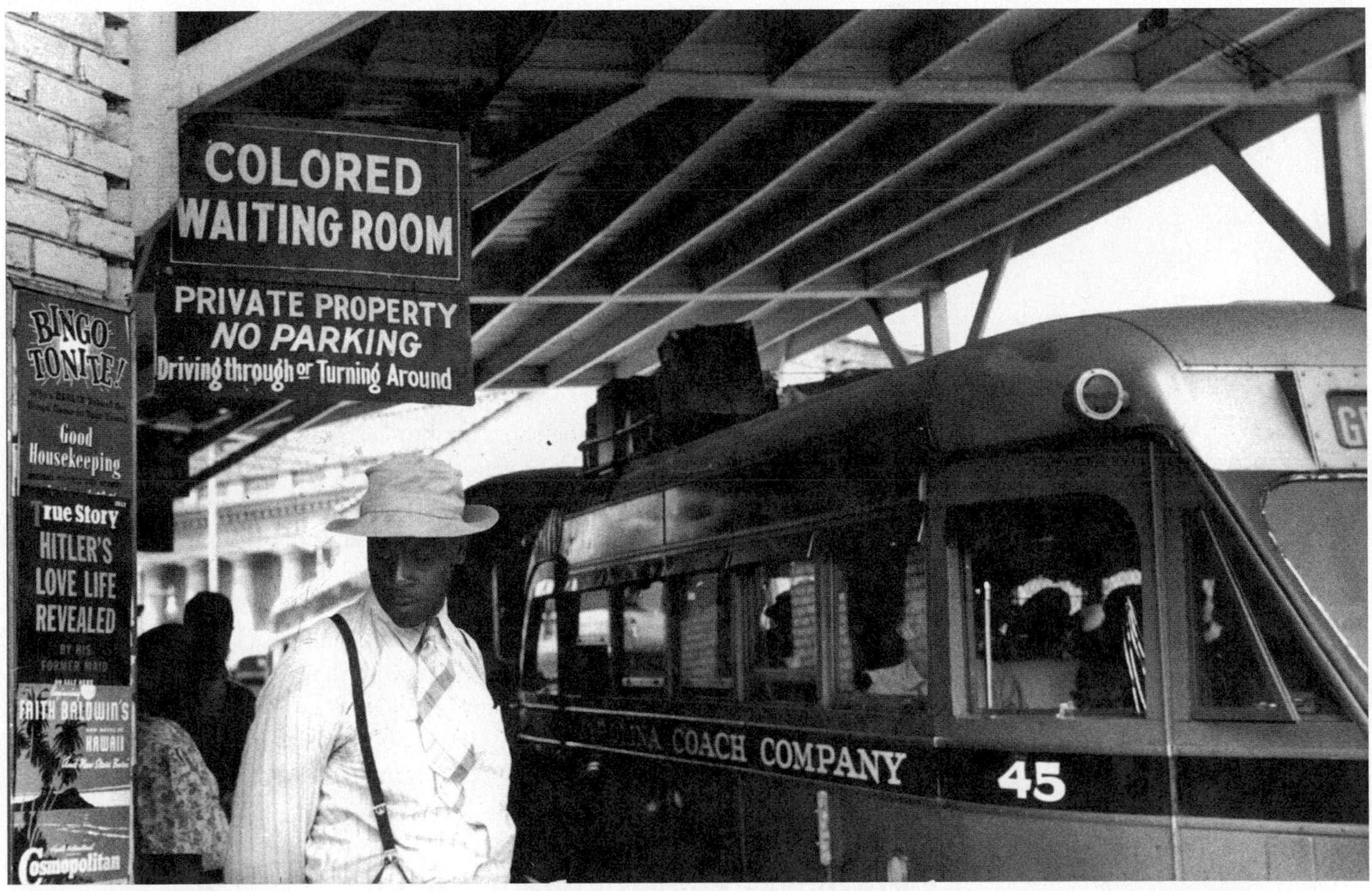

JIM CROW IN DURHAM, NORTH CAROLINA, 1940

The separate but equal doctrine was the cornerstone of racial segregation. The Supreme Court validated the doctrine in 1896, but in *Brown v. Board of Education* in 1954, it declared that mandatory racial separation is inherently unequal and unconstitutional.

6.1

6.2

6.3

6.4

Jim Crow
system of laws that separated the races in schools, public accommodations, and other aspects of daily life.

Plessy v. Ferguson
Supreme Court decision in 1896 upholding the constitutionality of laws and government policies that required segregated facilities for blacks and whites.

separate but equal doctrine
Supreme Court doctrine that laws or policies requiring segregated facilities for the races are constitutionally acceptable as long as the facilities are of equal quality.

dominated. Beginning in the late 1880s, southern states enacted laws that required blacks and whites to be separated when they used public accommodations. Referred to as **Jim Crow** laws, the statutes covered a wide range of circumstances. From parks to schools, hotels, restaurants, hospitals, prisons, funeral homes, cemeteries, sporting events, restrooms, entrances, exits, transportation, and more, the laws required separate facilities for blacks and whites. Blacks were prohibited from eating at whites-only restaurants, attending whites-only state universities, or riding in the front of public buses. African Americans had separate and usually unequal hospital and educational systems. In 1890, Louisiana passed a law requiring all railway companies to provide "equal but separate accommodations" for blacks and whites.

Homer Plessy was arrested in June 1892 after he boarded a train in New Orleans and refused to leave the car reserved for whites.[13] In ***Plessy v. Ferguson*** (1896), the Supreme Court ruled 8–1 that Louisiana's law was constitutional. Separate accommodations were not a "badge of servitude" akin to slavery, the Court ruled, so the Thirteenth Amendment did not apply. As for the Fourteenth Amendment, there was nothing inherently discriminatory in separating the races, the Court concluded, as long as each race was accommodated. The amendment intended to create equality before the law, not to abolish racial distinctions or enforce social integration. Indeed, the Court noted, Congress had passed acts requiring separate schools for blacks in the District of Columbia, so it would not likely disapprove of similar acts in the states. According to the **separate but equal doctrine,** it was constitutional to require separate facilities for the races, as long as the facilities were substantially equal, even though not identical. The Court interpreted Louisiana's law as a reasonable attempt to promote the public good as legislators saw it, not an attempt to oppress any group and not a violation of equal protection of the laws.

These late-nineteenth-century decisions limited national authority over race relations. Neither the president nor members of Congress were likely to address racial discrimination seriously. For southern politicians, such action would be career ending. For northern politicians, few constituencies pushed actively for integration. And the Supreme Court constitutionally protected segregation.[14]

Equal Protection of the Laws Gains Meaning

6.2 Explain the demise of the separate but equal doctrine and the creation of civil rights laws and regulations.

Segregation proved to be separate, but certainly not equal. Facilities and services provided to blacks were notably inferior in quality, quantity, and convenience. For nearly half a century after the *Plessy* decision, federal politicians did little to improve the political, economic, social, or legal status of blacks in the United States. Jim Crow continued unabated, and black voters in the South dwindled to just a small percentage of all blacks, because of discriminatory voting restrictions. Leaders of black civil rights organizations, however, continued to press for governmental action. After a long period, these efforts began to succeed. In fits and starts, the legal underpinning for segregation eroded. Finally, in 1954, the separate but equal doctrine came crashing down. Soon afterward, a wave of legislative and administrative changes would follow and advance civil rights, not only for blacks but for other groups of Americans as well.

Presidents Bypass Congress to Chip Away at Racial Discrimination

Black political activists knew that elected officials needed to consider the protection of civil rights as being in their own political interests, especially given the

Supreme Court's blunt acceptance of segregation. Over the first four decades of the twentieth century, activists formed organizations to represent black political interests, place pressure on politicians, and form a legal strategy for use in the courts. The most important of these organizations was the National Association for the Advancement of Colored People (NAACP), formed in 1909. The organization focused largely on legal strategies in its first two decades and began deeper consideration of legislative and administrative strategies in the 1930s. At the time of the NAACP's founding, white southern Democrats dominated Congress and thwarted any attempts to pass civil rights legislation. For this reason, the NAACP primarily concentrated its lobbying efforts on the president and the executive branch, and this strategy began to bear fruit during the presidency of Franklin Roosevelt (1933–1945).

Roosevelt used his unilateral executive powers to make some progress in civil rights. He appointed more blacks to his administration than any previous president. In June 1941, in part to forestall a massive March on Washington by blacks, but also because of the acceleration in military production brought on by U.S. assistance to Britain and China in mid-1941, President Roosevelt signed an executive order—a presidential proclamation with the force of law that does not require congressional approval—creating the Fair Employment Practices Committee (FEPC).[15] The order mandated an end to employment discrimination based on race, creed, color, or national origin in companies and U.S. government agencies involved in defense production, and it authorized the committee to punish offenders. The FEPC expired in 1946 when Congress refused to extend funding.

Following Roosevelt's death in April 1945, President Harry Truman (1945–1952) continued the use of executive orders to advance civil rights in the face of congressional opposition. Executive Order 9980 created the Fair Employment Board and forbade all racial discrimination in federal government hiring. Truman took his most dramatic civil rights action by integrating the armed forces through Executive Order 9981. Issued in July 1948, the order declared that regardless of race, color, national origin, or religion, there would be "equality of treatment and opportunity" for all members of the military. By October 1954, the last all-black military unit had been disbanded, and the military had become the most fully integrated institution in American society.

☐ Court Decisions Begin to Challenge Separate but Equal

Supreme Court decisions after 1937 began to challenge racial discrimination. Why this change at this time? In large part, the new perspective coincided with a major change in Court membership. Between 1937 and 1943, President Roosevelt appointed eight new justices; between 1945 and 1949, President Truman appointed three. And in education, blacks began to make some civil rights progress. Although the Court did not challenge the separate but equal doctrine during this period, it became more demanding in ensuring somewhat comparable conditions for black and white students. In 1938, the Court struck down Missouri's practice of paying blacks' tuition at out-of-state law schools rather than enrolling them at the University of Missouri Law School.[16] Although this decision did not result in integration of the law school—Missouri established a separate law school for minorities—it indicated that the Court was looking more carefully at how "equal" the conditions facing the races really were. Forcing students of one race to leave their state to attend school elsewhere was not, in the Court's view, comparable treatment. Following this victory, blacks in other states won similar victories at professional schools.

Engaging in lawsuits that challenged the system of segregation in American education was the strategy of the newly created legal arm of the NAACP, the NAACP Legal Defense and Educational Fund, formed in 1940. The organization sought first to win victories at specific schools around the idea of what "equal" meant. With successes in those cases on the state level, and in federal courts if those decisions were appealed, the organization could then move to challenge separate but equal as a principle.

6.1

6.2

6.3

6.4

Brown v. Board of Education
Supreme Court ruling in 1954 that in public education, mandatory separation of children by race leads to inherently unequal education. The decision overturned the separate but equal doctrine.

In 1950, the Supreme Court ruled that an alternative Texas law school for black students did not provide "substantial equality," and it ruled that a black student at the University of Oklahoma School of Education could not be separated from white students in classrooms, libraries, or cafeterias. For the first time, the Court hinted that separation itself was likely to damage the quality of a student's education.[17] Victories in these important cases convinced the organization that the time had come to challenge the *Plessy* decision.

The Supreme Court Declares Segregation Unconstitutional in *Brown v. Board of Education*

With these victories, the stage had been set for an assault on the separate but equal doctrine. Four cases in 1951 and 1952, from Kansas, South Carolina, Virginia, and Delaware, challenged the doctrine in education. The Supreme Court consolidated these cases and considered them together as ***Brown v. Board of Education*** *of Topeka, Kansas* (1954). The lead case was prompted when Oliver Brown attempted to enroll his daughter for third grade in an all-white school and was turned away. Arguing the case on behalf of Brown was Thurgood Marshall of the NAACP, who later became the first black Supreme Court justice.

AN INTEGRATION PIONEER IN LITTLE ROCK, ARKANSAS, 1957

Elizabeth Eckford arrives for her first day of class at Little Rock Central High School. A federal court ordered the school to enroll her and eight other black students. The court's order was prompted by a lawsuit filed by the NAACP.

Under the leadership of Chief Justice Earl Warren, the Court unanimously struck down the separate but equal doctrine. Avoiding any definitive stand on what the Fourteenth Amendment required in public education, the Court instead emphasized the importance of education in modern society and asked whether segregating the races provided equal opportunity for black children. In the Court's view, the answer was no. Referring to psychological studies, the Court concluded that segregation could generate a permanent "feeling of inferiority as to their status in the community." In public education, the Court famously ruled, "the doctrine of 'separate but equal' has no place. Separate educational facilities are inherently unequal."

The *Brown* decision brought down the legal and constitutional edifice of enforced segregation, as it struck down the laws of 21 states.[18] In practical terms, however, change was not as swift. Aware of the potential explosiveness of its decision, the Court did not set any timetable in *Brown*. In a follow-up opinion in 1955, referred to as *Brown II*, the Court stated that school districts should move with "all deliberate speed" to desegregate their schools.[19]

Massive resistance, especially in the South, blunted the speed of change. Many school boards preferred to go to court rather than voluntarily abide by the Court's ruling. Other districts sought to disband their public schools. Incidents of violence and intimidation to keep blacks from white schools were common. A decade after *Brown*, barely 3 percent of southern black children attended schools in which a majority of students were white.

In response to this foot dragging, the federal government began threatening to initiate lawsuits and withhold federal funds from states and districts that were not making progress in implementing desegregation. These tactics were effective. By 1970, about one-third of southern black children attended majority-white schools and 90 percent attended schools with at least some white students.[20]

de jure segregation
racial segregation that occurs because it is written into law, policy, or government procedures.

de facto segregation
racial segregation that results not because of explicit law, policy, or procedures, but from patterns of behavior that have the effect of segregating the races.

Civil Rights Activists Seek to Extend *Brown*'s Reach to Cases of De Facto Segregation

Activists in the black civil rights movement pushed courts to address instances both of de jure segregation and de facto segregation. **De jure segregation** refers to segregation explicitly written into laws and regulations—the kind of segregation outlawed by the *Brown* decision and common in southern states. **De facto segregation** occurs, in practice, because of patterns of behavior. If residential patterns are highly skewed racially, for example, and all children attend the school nearest to them, then schools would automatically remain highly segregated—a pattern common in the North. The issue became whether schools were required to desegregate, which could be achieved by repealing de jure segregation, or whether they were required to integrate, which would also entail challenging de facto segregation.

The Court's early decisions leaned toward integration.[21] "Busing," an especially controversial remedy, called for students to be bused from one part of a school district to another in order to achieve a particular racial balance, even if there had been no history of de jure segregation in the district. A later Court decision scaled back this remedy. In 1974, by a 5–4 vote, the Supreme Court concluded that the Fourteenth Amendment's equal protection guarantee did not extend to de facto segregation if there was no evidence that a school district intended to discriminate (see Table 6.1).[22] With this ruling in place, courts could not easily order school districts to use busing to remedy de facto segregation in the schools.

Nonetheless, school districts could voluntarily devise busing and other integration plans in order to achieve more diversity at their schools or to thwart potential lawsuits. For three decades, many districts did precisely that. In *Parents Involved in Community Schools (PICS) v. Seattle* (2007), however, the Supreme Court struck down such plans in Seattle, Washington, and Louisville, Kentucky, as an unconstitutional violation of equal protection.[23] In each city, white parents whose children were denied admission to a school on racial grounds brought the lawsuit against the school districts. The decision allowed districts to continue to find ways to make their schools more diverse,

TABLE 6.1 SIGNIFICANT SUPREME COURT DECISIONS ON SCHOOL DESEGREGATION

Case	Year of Decision	Decision
Brown v. Board of Education of Topeka, Kansas	1954	Segregated "separate but equal" schools are inherently unequal and unconstitutional.
Green v. County School Board of New Kent County	1968	Integration and not simply repeal of discriminatory laws and practices are necessary to comply with the "unitary system" of schools implied by *Brown*. Examination of student assignments, faculty assignments, staff assignments, transportation, physical facilities, and extracurricular activities will determine whether a school system is unitary or dual and separate.
Swann v. Charlotte-Mecklenburg Board of Education	1971	Busing is acceptable as a remedy to desegregate schools, as are quotas. The racial balance at a school need not be identical to the overall district balance. A school district's intent to discriminate by law or practice must be proven before a court imposes a desegregation plan.
Milliken v. Bradley	1974	Court-imposed busing cannot cover multiple school districts such as a city and its suburbs, unless intentional segregation is demonstrated in each district.
Freeman v. Pitts	1992	Federal courts can gradually withdraw from oversight of school districts as they are convinced that specific aspects of a desegregation plan are being met.
Parents Involved in Community Schools (PICS) v. Seattle School District No. 1	2007	Denying students enrollment in particular schools on the basis of their race, as part of a school district's voluntary integration or diversity plan, is unconstitutional.

through the drawing of school boundaries, magnet schools that specialize in a particular subject such as the arts or science and accept students from across an entire district, open enrollment in which students may enroll in any school in a district and perhaps in neighboring districts as well, and other such plans. School districts could not, however, make an individual student's enrollment in a school dependent on his or her race. Wrote Chief Justice John Roberts, "the way to stop discrimination on the basis of race is to stop discriminating on the basis of race." But as critics saw it, the decision effectively overturned *Brown* and would accelerate the resegregation of schools in the United States.[24]

Racial resegregation of schools had been on the upswing for at least 20 years prior to the decision—for example, the percentage of minority students in schools that were almost exclusively minority increased over this period (see Figure 6.1). In addition, the Court's restriction of voluntary desegregation plans such as those in Seattle and Louisville put pressure on those districts to find other ways to reverse resegregation without running afoul of the Supreme Court.[25]

The debate over how best—or whether—to achieve racial integration in education will continue as districts devise plans they hope will meet the Supreme Court's approval. In its *PICS* decision, the Court did not rule out using income and other socioeconomic factors as a basis for enrollment. Because minority status is often correlated with income and wealth, this approach achieves racial integration by increasing socioeconomic diversity. One challenge for architects of even the most creative integration and diversity plans will remain finding public support for their efforts. Although support for integration is certainly widespread in public opinion polls, some research suggests that surveys may overstate support on socially sensitive topics dealing with race, including integration. In addition, although the public considers diverse schools to be important, such diversity does not necessarily outweigh other considerations such as parents having some choice over school assignments and the quality of instruction and educational programs.[26]

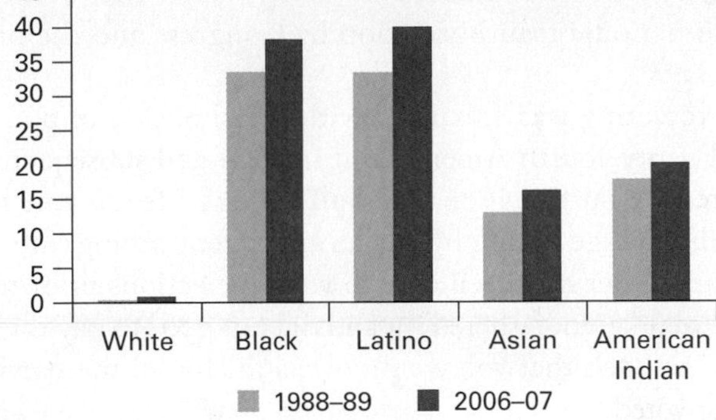

FIGURE 6.1 PERCENTAGE OF STUDENTS IN SCHOOLS OF 90 TO 100 PERCENT MINORITY ENROLLMENT.

Over a two-decade period prior to the *PICS v. Seattle* (2007) decision, the percentage of black, Latino, Asian, and American Indian students who attended schools with almost an entirely minority population increased.

Source: Gary Orfield, *Reviving the Goal of an Integrated Society: A 21st Century Challenge* (Los Angeles: University of California Civil Rights Project, 2009).

New Laws and Executive Orders Expand Civil Rights Protection

During the 1960s, civil rights also advanced in other spheres of public and private life. As with the education system, public officials employed both legislation and executive orders in this process.

LEGISLATION The Civil Rights Act of 1964 is the centerpiece of American anti-discrimination law. Work on the law began under President John Kennedy and, following his assassination, was completed by President Lyndon Johnson. The law prohibited discrimination in public accommodations and in private employment on the basis of race, color, religion, sex, and national origin.

On the surface, this law sounds similar to the 1875 Civil Rights Act that was struck down in the *Civil Rights Cases*—the decision ruling that the Fourteenth Amendment gave Congress the authority to regulate only government action, not private behavior. Significantly, however, Congress justified the Civil Rights Act of 1964 not in terms of the equal protection guarantee of the Fourteenth Amendment, but by linking the law to Congress's power to regulate commerce. The Supreme Court in 1937 established a generous definition of interstate commerce that vastly expanded the power of the federal government. As a result, if Congress could link discrimination to impediments and distortions in the flow of commerce, it could regulate discriminatory actions in the private sector.

Grounding Congress's action in an established constitutional power such as regulation of interstate commerce opened significant new horizons for civil rights legislation. The Civil Rights Act of 1964 also set the mold in another way: it denied federal funds to any program or activity that discriminated. After 1964, Congress justified all civil rights legislation that affected the private sector either on interstate commerce grounds or as an extension of Congress's control over federal spending.[27] By doing so, Congress bypassed the restrictions of the state action doctrine. The Civil Rights Act of 1968, which prohibited discrimination in the sale, rental, financing, or advertising of housing on the basis of race, color, religion, or national origin, is one key example.

Another signal legislative achievement was the Voting Rights Act of 1965. Earlier laws provided modest federal oversight of southern elections. The 1965 act was much stronger than these. It prohibited the use of discriminatory methods, such as literacy tests, intended to weaken the voting power of blacks. States or parts of states with a history of such methods were required to clear any changes in their voting laws with the Department of Justice. The same pre-clearance rule applied to laws that might affect the electoral power of minorities. For example, pre-clearance would be necessary if a city with a significant minority population wished to annex

6.1

6.2

6.3

6.4

poll tax
fee assessed on each person who wishes to vote; prohibited by the Twenty-fourth Amendment in 1964.

affirmative action
efforts to reach and attract applicants for jobs, college admissions, and business contracts from traditionally underrepresented groups, ranging from extensive publicity and outreach to quota plans.

neighboring suburbs that were almost completely white. The pre-clearance requirement is subject to periodic reauthorization by Congress and the president and remains in place today.[28]

Black access to voting was enhanced with the abolition of poll taxes in federal elections by the Twenty-fourth Amendment in 1964 and subsequently in state elections by the Supreme Court in 1966.[29] A **poll tax** was a fee to vote in an election. It was designed to discourage voting by blacks and recent immigrants. For example, if your father or grandfather had been able to vote in elections prior to the Thirteenth Amendment, you were "grandfathered" in and did not need to pay the tax. Some states had a cumulative tax, such that you would owe a fee for all the previous elections in which you had not voted.

These changes had significant effects. Voting by blacks surged and black candidates began winning elected office. The Supreme Court's "one person, one vote" mandates of the 1960s, which improved the representation of urban areas within states, further boosted black political participation and candidate success. Without these changes, Barack Obama's achievement would have been even more diffiicult. The groundwork to his victory in 2008 was laid in the victories for voting rights in the 1960s.

In recent years, one of the most hotly contested areas of election law concerns the requirement that voters show a photo ID, usually government–issued ID such as a driver's license, when they show up to vote. Proponents argue that the requirement is necessary to reduce the possibility of voter fraud. Critics reply that the degree of voter fraud is greatly exaggerated and that this particular method of addressing the problem most heavily impacts blacks and other minorities, the elderly, and the young, who are less likely to have a form of official photo identification that meets the standard. The laws have been introduced primarily by Republican legislators, but the few national surveys on the subject indicate bipartisan public support often near 80 percent.[30]

In *Crawford v. Marion County Board* (2008), the U.S. Supreme Court, in a 6–3 ruling, upheld the constitutionality of an Indiana photo ID law, concluding that the law imposed a slight burden on the right to vote that was outweighed by the state's interest in election integrity, and that the burden was neutral and nondiscriminatory. The Court's ruling does not give blanket approval to such plans—an overly burdensome arrangement might be struck down. In 2012, the Department of Justice launched an investigation into the voter ID laws in several states to assess whether they were overly restrictive of voting access. About a dozen states had photo ID laws in 2012 and another 18 required some form of ID at the polls.[31]

EXECUTIVE ORDERS As noted earlier, Presidents Roosevelt and Truman began using executive orders to advance civil rights—a practice continued by later presidents. Presidents Eisenhower and Kennedy, for example, used executive orders to activate National Guard units in Arkansas, Mississippi, and Alabama to enforce school desegregation. President Kennedy ordered the creation of compliance mechanisms for nondiscriminatory employment policies by federal contractors. Orders by later presidents enhanced these mechanisms. Additional categories of protection were added as well, including discrimination based on sex (President Johnson), disability and age (President Carter), and sexual orientation and status as a parent (President Clinton).[32]

AFFIRMATIVE ACTION Despite becoming one of the most controversial civil rights policies, affirmative action started out quietly in executive orders issued by Presidents Kennedy, Johnson, and Nixon in the 1960s to combat discrimination in federal hiring and contracts.[33] On its face, **affirmative action** calls for aggressive outreach efforts targeted to groups traditionally underrepresented in particular jobs and college admissions. Concerned that outreach might not be enough to satisfy the Supreme

Court, many employers, colleges, and government administrators interpreted affirmative action to require setting guidelines, such as quotas, for the recruitment of minorities. Some black leaders feared that quotas would lead to a white backlash.[34] For leaders such as Martin Luther King Jr., this was a dangerous risk. And to the extent that "affirmative action" was thought of strictly as "quotas," it was in fact highly unpopular among white voters (see *How Do We Know? Is White Opposition to Affirmative Action Racist?*).

Since 1989, the Supreme Court has been reining in the scope of these efforts. In *Richmond v. Croson* (1989), the Court struck down "set-aside" programs that required contractors on city projects to subcontract 30 percent of the project to minority businesses. The Court declared that state and local affirmative action such as that in Richmond could not be initiated as a response to racism in general—there had to be a specific discriminatory practice in a specific location to justify the need for the affirmative action policy. The Court further narrowed the scope of affirmative action programs in its 5–4 decision in *Adarand v. Pena* (1995), a case concerning extra payments supplied by the federal government to contractors who hired minority firms. The decision decreed that racial classifications at all levels of government would be subject to strict scrutiny, meaning the Court would need to be convinced that the classification was necessary to meet a compelling government interest, and that this interest was being achieved in the most targeted manner possible (was "narrowly tailored"). And a 5–4 decision in *Ricci v. DeStefano* (2009) concluded that New Haven, Connecticut, could not throw out the results of a firefighter promotion exam simply because officials feared being sued when few minorities did well.

Affirmative action affected college admissions as well. In ***Regents of the University of California v. Bakke*** (1978), the Court prohibited racial quotas for college admissions but ruled that race could be a "plus" factor considered along with other admissions criteria. In 2003, the Supreme Court in *Grutter v. Bollinger* upheld in a 5–4 vote the University of Michigan Law School's "holistic" use of race to foster viewpoint diversity at the school but rejected, in *Gratz v. Bollinger*, the University of Michigan's undergraduate admissions process. The college awarded 20 points—one-fifth of the total needed to guarantee admission—to every African American, Hispanic, and Native American applicant. Although again confirming that student diversity is a compelling government interest, the Court concluded that the college's automatic point system was not, as the*Bakke* decision called for, a narrowly tailored solution.

Regents of the University of California v. Bakke
Supreme Court decision in 1978 that a rigid quota plan for admissions violates the Constitution's equal protection guarantee, but race could be considered a "plus factor" in college admissions to increase student body diversity.

Voters in Arizona, California, Michigan, Nebraska, and Washington banned their state's use of affirmative action policies—usually defined in these constitutional amendments as discriminating against or granting preferential treatment in public hiring, contracting, and education. Oklahoma was the latest state to adopt such a ban, in 2012.

☐ Civil Rights Policies Vary Across Countries

The United States is not the only country to struggle with racial and ethnic conflict. European countries have faced tremendous electoral and policy tensions resulting from the diversity of their increasingly immigrant populations. The European Union in 2000 called for an end to discrimination in education, employment, housing, social welfare, and training, along the lines of American anti-discrimination law and policy. Countries remained free to add preference policies for groups long discriminated against. Progress has been uneven across Europe in implementing the decree.

Each country's particular political culture has shaped the extent to which it emphasizes two key tools: anti-discrimination laws and government programs. Compared to other countries, the United States has stronger anti-discrimination laws but less generous government benefits. Generous programs do not ensure nondiscrimination,

6.1

6.2

6.3

6.4

How Do We Know?

Is White Opposition to Affirmative Action Racist?

The Question

The opinions of whites and blacks are often far apart on policies such as affirmative action, school desegregation, and spending on social programs. Genuine principled opposition among whites to certain roles for government could explain such a gap. It could also be explained by white racism. If whites hold inherently negative and generalized views toward racial minorities, they might be more likely to oppose policies that seem to disproportionately benefit minority groups. Is white opposition to affirmative action racist? How do we know?

Why It Matters

Whether white opposition to policies benefiting minorities is based on bigotry or other factors matters for at least two reasons. First, political culture is negotiable. Advocates for a policy can try to convince people to balance beliefs in a new way or to redefine what they mean by particular beliefs. If policy opposition is based on political culture, there is some prospect that opponents and proponents can engage in dialogue. On the other hand, if policy opposition is based on racism, this more deep-seated resistance will be hard to change. Second, if bigotry, rather than different weighting of beliefs in the American creed, is the primary reason for opposition to certain policies, then the prospects for civil rights and racial and ethnic harmony would seem dim. The answer tells us something about how far the United States has evolved from the days of acute, public racism.

Investigating the Answer

Political scientists have explored this question largely through research on black and white public opinion, so that is the focus here.[a] The outcome analyzed is white opposition to affirmative action. The two competing factors that may explain the outcome are racist beliefs and general philosophical beliefs about government's appropriate role.

Public opinion data show substantial differences between whites and blacks on matters related to race, with whites often opposing the adoption of policies favored by blacks. The differences between the races' attitudes toward race-related policies, income redistribution programs, and the fairness of American life are often larger than those of class, gender, and religion.[b]

Exploring the extent to which racial considerations drive white opinion has been a large, complex, and heated area of debate in political science research.[c] One group of scholars points to the significance of what they call racial resentment.[d] Traditional racism was cruel and blunt and built around an explicitly stated belief in white racial superiority. The success of the civil rights movement, however, blocked that kind of racism from entering public discourse. Its public legitimacy evaporated: Words that were once commonly said could now no longer be said.

In its place, however, arose a more subtle racism in which blacks were not seen as inherently inferior but were critiqued for not making the best of the opportunities given to them. This racism blends traditional beliefs of American political culture, especially individualism, with disaffection for blacks or what is considered "black behavior." Discrimination, in this view, is not a significant problem and is used as an excuse by blacks for their failure to work and study hard and their expectation that government should take care of people even if they make poor choices in life. This racism is hard to detect in surface behavior, but underneath it are suppressed racist views. Extensive analysis of survey research has led scholars in this school to conclude that white attitudes toward affirmative action and similar programs are strongly determined by this racial resentment.

Another group of scholars believes the racial resentment argument goes too far in blaming racism for white opposition to programs such as affirmative action. This view claims that the impact of any white racism on policy attitudes has been overstated and is less important than general ideological predispositions about government. Whites are not averse to assistance for blacks, but they are, on average, less likely than blacks to support the types of assistance policies and programs favored by liberals. Opposition to certain programs would exist because of ideological positions favoring limited government, regardless of whether the beneficiaries were white or black. To the extent that the racial resentment argument presumes that liberal positions favor racial equality and conservative positions do not, white public opinion will be wrongly interpreted as racist when in fact whites are simply more ideologically conservative, on average, than blacks but no less committed to equality.[e]

One technique employed to test this possibility—the survey experiment—changes the wording of a public opinion survey question and compares responses. For example, in one study, whites were split into two groups. The first group was asked if, because of past discrimination, blacks should be given preference in college admissions. Only 26 percent of whites supported this idea. The second group was asked instead whether an extra effort should be made to ensure that qualified blacks applied for college admission. About 65 percent of whites supported this form of affirmative action specifically aimed toward blacks.[f]

Another experiment divided respondents into three groups. All three were asked about government assistance for those born into poverty. For the first group, the program was said to help blacks as a matter of racial justice for past wrongs: 31 percent of whites approved of such a program. For the second group, the program was said to help blacks,

---

[a] Vincent L. Hutchings and Nicholas A. Valentino, "The Centrality of Race in American Politics," *Annual Review of Political Science* 7 (2004): 383–408.

[b] Ibid., 389.

[c] Two pivotal figures in the debate have been Paul Sniderman and Donald Kinder. See Paul M. Sniderman and Edward G. Carmines, *Reaching Beyond Race* (Cambridge, MA: Harvard University Press, 1997); Sniderman and Thomas Piazza, *The Scar of Race* (Cambridge, MA: Harvard University Press, 1993); and Donald R. Kinder and Lynn M. Sanders, *Divided by Color: Racial Politics and Democratic Ideals* (Chicago: University of Chicago Press, 1996).

[d] A number of alternative terms have been employed, including new racism, symbolic racism, and covert racism. Examples of this work are found in David O. Sears, Colette Van Laar, Mary Carrillo, and Rick Kosterman, "Is It Really Racism?: The Origins of White Americans' Opposition to Race-Targeted Policies," *Public Opinion Quarterly* 61, 1 (1997): 16–53; and Donald R. Kinder and Nicholas Winter, "Exploring the Racial Divide: Blacks, Whites, and Opinion on National Policy," *American Journal of Political Science* 45, 2 (2001): 439–56.

[e] See, for example, Stanley Feldman and Leonie Huddy, "Racial Resentment and White Opposition to Race-Conscious Programs: Principles or Prejudice?" *American Journal of Political Science* 49, 1 (2005): 168–83; and Sniderman and Piazza, *The Scar of Race*.

[f] Paul M. Sniderman and Edward G. Carmines, *Reaching Beyond Race* (Cambridge, MA: Harvard University Press, 1997), pp. 25–27.

but the justification was equal opportunity rather than racial justice: 42 percent of whites supported this program. And for the third group, the program was said to help poor people as a matter of equal opportunity, with no race indicated: 49 percent of whites supported this program. This suggests that programs that are justified by reference to American creed beliefs and that do not single out particular racial or ethnic groups as beneficiaries receive greater support from whites.[g]

Finally, an experiment dividing white respondents into two groups asked one group about blacks and the other about new immigrants from Europe. Whites were equally likely to say these two groups should "work their way up without special favors," with about 80 percent giving this response. White views appeared more driven by ideology than by who benefited from government help. Views among blacks were similar, with 70 percent giving the "work their way up" response for blacks and for European immigrants.[h]

[g]Sniderman and Carmines, *Reaching Beyond Race*, pp. 126–29.
[h]Sniderman and Carmines, *Reaching Beyond Race*, pp. 136–37.

Survey Experiments on Affirmative Action Opinions

In a survey experiment, pollsters divide the respondents into two or more groups. Each group gets the same question wording except for one or a small number of wording differences. Comparing the group responses provides insight into the motivations behind public opinion. Wording differences appear in parentheses below.

Due to past discrimination, give blacks (preference/make extra effort to recruit) in university admissions

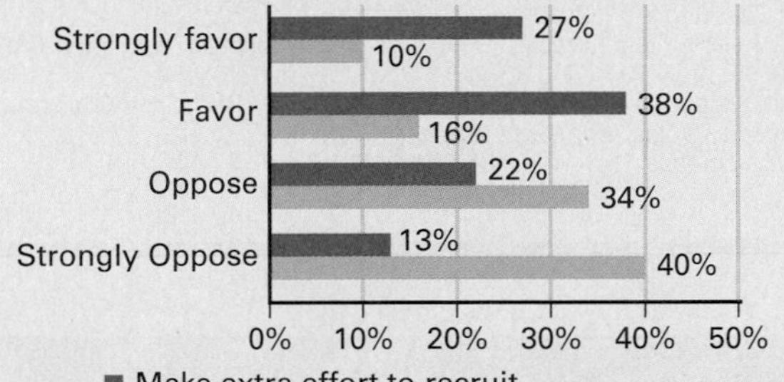

Whites are more supportive of making extra efforts to consider blacks for college admission than they are of preferential admissions for blacks.

Government should take responsibility for improving the social and economic conditions of (blacks/people) born into poverty because (everyone needs equal opportunity/of legacy of slavery and discrimination)

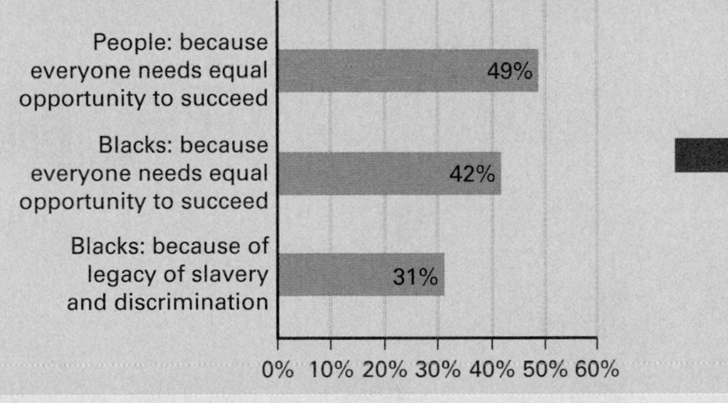

Whites are most supportive of programs that are broadly targeted and that are justified as promoting equal opportunity.

In the past, the Irish, Italians, Jews, and many other minorities overcame prejudice and worked their way up. (New immigrants from Europe/blacks) should do the same without any favors.

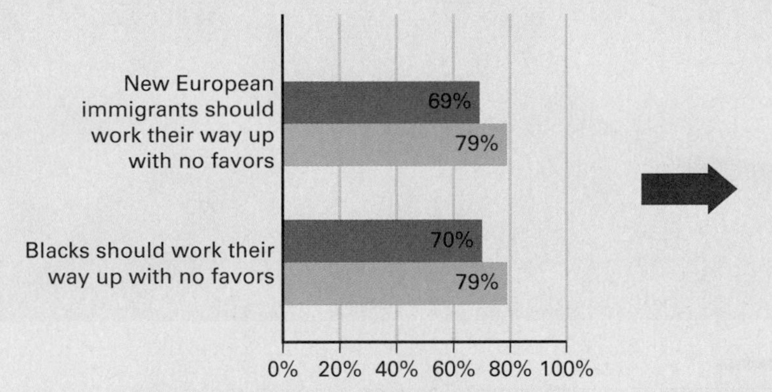

Whites, like blacks, are equally likely to disapprove of providing "favors" to blacks as to white European immigrants.

Source: Paul M. Sniderman and Edward G. Carmines, *Reaching Beyond Race* (Cambridge, MA: Harvard University Press, 1997).

The Bottom Line

The debate over racial resentment has been extensive, and studies continue to support each side in the argument—some finding that racial resentment is a key driver of white public opinion, and others finding that belief and ideology are more important than attitudes toward blacks.[i] Many Americans are conflicted in their views, believing that individuals are responsible for improving their condition, but also believing that society may need to provide assistance under certain circumstances.[j] Virtually all scholars agree that racism at some level remains a force in American society and that bigotry continues as an everyday problem facing blacks and other minorities, but clear evidence that racism is the predominant driver of white public opinion is lacking. Evidence in some studies shows that white public opinion is open to persuasion and appeals to principle, which seems unlikely if racism thoroughly dominated white opinion on racially oriented policies.[k] Scholars are careful to note, however, that such evidence does not mean that negative racial attitudes cannot be activated among some individuals by the way that issues are portrayed or symbolized, including in news coverage.[l] Nor does it mean that we can always be certain that the results obtained in experimental settings will apply directly to real-world situations.[m]

Thinking Critically

- In a survey experiment, participants are not saturated with the media messages they might receive in a real-world setting. Does this difference make these experiments more or less useful guides of individuals' true beliefs?
- When, if ever, are generalizations about a group's behavior acceptable in either designing or evaluating public policy?

[i]Steven A. Tuch and Michael Hughes, "Whites' Racial Policy Attitudes in the Twenty-First Century: The Continuing Significance of Racial Resentment," *The Annals* 634, 1 (2011): 134–52; Edward G. Carmines, Paul M. Sniderman, and Beth C. Easter, "On the Meaning, Measurement, and Implications of Racial Resentment," *The Annals* 634, 1 (2011): 98–116; and Michael Tesler, "The Spillover of Racialization into Health Care: How President Obama Polarized Public Opinion by Racial Attitudes and Race," *American Journal of Political Science,* http://onlinelibrary.wiley.com/doi/10.1111/j.1540-5907.2011.00577.x/full.

[j]Paul M. Kellstedt, "Media Framing and the Dynamics of Racial Policy Preferences," *American Journal of Political Science* 44, 2 (2000): 258; Kenneth Prewitt, "When Social Inequality Maps to Demographic Diversity, What Then for Liberal Democracies?" *Social Research* 77, 1 (2010): 1–20.

[k]A related area of study is whether diversity and interracial trust are connected. See Thomas J. Rudolph and Elizabeth Popp, "Race, Environment, and Interracial Trust," *Journal of Politics* 72, 1 (2010): 74–89.

[l]Paul M. Kellstedt, *The Mass Media and the Dynamics of American Racial Attitudes* (New York: Cambridge University Press, 2003); Rene P. Rocha and Rodolfo Espino, "Racial Threat, Residential Segregation, and the Policy Attitudes of Anglos," *Political Research Quarterly* 62, 2 (2009): 415–26.

[m]Jason Barabas and Jennifer Jerit, "Are Survey Experiments Externally Valid?" *American Political Science Review* 104, 2 (2010): 226–42.

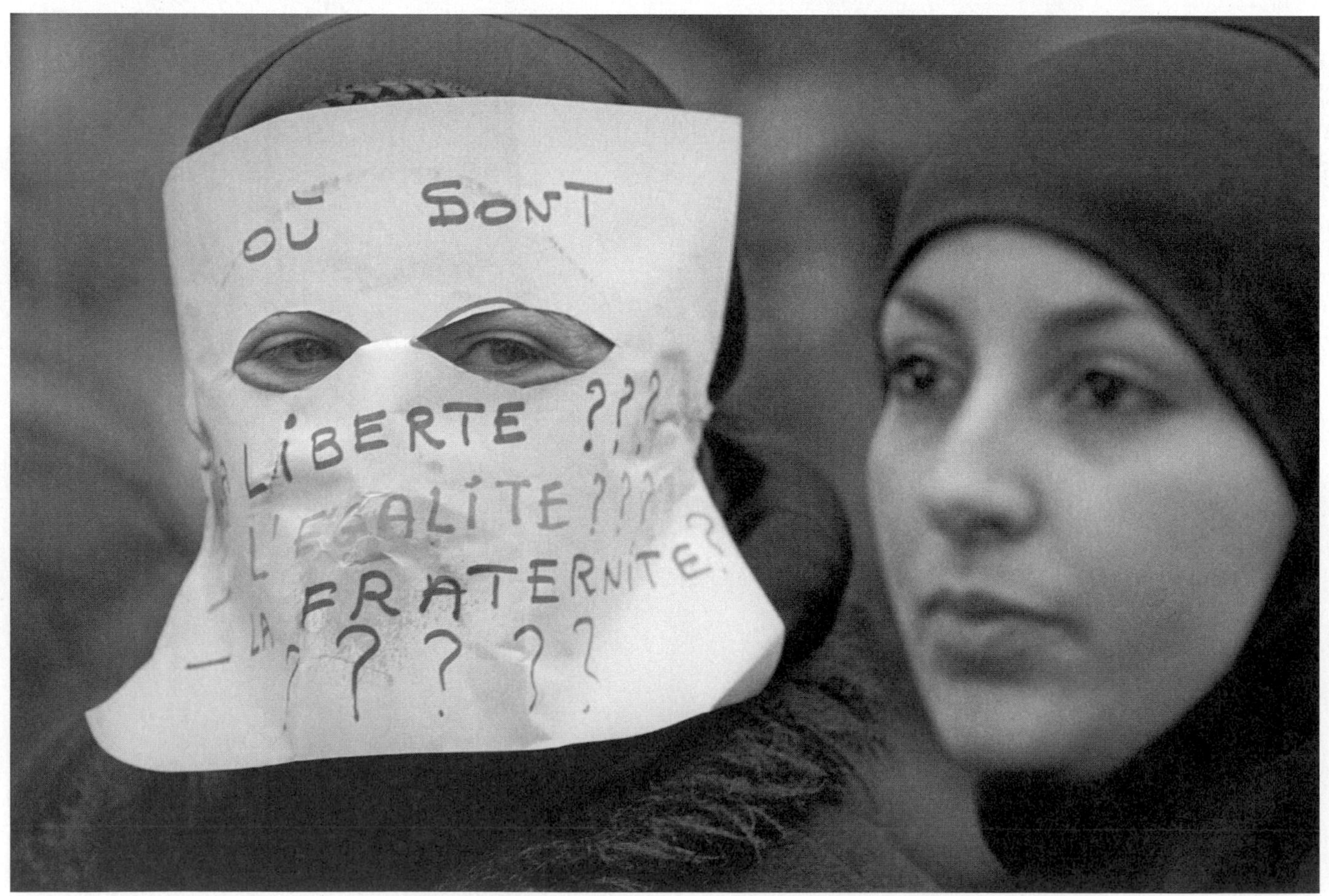

FRENCH STUDENTS PROTEST RESTRICTIONS ON WEARING RELIGIOUS SYMBOLS

To defuse ethnic and religious hostilities, students in French schools are prohibited from wearing religious symbols or clothing. These demonstrators in Paris ask, "Where are liberty, equality, fraternity?"—referring to the motto of the French Republic. Would the French model of deemphasizing group difference work effectively in the United States?

but they may reduce economic inequality between groups. On the other hand, those paying for these programs may oppose the high costs.

Two of America's allies have handled the civil rights challenge differently from each other and from the United States. Britain and France have sizable minority populations, both native and immigrant. Britain has leaned toward American-style anti-discrimination laws, but enforcement has been modest. Britain also has a more generous set of government services and benefits than the United States, some, such as worker training programs, tailored to particular racial and ethnic groups. France offers generous benefits, but not targeted toward particular minority groups. It has not focused as strongly as the United States or Great Britain on anti-discrimination law. Affirmative action has been most deeply embedded in the United States, while Britain has allowed affirmative action but not quotas, and France has prohibited any kind of affirmative action. However, racial and cultural divisiveness is highly monitored and frequently punished in France. For example, the wearing of religious symbols in public schools was outlawed in 2004 as divisive; Holocaust denial is illegal; convicted racists are stripped of some rights such as the ability to run for public office; and collection of economic, housing, educational, and other data by race and ethnicity is sharply limited, much more so than in the United States and Britain.[35] Variations in these countries' historical experiences, interest group pressures, and political cultures help account for these differences.

The Politics of Civil Rights

6.3 Analyze the changes that led to the success and splintering of the civil rights movement.

By the end of the 1960s, the United States had been through a civil rights revolution. The equal protection clause had been used to challenge discrimination by government. Congress advanced civil rights in the private sector through its commerce clause and spending powers. Presidents used unilateral executive power to prod civil rights in the federal government and among those doing business with it. Segregation had fallen, voting rights were expanded, and employment discrimination was prohibited. The Supreme Court added its first black justice, Thurgood Marshall, in 1967. In later years, blacks, women, Hispanics, and other minorities would reach the highest levels of American government. Barack Obama's election in 2008 provided an exclamation point to this journey. Inequities in quality of life remained then and remain today, but the country had changed radically (see *Unresolved Debate: Are Social Capital, Diversity, and Equality Linked?*).

How did these seismic changes happen? To understand, we need to explore the politics of civil rights in greater detail. Some political scientists argue that the success of civil rights resulted from political opportunities that created the possibility for change. Others focus on effective appeals to American creedal beliefs. Still others emphasize overcoming the difficulties in organizing people for political action. All of these factors are important, and their reversals featured prominently in the struggles civil rights advocates faced after these major successes.[36] As is common in politics, no single explanation is sufficient.

The Civil Rights Movement Leads to Civil Rights Successes for Blacks

The pressure created by the civil rights movement contributed to the legal, legislative, and administrative successes gained by blacks. As mentioned earlier, organizations

Unresolved Debate

Are Social Capital, Diversity, and Equality Linked?

Social capital refers to connections among people through volunteerism, community involvement, group membership, civic participation, and networks of friends and associates. Adding a number of these variables together, scholars create summary measures of social capital. One of social capital's possible attractions is that it might produce trust and solidarity among diverse individuals and lead to less unequal public policy outcomes. Are social capital, diversity, and equality linked?

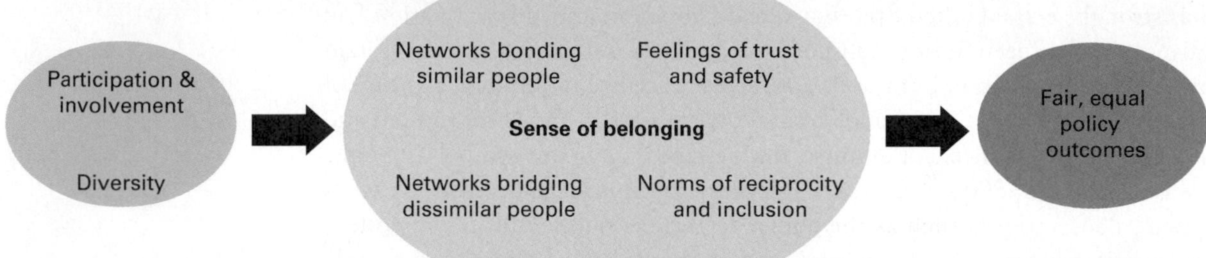

YES

*Despite optimistic findings from his earlier research, political scientist Robert Putnam later acknowledged, as other scholars had argued, that social capital actually appears to be **inversely** related with racial and ethnic diversity, dashing hopes that diversity and social capital would work together to produce more equal policy outcomes.[a] But Putnam argues there are grounds for optimism.*

- Comparing a large number of communities at one point in time might obscure improvements occurring over time in a single community.
- Settings other than cities, counties, and states might be fruitful arenas for positive relationships among diversity, social capital, and more equal outcomes.
- Integration in the U.S. Army, racial and ethnic integration at large evangelical churches, and widespread intermarriage and intergroup relations between the children of once highly separated immigrant groups from Europe show that over time diversity, social capital, and equal treatment can thrive.

NO

Political scientists Daniel Hawes and Rene Rocha are skeptical about purported linkages between social capital, diversity, and equality.[b] They provide the first analysis of state-level social capital, diversity, and policy outcomes over time rather than at one point in time. They find generally that diversity contributes to fair and more equal outcomes, but social capital does not.

- More social capital is related to more unequal outcomes; higher levels of racial and ethnic diversity tend to decrease them.
- Greater social capital is linked to more school suspensions for blacks and Latinos compared to white, non-Hispanic students, and to greater placement of Latino students in special education classes compared to whites. More diversity is associated with reduced disparity between black and white suspensions.
- Higher levels of social capital are associated with higher inequality in black and Latino incarceration rates relative to whites; increased diversity is associated with lower disparities.

CONTRIBUTING TO THE DEBATE

As the works above suggest, exploring how social capital, diversity, and equality work in different settings over time appears to be a promising research route. Researchers can also examine whether particular aspects of social capital and diversity might interact positively even though generally they might have an inverse relationship.

THINKING CRITICALLY

1. Is Putnam's example of integration and community among European immigrant groups a good guide to predict the future path present-day diversity and community?
2. How would you explain the findings by Hawes and Rocha that social capital was associated with less equal outcomes and diversity was associated with more equal outcomes?

[a]Robert D. Putnam, *Bowling Alone: The Collapse and Revival of American Community* (New York: Simon and Schuster, 2000). Robert D. Putnam, "*E Pluribus Unum*: Diversity and Community in the Twenty-first Century," *Scandinavian Political Studies* 30, 2 (2007): 137–74.
[b]Rodney E. Hero, "Social Capital and Racial Inequality in America," *Perspectives on Politics* 1, 1 (2003): 113–22; Daniel P. Hawes and Rene R. Rocha, "Social Capital, Racial Diversity, and Equity: Evaluating the Determinants of Equity in the United States," *Political Research Quarterly* 64, 4 (2011): 924–37.

advocating for black civil rights led to significant legal victories in the first half of the twentieth century, culminating in the dramatic victory in *Brown v. Board of Education* in 1954. In December 1955, the NAACP encouraged a yearlong boycott of the bus system in Montgomery, Alabama, to protest segregation of public buses. The boycott drew national attention. Rosa Parks, the NAACP member who refused to change her seat, became a household name. Martin Luther King Jr., a Baptist minister, similarly became nationally known. King and the organization he would soon head, the Southern Christian Leadership Conference (SCLC), advocated a strategy of **civil disobedience,** the use of nonviolent tactics such as sit-ins and demonstrations, in breach of the law, to sway public opinion and pressure public officials. Civil disobedience involves breaking the law and being willing to accept the penalties that some with such action, for the purpose of building public support change a law or policy.

civil disobedience
strategy of breaking law nonviolently in order to protest a law one considers unjust and draw attention to one's cause.

Prior to the late 1950s, mass protests had been infrequent. Inequalities and injustice were severe, but organizing and encouraging mass participation in the face of entrenched and powerful opponents were not easy. Participants risked their jobs and even their lives. Each victory was important, and each victory gave future participants the sense that direct political action could succeed. Mass political activity for the right to vote and for the repeal of Jim Crow restrictions did not become widespread until the 1960s, by which time the these forms of political action spread out across the country (see Figure 6.2).

One of the most important of these protests occurred in Alabama in 1963. That spring, the SCLC decided to target Birmingham—a center of segregation—for a series of protests and boycotts. The goal was not only to force downtown stores to desegregate and end discriminatory hiring practices, but also to focus national attention on similar situations throughout the South. Sheriff Bull Connors and his deputies quickly obliged civil rights leaders on the latter goal. The notorious chief of the Birmingham police unleashed fire hoses and police dogs on the peaceful protestors and jailed thousands. Many of the protesters were high school and even

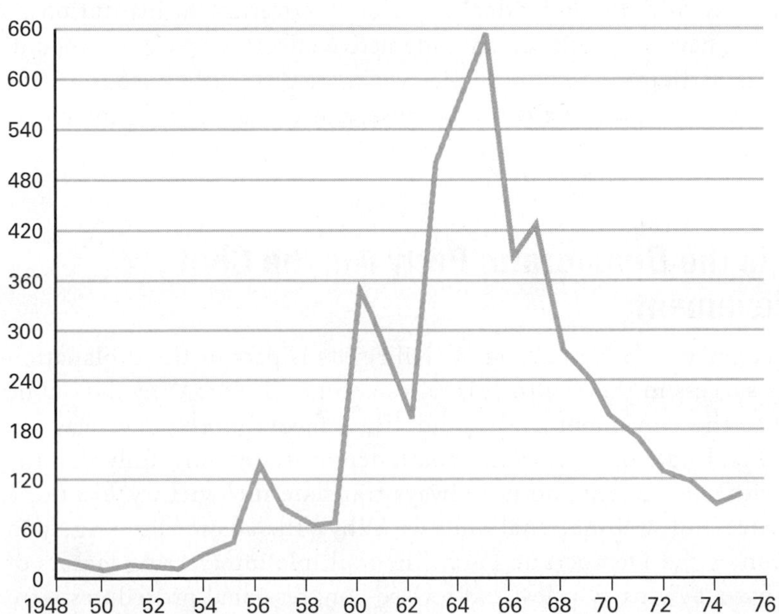

FIGURE 6.2 NUMBER OF CIVIL RIGHTS MOVEMENT MARCHES, SPEECHES, PROTESTS, SIT-INS, AND RELATED EVENTS ANNUALLY.

The number of events initiated by civil rights movement groups and organizations peaked from 1963 to 1965 and declined swiftly after that as the movement won major legislative victories and then splintered over goals and tactics.

Source: Doug McAdam, *Political Process and the Development of Black Insurgency 1930–1970* (Chicago: University of Chicago Press, 1982), p. 121. Copyright © 1982 by the University of Chicago. Reprinted by permission.

elementary school students. The national press and broadcast networks widely covered these harsh actions.

King and his deputies at the SCLC skillfully capitalized on the publicity and the images being transmitted to the rest of the country by raising money and galvanizing support in the North.[37] Their efforts even encouraged some northern whites, mostly college students and religious leaders, to go to the South to help organize voter registration drives and other acts of protest.

In retrospect, the success of the civil rights movement and the important role that mass protest played in breaking down barriers and winning African Americans the right to vote suggest that these activities were the obvious course for African Americans in the South and their supporters in the North. But rather than being obvious, they present a puzzle. Why would people risk their livelihoods, if not their lives, to register to vote or to get others to register to vote? Why would someone face police dogs to win the right to sit at a department store lunch counter or ride a bus? Why would individuals in the North bother to write letters to legislators and send contributions in support of the protests in the South?

The answers are complex and have been studied at great length. Political scientists, when looking at movements of collective action such as the civil rights movement, approach the subject from one of two directions. Some accounts provide a top-down view of mobilization, focusing more on actions of civil rights groups' leaders and political activists to build organizations and make demands on government. In the case of the civil rights movement, some individuals sincerely believed their actions could make a difference. Among these key political entrepreneurs and patrons were foundations that provided financial support to civil rights organizations, interest groups that focused on civil rights, ministers who motivated congregations to act, and government officials who promoted policy change. Other accounts offer a bottom-up view, focusing on how grassroots action changed public opinion about black civil rights and ultimately government policy. These accounts highlight those who participated to express their support for a cause and for the benefit of contributing to something important. These two types of explanations sometimes compete but can also be complementary, with each influencing different levels of society from the individual up through government institutions.[38] And movements can have a cumulative and interactive effect. As successes mount, as more individuals participate, and as public awareness grows, the incentives for others to participate, to be part of a winning cause, and to lead and organize that cause can also grow.[39]

Changes in the Democratic Party Aid the Civil Rights Movement

A wave of political action by supporters of civil rights is part of the explanation of the civil rights success in the 1960s. This raises another puzzle: Why did public officials respond to the movement as they did? Their favorable response was not guaranteed. Local and state officials in the South demonstrated forcefully that the demands of political movements do not always translate into victory. Yet these demands were successful with national officials. Why? The answer lies largely in the transformation of the Democratic Party. The multiple intersecting factors of a changed voter base, new party rules, and revised congressional procedures were key to public officials' political recalculations and their openness to movement demands.

In the period following the Civil War, the Democratic Party dominated politics in the South. The Republican Party, the party of the North and of Lincoln, remained almost invisible in the South, especially at the state and local levels. In many respects, the region had a one-party system with most outcomes essentially decided in the Democratic Party's primary election. Often, until outlawed in 1944 by the Supreme

Court, this was a **white primary,** in which—as the name implies—only white voters could cast ballots.[40] So even in the rare instances when blacks managed to register and vote in general elections, there were usually no contested races and no meaningful choices on the ballot.

white primary
primary elections in southern states in which only white voters were allowed to participate.

Just as the Democratic Party dominated southern politics, so the South dominated Democratic Party politics. Democratic Party politicians had to tread carefully around issues of race or risk disrupting the party coalition. At the national level, this power of the South over the Democratic Party played out in two ways. First, the Democrats required their presidential nominee to receive two-thirds of the delegate votes at the presidential nominating convention. This rule ensured that the South could thwart an undesirable contender for the Democratic nomination. A candidate who made civil rights a major goal would have no way to win the nomination. Second, in the Senate, the ability of a minority of senators to block action on bills—known as a filibuster—meant that civil rights legislation would face a difficult road to passage. Moreover, by the middle of the twentieth century, committee chairs were awarded almost exclusively on the basis of seniority. With no serious two-party competition in the South, Democrats from that region tended to be the committee chairs. Because chairs had great influence over when, if, and in what form bills would leave a committee and go to the full House or Senate, it was difficult to move civil rights legislation through Congress.[41]

The grip of the South over the Democratic Party began to weaken in the 1930s. The Great Migration of blacks from the South, where they typically could not vote, to the North, where they could, gave northern Democratic politicians increased interest in cultivating the black vote. But they had to proceed cautiously, because many northern Democratic constituencies did not embrace civil rights as an issue. After the Democrats swept through the country with a massive election victory in 1932, President Franklin Roosevelt was able to have the two-thirds rule removed in 1936 (this rule had required Democratic presidential nominees to receive two-thirds of the votes at the party convention). As a result, the South no longer had a veto over the Democratic presidential nomination. Recognizing that the party's geographical center was moving north, every Democratic presidential nominee after 1936 expressed support for civil rights, and the party added civil rights to its 1948 platform. Democratic Presidents Roosevelt, Truman, Kennedy, and Johnson all used executive orders and other unilateral powers to advance civil rights. For each, the calculation may have involved principle, but it certainly included a substantial amount of political pragmatism as well.

Southern Democrats' grip on Congress slowly weakened as well. With the northern share of congressional Democrats growing, and with this share dominated by urban, liberal representatives, support for civil rights increased. Even though southern Democratic senators could impede civil rights reforms by threatening or carrying out filibusters, the Senate modified the rule governing the termination of filibusters in the mid-1960s to make them easier to defeat. Subcommittees also gained additional independence to work around some of the tight control exerted by conservative southern committee leaders. All these factors combined to push the civil rights and voting rights acts through Congress in the 1960s.[42]

Obstacles in the Late 1960s Slow the Momentum of the Civil Rights Movement

The civil rights achievements of the 1960s were monumental. But as the decade wore on, the politics of gaining additional civil rights advances grew daunting. Why did the political environment become so unfavorable so quickly? Political scientists focus, with varying emphasis, on three igniters of this trend. First, unity in the civil rights movement disintegrated. Second, new issues raised by the movement troubled many whites who had supported, or at least not opposed, the breakthroughs of the early 1960s. Third, blacks had the support of the Democratic Party, and the party had the support of black voters, and this mutual support created challenges as well as opportunities. The combination of these three factors created particular problems for the civil rights agenda.[43]

COLLAPSE OF UNITY IN THE BLACK CIVIL RIGHTS MOVEMENT By the late 1960s, the black civil rights movement appeared to have peaked. Participation in civil disobedience events dwindled, as did the number of events. The ability of Martin Luther King Jr. and other black leaders to maintain nonviolent civil disobedience as the movement's central strategy came under increasing pressure after 1964. In the summer of 1964, massive violence directed at blacks and white civil rights activists in Mississippi shocked the country and inflamed black public opinion—80 civil rights workers beaten, 35 shot at, and 4 killed; 70 black homes, businesses, and churches burned; 1,000 activists jailed.[44] Similar scenes elsewhere shook faith in the effectiveness of nonviolent appeals. Riots sprang up in Los Angeles in 1965 and in many cities across the country following King's assassination in April 1968. Some in the civil rights movement, such as the members of the Black Panther party, believed that the violent resistance to civil rights should be met with a violent response. Black leaders including Malcolm X argued for a black nationalism that sought to advance black equality by withdrawing from white society and developing the black community rather than by focusing on integration.

The rupture in the movement was evident in 1966 when the Student Nonviolent Coordinating Committee (founded in 1960) and the Congress of Racial Equality (founded in 1942) embraced this notion of separationist black power. Two other prominent civil rights groups, the NAACP and the Urban League (founded in 1910), rebuked this goal. In part, these debates echoed those stretching back to the early twentieth century, when black leaders such as Booker T. Washington and W.E.B. Du Bois argued over the extent to which advancement and self-improvement were under blacks' control and to what extent they depended on major changes in white society. In the latter half of the 1960s, the consensus over political strategy had evaporated.

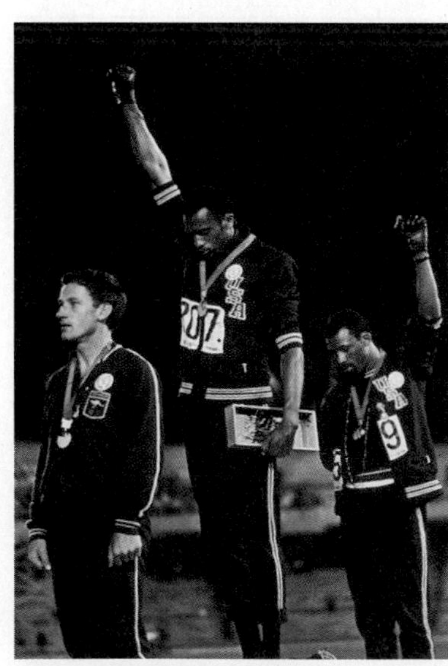

MEXICO CITY, 1968

Debate over how best to advance civil rights grew more fractious in the late 1960s. Leaders of some black organizations argued that the assassination of Martin Luther King Jr. earlier in 1968 was proof that civil disobedience was too passive an approach. Americans Tommie Smith and John Carlos shocked American television viewers of the 1968 Olympics by giving a black power salute while looking downward during the playing of the national anthem.

CHALLENGING ISSUES IN THE LATE 1960s Once the legal and political infrastructure of segregation and denial of voting rights had fallen, civil rights activists moved on to issues of social and economic equality. These issues were more difficult for many whites to support. As contentious as the issues of political equality were, they stood firmly within a political culture framework that was familiar to Americans and mostly consistent with their beliefs. Equal treatment under the law, equal opportunity, the freedom to hold a job and earn a living, the chance to go as far as one's talents allowed, to be judged not on the color of one's skin but on the content of one's character, as King preached, echoed familiar themes.

Newer issues, however, presented a greater challenge and a range of possible solutions. Some activists advocated reparations, the idea that blacks who were descendants of slaves needed to be compensated financially for the harsh deprivations imposed by slavery. Others advocated strong outreach efforts to bring minorities into colleges and the workforce, including the use of racial quotas if necessary. Yet others called for redistribution of wealth through government programs, benefits, and taxes to reduce economic inequality. In the eyes of many, these policies blatantly called for taking property and income from one group and giving it to another—always a controversial proposition. Many labor unions, because of the fear and opposition of their white members, struggled with civil rights issues. By the late 1960s, a backlash to the demands of the civil rights movement had set in.

CONSOLIDATION OF BLACK POLITICAL PRESSURE IN ONE PARTY Once the Democratic Party became the champion of black civil rights, black voter support for that party surged. In presidential elections, 90 percent or more of blacks typically voted for the Democrat. Black support for Democratic candidates at other levels was similarly high. Some scholars have suggested that this situation created a dilemma for black political power.[45] On the one hand, unified voting made blacks an important constituency for the Democratic Party and often an indispensable part of a winning coalition. On the other hand, such unified support can also be taken for granted by Democratic candidates, who might minimize blacks' concerns in order to avoid antagonizing white voters. The more that candidates highlight issues of particular interest to blacks, this argument suggests, the greater the risk of losing the votes of moderate whites and thus losing elections. And Republican candidates, given black voting patterns, might conclude they have relatively little to gain by making a strong pitch for the black vote, which would risk alienating other factions that do not favor expanding the scope of government spending, taxation, or redistribution. Thus, according to this argument, black political interests tend to be systematically underrepresented in electoral politics.

As the black vote became increasingly identified as Democratic, a causal chain of consequences followed. Support for Democrats in the white South, which had once been unshakable, began to wobble. Republican candidates began winning in the South, and the region became a key part of the Republican Party presidential election strategy. This created a dilemma for Democrats. The more they conceded the South to Republicans, the more difficult it would be to win the presidency. Republicans sought to link Democratic candidates to plans to redistribute wealth, bus students long distances, and base hiring on racial and minority quotas. Before Barack Obama in 2008, only two Democrats (Jimmy Carter and Bill Clinton) won the presidency from 1968 through 2004, both from the South and both considered relatively moderate compared to the party nationwide. They did not disavow civil rights, but they did not prominently campaign on this issue.

majority-minority districts
legislative districts in which district boundaries are drawn in a manner to ensure that a majority of the district residents are members of minority groups, intended to increase the probability of minorities being elected.

Debate Continues Over How to Enhance Minority Electoral Power

One question facing minority groups is how best to enhance their political power. Would an effective strategy be to spread minority voters out across districts so that they are a sizable and potentially influential bloc but not necessarily a majority of the district population? Or would minority interests be better served by concentrating minority voters in a small number of districts and virtually ensuring that a minority candidate would be elected who would then be able to negotiate on behalf of minority interests in the legislature?[46] Districts where boundaries are drawn to ensure that a majority of potential voters are minority—that is, a historically disadvantaged racial or ethnic group—are known as **majority-minority districts.** Starting in the late 1980s, the U.S. Supreme Court issued decisions in a series of cases that challenged the constitutionality of creating district lines for the express purpose of creating a majority-minority district. The conclusion of these decisions was that race or ethnicity could not constitutionally be the predominant factor in drawing district lines, but each could be taken into account as one of several factors.[47]

Whether the creation of majority-minority districts assists minority political influence has become hotly debated. The answer depends in part on the changing behavior of white voters.[48] One study suggests that although spreading minority voters across districts was not an optimal strategy for minority political influence in the 1970s or 1980s, it had become so by the 1990s. In part, reduced bloc voting by whites meant that even in districts where the minority population was 40 to 50 percent rather than a majority, a minority candidate could win about two out of three times.[49] This had not been true previously. Even if a minority does not win, this argument suggests, his or her strong share in the electorate may influence the winning candidate's voting

6.1

6.2

6.3

6.4

behavior as a legislator.[50] The debate over the "best" strategy for minority influence will continue, but this research suggests the answer may change over time.

The way forward will also depend on the Supreme Court. The Voting Rights Act required redistricting when a majority-minority district could be formed to address minority vote dilution, which refers to minority voting power and influence being reduced by spreading minority voters in small percentages across districts. But what about creating a district with a larger but not majority share of minority voters? In 2009, the Court decided 5–4 that the Voting Rights Act did not require redistricting to create a minority-influence district (sometimes called a coalition district) in which minority voting power would be enhanced but the minority presence would fall below 50 percent.[51] The dissenters in the Court's decision argued that minority-influence districts could be an effective counterweight to vote dilution.

Extension of Equal Protection to Other Groups

6.4 Describe legal and legislative actions to extend equal protection guarantees to other groups.

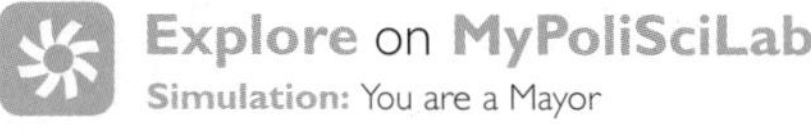

Governments classify individuals into groups and use these classifications to make decisions. Federal education assistance programs classify individuals as students and nonstudents. They classify students by full-time or part-time status, by the cost of their school, by the ability of their family to provide financial support, by whether or not they have a high school diploma or equivalent, and by whether they are dependent on their parents. The government uses these classifications to make decisions about who can receive a grant or loan and for what amount. Not everyone qualifies and not everyone gets the same amount. In short, the programs discriminate among groups, and most people have no problem with that.

Other discrimination, particularly as it pertains to race, ethnicity, sex, gender, sexual orientation, disability, or age, is different. How do the federal courts determine which group classifications resulting in differential treatment are acceptable and which are not? The courts divide these cases into three types.[52]

The first type concerns "suspect categories," namely race and ethnicity. Because of the country's struggle with slavery and the origin and history of the Fourteenth Amendment, the courts pay particularly close attention to laws and policies involving race and ethnicity. Selecting applicants for employment or government contracts on the basis of race or ethnicity is an example. The courts employ "strict scrutiny," meaning government officials would need to prove that there was a *compelling* governmental interest at stake that *required* the distinction between racial or ethnic groups. This is normally very difficult to prove. In one of the most controversial Supreme Court opinions, the Court ruled in *Korematsu v. United States* (1944) that the exclusion of Japanese Americans from the West Coast during World War II was subject to "the most rigid scrutiny," but was justifiable due to emergency national security concerns. A second type of case involves "quasi-suspect categories." Cases involving classification on the basis of sex are the prime example. Here the Court employs "intermediate scrutiny." Government would have to show that classifying by sex had a *substantial* relationship to an *important* government interest. In the decision that introduced this standard, the Court overturned an Oklahoma law that prohibited the sale of low alcohol beer to women under the age of 18 and men under the age of 21. The Court agreed that traffic safety was an important interest, but determined that the state failed to show that the law's gender distinction had a substantial relationship to this interest (*Craig v. Boren*, 1976) [53]

The third type of case involves most other classifications, such as age, income, and disability. They are evaluated on what the courts call a rational basis standard; that is, does the classification have some *rational* connection that *contributes* to the goal of the law or policy?[54] This is an easier test for government officials to meet, and the courts will be more easily convinced that these classifications were necessary than they will for race and ethnicity. For example, the courts allow the federal government to impose higher tax rates on wealthier individuals in order to fund programs and redistribute income across income levels, but it would not allow higher tax rates to be imposed on the basis of race. Overall, the courts demand the strongest justification from government officials for classifying by race and ethnicity, next so by sex, and the least stringent justification for other classifications.

Many racial, ethnic, and religious groups have faced severe discrimination throughout U.S. history. Legislation such as the landmark Civil Rights Act of 1964 and presidential orders such as the federal government's use of affirmative action in hiring and contracting were originally enacted primarily as a result of the black civil rights movement in the 1960s, but they also benefited these groups. The three mechanisms to advance black civil rights—equal protection clause cases, Congress's use of its commerce clause and spending powers, and the president's authority over the executive branch—were also used to advance the civil rights of other groups that have been victims of discrimination.

Latinos and Asians Face Special Challenges When Organizing for Political Purposes

According to the U.S. Census Bureau, Hispanics are the largest ethnic or racial minority group in the country, at 17 percent. Blacks are 13 percent of the population, Asians 5 percent, and Native Americans 1 percent.[55] Immigration has boosted the numbers of Asians and Hispanics in the United States. Since 2009, Asian immigration has led all other regions of the world, accounting for about 43 percent of all new legal permanent residents in 2011.[56] Immigration from Spanish-speaking regions was about 28 percent. After decades of a strong surge of authorized and unauthorized immigration from Mexico, in 2012 the Pew Hispanic Center reported that net migration from Mexico was effectively zero due to a range of factors including sluggish economic conditions in the United States, border control and deportations, and improved economic growth in Mexico.[57] Nonetheless, about 30 percent of all current immigrants in the United States are from Mexico. China is a distant second at 5 percent.

Because of the ways their histories in the United States differ from those of blacks—most notably the absence of slavery—the umbrella terms *Hispanic* and *Asian* may mean less for individuals in these categories than do national identities such as Mexican, Argentinean, Cuban, Japanese, Korean, or Chinese. "Hispanic" or "Latino" and "Asian" have not provided the same common identity and widely shared political outlook. That heterogeneity has made political organization more difficult, and cross-ethnic group coordination—black, Hispanic, Asian—has been minimal. On some issues, such as immigration and language accommodation, blacks, Hispanics, and Asians often see more conflict than commonality among their interests. Blacks and Latinos are disproportionately lower income compared to whites and Asians, for example, so more Latino immigration, particularly illegal immigration, has sometimes been seen by black advocacy groups as creating more employment competition.[58] Conflict has also simmered over affirmative action in college admissions, with some Asian American groups arguing that Asian enrollments are held back in order to accommodate students of other backgrounds.

DISCRIMINATION OF LATINO POPULATIONS AND IMMIGRATION IN THE SOUTHWEST As a consequence of migration patterns and the absorption of Texas and other territories in the Southwest into the United States, Latino

6.1

6.2

6.3

6.4

populations have historically been heaviest in the southwestern region of the country. Thus, segregation laws—similar to those laws affecting blacks—that called for separate accommodations, unequal or no access to restaurants and other businesses, employment discrimination, and restrictions on voting rights were particularly prominent in the Southwest. Cities and states in the Southwest were also actively involved in the return of Mexicans, including Mexican Americans, to Mexico during the Great Depression.

The issue of immigration became a nationally prominent one for Latinos with the U.S. government's adoption of the first national immigration quotas in 1924. These quotas identified specific numbers of immigrants who would be allowed from each country. The Immigration Act of 1965 and the Immigration Act of 1990 replaced this quota system. The 1965 law set a cap on total immigration with no more than 20,000 immigrants being allowed from any one country. The later law made the cap more flexible and provided more consideration for reuniting families in addition to the traditional emphasis on employment and skills. However, the number of those individuals who wished to enter the United States greatly outpaced the number who could be legally admitted under both these laws, leading to a decades-long struggle

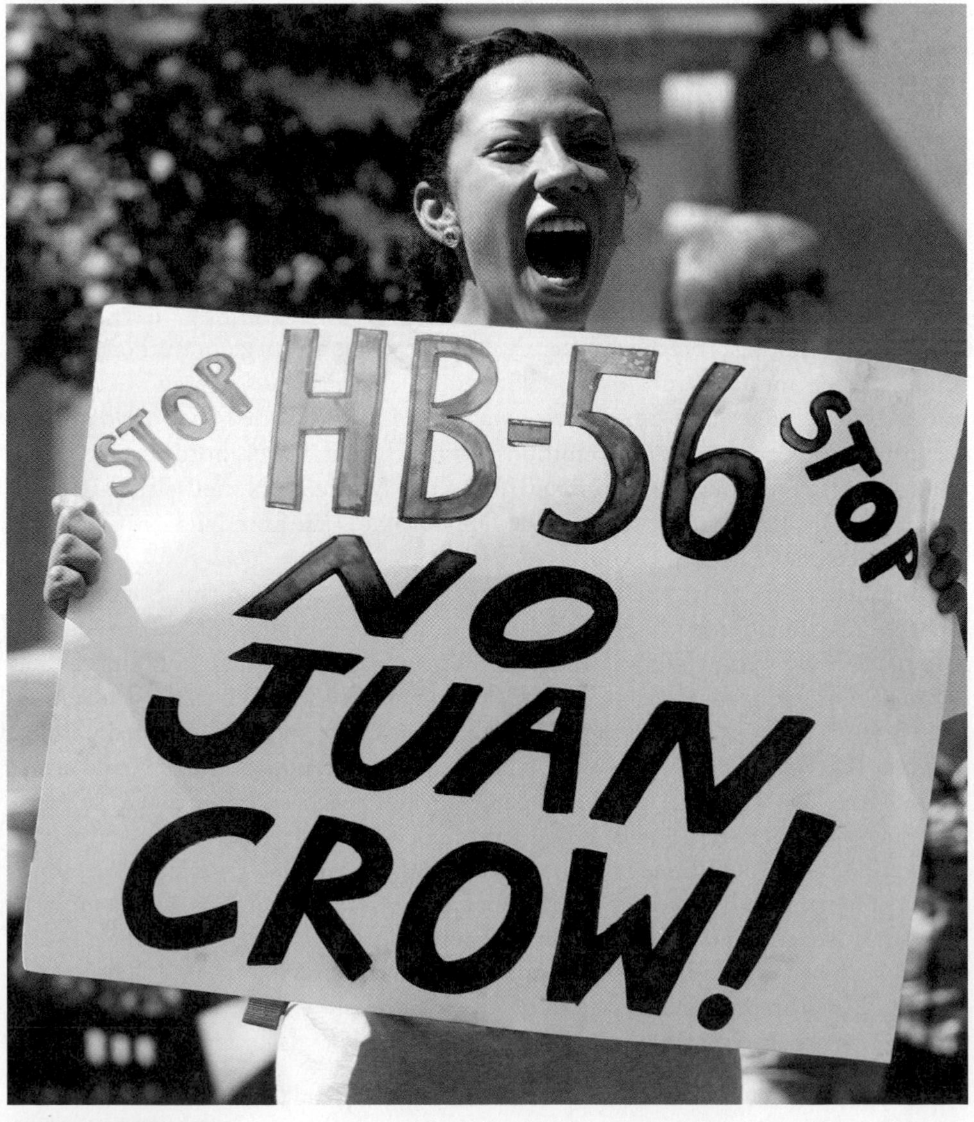

SEEING PARALLELS

Students at the University of Alabama protest against an extensive 2011 state law concerning illegal immigration. Most of the law's provisions were overturned by a federal appeals court in 2012.

and controversy over immigration law; its impact on families; and the impact of illegal immigration on various states and cities, particularly in the Southwest.

DISCRIMINATION OF ASIAN POPULATIONS IN THE WEST Asians were also the targets of many segregation laws, especially in the western United States where their population was heaviest. Alien land laws restricted property ownership by non-citizens. In 1880, San Francisco passed a law that required all laundries located in wooden buildings to obtain a permit from the city. Although 90 percent of the city's laundries had Chinese owners, none were given a permit. The U.S. Supreme Court in *Yick Wo v. Hopkins* (1886) unanimously struck down the law. Despite appearing neutral on its face, the justices viewed the law as designed to drive Chinese laundries out of business. The Fourteenth Amendment's guarantees of equal protection, the Court declared, "are universal in their application."[59]

Other laws and policies were created by the national government and so had nationwide impact, but because of residential patterns, they had their strongest effects in the West. As discussed at the beginning of this chapter, the national plan to move Japanese Americans into detention camps encompassed large numbers of individuals, especially in the West. The Chinese Exclusion Act of 1882 placed a 10-year ban on the immigration of Chinese laborers, as a response to fears about job shortages. The act was extended in various forms through 1943, when Congress repealed the exclusion act and included China in the system of national origin quotas established in 1924. Additionally in 1943, Congress for the first time allowed foreign-born Chinese the right to seek citizenship.

☐ American Indians Have Sovereign Nation Status

The experience of American Indians has its own distinctive features. Prior to the passage of the Indian Citizenship Act in 1924, American Indians were not considered U.S. citizens. As members of sovereign nations, they had to go through the same citizenship application procedures as individuals from other countries. Attempts to use the Fifteenth Amendment as a basis for the right to vote failed because of this lack of citizenship.[60] With the passage of the act, American Indians were considered U.S. citizens without any special procedure required. This status entitled them to the rights and responsibilities of U.S. citizenship, but as with other groups, rights did not instantly materialize. They required political action.

The case of American Indians differs from that of other groups in that they are considered U.S. citizens and also members of sovereign nations that exist within the United States. The anti-discrimination statutes and regulations that cover other groups also protect American Indians. In addition, they have tribal rights and responsibilities that differ among the various tribes and are determined by tribal authorities. Tribes have been actively involved in court cases and legislation seeking to preserve and restore their interests in land, mineral, and water resources and in defending traditional customs even if they conflict with state or national law.

☐ Pervasive Sex Discrimination in Law Has Eroded

The movement for women's equality had two distinct phases. The early phase culminated in 1920 with the Nineteenth Amendment, which gave women the right to vote. An extensive array of legal restrictions on women remained, however, and these became the focus of women's rights organizations in the second phase, beginning in the 1960s.

Like the civil rights movement, the women's movement used legal and legislative strategies to challenge laws and policies that differentiated between men and women. The women's movement also engaged in "consciousness raising" designed to help women understand their identity and their status in law and society. Sometimes criticized as being geared toward the needs of white upper-middle-class women, this self-awareness and its call for "women's liberation" likely generated important organizational benefits by contributing to fund-raising and support for the efforts of women's rights organizations.[61] These funds would be instrumental in filing court cases and lobbying for legislative changes. The National Organization for Women (NOW), one of the key organizations involved in these efforts, was founded in 1966.

SUPREME COURT RULINGS Prior to the 1970s, the Supreme Court tended to uphold gender-based distinctions in law. It sustained laws that denied women the right to vote prior to 1920, restricted their working hours to "protect the weaker sex," and prohibited admission to trades and professions. Fundamental rights and responsibilities of citizenship, such as participating on juries, were often denied to women.[62] After 1970, the Court overturned many gender-based state laws. Examples of the kinds of gender distinctions in law that the Court rejected included different treatment of men and women when calculating Social Security benefits, different ages for consuming alcohol, and permitting unwed mothers but not unwed fathers to withhold consent on the adoption of their children.

Most of the Court's discrimination-based decisions since the mid-1980s have been justified on the interpretation of civil rights statutes—what did laws mean and what did they require—rather than on Fourteenth Amendment equal protection grounds. For example, the Court ruled in 1986 that the Civil Rights Act of 1964 prohibited not only sex discrimination in hiring and firing, but also sexual harassment on the job.[63] Sexual harassment includes unwanted sexual attention, advances, or comments. The harassment can be directed toward a person or can be a part of the culture or environment of a workplace. A hostile environment on the job, whether general or targeted to a particular person, threatens the full participation in American commerce that is at the base of Congress's commerce clause justification for laws regulating discriminatory actions in the private sector.

Although striking down most sex distinctions, the Court has upheld those that it was convinced supported important government interests. It upheld limiting the military draft to men in *Rostker v. Goldberg* (1981), for example. The Court concluded that the exclusion of women from the draft was connected to military need: the draft was intended primarily to add troops for combat purposes, but women were prohibited from direct combat duty. (The combat prohibition itself was not under review in the case.) Congress argued that the draft needed to be limited to men for that reason, and that women could be recruited into noncombat positions through the regular channels of military recruitment. The ban on women in direct ground combat continues today. In 2012, the Pentagon opened up service in battalions—including key jobs near the front lines of combat such as radio operators, medics, and tank mechanics—to women. However, women remain prohibited from infantry, combat tank units, and Special Operations command units. Supporters of the combat ban point to physical concerns as well as perceived psychological concerns among men in those units fighting alongside women that would be detrimental to combat success in the heat of battle. Fifteen percent of the 1.5 million active military in 2012 were women.[64] Israel, France, Germany, Australia, Canada, and the Scandinavian countries, among others, include women more extensively in combat service than does the United States.[65]

The Supreme Court has also upheld the constitutionality of regulations and policies that do not formally distinguish between men and women but in practice will have the effect of doing so. Giving preferences to veterans in state and federal government employment will tend to advantage men disproportionately, but the Court has upheld these as being a reasonable inducement to the government's interest in recruiting and rewarding military personnel (*Personnel Administrator MA v. Feeney*, 1979). Job screening that requires the ability to lift heavy weights will tend to favor men, but if this skill is related to the job being performed, the Court has accepted the practice. However, the Court may also examine whether there is any prospect for restructuring the job to eliminate the need for heavy-lifting skill, so that these skill filters are not simply indirect ways to discriminate on the basis of sex.

WOMEN IN COMBAT ON THE FRONT LINES

U.S. Marines take a breather during a village medical outreach in Afghanistan in late 2010. About 50 women soldiers were working near the war's front lines, gaining access where men cannot. The deployment lasted about six months. The U.S. Military has been expanding the roles in which women can serve.

The Court determined in 2011 that class-action lawsuits have limits as a means to advance women as a class of individuals. In a class-action suit, a small number of individuals file a lawsuit, saying they represent a "class" of similar individuals. If approved by a judge, this class of individuals is then entitled to a share of whatever success is reached in the case. Betty Dukes was a Wal-Mart greeter who, along with five other women, filed a pay and promotion discrimination suit against Wal-Mart on behalf of all women employees at the company after 1998: a total of 1.5 million women in 2001 when the case was first approved as a class action by a federal judge. In its most significant class-action decision related to women, the Court in *Wal-Mart v. Dukes* (2011) unanimously agreed that the case could not go forward as a class action. The Court concluded that the suit in effect encompassed millions of employment-related decisions but did not provide any "connecting glue" that would show the women's situations were equivalent or that they had been subject to similar discriminatory rationales for employment decisions that affected them across the large number of Wal-Mart workplaces and the many different types of jobs in which the women were employed.

ACTIONS BY CONGRESS AND PRESIDENTS Congress and presidents have also addressed sex discrimination issues. The 1963 Equal Pay Act required equal pay for equal work, and the 2009 Lilly Ledbetter Fair Pay Act stated that the 180-day clock for filing a pay-bias case starts again with each new paycheck, not just the first one. The Civil Rights Act of 1964 prohibited employers, employment agencies, and labor unions from discriminating on the basis of sex. Amendments to the Higher Education Act in 1972, specifically that portion of the act known as Title IX, denied federal funds to universities that discriminated against women in any respect, including admissions, course availability, athletics, and advising.

Women's rights activists have argued that full equality sometimes needs to take account of differences. Expanded government support for child care, for example, has been advocated on gender equality grounds, so that women can more fully enter the workforce. In the United States, the need to accommodate the special demands placed on women inspired the Family and Medical Leave Act of 1993, which provides women with 12 weeks of unpaid leave following childbirth. New fathers can take this time off also, as can same-sex partners and individuals needing to care for a sick family member. France, Denmark, Austria, Spain, Germany, and India provide from 12 to 26 weeks of leave with 100 percent of wages paid. The United Kingdom, Italy, Greece, and Japan offer 14 to 22 weeks at 60 to 90 percent of one's wages. And Australia offers unpaid leave, like the United States, but for a one-year period.[66] Why such a range of policies? Differing political cultures in these countries in part are the causal forces behind these differences. Overall, social and welfare programs in the United States tend to be less comprehensive than those in other countries, partly because of the power of American creed beliefs about individualism and limited government. The organization of interest groups would be another key causal factor. In the United States, for example, if the government does not provide the funding, then the cost of a paid leave to accommodate new parents would likely fall primarily on employers. These employers are well organized and would push back on efforts to force them to absorb the cost of these leaves over and above the cost of holding open unfilled positions for three months or hiring temporary replacements for these positions.

EQUAL RIGHTS AMENDMENT Like the black civil rights movement, the women's rights movement lost strength over time. The difficulties facing the women's movement became apparent in the battle over adding an Equal Rights Amendment (ERA) to the U.S. Constitution. Introduced annually since 1923, the ERA finally passed both houses of Congress in 1972 after heavy lobbying by NOW and the National Women's Political Caucus. The proposed amendment stated, "Equality of rights under the law shall not be denied or abridged by the United States or by any State on account of sex." It was sent to the states for ratification, with 1979 set as the deadline. Twenty-two states ratified the amendment in the first year. By 1978, the amendment was three states short of the 38 needed for ratification. Congress controversially extended the ratification period through 1982. But by 1982, the amendment was still three states short, and five states that had approved the amendment rescinded their approval (see Figure 6.3). The constitutionality of the rescissions was unclear; nevertheless, the proposed amendment never obtained enough state approval to be added to the Constitution. Why not?

Three causal factors loom large in explaining what happened—the rise of a conservative opposition, division among women, and a legacy of prior success. First, the ERA faced concerted opposition by religious and conservative groups, which had used this issue to build very effective political organizations. Ironically, these groups may have actually benefited from the quick approval of the ERA in 35 states. They were able to concentrate their resources and lobbying on the remaining states, rather than fighting a national battle.[67] Second, division among women meant that the pro-amendment forces were unable to marshal the same focused intensity as the opponents. Some women thought the amendment did not go far enough. Others thought women would lose some rights in the workplace—for example, accommodations for pregnancy—or would not be able to obtain support from ex-husbands. The rise of a strong conservative Christian spiritual and political movement by the late 1970s also highlighted splits among women and raised the question of whether the women's movement allowed for only a single, narrow identity for women—pro-choice on abortion, career oriented, in the workforce, seeking jobs traditionally held by men, and believing that male-female distinctions were socially perpetuated rather than biological. Although often agreeing with the women's movement on economic and legal equality issues, women holding more conservative views did not

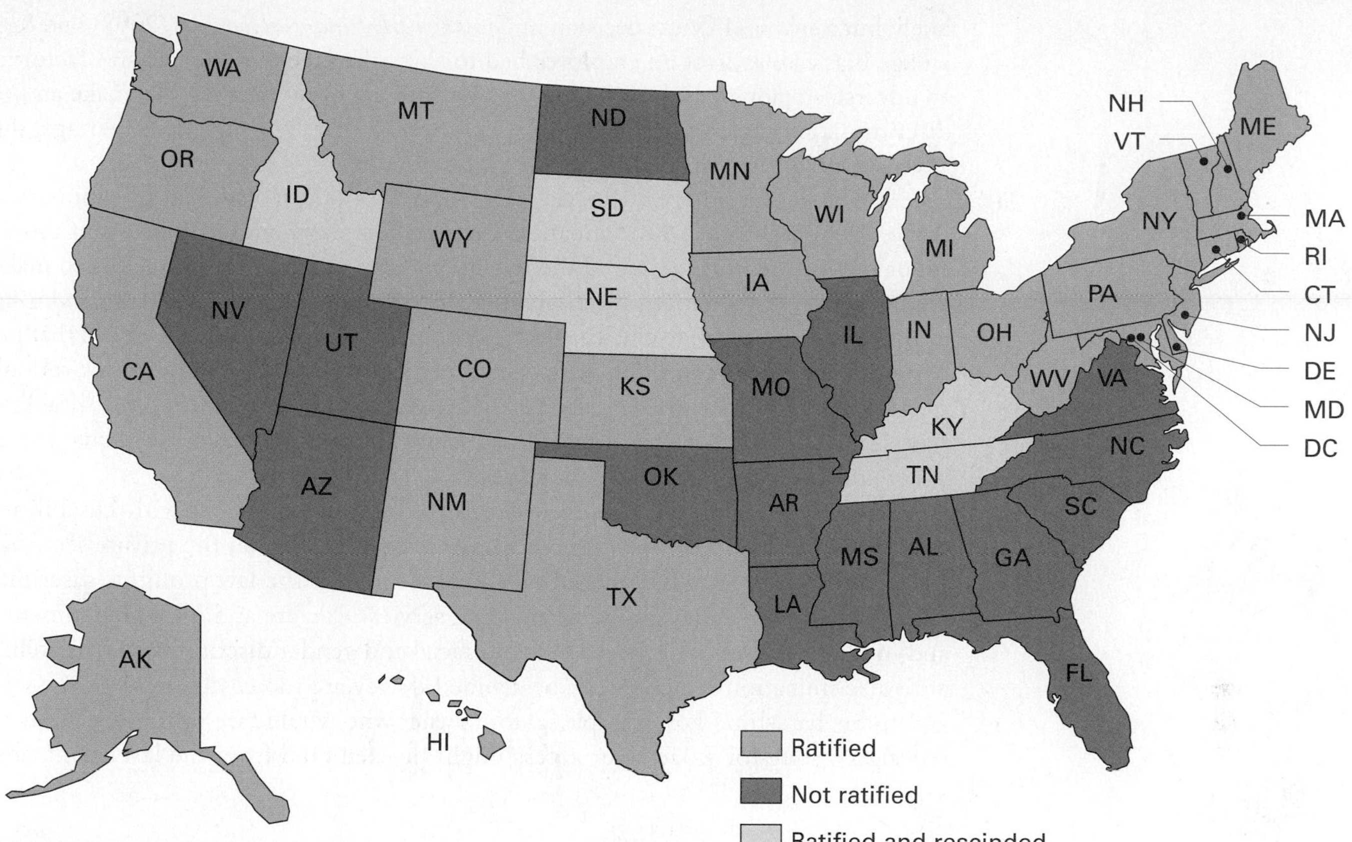

FIGURE 6.3 RATIFICATION OF THE EQUAL RIGHTS AMENDMENT.
Ratification by 38 states was necessary for the amendment to be added to the Constitution, but only 35 ratified the proposed amendment. Five of those 35 later sought to rescind their ratification. Opposition in the South was especially strong, most likely because of the greater degree of conservative political beliefs in that region of the country.

necessarily accept the other liberal views propounded by the major women's rights organizations or share the same priorities as the ERA. This split resembles the fissures that emerged between factions in the movement for black civil rights. Third, the amendment may have been weakened by a perception that much of what the amendment was intended to achieve had already been accomplished by law, unilateral presidential action, and Supreme Court application of the Fourteenth Amendment's equal protection guarantee and its interpretation of civil rights laws. Together, these factors stalled the drive for the ERA.[68]

Age and Disability Discrimination Are Subject to Standards of Review Different From Those for Race and Sex

Not considered suspect or quasi-suspect classifications requiring the Court's strict scrutiny, the use of an age or disability classification in law must have some rational connection to the goal of the law. If it does not, the law will be struck down as inconsistent with equal protection. If it does, the law can stand. For example, the Court in *Gregory v. Ashcroft* (1991) upheld Missouri's mandatory requirement that state judges retire at age 70. Employing a rational basis test, the Court concluded that because of the correlation between age and the decline of mental and physical capabilities, a rational connection existed between the state's goal of having competent state court judges and the age 70 retirement rule. Similarly, certain rights, such as voting, are limited to adults.

Laws passed by Congress and executive orders issued by presidents have also addressed discrimination based on age and disability. The Age Discrimination in Employment Act of 1967 prohibits employment discrimination against individuals between the ages of 40 and 70—the time when discrimination is considered more likely, but a split 5–4 Court decision in *Gross v. FBL Financial Services* (2009) said that an age bias case against an employer had to show that age was the decisive factor in an adverse employment decision, not just one among other factors.[69] To make an age discrimination case, an employee now has to show that "but for" his or her age, the adverse employment decision would not have occurred.

Two major laws have advanced civil rights for the disabled. The Rehabilitation Act of 1973 prohibited discrimination in federal employment on the basis of physical or mental disability, required the federal government and its contractors to make reasonable accommodations for disabilities, and mandated affirmative action in hiring in the form of outreach to the disabled to encourage job applicants and ensure that internal processes for promotion were open and inclusive and did not deter or overlook those with disabilities. The act also played a significant role in igniting the disability rights movement, which has fought for disability laws to be presented as civil rights issues and not as welfare or benefits issues.[70]

Years of lobbying, litigation, and protest led to the Americans with Disabilities Act (ADA) of 1990. This act placed the same requirements on the private sector as the Rehabilitation Act had placed on the government. The law prohibits discrimination in employment, in all programs and services of state and local governments, and in public accommodations. Unlike in racial and gender discrimination, disability anti-discrimination remedies can be avoided if they are too costly or would impose an "undue hardship." For example, a store owner who would face prohibitive costs to redesign a store for wheelchair access might be exempted from the law's demands.

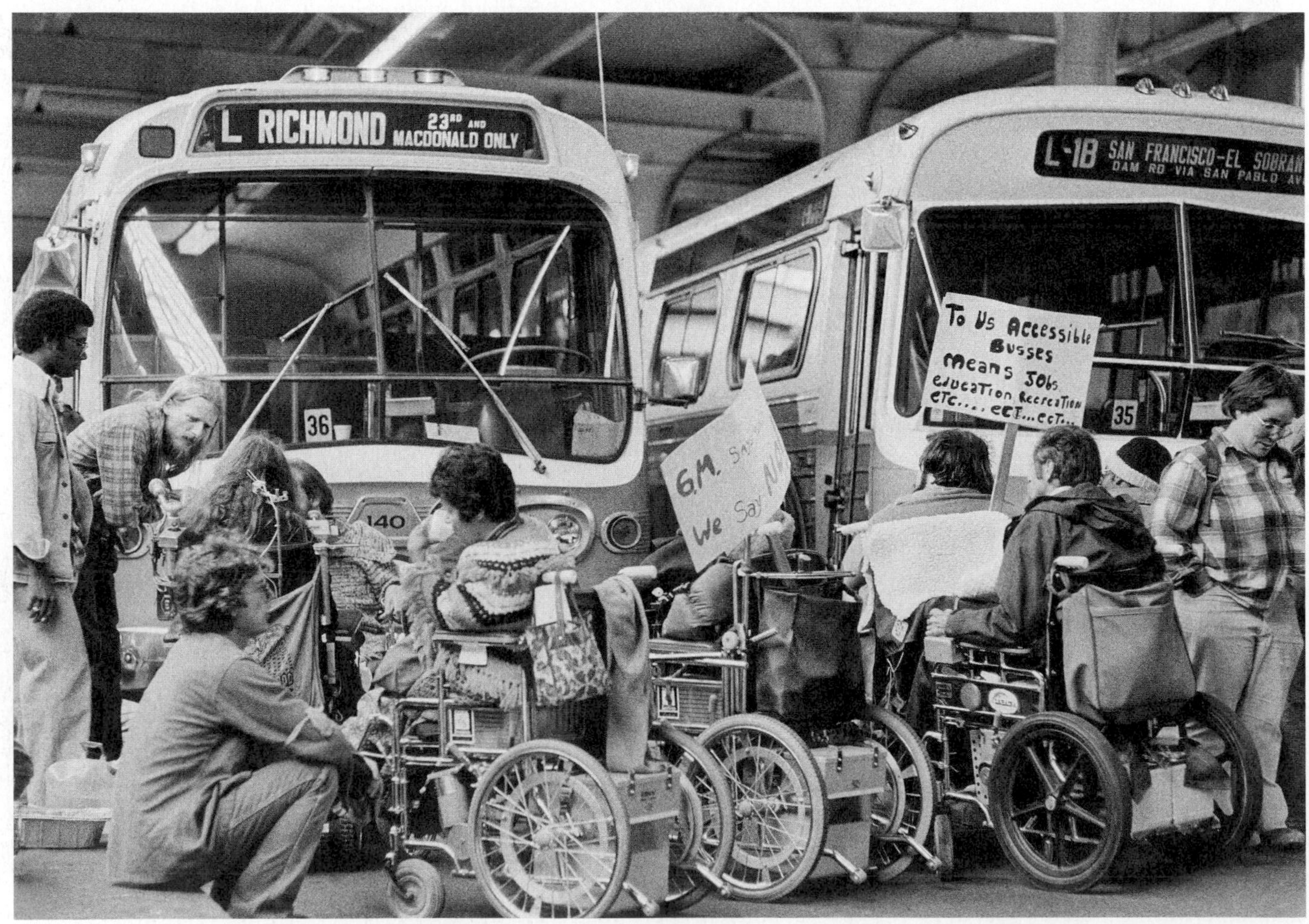

ACCESSING THE AMERICAN DREAM

Protesters demanding better access to public transportation in San Francicso, 1978. The 1990 Americans with Disabilities Act led to improved accommodations for individuals with physical or mental disabilities. The nature of the required accommodation has been a matter of ongoing legal dispute, as has the cost. How much is too much? Should cost be irrelevant?

Because of this possible exemption, and because "accommodation" and "disability" are subject to different interpretations, many cases have reached the courts in an attempt to sort out what is and is not reasonable with regard to accommodations and what type and severity of disability leave a person qualified or unqualified for a particular job. In response to court decisions, the ADA was amended in 2008 to clarify that Congress intended the courts to take a broad rather than narrow view of what constituted a disability under the law.

Since the passage of the ADA, the transformation of law concerning the disabled from a welfare and assistance orientation to a civil rights orientation—integrating the disabled as full participants in the economy and society—has occurred around the world. Australia and Great Britain enacted laws prohibiting employment discrimination and calling on employers to make efforts to accommodate the disabled. Several European countries have required quotas to move disabled people into the workforce. In Germany, employers who do not meet their quotas are fined, and the funds raised from these fines go to employers who meet or exceed their quotas. Generally, however, quota systems have yielded disappointing results. Some quota systems are not well enforced, and in other systems, like Germany's, the fines proved insufficient to motivate employers. Even so, the ADA anti-discrimination model has become attractive to many advocates for the disabled in countries with quota systems and has been endorsed by the European Union.[71]

The Movement for Gay and Lesbian Equality Has Promoted Change Through Legislation, Executive Branch Action, and the Courts

Rights campaigns for gays and lesbians, like other major social movements, have sought change through the legislative, executive, and judicial branches. Most states, many cities, and the federal government have adopted anti-discrimination hiring policies that include sexual orientation. These cover government employees and companies doing business with the government. Determining which aspects of federal civil rights law apply to gays and lesbians has been handled by the Supreme Court on an issue-by-issue basis. For example, the Supreme Court ruled in 1998 that the 1964 Civil Rights Act forbids same-sex sexual harassment.[72] On the other hand, the Court in 2000 upheld the Boy Scouts of America's right to prohibit gays from serving as troop leaders because doing so conveyed a message contrary to the organization's beliefs.[73]

As a presidential candidate in 2008, Barack Obama did not voice support for same-sex marriage, and once president, gay and lesbian groups were disappointed by his administration's initial defense of the Defense of Marriage Act in federal court. President Obama did, however, take a number of unilateral steps through executive orders, proclamations, and administrative rulings to promote lesbian, gay, bisexual, and transgender rights. As a result,

- sexual orientation is now a protected class under hate crimes law;
- hospital visitation is available to gay and lesbian partners at any facility taking Medicare dollars;
- the Family and Medical Leave Act applies to partners in a same-sex couple for care of a sick child or newborn;
- the Violence Against Women Act, which in practice also covers domestic violence against men, includes victims in same-sex relationships of either gender; and
- the Census Bureau is for the first time reporting the number of people in same-sex relationships.

In 2011, the Obama administration reversed course and announced that it would no longer defend the Defense of Marriage Act in federal court, and in 2012, the president announced that his position on same-sex marriage had shifted and that he now believed it should be allowed.

6.1

6.2

6.3

6.4

On the legislative side, in 2009, the president signed into law the Matthew Shepard and James Byrd, Jr. Hate Crimes Prevention Act, known as the Matthew Shepard Act, an expansion of the federal hate crimes statute. Hate crimes laws add an increased penalty to criminal acts such as murder. The bill was first introduced in the late 1990s and was considered several times by Congress over the next decade. The existing 1968 law considered hate crimes as those motivated by a victim's race, color, religion, or national origin; the expansion added a victim's sexual orientation, gender, gender identity, or disability as new hate crime categories. Almost every state has some form of hate crimes law, as do many countries. The federal law authorizes the federal government to investigate cases either not covered by a state hate crimes law or to complement state investigations.

At the national level, one of the most prominent civil rights issues for 20 years concerned homosexuals serving in the military. The ban on gays in the military became a major issue advanced by gay advocacy groups in the 1980s. The groups argued that the policy violated the civil rights of homosexuals by banning them as a class from this aspect of citizenship. They also argued that the policy was inconsistent, because thousands of gays had in fact served in the military without being discharged, whereas others were discharged or not allowed to enlist.

In his 1992 presidential campaign, Democratic nominee Bill Clinton advocated an end to the ban on gays serving in the military. The issue became one of the earliest and most controversial tackled by the Clinton administration upon taking office in 1993. When it became apparent that a complete removal of the ban was politically unlikely, the administration later in the year adopted a compromise policy known as "don't ask, don't tell." Under this policy, military personnel were not to be asked about their sexual orientation nor were they to disclose it, the logic being that unit cohesion and discipline would thus be protected. Although this policy allowed gays and lesbians to serve in the military, it did not allow them to do so openly.[74]

Public opinion on the issue has shifted over time. In December 2010, President Obama signed into law a repeal of the ban on openly homosexual individuals serving in the armed forces. Following Defense Department certification that the repeal would not harm military readiness or unit cohesion, the ban on gays in the military expired in September 2011.

☐ Noncitizens Share Some of the Rights of Citizens, But Not All

The U.S. Constitution confers rights on all persons in the United States, not just citizens. Whether citizen or not, legally in the United States or not, individuals are covered by the Constitution's due process provisions when charged with a crime, prohibition against cruel and unusual punishment, freedom to practice one's religion, equal protection of the laws, and so on.[75] The major provisions of the Bill of Rights apply to citizens and noncitizens alike.

Noncitizens are protected by First Amendment free speech rights in that they cannot be criminally prosecuted for speech, except in those same instances when speech is not protected for citizens, such as child pornography. Speech made prior to entry in the United States and speech deemed possible once a person arrives here can, however, be taken into account in the decision to grant entry. The courts will generally dismiss a claim that a noncitizen was selectively targeted with a technical violation of immigration law but that his or her speech was the real motive.[76] Although individuals who are in the United States illegally may have constitutional rights and may legally have access to certain services and benefits, they remain subject to deportation for having violated immigration law. For this reason, there has been great controversy around the country as to what extent government officials should, when they are not directly involved in immigration enforcement, inquire about citizenship status and whether an individual is in the United States legally.[77]

The simmering debate over this issue boiled over in 2010 with respect to a new Arizona law intended to increase these inquiries. The U.S. Justice Department responded by filing a successful lawsuit in federal district court to block implementation

Explore on MyPoliSciLab

Are All Forms of Discrimination the Same?

In the 1967 *Loving v. Virginia* decision, the Supreme Court ruled unconstitutional all laws that restricted marriage based solely on race. Today, a similar debate revolves around marriage for same-sex couples. Public opposition to interracial marriage declined dramatically after the federal government gave its ruling — as shown in the 1972 and 1988 data. Has opinion about same-sex marriage changed in a similar way?

"Should Interracial Marriage Be Legal?"

1972

REGION	YES	NO
Northeast	71%	26%
Midwest	62%	35%
South	43%	53%
Rocky Mountains	54%	41%
Pacifc Coast	74%	24%

1988

REGION	YES	NO
Northeast	85%	11%
Midwest	76%	21%
South	62%	35%
Rocky Mountains	89%	11%
Pacifc Coast	87%	12%

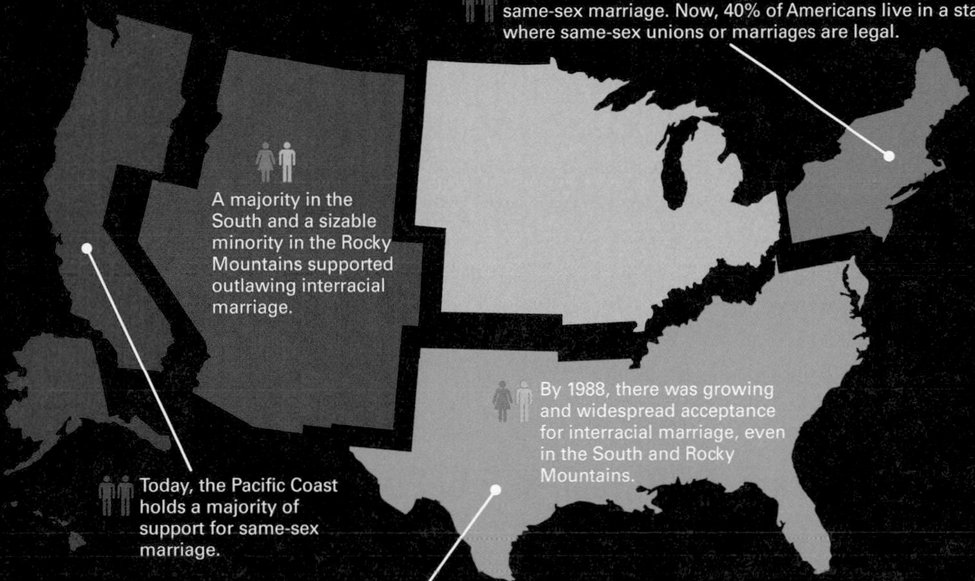

In 2004, Massachusetts became the first state to legalize same-sex marriage. Now, 40% of Americans live in a state where same-sex unions or marriages are legal.

A majority in the South and a sizable minority in the Rocky Mountains supported outlawing interracial marriage.

By 1988, there was growing and widespread acceptance for interracial marriage, even in the South and Rocky Mountains.

Today, the Pacific Coast holds a majority of support for same-sex marriage.

In 1988, solid majorities disagreed with same-sex marriage across the U.S. As of 2012, the strongest prohibitions to same-sex union are found in the South.

"Should Same-Sex Marriage Be Legal?"

1988

REGION	YES	NO
Northeast	13%	63%
Midwest	12%	66%
South	8%	78%
Rocky Mountains	12%	63%
Pacifc Coast	16%	62%

2010

REGION	YES	NO
Northeast	54%	30%
Midwest	50%	41%
South	38%	46%
Rocky Mountains	45%	44%
Pacifc Coast	52%	33%

SOURCE: General Social Survey data from 1972, 1988, and 2010.

Investigate Further

Concept How do we measure discrimination of interracial and same-sex marriage? Pollsters ask if a person agrees or disagrees with policy proposals, such as laws that recognize same-sex or interracial marriage. By watching the responses over time, we are able to determine change across the country.

Connection How does geography help predict public opinion on interracial marriage and same-sex marriage? The American South and Rocky Mountains are historically more conservative regions, and more resistant to changing definitions of marriage. But, even in these regions, opinion on marriage became more liberal over time.

Cause Does opinion about marriage influence policy or vice versa? After the Supreme Court settled the matter of interracial marriage in 1967, majority opinions followed suit across the country. Support for same-sex marriage has also changed over time, but policies vary by state. Legalization is more common where public opinion is most favorable, and bans are most common where support lags.

marriage, but residents are lessening their opposition to broadened marriage rights.

6.1

6.2

6.3

6.4

Racial profiling
law enforcement investigation of individuals at least in part because of their race or ethnicity rather than direct evidence of wrongdoing.

of the law, arguing that portions of the legislation violated the national government's supremacy in immigration policy. Arizona appealed the ruling and lost in the U.S. Court of Appeals, and it then appealed that ruling to the U.S. Supreme Court. In *Arizona v. United States* (2012), the Court struck down much of the Arizona law, concluding that federal immigration laws preempted Arizona's attempts to regulate in this area. Specifically, the Court struck down the portions of the law that made it a state crime to be in the United States unlawfully, made it a crime to work without appropriate legal authorization, and permitted arrests without warrants of individuals thought to be in the United States illegally. However, the Court upheld the provision of the law that had received the most public attention, the requirement that police determine the citizenship or residency status of individuals arrested or detained for other reasons, such as a traffic violation, if they have reason to suspect the person might be in the United States illegally. In the Court's view, this portion of the law acceptably made mandatory a power that police already had at their discretion. Throughout the controversy over the law, opponents expressed concern that despite the law's prohibition on **racial profiling**—detaining people because of their appearance to inquire into their immigration status—the law would in fact encourage profiling.[78] The Court left open the possibility that a further constitutional challenge could be made on civil rights grounds rather than the national supremacy grounds of its decision, if evidence suggested that police were implementing the law in a discriminatory fashion.

Noncitizens do not have all the same rights and privileges as citizens. They cannot, for example, run for certain public offices and they cannot vote in federal elections. Access to federal programs and funds may in some instances be limited to citizens. Because of national security concerns, limits are placed on noncitizens, including the length of time they can be in the United States and their access to certain jobs. Immigrants in the country illegally are subject to long detentions prior to hearings or possible deportation. Because violation of immigration rules is typically treated as an administrative and not a criminal matter, noncitizens do not have a right to have counsel provided during immigration proceedings.

At the state level, issues such as whether noncitizens can obtain driver's licenses, pay in-state tuition at public universities, and qualify for public assistance programs vary across the states. Generally, the Supreme Court has applied an intermediate to high level of scrutiny in examining cases concerning classification by citizenship status—the Court has approached such distinctions with skepticism and has frequently overturned them. The Court has ruled, for example, that public schooling cannot be denied based on whether or not one is a citizen.[79]

Who Bears the Burden of Proof in Discrimination Cases Is Controversial

Across all these various population groups, one of the issues considered by the Supreme Court and Congress is whether each individual who believes he or she has been discriminated against has to prove discrimination. In *Ward's Cove Packing Co. v. Atonio* (1989), the Supreme Court declared that the burden of proof was on the person alleging discrimination to show how an employment practice was, on its own, directly discriminatory toward that particular person. If each individual must prove intentional discrimination, rather than rely on statistical patterns that show disparity between groups, for example in pay, these cases would be much more difficult to win.

Congress responded to the Supreme Court in the Civil Rights Act of 1991. The act returned the burden of proof to the employer—the employer would have to defend a questionable pattern in employment and explain why it was not problematic. A Court decision in 1993 divided the burden of proof, concluding that each individual need not prove the employer set out to discriminate against him or her but would still need to demonstrate that any discriminatory impact between groups was intentional and unreasonable.[80] In civil rights, such seemingly technical distinctions are highly consequential and are the focus of substantial political and legal conflict.

Review the Chapter

 **Listen** to **Chapter 6** on **MyPoliSciLab**

Equality and Civil Rights

6.1 Trace the advances and setbacks in the quest for civil rights in the nineteenth century, p. 190.

Amendments to the Constitution during and following the Civil War, as well as legislation enacted during the period known as Reconstruction, began the process of national recognition of civil rights for blacks. The Fourteenth Amendment's guarantee of equal protection of the laws was interpreted by the Supreme Court to limit government discrimination, not private discrimination. And the Supreme Court concluded that mandating separate facilities for blacks and whites did not violate equal protection as long as the facilities were substantially equal.

Equal Protection of the Laws Gains Meaning

6.2 Explain the demise of the separate but equal doctrine and the creation of civil rights laws and regulations, p. 194.

In the twentieth century, black civil rights organizations began to challenge discriminatory laws in court, with some success, while presidents bypassed Congress to promote civil rights through executive orders and other unilateral actions. The rejection of the separate but equal doctrine by the Supreme Court in *Brown v. Board of Education* prompted a broader movement to press for civil rights. Major legislation challenging discrimination in the private sector and government, significant executive orders introducing affirmative action policies, and a constitutional amendment prohibiting use of the poll tax produced a civil rights revolution in the United States. Congress used its interstate commerce powers and spending powers to avoid Supreme Court concerns that the Fourteenth Amendment did not apply to the private sector.

The Politics of Civil Rights

6.3 Analyze the changes that led to the success and splintering of the civil rights movement, p. 205.

Civil rights successes depended heavily on the rise of a strategically effective civil rights movement, appeals to key beliefs in the American creed, and changes in the Democratic Party that focused the party more on its growing northern, urban, and minority constituency. The push for civil rights encountered difficulty when the movement splintered, policies and ideas became more controversial, and white backlash worried Democratic politicians about their chances to win the presidency.

Extension of Equal Protection to Other Groups

6.4 Describe legal and legislative actions to extend equal protection guarantees to other groups, p. 212.

Although covered by the same laws, court decisions, and presidential actions that aided black civil rights, groups based on ethnicity, gender, religion, age, and sexual orientation, among other categories, have each faced distinctive issues and formed their own organizations to challenge discriminatory laws and practices. The doctrine of equal protection extends to these groups, although the Supreme Court does not treat every classification the same. Race and ethnic classifications in laws and regulations are reviewed the most strictly, followed by gender classifications.

Learn the Terms

 **Study** and **Review** the **Flashcards**

affirmative action, p. 200
Brown v. Board of Education, p. 196
civil disobedience, p. 207
civil rights, p. 190
de facto segregation, p. 197
de jure segregation, p. 197
Dred Scott v. Sandford, p. 191
equal protection clause, p. 191
Jim Crow, p. 194
majority-minority districts, p. 211
Plessy v. Ferguson, p. 194
poll tax, p. 200
racial profiling, p. 224
Regents of the University of California v. Bakke, p. 201
separate but equal doctrine, p. 194
state action, p. 193
white primary, p. 209

Test Yourself

 **Study** and **Review** the **Practice Tests**

6.1 Trace the advances and setbacks in the quest for civil rights in the nineteenth century.

Starting in the late nineteenth century, the Supreme Court took a "state action" view toward the Fourteenth Amendment regarding civil rights. This meant that

a. The amendment concerned only discriminatory actions that involved an action of a government, not private individuals.
b. The amendment dealt with discriminatory actions that involved private individuals and not the action of states or the federal government.
c. Only the sate governments, not the federal government, had to honor the civil rights of blacks.
d. State and federal governments needed to take strong affirmative action to integrate newly freed slaves into American social and economic life.
e. Upon request by citizens, governments had to state in writing the actions they were planning to take to advance the cause of civil rights.

6.2 Explain the demise of the separate but equal doctrine and the creation of civil rights laws and regulations.

The Supreme Court's decision in *Brown v. Board of Education*

a. ruled that federal courts had no authority to rule in cases of de jure segregation.
b. affirmed the constitutionality of affirmative action in college admissions.
c. overturned the Court's decision in *McCulloch v. Maryland.*
d. ruled that the separate but equal doctrine was constitutional.
e. struck down the separate but equal doctrine.

6.3 Analyze the changes that led to the success and splintering of the civil rights movement.

All of the following are reasons why civil rights movement splintered EXCEPT

a. consensus over strategy evaporated.
b. the Republican Party began to take unified black support for granted.
c. issues of social and economic equality were more difficult for many whites to support, unlike the issue of political equality.
d. the Democratic Party began to take unified black support for granted.
e. participation in civil disobedience events dwindled.

6.4 Describe legal and legislative actions to extend equal protection guarantees to other groups.

How did the nation's civil right laws begin to apply to the private sector?

a. The Supreme Court overturned the state action doctrine.
b. Because the Senate represents the states, any law it passes must also apply to the businesses in those states.
c. Congress argued that private sector discrimination had a substantial negative effect on interstate commerce and therefore could be regulated through the commerce clause.
d. An agreement reached by civil rights groups, the federal government, and a dozen major business organizations included a promise that businesses would allow the civil rights laws to apply to the private sector.
e. The Supreme Court ruled on the constitutionality of the state action doctrine.

Explore Further

SUGGESTED READINGS BY TOP SCHOLARS

Angelo N. Ancheta. 2007. *Race, Rights, and the Asian American Experience*, 2nd ed. New Brunswick, NJ: Rutgers University Press. A compelling overview of Asian American civil rights. Emphasizes the importance of considering civil rights beyond the black-white relationship.

Claudine Gay. 2002. "Spirals of Trust: The Effect of Descriptive Representation on the Relationship between Citizens and their Government," *American Journal of Political Science* 46, 4: 717–33. Finds that constituents are more likely to contact representatives with whom they racially identify, but such racial identification does not affect citizens' perceptions of Congress as an institution.

Victoria Hattam. 2007. *In the Shadow of Race: Jews, Latinos, and Immigrant Politics in the United States*. Chicago: University of Chicago Press. Explores the distinction between race and ethnicity and how these have affected public policy and immigrant politics.

Ira Katznelson. 2005. *When Affirmative Action Was White: An Untold History of Racial Inequality in Twentieth-Century America*. New York: W. W. Norton. Argues that many of the public programs arising from the New Deal in the 1930s and 1940s were in effect affirmative action that benefited white Americans.

Richard M. Valelly. 2004. *The Two Reconstructions: The Struggle for Black Enfranchisement*. Chicago: University of Chicago Press. Examines movements for black enfranchisement, offering an explanation of why these efforts failed in the nineteenth century but were successful in the twentieth century.

SUGGESTED WEBSITES

U.S. Department of Justice, Civil Rights Division: www.usdoj.gov/crt

Provides links to presidential statements on civil rights, newsletters, Department of Justice special initiatives and court cases, and guidance on compliance with civil rights policy.

American Civil Rights Institute: www.acri.org
Website of an organization dedicated to ending racial and gender preference policies around the country and challenging the philosophy of other civil rights organizations.

National Association for the Advancement of Colored People: www.naacp.org
Website of the organization that played a crucial role in the rise of black civil rights. Provides information on the organization's major policy and legal concerns and its advocacy priorities.

National Council of La Raza: www.nclr.org
One of the major Hispanic/Latino civil rights and advocacy organizations.

Human Rights Campaign: www.hrc.org
One of the leading advocacy organizations for lesbian, gay, bisexual, and transgender rights.

Disability.gov: www.disability.gov/civil_rights
Access to information on civil rights in the United States and at the state level.

Listen to Chapter 7 on MyPoliSciLab

Public Opinion

GUESSING WEIGHTS

One day in the fall of 1906, British scientist Francis Galton left his home in the town of Plymouth and headed for a country fair. As he walked through the exhibition that day, Galton noticed a crowd forming around a fat ox. People were lining up to put wagers on how much the ox weighed.

Eight hundred people tried their luck. They were a diverse lot. Some were butchers and farmers, likely experts at judging the weight of livestock. But there were also many with no expertise at all. Galton described these nonexperts in the scientific journal *Nature* as "those clerks and others who have no expert knowledge of horses, but who bet on races, guided by newspapers, friends, and their own fancies."

When the contest was over and the winners received their prizes, Galton borrowed the tickets from the organizers and studied the guesses. He thought the average guess would be way off the mark. After all, mix a crowd of experts at guessing livestock weights with a slew of less well-informed folks, and it seems likely the result would be a wrong answer. But Galton was wrong. On average, the crowd guessed that the ox would weigh 1,197 pounds after it was slaughtered and dressed. The actual weight? 1,198 pounds. The crowd's judgment was right on the money.[1]

What Galton discovered that day was something of a paradox: A group of people, many of whom have little interest or expertise in a particular subject matter, can still, collectively, get it right. This is true of American politics as well. Although many Americans have no great interest or expertise in politics or policy, somehow they tend to make appropriate, reasonable, and logical judgments about political life. These judgments fall under the heading of "public opinion," one of the most commonly used phrases in any discussion of politics and policy.

Public opinion has great influence. We are constantly bombarded with the results of polls and surveys showing what Americans think about almost every issue imaginable. Politicians consider

7.1 Define public opinion and identify its four basic traits, p. 231.

7.2 Outline the process and agents of political socialization, p. 236.

7.3 Explain the basics of public opinion formation, p. 243.

7.4 Establish how American democracy functions despite the public's lack of sophisticated political knowledge, p. 245.

GUESSING WEIGHTS This team of oxen is not unlike those in the weight-guessing competition at the country fair. On average, a crowd not only may be very close to guessing an ox's correct weight but also may collectively exercise good judgment in a political context.

The Big Picture Imagine that all of the political considerations in your head about immigration, welfare, or abortion are ping pong balls. Author Kenneth M. Goldstein describes what happens to those ping pong balls when we are confronted with a political survey and why our responses tend to be so inconsistent.

The Basics How do people form opinions? In this video, we examine how we know what opinions the public holds, and how they come by those opinions. As we go along, you'll discover that Americans aren't always well-informed about government and policies, but that they share core values.

2
Are average folks informed about their government?

In Context How did the emergence of scientific polling in the twentieth century change our democracy? In this video, Columbia University political scientist Robert Y. Shapiro outlines the history of polling and the emergence of public opinion as a major factor in American politics.

Think Like a Political Scientist Uncover some of the new questions being asked by political scientists regarding public opinion. In this video, Columbia University political scientist Robert Y. Shapiro examines some of the new public opinion trends that are being researched.

In the Real World Should politicians listen more to their constituents (who may not be educated about all of the issues), or to their own sense of what is right and wrong? Hear real people weigh in on this question, and learn how presidents have dealt with it in the past.

So What? How can studying political science be applied to a career in journalism, marketing, business, or law? Author Kenneth M. Goldstein teaches students how to create a political poll and how to think critically about other surveys in the media.

these opinions as they form their stances on issues. The media reflect these opinions in the way they report news stories. And these political and media messages tend to influence what people think.

Frank Newport, editor-in-chief of the Gallup Poll, a prominent monitor of American public opinion, understands this cycle of influence firsthand. Consider how people think about the economy and government competence. Toward the end of 2011, although a sizable minority of people were still feeling the effects of the economic downturn and high unemployment rates, many more people were employed and healthy.

"We have a lot of economic anxiety," Newport explained. Despite the tough times, "most of us go through our daily lives OK. We have jobs. We have health insurance," he said. But because the media offer steady reports about high unemployment and home foreclosures, the public gets a certain message about how it should feel. According to Newport, "We're anxiety-ridden in part because the media [tell] us that we should be."

That anxiety translates into an overall feeling of pessimism and lack of confidence in the government. Newport explained that in a 2011 poll asking people to describe the federal government in a word or phrase, people often used words such as *incompetent, confused,* and *corrupt.*[2]

To manage public opinions such as these, political leaders and strategists focus on influencing the content and direction of what people think and know about politics. The fact that public opinion plays an important role in American politics comes from our political culture and the value it places on democracy, representation, and civil liberties. Compared to other political systems (even other democratic ones), the American system allows citizens many opportunities to express their own opinions—and to use those opinions to impact politics. This dynamic allows the public to shape public policy separate and apart from elections—a powerful force that no politician can afford to ignore.

The Nature of Public Opinion

7.1 Define public opinion and identify its four basic traits.

Public opinion is one of the most commonly used phrases in the discussion of politics and policy. It can be measured, obeyed, manipulated, ignored, and even misunderstood. But, what is public opinion?

Public opinion is the collection of "preferences of the adult population on matters of relevance to government."[3] Another definition provides a broader perspective: Public opinion is the collective political beliefs and attitudes of the public, or groups within the public, about issues, candidates, officials, parties, and groups. Although public opinion typically refers to the collective opinion of the public, it can also refer to opinions of groups within the public sphere.

public opinion
the collective political beliefs and attitudes of the public, or groups within the public, on matters of relevance to government.

salience
an issue's importance to a person or to the public in general.

stability
the speed with which the change will occur, and the likelihood that the new opinion will endure.

Public Opinion Has Four Basic Traits

In general, public opinion has four basic traits: salience, stability, direction, and intensity. **Salience** is how important an issue is to a particular person or to the public in general. An issue may be salient to the public, but an individual person might not find that same issue to be very important personally. Similarly, the public might mildly favor or mildly oppose an issue, but that issue might be quite salient to many individual people.

When politicians decide whether to attempt to change public opinion or whether to follow the public's lead on an issue, they need to consider the **stability** of public opinion. That means whether public opinion on an issue is likely to change. And, if public opinion does change, will that change be gradual or rapid? Once changed, will it change frequently, or will it solidify around that new position? These are crucial questions for politicians to consider. For example, are public attitudes about health care likely to change significantly in the short term? If they do, will those new opinions stay

direction
in public opinion, the tendency for or against some phenomenon.

intensity
the strength of the direction of public opinion.

the same or continue to change? The **direction** of the public's opinion refers to whether the public favors or opposes a particular point of view. Any indication of agreement or disagreement, approval or disapproval, favor or opposition is an example of direction.

The **intensity** of the public's opinion measures the strength of the direction. For example, some people strongly favor or oppose abortion rights, whereas others may not harbor such strong feelings on the issue. Some will favor abortion rights in most cases, but not strongly; some will oppose abortion rights in most cases, but not strongly.

Public opinion can also vary significantly among different groups within the population. It is important for politicians to recognize how public opinion breaks down among these various groups so they can better understand the impact of different policies on different demographics.

In 2008, when Californians voted on a measure to make same-sex marriage unconstitutional, liberals expected that overwhelming support for Barack Obama's presidential campaign would lead to a strong turnout of pro–gay marriage voters. Although the state did vote for Obama, it also voted against same-sex marriage. As it turns out, African American voters, who are overwhelmingly supportive of Obama but also socially conservative on several issues, came out largely against gay marriage.

Hispanics are another demographic group that can confuse politicians. Hispanics, particularly Evangelicals and church-going Catholics, tend to be conservative, especially on social issues. They generally oppose abortion and gay marriage. They are sympathetic toward Israel. On the other hand, they tend to be more liberal on economic issues. Many support government-provided services such as health care, even if they result in higher taxes. Many believe that the government should offer more benefits to help the poor.[4] Hispanics are also fairly liberal when it comes to immigration policy.

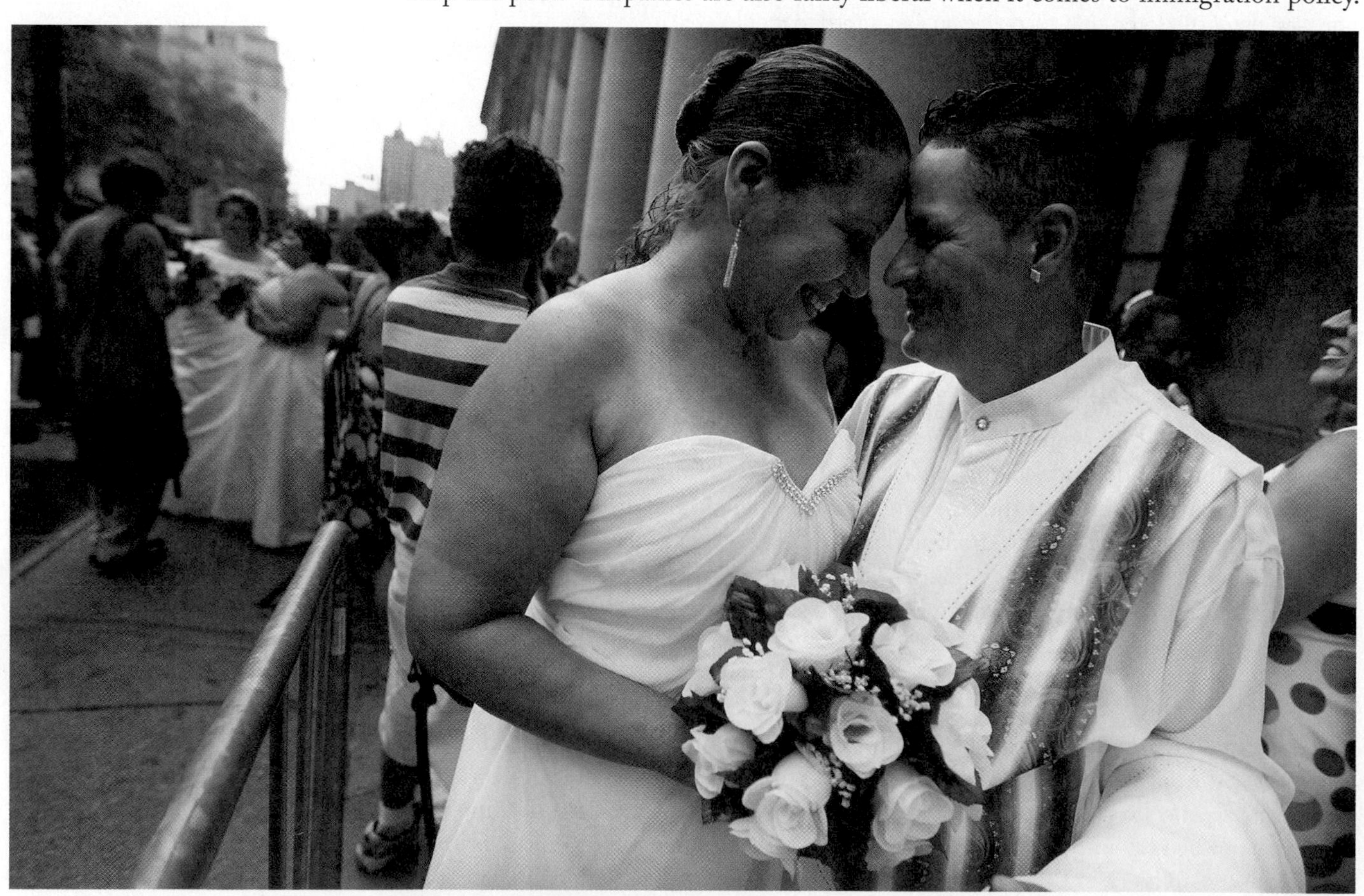

ATTITUDES ON GAY MARRIAGE DIFFER SIGNIFICANTLY ACROSS THE COUNTRY

Although acceptance of homosexuality is much greater now, there remains significant disagreement among Americans about whether or not same sex couples should be allowed to marry.

President Obama voiced his support for gay or same sex marriage over the summer of 2012, but marriage laws remain a state level responsibility with a handful of states permitting same sex couples to be wed. This picture shows same sex couples lining up at the city clerk's office in Brooklyn New York in July of 2011 on the first day that gay marriage was allowed in New York state.

For example, a December 2011 study by the Pew Research Center showed that Hispanics opposed President Obama's deportation policies by a 2-to-1 margin, despite supporting the president generally.[5]

Table 7.1 shows how public opinion on specific policy issues varies greatly among different demographic groups. Race, gender, income, and political affiliation are all factors in how an individual forms an opinion on a certain issue.[6] It is important for politicians to understand how opinions can differ among these groups—and even within them—so they can appeal more strategically to each group.

Understanding dynamics like these can help politicians gauge public opinion. But the forces that drive public opinion can change, as can the direction, intensity, and salience of public opinion. Politicians must follow these changes closely and constantly consider a variety of questions, including the following: Do my positions track public opinion now? What happens if public opinion quickly shifts in another direction?

TABLE 7.1 ATTITUDES ABOUT MAJOR POLICIES BY DIFFERENT DEMOGRAPHICS

Views on Health Care Legislation by Demographics

	Favor (%)	Oppose (%)	Don't Know/ Refused (%)
Gender:			
Men	57	35	7
Women	46	42	12
Race:			
White Non-Hispanic	53	37	10
Total Nonwhite	46	43	11
Black Non-Hispanic	47	43	10
Income:			
$75,000 +	61	32	7
$30,000–$74,999	53	40	7
<$30,000	41	47	11
Party ID:			
Republican	65	29	6
Democrat	45	44	12
Independent	49	41	9

Views on the Afghanistan War by Different Demographics

	Favor (%)	Oppose (%)	Don't Know/ Refused (%)
Gender:			
Male	35	50	14
Female	34	46	19
Race:			
White Non-Hispanic	30	55	16
Total Nonwhite	48	32	20
Black Non-Hispanic	61	18	21
Income:			
$75,000 +	37	54	8
$30,000–$74,999	36	49	15
<$30,000	36	43	20
Party ID:			
Republican	11	79	11
Democrat	59	20	21
Independent	32	52	16

Source: Pew Research Center for the People and the Press, "Unabated Economic Gloom, Divides on Afghanistan and Health Care." December 16, 2009, http://people-press.org.

7.1

7.2

7.3

7.4

sampling
taking a small fraction of something that is meant to represent a larger whole, for example, a group of people who represent a larger population.

random sample
a population sample in which it is equally likely that each member of the population will be included in the sample.

sampling error
the difference between the reported characteristics of the sample and the characteristics of the larger population that result from imperfect sampling.

margin of error
the range surrounding a sample's response within which researchers are confident the larger population's true response would fall.

nonresponse bias
a nonrandom error that occurs when people who choose to participate in a survey have different attitudes from those of people who decline to participate.

Do I attempt to move public opinion in a new direction or make it more intense or salient? How do I approach an issue that has great stability and is hard to change?

Answers to these questions cannot guide every decision a politician makes. Still, in a well-functioning representative democracy, policy making generally follows the contours of public opinion on most issues. Most politicians like to be on the "80 side of 80–20 issues." That means politicians tend to agree with the public when there is a large public consensus on an issue. Officeholders who end up on the wrong side of public opinion too often risk great political costs and face defeat come election time.

Politicians and Political Scientists Use Polls to Gauge the Opinions of the American Public

During election season, scores of polls report who is ahead and behind virtually every day. At other times, news reports frequently mention the public's perception of the president's job performance and whether the country is heading in the right direction. If the president or a member of Congress makes a significant policy proposal, major media outlets survey Americans for their reactions. A well-designed survey can provide accurate information on public opinion, but one that is poorly done can lead to faulty conclusions and mistaken actions.

Sampling Is the Process of Choosing a Small Group of People to Interview for a Survey

Imagine you are making a pot of soup for some friends. You add water, chicken, vegetables, and spices, and let the soup simmer for a couple of hours. Before serving it, you want to make sure it tastes good, so you take a small spoonful. If you take your spoonful from the top, you might think the soup needed more seasoning. If you take your spoonful from the bottom, you might think the soup needed more water. A good cook mixes the soup before taking a sample spoonful to make sure all parts are represented.

The same logic applies to survey **sampling**, the process of choosing a small group of people to interview for a survey. A survey sample should represent all elements of the population—men, women, young, old, Democrats, Republicans, and other groups—in rough proportion to their population percentages. Such representation is accomplished by using a **random sample**, a sample in which every member of the population has an equal chance of ending up in the sample.

A random sample captures people who will likely represent the total population in their personal characteristics, as well as in their views. That way, their answers will closely approximate those we would get if we asked everyone in the entire population.

Even in perfectly drawn samples, however, unavoidable **sampling error** occurs because no sample is an exact match for the entire population. Most surveys report this sampling error as the **margin of error**. To understand what this means, suppose that 55 percent of respondents in a survey approved of the president's job performance. If we had spoken to the entire population, we would have found that somewhere between 50 percent and 60 percent approved of the president's performance—that is, 55 percent plus or minus five percentage points. Those five percentage points are what the survey claims as its margin of error. That way, it accounts for any additional differences that would change the result if we had spoken with the entire population.

Surveys may also suffer from **nonresponse bias**, in which many chosen respondents decline to participate. This affects the reliability of the results. For example, a survey on Social Security would need to include opinions from younger workers, older workers, and retirees to reflect the general population. But if many young workers declined to participate in the survey, the results would have a disproportionate amount of input from older workers and retirees, who likely have very different views on the subject. So the greater the likelihood for a diversity of opinion, the more people a researcher needs to survey to be confident of the results. For more information on the challenges of conducting accurate surveys, see *How Do We Know? Can Surveys Accurately Gauge the Opinions of More than 300 Million Americans?*

How Do We Know?

Can Surveys Accurately Gauge the Opinions of More Than 300 Million Americans?

Discussions of public opinion are a routine part of American political life. Politicians use surveys to take the pulse of the nation before, during, and after a campaign; an important speech; or the introduction of a major policy initiative. Political scientists also use surveys to gauge the collective consciousness of the American people. Not all surveys are equal, however. The question is: Can surveys accurately gauge the opinions of more than 300 million Americans? How do we know?

Why It Matters

Agreement between public opinion and government action is one measure of a democratic government. However, it is not always a good one. Sometimes the opinion "snapshot" in a survey obscures momentum—at the time of the survey, government may be in the process of moving toward the public's position, or vice versa. And sometimes what the public wants may be ill advised or even unconstitutional. However, a critical starting point in our assessment is developing an understanding of how surveys work.

Investigating the Answer

A good survey sample is a random sample that reflects a true cross-section of the population being surveyed. Traditionally, telephone surveys were an excellent way to collect a random sample. During the post–World War II period, most Americans had access to a household telephone line. Surveys would draw a sampling of telephone numbers and then allow all adults living in each household an equal chance to be selected for the survey.

Today, because so many people use mobile phones—often instead of landlines—it is much more difficult to use land-based phone numbers to draw a random sample. The person who answers a mobile phone is generally its sole owner, which also makes him or her automatically the survey participant and does not offer an equal chance at participation to others. In addition, many people younger than age 18 use mobile phones, and they are not eligible to participate in political surveys. Finally, although area codes identify the geographical location of landlines, a person can have a mobile phone with an area code from one geographic location but actually live somewhere else. This makes it more difficult for surveys to ensure geographic diversity in drawing a random sample.

Some of these challenges also apply to Internet surveys, with which volunteers answer questions online in exchange for gifts or money. Even though Internet surveys have grown into a multi-billion-dollar industry, they are flawed. First, only people with Internet access can participate in these polls, which does not offer an equal chance at participation to the general population. As of August 2012, 85 percent of American adults used the Internet.[a] Internet users also tend to be younger, between the ages of 18 and 49, and have higher incomes.[b] Also, some demographic groups are online less frequently, even if they do have Internet access. This leads to significant underrepresentation of specific groups of people, and therefore, inaccurate results.[c]

Even if it were possible to draw a perfect random sample, sampling error would be unavoidable. A variety of factors can influence the extent of sampling error. One is the size of the sample: the larger the sample, the smaller the sampling error. If you flipped a coin several times, you should get a roughly equal proportion of heads and tails. The more times you flip the coin, the more likely the proportion of heads to tails will be nearly equal. Try it! The same applies to survey samples. If researchers picked just one person at random, or 10, or even 100, to represent the entire U.S. population, the sampling error would be enormous. But if they picked 1,000 people at random, the sampling error would be three or four percentage points, an acceptable margin for error. With 1,000 people in the sample, there would likely be a fair mix of men, women, young, old, Democrats, Republicans, whites, nonwhites, and so on to broadly represent the entire U.S. population.

Population diversity can also affect sampling error. To take an extreme example, suppose you knew everyone in a state had the same opinion on every issue. If you wanted to measure public opinion on an issue in that state, you would need to ask only one person. Now suppose everyone had a slightly different opinion on every issue. If you were to interview just one person, your sampling error would be unacceptably large. Surveys are also sensitive to the wording of survey questions, as well as to question order. For example, the way questions are worded can encourage a particular response. Consider the following questions:

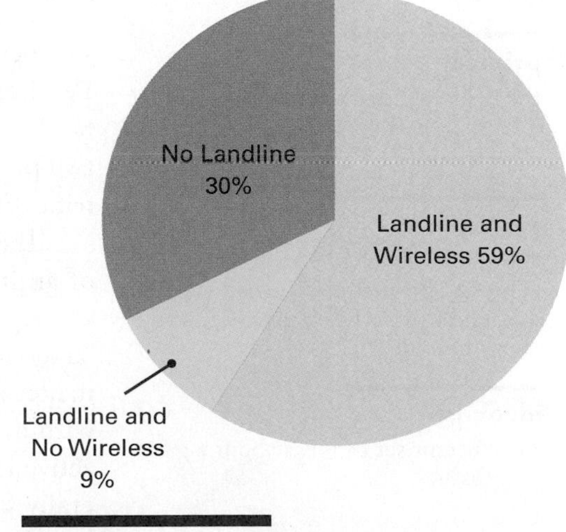

PHONE USAGE

One in Three Adults in the US only Has a Cell Phone

[a] Trend Data *http://pewinternet.org/Trend-Data/Online-Activites-Total.aspx* http://pewinternet.org/Static-Pages/Trend-Data-%28Adults%29/Whos-Online.asp

[b] Demographics of Internet Users *http://pewinternet.org/Trend-Data/Whos-Online.aspx* http://pewinternet.org/Static-Pages/Trend-Data-%28Adults%29/Whos-Online.asp

[c] AAPOR Report on Online Panels, 2010, http://aapor.org/AM/Template.cfm?Section=AAPOR_Committee_and_Task_Force_Reports&Template=/CM/ContentDisplay.cfm&ContentID=2223

7.1

- Given the recent series of murders in our state, some people say the state should reinstate the death penalty. Do you agree or disagree?
- Given the recent cases of police misconduct and the freeing of inmates who had been wrongly convicted, do you agree or disagree that the state should reinstate the death penalty?

7.2

The first question is structured to elicit pro–death penalty responses, whereas the second question is structured to elicit anti–death penalty responses.

Finally, the demographic characteristics of interviewers can also introduce error. Evidence shows that men reply differently to male interviewers than to female interviewers on issues such as abortion and birth control. Similarly, the race of an interviewer influences responses to questions about race.

7.3

7.4

The Bottom Line

Surveys can be an incredibly useful tool for journalists, political scientists, and politicians. However, identifying good survey methods and understanding how particular surveys are conducted are highly useful skills for citizens as well. Those skills will serve you well in other courses as well as enable you to think critically about poll results.

Thinking Critically

- Suppose you were in charge of designing a survey to gauge public opinion on certain major issues. How would you word your questions?
- Do you think polling via the Internet is as trustworthy as other, more established polling techniques? What are some problems Internet polls may have?

Political Socialization

7.2 Outline the process and agents of political socialization.

political socialization
the learning process in which individuals absorb information and selectively add it to their knowledge and understanding of politics and government.

primacy
the principle that what is learned first is learned best and lodged most firmly in one's mind.

persistence
the principle that political lessons, values, and attitudes learned early in life tend to structure political learning later on in life.

ideology
a consistent set of ideas about a given set of issues.

What is the source of public opinion? How do individuals acquire their political values and attitudes in the first place? The process takes place through what political scientists call political socialization. **Political socialization** is a learning process, one in which individuals absorb information about the political world and add it, selectively, to their core of knowledge.

This learning tends to be governed by two important principles: primacy and persistence. **Primacy** means that what you learn first, you learn best—it tends to stick. **Persistence** means that the political lessons, values, and attitudes you learn early in life tend to form the basis for your political learning later on in life. In keeping with these two principles, what young people learn about politics becomes an important determinant of the values, attitudes, and beliefs they will hold later in life.

The most common expression of values, attitudes, and beliefs is the identification of an individual's ideology. **Ideology** can be described as a consistent set of ideas about a given set of issues. The two most commonly used ideological categories are "liberal" and "conservative." Although there are no hard and fast definitions for what makes an individual liberal or conservative, certain beliefs are generally associated with one ideology or the other. A liberal would generally favor a government that is active in promoting social equality and economic welfare. A conservative would generally favor a smaller government that interferes minimally in the economic sphere but actively promotes social morality. Further, liberals are often said to fall to the "left" of the political spectrum, whereas the "right" is occupied by political conservatives. (The terms *right* and *left* refer to the ideologies of those who sat in the French National Assembly in the eighteenth century and have been appropriated for use in other countries.) Of course, many people do not fall squarely in either of the two camps. People who favor a smaller government that interferes minimally in the economy might be ordinarily lumped with the right, but sometimes they also oppose government involvement in matters of social morality and thus could be viewed differently. They are called "libertarians." Those who support an active government role in the economy tend to be on the left, but if they also favor governmental involvement in social morality, they might be comfortable on the right. They are dubbed "populists."

Political Sophistication Develops with Age and Maturity

Political socialization plays a crucial role in determining which ideology an individual will support. Children begin learning about politics and government surprisingly early. Preschoolers first encounter government often in the form of police officers. With some exceptions, preschoolers generally think of a police officer as a helpful, benevolent, authority figure.[7] Exceptions to this rule include African American; Hispanic; and low-income, white children of Appalachia,[8] who sometimes do not view political authority as favorably as the rest of the population.

As children enter elementary school, they also begin to recognize the U.S. president.[9] Children in early grade school generally view the president as positive, honest, trustworthy, and virtuous—similar to how preschoolers often view police officers.

As children advance through elementary school, they expand their awareness of political figures to firefighters, soldiers, mayors, and governors.[10] They also become more aware of government institutions, such as Congress and political parties, as well as political activities such as voting.[11]

EARLY INTERACTIONS WITH GOVERNMENT

Police and firefighters are often young children's first introduction to government. In later years, children learn about their president, mayor, and members of Congress.

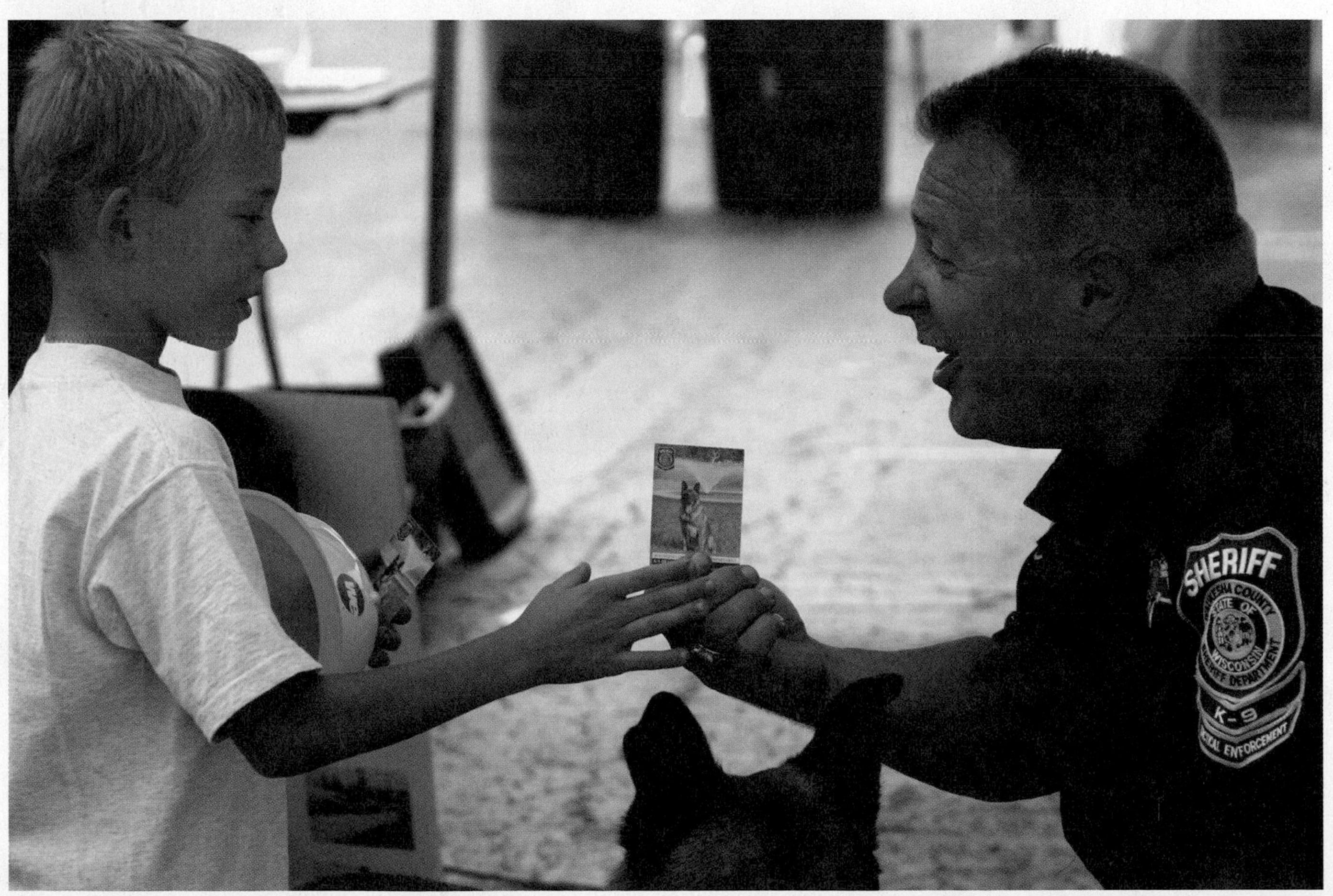

Explore on MyPoliSciLab

What Do Young People Think About Politics Today?

In recent years, attention has focused on the potential power of the youth vote. But in 2012, polls show that individuals between the ages of 18 and 25 are cynical about political leadership as well as their own ability to influence government. In a time when many are taking to the streets with the Tea Party and Occupy Wall Street movements, most young voters are not gravitating to either group. Here is how they responded to questions about leadership and participation.

How 18- to 25-Year-Olds Responded

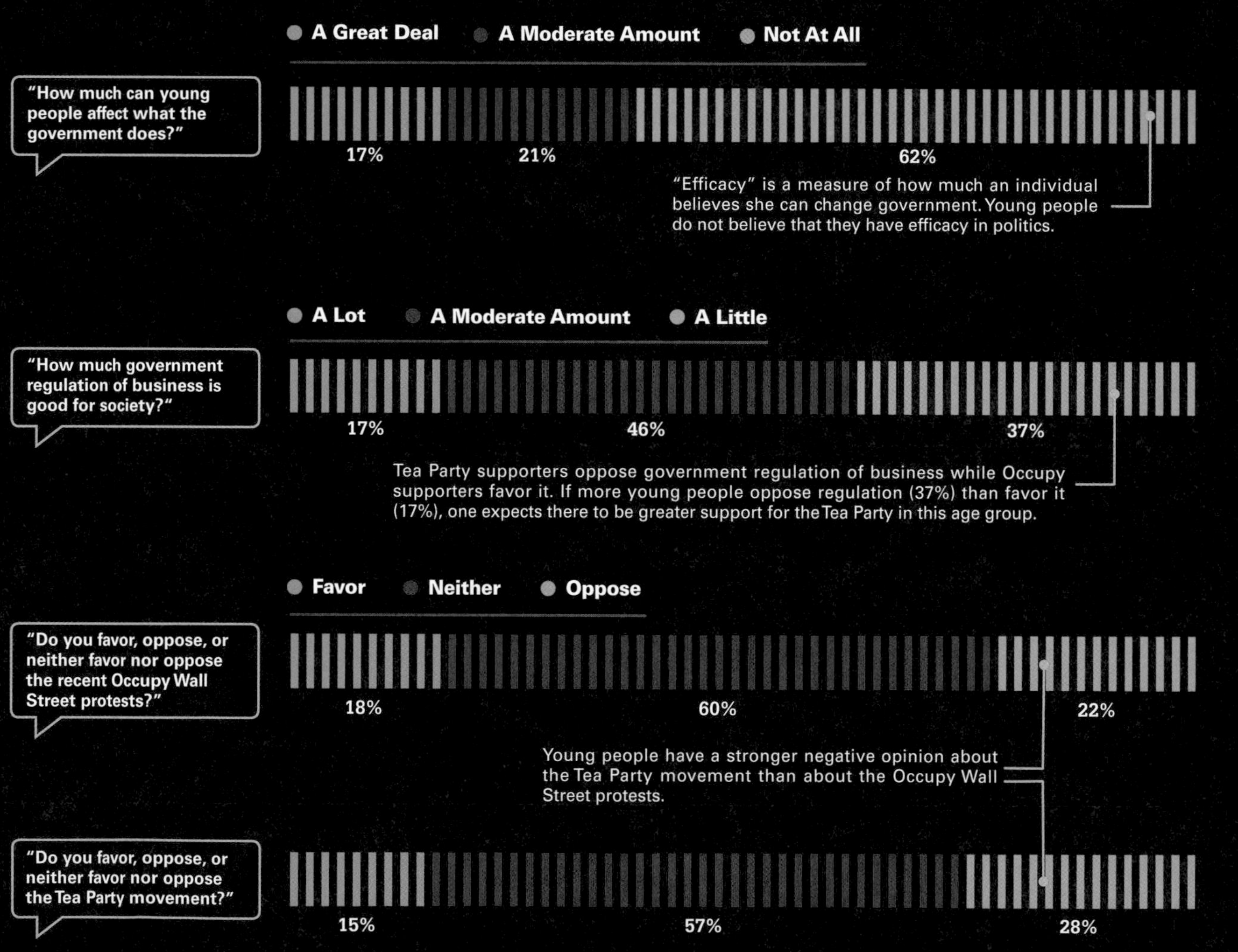

A Great Deal
A Moderate Amount
Not At All
"How much can young people affect what the government does?"
17%
21%
62%
"Efficacy" is a measure of how much an individual believes she can change government. Young people do not believe that they have efficacy in politics.
A Lot
A Moderate Amount
A Little
"How much government regulation of business is good for society?"
17%
46%
37%
Tea Party supporters oppose government regulation of business while Occupy supporters favor it. If more young people oppose regulation (37%) than favor it (17%), one expects there to be greater support for the Tea Party in this age group.
Favor
Neither
Oppose
"Do you favor, oppose, or neither favor nor oppose the recent Occupy Wall Street protests?"
18%
60%
22%
Young people have a stronger negative opinion about the Tea Party movement than about the Occupy Wall Street protests.
"Do you favor, oppose, or neither favor nor oppose the Tea Party movement?"
15%
57%
28%

SOURCE: Data from American National Election Study, "Evaluations of Government and Society Study," Release Wave 4, Winter 2012.

Investigate Further

Concept Why does efficacy matter? Questions that measure efficacy among Americans indicate that it is low among young voters because this group thinks they have no voice. This disengaged attitude is not indicative of a healthy democracy.

Connection Do opinions about Occupy Wall Street and the Tea Party relate to young people's economic beliefs? Like the Tea Party, young voters tend to oppose government regulation, while Occupy supporters favor government involvement. However, this shared belief between young people and the Tea Party does not translate to stronger Tea Party support.

Cause Does low efficacy among 18- to 25-year-olds fuel their desire to influence government and join popular political movements? No. Even though Occupy Wall Street is viewed more positively than the Tea Party among today's youth, feelings of low efficacy do not lead to widespread support for either movement.

7.1
7.2
7.3
7.4

In addition, children begin to show preferences for particular political figures. For example, they may like the president more than the police officer, and both more than the senator.[12] Overall, however, positive feelings toward various authority figures begin to decline during late childhood as kids begin to transition toward a more realistic, less heroic view of specific political figures.[13] During these years, children also begin to gain a basic understanding of political concepts such as policy, conflict over specific issues, and competition between the political parties.[14]

During elementary school, children also begin to understand what good citizenship means. First, they learn what it means to be a "good person." As they mature, they learn more about how the government works, and why it is important to participate in politics by voting.[15] They learn to support politicians who will perform well in office, regardless of their partisanship.[16] Children getting closer to middle school begin to understand that there are different political parties, and they may express a preference for one or the other but still have a hard time understanding the differences between them.[17]

In high school, teens begin to develop a substantially more sophisticated understanding of both political issues and the political process. High school students often become interested in issues such as the environment, the legal drinking age, and free speech, as well as other major policy issues. They understand the differences between Republicans and Democrats and begin to align themselves with one of the parties.[18] They also gain an understanding of the place of interest groups in the political process and can recognize which groups are involved with which issues.[19]

In addition, as teens grow and mature, they become less trusting of the political process and more able to view it critically and realistically. But this is an ongoing process. High school seniors tend to be less cynical about politics and government than their parents.[20]

What causes children to develop certain attitudes about politics? Political scientists point to agents of socialization. Agents of socialization include individuals, institutions, and events that help confer political knowledge and socialize people to politics.

FAMILY The single most important socialization agent is the family, particularly parents. Parents are likely to discuss their own political beliefs either in front of or with their children more frequently and openly than other socializing agents—including teachers and peers, for example.[21] Plus, given their close relationship, parents can have a significant influence on their children's opinions.

The most reliable area of transmission from parent to child is identification with a political party, that is, whether one considers oneself a Democrat, Republican, independent, or something else.[22] One reason that partisanship tends to be "inherited" more easily than specific issue positions is that a parent's partisanship is much easier for a child to grasp than a parent's position on, say, Social Security reform. (Consider "My mom's a Republican" versus "My mom thinks that if the government stopped indexing retiree earnings to account for increases in average wages, the financial problems with Social Security would be much more manageable.") Finally, partisanship is often deeply held and highly salient to adults. Such core beliefs tend to be transmitted most reliably.[23]

Of course, parental influence does not always translate into political agreement. Children and their parents often do not agree on political issues. A variety of factors explain this disparity. Chief among these is the communication between parents and children about politics—and specifically, the quantity, clarity, and importance of that communication.

For example, parents who do not often discuss politics in front of or with their children, do not watch or react to political programming on television, or do not teach political values are not likely to transmit particular political ideas to their children. Further, parents who are not sure of their own political beliefs or who disagree with their spouse on political issues are less likely to convey a specific political worldview to their children.

Of course, as children mature, they often simply develop their own opinions. They can sort through information about the political world and arrive at conclusions different from those of their parents. This is particularly true when they are exposed to events or influences unique to their generation. For example, young people of college or draft age were more influenced by the Vietnam War than their parents and grandparents were. In addition, children—especially teenagers—sometimes take pride in small acts of rebellion against their parents. These may include adopting divergent positions on the hot political topics of the day.

RELIGIOUS INSTITUTIONS AND TRADITIONS Family religious traditions may also influence how a child develops political views. Religious teachings are, of course, dedicated to the spiritual realm rather than the political. But different religions and denominations teach different values about issues such as punishment and mercy, social justice, the importance of law and authority, and equality. These values, especially understood from a religious perspective, can also play an important role in thinking about politics.

Furthermore, people of certain religions often affiliate with particular political parties.[24] Jewish people, for example, tend to be Democrats, whereas evangelical Christians are more likely to be Republicans. Often, as parents pass their religion on to their children, they also pass along political beliefs. These loyalties, however, are not set in stone.

PEER GROUPS Peer groups, or the friends that a child most closely associates with, can impact the development of a child's political views, especially during adolescence,

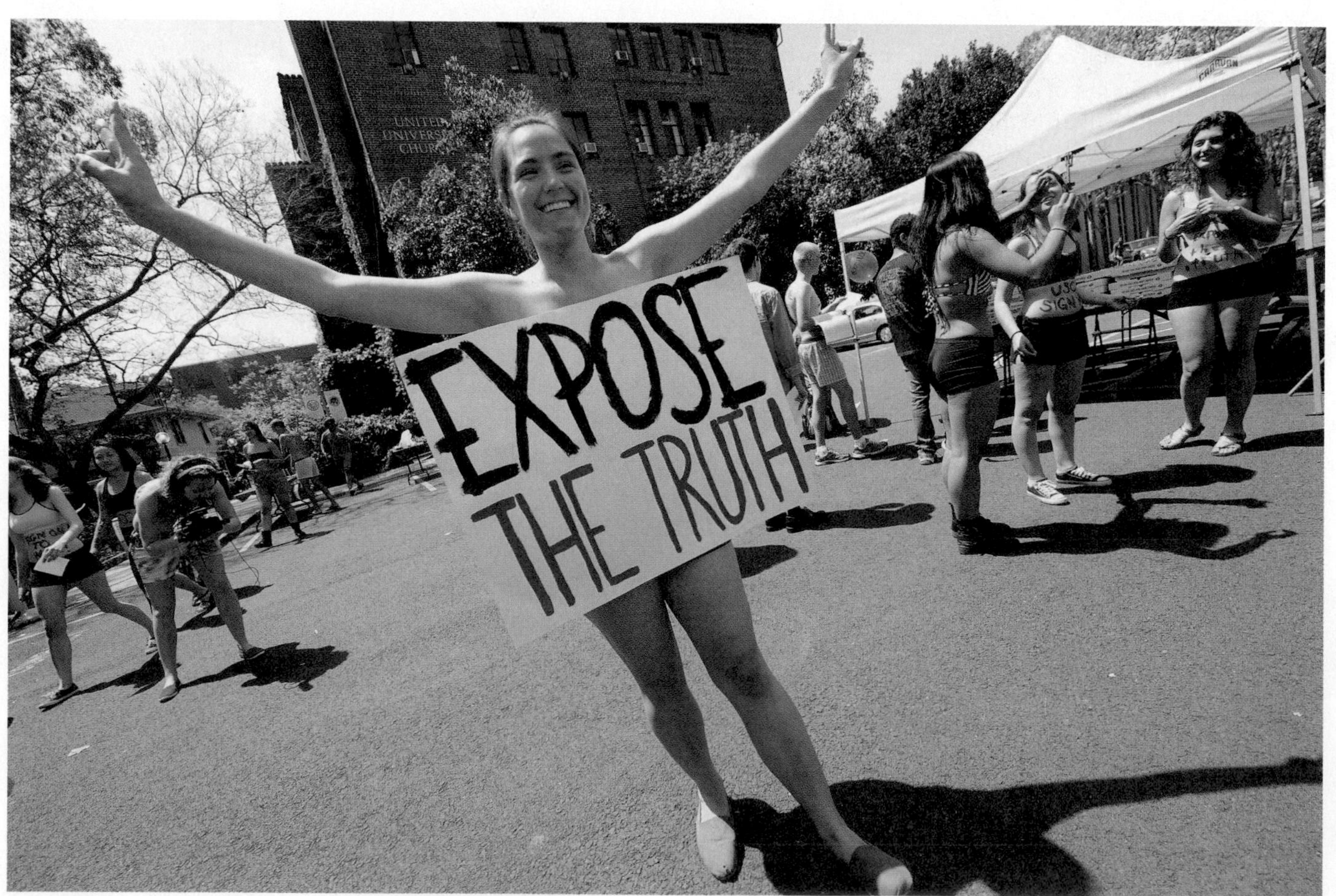

PEER GROUPS IMPACT POLITICAL VIEWS

Parents have by far and away the largest impact on the political views of their children. Still, attitudes and intensity can be influenced by the friends and peers. Here, University of Southern California students are shown demonstrating in support of workers rights in foreign factories that make athletic and other university apparel.

when teenagers spend more time with their friends and away from their parents. But it also depends on how much they discuss politics with their friends. Typically, the salience of politics to adolescents is low.[25] Therefore, political communication among adolescents is generally limited, and the resulting peer-to-peer socialization of political attitudes is similarly limited.[26]

generational effect
the situation in which younger citizens are influenced by events in such a fashion that their attitudes and beliefs are forever rendered distinct from those of older generations.

EDUCATIONAL SYSTEM Another potentially important socialization agent is the educational system. Public schools actively seek to inculcate students with a respect for the law, authority, and democratic values; an appreciation of the American political system; a sense of the meaning and importance of active democratic citizenship; and the political knowledge necessary for active, effective political participation. They also teach some of the rituals and symbolism of politics—flying the flag, reciting the Pledge of Allegiance, voting in student elections, writing to elected officials, and so on. Because schools are often homogenous, with children from similar backgrounds attending the same school, it is difficult to separate the impact of the education system from other socialization agents. Still, schools seem a very likely contributor to children's take on the American political system and the idea of good citizenship.[27] On the other hand, contrary to the claims of some partisans that teachers indoctrinate students with their own views, there is little evidence that school has a significant impact on partisan or issue attitudes.

THE MEDIA Political socialization depends on politically relevant information, often provided by the media. What the media choose to cover, how they choose to do so, and the accessibility of their coverage are all important political socialization questions.

Events that Socialize Can Have Generational, Period, or Life-Cycle Effects

As young people mature, they generally lose some of their childhood idealism about government. Nevertheless, most young adults support the American system of democratic government. Experiencing political events can contribute to how young people—and even adults—understand politics, and to their developing political beliefs. Political events can influence public opinion through a variety of ways.

GENERATIONAL EFFECTS Political events can cause younger members of the population to have different attitudes and beliefs than people in older generations. This is called a **generational effect**. For example, the tumultuous political period of the 1960s and early 1970s included the defining political events of the Vietnam War and the protest movement surrounding it. Young people growing up during that time, especially those who participated in protest politics, ended up with a distinctive—and more liberal—set of political beliefs.

One research study found that college-educated war protesters in the 1960s developed a distinctive political character.[28] Based on information the researchers collected, they knew that both the protesters and non-protesters had similar backgrounds. They concluded that it was participation in antiwar demonstrations that inspired a particular set of political attitudes.

POLITICAL EXPERIENCE OFTEN SHAPES POLITICAL BELIEFS

Those involved in the Vietnam War protest movement adopted a distinctive and more liberal set of political beliefs than others in their generation.

In 1965, the war protesters were quite similar to their college-educated, non-protesting peers on a number of demographic and attitudinal measures. By 1973, as the war protest movement had begun to wane, the protesters differed sharply from non-protesters in a number of ways:

- Protesters were much stronger Democratic partisans than non-protesters.
- Protesters showed much higher support for civil liberties than non-protesters.

period effect
an event that influences the attitudes and beliefs of people of all ages.

- Protesters showed much less support for conservative groups, and much more support for women, the poor, and minorities than non-protesters.
- Protesters espoused significantly more liberal positions than non-protesters.

A follow-up study in 1982 concluded that differences between the two groups persisted. Thus, those who received their "political baptism" via the Vietnam War protests maintained the distinctive set of political beliefs they learned during that period. Again, because these researchers had information on the attitudes and behavior of these students before they protested, we know that protesting was a decisive factor, and we can be confident that there was a causal relationship.

PERIOD EFFECTS Political events do not influence just younger generations. Sometimes, events exert a noticeable impact across political generations and affect the political socialization of all citizens. This is known as a **period effect**. Consider, for example, responses to the following survey question:

> There is much discussion as to the amount of money the government in Washington should spend for national defense and military purposes. How do you feel about this? Do you think we are spending too little, too much, or about the right amount?

Figure 7.1 presents the public's answers to this question from 1969 through 2011.[29] Consider only the "too little" responses given in Figure 7.1. Note that in the early 1970s, only a small percentage of Americans thought that the country was spending too little on national defense. By the mid-1970s, the number of Americans who held that belief doubled once, and then, surprisingly, doubled again. What caused this dramatic shift?

One political scientist suggests it was a combination of two factors. First, this period saw a substantial decline in defense spending as a percentage of the federal budget and as a percentage of gross domestic product. Second, a series of disturbing foreign policy events rocked the world: the fall of South Vietnam, Cambodia, and Nicaragua to communist forces; the Soviet military buildup and takeover of Afghanistan; and the hostage crisis at the American embassy in Iran.[30] Notice also the substantial increase in those who believed we were spending too little from 1990 to 2000. In 1990, only 7 percent believed we were spending too little on national defense. By August 2000, that number had grown to 40 percent. To produce such substantial shifts in public opinion, these events must have pushed virtually every age group in

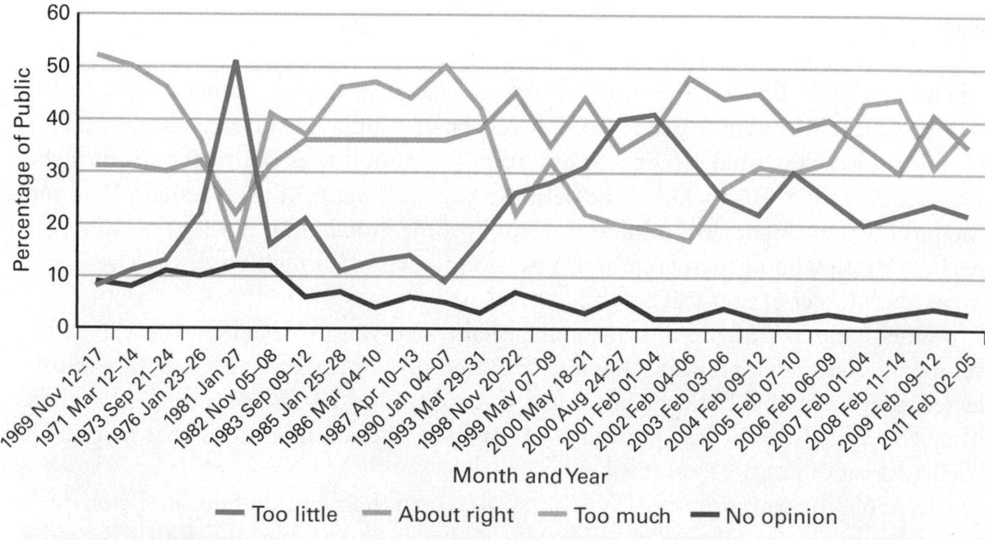

FIGURE 7.1 SUPPORT FOR DEFENSE SPENDING SHOWS A STRONG SURGE, 1969–2011.
After reaching a low point in the early 1970s, at the end of the Vietnam War, support for defense spending surged through the late 1970s and early 1980s with the election of Ronald Reagan. Public attitudes also shifted significantly in the 1990s as conflicts in the Middle East escalated.

Source: http://www.gallup.com/poll/146114/Americans-Remain-Divided-Defense-Spending.aspx

the same direction—toward support of more defense spending. Both of these examples are clear illustrations of the period effect.

LIFE-CYCLE EFFECTS The process of getting older can also have an impact on political opinions. In the **life-cycle effect**, individuals tend to get more conservative as they grow older and more secure in their political beliefs. Consider again the study of Vietnam War protesters and their non-protesting peers. As mentioned earlier, the impact of the war and protest politics appears to have made the protesters a substantially more left-leaning group than non-protesters of the same age. Even so, the study found both groups moving in a more conservative direction, with the protesters doing so at a more rapid pace. In other words, although protesters remained more liberal, the groups grew more alike, and more conservative, as they aged.

The same basic phenomenon is true for Americans generally. As they age, survey respondents are more likely to declare they are conservative—a classic life-cycle effect.[31] Americans also grow more secure in their partisan attachments as they grow older: They are increasingly likely to side with the Democratic or Republican Parties and less likely to say that they are politically independent.[32]

life-cycle effect
attitudes or physical characteristics that change as one ages, no matter the time period or generation. The graying of one's hair is a life-cycle effect.

DECLINING TRUST

Vietnam, Watergate, the protracted period of stagflation in the 1970s, the Iran-Contra affair in the late 1980s, and the Iraq War in more recent times may all have led to declining trust in government.

Public Opinion Formation

7.3 Explain the basics of public opinion formation.

People do not have perfectly formed attitudes that correspond to the specific answers required by survey questions (for a further examination of this issue, see *Unresolved Debate: Do American Citizens Have the Stable, Informed Opinions Necessary to Make Good Decisions About Politics?*). Instead, individuals embody a mix of considerations. Realizing that people do not have one solid opinion can help us understand how to measure and understand public opinion and how to devise a model of public opinion formation.[33]

Think of a bunch of ping-pong balls in your head, each with a competing thought about a particular issue. For some people, that mix of ideas might be more or less a 50–50 proposition. One person, for example, might have a head full of competing ideas on abortion rights. Half of those ideas suggest that abortion rights should remain legal. The other half suggests that all or most abortions should be against the law. Or maybe that mix of ideas is not divided evenly down the middle. On the one hand, someone might believe in the wisdom of tougher gun control laws. On the other hand, that person may also believe that in some cases, gun laws are either too restrictive or fine as they are.

What happens when someone with a head full of different, sometimes inconsistent ideas must answer a question in a survey? In general, a survey respondent offers answers based on whatever ideas are at the forefront of his or her mind at that moment.

Consider the case of the person with predominantly pro–gun control ideas but also a handful of ideas sympathetic to the gun rights movement. Under normal circumstances, we would expect her to answer a survey question about gun control sympathetically. Most of her ideas, after all, support more gun control. It is most likely that these more pro-gun control ideas will be at the top of her mind when the pollster calls.

This instability could suggest that many people simply "make up" a response on the fly, just to accommodate the interviewer. In other words, respondents might otherwise have no substantive thoughts on the issue. However, although survey respondents very often do not have complete, fully formed attitudes on public policy issues, this limitation is not the same as saying that they have "nonattitudes" and simply

Unresolved Debate

Do American citizens have the stable, informed opinions necessary to make good decisions about politics?

For democracy to succeed, it needs citizens who understand and care about political issues. Citizens with strong beliefs, or what some political scientists call "conviction," are more likely to participate in the political process. Citizens with conviction are more likely to influence the issues that float to the top of the political agenda. By taking action, citizens may sway the decisions the government makes. The push and pull between citizen participation and government action keep a democratic system healthy. But most citizens do not act with conviction. Many do not know much about politics at all, and many change their opinions on a dime. Given that, do Americans have the stable, informed opinions necessary to make good decisions about politics?

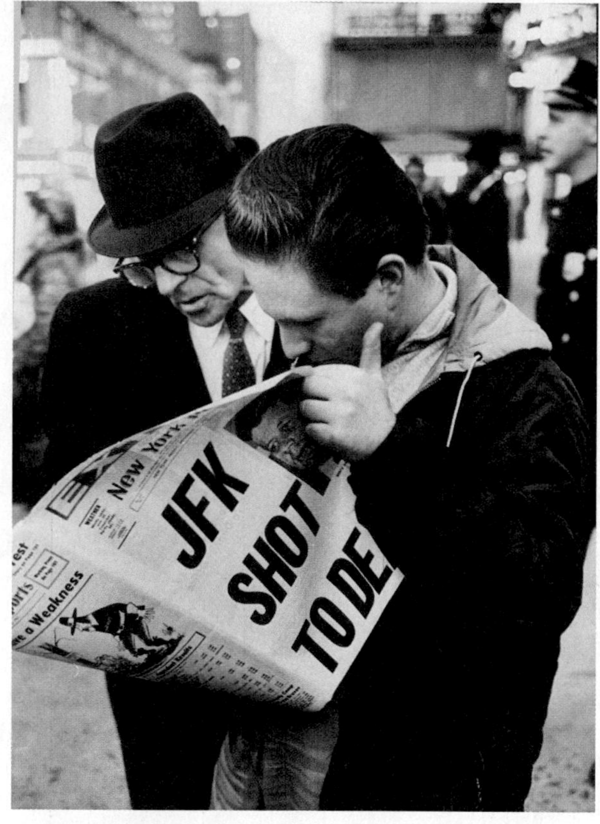

MAJOR EVENTS MAY CHANGE OPINIONS

Major events like the Kennedy assassination have a tendency to more actively engage people in politics.

NO

University of Michigan scholar Philip Converse addressed this question in his seminal study published in 1964.[a] His research remains the starting point for any discussion of the sophistication of political thinking among the public:

- Converse concluded that most Americans are ideologically innocent. They lack the capacity for well-developed, informed political thought and are not interested in political issues.
- Converse also maintained that most Americans change their attitudes and beliefs randomly and do not base their opinions on thoughtful reasoning. Converse demonstrated this ideological "coin tossing" by polling the same group of people on the same issue in 1956, 1958, and 1960. Generally, people had one attitude in 1956, changed that opinion in 1958, and then flipped back again by 1960. Converse termed these constantly fluctuating opinions "nonattitudes" and believed that Americans with nonattitudes were incapable of following or participating productively in politics.

YES

Other scholars insist that Americans are capable of making good decisions about politics:

- Political scientist Chris Achen argues that nonattitudes stem more from poorly worded survey questions than from any genuine randomness in people's beliefs. According to Achen, instability in survey responses does not occur because of fuzzy people; it occurs because of fuzzy questions. Achen insists that survey responses are not a good reflection of Americans' ability to understand and make good decisions about politics.[b]
- John Zaller, another political scientist, explains that people's nonattitudes can stem from the fact that they sample from competing considerations when they are asked to answer a survey question and may answer differently at different times. Zaller considers all of these opinions to be valid. For example, someone might not be sure how she feels about abortion. One morning, she reads a newspaper article about pro-life activists blocking access to a

family planning clinic. This action strikes her as inappropriate, as long as abortion is legal. That afternoon, she receives a call from a pollster asking about abortion rights. Her answers reflect more pro-choice opinions. Another day, she may offer more pro-life opinions.[d]

- More current research focuses on public opinion overall, rather than on how individuals form opinions. According to political scientists such as Benjamin Page and Robert Shapiro, collective public opinion is "rational" in the end.[e] The overall group generally cancels out incorrect or uninformed opinions. Taken as a whole, public opinion responds properly to social, economic, and political factors.
- Later political scientists confirmed Converse's findings. In 1978, a group of researchers asked people if they supported repealing a completely made-up piece of legislation. Rather than honestly admitting they never heard of the legislation, many respondents actually offered an opinion. Then researchers asked another group of people if they knew enough about the legislation to support or oppose it. Although respondents had an easy way out, 7 percent still insisted they had heard of the legislation and had an opinion about it.[c]

CONTRIBUTING TO THE DEBATE

What Americans know or do not know (and when they know or do not know something) remains a core question in the study of American public opinion. To characterize the contrasting conclusions, then, one might say that although Americans do not know as much about politics as they should in order to be highly effective democratic citizens, they do possess some substantial political knowledge—more, in fact, than is often alleged. The answers to this question have important empirical implications for those who try to measure and understand attitudes as well as important normative implications as we assess the health of our democracy. Although scholars now give Americans more credit than Converse's coin flippers, his work remains a touchstone in the study of public opinion and democracy. Using both panel studies that assess the same respondents over time and taking advantage of the huge proliferation of public polls, scholars will continue to examine the quality and consistency of public opinion.

WHAT DO YOU THINK?

1. Do people need to have stable opinions to make good political decisions? Why or why not?
2. Why might some people have trouble balancing competing considerations?

[a] Phillip Converse, "The Nature of Belief Systems in Mass Publics," in David E. Apter, Ideology and Discontent (New York: Free Press, 1964), 206–61.
[b] Christopher H. Achen, "Mass Political Attitudes and the Survey Response." *American Political Science Review* 69 (1975): 1218–31.
[c] George F. Bishop, Robert W. Oldendick, and Alfred J. Tuchfarber, "Pseudo-Opinions on Public Affairs," *Public Opinion Quarterly* 51 (Summer 1980): 198–209.
[d] John Zaller and Stanley Feldman, "A Simple Theory of the Survey Response: Answering Questions Versus Revealing Preferences," *American Journal of Political Science* 36, 3 (1992): 379.
[e] Donald Kinder, "Belief Systems Today," *Critical Review* 18, 1–3 (2006): 211.

invent answers to satisfy survey interviewers. Instead, they have a variety of ideas about a specific issue. Yet those ideas typically do not form a cohesive, stable stance that mirrors ideological categories—either on one particular issue or from one issue to the next.

Making Public Opinion Work in a Democracy

7.4 Establish how American democracy functions despite the public's lack of sophisticated political knowledge.

Although Americans may lack sophisticated political knowledge, some aspects of changes in public opinion are reassuring. For example, when a president performs poorly in office, the public usually recognizes this, reduces its collective approval of his job performance, and ultimately denies

7.1

7.2

7.3

7.4

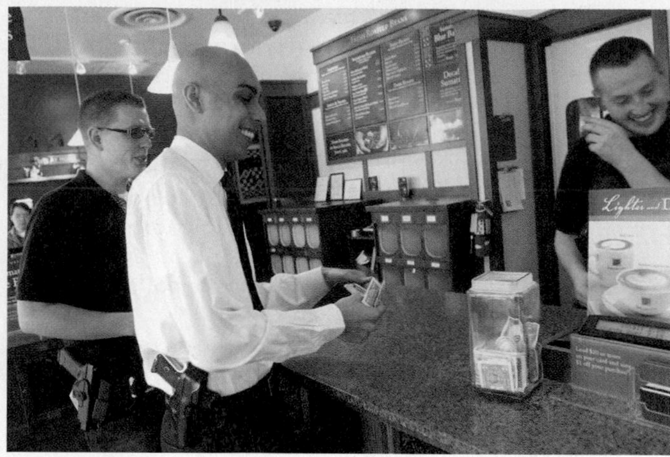

RECENT EVENTS MAY DRIVE SURVEY RESPONSE

Our views in combination with the stories and ideas that we have heard most recently will influence our response to a survey question on gun control. These pictures show a vigil after the shooting of Trayvon Martin by an armed neighborhood watch volunteer as well as citizens taking advantage of their right to openly carry arms—while purchasing coffee.

miracle of aggregation
the phenomenon that occurs when a group consists of individuals who are largely ignorant of a particular issue, but their collective opinion tends to makes sense.

him reelection. Likewise, when a president performs well in office, the public recognizes this, too, and typically rewards the president with high job approval numbers and another term. Similarly, the public will often react in orderly, predictable ways to shifts in public policy.

The Miracle of Aggregation Can Compensate for Low Levels of Information Among the Mass Public

Recall the example presented at the beginning of this chapter, in which non-experts collectively and accurately guessed the weight of an ox. It illustrates a paradox often referred to as the **miracle of aggregation**. The "miracle" is that even though a group of individuals can be largely ignorant of a particular phenomenon, when their opinions are aggregated, their collective opinion tends to make sense.

Here is how the miracle of aggregation works. Imagine an American public in which only 30 percent of the people paid close attention to politics and the other 70 percent were completely ignorant. Of that 30 percent that is knowledgeable, let's assume that two-thirds want Social Security reform and one-third does not. When politicians seek public guidance on whether to overhaul Social Security, they will find that 20 percent of the electorate favors reform, 10 percent opposes reform, and 70 percent have no idea.

Now what happens when the 70 percent of people who know nothing about the issue need to offer an opinion on it? Let's assume that 35 percent will support reform and 35 percent will oppose it. Now the picture of public opinion on the issue looks like this: 55 percent support reform and 45 percent do not. Notice what has happened: Opinion from the public as a whole, including the great mass of ignorant individuals, conveys the same message to policy makers as opinion from only the informed 30 percent—Americans want Social Security reform. A miracle!

As long as the random opinions of uninformed members of the public cancel one another out, policy makers will get a clear, meaningful signal that accurately reflects the wishes of those who are paying attention. This result may cause some anguish for those who would like the entire public to be aware, interested, and informed. However, the miracle of aggregation at least provides a way for the truly interested and informed to see their policy preferences accurately represented to decision makers.

"Look, we've got to improve our voter-tracking algorithms if we want to make more accurate wild-ass guesses."

BACK AND FORTH

Polls may reflect fuzzy people, fuzzy questions, or a more complicated underlying process for forming and reporting opinions.

Opinion Leaders Shape What the Public Thinks About and What They Think About It

opinion leaders
individuals with high levels of interest and expertise in politics who seek to communicate their political beliefs to others.

Studies of public opinion typically divide the American public into three segments: those who pay very close attention to politics, those who are generally indifferent to politics but pay attention sporadically, and those who pay no attention to politics at all. There are debates over the relative size of these segments, but the most attentive group is likely to be a small one, and on particularly obscure issues, extremely small.

That this most attentive group is small, however, does not mean that it lacks significant influence. In fact, many of the members of this group can be considered opinion leaders. **Opinion leaders** are people who can legitimately claim high levels of interest and expertise in politics and seek to communicate their political beliefs to others. This group may include political writers and journalists, politicians, political professionals (lobbyists, pollsters, campaign consultants, association executives), bloggers, academic political scientists, community activists, and garden-variety "political junkies."

Opinion leaders make it their business to send strong signals to the public regarding which political issues are important and what the public ought to think about them. An opinion leader can communicate with the public impersonally through television or intimately over a cup of coffee. Leaders also often communicate with people through e-mail, text messages, and social networking platforms such as Facebook and Twitter. Whatever the platform, opinion leaders can quickly and easily inform the mass public about their views.

You can see an example of opinion leadership by looking at the results of the "most important problem" question over the years. Periodically, polling organizations

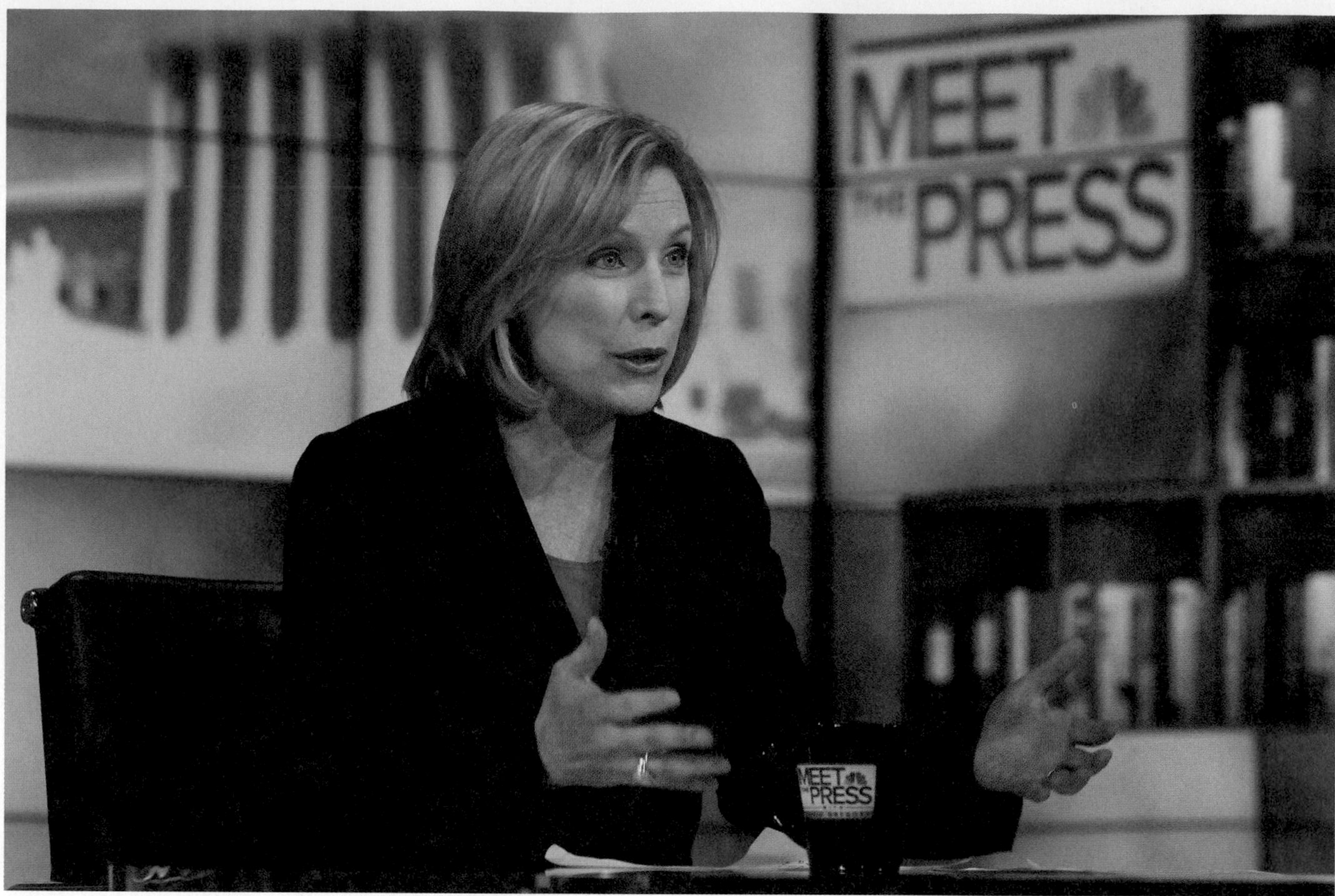

OPINION LEADERS INFLUENCE PUBLIC OPINION

New York Senator Kirstin Gillibrand appears on Meet the Press. Although the program does not have an enormous audience, opinion leaders across the country tune in and it is an important venue for political leaders to try to shape the public debate.

have asked the American public the following question: "What do you think is the most important problem facing the country today?" In April 2009, only 9 percent of the public identified health care as America's most important problem. A mere four months later, however, in August 2009, that number had risen to 20 percent. Clearly, the health care situation in the United States remained unchanged in those few months. What had changed, however, was that members of Congress began debating the urgent need for reform in the health care system. The media carried that message from the Congress through television and newspaper coverage of this debate, and through commentary and editorials of their own. Various opinion leaders continued this "trickle-down" process, discussing the issue in town hall meetings and personal conversations. The polling data indicate that at least part of the public ultimately received the message coming out of Congress.

More recently, opinion leadership has affected how people view the state of the economy. In 2007, only about 16 percent of Americans mentioned economic issues as the nation's most important problem. By 2008, as a financial crisis gripped Wall Street, about 49 percent of Americans identified it as the most important problem, and by 2009 the number was 86 percent. In early 2012, it dipped to 66 percent.[34] During these years, everyone was talking about the economy—not only the people personally affected by the mortgage crisis and high unemployment—but also the president, members of Congress, presidential candidates, and the media. As discussion of the economy by opinion leaders gave way to coverage of the presidential campaign and other issues, public concern over the economy dropped slightly.

Opinion leaders do not just influence *what* issues the public cares about, they also influence *how* people think about those issues. In one scholarly study, for example, researchers identified 80 questions that were asked at least twice on a variety of surveys from 1969 to 1983. In many cases, opinion had changed noticeably between the first time the question was asked and the second. In explaining these changes, the researchers found that changes in public opinion corresponded significantly with television news commentary—in other words, messages from opinion leaders.[35]

Partisanship Simplifies Political Judgments

Unlike many other aspects of public opinion, most voters have a self-defined, stable affiliation with a political party. In making judgments about the political world, then, they can use partisanship as a cue.[36] The partisan affiliation of a political candidate communicates a tremendous amount of information. If you are a Democrat, for example, you know that you are much more likely to agree with the policy preferences of Democrats than with those of Republicans, without having to sort through each and every position of a particular candidate. If you vote strictly along party lines, you may regret your choice occasionally. For the most part, though, a vote for your party versus the other party will tend to be consistent with your preferred outcome. Similarly, if you are a Republican, you know that most of the policy proposals from your party's leaders are likely to be more acceptable to you than proposals from the Democrats. Knowing that your party proposed them provides you with some assurance that you agree with the ideas.[37]

The same basic logic applies to your approval or disapproval of the job performance of policy makers, from the president on down. If they share your partisan affiliation, it is likely that you will agree, on the whole, with the policy choices they are making. You may not know the details of those choices, but because you are members of the same party, you know that you probably share the same broad set of beliefs. With that knowledge, you can have some confidence that if you could follow their performance closely, you would likely approve of the job they are doing.[38]

Moderately Attentive "Scorekeepers" Cause Most Aggregate Public Opinion Change

One political scientist proposes that the middle stratum of Americans referred to earlier—the group that is only moderately attentive to politics—serves an important "scorekeeping" function.[39] This group has little passion for politics and does not think about the political world in ideological terms. It pays just enough attention to politics to pick up on signals indicating big changes—for example, a change from peace to war, from recession to recovery, from bipartisan cooperation to acrimony and scandal, or from a conservative bent in social policy to a liberal one. The scorekeepers, in other words, keep a running tally of how things are going in very broad policy areas. When they pick up a signal that a noticeable change has occurred, they adjust their opinions accordingly. In this view, those changes account for most of the movement in aggregate public opinion. Furthermore, they are connected to real-world events in a fairly logical, orderly fashion that results in government accountability through elections.

These are just some of the shortcuts that help the public arrive at collectively rational opinions about politics and government. Certainly, these shortcuts help mitigate some of the potential consequences of low voter sophistication and keep policy makers aware of, and generally accountable to, the public. But American public opinion remains a very mixed picture, full of attitudes and nonattitudes, contradictory beliefs, loosely and fleetingly held considerations, authentic opinions, strong value commitments, vast stretches of ignorance and indifference, and isolated oases of knowledge, all mixed together.

On MyPoliSciLab

Review the Chapter

Listen to **Chapter 7** on **MyPoliSciLab**

The Nature of Public Opinion

7.1 Define public opinion and identify its four basic traits, p. 231.

Public opinion is a subject at the heart of democratic theory. It is the collective political beliefs and attitudes of the public, or groups within the public, on matters of relevance to government. Public opinion has four basic traits: salience, stability, direction, and intensity. It is challenging but crucial for leaders to know and understand public opinion in terms of all these traits and patterns.

Political Socialization

7.2 Outline the process and agents of political socialization, p. 236.

Political socialization is the process by which citizens acquire the values and attitudes that shape their thinking about politics. It tends to be governed by two important principles: primacy and persistence, both of which point to the importance of early childhood learning. There are several phases of socialization from early childhood all the way through young adulthood, and the development of ideological thinking demonstrates increased political sophistication. Socialization occurs through specific agents of socialization and socializing events. Although the family is foremost among agents of socialization, socializing events include generational effects, period effects, and life-cycle effects.

Public Opinion Formation

7.3 Explain the basics of public opinion formation, p. 243.

Political scientist Philip Converse's work has been a particularly important touchstone when it comes to public opinion formation. Although much subsequent research has taken issue with Converse's findings and not all of his conclusions hold today, a large proportion of what we know about public opinion has come about as scholars have addressed and often challenged the findings from the original work.

Making Public Opinion Work in a Democracy

7.4 Establish how American democracy functions despite the public's lack of sophisticated political knowledge, p. 245.

American public opinion collectively makes sense in many cases. Despite the lack of sophisticated political knowledge at the individual level, collective opinion is often rational, ordered, and predictable. A number of shortcuts and devices enable the American public to communicate to policy makers a collectively ordered, rational set of preferences.

Learn the Terms

Study and **Review** the **Flashcards**

direction, p. 232
generational effect, p. 241
ideology, p. 236
intensity, p. 232
life-cycle effect, p. 243
margin of error, p. 234
miracle of aggregation, p. 246
nonresponse bias, p. 234
opinion leaders, p. 247
period effect, p. 242
persistence, p. 236
political socialization, p. 236
primacy, p. 236
public opinion, p. 231
random sample, p. 234
salience, p. 231
sampling, p. 234
sampling error, p. 234
stability, p. 231

Test Yourself

7.1 Define public opinion and identify its four basic traits.

Which of the following are the four basic traits of public opinion?

a. Salience, stability, direction, and longevity.
b. Salience, stability, direction, and accuracy
c. Salience, intensity, direction, and accuracy
d. Salience, stability, direction, and intensity
e. Salience, direction, longevity, and intensity

7.2 Outline the process and agents of political socialization.

Which of the following is the most important socialization agent?

a. School
b. The family
c. Religious institutions and traditions
d. Peer groups
e. The media

7.3 Explain the basics of public opinion formation.

Which of the following statements is TRUE of public opinion formation?

a. Individuals do not have perfectly formed attitudes that correspond to the specific answers required by survey questions.
b. Individuals always have perfectly formed attitudes that correspond to the specific answers required by survey questions.
c. Once an individual forms an opinion about something, he or she will never change that opinion, even if faced with new information.
d. Once an individual forms an opinion about something, he or she will always change that opinion if faced with new information.
e. Once an individual forms an opinion about something, he or she will rarely change that opinion if faced with new information.

7.4 Establish how American democracy functions despite the public's lack of sophisticated political knowledge.

What is the miracle of aggregation?

a. When a group of individuals is ignorant of a particular phenomenon, their collective opinion is likely to make little sense.
b. When a group of individuals is knowledgeable about a particular phenomenon, their collective opinion is likely to make sense.
c. Even though a group of individuals can be largely ignorant of a particular phenomenon, their collective opinion tends to make sense.
d. Even though a group of individuals can be largely knowledgeable about a particular phenomenon, their collective opinion tends to make little sense.
e. Even though one individual may be largely knowledgeable about a particular phenomenon, a group of individuals can be largely ignorant.

Explore Further

SUGGESTED READINGS BY TOP SCHOLARS

We asked leading public opinion scholars to identify the most important readings of the past decade on the subject of public opinion, and what follows were their suggestions.

Robert Erickson and Kent Tedin. 2005. *American Public Opinion: Its Origins, Content, and Impact*. New York: Longman. An excellent text that covers a wide range of information about the measurement, nature, and importance of public opinion.

Morris Fiorina. 2006. *Culture War? The Myth of a Polarized America*. New York: Longman. Argues that Americans are not nearly as divided on major political issues as many commentators claim.

Paul M. Sniderman, Richard A. Brody, and Philip E. Tetlock. 1991. *Reasoning and Choice: Explorations in Political Psychology*. Cambridge: Cambridge University Press. Argues that ordinary citizens who pay little attention to politics can still make reasonable decisions based on particular shortcuts.

James Stimson. 2004. *Tides of Consent: How Public Opinion Shapes American Politics*. Cambridge: Cambridge University Press. Although the public rarely engages in politics, when public opinion is aroused, major changes in policy result.

Herbert Weisberg, Jon Krosnick, and Bruce Bowen. 1996. *An Introduction to Survey Research, Polling, and Data Analysis*. Thousand Oaks, CA: Sage. The basics of how to conduct and analyze survey research, with information on sampling, question writing, and interviewing techniques.

John Zaller. 1992. *The Nature and Origins of Mass Opinion*. New York: Cambridge University Press. Argues that people sample from a mix of political considerations in their head when confronted with the need to make political decisions or share political attitudes.

SUGGESTED WEBSITES

Gallup: www.gallup.com

Gallup conducts regular public opinion polls on timely topics. This site provides links to surveys on the 2008 elections.

The Pew Research Center for the People and the Press: www.people-press.org

The Pew center is an independent opinion research group that studies attitudes toward the press, politics, and public policy issues. Pew conducts regular national surveys to measure public attentiveness to major news stories. This site provides links to recent surveys.

Pollster.com: www.pollster.com

Taking advantage of the proliferation of publicly released polls, this site aggregates and tracks public opinion across a wide range of issues. It features expert commentary on the practice of polling and clear graphical presentation of data.

The Center for Information and Research on Civic Learning and Engagement (CIRCLE): www.civicyouth.org

CIRCLE conducts research on the civic and political engagement of Americans between the ages of 15 and 25.

Listen to Chapter 8 on MyPoliSciLab

8 Political Participation and Voting

LITERACY TESTS

Imagine that you want to participate in politics by voting in an election for president, governor, Congress, or a local office, but you are required to answer the following questions:

1. The only laws that can be passed to apply to an area in a federal arsenal are those passed by _____, provided consent for the purchase of the land is given by the _____.
2. Appropriation of money for the armed services can be for a period limited to only _____ years.
3. A United States senator elected at the general election in November takes office the following year on what date? _____

African Americans had to answer questions about obscure facts like these if they wanted to vote in southern states in the 1950s and 1960s. Although these were called "literacy tests," they did not aim to measure literacy. Rather, they were part of a larger effort to disenfranchise black citizens, depriving them of a vote and the power of the ballot box.

It took decades for African Americans to overcome the many obstacles preventing them from exercising their rights. They earned protections and political participation rights piecemeal. First,

8.1	8.2	8.3	8.4	8.5	8.6
Explain the costs and benefits of political participation for individuals and groups. p. 255.	Define the paradox of participation, and describe the different kinds of political activities in which Americans participate, p. 257.	Outline the main factors that influence political participation, p. 263.	Analyze voter turnout from comparative and historical perspectives, p. 270.	Describe the key factors that determine how voters make electoral choices, p. 275.	Assess whether political participation impacts governmental decisions, p. 282.

GAINING THE RIGHT TO VOTE A series of burdensome laws in addition to direct intimidation made it difficult for African Americans in the South to exercise their right to vote. Here, in the wake of the Voting Rights Act, women in Georgia register to vote for the first time.

The Big Picture Ever feel like your vote does not matter? Author Kenneth M. Goldstein explains why you are wrong and how this simple act of participation both strengthens our democracy and has real power to change it.

The Basics If you had lived during the early days of our country, would you have had the right to vote? In this video, you will find out how voting rights in America have evolved since its founding. You will also examine patterns in voter turnout and identify methods to increase turnout.

In Context Discover how voter turnout has changed over the course of American history. Has enfranchising women, African Americans, or young people increased turnout? Columbia University political scientist Donald P. Green addresses these and other questions in this video.

Think Like a Political Scientist Why has the United States experienced a surge in voter turnout? Columbia University political scientist Donald P. Green analyzes voter turnout trends, and takes a look at how research conducted by political scientists on this subject has contributed to increased voter turnout.

In the Real World Not every citizen of the United States has a photo ID. Should everyone be required to have one when they vote? Real people discuss the issue of voter fraud, and whether it is a serious enough problem to warrant possibly disenfranchising a large segment of the population.

So What? What effect does increased political participation have on who the president will be in the future? From the exclusion of women and minority groups to the unprecedented turnout of African American voters in the 2008 election, author Kenneth M. Goldstein traces the history of political participation.

the Civil War and the Emancipation Proclamation freed blacks from slavery. Then, in 1868, the Fourteenth Amendment to the U.S. Constitution conferred citizenship upon African Americans. It also served to protect civil and political liberties, although women were still excluded. Even though citizenship should include the right to vote, southern states nonetheless systematically turned black men away at the polls. Pressure mounted to provide a constitutional guarantee of black voting rights. Accordingly, in 1870, Congress passed the Fifteenth Amendment, which ensured that "the right of citizens of the United States to vote shall not be denied by the United States or by any state on account of race, color, or previous condition of physical servitude."

Despite the amendment, African Americans who wanted to vote still faced many barriers, including physical intimidation (even death), literacy tests, and poll taxes. These tactics resulted in very few black Americans registering to vote and actually participating in American democracy.

In 1960, nearly 100 years after the end of the Civil War, the number of African Americans registered to vote in some southern states was around one-tenth of the number of eligible voters. In Mississippi, for example, only 5.2 percent of blacks were registered, compared to 63.9 percent of white citizens. In Alabama, it was 13.7 percent of blacks compared to 63.6 percent of whites. In South Carolina, 12.7 percent of blacks were registered voters, whereas 57.1 percent of whites were. Overall, 29.1 percent of blacks were registered in the 11 original Confederate states, compared to 61.1 percent of white citizens.[1] This gap did not close until the 1965 Voting Rights Act gave the federal government new powers to enforce the promises made in the Fifteenth Amendment.

It took another 45 years for African Americans to overcome the next and perhaps greatest barrier to full political participation. On November 4, 2008, the culmination of a more than 200-year struggle to join the mainstream of American democratic life could be seen in the tears streaming down the cheeks of black leaders and notable personalities, such as Jesse Jackson and Oprah Winfrey, as they watched President-elect Barack Obama deliver his victory speech in Chicago. Until 2008, the cost of participating in the political process was not always outweighed by the benefits, perhaps explaining why blacks did not vote as actively as other American demographic groups. But in 2008, the prospect of the first African American president compelled many people to wait for 12 hours in line to vote and increased black voting participation by 4.9 percent. The cost was now worth the benefit for many. Recognizing how these costs and benefits interact is a major theme of political participation and helps political scientists understand why people choose to vote.

The Costs and Benefits of Political Participation

8.1 Explain the costs and benefits of political participation for individuals and groups.

olitical participation is the effort to influence what happens in the political world. We do this by voting or by taking action—writing letters, signing petitions, or attending demonstrations—with the intent of influencing political officials or the public at large. It is an important privilege, and our country was founded to protect this right. But, if you have ever voted on Election Day, volunteered for a political campaign, or contacted a public official advocating a certain position, you first had to decide whether taking these actions would be worth your time and effort. Many people in America engage in these sorts of activities, but just as many—and usually more—do not. In fact, about half of America's citizens engage only in voting, and most do not vote in all the elections available to them.[2]

Political scientists have studied why some people get involved in politics and others do not, borrowing language and ideas from another discipline—economics. These political scientists believe that decisions about whether or not to participate in politics

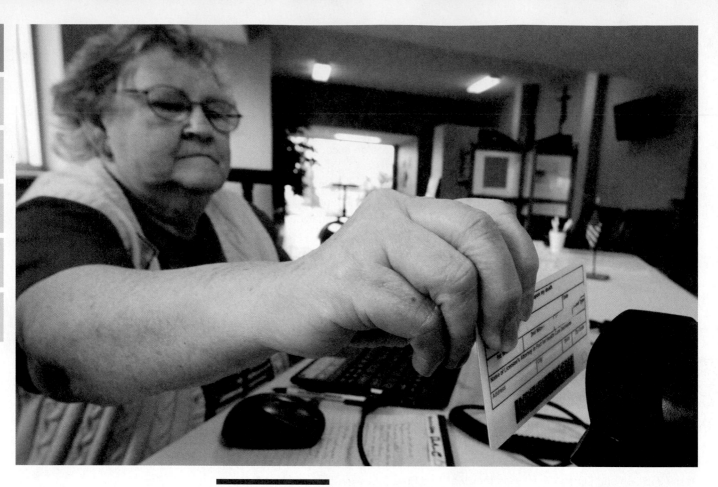

VOTING IS A TWO STEP PROCESS IN THE UNITED STATES

In the United States, unlike many other Democracies, citizens must register to vote before they can cast a ballot. Regulations vary from state to state. In this picture, a clerk in Missouri checks a driver's license before registering a new voter.

depend in large part on individual evaluations about the costs and benefits of political activity.

For most citizens, deciding whether or not to participate in politics depends on what the costs and benefits may be. Let's take voting, for example. First, consider the costs of voting. They include the time and effort required for you to register to vote or to update your registration, travel to a polling place, wait in line, and cast your vote. The costs also include the time you spent determining how to register or reregister; finding out where your polling place is; and perhaps the most time-consuming aspect, learning enough about the different candidates and issues to make educated choices. And some citizens prefer not to register, simply to avoid being called as a potential juror, because jury rolls typically are made up from registered voter lists.

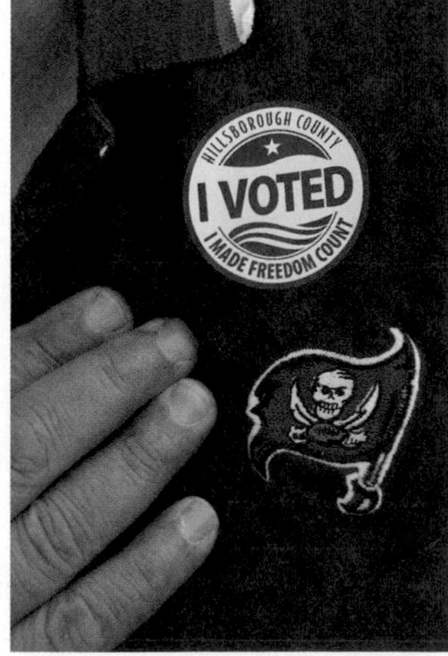

"I VOTED!"

For some, the sense of civic duty and the personal satisfaction gained from doing that duty motivate political participation.

Now, consider the benefits of voting. If your vote helps elect your preferred candidate, some or all of his or her policies—policies that you support—will be adopted. Depending on your political preferences, some of the benefits you would receive from voting might include lower taxes, more money for student loans, a new federal highway near your hometown, increased Social Security benefits for your grandparents, or other policy changes the candidate has promised.

Finally, you have to compare these costs and benefits. If the benefits to you outweigh the costs, you will vote. If not, you will stay at home. This is the same logic you would use to decide if any other form of political participation is worth it to you.

The Paradox of Political Participation

8.2 Define the paradox of participation, and describe the different kinds of political activities in which Americans participate.

lthough voting is the most common type of political activity, citizens can participate in politics in many other ways. Whereas voting involves the direct choice of political leaders, the goal of nonvoting activities is to try to influence the decisions of leaders who have already been elected.

Each year, Americans typically participate in a variety of political activities other than voting (see Table 8.1). These include signing petitions, attending demonstrations, organizing or attending community meetings, joining political organizations, contacting government officials, and volunteering for political campaigns. In addition, about 15 percent of Americans contribute money to political campaigns.

Social movement
an informal alliance of groups or individuals who join together for the purpose of enacting or resisting social change.

Another form of nonvoting political participation is the social movement. A **social movement** is composed of informal alliances of groups or individuals for the purpose of enacting or resisting social change. Such movements often include several types of the nonvoting behavior, such as joining and attending meetings of political organizations, contacting government officials, and participating in political protests. The civil rights movement of the 1950s and 1960s and the anti–Vietnam War movement of the 1960s and early 1970s were famously influential social movements. More recently, the Tea Party and Occupy Wall Street movements, which we discuss in greater detail later, have brought particular economic and social issues to the forefront of the political arena. These examples demonstrate the power of this type of political participation.

Americans typically have a reputation for being relatively inactive in politics in whatever form. But this reputation may be undeserved. Figure 8.1 compares levels of participation in various political activities across several countries. Only in voting do Americans lag substantially behind their peers in industrialized democracies. In the remaining four activities, American rates of participation either exceed or are roughly equivalent to those seen in other industrial democracies.

TABLE 8.1 PARTICIPATION IN POLITICS OUTSIDE THE VOTING BOOTH

Type of activity	Percentage of Americans participating in activity last year
Discuss politics with family or friends	77.7
Volunteer	39.2
Work at/join organization to deal with community problem	30.6
Attend community meeting about school or community issue	22.8
Participate in protest	19.1
Contact public officials	18.5
Campaign contributions to party, candidate, or other group	14.9
Campaign-related activities (attend meeting, put up signs, etc.)	8.5
Attend campaign meetings, rallies, speeches, and so on	8

Source: Authors' analysis of 2008 National Election Study, http://electionstudies.org.

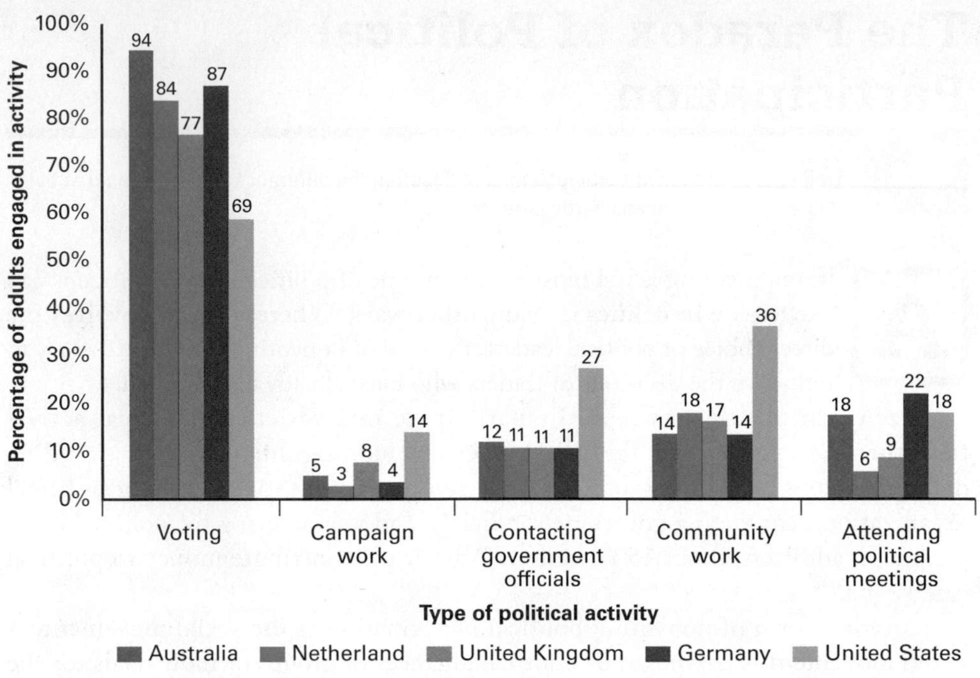

FIGURE 8.1 POLITICAL PARTICIPATION: HOW DOES THE UNITED STATES COMPARE TO OTHER COUNTRIES?

The United States has lower rates of voter turnout than most other industrialized Western democracies.

paradox of participation
The fact that people participate in politics, even though the impact of their individual participation would seem far too small to matter.

It Is Unlikely that a Single Individual Will Influence an Election Outcome or Political Decision

Even though many Americans choose not to vote, millions still do. Why do they make that choice? Primarily because they decide that the potential benefits of voting may likely outweigh the costs. For example, spending a half-hour figuring out how to register or using a lunch break or hiring a babysitter to be able to cast a ballot seems like a minor inconvenience compared to the benefits of more generous student loans, expanded health care, lower payroll taxes, and the other policy changes your candidate favors. But this calculation assumes that your candidate needs your vote in order to win.

What if your candidate could win without your vote? Then you could enjoy all of the benefits of voting—specifically, the policy changes that your candidate would bring about when he or she wins—without any of the burdens. If that were true, then why would you bother voting? The only case in which your vote would be decisive is if your vote causes or breaks a tie. In all other cases, whether or not you vote, the winner will be the same.

Looking at the history of elections, and even in local elections with very few voters involved, it is exceedingly rare that an election is decided by a single vote. In fact, you can safely assume before any particular election that your vote will not decide the outcome. Whether you stay home or cast your ballot, the election result will be the same. From this perspective, it makes no sense for you to vote ever. Yet every Election Day, Americans vote by the millions. That they do so, even though they could enjoy the benefits of voting without bearing the costs of casting a ballot, is the paradox of voting.

This paradox applies to other types of political participation, too, and so can actually be considered a **paradox of participation.** For example, in early 2010, in the midst of a major legislative and political battle over health care reform, many Americans contacted their members of Congress to express support or opposition. Suppose a friend asked you to call your member of Congress to request his or her support for the legislation. Faced with this situation, you might think through costs and benefits as described earlier. Before you even get there, though, you might consider the following: What if proponents of health care reform get 9,999 people to e-mail or call this same member of Congress? Is my one phone call, making it an even 10,000, really going to matter? Probably not. There is really no difference between 9,999 e-mails and phone calls and 10,000 of them. And what if only 100 people e-mail and call? If I make a call, then there will be 101. But there is no real difference between 100 and 101, either. So no matter how many people call in, whether or not I do will not likely be critical.

Your logic here would be exactly the same as the logic about whether or not to vote. The effect of your participation is unlikely to make any meaningful difference in the outcome either way, so why bother? If the member of Congress is going to vote against the Democratic health care bill whether or not you make a phone call, then you should not bother. And if the president is going to support the bill regardless of your opinion, the same approach—inaction—makes sense, too. After all, you get to enjoy the benefit of the bill's passing without putting forward any effort.

Some forms of political participation can make a more significant difference, though. For example, during the 2004 elections, financier and philanthropist George Soros donated more than $20 million to groups such as MoveOn.org to support Democratic candidates and to defeat incumbent President George W. Bush. In 2012, billionaire businessman and philanthropist Sheldon Adelson and his wife, Miriam, donated a total of $10 million to a political action committee supporting Newt Gingrich and reinvigorated his sinking presidential campaign. Although these donations did not change the outcome of either election, they brought attention to the issues and candidates in a way that just casting a vote could not.

Raising awareness about a candidate or an issue is what makes large political donations feel worthwhile to the donor, despite the fact that no matter how much a person donates to a campaign, his or her vote carries the same weight as a voter who donates nothing. Adelson's and Soros's votes are as effective in an election as the votes of your local trash collector or car mechanic who may never have donated a dime to

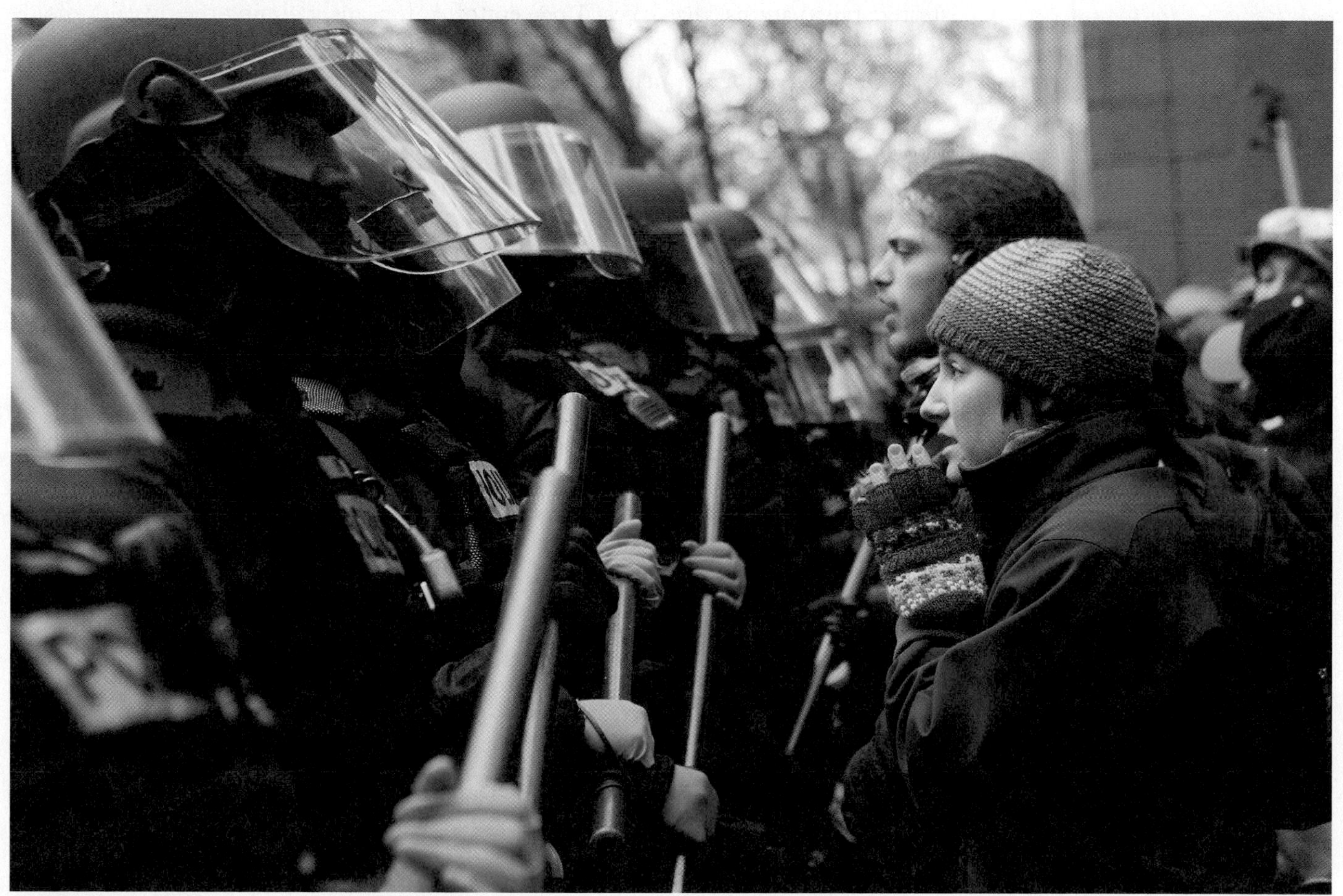

OCCUPY WALL STREET

In Fall of 2011, protests sprung up around the country, demonstrating against what some perceived to be the inordinate power of the financial sector in American life and politics. The protests often took the form of extended encampents in public parks. Here, demonstrators in Portland, Oregon confront police who are attempting to evict them from the park they were occupying.

8.1

8.2

8.3

8.4

8.5

8.6

any political campaign. Yale political scientist Robert Dahl called this "interchangeability." Votes are interchangeable with each other. Other forms of political participation, though, are not interchangeable. If an Adelson or a Soros writes a letter to a congressman in support of an issue, that letter is likely to have more influence than a letter from an unknown citizen.

If you do not have millions of dollars to donate to a cause or candidate but still want the same benefit of raising awareness about an issue or a candidate, you can join forces with like-minded others in a political movement. In recent years, two groups—the conservative Tea Party and the liberal Occupy Wall Street—have brought together citizens who want political candidates to pay more attention to their views.

The Tea Party has been more successful than Occupy Wall Street at turning political activity into a powerful political movement. When it began in 2009, the Tea Party held rallies opposing government spending, the federal deficit, increased taxes, and the 2009 stimulus package. These rallies—which took place in cities around the country—brought thousands into the movement, many of whom had never before participated in politics. CNN, Fox News, and MSNBC covered the rallies, and TV shows such as *The Daily Show* and *The Colbert Report* mocked them. More than garnering media, Facebook, and Twitter attention, however, the Tea Party also organized throughout the country, backing candidates on the local and congressional levels who supported their ideas. Tea Party supporters elected enough like-minded members of Congress that a Tea Party caucus formed in the House of Representatives, led by Michelle Bachman, who ran in the 2012 Republican presidential primaries. Americans became well aware of the Tea Party, its focused message, and its voting power.

Occupy Wall Street began in September 2011 with a protest and camp-out in a park in New York's financial district. With the slogan "We are the 99 percent," protesters railed against the richest 1 percent of Americans, claiming their wealth disadvantaged the rest of America's 99 percent. Over the next few months, the movement held demonstrations in major cities all over the country protesting against a wide variety of issues, including inequality, American financial policy, the mortgage crisis, police brutality, and high college tuition rates. The protests received a lot of media attention and public support, especially from celebrities including Dave Letterman, George Clooney, and Brad Pitt. The movement also received financial backing and fundraising help from donors such as Ben Cohen and Jerry Greenfield, of Ben & Jerry's Ice Cream. Websites, Facebook groups, and Twitter updates helped power the movement's popularity. Nevertheless, the movement lacked the internal organization and crystallized messaging necessary to substantially influence politics and elections. It never elected politicians who specifically supported its agenda, and so its political influence never reached the level of that of the Tea Party. Its supporters will have to decide whether the effort it takes to participate in Occupy demonstrations is worth it, especially because the movement's goals are still unclear.

No matter how much or how little these movements influence politics, however, they allow citizens to raise their voices in the public and political arena. Clearly, Americans value the ability to do this.

The Paradox of Participation Has a Number of Possible Solutions

Efforts such as Occupy Wall Street, as well as rallies and e-mails and phone calls to members of Congress on various other issues, leave it to political scientists to resolve the paradox of participation—the fact that people participate in politics even though the impact of their individual participation would seem far too small to matter. How have they attempted to resolve this paradox?

One argument is that citizens worry that other individuals will make the same decisions they make. That is, individuals might recognize that it is possible to collect benefits without paying the costs of participation. Also, they recognize that if all citizens made the same calculation, then no one would participate in democracy. Not wanting democracy to collapse, at least some citizens decide to participate.[3]

How Do We Know?

How Many People Vote on Election Day?

The Question

The 2008 presidential election is a great example of just how tricky it can be to get a precise figure on voter turnout. The Census Bureau's Current Population Survey included a Voting and Registration Supplement with information on voting behavior and trends. It shows that national turnout and registration rates decreased from 63.8 percent in 2004 to 63.6 percent in 2008. But aggregate findings, which take into account actual voters and estimates of the voting-eligible population (VEP), suggested that turnout rate actually increased from 60.1 percent in 2004 to 61.7 percent in 2008. Although both methods are reliable, they offer different conclusions about voter turnout trends. That 1.9 percent difference is actually significant—and it illustrates just how difficult calculating turnout rates can be. As we write this, 2012 Census voting estimates are not available, but initial estimates of aggregate turnout peg it at 54.9 percent of VEP—a big drop from 2008. Knowing how many people vote on Election Day indicates how healthy our democracy is. That is why after every national election, political scientists ask: How many people voted? How do we know?

Why It Matters

Voting is the most fundamental act of democratic citizenship. When voter turnout is high, we know citizens believe that their vote matters and that a particular outcome is worth their sacrifice of time and energy. When turnout is low, we can assume that citizens either do not believe their vote matters or are uninterested in voting because they do not believe the democratic system is going to change either way. In that case, we need to consider how to increase voter participation by increasing citizen engagement. But first, we need to construct a valid, reliable measure of voter turnout to assess our progress—actually a very challenging task.

Investigating the Answer

Voter turnout measurements need to be consistent and produce comparable results from one election to the next. Political scientists usually do not measure the absolute number of voters who show up on Election Day, but rather the turnout rate. Turnout rate is the number of people who voted in the election divided by the number of everyone who could have voted.

Turnout Rate = Actual Voters Divided by Potential Voters

For example, if 100 people could have voted in an election, but only 50 people actually did vote, the turnout rate would be 50 percent. But "potential voters" can be either only registered voters or registered voters plus anyone else eligible to vote, regardless of registration status. Which should it be?

If we count only registered voters, 90 percent of them could show up on Election Day, but they represent only 30 percent of the eligible voting population—including those not registered to vote. You could say turnout was 90 percent, but in reality, only 27 percent of people eligible to vote actually cast a ballot (30 percent multiplied by 90 percent). This also would not account for those voters historically excluded from voting. Using this method to calculate voter turnout in the 1960 presidential election would obscure the fact that many African Americans were prevented from voting.

Finally, measuring only registered voters makes it difficult to compare turnout rates in the United States with those in other countries. In the United States, citizens register themselves to vote, whereas in many foreign democracies, the government makes everyone eligible. To compare turnout, we would need to count the entire eligible U.S. voter population.

But how do we determine this number? Statisticians often use census data on the number of individuals age 18 or older living in the United States. But not everyone counted in that group can actually vote. Foreign citizens and in some states convicted felons are not legally eligible to vote. At the same time, legally eligible American citizens living overseas would not count. To account for these problems, researchers are developing better ways of measuring the U.S. voting-age population.[7] The Census Bureau, for example, has prepared an alternate measure that excludes noncitizens from the pool of potentially eligible voters.

There are also a variety of ways to measure the number of people who actually vote. The most common method is just counting each ballot. With one ballot per person, the number of ballots cast would represent the number of voters. It is surprisingly difficult, however, to get an accurate count of these ballots. There can be voter error, machine error, mistakes by poll workers, or a combination of these factors.

Political scientists and media outlets often use public opinion surveys to estimate voter turnout. These surveys could ask a nationally representative sample of voting-age adults if they are legally eligible to vote, and if they actually voted. Then, they could estimate turnout on the basis of the survey as follows:

Turnout Rate = Number of Survey Respondents Who Report Having Voted Divided by Number of Survey Respondents Legally Eligible to Vote

A downside to this approach, though, is that it does not draw a representative sample of the voting-age population. For example, telephone surveys exclude people without landline phones, including students and people who use only mobile phones. These groups are also less likely to vote. In addition, some people may say they voted when they did not.

The combination of these two problems—excluding low turnout and overstating the number of voters—can result in an inflated turnout estimate. Nevertheless, political scientists can use these estimates to compare behavior among different demographic groups and rates of turnout over time. It does not matter that the overall turnout rates are overstated, as long as they are overstated by the same amount in each survey.

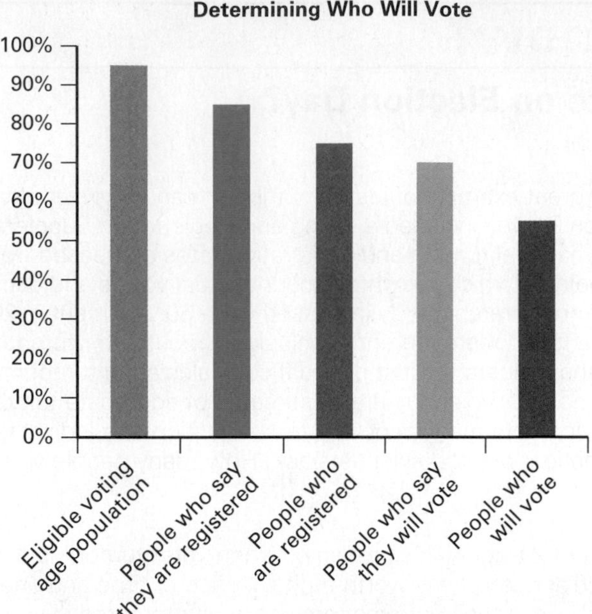

The Bottom Line

Even something as seemingly straightforward as measuring how many people vote in American elections presents difficult methodological issues. Nonetheless, recent work that accounts for the number of eligible voters—the voting-eligible population—makes us more confident that we are assessing the actual proportion of voters who vote in any particular election. Furthermore, although surveys almost definitely overstate turnout in any one election, they are a useful way to look at trends over time and assess how particular groups behave, such as the young, old, rich, poor, strong partisans, or weak partisans.

Thinking Critically

- Why might it be easier to calculate turnout rates in other countries?
- As a political scientist, what methods would you use to ensure that you counted as many voters, or eligible voters, as possible?

[1]United States Election Project, "2008 Current Population Survey Voting and Registration Supplement," November 20, 2009, http://elections.gmu.edu/CPS_2008.html.

[2]Michael McDonald and Samuel Popkin, "The Myth of the Vanishing Voter," *American Political Science Review* 95 (2001). [add pages]

collective benefit
a benefit all people enjoy, regardless of whether or not they contributed to its attainment.

selective benefit
benefit that only those who contributed to its attainment get to enjoy (compare to collective benefit).

Another possible resolution of the paradox is that individuals may think about benefits of voting other than the outcome of the upcoming election—that is, benefits beyond just the victory or defeat of their preferred candidate. A candidate's victory or defeat is what political scientists call a **collective benefit**—everyone gets to enjoy it, whether or not they vote. But political scientists have also identified what can be called **selective benefits** of voting—benefits that only voters get to enjoy.[4]

What might such a selective benefit be? Political scientists frequently point out that only those who vote get to experience the satisfaction of fulfilling their civic duty. An individual does not have to believe that he or she will be the deciding vote in order to receive this benefit, nor does it matter to that person whether other individuals vote. For those who actually show up to vote on Election Day, this benefit may be enough to outweigh the costs associated with voting.[5]

Cost-Benefit Analysis Can Help Us Understand Who Participates

The cost-benefit approach helps us understand why some people participate in politics and others do not. The argument is not that individuals are "computers" who put precise figures on costs and benefits and calculate expected outcomes. Rather, people behave as if they take costs and benefits into account, even if they do not make precise calculations about them in their heads. For example, in a large-scale survey of Americans who regularly participate in a variety of political activities, 61 percent said that one of the reasons they vote is "the chance to influence government policy."[6] To political scientists, it is absurd to think that one vote can influence government policy when more than 100 million votes may be cast in a given election. But if that idea makes sense to Americans who participate in politics, then political scientists need to take it seriously.

socioeconomic status (SES)
a combination of an individual's occupation, income, and education levels.

People are more likely to participate when expected costs are low. For example, it is easy to register to vote because registration deadlines are now closer to Election Day, and there are plenty of easy opportunities to register. People are also more likely to vote when they can easily absorb the costs of voting and afford the cost of the time it takes to become informed—for example, when they can afford to hire a babysitter so they can get to the polls or can afford to pay for media sources that will help them understand election issues.

As for expected benefits, participation in elections (typically dubbed *voter turnout*) is likely to be higher when the collective benefits are greater and lower when they are smaller. (For a discussion of how voter turnout is calculated, see *How Do We Know? How Many People Vote on Election Day?*) For example, when the election is for the county registrar of deeds, voters often do not really know why one candidate would be better than another. As a result, turnout will likely be lower. If candidates seem close on many issues, the expected benefit of voting will also be unclear, because the policy outcomes will be quite similar no matter who wins. If a particular candidate runs for office unopposed, the selective benefits derived from voting are negligible. Why? The sense of civic duty a voter feels and the satisfaction from doing one's duty are probably not as strong when the election has effectively been decided before Election Day.

Factors That Influence Participation

8.3 Outline the main factors that influence political participation.

Explore on MyPoliSciLab
Simulation: You Are a Voting Registration Volunteer

Political scientists have identified a number of factors that affect individuals' perceptions of the costs and benefits of participation, and therefore the likelihood that they will participate when presented with the opportunity. These include personal factors, legal factors, the political environment, and mobilization. Many of the factors we discuss in this section are related, and it is important for political scientists to take all into account when attempting to determine the impact of each.

Personal Factors Influence Participation

By a wide margin, the most important personal factor influencing political participation is **socioeconomic status (SES)**. This factor has turned up as a highly significant predictor of participation in study after study, election after election. SES influences participation directly, but also through its impact on other factors that influence participation. These other factors include education, income, and party identification. Table 8.2 indicates rates of voter turnout in 2008 among groups of individuals with varying personal characteristics.

SES is usually measured as a combination of an individual's occupation, income, and education levels. Someone with a high-ranking professional position, a high income, and an advanced education has a high SES. Someone who has a low SES has a poor education, minimal specialized skills, and a job with low earnings.

Explore on MyPoliSciLab

How Are People Involved in Politics?

According to the 2008 American National Election Study, there is significant variance in the sort of activities American report having done at some point in their life. The most prevalent are having attended a city council or school board meeting or signing a petition. Contributing money falls just below those two activities. Trust in government varies over time, but is one factor among many that can explain who participates and the nature of that participation.

Political Activity

Activity	Percent
Signed a paper petition	56%
Attended a city council or school board meeting	55%
Gave money to a social/political organization	42%
Attended meeting on a political or social issue	34%
Distributed social/political group information	21%
Joined a protest rally or march	19%

Do You Have a Say in Government?

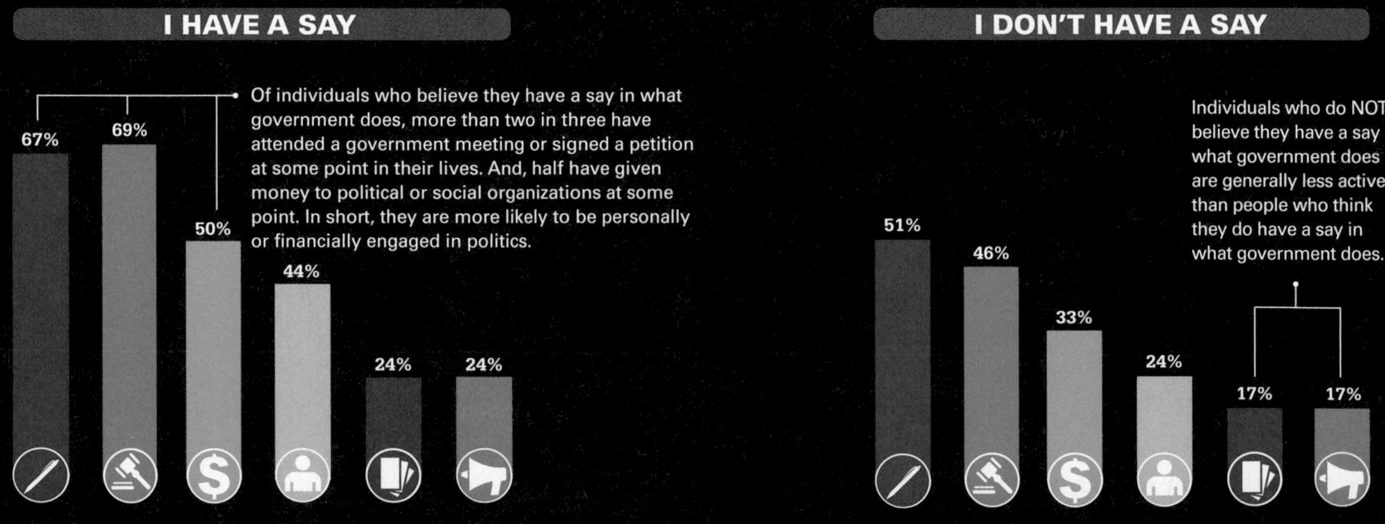

I HAVE A SAY
67%
69%
50%
44%
24%
24%
Of individuals who believe they have a say in what government does, more than two in three have attended a government meeting or signed a petition at some point in their lives. And, half have given money to political or social organizations at some point. In short, they are more likely to be personally or financially engaged in politics.
I DON'T HAVE A SAY
51%
46%
33%
24%
17%
17%
Individuals who do NOT believe they have a say in what government does are generally less active than people who think they do have a say in what government does.

SOURCE: Data from The American National Election Study, 2008 Time Series Study, post-election interview responses only.

Investigate Further

Concept What are the most frequent forms of participation? Americans most frequently participate by attending local government meetings and signing paper petitions. Attending protests and rallies and distributing political information are less common.

Connection How are city council and school board meetings different from protests and petitions? Council and board meetings can make policy for government. Protests and petitions are ways of communicating information about issues to people with authority to make policy.

Cause How is participation related to trust in government? Unlike voting, where those who trust government are more likely to report casting a ballot, in many cases, those who say they never trust government are more likely to report having participated in other sorts of activities at fairly high levels. These include attending local meetings, signing a petition, and even contributing money.

TABLE 8.2 OLDER, MORE EDUCATED, AND MORE PARTISAN VOTERS WERE MORE LIKELY TO VOTE IN 2008

Personal qualities or characteristics	Percentage who reported voting in 2008
Education	
Grade school/some high school	51.3
High school diploma	70.1
Some college, no degree	80.6
College diploma or advanced degree	90.2
Income	
1st quintile	71.1
2nd quintile	68.5
3rd quintile	75.2
4th quintile	83.8
5th quintile	90.2
Age	
29 and under	65
30–45	77.5
46–61	80.2
62–77	87
78 and over	84.1
Partisanship	
Democrats (incl. leaners)	78.5
Independents and apoliticals	48.4
Republicans (incl. leaners)	84.1
Ideology	
Liberals	85.5
Moderates	75.5
Conservatives	85.9
Region	
South	76.6
Non-South	78.5

Source: Authors' analysis of 2008 American National Election Study, http:www.electionstudies.org.

Why should occupation level have an impact on political participation? In a high-level professional position, one normally cultivates the skills of writing, speaking, analyzing, and organizing. These skills translate handily into the political arena, where political activists often have to speak, write, persuade others, think on their feet, and organize events and individuals. To someone with these **civic skills,** the costs of political participation seem lower. So the more advanced one's occupational level, the more likely one is to have the skills that make participation easier, and the more likely one is to participate in politics, other things being equal.

civic skills
the skills of writing, speaking, analyzing, and organizing that reduce the cost of political participation.

A large income clearly makes one type of political participation easier—contributing money to political campaigns. Moreover, a substantial income also may bring contact with certain institutions—philanthropies, social clubs, and civic organizations—where it is common to discuss and participate in politics. Involvement in politics in these ways lowers the cost of participation. This environment makes it easier to understand the political world and helps develop the skills that make political participation seem less daunting. Table 8.2 shows that among those in the highest income groups, nearly 90 percent turn out to vote on Election Day, or about 20 percent more than members of the lowest income groups.

A related factor is education, which is not only the most important component of SES, it is one of the most important determinants of political participation generally.

8.1

8.2

8.3

8.4

8.5

8.6

political efficacy
an individual's belief that he or she can influence what happens in the political world.

suffrage
the right to vote.

Voting Rights Act of 1965
legislation that abolished literacy tests as a requirement to register to vote.

For one thing, education tends to give people access to better jobs and to more income. And, as shown, those kinds of jobs, coupled with more money, can help increase participation by lowering its costs. The classroom also provides instruction and practice in the skills critical for taking part in political life—reading, writing, speaking, organizing, and critical thinking. So the better educated an individual is, the better developed these skills usually are, and the less costly participation seems. Lastly, a more advanced education level increases the likelihood that an individual has gained enough understanding of politics and government to believe that he or she can influence what happens in the political world, developing a sense of **political efficacy.**[7] You can see in Table 8.2 that someone with a college diploma or an advanced degree is nearly twice as likely to vote as someone with less than a high school education.

These qualities affect one's perception of the costs and benefits of political participation. Greater interest in politics results in more satisfaction from political activity. This is just another way of saying that more education brings greater benefit from political participation than does less education. A sense of political efficacy also raises an individual's assessment of the benefits of participation. The more effective and influential you feel, the more likely you are to believe that your participation will result in some collective benefit you value. Finally, the knowledge about politics that education brings can help reduce the costs of getting involved. If your education has made you conversant in political and policy issues, you can more readily participate in politics than someone with less education.

Finally, note in Table 8.2 the importance of party identification (party ID), the strength of one's attachment to one of the two major political parties. Citizens who strongly identify with either the Democratic or Republican parties are 30 and 36 percentage points, respectively, more likely to vote than citizens who consider themselves pure independents. In between these two groups are individuals who say they are independent but tend to lean toward one of the parties, and individuals who say that they identify with one of the two parties, but only weakly. Thus, according to these statistics, turnout increases across the spectrum from pure independents, to independent leaners, to weak partisans, to strong partisans. Citizens with strong partisan attachments are more likely to believe that they will enjoy meaningful benefits if their candidate wins, or that they will lose such benefits if their candidate loses. Therefore, the stronger the partisanship, the greater are the perceived benefits, and the greater the likelihood of voting on Election Day.

☐ Legal Factors Affect the Cost of Participation

Legal factors can make it more or less costly to participate in politics, particularly to vote. In the United States, **suffrage**, or the right to vote, has become available to all citizens relatively recently. At various points in U.S. history, wealth, gender, race, age, and property ownership all served as voting qualifications. Until the 1820s, laws prohibited most men who did not own land, regardless of their race or ethnicity, from voting. Although allowed to vote earlier in some states, women could not vote by federal law until ratification of the Nineteenth Amendment in 1920. Many blacks were effectively barred from voting in a large segment of the country until passage of the **Voting Rights Act of 1965.** Young people ages 18–20 were not allowed to vote until passage of the Twenty-sixth Amendment in 1970.[8] Today, convicted felons (in some states) and noncitizens are the only remaining groups of adults who do not have voting rights. Thirty-two states maintain some manner of prohibition on the casting of ballots by felons, and noncitizens are universally excluded from the franchise, with the exception of a limited number of municipal and school-board elections.[9]

Even for adults who can vote, however, the voting process followed in the United States is rare among other democracies because it requires a two-step process. Registration requirements vary from state to state. In some states, citizens can register at the polls on Election Day. In those states, turnout rates tend to be higher. But in those places where an individual has to register 10, 20, or 30 days before an election, a voter who get involved late in the campaign—the point when most campaigns actually get interesting—will be unable to cast a ballot. States that allow early voting or make absentee voting by mail easier also tend to see higher turnout. North Dakota is the only state that does not require that citizens register to vote before they cast a ballot.

Even with some states recently passing laws requiring voters to have approved IDs to vote, over time, the movement has been toward a reduction in the legal barriers to registration and voting. For example, thanks to the efforts of political parties, civic groups, and the courts, registration offices must now stay open during standard business hours. Also, since the passage of Motor Voter Law in 1993, citizens may register by mail and at various government offices (including motor vehicle agencies, which gave the law its nickname). Furthermore, the deadline for registration before an election is now 30 days, rather than 60 or 90 days, which had been the norm in some states.

GOTV (get-out-the-vote)
term used by campaign professionals to describe the various activities candidates, political parties, activists, and interest groups use to make sure their likely supporters go to the polls on Election Day.

The Political Environment Influences Voter Turnout Decisions

In addition to personal and legal factors, the nature of the candidates, campaigns, and issues in an election year can influence who turns out to vote. As noted earlier, people who have stronger attachments to one of the parties are more likely to participate in politics. This is another reason why the 2008 election stands as a watershed event in American political history. The first African American nominee of a major party, Barack Obama, created tremendous pride in African American voters, who cast ballots in record numbers and increased their share of the electorate from 11 percent in 2004 to 13 percent in 2008. Hispanics and young voters also voted overwhelmingly for Obama, greatly increasing their turnout by 2.7 percent and 2.1 percent, respectively, in the 2008 election.[10] The powerful image and message of a minority president likely presented the benefit that gave both groups the added incentive to cast their ballots.

Similarly, the presence on the ballot of more interesting or important contests and candidates can boost turnout. An election for president, governor, or U.S. Senate would likely motivate greater turnout than one for, say, state mine inspector (an elective position in Arizona), as the potential benefits of a victory or defeat for John McCain or Barack Obama in the 2008 contest for president exemplifies.[11] Having appealing, attractive, or even "star quality" choices on the ballot also appears to elevate turnout.[12] Voters seem to find politics more interesting, and therefore more worth their time, when they can vote for a candidate with the star power of an Arnold Schwarzenegger or an Obama. The presence of specific issues on the ballot may help some citizens find more benefits in participation that they might not otherwise see.

According to some research, voters turn out at the polls when they think it will be a close election.[13] Close elections stimulate more intense campaign activity and media coverage, which provide voters with more information about the campaign. Furthermore, citizens are more likely to discuss politics among themselves when an election is close. In the months preceding the 2012 presidential contest, newspapers, websites, and news broadcasts were full of stories about the battle between President Obama and Mitt Romney, as ads saturated the airways and the candidates barnstormed around the country. U.S. citizens, especially in competitive or battleground states, told various survey organizations that they were interested and engaged in the presidential election, and with other factors held constant turnout in these battleground states was higher than in states that were not as close and crucial to the respective campaigns. With all the attention given to the race, citizens could more easily access the information they needed and wanted in order to vote. Close elections can also convince citizens that their vote will count, increasing their perception that their vote may influence the outcome and, thus, determine whether they receive benefits.

Mobilization Efforts Increase Turnout

Mobilization efforts, often dubbed **GOTV (get-out-the-vote),** are activities by candidates, political parties, activists, interest groups, friends, and coworkers to induce others to participate in politics. These efforts can include phone calls, personal visits, direct mail, and even transportation to the polls on Election Day. If you have ever been called the night before an election and urged to vote or had someone stop you outside the library and ask you to sign a petition, you have been the target of mobilization efforts. In the 2012 elections, the Obama campaign had a particularly sophisticated mobilization or GOTV operation.

The campaign scored voters on both their likelihood of voting and their likelihood of voting for Obama. For those voters who they felt would vote for Obama, but needed to be encouraged to vote, the campaign made sure they got multiple different sorts of in-person contacts and follow ups over the course of the year. The campaign even had a team that just targeted people in beauty parlors and barber shops.

Mobilization can increase participation in three ways. First, mobilization efforts tend to provide information about the relevant candidates and issues, making it easier for people to learn what they need to know to make good voting decisions. In addition to simply asking you to help organize a community meeting on local crime, a neighbor would probably give you some background on the issue and tell you what a local meeting might accomplish. Second, mobilization efforts lower the costs of participation by providing information to individuals on exactly how to carry out the activity—where and when to vote, how to get to the rally, how to sign up to be heard at the committee hearing, and so on. In states with early and absentee voting, mobilizers can even arrange for ballots to be sent to citizens at home. Third, mobilization brings implicit social rewards for those

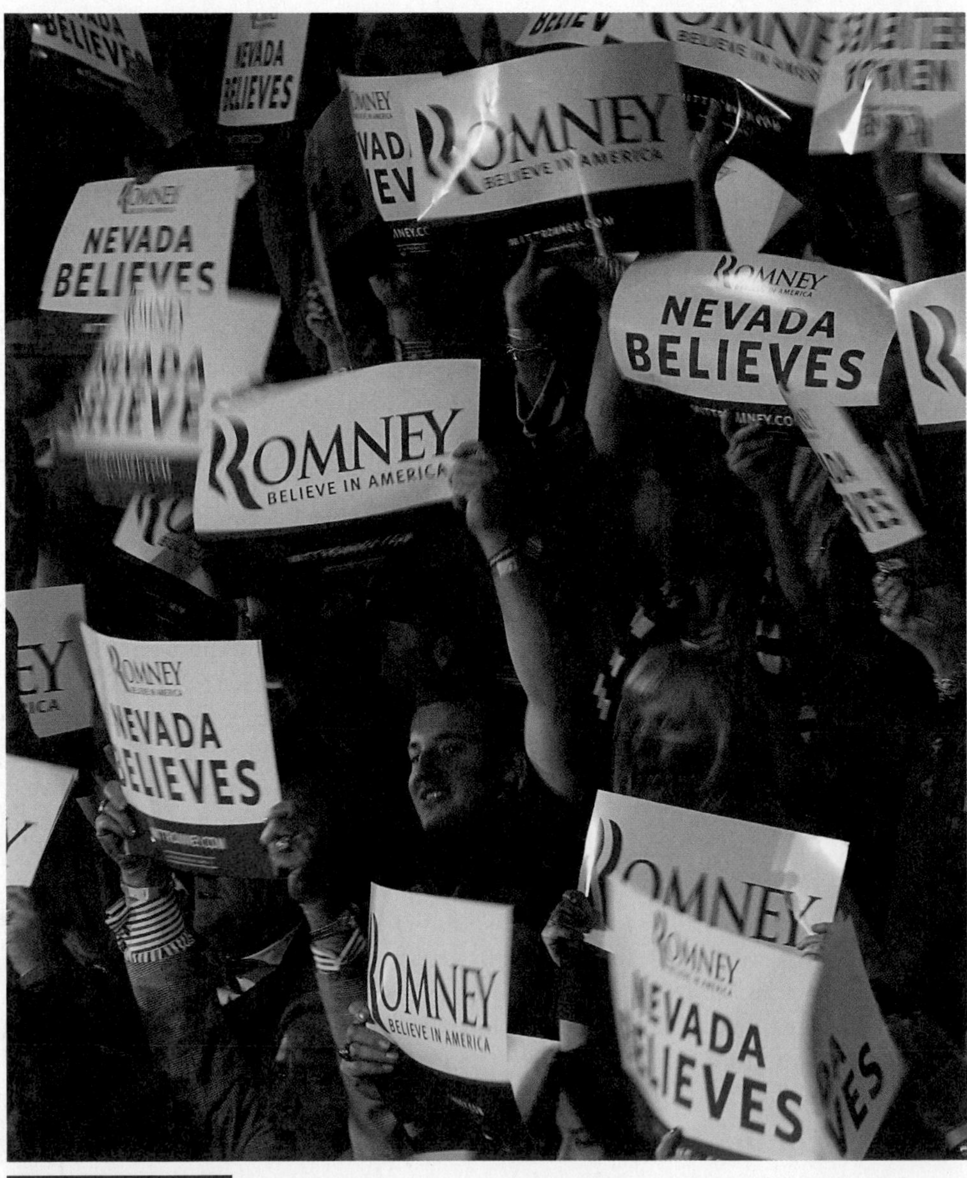

IMPORTANCE OF CAMPAIGN MESSAGE

Campaigns messages are delivered in various ways by candidates. They can be through television commercials or media interviews or delivered in front of supporters in venues designed to attract maximum media attention.

who agree to participate, and possibly negative consequences for those who do not. Individuals who become involved in politics at the behest of others will enjoy the gratitude and esteem of those who asked them to participate.[14] This benefit can be very important, considering that these individuals are often coworkers, neighbors, or fellow parishioners.

For mobilization to work, however, campaigns must first have the right message—one that convinces people to care and to show up at the voting booth. Then, campaigns, parties, and interest groups must also contact the most appropriate people—those who will be most motivated by the message to participate. A significant element of mobilization, therefore, requires that the "right" message be sent to the "right" people. Basing a campaign simply on the mechanical aspects of turnout is not sufficient. Although voter contact and organization do play a significant role in voter turnout, it is often the message of campaigns or the current political situation that ultimately leads voters to the booth. In 2008, the Obama campaign spent tens of millions of dollars on GOTV activity directed at African Americans. Although this activity might have spurred turnout, the presence of Barack Obama himself on the ticket was probably a greater mobilizing factor.

One of the big stories of the 2010 election was the enthusiasm gap separating Democrats and Republicans. Republicans were simply much more engaged and likely to vote than Democrats were in 2010. Samples of likely voters in preelection polls skewed strongly Republican, whereas surveys that included all registered voters or all adults had the Democrats doing better. Fundamentally, the 2010 electorate mirrored the 2008 election when Democrats were more energetic, engaged, and likely to vote. In 2012, there was much pre-election debate about what the composition of the electorate would be. In fact, what turned out to be misplaced confidence on the GOP side was based on their assumption that Republicans were enthusiastic and that the electorate would not be as Democratic as it was in 2008. However, exit polls in 2012 indicated that Democrats had virtually the same six to seven percentage point advantage that they had in 2008. Fewer voters cast ballots in 2012, but there was no difference in the shape of the electorate.

Typically, the mobilization efforts of Democrats and Republicans take different directions, based on their assumptions about their voters. Democrats usually focus efforts on voters with somewhat lower SES, whereas Republicans tend to mobilize suburbanites, church members, and hunters. In the 2012 election, both parties and their supporters engaged in massive mobilization and GOTV efforts along these lines. Democrats typically focus more of their energies than Republicans on mobilizing their voters with the assumption that their voters—who, on average, have lower SES than Republican voters—need more of a push to go to the polls.

In the 2008 election, Barack Obama took advantage of relatively new media and social networking sites such as Facebook, Twitter, and MySpace to mobilize millions of supporters. He effectively used online media to raise millions of dollars and generated a type of online activism never seen before. This online public engagement gave him a significant advantage over John McCain, who failed to mobilize a sizable number of people with his online outreach. Obama's use of online tools gave him an outlet for instant political mobilization, as well as a vehicle through which to easily and directly get his message across to millions of online followers. Many political pundits pointed out, and arguably overemphasized, Obama's aggressive use of online media as a major reason for his victory. Still, although many who participated in Obama's online outreach were already supporters, and the millions of text messages, tweets, and e-mails were "preaching to the converted," it nonetheless gave them an easy medium for communicating and a sense of community not realized in any previous presidential campaign. Social networking sites were crucial for generating hype and discussion, and they offered a significant number of people—especially younger people who otherwise would have lost interest—a chance to participate in politics.

Barack Obama's campaign also made the most productive use of another effective mobilization technique: phone banking, where people in non-battleground states such as California called people in Ohio and other key states. This gave people living in these noncontested states a chance to make a difference. Volunteers received lists of undecided, likely, and Democratic voters to call and persuade in key states, or they had the option of signing up online and calling people through a virtual phone bank. Obama supporters could volunteer their time at their convenience in the comfort of their own home. The Obama

8.1

8.2

8.3

8.4

8.5

8.6

data mining
a catch-all term that refers to analysts using increasingly powerful computers and statistical tools to extract useable information or insights from extremely large data sets.

campaign also used mass texting as a way to get out the vote. People could sign up to receive alerts from the campaign and then reminders to vote and information on the nearest polling station. Obama was not the only one to use such technology through the primaries and general election, but he certainly used it most effectively. In fact, one exit poll showed that Obama's team made as much as 37 percent more voter contacts than did McCain's team.[15]

In the 2012 elections, the Obama campaign spread its message beyond loyal supporters. The campaign spent millions of dollars to collect personal details about millions of American citizens from data brokers (vendors who sell information about people's individual consumer habits), voter files, and online resources. It then used this information to target potential voters with online ads and fund-raising materials personalized to their interests. So, rather than just preaching to the converted, the Obama campaign actively sought out new people to convert, based on the likelihood that they would sign on to their team. The Romney campaign used similar advanced online targeting strategies. Eventually, the public, politicians, and campaigns will need to determine how much personal **data mining** is necessary to attain the benefits of participation in our democratic system and how much is too much of an invasion of privacy.

All of these mobilization efforts tend to add to the already substantial influence of socioeconomic status in determining participation. If you really want someone to help advance a political issue you care about, you would be smart to pick someone with developed civic skills and a high-prestige job; someone with substantial amounts of money to give to the cause; someone with access to clubs and charities full of other people with money; and someone with a good education and all of the knowledge, skills, and confidence that education brings with it. In other words, you would ask a high-SES individual. In fact, high-SES individuals are the ones most likely to be asked to participate in political activities. So even though individuals who enjoy high SES are more likely to participate in politics in the first place, they are also prime targets for mobilization campaigns.

Comparative and Historical Puzzles of Voter Turnout

8.4 Analyze voter turnout from comparative and historical perspectives.

American rates of voter turnout lag behind those in a handful of Western European countries (refer again to Figure 8.1). Expanding the list of countries to include Canada, Japan, New Zealand, and Iceland yields the same result. Among the 21 countries included in this larger list, American voter turnout would rank next to last in recent years. Only the Swiss vote at lower levels. Even with all the excitement of the 2008 election and pictures of long lines of people waiting to vote, the participation levels in America remain low when compared with other countries.

Voter Registration Requirements Top the List of Reasons for America's Low Voting Rate

Why does America's voter turnout lag so far behind that of other democracies? Answering this question is a challenge because comparable data on some variables are unavailable from one country to the next. Although registering has gotten easier over time, some important reasons for this disparity include registration regulations, how often and when elections are conducted, the way votes are counted and apportioned, and America's two-party system.

REGISTRATION REGULATIONS First, voter registration requirements in the United States significantly depress turnout in comparison with other countries, where voter registration is a government responsibility and the registration process is effortless and free.[16] The United States has a personal registration requirement, meaning that

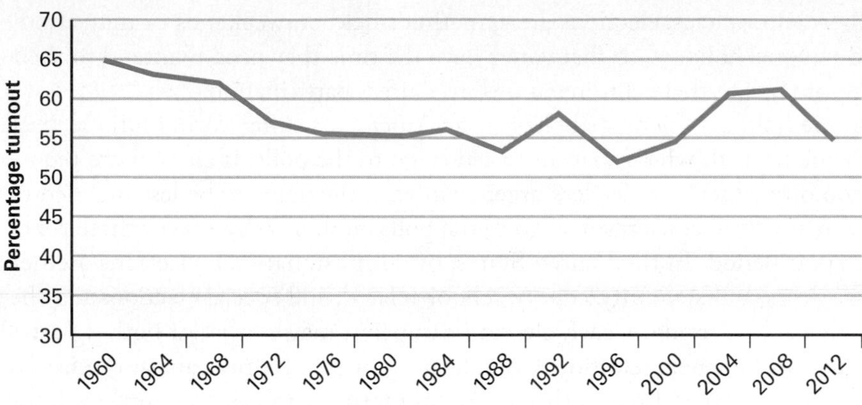

FIGURE 8.2 VOTER TURNOUT IN PRESIDENTIAL ELECTIONS, 1960–2012.

Voter turnout in presidential elections declined after 1960 but has shown an upturn in recent years.

Source: Social Science Research Council, http://election04.ssrc.org/research/csae_2004_final_report.pdf. Reprinted with permission.

Americans are personably responsible for registering to vote. Like buying a car, this is something most people do infrequently and so are less likely to know how to do. Some Americans, therefore, forget to register or do not realize that they need to; others attempt to register but fail to comply with state regulations or just give up in frustration over the process. As a result, tens of millions of Americans who are otherwise eligible to vote cannot do so, simply because they have not registered.

The personal registration requirement has significant consequences for voter turnout. Fully 30 percent of Americans who could register to vote have not done so and are thus not eligible to cast ballots. Among registered voters in the United States, turnout is about 85 percent in presidential election years (see Figure 8.2), a rate that is respectable in comparison with other Western democracies. In midterm elections, however, this percentage drops to 69 (see Figure 8.3).[17] On the basis of this comparison, then, it appears that if the United States adopted a European-style voter registration system, participation in American elections would come closer to matching rates in other countries.

ELECTION SCHEDULING The way we conduct elections is another legal factor with implications for U.S. voter turnout. Typically, American elections take place on a single day—a Tuesday—during which voters are expected to find time to participate amid their other personal and professional activities. Early and absentee balloting now gives many Americans the chance to vote over the course of days or even weeks. But the evidence on whether early voting increases turnout has been mixed. Most scholarly studies show that early voting has an insignificantly small impact on voter turnout.[18]

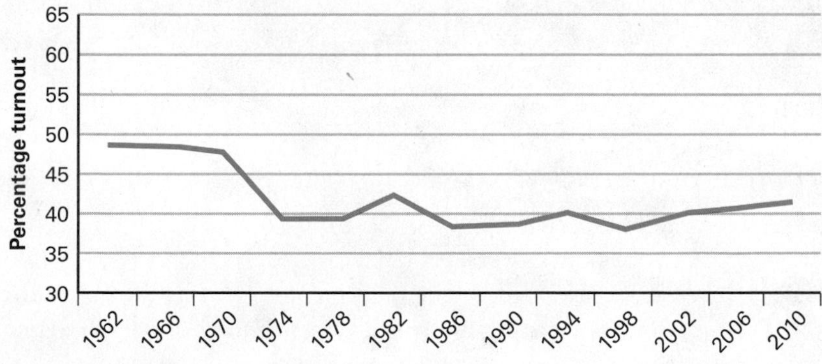

FIGURE 8.3 MIDTERM ELECTION TURNOUT, 1962–2010.

Midterm election turnout has also declined over the past 40 years. In the 1962 midterm elections, 47 percent of eligible Americans cast ballots. In the 2010 midterm elections, 41.5 percent of the eligible population cast a ballot.

Source: Center for the Study of the American Electorate, http://www.american.edu/ia/cdem/csae/pdfs/csae061109.pdf.

In other democracies, elections are sometimes held on weekends or may also be declared national holidays, so that voters have the time they need to attend to their civic obligations. All of these considerations may affect participation.

Some political scientists believe that Americans suffer voting fatigue, based on the frequency with which they are asked to go to the polls. If citizens are required to vote too often, they may see less urgency in each election and be less inclined to turn out. In many democracies, voters go to the polls no more than two or three times over a four-year period. In the United States, by contrast, national elections are held every two years, and state, city, county, school-related, and special elections may be held in between. Furthermore, each election campaign may consist of both a party-level (primary) and a general election. Complicating matters, Americans also must vote on many more offices and issues than their counterparts in other countries. Some European countries, for example, do not have or do not frequently use the ballot initiative process in which citizens vote directly on legislation (instead of just leaving such votes to elected legislators). Furthermore, many democracies have far fewer elected offices and far more appointed offices than the United States. As a result of both the frequency and the complexity of U.S. elections, then, the investment required to be an active voter in the United States is substantially more than in other countries.

PLURALITY DECISIONS The way votes are counted and apportioned in America may also depress voter turnout. Elections in the United States are predominantly plurality, or winner-take-all, affairs. Decision by plurality means that the candidate who receives the most votes wins the seat being contested; all other candidates lose. Imagine that you are a liberal Democrat living in Orange County, California, a bastion of conservative politics. In election after election, your district sends Republicans to

MULTIPARTY SYSTEMS ALLOW VOTERS MORE SPECIFIC CHOICES

When Islamic terrorists struck a central Madrid train station just days before an election, voter turnout surged. Spanish voters put the Socialist Party in office, and within a matter of weeks, all of Spain's troops serving in Iraq were brought home.

Unresolved Debate

Can Any One factor Explain the Decline in Voter Participation in the United States?

In the heated 1960 presidential race between Richard Nixon and John F. Kennedy, more than three-fifths of eligible Americans cast their ballots. In an equally competitive presidential race in 2000 between George W. Bush and Al Gore, only about half of all eligible Americans voted. There was modestly higher turnout in 2004 and 2008, but turnout hovers around 50 percent and has decreased significantly over the last 50 years.

This decline puzzles American political scientists. In particular, two factors strongly correlated with turnout—education and legal restrictions—changed over the past few decades in ways that should have boosted turnout. Can any one factor explain the decline in voter participation?

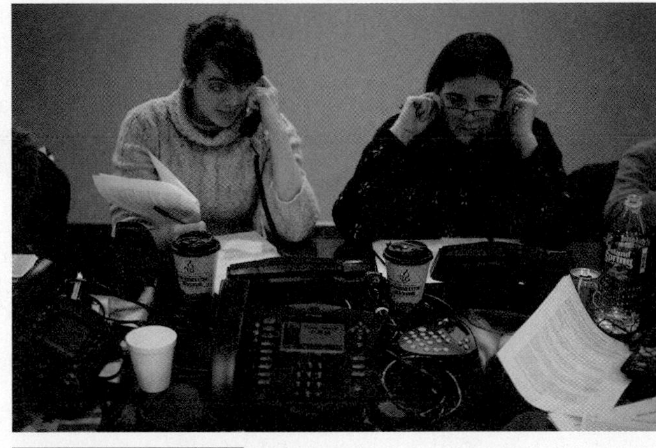

Campaigns and their party allies make millions of phone calls during an election year to identify supporters and encourage them to vote. Volunteers for John McCain's campaign in 2008 are shown here making get out the vote phone calls.

YES

Still other political scientists make the case that the decline in voter participation can, in fact, be attributed to specific factors:

- Paul Abramson, John Aldrich, and David Rohde argue that although the Twenty-sixth Amendment in 1970 extended the right to vote to 18- to 20-year-olds, young people are less likely to vote than older people, so the overall proportion of Americans voting decreased.[a]
- Samuel Popkin and David McDonald point to the way the voting age population has traditionally been measured as the reason for the apparent decline in participation. They argue that this number artificially inflates the number of people who are actually eligible to vote because it includes new immigrants who are not yet citizens as well as illegal immigrants, those currently serving prison time, and felons—all groups whose populations have been increasing. They argue that we should look at turnout as a proportion of the voting-eligible population (which removes those not eligible to vote from the denominator).[b]
- Steve Rosenstone and Mark Hansen insist that fewer people vote because mobilization efforts are weaker. In the past, mobilization meant friends, neighbors, and committed volunteers canvassed personally. Today, professional consultants and phone banks conduct voter mobilization operations.[c]

NO

Many political science scholars make the case that no one factor can explain the decline in voter turnout in the United States and that, in fact, several factors together provide a possible explanation:

- Margaret Conway argues that Americans have lower levels of political efficacy, trust in government, and attachment to political parties than they did 50 years ago and that, together, these factors account for as much as three-quarters of the decline in turnout since 1960.[d]
- Ruy Teixeira argues that both laws and attitudes explain the decline in voter turnout and proposes a set of registration and political reforms to make voting easier and increase efficacy.[37]

8.1

8.2

8.3

8.4

8.5

8.6

CONTRIBUTING TO THE DEBATE

Another factor that may affect voter turnout is social connectedness, or interactions outside of work. Over time, we've seen a decline in activities such as church attendance, civic organization participation, labor union membership, and socializing with family and friends. The more socially connected someone is, the more exposure he or she may have to voter mobilization efforts. Personalized mobilization efforts often encourage people to understand the importance of an election outcome—and want to vote.[e]

But scholars disagree about how to measure social connectedness, and how much it affects turnout. For example, online social networking often gives people an exaggerated feeling of connectedness. Even if you have 850 Facebook friends, how many of them do you see regularly? Could you convince all of them to attend a rally for a cause you believe in or vote for a candidate you support? What if a Facebook friend you haven't spoken to for years posted a status update that asked you to "Support lowering the minimum legal drinking age"? Would just reading that status motivate you to vote for a particular issue or candidate? Probably not. Would "liking" that status make a difference to a candidate's campaign? Definitely not. Over time, these trends may continue to evolve and further shape voter turnout.

WHAT DO YOU THINK?

1. Why has American voter turnout continued to decline even as the average American becomes more educated?
2. How can political scientists better measure social connectedness to determine its effect on voter turnout?

[a]Rosenstone and Hansen, *Mobilization, Participation, and Democracy in America.* [need full citation here]
[b]Popkin, Samuel and McDonald GET CITE
[c]Paul R. Abramson, John H. Aldrich, and David W. Rohde, *Change and Continuity in the 2004 Elections* (Washington, DC: Congressional Quarterly Press, 2006), 85.
[d]M. Margaret Conway, *Political Participation in the United States* (Washington, DC: Congressional Quarterly Press, 1991), 171.
[e]For a review of the existing literature and a report on some new research findings, see Alan S. Gerber and Donald P. Green, "The Effects of Canvassing, Direct Mail, and Telephone Contact on Voter Turnout: A Field Experiment," *American Political Science Review* 94 (2000): 653–63. [Citation will be at least 13 years old when book is published; not sure this qualifies for new research findings.]

Congress. You show up faithfully to vote in every election, but your candidate, the Democrat, always loses. Under the circumstances, it would not be surprising if you concluded, "Why bother?"

Many foreign countries—such as Israel—have a proportional representation system in which a party's share of legislative seats is proportionate to its share of votes. In such a system, even if the party you vote for finishes in second place or lower, it will likely win some seats in the legislature. As a voter, this system gives you an incentive to vote; at least some candidates of the party you favor can win seats, even if your party does not get the most votes. The net effect of this procedure is to increase the benefits of voting.

THE TWO-PARTY SYSTEM Finally, the U.S. system has only two major political parties, and two relatively centrist parties at that, both of them battling within the confines of the American creed. This situation may also result in lower rates of voter turnout. In multiparty parliamentary systems, the parties have more narrowly focused agendas and closer links to population groups. For example, in many European countries, environmentalists can find a comfortable home in various Green parties, which are devoted almost exclusively to environmental issues. In the United States, by contrast, voters who are environmentally conscious have to choose between Republicans and Democrats, neither of which places environmental politics at the center of its agenda. Thus, in a multiparty system, voters may believe that their vote can help deliver the specific kinds of collective benefits that interest them most. Naturally, this perception gives them a greater incentive to turn out on Election Day.

A variety of other factors might explain the turnout gap between the United States and other countries. Just remember two main points: First, the structure of America's government and of its election system tends to make casting a ballot more costly here than in other democracies. Second and specifically, the single largest determinant of the relatively low rate of American turnout in comparison with other countries is America's uniquely onerous voter registration system. For a further discussion of the decline in voter participation, (see *Unresolved Debate: Can Any One Factor Explain the Decline in Voter Participation in the United States?*)

Understanding Individual Vote Choice

8.5 Describe the key factors that determine how voters make electoral choices.

fter a potential voter weighs the costs and benefits of voting and decides that voting is worth it, then comes the really hard part: deciding who or what to vote for. In a presidential election, voters generally have two chances to cast a vote for a candidate—once in the primaries, and once in the general election. Once the campaigns are over, the advertisements have been aired, the debates have come and gone, and the media have made their endorsements, the voters must make a choice and cast a ballot. And because there are different processes for the primary election and the general election, the factors that determine those choices may be different.

Primary Voting Is Less Studied and Understood than General Election Voting

No single aspect of political behavior in America has been examined more often or more closely than the individual vote for president. Although political scientists know a great deal about individual vote choice during the November presidential election, they know relatively little about individual decision making among presidential primary voters.

Two reasons account for this discrepancy. First, the general election determines who will be president, and that choice, in turn, usually has major consequences in terms of domestic policy, the economy, and international affairs. But who wins a particular party's nomination may end up being little more than a historical footnote. The second reason for political scientists' greater attention to presidential elections is that party identification—not an issue in primary elections—is very much at play and provides a critical basis for understanding why voters go with one candidate rather than another.

In the 2012 general election, for example, more than 90 percent of Democrats voted for Barack Obama, and more than 90 percent of Republicans voted for Mitt Romney.[18]

In a primary, though, all of the candidates are of the same party. Political scientists, therefore, cannot explain the primary vote choice as well as they can explain the general election vote. They do, however, have some understanding of the outcome of the primary process as a whole—why a particular candidate ends up being the party's nominee.

Partisanship Can Both Influence and Be Influenced by the General Election Vote

In the 1950s, a pioneering study established enduring theories on the role of partisan identification in the behavior of individual voters. In their seminal work *The American Voter*, Angus Campbell, Philip Converse, Warren Miller, and Donald Stokes argued that in their pre-adult years, most voters adopt a partisan affiliation that becomes a psychological attitude akin to the attachment a person has to a religion or a racial identity.[20] Therefore, it tends to be highly stable over time (although slow change could occur), and it is the predominant force in determining most other political attitudes and behaviors—including voting. This view has come to be known as the "traditional" view of partisan affiliation.

DIRECTION AND STRENGTH OF PARTISAN IDENTIFICATION *The American Voter* identified two components in an individual's partisan attachment: direction and strength. Direction refers to whether a person identifies more with the Republican Party or with the Democratic Party. Strength refers to the intensity of that attachment. Accordingly, researchers typically measure partisan identification using a series of questions and a seven-point scale that captures both direction and strength, like the one in Figure 8.4.

Since the 1950s, relatively few party ID panel studies have tracked the same group of individuals over many years. Those few suggest that partisan affiliation is a stable attachment. For example, a panel study that looked at the same group of adults at three different times—1965, 1973, and 1982—found that nearly 80 percent of these individuals maintained the same partisan status from one period to the next. A majority of the rest only moved into or out of the independent category.[21]

DIFFERING VIEWS OF PARTY IDENTIFICATION The traditional view of partisanship sensibly emphasized party ID as a factor that determined other beliefs and behaviors—that is, as a causal factor. Because the average citizen pays little attention to the fine points of politics, the voter needs some way to simplify and make sense of the political world. Partisan affiliation is a highly effective mechanism for this. Supporting one's party and opposing the other party is a relatively simple way to organize the political world. Thus, it makes sense to think of partisanship as a lens through which one sees the political world, and a handy shortcut for arriving at opinions about specific political figures and issues.

Not all political scientists are completely satisfied with this view of party ID, however. In the "revisionist" view embraced by some scholars, party affiliation can certainly influence vote choice, issue stands, and evaluations of candidates; however, the reverse is also true; those same opinions about issues and candidates can influence party identification. Consistent with this view, political scientist Morris Fiorina[22] has argued that party identification is less a "standing decision" than a "mental tally" of party performance. Ronald Reagan, a Democrat who became a Republican in the 1950s, reflected this aspect of party identification when he stated, "I didn't leave the Democratic Party. The Democratic Party left me."[23]

Which view of partisan attachment makes more sense: the traditional or the revisionist? Consider that each explains some of the puzzle of partisan attachment.

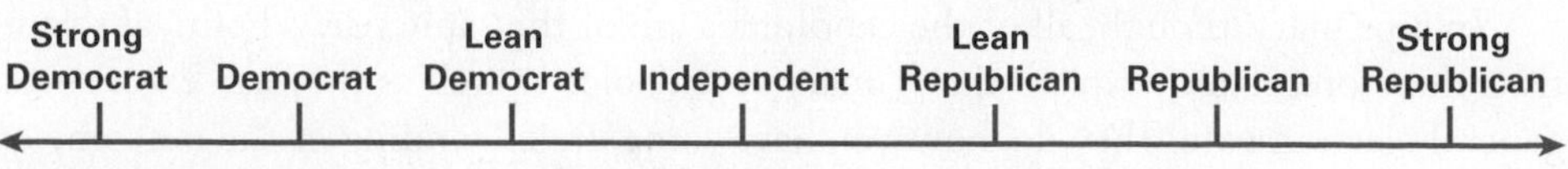

FIGURE 8.4 PARTISAN IDENTIFICATION ON A SEVEN-POINT SCALE.

Source: The American National Election Studies (www.electionstudies.org). The 1948–2004 ANES Cumulative File [data set]. Stanford University and the University of Michigan [producers and distributors], 2005.

Because of political socialization, most voters develop a partisan attachment long before they would be capable of assessing the parties' performance in office. Furthermore, there is little evidence that individuals switch from one party to another in reaction to party performance (with limited movement to the independent category).

PARTISAN CHANGE AND INSTABILITY At the same time, partisan affiliation is not always permanent or perfectly stable, nor need it be seen only as a causal agent. Partisans, especially weaker ones, sometimes do switch sides and affiliate with the other party—particularly when extraordinary political events upset existing political arrangements. During the civil rights movement of the 1960s, for example, the national Democratic Party adopted an agenda of federal intervention to promote political, social, and economic equality for blacks—leaving many white southern Democrats disenchanted (see Figure 8.5).

Another example of political attitudes affecting partisan affiliation instead of the reverse is the emergence in the 1980s of a group of voters known as "Reagan Democrats." These were generally white, working-class voters who had traditionally considered themselves Democrats but began to identify with the Republican Party on social issues. Accordingly, many of these individuals voted for Ronald Reagan in 1980 and 1984 and ultimately registered as Republicans. But, as the traditional theory would suggest, these conversions were not a simple calculation that it suddenly made more sense to identify with the Republican Party. These individuals had to overcome their strong, lifelong attachment to the Democrats.

The defection of previous partisans to the independent and "leaner" categories might raise some doubts about the traditional view of partisan stability. However, research suggests that two other factors have been more influential than partisan defections. First, individuals who came of political age in the late 1950s and early 1960s entered adulthood with weaker partisan attachments than their parents. Second, some individuals who typically would be expected to grow stronger in their partisan attachments over time, as a result of the life-cycle effect, did not do so. Therefore, defections among former Republicans and Democrats can account for only 30 to 40 percent of the reduction in partisan attachments.[24]

Although one is generally safe in assuming the durability and stability of partisan attachments, change can occur, as it did in the 2008 elections. In 2004, most polls showed relative parity in the number of voters identifying themselves as Democrats and Republicans. But by 2008, Democrats had a double-digit lead in party

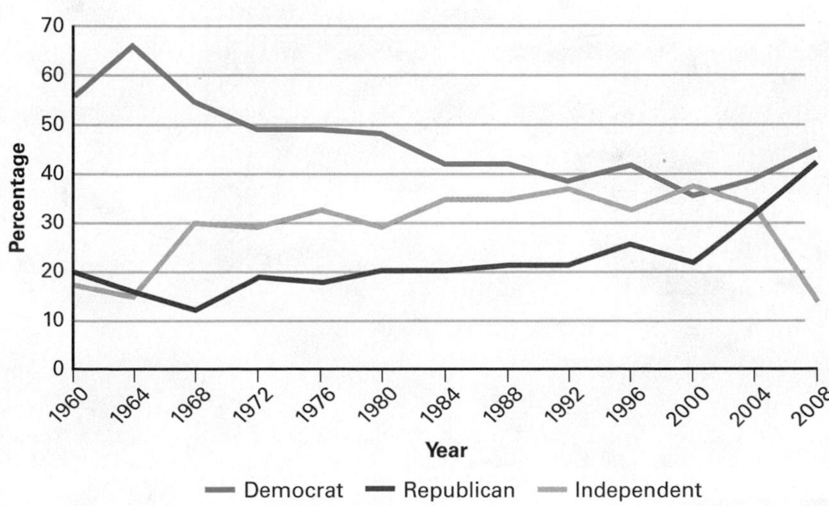

FIGURE 8.5 PARTISAN AFFILIATION AMONG SOUTHERNERS, 1960–2008.

Source: American National Election Study, Cumulative File.

issue voting
voting style in which the voter judges candidates based on the voter's and the candidates' opinions on specific issues and preferences for certain policies.

identification. Then, in the 2010 and 2012 elections, the pendulum swung back to a more even distribution of party identification. The swings that we have seen in recent years are some of the most dramatic that scholars have documented in the more than 60 years of tracking partisan attachments.

Regardless of one's precise view of partisanship and its durability and predictive value, partisan affiliation remains a singularly important predictor of vote choice in general and presidential voting in particular. In recent presidential elections, typically 90 percent or more of "strong" Democratic and Republican partisans have voted for their party's candidate. Among individuals who identify themselves as Democrats and Republicans, although not strongly, the loyalty rate is somewhat lower but still impressive—generally in the range of 70 to 85 percent.[25] In 2010, according to the exit polls, 92 percent of Democrats voted for Democratic candidates for Congress and 95 percent of Republicans voted for Republicans for Congress. Thus, knowing voters' partisan affiliations will yield tremendous insight into their probable vote choice.

Not all partisans are loyal to their party's candidate in every election, however. Furthermore, not every voter considers himself or herself a Democrat or Republican. Two other factors are thought to have an important influence on the individual vote—issue and policy preferences and candidate evaluations.

Issue and Policy Preferences Have a Complex and Uncertain Impact on Voter Choice

Most political scientists agree that voters' opinions on specific issues and their preferences for certain policies can and do affect their presidential vote. The shorthand phrase for this phenomenon in the research literature is **issue voting.** It makes sense intuitively. For example, if you are a strong supporter of universal, government-paid health care,

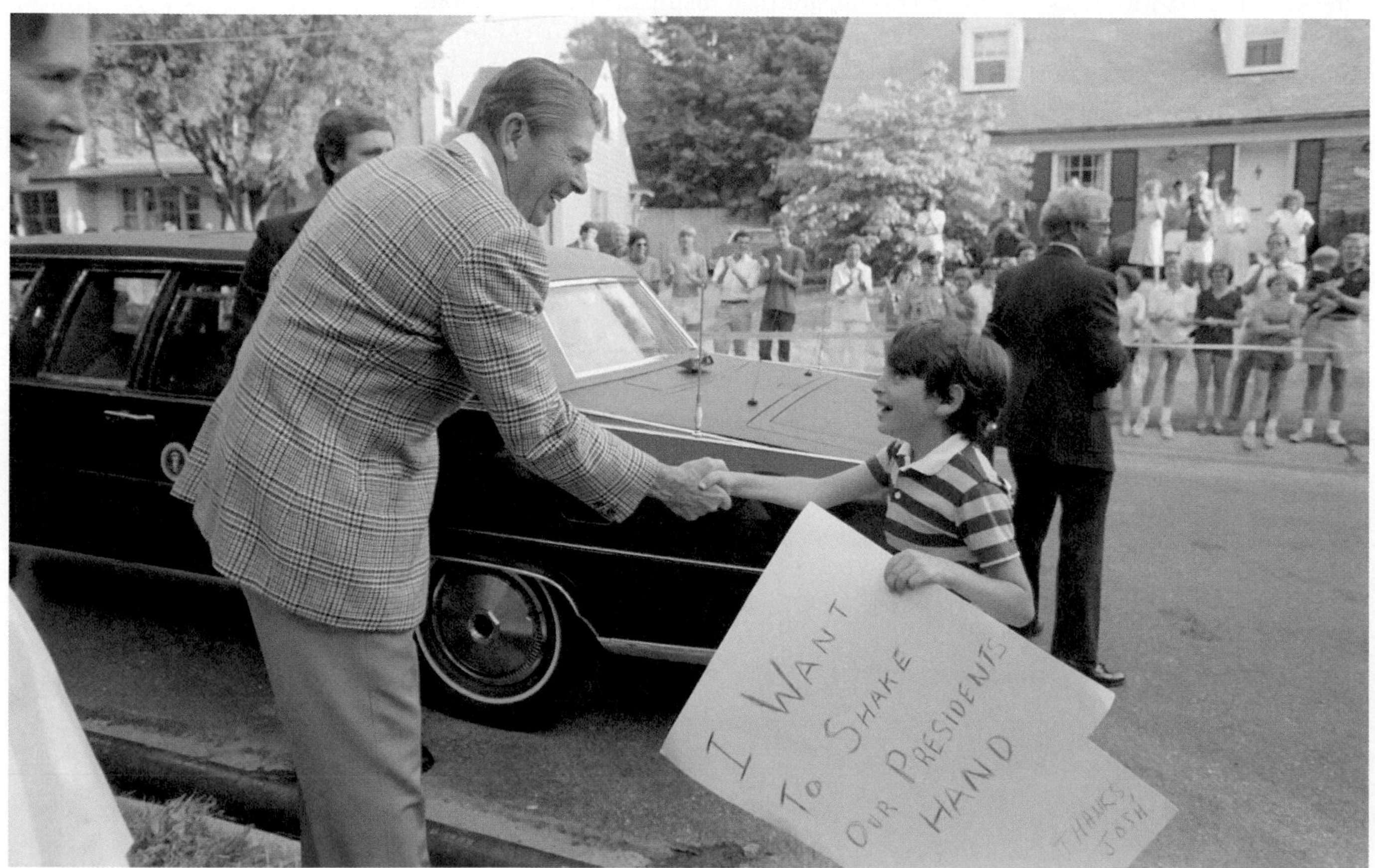

REAGAN DEMOCRATS

Ronald Reagan shakes hands with white working-class voters. Some of these voters followed him as he moved from the Democratic to the Republican Party.

you will likely be inclined to vote for a candidate who also supports that concept rather than one who opposes it (other things being equal). Political scientists also agree on certain preconditions that must exist in order for a voter to engage in issue voting:

- The voter must be aware of the issue and have an opinion concerning it.
- The issue must be at least minimally important to the voter.
- The voter must be able to identify the candidates' positions on the issue accurately.
- The voter must believe that one party or candidate represents the voter's own position better than the other party or candidate.[26]

Beyond these basics, political scientists disagree about the relative importance of issues in the voting decision, the precise mechanisms by which voters compare their issue positions to those of presidential candidates, the kinds of issues that are relevant to voters, and the best ways to study issue voting.

RETROSPECTIVE AND PROSPECTIVE VOTING Scholars also introduced another insight on issue voting. Voters do not only try to project how candidates will perform on important issues in the future—a process known as **prospective voting.** Rather, issue voting can also be **retrospective voting;** voters simply assess the performance of the party that has held the presidency for the past four years. If a voter believes the party has performed well on the issues the voter cares about, he or she will reward that party's candidate with a vote. According to this logic, presidential elections are considered more of a referendum on the incumbent party's stewardship of the country than a judgment about the relative strengths and weaknesses of two competing candidates. V.O. Key summed up the essence of this idea in fairly dramatic terms, describing the voter as "a rational god of vengeance and reward."[27]

Several twentieth-century presidential elections demonstrate the validity of Key's arguments. Presidents who presided over periods of recession or slow economic growth, found themselves mired in serious scandal or controversy, or were associated with conspicuous foreign policy failures did not win reelection—Herbert Hoover, Gerald Ford, and Jimmy Carter, among others. Presidents who served during eras of peace and general prosperity typically earned the reward of reelection, such as Dwight Eisenhower, Ronald Reagan, and Bill Clinton.

This same logic applies even when an incumbent president is not up for reelection. In 1988, for example, Reagan's vice president, George H. W. Bush, benefited from the peace and prosperity of the Reagan years, with a relatively easy path to the presidency. In 2008, the economic downturn and resulting anxiety people felt during George W. Bush's presidency clearly hurt the Republican candidates, John McCain and Sarah Palin, even though Bush himself was not even on the ballot. These patterns also hold in midterm elections, as we saw in 2010. Although he was not on the ballot, President Obama's plunging job approval numbers in the months leading up to the election hurt Democratic congressional candidates.

In the 2012 elections, for much of the year, President Obama's job approval rating was in a grey area—in the high 40s. A little bit higher and he certainly would have been re-elected and a little bit lower and re-election would have been all but impossible no matter the skill of their campaign. By Election Day, 53 percent of voters approved and 47 percent disapproved of the job Obama was doing as president. Obama won over 90 percent of the votes of those believing he was doing a good job and he was able to win a narrow victory.

One reason it is easier for people to follow this retrospective voting model is that it is much simpler to judge a party or candidate based on what has already been done than on what will be done. Prospective judgments require learning what the two presidential candidates say they will do on various issues if elected, and then comparing the candidates' positions with one's own. Retrospective voting, on the other hand, simply requires the voter to observe the results of the incumbent candidate's policies. As noted, voters tend to make retrospective judgments on the basis of "big" issues—for example, the state of the national economy; whether the

prospective voting
voting style in which voters judge a candidate based on their assessment of what the candidate will do in office if elected.

retrospective voting
voting style in which voters judge candidates based on the performance of the candidates or their parties rather than issue stands and assessments of what each candidate would do if elected.

valence issues
issues on which virtually everyone agrees.

country is at peace or at war; and if the latter, whether that war is being executed successfully.

DEVELOPING POSITIONS AND MAKING VOTING DECISIONS Some issues are relatively easy for voters to develop opinions on—and therefore to incorporate into their voting decisions—whereas others are much more technical and complex. For example, compare and contrast two issues: same-sex marriage and policy options in Afghanistan. With respect to the same-sex marriage issue, there are only two options: for or against. Developing a well-informed position on this issue might require nothing more than thinking through one's own existing beliefs and values. With respect to the Afghanistan situation, however, there are a number of policy options to consider:

- Maintain the status quo.
- Withdraw troops immediately.
- Withdraw troops over time while attempting to prevent the Taliban from taking over.
- Allow the army and police force to develop a new Afghan government.
- Use American dollars to develop infrastructure and technology within Afghanistan.
- Attempt to disrupt Afghanistan's alignment with Iran.
- Some combination of these steps.

Although many Americans have opinions, developing a well-informed position on the appropriate Afghanistan policy means thoroughly considering all these options and their potential costs and benefits. That requires analytical expertise beyond the reach of the vast majority of Americans. In general, one should expect a greater incidence of issue voting on issues that are relatively easy for the mass electorate to consider.[28]

Perhaps the "easiest" issues of all are so-called **valence issues**—issues on which virtually everyone agrees. Almost all voters agree, for example, that less crime is better than more, that peace is better than war, and that lower unemployment is better than higher unemployment. On these issues, most voters do not have conflicting preferences. However, voters do have distinct beliefs about which party is better able to deliver on such valence issues.[29] One voter might believe, for example, that the Democratic Party is more likely than the Republican Party to help achieve low unemployment. Another voter might believe precisely the opposite.

When this occurs, it does not necessarily mean that voters can explain why or how one party would do a better job managing the issue than the other, or what the voters themselves would like to see done on that issue. In fact, many voters would be unable to offer any such explanation. It does mean, though, that voters are engaged in issue voting of a sort. They care about a particular set of issues, and they will vote for the party that they believe would be more capable of addressing those issues. In 2012, jobs and the economy were clearly the valence issues.

Beyond these generalities, it is difficult to draw conclusions about when and why a particular issue will affect a given election outcome. This obstacle does not stop journalists, campaign consultants, and even political scientists from claiming that a specific issue—say, abortion, gun control, or "moral values"—influenced or even determined an election. When assessing such claims, keep in mind the prerequisites for issue voting identified earlier. When these circumstances do not hold, or when their applicability is open to debate, then any talk about issue voting is just that—talk.

☐ Voters Appraise Candidates in Three Big Ways

A final factor that many political scientists believe influences individual vote choice is candidate evaluation. This term does not refer to which candidate has the most winning smile, the most engaging wit, or the most photogenic family. Although democratic theorists worry that such superficial characteristics may influence the vote, very little research supports this. Rather, candidate evaluation includes how voters characterize candidate ideology and perceive their personality and policies. Examples of how voters evaluate candidates can include the following:

- Making open-ended comments about aspects they like and dislike about specific candidates.[30]
- Assessing whether particular presidential candidates have "the kind of personality a president ought to have."[31]
- Rating a presidential candidate with a "feeling thermometer" in which voters rate how they relate to a candidate on a scale of zero to 100. A zero rating might mean the candidate seems "very cold or unfavorable," and 100 may mean he or she is "very warm or favorable."[32]

Despite many studies regarding the effects of candidate evaluations on vote choice—some large, some very modest—there is no consensus on the best ways to measure candidate evaluations, or on the relative importance of candidate evaluations among other factors that influence the vote. Even so, it is reasonable to consider candidate evaluations, along with party ID and issue voting, as one of the "big three" determinants of vote choice.

Party Identification, Issues, and Candidate Appraisals Come Together to Produce a Vote Choice

How exactly do these three elements combine to produce an individual vote decision? This is a difficult question to answer. First, individual decision making inevitably includes elements of random, idiosyncratic behavior that are hard to identify and describe—even for voters themselves. Second, the three elements of voter choice interact in complex ways. Party identification (ID) can affect candidate evaluations, which in turn can affect a voter's thinking about the candidate's issue positions. Other things being equal, a Republican voter is more likely to evaluate a Republican candidate favorably and then to project his preferred issue positions onto that candidate. For example, "I like everything about Mitt Romney; I'm sure I agree with him on most of the important issues." The reverse is true as well—the voter's understanding of the candidate's issue positions can affect her evaluation of the candidate.

Despite the complexity of these interactions and the degree of randomness inherent in human decision making, a good, general rule that describes most presidential voting behavior might be the following:

> The voter canvasses his likes and dislikes of the two candidates involved in the election. He then votes for the candidate for whom he has the greatest net number of favorable attitudes. If no candidate has such an advantage, the voter votes consistently with his partisan affiliation, if he has one.[33]

One can test the accuracy of this rule by generating vote predictions from it using voter survey data. This basic rule, relying on candidate evaluation and party ID, can generate a correct prediction nearly 85 to 90 percent of the time (depending on the election). Thus, it would seem to be a good approximation of the way that voters actually arrive at a final decision.

You may have noticed, however, that the rule includes only two of the big three vote determinants: candidate evaluations and party ID. What about voter issue positions? Issue positions influence the vote by way of candidate evaluations. Specifically, the voter's assessment of candidates' issue positions affects the voter's candidate evaluation, which in turn affects the vote. Not surprisingly, party ID also affects voter evaluations of candidates. Because of these relationships, party ID influences the vote through candidate evaluation, and not just as a tiebreaker,

8.1

8.2

8.3

8.4

8.5

8.6

as the rule would seem to indicate. Finally, party ID also affects voter issue positions, which may indirectly affect the vote.[34]

Who Gets Heard? Does It Matter?

8.6 Assess whether political participation impacts governmental decisions.

In addition to the factors that influence how people decide to vote, other factors make certain types of people more likely to care about voting and actually show up on Election Day. These factors highlight an important and disconcerting fact of American political life: Participation in the political process is not equal among American citizens. As we well know, income, education, political attitudes, and opportunities for mobilization are not uniformly distributed across the demographic spectrum. Men and women; young and old; black, white, Hispanic, and Asian; wealthy and poor; and Republicans and Democrats all differ among the factors that help determine participation. The result is that these groups participate in American politics to very different degrees.

Political Participation Differs Considerably Across Demographic Categories

Consider the different rates of participation according to race (see Figure 8.6). Whites tend to participate to a greater extent than both blacks and Latinos, except in campaign work, protests, and community activity. Latinos, on the other hand, are not the most involved group in any of the activities indicated in the figure. Although they are as likely as whites to serve as board members, in all other categories they show the lowest rates of participation among the three groups.

Expanding this analysis to other demographic categories makes it clear that people who participate in American politics tend to be whiter, older, wealthier, better educated, more likely male, and more conservative than the populace at large. This fact has led some observers to complain that the American political system does not live up to its ideals—for example, that all have an equal say in

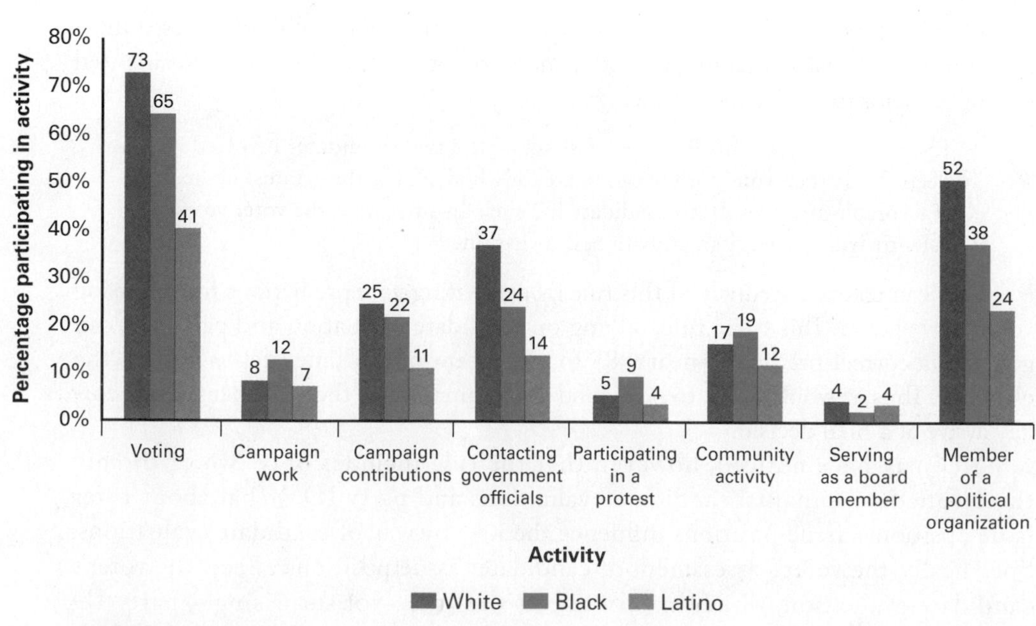

FIGURE 8.6 PARTICIPATION IN POLITICAL ACTIVITY BY RACE.

TABLE 8.3 THE OPINIONS OF BLACK AND WHITE AMERICANS DIFFER SIGNIFICANTLY ON IMPORTANT ISSUES

Issue	Whites	Blacks	Difference
Government should make every effort to improve the economic and social condition of blacks and other minorities	17%	47%	30%
Due to past discrimination blacks should be given preferences in hiring and promotion	11%	44%	33%
Affirmative action programs needed "as long as there are no rigid quotas"	43%	79%	36%
Government should provide more services and increase spending	47%	65%	18%
Government should guarantee food and shelter	62%	80%	18%
Favor death penalty for those convicted of murder	77%	45%	32%
War in Iraq was not worth fighting	38%	74%	36%
Government collects too much information about people like me	54%	74%	20%

Source: Robert S. Erikson and Kent L. Tedin, *American Public Opinion* (New York: Pearson Education, 2005), 201–3.

government—and that it caters disproportionately to the needs and demands of only a portion of the population.

Considering broad demographic categories, some of those needs and demands would appear to differ significantly from one group to the next. Table 8.3 compares opinions between whites and blacks on a variety of policy issues. The opinion difference between the groups in each issue area is substantial—between 18 and 36 percentage points. But if blacks are underrepresented in the political process and whites are overrepresented, that can affect what opinions policy makers hear the most.

Political participation also differs considerably according to another demographic category: age (see Table 8.4). Note substantial differences in the opinions of Americans under age 30 and those 55 and older. In all political activities, seniors participate at significantly higher rates than younger cohorts. And for virtually every issue,

TABLE 8.4 YOUNGER AND OLDER AMERICANS HAVE DIFFERING ATTITUDES ON VARIOUS ISSUES

Issue	Under 30	55 and over	Difference
Favor the U.S government paying for all necessary medical care for all Americans	59.7%	40.4%	19.3%
Government should provide more services than it does now	43.6%	34.4%	9.2%
Favor allowing Social Security funds invested in stock market	35.6%	23.8%	11.8%
Allow same-sex marriage	59.5%	21.8%	37.7%
By law, a woman should always be able to obtain an abortion	46.3%	29.9%	16.4%
Favor cutting the deficit by spending less on the military	47.6%	31%	16.6%
War in Iraq was not worth the cost	80.2%	74.2%	6%
Liberal	28.3%	16.7%	11.6%
Moderate	20.8%	21.8%	1%
Conservative	23.8%	37.5%	13.7%

Source: Authors' analysis of 2008 American National Election Study, http:www.electionstudies.org.

older Americans support the more conservative position. In the most extreme example, older Americans oppose same-sex marriage at a rate nearly 38 percentage points higher than their younger counterparts.

We could expand this analysis to other groups—the working class and the upper class, different religious groups, and so on. It would likely become obvious that different demographic groups sometimes hold very different opinions on policy issues. This fact, combined with varying rates of political participation, raises the concern that not all voices and positions get the hearing they deserve in America.

If Demographic Groups Participated in Proportion to Their Percentage in the Population, Collective Opinion Would Change Little

Some researchers have attempted to determine the message policy makers would hear from the American public if various demographic groups participated in politics in proportion to their percentage of the population. They have analyzed, for example, whether policy makers would get a different message if African Americans, who constitute approximately 12 percent of the population, also constituted 12 percent of the individuals engaged in various forms of political participation. Researchers have extended this analysis to all major population groups and compared opinions of people who actually participate in politics with those of people who would participate if all groups participated at rates equal to their population percentages.

According to researchers, this hypothetical public holds only a mildly more liberal set of beliefs than the actual participating public. But how can this be true, given the very sharp differences in opinion shown earlier? In general, the groups that tend to be most underrepresented also tend to be small. African Americans and the poor, for example, each constitute no more than about one-seventh of the American public. Thus, even if they participated at full strength, it would be hard for them to change collective opinion considerably. However, they certainly could gain influence at the margin in some competitive congressional districts and states.

Other groups, such as women, are underrepresented as well. However, their opinions tend to align more closely with the groups that are overrepresented. Again, even if women were to participate in politics at rates equivalent to their population percentages, they would not dramatically change opinion.

The most persuasive critique of this conclusion comes from those who argue that comparing responses to survey questions from political participants and nonparticipants is not the best approach. After all, one does not write a letter to a public official simply requesting "more services and increased spending," which would be a typical survey question. Usually, an individual's interests in policy are highly specific. When it comes to these more specific policy preferences, the distortion created by underrepresentation of some groups may be far more significant than the survey data indicate.

Another difficulty with opinion comparisons based on surveys is that they fail to indicate the different issue agendas that various groups might bring before government. Imagine that the wealthy and the poor had precisely the same opinions on school voucher programs—programs that provide government funds for parents to send their children to private schools. Such agreement might provide some comfort to those who worry that the poor are underrepresented in politics and the wealthy overrepresented. But imagine further that a federal voucher program is the number-one priority for the poor and at the bottom of the list for the wealthy. The wealthy are unlikely to bring this issue to the attention of policy makers, whereas the poor would do so if they were actively participating. In politics, as we discuss in chapters on public opinion and interest groups, who controls the agenda is a vitally important question.

"HOOVERVILLE"

Shantytowns of the 1930s were called Hoovervilles by those frustrated and disappointed with President Hoover's involvement with the relief effort for the Great Depression.

☐ Does Participation Matter?

This discussion about differential participation rates is entirely academic if participation does not influence the decisions that policy makers make. Does participation matter? Considered at the level of the individual, it would be hard to argue that participation matters much. As noted, the impact of an individual's participation in politics is minimal. Someone engaging in a one-person protest outside the offices of a business guilty of polluting the environment, or at a clinic that provides free contraceptives, or at a school that does a poor job educating its students would be fighting a lonely battle. Being the one-hundred-thousandth marcher in a demonstration will not materially affect its impact. We would expect these behaviors to have no impact. This is part of the paradox of participation.

Yet the collective actions of individuals, whether coordinated or not, clearly do have an impact on political outcomes. In the 1932 presidential election, for example, a surge in voter turnout ousted the conservative Herbert Hoover and swept in the progressive New York governor, Franklin D. Roosevelt. This vote was largely a response to the dire economic conditions gripping the country in 1932, the height of the Great Depression. The coalition that came together to support Roosevelt dramatically changed the shape of American public policy in ways that continue to affect the country today through programs such as Social Security, welfare, unemployment compensation, housing assistance, and labor union protections.

grassroots lobbying
efforts to persuade citizens to contact their elected officials regarding a particular issue or piece of legislation.

Perhaps a less momentous, but equally dramatic, result of participation can be seen in the presidential election of 2000. The result in Florida, and therefore the outcome of the presidential election, came down to slightly more than 500 votes. If a relative handful of people had voted differently that day, or decided not to vote at all, the result of the election—and perhaps of American history—would have been different. Furthermore, the voting behavior of those few hundred people may have been influenced by others' participation—mobilizing them to vote, for example, or to vote one way rather than the other. Although in 2004, the margin was more decisive, the presidential election again came down to one state, and George W. Bush won Ohio and the presidency by a little more than 120,000 votes. Again, the impact of citizen participation in the election was unmistakable and decisive. In 2006, the Democrats took control of the Senate by narrow victories in two states, Virginia (where Democrat James Webb won by about 9,000 votes) and Montana (where Democrat Jon Tester won by 3,500 votes).

The impact of voter participation is also apparent from the election-year activities of political parties and organized interests. For example, the Democratic and Republican Parties, as well as their interest-group allies, spent hundreds of millions of dollars on voter mobilization efforts in the 2012 election. The parties and the groups that support them obviously believe that who shows up on Election Day, and how they vote when they show up, can determine an election outcome. Otherwise, why invest such significant resources in get-out-the-vote efforts?

Measuring the impact of nonvoting forms of participation, such as contacting elected officials or joining a protest, is more difficult. The evidence concerning the impact of such participation is often less systematic. That does not necessarily make it less persuasive, however. For example, we know that the Clinton health care plan went down in defeat in 1994. We also know that in the battle leading up to that defeat, opponents of the Clinton plan were much more likely than supporters to contact Congress. Moreover, many of those active in the fight over Clinton's plan believed that this **grassroots lobbying** was decisive. One key architect of President Clinton's health care policy claimed, "the most effective tactic against our program was grassroots lobbying and phone banks in selected districts."[35] With this in mind, the Obama administration and the Democratic National Committee orchestrated huge efforts to get constituents to contact members of Congress in the days leading up to the final health care vote in Congress in spring 2010.

If grassroots mobilization and phone banks—selectively used—are not effective tactics, then the tens of millions of dollars that interest groups spent on those tactics did not work. More broadly speaking, if nonelectoral forms of political participation do not matter, we have to ask why millions of individuals and organized interests spend countless dollars and hours participating in politics, and why political insiders routinely report that these nonelectoral forms of participation do have an impact. Either participation matters, or those who act as if it matters and those who report that it matters are simply fooling themselves. We can find examples, of course, in which the impact of nonvoting forms of participation is undisputed.

Two Key Examples Demonstrate How Much Participation Matters

Extension of the franchise to women and minorities is a relatively new development in the United States. Women were not guaranteed a constitutionally protected right to vote until 1920. And in 1963, there were essentially no federal protections for the voting rights of African Americans. The women's suffrage movement and the civil rights movement worked to enfranchise women and minorities and, in the process, demonstrated that participation matters.

THE WOMEN'S SUFFRAGE MOVEMENT The women's suffrage movement was launched with a convention at Seneca Falls, New York, in 1848, and it took roughly 70 years for the movement to achieve its goal of enfranchising women. In the second half of the nineteenth century, women volunteered in the antislavery movement, the temperance movement (advocating the abolition of liquor), the settlement house movement (which provided educational, health, and cultural programs for the urban poor), and assorted organizations promoting better working conditions for women and children. In the course of this work, they came to see the franchise as indispensable in promoting their concerns on a broader scale.

In 1869, therefore, leaders founded two organizations promoting women's suffrage: the National Woman Suffrage Association (NWSA) and the American Woman Suffrage Association (AWSA). After two decades of pursuing separate agendas, the groups merged in 1890. The new organization was named the National American Woman Suffrage Association (NAWSA). Its leader was Susan B. Anthony.

Women who worked for causes such as prohibition; abolition of slavery; and improved living and working conditions for the poor, women, and children brought their skills and relationships to the suffrage movement. Women's participation in social clubs also strengthened their ties to other women and helped create an organizational base for the movement. As the suffrage movement grew in size and success by securing the franchise at the state level, other women's groups joined the cause. These included the General Federation of Women's Clubs and assorted professional organizations. Eventually, both the size of the movement and its success in securing the franchise at the state level created an irresistible momentum for a constitutional amendment guaranteeing women the right to vote. Congress proposed that amendment in 1919, and it was ratified by the required 36 states in 1920.[36]

SUFFRAGISTS MAKE HISTORY

This poster promotes a rally in support of giving women the right to vote. In 1920, the Nineteenth Amendment granted all American women the right to vote.

THE CONGRESSIONAL BLACK CAUCUS

The Congressional Black Caucus was established by African American members of Congress in 1971 to "positively influence the course of events pertinent to African Americans and others of similar experience and situation [and] achieve greater equity for persons of African descent in the design and content of domestic and international programs and services."

THE CIVIL RIGHTS MOVEMENT The story of the civil rights movement is similar in many respects to the women's suffrage movement. In 1963, no federal voting rights protections existed for African Americans. As a result, there was not a single African American member of the House of Representatives from the South, and only a handful of state and local officials such as mayor or sheriff. In Birmingham, Alabama, thousands of protesters hit the streets.

By the year 2010, thanks to civil rights legislation and court decisions protecting the voting rights of African Americans, 41 members of the U.S. House of Representatives were African American, and thousands were elected to serve at the state and local levels. Although African Americans have been disproportionately underrepresented in the Senate, they have been crucial in electing Democratic governors and senators throughout the South. And in the 2008 election, Florida, North Carolina, and Virginia went to Barack Obama. The civil rights movement, a form of mass, nonelectoral participation, created irresistible pressure on policy makers to guarantee voting rights to African Americans. With those voting rights in place, African Americans had a major impact on the American political landscape.

Finally, participation also matters in a broader sense than the outcomes it produces on a particular issue. The health of representative democracy demands that citizens choose their leaders, monitor their work, and provide feedback both at the ballot box and through nonelectoral forms of participation. This is how Americans should act as responsible stewards of democratic government. Furthermore, the act of citizen participation can be beneficial to the individual citizen. It can provide skills, experience, knowledge, and a sense of efficacy that will enable individuals to play a more active, constructive role in the workplace, the church, and the community—or even in politics.

Review the Chapter

Listen to Chapter 8 on MyPoliSciLab

The Costs and Benefits of Political Participation

8.1 Explain the costs and benefits of political participation for individuals and groups, p. 255.

People analyze the costs and benefits of voting in any particular election and decide whether or not to vote based on these perceived costs and benefits. For example, the costs of voting can include the time and effort required to participate, such as determining how to register to vote, updating registration, traveling to a polling place, waiting in line to cast a ballot, and learning enough about the candidates and issues to make an informed choice. Benefits may include electing a preferred candidate, which in turn results in the policies the voter supports being adopted. Citizens compare these costs and benefits and make a determination about whether voting, specifically, or participation, in general, is worth it.

The Paradox of Political Participation

8.2 Define the paradox of participation, and describe the different kinds of political activities in which Americans participate, p. 257.

Many Americans vote even though a rational analysis suggests they will not—this is the paradox of participation. As the incremental benefit of participation is often quite small, a confusing situation arises in which the costs often seem to outweigh the benefits of participation. Yet, millions of people vote in elections and participate in politics in some capacity or another. Citizens can participate in politics in America in many ways. Although voting is the type of participation that first comes to mind, signing petitions, attending demonstrations, organizing community meetings, joining political membership organizations, volunteering for political campaigns, and contacting elected officials are examples of other sorts of political activities. Although Americans tend to vote at lower rates than citizens in other countries, they also engage in these other activities at higher rates.

Factors That Influence Participation

8.3 Outline the main factors that influence political participation, p. 263.

Personal factors, legal factors, the political environment, and mobilization efforts are key elements that influence political participation. By a wide margin, the most important personal factor influencing political participation is socioeconomic status. The civic skills SES implies make the costs of political participation seem lower, and levels of political efficacy are generally higher for those with higher socioeconomic status. Legal factors, like poll taxes and literacy tests, also play an important role in participation decisions. The twentieth century brought an end to a number of legal barriers that prevented women and African Americans from voting. The competitiveness of a race and the efficacy of mobilization efforts also affect participation: the more competitive the race and the more effective the mobilization, the higher the levels of political participation.

Comparative and Historical Puzzles of Voter Turnout

8.4 Analyze voter turnout from comparative and historical perspectives, p. 270.

There are many comparative and historical puzzles of political participation. One comparative puzzle is the fact that America's voter turnout lags far behind that of other democracies. Reasons may include America's personal registration requirement, which makes it inconvenient for citizens to register to vote. Other factors may include voter fatigue (as a result of the relative frequency of American elections), plurality decisions, and the two-party system. Nevertheless, the United States has high levels of nonvoting political participation relative to other advanced democracies. Historically, the United States is in a puzzling situation: Both the costs and levels of participation in the United States have decreased with time. Participation should increase as costs decrease, but other reasons, including younger eligible voters, decreases in political trust and efficacy, and ineffective mobilization, may explain the puzzle.

Understanding Individual Vote Choice

8.5 Describe the key factors that determine how voters make electoral choices, p. 275.

Partisanship is the predominant force in determining most other political attitudes and behaviors—including voting. There are two components to an individual's partisan attachment: direction and strength. Nevertheless, partisans sometimes do switch sides and identify with the other party, particularly when extraordinary political events upset existing political arrangements. In addition, issue and policy preferences have a complex and uncertain impact on voter choice. Voters can switch parties if they agree with a different party on an issue that is very important to them, and if they believe the other party better represents their views. Issue voting can also be retrospective. If a party performs well on issues a voter cares about, the voter will reward that party with a vote. Voters also vote for the party they believe will perform the best on valence issues. Finally, voters make decisions based on candidate evaluation, which is an intuitive sense of whether they like the candidate and think the candidate will do a good job.

Who Gets Heard? Does It Matter?

8.6 Assess whether political participation impacts governmental decisions, p. 282.

Questions of whether political participation matters and whether it affects the decisions of government are particularly important because participation in the political process is not equal across demographic groups. Whites, men, and upper-class individuals tend to have higher levels of participation than their counterparts in nearly every category. Ironically, however, if demographic groups participated in proportion to their percentage in the population, there would be little change in collective opinion. This would likely occur because underrepresented groups are either relatively small or have opinions similar to those of the overrepresented groups. Finally, although individual participation is unlikely to cause great change, political participation collectively can alter the American political landscape in vast and meaningful ways. The women's suffrage movement, the election of Franklin Roosevelt, and the civil rights movements are just a few such examples.

Learn the Terms

 **Study** and **Review** the **Flashcards**

Test Yourself

 **Study** and **Review** the **Practice Tests**

8.1 Explain the costs and benefits of political participation for individuals and groups.

Which of the following is a benefit associated with voting?

a. Registering to vote
b. Waiting in line to vote
c. Learning about different candidates and issues
d. Seeing a preferred candidate elected
e. Getting to a polling place

8.2 Define the paradox of participation, and describe the different kinds of political activities in which Americans participate.

What is the paradox of participation?

a. People do not participate in politics, even though the impact of their individual participation would matter a great deal.
b. People participate in politics, even though the impact of their individual participation would seem far too small to matter
c. People have only just begun to participate in politics in great numbers.
d. Political participation has continued to decline despite the growing interest in politics generated by the media.
e. There is no such thing as a paradox of participation.

8.3 Outline the main factors that influence political participation.

What is the most important personal factor influencing political participation?

a. Education
b. Income
c. Party identification
d. Race
e. Socioeconomic status

8.4 Analyze voter turnout from comparative and historical perspectives.

Which of the following is NOT a reason for America's low voting rate?

a. The way elections are conducted
b. Voter registration requirements
c. The proportional system of apportioning votes
d. The winner-take-all system of apportioning votes
e. America's two-party system

8.5 Describe the key factors that determine how voters make electoral choices.

Which of the following is a precondition that must exist for a voter to engage in issue voting?

- **a.** The voter must be aware of the issue and have an opinion concerning it.
- **b.** The issue must not be important to the voter.
- **c.** The voter must believe that no party or candidate represents his or her position well.
- **d.** The voter must believe that both parties represent his or her position well.
- **e.** The voter must like the personal characteristics of the candidate.

8.6 Assess whether political participation impacts governmental decisions.

Does participation by individuals matter?

- **a.** Never
- **b.** Only when it is considered at the level of the individual
- **c.** Always
- **d.** Sometimes when individuals act collectively
- **e.** Always when individuals act collectively

Explore Further

SUGGESTED READINGS BY TOP SCHOLARS

James Fowler. 2008. "Genetic Variation in Political Participation." *American Political Science Review*. 102:2. 233-249. Ethics are being shown to be powerful predictors of a wide range of behaviors, and political participation is no exception. Genetic studies will become increasingly important in studies of political participation.

Donald Green and Alan Gerber. 2008. *Get Out the Vote: How to Increase Voter Turnout*, 2nd ed. Washington, DC: Brookings Institution. Uses results from random experiments to identify the factors that influence participation and how these factors can be influenced to increase turnout.

D. Sunshine Hillygus and Todd Shields. 2008. *The Persuadable Voter: Wedge Issues in Presidential Campaigns*. Princeton, NJ: Princeton University Press. Looks at why strategists employ wedge issues such as abortion, gay marriage, and immigration in many political campaigns and what impact these issues have on swing voters.

Richard Lau and David Redlawsk. 2006. *How Voters Decide: Information Processing During Election Campaigns*. New York: Cambridge University Press. Uses experiments to test a number of different models of voter decision making and examines how voters make sense of all of the information that comes at them during a campaign.

Steve Rosenstone and Mark Hansen. 2002. *Mobilization, Participation, and Democracy in America*. New York: Longman Classics. Argues that people participate in voting based on the perceived costs and benefits of doing so and because politicians mobilize them, but that costs and benefits may depend on one's income, education, age, race, efficacy, and social networks.

SUGGESTED WEBSITES

The United States Elections Project: http://elections.gmu.edu/index.html

The United States Elections Project provides a wide variety of data on voter turnout in the United States. It has detailed tables on voter participation and the eligible electorate in each state for recent elections as well as data and commentary on early voting and other new trends. It also links to important scholarly articles on participation.

HuffPost Pollster: http://www.huffingtonpost.com/news/pollster/

One of the first sites to aggregate polling results, pollster.com is a great one-stop source for survey results around the country. In addition, it has constant commentary and analysis of polling trends and technical issues going on in the survey industry.

Real Clear Politics: http://www.realclearpolitics.com/

Real Clear Politics aggregates political analysis and commentary from a variety of sources. Its sister web sites also provide compilations of analysis and commentary on everything ranging from the stock market to sports.

Politico: http://www.politico.com/

Politico is a web based political media site that intensely covers politics and elections. Founded by former print reporters, its goal is to combine the original reporting and editorial quality of traditional media with the speed of the internet and the new media. It's daily "Playbook" compilation is an excellent way to get caught up and know what's coming down the pike every day.

ABC News: http://abcnews.go.com/Politics/Elections

Maps, vote totals and exit poll results are all accessible from this site run by ABC News. There are also links here to other ABC News political unit analysis and commentary of politics and elections.

The Wesleyan Media project: http://mediaproject.wesleyan.edu/

The Wesleyan Media Project gathers and codes data on political advertising. During the course of an election year, it releases its findings and is a great source for information on the single largest expenditure in modern elections—local television advertising.

Listen to Chapter 9 on MyPoliSciLab

Campaigns and Elections

THE PUZZLE OF THE 2000 ELECTION

When Americans woke up on the day after the 2000 election, they did not know who their next president would be. It was not until 36 days after Election Day that Democratic Vice President Al Gore conceded the election to Republican George W. Bush. That occurred only after a deeply divided Supreme Court denied Gore a statewide vote recount in Florida.

Following that election, some people had a lot of explaining to do. Television network executives had to explain why they first mistakenly called Florida for Gore, and then for Bush. Voting machine manufacturers and election officials had to explain the high number of uncountable ballots across the entire country, but especially in Florida. The Democratic election supervisor in Palm Beach County, Florida, had to explain the confusing ballot design, which caused many voters to choose independent candidate Pat Buchanan when they meant to choose Democrat Al Gore. Supreme Court justices had to explain their controversial ruling ending the Democrats' legal challenges. And Al Gore had to explain why he had not won the election in a landslide given his association with eight years of peace and prosperity under the Clinton administration.

Lost among these issues was another embarrassing fact—embarrassing at least for a panel of top political scientists. At an American Political Science Association conference prior to the election, this panel predicted that Gore would beat Bush. Panel members used an analytic method known for reliably predicting presidential election outcomes.[1] This panel also had some explaining to do.

Political scientists can use different types of analysis to predict election outcomes, but most share some basic characteristics. First, they assume that party identification determines individual vote choice. Citizens tend to identify with one of the two major political parties. When more

9.1 Outline election procedures, including how candidates are nominated and how winners are determined, p. 295.

9.2 Explain the key factors that determine the outcome of presidential elections, p. 306.

9.3 Analyze the methods candidates use to conduct election campaigns, p. 309.

9.4 Describe how election campaigns are funded, p. 316.

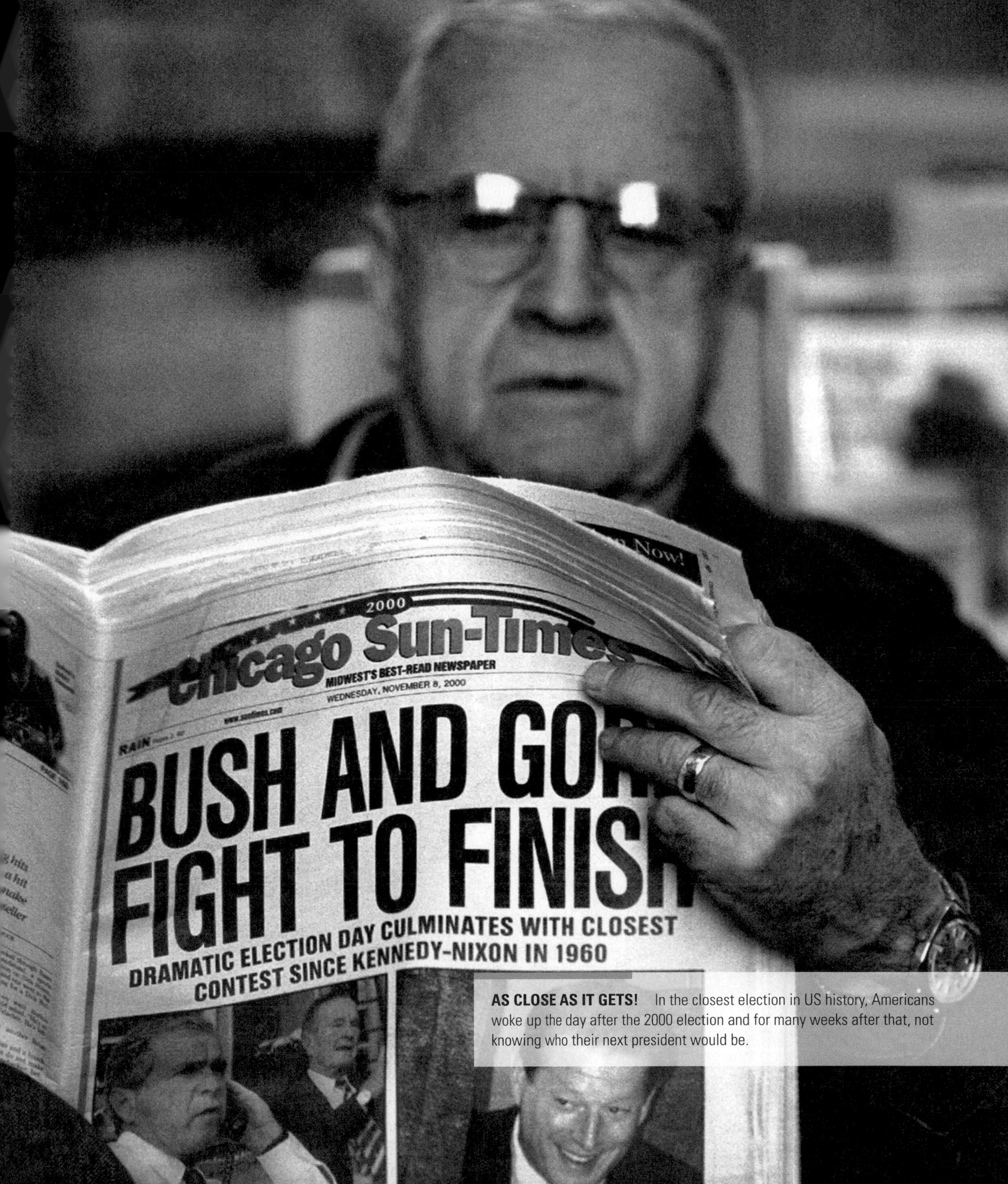

AS CLOSE AS IT GETS! In the closest election in US history, Americans woke up the day after the 2000 election and for many weeks after that, not knowing who their next president would be.

The Big Picture Find out how political scientists can predict the outcomes of elections without even analyzing the candidates. Author Kenneth M. Goldstein reveals the factors that really drive election decisions (hint: it isn't the amount of money a candidate spends on television commercials).

The Basics Do you have trouble figuring out when all the elections are and who you should vote for? If you do, you are not alone. This video will help you understand why the United States has so many types of elections, what purposes they serve, and whether money and campaign staff is vital to campaign victories.

Do you think money is important in electio

In Context Discover why voting and elections are essential to a democracy. In this video, Fordham University political scientist Costas Panagopolos discusses why voting is important in the United States. He also explains how electoral reforms have expanded the voting population throughout the years.

Think Like a Political Scientist Discover how scholars respond when voter turnout – even in presidential elections – declines, as it did during the last half of the twentieth century. Fordham University political scientist Costas Panagopolos explorers the research behind this issue, recent trends, and factors that may explain these outcomes.

In the Real World In its controversial Citizen's United decision, the Supreme Court ruled that money is speech and thus the courts cannot put a limit on the amount of money an individual—or a corporation—spends on an election. Real people decide whether or not they agree with that decision, and they consider some of its long-term implications.

So What? "Democrats vote for Democrats and Republicans vote for Republicans." Sound too simple? Author Kenneth M. Goldstein describes how television advertisements, the economy, and other variables can impact voters at the polls.

voters identify with one party, that party gets the advantage. In 2000 (as in 2008), more voters identified as Democrats. In 2010, more voters identified as Republicans.

Second, the models also assume that voters choose candidates using a retrospective perspective. This means they select a candidate based on what the candidate, or the candidate's party, achieved in the past, rather than by comparing what each candidate would do if elected.

The 2000 elections capped off nearly a decade of robust economic growth, presided over by a Democratic administration. Voters were happy with the Democrats, and political scientists expected the popular vote to reflect that satisfaction—so the results were surprising. In 2008, by contrast, voters were dissatisfied with the Bush administration and the sinking economy. They wanted something new. They chose Obama—less because of his good looks, inspiring personal story, and message of hope and change—and more because he was a Democrat. In all likelihood, any Democrat would have won the 2008 election. By 2010, voters held the Obama administration and the Democrats accountable for high unemployment and continued difficult economic times. The 2008 and 2010 elections show a causal relationship between how voters feel about a party and whether that party wins its next election. But what happened in 2000? In this chapter, we will examine the factors that determine the outcome of presidential elections. These include party identification and incumbent performance, as well as the nature of the candidates' campaigns, their issue positions, and voter assessments of them as individuals. We will also discuss the rules that structure and finance campaigns and elections.

The Basic Rules Governing American Elections

9.1 Outline election procedures, including how candidates are nominated and how winners are determined.

The rules governing elections shape the choices voters have on Election Day; they also shape how candidates run their election campaigns. For example, if we decided presidential elections on the basis of the popular vote rather than on who wins an Electoral College majority, presidential candidates would probably conduct their campaigns differently. Furthermore, the rules that govern U.S. elections differ from those in most other democracies around the world. Most parliamentary democracies, for example, employ a system known as proportional representation. In this system, each party's vote share determines the number of its seats in the legislative body. Therefore, a party whose candidate came in second place would still earn a significant number of seats in the legislature. In the United States, we use a winner-take-all approach, which means that the candidate who gets the most votes wins, whereas any other candidate loses and receives nothing.

delegates
individuals who represent a state's voters in the selection of a political party's presidential candidate.

A Candidate Running for President Seeks His or Her Party's Nomination Through Caucuses and Primaries

State ballots list one Democratic candidate for president, one Republican candidate, and one candidate for each House and Senate seat.[2] These are the candidates who receive their party's nomination. Candidates who run under the party label receive "built-in" support from the party's members in the electorate and may also receive substantial financial and logistical help from the state and national party organizations.

How does a candidate receive the nomination of his or her party? In the presidential race, a successful candidate needs to accumulate a majority of **delegates**—representatives of the voters—at the party's nominating convention in the summer before the November election. Candidates earn delegates' support primarily by competing in state primaries and caucuses. All of the primaries and caucuses for presidential elections are held during a five-month period of each election year—from late January or early February through

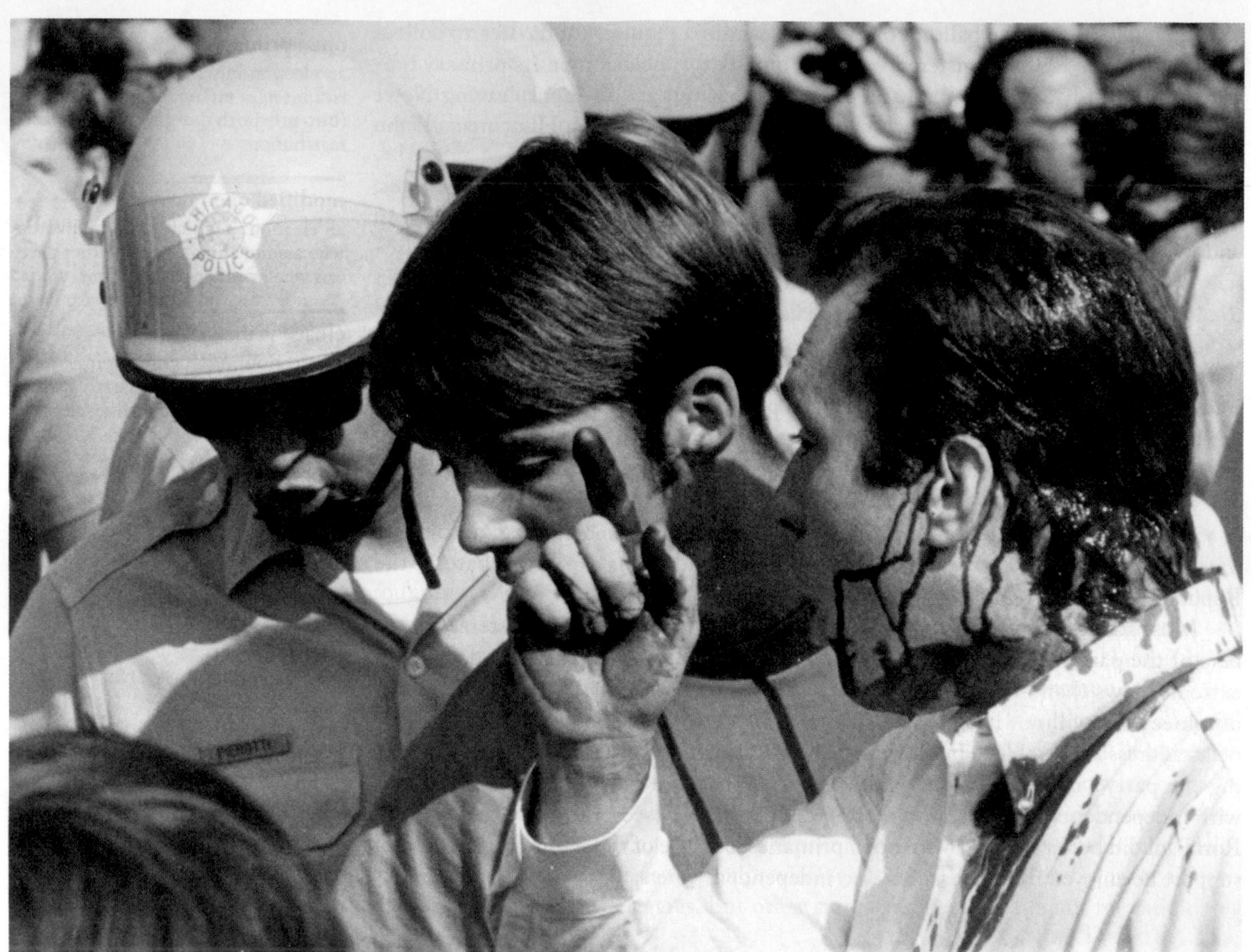

CHAOS AT THE CONVENTION

Police and protesters collide in the streets of Chicago following the Democratic convention of 1968.

Even though Humphrey had not campaigned in any of the Democratic primaries, party leaders supported his candidacy. Therefore, Humphrey arrived at the 1968 Democratic convention in Chicago with a sufficient number of delegates to win the nomination. Antiwar activists, including McCarthy and Kennedy supporters, opposed Humphrey's bid because they knew he would continue the current Vietnam policy. Their anger boiled over into the streets of Chicago. The rest of the country watched on live television the violent demonstrations and clashes between police and protesters. Ultimately, Humphrey lost a close election in November to Republican Richard Nixon; independent candidate George Wallace picked up 13 percent of the popular vote and 46 electoral votes.

DEMOCRATIC REFORMS To avoid a repetition of these events, the Democratic Party appointed a commission to study ways to give rank-and-file party members a greater voice in choosing the party's nominee. South Dakota Senator George McGovern, who became the Democratic Party's nominee for president in 1972, chaired the commission. The recommendations of the McGovern commission led to the system of delegate selection described earlier—one in which candidates accumulate delegates chiefly through primary and caucus votes, rather than through the backroom dealings of party leaders.

The Democratic reforms led to a proliferation of presidential primaries. In 1968, 17 states held Democratic primaries, and 16 held Republican primaries. By contrast, in 2008, 38 states held Democratic primaries, and 34 states held Republican primaries. In 2012, 38 states held Republican primaries. Caucuses determined the remaining delegates. Delegates whom voters choose in primaries and caucuses are dubbed

"How did you find out I was a superdelegate, Irene?"

THE SUPERPOWERS OF SUPER-DELEGATES

Super-delegates have the power to vote for whomever they choose at the Democratic convention. They often express their support for a particular candidate beforehand. Hillary Clinton and Barack Obama competed for the votes of these all-powerful few throughout the primary season.

"pledged delegates." They must vote for the candidate they pledged to support on the first ballot at the nominating convention.

SUPER-DELEGATES AND BROKERED CONVENTIONS One exception to the trend toward the increasing importance of primaries is the creation of "super-delegates." In the 1980s, the Democratic Party—though not the Republican Party—began to select a bloc of about one-fifth of its convention delegates outside the primary and caucus process. These super-delegates included the following:

- Members of the Democratic National Committee (DNC)
- Democratic members of the U.S. House and Senate
- Sitting Democratic governors
- Other distinguished Democratic party leaders, such as former presidents, vice presidents, and DNC chairs

Super-delegates may vote for whomever they choose at the convention, but they are typically expected to vote for the front-runner of the primary and caucus season. If a single candidate does not emerge with a majority of the delegates, however, there can be a "brokered convention," in which party leaders choose a candidate to carry their party's banner in the fall election. In a brokered convention, the party expects super-delegates to support the most electable candidate and encourage other convention delegates to follow their lead. Journalists, political scientists, and other political junkies like to entertain the possibility of a brokered convention, but it has never happened. However, in 2008, when Barack Obama had a lead but not a majority of pledged delegates, superdelegates actually decided the battle for the Democratic nomination. During the spring primary season, both Hillary Clinton and Obama fought hard to convince these Democratic Party leaders that they were the more deserving and more electable.

MORE PRIMARIES, EARLIER PRIMARIES In 1968, fewer than 10 percent of states held their primaries by the end of March. By contrast, in 2012, almost 75 percent of states held their primaries by then. Over the past 40 years, more states have held primaries and moved them earlier in the year. For example, New Hampshire held its primary on March 7 in 1972, but the primary was held on January 10 in 2012. Early primaries such as this one and the Iowa caucuses attract a lot of attention and campaign spending dollars. To take advantage of these benefits, other states have moved up their contests to earlier in the season.

The parties, however, discourage this tinkering. In 2006, the Democratic Party issued a ruling saying that only four states—New Hampshire, Iowa, Nevada, and South Carolina—could hold primaries before February 5, 2008. When Florida and Michigan moved up their primary days to January anyway, the Democratic Party penalized the two states by taking away their delegates.[5] Ironically, in 2008, primaries late in the season that few thought would matter—Ohio and Texas on March 3, Pennsylvania on April 22, and North Carolina and Indiana on May 7—became crucial and received immense attention from the campaigns and the media.

In 2012, Florida and Michigan moved their primaries up again, and New Hampshire, Arizona, and South Carolina joined them. The Republican Party penalized these states by cutting the number of their delegates in half.[6]

With a shorter primary calendar, many states now hold primaries on the same day. In the 1980s, Democrats in southern states sought to turn this situation to their advantage. They were concerned about what they considered to be the liberal tilt of the national Democratic Party and were eager to avoid a repeat of Walter Mondale's 49-state loss to Ronald Reagan in 1984. As a result, southern Democrats united to create a regional primary dubbed Super Tuesday. The first Super Tuesday primary was held on March 9, 1988. The results of that contest were mixed. The Reverend Jesse Jackson, Senator Al Gore, Governor Michael Dukakis, and Representative Richard Gephardt each won at least one state. Although the nomination went to Governor Dukakis, who represented the liberal wing of the Democratic Party, Super Tuesday also boosted the candidacy of moderate Democrat Al Gore. In the next Super Tuesday contest in 1992, Arkansas Governor Bill Clinton—the consummate Democratic centrist—swept the day's primaries and became unstoppable in his quest for the nomination.

□ Presidential Election Rules Are Complicated

Determining winners and losers in presidential elections is complicated. In the fall general election for president, the winner of the popular vote may or may not win the presidency. In 2000, for example, Al Gore won the national popular vote, but he lost the presidential election to George W. Bush. To win the presidency, a candidate must win a majority in the Electoral College—regardless of the popular vote total. Gore did not. A similar situation occurred in the highly controversial election of 1876. Despite winning the popular vote by more than 200,000 ballots, Samuel J. Tilden lost the Electoral College and the presidency to Rutherford B. Hayes by one vote, 185 to 184.

The decision to select the president via the Electoral College rather than by popular vote resulted from a compromise during the Constitutional Convention in Philadelphia in 1787. Delegates at the convention considered two options for selecting the president—popular vote and selection by members of the House of Representatives. Representatives of smaller states opposed the popular vote idea. They feared that larger states might overwhelm their smaller states' influence.[7] At the same time, some

Explore on MyPoliSciLab

Is the Electoral College Democratic?

In 2000, George W. Bush won the presidency despite the fact that over 500,000 more Americans voted for Al Gore. The result set off a renewed debate about the Electoral College's role in presidential elections. In the Electoral College, each state is assigned a number of "electors" equal to the total number of state senators and Congressional representatives. In most states, the winner of the state's popular vote takes all of the electoral votes. The candidate with the most *electoral votes* becomes president. In 2000, the presidential election came down to the state of Florida which Bush won by 537 popular votes.

The Electoral College Across the United States in 2000

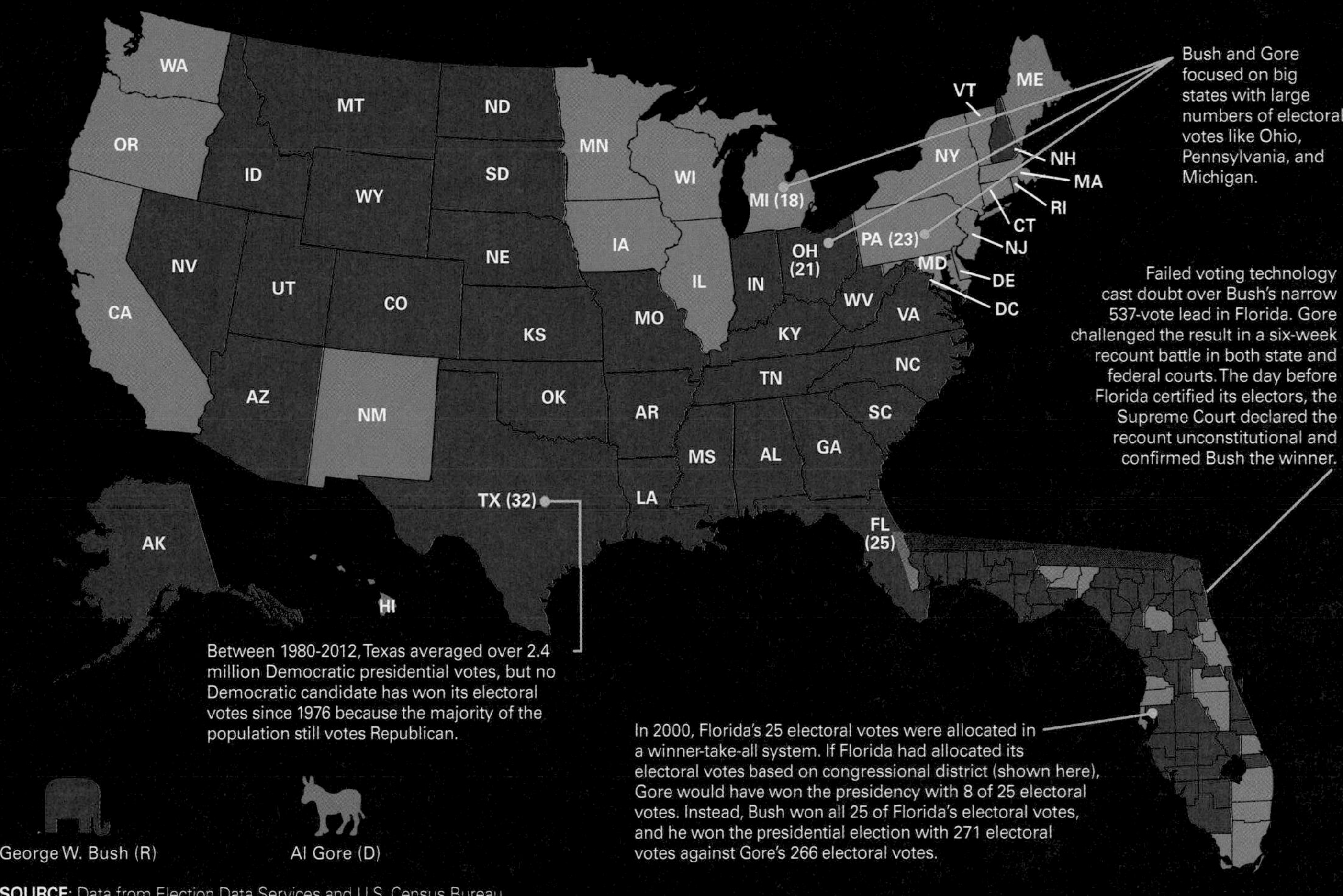

WA
OR
CA
ID
NV
MT
WY
UT
AZ
CO
NM
ND
SD
NE
KS
OK
TX (32)
MN
IA
MO
AR
LA
WI
IL
MS
MI (18)
IN
OH (21)
KY
TN
AL
GA
FL (25)
SC
NC
VA
WV
PA (23)
NY
VT
ME
NH
MA
RI
CT
NJ
DE
DC
MD
AK
HI
Bush and Gore focused on big states with large numbers of electoral votes like Ohio, Pennsylvania, and Michigan.
Failed voting technology cast doubt over Bush's narrow 537-vote lead in Florida. Gore challenged the result in a six-week recount battle in both state and federal courts. The day before Florida certified its electors, the Supreme Court declared the recount unconstitutional and confirmed Bush the winner.
Between 1980-2012, Texas averaged over 2.4 million Democratic presidential votes, but no Democratic candidate has won its electoral votes since 1976 because the majority of the population still votes Republican.
In 2000, Florida's 25 electoral votes were allocated in a winner-take-all system. If Florida had allocated its electoral votes based on congressional district (shown here), Gore would have won the presidency with 8 of 25 electoral votes. Instead, Bush won all 25 of Florida's electoral votes, and he won the presidential election with 271 electoral votes against Gore's 266 electoral votes.
George W. Bush (R)
Al Gore (D)

SOURCE: Data from Election Data Services and U.S. Census Bureau.

Investigate Further

Concept What is the difference between the popular vote and the Electoral College vote? The popular vote is an example of a direct democracy in which every citizen's vote makes a difference. If more people vote for one candidate, then that candidate becomes president. The Electoral College vote is an example of indirect democracy, in which the presidency is voted on by representatives.

Connection How do electoral votes lead to controversy? Using the Electoral College in winner-take-all elections makes candidates focus on large states with more electors. Winner-take-all allocations in large states can also result in millions of individual votes having no direct impact on the election outcome. People vote, but there is no chance of directly influencing the result if the majority of the population votes for the other candidate.

Cause How might the Electoral College be more democratic? Allocating electoral votes in winner-take-all systems silences minority voters. If more states were to allocate electoral votes via congressional district, political minorities would have a greater impact on the presidential race. In states like Florida, where hundreds of thousands of voters get no chance to contribute to their candidate's potential success, district voting would allow them some influence on the election.

Electoral College
the meeting, in each state and the District of Columbia, of electors who cast votes to elect the president.

convention members questioned whether the largely uneducated populace could make a wise choice for president. Others worried about logistical issues involved in holding a single nationwide election on a specific day.[8]

The other option—selection by the House of Representatives—also raised concerns. The biggest worry was that if the House put a president in office, the president might feel the need to side with the House on legislative issues, which could violate the sacred principles of separation of powers and checks and balances and lead to the very tyranny the new system was intended to prevent.[9]

The convention reached a compromise solution by creating the **Electoral College,** which addressed some of these concerns, albeit imperfectly. The compromise allowed citizens to vote for electors, or people who would then represent each state in the national election. Small states received disproportionately high representation in the Electoral College relative to their population. Each state received one elector for each member it sent to the House of Representatives and one for each of its two senators.

For those who worried about the capacity of the people to pick an appropriate president, the Electoral College offered an assembly of "wise men" who would choose

COUNTING ELECTORAL COLLEGE VOTES

It is the electoral votes of each state, awarded to the winner of a state and not the raw vote of the entire country that selects the president. The electors from each state meet to cast their ballots and then officially report their results to Congress for certification. Here, the results of the 2008 election are reported to Speaker of the House, Nancy Pelosi, and to Vice President Dick Cheney, in his role as President of the Senate.

a president more carefully than the masses. The electors from each state would meet in their respective states about a month after Election Day and vote for the presidential and vice presidential candidates of their choosing. If no candidate received a majority of the delegates' votes, then the House of Representatives would determine who would be the president.[10] We continue to use this system today. Many voters do not realize that during presidential elections, they actually cast their ballots for a party's slate of electors to the Electoral College and not directly for the president.

All states except Maine and Nebraska assign their electoral votes on a winner-take-all basis. In Maine and Nebraska, the winner of a state's popular vote receives two electoral votes. The remainder of the electoral votes is then allocated by congressional district, but the popular vote winner in each district receives one electoral vote. In 2008, Barack Obama won one of Nebraska's Electoral College votes.

The modern Electoral College consists of 538 electors, representing the 50 states and the District of Columbia. Each state's number of electors is equivalent to its combined number of House and Senate members. (The District of Columbia does not have voting representatives in the House or Senate, but it has three electors in the Electoral College.) In 2000, for example, Florida had 23 members in the House of Representatives and, like every other state, two senators for a total of 25 votes in the Electoral College. In the 2000 presidential election, George W. Bush earned 246 electoral votes, and Al Gore earned 266, not counting Florida. (One elector abstained in protest.) The winner of the Florida race would earn the 270 electoral votes needed to win a majority of the Electoral College and clinch the presidency. In 2004, John Kerry lost the national popular vote by 2.5 percentage points or about 3 million votes. But in Ohio, he lost to Bush by only 120,000 votes. If Kerry had won Ohio's 20 electoral votes, he would have won the presidency.

The evolution of the modern party system—dominated by two political parties, the Democrats and the Republicans—changed the Electoral College in a way America's founders never envisioned. Local political parties and the presidential campaigns now select the electors who will participate in the Electoral College vote. Selection is based not necessarily on wisdom or experience, but on service to the party, political contributions, and other demonstrations of party loyalty. Thus, the Electoral College no longer serves as a deliberative body, consisting of wise men and women who will choose the best-qualified candidate. Instead, electors are expected to vote for their party's nominee for the presidency—whether or not they believe that nominee is the best-qualified person. In fact, in most states, they are required to do so or they face a fine.

Congressional Election Rules Are Much More Straightforward

The processes for securing the nomination for a House or Senate seat and for determining a winner in the general election are much more straightforward than the processes for securing a presidential nomination. A congressional candidate must win the party's primary election to run as the party's candidate in the fall election. In state congressional primaries, the candidate who wins the most votes receives his or her party's nomination. This is in contrast to the lengthy and complex presidential primary process.

In the United States, parties have less control over who can run under their party label than do parties in other countries. In many countries, party leaders or party committees choose the nominees to run in the general election. In Great Britain, for example, when someone wants to run for Parliament under the Labour Party banner, a small committee of Labour Party leaders or members must approve that candidacy. In the United States, voters make the ultimate decision.

The 2010 elections are just one example of when the voters had more control over congressional candidates than the party. That year, the favorites of Republican Party leaders lost primaries in Colorado, Delaware, Kentucky, and Nevada. When

9.1

9.2

9.3

9.4

How Do We Know?

How Much Does Congressional Candidate Campaign Spending Affect Election Outcomes?

The Question

Running for Congress can be very expensive. The Federal Election Commission reported that Democratic and Republican candidates spent nearly $1.5 billion on congressional campaigns in 2010.[1] Critics claim that candidates often spend huge sums of money to buy their congressional seats. Political scientists want to know if claims like this are really true. How much does spending by congressional candidates—both incumbents and challengers—affect who wins elections? How do we know?

Why It Matters

Many worry that candidates rely too much on private donations to keep pace in a campaign and win election. Successful candidates may then feel obligated to agree with their financial supporters on political issues. One possible solution is to limit how much money candidates can spend on campaigns. But such a restriction could disadvantage one particular group of candidates—the challengers. Challengers rely on high campaign spending to level the playing field with incumbents who enter election season with certain advantages. The reelection rates of incumbent members are already sky high. So limiting campaign spending could make it even easier for incumbents to win reelections and reduce the competitiveness of congressional elections overall.

Investigating the Answer

One way to investigate how spending affects election outcomes is to determine whether candidates who spend more money than their opponents actually win. Most of the time, they do. In 2010, for example, House incumbents who won with more than 60 percent of the vote spent nearly 10 times more on their campaigns on average than did their challengers. Incumbents who won with less than 55 percent of the vote spent $1.50 for every $1 spent by challengers.[2] A clear correlation exists between the amount of campaign spending and the probability of an election victory. But a political scientist would ask whether that correlation reflects causation—that is, whether candidates who spend more win because they spend more. Can other variables affect the election result?

To determine the relative influence of different variables on election outcomes, political scientists build statistical models that measure the incumbent candidate's share of the two-party vote in the election. The purpose of this model is to determine how much campaign spending affects election outcomes relative to other variables. The two causes that together represent the campaign-spending variable are (1) the amount of money the incumbent candidate spent on the campaign and (2) the amount of money the challenger spent on the campaign. Other variables can include the party identification composition of the electorate, the challenger's political positions, and the incumbent candidate's past performance.

What have political scientists learned about the impact of campaign spending on election outcomes from these models? Challenger spending does appear to exert a large and consistent impact on election results. Other things being equal, when a challenger spends more money on an election campaign, he or she is likely to get a higher percentage of the vote. Unlike incumbents, challengers often begin the election cycle at a disadvantage. That is because they have little name recognition among voters and do not share any of the incumbent's advantages of office. Yet by spending large amounts of money during the campaign, challengers can raise their name recognition dramatically. They can buy some of the familiarity, respect, and goodwill that incumbent office holders get for free. Those benefits can then translate into votes for the challenger on Election Day.

These arguments make sense intuitively, and political science research supports them in most circumstances. For example, imagine that an incumbent is facing a very strong challenger—someone well known and well liked and who has either raised a significant amount of money or who already has a large personal fortune available to finance a campaign. This type of challenger will make the campaign competitive and likely result in a close election. When an incumbent expects an election to be close, he or she will usually raise and spend significant sums of money to fend off the challenge. If the incumbent faces an unknown challenger waging a largely symbolic campaign with little or no money to spend, the incumbent has every reason to expect an easy victory. Under those circumstances, he or she usually will raise and spend relatively little money. Incumbents often spend more on races that are close. Less spending frequently means the incumbent will have a greater margin of victory. This is somewhat counterintuitive; one might expect that when incumbents spend a lot of money, they should win big, and when they spend only a little money, the race will be close. This paradoxical result occurs, however, because the same factors—the challenger's strength, experience, and quality—influence how much money the incumbent spends and the closeness of the outcome on Election Day.

The Bottom Line

Clearly, campaign spending can influence the outcome of an election. A number of studies demonstrate that challenger spending is likely to matter more than incumbent spending, and that even incumbent spending can matter at the margin—which can make all the difference in a close election. In 2010, an unusually large number of races were decided by less than 2 percent, including the Senate races in Washington and Colorado. In addition, about 10 House races were too close to call even weeks after the election.

[1] "Stats at a Glance," OpenSecrets, http://www.opensecrets.org/overview/index.php.
[2] http://www.cfinst.org/pdf/federal/PostElec2010_Table4_.pdf.

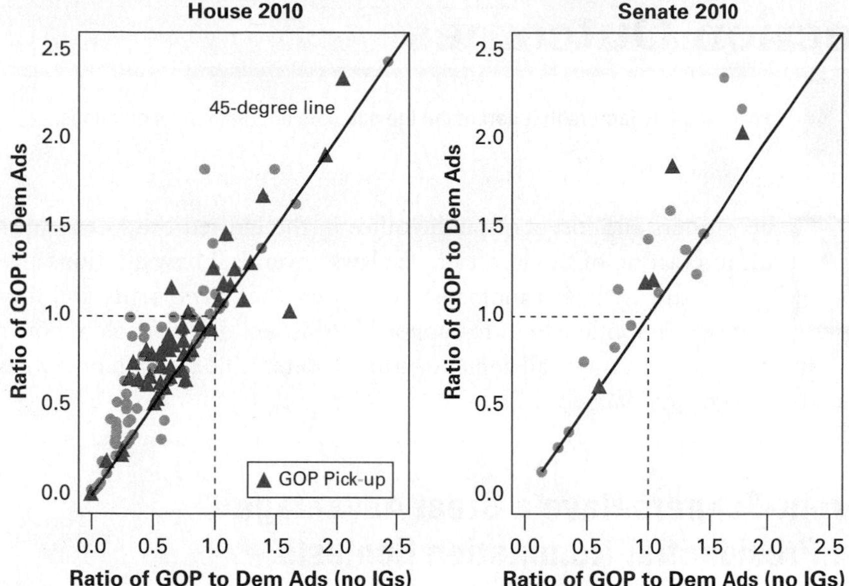

Spending by House Incumbents and Challengers, 2000–2010

Thinking Critically

- What kind of impact does the rise of campaign spending have on elections overall? In particular, do you see any problems with such a dramatic rise in campaign expenditures?
- Besides those mentioned in the previous paragraphs, what other factors may cause a rise in incumbent spending? In challenger spending?

---

three of the winning candidates in those primaries went on to lose in the general election, the Republican Party also lost three potential Senate seats. In addition, incumbent Republican senators from Alaska and Utah lost their renomination bids as well.

plurality rule
a candidate wins office by getting more votes than his or her opponent, even if that candidate does not receive an absolute majority of the votes.

Determining the winner in U.S. congressional elections is also easy; in most cases, winners are determined based on the plurality rule. The **plurality rule** means that the candidate who receives the most votes wins the office—even if that candidate does not receive an absolute majority. There are a few isolated exceptions to the plurality rule. Some elections have two rounds of voting: If no candidate receives a majority of the vote in the first round, the contest goes to a second round, or to a runoff election in which the top two candidates face off against each other. In 2008, for example, Georgia Senator Saxby Chambliss received 49 percent of the vote on Election Day, beating his Democratic opponent and a weak third-party challenger. Because Chambliss failed to get an absolute majority of the vote, he competed against the second place finisher—Democrat Jim Martin—in a runoff election. Chambliss won.

Those who oppose the winner-take-all format argue that proportional representation produces a legislature that more accurately represents the various opinions of voters. In the U.S. system, they argue, the winner-take-all format leads to two major parties rather than multiple parties. This can cause large groups of minorities to feel unrepresented in Congress. Supporters of the winner-take-all format argue that a two-party system avoids the factionalism caused by having competing parties in the legislature, as is the case in Israel or Italy. Also, in parliamentary systems, smaller parties often have to form coalitions after the election to create a governing majority. In the United States, by contrast, the major parties themselves represent coalitions.

Understanding Presidential Election Outcomes

9.2 Explain the key factors that determine the outcome of presidential elections.

invisible primary
the race to raise the most money and achieve front-runner status before the primary season begins.

momentum
the boost in media coverage, name recognition, fund-raising, and perceptions of electability that accompanies unexpected and repeated primary success.

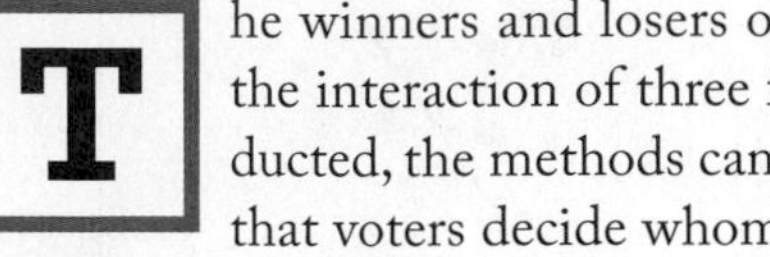

The winners and losers of public office in the United States emerge from the interaction of three factors: the laws governing how elections are conducted, the methods candidates use to wage their campaigns, and the ways that voters decide whom to support. In this section, we explore how rules, campaigns, and voters' decisions all come together to determine election outcomes and the leaders who govern us.

Front-Runners Have a Great Advantage in Presidential Nomination Contests

Even if political scientists do not understand all the ins and outs of voters' choices, they do understand the primary election process and how it produces a particular nominee. This understanding has changed significantly over the past generation.

THE PREPRIMARY SEASON A candidate hoping to win the party's nomination needs to prepare a competitive campaign strategy in multiple states before the primary season even begins. This includes raising substantial funds, earning front-runner status in preprimary polls, or preferably both. These milestones are part of what is called an **invisible primary.** Invisible primary winners almost always go on to win their party's nomination.

IMPORTANCE OF MOMENTUM IN PAST PRIMARIES Until the early 1980s, the key to understanding the primary process was one word: **momentum**—that is, media coverage, name recognition, fund-raising, and a public perception of electability. Forty years ago, there were fewer primary contests, and they were spaced far enough apart that even long-shot candidates had time to build a credible campaign over the course of a primary season. An early success in Iowa or New Hampshire gave candidates a coveted shot of momentum. They could convert this asset into a successful campaign in the next primary. Going forward, these benefits would keep on building. By exceeding expectations in an early caucus or primary, a long-shot candidate such as George McGovern in 1972, Jimmy Carter in 1976, and Barack Obama in 2008 could leverage the primary process itself to become a formidable candidate for the nomination.[11]

Today's crowded primary calendar leaves little time to raise money, organize local volunteers, attend campaign events, and develop and implement state-specific media strategies while the campaign is in progress. A candidate could work hard to win in just one or two early states and then build these wins into sustained success in later contests. But this strategy takes too long to work, as Rick Santorum demonstrated in the 2012 presidential campaign. Santorum campaigned vigorously in Iowa—inspiring blue-collar and Tea Party voters in public libraries and diners throughout the state. He picked up enough support to win the state, although narrowly, which helped make him a top rival for front-runner Mitt Romney. However, because the win was somewhat unexpected, his campaign was not sufficiently organized to capitalize on the Iowa momentum. Although Santorum won other primaries, his small team; comparatively low fund-raising; and inability to get on the ballot in many districts and some states, such as Virginia, eventually prevented him from overtaking Romney. He dropped out right before the primary in his home state of Pennsylvania, when it was unclear whether he had enough momentum left to win there.

EMERGENCE OF THE FRONT-RUNNER The preprimary period often creates a clear front-runner for the nomination, although in some cases this does not happen until late in the primary season. In 2012, for example, Mitt Romney was generally considered the front-runner, but he had stiff competition at different times from both Newt Gingrich and Rick Santorum. As in other years, the 2012 presidential primaries offered twists, surprises, tension, and drama among the candidates, although Romney ultimately prevailed. Why? As we have noted, the compressed primary calendar rewards candidates who can run a credible campaign in multiple states in a very short span of time. The candidate best equipped to do this is the one who has abundant resources and support in place before the primaries begin. When all is said and done, the candidate prepared to win from day one usually wins.

THE EMERGENCE OF A FRONT-RUNNER

Although it took longer than some media pundits had expected and than his campaign had hoped, Romney's lead in fundraising and in early polls suggested that he would emerge as the frontrunner and eventual GOP nominee in 2012.

Despite the relative accuracy of this claim, there is still something unsatisfying about it. Note that it says nothing about how or why a particular individual comes to win the invisible primary in the first place. The reason they have neglected this topic is that political scientists do not fully understand invisible primary dynamics—specifically, how one builds momentum in the preprimary period. They do know that early fund-raising success leads to favorable media coverage, which in turn leads to greater name recognition and a higher standing in the polls. All this can then lead to more successful fund-raising and so the cycle continues. But these relationships raise a critical question: Why are some candidates more successful than others at raising money?[12] And why do some candidates who raise large sums of money—such as businessman Steve Forbes in 1996 and 2000 or Mitt Romney in 2008—not succeed? Even if political scientists could answer these questions, they would still find it difficult to predict winners of the invisible primary. Those kinds of predictions, however, are the hallmark of good political science theory.

Beyond this gap in our understanding of the invisible primary, the evolution of the Internet as a political tool and communications medium has changed the way the primary process works. Candidates can now instantaneously raise and spend large sums of money. They can communicate inexpensively with voters round-the-clock through websites, Twitter, Facebook, and e-mail. The Web has also changed the news cycle significantly. Stories used to be updated once a day in the morning paper or on the evening news. Now, we have access to continuous online updates. Twenty-four-hour news channels and the proliferation of nationwide talk-radio programming also contribute to our constant access. Thus, candidates who need to raise money, communicate with millions of supporters, recruit volunteers, raise media awareness, and get their message out in a hurry now have tools that were not available to them even a few years ago. Eventually, these factors may change the existing primary season dynamic. But, for now, candidates who start behind almost always end behind.

Key Factors Allow Political Scientists to Accurately Forecast Presidential Election Results

In 2008, the American Political Science Association solicited election forecasts from nine teams of top scholars. These scholars completed their forecasts several months before the fall election. In six out of nine cases, they predicted that Barack Obama would be the new president. On average, the forecasters predicted that Obama would receive 52 percent of the two-party vote.[13] In actuality, Obama received just over 52 percent of the vote. In this instance, the forecasters were amazingly accurate, signifying the reliability and accuracy of these forecasting models.

FACTORS IN FORECASTING To predict presidential election outcomes, the political scientists' models generally take into account four factors:

- The partisan orientations of the electorate
- The job approval rating of the incumbent party president
- The performance of the economy during the first half of the election year
- Incumbency, that is, whether an incumbent president is running for reelection, and if so how long his party has held the presidency

These factors combined with partisan orientations are a critical influence on individual electoral choices. The incumbent president's job approval gives a rough sense of what retrospective judgments voters will make about the performance of the party in power, about voters' comfort level with that party's issue positions, and about their personal feelings toward the party's leader (the president). Whether or not the incumbent president is running for reelection, all of these factors can influence voters' evaluation of the party's candidate in the general election. The strength of the economy is the single most important issue to voters in election after election. When the economy is performing well, the party in power tends to win. The economy was doing well in 1996 and Bill Clinton easily won reelection. When the economy is not doing well, the party in power tends to lose. The economy was slowly coming out of recession in 1992, but George H. W. Bush lost the contest to serve another term. Finally, the incumbency factor shows that voters generally recognize the name of the president in power and feel more comfortable with him than with a lesser-known challenger. However, incumbency can operate in reverse; the longer the same party holds the presidency, the more likely the voters will become disenchanted with its candidates and policies and vote for a change.

From one election to the next, the factors that are most likely to sharply influence election outcomes are presidential approval ratings and economic performance. These factors help predict results before an election and explain results afterward. In presidential elections since 1952, we have seen that when the incumbent party's president has an average approval rating of 49 percent or better in April, May, and June of the election year, that party's candidate wins the general election. When approval is 46.7 percent or lower, the incumbent party's candidate loses.[14] Approval that falls in between these extremes is in a sort of limbo—an area of uncertainty. George W. Bush was dangerously near this place in 2004, barely achieving an approval rating of 49 percent during the second quarter of the election year. Predictions based on his approval rating showed that Bush was vulnerable, but with a slightly better chance of winning than losing.

Economic performance is another predictor. In election years between 1952 and 2008, when gross domestic product (GDP) grew at an annualized rate of at least 2.6 percent in the second quarter of the election year, the incumbent party won. When growth was 1.5 percent or less, the incumbent party lost. Growth rates in between are inconclusive. Richard Nixon, for example, saw 6.9 percent GDP growth in 1972 and won reelection overwhelmingly. Ronald Reagan and Bill Clinton benefited from growth rates of 6.5 percent and 3.7 percent, respectively, during their reelection years. Both were rewarded with a second term (see Figure 9.1).[15]

Party attachment in the electorate typically change at a snail's pace and were essentially even in 2000 and 2004. By 2008, however, the Democrats had a healthy advantage in party identification. Furthermore, with the economy in trouble and the war in Iraq moving into its fifth year, as well as presidential approval numbers in record low territory, all the fundamental factors seemed to be with the Democrats in 2008.

Still, although the Democrats enjoyed these advantages in 2008, Barack Obama was not guaranteed a win. The party still needed to convince so called swing voters, those voters without strong leanings toward either party. In 1980, the fundamental factors advantaged the Republicans, but it was not until late in the campaign that Ronald Reagan achieved enough credibility with key blocs of voters to win the election. In 2004, even with President Bush's approval level in a dangerous zone for an incumbent, John Kerry was not quite able to reach a threshold level of credibility with key swing

Economic Indicators and Presidential Outcomes

	1980	1984	1992	1996	2004	2012
Unemployment Rate (%)	7.18	7.51	7.49	5.41	5.53	8.3
GDP Growth (%)	−2.4	6.5	3.4	3.7	3.6	2.3
Consumer Confidence	87	105	66	110	93	69.2

FIGURE 9.1 ECONOMIC INDICATORS AND PRESIDENTIAL OUTCOMES
Basic gauges of the state of the economy and consumer sentiment are very strong predictors of whether an incumbent president is re-elected.

Source: Kantar Media.

voting blocs. In 2008, Barack Obama did reach that threshold level of credibility. He got the advantage of the factors giving any Democrat nominee the winning edge.

retrospective voting
voters judge candidates based on the performance of the candidates or their parties rather than issue stands and assessments of what each candidate would do if elected.

THE REWARD/PUNISHMENT EQUATION What all of these voting considerations suggest is that a basic way to understand election outcomes is through a "reward/punishment" or **retrospective voting** model, combined with the importance of partisanship. Every election year starts with the electorate divided into three camps: Republicans, Democrats, and independents. Some movement occurs among these groups during the year, but their proportions are expected to remain fairly stable. Naturally, the vast majority of strong partisans vote loyally. But some of the weaker partisans and most of the independents will likely decide by comparing candidates to the performance and leadership of the party in power. Based on the political scientists' predictive models, if voters are generally pleased with the incumbent party and its president—as indicated in presidential approval ratings—they will likely support the party's candidate for president. Likewise, if the economy performed well with the incumbent party in charge, voters will probably reward that party's candidate for president with a win.

If you are not a political scientist, you may think that these predictive models omit many important factors. In early 2012, for example, many Americans worried deeply about skyrocketing gas prices. In March, gas in some places cost more than $4.00 a gallon. Many voters blamed Obama for the increases. A *New York Times*/CBS News poll showed that 54 percent of respondents believed that presidents could control gas prices. Forecasting models take important voter concerns such as these into account through presidential approval ratings. Voter fears about gas prices showed in Obama's approval ratings, which dropped four points between February and March 2012 to hit a dangerously low 46 percent.[16]

Conducting Campaigns

9.3 Analyze the methods candidates use to conduct election campaigns.

Aside from predictions, a lot of work goes into determining election outcomes through campaigns. In the most recent presidential campaign, candidates, campaign organizations, and interest groups spent hundreds of millions of dollars on television advertising. The parties held national conventions, and the candidates participated in debates and made visits to key states such as Florida, Ohio, and Pennsylvania. Did all of this hard work matter? (See Unresolved Debate: Do Presidential Campaigns Matter?)

9.1

9.2

9.3

9.4

Unresolved Debate

Do Presidential campaigns matter?

In 2012, the most expensive campaign to date, candidates spent seven billion dollars with almost three billion dollars spent just on the presidential race. Various Republican outside groups were especially active assuming that the more resource they were able to put toward the campaign, the more likely it was that their favored candidates would win election. The Obama campaign got a lot of credit from pundits and analysts for running a smart campaign. But is an expensive, well-run campaign the secret to an election win? Do campaigns really impact who wins elections? Do presidential campaigns matter?

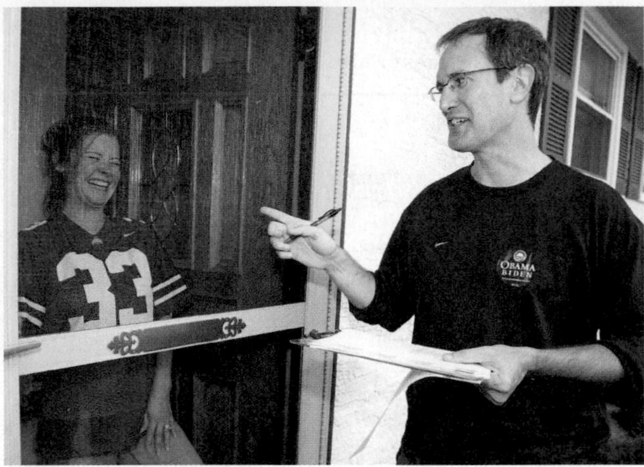

CAMPAIGNS MATTER AT THE MARGINS

Although it is hard to measure the impact of GOTV efforts, political scientists believe that campaigns matter for electoral outcomes.

YES

While other scholars accept that long standing party attachment and fundamental factors like the economy explain most of the variance when it comes to individual voting behavior and election outcomes, they argue that campaigns have the potential to play a small, but decisive role.

- Steven Finkel found that relatively few voters change their minds over the course of a campaign and that most votes can be explained by the state of the economy. Still even though he argued that relatively few voters can be or are influenced by campaigns, campaigns can matter at the margin and it is the margin that may matter in some important contests.[17] For example, even just a few percentage points—or a few hundred votes—can make a difference, as the 2000 election illustrated when a few hundred voters in Florida cost Al Gore the presidency. In 2002, Republicans gained a majority in Congress because they won by 20,000 votes in Missouri and another 20,000 votes in Minnesota. In 2004, the presidential election came down to which candidate took Ohio. George W. Bush won the state and the presidency. If John Kerry had earned more votes in that state, he would have been the president.
- Andrew Gelman and Gary King are also strong proponents of the notion that election outcomes are predictable from fundamental factors. Still, in their article that looks at why early polls are so unstable, they argue that campaigns play an important role in getting voters the needed information in order for them to vote in the ways political scientists would forecast. In other words, campaigns activate predisposition and absent a campaign that

NO

Many political scientists believe that campaigns have only a minimal effect on the outcome of elections. Political scientist Steven Rosenstone argued in 1983 that campaigns matter little and that the factors determining the election are in place long before people hear of the candidates or before the candidates face off in front of the cameras.[2] Rosenstone and others believe this is true for elections generally for a number of reasons:

- Campaigns cannot do much to change people's identification with a particular party. Republicans vote for Republicans and Democrats vote for Democrats. Independents end up somewhere in the middle. In addition, campaigns cannot control or change two factors that often influence elections: the state of the economy around Election Day and the current president's approval ratings.
- A winning candidate needs to have a competitive edge over his or her opponent. In general, presidential candidates run equally strong campaigns. They all participate in debates, raise campaign funds, and advertise in the media. According to political scientist James Campbell, running equally competitive campaigns puts candidates on "equal footing" and "narrows the gap between the candidates." So in the end, the campaigns cancel each other out and no one earns an advantage.
- In general, people who follow a presidential campaign are interested in politics. They are the ones watching the debates and reading the latest blog posts, and they are generally not undecided. Innovative campaign messages and tactics will not sway them.

provided information, voters would not behave in the ways we predict.[18]

- Also, even when all the fundamental factors are in their favor, candidates need to reach a certain threshold of credibility. So, in both 1980 and 2008, voters were predisposed to vote out the incumbent party and Ronald Reagan, in 1980, and Barack Obama, in 2008, went into the campaign with the wind at their backs. Still, they needed to convince voters they were up to the job and when they did, both contests swung decisively.

CONTRIBUTING TO THE DEBATE

Measuring the effectiveness of a campaign can be difficult. One way to find out if a campaign is effective is to ask people how and what they know about a candidate. But people often misreport their answers. For example, one study asked people where they obtain political information. Many said they read the *New York Times* or listen to National Public Radio. But these same respondents could not answer basic questions that anyone familiar with these outlets would know. Even if they were telling the truth about where they got their political information, these respondents did not absorb the political or campaign messages. Effective campaign messages must not only reach voters, they must also reach the right voters. The right voters have enough interest in the campaign to absorb the message—and act on it come Election Day.

WHAT DO YOU THINK?

1. Why are informed voters least likely to change their opinion?
2. Why is it difficult to measure the effect of campaign messages?

[1]2008 Campaign Costliest in U.S. History, http://www.politico.com/news/stories/1108/15283.html.
[2]Steven J. Rosenstone, *Forecasting Presidential Elections* (New Haven, CT: Yale University Press, 1983).

The short answer is yes; it did matter. Imagine a hypothetical election year in which one party built an election campaign, but the other party did not. One party held a national convention, ran television and radio advertisements, conducted a **direct mail** campaign, organized get-out-the-vote (GOTV) efforts in important states, showed up for the debates, and traveled around the country to motivate and mobilize local party activists. The other party did none of these things. Would it matter? Almost certainly. The party that ran a campaign could expect a higher turnout rate among partisans than the party that did nothing. The party that ran a campaign could expect more loyalty among its partisans—that is, fewer voter defections to the other party's candidate—than the party that did nothing. Finally, the party that ran a campaign could expect a higher vote among weak partisans and independents than the party that did nothing.

direct mail
political advertising in which messages are sent directly to potential voters in the form of mail or e-mail, rather than using a third-party medium.

In the real political world, though, both sides run active and aggressive campaigns, especially in competitive races. In that way, each party's efforts can offset those of the other. But the parties' and candidates' efforts are not always equally effective. In a close race, a particularly good campaign or a particularly inept one might make the difference between winning and losing.

What elements make a campaign successful? One is voter turnout. A successful campaign gets as many loyal voters as possible to show up on Election Day and vote for its candidate. It also persuades voters who identify with a different party to vote for its candidate. It wins over undecided voters. Another is messaging. A successful campaign crafts powerful messages and targets them to a wide range of voters. A third critical factor is advertising. Although GOTV efforts, newspaper coverage, debates, and personal campaign tours can help make a campaign successful, nothing is more effective than television advertising.

Turnout, Loyalty, Defection, and Persuasion Are the Ingredients of a Successful Campaign

Consistent with the arguments presented earlier, candidates and their campaign managers know that to win any election, they must successfully achieve as many of the following objectives as possible:

- Achieve high turnout among their own party's identifiers.
- Win a large share of the vote from their own party's identifiers.
- Encourage some of the other candidate's partisans to defect.
- Reduce turnout among the other candidate's identifiers.
- Win independents.

A winning campaign equation based on these objectives would look something like this:

$$\text{Turnout} + \text{Loyalty} + \text{Defection} + \text{Persuasion} = \text{Victory}$$

The equation begins with turnout—getting large numbers of your own partisans to show up on Election Day, and if possible, demoralizing the other candidate's partisans so that they do not vote. Loyalty is next—ensuring that the highest possible percentage of your partisans vote for your party's candidate. Defection is the reverse of loyalty—getting some of the other party's voters to cast their ballots for your party's candidate. Last comes persuasion—convincing independent voters that they should vote for your candidate rather than the other party's. Put all of these elements together, and they add up to victory.

Campaign Messages Are Meticulously Researched and Targeted

How do campaigns pursue the elements of victory? First, they develop messages or themes beneficial to their candidate. Effective messages may encourage voters to support a candidate, generate enthusiasm among partisans, and inspire them to vote. They may also demoralize the other party's voters and discourage them from voting. Voters hear these messages and themes repeated endlessly in debates, campaign appearances, and television and radio advertising.

The fundamental factors mentioned earlier—the state of the economy and presidential approval—render some messages more effective than others. A shaky economy, for example, set the stage for Bill Clinton's successful campaign to unseat George H. W. Bush in 1992. With its mantra of "It's the economy, stupid," the Clinton team continually reminded voters of the country's sluggish employment situation, placing the blame squarely on Bush's shoulders.

In other cases, the political environment significantly constrains the message options available to candidates. In 1980, an election-year recession and a series of foreign policy crises hindered Jimmy Carter's reelection bid. A "You've never had it so good" campaign did not fit the facts or the national mood. Although he tried, Carter could not raise serious doubts about his opponent, Ronald Reagan, and conservative Republicans. Here is one of his unsuccessful attempts:

> The Republican nominee advocates abandoning arms control policies which have been important and supported by every Democratic President since Harry Truman, and also by every Republican President since Dwight D. Eisenhower. This radical and irresponsible course would threaten our security and could put the whole world in peril. You and I must never let this come to pass.[19]

LOOKING FORWARD TO LOOKING BACKWARD

In the 2012 election, the Romney campaign wanted to frame the contest as a referendum on President Obama's performance over the last four years. The Obama campaign wanted to make the election more of a choice and frame it as what policies the respective candidates would implement if elected.

How do campaign managers develop such messages? They gather information on their opponents' views and compare them to the positions of their own candidate. They identify the most persuasive arguments for their side and against their opponent. They use the most compelling language to convey their message. As part of the development and testing of their messages, campaign managers also use **focus groups**—in-depth interviews with a small number of people representing important voter constituencies, such as undecided voters.

focus group
in-depth interview with a small number of people representing important voter constituencies.

TELEVISION ADVERTISING Once campaigns develop and test their messages, they can deliver them to the public. Television advertising is one major way that political campaigns deliver their messages to the widest audience. In the 2012 presidential campaign, more than one billion dollars was spent on television advertising (see Figure 9.2). Campaigns spent tens of millions more on radio and direct mail ads. Television advertising is effective because it can reach so many people. You do not have to be interested in politics or know anything about the candidates to see a commercial while you watch *Jeopardy!* or *Modern Family*. If the commercial you happen to see is powerful enough, it might even inspire you to vote for that candidate. By contrast, information on a candidate's website, Twitter feeds, or political blogs generally does not sway new voters because most of the people exposed to those messages are already supporters.

Advertising is most effective at convincing people who do not already have strong views about a candidate or a party. Chances are that a strong Republican or Democrat will not change his or her mind after watching a commercial. But someone on the fence—who pays attention only occasionally—is much more likely to vote based on

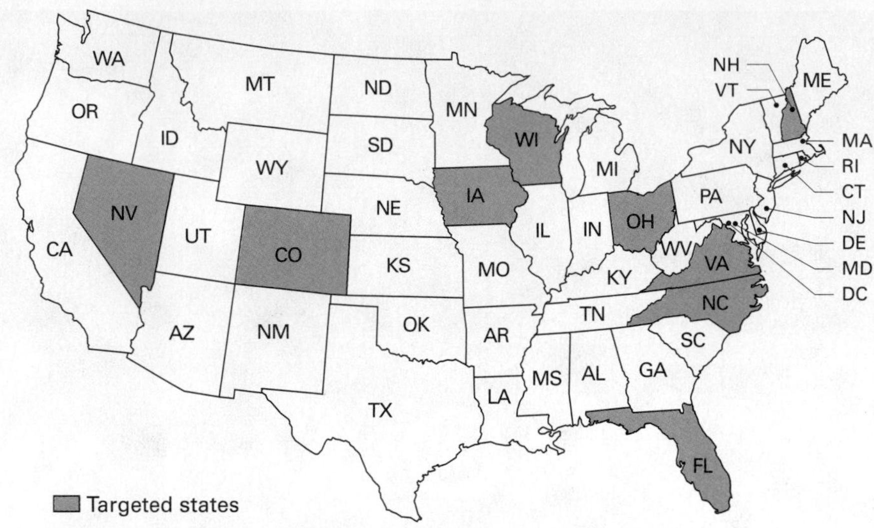

FIGURE 9.2 MAP OF ADVERTISING BUYS IN 2012.

Television advertising in the presidential race in 2012 was highly focused with only nine states getting any sustained and significant attention.

battleground states
competitive states in which no candidate has an overwhelming advantage, and therefore Electoral College votes are in play.

red states
largely uncontested states in which the Republican candidate for president is very likely to win.

blue states
largely uncontested states in which the Democratic candidate for president is very likely to win.

effective television advertising. Therefore, candidates tend to focus their advertising efforts on states expected to have very close elections. With winner-take-all rules for assigning the vast majority of electoral votes, it makes little sense for candidates to invest resources in states that they can safely expect to win or lose. There is no "extra credit" for an especially large victory margin, and no credit at all for coming in second. Persuading swing voters in competitive states can make the difference between losing or winning the primary nomination. Campaigns spend advertising dollars accordingly.

In the 2008 election, for example, the McCain and Obama campaigns bought no political advertising at all in the country's three largest states: California, New York, and Texas. Both camps were confident that Obama would win California and New York and that McCain would triumph in Texas. Neither felt compelled to advertise there. But both the McCain and Obama campaigns invested heavily in television advertising in three states that had a lot of electoral votes and were competitive: Ohio, Florida, and Pennsylvania. Obama won all three.

In recent years, competitive or **battleground states** and states that are reliably Republican or Democrat have remained fairly stable. Republican states are called **red states** because media graphics use the color red to show them on election maps. For the same reason, reliably Democratic states are called **blue states.** Media graphics usually show competitive, swing, or battleground states in white, yellow, or gray. In 2008, the battlefield expanded when traditionally red states such as Indiana, Virginia, and North Carolina became battlegrounds. Ultimately, Obama won all three of these states. Figure 9.3 offers one picture of the states considered red, blue, and competitive prior to the 2012 election. Figure 9.4 shows the actual results of the 2012 election.

THE ROLE OF DEBATES The modern television era helped increase the importance of debates in presidential campaigns. Debates offer candidates a particular kind of free advertising. They receive three days' worth of media coverage for every debate—the day before in anticipation of the debate; the day of the debate itself; and the following day, as media pundits analyze the answers and outcome.

Campaigns spend countless hours preparing for debates. They can sometimes play a pivotal role in shaping the outcome of a race. They certainly did in the first ever nationally televised debate in the 1960 presidential election between Vice President Richard Nixon and Senator John Kennedy. About 70 million viewers tuned in to see a pale and sickly looking Nixon side by side with the tan and telegenic Kennedy. This contrast helped Kennedy win the "image" battle, and many point to this as a significant catalyst in Kennedy's victory. This first debate offered an important lesson for future campaigns: Debates can often swing a campaign just enough to make a difference.

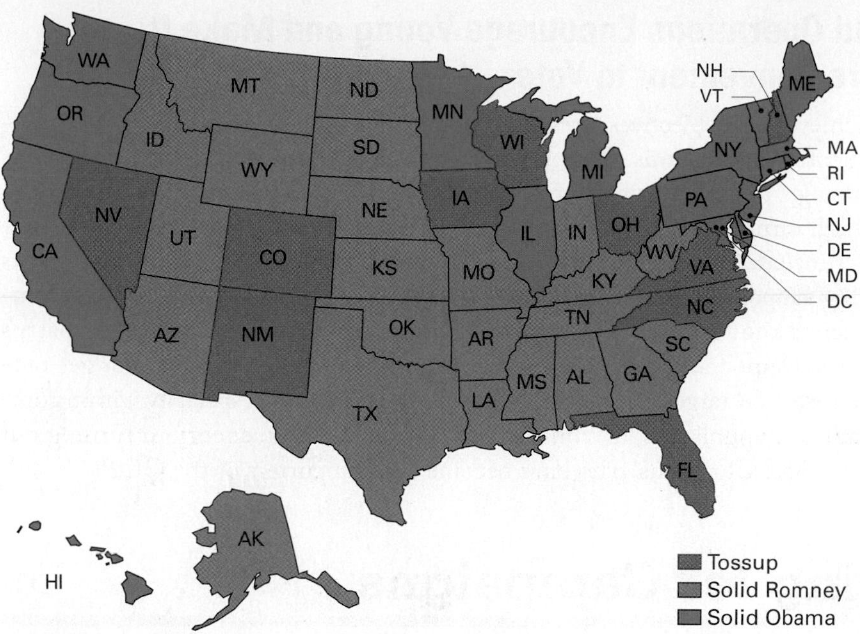

FIGURE 9.3 CLASSIFICATION OF STATES ACCORDING TO COMPETITIVENESS: SOLID ROMNEY, SOLID OBAMA, TOSS-UP.

The Obama campaign had more paths to victory in 2012 than the Romney campaign. They started with a base of more Electoral College votes and the Romney campaign need to win almost all the battleground states.

After all, in 2000, Al Gore needed only 269 more Florida voters to choose him over Bush and he would have won the presidency. Could a better campaign have made that difference? Possibly. Political scientists do not consider the campaign—or debates, for that matter—as routinely decisive. But they do recognize that they can be, especially when the country is closely divided politically. They also freely admit that their forecasting models, which do not explicitly account for campaign effects, often miss the mark in their predictions by a few percentage points. These misses could be a result of unmeasured campaign effects. In a close election, those effects can make the difference between winning and losing.

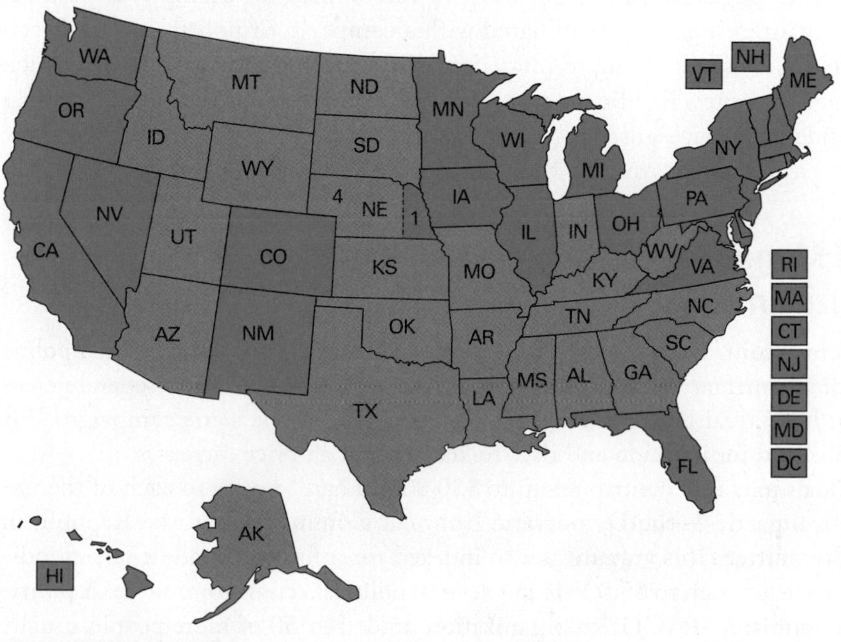

FIGURE 9.4 STATE-BY-STATE RESULTS FROM THE 2012 ELECTION.

In 2012, the only two states to change from their 2008 outcome were North Carolina and Indiana. Romney put both of those back in the Republican column, but that was not near enough to get to 270 Electoral College votes.

field operations
the "ground war" intended to produce high turnout among party loyalists, particularly in battleground states.

hard money
funds to be used by candidates or parties for the express purpose of running an election campaign, or by PACs for contributing to candidates.

soft money
funds to be used for political purposes other than running a campaign, for example, get-out-the-vote efforts; or by some interest groups for political ads praising or attacking candidates.

public money
taxpayer funds used to help finance presidential campaigns.

political action committee (PAC)
a group that collects money from individuals and makes donations to political parties and candidates.

Explore on MyPoliSciLab
Simulation: You You Are a Camaign Shrategist

Field Operations Encourage Voting and Make It More Convenient to Vote

To help achieve their objectives, presidential campaigns pursue one final type of campaign tactic: **field operations.** If television advertising constitutes the air war in a political campaign, then field operations are the ground war. Field operations attempt to produce high turnout among party loyalists, particularly in battleground states. Specific tactics include phone calls, letters, e-mail, social networking, and personal visits encouraging supporters to vote and offering resources to help them do so. For example, Democrats know that African Americans in most cases will support their party's nominee. The Democratic Party traditionally invests significant resources for get-out-the-vote efforts that target black neighborhoods in large cities, especially within competitive states. Republicans, by contrast, invest considerable energy in turning out white, evangelical Christians, who have become core supporters of the GOP.

Paying for Campaigns

9.4 Describe how election campaigns are funded.

Running a modern campaign for the presidency or for Congress is extremely expensive. In the 2008 election, Barack Obama spent more than $650 million on his campaign. His GOP opponent, John McCain, spent more than $350 million. Candidates in competitive Senate races in 2010 typically spent more than $20 million, and some House candidates spent more than $5 million. Before they can spend money, however, campaigns first have to raise it. The rules governing campaign fund-raising are complex, and they have changed considerably in recent years.

Three kinds of monies fund federal campaigns: hard money, soft money, and public money. **Hard money** refers to funds designated for the express purpose of running an election campaign, and such money is subject to strict limits on size and source. Federal candidates and political parties may use only hard money. **Soft money** refers to funds designated for political purposes other than running a campaign—voter registration and get-out-the-vote efforts, for example, or political advertising by interest groups unaffiliated with a campaign or political party. It can also refer to money spent trying to influence political or legislative decisions, which is called issue advocacy. **Public money** refers to taxpayer funds designated to help finance presidential campaigns, both in the primary season and in the general election. The laws and regulations governing these three kinds of monies differ substantially.

Hard Money Is Subject to Strict Limits on Size and Source

Individuals may contribute up to $2,500 in hard money to candidates for each political election. The primary election and general election are considered separate elections, so an individual may contribute $5,000 per year to the same campaign. This amount is indexed for inflation and rises to keep pace with price increases.

Individuals may also contribute up to $30,800 in hard money to each of the national political parties—the Democratic National Committee and the Republican National Committee. This amount is also indexed for inflation. In addition, an individual may contribute up to $5,000 to any federal political action committee. A **political action committee (PAC)** is an organization funded by 50 or more people, usually affiliated with a corporation, labor union, or some other special interest group. The PAC combines individual contributions to donate campaign funds to federal candidates. This allows individuals to pool their resources and have greater influence on a campaign than they could on their own. Table 9.1 summarizes the amount of hard

TABLE 9.1 HARD MONEY CONTRIBUTION LIMITS

	To any candidate campaign	To a national party	To a political action committee
An individual can give	$2,500 per election, indexed to inflation	$30,800 per year, indexed to inflation	$5,000 per year
A PAC can give	$5,000 per election	$15,000 per year	$5,000 per year
A national party can give	$5,000 per election in the House; up to $43,100 for a Senate campaign	Not applicable	$5,000 per year

Source: www.fec.gov/pages/brochures/contriblimits.shtml.

money or express advocacy funds that an individual, PAC, or national party can give directly to a campaign, national party, or PAC.

independent expenditures
funds spent to elect or defeat candidates but not coordinated with any candidate's campaign.

coordinated expenditures
legally limited purchases or payments made by a political party on behalf of, and in coordination with, a specific campaign.

matching funds
public monies given to qualifying candidates to match a certain percentage of the funds they have raised from private donors.

Soft Money May Be Used for Political Purposes Other than Running a Campaign

Previous campaign finance law prohibited corporations and unions from contributing soft money directly from their treasuries to a political campaign. They were also not allowed to fund television advertisements for a candidate that aired within 60 days of a general election or within 30 days of a primary. This advertising is called "electioneering communication." In 2010, however, in *Citizens United v. Federal Election Commission*, the Supreme Court declared these restrictions unconstitutional. Now, corporations and unions, which often unify through a PAC, may spend unlimited funds on advertisements and air them throughout an election season.

Rather than representing a particular candidate, PACs often support particular issues. With more advertising power, these special interest groups can reach a more diverse audience with their views. They can also encourage candidates to address issues they find important. As a result, special interest groups now play a more prominent role in elections.

Both parties and interest groups may also make unlimited **independent expenditures.** These are expenditures on behalf of a candidate, but without any coordination between the party and the candidate's campaign. For example, a group might wish to pay for a campaign advertisement in a local newspaper or on a local television station. However, checking with the candidate's campaign on the wording of the ad would constitute a **coordinated expenditure**, which is prohibited.

Candidates Who Accept Public Money or Matching Funds Must Abide by Spending Limits

In addition to hard money and soft money, public money has been a major source of funding in presidential campaigns. The funding structure in the primary election process is different from that used in the fall general election.

PRIMARY SEASON FUNDING During the primary season, candidates for their party's nomination can qualify for **matching funds,** which are public monies candidates receive to match a certain percentage of the funds they have raised from private donors. To qualify for matching funds, a candidate must raise at least $5,000 in individual contributions of $250 or less in at least 20 states. The candidate must also agree to adhere to both state-specific and total spending limits during the primary season. Finally, candidates who fail to receive at least 10 percent of the vote in two successive primaries lose eligibility for matching funds.

Candidates who can clear the fund-raising hurdle, agree to the spending limits, and continue to receive at least 10 percent of the vote in party primaries will receive

SUPERPACS

Outside groups are becoming increasingly powerful forces in elections. Late night Comedy Central host Stephen Colbert taught many of his viewers about the phenomena and even started his own Super Pac.

matching funds. Specifically, the federal government will provide a dollar-for-dollar match for each individual contribution received by the candidate up to certain limits.

Candidates are not required to receive public money. If they do accept it, though, they must abide by the spending limits. If they do not accept public money, they are free to spend what they wish. This format is consistent with the Supreme Court's rulings on campaign finance—namely, that spending limits on campaigns are unconstitutional unless they are voluntary. Government, therefore, has to offer something to get candidates to agree to limit their spending. Candidates have to decide whether taking the government funds is worth abiding by these regulations. They must determine if they can win the nomination if they abide by the federal spending limits or if they can raise the funds they need without the help of public financing. Furthermore, candidates often want to spend money after the primary season is over—to keep their names on voters' minds before the national conventions and fall campaigns take place. Candidates then have to decide whether the federal spending limits will prevent them from funding a postprimary media campaign.

In recent years, most major candidates declined to take public financing during the primaries. In 2000, for example, George W. Bush became the first eventual party nominee to refuse matching funds. In 2004, he refused again, as did Democratic Senator John Kerry, who went on to become his party's nominee. In 2008, none of the major candidates accepted matching funds in the primaries. The Democrats raised substantial funds—Hillary Clinton raised more than $200 million and Barack Obama raised more than $250 million. The campaigns raised their money in significantly different ways from one another, however. The majority of Clinton's contributions came from donors giving the maximum amount. Obama relied on many more contributors—more than 3 million—who gave smaller amounts, often online. In 2012, the candidates again refused to accept federal campaign funding.

GENERAL ELECTION FUNDING Once the parties select their nominees, the federal government provides financing for the fall general election campaign. In 2004, the Democratic and Republican presidential nominees each received about $75 million to spend on the presidential campaign. As a condition of receiving this money, however, the candidates had to agree that (1) their campaigns would not seek to raise or spend any additional funds from private individuals, and (2) they would not spend any more than $50,000 of their own personal funds on the campaign. If candidates agree to these terms, they can spend the campaign funds as they see fit, with no state-specific limits on spending. In 2008, Barack Obama refused public funds for the general election campaign, whereas the Republican nominee, John McCain, took the $84 million offered. This decision allowed the Obama campaign to vastly outspend the McCain campaign and control the campaign message.

Third parties—parties other than the Democratic and Republican Parties—may qualify for full general election campaign funding only if they received at least 25 percent of the vote in the previous presidential election. Parties that meet this threshold can retroactively receive the same amount that the two major parties received that year. Also like the other major parties, they can receive an equal share in the next presidential election at the outset of the general election campaign, not after the election. No third party has received full public funding, but they can receive limited public funding if they earn at least 5 percent of the national vote in the preceding election. For example, the Reform Party qualified for partial general election funding in 1996 and 2000 based on the performance of presidential candidate Ross Perot in 1992 and 1996.

On MyPoliSciLab

Review the Chapter

Listen to **Chapter 9** on **MyPoliSciLab**

The Basic Rules Governing American Elections

9.1 Outline election procedures, including how candidates are nominated and how winners are determined, p. 295.

The first objective of a candidate running for office is to receive his or her party's nomination. In the presidential race, the candidate does so by winning a majority of delegates to the party's nominating convention during the state primary elections. The Electoral College and the winner-take-all system do much to define the American political landscape.

Understanding Presidential Election Outcomes

9.2 Explain the key factors that determine the outcome of presidential elections, p. 306.

In order to succeed in presidential primaries, it is crucial to win the invisible primary. This includes leading the field in public opinion polls, in fund-raising, or in both at the end of the preprimary period. Candidates who begin the primary season in the lead often go on to win. Primaries now follow each other too rapidly for underdog candidates to devote resources to multiple races and build the momentum necessary to win the nomination. In general elections, presidential approval ratings and economic performance are the two variables most often included in election forecasting models—and they have excellent predictive power. The partisan orientations of the electorate, an incumbent president running for reelection, and how long the party has held the presidency are also significant factors. Campaign tactics can make a difference in close races, as well.

Conducting Campaigns

9.3 Analyze the methods candidates use to conduct election campaigns, p. 309.

Understanding the "victory equation" and its components—turnout, loyalty, defection, and persuasion—is crucial to understanding how presidential candidates wage a campaign. Candidates secure these components by developing messages or themes beneficial to the campaign and by effectively managing field operations. The messages and field operations are carefully planned and targeted almost exclusively to battleground states. Forecasting models and candidates are not perfect, however, as demonstrated by the failed forecasts of the 2000 presidential election.

Paying for Campaigns

9.4 Describe how election campaigns are funded, p. 316.

Running a modern campaign for the presidency or for Congress is extremely expensive, and campaign finance laws dictate how money may be raised and spent by candidates. Campaign finance laws distinguish between hard, soft, and public money. In addition, in 2010, the Supreme Court lifted restrictions on corporations and unions seeking to place television advertisements for issues or candidates.

Learn the Terms

Study and **Review** the **Flashcards**

battleground states, p. 314
blue states, p. 314
caucus, p. 296
closed primary, p. 297
coordinated expenditures, p. 317
delegates, p. 295
direct mail, p. 311
Electoral College, p. 302
field operations, p. 316
focus group, p. 313
hard money, p. 316
independent expenditures, p. 317
invisible primary, p. 306
matching funds, p. 317
modified open primary, p. 297
momentum, p. 306
open primary, p. 297
plurality rule, p. 305
political action committee (PAC), p. 316
primary, p. 296
public money, p. 316
red states, p. 314
retrospective voting, p. 309
soft money, p. 316
winner-take-all, p. 296

Test Yourself

Study and **Review** the **Practice Tests**

9.1 Outline election procedures, including how candidates are nominated and how winners are determined.

Which of the following best exemplifies the plurality rule?

a. The congressional candidate who receives the most votes in the primary must participate in a runoff election.
b. The presidential candidate who receives a majority of the popular votes wins a majority, but not all, of the Electoral College delegates.

c. The congressional candidate who receives the most votes wins office.
d. The presidential candidate who ties with another candidate in the primary, must participate in a runoff election.
e. The congressional candidate who ties with another candidate in the primary election must participate in a runoff election.

9.2 Explain the key factors that determine the outcome of presidential elections.

Which of the following is NOT a factor that political scientists generally take into account when predicting presidential election outcomes?

a. The demographics of the electorate
b. The partisan orientations of the electorate
c. The job approval rating of the incumbent party president
d. The performance of the economy during the first half of the election year
e. Incumbency

9.3 Analyze the methods candidates use to conduct election campaigns.

All of the following are objectives that campaign managers and candidates seek to achieve EXCEPT

a. Votes from independents
b. High turnout among their own party's identifiers
c. Defection by some of the other candidate's partisans
d. Reduced turnout among the other candidate's identifiers
e. High turnout among the other candidate's identifiers

9.4 Describe how campaigns are funded.

Which of the following statements is TRUE about presidential campaign funding?

a. There are no restrictions on the size and source of hard money.
b. In recent years, most major presidential candidates have declined to take public financing during the primaries.
c. Corporations and unions may not make unlimited independent expenditures.
d. Candidates who accept public money have no spending limits.
e. All recent presidential candidates have accepted public money.

Explore Further

SUGGESTED READINGS BY TOP SCHOLARS

Paul Abramson, John Aldrich, and David Rohde. *Change and Continuity in the 2008 Elections*. Washington, DC: CQ Press, 2007. Straightforward and accessible analysis of the 2008 election, evaluating campaign strategies and their impact on the outcome of the midterm elections.

Gary Jacobson. *Politics of Congressional Elections*. New York: Longman, 2008. A comprehensive review of the current literature on congressional elections: why people vote as they do, variance in outcomes across districts and states, changes over time in aggregate representation (who has power), and the implications for democratic governance.

Richard G. Niemi and Herbert F. Weisberg, eds. *Controversies in Voting Behavior*, 5th ed. Washington, DC: CQ Press, 2010. Examines the key questions in political science: Why is voter turnout low and declining? Does the public's lack of political information or expertise matter? What determines vote choice? Do campaigns matter? Do voters intentionally elect a divided government? How much does politics affect party identification? Are parties changing? Also includes essays on party realignment and the polarization of the American electorate.

Jan Leighley. *The Oxford Handbook of American Elections and Political Behavior*. New York: Oxford University Press, 2010. Describes the various approaches and issues in research design, political participation, vote choice, and the influences on individuals' political behavior.

David Plouffe. *The Audacity to Win.* New York: Viking, 2009.

Karl Rove. *Courage and Consequences.* New York: Threshold Editions, 2010. Pick your party. Both books discuss how political scientists view elections, from the campaign managers who ran the Barack Obama (Plouffe) and George W. Bush (Rove) presidential campaigns.

SUGGESTED WEBSITES

Democratic National Committee: www.democrats.org
Provides links to the Democratic National Convention, action plans, and agenda as well as opportunities to register to vote and contribute to current campaigns or the party.

Republican National Committee: www.rnc.org
Offers links to blogs, calls to action, groups affiliated with the party, party issues, and state parties.

Political Maps: politicalmaps.org
The best and most interesting political maps. Site managers update the site regularly during election season.

Federal Election Commission: www.fec.gov/law/feca/feca.shtml
Congress created the FEC in 1975 to administer and enforce the Federal Elections Campaign Act (FECA). The FEC hosts this campaign finance law site, which provides links to statutes, legislative recommendations, campaign finance reports and data, committee meetings, enforcement matters, and help with reporting and compliance.

National Institute on Money in State Politics: www.followthemoney.org/index.phtml
The institute is a nonpartisan, nonprofit organization that examines the influence of campaign money on state-level elections and public policy throughout the United States. This site provides access to the institute's data, research, and reports.

10

Listen to Chapter 10 on MyPoliSciLab

Media and Politics

TOM BROKAW, POLITICIAN

One of the most important endorsements of the 2012 presidential election came from someone who holds no political office and never has. He has no political party affiliation, and many Americans believe him to be objective, impartial, and independent of the political process. What is perhaps most unusual is that he issued his endorsement a decade and a half earlier, when the candidate he attacked was not running for president and the candidate he indirectly endorsed still had not taken the helm of the Salt Lake City Winter Olympics.

The endorsement came in the midst of the 2012 Republican primaries, as Newt Gingrich—a former Speaker of the House of Representatives—was coming off an impressive win in South Carolina and was ahead in polls over Governor Mitt Romney heading into an all-important primary in Florida.

Romney's campaign then issued an unusual advertisement. It featured a nearly uninterrupted 30-second clip of longtime NBC News anchor Tom Brokaw opening his January 21, 1997, broadcast. In the clip, Brokaw reports that Speaker Newt Gingrich's House colleagues had, "by an overwhelming vote," found him guilty of ethics violations. The report was 100 percent accurate. And it was 100 percent effective as a political endorsement of Romney, and a political attack on Newt Gingrich's fitness to serve as the Republican presidential nominee. The ad played 2,225 times in the five days leading up to the Florida primary. And Gingrich lost the state to Romney by 14 points.

The Romney campaign repeated the strategy just a few weeks later, as Romney sought a knockout punch on former Senator Rick Santorum in the Pennsylvania primary. On April 9, just

10.1 Evaluate the unique role that the media play in American politics and society, p. 326.

10.2 Identify the legal constraints under which the American media operate, p. 333.

10.3 Explain how technological changes have impacted patterns of media use, p. 335.

10.4 Determine whether the media are biased, p. 341.

10.5 Assess the effect of the media on political attitudes and behaviors, p. 344.

NOW STARRING One twist that appeared in the 2012 air wars was the use of clips of journalists in political ads. Tom Brokaw starred in one of the most prominent ads of the cycle that replayed his reporting of Newt Gingrich's censure by the House in 1998.

The Big Picture Is the media influencing your political opinions, or is it just reinforcing opinions that you already have? Author Kenneth M. Goldstein discusses how Americans seek out news that they agree with—and block out the information that they do not want to hear.

The Basics How do the media help support our democratic institutions? In this video you will find out how a free press functions not just as a source of knowledge, but also as a public forum and a government watchdog. You'll also analyze how private ownership and partisanship impact the ability of the media to do its job.

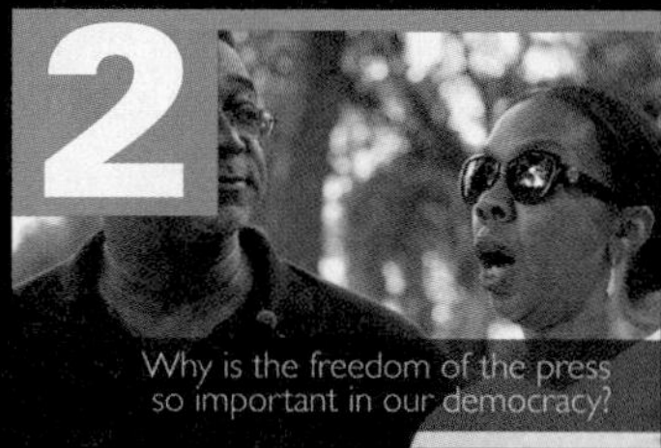

2
Why is the freedom of the press
so important in our democracy?

3

In Context Trace the evolution of media outlets from newspapers to the new media that exists today. In this video, University of Oklahoma political scientist Tyler Johnson examines the history of media outlets and the effect of both traditional and new media on the political information and messages that reach the public.

Think Like a Political Scientist How does the media shape public opinion? In this video University of Oklahoma political scientist Tyler Johnson discusses how media framing works and what market factors are influencing this process.

In the Real World What is the ideal relationship between the government and the media? Real people consider whether leaks of confidential government information to the press is good for democracy or whether leaks give the government too much control over the stories being told in the newspapers.

So What? Which came first—the tweet that Osama bin Laden was killed or the New York Times headline? Author Kenneth M. Goldstein explains how a basic understanding the media will help students evaluate the news no matter where it comes from in the future.

15 days before the Pennsylvania primary, a new Romney campaign ad opened with the voiceover by then *CBS Evening News* anchor Katie Couric reporting Santorum's loss of his Senate seat on election night in 2006. National political correspondent Gloria Borger remarked that Santorum lost "among Democrats and independents, women and men, young and old, blacks and whites, rich and poor." The message was clear: Santorum lost his own state and lost across the board. The ad aired 177 times that day. Within days, Santorum's position in the race began to flag, and facing likely defeat in his home state, Santorum suspended his campaign. Romney knocked him out.

Two of the most effective political ads of the year featured not partisan attacks, not highly produced visuals, not new attacks lines, but the simple replaying of past broadcasts of the news. These accounts, presented originally as objective observations of events, suddenly had all the muscle of a highly charged political attack ad.

Although media companies and journalists protested the use of their images, voices, and reports in political ads, the practice is unlikely to end. Similar ads were used in a high-stakes gubernatorial recall campaign in Wisconsin and in the 2012 presidential general election. Such ads have proven their effectiveness, for reasons that the news media may well cheer. Neutral-toned, objective journalism has special cachet in today's political environment. Even if many politically active citizens regard the media as biased against their viewpoints (a common conceit among voters on both the left and the right), the mainstream media retain special power to influence voters, affect the debate, and deliver political messages in ways that they never anticipated. This happens because those voters most important in elections—swing voters who are not closely aligned with one political party or another—are especially affected by messages delivered by sources they regard as objective and independent.

The "Brokaw ad" is, therefore, an ironic twist on the conventional wisdom about media effectiveness. For many years, campaign officials had a difficult time using independently produced news to influence voters, because most media resist stories with the kind of one-sided perspectives known to influence minds. Media outlets delivering more one-sided messages, on the other hand—such as FOX News Channel or MSNBC, are watched mainly by people who have already made up their minds. Yet those voters who are most influential in securing a political victory are those in the middle, and these people tend to resist such one-sided telecasts. By using relatively neutral broadcasts as a reminder of the failures of an opponent (or conversely, the strengths of their candidate), a campaign can deliver a highly charged message in a wrapper that is welcome to swing voters.

The Brokaw piece and its cousins have the added strength of delivering in video a message that would otherwise have to be read. Political ads for years have featured newspaper headlines floating through the screen. But even casual voters have long learned to doubt such floating headlines, because they cannot be sure of where they first appeared or whether they represent a news story or an editorial. They also have to be read quickly, which is not as easy as simply listening to a familiar anchor.

For advertisers, the tactic of using objectively reported news footage is low risk with a high reward. But the practice is perilous for broadcast journalists, whose reputations for objectivity are put at risk. Being used in political ads, even against their wishes and from footage shot many years earlier, subtracts from future perceptions of their objectivity. Networks are loathe to see their top journalists and news programming used this way, but they have little recourse. When they protest, advertisers claim "fair use," a tenet of U.S. copyright law allowing limited use of copyrighted material without the owner's permission. Television stations are especially leery of appearing to try to censor candidates by pulling their ads.

In 2006 and 2008, a standard tool of political campaigns was to send volunteers with digital video cameras to every public event of the opponent and simply record what was said and done, in the hope of a single slip of the tongue that could be used in a new campaign ad. Today, campaigns scour the traditional media for broadcasts of a relatively objective nature to use in attack ads. The TV news coverage may be days, weeks, or years old. It doesn't matter. What matters is that such programming can populate their own ad narratives with the anchors and reporting that best serve their political messages. News divisions are scrambling to protect their independence from the campaigns, but to little avail.

In the end, the one thing that American media did not expect—to see its mainstream outlets become tools of political warfare—was a central new development of the 2012 campaign. The power that American journalists had hoped to wield through their objective and dispassionate reports had suddenly been turned into effective political weapons. And with this development, the American media's most cherished quality—independence—was at risk of being overrun by a trend far more worrisome than irrelevance or declining audiences both of which had seemed, in 2010, like the most likely threat to the mainstream media's future.

The Unique Role of the American Media

10.1 Evaluate the unique role that the media play in American politics and society.

mass media
various modes of communication intended to reach a mass audience—including television, radio, newspapers, newsmagazines, and the Internet.

One of the central freedoms Americans enjoy is free speech—the almost unfettered right to say and print whatever one wants. This freedom has made possible one of the world's most vibrant mass media markets. Whether in the form of television, radio, newspapers, news magazines, or the Internet, America's **mass media** is commonly viewed as a central pillar of U.S. political life. Although journalists are not licensed, elected, or appointed by any authority, they wield significant influence over the U.S. government through multiple channels of activity. It is impossible to understand American political life or government without understanding its media.

When we discuss the media, we refer not only to those forms of distribution of news, opinion, and other content, but also to the individuals responsible for producing the content. Thus, when this chapter refers to "the media," it may be referring to the actual communications of the media themselves (newspapers, for example) or to the people who are responsible for their content (such as newspaper reporters and editors and news-focused bloggers and independent journalists).

Freedom Is the Defining Characteristic of the American Media

The press's ability to publish what it deems appropriate without government restriction has come a long way over the course of American history. Members of the modern media have few of the restraints faced by their earliest forebears. However, contemporary political journalists in the United States do face some constraints on what they can air or publish.

At the time of its passage in 1791, the First Amendment was thought to guarantee freedom of the press only from prior restraint by government. Expansions of freedom were won through ongoing battles among the press, the government, and public figures; many of which the press lost.

EARLY RESTRICTIONS ON THE PRESS The most famous early restriction on the press was the Sedition Act, a federal law passed in 1798. The act effectively criminalized criticism of Congress and the president:

> If any person shall write, print, utter or publish . . . any false, scandalous and malicious writing or writings against the government of the United States, or either house of the Congress of the United States, or the President of the United States, with intent to defame the said government, or either house of the said Congress, or the said President, or to bring them, or either of them, into contempt or disrepute; or to excite against them, or either or any of them, the hatred of the good people of the United States . . . then such person, being thereof convicted before any court

of the United States having jurisdiction thereof, shall be punished by a fine not exceeding two thousand dollars, and by imprisonment not exceeding two years.[1]

Presumably, the act was designed for national security purposes—to silence American supporters of France, a country with which President John Adams feared the United States might soon be at war.[2] Critics argued, however, that the act was intended instead to quiet the critics of President Adams and his Federalist Party allies in Congress.[3] And, in fact, all 14 individuals indicted under the act (10 of whom were convicted) were members of the Anti-Federalist opposition—mostly editors of opposition newspapers.[4]

When Thomas Jefferson, leader of the Anti-Federalists, was elected president in 1800, he freed those still serving prison sentences because of Sedition Act convictions. The Sedition Act itself was allowed to expire in 1801, but the struggle for a free press was far from over. During the Civil War, the federal government limited telegraph transmissions from Washington, D.C., arguing that some of these transmissions might compromise the successful planning and prosecution of the war. During the post–Civil War era, the federal government jailed reporters who were critical of the program of southern Reconstruction. Reporters were also cited for contempt of court for describing pending legal cases, particularly if they criticized presiding judges.

By the turn of the twentieth century, press outlets were being sued, successfully, for printing photographs of and intimate gossip about figures of interest to the public. Legislation was enacted to restrict the ability of the press to "invad[e] the sacred precincts of private and domestic life."[5] Further restrictions on the press were enacted during World War I. The Espionage Act, passed in 1917 and expanded in 1918, made illegal any "seditious expression"—in particular, publications that might undermine military recruitment or weaken support for the military draft. Nearly 1,000 individuals ultimately were convicted for engaging in such expression.[6] A similar law, the Smith Act, was passed as World War II loomed. Although it was rarely enforced during the war, it was used in the early postwar years to prosecute American communists.

ESTABLISHMENT OF PRESS FREEDOMS IN THE TWENTIETH CENTURY A countervailing trend began during the 1930s, when the Supreme Court developed a more expansive interpretation of the First Amendment. The trend took decades to reach maturity, but by the end of the 1970s, the press freedoms that we recognize today had largely been established in case law and federal statute. Eventually, the press—and private individuals who wished to publish information for mass distribution—won important decisions expanding its freedom to criticize the government and public officials, guaranteeing the right to cover criminal trials and aspects of individuals' private lives, setting highly restrictive limits on prior restraint in cases related to national security, and granting access to government information that was once off-limits. Thus, in the twenty-first-century, the American press operates with substantially more latitude than it did in the first 200 years of the nation's history.

□ American Media Are Largely Privately Owned

Unlike in other industrialized democracies, the largest media outlets in the United States are owned and operated by the private sector, rather than by the government. Public broadcasting in the United States receives only a small share of its funding from the government and accounts for about 2 percent of the total television audience share.[7] By contrast, in the vast majority of European countries and the democratic countries of Asia and the Pacific, the government owns at least one major television outlet.[8] Government-owned outlets in these areas typically have at least a 30 to 40 percent audience share.[9]

Still, the U.S. government maintains controls over media ownership and some forms of distribution. Prior to the 1980s, government restrictions determined how many news and broadcast outlets one company could own. Each of the networks could own only three local stations. After these limitations were lifted, the United States saw

10.1

10.2

10.3

10.4

10.5

prior restraint
government intervention to prevent the publication of material it finds objectionable.

a wave of takeovers and mergers. The News Corporation, a global media enterprise under the ownership of Rupert Murdoch, added Fox News and the *Wall Street Journal* to its holdings. CNN and Time Warner merged. Disney bought ABC. Westinghouse purchased CBS, which was then placed in the hands of Viacom. All media outlets using the public broadcast spectrum, which is considered public property, must pay for the privilege and are also subject to significant government restrictions over content. These restrictions typically keep major networks from airing content considered profane or offensive to members of the public.

Newspapers are a different story. In the industrialized democracies, including the United States, government ownership of print media is highly unusual. Many other countries, however, have a print tradition that is not as well established as in the United States—that of the national newspaper. Most American newspapers are tied to a particular city, state, or region—the *San Francisco Chronicle, New York Post, Des Moines Register*, and *Denver Post* are examples. Although *USA Today* attempted to change that, producing a national daily paper in 1982, the majority of Americans continued to rely on their local papers. The *Wall Street Journal* also turned its business format into a national daily as well, especially under the ownership of Murdoch. In other countries, though, some of the oldest, most respected, and most widely read newspapers are national in scope. These include the *Sun* in the United Kingdom, *Le Monde* in France, and *Die Zeit* in Germany.

American Media Operate Largely Unfettered by Government Restriction

Unlike media in other countries, those in American are largely unrestrained by government interference. Most significantly, U.S. media are allowed to publish or broadcast free from the threat of **prior restraint**—that is, government intervention to stop the publication of material it finds objectionable. This freedom has never been absolute, however. The Supreme Court has ruled that if publication of certain information "will surely result in direct, immediate, and irreparable harm to our nation or its people," then prior restraint can be exercised.[10] For instance, the government often tries and sometimes succeeds in exercising prior restraint in cases involving national security. A broadcast or print outlet could be restrained from publishing the secret locations of U.S. armed forces in enemy territory or the names and addresses of intelligence agents overseas. Significantly, however, the Supreme Court has made it clear that the burden rests with government to demonstrate that publication would be harmful, rather than with the media to show why the information merits a public airing.

This principle grew out of the Pentagon Papers case in June 1971, when the *New York Times, Washington Post*, and *Boston Globe* published excerpts of a top-secret government study of U.S. involvement in Vietnam. Daniel Ellsberg, a former government employee who had worked on the study and had become disenchanted with the Vietnam War, provided the excerpts. Initial excerpts cited repeated examples of poor presidential decision making and failures to deal honestly with both Congress and the American public. Claiming a threat to national security, the Nixon administration sought an injunction to prevent publication of further installments. The administration won an injunction, but the victory was short lived; the U.S. Supreme Court ultimately ruled in favor of the newspapers and argued that the government did not meet the extraordinarily high burden of proof necessary to justify such a restraint.

The media will sometimes voluntarily hold off publishing or broadcasting information. In 2005, the *New York Times* learned of a covert program in which American scientists and Special Forces helped guard Pakistani nuclear material. Because of the fear of adverse reaction in Pakistan and the Muslim world if word got out about the top-secret program, the Bush administration asked the *New York Times* not to reveal its existence. The paper agreed and held the information for more than two years. In this case, the key point was that the paper's restraint was voluntary. There was virtually nothing the Bush administration could have done to prevent the paper's publishing the information.

With the ease of digital publication, the discretion exercised by working journalists in publicizing sensitive information has declined markedly. In 2011, the website Wikileaks received and published a trove of classified diplomatic cables detailing a variety of communications to and from the U.S. government and its diplomats around the world, as well as secret correspondence to and from the U.S. government and its foreign counterparts. The leaks included the names of individuals who had cooperated with the United States in sensitive military and nonmilitary operations, as well as valuable intelligence on America's known enemies. If an American media outlet had received such documents, it might have been restrained from printing them by the US government. However, because Wikileaks is a website located and controlled outside the United States, it was not subject to such restrictions. The ramifications of the Wikileaks scandal are significant. In a media world that operates without the restrictions imposed by national boundaries, there is little to prevent any media outlet from publishing what it wants, when it wants, and how it wants.

American Media Pursue Objectivity . . . but This Is Changing

American media aspire to present the news in an objective and nonpartisan way. Their pursuit of accuracy, fair-mindedness, and independence from special interests are considered central characteristics of working reporters and producers. It was not always this way. William Randolph Hearst created one of the most powerful and successful newspaper chains in the 1890s; by the mid-1920s, he owned 28 of the most influential papers in the country, with a brand of titillating and sometimes even

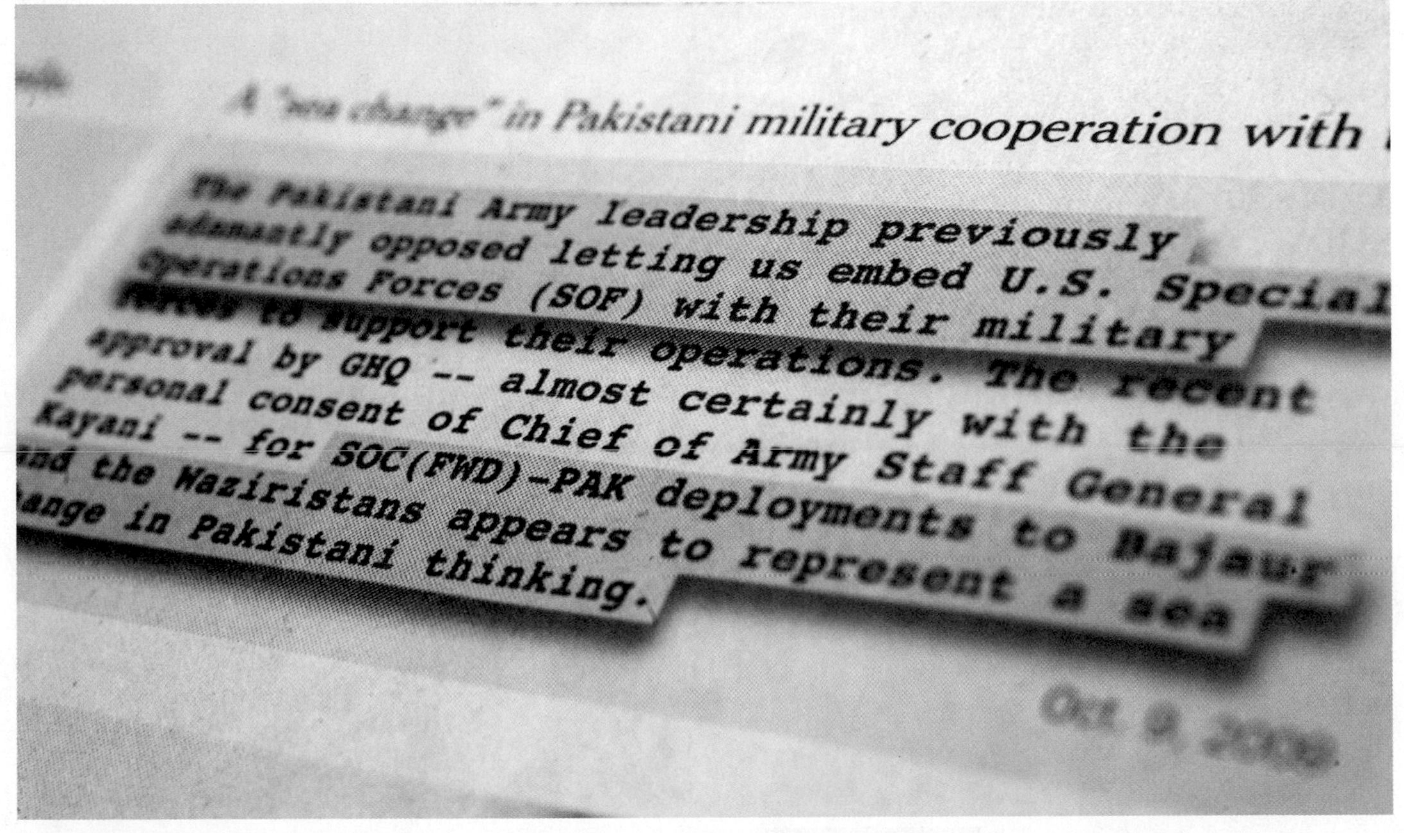

INSIDER INFORMATION

Secret memos like the one on the Pakistani military were leaked to Wikileaks and were immediately available for all to see.

advocacy journalism
news outlets that present news with either an explicit or implicit point of view favoring certain political positions.

false but sensational stories known as yellow journalism. These papers were far from objective. But, by the 1940s, newspapers and radio networks strived to play it fair. Despite criticism, most journalists have aspired to practice the values of objectivity and accuracy.

However, American media are shifting in this regard. In the 1990s, with the advent of cable television and conservative talk radio, personalities such as Rush Limbaugh, Sean Hannity, and Bill O'Reilly argued that the mainstream media or "MSM," which included the *New York Times* and CBS, NBC, and ABC news programs, may have claimed to be unbiased but showed a fondness for reports that favored liberal viewpoints.

This perception led to the proliferation of **advocacy journalism**—news outlets presenting news with an either explicit or implicit point of view favoring certain political positions. News outlets pursue advocacy journalism because audiences are likely to see information that comes from sources that are consistent with their existing beliefs (from a conservative source if they have conservative beliefs or from a liberal source if they have liberal beliefs) as more credible.[11] This model has proven to be effective, from the point of view of building audience loyalty. Fox News, with its conservative focus, quickly outpaced the older and established CNN. MSNBC countered with a left-of-center point of view and proved resilient. At the end of 2012, CNN had fallen far behind its more partisan competitors, leading many critics

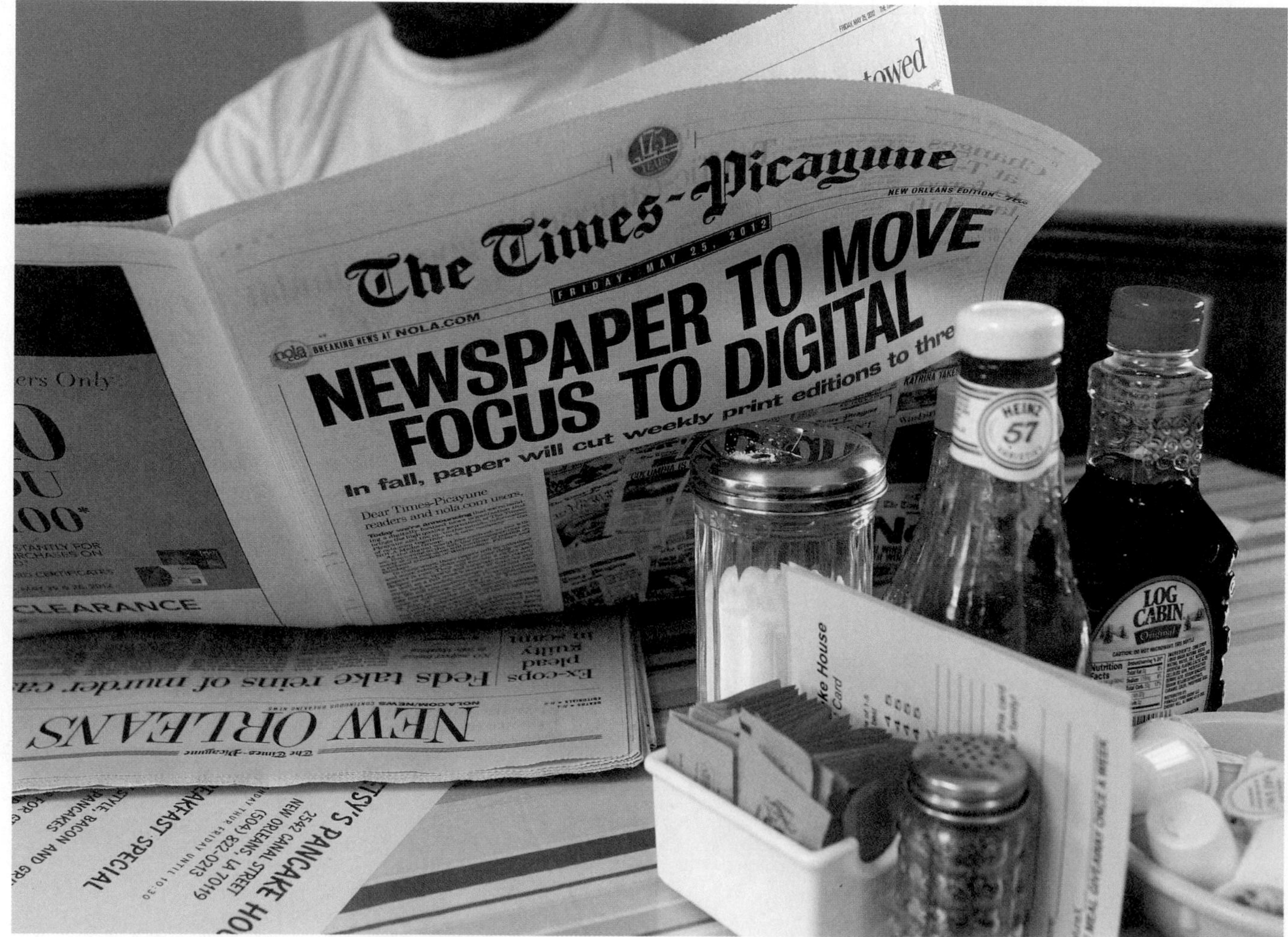

MOVING TO DIGITAL

Newspaper around the country are seeing significant declines in profits as readership migrates to the web. In many cases, like in New Orleans, newspapers have stopped publishing hard copies of the paper and have migrated their entire operation to the web.

and observers to wonder whether there is a future for relatively down-the-middle journalism in cable news.

At the same time, the major sponsors of most efforts at objective journalism—newspapers—were in a free fall in both circulation and advertising. Many major newspapers, such as the *Los Angeles Times*, *Boston Globe*, *Philadelphia Inquirer*, and *Chicago Tribune*, have seen their circulation figures drop by half since 1990. Several small and mid-sized newspapers have gone out of business altogether, leaving some cities without a local daily newspaper for the first time in their history. Only a small handful of publications have been able to resist this trend, and their success appears to be closely tied to their focus on coverage of business and financial matters (e.g., the *Wall Street Journal* and *The Economist*) or their close focus on specific areas of U.S. political life (e.g., *Politico*).

The combination of the decline in print newspapers and the rise of partisan or advocacy journalism raises a significant question about the future championing of objectivity by the American media. One of its hallmarks—being a reliable source of accurate and relatively unbiased reporting of the day's events—appears to be in broad decline, sustained only in a few select places, and largely replaced by advocacy media.

watchdog
the media's role in keeping a close eye on politicians and presenting stories and information that politicians might not willingly reveal to the media on their own.

American Media Aim to Play a Watchdog Role in Government and Politics

American journalists like to believe that they serve a **watchdog** function. By attending public meetings, holding elected and appointed leaders accountable for their promises, reviewing public documents, and asking questions about the future course of American society, they can provide a check on the workings of American government. And some of the most famous journalists in American history are honored precisely because they performed this duty. Perhaps the most famous of these journalists were two reporters with the *Washington Post*, Carl Bernstein and Bob Woodward. They worked on the Metro desk of the *Post* when they were assigned to report on the botched Watergate burglary in 1972. By closely following the string of connections between the burglars and the campaign committee for President Richard Nixon, Bernstein and Woodward demonstrated that the burglary had been done for political purposes, and that a vast cover-up orchestrated within the White House had sought to obscure that fact. The stories, and the coverage that followed, eventually led to the resignation of President Richard Nixon on August 9, 1974.

Reporters have always been willing to challenge those in authority, and within the American media, it is a badge of honor to be disliked and feared by the powerful. Yet, there are significant questions about whether the American media continue to act on this impulse and the degree to which they are successful. Many critics believe that the U.S. political press corps did not raise enough questions about the intelligence used to justify the 2003 invasion of Iraq. And in the wake of the 2008 election of Barack Obama, many critics (including many Democrats) said that American reporters were insufficiently critical of Obama's background and policy positions because of their own personal sympathy for his candidacy. Some anecdotal evidence exists to show that coverage of Obama was far more positive than that for his predecessors.[12]

Critics of the media on both the left and the right are increasingly wondering aloud whether mainstream reporters have become detached from their watchdog role. They question whether the significant corporate ownership of major media has made editors and producers more cautious about pursuing stories that question major political, corporate, and nongovernmental organizations. They question whether the declining business fortunes of many media make investigative journalism—a staple of the watchdog role—increasingly difficult to support and pursue. They worry that the demographic qualities of many leading journalists—often elite, educated at Ivy League universities, based in New York or Washington, and former political figures themselves—make them unwilling to criticize people who may well be their friends and who happen to be in political office.

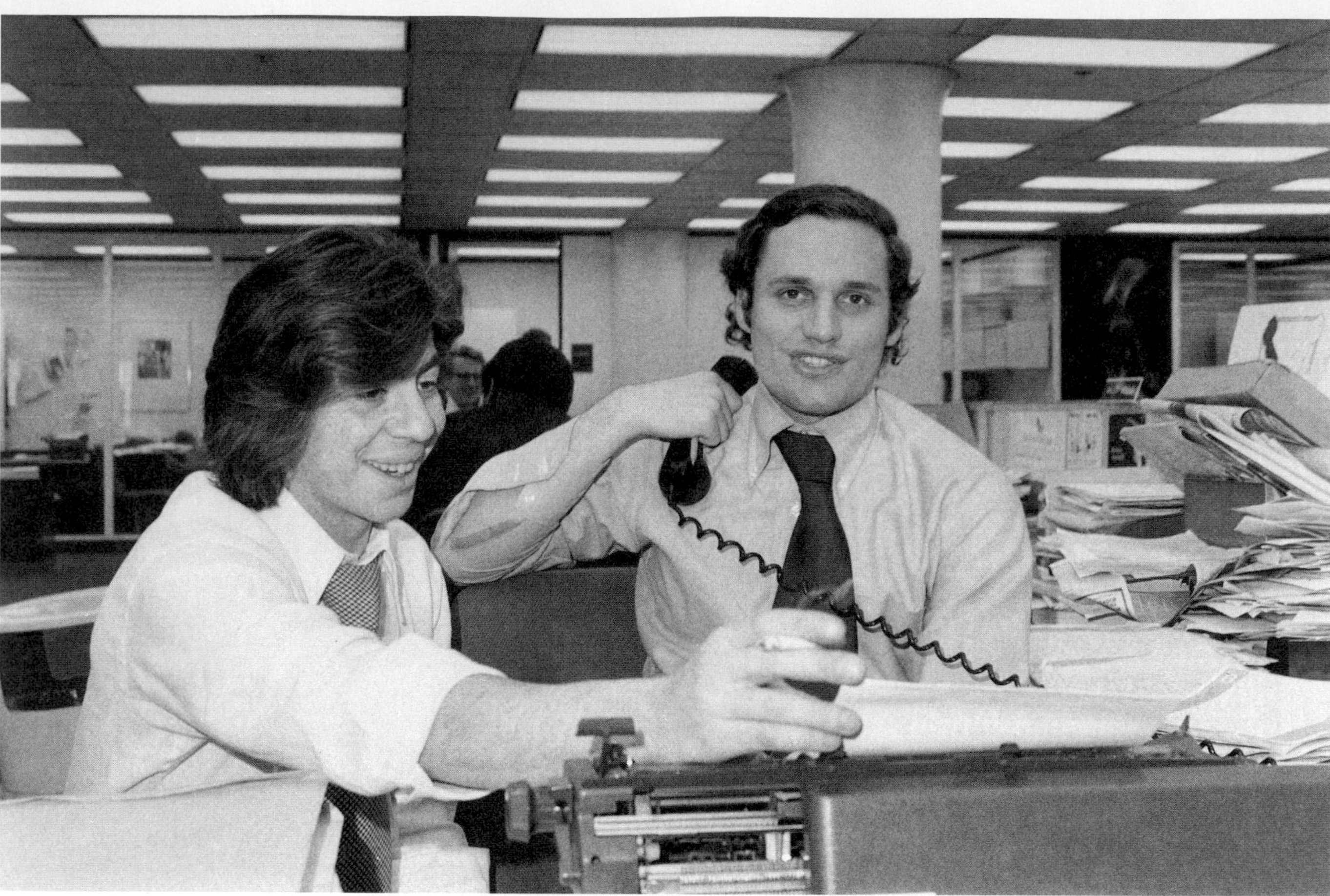

TAKING DOWN A PRESIDENT

Washington Post Reporters Bob Woodward and Carl Bernstein achieved legendary status among journalists for their work in investigating the Watergate scandal and the other illegalities practiced by the 1972 Nixon campaign.

The "revolving door" that exists, particularly in cable news and on opinion pages, whereby political figures become talking heads on news shows, contributes to the impression that the media are, in fact, part of the political power structure. This impression, too, has opened up the media to further criticism and cynicism. It has also led to competition from reporters, writers, and others who proclaim themselves to be truly independent and unconcerned with the upset they cause with their reports. And because no one has to be licensed or specially educated to be a member of the media, the barrier to entry is low—and lower still in an age when a single individual can set up a news website in a matter of hours.

The moment when this first became clear to the mainstream media was 2004, when a single blog controlled by several authors first raised questions about a report by CBS News anchor Dan Rather that suggested George W. Bush had been spared a combat role during Vietnam because of political interference. The bloggers pointed out with careful and painstaking analysis (not done by CBS) that documents used by Rather were likely to have been forged. Examples of bloggers poking holes in mainstream media accounts have since become commonplace. In a unique twist, reporters and producers have become avid contributors to the kinds of social media networks that once were themselves held at arm's length by the mainstream media. Now, it is not uncommon for reporters covering the White House to engage in direct discussion with their Twitter followers on questions they might ask the president at his next press conference. Many major publications now offer lightly edited blogs on their websites; one, *The Atlantic*, has reinvented itself significantly from a monthly issues-rich publication to a digital one focused significantly on provocative opinions. This trend of participatory journalism has opened up a new chapter in the American media experience, and where it will lead is not immediately understood.

Constraints on American Media Freedom

10.2 Identify the legal constraints under which the American media operate.

Can the Media Be Held Accountable, Censored, or Coerced?

Even in situations not related to national security, the media are not free to say whatever they want, despite the broad protections they enjoy. For example, if the media pursue a false or unsubstantiated attack on someone's good name or reputation, they can be accused of defamation and be liable for significant financial damages. To be considered defamation, an attack must be false. In the case of a public figure, the media have greater latitude to publish or broadcast criticisms of a person's character. A public figure accused of something outrageous can generally sue only if he or she can prove malice (a motive on the part of the media outlet to publish a falsehood in order to damage the individual). This is a harder allegation to prove than mere falsehood and defamation, and most public figures are unsuccessful in their suits.

Authoritarian governments handle the problem of pesky journalists in a less nuanced way. In Cuba, Saudi Arabia, and other restrictive countries, for instance, the governments prohibit dissident newspapers, and independent journalists are jailed and sometimes executed. Even after the fall of Soviet communism, Russian journalists who were critical of the government were killed, and their murders were never solved. The government of Iran not only prohibits criticism from its own journalists but has threatened foreign journalists as well.

In the United States, the media are not obligated to print facts that are beyond doubt or to defer to perspectives held by some experts to be accurate. On both sides of the climate change debate, for example, some believe the media should not treat as fact the core principles, beliefs, or conceits of the other side. Thus, the media sometimes operate as a self-policing "pack," whereby those who do not subscribe to a dominant worldview are cast out or otherwise diminished. As new forms of media have sprung up, especially independent journalists operating blogs and their own websites, the effectiveness of self-policing by the pack has decreased significantly and opened up the mainstream media to charges of bias and self-censorship.

We have addressed issue of whether the government or any other institution can prevent the media from publishing or broadcasting certain information. But can the media be compelled to publish something it would otherwise choose not to? With respect to print media, the answer is no. The courts have ruled that no individual or institution has a right to receive coverage of an opinion or pet issue in the print media. The broadcast media, on the other hand, are treated differently. The broadcast spectrum is considered a public asset; those who use the spectrum must provide a public benefit through public access channels, adhering to certain standards, and/or equal access to political figures. The federal government acting through the Federal Communications Commission (FCC) is able to exert significant control over any news organization that uses a piece of the public spectrum to broadcast. Those who do not use any spectrum—cable or Internet-only news networks, for example, do not have the same responsibilities.

Reporters May Be Compelled by the Government to Reveal Their Sources

Despite their resistance to the idea, reporters can be compelled to reveal the names of confidential sources. This mandate can become an issue when the information provided by a source is relevant to a legal matter. In 2003, for example, *Time* magazine

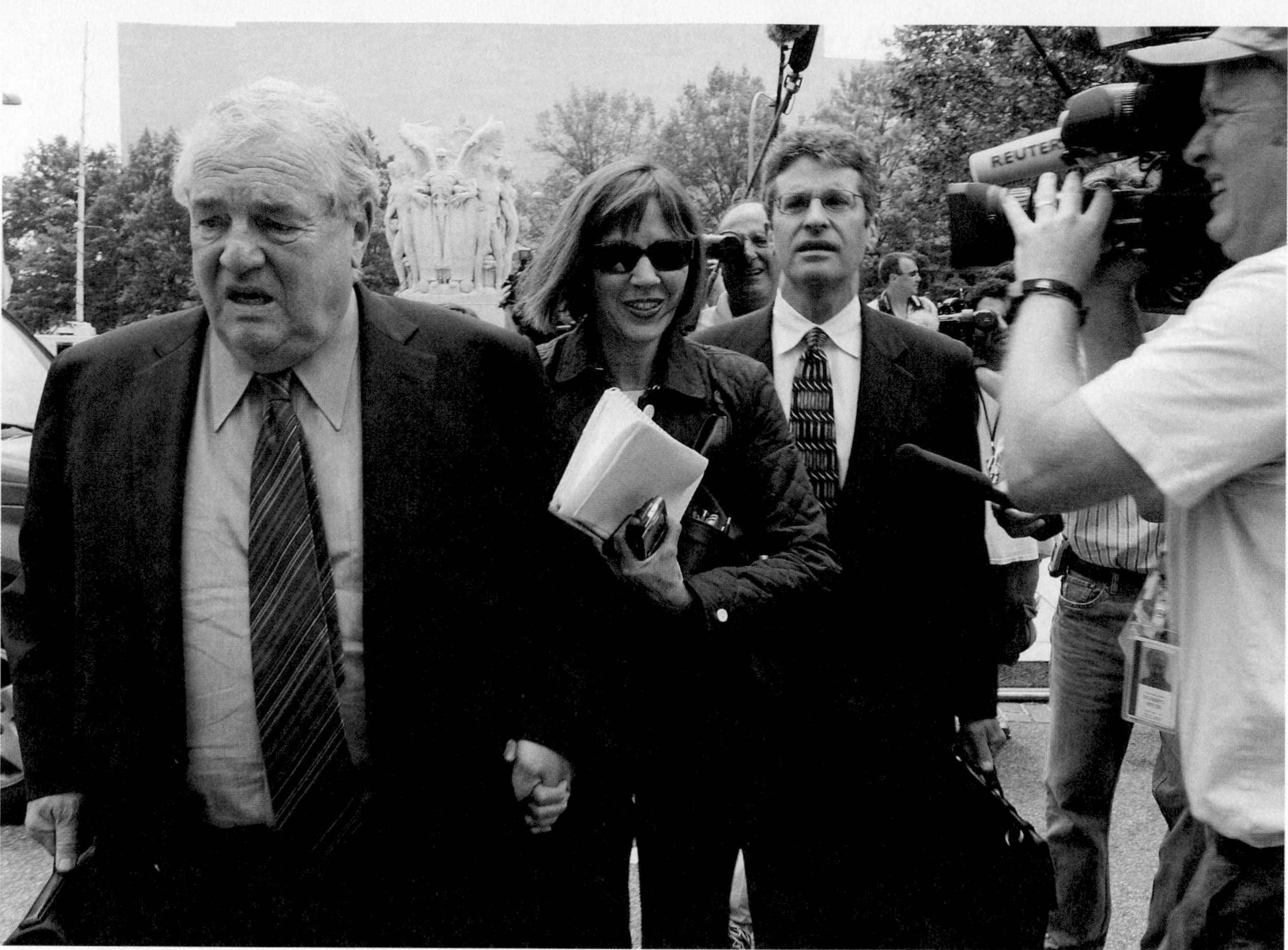

PROTECTING CONFIDENTIAL SOURCES

New York Times reporter Judith Miller received information on the identity of CIA official Valerie Plame from a government source but refused to identify the source to a grand jury investigating who leaked the sensitive information. Why would the federal government be resistant to shield laws?

published an article revealing the name of CIA officer Valerie Plame. The reporters involved in the story did nothing illegal by revealing Plame's identity, but it is illegal for a government official with authorized access to a covert agent's identity to deliberately reveal that information to a reporter. Accordingly, a federal grand jury was assembled to determine whether any criminal wrongdoing had taken place.

At the heart of the investigation was one question: Who revealed Plame's identity to reporters? Two reporters involved in the story, Matthew Cooper of *Time* magazine and Judith Miller of the *New York Times*, were called to testify. Having received permission from his source to reveal the name, Cooper identified presidential adviser Karl Rove. But Miller either received no such permission from her source or chose not to exercise it; she would not reveal her source in testimony before the grand jury. For her refusal, she was sentenced to remain in jail until the grand jury was dismissed. She eventually revealed her source—Lewis Libby, Vice President Dick Cheney's chief of staff—when he released her from her pledge of confidentiality. But this disclosure happened only after she spent 85 days in jail.

In order to avoid the choice between spending time in jail and revealing a confidential source, reporters have advocated shield laws. These laws grant journalists certain exemptions from having to testify in legal matters. Just as a priest cannot be compelled to testify against a penitent, or one spouse against the other, shield laws protect journalists from having to reveal the name of a confidential source in a legal proceeding. Most states have adopted shield laws of varying leniency, but the federal government has not. However, both federal and state courts have recognized limited exemptions from the normal requirement that a reporter testify when subpoenaed—even when no explicit statutory exemption exists.

In summary, then, reporters have some protections against compelled testimony, but those protections are far from absolute. Reporters argue they need this protection—without it, sources would fear to come forward and reveal crimes. Despite these various restrictions, the American media are still among the freest in the world. According to Freedom House's ranking of Global Press Freedom, the United States ranks 22nd out of 195 countries.[13] Even though American journalists sometimes complain about government restrictions on their activities, they operate with significant latitude. Very few journalists around the world enjoy similar freedoms.

Patterns of Media Use

10.3 Explain how technological changes have impacted patterns of media use.

The difference between today's media environment and that of the nation's first days can be illustrated with a simple anecdote: The first news report of the killing of Osama Bin Laden, in 2011, came not from a news organization but from a Twitter feed of a non-journalist. The noise from the attacks alerted a Pakistani man, who tweeted what he had heard as sounding like a combat helicopter. The political staffers and reporters who first confirmed the killing broke the news on their own Twitter and social media feeds before the accounts were given official confirmation by any government spokesperson or network news anchor.

In this sense, the media reflect the technology that permits information to spread. The quality, quantity, diversity, and power of media are directly correlated to the means of its creation and distribution. This has been true for all of American history. The political press of the Revolutionary Era was highly partisan because it was relatively easy for political partisans to launch and publish a document suited to their interests. The idea that a newspaper was expected to deliver news in some kind of neutral, fact-based way simply did not exist in any meaningful sense.

The media were not counted on to deliver news quickly or efficiently until 1837, when Samuel F.B. Morse, an American, sent the first electronic telegram using his code of dots and dashes. With the installation of the transatlantic cable in 1866, Americans could learn the news from Europe in minutes, as opposed to weeks when messages came by ship; soon both coasts of the United States were connected via telegraph wires. The speed of news delivery quickened further in the 1920s, when radio offered instant and immediate news to the entire nation, followed 20 years later with pictures in a device called television. And at the dawn of the 21st century, the spread of social media, married to Internet technology, allowed news consumers to not only share information more quickly, but also create their own news and make their own news judgments. In this last major technological shift, the audience superseded and often replaced working journalists, who had served as both gatekeepers and content creators.

Audiences began to get their news for free and to bypass the classifieds and advertisements that had once supported most media enterprises, thus disrupting the business model of many newspapers, magazines, and news shows. Audience participation in the news (or consumer-created content) has also brought a level of scrutiny that many reporters have never before experienced. And because the cost of creating content and building distribution through the Internet is far below that of purchasing broadcast licenses, the American public now has far more options in their news outlets and news choices. They may self-select what they want to hear and watch and avoid exposure to other viewpoints. All of these factors are having a major impact on U.S. civic life and forcing change in politics, government, and the media itself.

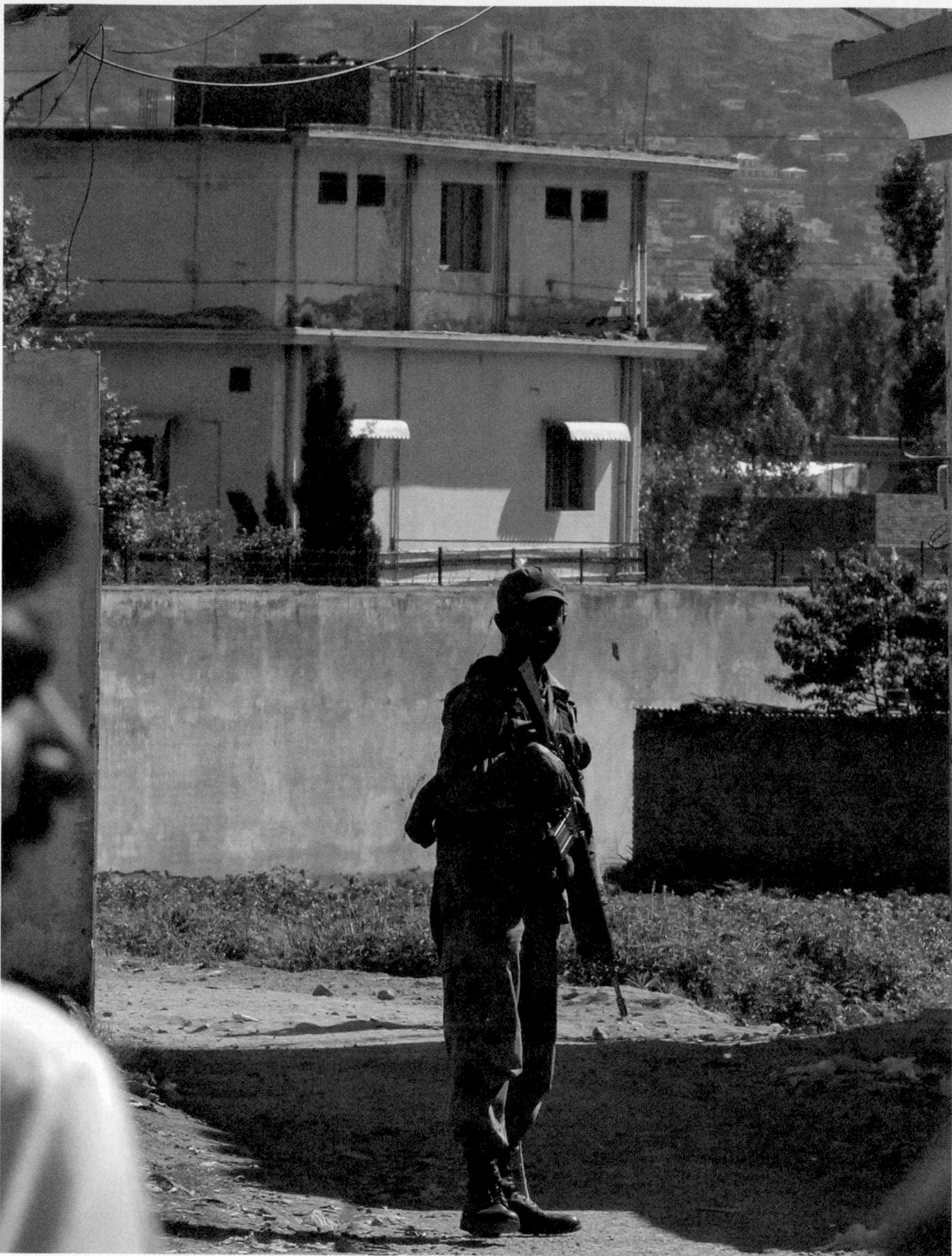

BIN LADEN KIA

Hours before President Obama announced that Navy SEALS had killed Osama Bin Laden, social media was abuzz with real time reports of the attack on a house in Abotobad.

The Media Often Focus on Strategy Over Substance

The decline in newsroom budgets, the rise of consumer-created media content through social media, and the increase in advocacy or agenda-driven journalism have meant that the once-standard work habits of journalists have changed. Reporters in both newsroom and broadcast outlets are increasingly tasked with monitoring first-person reports of news rather than observing news themselves. It is entirely possible, for example, to cover a political revolution half a world away simply by reading Twitter and Facebook feeds. Journalists covering political campaigns still follow candidates closely, but many are now relatively inexperienced compared to those who staffed campaign buses just two decades ago.

Consumers of media are often under the impression that those reporting and writing stories are close to the news and responsive to what the facts tell them. Although such reporters and producers do exist, they are increasingly rare. What often happens is that an editor or senior producer decides that a story is needed on a specific topic, with a specific angle, and even with a specific conclusion. Reporters are then assigned to collect the materials, either firsthand or through a network of freelancers and "stringers" who find whatever facts, quotes, and sound bites will support the thesis of the story. Someone who "hasn't been within 500 miles of the story" narrates the final piece.[14]

horse race
a focus in election coverage on who and what are up or down in the latest poll numbers.

This dynamic often dominates political coverage, with senior producers and editors deciding what to cover based on their own agendas, rather than on actual developments near a campaign. With less focus on issues of substance, and more on the theater of political campaigns, most media have resorted to covering the **horse race** of elections—who is winning, what is happening behind the scenes, who has committed the latest gaffe or landed a rhetorical blow, and which candidates are winning a competitive advantage. Such reporting is also referred to as "strategy frame coverage" because it sometimes treats elections purely as a competitive game for power or a contest of political strategies rather than policy ideas.

Why do television reporters, in particular, prefer this kind of coverage? It may simply be that reporters and viewers find such stories more entertaining than the dry stuff of policy papers and voting records.[15] Such coverage may also reflect cynicism about the authenticity of the candidates' views or even the meaning attached to the candidacies by supporters.[16] Reporters may believe that stories on tactics and behind-the-scenes discussions shed light on what is really driving a campaign (as opposed to what candidates and their handlers say is doing so). Furthermore, whereas candidates' issue positions and policy proposals do not change from day to day, poll numbers, political tactics, and politicians' behavior can change on a daily basis and get reported as news.

The risks in such coverage are manifold, chief among them the possibility that the public will know a great deal about the mechanics of a winning campaign, but not much about its substance. In 2008, Barack Obama spoke openly about his desire to address health care reform, strengthen financial markets regulations, and end America's involvement in Iraq. When he came to office and pursued these three goals, no one should have been surprised, but many people were. This may have been as much a failure of the media to publicize the content of Obama's speeches and policy papers as it was a failure by Obama to make clear his agenda once in office.

A Large Percentage of the Population Gets Its News from the Web

Despite the continued dominance of television as a news source, in recent years, its control has begun to weaken—particularly in broadcast television and the network news programs. Although cable news networks such as CNN and Fox News remain the most common source of news for Americans, since 2002, the Web has become an increasingly popular source of news information. That reality is reinforced by the decline in the percentage of individuals who rely primarily on national and international news from the networks' nightly news programming over the same period.[17]

Where have those who fled television news gone? Not to daily newspapers, as we have already noted. Some have turned to cable television. CNN, MSNBC, and Fox News all offer news programming in direct competition with the networks. Some former network viewers also appear to be tuning in to public radio and talk radio for their news. One broadcaster alone—Rush Limbaugh—attracts more than 13 million listeners per week, and the number could be much more according to some estimates.[18] Local television news has also managed to fill part of the role of the networks. Satellite technology now makes it possible for local news stations to cover national and international stories that formerly only the "big three" networks could cover.[19]

An increasingly large percentage of the population obtains its news from the Web. In 1995, the Web was still unfamiliar to most Americans; by January 2011, 41 percent of the U.S. population was going online to obtain most of their national

Explore on MyPoliSciLab

Where Do You Get Your Political News?

Politically-interested people get their news from four news outlets—television, the Internet, print, and radio. Among these media sources, no single one dominates the others, but partisan trends do exist. Republicans more often go to Fox News, while more Democrats go to NPR's "All Things Considered".

Americans Go To These News Sources

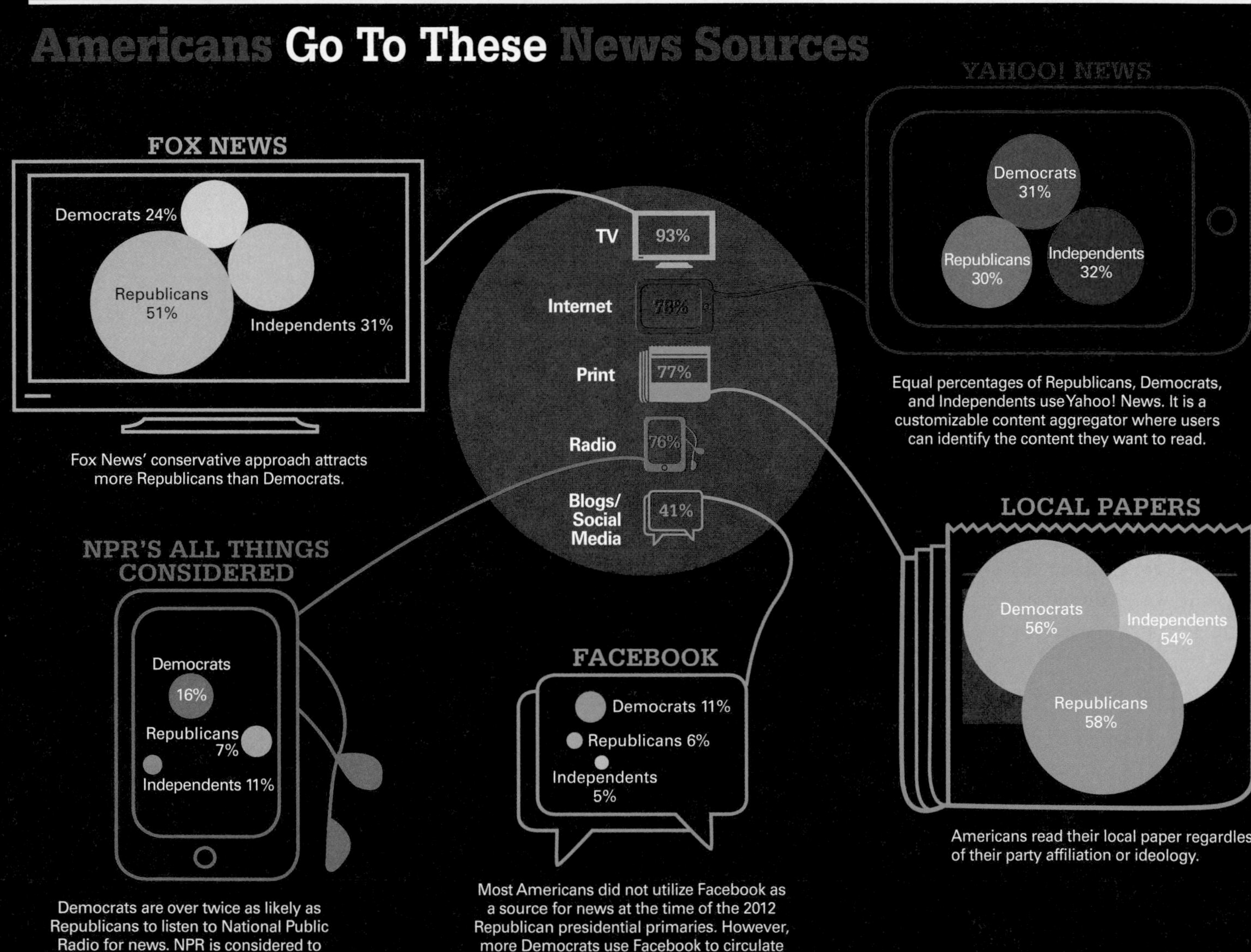

YAHOO! NEWS
Democrats 31%
Republicans 30%
Independents 32%
Equal percentages of Republicans, Democrats, and Independents use Yahoo! News. It is a customizable content aggregator where users can identify the content they want to read.
FOX NEWS
Democrats 24%
Republicans 51%
Independents 31%
Fox News' conservative approach attracts more Republicans than Democrats.
TV 93%
Internet 78%
Print 77%
Radio 76%
Blogs/ Social Media 41%
LOCAL PAPERS
Democrats 56%
Independents 54%
Republicans 58%
Americans read their local paper regardless of their party affiliation or ideology.
NPR'S ALL THINGS CONSIDERED
Democrats 16%
Republicans 7%
Independents 11%
Democrats are over twice as likely as Republicans to listen to National Public Radio for news. NPR is considered to have a "center left" approach.
FACEBOOK
Democrats 11%
Republicans 6%
Independents 5%
Most Americans did not utilize Facebook as a source for news at the time of the 2012 Republican presidential primaries. However, more Democrats use Facebook to circulate political content than Republicans.

SOURCE: Data from American National Election Survey, "Evaluations of Government and Society Study," Release Wave 4, February 2012.

Investigate Further

Concept Where are people getting their political news? Politically-interested Americans go to several types of outlets for political news. Television is still the most popular news source, but the Internet, print, and radio hold substantial ground. Despite widespread popularity among youth, social media—like Facebook—is not a dominant source for political news.

Connection How is politics related to media choices? In general, Americans tend to seek information that reinforces their politics. The rise of cable television and Internet sources compartmentalized information. People can't read or watch all the news, so they choose a few "comfortable" content providers who reinforce their opinions and beliefs.

Cause Do the major parties exhibit particular media consumption habits? Both parties have certain news sources that they favor over others. For example, Republicans rely more on Fox News while Democrats tend toward NPR's "All Things Considered". However, party crossover in media use does exist, particularly for Internet and social media sources.

and international news.[20] Ten years ago, the idea of going online to get news was regarded as foolish. Today, however, rapid download and upload speeds, high-definition tablets, video streaming, social media, mobile video capture, and broadcast in real time make possible access to the news without subscribing to a newspaper or owning a television or a radio. Less than a decade ago, a person could demonstrate familiarity with the news by quoting the number of his or her newspaper and magazine subscriptions. Now, that person can be exceptionally well informed by simply owning a smartphone.

As it happens, this trend has deepened the possibility for an informed population. News operations often use the Web to post materials or provide information that cannot be shown on their broadcasts or in print because of limited time and space. The *New York Times* regularly links readers of its paper or Web edition to additional material, such as a video interview of the reporter who wrote the story. ABC might lead its nightly newscast with results of a poll about attitudes toward the economy and the president. Although only a few seconds of airtime will be devoted to the results, the network will post additional analysis, commentary, and a full copy of the poll on its website. The depth and range of news coverage have therefore increased significantly. While the major media struggle to build an online business model, there is little doubt that the audience for news has not decreased, even as the audience for traditional news continues to do so.

In addition to online news channels, social media have increasingly become a way to produce and obtain news. In its most dramatic form, social media sites can allow participants in news events, such as disasters and political revolutions, to deliver first-person accounts in real time. Other social media allow users to post photos and links and other tidbits of news and opinion that together create an impression of reliable and accurate information. Again, although traditional journalists saw these initial trends as threats, they have come to embrace them. It is not unusual for a journalist at a major news outlet to preview a story they're working on by tweeting some of its details; responding to reader questions; going on alternative media to promote the story; and reporting the story in print, radio, and television. The distinctions among print, broadcast, and online journalists—once important within media organizations—have ceased to exist in any meaningful sense. What distinguishes journalists from one another is not the medium in which they work, but the audience they reach.

earned media
news coverage that is determined to be important to a news outlet's audience, solely by virtue of the news story's content.

paid media
advertising

microtargeting
campaign efforts that aim to hit particular voters with very specific messages tied to their individual demographics and attitudes.

Campaigns Use Microtargeting in Advertising to Reach Voters

To this point, we have discussed press coverage that is event driven. For better or worse, when a public figure says or does something that the press believes would be interesting to its audience, the remark or action is reported. In this context, the media are the sole arbiters of what events are worthy of coverage. Such **earned media** are distinguished from **paid media**—better known as advertising. Paid media can be purchased; earned media cannot.

In addition to generating revenue for news outlets, advertising is an integral part of the media's political impact: "In modern presidential campaigns, television advertising accounts for more spending than any other campaign expenditure."[21] Intuitively, one might assume that political advertisers employ a scattered or "shotgun" approach—that campaigns simply blast out as much advertising as financially possible seeking to reach as many voters as they can regardless of the audiences' demographic or socioeconomic characteristics. But the truth is more complex. Campaign advertisers most often employ a tactic known as **microtargeting,** whereby strategists identify persons open to a particular message based on such factors as election turnout, political party identification, and detailed information on spending habits. The campaigns then poll voters in order to be able to classify each voter in their files (e.g., as a soccer mom, NASCAR dad).[22]

FIGURE 10.1 DATA WARS

While campaigns still spend enormous amounts on television commercials, they are increasingly using a variety of data to pin point particular messages to particular sorts of voters. As this figure shows, campaigns not only know voters' age and gender, but their likely voting habits and issue concerns.

Although microtargeting has been traditionally discussed and used in relation to electoral campaign strategies such as the use of direct mail or phone banks, campaigns are increasingly using microtargeting in television advertising as well. Once media consultants have the data on the demographics of a show's audience, for example, stay-at-home moms or sports-fanatic single men, they can use that information to create advertising tailored to appeal to these demographics, rather than sending a generic message to everyone. According to political scientists, "although airing television advertising may still be a 'shotgun' approach, media consultants increasingly believe that more precise targeting and tailored appeals can increase the efficiency of a 30-[second] campaign ad."[23]

Microtargeting goes beyond simply putting ads on Fox News or MSNBC. Surveys indicate that Republican-leaning voters are more likely than Democratic-leaning voters to watch sports programs and national news.[24] Democrats by contrast make up a greater share of the audience watching science fiction and dating shows. By learning which television programs' audiences consist of individuals more or less likely to vote and how they are likely to vote, advertisers can focus on those audiences they deem to be most strategically significant.

Microtargeting enables campaigns to focus their advertising on voters who fall into three distinct categories: those most likely to support their candidate (rallying the base); those, such as independent voters, who are least likely to have decided whom they will support in the election; or those likely to support their opponents.[25] Research examining where the campaigns advertised during the 2008 presidential campaign gives a glimpse into the microtargeting strategies employed:

> In 2008, [Sen. John] McCain devoted relatively more resources to programs with a large religious audience, and [then Sen. Barack] Obama placed more ads (relative to McCain) during programs with larger audiences of Blacks and Hispanics. . . . But contrary to our findings from 2000 and 2004, the Democratic nominee in 2008 actually devoted relatively more resources to programs that featured larger Republican audiences than did the Republican nominee. The Obama campaign also placed disproportionately more ads during programs with higher turnout than did the McCain campaign. These programs with high-turnout audiences generally attract a greater proportion of Republican viewers. Finally . . . we see that both candidates were speaking to independents . . . and McCain did not target genres with Republican audiences any more than genres with Democratic audiences.[26]

Are the Media Biased?

10.4 Determine whether the media are biased.

Explore on MyPoliSciLab
Simulation: You Are a Newspaper Editor

One enduring debate among observers of American politics is whether media coverage of politics and government exhibits **bias,** that is, favorable treatment to certain politicians, policy positions, groups, or political outcomes. Certain aspects of the American media are decidedly and unapologetically partisan. Radio hosts Rush Limbaugh and Sean Hannity, for example, are openly conservative and are far more critical of Democrats than Republicans in their daily monologues. Similarly, Chris Matthews and Rachel Maddow of MSNBC are clearly left of center and often criticize Republican politicians and conservative viewpoints. But these media figures, who are unabashedly one-sided and do not subscribe to any notions of fairness, do not reflect instances of media bias. The question of media bias depends entirely on the particular medium's own definition of objectivity—its stated commitment to avoid partisan or political bias.

bias
favorable treatment to certain politicians, policy positions, groups, and political outcomes.

Against this definition, bias may depend significantly on who decides. Many critics say that the corporate ownership of major media outlets renders their news accounts subtly, if not exclusively, biased. Others say that the major media's political habits—most working journalists vote for Democrats rather than Republicans—are enough proof of bias, regardless of the work these same journalists produce. Regular consumers of media may perceive no bias whatsoever in most of the news stories they read or see. But on occasion, they will have firsthand knowledge of an event or an issue that is the subject of a news story. In that instance, they may see bias creep into the report. They may wonder: Does this bias affect everything else I am reading and seeing? If so, what does that mean?

The Implications of a Biased Media Are Significant

A biased media could result in several negative outcomes. First, it could lead to a distorted democratic process—one in which the public makes up its mind on the basis of incomplete and possibly misleading information. Second, it might contribute to a climate in which the public is less informed about matters of politics and government than it could be. Third, it may lead to public cynicism about all information, resulting in greater public consumption of news from alternative and perhaps even less accurate news outlets, or consumers might switch to more entertainment-oriented "news light" programs, such as the early morning network offerings including *Good Morning America*. Fourth, politicians themselves might begin to ignore the news media and move to more controlled and friendlier media outlets.

In truth, some or all of these outcomes have materialized in certain respects in recent years, and it is unknown whether they have occurred because of rising public perception of media bias or independent of such perceptions. For instance, the rise of comedy shows such as *The Daily Show* or *The Colbert Report* as a source of news may be a simple outgrowth of the quality of the writing on such shows, as opposed to greater cynicism about the mainstream media, or viewers could be attracted to the sarcasm and bite of such shows, preferring their news with more bias and point of view. This is an area ripe for potential scholarly inquiry into the extent of media bias and the implications of such bias and whether bias drives audiences away from mainstream media outlets or whether audiences prefer their news delivered differently regardless.

Anecdotal Evidence of Bias in the Media Is Mixed

In the debate over media bias, much of the evidence is anecdotal—that is, it is based on a few isolated examples that may or may not represent overall media coverage. Some studies have sought to isolate specific examples of potential bias. An organization called Fairness and Accuracy in Reporting (FAIR), for example, has produced studies indicating that conservative think tanks are cited more often in the media than left-leaning ones.[27] On the other hand, the Center for Media and Public Affairs found that in the 2008 election, Barack Obama received the most favorable coverage of any general election candidate for the presidency since 1980.[28]

☐ Media Content Shows Little Evidence of Bias

Obviously, by choosing issues, media outlets, and time periods selectively, one can produce evidence of both liberal and conservative media bias. The question, however, is whether a comprehensive analysis across a broad range of issues, a wide variety of media outlets, and a substantial time period would indicate systematic bias. Ultimately, the proof is in the actual content of media reporting.

SELF-ASSESSMENT One way to assess the content is to ask journalists themselves what they think of it. In a survey of more than 1,700 newspaper journalists, the American Society of Newspaper Editors asked the following question: "Thinking about how your newspaper tends to cover particular social or political groups, is that coverage sometimes too favorable or sometimes unfavorable?"

At first glance, the figures suggest a bias against conservatives; the reporters indicated that they report less favorably on conservatives than on liberals. This finding is not consistent throughout, however. For example, the same reporters indicated that the military and the wealthy, two groups usually associated with the American right, received overly favorable coverage. Similarly, poor people and labor union members, groups usually associated with the left, appeared to receive disproportionately unfavorable coverage. Then again, gun owners—another group associated with political conservatives—also seem to receive unfavorable coverage.

More generally, a series of surveys conducted over more than 40 years has shown journalists to be more liberal than conservative, and to be more liberal than the average American.[29] A survey of Washington, D.C.–based reporters indicated that 89 percent had voted for Democrat Bill Clinton in the 1992 election—compared with only 42 percent of the American public. Although that survey was criticized for its low response rate, the reality remains: Journalists lean left.[30]

Prior to the 2008 election, 55 members of the staff of *Slate* magazine were asked whom they would vote for. All but two said they would vote for the eventual winner, Barack Obama. Another 2008 survey indicated that whereas the majority identified themselves as moderate, those journalists who identified themselves as liberal outnumbered those identifying themselves as conservative by a significant margin, and that journalists were much more liberal in their political orientations than the public as a whole (see Table 10.1 for this breakdown).[31]

Some argue that such results are evidence that reporters' political predispositions inevitably make their way into news stories, leading to biased reporting. Others argue that there is no correlation between journalists' personal beliefs and the content of their reporting. First, they note that journalists are trained to set aside their personal predispositions when reporting on politics and government. A Democratic journalist reporting on a Republican administration, they say, is no different from a Democratic

TABLE 10.1 *NEWSPAPER JOURNALISTS' SELF-ASSESSMENTS.* JOURNALISTS ARE MORE LIKELY THAN THE GENERAL PUBLIC TO CALL THEMSELVES LIBERAL.

Ideological self-rating	General public*	National press	Local press
Liberal	20%	32%	23%
Moderate	35%	53%	58%
Conservative	35%	8%	14%
Don't know	10%	7%	5%
	100%	100%	100%

*Public figures from August 2008 Pew Media Believability Study (N=1800).
Source: http://www.stateofthemedia.org.

doctor operating on a Republican patient. Second, they say that the economics of the media industry are designed to drive out biased coverage. Newspapers, television and radio programs, and newsmagazines that allowed bias to enter their coverage of politics and government would risk offending paying customers and advertisers who did not share their opinions. If for no other reason than the "bottom line" then, the media must work to keep their products bias free. Third, even though many reporters may exhibit liberal tendencies, publishers and owners of radio, television, and print media outlets, being businesspeople, are presumed to exhibit more conservative leanings. Indeed, many newspapers have been known to feature slightly liberal-leaning news coverage but strongly conservative editorials. Somewhere, then, in the balance between reporters' and owners' politics, the media generally get the story right. In the final analysis, it is difficult to discern whether bias actually exists in U.S. newsrooms, and if so, in what form.

CONTENT ANALYSIS Given the mixed nature of these findings, political scientists and other researchers have moved beyond examination of survey data into actual content analysis of media reporting. Content analysis is a technique for identifying themes, categories, and logical groupings in written material or material that can be converted into a written transcript. This could include television programming, newspaper and magazine reporting, and radio broadcasts. The methods of content analysis, therefore, can be applied to the study of media bias.

Because presidential elections are the great spectator sport of American politics, scholars have studied media bias primarily in the context of presidential election coverage. A 2000 meta-analysis examined 59 studies of media bias in presidential election coverage from 1948 to 1996 that included analysis of television, newspaper, and weekly newsmagazine reporting on the presidential election. They investigated three kinds of bias:

- **Gatekeeping bias:** presenting news stories that cast a favored party or politician in a positive light while ignoring stories that would cast the party or politician in a negative light.
- **Coverage bias:** providing more news coverage to a favored party or politician and less to opponents.
- **Statement bias:** making positive statements about a favored party or politician and negative ones about opponents.

In analyzing the results of the 59 studies addressing these three kinds of bias, the authors concluded that "the results indicate an aggregate, across all media and all elections, of zero overall bias."[32]

This conclusion does not indicate that every media outlet was bias free in every presidential election conducted between 1948 and 1996. First, the number of studies of gatekeeping bias in newspaper and television news coverage of presidential elections was too small to draw any definitive conclusions.[33] Second, bias in one medium in one election can be offset by an opposing bias in another medium and in a different election. For example, the study identified small pro-Democratic coverage and statement biases in television news covering presidential elections, and even smaller pro-Republican coverage and statement biases in weekly newsmagazine reporting of the same elections. These two results effectively canceled each other, leading to a finding of zero "net" bias.

Recall, however, that even with the rise of the Internet, Americans' consumption of the news still tends to come disproportionately from television. Thus, "a little" bias in television news coverage could have a big impact on viewer beliefs. The researchers recognized that possibility but found it irrelevant. Specifically, they acknowledged that Democratic candidates received just over 10 percent more television coverage than Republican candidates, but they claimed this difference was "almost certainly undetectable by the audience." (Were they right? We discuss the impact of the mass media on public opinion in the next section.)

Presidential elections, as interesting and exciting as they can be, are not the only setting in which biased media coverage may occur. What about the day-to-day media coverage of Congress, the presidency, and current events? Is that coverage biased and, if so, in what direction? Political scientists have not reached a consensus on the answers to these questions. The existing studies are too few, too limited in scope, and too contradictory in their conclusions to provide any definitive answers. Perhaps after another generation of scholarship, it will be possible to conduct a meta-analysis of the sort described earlier in the context of election coverage. Until then, the jury is out.

Media Effects on Public Opinion

10.5 Assess the effect of the media on political attitudes and behaviors.

To what extent does the content of media coverage affect public opinion? Startling demonstrations of the power of mass media in the 1920s, 1930s, and 1940s prompted the early research on this subject. One early indication of this impact was the panic following news of the stock market

THE POWER OF THE MEDIA

When Orson Welles performed the radio play *War of the Worlds,* millions of Americans heard the broadcast and actually thought the United States was under alien invasion. This event and the massive newspaper coverage that it received suggested that people could be moved by the media to believe just about anything. How much do you think you are influenced by mass media?

crash in 1929. Prior major declines in the stock market had not induced as strong a public reaction. But the rise of radio accelerated the awareness of the 1929 decline and set off a major panic. During the 1930s, two European fascist dictators, Benito Mussolini in Italy and Adolf Hitler in Germany, cultivated popular support through radio addresses and newsreels that carried their fiery speeches to enraptured crowds. Hitler's political party, the Nazis, distributed radios to the public for free—the radios were programmed to receive the signal from only a Nazi-controlled station. In 1938, Orson Welles's dramatic radio broadcast of H. G. Wells's science fiction book *War of the Worlds* set off a panic among a million Americans who mistook the dramatization for an actual news broadcast of an alien invasion.[34]

Observing these events, scholars worried that clever use of the mass media could enable leaders to inject the masses with supportive attitudes the way a hypodermic needle injects a patient with medicine. One researcher warned that "one persuasive person could, through the use of mass media, bend the world's population to his will."[35]

minimal effect
the theory that change in voting intent as a result of mass media exposure was relatively rare.

agenda setting
the media's role in determining which issues the public considers important, by covering some issues and ignoring others.

Early Research into the Impact of Media Pointed to Minimal Effects

But whether the media can be used so effectively and directly is not clear. Researchers in the United States first investigated the effects of the mass media on voting behavior. These seminal voting studies conducted in the 1940s and 1950s revealed an electorate surprisingly unaffected by media coverage. The studies found most voters were party loyalists whose votes could not be swayed by media messages. A number of group and personal characteristics—particularly religion, social status, and place of residence—also strongly dictated political predispositions. Partisanship and other political predispositions were so strong, in fact, that large majorities of voters in the 1950s and 1960s made their voting decision before the general election campaign and the related media coverage even began.[36] Thus, changes in voting intent as a result of mass media exposure were relatively rare.

This finding in the early literature came to be referred to as **minimal effect.** For years, media scholars accepted the minimal effect conclusion, although many found it unsatisfying. One researcher explained the scholars' dilemma as follows:

> The mass media have been a source of great frustration to social scientists. On one hand, citizens in modern democracies routinely develop opinions about political events and personalities far beyond their direct experience. It is hard to imagine where many of these opinions come from if not from the mass media. And yet it has proven maddeningly difficult to demonstrate that the mass media actually produce powerful effects on opinion.[37]

Ultimately, scholars were able to demonstrate that the media's effect is more than minimal. But to do so, they had to overcome certain assumptions about the kinds of effects they should be looking for and how such effects might work.

The Media May Exert Influence Through Agenda Setting, Priming, and Framing

Early research into media effects focused on persuasion, or changing someone's mind about an issue, person, or group. But the media can also play a role in political socialization: in educating the public with basic information about politics, government, issues, groups, and candidates; in stimulating or discouraging political participation among the public; in helping crystallize or reinforce existing beliefs and predispositions; and in determining which issues the public and policy makers consider important, known as **agenda setting.**

What the media focus on, the public tends to treat as most important. A classic example of this is crime. When crime is covered extensively, the public begins to believe that there is a crime wave. Certain kinds of crime, such as random acts of violence on innocent bystanders, will garner significant coverage, making people fear for their lives at

10.1

10.2

10.3

10.4

10.5

priming
a media effect in which the public assesses the performance of politicians and candidates in terms of the issues that the media have emphasized.

framing
a media effect in which a journalist simplifies and condenses information in a story in order to put the issue into clear focus for the audience.

selective exposure
the tendency of people to expose themselves to information that is in accord with their beliefs.

all times of day. In reality, the most common forms of crime—especially those involving assault and murder—occur among people who already know each other, often during domestic disputes. Yet, such crimes often do not garner as much coverage. The public is therefore conditioned to believe that the greatest threat to life and limb comes from complete strangers when the truth is that the greatest threats may come from people we already know. The media's overplaying one story and underplaying another can shape the public's perceptions significantly and create an agenda to solve one problem when another related problem is more urgently in need of public engagement and solution.

Researchers have also demonstrated **priming,** a media effect in which the public assesses the performance of politicians and candidates in terms of the issues that the media have emphasized. Finally, **framing,** defined as how a story is reported (as opposed to the substance of the story itself) is another way in which the media can influence its audience.[38] Journalists work under a number of constraints, including how much time/space can be devoted to a given story and the level of knowledge the audience may have about a given issue. Stories must be framed to adhere to these constraints.

Imagine, for example, that the media devote extensive coverage to the issue of religiously motivated terrorism. If the public begins to consider terrorism as an important problem because of this media coverage, this is evidence of agenda setting. If the public also begins to evaluate the performance of the president in terms of what he is doing or not doing to combat terrorism, that is evidence of priming. And, if in their coverage journalists decide not to distinguish among different religious denominations when reporting on people's attitudes toward terrorism, that is framing. The experiments described in *How Do We Know? Do People React to Coverage of Events or the Events Themselves?* demonstrate that people exposed to extra stories on defense preparedness tended to evaluate the president more heavily in terms of his performance in addressing defense preparedness. The same held true for the pollution and inflation issues. Thus, the media appear to have a priming effect on public opinion.

The media draw the attention of policy makers as well. For example, studies have shown that policy makers' attention to the issues of global warming, the North American Free Trade Agreement, and the Clinton administration's Whitewater scandal increased, in part, as a result of intensive media coverage of these issues.[39] The research in this area has not been as thorough, and the conclusions not as strong, as in studies of the effect that the media have on what gets on the public's policy agenda. Furthermore, the research often suggests a two-way relationship: Media coverage affects policy makers' agendas, but policy makers' agendas also affect what the media cover. Still, most of the research on the agenda-setting power of the media among policy makers, and particularly the most recent research, indicates that the media can exhibit a strong influence on the issues that policy makers choose to pay attention to.[40]

Three Primary Phenomena May Limit the Media's Influence on Attitudes and Behaviors

The early media effects research tended to assume that with enough exposure to a particular media message, individuals would eventually accept it. But this assumption was inconsistent with theories and findings from the fields of communications and psychology. Three phenomena limit the ability of media to influence attitudes and behaviors. The first is **selective exposure,** the tendency of people to expose themselves to information that is in accord with their beliefs. As we discussed earlier in this chapter, the fragmented and increasingly partisan world of cable and Internet coverage of politics enables people to avoid information and arguments that might upset their belief system—and potentially change their opinions. Unlike an advertisement on television, individuals deliberately expose themselves to or actively seek out information from the Web or from a talk radio station. These sources may mobilize and energize base supporters (Republicans through talk radio, for example, and Democrats through liberal blogs), but because people probably already agree with the source, the persuasive effects are likely to be severely limited.

How Do We Know?

Do People React to Coverage of Events or to the Events Themselves?

The Question

Media outlets are profit-oriented businesses that must sell advertising and subscriptions. To do so, they must make their content appealing, and a good way to ensure that appeal is to cover issues their audience considers important. The media will cover the economy during a recession. At the same time, many people will lose a job, know someone who has lost a job, or witness local companies going out of business. They have an understanding of the problems in the economy through direct, personal experience and through media coverage of the recession. So, when people tell researchers that they believe the performance of the economy is an important issue, are they reflecting their own experience or are they responding to media coverage? More generally, when it comes to measuring the agenda-setting power of the media, do people react to media coverage of events or to the events themselves? How do we know?

Why It Matters

Even though most people and politicians assume that the media have extraordinary power to shape mass opinions and influence political behavior, scholars have had a hard time finding evidence of significant effects. The failure to find media effects has been described by one scholar as "one of the most notable embarrassments of modern social science."[a] The implication of this failure is significant. If the media have the ability to shape mass opinions and influence political behavior, any instances of bias could induce the public to believe something they would not ordinarily believe. By the same token, if the media's ability to influence public opinion is either nil or severely limited, the overriding concern for objectivity in American media may be entirely misplaced.

Investigating the Answer

Experiments have been designed to disentangle the sort of "chicken or egg" causal puzzle that exists when examining the potential agenda-setting power of the media. The 1989 book *News That Matters* offered an experimental research approach that addressed concerns about both determining causality and accurately measuring exposure to particular media sources.[b] The researchers recruited hundreds of volunteers to participate in their experiment. They asked participants to complete a questionnaire covering a variety of topics relevant to politics and current events. Participants were then randomly divided into groups.

Over the next four days, each group gathered and watched what participants were told were recordings of the previous evening's network news. The researchers, however, had manipulated the news broadcasts to emphasize certain issues. For example, one group saw broadcasts with a few added stories on American defense preparedness. Another group saw broadcasts with extra stories on pollution. Another saw additional stories on inflation. Because the groups were kept separate, they did not realize they were watching slightly different versions of the news. All assumed they were watching the same newscast.

To make the experience of watching the television news more realistic, the researchers sought to create a comfortable, homelike atmosphere for participants. They provided newspapers, magazines, and refreshments and asked questions in the survey that were designed to mask the true goal of their research.

After the groups had watched the manipulated broadcasts on four consecutive nights, the researchers again administered a questionnaire to participants. Answers to this second questionnaire revealed that individuals who had seen the broadcasts with added stories on defense preparedness considered that issue much more important than they had before the experiment began. The same held true for pollution, though not for inflation. (The authors argued that participants considered inflation such an important issue before the experiment that there was little room for them to show more concern after the experiment.) Thus, the agenda-setting hypothesis was largely supported; media emphasis on an issue could elevate the salience of that issue in the public mind.

The Bottom Line

The finding that media emphasis could elevate the salience of an issue was important. But just as important was the fact that this hypothesis was supported in an experimental setting. This controlled group could not in any way influence the way the news broadcasts were shaped—therefore, there was no chicken-egg problem. The news broadcast determined the news agenda that was presented to the audience; the audience did not determine the news agenda (nor did any politicians). Therefore, it could not be argued that the media coverage reflected audience concerns. Given the difficulties in systematically measuring what the media cover and what people are exposed to in the real world, experiments such as this have become a useful way for scholars to study media effects.

Thinking Critically

1. Ultimately, what effect do you think that the media's agenda setting power has on influencing public opinion and policy outcomes?
2. How much variance is there in the sorts of things that different media outlets cover and how does this lead to different sorts of public concerns?

---

[a]Larry Bartels, "Messages Received: The Political Impact of Media Exposure," *American Political Science Review* 87, 2 (1993): 267.
[b]S. Iyengar and D. R. Kinder, *News That Matters: Television and American Opinion*, American Politics and Political Economy Series (Chicago: University of Chicago Press, 1989).

10.1

10.2

10.3

10.4

10.5

selective perception
the tendency of individuals to interpret information in ways consistent with their beliefs.

selective retention
the tendency of individuals to recall information that is consistent with existing beliefs and to discard information that runs counter to them.

cognitive dissonance
a state in which some of one's attitudes, beliefs, or understandings are inconsistent with others.

The second phenomenon is **selective perception,** the tendency of individuals to interpret information in ways consistent with their beliefs. Imagine, for example, a television news story depicting President Barack Obama talking to troops returning home from Afghanistan. An Obama supporter likely would see this as evidence of the president's patriotism and support for the military. An Obama detractor, on the other hand, might see it as a politician seeking to obscure the fact that he is pulling troops out of a country still at war, with American goals unmet.

Consider what happens after a presidential debate. Republicans and Democrats watch the very same debate, but Republicans inevitably conclude that the Republican performed better, and Democrats conclude that the Democrat performed better. In part, this is a consequence of selective perception.

Finally, there is **selective retention,** the tendency of individuals to recall information that is consistent with existing beliefs and to discard information that runs counter to them. An admirer of President Ronald Reagan and his supply-side economics, for example, would recall the significant tax cuts enacted in Reagan's first and second terms but might well forget the substantial tax increases that were also enacted during Reagan's first term. A critic of President Obama's handling of the war in Afghanistan might forget that he ordered a surge of troops into Afghanistan in his first year in office, an effort that proved successful in putting down a Taliban offensive there.

Note that there is a common element in these phenomena that limits the ability of the media to influence attitudes and behaviors. All represent efforts by individuals to avoid or reduce cognitive dissonance. **Cognitive dissonance** is a state in which some of one's attitudes, beliefs, or understandings are inconsistent with others. This

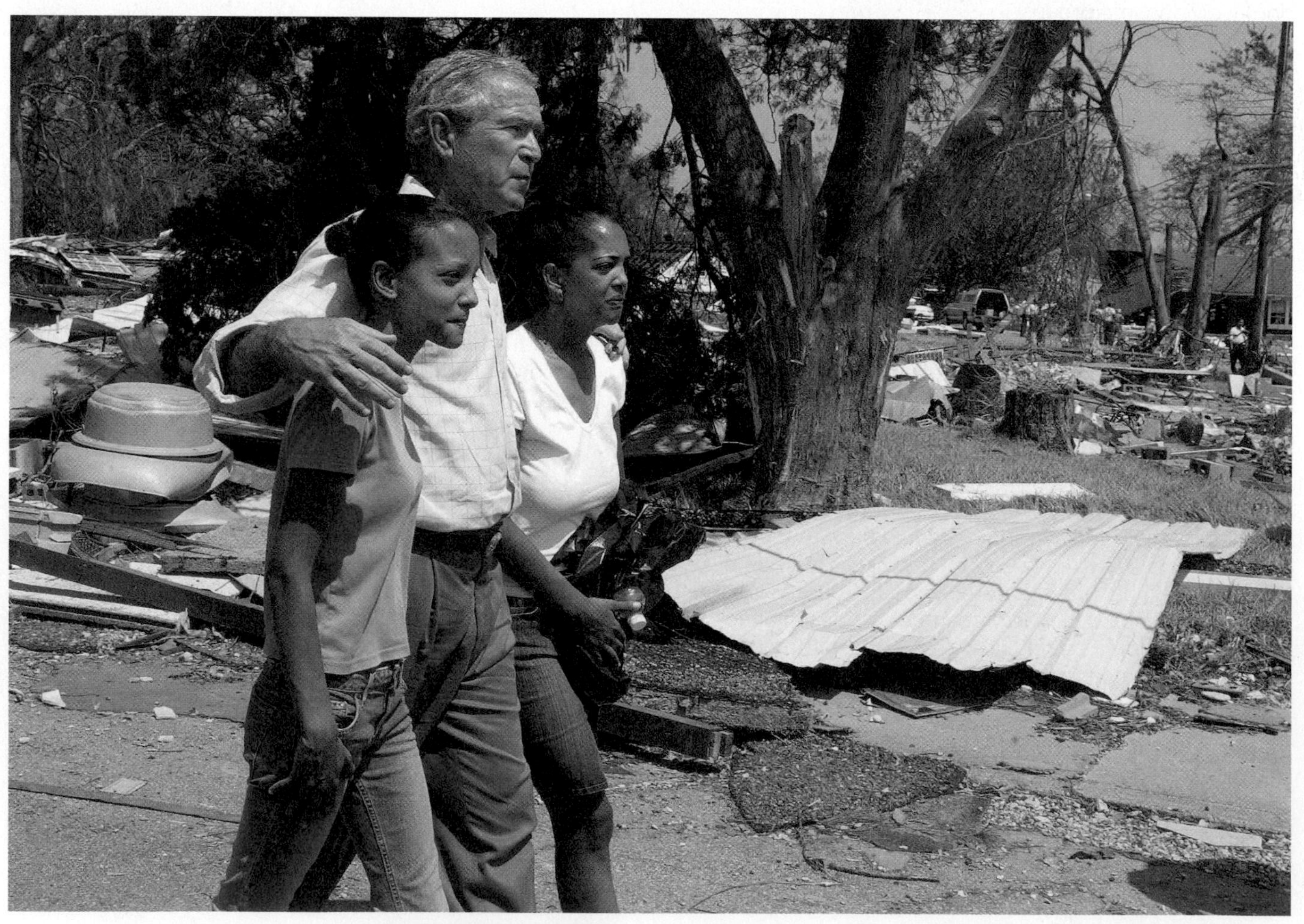

SELECTIVE PERCEPTION

As a result of selective perception, your previous attitudes toward President George W. Bush would likely influence what you think of this picture of the president inspecting Hurricane Katrina damage with two people affected by the disaster.

dissonance leads to psychological discomfort, which people normally try to avoid or remedy.[41] The effect of selective exposure, selective perception, and selective retention is to render the information inside one's head more internally consistent.

Think again about the example of selective exposure. If a conservative reader suddenly stopped listening to Rush Limbaugh and started reading the Daily Kos, she would be exposed to a number of arguments and ideas that were inconsistent with her existing worldview. This exposure might force her to question some of her beliefs. She might end up having doubts about matters on which she had held a settled opinion for years. On some issues, she might even be forced to change her mind. All of this could cause psychological discomfort. A sure way to avoid that discomfort, however, would be not to read the Daily Kos in the first place.

Selective exposure, selective perception, and selective retention all limit the impact that the media can have on individual attitudes. If people are inclined to see, hear, interpret, and retain only information that reinforces their existing beliefs, the media's ability to influence attitudes is limited to the audiences it has. A media outlet is unlikely to influence, through deliberate efforts, those audiences that already avoid that outlet.

political attentiveness
an individual's general attention to and knowledge of politics.

political predisposition
the interests, values, and experiences that help organize one's thinking about politics.

Exposure, Comprehension, and Receptivity Are Preconditions for Media Effects

Discovering the consequences of selective exposure, perception, and retention led political scientists to approach the study of media effects differently. Rather than simply assuming a direct link between the content of media messages and public opinion, they began studying the necessary preconditions for a message to change opinion. One of these is *exposure*—whether a person actually sees, hears, or reads a particular media message. Another is *comprehension*, understanding a message to which one has been exposed. A third is *receptivity*, which refers to an individual's openness to accepting a message communicated through the media.

Without exposure, comprehension, and receptivity, an individual cannot be influenced by a media message. If we look for media effects on public opinion among the public at large, we will probably be disappointed because many people, perhaps most, will not have been exposed to a particular media message, will not have comprehended it, or will not have been receptive to it. But if we look for effects among individuals who have been exposed to a message, who have comprehended it, and who are at least potentially receptive to it, then our search is likely to be more fruitful.

Moderately Attentive and Predisposed Individuals Are Most Likely to Feel Media Influence

In *The Nature and Origins of Mass Opinion*, political scientist John Zaller argues that the likelihood of exposure to and comprehension of a media message depends largely on **political attentiveness**, an individual's general attention to and knowledge of politics.[42] An individual who is highly attentive to and knowledgeable about politics is likely to be exposed to, and understand, most politically oriented media messages. On the other hand, someone who pays little attention to politics and understands little of the political world will either miss most political messages in the media or fail to understand them if he or she should happen to come across them.

Receptivity also depends on **political predisposition**—the interests, values, and experiences that help organize an individual's thinking about politics. Someone who has very strong political predispositions is unlikely to be receptive to media messages that contradict those predispositions. For example, someone who is firmly convinced that U.S. troops should be used only to guard America's borders is unlikely to be receptive to media messages indicating the need for a deployment of troops to, say, the Middle East.

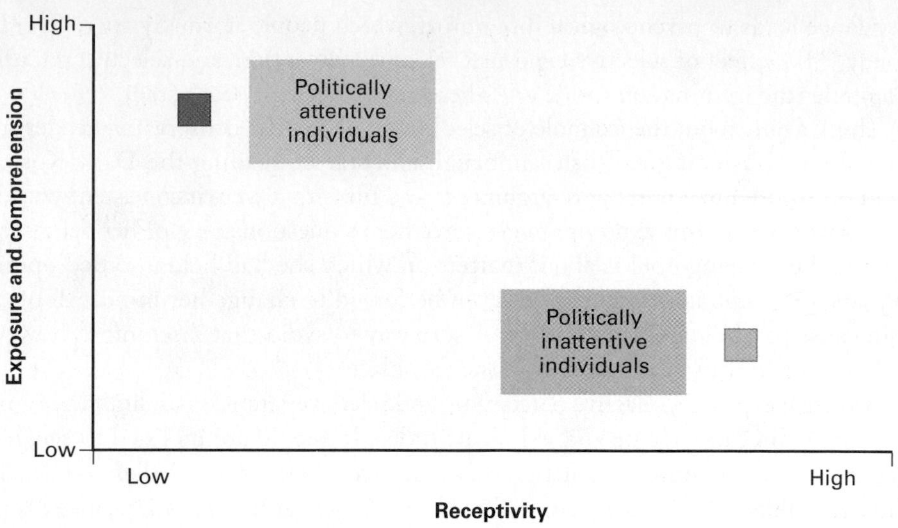

FIGURE 10.2 EXPOSURE TO AND INFLUENCE OF MEDIA MESSAGES

Those most likely to be influenced by the media are less likely to be exposed to and understand media messages.

These insights have many interesting implications. Data indicate that the most politically attentive individuals also tend to have the strongest political predispositions; therefore, individuals who are most likely to be exposed to and comprehend media messages (people who are most politically attentive) are least likely to be persuaded by them (because they have the strongest predispositions). The reverse is also true—the least politically attentive individuals tend to have the weakest political predispositions. Although the latter are most likely to be persuaded by media messages (because they have the weakest political predispositions), they are least likely to be exposed to and comprehend media messages (because they are least politically attentive). Figure 10.2 illustrates these relationships.

Who, then, are the most likely candidates for political persuasion by the media? People right in the middle—that is, individuals with a medium level of political attentiveness and political dispositions of medium strength. They will not be exposed to and comprehend every message that comes through the media, but they will encounter and understand many of them. And when they do, their political predispositions will be flexible enough to accept many of these messages. These realities suggest that part of the failure by political scientists to find strong media effects in the past was a failure to focus the search on this middle group.

Zaller does not argue that this middle group is the only one that can be influenced by the media or that the media always influence this middle group. In some cases, when a message is particularly prominent (such as the coverage of Osama Bin Laden's death), even the least attentive person will be unable to miss it. The massive increase in President George W. Bush's job approval ratings after the September 11, 2001, terrorist attacks reflected the fact that everyone—from the most politically attentive to the least—had gotten the message about the attacks and the administration's strong response.

If a message is relatively "quiet," opinion change can still take place, but it will bypass all but the most politically attentive. Between 1964 and 1966, for example, press coverage of the Vietnam War became more negative. During that same period, some highly politically attentive individuals—but only highly politically attentive individuals—grew less supportive of the war. Why? Because only the highly attentive were exposed to and able to comprehend the change in the tone of media coverage. Individuals of middle and low attentiveness missed this shift, so their support for the war remained strong.

If we think in these terms, it becomes relatively easy to identify areas in which the media can have a large impact and those in which the impact is likely to be limited. For example, we know now that predispositions limit people's receptivity to media messages. If we want to look for media effects, then, we should look for cases in which predispositions are weak. Think, for example, about primary elections in which no incumbent is running—the 2008 Republican and Democratic presidential primaries, for example. In each primary race, all of the candidates were of the same party. Party identification, therefore, was useless as a tool for judging candidates. Furthermore, many of the candidates were unfamiliar to the public at large when the primary season began. Without partisanship and previous information about the candidates to draw on, voter predispositions toward candidates were weak. Accordingly, the potential for media influence was greatly enhanced. In fact, research has shown that the media do exert a strong influence on voter judgments during the presidential primary process.[43]

On the other hand, consider a case in which policy maker and media discussions of an issue are largely balanced between a "pro" side and a "con" side. The general election between Republican and Democratic candidates for president usually fits this model. Campaigns and their supporters have roughly equal amounts of money to spend on their message and, as discussed earlier, the mainstream media present broadly balanced coverage of presidential election campaigns. Under these circumstances, even if there were universal exposure to "the message," a balanced message would not challenge anyone's political predispositions because it would not convey a strong point of view. It would be unlikely, therefore, to result in large-scale opinion change.[44] Note, however, that in a country as closely politically divided as the United States, even small shifts in public opinion can have significant consequences. Thus, even if the minimal effects perspective were still considered accurate, "minimal" would not necessarily mean "inconsequential."

Media Effects Can Be Found if You Look in the Right Places

Scholars may have failed to find large media effects because they have been looking in the wrong places. First, we now know that to find media effects, they should look for opinion change among people with moderate levels of political attentiveness and only moderately strong political predispositions. These people are likely to be exposed to most media messages, to have at least some comprehension of them, and to be somewhat receptive to them, even if the messages contradict their beliefs.

Second, opinion change occurs most often when the message is "loud," that is, when it is covered thoroughly by a number of media outlets for a long period of time. This tactic maximizes the chances of broad exposure to the message, which in turn maximizes the chances of broad-based opinion change. Recall the example of media coverage of the 9/11 terrorist attacks and the Bush administration's response.

Third, a media message that carries a largely one-sided point of view is more likely to lead to opinion change than balanced coverage. During the 1992 general election campaign between Bill Clinton and George H. W. Bush, for example, 90 percent of network news references to the economy were negative.[45] This kind of coverage can shift public opinion. On the other hand, coverage that is balanced—"some believe the economy remains weak, whereas others point to signs that it is in recovery"—would be unlikely to change opinions because it does not convey a particular point of view.

Fourth, opinion change occurs when media messages do not fit neatly with existing political predispositions. Recall the example of media coverage of presidential primary elections, in which partisanship and thorough knowledge of the candidates are generally not available to bolster predispositions. Another example would be media coverage of new or particularly complex issues, such as health care reform. The public can have difficulty determining how new or complex issues fit with their predispositions. With predispositions less of a factor, the chances for media influence on opinion are greatly enhanced.

Fifth, opinion change results from media messages to which people are most likely to be exposed. Recall that most Americans get their news from local television stations. Most studies of media influence, however, focus on messages delivered by network news and major newspapers, such as the *New York Times* and *Washington Post*. Why? Network news and newspaper content are monitored by various archiving and indexing services that are accessible online. Similar technology for archiving and tracking local news content is only beginning to be put in place. But local television news content likely holds the most promise for demonstrating the influence of media messages.

Sixth, opinion change takes two forms—gross and net. In an extreme example, imagine a society divided into two equal-sized groups—Group A and Group B. One hundred percent of Group A approves of the job the president is doing, whereas zero percent of Group B approves. This equal split puts the president's overall job approval at 50 percent. Imagine, though, that in a moment of weakness, the president reveals to reporters that he finds members of Group A annoying and unattractive but finds members of Group B delightful and easy on the eyes. The media provide blanket coverage of the president's verbal indiscretion and the president's job approval falls to zero in Group A but rises to 100 percent in Group B. The president's overall approval rating remains at 50 percent, so there has been no net change, but there has been massive gross change, that is, change within both Group A and Group B. By concentrating solely on net change, researchers can miss large but offsetting gross changes in opinion within subgroups of the population.

Finally, if a media message is particularly quiet or largely balanced between two sides, look for opinion change only among the most politically attentive. This is the only group likely to pick up on a quiet message in the first place, and the only group sophisticated enough to notice any subtle cues amid the largely balanced coverage that might induce a change in opinion.

On MyPoliSciLab

Review the Chapter

Listen to **Chapter 10** on **MyPoliSciLab**

The Unique Role of the American Media

10.1 Evaluate the unique role that the media play in American politics and society, p. 326.

The U.S. mass media differ from the media in other countries in several key ways. In the United States, the media are largely privately owned, views differ about objectivity and taking sides, and the American media aim to play a watchdog role. The American media also operate with relative freedom, and freedom from prior restraint is a particularly noteworthy characteristic.

Constraints on American Media Freedom

10.2 Identify the legal constraints under which the American media operate, p. 333.

Despite their relative freedom, the American media do operate under some constraints, including laws against defamation and the limited protection of shield laws. These limits are minor compared to those faced by American journalists in earlier centuries, when the media operated under much stricter government control. Beginning in the 1930s, this changed dramatically with a series of U.S. Supreme Court decisions expanding press freedoms.

Patterns of Media Use

10.3 Explain how technological changes have impacted patterns of media use, p. 335.

Americans acquire information on politics and government from various types of media. Whereas newspapers once dominated, they were supplanted by broadcast television in the second half of the twentieth century. However, broadcast news has been in decline in recent years, with cable television, talk radio, and the World Wide Web gaining popularity as alternate news sources.

Are the Media Biased?

10.4 Determine whether the media are biased, p. 341.

Several kinds of evidence—anecdotal, survey data on journalists' beliefs, and the actual content of reporting—can be brought to bear on whether the media are biased. The best available evidence indicates a lack of bias in press reporting of presidential elections, but there is insufficient information to draw conclusions about other kinds of coverage.

Media Effects on Public Opinion

10.5 Assess the effect of the media on political attitudes and behaviors, p. 344.

Early studies of media influence focused on voting behavior and produced evidence of only minimal effects. More recent studies of agenda setting, framing, and priming have revealed more effects of media influence. However, selective exposure, selective perception, and selective retention limit media influence on attitudes and behavior. Research has also shown that individuals who are only moderately attentive to media coverage are likely to be the most influenced.

Learn the Terms

Study and **Review** the **Flashcards**

advocacy journalism, p. 330
agenda setting, p. 345
bias, p. 341
cognitive dissonance, p. 348
earned media, p. 339
framing, p. 346
horse race, p. 337
mass media, p. 326
microtargeting, p. 339
minimal effect, p. 345
paid media, p. 339
political attentiveness, p. 349
political predisposition, p. 349
priming, p. 346
prior restraint, p. 328
selective exposure, p. 346
selective perception, p. 348
selective retention, p. 348
watchdog, p. 331

Test Yourself

10.1 Evaluate the unique role that the media play in American politics and society.

What is the defining characteristic of the American media?

a. Anti-government
b. Pro-government
c. Fairness
d. Objectivity
e. Freedom

10.2 Identify the legal constraints under which the American media operate.

Which of the following is TRUE about a journalist's ability to protect sources?

a. A journalist is protected through shield laws at both the state and federal levels.
b. A journalist is protected from being compelled to testify at all levels of government.
c. A journalist has some protections against being compelled to testify, but those protections are far from absolute.
d. A journalist has no protections against being compelled to testify.
e. A journalist may never be compelled to reveal a source.

10.3 Explain how technological changes have impacted patterns of media use.

How does microtargeting work?

a. Voters send messages directly to politicians online.
b. Campaign consultants use demographic information on specific voting populations to tailor advertising messages to those specific populations.
c. Politicians use information gleaned from polls in a shotgun approach to television advertising.
d. Media consultants create advertisements that appeal to no one.
e. Media consultants create advertisements that appeal to everyone.

10.4 Determine whether the media are biased.

All of the following are implications of a biased media EXCEPT

a. A distorted democratic process.
b. A climate in which the public is less informed about politics than it could be.
c. Public cynicism about all information.
d. A climate in which the public is more informed about politics.
e. A move by politicians to less controlled and friendlier media outlets.

10.5 Assess the effect of the media on political attitudes and behaviors.

The media exert influence through

a. agenda setting, priming, and framing.
b. selective exposure, selective perception, and selective retention.
c. priming, selective perception, and selective retention.
d. cognitive dissonance, priming, and selective retention.
e. agenda setting, priming, and cognitive dissonance.

Explore Further

SUGGESTED READINGS BY TOP SCHOLARS

Brader, Ted. 2006. *Campaigning for Hearts & Minds.* University of Chicago Press. Examines how nonverbal information (music and imagery) in ads affect emotions and consequently political attitudes.

Druckman, Jamie. 2004. Political preference formation: Competition, deliberation, and the (ir)relevance of framing effects. *American Political Science Review*, 98, 671–686. Although framing effects have been identified in a variety of environments, this article identifies the mix of individual characteristics and contextual effects that influence their magnitude.

Groseclose, Tim and Jeffrey Milyo. 2005. "A Measure of Media Bias." *Quarterly Journal of Economics* 120(4): 1191–1237. While many people claim media bias, actually measuring it in a rigorous fashion has been an ongoing challenge for social scientists. This article proposes a methodology to gauge whether media bias exists.

Prior, Markus. 2007. Post-Broadcast Democracy: How Media Choice Increases Inequality in Political Involvement and Polarizes Elections. Cambridge University Press. Examines the consequences of media fragmentation and the fact that people are less likely to be exposed to information that contradicts their predispostions.

John Zaller. *The Nature and Origins of Mass Opinion.* Cambridge University Press. 1992. How people acquire political information from the mass media and convert that information into political preferences.

SUGGESTED WEBSITES

ABC News The Note: http://abcnews.go.com/blogs/politics/the-note/

A political blog by ABC News' political unit that includes a daily round of political coverage along with original reporting and commentary.

PoliWatch, Political Meanings: poliwatch.org/

A multi-partisan political blog, with insight into political blogger assistance and training, publishing both experienced and newbie political bloggers. Also gives political news, research, polls, and more.

Mashable, The Social Media Guide: mashable.com/

Real-time updates on social media, including Facebook and Twitter, and reports on current issues in technology and the Internet, giving substantial coverage to the changing information age.

Daily Kos: www.dailykos.com

A left-leaning daily political blog.

Hugh Hewitt: A Blog of Townhall: www.hughhewitt.com/blog

A right-leaning daily political blog.

Listen to Chapter 11 on MyPoliSciLab

Political Parties

GETTING TO KNOW VOTERS, ONE BY ONE

The GOP Knows You Don't Like Anchovies.[1]

And they know much more about you than that. Republican researchers found, for example, that viewers of Fox News or the Golf Channel, BMW drivers, health club visitors after work hours, and bourbon or Coors beer drinkers were more likely to support Republicans than Democrats.

Both major political parties engage extensively in microtargeting, an effort to collect information on voters in order to send specific messages to them. Political parties today know a lot about you, and they hope to convert that knowledge into votes.

One feature of the so-called "party machines" present in big cities in the early twentieth century was their tight connections with voters. Machine precinct leaders knew each supporter in their area, checked in on them, and helped them navigate through city government. Having legal trouble? Need some help getting through a rough patch? The party machine could help you, providing services such as obtaining legal assistance, finding a doctor, and arranging for groceries during tough times. The machine was, in part, a social service or welfare agency. In exchange, the machine wanted your loyalty and your vote. It knew its voters personally and individually.

Political parties today are not in the business of leaving groceries at your door. But through microtargeting, they try to understand voters one by one to target messages to each. The hope is to persuade the undecided to support the party's candidate and to motivate the already decided to get out to vote.[2]

11.1 Analyze the functions of political parties in American politics, p. 360.

11.2 Determine why American electoral competition is dominated by two political parties rather than multiple parties, p. 369.

11.3 Trace the evolution of American party organizations and their expanding role in campaigns, p. 377.

11.4 Explain how parties achieve electoral success by building and maintaining coalitions of supporters, p. 383.

TARGETING AND PERSUADING Microtargeting relies on analyzing hundreds of data points of information on each potential voter to help candidates and parties identify potential voters who should be contacted and what issues would matter to those voters. The purpose of a contact might be to generate support for a candidate among voters open to persuasion, or to motivate those who are already supporters to vote. Contacts are usually made by a volunteer or a paid campaign worker, but here Barack Obama makes individual voter contacts in Philadelphia, Pennsylvania.

MyPoliSciLab Video Series

Watch on MyPoliSciLab

The Big Picture Are political parties good for anything besides bickering and stalling legislation? Author John J. Coleman argues that that they actually serve important functions for both voters and politicians.

The Basics Why do we have political parties in America? In this video, you will learn about the rise of political parties in the United States, the reasons why the two-party system continues to dominate American politics, and how the major parties differ from one another.

In Context Trace the development of political parties in the United States from the time of the ratification of the Constitution. Oklahoma State University political scientist Jeanette M. Mendez explains why political parties emerged and what role they play in our democratic system.

Think Like a Political Scientist How can we tell that Americans are increasingly polarized and what are the implications of this trend? In this video, Oklahoma State University political scientist Jeanette M. Mendez reveals how scholars measure party polarization at the elite and mass level and who is behind this phenomenon.

In the Real World Why do Americans only have two party choices—Democrats and Republicans? Real people evaluate the effectiveness of the "winner takes all" electoral system in the United States, and they weigh in on whether third parties—such as the Libertarians and the Green Party—should have more representation in national elections.

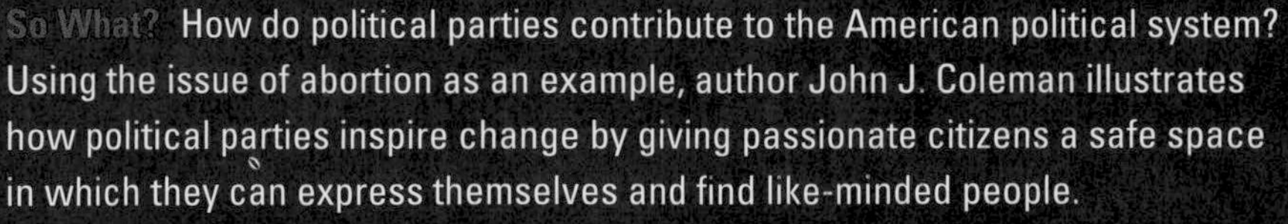

So What? How do political parties contribute to the American political system? Using the issue of abortion as an example, author John J. Coleman illustrates how political parties inspire change by giving passionate citizens a safe space in which they can express themselves and find like-minded people.

Modern microtargeting consists of building huge databases of information about voters. For each potential voter, party workers enter hundreds of bits of information, ranging from neighborhood characteristics available from the U.S. Census to consumer characteristics, such as purchasing habits, brand of car owned, television networks watched, magazine subscriptions, gun ownership, sports preferred (those who prefer football lean Republican, those who prefer basketball lean Democratic), type of musical preference, and much more. Most any contact you have with a party or candidate will likely make its way into a database. Diet Dr. Pepper drinkers tend to be Republicans who vote; Democrats who vote infrequently opt for 7Up. Phone or direct contact with you from a party staffer or volunteer—known as party canvassing—might extract some additional information for the database.[3]

Republicans in 2002 were the first to use microtargeting in a systematic way, and it was a prominent part of the party's campaign effort in 2004. The Republican National Committee, in coordination with the Bush campaign and Republican state and local party organizations, purchased commercial databases that held hordes of information on individuals. The party also purchased or received from supporters the membership information from organizations expected to lean toward the party's positions, including the National Rifle Association, churches, and clubs. All this information was entered into the national Republican database known as Voter Vault, which holds information on more than 170 million voters.

The Democrats microtargeted extensively in 2006 as they regained majorities in the U.S. House and Senate. By 2008, the Democratic National Committee had built a national voter database known as DataMart that had grown tenfold since 2004 and that matched the Republicans' in size. Volunteers could log into the database over the Web and provide real-time updates to the information collected on potential voters. The database is also updated after primary elections, as candidates add new information they have collected over the course of the campaign. The Democrats' database benefited from the Obama campaign's heavy use of technology and social media to reach volunteers and supporters. The Obama campaign organization's outreach continued during his presidency in the form of Organizing for America, further boosting Democrats' data gathering.[4] Private microtargeting firms also provide data collection and analysis for the parties.

Examining voter databases, which are readily available from states, provides information to the party on the voter's turnout history, party registration, and possibly which party primary she or he voted in. Voter visits to the party's website or, for example, its Facebook profile provide additional information, as does a voter's web browsing history in general. The more information acquired about the voter, the better.[5] Public opinion data are then merged into the file, allowing data analysts to unearth connections between demographic, consumer, and other information and views on public issues.

These data are then analyzed to produce a specific message tailored to a voter's key interests. Targeted appeals will appear in the parties' ad campaigns. Democrats in 2008 advertised far more on *Tyler Perry's House of Payne* than did Republicans. The GOP advertised much more heavily than Democrats during broadcasts of the *Country Music Association Music Festival*. Each party knew the demographics of the viewers of those programs and the issues that concerned them.[6] The same principle applies to the Web. In 2012, two Republican primary voters visiting the same website would see different ads for Mitt Romney, based on their browsing history and other information.[7]

Beyond television, the voter database helps generate sophisticated and narrowly targeted mailings, brochure drops at the door, phone contact, personal contact, and get-out-the-vote drives on behalf of a range of party candidates.[8] Analysts compute scores for each individual to estimate his or her likelihood of supporting the party's candidates, so the party can target its outreach efforts efficiently. As a result of these efforts in previous elections, both parties in the 2012 elections had billions of bits of voter information at their disposal.

Do these new and highly sophisticated targeted efforts create their desired result? Do they persuade voters and convince them to vote? Political scientists are beginning to explore whether and if so, how these efforts have their desired causal effects. Perhaps voters will be less moved by targeted appeals than by general appeals. Perhaps the messages will not have much effect in persuasion but rather in mobilization or for some groups only.

11.1

11.2

11.3

11.4

political parties
organized groups with public followings that seek to elect officeholders who identify themselves by the group's common label, for the purpose of exercising political power.

For example, one experimental study found that targeted Republican appeals to Christian voters and Latinos were effective, but they also created a loss of support for other non-group members who might see the appeals.[9] None of these causal questions addresses whether the appeals are desirable, but that is a fair question: Are there problems for governance that result from assembling coalitions of voters based on narrow messages?

Parties are everywhere in the American political system, from the local level to the national and in all branches of government. Affinity with a political party is the most prominent political attachments of the typical voter, and it is usually the strongest influence on their voting choices. This chapter explores the roles played by political parties in American politics, the coalitions of voters that support each party, and how the parties work.

What Political Parties Do

11.1 Analyze the functions of political parties in American politics.

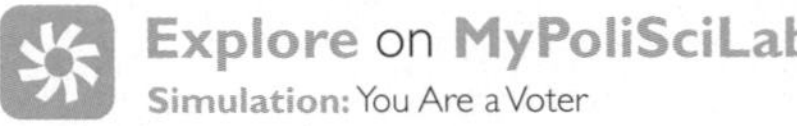
Explore on MyPoliSciLab
Simulation: You Are a Voter

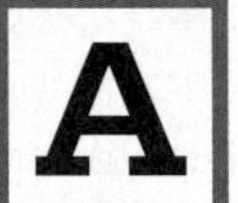

Americans' views of parties have changed over time from fearful, to supportive, to skeptical. President George Washington, in his Farewell Address, warned Americans about the dangers of political parties. By the late nineteenth century, however, partisanship was a central aspect of Americans' identity, mentioned right alongside ethnicity, region, and religion. Today, Americans still have strong attachments to parties and do not fear them, but there is a pervasive skepticism that parties confuse issues more than clarify them—or alternately, that they are too polarized and stubborn and refuse to work together. What provokes these strong reactions? What are political parties and what do they do?

Political parties are organized groups that seek to gain office and exercise political power through legislation, executive action, and control of government agencies, among other means. They aim to elect officeholders who associate with the group and identify themselves by the group's common label. Candidates rally voters to their side who share the outlook or background of other supporters of the party.[10] Party activity occurs at all levels in American politics: from the individual voter who feels close to a party; to the candidate at the local, state, or national level who runs on the party label; to the public official who tries to rally fellow partisans around a policy proposal.

Defined narrowly, "the party" usually refers to its elected officials and the individuals working for official party organizations. More broadly, political parties are *networks* of people and groups who share common policy goals. The leadership of labor unions, trial lawyers, environmental groups, teachers, pro-choice groups, liberal think tanks, and the liberal blogosphere tend to align with the Democratic Party. The National Education Association (teachers' union), NARAL (pro-choice group), Center for American Progress (liberal think tank), and MoveOn.org (online liberal ideological group) are examples. Leaders of libertarian-leaning groups, business associations, gun rights groups, veterans, pro-life groups, conservative think tanks, and conservative talk radio outlets tend to align with the Republican Party. The U.S. Chamber of Commerce (business group), the National Rifle Association (gun rights association), National Right to Life (pro-life group), and Heritage Foundation (conservative think tank) are examples. Dozens of other issue advocacy groups have close ties with one of the two major parties and actively seek to help the party's candidates win. These groups also expect that their voices will be heard as their party debates policy options. The party network thus involves the ongoing dialogue and mutual support among the party organizations, elected officials, party candidates, and political activists. In thinking of "the Republican Party" or "the Democratic Party," it is useful to keep in mind this entire party network of influence and conversation.[11]

Despite the negative attitudes the public often expresses about parties, political scientists generally offer a more positive assessment. Although not discounting parties' shortcomings, scholars see them as a vital part of democratic politics. Parties perform many roles in American politics, reflecting their construction as networks and their activity at all levels of politics. These roles serve the self-interest of party members, but they also produce benefits for the operation of American government and for the public.

Parties Fill Gaps Left by the Constitution

The Constitution provides the basic structure for the selection of public officials. Elections determine the president, members of the House of Representatives, and U.S. senators. But the Constitution stops there. To say that elections are the selection mechanism is one thing; for candidates and voters to make it work is quite another. For the system established by the Constitution to gain credibility and legitimacy, some way had to be found to staff the offices of government and involve the public in politics.

Political parties filled this void. They were created by ambitious, hardheaded politicians to solve particular problems of candidate recruitment, to increase the likelihood of winning debates in the legislature, and to mobilize enough voter support to win elections.[12] They also serve as a vehicle for competing groups in the public—for example, a group advocating for more solar energy development and another advocating for more oil drilling—to influence the policy-making process. In serving the purposes of politicians and political activists, parties also assist political system legitimacy by contributing to a functioning system of electoral politics beyond what is specified in the Constitution.

Parties Recruit Candidates Into the Electoral Process and Nominate Them for Office

Nationally and in most states, political parties take an active role in identifying promising individuals and recruiting them to run for office. In the course of doing this, the party will assist both first-time and seasoned candidates with the various aspects of running a campaign, including raising money, dealing with the media, identifying potential supporters, developing positions on issues, and putting together a campaign organization to contact citizens and research opponents. In addition to the parties themselves, affiliated groups in the party's network contribute to candidate recruitment and training. For example, Emerge America is a group dedicated to recruiting and training women to run as Democratic candidates. The National Federation of Republican Women is its counterpart on the Republican side.

Parties also provide a ladder of opportunity up which candidates can climb, guiding them through a political career path. This helps sort out the potentially competing ambitions of many individual candidates by providing them with various offices to run for and a structure for moving up the party rungs to the next level of offices. Sometimes, at the request of party leaders, a potential candidate will agree to step aside and run for office later or run for a different office.

Parties engage in finding candidates so that the party can increase its power. The party has the incentive to run as many candidates as it can in order to win control of as many offices as it can. But this self-interest also serves a social interest. Parties provide voters with choices, which are the key to generating a sense of legitimacy for American politics. Elections with choices make voters feel empowered. The Constitution could appear an empty promise if there were elections, but few candidates on the ballot.

After recruiting candidates, parties nominate them and put them on the ballot. Around the world, control of the nomination process is among the most significant powers of political parties: the power to filter who is elected to public office. In the United States, at first party leaders controlled the nomination of candidates; then delegates began to make the selection at party conventions; and now, in most cases, state-mandated primary elections serve to nominate candidates.

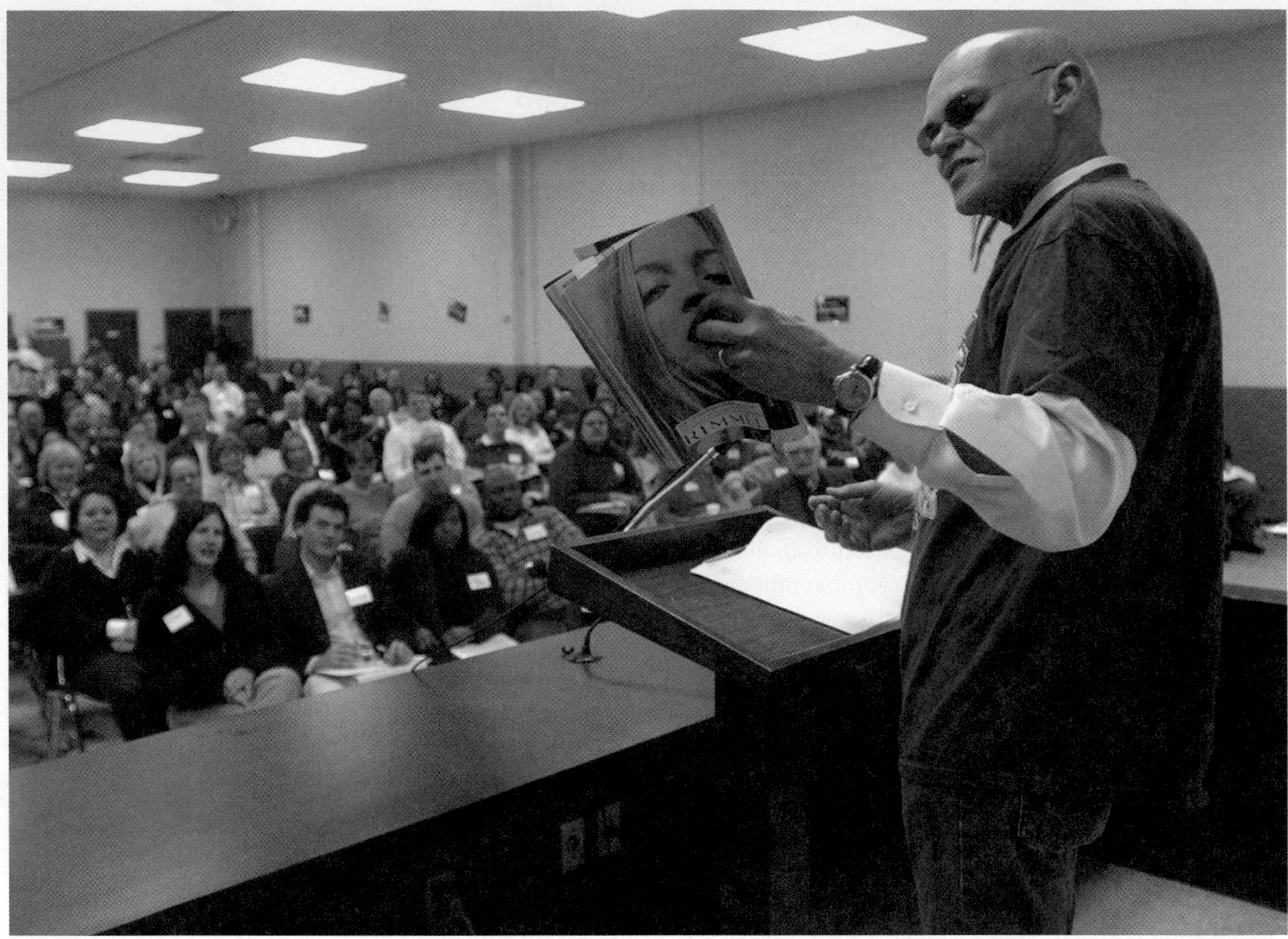

PARTY SCHOOL

Political party campaign schools teach candidates how to run for office and teach party workers and volunteers how to increase support for the party's candidates. James Carville, one of the best-known Democratic political consultants, spoke to participants at the Georgia Democratic Party's Grassroots Training program.

☐ Parties Bridge Constitutional Gaps Between Institutions

The Constitution deliberately spreads power across institutions, across two houses of the legislature, across elected and unelected offices, and across the federal and state governments. It creates a governing system that makes the abuse of power difficult, but it also makes lawmaking difficult. This diffusion of power is consistent with the limited government ethos of the American creed.

Political parties bridge these institutional gaps by providing incentives for officials to cooperate in policy making, as shown in Figure 11.1. Officials who share a party label share a "brand name." When a president does well, members of his party in Congress enjoy some of the glow of that success. If he suffers from low approval ratings, the public's critical view can carry over to his fellow partisans in Congress. In 2010, with President Obama's approval low, health care reform unpopular, and the economy struggling, voters flipped over 65 House and Senate seats from Democratic to Republican control, and Republicans also made big gains at the state level. Officials who share a party's brand name have an interest in seeing fellow partisans govern successfully.

This common bond does not undermine the Constitution's separation of powers, checks and balances, or federalism, but it does increase the ability to get things done. Because members of a party will usually share general goals and approaches, they start from a base of support when trying to enact policy. In that way, political parties contribute to governing by reducing some of the challenges to lawmaking in the

A. Institutional walls of separation in the Constitution

President

House

Senate

States

B. The party brand name provides incentives for coordination and cooperation across the constitutional walls

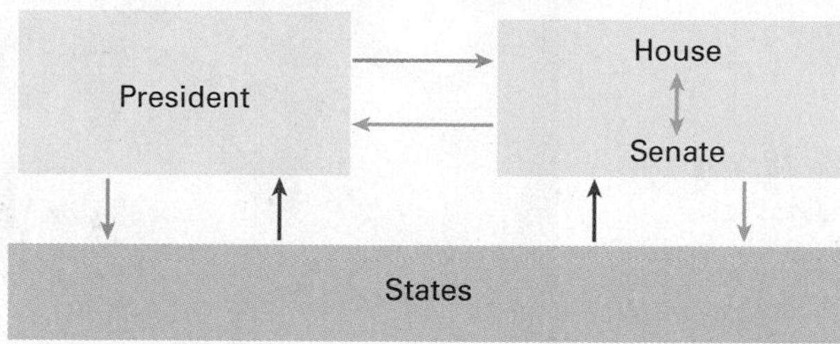

FIGURE 11.1 POLITICAL PARTY ASSISTANCE TO POLICY-MAKING.

The Constitution created a set of institutions that would be involved in policy making. It focused on the way these institutions could check one another's use of power. Left unstated was how the individuals in these institutions might work together. A political party provides a common "brand name" that encourages cooperation across institutional boundaries. Politicians know that when other members of their party are successful, the party brand name is enhanced and public approval and the probability of future election victories increase.

American system. Members of a party do not always agree—but the shared party label increases the probability of cooperation. Without the connecting glue of partisanship, government might be even more hamstrung in acting.

This logic would seem to suggest that government gets more "big things" done when one party controls both Congress and the presidency—**unified government**—rather than when different parties control each of these branches—**divided government**. Does it? Certainly the passage and content of some of President Obama's major legislative victories—economic stimulus, health care reform, and financial industry reform—depended in part on his party's unified control of government in 2009 and 2010. In 2011 and 2012, conversely, when the president faced a Republican House and a smaller Democratic majority in the Senate, he struggled to advance his agenda on tax increases for high-income Americans and in other areas. Political scientists have extensively studied the causes and consequences of unified and divided government and the contributing factors to legislative productivity. To determine whether unified government increases the probability that the president and Congress will enact major legislation, scholars have to take into account other factors that could lead to the government accomplishing more or less. A sense of crisis might inspire action; a shortage of revenue might discourage it. Public opinion may be calling for government action, or it might be calling for government to pull back. A president with high approval ratings might get more support from Congress, regardless of which party controls the House and Senate. A party with unified control of government might accomplish more early in its tenure rather than later. A president in his final years might find it difficult to get Congress to go along with him. And it matters whether a party is ideologically cohesive—a party can control the presidency and Congress, but if it suffers from internal dissension, legislative action will be difficult.

unified government
the presidency and both houses of Congress are controlled by the same party.

divided government
the presidency is held by one party and at least one house of Congress is controlled by a different party.

Studies by political scientists that take these and other factors into account generally conclude that unified government tends to increase the number of important laws enacted and reduces delay in various facets of legislative activity. The number is not large, maybe two or three additional significant enactments during a two-year congressional term. Over time, however, this can add up to a large number of enactments that may not have been possible under divided government.[13] Whether this increased legislative

11.1 11.2 11.3 11.4

Unresolved Debate

Is Divided Government Intentional?

Since 1993, party control of government has been unified for 9 years and divided for 11 years. Why does divided government occur? One idea is that voters split their tickets—vote for candidates of different parties for different offices—to check and balance each each party's influence. A related idea is that voters try to produce ideologically moderate public policy by dividing control between the parties. Other scholars believe divided government occurs for reasons other than voter intent. Is divided government intentional?

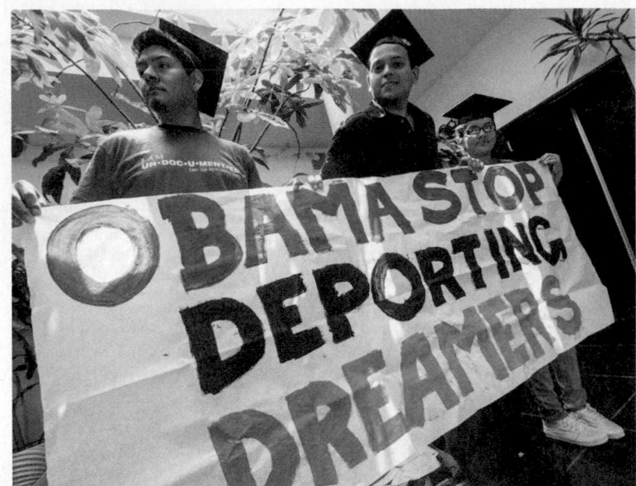

UNILATERAL ACTION

Stymied in his efforts to push immigration reforms through a Congress controlled by Republicans in the House and Democrats in the Senate, President Barack Obama in 2012 took unilateral steps to block the deportation of students who were the children of illegal or undocumented immigrants? Is it proper for presidents to act unilaterally when they cannot get congnressional support?

YES

Political scientists Michael Lewis-Beck and Richard Nadeau argue that a sizable portion of the electorate, perhaps one-quarter, are "cognitive Madisonians" who, in the spirit of the Framers, deliberately seek to check and balance power and policy through split-ticket voting[a]. Divided government is intentional.

- Those who said they preferred divided government in 1992 and 1996 were more likely to split their tickets than were other voters, showing that they did act on their beliefs.
- Cognitive Madisonian voters were more likely to vote a split ticket when they perceived themselves to be about equally distant ideologically from the two parties and when the distance is not great trying to balance policy by electing moderates.
- Voters preferring divided government and ideologically close to their less preferred party were 10 times more likely to split their tickets than were unified government supporters.

NO

In 1988, voters elected Republican George H.W. Bush as president and elected Democrats to House and Senate majorities. Political scientists Barry Burden and David Kimball reject the idea that voters were intentionally trying to create divided government by splitting their ticket.[b] Divided government is unintentional.

- Voters split their ticket because they had much more knowledge about the Democratic congressional candidate than the Republican.
- Split-ticket voting increased when the incumbent House or Senate member was a Democrat voters reward incumbents' high name recognition and known record of accomplishment.
- Voters were more likely to split their ticket when the ideological gap between the Republican Bush and the Democratic House or Senate candidate was relatively small so they were not trying to balance ideological extremes.

CONTRIBUTING TO THE DEBATE

Voters in a midterm election are not making any decision about who to vote for president, because that office is not on the ballot. Research could exploit this electoral feature of American government. The president's party nearly always loses seats in the midterm election. Is that a result of voters intentionally pursuing divided government, or of something else?

THINKING CRITICALLY

1. Would you consider it a serious flaw in the American political system if divided government occurred unintentionally?
2. Many voters say they prefer divided government, but they are displeased with partisan conflict. Is it inconsistent for voters to hold these views simultaneously?

[a]Michael S. Lewis-Beck and Richard Nadeau, "Split-Ticket Voting: The Effects of Cognitive Madisonianism," *Journal of Politics* 66, 1 (2004): 97–112.
[b]Barry C. Burden and David C. Kimball, "A New Approach to the Study of Ticket Splitting," *American Political Science Review* 92, 3 (1998): 533–44.

productivity is a good thing or not is a matter of one's personal political philosophy. For political scientists, the potentially different policy outcomes of unified and divided control raise an important companion question: What causes unified and divided government? In particular, scholars have asked whether divided government is the result of intentional voter behavior or happens because of other features of the American electoral system (see *Unresolved Debate: Is Divided Government Intentional?*).

☐ Parties Bring Citizens Into the Electoral Process

Parties are self-interested bodies. They seek power to pursue their goals. To gain and assert power, parties need to win offices. To win offices, they need to win elections. And to win elections, they need more votes on Election Day than their opponents. Parties therefore have an incentive to get voters involved, and they do so in a number of ways.

EDUCATE AND INFORM VOTERS Historically, political parties have played a significant role in educating voters about candidates. In the nineteenth century, parties staged parades, festivals, and other events to attract a crowd to listen to candidates and party supporters deliver speeches. Given the limited entertainment options in the nineteenth century, these events were a big deal for a small town or city neighborhood. Voters would be entertained and energized by listening to detailed speeches explaining how the party was superior to its opponents.

In addition, political parties controlled much of the mass media of that era, newspapers in particular. Major party figures often urged the creation of newspapers as a means to communicate the party's message and assail the opposition. Publishers and editors had strong political and partisan views and saw the paper as a means to advance those views. The parties and the press were deeply intertwined, and the notion of "objective journalism" was still far in the future. So the positions of the party and its candidates were prominently available for citizens on a daily basis.

Parties today do not have the same kind of monopoly on information about their candidates. Nonetheless, they still attempt to educate voters through campaign advertisements, leaflets and other literature, websites and blogs, e-mail, video, tweets, and frequent appearances by party officials and important party members on television and radio news and talk shows. They may coordinate candidate issues and messages across the country through advertising.

DELIVER PEOPLE TO THE POLLS Parties work hard to convince supportive voters that something is at stake in the election and that the benefits of voting are so important that the voter best not stay at home. A party will point out to its supporters not only its positions and candidates, to show them the benefit of voting, but also the positions and candidates of the other party, to show them the dire repercussion of failing to vote. More directly, with their get-out-the-vote (GOTV) efforts, party supporters—or sometimes hired telemarketing firms—make phone calls, send e-mail, and go door to door to remind people to vote and ask if they need assistance getting to the polling place. These activities may also inspire supporters of the opposing party to increase their efforts to get voters to the polls. Helping motivate people to get out and vote is a major way for young people to be involved in party politics.

An individual voter might get a number of these reminders. Do any of these efforts matter? Studies show that individuals who are contacted by political parties or by other groups are more likely to say they voted than individuals who were not contacted. This correlation is not proof of causation, however. It is also the case that parties target their contacts to those individuals who they have reason to believe are more likely to vote. Spending a significant amount of staff time and financial resources in the midst of a campaign to reach out to perpetual nonvoters or individuals highly uninterested in politics would rarely be a wise use of time and money. As communication costs drop significantly as a result of advances in technology, it may be that parties and candidates can increasingly reach out to a wider audience. In 2008 and 2012, Barack Obama's campaign made extensive use of newer technologies and, especially in 2008, also used large rallies effectively to recruit new GOTV volunteers. In addition, it placed many well-staffed local field offices around the country, generally in places where the race was expected to be close. These offices located and trained volunteers who would contact voters, and in 2008 they appear to have boosted Obama's vote total significantly in these areas.[14]

Sometimes parties take on a longer process of engaging new voters, conducting outreach regularly rather than only during campaigns. Generally, though, during the heat of a campaign, it is sensible for parties, with their limited resources, to contact individuals with a prior history of voting or some other expression of strong interest. A better way to think of this relationship between contact and voting is that it is mutually reinforcing. Parties are likely to contact individuals with a higher than average likelihood of voting. The party contact can further increase this probability by stressing the importance of an election and the closeness of a contest. Research controlling for this possible reverse causation suggests that the contacts do indeed have an effect on driving up turnout.[15] Party contact is unlikely to turn a habitual nonvoter into a voter, but it can prompt an occasional voter to turn out.

INTEGRATE NEW SOCIAL GROUPS Political parties have an incentive to bring new groups into the political process, but they are selective about which groups to approach. In order to win elections, their main goal is to maximize the turnout of people who will vote for them, not to maximize overall turnout. The logic of competition suggests that if one party pushes a group away, the other major party would have an interest in integrating that group into American politics, especially if it can do so without unduly alarming groups that already support the party. The Republican Party received strong support from black voters up through the 1950s, earning black votes because of its legacy as the party that ended slavery and began integrating blacks into the country's political life. In contrast, parties may invest resources in keeping a group out of politics—especially if the group is likely to support the opposing party—as southern Democrats did with blacks through the early 1960s. Parties also saw other newly enfranchised groups, such as women after 1920 and young voters after 1971, as opportunities for support.[16]

This process of reaching out to new social groups can also be seen in immigration. In the waves of immigration across American history, the two major parties vied with each other to bring members of these groups into the electoral process and make them believe that the party represents them and cares about them.[17] Since the late twentieth century, the parties have reached out to different Hispanic groups. Cuban immigrants, many of whom strongly opposed the communist regime in Cuba, have tended to support the Republicans because of their perception that the party was more committed to challenging the actions of the Cuban government. Mexican immigrants have shown stronger support for the Democrats, partly due to the Democratic Party's economic and immigration policies. One scholarly examination suggests that immigrant groups today, in particular Latinos and Asians, have not yet been well integrated into the American party system. More so than for other groups, members of these groups are less inclined to think of politics or themselves in partisan terms. This disconnect from politics may in part explain the low registration and voting rates among Hispanics compared to both non-Hispanic whites and blacks.[18]

When it has suited their purpose, parties have also sought to make it hard for immigrant groups to enter politics. For example, in the 1890s, virtually every state enacted some form of personal voter registration. At first, registration often applied only to urban areas, where immigrant groups were concentrated. Although personal voter registration could make good policy sense—perhaps the risk of voter fraud is greater in areas of higher population—reformers also believed it would reduce immigrant influence in elections, and immigrant groups were thought to be unduly influenced by party "bosses" in the big cities.[19] Today, some observers lodge the same charge at state laws that require photo identification prior to voting. Although reducing the potential of fraud is undoubtedly a good thing, these observers contend that one of the results of requiring a photo ID is to harm Democratic Party electoral prospects by discouraging voting by legal immigrants who are wary of U.S. authorities, and by minority groups that are

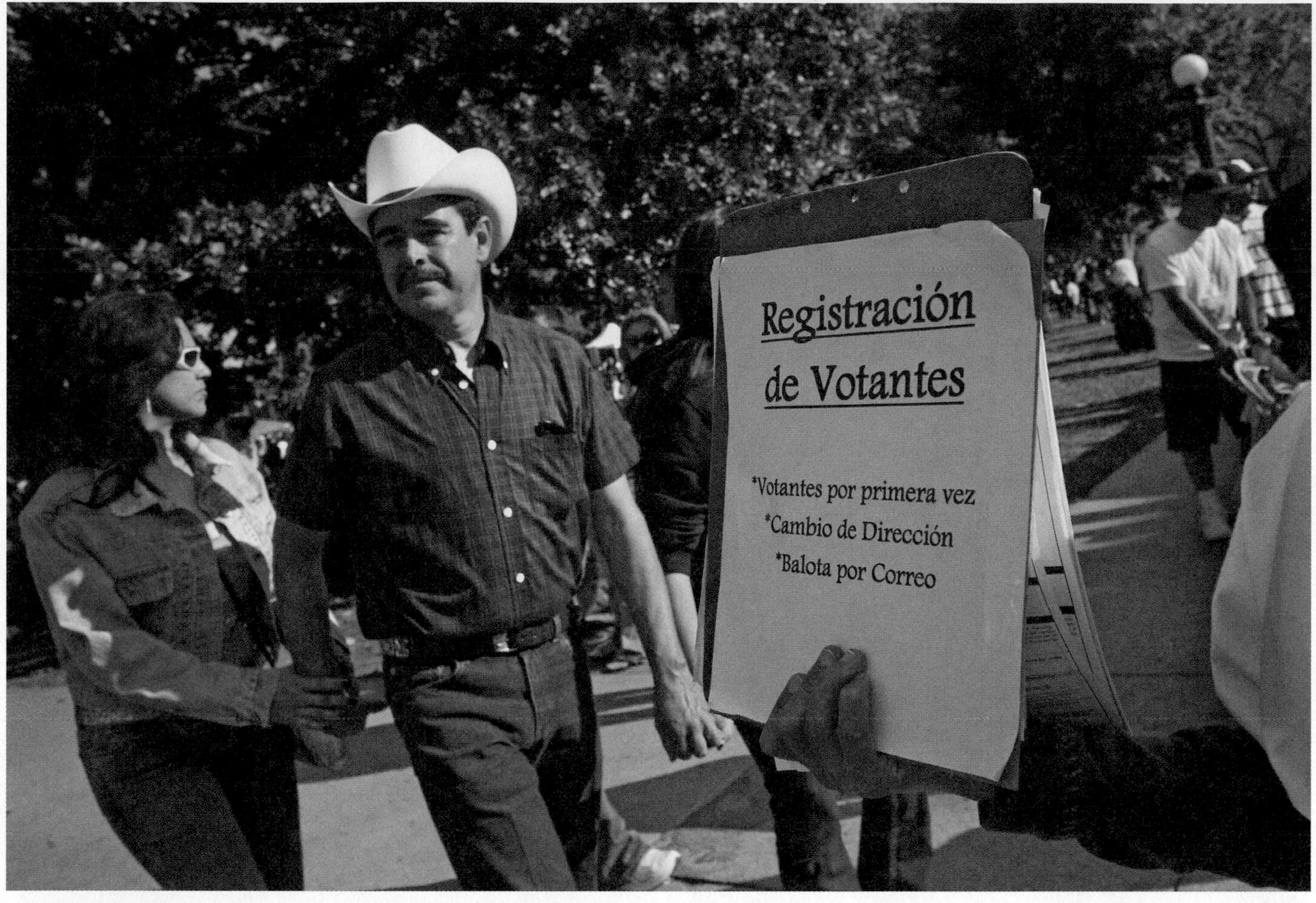

JOIN THE PARTY

Parties seek to enlarge their vote totals by adding new groups of supporters. Here, Democratic party workers in Denver, Colorado, sign up new voters on Mexican Independence Day.

disproportionately less likely to have a form of government-issued photo identification. Supporters of the policy argue that acquiring a photo ID does not create a significant hurdle to voting and increases public confidence in the integrity of the voting process.[20] Figure 11.2 shows the voter identification requirements in states across the country.

In recent elections, with the balance of power close in Congress and presidential elections hard fought, both major parties have worked to pull young adults into politics as volunteers and as voters. In the 1990s, the Republican Party was especially effective in reaching out to young adults through its network of support from church groups in rural areas. More recently, both the Democratic and Republican Parties and their supporters have used new technologies to reach out to young people. This trend was inaugurated in 2008 primarily by people in their twenties who launched blogs, political meet-up and fund-raising sites, and social networking sites in support of Barack Obama's presidential campaigns. In 2010 and 2012, Republican candidates made more use of these technologies. This pattern of one party initiating new campaign techniques and the other following is common throughout the history of American parties.

The Public Exerts Leverage Over Public Officials Through Use of the Party Label

Parties benefit from the attachments and loyalty of the public. Candidates know they can count on 80 to 90 percent, or more, of their party loyalists to vote for them. They will need to spend some time energizing these loyalists and convincing them to vote,

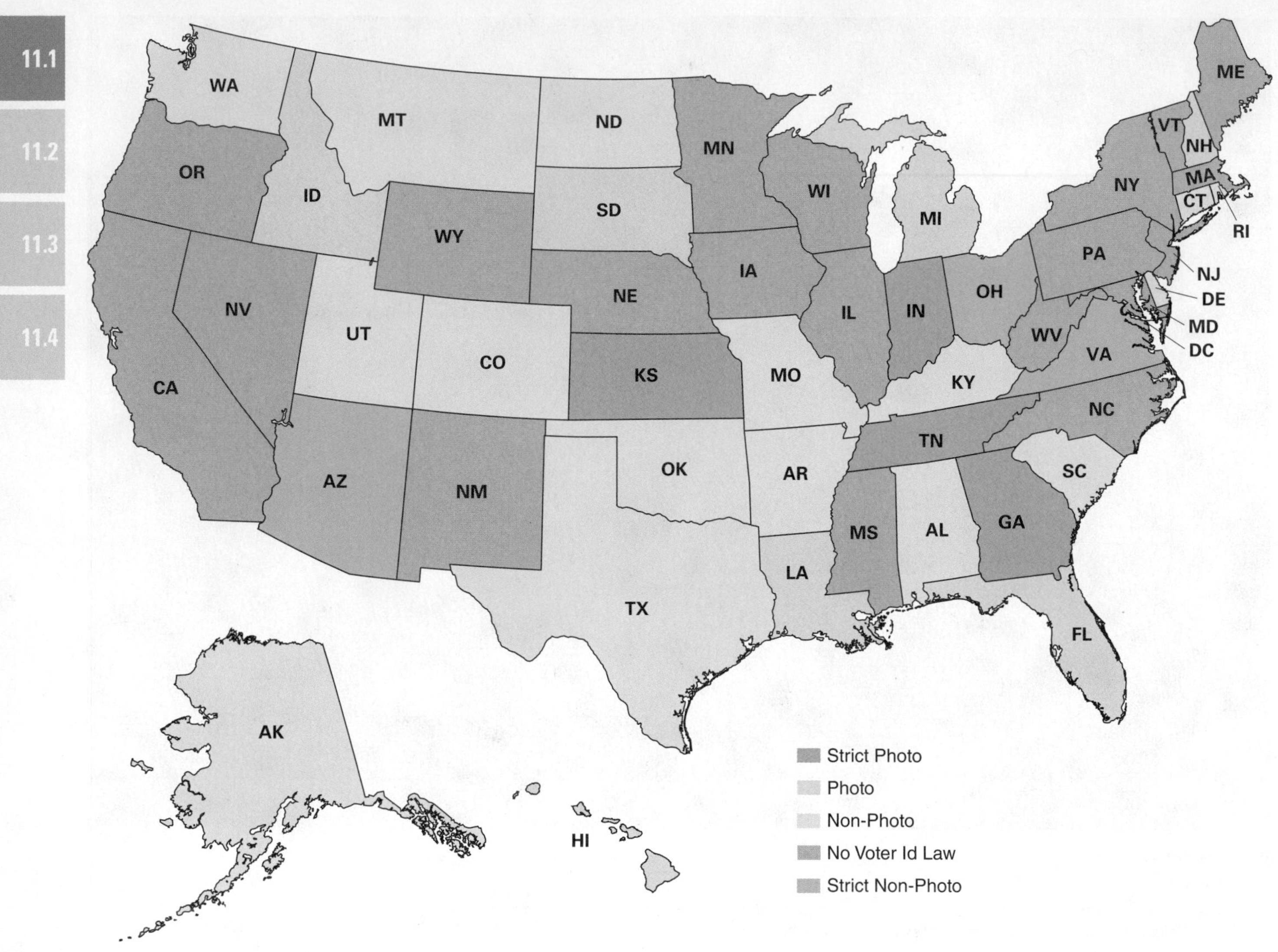

FIGURE 11.2 VOTER ID REQUIREMENTS IN EFFECT FOR 2012.

Over 30 states now require some form of voter identification at the polls. Most controversial have been photo-ID requirements. Critics argue that certain groups such as racial and ethnic minorities, the elderly, and low-income voters are less likely to have valid photo ID than are other groups. Supporters argue the measures are necessary to prevent fraud and reinforce voter confidence in the voting process. Strict ID requirements allow a voter to fill out a provisional ballot that will not be counted until the voter provides the required identification within a few days. Non-strict requirements generally allow the voter to cast a ballot, but require election officials to make a note that the voter did not present appropriate ID when casting a vote.

Source: http://www.ncsl.org/?tabid=16602

but the guaranteed support means they can devote more of their resources to appealing to undecided voters who do not have strong partisan leanings. Thus, party candidates benefit from having the party label.

Voters, in turn, can also use the party label to increase their leverage over public officials. The party label is a powerful tool for those voters with strong views who are highly attentive to politics. If voters believe that the parties are substantially different in their policy priorities and preferences, they can consider this distinction when voting.[21] By voting for a Democrat, for example, they are roughly endorsing a particular approach to public policy. A Democratic public official seen as straying from this approach may face vigorous criticism from this attentive public. Thus, voters use the party label to hold officials accountable. All voters, whether highly attentive or not, can use the party label to sweep one party out of office and put the other party in. This happened in 1994, when voters put Republicans in control of both the U.S. House and Senate for the first time in 40 years. In 2006, voters turned the tables and put the Democrats in control. Voters changed course again in 2010, giving Republicans big gains in the Senate and control of the House.

The party label provides Americans with the simplest and most practical tool they have to make wide-ranging changes in the personnel of government and a possible new direction in public policy. The label frees voters from needing to know extensive information about each candidate, which is a hurdle relatively few voters could surmount. Although voting for a candidate because of his or her party label is often frowned upon in the media and popular culture—"I vote for the person, not the party" is a common refrain—political scientists have found the party label to be an effective, powerful, and usually accurate information shortcut.

two-party system
a system of electoral competition in which two parties are consistently the most likely to win office and gain power.

The Two-Party System

11.2 Determine why American electoral competition is dominated by two political parties rather than multiple parties.

merican electoral competition usually takes place between two major political parties. A major party has a large following; has endured over time; and is perceived to be electorally competitive by the public, potential candidates, and political observers. Minor parties, or "third parties," lack these features.

To say there is a **two-party system** in the United States does not mean that only two parties can compete but, rather, that it is a system of electoral competition in which two parties are consistently seen as the most likely to win office and gain power. If you were to predict who was going to win an election, and you predicted it would be either a Democrat or a Republican, you would be right nearly every time.

Electoral systems outside the United States differ. In multiparty systems based on proportional representation, as discussed later, there might be several—not just two—parties that, in one election year or another, could potentially finish with the most votes. In addition, in those systems, a party need not finish in first place to win seats in the legislature. Therefore, even smaller parties can be genuine contenders for power. To consider just a few examples, in their most recent legislative elections, Germany, Italy, Sweden, and Mexico each had six or more parties win seats in the national legislature, and in the 2012 elections, 12 parties in France won seats in the National Assembly. Each uses an electoral system based on proportional representation.[22]

Hundreds of political parties have competed over the years in the United States, but competition nationally has almost always been between two major parties. Across American history, there have been five major political parties: the Federalists (1789–1816); the Democratic-Republicans (1790–1824); the Democrats (1828 to the present); the National Republicans, later Whigs (1824–1854); and the Republicans (1854 to the present). Third parties have included those organized around ideology (Socialist Party, Progressive Party, Green Party, Libertarian Party), particular issues (Prohibition Party, Greenback Party), and defection from a major party (States' Rights, also known as Dixiecrats), and parties built initially around a single presidential candidacy (American Independent Party for George Wallace in 1968; National Unity Party for John Anderson in 1980; United We Stand for Ross Perot in 1992, which led to the Reform Party in 1996). Wallace, Anderson, and Perot in 1992 were independents, and the parties were built up around them after they had started running, rather than their candidacies emerging from the parties.

At its very beginning, the Republican Party was a third party, but it quickly rose to ascendancy over the Whigs, which disbanded. Today, the most significant third parties nationally are the Green Party and the Libertarian Party. These two parties contest a large number of offices, occasionally win elections, and have organizational structures from the local level to the national level that are somewhat similar to but not as extensive as those of the major parties.[23] Despite its name, the Tea Party, which was active in the 2010 and 2012 elections in promoting the nomination and election of conservative candidates, is not a formal political party. Rather, it can be thought of as a faction within the Republican Party or more accurately a network of activists seeking the election of more conservatives to office, first through the nomination process in the Republican Party and then through general election support of conservative candidates—who are in almost all cases Republicans.

Third Parties Are Rarely Successful Electorally But May Be Influential in Other Ways

The electoral performance of American third parties can be summed up in one word: dismal. Third-party candidates rarely win elections and usually do not garner a significant share of the vote. Over the past 50 years, they rarely have received more than a few percentage points of the total national congressional vote. Their performance was strongest in the nineteenth century, with about 5 percent of House seats in the period from 1830 to 1870 held by third-party members. Since 1970, by contrast, a non-major party candidate has held a seat in the House only 11 times, but all of these candidates ran as independents rather than members of a political party. Former Representative Bernard Sanders of Vermont, currently a U.S. Senator, accounts for 8 of the 11 victories.[24]

Similarly, in presidential elections, third-party candidates rarely win many votes or win a state. Since Ralph Nader won 2.7 percent of the national vote in 2000, no third party or independent candidate has received more than 1 percent of the vote. No state has sided with a third-party candidate since 1968, when five southern states backed Alabama's Democratic governor, George Wallace, who was running as an independent candidate with the newly created American Independent Party.

Although third parties do not often win elections, they can still play significant roles in elections. Probably the most important of these roles is that third-party candidates, or independent candidates more generally, can introduce ideas and issues into the campaign that the major-party candidates might be neglecting or avoiding. Some analysts believe Democrat Al Gore struck a more populist tone in 2000 because of the solid showing of Green Party candidate Ralph Nader in polls.[25] Given this ability to introduce new ideas, one positive sign for third parties is that more voters today have the opportunity to hear from them in congressional elections (see Figure 11.3), in large part because of ballot access lawsuits Perot filed in 1992.

Another possible but controversial role for third parties is to alter the election outcome between the major parties. It was easy for Democrats in 1968 and Republicans in 1992 to blame George Wallace and Ross Perot for the defeat of Democrat Hubert

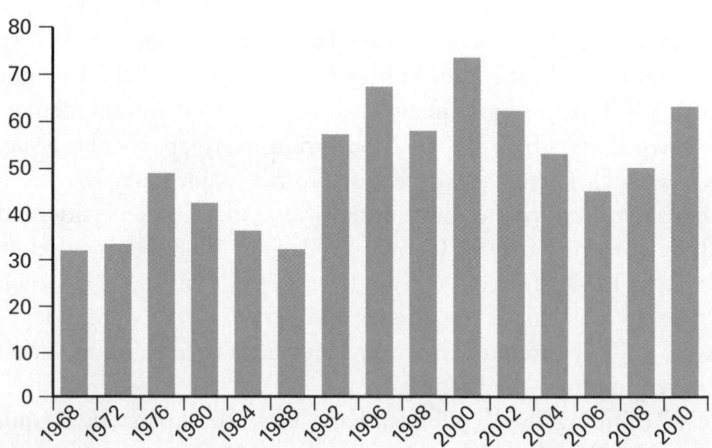

FIGURE 11.3 PERCENTAGE OF U.S. HOUSE DISTRICTS WITH A MINOR-PARTY OR INDEPENDENT CANDIDATE RUNNING.

Since 1992, voters in U.S. House elections have been more likely to see a third-party or independent candidate on the ballot than was true previously, with more than half of all districts featuring a third-party or independent candidate. Prior to 1992, the proportion was more typically around 30 to 35 percent.

Source: (for data through 1992) Christian Collett and Martin P. Wattenberg, "Strategically Unambitious: Minor Party and Independent Candidates in the 1996 Congressional Elections," in John C. Green and Daniel M. Shea, eds., *The State of the Parties: The Changing Role of Contemporary American Parties* (Lanham, MD: Rowman and Littlefield, 1999). Reprinted with permission.

Humphrey and Republican George H. W. Bush, respectively. Wallace and Perot received a large number of votes, and Humphrey and Bush lost; therefore, the argument goes, these third-party candidates cost Humphrey and Bush their elections by diverting votes from these two major party candidates. Many Democrats remain angry with Ralph Nader for his run in 2000, believing he cost Al Gore the presidency. However, instances in which Democrats and Republicans place blame on third parties for causing an election loss are usually cases in which correlation is mistaken for causality. First, these third-party candidates emerged and did well because of weaknesses in the major parties and their candidates. They may take advantage of those weaknesses, but they did not necessarily create them. Strong major-party candidates discourage serious third-party challenges and deflate third-party performance. Humphrey in 1968, Bush in 1992, and Gore in 2000 failed to do so. The leap from correlation to causation also assumes that third-party candidates deliberately employ a spoiler strategy—seeking to cause the defeat of the major party they are ideologically closer to. Angry Democrats made this contention especially loudly about the Nader candidacy in 2000, but it is not well supported by political science research.[26] If Nader's goal was to contribute to Gore's defeat, he should have spent most of his time campaigning in states where the race between Bush and Gore was known to be close, in order to deny Gore victories in those states. Analysis of Nader's campaign travel and activity, however, found that he spent his time in states where he thought he could accumulate a large number of votes, not necessarily in states where the competition between Bush and Gore was expected to be tight. This pattern of campaign activity suggests that Nader's main goal was to reach 5 percent of the national vote to qualify the Green Party for public campaign financing, not to deny Gore the presidency.

single-member districts
electoral districts in which only one person is elected to represent the district in a representative body.

plurality elections
elections in which the candidate with the most votes, not necessarily a majority, wins.

Single-Member Districts with Plurality Elections Favor Two-Party Competition

Certainly there is no constitutional prohibition on significant third parties. Indeed, the Constitution, unlike newer constitutions in many other countries, does not mention political parties at all. And Americans often say in surveys that they would welcome another major party—half the public supported the idea in early 2012, similar to the level seen for at least a decade.[27] Why would America's electoral competition tend to feature only two major parties as serious competitors? No single-factor explanation is sufficient. Rather, political scientists have identified a number of factors that push American party competition toward a two-party model.

In U.S. House elections, as with most American elections, **single-member districts** are the norm: voters elect one candidate to represent each congressional district. In addition, the candidate with the most votes (but not necessarily a majority) wins: these are **plurality elections**, sometimes referred to by scholars as first-past-the-post elections. As in a race, the image suggests, what matters in an election is who crosses the finish line first, not how much she wins by or how long it took. Being first means you and only you win. Assume that politicians are ambitious and want to increase their chances of consistently winning office. What would be the best strategy: to remain in a small party that has the support of 5 percent of the population or to join a larger party that can potentially obtain majority support? Joining a larger party is the likely answer, and two large, roughly evenly sized parties are the likely result.[28]

This line of argument holds up generally but not in every case. Canada and the United Kingdom, for example, have plurality elections but more than two major parties. Each has three major parties that are national in scope. In addition, each has parties strong in particular regions for reasons of nationality or language. Because of their strength in these regions, they earn seats in the national legislature. Within any particular district, competition might be primarily between two parties, but when summing the effects across the country, multiple parties win seats in the legislature. In the United Kingdom's 2010 elections to the House of Commons, the performance of the Liberal Party was so strong that it denied a majority to either the Conservative or the Labour Party. The Liberals joined a coalition government with the Conservatives and extracted promises of future electoral reforms, including a national referendum that

11.1

11.2

11.3

11.4

proportional representation
an election system in which candidates are elected from multimember districts, with a party's share of seats from a district being roughly proportional to their share of the popular vote.

would eliminate the system of plurality elections. In May 2011, nearly 70 percent of voters chose to stay with the current system.

The idea that single-member districts and plurality elections push toward two-party politics in the United States assumes that parties have a way to nominate candidates to be on the November general election ballot. Nearly all states allow for party nominations, usually through a primary election or party convention. Louisiana and Washington, however, employ nonpartisan blanket primaries, in which all the candidates for an office, regardless of party, are in the same primary. Under this system, two candidates from the same party could win the primary and then face off in the next round of elections. California voters adopted Washington's version of this system in a 2010 referendum. Political scientists will need to wait for more election results from these states, and from other states that might adopt a form of nonpartisan blanket primary, before they can determine the long-term consequences for two-party competition and the fate of minor parties.

An alternative to the single-member plurality model is a system of **proportional representation** (PR), common in Europe and in many other democracies around the world. In this system, voters elect many representatives from the same district. The district, in fact, might be the entire country, as is the case in Israel. Depending on the procedure used, voters may vote for a party but not specific candidates. Or, more commonly, they may be able to vote for specific candidates from a party's list. The number of representatives elected from a particular party will depend on that party's percentage of the vote on Election Day. If a party receives 35 percent of the vote in a district, it will send roughly 35 percent of the legislators from that district.[29] What this means is that the second- or third-place parties, or even more, may also be sending representatives to the legislature. Thus, in a PR system, an ambitious politician can remain in a smaller party and still have a chance to be elected to the legislature. Because there is a significant likelihood that no party will win a majority of the legislative seats, a majority coalition will need to be forged, further empowering smaller parties. Some countries, including Germany, use a mixed model, electing some seats by PR and some by the plurality system.

If single-member districts with plurality elections are generally found in countries with predominantly two-party competition, a puzzle remains: Is the two-party competition a consequence of these election rules or a cause of them? One study of the adoption of proportional representation systems found that countries with a prior history of diverse political competition between multiple groups adopted PR. In other words, the PR system was adopted as a result of what was effectively multiparty competition, rather than being the cause of that competition.[30] Iraq, for example, has numerous divisions among class, ethnic, religious, and regional lines. When devising Iraq's election rules in recent years, the writers of the new constitution created a system that gives a large number of parties a chance for representation in the legislature. Once in place, such a PR system would tend to encourage continued multiparty competition. In 2010, nine parties in Iraq won seats in the national legislature.

In the United States, on the other hand, political scientists have suggested that early political discourse was strongly oriented around fundamental debates about the proper role of government, and these debates tended to feature two competing views, one advocating a bigger role for the national government and the other a smaller role. Single-member districts with plurality elections work well in such an environment, reflecting rather than creating the nature of political competition between two predominant opposing viewpoints.[31] Overall, the research suggests that new electoral rules certainly can change outcomes—place a proportional representation system in the United States and it is feasible that third parties would win seats—but a society such as Iraq with a history of multiple, deep political cleavages may be more likely to experience the political pressure to create rules that would encourage multi-party competition.

The Winner-Take-All System in Presidential Elections Favors Two Major Parties

Presidential elections pose a similar challenge to third parties. With the exception of Maine and Nebraska, all states allocate their electoral votes on a winner-take-all basis.[32] The popular vote winner of the presidential contest in these 48 states wins all the electoral votes from the state, no matter what the size of the popular vote victory. For a third-party candidate, this system makes it difficult to win electoral votes. Because a third party is not likely to be the leading vote winner in a state, it will win no electoral votes. With the winner of the presidency needing to win a majority of the electoral vote, the third-party path to the presidency is very challenging. And with the presidency and national government growing in stature and influence over the course of American political history, politicians throughout the country would want to be affiliated with a party that has a chance to win that powerful office. Voters also would want to have a say in choosing the president by voting for one of the major-party candidates who has a plausible chance at victory.[33]

The structure of the presidential election process benefits third parties with strong regional appeals while hurting those with substantial national appeal. George Wallace in 1968 won 13 percent of the popular vote nationally, but he was the popular vote leader in five southern states and won their electoral votes over Republican Richard Nixon and Democrat Hubert Humphrey. In 1992, Ross Perot did even better nationally than Wallace, winning 19 percent of the popular vote, but he did not win a single electoral vote. He had broad national appeal but not a strong enough appeal in any single state or region to win electoral votes.

fusion
a strategy in which third parties endorse a major party candidate but list that candidate separately on the ballot so that voters can vote for the candidate under the third-party label.

Australian ballot
an official government-produced ballot for elections that lists all offices and all the candidates and parties that have qualified to be on the ballot.

Legal and Behavioral Features of American Elections Reinforce Two-Party Competition

In addition to the basic structural features of American politics already discussed, statutes affecting elections, as well as the behavior of voters, politicians, and the media, reinforce the tendencies toward two-party politics.

ANTI-FUSION LAWS Anti-fusion laws prohibit third parties from practicing fusion with a major party. **Fusion**, a common and successful strategy until banned in nearly all states around the turn of the twentieth century, means that a candidate's name appears on the ballot more than once, allowing voters to vote for the candidate under either the third-party label or the major-party label. The strategy was intended to make voters comfortable voting for third-party candidates and to increase the influence the third party could exert on the candidates once they were in office.[34] Currently, only seven states allow fusion, also known as cross-filing: Connecticut, Delaware, Idaho, Mississippi, New York, South Carolina, and Vermont. In *Timmons v. Twin Cities Area New Party* (1997), the U.S. Supreme Court rejected a challenge to the constitutionality of anti-fusion laws. The New Party argued that such laws infringed on its First Amendment rights to freedom of association, but the Court concluded that on balance the state of Minnesota's interest in reducing ballot clutter (referred to as "ballot integrity") and voter confusion outweighed the infringement on free association, particularly because a candidate would still appear on the ballot, just not multiple times.

BALLOT ACCESS Prior to the 1880s, ballot access was not an issue. Parties printed their own ballots, which voters took to the polling place and dropped into the ballot box. Ballots could be a variety of shapes, sizes, and colors, and it was often easy to identify which party's ballot a voter was casting. Over a short period in the 1880s and 1890s, nearly every state adopted the **Australian ballot**, named for its country of origin. This is the ballot as we know it today—an official ballot printed by the government, provided at the polling place, listing all the candidates for every office, and cast secretly.

As soon as the ballot became an official, standardized government document, questions emerged: Would every candidate from every party, no matter how small, appear on the ballot? Or would the ballot list a limited set of candidates to prevent ballot clutter? Every state opted for the limited, clutter-free version and created rules to determine which candidates qualified for inclusion on the ballot. In most states, parties could gain automatic ballot access if they did sufficiently well in prior elections—this

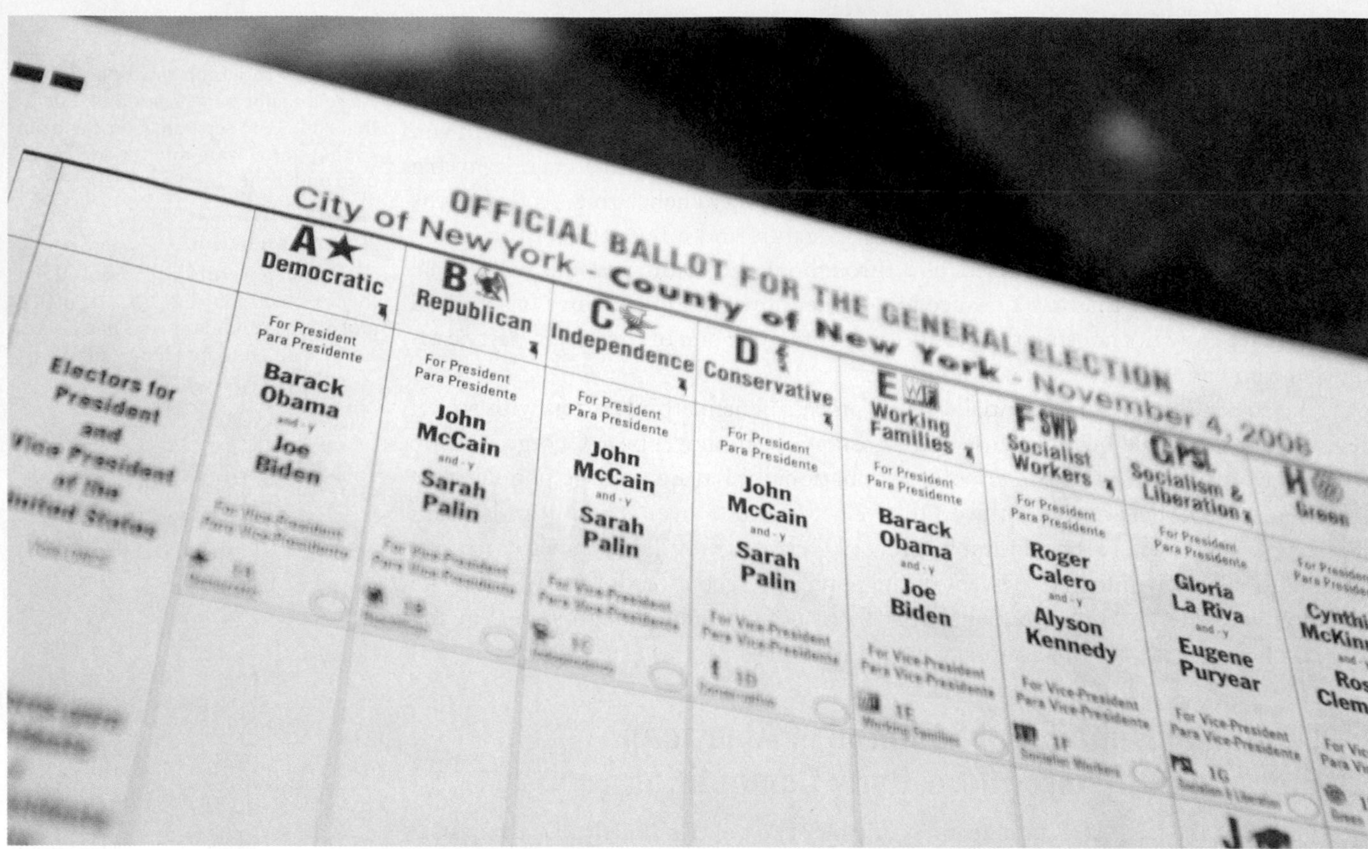

FUSION BALLOT

New York State allows fusion, also known as cross-filing, in which a candidate can appear on a ballot separately as more than one party's nominee. Advocates of third parties hope fusion ballots will make voters comfortable with third-party candidates and that victorious candidates will realize they earned some of their votes as the nominee of a third party.

rule largely benefited the major parties. Requirements to collect a large number of signatures to earn a spot on the ballot created a hurdle for minor parties. Over time, these restrictions have relaxed somewhat, usually as a direct result of lawsuits filed by third-party candidates.

CAMPAIGN FINANCE Running for office is expensive. Third-party candidates suffer from the fact that donors are usually not interested in contributing money to candidates they perceive as having no chance of winning. The public financing system for presidential candidates is also geared toward the major party candidates. Parties whose candidates received at least 25 percent of the vote in the prior presidential election get a full share of public financing for the general election in the fall. If a candidate received between 5 and 25 percent in the previous election, his or her party is entitled to a proportional share of public financing in the current election. Candidates falling below 5 percent, which is nearly always the case for third-party candidates, do not earn their party any share of public financing. Thus, third parties rarely qualify for public financing in presidential campaigns. The last one to do so was the Reform Party, as a result of Ross Perot's success in 1992 and 1996.

The two major parties also benefit from independent spending by groups and individuals and, following the Supreme Court's ruling in *Citizens United v. Federal Election Commission* (2010), by corporations, unions, and nonprofit incorporated organizations. In the same way that donors are unlikely to see a contribution to a third-party candidate as a wise use of their resources, they are unlikely to see spending money independently on behalf of a third-party candidate as a sensible investment. The funds spent on independent expenditures in the 2012 elections went almost exclusively to promoting candidates of the major parties.

VOTER, MEDIA, AND CANDIDATE BEHAVIOR The ways in which voters, the media, and candidates respond to the incentives created by these structural and legal aspects of American politics reinforce the tendency toward two-party politics. Voters unhappy with major-party candidates often choose not to vote rather than vote for a third-party candidate who is likely to lose.[35] Other voters fear that voting for a third-party candidate amounts to throwing their vote away and helping their least favored of the two major-party candidates—by denying a vote to one major-party candidate, voters calculate, they are implicitly helping the other. Third parties face a difficult time breaking through the psychology of not voting and the fear of the wasted vote.[36]

Media coverage is also problematic for third parties. Third-party officials often complain that if the media paid more attention to third parties, they would do better electorally. Media representatives respond that if third parties did better electorally, the news media would pay more attention to them. Each side is right. A media outlet that focuses a lot of attention on relatively obscure candidates may well find its readers, viewers, or listeners drifting to other media outlets. But more attention from the media would, overall, be at least marginally helpful for third-party candidates.

Ambitious, qualified candidates are much more likely to run for office as a Democrat or Republican than as a third-party candidate. Someone wanting to maximize her probability of winning, certainly someone who would like to make a career of elective office, is highly likely to affiliate with one of the major parties. Most voters, guided by their party identification with one of the major parties, are reluctant to vote for third-party candidates. Further, each major party has a network of supporters, consultants, experts, and fund-raisers to draw on. Running as a major-party candidate has huge built-in advantages.

Occasionally, third parties overcome these difficulties. Third-party candidates who have already become nationally visible as a former member of a major party or in some other way will often be talented, strong candidates (see Table 11.1). Theodore Roosevelt, George Wallace, and Ralph Nader all had significant name recognition. For some wealthy candidates, such as Ross Perot in 1992, campaign financing is not an obstacle.[37] Perot self-financed his campaign in 1992 and accepted public funding in 1996.

TABLE 11.1 MOST SUCCESSFUL THIRD-PARTY PRESIDENTIAL CANDIDATES, 1900–2012

Year	Candidate	Party	Percentage of popular vote	Number of electoral votes
1912	Theodore Roosevelt	Progressive	27.4	88
1992	Ross Perot	Independent/ United We Stand	18.9	0
1924	Robert La Follette	Progressive	16.6	13
1968	George Wallace	American Independent	13.5	46
1996	Ross Perot	Reform	8.4	0
1980	John Anderson	Independent/ National Unity Party	6.6	0
1912	Eugene Debs	Socialist	6.0	0
1920	Eugene Debs	Socialist	3.4	0
1916	Allan Benson	Socialist	3.2	0
1904	Eugene Debs	Socialist	3.0	0
1908	Eugene Debs	Socialist	2.8	0
1948	Henry Wallace	Progressive	2.8	0
2000	Ralph Nader	Green	2.7	0
1948	Strom Thurmond	States' Rights	2.4	39
1932	Norman Thomas	Socialist	2.2	0

Source: Dave Leip's Atlas of U.S. Presidential Elections, www.uselectionatlas.org.
Note: Includes all third-party presidential candidates who received at least 2 percent of the national vote.

Alternative Voting Rules Might Assist Third-Party Electoral Fortunes

Supporters of an enhanced role for third parties argue that changes in voting rules could give these parties a better chance of winning elections. Whether this claim is accurate is difficult to determine because these alternative rules are not in wide use in the United States.[38] Moreover, it may be that these reforms tend to be enacted in places already friendly to third parties—that is why they are enacted—rather than that they lead to support for third parties. Nonetheless, it seems plausible that these rules would have some minor benefit for third parties.

Unlike full proportional representation, which would require the dismantling of single-member districts, preference voting and approval voting work within the American single-member district format.[39] Each aims to overcome the voter psychology that reinforces the two-party system and discourages casting a vote for a third-party candidate.

PREFERENCE VOTING In American elections, voters select their favored candidate among those on the ballot. An alternative arrangement would allow voters to rank their choices, indicating which candidate is their first pick, second, third, and so on. The idea is that voters could express support for a third-party candidate but need not indicate support for only that candidate.

Of the several varieties of preference voting arrangements, instant runoff voting, also known as ranked choice voting, is one that a handful of cities in the United States, including San Francisco; Minneapolis; and Portland, Maine, have adopted. In this system, voters rank their choices. If no candidate receives a majority of the first-place

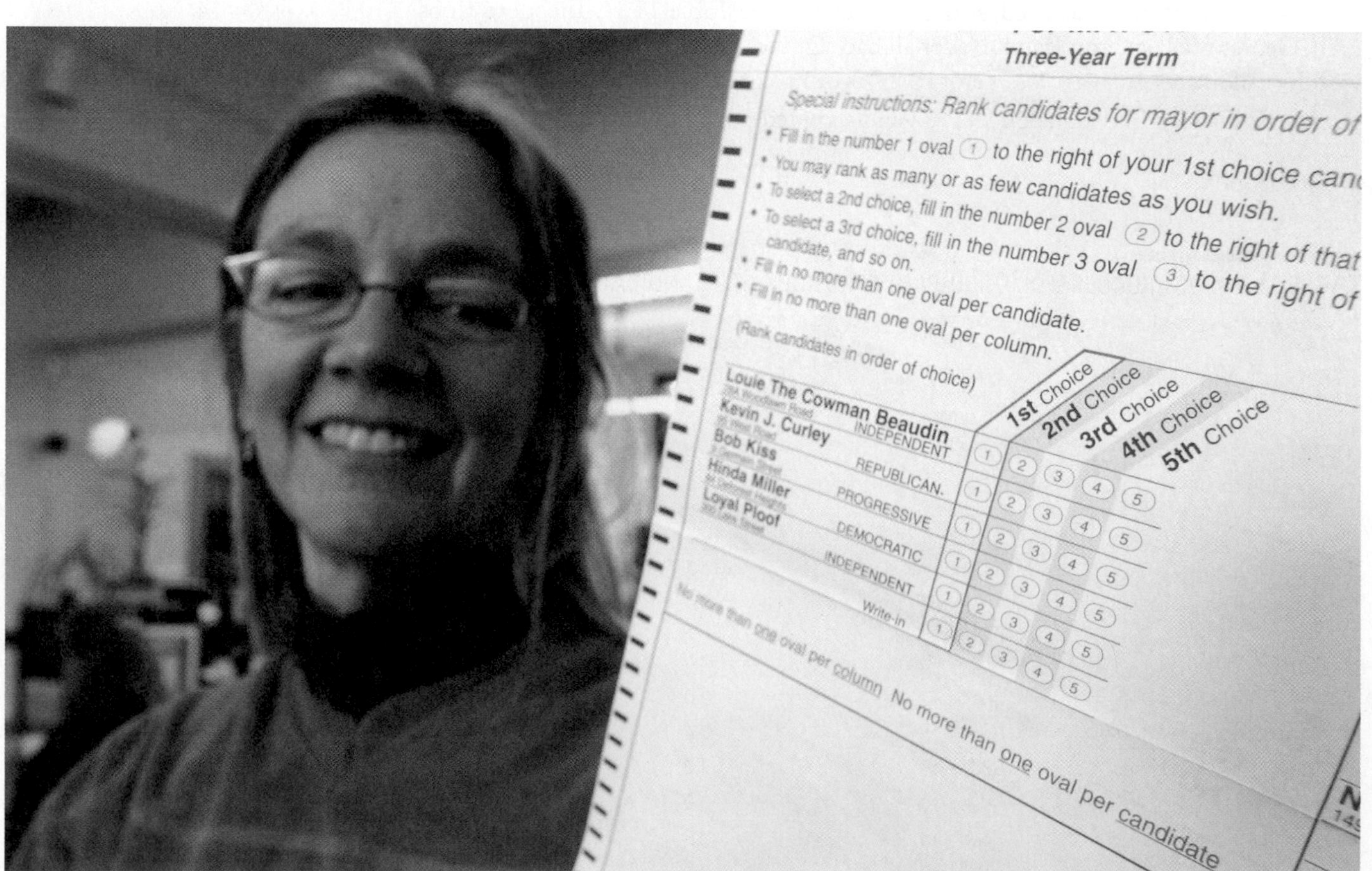

INSTANT RUNOFF VOTING BALLOT

Instant runoff voting (IRV)' has voters rank their preferences. If your top-ranked candidate finishes last in the first round of voting, your vote is reallocated to your second choice. This procedure continues until one candidate has received a majority of the votes. Burlington, Vermont uses this system for local elections. Should more cities and states be encouraged to adopt IRV?

votes, the candidate receiving the fewest first-place votes is eliminated, and the votes cast for him or her are redistributed to other candidates based on the preference ranking indicated by those voters. If a candidate now has a majority, he or she wins. If not, the last-place candidate is again removed and the votes redistributed. This process continues until a candidate has received a majority of the votes.

APPROVAL VOTING Rather than ranking candidates, approval voting allows voters to indicate all of the candidates who meet their approval. The candidate receiving the most votes wins. As with preference voting, the logic is that voters might be interested in a third-party candidate but, because of their fear of wasting their vote, they would not want to commit their only vote to that candidate. Instead, with approval voting, they could vote for a third-party candidate and other candidates of their choosing—they would not have to worry about wasting their vote. Cumulative voting is a form of approval voting used primarily when voters elect more than one official. For example, if a five-member school board is being elected, you as a voter could distribute votes as you please, ranging from giving all five of your votes to one candidate to casting one vote for each of five candidates, or any distribution of votes between those extremes. Currently, cumulative voting is used mainly in nonpartisan races such as those for school boards in which multiple members are elected district wide.

Whether promoting multiparty democracy in the United States through alternative voting rules is a good idea or not is a matter of dispute. To some political observers, multiparty democracy is more inclusive and produces higher voter turnout. To other observers, a two-party system produces more focused debates and a greater probability of decisive, majority victories rather than the plurality victories common to multiparty systems.

Party Organization

11.3 Trace the evolution of American party organizations and their expanding role in campaigns.

Scholars sometimes describe American political parties as a three-legged stool. The first leg is the party in the electorate: the party identification of voters, changes in their party attachments over time, and the influence of these attachments on political behavior. The second leg of the stool is the party in government: the role of political parties in structuring the behavior, influence, and success of Congress, the president, the courts, and the bureaucracy. The third leg of the stool is party organization, which is defined in different ways, but generally it refers to the formal structure that sets rules for party operations and provides services for various party units and candidates.

Party Organization in the Nineteenth Century Was Informal

Political parties in the early nineteenth century did not have large, official organizations. Prominent elected officials such as governors or members of Congress usually held great sway over party activities. They would meet informally in small caucuses to select the party's candidates. In later years, parties sent large numbers of delegates to nominating conventions to select candidates, but elected officials still often hand-picked the delegates to the conventions.

During this era, the control was relatively tight over which candidate could claim the party label. Once candidates were in place, party workers organized parades, rallies, marches, and other events to motivate voters to get involved and support the ticket. These motivational efforts had the feel of "us against them" military campaigns and worked tremendously well. Voter turnout rates in the nineteenth century, especially in the later decades, were often in the range of 80 percent or more.[40]

THE "BRAINS"
THAT ACHIEVED THE TAMMANY VICTORY AT THE ROCHESTER DEMOCRATIC CONVENTION.
Th: Nast.

MONEY MAKES THE MACHINE GO 'ROUND

Cartoonist Thomas Nast was a vigorous critic of party machines. Here he pans them as nothing more than corrupt organizations that bought the support of delegates at nominating conventions in order to get their favored candidates nominated.

party machine
disciplined local party organizations that selected candidates; got out the vote; provided benefits to supporters including government workers, local constituents, and businesses; and served as social service agencies for their followers.

□ Party Machines Provided Organization in Urban Areas

The era from 1870 to 1920 was the heyday of the local **party machine**. These organizations did not disappear entirely after that point, but they became less common and less powerful. One of the best-known political machines to survive was that of Mayor Richard Daley of Chicago from 1955 to 1976. Daley combined his roles as mayor and as chair of the Cook County Democratic Party to wield tremendous influence on city affairs.

The word *machine* gives some hint as to its nature. Unlike the somewhat informal party organization common earlier in the nineteenth century at the state and national levels, machines were disciplined organizations that selected candidates, got out the vote, and provided benefits to loyal constituencies. The leader of the machine was usually an elected official, typically a mayor, but not always. Machines were hierarchical organizations with a reach all over a city, so that each precinct (usually a few city blocks) had a machine representative in charge, who reported to a ward boss. They were intensely local in focus, but they were willing to offer the backing of the machine and its supporters to a state or national politician who could return the favor in some way.

The machine spread benefits broadly. As a candidate or officeholder, you knew that affiliation with the machine increased your likelihood of victory. Kicking back a portion of your salary to the machine would be an acceptable price to pay—it beat losing. As a worker, the promise of a city job awarded to you for your loyalty, known as

patronage, made the machine a path to upward mobility. This was especially true for immigrants who might otherwise find it difficult to advance in the American economy. Businesspeople, lawyers, and bankers knew they would prosper through government contracts and favorable regulations if the machine were electorally successful. And precinct captains catered to individual voters by providing them with groceries, financial and legal assistance, job contacts, help renting a facility for a wedding, or any other kind of assistance that would cement the voter's loyalty to the machine.

patronage
awarding jobs in government on the basis of party support and loyalty rather than expertise or experience.

Progressive reforms
a set of political and electoral reforms in the early twentieth century that had the combined effect of weakening political parties.

Party Organizations Were Reformed at the Beginning of the Twentieth Century

Despite building deeply personal alliances with their supporters and serving important social service functions, machines had problems. Fiscal discipline was not one of their hallmarks. Nor were open and fair bids for contracts. The patronage system rewarded loyalty more than competence.

With the rise of professions and the middle class at the turn of the twentieth century, machines came under strong attack. Businesses that were not favored by the machines, rival politicians, and middle-class reformers joined forces in what became labeled the Progressive movement to change civil service laws at the national, state, and local levels. These **Progressive reforms** protected government workers from removal when a new party came into power.

Parties at the state and local levels were the subject of a wide range of Progressive reforms during the first two decades of the twentieth century. Reforms included the introduction of nonpartisan elections; citywide rather than ward-based elections to city councils; the development of separate and often appointed rather than elected governing districts for services such as water, transportation, and schooling; and the hiring of city managers to run much of the day-to-day business of the city, taking that job away from elected mayors. At the state level, reforms included the widespread adoption of personal registration requirements for voting, requirements that primary elections determine party nominations, and the increased use of nonelected boards and commissions to make public policy. Reformers expected these changes to weaken political parties, or at least to weaken the control of their opponents over the parties and government. In this way, reformers and machine politicians were alike: Each group wanted to make it more difficult for its opponents to hold office and wield power.

As one political scientist suggests, it is misleading to describe machine politicians as determined to hoard power and reformers as determined to spread it widely. Instead, both represented coalitions of supporters who preferred that they hold power rather than their challengers. Each took advantage of opportunities to revise rules, laws, and political processes to create "political monopolies." And, by increasingly serving the narrow needs of its coalition while cities changed around them, each created the conditions for opposition to arise and lead to the monopoly's collapse.[41]

Because it was ardently pursued by reformers, the adoption of the primary election has usually been thought of by political scientists as an assault on a party's most defining power: control over nominations. Certainly, primaries do present challenges, as they create strife within parties and risk the nomination of weak candidates. There is also the curious fact of using a public process to select the candidates of a private organization, which political parties legally are—it is as if nominations to the board of directors of the Sierra Club were a matter of a public vote rather than being left to the Sierra Club. The correlation between the support of reformers and the adoption of the reform, however, is somewhat misleading. More recent research shows that major party officials welcomed the primaries in part because they had increasingly struggled to maintain control over their growing organizations and the conflicts about who "deserved" a nomination. Factional disputes within parties became common, and primary elections were seen as an easier method of sorting out these disputes.[42] Reformers advocated for primary elections, but party leaders also accepted primaries as a way to address serious organizational challenges.

The adoption of primaries as the dominant form of party nomination was part of a broader trend of state government regulation of political parties.[43] States established laws and rules concerning party committees, the process of selecting party officials, how parties could raise and spend money, in what ways they could assist their candidates, how candidates would qualify for the party primary ballot, and who could vote in the primaries.

Party Organizations Have Become More Active in Recent Decades

For decades after the introduction of Progressive movement reforms, party organizations were largely ineffective and inactive. The threadbare organizations rarely had a headquarters and seemed to disappear between elections. Party functions such as recruiting, training, and assisting candidates fell by the wayside as candidates built their own campaign organizations, became less reliant on the resources of the formal party organizations, and deemphasized their link to their political parties. Voter mobilization by parties lagged in many areas. Organizations today have reversed these trends.

STATE PARTY ORGANIZATIONS State parties challenged legal restrictions by arguing that they were not quasi-public utilities, but rather were private associations entitled to set their own rules. In a series of decisions beginning in the late 1980s, the Supreme Court agreed and granted state party organizations more autonomy from government regulations.[44]

In *Tashjian v. Connecticut* (1986), the Court determined that political parties did not have to agree to hold primaries in which individuals not affiliated with the party were allowed to select a party's nominees. And, the Court's decision in *California Democratic Party v. Jones* (2000) struck down the mandatory partisan blanket primary, in which voters could choose office by office in which party's primary to participate. As private associations, the Court argued, political parties had a right to decide who could be involved in selecting their nominees for office.

With a mandatory partisan blanket primary now off limits, the state of Washington devised a modified version, referred to as a nonpartisan blanket primary or a "jungle" primary. Based on the primary process used in Louisiana, in a nonpartisan blanket primary, candidates can choose to have a party label listed on the ballot for informational purposes, but they are not officially selected by the parties in any way. In this system, later adopted by California as the "top two" system, the top two finishers in the primary go on to the general election, and both of these candidates might have the same party affiliation—parties would not be guaranteed a spot on the general election ballot. Washington's system won the Court's approval in *Washington State Grange v. Washington State Republican Party* (2008), with the Court's majority concluding that the primary was in effect nonpartisan and so did not violate the parties' private associational rights.

In terms of funding, the Court upheld the right of parties to spend unlimited sums on behalf of candidates in *Colorado Republican Federal Campaign Committee v. FEC* (1996), so long as candidates had no say in how the money was spent. If the spending was coordinated with a candidate, the amount the party spent could be limited (*FEC v. Colorado Republican Federal Campaign Committee*, 2001).

To respond to the competitors for some of their key functions, state party organizations and legislative campaign committees increased their professionalism. They hired new staff and experts to recruit, train, and help finance candidates, and they worked more closely with the new web of pollsters, consultants, and media advisers.

NATIONAL PARTY ORGANIZATIONS The national party organizations include the Democratic and Republican national committees and the campaign committees for each party in the House and Senate, referred to as the Hill committees (Democratic Congressional Campaign Committee, National Republican Congressional Committee, Democratic Senatorial Campaign Committee, National Republican Senatorial Committee).

Starting in the mid-1970s, both parties began modernizing their operations and becoming more active in presidential campaigning, with the Republicans moving first. As the parties became more proficient at raising large sums through new methods—initially direct mail and later through the Web—and as major changes in society (civil rights, the women's movement, evangelical Christianity), the economy (high unemployment, inflation, and changes in interest rates), and the international scene (the Vietnam War and its aftermath, Americans taken hostage in Iran, the Soviet Union intervening militarily in Afghanistan, and the buildup of nuclear arsenals) raised the stakes of government action, both parties expanded their funding and staff. Parties had the means to raise more funds, and voters and activists had the motives to contribute. Voter contact, fund-raising, polling, advertising, candidate recruitment and training, opposition research, internal party communications, and fund transfer arrangements between the national and state parties all increased markedly. The key to this revival was that parties benefited from the complexity of campaigning in an era of high technology, constant media, large fund-raising demands, and intense demands from issue activists. Some candidates—especially new ones—simply could not assemble on their own the necessary money and expertise needed to run a modern campaign, thus opening the door to national party organization involvement.[45]

In addition to contributing funds and providing services to their candidates, the national party organizations also acted independently. The national party committees spent anywhere from 3 to 15 times as much money in their independent spending than in their contributions to the party's candidates.[46] In total dollars, independent party expenditures were well over 100 times higher in 2010 than they had been in 2002.[47] In competitive congressional races, it was not unusual for the party organizations to spend more on a campaign than either of the candidates. The Hill committees expected safe incumbents to contribute some of their campaign funds to the party so the party could redeploy these funds to other contests. An expectation like this signals how far the national party organizations have come in increasing their discipline and focus.

PARTY CHIEFS

The national party committee establishes rules by which the party's business is conducted and provides support for recruiting, training, and financing candidates. The party chairs, such as Debbie Wasserman Schultz and Reince Priebus, 2012 chairs of the Democratic and Republican National Committees, respectively, are usually the most visible spokespersons for the national party organizations.

national party convention
a meeting held over several days at which delegates select the party's presidential nominee, approve the party platform, and consider changes in party rules and policies.

party platform
a document expressing the principles, beliefs, and policy positions of the party, as endorsed by delegates at the national party convention.

The 2010 and 2012 election cycles featured a large role for so-called Super PACs, with more than 500 Super PACs registered with the Federal Election Commission in 2012. These organizations emerged in part out of the Supreme Court's decision in *Citizens United v. Federal Election Commission* (2010) and even more so out of a federal court's decision in *SpeechNow.org v. Federal Election Commission* (2010).

Citizens United established that many corporate entities—nonprofit incorporated organizations and associations, unions, and business corporations—could, if allowed by their tax status, use their treasury funds to spend independently on campaign advocacy or contribute those funds to an organization (a Super PAC) that would do so. *SpeechNow* established that individuals could similarly contribute as much as they wish to these organizations, and individual contributions rather than corporate entities have driven most of the growth in Super PAC spending.

For the party organizations, Super PACs present an opportunity and a challenge. The opportunity is that Super PACs can be helpful in promoting a party's candidates, and because they are not subject to contribution limits from their donors, they can quickly assemble large war chests. The challenge is that the candidates might find themselves spending valuable time distancing themselves from provocative Super PAC attack ads against an opponent. Super PACs are not parallel organizations to parties—they are thinly staffed and engaged almost exclusively in running campaign ads. Nonetheless, they can shape a party's public image by magnifying the influence of particular factions within a party.

Like political parties in the United States, parties in the Western European democracies traditionally relied on private funds from wealthy donors, trade unions, and party members to finance their campaigns. Over the past two decades, in contrast to the United States, government funding for party campaign activity has grown significantly in Europe at the national level. In the United States, only when candidates opt into the presidential public financing system do national tax dollars finance party campaign activity or, more precisely, the campaign activity of the party's nominee. Although especially a practice in the new democracies of Eastern Europe, western and southern European countries such as Germany, France, Italy, Spain, and Portugal also now provide large sums to parties. Many of the newer democracies explicitly provide for political parties in their constitutions, and they support that guarantee through financial assistance.[48]

For most Americans, the most visible activity of the national party organizations is running the **national party convention** held every four years to select the party's presidential and vice presidential nominees. The convention delegates pass the **party platform**, a statement of the party's principles, goals, and plans, and settle rules controversies within the party. Up through the mid-twentieth century, rival factions within a party battled to select the party's presidential nominee at the conventions. Multiple ballots were sometimes needed to determine the nominee; the Democrats famously took 104 ballots to select John Davis in 1924. Today, however, largely because of the reforms to the nominating process after 1968, the nominee is usually known well in advance of the convention. The convention is a televised spectacle as well, and neither party wants a divisive internal battle broadcast across television screens like a bad reality TV show.

☐ A New Federalism of the Parties Now Exists

Today, the national party organizations have more influence on the state organizations than was true previously. The Democratic and Republican national party organizations provide financing and technical assistance for their state parties. Each national party channels contributions to the state parties—when an individual or organization has maxed out on allowable contributions to the national party—with directions about how to employ these funds to benefit candidates for national office.

Both parties, but especially the Democrats, set mandatory rules at the national level. The Democrats have established rules for how delegates are apportioned among candidates in presidential primaries and caucuses, the demographic composition of state delegations to the national convention, and the procedures by which caucuses are run. The Republicans have traditionally left more of these matters to the state parties to determine. In 2012, however, the Republican national party imposed rules on state parties that held their nomination contest too early. State parties in some cases lost half their delegate seats to the national convention; in other cases, states could not opt for winner-take-all arrangements (in which the candidate winning a primary would receive all the delegates from that state) unless they waited until April to hold their nomination contest. The intent was to encourage states to move their contests later into the spring and stretch out the nomination calendar for a variety of reasons, such as reducing the likelihood of a quick coronation of a weak nominee. The plan worked. In 2008, 32 states held nomination contests in January and February. In 2012, that number was 11.

As part of their increased activity in recent elections, national party organizations have created coordinated campaigns with state party organizations in which the national party provides financial resources, expertise, and staff to help a state party's effort to win a congressional or other seat. Howard Dean, chair of the Democratic National Committee in 2006, adopted the "50-State Strategy" to signal to state party organizations that this kind of national assistance was possible across the country, not just in traditional Democratic strongholds. Rahm Emanuel, then the head of the Democratic Congressional Campaign Committee and more recently President Obama's chief of staff for two years, blasted the plan as squandering resources rather than focusing them on voter turnout in the most competitive races. Even after the Democrats' success in 2006, the 50-State Strategy remained controversial, but Barack Obama in 2008 followed Dean's lead by placing staff across the country, not just in loyal Democratic states and swing states.

The Evolution of Party Competition and Party Coalitions

11.4 Explain how parties achieve electoral success by building and maintaining coalitions of supporters.

ith two major parties in the United States, winning an election means getting more votes than the opponent, typically more than 50 percent. American parties, therefore, are large coalitions that bring together a wide range of groups with varied interests and policy perspectives under the same umbrella. Groups benefit by associating with a winning party because it increases the likelihood of action on the groups' key issues. The collection of groups under the party umbrella assists governing, because it forces some compromise among these groups—not every group's interest can be the top priority of the president and legislators. And bringing groups under the umbrella benefits parties, because it helps them win.

Bringing interests together does pose challenges, however. The larger the party, the more factions it is likely to have. For a while, these factions can reside in peaceful coexistence, but as groups in the coalition begin to believe that the party is marginalizing their issues and concerns, the coalition comes under strain. Coalition management presents complex challenges to party leaders.

Once in office, President Obama confronted the problem of keeping Democratic coalition members satisfied. Unions, for example, pushed hard with the president and Democratic leaders to pass "card check," in which a worker could indicate his support for creating a union by signing a card rather than voting in a certification election. Unions were unsuccessful while the Democrats controlled the House, the Senate, and

responsible party model
the idea that political parties should run as unified teams, present a clear policy platform, implement that platform when in office, and run on their record in the subsequent election.

the presidency in 2009–2010, and when Republicans gained a majority in the House in 2011, card check effectively died.[49] On the Republican side, House Speaker John Boehner of Ohio faced blistering criticism in 2011–1212 from Tea Party activists, media figures, and members of Congress who believed he did not do enough to force President Obama and Democrats to accept major spending cuts. To these conservative activists, too many Republican elected officials are RINOs (pronounced rhinos, meaning Republicans In Name Only).

The fact that American party coalitions need to be large has been the basis for a long-standing debate about American parties. Some analysts have called for candidates from a party to run as a team that offers a clear platform of proposals; works in a highly unified, disciplined fashion to enact them; and then runs on its record. Many political activists wish for the same. This is the **responsible party model**. One attraction of this model is that it improves accountability by forcing politicians to act in a cohesive way and then defend their record. Voters know where to point the finger of blame if things go wrong or whom to credit if they go right.

Some analysts, however, have said that the broad nature of American party coalitions makes this kind of party behavior unlikely over an extended time because parties constantly need to adjust their positions to either become or maintain a majority. They need to respond to events and to the tactics of the other major party. And because some positions might be more popular in one part of the country than another, candidates of the same party from different regions will differ in their views. The practical reality, these critics say, is that successful parties will usually have to compromise and adjust their positions more than their most fervent supporters would like.[50]

☐ Coalitions are Dynamic, not Static

"The party coalition" is a general term that obscures the complicated nature of holding together a coalition. Coalitions come together in a wave of optimism—and perhaps in a wave of relief from removing the other party from power—because their members believe that their goals will be better achieved by joining forces. In general, they believe the party's approach to issues will advance their cause. They might even be willing to defer pressing their cause for a while as other coalition members take their turn.

A victorious party might wish for time to stand still while it revels in its unity—its coalition intact and the party a national majority. This is impossible. Party coalitions are always changing and facing strains. Like tectonic plates, the factions within a party shift and collide, sometimes creating minor rumbles, sometimes earthquakes. The intense preferences and demands of a party's factions can play a strong role in demanding that a party remain on the same policy and strategic path or that the party shift its direction and focus to new issues, perspectives, and voters. Cracks in the party foundation may appear immediately. At other times, they may build up over decades. Unity tends to fracture. Waiting becomes less palatable, and the various parts of a coalition want their issues to be the party's primary concerns.

If a party knows that its success depends on serving the members of its coalition, what might prevent it from doing so? Media personalities, newspaper columnists, and bloggers often solve this puzzle by pinning the blame on unprincipled and spineless politicians. This explanation ignores the significant difficulty involved in holding together diverse coalitions of dozens of interest groups, hundreds of elected officials, and tens of millions of voters spread coast to coast. The explanation is appealing in its simplicity by focusing on character and personality, but it is misleading for that very reason. It ignores or wishes away the political realities faced by party leaders. Good analysis requires understanding these realities. Several strategic factors explain why a party might not serve all parts of its coalition equally.

First, a group might be so loyal to the party that it seems to have no serious options politically, which could reduce pressure on the party to advance the group's agenda. Leaders of black and labor organizations have had such complaints about the Democratic Party.[51] Second, one group's interests might clash with the interests of other groups in the coalition—someone will have to be disappointed. Some of the desires of the Republican Party's conservative Christian followers, for example, would be objectionable to those Republicans who define themselves as libertarians and argue that government needs to stay out of individuals' decisions as much as possible. Third, as the mix of voters supporting a party changes over time, a group may become a smaller share of a party's voters and therefore be less central to the party's electoral strategies.

Lastly, a party that has lost recent elections will have conflicting internal interpretations about what lessons to learn from these defeats. The winning interpretation will favor some party groups and their issues more than others.[52] After the Republican Party's defeats in the 2006 and 2008 elections, the party's factions sparred over whether the party had pushed too far in a conservative direction or had strayed too far from conservative principles. By 2010, with the rise of the Tea Party movement, the argument that the Republican Party had drifted too far from conservative thinking dominated. Candidates supported by Tea Party followers captured Republican primaries in 2010, sometimes with the support of prominent Republican elected officials and sometimes in defiance of them. This pattern continued in 2012 when the Tea Party pushed traditional Republican candidates in a more conservative direction. For instance, Mitt Romney presented a more thorough conservatism in his 2012 bid for the Republican nomination for president than he had in his 2008 effort. In these elections, Tea Party supporters and organizations were the most active grassroots elements in the Republican Party and also received significant organizational and financial support from wealthy benefactors, not an unusual combination in activist politics.[53]

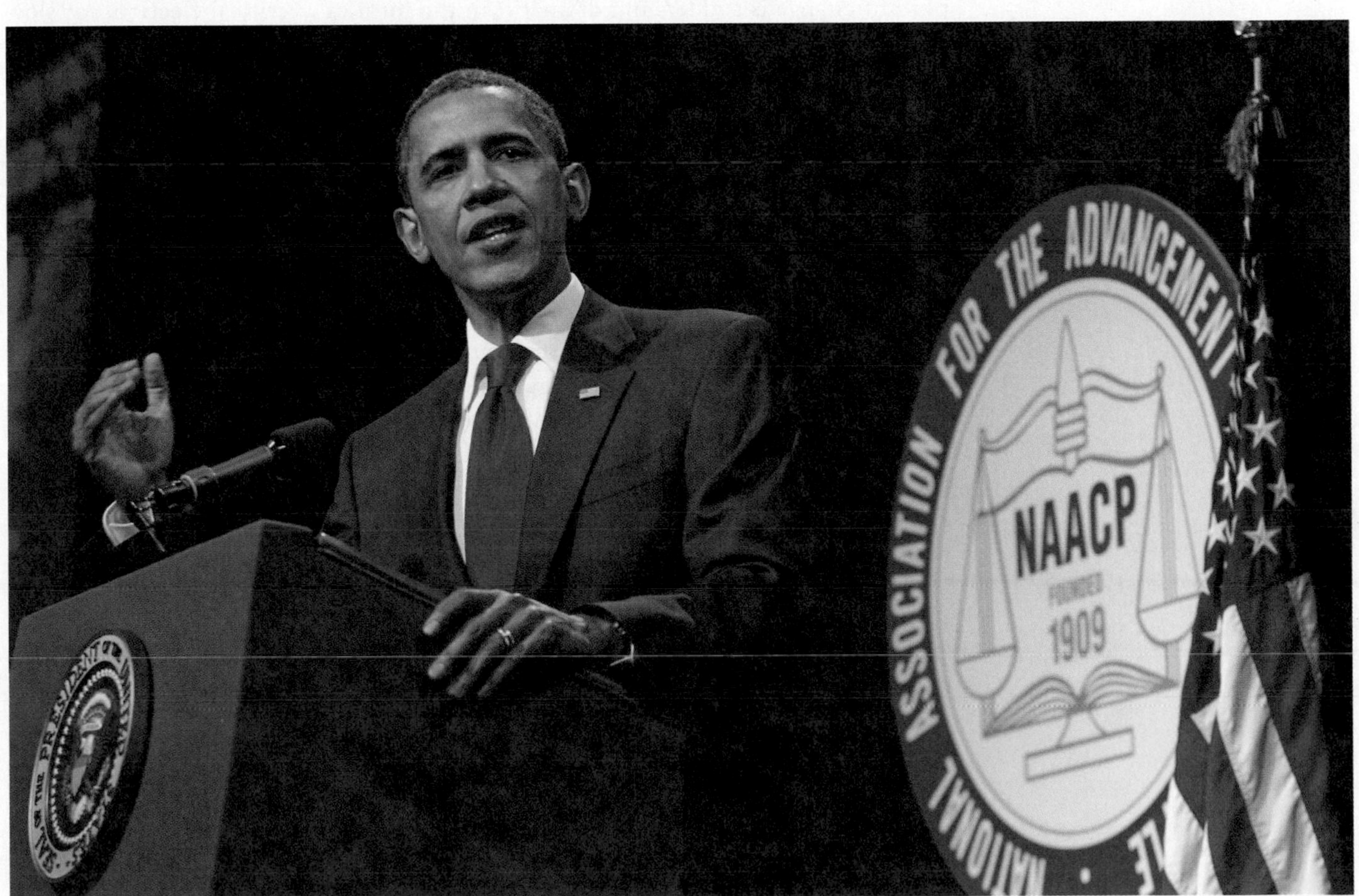

BALANCING PARTY AND INTEREST GROUP AGENDAS

Politicians want to appear responsive to their support groups, but they do not want to create the impression that they are controlled by a group's agenda. For national Democrats, signaling support for the NAACP's priorities at its annual national convention is a long-standing tradition. President Barack Obama spoke to the group in July 2010.

issue evolution
a change in the partisan base of support for an issue over time, such that the positions of Democrats and Republicans switch.

electoral realignment
a shift in the composition of party coalitions that produces a new, relatively durable pattern of party competition.

All four of these factors contribute to parties changing their emphasis on particular issues, perhaps to the chagrin of some coalition members. At the extreme, a party might even reverse its position on an issue. Political scientists refer to flips in party positioning as **issue evolution**. Some examples of issue evolution are the support of civil rights by the Democratic Party beginning in the 1960s, a stance previously taken by Republicans, and the move by Republicans to a free trade position in the 1970s, after having been the party more supportive of protectionism since its founding in 1854. Another form of issue evolution occurs when an issue moves from being one that does not have strong partisan differences to one that does. Over the past few decades, abortion has gone from being an issue where party differences were absent to one that is seen as one of the central defining differences between the parties. Issue evolution is a dramatic illustration of how party coalitions always evolve. Sometimes party leaders calculate that maintaining and enlarging the party's base of support requires setting aside some groups' concerns or revising or even reversing a long-standing party position.[54]

American Parties Have Evolved Through Six Periods of Party Competition

Over time, the key issues and relative strength of the two major parties have changed. Political scientists refer to the switch from one period of competition to another as **electoral realignment**—the shifting of support groups between the parties, the addition of new groups, and the rise of a new set of prominent issues. Political scientists dispute the process by which electoral realignment occurs and whether the most important change is sudden and dramatic, in the form of a "critical election," or slow building and gradual.[55] They more widely accept the view, however, that there are some roughly demarcated periods of competition.

A common perspective among political scientists is that the United States has experienced six periods of party competition. The first was from 1801 to 1828. The Federalist Party of the 1790s, led by John Adams and Alexander Hamilton, advocated a larger, more active national government. Its support was strongest in the Northeast, among businesspeople and those of higher incomes. The Democratic-Republican Party, represented by Thomas Jefferson and James Madison, pushed to protect states' rights and limit national power. It prospered in the South and Mid-Atlantic states. The Democratic-Republicans were the dominant party and effectively the only major party for much of this period (see Figure 11.4).

The Democratic-Republican Party split in two, inaugurating a new period of party competition from 1829 to 1860. The Democratic Party, represented by Andrew Jackson, continued the tradition of representing rural, low-income, and southern voters, but it also added support among the urban working class. It was the dominant party during this time. The National Republican Party, which would become the Whig Party, argued for an expansion of the national government's economic powers through such measures as funding railroad building and reestablishing the Bank of the United States after Jackson vetoed its renewal. It fared better among wealthier voters. John Quincy Adams was a major figure in this party.

The Whig Party collapsed when it was unable to heal internal divisions over the slavery issue. In 1854, the Republican Party, represented by Abraham Lincoln, emerged and quickly moved to major party status as the Whigs disappeared. The years 1861 through 1896 marked a third period of party competition. Slavery and then the Civil War and Reconstruction became the central issues. Party success was strongly regional, with Democrats prevailing in the South and Republicans in the Northeast and Midwest. The national government's role in economic development, and particularly its promotion of industrial capitalism through tariffs and other measures, also strongly divided the parties, with Republicans advocating a stronger government role and Democrats arguing for the primacy of states' rights and local economic development.

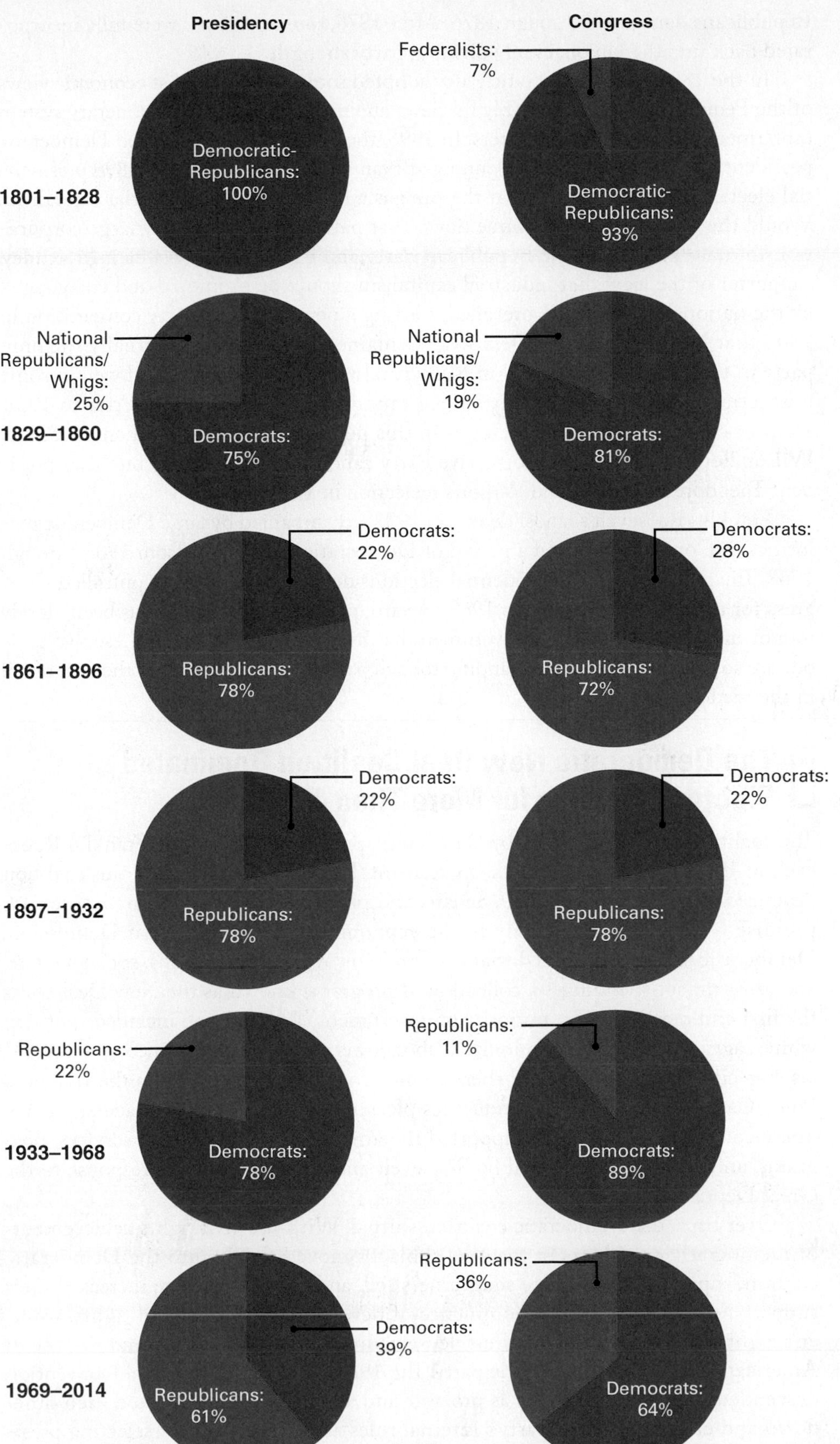

FIGURE 11.4 PARTY CONTROL OF CONGRESS AND THE PRESIDENCY, 1802–2014.

Most periods of American party completion have featured one clear majority party in presidential, Senate, and House elections. The period since 1969 is the only one in which each of the two major parties has at least one institution that it has controlled for the majority of years. Divided government has also been more common in this most recent era than in the preceding eras.

11.1

11.2

11.3

11.4

Republicans dominated through 1876. After 1876, southern states were fully incorporated back into the Union, evenly dividing party strength.

In the 1890s, the Democratic Party adopted some of the populist economic views of the People's Party, most notably its views about the impact of the monetary system on farmers and agricultural workers. In 1896, the People's Party endorsed Democratic presidential candidate Williams Jennings Bryan on a fusion ticket. The 1896 presidential election was widely viewed at the time as a referendum on industrial capitalism. Would the United States continue down that path, with increasingly large corporations of national scope? The Republican Party and its candidate William McKinley, supporter of the view that industrial capitalism should be promoted and encouraged by the national government, prevailed, starting a new period of party competition in 1897 that lasted until 1932. Democrats remained the dominant, virtually the only, party in the South, and did well in many rural western states. They did well in some northern cities as well, especially among immigrant Catholic voters. Prior to 1932, Democrats' only presidential victories in this period came in 1912, when Woodrow Wilson benefited from the Progressive Party candidacy of former Republican president Theodore Roosevelt, and Wilson's reelection in 1916.

Franklin Roosevelt's landslide win in 1932, accompanied by large Democratic majorities in Congress, initiated a period of Democratic dominance from 1933 through 1968. The party won most presidential elections during this time and controlled Congress for all but four years. From 1969 onward, political competition has been closely fought, and divided control of government has been common. Because these two periods are so important for understanding today's party politics, we discuss them in detail in the sections that follow.

The Democratic New Deal Coalition Dominated Electoral Politics for More Than 40 Years

The coalition brought together by Democratic presidential candidate Franklin Roosevelt in 1932 proved to be remarkably resilient. For more than 40 years, this coalition produced victories in the House, Senate, and presidency. Galvanized by Roosevelt's promise to respond aggressively to the economic stress of the Great Depression, Democratic supporters agreed that economic recovery through jobs, social welfare, and government spending—a collection of programs known as the New Deal—was the first and most important priority of government. The coalition included southern whites, agricultural workers, unionized labor, lower to lower-middle income individuals, big-city public officials and their ethnic group supporters such as the Irish and Poles, Catholics and Jews, and industries pleased by Roosevelt's free trade approach. These constituencies strongly supported the array of new government services, programs, and entitlements created by Roosevelt and the Democrats in response to the Great Depression.

Over time, the Democratic coalition shifted. With the civil rights achievements of Democratic presidents in the 1960s, blacks moved firmly into the Democratic column, support among white southerners fell, and Hispanic voters increased their support for Democrats. The prominence of new issues based on civil rights, women's rights, environmentalism, lifestyle, sexuality, the Vietnam War, and the use of American military power split the party. The 1968 Democratic National Convention descended into televised chaos as pro-war and antiwar factions shouted each other down and clashed over the party's internal rules and procedures for selecting presidential nominees.

After 1968, upper-middle-class professionals, particularly in government, the nonprofit sector, law, the media, and academia, along with upper-income voters and college graduates, became a larger share of the Democratic Party coalition. Meanwhile, support began to wane among the original members of the New Deal coalition.[56] About 70 percent of Catholics favored Democratic candidates in the 1950s; by the 1980s, a little over 50 percent did. Support among white working-class voters—non-college-educated workers engaged in manual labor—also dropped.[57] And as union membership declined after the 1950s, especially in the private sector, the proportion of Democratic voters who were from union households dropped from nearly 35 percent to less than 15 percent.[58]

dealignment
a substantial reduction in the proportion of the voting population consistently voting for and identifying with one party.

The Coalition Crafted by Ronald Reagan Brought the Republicans to National Parity

In 1980, Ronald Reagan built a coalition that brought the Republicans to parity with Democrats nationally. In the wake of bad economic times and struggling U.S. foreign policy, Reagan encouraged new identities for disgruntled groups. He asked middle-class and working-class voters to think of themselves not as the beneficiaries of government programs, but as the taxpayers bearing the heavy cost of supporting these programs. Blue-collar workers were asked to focus not only on their economic concerns, but also on their patriotic concerns for the United States and their values that were "looked down on" by media and liberal elites. These "Reagan Democrats" joined conservative white southerners, conservative Christians, business owners and executives frustrated by high taxes and regulation, and the Republicans' traditionally strong support groups of middle- to high-income individuals and small-town and rural residents.[59]

This coalition of voters produced presidential victories for Republicans Reagan (1980, 1984), George H. W. Bush (1988), and George W. Bush (2000, 2004). In 1994, Republicans gained control of the House and Senate for the first time in 40 years. Representative Newt Gingrich of Georgia played a leading strategic role in this electoral success. For more than a decade, he had been pushing the party to take a more combative and conservative stance in Congress, encouraging conservative candidates to run, and providing them with financial assistance and training. The Republican congressional majority lasted until 2006 when the party lost its control of both the House and Senate because of economic concerns, the Iraq War, a series of scandals, and President Bush's low approval ratings.[60]

Divided Control of Government Has Been Common in Recent Decades

Whereas the years from 1933 through 1968 consistently featured a Democratic majority, party competition since 1969 has been more complex. Divided government has been common. Rather than a party realignment, some analysts argue that the first half of this period featured **dealignment**, with voters splitting tickets, feeling less attachment to the parties, increasingly identifying themselves as independents, and turning out in lower numbers to vote. These behaviors peaked in the mid-1980s. After that, ticket splitting dropped: Voters who identified as Democrats were increasingly likely to support the Democratic candidate for the House, Senate, or presidency, and similarly for Republicans. Generally, the Democrats were stronger in the Northeast and Pacific Coast, Republicans prevailed in the mountain and western states and the South, and the Midwest was a battleground between the two parties.[61]

This geographical pattern presents a puzzle: Republicans were winning relatively poorer states, and Democrats wealthier ones. Yet, we tend to think of wealthier voters supporting Republicans and poorer voters supporting Democrats. How can it be that Republicans won the votes of better-off voters but Democrats won better-off states? One prominent explanation, popular among Democrats, is that lower-income voters had been misled into voting against their economic self-interest by the Republicans' focus on social and cultural issues.[62] However, one extensive study of this puzzle concludes that the Democratic conventional wisdom leaves out one key factor: political behavior can vary from state to state. The study finds that across all states, a majority of less-well-off voters *do* mostly support Democrats. In poorer states, better-off voters do reliably vote Republican. Adding lower-income Republican votes to the reliable higher-income votes

11.1

11.2

11.3

11.4

for the party can produce wins in poorer states. On the other hand, in wealthier states better-off voters lean more heavily Democratic than one might expect, primarily because of their social and cultural liberalism. Adding the votes of lower-income Democratic supporters to the higher-income Democratic voters was enough to produce victories for the party in these states. In sum, Republicans could win in poorer states and Democrats could win in wealthier states. Social and cultural issues did play a role, not among "misled" low-income voters, but among better-off voters in high-income states.[63]

Barack Obama's victory in 2008, coupled with Democratic gains in the House and Senate, had many Democrats hopeful that the chapter had closed on the long period of balanced party competition from 1968 through 2008, signaling a realignment and the beginning of a seventh period of party competition. They pointed to the size of Obama's victory, the succession of two congressional elections with significant gains for Democrats, and 90 percent of the public in 2008 saying the country was headed in the wrong direction as possible signs of an enduring sea change in American politics that would establish Democrats as a long-lasting majority party.

By 2010, however, Republicans made sweeping gains at the state level by flipping many governorships and state legislative chambers to Republican control. Nationally, they gained a majority in the House while gaining seats in the Senate. The 2012 elections were a pause from these dramatic swings. Divided government continued. Barack Obama was reelected president, but was the first president since 1832 reelected to his second term with a lower share of the vote than in his first election. Democrats kept their majority in the Senate, and Republicans kept their majority in the House. Top support groups provided no surprises (see Table 11.2). Changes in the states were also modest. Because of their loss to Obama and their loss of seats in the House and Senate, Republicans soon began the internal debates typical when a party believes it could have done better.

DIVIDED GOVERNMENT

The 2012 elections kept a Republican majority in the House of Representatives, where John Boehner became Speaker of the House after 2010. Since 1969, control of the presidency and Congress has more often been split between the two parties, rather than resting entirely in one party's hands as it did after the 2008 election. What might be the advantages and disadvantages of divided control of government?

TABLE 11.2 TOP TEN SUPPORT GROUPS FOR BARACK OBAMA AND MITT ROMNEY IN 2012

Group (size in electorate)	Percentage voting for Obama	Percentage voting for Romney	Pro-Obama gap (% points)	Pro-Romney gap (% points)
African American (13%)	93	6	87	—
Democrat (38%)	92	7	85	—
U.S. economy in excellent/good condition (23%)	90	9	81	—
Oppose Tea Party (30%)	89	9	80	—
Expand 2010 health care law or leave as is (44%)	87	11	76	—
Liberal (25%)	86	11	75	—
Government should do more to solve problems (43%)	81	17	64	—
Abortion should be legal in all cases (29%)	76	22	54	—
Hispanic/Latino (10%)	71	27	44	—
No religious affiliation (12%)	70	26	44	—
Repeal all of 2010 health care law (25%)	3	93	—	90
Republican (32%)	6	93	—	—
U.S. economy getting worse (30%)	9	90	—	81
Support Tea Party (21%)	11	87	—	76
Repeal some or all of 2010 health care law (49%)	15	83	—	68
Conservative (35%)	17	82	—	65
White evangelical or born-again (26%)	21	78	—	57
Abortion should be illegal in all or most cases (36%)	21	77	—	56
U.S. economic system is fair to most people (39%)	22	77	—	55
Government does too much better left to individuals and businesses (51%)	24	74	—	50

Source: Edison Research exit polls, total 26,517 respondents. Data available at www.cnn.com/election/2012. Groups 5% or less of electorate omitted.

These debates will guide the parties' policy and electoral strategies in the run-up to the 2012 elections (see Table 11.2).[64]

Democrats and Republicans today differ significantly Over public policy

Despite the common criticism that they are just two peas in a pod, the two major parties do differ significantly on many policy issues. Indeed, if this were not so, it would be difficult to understand why the parties have different voting coalitions, different alliances of interest groups that support them, and different campaign contributors. Presumably, voters support candidates in part for their issue stances. Even if voters support party candidates for reasons of group affiliation—a sense that the party is friendly to "people like me"—that, too, is rooted in some sense that the party will behave in a way that voters will tend to approve.

There is strategic sense to the idea that parties will somewhat skew toward the center of public opinion, if that is where most of the voters are, rather than to the most extreme ends of the ideological spectrum. But parties also have an incentive to maintain the ideological distance between them. This distance keeps them attractive to supportive interest groups and voters, so that the party can count on, although not assume, their support in upcoming elections. This allows the party to focus its efforts on turnout and on persuading undecided voters. Like a business, a party wants to have "repeat customers" whom it can count on—it will not achieve this goal by making its "product" a copycat of that of the other party.

Party differences vary at the national and state levels. Within a particular state, parties may adjust their position to be competitive. Republicans in the Northeast, for example, are generally more liberal than Republicans in the Southwest. Democrats in the South are generally more conservative than Democrats in the Pacific Northwest.

Which Party Governs Better?

When asked whether they trust government to do the right thing Americans are guided by partisanship—Democrats and Republicans each think government runs better when their party is in charge. But dissatisfaction with both major parties exists and many Americans believe that a third party option is needed in the United States.

Your Level of Trust Depends on Your Party

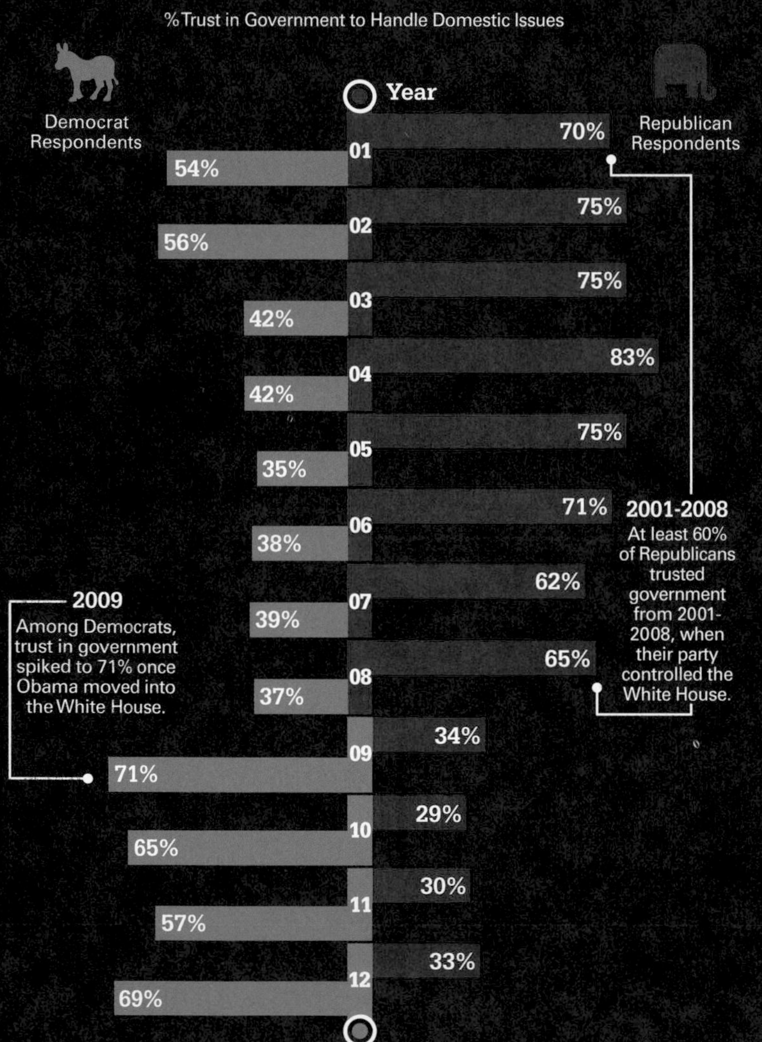

% Trust in Government to Handle Domestic Issues

2001-2008

Among Democrats, trust in government spiked to 71% once Obama moved into the White House.

SOURCE: Data from Gallup.

Does the United States Need a Third Party?

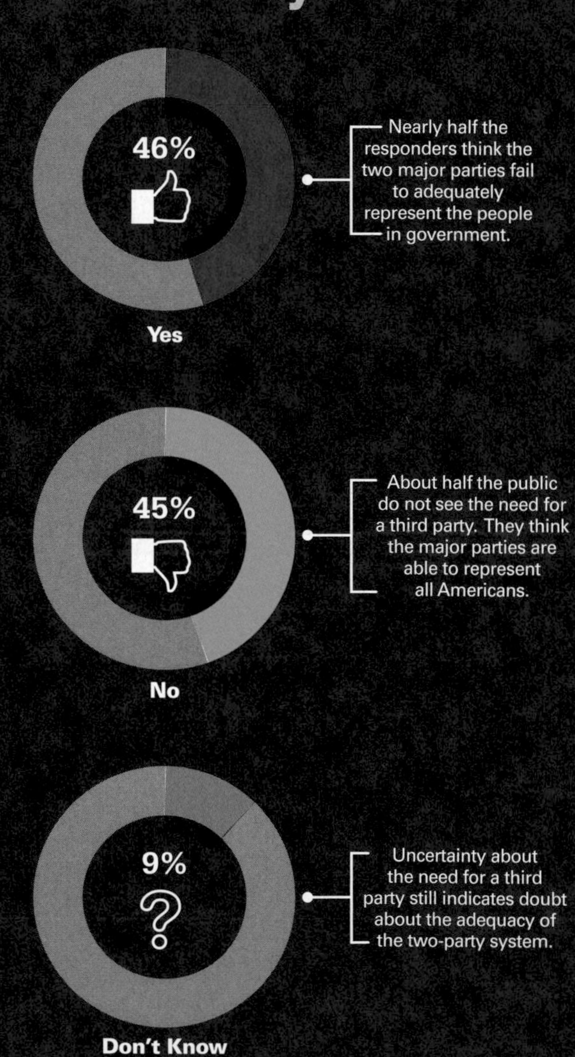

46%
Yes
Nearly half the responders think the two major parties fail to adequately represent the people in government.
45%
No
About half the public do not see the need for a third party. They think the major parties are able to represent all Americans.
9%
Don't Know
Uncertainty about the need for a third party still indicates doubt about the adequacy of the two-party system.

Investigate Further

Concept How do we measure which party governs better? Survey research allows us to track public opinion on party performance on certain issues. Historically, when it comes to trusting government, partisans trust their party to govern, but not the other. Partisanship is a lens through which voters evaluate and determine trust of parties and government.

Connection Which party do Americans think governs better? *Their* party. Democrats think government is more trustworthy when Democrats rule. Republicans think the same when Republicans rule. The parties represent different governing philosophies, so each party has a different definition of what it means to govern better.

Cause When do third parties become viable? Third parties become viable when major parties fail on divisive issues that matter to the public, like the economy or racial issues. Third parties emerge to address those issues and may capture some support. However, the third party is usually absorbed by a major party that co-opts their issues and supporters.

Nationally, Democrats tend to argue for a more expansive use of government in addressing social and economic problems. They are more inclined to define these problems as ones requiring a government solution. Republicans will lean toward a market-based, private-sector solution to the problem and ask whether government policies are obstacles to individuals and businesses seeking to undertake desired behavior. When Democrats proposed a $787 billion economic stimulus plan in 2009, every Republican in the House and nearly all in the Senate rebelled at the size and scope of this government intervention. On social issues such as abortion, however, Democrats are less inclined to involve government in individual decision making, whereas Republicans are more inclined to support government restrictions on abortion access. Democratic rhetoric will more often invoke equality and fairness, whereas Republican language will refer to individual opportunity and freedom. Democrats, for example, tend to consider tax arrangements that take a larger percentage of one's income as income rises to be a matter of fairness; Republicans argue that increased tax rates amount to a penalty for individual hard work and success.

Although cultural and social issues such as abortion or same-sex marriage receive significant attention in public discussion of parties and candidates, the contrasting agendas of the parties focus much more on economic, financial, and regulatory matters, including economic growth, prices, employment, taxes, regulating business, health care, retirement, and other issues such as education that can be defined as having economic significance.[65] And, in foreign policy, Republicans have generally supported a more aggressive use of military force to obtain desired goals, whereas Democrats have expressed more reluctance in this area.

In addition to different views on issues, party supporters also prioritize some issues differently. In early 2012, Republican and Democratic survey respondents agreed that strengthening the economy, improving the jobs situation, and defending against terrorism were top national priorities, with lesser but strong agreement that securing Social Security and Medicare were also key concerns. Respondents of neither party ranked campaign finance, global warming, or reducing the influence of lobbyists as high on their priority lists. Republicans named reducing the federal budget deficit and addressing the nation's moral problems as important priorities; Democrats named improving education, reducing health care costs, and making the tax system fairer as high priorities. Independents agreed on the leading importance of the economy, jobs, and terrorism; on other issues, they tended to fall in between Democrats and Republicans regarding the percentage who saw the issue as a top national priority.[66]

Voters identify some issues so strongly with one party that scholars say the party "owns" these issues. For example, the public has long identified Social Security as a Democratic strong suit while giving the Republicans a similar advantage on foreign policy. Not every issue is owned by a party—some bounce back and forth between them.[67]

These owned issues will shape party competition. The party that owns an issue will emphasize the issue to maximize its advantage on it. Republicans in 2012 hammered away on the issues of the power of the federal government and the size of federal debt, issues that appealed to Republicans, independents, and some Democrats, and on which the Republicans held an advantage. Democrats sought to focus public attention on the benefits of health care and financial reform and the reasons to increase taxes on the affluent, and portraying Republicans as too cozy with big corporation, all issues owned by Democrats. Candidates may also try to deflect the other party's advantage on an issue, as when George W. Bush emphasized education reform in 2000 and Barack Obama emphasized his foreign policy record in 2012.

In recent years, observers have suggested that party differences have become extreme. They depict this competition as a clash of values and culture between red America and blue America, or red states (Republican) and blue states (Democratic). Some observers, such as television commentator Bill O'Reilly, refer to it as a culture war. To other observers, though, the nature of American public opinion and the breadth of party coalitions mean there is at best a culture skirmish rather than a culture war (see *How Do We Know? Is America Polarized?*).

How Do We Know?

Is America Polarized?

The Question

For many Americans, politics in the United States has become nasty, bitter, and rife with conflict. "Red and blue America" and "culture war" are labels said to define current American politics. But, is America polarized? How do we know?

Why It Matters

Both for citizens and for politicians looking to influence the policy process, it matters whether Americans are in two different worlds politically or have political differences that are modest in degree. If the country is polarized, then political success will depend on highly charged mobilization based on strong rhetoric. If the country is not, then success will depend more on persuading and mobilizing the support of those whose views are relatively moderate.

Investigating the Answer

Television election result maps in 2000 and 2004 showing the country divided sharply into regions of Republican support (colored red) and Democratic support (colored blue) helped popularize the idea that Americans live in polarized worlds politically, with a vast gulf in their cultural values and political preferences.

Closer examination, however, showed that the maps were misleading. Some red states were barely red, and some blue states barely blue, and some red states flipped to blue in 2008. Moreover, blue states nationally might have Republican governors, whereas red states might have Democratic state legislatures.[a]

Perhaps the place to look for polarization is not in the state-level pattern of party victories, but in public opinion. Does public opinion show more polarized views?

One prominent study examines public opinion on a range of "hot button" issues such as abortion and gay rights. The authors find that when given the option, most Americans place themselves toward the middle of the scale rather than taking a position on the far left or far right. Even where opinion has become more polarized over time, the difference is not that great. On a seven-point scale used by the National Election Studies, the average difference between Democrats and Republicans has increased since the early 1970s, but only modestly. Public opinion among Democrats and Republicans is distinctive, but they are separated on average by only one point on the seven-point scale.[b]

Another study confirms that differences between Democrats and Republicans have grown—and uniquely so. From 1972 through the mid-1990s, on 35 issue areas, public opinion differences across age, education, race, religious affiliation, region, and gender had dropped or been stable. Partisanship was the exception. Only on this measure had opinion grown further apart.[c] Survey data published by the Pew Research Center confirm this pattern continuing from the mid-1990s to the present.[d] This research suggests that public opinion overall may not be much more polarized, but that today's parties more precisely reflect and articulate the differences that do exist. Political scientists refer to this as ideological sorting, meaning that the correlation between one's ideology and party identification is stronger today than previously: liberals are increasingly likely to identify with Democrats and conservatives with Republicans.[e]

Partisans at the elite level have also moved further apart. Numerous studies of legislative roll call voting show Democrats and Republicans in Congress are more ideologically distinct now than previously, with polarization of party voting patterns in the House and Senate at the highest levels since the end of Reconstruction.[f] Ideological sorting is even more pronounced than in the public. The opinion of party activists, as measured by a survey of delegates to the two parties' national conventions in 2008, is also strongly divergent, more so than among the public.[g]

So, both elites and the public are better sorted ideologically into parties. That is the correlation. But what is the causality—what led to what? Did liberal and conservative voters begin the process by flocking more consistently to the Democratic and Republican Parties, respectively, forcing the parties' candidates to respond by taking more extreme views? Or did candidates start the process by taking more extreme views, leading voters to respond by shifting and strengthening their party allegiance?

Political scientists have wrestled with these questions. Perhaps redistricting created safe partisan districts that encouraged legislators to behave in a more ideological fashion. Or, perhaps the story is really about the South and its emergence out of one-party political competition in which nearly every voter, whether liberal or

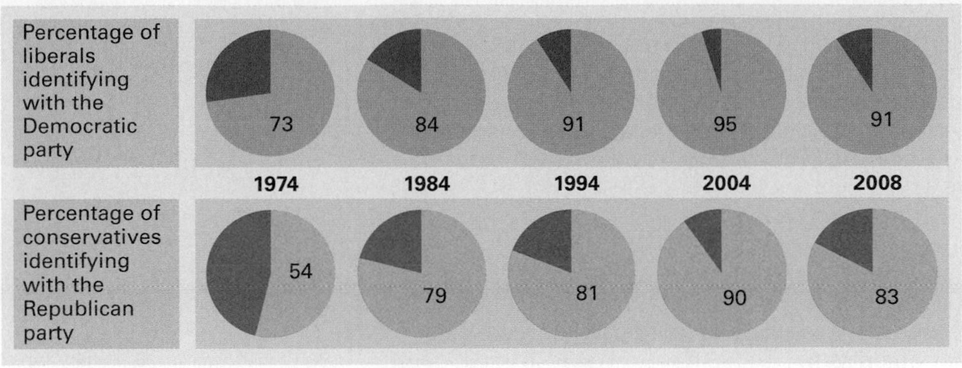

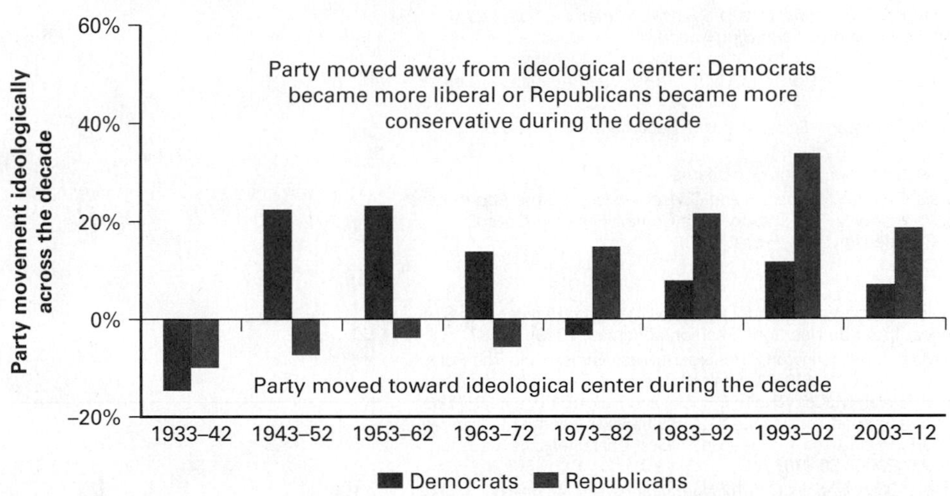

Note: Chart tracks movement away from or toward ideological center as measured by DW-NOMINATE scores. A negative score of −10%, for example, means a party moved 10 percent closer to the ideological center. Similarly, a positive score of 20% means a party has become 20% more liberal (Democrats) or conservative (Republicans). Both parties have been moving away from the ideological center since 1983.

Source: Keith Poole and Howard Rosenthal, http://voteview.com.

PARTISAN AND IDEOLOGICAL SORTING, 1974–2008.

Over time, liberals became more likely to identify with the Democratic Party and conservatives with the Republican Party. Liberal identification with the Democrats rose from 73 percent in 1974 to 95 percent in 2004, a 22 percentage point rise. Conservative identification with the Republicans rose from 54 to 90 percent over the same period, a 36 percentage point increase. Ideological sorting dropped slightly in 2008.

conservative, supported Democratic candidates. Scholars have tested many more possible explanations.[h]

Although the data are mixed, overall it appears that elites led and the public followed. As political activists within the party networks—representatives of business groups, advocacy groups, nonprofits, unions—became better organized and more involved, candidates increasingly took the positions that would garner their support. With this relationship between activists and candidates occurring in both parties, the public faced candidates taking stronger ideological stances, and individual voters sorted themselves into the party closer to them ideologically and voted more consistently for the candidate of that closer party.[i]

The Bottom Line

Public opinion overall is not dramatically more polarized now than previously. What has changed is that for both voters and politicians, opinion differences are now more sharply lined up by political party—fewer conservatives are aligned with the Democratic Party and fewer liberals identify with the Republican Party. Ideological sorting has led to a bigger philosophical gap between the typical Democratic and Republican politicians and to a bigger gap between the typical Democrat and Republican in the public. Because of these trends, the cultural, economic, and other differences among Americans have become a more significant part of political debate, and public approval of Presidents Clinton, Bush, and Obama diverged greatly based on partisanship.

Politics is a battle over big stakes and big outcomes. Issues matter. Because people do see the world differently, ideological sorting is likely to remain. Some observers say these developments in partisanship artificially create more conflict in government and leave moderate voters with unappealing choices. But others counter that ideological sorting has led to party competition that gives voters real choices, gives them a reason to vote, and encourages fellow partisans in government to work together.[j]

Thinking Critically

- Is the trend toward greater ideological sorting among voters something to be applauded or feared? Why?
- Would electoral reforms that increased the possibility for third-party success be likely to exacerbate or reduce polarization? Why?

---

[a]Pietro S. Nivola and David W. Brady, *Red and Blue Nation? Characteristics and Causes of America's Polarized Politics* (Washington, DC: Brookings Institution Press, 2006); and *Red and Blue Nation? Consequences and Correction of America's Polarized Politics* (Washington, DC: Brookings Institution Press, 2008).

[b]Morris P. Fiorina, Samuel J. Abrams, and Jeremy C. Pope, *Culture War? The Myth of a Polarized America*, 3rd ed. (New York: Longman, 2010).

[c]Paul DiMaggio, John Evans, and Bethany Bryson, "Have Americans' Social Attitudes Become More Polarized?" *American Journal of Sociology* 102, 3 (1996): 690–755.

[d]http://www.people-press.org/2012/06/04/partisan-polarization-surges-in-bush-obama-years/

[e]Matthew Levendusky, *The Partisan Sort: How Liberals Became Democrats and Conservatives Became Republicans* (Chicago: University of Chicago Press, 2009); Alan I. Abramowitz, *The Disappearing Center: Engaged Citizens, Polarization, and American Democracy* (New Haven, CT: Yale University Press, 2010).

[f]www.voteview.com/polarized_america.
htm#Politicalpolarization

[g]CBS News/*New York Times* Poll, August 31, 2008, www.cbsnews.com/htdocs/pdf/RNCDelegates_issues.pdf. See also Marjorie Randon Hershey, *Party Politics in America*, 13th ed. (New York: Pearson Longman, 2009), p. 187.

[h]For a small sample of this large body of studies, see Marc J. Hetherington, "Resurgent Mass Partisanship: The Role of Elite Polarization," *American Political Science Review* 95, 3 (2001): 619–31; Sean M. Theriault, *Party Polarization in Congress* (New York: Cambridge University Press, 2008); Nolan McCarty, Keith T. Poole, and Howard Rosenthal, "Does Gerrymandering Cause Polarization?" *American Journal of Political Science* 53, 3 (2009): 666–80; Geoffrey C. Layman, Thomas M. Carsey, and Juliana Menasce Horowitz, "Party Polarization in American Politics: Characteristics, Causes, and Consequences," *Annual Review of Political Science* 9 (2006): 83–110.

[i]Seth E. Masket, *No Middle Ground: How Informal Party Organizations Control Nominations and Polarize Legislatures* (Ann Arbor: University of Michigan Press, 2009); Fiorina, Abrams, and Pope, *Culture War?*; Morris P. Fiorina, "Parties and Partisanship: A 40-Year Retrospective," *Political Behavior* 24, 2 (2002): 93–115.

[j]Matthew Levendusky, *The Partisan Sort: How Liberals Became Democrats and Conservatives Became Republicans* (Chicago: University of Chicago Press, 2009).

On MyPoliSciLab

Review the Chapter

 **Listen** to **Chapter 11** on **MyPoliSciLab**

What Political Parties Do

11.1 Analyze the functions of political parties in American politics, p. 360.

Political parties play a variety of roles. The Constitution provided for an electoral system but did not say how a sufficient number of candidates would emerge or how citizens would become engaged in the electoral process. Parties fill these roles. These functions of candidate recruitment and citizen mobilization, intended largely to advance the interests of the parties and their candidates, also enhance the legitimacy of American politics and government by bringing into practice the promise of electoral competition that was implicit in the Constitution. Political parties also contribute to American governance by giving public officials in different institutions and at different levels of government incentives to cooperate with one another to make public policy.

The Two-Party System

11.2 Determine why American electoral competition is dominated by two political parties rather than multiple parties, p. 369.

Two-party electoral competition has dominated American politics since the very beginning of the party system. The structure of American government, including single-member districts, plurality elections, and winner-take-all electoral votes in presidential elections, pushes electoral competition toward a two-party model. In addition, a number of laws as well as the behavior of voters, the media, and candidates, reinforce the tendency for two parties to be the serious competitors. Third parties are only rarely successful electorally, but they can make a mark in other ways, such as introducing issues to the campaign that the major party candidates have ignored.

Party Organization

11.3 Trace the evolution of American party organizations and their expanding role in campaigns, p. 377.

Party organization has gone through several phases. In early American history, party organizations were informal and largely implemented the wishes of important political leaders, especially regarding candidate nomination. Party machines emerged in the late nineteenth century. Machines thrived by developing a very personal form of politics but ran afoul of reformers who saw them as bastions of corruption. Progressive reformers passed a series of laws that weakened and regulated political parties in the early twentieth century. In recent decades, party organizations have become more active, especially by providing campaign services to party candidates.

The Evolution of Party Competition and Party Coalitions

11.4 Explain how parties achieve electoral success by building and maintaining coalitions of supporters, p. 383.

The broad and diverse nature of coalitions necessary to produce a majority and win elections creates a difficult job of political management for party leaders. They play the balancing act of maintaining the coalition and focusing on the key public policy concerns of coalition members, while also adapting to new circumstances and trying to keep the coalition growing. As they accommodate new issues and new groups, they risk unraveling the coalition by driving current supporters away. Neither party can produce victories today by simply relying on the coalitions of the past. American parties have evolved through six periods of party competition, with different issues and different major parties dominating in each.

Learn the Terms

 **Study** and **Review** the **Flashcards**

Australian ballot, p. 373
dealignment, p. 389
divided government, p. 363
electoral realignment, p. 386
fusion, p. 373
issue evolution, p. 386
national party convention, p. 382
party machine, p. 378
party platform, p. 382
patronage, p. 379
plurality elections, p. 371
political parties, p. 360
Progressive reforms, p. 379
proportional representation, p. 372
responsible party model, p. 384
single-member districts, p. 371
two-party system, p. 369
unified government, p. 363

Test Yourself

Study and **Review** the **Practice Tests**

11.1 Analyze the functions of political parties in American politics.

Political parties do all of the following EXCEPT

a. Deliver people to the polls.
b. Integrate new social groups.
c. Educate and inform voters.
d. Discourage voter participation.
e. Recruit and nominate candidates for office.

11.2 Determine why American electoral competition is dominated by two political parties rather than multiple parties.

Why are third parties rarely successful in American electoral politics?

a. The proportional representation system used
b. They put forward issue agendas that no one really cares about
c. The Constitution prohibits more than two political parties
d. The use of preference voting in elections
e. The use of single-member districts and plurality elections

11.3 Trace the evolution of American party organizations and their expanding role in campaigns.

Why have party organizations become more active in recent decades?

a. Progressive movement reforms
b. Patronage
c. Modernization of operations and Supreme Court decisions
d. The party machine
e. The elimination of a party platform

11.4 Explain how parties achieve electoral success by building and maintaining coalitions of supporters.

All of the following are reasons why party coalitions may be dynamic EXCEPT

a. Internal strife is rare in a political party, and many groups enjoy conflict.
b. Group loyalty reduces the pressure on a party to advance the group's agenda.
c. One group's interests might clash with the interests of other groups in the coalition.
d. As the mix of voters supporting a party changes over time, one group may become a smaller share of a party's voters and less central to the party's electoral strategy.
e. When a party loses an election it will have conflicting internal interpretations about what lessons to learn from the defeat.

Explore Further

SUGGESTED READINGS BY TOP SCHOLARS

John Aldrich. 2011. *Why Parties? A Second Look.* Chicago: University of Chicago Press. Examines the development of political parties across American history, arguing that political elites built parties to address basic problems facing a competitive democratic political system.

Marty Cohen, David Karol, Hans Noel, and John Zaller. 2008. *The Party Decides: Presidential Nominations Before and After Reform*. Chicago: University of Chicago Press. Argues that political parties, conceived as a network of interest groups, activists, and elected officials and members of official party organizations, remain the dominant force in selecting presidential nominees.

Daniel DiSalvo. 2012. *Engines of Change: Party Factions in American Politics, 1868–2010.* New York: Oxford University Press. Argues that party factions play a key and overlooked role in nominations, governance, and policy direction.

Morris P. Fiorina, Samuel J. Abrams, and Jeremy C. Pope. 2010. *What Culture War? The Myth of a Polarized America*. New York: Longman. The most prominent statement of the view that opinion polarization in the United States is more modest than conventional wisdom suggests, and that voters have become more consistently partisan because of the candidates they have to choose between rather than any increase in voters' ideological extremism.

Jessica Trounstine. 2008. *Political Monopolies in American Cities: The Rise and Fall of Bosses and Reformers*. Chicago: University of Chicago Press. Uses case studies from Chicago and San Jose, and statistical analysis of a large number of cities, to argue that both party machines and reform movements seek to create uncompetitive political monopolies.

SUGGESTED WEBSITES

FairVote: www.fairvote.org
Advocacy group for proportional representation and alternative voting systems. Site provides explanation of various voting reforms.

Real Clear Politics: www.rcp.com
Analysis of politics and news featuring a good array of conservative and liberal writers.

Politics 1: www.politics1.com/parties.htm
Comprehensive list of links to political party websites, including capsule descriptions of third parties.

American Presidency Project: Political Party Platforms: www.presidency.ucsb.edu/platforms.php
Full text of platforms of all parties receiving electoral votes since 1840.

Campaign Finance Institute: www.cfinst.org
Extensive databases and helpful analysis of campaign finance, especially party revenues and spending.

ANES Guide to Public Opinion and Electoral Behavior: www.electionstudies.org/nesguide/nesguide.htm

Collection of tables presenting more than 40 years of data on partisanship, evaluation of candidates, participation, and public opinion from the premier academic election survey.

Dave Leip's Atlas of U.S. Presidential Elections: www.uselectionatlas.org

Excellent collection of tables, data, graphs, and maps related to presidential election outcomes throughout American history. Also covers gubernatorial, U.S. Senate, and U.S. House elections.

12

Listen to Chapter 12 on MyPoliSciLab

Interest Groups

OPPOSITE OUTCOMES ON HEALTH CARE REFORM

Americans have debated the concept of national health insurance since the New Deal. But proposals in recent years demonstrate how lobbying and interest groups can play a significant role in shaping national policy.

When he first stepped into office in 1993, President Bill Clinton made offering health care to all Americans his top priority. Although most Americans had health care coverage through their job, many did not. For some, a catastrophic illness could wipe out their entire savings. Clinton's proposed legislation sought to address these problems. And in response, a grassroots lobbying campaign developed. Some efforts focused on convincing members of Congress to support the measure. But a much stronger effort sought to warn Americans about the dangers of a government-run plan.

One particularly effective element in the grassroots lobbying effort was a television commercial financed by the Health Insurance Association of America, a trade organization of health insurance providers. The commercial showed a typical married couple, Harry and Louise, sitting in their kitchen poring over a pile of papers. They worried aloud about Clinton's plan. Would the bill create a government monopoly over the health industry? Would accessing health care mean battling a huge, intrusive, impersonal federal bureaucracy? These were the same questions many Americans were asking themselves. The commercial—targeted to the districts of influential members of key committees in Congress—asked constituents worried about the changes to reach out to their congressional representatives.

The commercial was a huge success. It generated hundreds of thousands of phone calls and mobilized activists in the districts of key members. As important, the ad also earned tremendous media coverage in newspapers, on television, and on the radio. It sparked other groups to

12.1 Distinguish between pluralist theory's and James Madison's interpretation of the role of interest groups within American politics, p. 403.

12.2 Describe how critics of pluralist theory view the role of interest groups today, p. 404.

12.3 Explain how interest groups form and attract members, p. 408.

12.4 Analyze the strategies and tactics interest groups use to impact elections and public policy, p. 413.

12.5 Assess how much influence interest groups have over policy outcomes, p. 422.

FACING OFF The battle over health care reform generated intense interest group activity and strong passions on both sides. Here opponents and proponents of the Affordable Health Care Act or "Obamacare" demonstrated in front of the Supreme Court.

The Big Picture Do interest groups benefit the collective good or are they just selfish? Author Kenneth M. Goldstein discusses how the Founders believed that competition between interest groups would lead to the best policies, and he considers the strategies of successful interest groups.

The Basics What are interest groups and what role do they play in our democracy? Listen to real people tackle these and other questions. Learn what types of interest groups exist in our country, what tactics they use to achieve their goals, and why interest groups matter.

In Context Examine the emergence of interest groups in American politics. In this video, Boston College political scientist Kay Schlozman traces the roots of interest group involvement in American politics and why they are an important part of the political process today.

Think Like a Political Scientist Do interest groups have an impact on policy? Boston College political scientist Kay Schlozman explains why this is not an easy question to answer. She also discusses how scholars determine which groups are represented and which groups are not.

In the Real World Is pizza a vegetable? This video illustrates the difference between elitist and populist theories of interest groups by examining real people's reactions to the recent debate over whether school cafeterias should count pizza sauce as a full serving of vegetables.

So What? What is the Collective Action Problem and how does it relate to political interest groups? Using AARP as an example, author Kenneth M. Goldstein explains how to create an interest group with members who are invested in the organization's collective agenda.

promote their own ads warning against the new legislation and asking listeners to call their members of Congress and ask them to vote against the Clinton health care plan.[1]

These ads targeted a particular audience of constituents most likely to win over Congress. Unlike votes, letters and phone calls from citizens do have different levels of influence. Input from local civic, business, or political leaders often have the most sway. So does input from individuals or groups with a particular interest or expertise in an issue. A "grass tops" strategy seeks to mobilize people with the most potential influence with their elected representatives.

Data indicate that those opposing the Clinton health plan successfully implemented a grass tops strategy. These efforts caused policy makers to address the issues raised by the Harry and Louise commercial. As a result, the Clinton bill ended in a humiliating defeat. It set back Clinton's entire legislative agenda and hurt him in the polls.

Sixteen years later, President Barack Obama tried again. But this time, the political landscape was different, and so was Obama's strategy. Clinton did not enter office with a mandate for health care change; Obama did. He also had a super majority of 60 Democrats in the Senate and strong Democratic control of the House.

As for strategy, Obama took his cues from where Clinton lost out. Early on, he worked to bring the adversaries of the Clinton plan on board. He struck a deal with the large and powerful pharmaceutical industry. He promised drug companies that his bill would help sell more drugs to prevent their lobbyists from opposing it. He coordinated with the American Medical Association (AMA) so it would appear that all doctors supported his plan.

Henry and Louise even returned to television screens. The couple, now older, was still worried about health care. But this time their concern was for all of their fellow Americans who lacked health insurance. Now, Obama's health care plan was the solution—not the problem.

In the final vote, not one Republican supported the measure and even 34 Democrats opposed it. The bill passed in the House by 7 votes, 219 to 212. President Obama won his first significant victory and boosted his falling approval numbers. Although a variety of factors made it possible for Obama to succeed where Clinton had failed, enlisting interest groups and employing or neutralizing lobbyists was critical to his success.

Ironically though, Obama is also a sharp critic of these sorts of groups and activities. In his first State of the Union Address, Obama told the American public that "We face a deficit of trust—deep and corrosive doubts about how Washington works that have been growing for years. To close that credibility gap, we have to take action on both ends of Pennsylvania Avenue—to end the outsized influence of lobbyists; to do our work openly; to give our people the government they deserve."[2] This rhetoric has fueled much of the debate over how powerful and trustworthy lobbyists and interest groups are.

Organized interests contributed to one outcome in the Clinton administration and the opposite outcome in the Obama administration. These competing narratives lead to important questions about the role of organized interests, or interest groups, in American politics. Are they active and powerful? Are they passive? Are they a positive or negative influence on American democracy? Do they encourage a healthy, broad-based consideration of a variety of interests, or do they promote the pursuit of narrow self-interest? Guided by these questions, this chapter examines the role of interest groups in America.

The Problem of Factions and the Pluralist Answer

12.1 Distinguish between pluralist theory's and James Madison's interpretation of the role of interest groups within American politics.

lmost every discussion of group politics in the United States begins with *Federalist 10* by American founding father James Madison. It is part of Madison's larger work, *The Federalist Papers,* and one of the most famous pieces of political rhetoric ever written by an American. In it, Madison

interest groups
organizations that seek to influence government decisions.

pluralism
the theory that all groups are well represented and no single interest controls government decisions.

notes the capacity of the proposed federal republic "to break and control the violence of faction." By *faction*, Madison meant a group of individuals who share a belief that could potentially jeopardize the rights of individuals outside the group. It could also conflict with the interests of the community as a whole. Madison worried about the potential influence of factional interests on individual rights and the collective well-being of the country. But he also believed the American system was sufficiently well designed to guard against the potential problems these interests could cause.

Madison's view on factions prevailed until the 1950s. Then, political scientists began to examine both normatively and empirically the place of groups in politics. Rather than faction, these scholars used terms such as *groups*, *interests*, *organized interests*, or **interest groups.** They accepted the role of groups as a healthy, legitimate part of democracy. In fact, they believed that groups and group struggle were the essence of politics. For these scholars, politics is the organized effort to resolve conflicts among competing group interests.[3] This perspective, called **pluralism**, means that multiple groups and interests can make demands on government, even if government ignores the demands. Pluralists see political power and resources dispersed widely throughout society. Some groups have influence on particular issues. Other groups influence different issues. Because of this dispersion of power and resources, no one group or set of groups can achieve long-term supremacy across a significant number of issue areas.

Pluralists also believe that groups can influence the political system through multiple access points. Groups are free to petition government at the local, state, and national levels and through the offices of the executive, the legislature, and the judiciary. A group denied its policy preferences in one venue or at one level of government may take its argument to a different venue or to another jurisdiction—local, state, or federal. Some branch of government will always be available to hear a group's concerns. Pluralists believe this empowers groups.[4]

Finally, pluralists argue that politics can also support individuals with a common interest, even when they do not organize into a formal group. Policy makers must recognize that these loosely formed groups can become actual groups if the government does not meet their needs, which could upset existing political arrangements. Elected officials have an incentive to manage the needs of unorganized interests, so they do not become organized groups.

Criticisms of Pluralism

12.2 Describe how critics of pluralist theory view the role of interest groups today.

Pluralism has influenced how political scientists understand American politics and government since at least the 1950s. Along with influence, however, comes scrutiny. Critics of pluralism argue that the American political system is inherently resistant to change, political resources are not distributed equally, many important issues never make it onto the agenda, and groups do not automatically form.

The American Political System Is Resistant to Change

A fundamental critique of pluralism is that the American political system is resistant to change. The checks and balances designed by the Framers coupled with the multiple decision points in the system make it much more difficult to change the status quo than to defend it. There are many ways for an individual or group to defeat a new policy proposal. Opponents of a measure can stop it from being

- introduced as a bill in the first place
- heard in committee

- approved in committee
- reported out of committee
- heard on the House floor
- heard on the Senate floor
- approved by the House
- approved by the Senate

If a bill makes it over these hurdles, opponents can still stop the

- reconciliation of any differences between the Senate and House versions of the bill
- House from voting on the reconciled version
- Senate from voting on the reconciled version
- House from approving the reconciled version
- Senate from approving the reconciled version
- president from signing the reconciled version

But even this list does not exhaust the possibilities for defeating a policy proposal. Programs and initiatives that make it through the legislative process can also be challenged in the court system, denied necessary funding in the appropriations process, or watered down or ignored by bureaucrats or state and local officials.

The bias against change in the American system is clear. Someone wishing to preserve the status quo need only succeed at one point to kill a policy initiative. Someone wishing to change the status quo must succeed at every point.

Because of this power to obstruct, critics of pluralism argue that the apparent openness of the American political system may not count for much. If a group succeeds in getting its policy preferences adopted, other groups with different preferences will have difficulty coming along later and altering the status quo. Thus, although the complex machinery of American government protects citizens against tyranny and factions, it also makes it hard for organized interests to bring about change.

☐ Political Resources Are Distributed Unequally

Critics of pluralism also argue that many people face significant barriers to joining a group. In the pre–civil rights era, for example, participation in politics by African Americans was strikingly low. The political system deliberately excluded African Americans from the political system for much of American history. It was not because African Americans were content with the status quo or did not think politics was relevant to their own interests.[5]

Although the political history of African Americans in the United States is an extreme case, other, less extreme cases of political exclusion have occurred. According to the most recent data, for example, more than 46.2 million Americans live below the poverty line.[6] Many of the impoverished are children. But there are no vocal, highly successful interest groups that defend poor kids. By contrast, many such groups support gun owners, nurses, attorneys, teachers, and the elderly.

There are many reasons for this inequity. One is that effective political organization requires resources that the poor often do not have: money, time, knowledge, education, personal relationships, and political experience, among others. Critics of pluralism argue that this unequal distribution of political resources biases the interest group system in favor of upper-and middle-class groups. These have relatively easy access to the most important political resources and assets.

Pluralists acknowledge this imbalance. As political scientist E. E. Schattschneider famously said, "public activity of all kinds is a habit of the middle and upper classes."[7] Fellow political scientist Jack Walker determined that among all organized groups with a presence in Washington, D.C., 70 percent represented business interests trying to increase profits. Fewer than 5 percent represented civil rights groups; minority

12.1

12.2

12.3

12.4

12.5

nondecisions
decisions not to consider particular issues or incorporate them into the policy agenda.

policy agenda
the set of issues under consideration by policy makers.

disturbance theory
the theory that when social, political, and economic relationships change, individuals form groups in response.

free-rider problem
a barrier to collective action because people can reap the benefits of group efforts without participating.

collective action problem
This situation arises when many or all members of a population would benefit from some sort of activity or a policy that activity is trying to influence, even if they did not not actively participate in the effort.

organizations; social welfare groups; poor people's organizations; and groups advocating on behalf of the handicapped, gays, and women.[8]

☐ Many Important Issues Never Make It Onto the Agenda

Another critique of pluralism is that political elites set the issue agenda. Issues they care about get the most attention. Issues not so important to them get very little.[9]

Consider poverty as a political issue. The plight of the country's poor was at the top of our national agenda during the Great Depression of the 1930s, and then again with Lyndon Johnson's declaration of a War on Poverty in 1964. Between these two periods—in the 1940s and 1950s—poverty virtually disappeared as a topic on the public policy agenda. Policy makers simply assumed (wrongly, as it turns out) that the nation conquered poverty with its return to prosperity in the 1940s Thus, the attention of government decision makers turned to other issues.

This example illustrates the importance of what political scientists call nondecisions.[10] A **nondecision** is a decision not to put a particular issue on the **policy agenda,** which is the set of issues actively under consideration and discussion by policy makers. Pluralists emphasize group participation in the decision-making process. Critics assert that nondecisions play a role as well. As E. E. Schattschneider quipped, "Some issues are organized into politics while others are organized out."[11]

When government shunts some issues aside, the pluralist model breaks down. Policy makers cannot take group preferences on a particular issue into account if they choose not to address it at all. For more on this issue, see *How Do We Know? Is It Possible to Measure the Impact of an Issue's Absence from the Policy Agenda?*

☐ Groups Do Not Automatically Form

Pluralism best supports democracy when groups champion interests the government can address. The political world is full of groups and associations actively pursuing agendas at all levels of government. Pluralists tend to take this trend for granted. Pluralists explain the formation of groups through the **disturbance theory**, which holds that when social, political, and economic relationships are upset by some outside force, affected individuals often form a group in response.[12]

Groups do not always form in response to a disturbance. In fact, when too many people stand behind a cause, it can be even more difficult to form a productive group. In 1965, economist Mancur Olson argued that "rational, self-interested individuals will not act to achieve their common or group interests."[13] Why? Because an individual's own efforts "will not have a noticeable effect on the situation of his organization, and he or she can enjoy any improvements brought about by others whether or not he has worked in support of his organization."[14]

Olson's argument is also known as the public goods problem, the **free-rider problem**, the prisoner's dilemma, the tragedy of the commons, and the **collective action problem.** College students as a whole may support increasing the pool of government scholarships available. But an individual student would probably not contribute time or money to help convince legislators to increase scholarship options. Furthermore, not taking action will probably not affect the amount of funds available. Plus, students who do not try to convince the government to fund higher education are still eligible for such funding and could enjoy its benefits anyway.

What does this example have to do with group formation? Imagine that you and your fellow students wish to have the school year shortened by two weeks. This requires a decision by school administrators. The best way of getting the decision you want is to form a group, organize rallies and e-mail campaigns, and lobby the relevant decision makers. From your perspective as an individual, however, it would be ideal if other students did all of the work and left you in peace. If the group consisted of, say, 500 active participants, your individual effort probably would not be missed anyway. Furthermore, if you failed to participate and the group succeeded without you, you would reap all of the benefits without having to give up any of your own time, money, or energy. What a great deal for you!

How Do We Know?

Is It Possible to Measure the Impact of an Issue's Absence from the Policy Agenda?

The Question

Sometimes in politics, things that do not happen are just as important as things that do. But if they don't happen, how can we account for them? Things that do not happen are very difficult, if not impossible, to study. So how can critics of pluralism argue that nondecisions play a role in politics? Is it possible to measure the impact of an issue's absence from the policy agenda? How do we know?

Why It Matters

The power of interest groups stems from their ability to put issues on the national agenda. When groups fail to advance their interests, these issues fall off the agenda and become nondecisions. It is important to understand why some issues advance and some disappear. It offers key insight into how groups wield power in the United States.

Investigating the Answer

In *The Un-politics of Air Pollution,* Matthew Crenson examined why some cities take aggressive action against local pollution whereas others neglect the issue. He analyzed a survey of community leaders in 51 cities. Then, he identified which cities put pollution on their policy agenda, which cities did not, and what accounted for the difference. He found that cities that care about pollution have bad pollution problems, whereas cities that do not care as much are cleaner. But Crenson also examined pollution measures for each city and concluded that this is not the whole story.[30]

He compared two cities in the survey that both have bad pollution problems. East Chicago, Indiana, takes swift action to address the problem. Gary, Indiana, takes its time. Why? Industrial interests in Gary failed to oppose or support the city's antipollution plans. Other local stakeholders looked to industry to stake out a clear position. When no group expressed a strong interest one way or the other, the issue remained unresolved.

Based on this finding, Crenson hypothesized that cities with strong, vocal business interests respond more slowly to pollution problems than cities with weaker business communities. To back up his claim, he compared data from two relevant surveys. One polled local public figures on the influence of local business. The other assessed how seriously different communities consider the issue of air pollution. Crenson concluded that the stronger the business community in a high pollution city, the less likely that city is to elevate the problem of air pollution to the public policy agenda.

In *Power and Powerlessness,* John Gaventa offered another example of political inaction. He explored why miners in Middlesboro, Kentucky, never opposed severe economic inequalities and poor working conditions. Gaventa argued that powerful economic and political interests set the value system for the town, which kept the miners quiet and powerless.[31]

First, Gaventa compared how miners in nearby communities reacted to inequality. Economic interests in these towns were not as strong as in Middlesboro, and he found that these other towns conducted more protests, strikes, and even insurrections than Middlesboro. Second, Gaventa analyzed how Middlesboro townsfolk responded when the power of the mining interests weakened. Gaventa suspected the townsfolk had internalized the idea that their "natural" role was subordinate to that of the town's economic and political leaders. He thought that even with a change in power, the miners would still not speak out. Gaventa found that both possibilities emerged. When the power of the mine owners weakened, the miners demanded some changes. But they were not as numerous or as vocal as we might expect if the miners tried wholeheartedly to advance their own interests.

The Bottom Line

By definition, studying nonevents or nondecisions is difficult. But these two studies show how it is possible to study political power even when groups do not wield it directly. This is crucial; for if we study only the winners and losers in battles that we can see, we miss two fundamental ways that groups use power. One is through inaction and another is through the internalization of powerlessness by groups that fail to organize.

Thinking Critically

- Can you think of any examples of groups holding little to no power that were able to convince powerful interests to enact change?
- Explain how a nonevent can sometimes be more important than an actual event.

12.1

12.2

12.3

12.4

12.5

selective benefit
benefit that can be accessed only by those who participate in or contribute to group activity.

material benefit
a good or service offered to encourage participation in group activity.

The obvious problem is that if everyone thought this way, groups would never form, bring attention to issues, or lobby decision makers. In this last example, a large group wanted a shorter school year. But if individual interests prevented anyone from taking action, the school year would remain two weeks longer. This is a simple statement of the collective action problem. But the collective action problem is a shot right at the heart of pluralism. If individuals with a common interest fail to organize to pursue that interest, they cannot compete for the government attention that defines pluralism. If this happens often enough, the pluralist model collapses.

Solving the Collective Action Problem: Group Formation and Maintenance

12.3 Explain how interest groups form and attract members.

Political scientists have identified a variety of ways groups can overcome the collective action problem. These include (a) selective benefits provided to group members, typically material or monetary, but also social or ideological; (b) individual entrepreneurship, which can motivate individuals to get involved and stay involved in a group's activities; and (c) patronage from outsiders who support the group's mission.[15]

Selective Benefits Are Available Only to Those Who Contribute

Groups often provide contributors with **selective benefits,** benefits available only to those who contribute. Remember, one of the key parts of the collective action problem is free riding: In certain circumstances, individuals can enjoy the benefits of group activity without bearing any of the costs. Providing selective benefits is a way for groups to get around the free-rider problem.

MATERIAL BENEFITS **Material benefits** are the easiest to provide and include publications, goods and services, discounts on products, and professional advice. For example, individuals who join the American Association of Retired Persons (AARP) become eligible for dozens of benefits. These include discounts on hundreds of consumer products, members-only insurance plans, a subscription to AARP's monthly magazine, health and fitness tips, exclusive investment products, credit cards, financial advice, and tax preparation assistance. You get it all for as little as $16 a year just for being 50 years old or older.

Considering the low cost of membership, millions of AARP members undoubtedly join the group for the benefits alone. In fact, a 1982 survey found that only 17 percent of members joined primarily because of the group's work on behalf of the elderly. The rest were more interested in the material benefits.[16]

Professional associations for groups including doctors, lawyers, teachers, nurses, accountants, and social workers provide similar material benefits. They also offer critical professional certification and credentialing. Attorneys cannot practice law without first being admitted to their state bar. To remain bar members in good standing, they must meet continuing legal education requirements. State bar associations regulate all of these processes. Members must pay a fee for the services. The fees help subsidize the bar organizations' considerable government-relations activities. Attorneys who do not want to subsidize group political action by paying these fees simply cannot practice law. A state bar's control over this highly important selective benefit is one way it overcomes the collective action problem and can participate actively and effectively in the political process.

STAYING ACTIVE . . .

And solving the collective action problem. These seniors practice fitness tips available to members of AARP. This benefit, among others, can help the group combat problems often associated with group formation and maintenance.

SOCIAL BENEFITS A group also can provide its members **social benefits.** Joining the Sierra Club, Greenpeace, or the Nature Conservancy allows avid environmentalists to interact with others who are passionate about the environment. Small business owners who join the National Federation of Independent Businesses can connect with others who share many of the same challenges and successes.

social benefit
benefit that encourages individuals to join a group in order to enjoy the company of those who share similar opinions and interests.

purposive benefit
benefit that encourages group participation by connecting individuals to an organization's political purpose.

Group participation allows you to socialize with people who have similar interests. You benefit from the camaraderie and connections with people who share your beliefs or values. If, for example, you are a member of the College Republicans or a contributor to EMILY's List (an organization that raises money for pro-choice women candidates), you receive the social benefit of solidarity while also working on behalf of group interests.

PURPOSIVE BENEFITS Perhaps most important, millions of people join groups to demonstrate support for a cause. These people enjoy **purposive benefits,** or the satisfaction of contributing to a purpose or cause they support. This volunteer expresses the purposive benefits of participating in Compassionate Action for Animals (CAA), an animal rights advocacy group:

> Through CAA I've come to realize that every little bit I do to end the suffering of animals makes a difference. But my efforts combined with others [set] an example for a whole new generation, offering knowledgeable support in everything from raising positive awareness of farming to maintaining nutrition as a vegan. Through CAA I believe people give animals and our society a brighter, more socially responsible future. CAA has definitely given me hope for a better tomorrow.[17]

This person clearly derives satisfaction from helping promote animal rights. Of course, individuals do not need to volunteer or join a group to support a cause. But

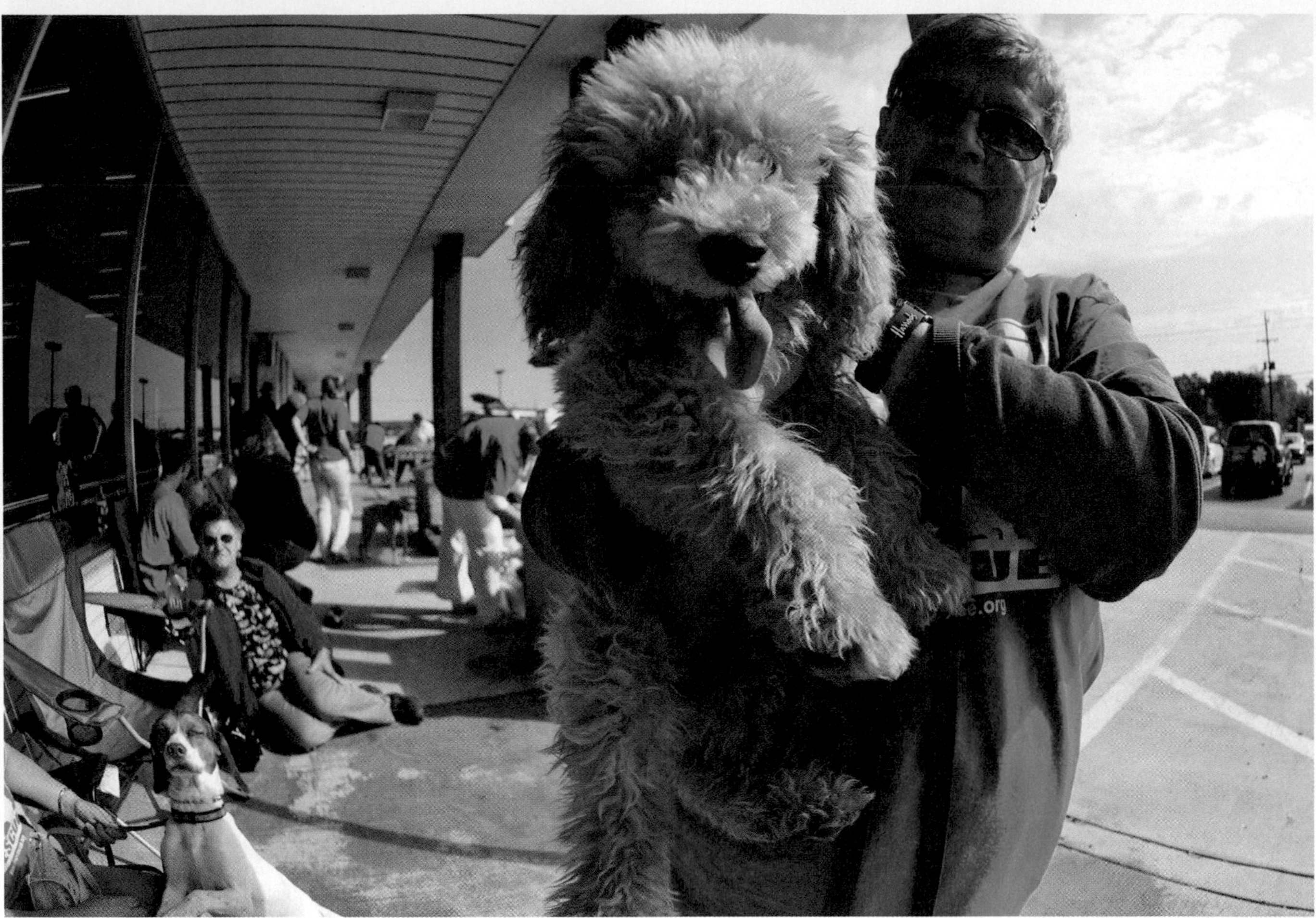

DOGGIE GROUP

Often people join groups that provide a benefit to society as a whole because of social reasons. Dog rescue volunteers, shown here, certainly provide a valuable service to society—and the dogs they rescue. Volunteers may be active because of their belief in the cause, but also because it gives them the opportunity to socialize with other people with similar interests.

interest group entrepreneur
one who overcomes the costs of collective action by launching and managing an interest group.

groups offer the structure and opportunities that make getting involved easier. Members then enjoy unique purposive benefits not available to nonmembers.

Individual Entrepreneurship can Motivate Individuals to Get Involved and Stay Involved in a Group's Activities

Before a group can offer selective benefits, someone has to create the group. This takes significant organizational work. Some political scientists argue that the collective action problem asserts itself at this point, as well. Wouldn't everyone with a potential interest in organizing a group prefer to let others bear the burden of group formation? But if everyone tried to free ride this way, groups might never form. Often, the efforts of an **interest group entrepreneur,** the person who launches and manages an interest group, make it all happen.[18]

One of the most effective and well-known interest groups in America is the National Rifle Association (NRA). Today, it works to promote and protect the rights of gun owners. But the NRA began with a very different agenda. Two Civil War veterans, William Conant Church and George Wood Wingate, worried that the Union troops lacked shooting skills. Church and Wingate took action to address this perceived problem. They sought a charter and $25,000 from the New York legislature to purchase land and develop shooting ranges. Church urged New York's "citizen soldiers" to write to their legislators and encourage them to approve a charter and funding. Ultimately, the legislature agreed to the demands and the NRA was born.[19]

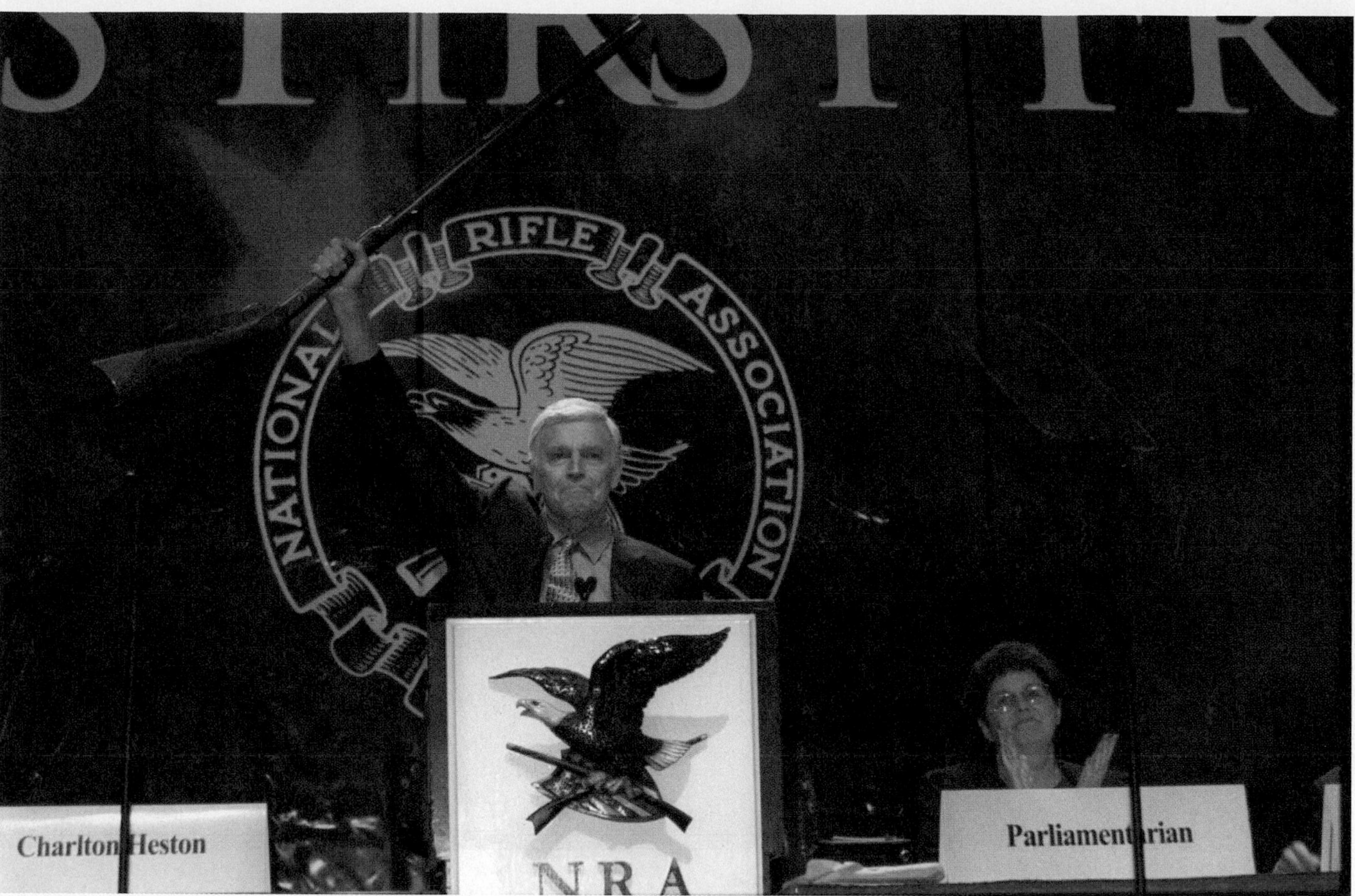

AIM HIGH
Interest group entrepreneurs such as the late actor Charlton Heston, former president of the NRA, help launch or manage interest groups.

Church and Wingate are perfect examples of interest group entrepreneurs. They invested the initial time, energy, and even cash to get the NRA off the ground. Like business entrepreneurs, they took a risk. They hoped their efforts would pay off so they could get back their initial investment along with some "profit." Their entrepreneurship allowed the NRA to form in the successful way it did.

patron
an individual who supports an interest group by providing the resources needed for it to organize and flourish.

Patronage Provides the Resources Groups Need to Organize and Flourish

Church and Wingate's biggest hurdle was getting $25,000 in start-up funds from the New York legislature. Back in 1871, it would have been hard to convince prospective NRA members to put up that amount of money—about $400,000 in today's dollars. Many would have balked at the price tag. Others would have chosen to free ride: "Why should I contribute? Let others pick up the tab, and I'll just enjoy the benefits."

This is where patrons come into play. **Patrons** provide groups with the resources they need to get started. Patrons may work with an interest group entrepreneur to establish a group, or they may launch the group themselves but leave its management to others. Either way, they eliminate the need for groups to try to cobble together small contributions from potential members, all of whom are susceptible to free-rider thinking.

Sometimes a patron is a single individual with a passion for an issue and with resources to share. In 2004, for example, billionaire financier George Soros learned of a new organization called America Coming Together (ACT). The objective of this group was to increase voter turnout in an effort to defeat President George W. Bush's bid for reelection. Soros, who described the defeat of President Bush as "the central focus of my life," was intrigued. He knew that it would take a massive effort for ACT to succeed. It would have to reach into key electoral battlegrounds across the United

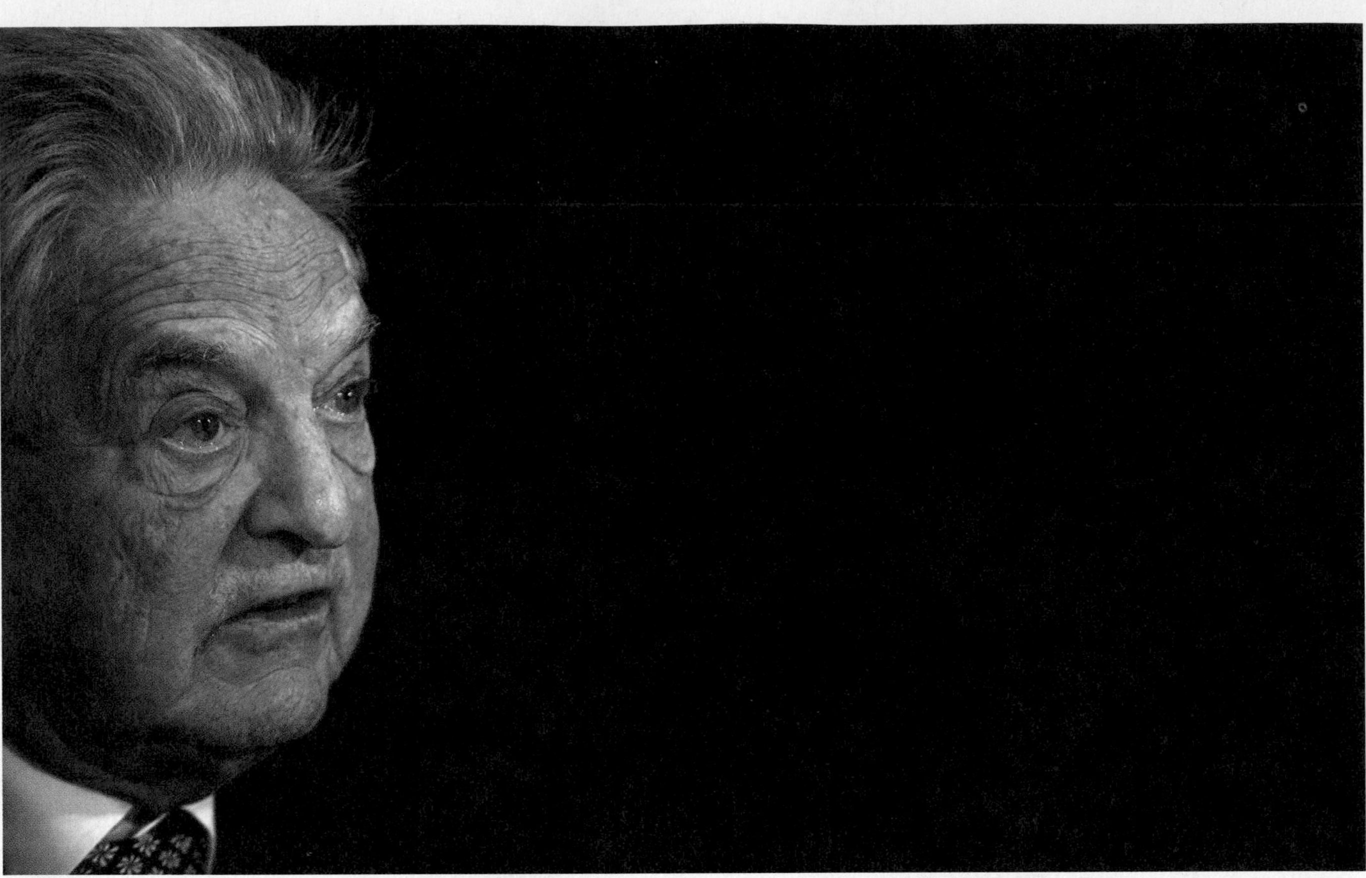

PUT YOUR MONEY WHERE YOUR MOUTH IS

Although big givers to Republican groups like Sheldon Adelson got a lot of publicity in 2012 and many considered the practice novel, Democrats like George Soros (pictured here) contributed enormous sums to Democratic groups in 2004 in a bid to defeat George W. Bush.

States. Accordingly, he pledged $10 million to help get the group up and running. With a stroke of his check-writing pen, he effectively shifted ACT from idle to fifth gear.[20] More recently, billionaire donors, including industrial tycoons David and Charles Koch, gave the conservative Tea Party group the financial boost it needed to transition from a grassroots effort into a politically influential powerhouse.

Patrons need not be autonomous individuals. Corporations, units of government, foundations, and even other interest groups can found new groups or help start-ups get off the ground. Patronage from county governments created the National Association of Counties, which represents the interests of the nation's counties "on Capitol Hill and throughout the federal bureaucracy."[21]

In 1912, Secretary of Commerce and Labor Charles Nagel's patronage helped create the U.S. Chamber of Commerce, a membership group of businesses; associations; and state, local, and international chambers of commerce. Nagel suggested the idea for a national business organization to President William Howard Taft. He encouraged Taft to publicly support a commercial group to speak to Washington policy makers with a single voice. Nagel also invited about 1,000 diverse business executives from all over the country to a national conference. He used his own department's resources to support the conference. Both Nagel and Taft spoke at the conference. They promoted the importance of a consolidated national business group and encouraged attendees to take advantage of the rare gathering. With the president on board, business had a strong incentive to act. By the time the conference adjourned, a new, nationwide business organization had been born: the U.S. Chamber of Commerce.[22] Today, the Chamber of Commerce is a highly influential group and continues to be a major political player in American politics.

Even a casual observer of American politics can see that tens of thousands of groups have succeeded in overcoming the collective action problem (Figure 12.1). The challenges inherent in group formation and maintenance are not the same for

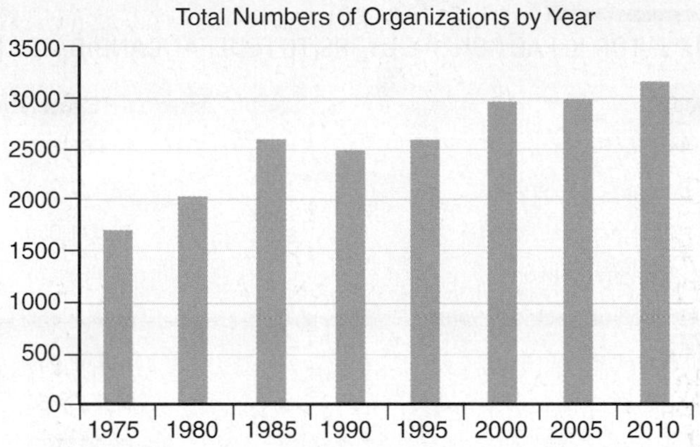

FIGURE 12.1 RISE IN THE NUMBER OF INTEREST GROUPS.
In spite of the collective action problem, the number of interest groups in Washington has nearly doubled in the past 40 years.

all groups, however. Some groups have ready access to desirable selective benefits, dynamic entrepreneurs, or resource-rich patrons. Some have access to all three. Some have access to none. Some groups are small and do not struggle with the free-rider problem. Some are so large they must continually work to keep their members engaged. Some are organized around simple, high-profile, ideologically charged issues that naturally incite passions and attract attention. Others focus on technical, abstract, nuanced issues that make the general public yawn.

political action committee (PAC)
a group that collects money from individuals and makes donations to political parties and candidates.

In short, different groups face different challenges and have strengths and weaknesses in different areas. Thus, groups must choose among various potential strategies and tactics to achieve their ends. We explore some of these choices in the next section.

What Groups Do, and Why They Do It

12.4 Analyze the strategies and tactics interest groups use to impact elections and public policy.

The ultimate goal of most politically oriented interest groups is to shape public policy in support of the group's interests, values, and beliefs. In general, groups use two primary strategies to do this: An electoral strategy attempts to influence the selection of public officials, and a legislative strategy attempts to influence the decisions that elected officials, bureaucrats, or members of the judiciary make. Of course, groups can pursue both strategies at once. Furthermore, the two strategies often intertwine.

Explore on MyPoliSciLab
Simulation: You Are a Lobbyist

☐ An Electoral Strategy Consists of a Variety of Tactics

Interest groups that pursue an electoral strategy may use a number of different tactics. These can include campaign spending, endorsements, voter mobilization and education, and volunteering.

CAMPAIGN SPENDING Many groups interested in election outcomes form **political action committees (PACs).** A PAC is an organization funded by 50 or more people, usually affiliated with a corporation, labor union, or some other special interest group. The PAC collects donations from individuals and then turns those donations into contributions to political parties and candidates for election (see Table 12.1). Groups may also encourage their members to donate to other PACs.

PACs allow individuals to multiply the effect of a campaign contribution. An individual $50 contribution to a Senate campaign might not do very much. But when you contribute that same $50 to a PAC, it combines with many other individual

12.1

12.2

12.3

12.4

12.5

TABLE 12.1 TOP 10 PAC CONTRIBUTORS TO FEDERAL CANDIDATES IN 2010

PAC	Amount Contributed
National Assn of Realtors	$2,886,331
National Beer Wholesalers Assn	$2,721,000
Honeywell International	$2,671,659
Operating Engineers Union	$2,486,110
Intl Brotherhood of Electrical Workers	$2,298,850
American Assn for Justice	$2,264,000
AT&T Inc	$2,235,050
American Bankers Assn	$2,217,950
Plumbers/Pipefitters Union	$2,007,000
Northrop Grumman	$1,984,400

*From http://www.opensecrets.org/pacs/toppacs.php
** Based on data released by the FEC on XXX

bundling
the practice of collecting individual checks and presenting them to a candidate at one time.

527 committee
an independent, nonparty group that raises and spends money on political activities.

contributions. You become part of a group collectively contributing much more (say $10,000), and in that way, you get more bang for your buck.

PACs are very popular donation vehicles. In the 2010 election, PACs contributed almost $375 million to candidates running for the House and Senate.[23] This represents about one-fourth of the funds that candidates for Congress raised during the 2009–2010 election cycle.

Competitive campaigns for Congress can be extraordinarily expensive. In 2010, the most expensive House campaign cost more than $8.5 million (Michelle Bachmann, R-MN), and the most expensive Senate campaign cost more than $41 million (Linda McMahon, R-CT).[24] In a very costly race, then, the maximum PAC contribution of $5,000 will comprise a trifling amount of the total the campaign will spend.

Groups can also request that members write checks directly to a candidate's campaign. The group can then collect the individual checks and present them to the candidate all at once. This practice is called **bundling.** Considering that individuals can contribute up to $2,500 for each election, a bundle of checks from dozens of well-heeled donors can make quite an impression. In the 2008 presidential campaign, Barack Obama raised large sums of money in small amounts over the Internet. But the backbone of his fund-raising efforts was a group of supporters who gathered or "bundled" contributions to his campaign.

Groups may also form and raise funds for **527 committees,** also called "527s," named for the relevant section of the Internal Revenue Code. A 527 is a tax-exempt,

TABLE 12.2 SUMMARY OF CAMPAIGN DONATION LIMITS

2012 Contribution Limits	
Individuals can give:	
To candidate	$2,500
To national party committee	$30,800
To PAC/state or local party	$10,000 to state or local party
	$5,000 to each PAC
Aggregate total	$117,000 per two-year election cycle
	$46,200 to candidates
	$70,800 to all national party committees of which no more than $46,200 per cycle can go to PACs
Multicandidate PACs can give:	
To candidate	$5,000
To national party committee	$15,000
To PAC/state or local party	$5,000
Aggregate total	No limit

Source: Federal Election Commission: http://www.fec.gov/pages/brochures/contrib.shtml.

OUTSIDE GROUPS

Groups comprised an increasingly large share of campaign spending in 2012—especially on the Republican side. Here, Democratic Senators Charles Schumer and Al Franken question the source of funds contributed to Crossroads, one of the biggest groups supporting GOP candidates.

nonparty group that can raise and spend money on political activities and advertising with no effective limits.

The decision by the Supreme Court in *Citizens United v. FEC* (2010) permitted groups such as unions and corporations to have a much more direct role in campaigns. They could now air ads within 30 days of a primary and 60 days of a general election, which had been previously prohibited. They could now endorse candidates in issue advertising using "magic words" (words such as "vote for" or "vote against") to directly advocate for or against a particular candidate. Previously, in *Buckley v. Valeo* (1976), the Supreme Court had banned the use of such magic words in issue advertisements.

President Obama harshly criticized *Citizens United,* fearing that corporations would take advantage of the decision. In the 2010 and 2012 elections, although no television commercials said "Defeat Jones, paid for by Gillette Shaving Cream," corporations did fund advocacy groups that aired ads praising or attacking candidates. Groups often aired these ads without disclosing their donors, which made it hard to track the true extent of corporate activity. Unions took advantage of *Citizens United* as well. They funded a lot of their election activities with resources from outside their PACs.

In many ways, the *Citizens United* decision strengthened groups by allowing them to fund ads that expressly support candidates with unregulated funds. At the same time, it weakened political parties. As a result of the decision, the proportion of campaign spending parties devote to advertising has decreased significantly, from about 25 percent in 2006 to 15 percent in 2010. By contrast, the proportion of campaign spending groups now devote to advertising has increased significantly, from about 25 percent in 2006 to 50 percent in 2010. In 2012, groups played an even bigger role, airing xx percent of all advertisements. Still, the *Citizens United* decision did not transform the overall look of campaigns. For years, organized interests used loopholes to invest unregulated money into the electoral process. No matter what the Court had decided, competitive races would have cost a lot of money, interest groups would have found ways to invest in their preferred candidate, and voters would have seen an abundance of political ads on television.

OTHER ELECTORAL TACTICS Although campaign spending is probably the most high-profile and controversial tactic that interest groups use to pursue their electoral goals, it is just the beginning. Groups interested in electoral outcomes have a number of other tactics at their disposal, including the following:

Endorsements: Groups often publicize their support for a candidate. This provides a valuable voting cue for anyone sympathetic to the group's mission.

Voter mobilization: As noted earlier, interest groups often dedicate themselves to increasing voter registration and turnout. This is especially true for competitive congressional races in important battleground states that decide presidential elections.

Voter education: Sometimes groups seek to influence elections by disseminating educational materials to prospective voters. These materials may discuss a candidate's background, beliefs, or record; compare and contrast competing candidates; or rate a whole slate of candidates according to their votes or positions on various issues. Conservative Christian groups often use this approach by distributing voter guides in evangelical churches every election year.

Volunteer work: Groups provide volunteers to do some of the necessary day-to-day work on behalf of candidates they favor. This can include answering

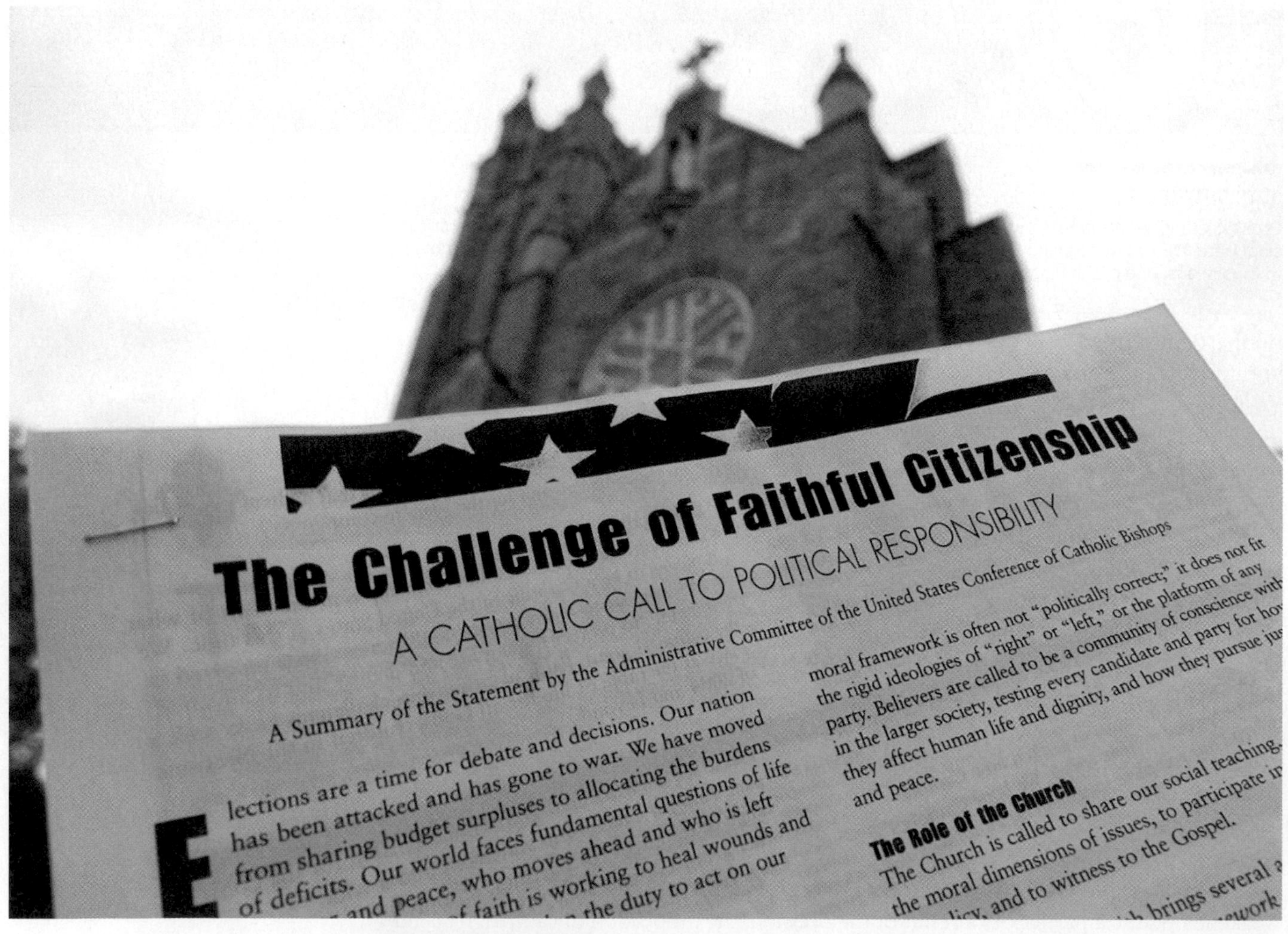

COMMUNICATION WITH THE FAITHFUL

Although they needed to refrain from direct endorsements of candidates, clergy and religious organizations are able to communicate with their followers and often frame these communications in ways that strongly benefit one candidate or another.

Explore on MyPoliSciLab

Can Interest Groups Buy Public Policy?

Interest groups such as banks and labor unions participate in activities that influence legislation their members care about, such as tax policy or social benefits. During the election season, interest groups team up with political action committees (PACs) to finance different campaigns. Directing contributions to the party in power, and specifically to committee members who write legislation, is a common practice in American politics. Both labor unions and banks donate similar amounts of money to candidates, but they have different contribution strategies.

Banks and Labor Unions Have Similar Campaign Funding

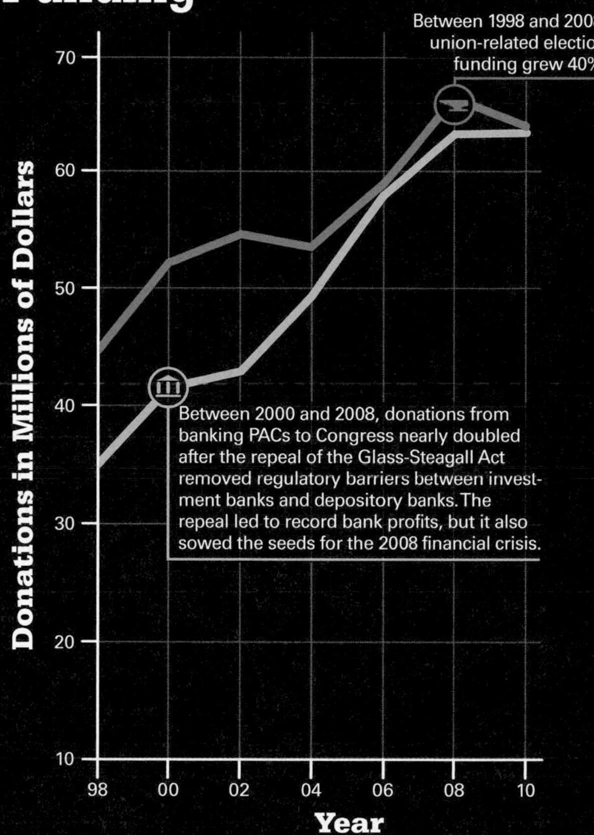

Between 1998 and 2008, union-related election funding grew 40%.
Between 2000 and 2008, donations from banking PACs to Congress nearly doubled after the repeal of the Glass-Steagall Act removed regulatory barriers between investment banks and depository banks. The repeal led to record bank profits, but it also sowed the seeds for the 2008 financial crisis.
Donations in Millions of Dollars
70
60
50
40
30
20
10
98
00
02
04
06
08
10
Year
Labor donations to all candidates
Banking donations to all candidates

SOURCE: Data from the Federal Election Commission, www.fec.gov.

Banks and Labor Unions Have Different Party Priorities

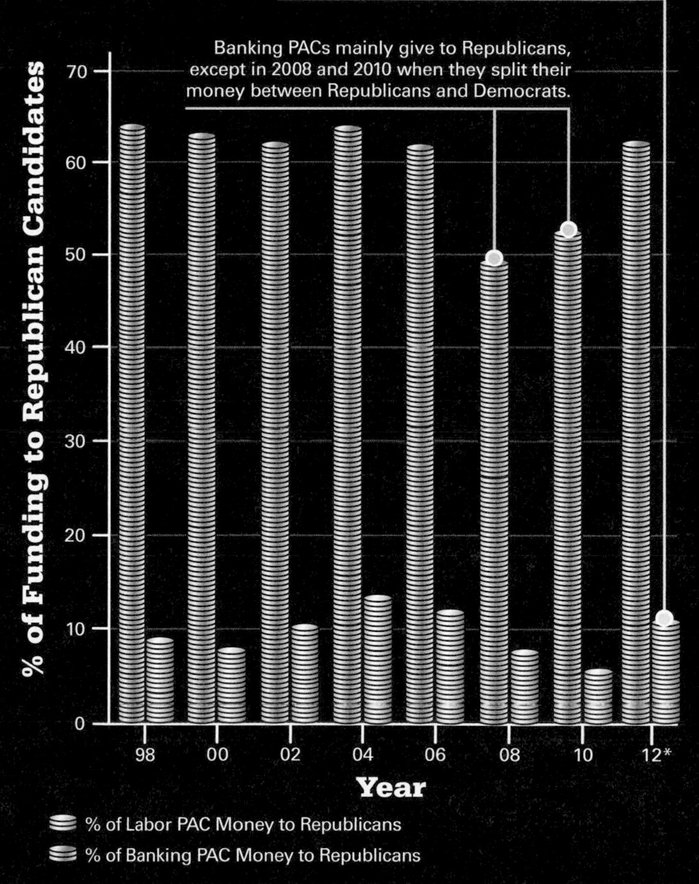

Labor PACs consistently give less than 20% of their money to Republicans no matter which party is in power.
Banking PACs mainly give to Republicans, except in 2008 and 2010 when they split their money between Republicans and Democrats.
% of Funding to Republican Candidates
70
60
50
40
30
20
10
0
98
00
02
04
06
08
10
12*
Year
% of Labor PAC Money to Republicans
% of Banking PAC Money to Republicans

* As of reporting period ending October 1, 2012.

Investigate Further

Concept Are banks or labor unions giving more money to politicians through their PACs? They are giving roughly similar amounts of money. In fact, labor PACs donate more money than banking PACs.

Connection How are labor unions' donation strategies different from those of banks? Labor PACs consistently give the majority of their PAC money to Democrats even when Republicans control Congress. Banking PACs give more strategically. During most years, they focus their money on Republicans, but when Democrats are in power they split their donations between both parties.

Cause How do interest groups buy policy? Interest groups use PACs and campaign financing to reinforce political friendships with legislators. Labor PACs use their donations to support Democrats who share their ideological values, while banking PACs change their donation strategy depending on which party is in power.

12.1

12.2

12.3

12.4

12.5

lobbying
communicating with government officials to persuade them toward a particular policy decision.

inside lobbying
meeting directly with public officials to influence political decisions.

phones, preparing campaign mailers, coordinating local meetings, reminding voters to do their civic duty on Election Day (for the preferred candidate, of course), and even driving voters to the polls.

☐ Legislative Strategies Include Lobbying

As with the electoral strategy, groups that pursue a legislative strategy use a variety of tactics. The most familiar of these is **lobbying**: communicating with government officials to persuade them to support a particular policy decision. Lobbying and lobbyists are sometimes stigmatized as sleazy, unseemly, and even undemocratic. For example, in his 2008 presidential campaign, then-Senator Barack Obama said:

> I am in this race to tell the corporate lobbyists that their days of setting the agenda in Washington are over. I have done more than any other candidate in this race to take on lobbyists—and won. They have not funded my campaign, they will not get a job in my White House, and they will not drown out the voices of the American people when I am president.[25]

As president, Obama had to relax his stance somewhat. When pursued legally and ethically, lobbying is a legitimate tactic used to achieve a legitimate democratic end: influencing the deliberations, decisions, and actions of government officials. In fact, the right to lobby is guaranteed by the First Amendment, which prohibits Congress from interfering with the right of the people "to petition the government for a redress of grievances." Lobbying takes two general forms, inside lobbying and grassroots lobbying.

INSIDE LOBBYING AND CONGRESS What most people think of as lobbying is technically called **inside lobbying,** which occurs when a group's representatives meet with public officials or their staff members. The lobbyist's job in these meetings is to present specific, evaluative information to the public official and to request an action or a decision based on that information.

The lobbyist does not simply say, "We want you to know that our group is pro-environment, and we hope you will be, too." Instead, the lobbyist presents the group's position on a specific bill, amendment, nomination, budget item, or issue along with the reasons for that position: "The Sierra Club is opposed to this amendment because we think it will undercut some major provisions of the Clean Air Act that have nearly universal public support." To this statement, the lobbyist adds his or her request for action by the public official: "Because of that, we are asking that you vote against the amendment."

There are, of course, dozens of variations on this basic information/request-for-action two-step. Lobbyists recognize that public officials have a variety of goals. Members of Congress value good public policy; reelection; and advancement within the institution, such as chairing a desirable committee or earning a spot in the party leadership. Lobbyists make their case to these officials with these goals in mind. In the previous example, the Sierra Club presented an evaluation of an amendment in terms of its soundness as public policy. Recognizing that members of Congress are interested in reelection, too, the lobbyist might have added: "Furthermore, our research shows that the substance of this amendment is immensely unpopular within your district. If you vote for it, an opponent in the next election may beat you over the head with this issue all the way to November."

The type and amount of information that lobbyists provide varies from situation to situation. Some policy makers want to see detailed studies supporting a group's position. Others are more interested in expressly political information on the issue: polling data, communications from voters, and activities of opposing groups. Some legislators want to know what recognized experts think. Some simply want a short list of talking points they can use to explain their vote. Others want to know what kind of media coverage the issue has received in national and hometown newspapers. Still others want to talk through hypothetical scenarios: "What if, instead of just voting against the amendment, we sent it back to committee for reconsideration with some specific suggestions for improving it?"

The lobbyist must be prepared to answer all such questions and provide supporting information when meeting with public officials or soon after. Lobbyists' ability to do so makes them immensely helpful to members of Congress. Faced with dozens of high-profile issues, each of which must pass through a long series of meetings, hearings, decisions, discussions, negotiations, and votes, representatives and senators cannot become experts in more than two or three issue areas. Having lobbyists available to provide information on other issues is like having a public policy encyclopedia at the ready.

Unlike an encyclopedia, however, a lobbyist has a point of view and a position to promote. Often, lobbyists have a broad philosophical orientation, such as being "pro-labor" or "pro-business." This helps public officials. They are far too busy to listen to lobbyists who present both sides and leave it up to the official to decide. Instead, they can hear the strongest arguments from the most passionate, well-informed advocates on both sides. The lobbyists' information, expertise, and familiarity with an issue help public officials evaluate it in ways that they otherwise could not.

Lobbyists' requests can vary tremendously from situation to situation. A lobbyist could ask a member of Congress to sponsor, amend, rewrite, or vote for or against a piece of legislation; talk to colleagues; hold hearings (or decline to hold hearings); take a stand regarding an issue; support or oppose a nominee; or intervene with an agency.

Members of Congress may agree to do such work on behalf of an interest group for a variety of reasons. It may be consistent with their goals. They may be grateful for the lobbyist's or group's support in the past. They may want to build goodwill in anticipation of a request for support in the future. Whatever the case, by helping the lobbyist and the group the lobbyist represents, members of Congress generally help themselves.

This kind of help is not a one-way street. A lobbyist who asks a member to sponsor a piece of legislation often provides a draft bill that the member can use as a starting point. The lobbyist might also volunteer to answer any questions on the legislation from the member's colleagues. If the member agrees to meet with a regulatory agency, the lobbyist might offer to help set up the meeting and preview the major issues and arguments.

Furthermore, once a lobbyist establishes a trusted relationship with a public official, that official may seek out the lobbyist for help. An official working on a pet issue may ask the lobbyist for information or to provide a subject-matter expert who can give congressional testimony. The official may want the lobbyist to talk to other groups involved with the issue to scope out their position. Lobbyists are normally happy to oblige. They know that a close, trusting, and mutually supportive relationship will benefit the groups they represent.

INSIDE LOBBYING AND THE EXECUTIVE BRANCH Although inside lobbying most often occurs with members of Congress and their staff, interest group lobbyists also devote resources to the executive branch. In some cases, this means the president and White House personnel, but more often these lobbying efforts focus on executive branch agencies. These agencies issue regulations, statutory interpretations, and quasi-legal decisions on issues as diverse as endangered species protection, the content of television and radio advertising, business accommodations for individuals with disabilities, and interstate speed limits. They also participate in the executive branch budget process. They can support maintaining, increasing, reducing, or eliminating funding for various programs. Executive agencies also administer major federal programs and tax credits. Finally, they pursue policy agendas of their own, encouraging the president to promote and fund certain policy initiatives and to abandon others.

Obviously, interest groups and their members can have a significant stake in these executive agency decisions and activities. Some groups, therefore, devote major lobbying resources to the executive branch.

INSIDE LOBBYING AND THE JUDICIARY Inside lobbying of the judicial branch takes two primary forms. When a court case involves an issue relevant to a group, it can file an *amicus curiae*, or friend of the court, brief. Essentially, these briefs present the group's analysis of legal or factual questions in the hope that judges, justices, or their clerks will consider arguments when deciding the case.

12.1

12.2

12.3

12.4

12.5

grassroots lobbying
efforts to persuade citizens to contact their elected officials regarding a particular issue or piece of legislation

outside lobbying
lobbyng that takes place outside washington dc

Several groups filed *amicus* briefs in the U.S. Supreme Court case of *Morse v. Fredrick* (2007). Fredrick, a high school senior, was suspended from school for hanging a banner school officials found offensive. Fredrick claimed this was a violation of his First Amendment rights. When the case made its way to the Supreme Court, a number of groups, including the National Coalition Against Censorship, the Christian Legal Society, and Students for Sensible Drug Policy, filed briefs supporting Fredrick's position. They saw the case as an opportunity to establish important principles regarding freedom of speech in a public school setting. In the end, however, the Supreme Court ruled that Fredrick's First Amendment rights had not been violated by school administrators.

The other judiciary-related tactic available to interest groups is litigation. Although this is not lobbying per se, it can have important policy implications. During the 2004 Senate race, for example, Wisconsin Right to Life, Inc. (WRTL), an anti-abortion group, challenged the Bipartisan Campaign Reform Act (BCRA) of 2002, also known as the McCain-Feingold Act. BCRA prohibited a union or corporation from using general treasury funds to sponsor advertisements that mention a federal candidate by name within 30 days of a primary election. WRTL believed these restrictions were unconstitutional and directly violated the act. It used funds from its general treasury to broadcast television advertisements mentioning Wisconsin senators Herb Kohl and Russ Feingold by name within a month of the election. WRTL then sued the Federal Elections Commission, the agency responsible for administering BCRA. The U.S. Supreme Court decided in favor of WRTL, effectively modifying a law enacted by Congress and signed by President Bush. Ultimately, this decision paved the way for the Supreme Court's decision in *Citizens United v. FEC*, which further loosened campaign finance laws for corporations and unions.

GRASSROOTS LOBBYING The other major tactic that groups use is **grassroots lobbying,** which is also called **outside lobbying.** In this form of lobbying, rather than advocating directly with decision makers in government, interest groups and their lobbyists seek to influence opinion and stimulate action by the general public, specific groups, and the media. Groups generally begin a grassroots lobbying effort by reaching out to their own members through established communication channels. They can depend on members to agree on the issues and take action if necessary. Leaders bring new issues to members' attention; try to shape opinions on existing issues; and ask members to call, e-mail, and write letters to policy makers in positions of influence.

Consider the example of LEAnet, a nationwide coalition of special education professionals and school administrators. LEAnet routinely notifies members of pending congressional actions that may affect group members' interests. This often includes advocating for preserving Medicaid funding for special needs students in public schools. These communications are often a call to action that asks members to e-mail or call a congressperson's office immediately, and they provide a sample message of what to say.[26]

Some groups go further and encourage, or even arrange for, their members to meet policy makers in person. The American Public Health Association (APHA), for example, touts the value of such meetings on its website: "One of the most effective ways to influence the policymaking process and make a lasting connection is to visit with your Senators and Representative, or their staff, in person."[27]

Interest groups know that government officials respond to public opinion broadly, not just to opinions expressed by group members with an interest in a particular issue. They know, too, that policy makers react to what they see, hear, and read in the media. Because of these characteristics, a grassroots lobbying campaign may be both extensive and multifaceted.

In 2005, Progress for America (PFA), a group that often advocated on behalf of President Bush and various Republican candidates and initiatives, launched a multifaceted campaign to support Samuel Alito, a Bush nominee to the U.S. Supreme Court. Efforts included putting up a website and airing about $500,000 worth of television advertising. PFA also hired consultants in 20 swing states to speak with newspaper editorial boards and sent more than 10 million e-mail messages to Republican Party lists. In addition, the group arranged for Judge Alito's former law clerks to visit Washington and lobby senators for their former boss. To generate favorable news stories, PFA even sought out people from Judge Alito's past, including former teachers, coaches, and neighbors.[28]

This example illustrates many of the hallmarks of a textbook grassroots approach to lobbying. PFA attempted to influence the general climate of opinion through paid advertising. It sought to educate and mobilize individuals willing to take action on behalf of Judge Alito. It tried to generate favorable stories and friendly interviews about him in mass media outlets. It arranged for meetings between lawmakers and Alito's former clerks, rather than meetings between lawmakers and paid professional lobbyists. In short, instead of using Washington-based, lobbyist-centered inside tactics, PFA tried to give senators (who had to vote on Alito's nomination) the impression that Alito had significant support outside Washington. Ultimately, Alito won confirmation. Although PFA's campaign was not the sole reason for Alito's Senate confirmation, it is a great example of grassroots lobbying. Former Illinois Senator Everett Dirksen summed up the logic that drives grassroots lobbying this way: "When politicians feel the heat," Dirksen said, "they begin to see the light."

The Electoral Strategy and the Legislative Strategy Intertwine

Groups need not choose between an electoral strategy and a legislative strategy. Many pursue both at once and one often reinforces the other. A member of Congress elected with the support of a particular group may be more open to entertaining that group's viewpoints on policy issues. The member needs to maintain a friendly relationship with that group if he or she wants its support in the next election cycle. That keeps the member's ears open to the group's needs. This is how a group's electoral strategy can support its legislative strategy.

The reverse can be true as well. A group that wants a member of Congress to vote its way on a bill can point out the political appeal of that vote (or the political damage of opposition) in the next election. A group that uses an outside lobbying strategy such as encouraging communications to a legislator is registering its viewpoints on issues. At the same time, it is showing the kind of muscle it can flex—on behalf of the legislator or an opponent—in the next election.

In a similar vein, an interest group might seek to support legislation because it causes problems for political opponents. Pro-life members of Congress proposed the "partial birth abortion" ban in 1995 in part to force pro-choice legislators to take a public position on a procedure many Americans oppose. Legislators used the same tactic in proposing the federal assault weapons ban, which passed in 1994. Most of the public approved of the ban, which put gun rights enthusiasts who opposed it in an awkward position.

Interest Groups Have a Wide Variety of Tactics in Their Toolkits

As the preceding discussion indicates, interest groups have a wide variety of tactics they can choose from to try to influence the policy process. Their choice of tactics depends on their goals. All the various tactics try to convey some sort of information to policy makers—either on the substantive merits of their position or on the political consequences of a particular course of action. Table 12.3 summarizes the various tactics and how often they tend to be used.

TABLE 12.3 LOBBYING TECHNIQUES AND THEIR PREVALENCE

Legislative Branch	
Doing favors or providing gifts for legislators	–
Meeting personally with legislators or their aides	very often
Testifying at legislative hearings	very often
Executive Branch	
Interacting with special agencies that advise the chief executive	–
Interacting with special liaison offices within the chief executive's office	–
Meeting personally with chief executive or aides	seldom
Meeting personally with executive agency personnel	very often
Serving on executive agency advisory boards or committees	occasionally
Submitting written comments on proposed rules or regulations	very often
Testifying at executive agency hearings	–
Judicial Branch	
Attempting to influence judicial selections	–
Engaging in litigation	occasionally
Submitting *amicus curiae* ("friends of the court") briefs	occasionally
Grassroots	
Arranging face-to-face meetings between group members/supporters and government officials	–
Dispatching a spokesperson to the media	–
Engaging in e-mail, letter, telegram, or telephone campaigns	very often
Engaging in demonstrations or protests	seldom
Running advertisements in the media	seldom
Direct Democracy	
Attempting to place an initiative or referendum on the ballot	–
Campaigning for or against an initiative or referendum	–
Electoral	
Campaigning for or against candidates	seldom
Endorsing candidates	seldom
Engaging in election issue advocacy	seldom
Making in-kind contributions to candidates	seldom
Making monetary contributions to political parties	seldom
Making monetary contributions to candidates	occasionally
Mobilizing activists to work on a candidate's behalf	–
Issuing voter guides	seldom
Other	
Joining coalitions with other organizations or lobbyists	very often

Note: Dashes (–) indicate that there is little evidence with which to judge the frequency of such activities.

Do Groups Matter?

12.5 Assess how much influence interest groups have over policy outcomes.

igh-profile corruption cases often receive significant media attention. In the past, some interest groups went well beyond the sorts of activities we have outlined here and attempted to bribe members of Congress. Randy Cunningham, a former representative from California, received a Rolls Royce and a yacht for steering Defense Department business toward a particular contract. Cunningham is currently biding his time in prison. Jack Abramoff, a well-known

Unresolved Debate

Do Interest Groups Influence Legislative Decisions?

Most researchers agree that interest groups make a difference when it comes to which candidates win elections and what issues appear on the public agenda. But rarely is there clear evidence showing a specific group activity caused a particular political outcome. Even more difficult to generalize about is the impact of political action committee (PAC) contributions on legislative outcomes. Journalists note that legislators who receive large PAC contributions often vote to please their donors. In contrast, political scientists explain that PACs often give money to legislators who support their agendas. Which group has it right? Do interest groups influence legislative decisions?

YES

Although the influence of interest groups may not necessarily buy votes, political scientists Richard Hall and Frank Wayman argue that it can still buy time—that is, the time a targeted legislator may spend to incorporate group preferences into legislation. In addition, political scientists Kenneth Godwin and Barry J. Seldon believe that the added time can lead to advantages for interest groups that go beyond floor votes.

- Hall and Wayman found that legislators who received campaign funds from an interest group were more likely to support that group through numerous methods including negotiating compromises behind the scenes, offering friendly amendments or actively opposing unfriendly ones, lobbying colleagues, and showing up to vote in favor of the interest group's position. They argued that these activities, rather than floor votes, were more likely to show evidence of group influence.[a]
- Godwin and Seldon also argue that these additional activities can result in advantages that include government contracts, price increases, tax breaks, earmarked funds, and exemptions from certain statutory provisions.[b]
- Legislators often distribute these kinds of private goods to interest groups behind the scenes—away from reporters and without a formal vote. Massive appropriations bills can bury them in the fine print so they are easily missed—even by political scientists.

NO

Most research finds that interest groups do not influence legislative decisions through their PAC contributions.

- A floor vote on a piece of legislation comes at the end of the legislative process. Before a bill gets to a floor vote, it has already endured important decisions, hearings, committee votes, negotiations, and coalition building. An interest group trying to buy influence after all these steps would be as effective as a football fan who pays full price for a Super Bowl ticket with only two minutes left in the game.
- Members of Congress face many other influences on their vote aside from campaign contributions, including their own policy preferences, constituents' preferences, the dictates of party leaders, and their voting records.
- The multitude of other influences on members of Congress tends to be so strong that it is unlikely that an interest group contribution could override them enough to change votes.

CONTRIBUTING TO THE DEBATE

Political scientists and journalists generally study issues that are hotly contested. But groups may have the greatest influence when the outcomes they seek are much lower profile. These can include outcomes that are uncontested or decided in low-profile settings, do not have a significant impact outside the groups affected, and are not of interest to causal political observers. For example, if 10 out of 11 committee members had hard-line positions on an issue, interest groups would likely focus their lobbying efforts on the undecided member. A scholar looking for influence on all 11 committee members would likely come up empty handed. Reorienting interest group research in this way would undoubtedly demonstrate interest group influence in a wide range of legislative activity, as well as executive, judicial, and electoral activity.

WHAT DO YOU THINK?

1. How can interest groups influence legislation without changing legislative votes?
2. Why is it harder to discern interest group influence on low-profile issues than it is on high-profile issues?

---

[a]Richard L. Hall and Frank W. Wayman, "Buying Time: Moneyed Interests and the Mobilization of Bias in Congressional Committees," *American Political Science Review* 84, 3 (1990): 802.

[b]R. Kenneth Godwin and Barry J. Seldon, "What Corporations Really Want from Government," http://72.14.253.104/search?q=cache:nartLRj_rsYJ: www.politicalscience.uncc.edu/godwink/RecentPublications/What%2520Corporations%2520Really%2520Want%2520from%2520Government.pdf+%22what+corporations+really+want+from+government%22&hl=en&ct=clnk&cd=1&gl=us (accessed August 11, 2008).

lobbyist in D.C. for many years, also earned prison time for his role in orchestrating bribes to members of Congress.

These sorts of blatant and illegal activities are rare, and as we have argued, interest groups and lobbyists play an important role in our political system. But given what we now know about groups, we are left with a final question: Do groups matter? That is, do group activities influence election results and public policy outcomes in the ways that groups intend? The answer to that question is surprisingly murky (see *Unresolved Debate: Do Interest Groups Influence Legislative Decisions?*).

On MyPoliSciLab

Review the Chapter

Listen to **Chapter 12** on **MyPoliSciLab**

The Problem of Factions and the Pluralist Answer

12.1 Distinguish between pluralist theory's and James Madison's interpretation of the role of interest groups within American politics, p. 403.

Founder James Madison was concerned about the negative influence of factions on individual rights and the collective good. However, he concluded that the American system was well designed to mute the influence of factions. The pluralists viewed politics as an organized effort to resolve conflicts among competing group interests, and they attempted to demonstrate empirically what Madison had argued theoretically. They concluded that interest groups share political power and resources widely. Some have influence and resources for certain issues, whereas others have more control over different issues.

Criticisms of Pluralism

12.2 Describe how critics of pluralist theory view the role of interest groups today, p. 404.

Critics of pluralism argue that the American system is resistant to change and prevents certain issues from getting on the agenda. Furthermore, the free-rider or collective action problem questions the assumption that groups automatically form and suggests some types of groups are more able to form than others.

Solving the Collective Action Problem: Group Formation and Maintenance

12.3 Explain how interest groups form and attract members, p. 408.

Groups pursue a variety of strategies to get around the collective action problem. They provide selective benefits and material benefits, which members receive in return for joining. They also provide social benefits, in which members enjoy the camaraderie of being part of a group. And they provide purposive benefits, in which those who join receive satisfaction from being involved in an important political struggle.

What Groups Do, and Why They Do It

12.4 Analyze the strategies and tactics interest groups use to impact elections and public policy, p. 413.

Groups try to influence public policy in two ways. Using an election strategy, groups try to influence which leaders achieve power and make public policy. Using a legislative strategy, groups try to influence the behavior of elected officials, bureaucrats, and judges who are already in power.

Do Groups Matter?

12.5 Assess how much influence interest groups have over policy outcomes, p. 422.

Media coverage and public opinion suggest that interest groups are too powerful and often malevolent. They are neither. Although particular lobbyists and legislators sometimes cross the line, groups in general play an important role in American politics, even though they are more likely to influence policy making in small and subtle ways.

Learn the Terms

Study and **Review** the **Flashcards**

527 committee, p. 414
bundling, p. 414
collective action problem, p. 406
disturbance theory, p. 406
free-rider problem, p. 406
grassroots lobbying, p. 420
inside lobbying, p. 418
interest group entrepreneur, p. 410
interest groups, p. 404
lobbying, p. 418
material benefit, p. 408
nondecisions, p. 406
outside lobbying, p. 420
patrons, p. 411
political action committee (PAC), p. 413
pluralism, p. 404
policy agenda, p. 406
purposive benefit, p. 409
selective benefit, p. 408
social benefit, p. 409

Test Yourself

12.1 Distinguish between pluralist theory's and James Madison's interpretation of the role of interest groups within American politics.

James Madison assumed that competing factions

a. Would set the agenda.
b. Would form and compete resulting in a collective good for society.
c. Were dangerous by definition and should be banned.
d. Were unlikely to form.
e. Would ally in the Electoral College.

12.2 Describe how critics of pluralist theory view the role of interest groups today.

Which of the following is NOT a criticism of pluralism?

a. The American political system is open to change.
b. The American political system is resistant to change.
c. Some examples of nonparticipation are a result of insurmountable obstacles to participation, rather than a lack of interest.
d. Pluralists ignore the same issues that policy makers ignore.
e. Groups do not automatically form when there is a disturbance.

12.3 Explain how interest groups form and attract members.

How do groups overcome the collective action problem and attract members?

a. They promote the idea that others will act, and that there is no need for active participation by group members.
b. They disdain leaders and prefer, instead, a flat organizational structure in which no one manages the group.
c. They decline patronage and rely on the small donations of many group members.
d. They offer material benefits to group members and non–group members alike.
e. They offer selective benefits to members only.

12.4 Analyze the strategies and tactics interest groups use to impact elections and public policy.

All of the following are electoral tactics used by interest groups EXCEPT

a. Volunteer work.
b. Bundling of individual checks for a candidate.
c. Filing of *amicus curiae* briefs.
d. Endorsements.
e. Voter mobilization.

12.5 Assess how much influence interest groups have over policy outcomes.

What is TRUE of the influence of interest groups on legislative decisions?

a. Interest groups have no influence on legislative decisions.
b. Legislators will almost always vote the way an interest group wants, if the interest group contributes a significant amount of money through its PAC.
c. Interest groups have the greatest amount of influence at the end of the legislative process.
d. Interest group influence on legislative decisions can be seen most clearly by looking at floor votes.
e. Interest group influence can often be seen by the time a legislator spends to incorporate interest group preferences into legislation.

Explore Further

SUGGESTED READING BY TOP SCHOLARS

Esterling, Kevin M. 2007. "Buying Expertise: Campaign Contributions and Attention to Policy Analysis in Congressional Committees." American Political Science Review. 101:93–109. This innovative study posits that members with more analytical ability, who are likely to take an more active role in shaping legislation, are more likely to draw campaign contributions from organized interests.

Hall, Richard L., and Alan V. Deardorff. 2006. "Lobbying as Legislative Subsidy." American Political Science Review. 100:69–84. This article views lobbying as not so much targeted at swaying undecided legislators or convincing opponents, but as providing support and information for allies.

Baumgartner, Frank R., Jeffrey M. Berry, Marie Hojnacki, David C. Kimball, and Beth L. Leech. 2009. Lobbying and Policy Change: Who Wins, Who Loses, and Why. Chicago:

University of Chicago Press. Although most politicians and pundits consider them to be all powerful, this study actually questions when and if lobbyists are particularly powerful.

Jeffrey Berry and Clyde Wilcox. 2008. *Interest Group Society*, 5th ed. New York: Longman. A comprehensive summary of what scholars know about the role of interest groups in American politics, putting interest groups into context and discussing their strategies and tactics.

Michael Franz. 2008. *Choice and Changes*. Philadelphia, PA: Temple University Press. The impact of interest groups on electoral politics, with a particular focus on "soft money" contributions, issue ads, and "527s".

SUGGESTED WEBSITES

AARP: www.aarp.org

The AARP website offers members tips on managing money, health care, family, and leisure and links to various resources related to these and other concerns of the retirement-age population.

Sierra Club: www.sierraclub.org

The Sierra Club is dedicated to protecting communities and the environment. It is America's oldest, largest, and most influential grassroots environmental organization.

EMILY's List: www.emilyslist.org

An acronym for "Early Money Is Like Yeast" (it makes the dough rise), EMILY's List has become the nation's biggest political action committee. Members work to elect pro-choice Democratic women to office by recruiting and funding viable women candidates, helping these women build effective campaigns, and mobilizing women voters.

College Republican National Committee: www.crnc.org

The College Republican National Committee recruits and trains conservative student leaders to build a conservative movement to "fight against the radical left on campus."

College Democrats of America: www.collegedems.com

The College Democrats of America is the college outreach arm of the Democratic Party. It focuses on electing Democrats to offices at all levels of government. This site offers links to local chapters and voter registration.

National Rifle Association: www.nra.org

The NRA represents millions of Americans who "believe in the Constitution" and "actively pursue some of the country's finest traditions—Hunting and Sports Shooting."

American Veterinary Medical Association: www.avma.org

The AVMA is a nonprofit association representing more than 76,000 veterinarians.

National Federation of Independent Businesses: www.nfib.com

The National Federation of Independent Businesses is a network of grassroots activists who send their views directly to state and federal lawmakers through member ballots.

13

Listen to Chapter 13 on MyPoliSciLab

Congress

DISTRIBUTING HOMELAND SECURITY FUNDS

In fiscal year 2010, the federal government spent $842 million on domestic counterterrorism.[1] On a per capita basis, though, these funds were not distributed equally across the country. Rather, one of the least populous states received one of the largest per capita shares of federal antiterrorism funds. Wyoming, not generally considered to be a terrorist target, secured funds amounting to $12.15 for each of its half-million residents from the Homeland Security Grant Program. New York, by contrast, received just $5.80 per resident, in spite of the fact that it was a site of the September 11, 2001 terrorist attacks.[2]

How did Wyoming manage to secure such a large chunk of federal funds to fight terrorism? The answer lies in the USA PATRIOT Act, more commonly known as the Patriot Act, which Congress passed in the aftermath of September 11, 2001. Among other provisions, the Patriot Act established a federal grant system to help state and local governments prepare for and respond to terrorist attacks. Eager to demonstrate their resolve to fight terrorism, members of Congress provided money for states to train first responders, purchase security equipment, and develop plans for emergency situations. However, the Patriot Act required the State Homeland Security Program (SHSP) to distribute almost 40 percent of its funds evenly among the 50 states, regardless of their population, size, or risk of being a terrorist target.[3]

When Congress passed the act in late October 2001, no one objected to the funding distribution formula. In fact, members of Congress were eager to offer a swift, bold response to the September 11 attacks. The chair of the powerful Senate Judiciary Committee, Senator Patrick

13.1 Outline the basic structure of Congress, p. 432.

13.2 Analyze the relationship of members of Congress to their constituencies, and distinguish between the trustee and delegate models of representation, p. 435.

13.3 Assess the challenges that emerge when members of Congress set about working together, p. 443.

13.4 Identify the resources and the committee and party structures that help Congress address its challenges, p. 447.

13.5 Explain the lawmaking process in Congress, p. 454.

13.6 Describe the appropriations process, p. 459.

OUTFITTING STATES TO FIGHT TERRORISM In the aftermath of September 11, 2001, Congress distributed funds to every state in the country to combat terrorism. More than a decade later, funds still are not allotted strictly according to assessed risk of a terrorist attack. In addition, many funds have been wasted on unusable equipment. In June 2011, Hawaii purchased a $75,000 drone to patrol Honolulu's harbors, but a year later, it had yet to take flight because the state had never cleared it with the FAA before making the purchase.

The Big Picture Did you know that the Founders created Congress to be the center of government activity? Author William G. Howell describes the responsibilities of Congress, but argues that what really matters today is how the 245 members of Congress interact with each other and with the other branches of government.

The Basics Why do we have two houses of Congress? This video reveals the answer this question and explores the differences are between the two houses in their organization and procedures. You will also learn how a bill becomes a law, how Congress is organized, and how members of Congress represent you.

In Context Discover the role that the framers expected Congress to serve in the U.S. government. Columbia University political scientist Greg Wawro discusses how Congress has become more expansive in its powers. Listen as Greg Wawro also delves into the process of creating coalitions in Congress to achieve policy results.

Think Like a Political Scientist Why has the United States become more polarized in the last decade? Columbia University political scientist Greg Wawro examines this central question and explains why polarization may be correlated to the income gap between the wealthy and the poor. He also explores recent research on the Senate as a super-majoritarian institution.

In the Real World Congress today is the most divided it has been since the end of WWII. It is also the least effective. Is compromise the answer? Real people consider the benefits and the dangers of compromise, and they discuss issues—like abortion—where compromise seems impossible.

So What? Why is congress so dysfunctional? Author William G. Howell considers how representatives from different districts with conflicting priorities are expected to not only get along, but create national policies together.

Leahy of Vermont, included in the state antiterrorism program a distribution formula that would benefit the citizens of the small state he represented, and others just like it.

As the Department of Homeland Security devoted increasingly large sums of money to helping state and local governments prepare for a possible terrorist attack, the wastefulness of the Patriot Act's fund distribution formula became apparent. Common sense probably tells you that helping North Dakota buy a $200,000 remote-control bomb-disposal robot is not the most effective way of preparing the nation for a terrorist attack. Thomas H. Kean, chair of the September 11 Commission, agreed: "We've had some of this money spent to air condition garbage trucks. We've had some of the money spent for armor for dogs. This money is being distributed as if it's general revenue sharing."[4] Kean recommended that antiterrorism funds not be distributed evenly among the states, but on the basis of threat and vulnerability.[5] Michael Chertoff, homeland security secretary at the time, further acknowledged that a uniform distribution of funds across states was not a good policy.[6]

Yet when Representative Christopher Cox of California tried to craft a new law in 2005 that would distribute antiterrorism funds on the basis of threat and risk, he could not get enough support from members of the Senate. Senators from smaller, less populous states lined up against the proposed measure, hoping to preserve the funding going to their states under the existing law. Senator Leahy argued that distribution based on the degree of terrorist threat would "shortchange rural states."[7]

As a result, for fiscal year 2006, the Department of Homeland Security had a budget of $41 billion with, according to one analysis, only $27 billion directed toward "activities that meet the executive branch's definition of homeland security."[8] Another study documents that local appropriation of antiterrorism funding has

> "resulted in such imaginative spending as $180,000 to a port that receives fewer than twenty ships a year, $30,000 to buy a defibrillator for use at a high school basketball tournament, $100,000 to fund a summer jobs program in Washington, D.C., . . . $200,000 for a drug prevention program, $100,000 for a child pornography tip line, . . . and $63,000 for a decontamination unit that sits gathering (hopefully uncontaminated) dust in a warehouse in rural Washington, because the state does not have a team that knows how to use it."[9]

The failure of Congress to route out these clear inefficiencies in the distribution of federal anti-terrorism funds seems to make little sense. When we think about the incentives that motivate individual members of Congress, however, their behavior is easier to understand. Opponents of the Cox proposal were representing the interests of the voters who put them into office. Whereas Cox represented an urban district outside of Los Angeles, Leahy spoke for a rural state. By arguing that Vermont *did* need to protect itself from terrorist attacks, he hoped to secure federal funds for improving the state's police and fire protection services. Other members of Congress also wanted to secure funding to please voters who had the power to reelect them, even if it was not best for the country as a whole. As of 2010, SHSP antiterrorism funds continued to be distributed by the same basic formula established by the Patriot Act.[10]

Neither irrationality nor happenstance is primarily responsible for the existing distribution of federal antiterrorism funds. Rather, its origins lie in the strategic negotiations that occur every day on Capitol Hill. Congress is a collective decision-making body whose structure sometimes inhibits effective problem solving. The individual members who serve in Congress work hardest on behalf of those who elected them. The laws they write represent compromises among hundreds of individuals fighting on behalf of districts and states. Sometimes, the final result is legislation that serves the interests of the country as a whole. Often, though, the pressure of pleasing the voters results in laws that do not address problems as effectively, or as efficiently, as many would like. To understand why these inefficiencies occur, and what might be done about it, we need to think about the structure of Congress and the incentives it creates for those who work within it.

An Institution with Two Chambers and Shared Powers

13.1 Outline the basic structure of Congress.

bicameral
an institution consisting of two chambers.

impeachment
performed by the House of Representatives, the act of charging government officials with "treason, bribery, or other high crimes and misdemeanors." The Senate then decides whether to convict and remove the official from office.

ongress is a **bicameral** institution—that is, it consists of two chambers, a House of Representatives and a Senate. In the House, the 435 voting members (and the five nonvoting delegates)[11] are elected every two years and represent state districts, which are remade after the census to reflect changes in the number of people living in different regions of the country. On average, each member of the House represents roughly 600,000 voters. In the Senate, the 100 members serve six-year, staggered terms and represent entire states.[12] Obviously, the size of states varies tremendously. As a consequence, senators from larger states such as New York, Texas, and California represent tens of millions of voters, whereas senators from smaller states such as North Dakota, Wyoming, and Montana represent far fewer.

For the most part, members of the House and Senate do similar things. As we discussed in Chapter 3, most powers enumerated in Article II of the Constitution, which concerns Congress, do not differentiate between the Senate and House. Both the chambers have the responsibility of overseeing the bureaucracy, declaring war, regulating interstate commerce, raising and supporting armies, and most importantly, writing "all Laws which shall be necessary and proper for carrying into Execution the foregoing powers." Later in this chapter, we will consider the lawmaking process in detail.

There are some important differences, however, between the two chambers. In terms of duties, the Senate has the responsibility of ratifying foreign treaties. When brokering deals with foreign nations, presidents need anticipate the reactions of only senators, not representatives. Additionally, senators are charged with approving presidential appointments to the federal judiciary and executive branch. Therefore, before selecting federal judges, ambassadors, and members of their cabinet, presidents try to calculate their chances of securing the necessary approval of the Senate.

As part of the nation's system of checks and balances, Congress has the power to remove from office the president, vice president, and others immediately under their command. The removal process, however, is divided into two separate phases. In the first, members of the House decide whether to **impeach** the president—that is, determine that the charges against him are sufficiently credible and meet the standards laid out in the Constitution of "treason, bribery, or other high crimes and misdemeanors." Should the House impeach the president, the case goes before the Senate, with the chief justice of the Supreme Court presiding. For a conviction, two-thirds of the senators must vote against the president. In the nation's history, two presidents (Andrew Johnson in 1868 and Bill Clinton in 1998) have been impeached. The Senate, however, refused to convict either president. (See Chapter 14 for more on the impeachment process.)

Members of the House and Senate also have different relationships with the people they represent. Because representatives are elected every two years and usually face a smaller (and typically more homogenous) group of voters than do senators, they tend to maintain closer relationships with the voters and work on behalf of a narrower band of interests. Senators, by contrast, hold office for six-year terms and represent larger (and typically more heterogeneous) populations. Senators, therefore, have more freedom to exercise their own judgment on policy matters and are less beholden to a small group of people.

This difference is no accident. The Framers of the Constitution envisioned the House to be the "People's Chamber," in which the interests of specific groups would be aired. The Senate was intended to be more deliberative than the House, allowing elected officials to reflect upon issues with national implications. Therefore, senators are more

How Do We Know?

Has Congress Abdicated Its War-Making Authority?

The Question

The Constitution gives most war-making powers to Congress. Article I says that Congress shall have the power to declare war, raise and support armies, appropriate funds for war, and regulate the conduct of ongoing wars. By contrast, the war powers granted to the president in Article II merely identify the president as the commander in chief and authorize him to "receive ambassadors and other public ministers."

Today, though, the practice of war would not appear to follow the principles laid out in the Constitution. Most decisions about war are made by the president. And rarely does Congress formally restrict the president's ability to wage war abroad. Has Congress abdicated its war-making powers? How do we know?

Why It Matters

There is no greater government power than the ability to send citizens abroad to fight, kill, and perhaps die. For precisely this reason, the Founders worried a great deal about which branch of government would have the authority to wage war. If they vested too much authority in the president, the Founders worried that the system of checks and balances might one day collapse. The Founders therefore looked to the legislative branch, which could be expected to better represent the will of the people in making decisions about war.

For much of U.S. history, this is exactly how decisions about whether to go to war were made. From the founding of the Republic to the mid-twentieth century, most major uses of force were approved by Congress. In the past half-century, though, the president has made most decisions involving war, and Congress has been pushed to the sidelines. If the Founders were right that war-making powers should not be entrusted to a president, then citizens ought to be greatly concerned about contemporary practice.

Investigating the Answer

One way to determine whether Congress has abdicated its war-making powers is to examine the declarations and actions of presidents and members of Congress. Who is setting the agenda, and who is following? Not since World War II has Congress formally declared war. It has authorized some wars (including the Vietnam, Persian Gulf, and Iraq wars) but not others (including the Korean War and conflicts in Panama, Kosovo, Bosnia, and Haiti). Congress also has been reluctant to exercise its formal legislative and appropriations powers to influence wars that are underway. Although it has the constitutional authority to cut funding for a war, issue regular reports about a war's progress, and demand a withdrawal, Congress rarely takes advantage of these options—even when wars are unpopular.

In 1973, frustrated with the progress of the Vietnam War, members of Congress attempted to reassert their authority by passing the War Powers Resolution, which gave the president 60 to 90 days to secure formal authorization of a military deployment before troops would have to be withdrawn. Advocates believed the resolution would stop presidential incursions on congressional war powers and put members of Congress back in charge of decisions involving the use of military force. Instead, every president since the resolution was passed has refused to recognize its constitutionality. These presidents have launched one military initiative after another without securing congressional authorization.

More recently, political scientists have begun to examine subtle ways in which Congress nonetheless influences decisions about war. Although the president makes the case for war, members of Congress are not altogether silent. During the first three years of the Iraq War, for instance, members gave 5,000 speeches on the floors

The War Powers Resolution (WPR)
A Brief History of Presidential Actions

Oct. 24, 1973

President Nixon vetoes the WPR, but Congress overrides the veto, and it passes on November 7.

May 13–15, 1975, Cambodia

President Ford orders the U.S. military to rescue U.S. cargo ship SS *Mayaguez*, which had been seized by Cambodian forces on May 12. President Ford reports to Congress about the rescue operation on May 15, per section 4(a)(1) of the WPR—the only time a President has officially started the WPR clock; withdrawal has already commenced by the time of the report.

July 6, 1982, Lebanon

President Reagan publicly announces plans to take military action in Lebanon and commences discussions with congressional leaders (although a media leak indicates the president had approved U.S. military action in Lebanon on July 2).

Aug. 24, 1982, Lebanon

President Reagan reports to Congress about the dispatch of 800 marines to Lebanon; forces start to land in Lebanon on Aug. 25.

Aug. 30, 1983, Lebanon

President Reagan reports to Congress that US Marines in Lebanon had been fired upon since Aug. 28, with casualties sustained on Aug. 29.

Sep. 29, 1983, Lebanon

Congress passed the Multinational Force in Lebanon Resolution authorizing forces to remain in Lebanon for 18 months and determines that the WPR clock in section 4(a) started on Aug. 29, 1983—the only time that Congress has officially started the WPR clock.

Oct. 12, 1983, Lebanon

President Reagan signs the Multinational Force in Lebanon Resolution into law. On March 30, 1984, he reports to Congress that U.S. military involvement in Lebanon has ended.

Oct. 25, 1983, Grenada

President Reagan reports to Congress that he has ordered a military invasion of Grenada on Oct. 24, which commences on Oct. 25.

April 13, 1993, Bosnia

President Clinton reports to Congress regarding fighter aircraft enforcing a no-fly zone over Bosnia-Herzegovina as of April 12—Congress attempts but fails to authorize or prohibit military action in Bosnia between 1993 and 1998.

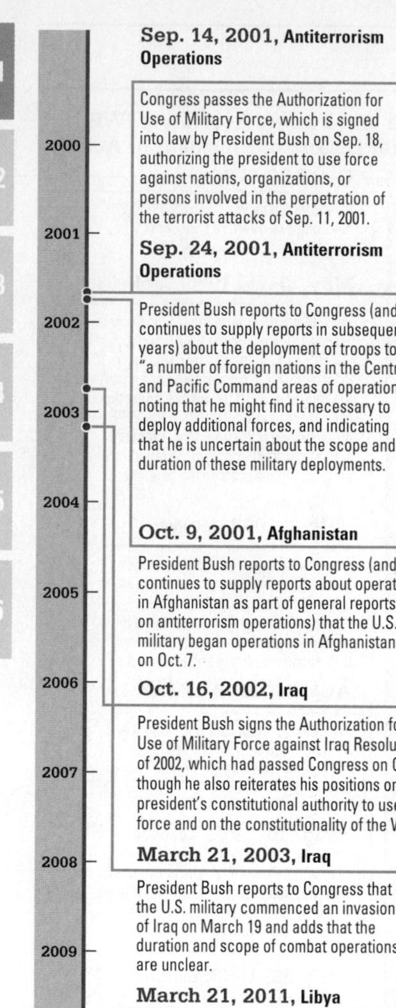

of the House and Senate. Such speeches, political scientists have shown, can have a profound impact on the ways in which the media cover a war, influencing the tone and content of news stories. By influencing the media, these speeches can also affect public opinion. And, over time, changes in public opinion can yield new governing majorities.[a]

Recent research also demonstrates that the partisan composition of Congress has important implications for the president's ability to wage war. Political scientists have observed the following patterns in military deployments following World War II: Presidents whose party holds a large number of seats in the House and Senate tend to wage war more often than those whose party holds relatively few seats, and presidents who enjoy lots of support within Congress tend to take military action more quickly.[b] The checks that Congress places on the president, then, are not constant. Rather, they vary according to the level of support that the president has.

Sep. 14, 2001, Antiterrorism Operations
Congress passes the Authorization for Use of Military Force, which is signed into law by President Bush on Sep. 18, authorizing the president to use force against nations, organizations, or persons involved in the perpetration of the terrorist attacks of Sep. 11, 2001.
Sep. 24, 2001, Antiterrorism Operations
President Bush reports to Congress (and continues to supply reports in subsequent years) about the deployment of troops to "a number of foreign nations in the Central and Pacific Command areas of operations," noting that he might find it necessary to deploy additional forces, and indicating that he is uncertain about the scope and duration of these military deployments.
Oct. 9, 2001, Afghanistan
President Bush reports to Congress (and continues to supply reports about operations in Afghanistan as part of general reports on antiterrorism operations) that the U.S. military began operations in Afghanistan on Oct. 7.
Oct. 16, 2002, Iraq
President Bush signs the Authorization for Use of Military Force against Iraq Resolution of 2002, which had passed Congress on Oct. 11, though he also reiterates his positions on the president's constitutional authority to use force and on the constitutionality of the WPR.
March 21, 2003, Iraq
President Bush reports to Congress that the U.S. military commenced an invasion of Iraq on March 19 and adds that the duration and scope of combat operations are unclear.
March 21, 2011, Libya
President Obama reports to Congress about the commencement of U.S. military operations and air strikes in Libya from March 19, adding that "these strikes will be limited in their nature, duration and scope."
2000
2001
2002
2003
2004
2005
2006
2007
2008
2009
2010
2011

The Bottom Line

The president's power to make decisions involving war has expanded dramatically during the past half-century, and congressional involvement in decisions involving war has declined. Congress, however, still represents an important check—arguably the most important check, at least domestically—on presidential war powers.

Thinking Critically

1. Has the emergent threat of terrorism made it more or less difficult for Congress to influence national decisions about the U.S. military?
2. What sort of evidence might demonstrate whether the work of individual members of Congress has influenced the content of U.S. foreign policy?

[a]Louis Fisher, *Congressional Abdication on War and Spending* (College Station: Texas A&M University Press, 2000), 65.
[b]William Howell and Douglas Kriner, "Political Elites and Public Support for War," University of Chicago typescript, 2007.

concerned with whether proposed legislation is consistent with long-standing principles of equality and individualism. Senators also reflect on the pros and cons of legislation for longer periods of time. "The use of the Senate," wrote James Madison in *Notes of Debates in the Federal Convention of 1787*, "is to consist in its proceedings with more coolness, with more system and with more wisdom, than the popular branch."[13] By "the popular branch," of course, Madison was referring to the House.

Congress is not the only bicameral legislature around. In fact, 49 of the country's 50 state governments have legislatures with two chambers. (The one exception is Nebraska.) Most large democracies around the globe also have bicameral legislatures, which go by many names. India's parliament, for instance, consists of the Lok Sabha (House of the People) and the Rajya Sabha (Council of States). Japan's parliament, which is called the Diet, contains the House of Representatives and the House of Councillors. Switzerland's Federal Assembly contains the National Council and the Council of States.

To be sure, the U.S. Congress distinguishes itself from other bicameral legislatures in important ways. For instance, the upper chamber of Congress (the Senate) is composed of elected representatives, whereas the members of the upper chambers of many European legislatures are appointed. Important similarities, nonetheless, persist. In most countries with bicameral legislatures, the lower chamber tends to have more individuals who represent smaller constituencies and who serve for shorter intervals, whereas the upper chamber tends to have fewer individuals who represent larger constituencies and who serve for longer intervals. The main reason for designing legislatures in this way is to promote competing notions of representation, the topic to which we now turn.

Principles and Dilemmas of Representation

13.2 Analyze the relationship of members of Congress to their constituencies, and distinguish between the trustee and delegate models of representation.

By design, the two chambers of Congress represent the people like no other branch of government. The federal judiciary is not elected—all judges are appointed. The executive branch sponsors just one election (for president and vice president) every four years—and because they can serve only two terms, presidents usually run for reelection at most once. Everyone else in the executive branch is either appointed or a civil servant. Congress, meanwhile, sponsors hundreds of elections. The public has more opportunities to evaluate members of Congress than any other group of politicians in the federal government. It should come as little surprise, then, that members of Congress are always focused on the next election.

constituents
the people who reside within an elected official's political jurisdiction.

Members of Congress Share One Objective: Getting Reelected

Members of Congress are a diverse bunch, coming from all walks of life. But they have one thing in common. As David Mayhew, a political scientist who wrote one of the most influential books on Congress, writes, members are "single-minded seekers of reelection."[14] Every vote they cast, speech they write, argument they advance, favor they offer, and bill they sponsor happen with an eye toward the next election—and the one after that, and the one after that.

Of course, members of Congress have other objectives as well. Some want to make a difference by reforming health care or pushing for prayer in public schools or cracking down on illegal immigration. Others want to direct government benefits to a particular population, such as college students, the poor, African Americans, or farmers. Others want to make names for themselves, and still others just enjoy sitting in a position of power. The mix of policy and personal objectives in Congress is as varied as the members.

To attain their individual goals, though, members must first win a seat and then hold onto it. In 2010 alone, in terms of spending, the top 10 interest groups contributed between $20 million and $132 million each to the reelection campaigns of representatives.[15] Hence, the motivation to be reelected precedes all other motivations. As Mayhew notes, reelection "has to be the proximate goal of everyone, the goal that must be achieved over and over if other ends are to be entertained."[16]

To Improve Their Reelection Prospects, Members Serve Their Constituents

Chapter 9 discussed the elections that determine who serves in Congress. In this chapter, we focus on what members of Congress actually do while they are in office in order to maximize their chances of winning the next election. More than anything else, successful members work hard on behalf of their **constituents**—that is, the individuals who reside within their political jurisdictions. To convince these people to vote for them, members generally support legislation that is popular in their home states or districts. Thus, members from the Midwest stand up for farm subsidies, members from Michigan advance the interests of autoworkers, and representatives in Florida attend to the elderly. For each, their political lives depend upon the voting habits of these populations.

13.1
13.2
13.3
13.4
13.5
13.6

incumbent
the individual in an election who currently holds the contested office; as distinct from the challenger, who seeks to remove the incumbent from power.

Political scientists have shown that members' electoral fortunes critically depend on how well they represent their constituents. Members who represent liberal populations but who support conservative bills, and vice versa, are more likely to lose the next election than members who faithfully represent the interests of their constituents. The basic lesson: "out of step, out of office."[17]

Although political scientists have documented a clear link between the preferences of voters and the actions of members of Congress, the exact nature of this link is less clear. It may be that individuals who share the policy objectives of most people in their districts or states are more likely to run for office; for the same reason, when they run, they are more likely to win. On the other hand, members may adjust their views according to the opinions of those citizens who will shortly decide their political fate.

It stands to reason that **incumbents**—individuals who currently hold office—have more freedom to do as they please. It turns out that, on average, 90 percent of Congress members are reelected, and they are usually reelected by large margins. In 2012, 86 percent of incumbents in the House and 84 percent of incumbents in the Senate were reelected. Incumbents who are confident of reelection might feel less bound by their constituents' views. We need to be careful, however, about the causal interpretations we draw from incumbent reelection rates. After all, does the fact that voters overwhelmingly approve of their representatives free them to do as they please, or are representatives reelected because they reflect the voters' views? If the latter is true, then members do not have that much freedom. When they disagree with large portions of their constituents, members may well face a tough challenge at the next election.

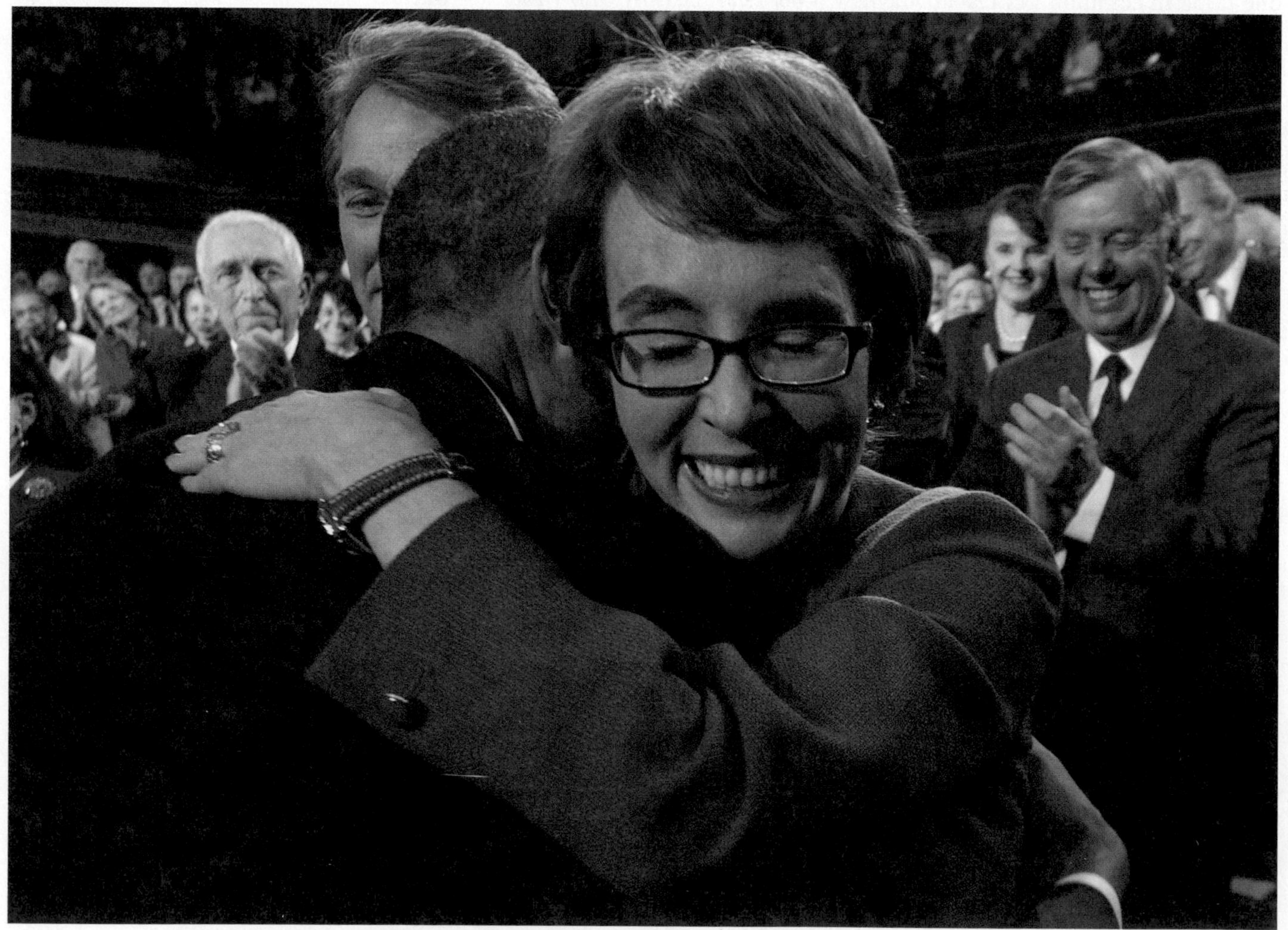

WHEN NO LONGER ABLE TO SERVE

Before his 2012 State of the Union Speech before Congress, President Barack Obama embraced retiring Representative Gabrielle Giffords, who was recovering from gun shot wounds from an attack that killed six people the previous year. At the time of the attack, Giffords was meeting with constituents about their concerns in Arizona.

Beyond the positions they take on the issues of the day, members of Congress also serve their constituents through **casework**—direct assistance to individuals and groups within a district or state. The staffs that work for members of Congress will help constituents locate missing Social Security checks, direct constituents to federal agencies, and provide procedural support for dealing with these agencies, among other services. Obviously, members of Congress cannot address the individual needs of every constituent. In the House, after all, members serve hundreds of thousands of voters; most senators represent many more. Still, by performing casework for at least some of these constituents, members can hope to secure their votes (as well as those of their friends and families) at the next election.

To enhance their reelection prospects, members of Congress also direct federal benefits to their home districts and states. When new legislation is being considered that is intended to clean up the nation's streams, reduce poverty, or provide health insurance to children, members of Congress work hard to ensure that their own constituents reap the benefits of these initiatives. And as we saw at this chapter's outset, this also applies to legislation designed to combat terrorism. Rather than building a comprehensive program that devotes resources to cities in direct proportion to the threat of terrorism, members of Congress built one that ensured every district and state received a sizable chunk of the federal government's funds.

casework
the direct assistance that members of Congress give to individuals and groups within a district or state.

delegate model of representation
the type of representation by which representatives are elected to do the bidding of the people who elected them; representatives are "delegates" in that they share the same policy positions as the voters and promise to act upon them.

trustee model of representation
the type of representation by which representatives are elected to do what they think is best for their constituents.

To Serve Their Constituents, Members of Congress May Act as Delegates or Trustees

The structural differences between the House and Senate reflect two broader conceptions of representation. According to the **delegate model of representation**, successful members of Congress share the same policy interests as the voters and promise to act upon them. If a majority of constituents support affirmative action, then so will the member of Congress; if a majority subsequently opposes the same policy, that member will switch his or her position. Delegates must vote according to the expressed interests of their constituents even when their conscience or personal preferences dictate otherwise.

In contrast, according to the **trustee model of representation**, members of Congress are chosen for their judgment, experience, and skill to do what they think is best for their constituents. As Edmund Burke, an eighteenth-century Irish philosopher and member of England's Parliament, put it, voters ought to choose a legislator for "his unbiased opinion, his mature judgment, his enlightened conscience."[18] Rather than simply mirroring their constituents' opinions, trustees reflect deeply on the arguments for and against different policies before taking a position. They still represent their constituents, but they do so by thinking about the longer-term implications that policies have both for their constituents and for the nation as a whole.

Roughly speaking, members of the House tend to act more like delegates, and members of the Senate behave more like trustees. They do so because of the electoral incentives they face. Because members of the House face more homogenous constituents at more regular intervals, they have stronger incentives to act on behalf of their public's current preferences. But senators, because they face more heterogeneous constituents over longer periods of time, can reflect on the deeper interests of a citizenry.

Not All Constituents Are Represented Equally Well

Although all members have powerful incentives to represent their constituents, not all constituents are represented equally well. Instead, constituent groups that are likely to have a greater impact on a member's reelection bid tend to receive greater consideration on Capitol Hill.

IN POLITICS, NOT EVERYONE IS REPRESENTED WELL

Members of Congress tend not to represent the interests of people who do not, or cannot, vote. Caught in the juvenile justice system, these youths cannot vote and have significantly fewer opportunities to put political pressure on members of Congress. In your view, should individuals who are incarcerated have the right to vote?

Some constituents are less important because they cannot vote and therefore have fewer opportunities to influence the outcome of an election. Consider, for instance, the differences between the elderly and children. Older Americans tend to monitor the behavior of members of Congress quite closely and to vote in high numbers. Children, by contrast, pay little attention to politics. And even if they wanted to, children could not vote until they officially become adults at age 18. Thus, it is not surprising that members of Congress tend to work harder on behalf of the elderly than they do on behalf of children. For every federal dollar spent to reduce poverty and poor health among children, four dollars are spent to accomplish the same objectives among the elderly.[19]

The citizens who organize, fund, and participate in interest groups also figure prominently in members' reelection strategies.[20] Through financial contributions and endorsements, interest groups can influence both the number of people who come out on Election Day and the candidates they choose. In 1998, lobbyists spent $1.4 billion in their efforts to court members of Congress. A decade later, as shown in Figure 13.1, that number jumped to $3.5 billion. During this period, the number of congressional lobbyists also increased by roughly 30 percent.[21]

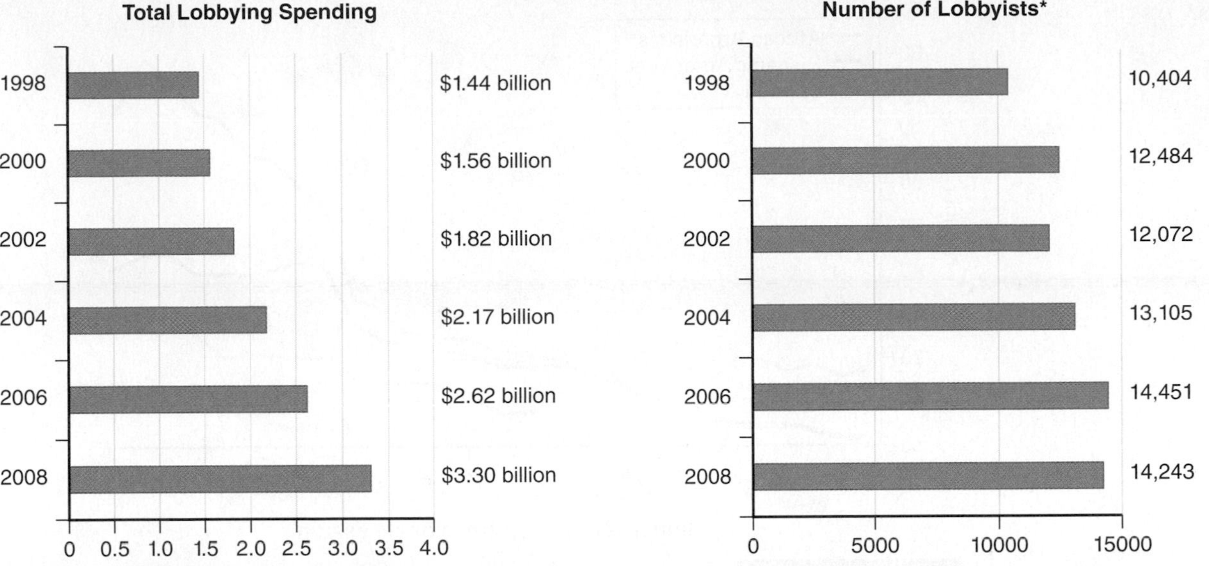

FIGURE 13.1 INCREASE IN CONGRESSIONAL LOBBYING AND LOBBYISTS.

In any given year, thousands of lobbyists, backed by billions of dollars, descend upon Capitol Hill. And there are few signs of their abatement. Over the past decade, the number of lobbyists has increased by 30 percent, and the total amount of money spent on lobbying has nearly tripled.

*The number of unique, registered lobbyists who actively lobbied during the indicated years.

NOTE: Figures in this figure are calculations by the Center for Responsive Politics based on data from the Senate Office of Public Records.

SOURCE: Reprinted by permission of Center for Responsive Politics—from http://www.opensecrets.org.

With the upsurge in interest group activity, members of Congress have stronger incentives to act on their behalf. Sometimes members do so by voting in ways that support these groups. More often, though, the influence of interest groups is subtler, affecting which bills Congress considers, the amendments that are made to these bills, and the speed at which members deliberate.[22] Members of Congress also have strong incentives to listen to their core supporters and those who can be persuaded to vote on their behalf. By contrast, members have less incentive to work on behalf of those individuals who would not, under any circumstances, vote for them. Consequentially, a Republican would likely support different policy proposals than a Democrat who came from the same district two years earlier, despite the fact that they both technically represented the same people.[23] The Republican representative will tend to support policies that help the district's Republican citizens, and the Democratic representative will generally try to help the district's Democratic citizens. For example, when the Republican Party secured a majority of seats in Congress after the 1994 election, Republican members, many of whom had just won seats held by Democrats, worked to increase federal insurance and loan program funding, a type of government benefit that helps the farmers, entrepreneurs, and small businesses that form a core constituency of the Republican Party.[24]

Political scientists have also examined the ways in which people of different genders, races, ethnicities, and incomes are represented by members of Congress. Some argue that citizens are best represented by members who have much in common with them: Women are best represented by women members, African Americans by African American members, and so forth.[25] And there is something to this claim. Female members, for example, are more likely than male members to sponsor laws concerning reproductive rights, women's health, and domestic violence.[26]

If the findings from these studies apply more generally, then recent Congresses should be doing a better job than past ones of representing the full spectrum of interests around the country. As Figure 13.2 shows, members of Congress are reasonably

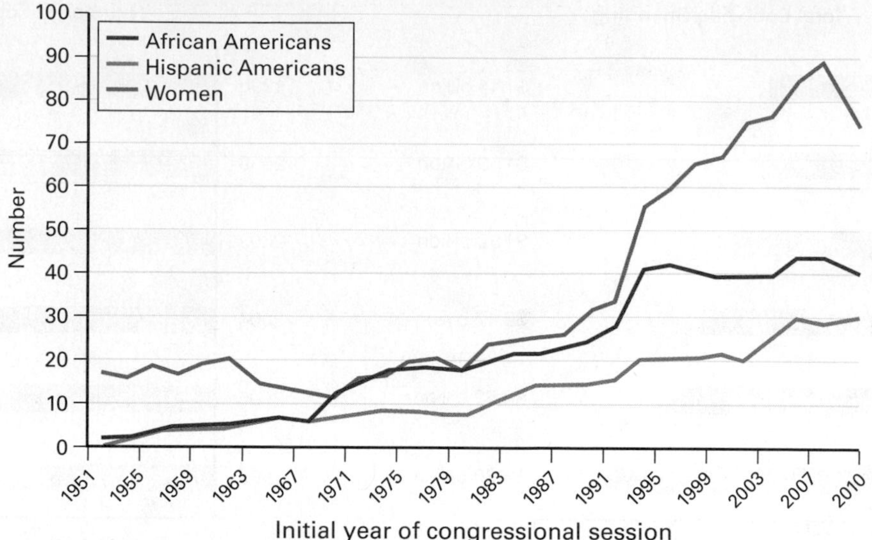

FIGURE 13.2 AFRICAN AMERICANS, WOMEN, AND HISPANIC AMERICANS IN CONGRESS, 1951–2010.

In 1951, just 2 African Americans, 3 Hispanics, and 11 women served in Congress. Two decades later, 11 African Americans, 6 Hispanics, and 11 women were serving. By 2010, there were 43 African Americans, 30 Hispanics, and 91 women in the House and Senate.

NOTE: Numbers include delegates, such as those from Washington, D.C., who do not have formal voting rights.

SOURCE: Mildred L. Amer, Congressional Research Service Report for Congress, *Membership of the 109th Congress: A CRS Profile,* May 31, 2006. Mildred L. Amer. CRS Report for Congress: Black Members of the United States Congress, 1870–2007. Washington, DC: Congressional Research Service; Carmen E. Enciso, 1995. Hispanic Americans in Congress, 1822–1995. Washington, DC: Library of Congress. Updated information, through 2011, is available at http://www.loc.gov/rr/hispanic/congress/chron.html. Accessed April 12, 2012.

diverse and are getting more so over time. The 112th Congress had a total of 91 women. Seventeen of these women served in the Senate, and 74 served in the House of Representatives.

redistricting
the drawing of boundaries around legislative districts, generally every 10 years after the U.S. Census; each district elects one legislator.

gerrymandering
the majority party in Congress draws lines around districts in such a way as to maximize the number of seats that party will win; this process often produces districts with contorted boundaries.

Redistricting Can Be Used to Empower Certain Constituent Groups

Congressional constituencies are not static. They change over time, most commonly because of redistricting. **Redistricting** refers to the drawing of boundaries around legislative districts, each of which elects one representative.[27] In 1964, the Supreme Court, in two famous decisions, concluded that democracy hinges on the principle of "one person, one vote," meaning that every citizen has one vote, each voter is equally powerful in selecting legislators, and each voter is equally represented in the legislature.[28] If one district had 1,000 potential voters and another had 600,000, the power of each voter in selecting a representative in the first district would be 600 times greater than in the second. Such unequally sized districts, which were common around the country, violated constitutional norms of equality that were fundamental to the American democratic process.

The Court's one person, one vote principle provides no explicit guidance about how to draw the lines that separate districts. Every 10 years, after the U.S. Census, therefore, states redraw their district lines to ensure that populations are approximately equal in House districts (if the state has more than one representative in the U.S. House) and in state legislative districts. Thus every decade after the U.S. Census finishes, bitter battles ensue to draw up district lines. In most states, the job falls to the legislature. And, most often, the pattern is predictable.

First, lines are drawn in a way to protect incumbents of both major parties. Then, the majority party seeks to draw lines around remaining districts in such a way as to maximize the number of seats the party will win. This process, known as **gerrymandering,** often produces districts with contorted boundaries. And last, the minority party might file suit against the new district lines, usually to no avail.

Unresolved Debate

Do Majority-Minority Districts Improve Minority Representation in Congress?

Since the passage of the Voting Rights Act in 1965, minorities in the United States have been legally entitled to equal representation at all levels of government. The defining characteristics of minority representation, however, remain a subject of much dispute. Civil rights leaders in the 1980s and 1990s began advocating for redistricting maps to be drawn in such a way as to create majority-minority voting districts. Such districts, their proponents argue, make it far more likely that minority representatives will be elected to Congress, thereby ensuring that the minority's interests are represented. But do majority-minority districts actually improve minority representation in Congress?

THE PRESIDENT MEETS WITH THE HISPANIC CAUCUS
In the summer of 2008, then-Democratic Presidential Nominee Barack Obama met with members of the Congressional Hispanic Caucus to strategize on how best to strengthen party unity in the upcoming general election.

YES

Political scientist David Lublin has disputed the findings presented by Cameron and his coauthors.[a] Lublin concedes that there is a trade-off between electing minority representatives and achieving minority legislative priorities by electing Democratic members of Congress more generally. According to Lublin, however, Cameron, Epstein, and O'Halloran neglect to include the presence of Latino voters in certain districts. When Latinos are included in the analysis, he finds that African American members of Congress are almost never elected from majority white districts. Rather, almost all of them are elected from districts with minorities (African Americans and *Latinos) in the majority. Moreover, Lublin is more sympathetic to the idea that a robust minority representation requires there to be actual minority representatives in Congress, as opposed to merely Democratic representatives with minority-favored legislative preferences.[b]*

- Although eight of the African American members of Congress studied by Cameron and his coauthors come from districts in which African Americans are the minority, seven represent districts in which African Americans and Latinos taken together constitute more than 55 percent of the population.
- Although minority populations may combine African American and Latino voters, the only way to ensure that minorities are regularly elected to Congress is to create at least some majority-minority districts.
- The ideal form of minority representation would combine majority-minority districts with a more even allocation of minorities across neighboring districts, thereby, ensuring the election of a greater number of Democrats sympathetic to minority policy preferences.

NO

According to political scientists Charles Cameron, David Epstein, and Sharyn O'Halloran, creating majority-minority districts actually has a negative effect on minority representation overall.[c] By taking a large group of minority voters from several districts and placing them all in a single district, they argue, redistricting efforts aimed at creating majority-minority districts make the surrounding districts less supportive of minority candidates and causes.[d] Cameron, Epstein and O'Halloran use statistical techniques to identify the percentage of African American voters that is needed to enable minority candidates to be elected in different districts around the country. In addition, the authors examine the advantages to African Americans, who are overwhelmingly Democratic, of electing an African American Democrat rather than a white one.

- In order to achieve a 50 percent chance of an African American black candidate being elected, a district in the South must be 40.3 percent African American; a district in the Northwest must be 47.3 percent African American; and a district in the Northeast need be only 28.3 percent African American.
- On legislative bills of particular relevance to minorities and minority rights, there is not a significant difference between how African American members of Congress vote and how a typical Democratic member votes.
- Therefore, although it may be beneficial to have a higher concentration of African Americans in certain southern districts, in general African American interests are best represented when African American voters are spread out across districts, where they can elect a greater number of Democratic members of Congress overall.

CONTRIBUTING TO THE DEBATE

At its heart, this debate rests on a disputed notion of what constitutes "representation." In one camp are those who believe that representation should be viewed purely in substantive terms. They argue that minorities should be concerned only with achieving their preferred policy outcomes—the actual race or ethnicity of a specific Congress member is not important. In the other camp are those who believe primarily in descriptive representation, who assert that minorities are best represented by members of Congress from their own racial or ethnic group, and that Congress as a whole ought to accurately reflect the diversity of America's population.

As a thought experiment, imagine a Congress in which a large majority of representatives are all white Democrats sympathetic to minority issues. Would such an elective body accurately "represent" minority voters in America? On the other side of the issue, it is worth considering where the line is drawn when it comes to descriptive representation. Lublin, for example, lumps African American and Latino voters together under a single "minority" banner. Historically, however, African American and Latino voters have not always had the same legislative preferences, especially on some hot-button issues such as immigration. Does an African American member of Congress necessarily "represent" a Latino voter better than a white representative does? The answer is unclear.

WHAT DO YOU THINK?

1. What is the trade-off between electing minority representatives and achieving minority-favored policy outcomes?
2. Should Republican politicians support majority-minority districts? Why or why not?

[a]David Lublin, "Racial Redistricting and African-American Representation: A Critique of 'Do Majority-Minority Districts Maximize Substantive Black Representation in Congress?" *American Political Science Review*, 93, 1 (1999), 183–86; see also David Lublin, *The Paradox of Representation: Racial Gerrymandering and Minority Interests in Congress* (Princeton, NJ: Princeton University Press, 1999).

[b]Ibid., 183.

[c]Charles Cameron, David Epstein and Sharyn O'Halloran, "Do Majority-Minority Districts Maximize Substantive Black Representation in Congress?" *American Political Science Review*, 90, 4 (1996), 794–812.

[d]Ibid., 810.

---

majority-minority voting districts
legislative districts in which district boundaries are drawn in a manner to ensure that a majority of the district residents are members of minority groups, intended to increase the probability of minorities being elected.

In a split decision in 2004, the U.S. Supreme Court declined to intervene in a case involving partisan bias in congressional redistricting in Pennsylvania. The Court concluded it had no clear standard to apply to determine how much partisan bias is "too much" and is contrary to democratic principles and equality. But it did not rule out the possibility that it might determine such a standard in the future.[29]

The most widely publicized dispute in recent years over district lines occurred in Texas. Following the 2000 census, the Texas legislature, with one house controlled by each party, was unable to agree on a new districting plan and, under state law, the districting process went before a panel of federal judges. The judges drew new lines that kept in place a Democratic majority in the Texas delegation to the U.S. House. In the 2002 Texas state legislative elections, however, Republicans gained control of the legislature and in 2003 passed a new district map much more favorable to Republican candidates. Predictably, in the 2004 U.S. House election, the Republicans won 21 seats, compared to 15 in 2002.

Challenges to the new Texas district lines landed in the U.S. Supreme Court in 2006.[30] Democrats charged there was no lawful reason to change the lines that had just been established in 2001. The mid-decade redrawing, the suit argued, was done solely for partisan advantage. Rather than treating individuals equally under the law, the suit alleged, the redistricting targeted and discriminated against Democratic voters for their political viewpoints. Moreover, minority groups claimed that the Texas legislature illegally sought to distribute Hispanic and black voters across districts in order to decrease the likelihood of electing Democrats to the House. In 2006, the Court concluded that the critics of the plan had not established that the partisan rearrangement was inherently unequal or undemocratic, but it did strike down one district for unconstitutionally weakening minority voting power.

Beginning in the 1980s, civil rights leaders began pushing state legislatures to draw redistricting maps in such a way as to create **majority-minority voting districts.**

In a majority-minority district, a constituency that is a minority of the overall population, such as blacks, makes up a majority of the voters in the designated jurisdiction. However, the Supreme Court has frowned on using race as a primary factor in drawing district lines since the late 1980s, including deliberate attempts to weaken the voting clout of minority groups (see *Unresolved Debate: Do Majority-Minority Districts Improve Minority Representation in Congress?*).

How Members Make Group Decisions

13.3 Assess the challenges that emerge when members of Congress set about working together.

embers of Congress do not work alone. To do so, in fact, would be foolhardy. Bills that rally the support of just a handful of other members are unlikely to impress most voters. To stand with confidence before their constituents, members of Congress must find ways to work together. For a variety of reasons, however, working together can be immensely challenging.

Members of Congress Often Disagree with One Another

Members of Congress hail from different regions of the country. They have wildly different views about the purposes of government. They represent different genders and ethnicities. They even follow different electoral calendars. To understand how Congress functions, it is vital to recognize the diversity of its membership.

Members' differing views reflect in part the districts they serve. Members serving districts in northern California, Massachusetts, New York City, and Chicago are reliably much more liberal than are members serving districts in eastern Oklahoma, Utah, Orange County in southern California, and Dallas. The set of issues on which Barbara Boxer (a Democratic senator from California) and Jim DeMint (a Republican senator from South Carolina) agree is small indeed. But even senators representing the same state often disagree about public policy. In the 112th Congress, 19 states had senators from different parties. Members who represent the same state and come from the same party regularly disagree about all sorts of issues. For example, Lindsey Graham and Jim DeMint, both Republican senators from South Carolina, differ on issues ranging from immigration to the maintenance of the Guantanamo Bay detention facility.

Even members who share a common ideological orientation may disagree about what constitutes the most pressing issue of the day. For example, Phil Roe and Don Young are conservative Republican congressmen. Roe, though, represents the first district in Tennessee, whereas Young represents the entire state of Alaska.[31] For Roe, the key issues include spurring economic growth in rural communities, maintaining the support of the Tennessee Valley Authority (one of the nation's largest government corporations) and tobacco farmers, and calling greater national attention to Great Smoky Mountains National Park. For Young, the protection of the Tongass National Forest, the protection of citizens' rights to bear arms, the regulation of the fishing industry, and the right to drill for oil in the Arctic National Wildlife Refuge stand out as the most important issues. Disagreements between Roe and Young have considerably less to do with their political outlooks or party affiliations. Rather, they concern the importance of local issues and the legislative priorities of Congress.

There are even differences in members' concerns about reelection—the core issue that supposedly unites them. As previously mentioned, some members come from less competitive states and districts, whereas others expect to face stiffer competition at the next election. In addition, members of Congress come up for reelection at different times. Every two years, all House members must face the electorate. Senators, however, serve six-year, staggered terms, with one-third up for election in each election year. Senators from the same state never come up for reelection in the same year, which means that every other year, one-third of the Senate's members are distracted by an election, whereas the other two-thirds can afford to focus on the obligations of governance. House members, by contrast, follow the same electoral calendar and therefore find it easier to coordinate their activities with one another.

☐ Members of Congress Confront Basic Challenges

Although all members of Congress care greatly about their reelection prospects, the factors that help one member get reelected are not the same as those that help another. Members must find ways of sorting through their differences in order to satisfy their different constituents and thereby retain their seats. Unfortunately, members of Congress—like members of any collective decision-making body—confront a set of problems that makes it difficult to work together.

COLLECTING INFORMATION Imagine the challenges facing members of Congress each session. They must keep track of changes in everything from the domestic economy to crime to international trade to transportation networks to wars around the world. Having canvassed all of these and many more policy domains, members then must identify the biggest problems facing the country and the best solutions. To do this, they need information—and lots of it.

Take, for example, the minimum wage. This would appear to be a simple issue, requiring members only to figure out whether they think it ought to be increased or decreased. Minimum wage legislation, however, consists of much more than a single line identifying the lowest hourly wage that employers can pay their workers around the nation. It is filled with exemptions and qualifications.[32] To complete the

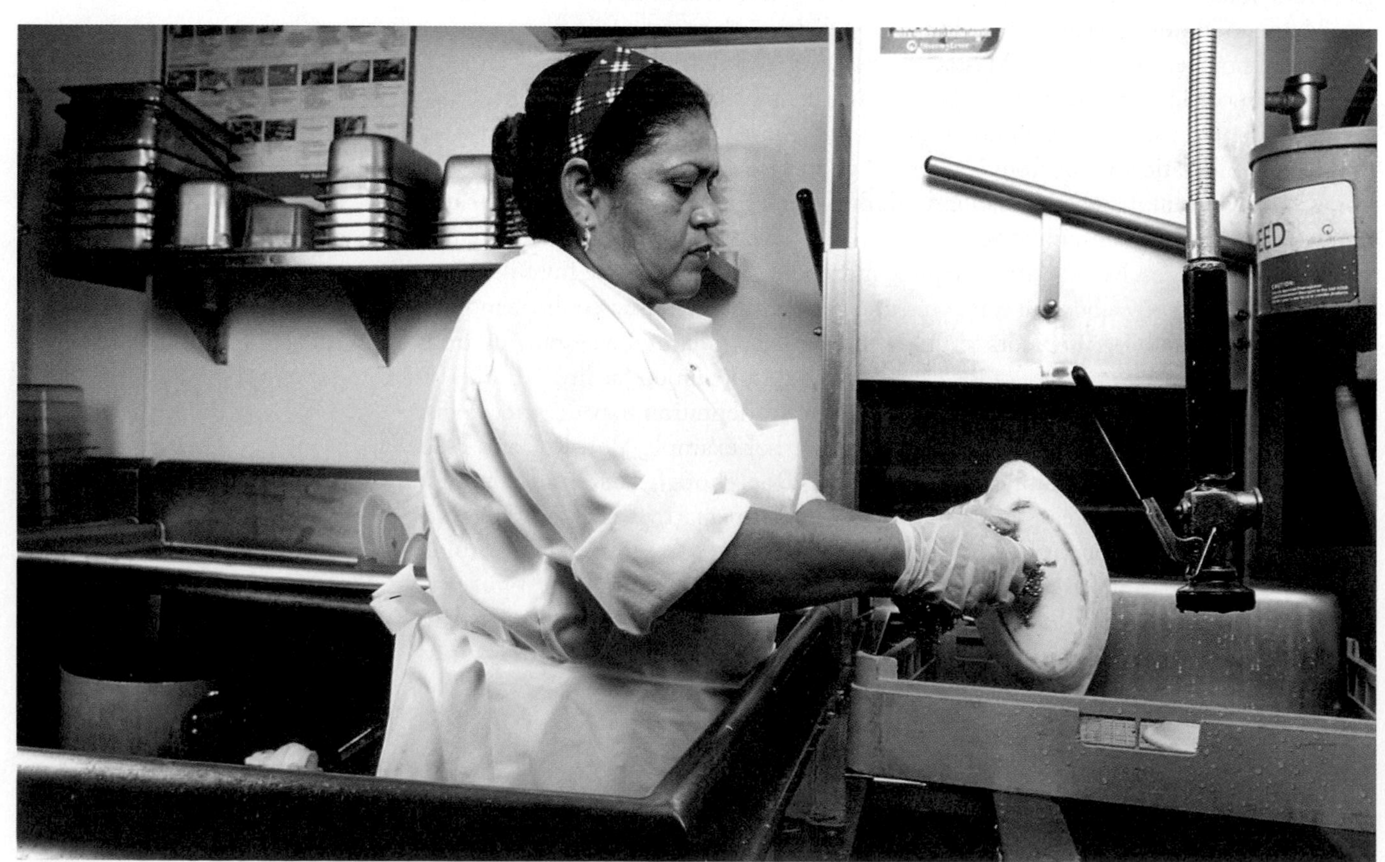

SETTING A MINIMUM WAGE

For many, minimum wage legislation strictly defines the hourly earnings they can expect to receive. The legislation itself, though, is extraordinarily complex, requiring members of Congress to develop and analyze lots of information about different industries.

legislation, members must address all kinds of questions: Should there be a different minimum for teenagers and for adults? What about for those who rely on tips for much of their earnings? What about for noncitizens? Should the government provide financial assistance to industries, such as hotels and restaurants, which rely on large numbers of low-wage workers? If so, then how much and for how long? Should new rates take effect immediately or be phased in? What kinds of penalties should apply to employers who fail to pay at least a minimum wage? Should the rate depend on the cost of living? If so, how should it be calculated and how often should it be updated?

collective action problem
a problem that arises when individuals' incentives lead them to avoid taking actions that are best for the group as a whole, and that they themselves would like to see accomplished.

Lawmakers must consider myriad issues when they do something seemingly as simple as changing the minimum wage. Imagine, then, the challenges of writing laws that address U.S. trade relations with China, immigration reform with Mexico, or urban redevelopment. Individually, members of Congress would appear ill equipped for the challenge. Although they may have some expertise in a handful of issues—typically ones that directly concern their constituents—members often know very little about most substantive issues they must confront. They must first collect the information they need to write the nation's laws.[33]

Having collected the relevant information, lawmakers find that the legislative process has just begun. To enact legislation, members must convince one another about the benefits of their preferred policies. They must bargain and negotiate with one another. To do this effectively, members need to learn about one another's preferences, which we now know can differ dramatically. Members need to anticipate what others will accept, what they will reject, and what they are willing to compromise over. Lacking this additional information, members of Congress would find it virtually impossible to legislate.

ACTING COLLECTIVELY It takes time and money to collect the information needed to write laws and evaluate how they will affect districts, states, and the nation at large. Because members of Congress have a relatively short period of time to build a record of accomplishments, they must decide how to allot their scarce resources. Not surprisingly, some would prefer to let other members commit the resources and then take undeserved credit for the solutions.

Even though the benefits of lawmaking generalize to all members of Congress, the costs do not. Specifically, the costs fall disproportionately on those who devote their own resources to researching an issue, devising possible solutions, and then building the coalitions needed to enact a policy. This, though, creates a basic **collective action problem,** which arises from the mismatch of individual and group incentives. As a group, members of Congress want to devise solutions for the nation's problems; individually, though, members would prefer that others pay the costs of formulating these solutions. And, because every member, individually, would prefer that other members pay these costs, there is a substantial risk of inaction.

A simple example serves to illustrate the point. Picture a common college student housing arrangement: four students, four bedrooms, a shared living area, and a very messy kitchen. Each of the students would prefer that the kitchen be cleaned. If all four students committed to cleaning the kitchen on any given evening, they could complete the job in relatively short order. The trouble is that each one of these students would be even better off if the other three did the work, leaving the fourth free to watch television. Because this basic incentive incompatibility applies to all of the housemates, the dishes just pile higher and higher. The collective benefit of a clean kitchen is never realized because the costs fall on the poor loser who finally gives up and begins scrubbing. Herein lies the tragedy of collective action problems. All four students would be better off if they all chipped in; however, because each one would be even better off reaping the rewards without doing the work, the dishes are never done.

So it is with lawmaking. Collectively, members of Congress would be better off if everyone contributed equally; individually, though, each member would be even better off if everyone else did the work, leaving her or him free to pursue a personal agenda.

Explore on MyPoliSciLab

Can Congress Get Anything Done?

A government cannot operate without a budget, revenue, or appropriations. But over the past thirty years, members of Congress have grown so polarized that they cannot agree on a budget or much of anything else. Polarization occurs when members of both parties move away from the moderate middle and share increasingly less common ground. Since 2001, Congress failed to pass a budget eight times, succeeding only in approving temporary budgets to keep government running. As the parties grow more polarized, Congress is less able to pass a permanent budget and the national debt increases.

Party Polarization

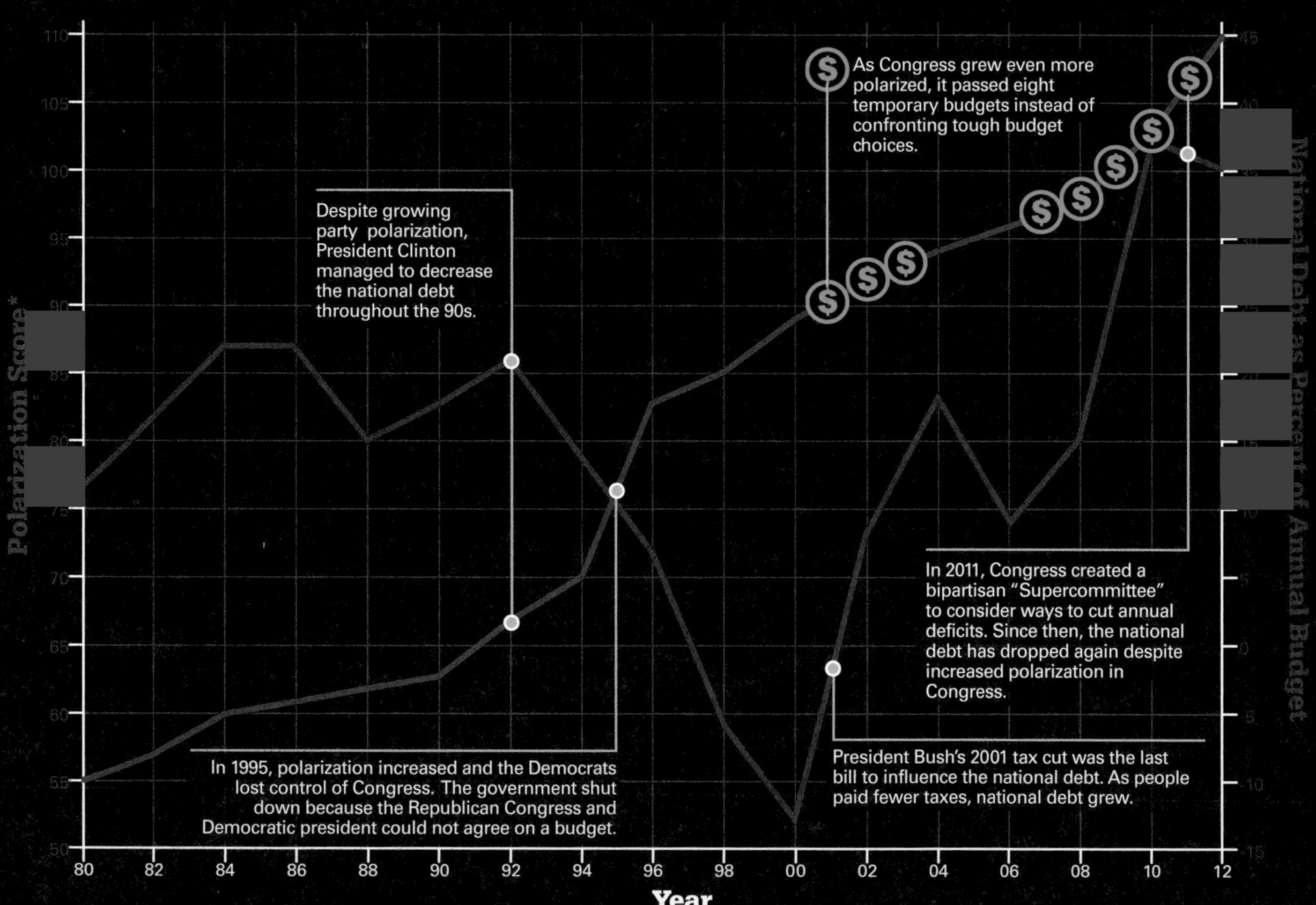

Polarization Score*
National Debt as Percent of Annual Budget
Year
As Congress grew even more polarized, it passed eight temporary budgets instead of confronting tough budget choices.
Despite growing party polarization, President Clinton managed to decrease the national debt throughout the 90s.
In 2011, Congress created a bipartisan "Supercommittee" to consider ways to cut annual deficits. Since then, the national debt has dropped again despite increased polarization in Congress.
In 1995, polarization increased and the Democrats lost control of Congress. The government shut down because the Republican Congress and Democratic president could not agree on a budget.
President Bush's 2001 tax cut was the last bill to influence the national debt. As people paid fewer taxes, national debt grew.

*** Polarization is measured as the distance between the two parties' ideological scores as computed from data at Voteview.com.**
SOURCE: Data from Voteview and the U.S. Government Accountability Office.

Investigate Further

Concept What is political polarization? Polarization occurs when members of both political parties consistently vote along ideological lines. Political scientists track polarization because it has nearly doubled in the past thirty years, and it tends to impede the government's ability to function.

Connection Is polarization related to greater annual debt? On a yearly basis, polarization is largely independent of the debt incurred by the United States—notice, for example, during the Clinton presidency how polarization grew even as debt decreased. However, as a long-term trend, both national debt and polarization in Congress do increase together.

Cause Does polarization impede Congress's ability to create annual budgets? Yes. The more polarized Congress becomes, the more likely the disagreements over permanent budget solutions lead to temporary resolutions that barely stave off government shutdown.

The problem is even more acute than the simple example of a dirty kitchen. Whereas the average dorm houses a handful of students, Congress houses hundreds of members, whose behavior is difficult to monitor. Some may claim to be working on comprehensive tax reform, for example, when they are actually focused on projects that will benefit one or two powerful interests in their districts. Without a clear and effective way of monitoring behavior, it is extremely difficult to overcome collective action problems.[34]

CYCLING Members have very different ideas about what constitutes good public policy. Consequently, they often have a difficult time making final decisions about public policy. A majority of members—that is, a group of at least 50 percent—would prefer some alternative to the existing policy. A second majority—that is, a different group that contains at least some members from the first majority—will then prefer a different alternative to the one first proposed. Yet a third majority will prefer still another alternative to the one proposed second. The result, which political scientists refer to as **cycling,** is that members cannot settle on a single change to existing policy.

In the world of lawmaking, the list of possible policy alternatives is seemingly limitless. And because it is almost always possible to identify another version of a policy that a majority might prefer, debate could go on and on without a decision ever being reached. Members therefore must figure out a way to conclude debates so laws can be written and enacted.

cycling
a phenomenon that occurs when multiple decision makers must decide among multiple options and cannot agree on a single course of action.

standing committee
a permanent committee with a well-defined, relatively fixed policy jurisdiction that develops, writes, and updates important legislation.

select committee
a temporary committee created to serve a specific purpose.

Imposing Structure on Congress

13.4 Identify the resources and the committee and party structures that help Congress address its challenges.

o effectively do their jobs, members of Congress must find ways of collecting information, making sure everyone does her or his part, and resolving differences. When members are left to their own devices, too often they work at cross purposes and fail to satisfy their constituents. Members have devised structural solutions to make Congress in many ways ideally designed to deal with the problems of information, collective action, and cycling.

Committees Establish a Division of Labor

In both the House and Senate, members are assigned to committees that oversee distinct policy areas. These committees draft versions of bills, hold hearings about policy issues, and investigate activities in the executive branch. The names of these committees suggest the policy issues that their members focus on: Agriculture, Nutrition, and Forestry; Armed Services; Environment and Public Works; Foreign Relations; Health, Education, Labor, and Pensions; and Veterans' Affairs, to name but a few in the Senate.

TYPES OF COMMITTEES In the 112th Congress, there were 16 standing committees in the Senate and 20 in the House. **Standing committees** have well-defined policy jurisdictions, which do not change markedly from Congress to Congress. Standing committees are also the real workhorses of Congress, developing, writing, and updating the most important legislation. Table 13.1 lists all the standing committees in the 112th Congress. **Select committees,** by contrast, are designed to address specific issues over shorter periods of time. Typically, they cease to exist once their members have completed their assigned task—or when they no longer have the political support of the majority party. In 2007, for instance, incoming Speaker of the House Nancy Pelosi created the House Select Committee on Energy Independence and Global Warming. Upon retaking the majority in the House in the 2010 midterm elections, however, Republicans immediately disbanded the committee.

TABLE 13.1 STANDING COMMITTEES OF THE 112TH CONGRESS.

Committees divide the labor of lawmaking across members of the House and Senate.

Committee	House of Representatives Subcommittees	Members	Committee	Senate Subcommittees	Members
Agriculture	6	46	Agriculture, Nutrition, and Forestry	5	21
Appropriations	12	50	Appropriations	12	30
Armed Services	7	62	Armed Services	6	26
Budget	0	38	Banking, Housing, and Urban Affairs	5	22
Education and the Workforce	4	40	Budget	0	23
Energy and Commerce	6	54	Commerce, Science, and Transportation	7	25
Ethics	0	10	Energy and Natural Resources	4	22
Financial Services	6	61	Environment and Public Works	7	18
Foreign Affairs	7	46	Finance	6	24
Homeland Security	6	33	Foreign Relations	7	19
House Administration	2	9	Health, Education, Labor, and Pensions	3	22
Judiciary	5	39	Homeland Security and Governmental Affairs	5	17
Natural Resources	5	48	Judiciary	6	18
Oversight and Government Reform	7	40	Rules and Administration	0	18
Rules	2	13	Small Business and Entrepreneurship	0	19
Science, Space, and Technology	5	40	Veterans' Affairs	0	15
Small Business	5	26			
Transportation and Infrastructure	6	59			
Veterans' Affairs	4	26			
Ways and Means	6	37			

joint committee
a committee made up of members of both chambers of Congress to conduct a special investigation or study.

subcommittee
a smaller organizational unit within a committee that specializes in a particular segment of the committee's responsibilities.

Whereas separate standing and select committees operate in the House and Senate, **joint committees** draw members from both chambers. Similar to select committees, joint committees focus on fairly narrow issue areas, but unlike select committees, they are permanent. For example, the Joint Committee on the Library oversees the Library of Congress, and the Joint Committee on Taxation monitors tax policy. Joint committees tend to be weaker than either standing or select committees. Rather than develop bills that either the House or Senate subsequently considers, a process we consider in detail later, joint committees typically act as fact-finding entities. As such, the primary purpose of joint committees is to address Congress's need to collect information.

Committees consist of smaller, and more specialized, **subcommittees.** For example, the U.S. Senate Committee on Banking, Housing, and Urban Affairs has five subcommittees: Economic Policy; Financial Institutions; Housing, Transportation, and Community Development; Securities, Insurance, and Investment; and Security and International Trade and Finance. Subcommittees allow for an even greater division of labor, which encourages the production of still more information. Because of their small size, it is easier to monitor members' behavior within subcommittees, improving the chances that all members do their share of the work.

Legislatures in many other countries are organized much the same way. The organization of Britain's Parliament, in fact, looks quite like Congress. Parliament consists of two chambers, the House of Commons (akin to the House of Representatives) and the House of Lords (akin to the Senate). Within each chamber are a variety of standing and select committees, whose purposes are defined by the types of policy that they write and oversee. Like Congress, Parliament has committees that focus on education, health, foreign affairs, and public works. Parliament also has committees devoted to issues that are particularly important to the United Kingdom, such as the Northern Ireland Affairs Select Committee and the European Union Select Committee. British Parliament has served as a model for the national legislatures of many other countries that, like the United States, were once colonies of Great Britain. India's parliament, for example, also has a variety of standing and ad hoc committees that address unique national issues, such as the Joint Committee on Food Management.

COMMITTEE MEMBERSHIP On average, senators serve on four committees and representatives serve on two. Committee members develop expertise in a handful of policy areas that they can share with their colleagues, who develop expertise in other policy areas. With such a division of labor, Congress as an institution is able to collect more and better information.

Given what we know about members' concerns about reelection, it should not come as a surprise that members of Congress try to serve on committees that oversee policies that their constituents care the most about. Members who have large concentrations of veterans and active military personnel in their districts will often serve on the Veterans' Affairs or Armed Services committees; members from the Midwest who represent farming interests will tend to serve on the Agriculture or Agriculture, Nutrition, and Forestry committees.[35]

Other committees attract members not because of the policies that they oversee, but rather because of the power that they wield. The appropriations committees—Ways and Means in the House and Finance in the Senate—deal with tax and

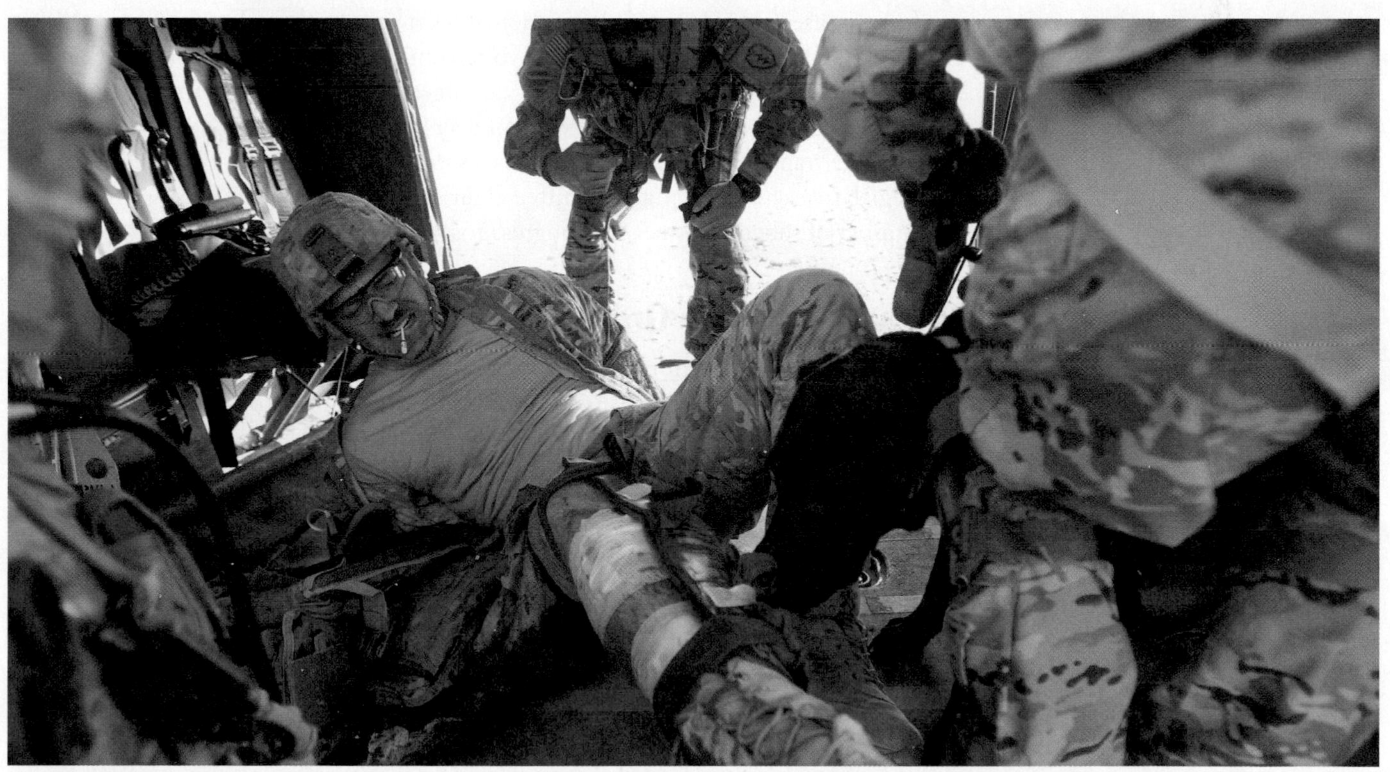

COLLECTING INFORMATION IN HEARINGS
After Colonel Daniel Davis issued a report in early 2012 that accused the President's administration of misleading the American public about the military venture in Afghanistan, members of Congress called for hearings. In a photo taken just months after Davis's report, injured U.S. Army dog handler Aaron Yoder and his dog Bart are shown being evacuated during a fire exchange with Taliban fighters while on a mission in southern Afghanistan.

13.1
13.2
13.3
13.4
13.5
13.6

seniority
the length of time a legislator has served in office.

party caucus
the gathering of all Democratic members of the House or Senate.

party conference
the gathering of all Republican members of the House or Senate.

Speaker of the House
the person who presides over the House and serves as the chamber's official spokesperson.

majority leader
the individual in each chamber who manages the floor; in the Senate, he or she is the most powerful member in the chamber; in the House, he or she is the chief lieutenant of the Speaker.

minority leader
the individual who speaks on behalf of the party that controls the smaller number of seats in each chamber.

spending issues, which concern all sorts of government programs. Similarly, the Energy and Commerce Committee in the House provides members with lots of opportunities to influence a broad array of public policies. Joining these committees gives members prestige and influence that can serve them well at the next election.

A chair, who is always from the party with a majority of seats in his or her chamber, oversees each committee and subcommittee. Because they set the agenda, schedule hearings, and call meetings, chairs often exert special influence. For much of the twentieth century, chairs were selected on the basis of **seniority**—that is, the length of time that they had served in office. From the perspective of information gathering, this makes perfect sense. The persons who had served the longest on a committee tended to have the most expertise.

Historically, though, the process of selecting chairs attracted some controversy. For most of the post–World War II period, the Democratic Party retained control of the House and Senate. In part, this occurred because the South was essentially a one-party region, electing Democrats year in and year out. Because they did not face substantial competition, southern Democrats tended to hold office for longer periods of time than northern Democrats. Committee chairs, therefore, were usually southern Democrats. These southern Democrats also were much more conservative than their northern brethren, and they often used their powers as chairs in order to kill bills that they did not like. For example, in 1962, House Rules Committee Chair Howard W. Smith (D-VA) led a coalition of Republicans and fellow southern Democrats in undermining legislation that would have created a Department of Urban Affairs. Southerners joined their GOP colleagues in expressing opposition to bigger government. The southerners also appeared to have worried about the possibility that President John F. Kennedy, a Democrat, would nominate an African American for the new cabinet-level post. Kennedy attempted to create the department with an executive reorganization order, which automatically would have gone into effect if neither chamber had vetoed it within 60 days. The coalition of Republicans and southern Democrats in the House of Representatives, however, swiftly rejected the plan by a vote of 262 to 150.[36]

In response to this kind of obstructionist behavior, northern Democrats in the late 1960s and early 1970s forced through two reforms. First, the senior committee member of the majority party was no longer guaranteed to be chair; thus, it became possible for northern Democrats to assume control over some committees. Second, important powers were transferred from committees to subcommittees, making it easier to jump-start legislative activity that a committee chair might not support. During this period, the number of subcommittees in Congress rose from roughly 40 to more than 300.

□ Parties Impose Order on Their Members

As the discussion of committee organization makes clear, the two major parties in the United States, Democratic and Republican, provide still more order to Congress. The parties determine who will control the various committees and subcommittees and thus determine which core issues Congress will consider, which it will disregard and how the debate will proceed. Through parties, coalitions in favor of one policy or another are formed. And within parties, strategies are developed to promote the policies that best serve their members' reelection prospects. Parties, in short, help overcome the collective action and cycling problems that otherwise would cripple Congress.

PARTY LEADERSHIP At the beginning of each term, congressional Democrats and Republicans gather to select their leadership. For Democrats, the gathering is called the **party caucus**; for Republicans, it is the **party conference.** In the House, the party with the most seats elects the **Speaker of the House,** which is the only position in the House that the Constitution specifically mentions. In the Senate, the majority party selects the **majority leader,** while in the House this title is given to the Speaker's second in command. In both chambers, the party with fewer seats selects the **minority leader.**

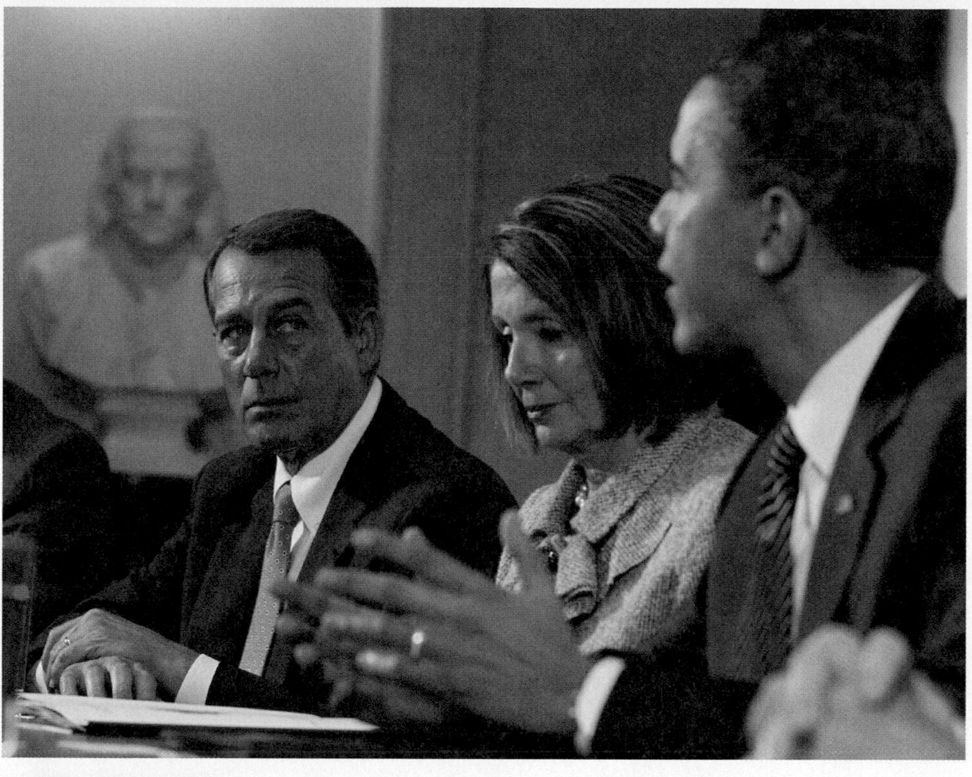

THE PRESIDENT AND PARTY LEADERS
In 2010, Republican House Minority Leader John Boehner of Ohio and Democratic House Speaker Nancy Pelosi of California joined President Barack Obama to discuss the Wall Street reform. Later that year, the Republicans would re-take control of the House, and Boehner and Pelosi would swap positions as Minority Leader and House Speaker.

whips
designated members of Congress who deliver messages from the party leaders, keep track of members' votes, and encourage members to stand together on key issues.

The Speaker of the House and the majority leader of the Senate perform many of the same functions. They preside over their chambers when they are in session, communicate with the White House about the progress of different bills, and act as congressional spokespersons. Because they decide which committees will consider which legislative proposals, they also help set the legislative agenda. If they strongly oppose a particular proposal, they often find ways of delaying its consideration by Congress as a whole.

For the most part, the Speaker of the House plays a more important role in overseeing affairs in the House than the majority leader does in the Senate. The reason has to do with the differences in the size and culture of the two chambers. Because the House has 435 voting members whereas the Senate has just 100, it is much more important to have a stronger leader in the House overseeing the business of the day.

PARTY DISCIPLINE Second in command in the House is the House majority leader, whose responsibility is to unify the party and help deliver the party's message to the public. The majority and minority party leaders of both parties also have **whips** who deliver messages from the leaders to the rank-and-file members, keep track of their votes, and encourage them to stand together on key issues. The term comes from "whippers-in," whose job it is to control the dogs in a fox hunt.

The efforts of the House majority leader and whips to get party members to vote together are generally successful. Over the past half-century, fewer than 30 percent of Republicans and Democrats have voted against their parties on so-called "party votes," votes on issues that are especially important to their leaders. In recent years, members have proved even less willing to break from their party leaders. In 2008, fewer than 10 percent defected on party votes.

Political scientists debate how party discipline is achieved. Some emphasize the powers of the party leadership to direct their members to vote in certain ways.[37] Leaders have a variety of means by which to punish members for defecting, such as cutting off financial aid to reelection campaigns. And, by controlling the legislative agenda, party leaders can keep divisive issues from ever coming up for a vote. Moreover, these scholars argue, members benefit from party discipline, because it helps them achieve their goal of enacting laws that will satisfy constituents.

Other scholars suggest that party leaders have very little to do with the decline of party defections.[38] Instead, party members vote together because they agree with one another. These scholars argue that there is little evidence that members of Congress systematically vote against their constituents' interests in order to toe the party line. Nor should members vote this way. After all, to vote against one's constituents is to reduce one's chances of being reelected. By this account, the correlation between party positions and individual voting behavior is not causal but simply reflects the shared views of members of the same party.

In the United States, different parties can control the legislative and executive branches of government. In some other systems of government, however, they cannot. In the United Kingdom, for instance, executive and legislative powers are shared by one party. The party holding the majority of seats in the House of Commons (the lower chamber of Parliament) selects the nation's prime minister from within its own ranks, and the prime minister, in turn, often uses valuable positions in the cabinet to reward loyal party members. Furthermore, the leaders of the Labour, Conservative, and Liberal Democratic Parties wield substantial control over the distribution of campaign funds and the list of candidates who appear on the ballots. Although individual legislators occasionally defect on party votes, such defections are rare in the United Kingdom.

☐ Party Polarization Is Increasing

One of the most striking trends in Congress during the past 30 years has been the increase in party polarization. As members have increased their tendency to vote together with their partisans, they in turn vote less frequently with members of the opposition party. As Figure 13.3 shows, congressional Republicans in 2011 were significantly more conservative than they were in 1970. Northern congressional Democrats are slightly more liberal than their predecessors, and southern Democrats are much more liberal—largely because conservative southern Democrats, starting in the mid-1970s, switched parties and became Republicans.[39]

Why are Republican members of Congress more conservative, and Democratic members more liberal, than they were a generation ago? The question is especially puzzling because very little evidence shows that citizens today are any more conservative or liberal than they were in 1970. According to one study, the root cause of this phenomenon is

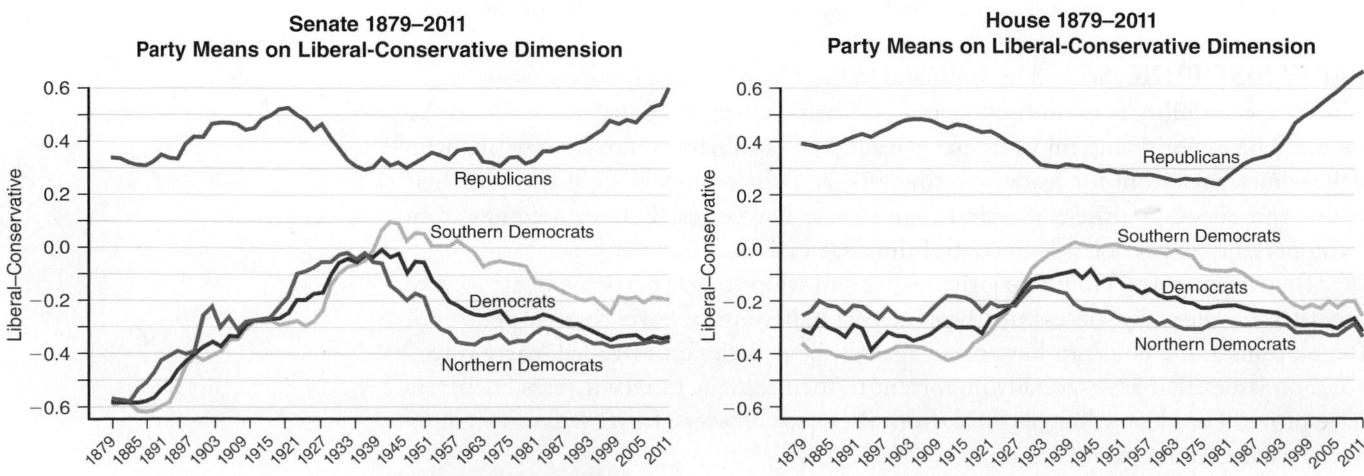

FIGURE 13.3 POLARIZATION OF DEMOCRATIC AND REPUBLICAN MEMBERS OF CONGRESS, 1879–2011.

The two major parties are more polarized today than they have been in almost a century. Here, we plot the average ideological score for Democratic and Republican members of Congress. Positive values indicate greater conservatism, and negative values indicate greater liberalism.

Source: http://voteview.com/political_polarization.asp

the rise in inequality around America.[40] Over the past century, partisan polarization has increased along with income inequality. It remains less clear, though, whether inequality and polarization are causally related. Just because the two trends move together does not mean that inequality causes polarization. The authors of this study, in fact, recognize that the opposite might be true—polarization might generate inequality. They characterize the relationship between the two phenomena as one of "back and forth causality."

It is not clear whether party polarization strengthens or weakens democratic governance. On the one hand, polarized parties present voters with clear choices about different policy issues. And, with these clear choices, voters can more easily hold members of a party accountable for their performance in office. If they do not like the policies advanced by an incumbent, voters can shift their support to a challenger with reliably different policy positions. On the other hand, polarized parties can impede legislative processes. As William Galston laments, under conditions of rising polarization "Congress can become a haven for obstruction and gridlock rather than deliberation and compromise."[41] Moreover, as the two majorities drift to the extremes of the ideological spectrum, a rising share of the American public refuses to affiliate with either of them. Whereas 28 percent of the American public self-identified as independent in 1970, fully 39 percent did so in 2011.[42]

Although the rift between the Republican and Democratic parties in the United States has grown starker in recent years, polarization is not an overarching trend within democracies worldwide. In fact, a number of countries sustain three or more parties, offering different platforms in order to provide representation to diverse opinions about key political issues. The particular mix of parties in these democracies is constantly changing. Israel provides a prominent example. In 2005, amid disagreements over his proposal to evacuate Jewish settlements in the Palestinian territories, then-prime minister Ariel Sharon withdrew from the conservative Likud Party and, with Shimon Peres of the liberal Labor Party, formed the backbone of a more centrist party called Kadima. More recently, Bob Katter, an independent but prominent member of the Australian House of Representatives and former National Party politician, shook up Australian national politics in 2011 when he filed papers to form his own political party—appropriately named "Bob Katter's Australian Party." Other democracies—such as France, Germany, and Canada—also sustain multiparty systems that offer voters wider options than does the United States.

Staff and Support Agencies Help Collect and Analyze Information

Members of Congress are assisted by roughly 11,000 staffers who perform all sorts of tasks, many of which concern the collection and analysis of information. On average, each senator has about 40 staffers working for him or her, and each House member has 17.[43] Some staffers work in a member's Washington, D.C., office, and others work back in the member's district or state. Those in D.C. tend research public policies, write briefs, draft proposals, organize hearings, and interact with lobbyists. They also communicate with staffers for other members, helping build coalitions in support of various policy initiatives. Staffers back home, meanwhile, interact with constituents about their concerns, their interests, and their ideas. These staffers then communicate this information back to the D.C. office.

Members also have access to several administrative agencies that provide vital information about public policy matters. The Congressional Research Service (CRS), established in 1914, handles hundreds of thousands of requests each year from members seeking information. Employees at CRS also inventory all the bills introduced in Congress and track their progress through the legislative process. The Government Accountability Office (GAO) studies policy issues upon congressional request. Established in 1921, the GAO acts as an investigatory body for members who wish to know more about the spending habits of bureaucratic agencies. The Congressional Budget Office (CBO), established in 1974, provides members with information about the costs of policies that they are considering, the economic implications of different budget proposals, and the general state of the economy.

13.1

13.2

13.3

13.4

13.5

13.6

Lawmaking

13.5 Explain the lawmaking process in Congress.

sponsor
a member of Congress who introduces a bill.

markup
the process by which the members of a committee or subcommittee rewrite, delete, and add portions of a bill.

open rule
the terms and conditions applied to a particular bill that allow members of Congress to make a wide range of amendments to it.

closed rule
the terms and conditions applied to a particular bill that restrict the types of amendments that can be made to it.

filibuster
a procedure by which senators delay or prevent action on a bill by making long speeches and engaging in unlimited debate.

cloture
a mechanism by which 60 or more senators can end a filibuster and cut off debate.

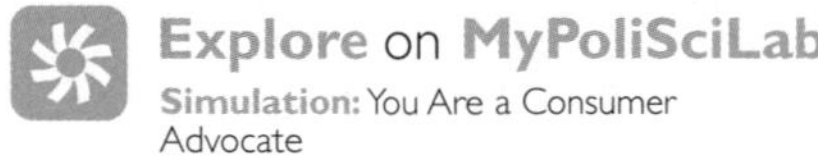

Explore on MyPoliSciLab
Simulation: You Are a Consumer Advocate

Members of Congress perform a variety of functions. They hold hearings and launch investigations to monitor goings-on in the executive branch. They help educate the public about the major issues of the day. They communicate with constituents and help resolve their problems. The single most important function that Congress serves, however, is to write the nation's laws.

The Legislative Process Is Long

To become a law, a bill must travel a long road, which is outlined in Figure 13.4. To begin the process, a **sponsor** introduces a bill into either the House or Senate. Any member of Congress can serve as a bill's sponsor. A bill can originate in either chamber, and sometimes equivalent bills are introduced simultaneously to both.

Subsequently, the bill must be referred to the appropriate committee for consideration. In the House, the Speaker decides which committee will take up the bill. In the Senate, the bill is assigned to a committee by the chamber's presiding officer, either the vice president or, more commonly, the president pro tempore, who is the most senior member of the majority party.

Bills typically are assigned to the committees that oversee the relevant policy domain. For example, bills on foreign conflicts are generally assigned to the Foreign Relations committee in the Senate and the Foreign Affairs committee in the House. Some bills are assigned to more than one committee—a practice called multiple referral.[44] In 2009, for example, the health care legislation that would mark the most significant legislative enactment of the 111th Congress was referred to three House committees: Education and the Workforce, Energy and Commerce, and Ways and Means. After assignment to one or more committees, a bill then is assigned to one or more subcommittees. The substance of a bill is typically first considered at the subcommittee level. Members of subcommittees carefully review the bill, holding hearings and conducting research on how it will likely affect their constituents and the nation as a whole. In a process called **markup,** members rewrite portions of the bill, delete others, and add still more. Once satisfied, the members then report the bill back to the full committee, whose members review the subcommittee's work and offer revisions of their own.

What happens next depends on which chamber is considering the bill. In the Senate, bills move straight from the committee of origin to the Senate floor, where the entire assembly of senators is given an opportunity to debate the merits of the proposed legislation. In the House, though, most bills coming out of committee are referred to the Rules Committee.[45] The Rules Committee decides how a bill will be debated on the floor by the entire membership of the House. It decides when the bill will go to the floor, how long members will debate the bill, and what kinds of amendments (if any) can be offered. When assigning an **open rule** to a bill, the Rules Committee allows for a wide range of amendments. Under a **closed rule,** the number and types of possible amendments are more restricted. Because bills assigned under an open rule can be altered significantly on the floor, supporters typically prefer a closed rule. Sometimes, however, a bill's supporter may assign an open rule to ensure that an important bill is amended rather than being rejected outright. Having completed its business, the Rules Committee then refers the bill to the House floor.

On the floors of both the House and Senate, members typically give speeches about the bill, offer amendments (rules permitting, at least in the House), and eventually vote. To pass the House, a bill must receive the support of a majority of votes. In the Senate, however, the threshold is somewhat higher. Technically, only a majority is needed to pass a bill. Any senator, though, may choose to **filibuster** a bill, which allows for indefinite debate. To end a filibuster—a process called invoking **cloture**—a

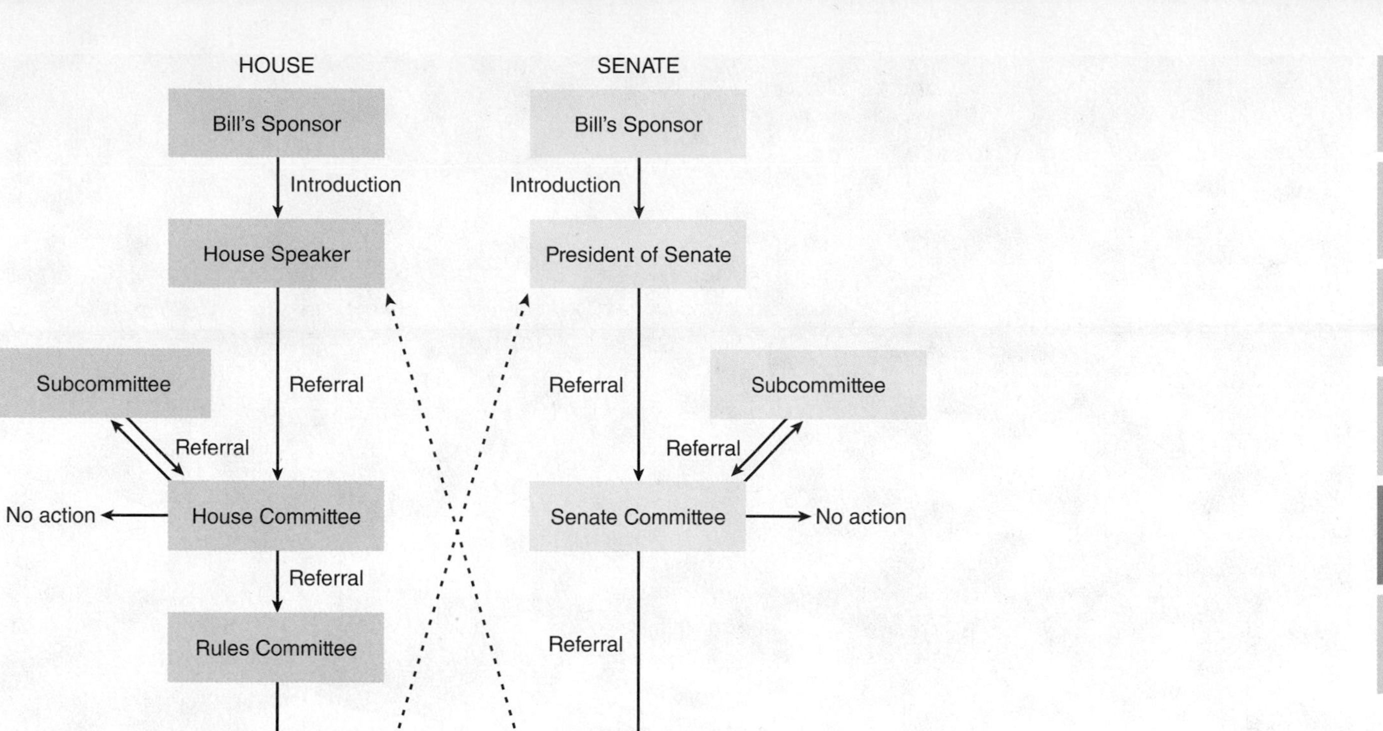

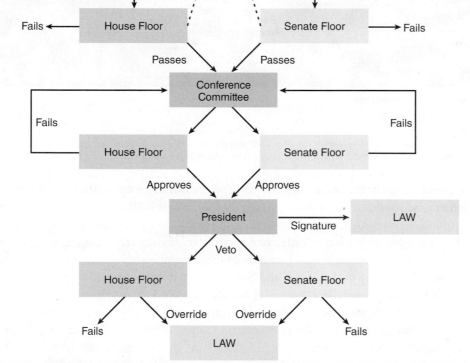

FIGURE 13.4 HOW A BILL BECOMES A LAW (OR NOT).

The lawmaking process is long, and most introduced bills fail to become laws.

supermajority of 60 votes is needed. Even if a majority of senators support a filibustered bill, it may not pass; it now requires a supermajority of 60 votes."[46]

To become law, a bill must pass both chambers of Congress. But having gone through markups in subcommittees and committees and then having been subject to further amendments on the floor, Senate and House versions of the same bill often look quite different from each other at this stage. During the summer and fall of 2009, for example, Congress considered health care reforms that would increase coverage while curbing rising medical costs. The House version of the bill had language allowing government-provided insurance, requiring employer responsibility, and creating subsidies for lower-income people, whereas the Senate's version did not. Such differences must be resolved before a bill becomes a law. Senators and representatives often reconcile their differences informally. Party leaders play an important role in such negotiations, recommending elements of a bill to keep, to discard, and to amend. More formally,

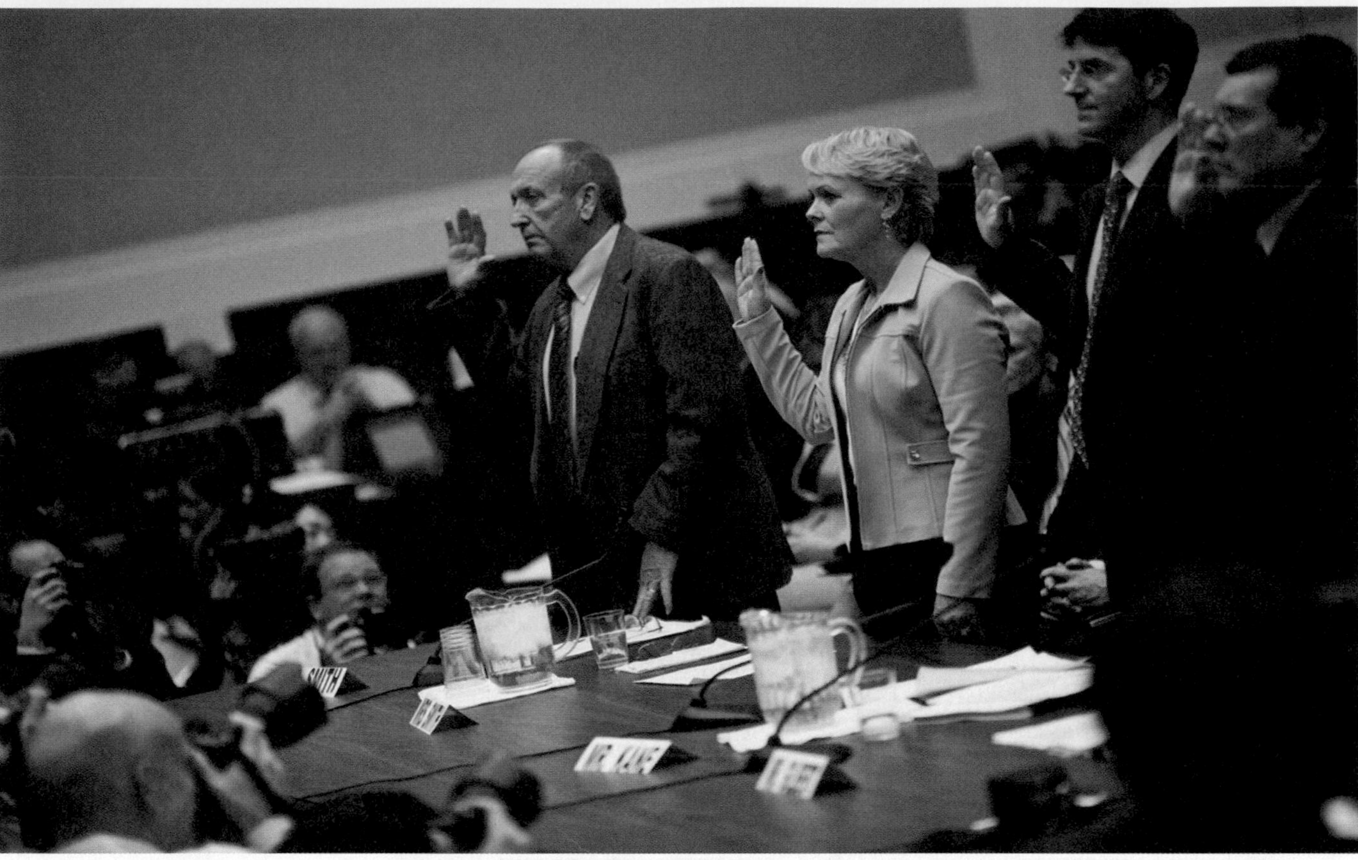

MEETING THE PEOPLE

Although congressional committees often solicit testimony from experts, they also meet with average citizens. In 2010, in the aftermath of a spate of accidents caused by sudden unintended acceleration in Toyota vehicles, a number of victims testified before the House Committee on Energy and Commerce.

conference committee
a committee made up of members of both chambers that is responsible for ironing out the differences between House and Senate versions of a bill.

veto
the president's rejection of a bill passed by both chambers of Congress, which prevents the bill from becoming law.

appointed members of each chamber serve on a **conference committee,** which has the job of producing a compromise version of the bill. Simple bills may have a relatively small conference committee, whereas complex and significant legislation may have hundreds of members serving on the conference committee. If conference committee members can come to an agreement—and sometimes they cannot—they send a revised version of the bill to the floors of the House and Senate, where it is subsequently voted on.

If the bill passes the House and Senate, it travels down Pennsylvania Avenue to the White House. The president can sign the bill, in which case it automatically becomes law. Alternatively, the president may **veto,** or reject, the legislation. Members can respond to a veto in three ways. First, they can refuse to reconsider the bill, in which case it dies. Second, they can make concessions to win over the president. In this case, both the House and Senate then vote on a new version of the bill, which is sent back to the president. Third, members can try to override the president's veto by securing the support of two-thirds of both houses. If they fail, the veto is sustained. Members of Congress may also select a combination of approaches. They might first write a revised version of a bill; if the president vetoes the bill again, they then might try to override him. If this fails, they may simply give up and move on to other issues.

□ Most Bills Are Not Enacted Into Law

While travelling down this long legislative road, it is not surprising that bills often hit a pothole and veer onto an embankment. There are, after all, plenty of opportunities for a strategic politician, either working alone or with others, to derail a bill. Committees, minority factions in either the House or the Senate, and the president, too, can undermine the prospects of even those bills that enjoy the support of congressional majorities.

Let's begin with committees. Committee members who are assigned a bill they oppose could try to tailor the bill more to their liking or could refuse to do anything at

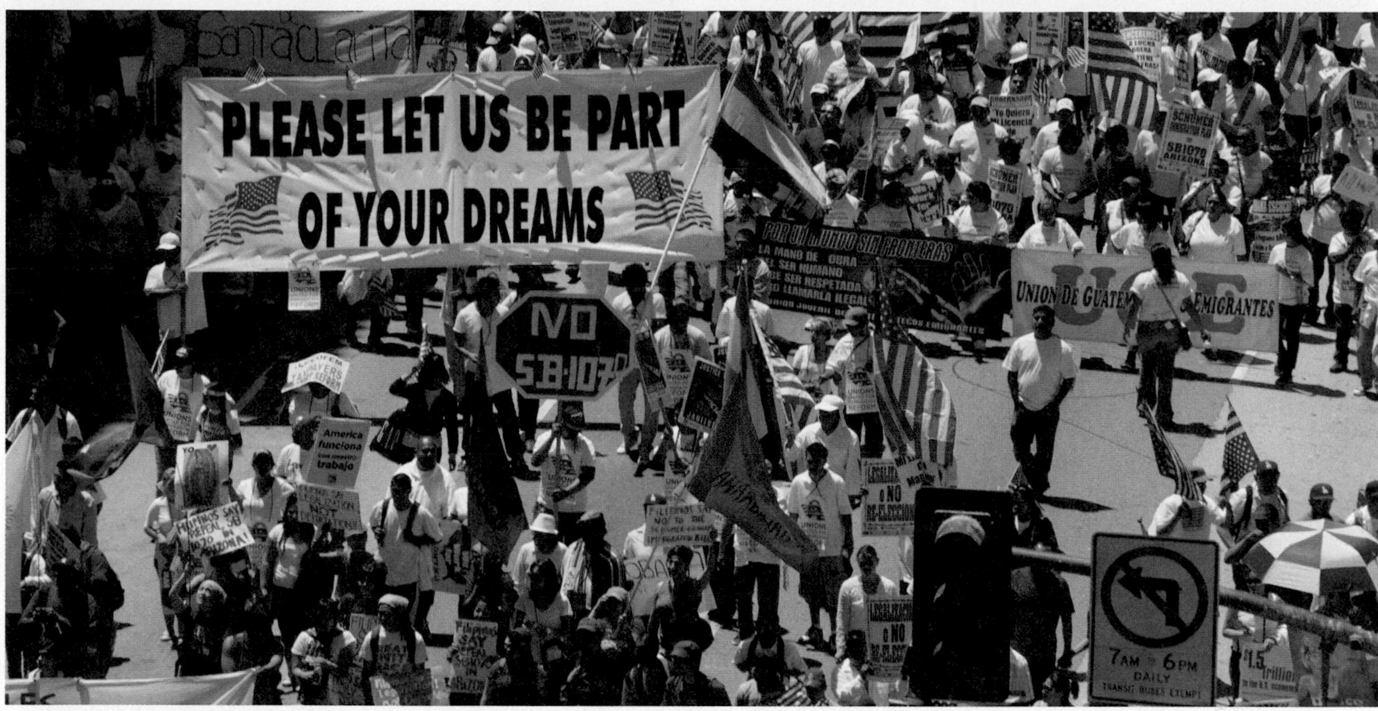

FAILING TO ACT

To date, Congress has failed to pass comprehensive immigration reform of any kind. As a result, some states have taken it upon themselves to do so. Arizona's action in 2010 evoked widespread protests from supporters of immigration. How do you think Congress should address the issue of immigration? And should the states have any say in the matter?

all and "table" the bill indefinitely. This **gate-keeping authority** can give committees substantial power over the kinds of bills that come before the floor of either chamber. Despite the fact that a majority of either the House or the Senate, presumably, would like to see at least some of these bills enacted, in most congresses, upward of 80 percent of all introduced bills never make it out of committee.[47]

gate-keeping authority
the power to decide whether a particular proposal or policy change will be considered.

Using a filibuster, just 41 opponents in the Senate can kill a bill—even if the other 59 senators and all 435 members of the House prefer to see it enacted. The filibuster is a powerful tool for minorities within Congress to check the powers of majorities and achieve desired policy aims, and minorities are making increasing use of it. During the first half of the twentieth century, only a handful of bills in each congressional session were subject to a filibuster. Beginning in the early 1970s, however, the average number increased to 22; during the 1990s, it increased to more than 40.[48] During the 111th Congress, Senators voted on whether or not to end filibustering on a bill 91 times. In December 2010, for example, because they objected to the high costs, Republicans in the Senate successfully filibustered a bill to provide medical benefits and compensation to emergency responders who were first on the scene of the September 11, 2001 terrorist attacks. Despite the fact that Democrats had the numbers to pass the bill should it have come to a vote, Republicans used a coordinated filibuster to prevent such a vote from ever taking place. Forced to compromise, Democratic and Republican senators eventually agreed upon a bill with significantly lower payouts. In this way, a minority (42 percent) of the Senate effectively passed its preferred bill against a much larger majority's wishes.

The president, too, can often thwart the general interests of majorities in both chambers of Congress. If either chamber fails to override a presidential veto, a proposed bill fails to become law. During the nation's history, presidents have used this power with greater and greater frequency to influence the content of legislation. During the first half of the nineteenth century, presidents tended to use the veto power sparingly, and then only to ward off congressional efforts to usurp executive powers. By the middle of the twentieth century, however, presidents were not at all shy about vetoing bills they objected to on policy grounds. Not surprisingly, the vast majority of these vetoes were sustained. Almost every president has succeeded in having more than 75 percent of his vetoes upheld in Congress.[49]

Because lawmaking is so difficult, most bills are not enacted into law. As Figure 13.5 shows, between 1981 and 2004 roughly 10 percent of bills introduced to the House passed; even fewer were enacted into law. Although the figures fluctuate somewhat, enactment rates peaked at 11.4 percent (in 1987–1988), and bottomed out at 4.8 percent (in 1997–1998). The root causes of these specific passage rates are particularly difficult to discern. In 1987, after all, Democrats had large majorities in the House, whereas in 1997, Republicans held control by the slimmest of margins. Yet, it seems implausible that smaller majorities increase passage rates. Rather, differences in the types of bills being considered may constitute the key reason why some Congresses pass higher percentages of bills than others.

Not all bills that are enacted into law, however, follow the traditional path outlined in Figure 13.4.[50] Indeed, a variety of parliamentary procedures enable members to occasionally circumvent the conventional approach. One such procedure is the "self-executing rule," colloquially called "deem and pass." First formulated in the House Rules Committee in the 1930s, deem and pass is a way of indirectly passing a bill through Congress without ever actually voting on it. If prior to the consideration of a bill, the House votes in favor of a rule containing a self-executing provision, then passage of that rule ensures passage of the bill that it references. In other words, by adopting rules on how a bill would be debated on the floor, the House can treat the bill as if it had actually been voted on.

Since the 1930s, Republicans and Democrats alike have employed the self-executing rule. Although it was initially used as a way to make minor modifications to bills, deem and pass soon became a partisan tool to promote specific policies concerning immigration, smoking regulation, and the Internal Revenue Service.[51] Since the 95th Congress, more than 200 self-executing rules have been used.[52] Most recently, during the 2010 congressional debate over the health care bill, House Democrats toyed with the idea of using the self-executing rule in order to approve the Senate's version of the bill without ever voting on it. Ultimately, however, Speaker Pelosi opted against the measure, as Democrats realized that the scope of the bill was too broad for such maneuvers.[53]

☐ Laws, Nonetheless, Are Enacted

Just because lawmaking is difficult does not mean that it is impossible. In a typical year, Congress enacts several hundred laws. Although most of these laws concern rather mundane affairs, at least some have profound policy consequences. According to one study that categorized legislation into four categories of significance, Congress each year enacts roughly 5 "landmark" laws, 6 "major" laws, 36 "ordinary" ones, and no less than 314 "minor" laws.[54]

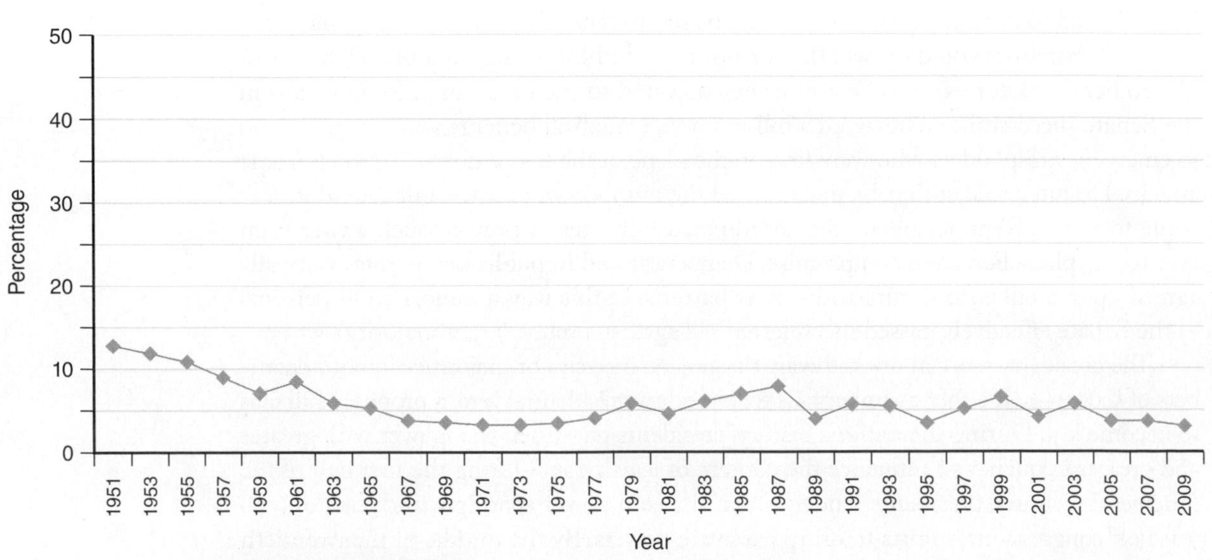

FIGURE 13.5 SUCCESS RATES FOR BILLS INTRODUCED IN THE CONGRESS.
The vast majority of bills introduced in Congress fail to become law.

Political scientists have tried to determine the mix of political factors most likely to result in successful legislation. One of the most powerful predictors is the strength of the majority party's control in the House and Senate. When Democrats or Republicans control both chambers of Congress by wide margins, they find it much easier to overcome the various institutional challenges that derail so many bills. The single most productive Congress during the past half-century operated from 1965 to 1966. During this period, when Democrats held a whopping 295 seats in the House and 68 in the Senate, Congress enacted such landmark legislation as Medicare and Medicaid, the Immigration Act, the Elementary and Secondary Education Act (ESEA), the Housing and Urban Development Act, the Voting Rights Act, the Freedom of Information Act, and the National Traffic and Motor Vehicle Safety Act, to name but a few.

Although most laws live on indefinitely, laws with **sunset provisions** must be reauthorized after a specified number of years, as in the Elementary and Secondary Education Act, first enacted in 1965, and most recently reauthorized in 2002 as No Child Left Behind. Given that existing laws maintain programs that are already up and running, that they have received political support in the past, and that they come up for formal consideration in a specified year, they are more likely to pass than other legislation. Moreover, Congress need not reauthorize these laws for full terms.

sunset provision
a condition of a law that requires it to be reauthorized after a certain number of years.

authorization
the granting of legal authority to operate federal programs and agencies.

appropriations
the granting of funds to operate authorized federal programs and agencies.

13.1 13.2 13.3 13.4 13.5 13.6

The Appropriations Process

13.6 Describe the appropriations process.

The work of Congress is not complete after it enacts a law. It subsequently must commit funds so that the law can be set in motion. Every year, Congress uses money from the Treasury Department to fund federal agencies and programs.[55] According to Article I, section 9, of the Constitution, "no Money shall be drawn from the Treasury, but in Consequence of Appropriations made by Law." But besides stipulating that "a regular Statement and Account of Receipts and Expenditures of all public Money shall be published from time to time," the Constitution has left most of the specifics to the legislature itself.

Spending Is a Two-Step Process: Authorization and Then Appropriations

Two steps must be taken for monies to make their way to different agencies and programs. First, these programs and agencies must receive **authorization** by the legislation that serves as the legal basis for their continued operation. The second step is **appropriations,** the actual granting of funds to federal agencies and programs. Authorization committees help determine the kinds of programs within their legislative jurisdiction that will be funded; appropriations committees determine the exact amounts of monies to be disbursed.

In principle, authorizations and appropriations are kept separate in order to reduce the chances that members of Congress will use federal monies to alter the actual operations of federal agencies and programs. In practice, though, the distinction between authorizations and appropriations often blurs—in part, because appropriations committee members make quite a habit of using limitations on the use of funds as a way to legislate indirectly. The phrase "none of the funds shall be used for . . ." has become an increasingly prominent feature in appropriations bills, effectively changing policy in spite of the prohibition against writing legislation in appropriations committees.[56]

Nonappropriations committees also use authorizing legislation to grant permanent budget authority to programs and agencies. As a result, a sizable fraction of each year's federal budget is dedicated to mandatory spending (often called entitlements) on these past obligations. The largest entitlements include such massive programs as Social Security, Medicare, and Medicaid, all of which are discussed at length in

13.1

earmarks
federal funds that support specific local projects.

13.2

regular appropriations
the standard mode by which federal moneys are allotted to programs.

13.3

continuing resolution
funds used to keep programs up and running when regular appropriations have not been approved by the end of the fiscal year.

13.4

13.5

13.6

Chapter 17. The remainder of the budget—the portion not already promised elsewhere and therefore available for discretionary spending on new obligations—is the subject of deliberations within the appropriations committees. Over time, a rising tide of entitlements has steadily shrunk the discretionary portion of the budget, reducing it to approximately one-third of total expenditures in fiscal year 2012.[57] Given that the federal budget is well over $3.5 trillion, however, this still leaves appropriations committees with a considerable amount of money to disburse.

Members also use **earmarks** to bypass executive agencies altogether and direct funds straight to their constituents. According to one watch-dog organization, Congress disclosed nearly 9,500 earmarks worth almost $16 billion in the 2010 fiscal year.[58] Texas alone received $1.6 billion in earmarks, despite the fact that four House Republicans from Texas refused to seek earmarks entirely, citing budget concerns.[59] Many legislators argue that earmarks support vital public works projects. Constituents benefit when their representatives obtain money to repair their roads and bridges or to fund state colleges and universities and community recreations centers. The positive aspects of regular earmarks, however, are occasionally outshined by reports of abuse. An infamous example from the 2008 presidential election is the Alaskan "Bridge to Nowhere" project that would have cost $398 million to connect the 50 residents living on Gravina Island to the mainland.

Facing substantial criticism for funding these "pork barrel" projects, in 2006, Congress passed the Federal Funding Accountability and Transparency Act that, among other things, established a searchable database of earmarks,[60] and in 2007, the House passed rules requiring public lists of every earmark, the recipient's name and address, and the individual who requested it.[61] Amid mounting criticism from President Obama and the public, the Senate Appropriations Committee eventually announced a two-year moratorium on all earmark spending in February 2011.

Yet, despite the moratorium on earmarks, there is evidence that members of Congress have found more indirect means of channeling money to their home districts. In May 2011, for example, the House passed a spending bill that created a special "Mission Force Enhancement Transfer Fund," with a budget of roughly $1 billion. Much of this money appears to be allocated for specific projects within certain members' districts. Rep. Steve Palazzo of Mississippi, for instance, requested that the fund allocate $19 million for Navy ship preliminary design and feasibility studies. The largest employer in Palazzo's district is Ingalls Shipbuilding, which is a major producer of Navy ships and would presumably receive at least a portion of that allocation. As one government watchdog group put it, "These amendments may very likely duck the House's specific definition of what constitutes an earmark, but that doesn't mean they aren't pork."[62]

Appropriations Come in Three Forms: Regular, Continuing Resolution, and Supplemental

There are three main types of appropriations. **Regular appropriations** are the main source of revenues that are disbursed to agencies and programs. Regular appropriations contain three standard features: an enacting clause that designates the fiscal year for which funds are given, a breakdown of budget authority by accounts, and general provisions that apply to all of the accounts. Small agencies might possess only one account, but larger ones are usually financed by several distinct accounts, designated with names such as "procurement" or "salaries and expenses." In general, agencies can "reprogram" funds (shift budget authority from one activity to another within a single account) by going through the proper notification and oversight channels. However, they cannot "transfer" funds (shift budget authority from one account to another) without statutory authorization.

A second type of appropriations is a **continuing resolution,** which disburses funding when regular appropriations have not been set by the close of the fiscal year on October 1. Continuing resolutions have become quite common. In fact, between 1977 and 2006, Congress and the president completed all of the regular appropriations on schedule only four times.[63] Traditionally, continuing resolutions were brief measures listing the agencies that had not yet received their regular funding and providing temporary assistance at the previous year's level or the president's budget request, whichever was lower. Today, however, continuing resolutions increasingly include omnibus measures that cover several of the regular appropriations bills at once.

Congress also provides **supplemental appropriations,** the third type, when regular appropriations do not cover certain activities or are deemed insufficient. In order to evade spending caps, Congress sometimes designates supplements as emergency funds. Franklin D. Roosevelt's New Deal used supplemental appropriations to create new government agencies and create new jobs. During World War II, the government used this type of appropriation to accelerate the production of fighter planes and other war weapons. In 2009, President Obama's economic stimulus package contained supplemental appropriations to stabilize the economy and preserve jobs. Much of the Iraq War was funded not through regular defense appropriations but through a series of supplemental appropriations.[64] Many of the appropriations went toward operational costs, replacing military equipment, and caring for veterans.[65]

supplemental appropriations
the process by which Congress and the president can provide temporary funding for government activities and programs when funds fall short because of unforeseen circumstances.

The Appropriations Process Is Streamlined and Generally Follows a Strict Timetable

The process of appropriating federal funds looks quite a bit like the legislative process. Suggested appropriations are debated and marked up within committees, considered on the floors of the House and Senate, reconciled across chambers, and eventually sent to the president. In two important respects, however, the appropriations process differs from the lawmaking process.

First, appropriations are purposefully streamlined. Whereas a failure to legislate may disappoint key constituencies, a failure to appropriate funds can bring the federal government to a grinding halt. And because appropriations are required every year, members of Congress have a vested interest in minimizing the procedural roadblocks—such as the Senate filibuster—that they are likely to encounter.

Second, the appropriations process is supposed to follow a strict timetable. The president initiates the process by submitting his annual budget proposal to Congress on or before the first Monday in February. The full House and Senate appropriations committees then have the option of conducting overview hearings to discuss the proposal with the Office of Management and Budget. From February to April, agencies meet with the relevant appropriations subcommittees to justify the difference between their newly requested amounts and the previous year's allotments. By April 15, Congress passes a resolution that determines the federal budget for the next five fiscal years and allocates that year's budget among all of its committees.

In May and June, the committees, subcommittees, and lastly the full appropriations committee mark up the proposals, reporting regular bills to the entire House by July. The House debates, considers amendments, passes the bills, and sends them to the Senate, which passes the bills (perhaps with amendments) before the August congressional recess. In September, members of both chambers' appropriations committees hold conferences to resolve any remaining differences. Usually the House considers the conference report first, and the Senate decides whether to accept or reject the House's report. Once the two chambers have settled on the final appropriations bills, they are sent to the president, who has 10 days to sign or veto them in their entirety.

In practice, Congress and the president rarely abide by this strict schedule. In some years, the legislature does not pass the budget resolution by the April 15 deadline, delaying transmittal of explicit spending ceilings to the appropriations committees. In fact, in fiscal years 1999, 2003, and 2006, Congress did not complete the resolution at all. Rather than responding to the House's passed bills, the Senate sometimes creates its own proposals, which are inserted into the House bills as "amendments." Hampered by the August recess, the chambers might not resolve their differences by October 1. Last but not least, the president could kill the bill, either explicitly or, if Congress has adjourned, by taking no action within the 10-day time frame. In December 1995, for example, Bill Clinton vetoed the reconciliation bill that would have enacted Republican-backed tax cuts and curtailed spending on social programs. When Congress failed to override the president's veto, portions of the federal government temporarily shut down.

A THREATENED GOVERNMENT SHUTDOWN

When the president and Congress fail to settle their differences and pass a budget, the consequences can be dramatic. At the extreme, federal employees cannot be paid and the government faces the prospect of shutting down.

In recent years, budget battles have reached a feverish pitch, thanks in large part to the very mechanisms meant to streamline the process. Given the extraordinary difficulty of passing a single piece of legislation under normal circumstances, members of Congress have increasingly sought to roll individual bills into the larger omnibus budget bill to bypass a protracted fight over their proposed legislation and avoid a Senate filibuster. As a consequence of this tactic, however, the budgetary process itself has become subject to the same protracted political fights that normally plague bills focused on more hot-button political issues. And because the entire budget is subject to a single up or down vote, these controversial elements of the budget prevent Congress from approving spending on essential government programs that enjoy near unanimous support.

This budget difficulty was on display in the summer of 2011, when budget battles between Democrats and Republicans nearly led to a government shutdown. Republicans, fresh off victories in the 2010 midterm elections, used their political momentum to push for a dramatic reduction in government spending. As new House Speaker John Boehner told reporters, "When we say we're serious about cutting spending, we're damn serious about it."[66] Many of Republicans' proposed cuts, however, targeted the specific appropriations that had been rolled into the larger budget by Democrats. Whereas conservative Republicans insisted on cutting government funding for favorite liberal organizations such as Planned Parenthood and government agencies like the Environmental Protection Agency, Democrats insisted Republicans were dismantling the welfare state and helping private corporations avoid pollution regulations. Issues such as abortion that were only tangentially related to the budget process ended up front and center in the public eye. Both sides agreed that a budget had to be passed to avoid a federal shutdown; yet, neither side was willing to budge on its position. Ultimately, Congress reached an agreement on April 8, mere hours before the scheduled shutdown. The final deal cut domestic federal spending by $40 billion but protected many of the most sacred Democratic priorities. In addition, the final bill included numerous new appropriations, such as an initiative supported by Speaker Boehner to provide federally funded vouchers for District of Columbia students to attend private schools.

On MyPoliSciLab

Review the Chapter

 **Listen** to **Chapter 13** on **MyPoliSciLab**

An Institution with Two Chambers and Shared Powers

13.1 Outline the basic structure of Congress, p. 432.

As a bicameral institution, the U.S. Congress has two chambers: the House of Representatives and the Senate. Members in the House serve for two years, and senators serve for six. Whereas members of the House represent congressional districts, senators represent entire states. The Senate also has some duties (such as the ratification of treaties and approval of Supreme Court nominees) that members of the House do not have.

Principles and Dilemmas of Representation

13.2 Analyze the relationship of members of Congress to their constituencies, and distinguish between the trustee and delegate models of representation, p. 435.

Congress represents the interests of some citizens more than others. Above all, members of Congress want to be reelected, and to be reelected, they must adequately represent the interests of their constituents. Depending on whether members follow a trustee or delegate model of representation, their relationship with their constituents will differ dramatically. Moreover, members do not represent all constituents equally. Depending on whether they vote, are organized, are Democrats or Republicans, or fit a certain demographic profile, some constituents receive more or less representation by the member of Congress who serves their district or state.

How Members Make Group Decisions

13.3 Assess the challenges that emerge when members of Congress set about working together, p. 443.

Members of Congress face important challenges when working together. They have different interests, priorities, and worldviews. To build a record of accomplishments that will serve them well at the next election, members of Congress must effectively navigate these differences. Additionally, they must overcome problems of information, collective action, and cycling that emerge when decisions require the participation of multiple members.

Imposing Structure on Congress

13.4 Identify the resources and the committee and party structures that help Congress address its challenges, p. 447.

The resources and structures that define Congress as an institution alleviate the challenges. Members of Congress have staffs that help collect information. They serve on committees and subcommittees that establish a division of labor. And most members belong to one of the two dominant parties, which provide further structure.

Lawmaking

13.5 Explain the lawmaking process in Congress, p. 454.

The lawmaking process is long and difficult. To become a law, a bill must pass through multiple committees and subcommittees in both the House and Senate, the floors of both chambers, and a conference committee, before it lands on the president's desk for signature. Even then, though, the president may veto the bill, in which case it returns to Congress for reconsideration. Not surprisingly, most proposed bills fail to become law. Nonetheless, Congress does manage to enact laws on a regular basis—sometimes because its members agree about the solution to a particular problem, and sometimes because the business of the day (appropriations and reauthorizations) requires them to set about finishing the task.

The Appropriations Process

13.6 Describe the appropriations process, p. 459.

The appropriations process differs from the lawmaking process. Because budgets must be approved every year, appropriations are usually easier to set than laws are to enact. Some of the roadblocks to lawmaking are eliminated, the budget has a permanent place on the congressional agenda, and the processes themselves are routinized. Still, delays are common. Increasingly, Congress has had to rely on continuing and supplemental appropriations to keep the government running.

Learn the Terms

 **Study** and **Review** the **Flashcards**

appropriations, p. 459
authorization, p. 459
bicameral, p. 432
casework, p. 437
closed rule, p. 454
cloture, p. 454
collective action problem, p. 445
conference committee, p. 456
constituents, p. 435
continuing resolution, p. 460
cycling, p. 447
delegate model of representation, p. 437
earmarks, p. 460
filibuster, p. 454
gate-keeping authority, p. 457
gerrymandering, p. 440
impeachment, p. 432
incumbent, p. 436
joint committee, p. 448
majority leader, p. 450
major-minority voting districts, p. 442
markup, p. 454
minority leader, p. 450
open rule, p. 454
party caucus, p. 450
party conference, p. 450
redistricting, p.440
regular appropriations, p. 460
select committee, p. 447
seniority, p. 450
Speaker of the House, p. 450
sponsor, p. 454
standing committee, p. 447
subcommittee, p. 448
sunset provision, p. 459
supplemental appropriations, p. 461
trustee model of representation, p. 437
veto, p. 456
whips, p. 451

Test Yourself

 **Study** and **Review** the **Practice Tests**

13.1 Outline the basic structure of Congress.

Congress is a bicameral institution, which means that

a. it consists of three chambers.
b. it consists of one chamber.
c. it consists of two chambers.
d. it consists of one chamber elected by the people, and another chamber elected by the House.
e. it consists of one chamber elected by the people, and another chamber elected by the Senate.

13.2 Analyze the relationship of members of Congress to their constituencies, and distinguish between the trustee and delegate models of representation.

In the trustee model of representation, members of Congress____; whereas, in the delegate model of representation, members of Congress_______.

a. sometimes do what they think is best for their constituents and sometimes vote according to the expressed interests of their constituents; vote according to the expressed interests of their constituents
b. do what they think is best for their constituents; sometimes do what they think is best for their constituents and sometimes vote according to the expressed interests of their constituents
c. vote according to the expressed interests of their constituents; sometimes do what they think is best for their constituents and sometimes vote according to the expressed interests of their constituents
d. vote according to the expressed interests of their constituents; do what they think is best for their constituents
e. do what they think is best for their constituents; vote according to the expressed interests of their constituents

13.3 Assess the challenges that emerge when members of Congress set about working together.

All of the following are challenges that members of Congress confront when working together EXCEPT

a. Most members of Congress know a great deal about the substantive issues they confront.
b. The factors that help one member get reelected are not the same factors that help another member get elected.
c. Though they may have some expertise in a handful of issues, most members of Congress know little about the substantive issues they confront.
d. The collective action problem often leads to inaction on the part of members of Congress.
e. Members of Congress have different ideas about what constitutes good public policy.

13.4 Identify the resources and the committee and party structures that help Congress address its challenges.

Which of the following is NOT a type of congressional committee?

a. standing committee
b. seniority committee
c. select committee
d. joint committee
e. subcommittee

13.5 Explain the lawmaking process in Congress.

Which of the following represents a step that occurs in the lawmaking process in the House of Representatives but not in the Senate?

a. A bill is introduced.
b. A bill is referred to a conference committee.
c. A bill is referred to a subcommittee.
d. A bill is referred to the Rules Committee.
e. A bill is referred to a standing committee.

13.6 Describe the appropriations process.

What happens in the appropriations process?

a. Congress grants funds to federal agencies and programs.
b. Congress makes laws.
c. Congress eliminates redundant or useless federal agencies.
d. Congress instructs the president to eliminate federal agencies.
e. Congress creates new federal agencies.

Explore Further

SUGGESTED READINGS BY TOP SCHOLARS

Richard L. Hall and Alan Deardorff. "Lobbying as Legislative Subsidy." *American Political Science Review* 100 (2006): 69-84. Provides a new theory of lobbying that has less to do with vote buying and information signaling, and more to do with the support of like-minded legislators on shared policy objectives.

William G. Howell and Jon C. Pevehouse. *While Dangers Gather: Congressional Checks on Presidential War Powers*. Princeton, NJ: Princeton University Press, 2007. Identifies how members of Congress can influence presidential decisions about military action through public appeals and hearings.

Gregory Koger. *Filibustering: A Political History of Obstruction in the House and Senate*. Chicago, 2010: University of Chicago Press. Provides historical overview of the use of obstructionist tactics in the Senate, and the rising frequency with which its members have used and threatened to use the filibuster.

Frances Lee. *Beyond Ideology: Politics, Principles, and Partisanship in the U.S. Senate*. Chicago, 2009: University of Chicago Press. Examines how many partisan battles within Congress reflect contestations over power rather than ideological disagreements.

Keith Poole and Howard Rosenthal. *Ideology and Congress*. New York, 2007: Transaction Press. Draws upon patterns in roll call votes to discern historical changes in the ideological composition of Congress.

SUGGESTED WEBSITES

Library of Congress, Thomas: thomas.loc.gov
Includes a tremendous amount of information about the legislative process, including a searchable database of bills introduced to the House or Senate in recent congresses.

U.S. Senate: www.senate.gov
Official website of the U.S. Senate.

U.S. House: www.house.gov
Official website of the U.S. House.

C-SPAN: www.c-span.org
Includes a rich array of video footage of congressional debates, hearings, and investigations.

Congressional Research Service: opencrs.com
Access to reports on a wide range of policy and political issues that are produced for members of Congress.

Listen to Chapter 14 on MyPoliSciLab

14 The Presidency

SURROUNDED BY CHALLENGES

"It has been a long time coming, but tonight, because of what we did on this date, in this election, at this defining moment, change has come to America." President-elect Barack Obama's words soared out to the crowd of 125,000 people gathered in Grant Park, Chicago, to celebrate the election of the new president of the United States. With the election of the nation's first African-American president, expectations, particularly among young voters and intellectuals, ran high.

As Obama concluded a campaign whose signature theme was "change," the nation remained mired in two wars and confronted by a domestic economy in freefall. Much as he might have liked, he could not turn immediately to the policy reforms that had figured so prominently in his campaign. He would admit this one year later, "We have inherited the biggest set of challenges of any U.S. president since Franklin Delano Roosevelt." In politics, the urgent often trumps the favored.

Presidents must manage their agendas in an uncooperative political world. They are responsible for setting and striving to meet the goals they campaigned on, while dealing with all the other issues that emerge when they are in office. By both today's public and tomorrow's historians, presidents are judged on how they balance their promises with their obligations.

In his first inaugural address in 2008, President Obama outlined his plan for the nation. America, he promised, would rise from the ashes of the previous presidency and return to the world scene with a renewed image and reputation. By ending military operations in Iraq and Afghanistan, reaching out to the Muslim world, and increasing aid to the world's poorest, the United States would usher in a new era of peace. Domestically, Obama promised to create jobs and rebuild the economy. He also reiterated a theme of his campaign, asserting that his administration would seek to bridge partisan differences and work with opposition leaders to put the country on the right path. "Only then," the new president declared, "can we restore the vital trust between a people and their government."[3]

14.1 Trace the constitutional origins and historical expansion of presidential power, p. 469.

14.2 Distinguish between the formal and informal powers of contemporary presidents, p. 481.

14.3 Analyze how presidents use public support, electoral victories, and congressional allies to push through their policies, p. 488.

14.4 Assess the role of the cabinet, the Executive Office of the President, and the White House staff in assisting the president, p. 494.

14.5 Describe how party identification, the economy, and other factors shape how the president is perceived by the American public, p. 499.

INUNDATED WITH CHALLENGES The president is inundated with challenges, both at home and abroad. Such challenges can even come from those who are supposed to protect him. In the Spring of 2012, the secret service assigned to the president were enmeshed in a scandal involving Colombian prostitutes.

The Big Picture How does the President affect change? Author William G. Howell considers the range of problems that the public expects the president to fix—from human rights issues to our relationship with China—and argues why the president does not stand a chance of fulfilling those high expectations.

The Basics What do presidents do? The simple answer is "an awful lot." In this video, you'll hear what ordinary people think about what presidents should do. In the process, you'll discover why there is often a gap between what we expect and what we get.

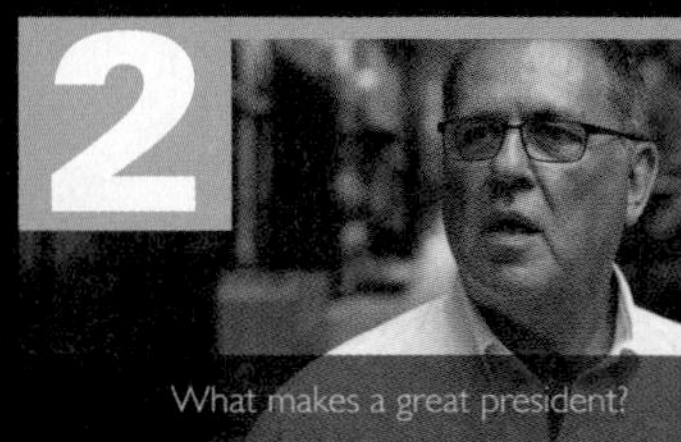
What makes a great president?

In Context Uncover the historical context that led the framers to fear a strong executive. In this video University of Oklahoma political scientist Glen Krutz not only reveals the reason behind the framers' apprehension, but also explores how this fear still restricts presidents today as they struggle to create new policies.

Think Like a Political Scientist Why do presidents try to persuade you to support their policies? In this video, University of Oklahoma political scientist Glen Krutz discloses why persuasion is vital to a president's success and how technology has created obstacles and opportunities for presidents.

In the Real World Should President Obama have used an executive order to change immigration policy? The president bypassed Congress to implement his own agenda. Find out why some people believe the president abused his powers and others think he was entirely justified.

So What? How should you judge the president? In this video, author William G. Howell examines the conflicting views citizens have of the president, and suggests methods for evaluating him that are more useful and more meaningful than the extent to which they fulfill campaign promises.

During the years that followed, the president struggled mightily to make good on his inaugural address. Obama faced a continually lagging economy, turmoil in the Middle East, and staunch political opposition to his proposed policy agenda. In his first term, Obama's administration witnessed the rise of the Tea Party and the retaking of the House of Representatives by Republicans. In some arenas, Obama successfully carried out his stated priorities: He signed a $787 billion economic recovery act and a comprehensive health care reform bill, killed Osama bin Laden, and ended the secret government surveillance program on American citizens. Yet, many other pieces of his purported policy agenda—immigration reform and the creation of a far-reaching jobs act—have come to naught. And, far from heralding a new post-partisan era in Washington, the Obama administration has presided over one of the most rancorous political climates in American history. Perhaps most fundamentally, the president has failed to restore Americans' trust in their government: A CNN poll in 2011 found that trust in the federal government was at an all-time low of 15 percent.[4]

President Obama's inability to deliver on all of his first campaign's promises, and the equally daunting challenges he faces in doing so during his second term, largely stems from the paucity of formal powers granted to the president. For the most part, individuals outside the White House hold the responsibilities for writing, interpreting, and implementing the laws. Thus, to get things done, President Obama, like all presidents who preceded him, must curry their favor. In addition, our perception of "failures" points to the incredible expectations we place at the president's feet.

Upon entering the White House, President Obama's supporters anticipated that he would restore the economy, fix the health care system, end two wars, and decrease America's dependence on oil, among a host of other issues. The sheer breadth of expectations placed upon the president has two major consequences. First, presidents' attention is divided among myriad priorities, virtually guaranteeing that they will not be completely effective in solving any one. Second, as modern presidents maneuver to solve these problems, they can be sure their every action will come under the highest scrutiny. Every appointment, speech, veto, executive order, and official visit attracts attention and debate. Like it or not, the president is the figurehead of the federal government—and no matter how much praise he may garner for one decision, he always risks shouldering blame the moment things go wrong.

As we will learn in this chapter, presidents must display a host of qualities, both formal and informal, to be successful. And, even more important, effective leadership and the realization of change depend upon the president's ability to rally support among the public and political actors who themselves have their own independent bases of authority.

Presidential Authority and Leadership

14.1 Trace the constitutional origins and historical expansion of presidential power.

Americans project their hopes onto the presidency. They expect their president to develop a legislative program and convince others to enact it. They demand that the president have, articulate, and defend policy ideas, all while unifying the country. They require him (someday her) to provide peace, prosperity, stability, and security. People want to feel that the country's leader has a plan, and they will credit him with good leadership if they believe that events are occurring in line with his plan. The plan must convey not only a sense of direction, of goals and priorities, but also a set of principles underlying those priorities. And perhaps most important, the plan must use the authority granted the president by the Constitution and historical precedent to act with certainty. Americans want to believe their presidents are acting decisively, that they are, in essence, masters of the universes that they inhabit.

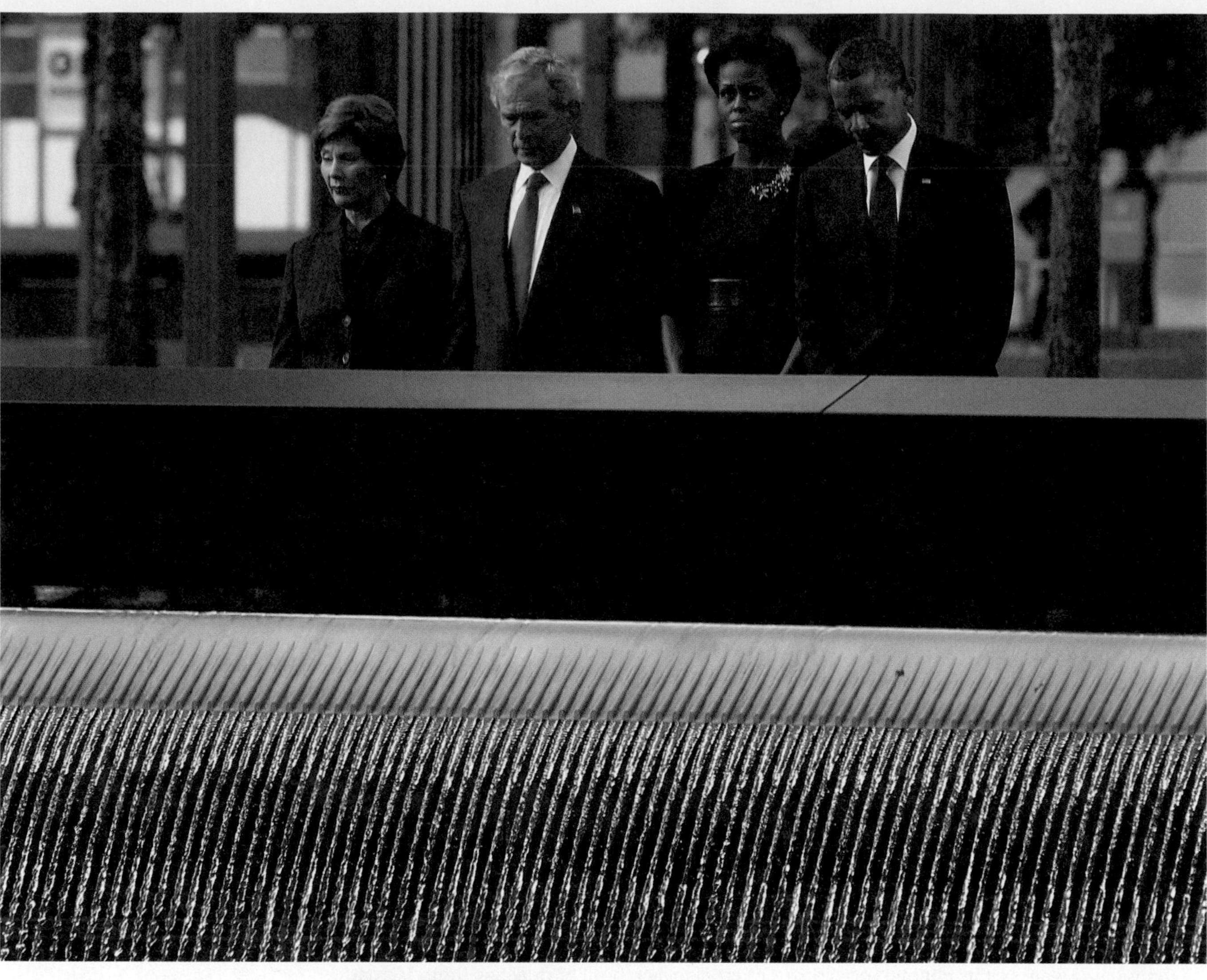

BUSH AND OBAMA AT GROUND ZERO

The terrorist attacks of September 11, 2001 singularly altered U.S. foreign policy. Marking the event's 10th anniversary, President Barack Obama and first lady Michelle Obama are joined by former President George W. Bush and his wife Laura Bush at the 9/11 memorial at the site of the World Trade Center.

In the past half-century, an avalanche of expectations has fallen at the White House doorstep. When the *Challenger* space shuttle exploded in 1986, when terrorists attacked on September 11, 2001, when Hurricane Katrina devastated New Orleans and the Gulf Coast in 2005, and when hundreds of thousands of gallons of crude oil poured out of a busted British Petroleum rig in the Gulf of Mexico in 2010, Americans turned to the president for reassuring words, for expressions of outrage, for signs that the country was strong and would persevere. And in calmer times, citizens look to the president, more than anyone else, for guidance on the basic policy priorities that are needed to address the challenges of the day.

In the United States, the president is both the "head of state" and the "head of government." As the head of state, the president is the embodiment of the popular will, and he represents the face of the federal government both within the country and in diplomatic relations with the outside world. And, as the head of government, the president must run the day-to-day operations of the country, interacting with Congress to create budgets, propose new laws, and make specific policy decisions as they arise. In many other countries, however, the head of state and head of government are two distinct offices held by two individuals. The manner in which these individuals are selected and the relative power they wield varies widely, though. The United Kingdom, for example, is a "constitutional monarchy." The monarch, currently Queen Elizabeth II, is the official head of state with mainly ceremonial powers. In practice, the government is led by the prime minister, currently David Cameron, who is generally the head of the majority party in Parliament (the legislature) and who answers to Parliament, not the queen.

In some other countries, the head of state and head of government are both elected or appointed positions. The head of state in these countries can sometimes have significant responsibilities, particularly in the realm of foreign affairs. France, for example, operates under a "semi-presidential" system. According to the French constitution, the president (head of state) is an elected position charged with making treaties and military decisions and generally representing France to the world. The president then chooses a prime minister (head of government) to run many of the daily government operations. The National Assembly (legislature) must approved the president's choice, however, and the prime minister is ultimately responsible to the legislature.

Electoral College
the meeting in each state and the District of Columbia of electors who cast votes to elect the president.

The Constitution Created the Office of the Presidency

How do presidents meet the extraordinary expectations laid before them? To begin to answer this question, we must first consult the document that created the presidency: the U.S. Constitution. When the delegates met in Philadelphia in 1787, they struggled mightily to create an executive office that would provide the needed "energy and dispatch" that was so sorely lacking in the Articles of Confederation, while also guarding against the very kinds of monarchical tendencies that led to the American Revolution.

CREATING THE PRESIDENCY Wary of giving too much power to one individual, the Framers wrestled with whether one person should hold the office of president or whether an executive committee or council was more appropriate. Some delegates initially lined up behind the Virginia Plan, which called for a congressionally appointed executive council. The executive would not have any specific powers granted in the Constitution, and members of the council would serve for a single seven-year term. A special body would be created that included the executive council and the Supreme Court. This body, known as the council of revision, could veto (reject) bills passed by Congress, with Congress in turn able to override the veto.

Other delegates argued that accountability would be stronger and more focused if a single individual held the office. These delegates, however, differed among themselves about the relationship between the president and Congress. Some wanted the president to be selected by Congress and have no independent authority. To other delegates, the presidency needed to have its own set of constitutionally enumerated powers. The delegates generally agreed, however, that the president would need to be able to check Congress, primarily through the veto power.

SELECTING THE PRESIDENT After deciding that one person would hold the position, the Framers debated how to select that person. Direct election by the public had little support. Instead, indirect election, in which the public selects other individuals who, in turn, elect the president, dominated the discussion. Indirect election was intended to prevent the president from becoming an extension of public passions. One plan called for election of the president by Congress for a single term. The person chosen would gain office by appealing not to the public, but to members of Congress. With a one-term limit, his actions would not be geared toward reelection. Most delegates, however, believed this system would make the president too dependent on Congress.

THE ELECTORAL COLLEGE

The Electoral College has often been criticized as undemocratic because it is possible for the person receiving the most popular votes nationally, as Democrat Al Gore did in 2000, to fall short in electoral votes and lose the election. Here, Gore concedes defeat to Republican George W. Bush with Democratic vice presidential candidate Joe Lieberman standing by.

The indirect election plan that prevailed was the **Electoral College**. In this system, electors from each state cast votes to elect the president. At first, each state legislature could choose how to select the state's electors. In some states, the state legislatures chose the electors; in others, the people voted for them. By 1856, however, every state allowed the people to vote for their electors. By not having Congress vote for the president and by allowing the president to run for reelection, the president's independence from the legislature increased. If no individual received a majority of the electoral vote, only then would Congress have a say, with the House of Representatives choosing the president.

14.1

14.2

14.3

14.4

14.5

The Electoral College was initially thought of as a way for the country's leaders in each state to meet, deliberate, and use their knowledge and wisdom to vote for the president, thereby insulating the selection of the president from direct public pressure. Today, this distinction between the electors and the people is meaningless—electors almost always are required by state law to vote for the candidate who won the presidential popular vote in that state. Electors do not play the role of wise sages originally anticipated by the Framers.

REACHING COMPROMISE OVER THE PRESIDENCY The American presidency as we know it today was a compromise that left no one at the Constitutional Convention entirely satisfied, but it contained elements that appealed to most delegates. The Constitution limited the presidency to individuals at least 35 years of age, born in the United States (or born abroad as the child of American citizens), and a resident of the United States for at least 14 years. The office was made more independent of the legislative branch than in earlier proposals. Indirectly elected by the people via the Electoral College, the president would serve a four-year term with the possibility of reelection.

Table 14.1 identifies the president's powers that are enumerated in Article II of the Constitution. Some constitutional powers, such as making treaties and appointing ambassadors and judges, are shared with the Senate. In these cases, the Senate must approve treaties negotiated by the president or confirm his nominees. Other powers are reserved for the president alone. These include the power to commission officers in the military, to grant pardons to those convicted of crimes (or, preemptively, to those who might be charged with a crime), to receive foreign ambassadors, and to convene sessions of Congress.

TABLE 14.1 IMPORTANT PRESIDENTIAL POWERS ENUMERATED IN THE CONSTITUTION

With the exception of the veto power, which is mentioned in Article I of the Constitution, all important sources of presidential authority are found in Article II.

Exclusive Powers of the President
Pardon
The president can personally exonerate any individual from criminal charges or judicial pursuit. "He Shall have Power to grant Reprieves and Pardons for Offences against the United States."
Commander in Chief
The president is the ranking officer of the U.S. Armed Forces. He directs the military and is responsible for military strategy. "The President shall be Commander in Chief of the Army and Navy of the United States, and of the Militia of the several States."
Implement Laws
The Constitution gives the president the power and responsibility to oversee the execution of laws passed by Congress. He does so through his cabinet and its bureaucracy. "He [the President] shall take Care that the Laws be faithfully executed."
Executive Power (the Vesting Clause)
The president holds the "executive power," the exact meaning of which continues to be debated to this day. "The executive Power shall be vested in a President of the United States of America."
Powers Shared with Congress
Veto
The president can send a bill he is unsatisfied with back to Congress for reconsideration. "Every Bill which shall have passed the House of Representatives and the Senate, shall, before it becomes a Law, be presented to the President of the United States: If he approve he shall sign it, but if not he shall return it, with his Objections to the House in which it shall have originated."
Treaties
Through the State Department, the president can negotiate treaties with other countries. However, they take effect only after they are ratified by a two-thirds vote of the Senate. "He shall have Power, by and with the Advice and Consent of the Senate, to make Treaties."
Appointments
The president has the power to nominate and appoint U.S. officials, subject to Senate approval. "He shall nominate, and by and with the Advice and Consent of the Senate, shall appoint Ambassadors, other public Ministers and Consuls, Judges of the supreme Court, and all other Officers of the United States."

The Constitution grants only limited specific powers to the president independent of Congress, but it includes some open-ended and potentially power-enhancing clauses. One clause directs the president to "from time to time give to the Congress information of the State of the Union, and recommend to their Consideration such Measures as he shall judge necessary and expedient" (Article II, Section 3). The first half of this statement was intended to ensure that the president did not remain aloof and distant from Congress. The second half provided an opening for presidential leadership of Congress. The **necessary and expedient clause**, which echoes the "necessary and proper" clause related to Congress, validates the president as a significant legislator—not merely an executive who implements and enforces the law, but one who plays an instrumental role in creating and promoting legislation.[5]

The Constitution also specifies that the president "take Care that the Laws be faithfully executed." The vagueness of this **take care clause** allows strong independent action, particularly if the president believes laws are being ignored. For example, in 1981, President Ronald Reagan fired all the federal air traffic controllers who had, in violation of their contract, gone on strike.[6] The clause also invites the president to interpret exactly what would be necessary to "faithfully execute" a law passed by Congress, which means he might take much bolder, or much less bold, action than Congress would like.

Finally, the Constitution gives the president "executive power." Debates continue about the exact meaning of this clause. Advocates of the unitary theory of the executive, for instance, suggest that this clause gives the president complete control over the departments and agencies that operate in the executive branch and, moreover, that the formulation and implementation of most U.S. foreign policy falls within its domain.[7] Others, by contrast, argue that this clause merely recognizes the president's responsibility to execute those laws enacted by Congress.[8] As we will see, the flexibility of this clause's interpretation has allowed presidents to expand the powers of their office over time.

necessary and expedient clause
a clause in Article II, Section 3, of the Constitution that authorizes the president to recommend legislation to Congress.

take care clause
the constitutional clause that grants the president the authority and leeway to determine if laws are being "faithfully executed" and to take action if in his judgment they are not.

Presidents Have Stretched the Language of the Constitution to Expand Their Influence in American Government

In addition to the authority granted to them in the Constitution, presidents have experimented to define the parameters of the office. A comparison of Article I in the Constitution (which concerns Congress) and Article II (which concerns the president) shows that the Framers had a much more detailed sense of the responsibilities and duties of Congress than they did of those of the president. Because Article II was written loosely, enterprising presidents have found ways to enlarge the powers and responsibilities of the office.

Put bluntly, presidents have had to stretch a few constitutional clauses here and there to see what Congress, the courts, and the public would accept as legitimate exercises of presidential authority. Does being commander in chief, for instance, mean that the president can take the country into war? Does the power to appoint bureaucrats also imply the power to fire them? Can presidents refuse to implement laws that they think are unconstitutional? Does the power to "execute" laws include the power to interpret them? Presidents pushed, other institutions responded, and over time the office became more clearly defined and more powerful; the process continues to this day. But what some in Congress and the public might see as an expansion of presidential power, presidents are inclined to see as a practice of the office's inherent power—the chief executive intrinsically has certain authority because of the nature of the job that need not be spelled out explicitly in the Constitution.

THE EARLY PRESIDENCY When George Washington took the oath of office as president in 1789, he began with the job as defined in the Constitution. Washington

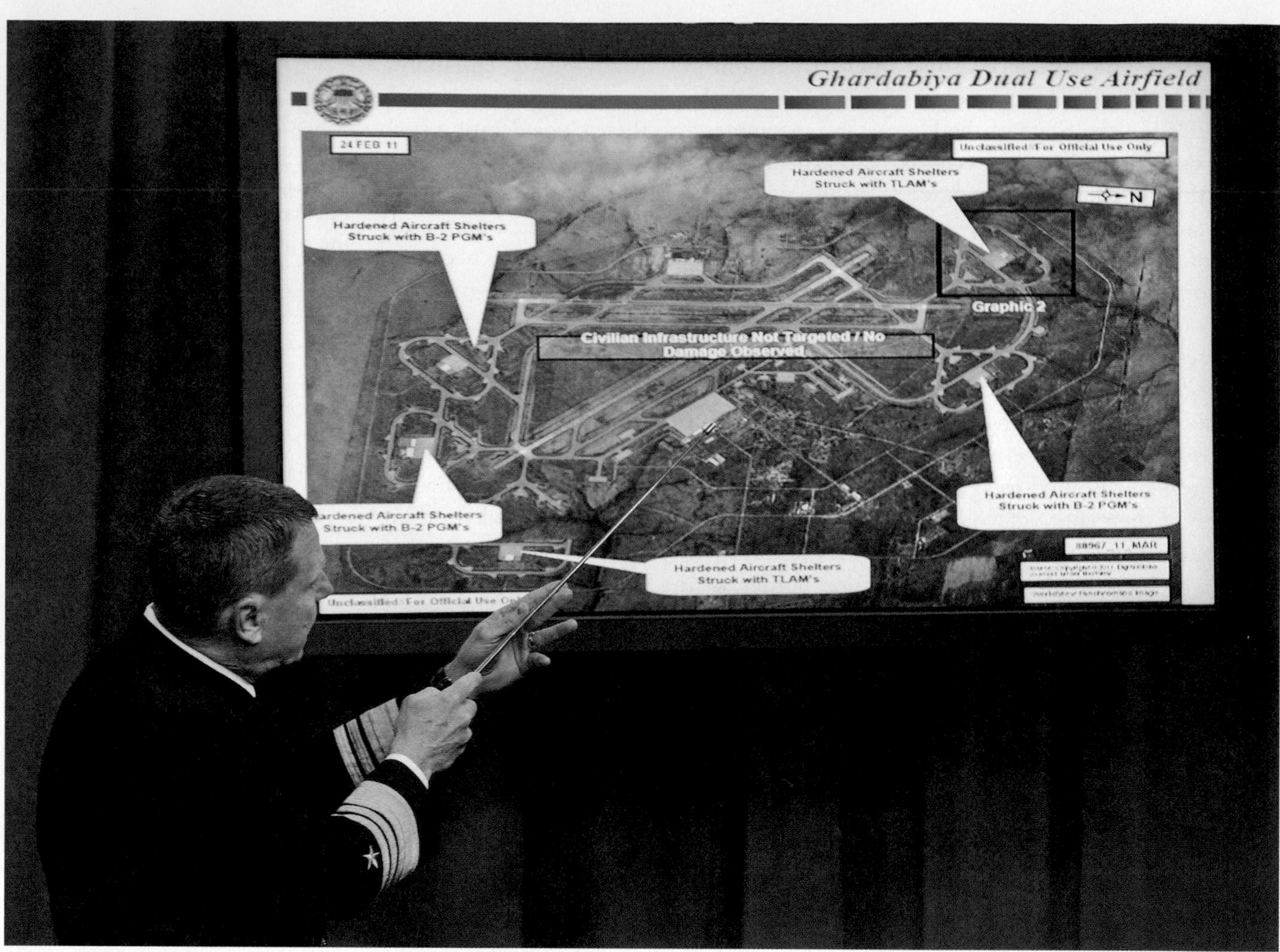

MILITARY ENGAGEMENT

President Obama did not merely inherit ongoing war in Iraq and Afghanistan. He also initiated military initiatives of his own. Above, Navy Vice Adm. William E. Gortney, director of the Joint Chiefs of Staff, briefs the press on "Operation Odyssey Dawn," in which U.S. and its allies targeted the Libyan government then ruled by Muammar Gaddafi.

(1789–1797) was determined to protect the president's independence. For example, he was adamant that the Senate's job was to confirm his nominees to the courts and not to dictate who those nominees should be; he even "politely" refused to give the Senate background information on his selections.[9] Washington immediately established the president's key role as head of state. Indeed, selected for the office primarily because of his enormous reputation throughout the country, most Americans viewed Washington as the one figure to whom the early nurturance of this new political office could be entrusted. Although he clearly led government during many heated political and legislative battles, Washington established the symbolic importance of the office as a representative of the nation, and he began the two-term president tradition. Until 1951, the Constitution did not require a president to step down after a maximum of two terms, though all but one (Franklin Roosevelt) did. Washington began the tradition, in part, to establish the practice of shifting power and to reassure Americans that the presidency contained no concentrated monarchical powers.[10]

Other early presidents promoted the office's independence and made clear that the president would not simply be implementing congressional legislation. Thomas Jefferson (1801–1809) actively engaged in legislative matters. He arranged the Louisiana Purchase, which vastly expanded the geographical reach of the United States, with no congressional consultation. Andrew Jackson (1829–1837) aggressively used vetoes to reject legislation that he found flawed as policy, and in so doing established the use of the veto as a key tool of presidential power. Before Jackson, presidential vetoes had been few and had centered on constitutional objections to legislation.

During the Civil War, Abraham Lincoln (1861–1865) took an expansive view of the authority of the presidency. To many of his critics, Lincoln's actions assaulted the nation's long-standing commitments to liberty and property rights. But in an emergency, Lincoln argued, Article II clauses concerning "executive power," "necessary and expedient," and "take care" had to be given very broad interpretations. Therefore, Lincoln initiated measures restricting civil liberties, including eavesdropping on telegraph lines and allowing prisoners to be held without charge.[11] To support the war effort, he launched the first national income tax not only in the absence of any constitutional language allowing such a policy but, in the eyes of many, directly contrary to constitutional language that seemed to prohibit this tax. It was not until 1913 that the Sixteenth Amendment would specifically allow the federal government to collect an income tax. Lincoln also created a national army that exceeded the size previously approved by Congress, helped establish the state of West Virginia, declared a boycott of southern ports, and authorized the construction of warships, all without congressional approval. In most instances, though, Congress ultimately granted its approval subsequent to these actions.

CREATION OF THE MODERN PRESIDENCY Theodore Roosevelt (1901–1909) was the first president to travel abroad during his term in office, cementing the president's role as the nation's chief diplomat. Roosevelt coupled this action with a foreign policy that sought to pull the United States more tightly into global politics and economics, including construction of the Panama Canal and a declaration that the Caribbean and Latin America were within the American sphere of influence. Roosevelt also pioneered the tradition of the president communicating directly to the public in easy-to-understand speeches about specific policy and legislative goals. In the nineteenth century, presidential speeches tended to be on broad topics that avoided controversy, rather than on specific legislation. Presidents presented themselves primarily as the head of state in their speaking tours around the country. Roosevelt, however, sought to influence public opinion by using his "bully pulpit," a term he coined to describe the president's direct connection with voters (Roosevelt used "bully" as a positive adjective, meaning roughly "wonderful"). This public influence, he believed, would in turn influence members of Congress.

In the 1930s, crisis again dramatically reshaped the presidency—this time the economic crisis of the Great Depression. "This country wants action, and action now," new President Franklin Roosevelt declared in 1933, and he had no doubt that he was the one to provide it. At one time, Americans would have recoiled from a president so determined to promise "action," but by the twentieth century, the idea sat more comfortably in people's minds—indeed, many saw the president's determination to act as a welcome change from previous presidents' cautious responses to the problems of the day.

Roosevelt (1933–1945) initiated a vast array of federal programs to deal with the collapse of the economy. In his inaugural address in 1933, he bluntly declared that he was willing to work with Congress, but that if Congress failed to act, he would seek "broad executive power" to address the emergency. Roosevelt put the nation on notice that he intended the presidency to be the leading political institution in the United States. He experimented in bold ways to redefine the presidency through active involvement in legislation and the creation of a set of supporting institutions in the Executive Office of the President. With a much larger staff at his disposal, the president could be even more active in policy making, using government agencies to carry out his wishes, and communicating to the public, legislators, and interest groups.

Roosevelt also revolutionized the relationship between presidents and the people they represent. From the moment he assumed office, Roosevelt expressed a commitment to harnessing the powers of the federal government to promote the welfare of average citizens. And over the course of his presidency, Roosevelt made a habit of

executive privilege
the idea that executive branch officials need to be able to advise the president in confidence, and that the president has a right to prevent that advice from becoming public.

speaking directly to his constituents. Through his weekly radio addresses, commonly referred to as "fireside chats," the president's voice entered the living rooms of citizens across the nation, speaking to their everyday concerns and the government's efforts to address them.

Roosevelt's presidency, though, was not without its share of controversy. The Supreme Court later declared several of the laws that he pushed through Congress unconstitutional. In response, Roosevelt proposed a plan that would give him a more favorable mix of justices on the Court. Rather than simply accept the Court's rulings, Roosevelt railed against justices who, in his view, remained out of touch with Americans' concerns. In response, he proposed to increase the size of the Supreme Court, a plan that would allow him to appoint justices who would look more favorably upon his domestic policy agenda. Neither the public nor Congress supported this perceived power grab, and the Court's membership remained fixed at nine Justices.[12] Despite the setback, the Court promptly shifted course and supported Roosevelt's policy agenda.

THE POSTWAR PRESIDENCY When the United States emerged from World War II as a world superpower, the president's power grew accordingly. During the Cold War between the United States and the Soviet Union, the president not only was the single most important person in American government but also was commonly seen as the most powerful person in the world. This enormous stock of prestige helped the president domestically. Increasingly, his actions were portrayed as connected to and vital for national security. To protect America's national interests, presidents declared that they needed to act swiftly and forcefully around the world. Domestic policy became entwined with foreign policy—as the world's economic leader, actions of the U.S. government could have significant repercussions for allies and potential allies.

One area in which all presidents have expanded the boundaries of the office is the control of information, and the postwar presidency continued the trend. The administration of Dwight Eisenhower (1953–1961) was the first to use the now common phrase **executive privilege** to refer to the idea that executive branch officials need to be able to advise the president in confidence, and that the president has a right to prevent that advice from becoming public. The withheld information usually involves discussions in the White House. When invoking executive privilege, the president usually argues that if members of Congress have access to private discussions, he and his staff are less likely to be fully forthcoming with one another. Moreover, if executive privilege is not permitted, Congress can request information merely out of a desire to discredit the president.

The most famous, or infamous, proponent of executive privilege was Richard Nixon (1969–1974) during the Watergate scandal. In June 1972, five men with ties to President Nixon's reelection campaign were arrested for breaking into the Democratic National Committee headquarters in the Watergate office building in downtown Washington, D.C.[13] Subsequent investigations into the incident uncovered a wide-reaching cover-up operation that implicated senior members of the Nixon administration, including the president himself. In their investigation of the president, prosecutors demanded that the White House release taped conversations between the president and his chief aides. Nixon refused, claiming that he had the right to withhold from the public any private notes, papers, and tapes of discussions in the White House. This invocation of "executive privilege" rested on Nixon's claims that a free flow of information and opinion was essential to the White House's ability to function, and that such freedom could exist only if private conversations remained classified. However, in *U.S. v. Nixon* (1974), the Supreme Court rejected Nixon's claim of executive privilege. In this first judicial test of executive privilege, the Court agreed that presidents had such a privilege, but that it was not absolute and needed to be weighed against the public interest. This ruling clarified that presidents cannot be assumed to always act in the public's best interests.

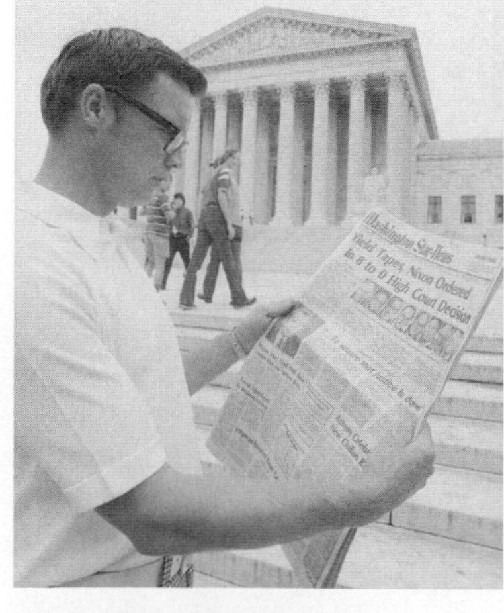

EXECUTIVE PRIVILEGE IS NOT ABSOLUTE

The Supreme Court ruled unanimously in 1974 that Richard Nixon's executive privilege did not allow him to withhold recordings of his conversations in the Oval Office. Two weeks later, Nixon became the only president to resign his position.

The George W. Bush administration expanded executive privilege by arguing that it applied broadly throughout the executive branch, not just to the president or vice president. President Bush used the take care and vesting clauses in Article II of the Constitution (Table 14.1) to argue for a view of the presidency known as the *unitary executive*. This doctrine, which the Bush administration propounded more strongly than any previous administrations, argues that the president is in direct, hierarchical control of all executive power in American government.[14] Thus, in 2007 and 2008 when Congress sought to investigate the firing of nine U.S. attorneys in the Justice Department, the Bush administration would not comply with requests for information that it believed were covered by this broader view of executive privilege.

Bush's and his advisors' conception of the unitary executive met with significant criticism. Legal scholar Jeffrey Rosen, for instance, argued that the doctrine set a dangerous precedent for the expansion of presidential powers.[15] And future Obama appointee to the top spot at the Office of Information and Regulatory Affairs Cass Sunstein wrote that although the unitary executive notion of a president maintaining hierarchical control over the executive branch was valid, it could not be distorted to mean that "the president can defy the will of Congress, or torture people, or make war on his own."[16]

As a candidate on the campaign trail in 2008, Barack Obama took particular exception to the Bush administration's articulation of executive power, and yet, as president, he has at times articulated a conception of presidential authority that is remarkably similar to Bush's unitary executive doctrine. For example, when Congress used a 2011 budget bill to defund several White House staff positions, Obama protested, arguing that the legislative language violated "the separation of powers by undermining the President's ability to exercise his constitutional responsibilities and take care that the laws be faithfully executed."[17] And when, in the early summer of 2012, Congress subpoenaed internal documents from the Justice Department relating to a gun-trafficking investigation, Obama invoked executive privilege.[18]

Despite these signs of increased strength, postwar presidents have faced significant obstacles to exercising power. The country has grown in population and complexity. The political environment contains powerful organized groups with diverse policy concerns. Numerous governmental programs are already in place, and attempts to remove them generate howls of protest. The federal budget is not limitless, neither is the public's willingness to tolerate increasing tax burdens. Presidents, therefore, often find themselves shackled by preexisting policy commitments that they inherit upon taking office. They cannot simply erase decades of history and start fresh. Indeed, once many laws go into effect, they become very difficult to repeal politically, especially if they provide additional services or cut taxes. For example, despite repeatedly stating his opposition to the Bush administration's tax cuts for the wealthiest 2 percent of Americans, President Obama extended the tax cuts in 2010 rather than let them expire under his watch; and in the summer of 2012, Obama called for yet another extension for all except the wealthiest Americans, reigniting partisan battles.

In addition, as members of Congress forge their own power during long careers, presidents also confront congressional challenges to their leadership. Unlike many members of Congress in the nineteenth century, who were content with one or two terms in Washington, members in more recent eras have been inclined to make Congress a career. Characteristically, the top four longest-serving senators in history all served part of their terms in the twentieth century.[19]

☐ Congress Delegates Authority to the President

In addition to the provisions in the Constitution, Congress yields additional authority to the president. Congress often defers to the president, either explicitly delegating policy-making tasks to him or deferring action until the president takes the initiative. Either way, the effect is to direct more public attention to the president as a leader. Through **delegation** of this sort, Congress gives the president discretion to act in a

delegation
the granting of authority by Congress to the president to be the first or main actor in a policy area, usually with implicit or explicit limits on actions that Congress would find acceptable.

particular area, typically within broad parameters of what is acceptable. If the president goes beyond these boundaries, Congress can find ways to indicate its displeasure by refusing to fund the implementation of the president's plan, setting stricter boundaries around future presidential action in this area, or being less cooperative in considering and passing a bill that is important to the president.

Congress has delegated especially vast powers in foreign affairs. For instance, beginning in 1975, Congress delegated to the president the authority to negotiate foreign trade agreements, limiting itself to a single vote on the agreement without the possibility of amending its language or engaging in a filibuster. Known as *fast-track authority*, this was a significant concession of congressional power. Fast-track authority expired in 1994, was renewed in 2002, but expired once again in 2007. What caused legislators to give up their ability to amend trade agreements? Political scientists have offered several possible explanatory factors. Legislators may have believed that negotiation with other countries works better when the United States presents a unified voice. Perhaps some of them feared that other members of Congress would be eager to protect industries in their districts, and the negotiations would unravel if the president then had to go back to other countries with a revised version of the treaty. Others might have considered trade to be a controversial subject and have wanted the president to take the criticism. Because some of these reasons put the president at political risk, even a Congress controlled by the opposition party might have granted presidents this authority.

Rather than pushing to revive fast-track authority, President Obama appointed Ron Kirk, a staunch opponent of the process, to the position of U.S. trade representative. Taking a more deliberate approach to drafting trade agreements, the Obama administration solicited input from union leaders (part of the Democratic base) before putting agreements up for a vote in Congress. In 2011, Obama signed into law four trade agreements that had been pending since the start of his administration. Critics of Obama's and Kirk's strategy argued that the trade agreements took far too long to come to fruition, wasting American resources and limiting efficiency in production. Kirk countered that by working carefully with Congress and interested parties; the resulting bills more effectively served the country's interests and, therefore, received rare bipartisan support in Congress.[20]

Congress also delegated to the president significant powers in the federal budget process. In part to help the president control executive branch agencies more effectively and in part to help Congress think more systematically about the budget, Congress after 1921 required the president to submit an annual overall budget as a framework for congressional deliberation. In practice, this meant that the president set the parameters in which the federal budget and Congress worked. The overall budget, as passed by Congress in a series of separate spending bills, typically looked very much like the president's original plan. In 1974, Congress passed the Congressional Budget and Impoundment Control Act to return some of the leverage to Congress. From then on, Congress passed budget resolutions that established targets for revenue and spending across all policy areas. But the president's budget was still the first to reach Congress, so even budget resolutions were a response to the president's plan.

Successful Leadership Entails Convincing People to Do What the President Wants Them to Do

Broadening interpretations of the president's constitutional authority, coupled with the growth in Congress's delegation of power to the president, have increased public expectations about the president's ability to lead. These expectations can be a burden for the president: A president seen as falling short may find that a growing proportion of the public disapproves of his performance in office. But public expectations can be a blessing, too. Higher expectations may enhance the president's leadership potential by forcing him to pressure Congress for cooperation. The president can appeal directly to the public, indicating that he wants to meet their expectations but Congress is obstructing him. Such appeals might generate public pressure on Congress to act and contribute to successful presidential leadership.

How Do We Know?

What Makes a President a Successful Leader?

The Question

For all that we expect of presidents, and for all that presidents do, it is difficult to determine whether any single president, in any important respect, succeeds. To be sure, no president fulfills all that the public expects of him or even all that he may have promised while on the campaign trail. But neither is any single president utterly ineffectual. Success is a matter of degree, not kind. So, what makes a president a successful leader? How do we know?

Why It Matters

Most Americans consider the election of the president to be among their most significant political acts. The more clear-headed and accurate we can be when casting these votes, the better. If we as citizens say we want strong and successful leadership, it helps to have standards by which to predict who will be the better leader or to determine whether a president has been a successful leader.

Investigating the Answer

Before researchers can determine whether a president is a strong leader, they first have to determine how to define and measure successful leadership. The public most often tends to think about presidential leadership in terms of impact: Did the president's action alleviate a problem, have no impact, or make things worse? These assessments matter electorally.

To political scientists, however, measuring success by impact is problematic for several reasons. First, whether the impact of a policy has been positive or negative can take a long time to determine and may change over time. Second, drawing the line between success and failure can seem arbitrary. What if the economic growth rate increases by 0.1 percent? By 1 percent? By 4 percent? Where does a researcher draw the line between success and failure, and why? Third, measuring presidential leadership by impact can be unreliable because the evaluation may be biased by political ideology. Consider Iraq. Iraq has deposed a dictator, held free elections, and written a constitution. It has also experienced brutal ongoing violence and a surge in terrorist activity, which has damaged the image of the United States among our allies. Given the mixed results, your ideology might dictate whether you judge the president's actions as having an overall positive or negative impact. Lastly, the impact you see may not be the result of presidential action: The correlation of the president's action with a particular outcome does not prove causation.

Therefore, political scientists tend to define presidential leadership in terms of outcome rather than impact. They look at what the president has attempted to accomplish and they evaluate his success in those areas. Some researchers have compared the president's campaign promises with his actual performance. Others have studied the president's State of the Union Address as a measure of his highest priorities and tracked what he accomplished legislatively in those areas. Both of these methods are attractive because of the available data on campaign promises or State of the Union Addresses across several presidencies. Other researchers have chosen a broader measure, comparing the president's preferences on roll-call votes taken in Congress and calculating how often Congress agreed with the president's position. The focus in these outcome-oriented studies of leadership is not on whether the president's policies "worked," but on whether he was able to persuade Congress to enact them.

The most common political science measure of successful presidential leadership is the frequency with which Congress votes in accord with the president's preferences. The measure is not a perfect indicator of leadership success—the president might not have done much to produce the outcome in Congress, and the final outcome on a vote does not tell us whether the president had to abandon major aspects of his policy in the days or months leading up to it. One especially attractive feature of this measure, though, is that the president typically takes a position on hundreds of congressional roll-call votes; thus, the frequency of presidential success can be calculated across time, across issue areas, and across different presidents, a method aiding political scientists in the kind of systematic analysis they prefer.

The Bottom Line

When assessing presidential leadership, political scientists focus on tangible outcomes. This method avoids the ideological bias that influences the assessments made by political activists and zealous partisans. By this measure, both Presidents Obama and Bush can be considered successful leaders, despite their low approval ratings. Focusing on other outcomes, however, such as their inability to get Congress to act on their jobs and Social Security reform initiatives, respectively, supports different conclusions.

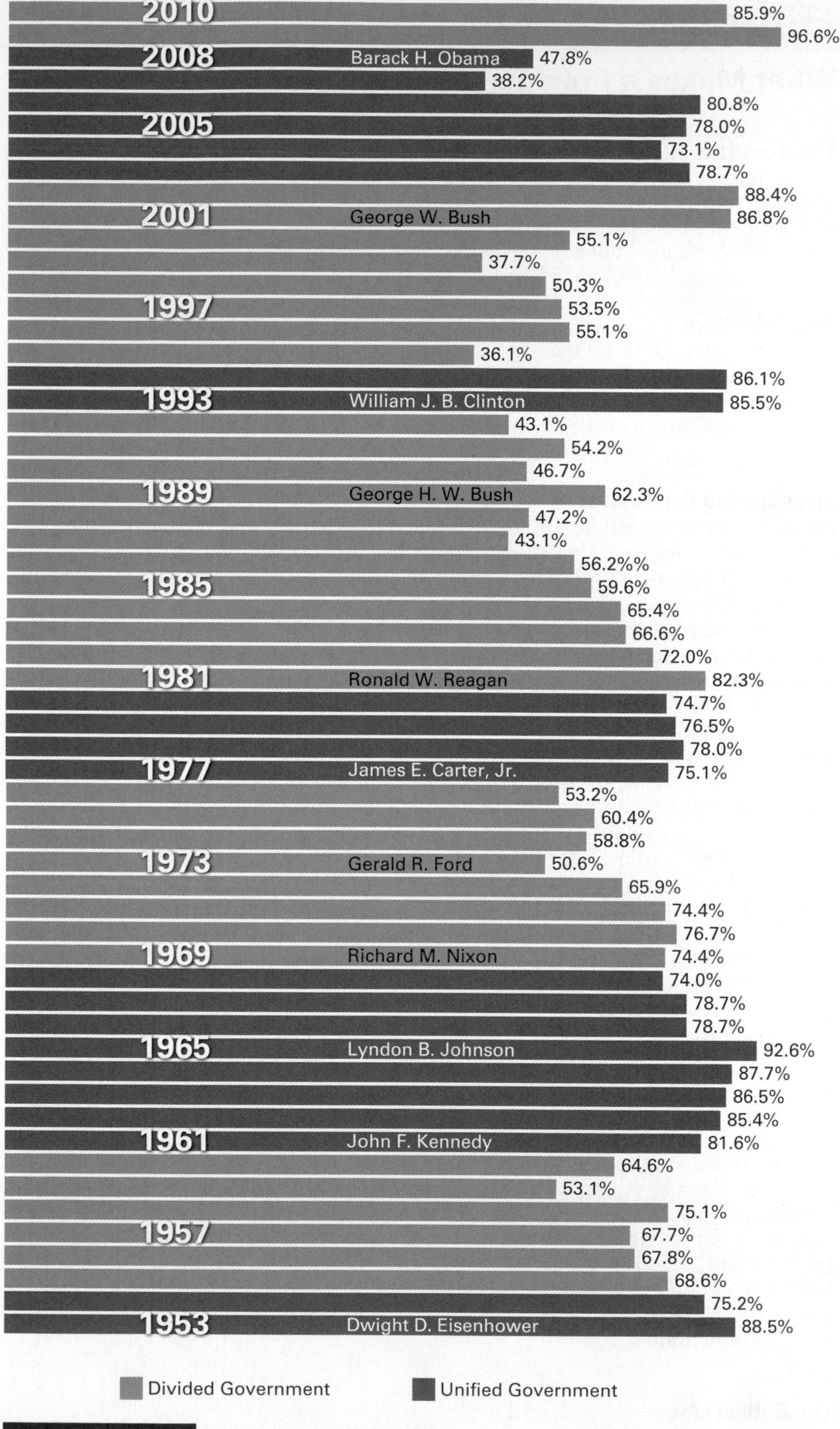

PRESIDENTIAL VICTORIES ON ROLL-CALL VOTES

Thinking Critically

- How should we compare the success rates of two presidents, one who has an aggressive and far-reaching domestic policy agenda, and the other who has only a modest set of proposals that he would like Congress to enact?
- How would you compare the legislative accomplishments of Bush's last year in office with Obama's first year? What accounts for the differences you observe?

Leadership can be evaluated in terms of outcome (Did the president succeed in getting Congress to pass his plan to reduce crime?) or in terms of impact (Did the plan actually reduce the crime rate?).[21] Political scientists tend to focus more on the outcome side of leadership. Thought of this way, leadership involves convincing the public that action is needed and getting a favored piece of legislation passed in Congress. It can also involve stopping action in Congress or influencing the content of legislation. Thus, to political scientists, **leadership** means the ability of a president to influence and guide others to achieve some desired policy or action. (See *How Do We Know? What Makes a President a Successful Leader?*)

Of course, it is easier to convince people to do what they are already inclined to do. In some situations, the president must use his skills to bring people together to do what, in effect, they already want to do but have not quite figured out how to do. Alternatively, the president can attempt to lead while rebuking public and congressional opinion. Here, the president tries to push the nation in a new direction and is often criticized for not being responsive to public opinion. This type of leadership is easier to pull off on matters of foreign policy, for which the president sets the agenda and often has the authority to act unilaterally. In the domestic policy arena, taking an unpopular stance can often prove more difficult.

In 2011, for example, President Obama advocated two major policy initiatives. Both initiatives met with stern opposition from Republicans. On the first initiative, the president undertook a very public campaign to persuade Congress to pass his proposed jobs bill. Yet, despite polls indicating that Obama had successfully convinced the public of his plan's merit, Republicans in Congress united to vote against the bill's passage. At the same time, President Obama announced his decision to withdraw nearly all American troops from Iraq by the end of 2011, without seeking approval from Congress. In August 2010, a majority of Americans (63 percent) had opposed staying the course in Iraq. But after Obama took to the bully pulpit, the number of Americans favoring withdrawal jumped 12 percentage points to 75 percent, making withdrawal the overwhelmingly popular option.[22] Though it is certainly possible that the president, at least in part, was taking his cues from the public, the abrupt shift in opinion observed shortly after the president's announcement suggests that Obama also did his part to shape public opinion on the Iraq War.

leadership
the ability to influence and guide others to achieve some desired policy or action.

formal powers
specific grants of authority defined in the Constitution or in law.

Powers of the President

14.2 Distinguish between the formal and informal powers of contemporary presidents.

Presidents invoke various powers in their efforts to set policy. Law and/or the Constitution designate some of these formal and expressed powers. Others—informal and inherent powers—derive from the unique advantages of the president as the sole public official in the United States elected by a national constituency. Presidential power is not limitless, however, and Congress and the courts can challenge its use.

Formal Powers Are Defined in the Constitution and in Law

As we have discussed, the president's **formal powers** are specific grants of authority defined in the Constitution or delegated by Congress. Others, though, were created through independent presidential initiative. The resulting mix of formal powers currently available to presidents establishes the first basis for leadership.

NEW LEGISLATION The president shares with Congress the role of enacting new legislation. In his role as "chief legislator," a president engages in every part

14.1

14.2

14.3

14.4

14.5

veto
the president's power to reject legislation passed by Congress; Congress can override a veto with a two-thirds vote in both the House and Senate.

pocket veto
the president's veto of a bill without the opportunity for Congress to override the veto; it occurs if the president does not act on a bill within 10 days after passage by Congress and Congress adjourns during that time.

line-item veto
the authority of a chief executive to reject part of a bill passed by the legislature.

of the process. He and his staff can draft bills, although the president cannot himself introduce a bill in Congress; a member of Congress must do that on the president's behalf. During deliberations over the bill, the president and his staff typically contact members of Congress and encourage them to vote with the president. They will also appeal to the media, interest groups, and the public itself to apply pressure on Congress. If the bill passes, the president must sign it before it can become law.[23]

PRESIDENTIAL VETO One of the most important formal powers is the **veto**, which allows the president to reject bills enacted by Congress: The veto is the president's power to say no. When the president vetoes a bill, Congress can override the veto with a two-thirds vote of each chamber, but this step typically proves very difficult to do. In the case of a **pocket veto**, Congress does not have even that opportunity. The Constitution gives the president 10 days either to sign or to reject a bill. If he does neither, the bill becomes law. If, however, Congress has adjourned (i.e., is not in session) during those 10 days and the president does not act, the bill is rejected—the president kills the bill by keeping it "in his pocket." Presidents can use their veto power to extract legislation more to their liking from Congress.[24]

The veto is powerful not only when it is used, but also when the president threatens its use. When the president threatens to veto a bill, members of Congress, particularly those who are not in the president's party, must decide whether they want to revise the bill according to the president's preferences or to refuse a compromise. If the bill is unchanged, the president will reject it. If they agree to revise the bill, the legislation will pass, but congressional members may be dissatisfied with the compromised version of the original bill. If they decide to allow the president to veto the bill, they are hoping that the public opinion backlash will force the president to reevaluate his stance or, if an election is near, that the president's position might hurt him or his fellow partisans running for office.

Over the course of the last half century, different presidents have exercised their veto powers with variable frequency. Presidents from John Kennedy through Bill Clinton vetoed legislation an average of nine times per year, but President George W. Bush made rare use of the veto power, issuing only 11 vetoes during his two terms in office. As of mid-2012, President Obama had issued just two formal vetoes during his first three and a half years in office—the lowest veto rate for a president since James Garfield in the nineteenth century.[25] In an effort to influence the legislative process, however, Obama made his willingness to exercise his veto power known, particularly after Republicans gained control of the House of Representatives in the 2010 midterm elections. [26]

A veto is a big knife, but sometimes what the president really wants is a scalpel. Presidents have long sought a more delicate device for fine-tuning bills in the form of the **line-item veto,** which would allow them to veto portions of bills rather than entire bills. A 1996 law gave this power to presidents, but President Clinton enjoyed it for only a short time. In 1998, the U.S. Supreme Court ruled that the line-item veto unconstitutionally added to the president's powers by, in effect, allowing him to amend proposed legislation—a task limited to Congress in the Constitution. The president could only approve or reject proposed legislation in its entirety: If he wanted the power to approve legislation in part, the Court ruled, a constitutional amendment would be needed.

COMMANDER IN CHIEF The president serves as the commander in chief of all the military services—the U.S. Army, Navy, Marines, Air Force, and Coast Guard. As commander in chief, the president has the authority to move American troops into combat. Being commander in chief requires the president to work in concert with Congress, but in this role the president tends to lead while Congress follows. This presidential authority is not clearly spelled out in the Constitution. Rather, it is one of those areas that presidents claimed over time, often over the vigorous protest of partisan opponents and constitutional scholars.

As commander in chief, presidents have argued that they have inherent powers to respond to emergencies and protect the safety of Americans and the security of the United States. George W. Bush's administration took controversial actions in response to terrorism, including indefinite detention of enemy combatants, denial of civilian court review of cases involving detainees, and surveillance of communications without prior judicial authorization. In defending these actions, President Bush and his spokespeople frequently argued that they fell squarely within the inherent powers of the president as commander in chief. Moreover, despite his initial opposition to this articulation of presidential power, President Obama has taken many of the same antiterrorism actions as his predecessor, highlighted most clearly in his refusal to shut down the government detention center at Guantanamo Bay, despite his 2008 campaign pledge.

Although the Framers intended the president to be in charge of the armed forces and guide their conduct during war, they also intended that Congress have the power to declare war. Fearing that the president had become too dominant in this area and had turned a shared power into a presidential one, Congress passed the War Powers Act in 1973. This act requires the president to notify Congress and receive its approval within 60 days when he deploys American troops militarily. As a practical matter, however, Congress usually finds that by that time it is too late to change course, and the president's decision stands. For example, when President Obama ordered American planes to assist NATO forces in bombing Libya in 2011, he did not seek congressional approval, arguing that the move did not constitute a true military action. Although members of Congress from both parties expressed public outrage over the president's refusal to heed the War Powers Act, the House ultimately voted to continue funding the bombing campaign, which was already in progress.

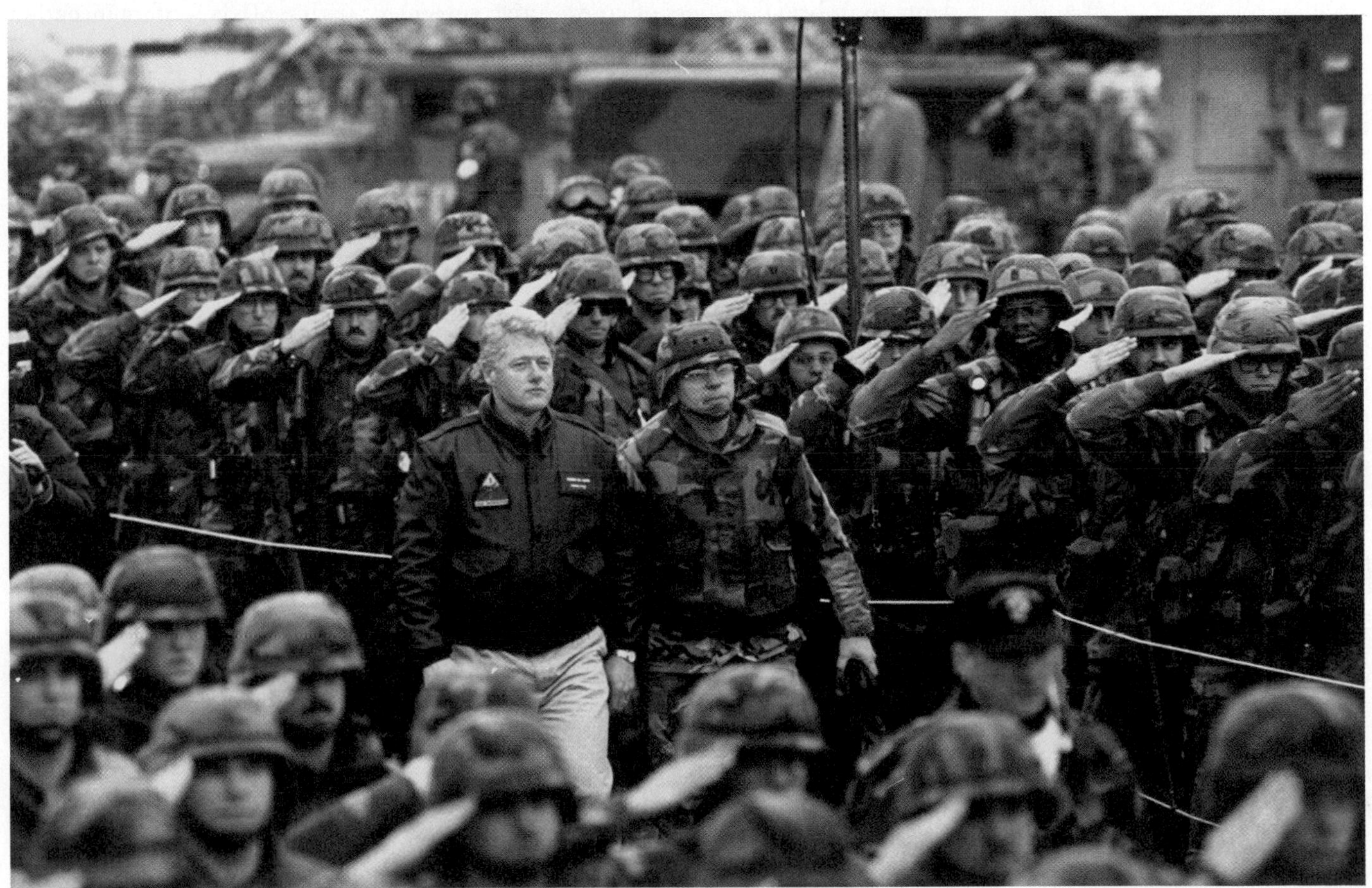

COMMANDER IN CHIEF

The president's commander-in-chief role over the world's largest military is a major part of his constitutional authority. Here, President Clinton visits with troops in 1996.

executive agreement
an international agreement in which the United States becomes a party once the president has signed it, without requiring approval from two-thirds of the Senate.

executive order
a presidential directive or proclamation that has the force of law.

EXECUTIVE AGREEMENTS AND EXECUTIVE ORDERS Two other formal powers available to presidents—the executive agreement and the executive order—enable them to enact public policy without the direct cooperation of Congress. These powers are not found in the Constitution but instead arise out of presidents' entrepreneurial efforts to expand their base of authority through claims of inherent powers.

With an **executive agreement**, a president can negotiate an arrangement with a foreign government without formal approval by Congress. These agreements cannot require changes in U.S. law—in those instances, Congress must sign off on the change through a treaty. But many subjects of international diplomacy do not require such changes. Not surprisingly, then, presidents often substitute executive agreements for treaties. Whereas the annual number of treaties ratified by Congress in the 19th Century regularly outnumbered the annual number of executive agreements issued by the president, today executive agreements outnumber treaties by a factor of roughly ten.[27] And they do so in lots of policy areas. In 2002, the Bush administration approved an executive agreement that committed the United States and Russia to specific nuclear arms reductions. In 2003, the United States and Vietnam reached an agreement to raise Vietnamese textile exports to the United States. And in 2009, President Obama and President Medvedev of Russia brokered an executive agreement to further reduce strategic offensive arms.

Executive agreements are not meant to be hidden from Congress and the public, although sometimes presidents have used them that way. A series of executive agreements between the United States and South Vietnam drew the United States more heavily into military involvement in Vietnam. Although the first of these agreements went into effect in the late 1950s under the administration of Dwight Eisenhower and continued through the 1960s under the administrations of John Kennedy and Lyndon Johnson, Congress was unaware of them until 1969. To forestall secret use of executive agreements in the future, Congress passed the Case Act in 1972, which requires presidents to inform Congress of an executive agreement within 60 days of its inception (amended to 20 days in 1977).

Executive orders (as well as proclamations, memoranda, and other directives) are presidential commands that have the force of law. Like executive agreements, they do not require Congress's approval; unlike executive agreements, they do not involve a foreign government. Executive orders apply to the executive branch and its employees, so the president, as head of the executive branch of government, is allowed to issue these, as would the chief executive of any organization. They can affect the private sector because private organizations interact with government, usually through contracts. For example, an executive order might state that companies wishing to provide goods or services to the government must have certain equal opportunity hiring policies in place. Although most orders are fairly routine matters of administrative procedure, the president can also use this tool to implement a wide range of policies, some of which aid constituencies important for the president's political success (see Table 14.2).[28]

In December 2002, for example, President Bush issued Executive Order 13279, designed to ensure that faith-based organizations—churches, synagogues, mosques, and other religious institutions—could compete for federal financing for programs that provide social services to the local community. Technically, the president required executive branch employees to treat these groups no differently from any other group applying for federal funding. By issuing the directive as an executive order, the president sidestepped potentially contentious congressional debate about the constitutionality of federal funding for religious organizations. Supporters saw the president's action as a vindication of the cultural support for religious rights and equality; opponents saw it as violating the American creed by forging too close a governmental link with religion.[29]

The president's power to use executive orders can be limited by Congress or by the U.S. Supreme Court. If a challenge is brought before it, the Supreme Court can declare an executive order void if it finds that the president's action exceeded his statutory authority or is contrary to the Constitution. As with executive agreements, Congress can weaken executive orders by cutting off their funding. Congress can also define areas that require prior congressional approval, thus negating the possibility of an executive

TABLE 14.2 EXAMPLES OF POLICY INITIATIVES IMPLEMENTED USING EXECUTIVE ORDERS

Executive order	Date	Subject	Issued by
9066	February 19, 1942	Internment of Japanese American citizens	F. Roosevelt
9981	July 26, 1948	Segregation in the armed forces ended	Truman
10730	September 23, 1957	Enforcement of school desegregation using National Guard	Eisenhower
10925	March 6, 1961	Affirmative action to be used by government agencies and contractors to ensure nondiscriminatory hiring practices	Kennedy
11615	August 15, 1971	Wage and price controls	Nixon
13158	May 26, 2000	Development of national environmental system of marine protected areas	Clinton
13379	December 12, 2002	More participation by faith-based organizations in federal social programs	G. W. Bush
13507	April 8, 2009	Creation of a White House Office of Health Reform	Obama

order. A future president also can overturn a prior executive order, as President Obama did with President Bush's order restricting federally funded stem cell research.

FORMAL POWERS COMPARED TO THOSE OF FOREIGN PRESIDENTS Although dozens of countries around the world have systems of government headed by presidents, the exact form of the presidency and its power vary. Compared to other presidential systems, an American president's powers fall around the middle of the range. For example, like the American president, presidents in Russia, Peru, and elsewhere can issue a unilateral directive similar to an executive order and then veto legislative attempts to repeal it. Although the legislature can check presidential behavior, presidents in these countries are more powerful than those in countries where unilateral action is not possible. On the more powerful end of the range, in some countries presidents have the exclusive right to introduce policy in particular areas. Taiwan and South Korea, among others, constitutionally limit the legislature's ability to refine the president's budgetary allocations. In these countries, the president has far more control over how money is spent, with the legislature's role being merely to accept or reject the president's overall plan.

Presidential vetoes are particularly prone to international variation. In some systems, a president's veto power may be limited to particular forms of legislation. The Mexican president, for example, cannot veto the annual appropriations bill that sets government spending. And the strength of the veto also varies across countries. In Venezuela, an override requires only the same number of votes that originally passed the bill. In other countries, such as Colombia, an absolute majority is necessary. In the United States and Argentina, among others, a two-thirds vote of the legislature is required to override a presidential veto. Although this authority gives the U.S. president a relatively powerful veto, he does not have the line-item or partial veto available to presidents of some countries, such as Argentina and Brazil.

☐ Informal Powers Include the Power to Persuade

Presidents also have informal powers, which are not the result of an established rule, policy mechanism, or constitutional assignment of authority. Rather, informal powers derive from a president's personal experience, leadership style, reputation, or prestige. Most famously in the category of informal powers, presidents have the "power to persuade." Some political scientists go so far as to say that the president's power *is* the power to persuade. Presidents devote considerable resources (financial and otherwise) toward persuading elected officials and the public about the merits of their policy positions. Some presidents, such as Lyndon Johnson and Franklin Roosevelt, had legendary bargaining skills. Others, such as Jimmy Carter, struggled to compromise and understand the political pressures faced by members of Congress.

Presidents often need the cooperation of members of Congress, aides and advisers, officials in federal agencies, and fellow politicians on the state and local levels. On some issues, they will be more passionate and involved and less willing to see their plans thwarted. Despite decreasing public and congressional support for the Iraq War, for example, President Bush was determined to defend his strategy.[30] A president may trade success on more peripheral issues to defend his position on the key issue. To secure cooperation, a president tries to persuade other policy makers that his position is right. He may offer them some benefit if they will cooperate—perhaps federal funds for a favorite project or fund-raising for a legislator facing reelection. He might threaten to withhold something from the legislator's district or indicate that he will not throw his support behind one of the legislator's priorities. Presidents will also try to put pressure on a recalcitrant member of Congress by appealing directly to his or her constituents.[31]

Signing statements, which presidents can issue when they sign legislation, are one way of persuading bureaucrats and judges. Most statements do little more than praise Congress for a job well done or emphasize the importance of the law itself. Increasingly, however, presidents have used these statements to reinterpret legislation in meaningful ways. In a budget bill designed to avoid a government shutdown in April 2011, Congress forbade the president from using discretionary money to fund four "czar" positions: the health care czar, climate change czar, urban affairs czar, and auto industry czar. Rather than accept Congress's orders, however, President Obama used a signing statement to defend his right as president to appoint such czars, which are not subject to Senatorial confirmation, to oversee his specific policy objectives within the executive branch.[32] It is important, however, not to overstate the influence presidents glean from signing statements. Such statements do not afford the presidents an opportunity—as some have charged—to actually rewrite the content of the law. Rather, they are attempts to persuade the bureaucrats who implement laws and the judges who may someday be called upon to interpret them.

Do signing statements cause bureaucrats to change their behavior? A congressional investigation in 2007 found some correlation between concerns raised in presidential signing statements and portions of legislation not implemented by federal agencies.[33] Although critics quickly asserted a direct causal relationship between statements and bureaucratic inaction, the facts at hand were more nuanced. It is not clear whether agencies ignored provisions of laws because of the signing statements or whether the statements were simply a convenient justification after the fact. It might also be true that the president was more likely to issue a signing statement when an agency had already signaled its predisposition to ignore some aspect of a law. In that case, it would be the agency's planned behavior that caused the signing statement, rather than the other way around. Because the report did not examine laws passed without signing statements, there was no way to know whether bureaucratic inaction was more frequent when signing statements were issued than when they were not.

Ultimately, the success presidents have in persuading other political actors often depends upon the degree to which they must rely on other actors to achieve their policy aims. If the president can act unilaterally, as Obama did to withdraw troops from Iraq in 2011, he may have an easier time subsequently persuading both Congress and the public to back his policy agenda. On the other hand, if the president must rely on Congress to pass enabling legislation, he may have a more difficult time convincing Congress to support his proposals. As a case in point, consider a showdown between the president and Congress that occurred at the beginning of the twentieth century. President Theodore Roosevelt wanted to show off America's newly acquired naval might by sailing his fleet around the world. Congress, however, rejected the plan as a waste of money. Rather than give up, Roosevelt famously ordered the fleet to start sailing anyway. Once the navy made it halfway around the world, the president approached Congress again and demanded that it cough up the money to bring the ships home. Backed into a corner, Congress had no choice but to acquiesce.

□ Congress and the Courts Can Check Presidential Power

Both Congress and the courts serve as a check on presidents who try to expand their authority too aggressively. When someone challenges a policy, ruling, or other action taken by the executive branch, the courts might declare it illegal or unconstitutional and therefore void. One of the most famous examples of the judicial branch checking the power of a sitting president occurred in the Supreme Court ruling *Youngstown Sheet & Tube Co. v. Sawyer* in 1952. The case arose out of a dispute between the federal government and the steel industry. Steel companies refused to increase workers' wages without also increasing the price of steel. But with the country in the midst of the Korean War, the Truman administration believed that an increase in steel prices would adversely affect America's military contractors. The United Steel Workers union, for its part, threatened to strike and halt steel production entirely unless wages were increased. Viewing a halt in production as a grave threat to the military, Truman ordered Secretary of Commerce Charles Sawyer to temporarily seize control of the steel companies' production facilities and keep the plants open. The steel companies argued that Truman's seizure was unconstitutional, and in a 6–3 decision, the Supreme Court ruled in their favor. In addition to establishing an important precedent concerning the limits of presidential power to seize private property during a state of emergency, this ruling—or more exactly, Justice Jackson's concurring opinion—established a framework for adjudicating disputes involving presidential power more generally.

Congress can check the president's power through the normal legislative process by not acting on legislation he desires, refusing to approve judicial and other nominees, designing agencies to have some independence from presidential control, and withholding funding and thereby prohibiting the executive branch from taking certain actions of which Congress disapproves. The threat of these actions often leads presidents to adjust their plans and soothe congressional objections.

The most severe congressional check on presidential power is **impeachment**, a process through which the House of Representatives can vote to initiate a trial conducted by the Senate that can lead to the removal of the president from office.[34] Under the Constitution, impeachment is the appropriate remedy for presidents who have committed "high crimes and misdemeanors," treason, or bribery. The exact meaning of "high crimes and misdemeanors" is left for members of Congress to decide. For guidance, members can look to the discussions among the Framers of the Constitution, previous impeachment efforts, and previous incidences of presidents who seemed to exceed their authority.

The process of impeachment begins in the House of Representatives, based on "articles of impeachment" that describe the charges against the president. Leaders in the opposition party, following a long period of strained relations with the president, usually draft these articles. The case against the president is first heard in the House Judiciary Committee. If that committee votes that there is a credible case against the president on all or some of the charges, it sends those articles to the full House to vote whether to proceed with impeachment. The Senate then holds the impeachment trial, and senators vote to determine whether the president is guilty and must be removed from office. Conviction in the Senate, not impeachment in the House, removes the president from office.

Two presidents, Andrew Johnson in 1868 and Bill Clinton in 1998, have been impeached. In both cases, the Senate acquitted them. Johnson had antagonized congressional Republicans with his too lenient (in their view) approach toward the former Confederate states and with his attempts to derail Republican plans for reconstruction of the South. The impeachment case was based largely on his violation of the Tenure in Office Act, which required the president to receive the Senate's approval before dismissing any office holders, and which had been passed largely to keep reins on Johnson. The case against Clinton was based largely on the charge that he had lied to a federal grand jury about his sexual involvement with White House aide Monica Lewinsky, and that he had obstructed justice by stonewalling the case.

Two other presidents, John Tyler and Richard Nixon, were nearly impeached. Tyler was "censured" in 1843 by the Senate for alleged misuse of power.[35] Nixon resigned in

impeachment
performed by the House of Representatives, the act of charging government officials with "treason, bribery, or other high crimes and misdemeanors"; the Senate then decides whether to convict and remove the official from office.

14.1

14.2

14.3

14.4

14.5

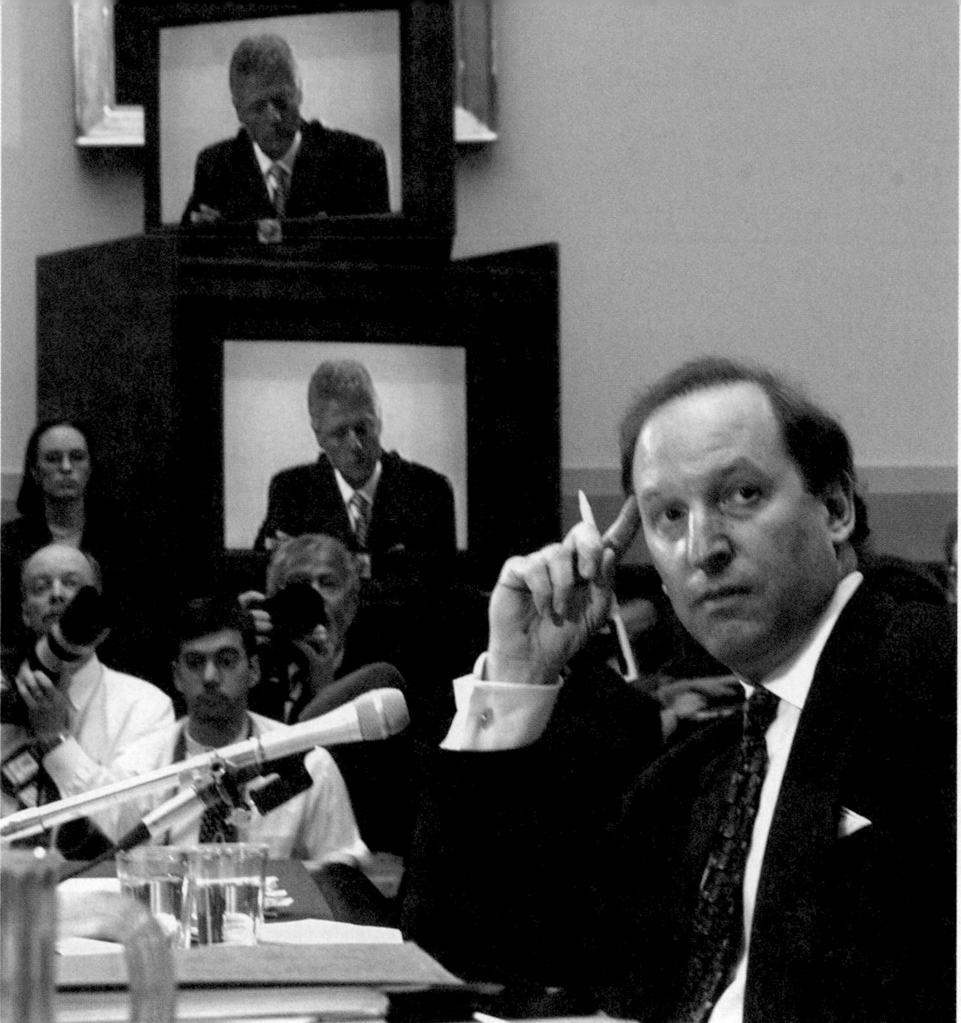

IMPEACHMENT

Minority Chief Investigative Counsel Abbe Lowell watches Bill Clinton's testimony to the House Judiciary Committee in 1997 during the president's impeachment hearings.

1974 after the House Judiciary Committee voted to send articles of impeachment to the full House. The committee charged the president with obstructing justice in the Watergate investigation and with abuse of power by using agencies such as the Federal Bureau of Investigation and the Internal Revenue Service to intimidate opponents. Technically, then, Nixon was not impeached, but it was all but certain that he would have been both impeached and convicted had he not voluntarily resigned from office.

Public, Electoral, and Contextual Resources for Presidential Leadership

14.3 Analyze how presidents use public support, electoral victories, and congressional allies to push through their policies.

Explore on MyPoliSciLab
Simulation: You Are a First-Term President

American presidents have varying degrees of success in leading the country, dealing with Congress, and achieving their goals. What explains these differing levels of success? Popular accounts often focus on a single factor—a president speaks well on television, he is fortunate to oversee a growing economy, or he receives overwhelming support from partisans in Congress.

Political science research, in contrast, shows that multiple factors contribute to presidential leadership success.[36] Pointing to just one factor can result in misleading interpretations. A president might preside while the economy is growing but still have trouble passing his program. This coincidence, however, does not mean that economic growth leads to presidential weakness. Rather, it suggests that other factors that are less favorable may be overwhelming the generally positive impacts of economic growth.

Successful leadership often depends on the resources available to the president. These resources include the president's relationship with the public, electoral factors such as the strength of the president's victory and the size and support of his party in Congress, and historical and policy contexts such as presidential advantages in foreign policy. A president who has an abundant supply of these resources should be more successful with Congress than a president who does not.[37] But success is not automatic. A president with a favorable political environment must still manage that environment with skill.

going public
activities of presidents such as highly visible trips, press conferences, interviews, speeches, and public appearances in an attempt to raise public support for a policy agenda.

☐ Presidents Seek Popular Support by "Going Public"

When **going public**, a president engages in a highly visible campaign of trips, press conferences, interviews, speeches, and appearances designed to galvanize support around his agenda. These campaigns are precisely plotted, scripted, choreographed, and timed to elicit a favorable response from the public and the media. Every symbol and prop on the platform from which the president speaks is carefully chosen. But whether going public is an effective political strategy is hotly debated by political scientists. (See *Unresolved Debate: Do Presidential Public Appeals Work as a Political Strategy?*)

In these public appeals, the president has strong advantages over members of Congress. Simply put, he is more likely to attract media attention than they are. In part, the inherent significance of the presidency leads journalists to focus on this office. It is also due to the power of one—the president provides a single focal point that simplifies the task of presenting the news. Unlike the 535 voting members of Congress, the president gives a journalist one story to tell.[38]

The trend of going public dates back to Teddy Roosevelt, who saw the presidency as a bully pulpit through which the executive could use public opinion to put pressure on Congress. In 1906, Roosevelt proposed legislation that would empower the Interstate Commerce Commission (ICC) to regulate shipping rates for railroads. When members of Congress loyal to the railroad industry opposed his proposal, Roosevelt went public with his plan, orchestrating an unprecedented speaking tour of the American West to appeal directly to voters. The move seemed to work: The Senate approved his legislation, and the resulting Hepburn Act was seen as a major victory for the Roosevelt administration.

More recently, President Obama used the strategy of going public to successfully pass his health care reform proposal through Congress. During the 2008 presidential election, Barack Obama promised sweeping changes to the American health care system. And, in his first year in office, he called for legislation that would impose new regulations on the insurance industry, control rising health care costs, and ensure quality and affordable health care for all Americans. To build public support for reform, Obama employed many of the grassroots organizing strategies from his 2008 presidential campaign, using a spin-off of his campaign organization to hold small rallies around the country. Obama spoke at length about the responsibility that members of Congress had to their constituents to bring about real change.[39] The president even called on bloggers to pressure their representatives to support health care.[40] This pressure ultimately proved successful: On March 23, 2010, the president signed health care reform into law. Although health care reform obviously cannot be attributed solely to President Obama's efforts, it is unlikely that passage would have been possible absent the president's vigorous public campaign for the issue.

What Influences a President's Public Approval?

Political scientists watch a president's approval because it shows how much political capital is available to him, indicates how much the public endorses the executive's performance, and helps us relate popular support to policy success, such as dealing with foreign crises or managing the economy. Gallup approval ratings of two recent presidents are shown below; you can see how presidential approval can be shaped by the economy and by events.

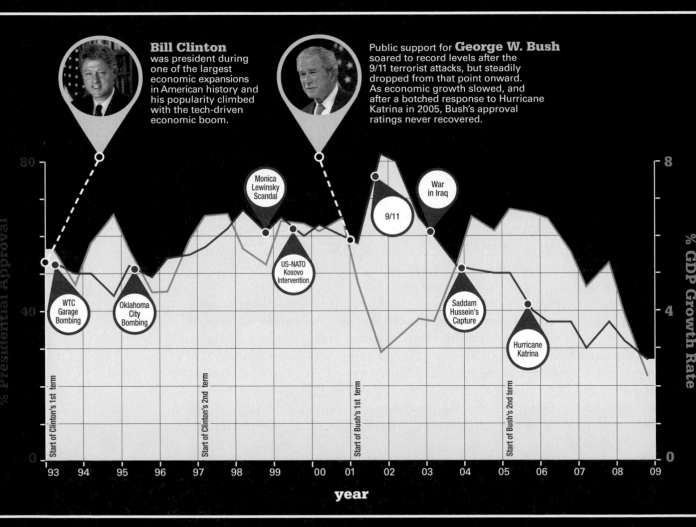

Bill Clinton was president during one of the largest economic expansions in American history and his popularity climbed with the tech-driven economic boom.

Public support for **George W. Bush** soared to record levels after the 9/11 terrorist attacks, but steadily dropped from that point onward. As economic growth slowed, and after a botched response to Hurricane Katrina in 2005, Bush's approval ratings never recovered.

Investigate Further

 **Explore** on **MyPoliSciLab**

Concept Do presidents gain or lose popularity over the course of their term? For President Clinton, an initial loss of popularity—due in part to economic recession—was followed by durable gains in public support. George Bush's popularity peaked with the 9/11 attacks then systematically fell off.

Connection Is popularity tied to economic performance? Clearly Bill Clinton's popularity moved with the economy. As it grew, so too did Clinton's job approval. For President Bush, there may be correlation between economic approval and popularity, but it is masked for much of his term by the effects of war on public opinion.

Cause How do events shape the popularity of President Bush? The 9/11 terrorist attacks led to a rally-round-the-flag effect which defined George W. Bush's presidency. For a brief period, success in the Iraq war boosted Bush's popularity until war fatigue and failure to manage other crises pulled his approval ratings to record low levels.

Unresolved Debate

Do Presidential Public Appeals Work as a Political Strategy?

For at least the past half-century, presidents have directly appealed to the public to rally support for their policy agendas. With ever-greater frequency, presidents have used television broadcasts, stump speeches, town-hall meetings, online appearances, and social media to make their case to the American people. But do these appeals work? Do presidential appeals cause people to change their views about policy matters?

APPEALING TO THE PUBLIC

During his time in office, Theodore Roosevelt forged a direct connection between the American public and its president. Here he acknowledges a crowd of supporters in Detroit.

YES

Although presidential appeals may not lead to widespread opinion change, they may increase the importance of issues and thereby lead some citizens to pressure Congress for policy changes that they, like the president, already supported. To explore this possibility Brandice Canes-Wrone, another noted presidency scholar, uses a wide variety of statistical techniques to show the influence of presidential appeals on spending in the federal budget:[a]

- Congressional appropriations more closely reflect the president's policy preferences on budgetary items that are the subject of public appeals.
- Domestic policy successes do not depend on the content of public opinion changing. Rather, presidential appeals turn latent public support into active support for elements of the president's agenda.
- On foreign policy, for which the public's preferences are less well informed, it may be possible for presidential appeals to change people's minds about specific issues.

NO

According to George Edwards, a noted presidency scholar, presidential appeals almost always fall "on deaf ears."[b] *Edwards argues that presidents, for the most part, are stuck with the political universe that they inherit. Try as they may, presidents can do very little to remake this universe in ways that benefit their particular policy goals. Edwards draws upon a wide array of quantitative and qualitative evidence to make his case that presidential appeals do little to generate support for the president's policy agenda:*[c]

- Public support for elements of the president's policy agenda changes hardly at all in the aftermath of prominent presidential speeches.
- When public support does change, it is just as likely to decline as to increase.
- Public reactions to some of the greatest presidential orators—Abraham Lincoln, Ronald Reagan, Barack Obama—indicate presidential influence runs in remarkably short supply.

CONTRIBUTING TO THE DEBATE

Efforts to assess the influence of presidential appeals face two core challenges. The first is that presidents do not issue public appeals randomly. Rather, they pay close attention to how their messages are likely to be received, which makes it difficult to isolate and assess the independent effects of appeals. Second, presidents are not the only political actors issuing appeals. Members of Congress, interest groups, and any number of media outlets issue appeals of their own. Trying to discern the unique effects of the president can be extraordinarily challenging.

Therefore, to make headway on this problem, political scientists must conduct survey experiments of their own in which they manipulate both the timing and content of messages sent by different political actors. This type of research may overcome the challenges of causal inference and provide clarity on a rich and ongoing debate within political science.

WHAT DO YOU THINK?

1. Under what conditions are presidents most likely to issue public appeals? What implications does this have for understanding whether public appeals change public opinion one way or another?
2. If presidential appeals do not generate wholesale changes in public opinion, why do presidents issue them so often?

[a] Brandice Canes-Wrone, *Who Leads Whom? Presidents, Policy, and the Public* (Chicago, IL: University of Chicago Press, 2006).

[b] George Edwards, *The Strategic President: Persuasion and Opportunity in Presidential Leadership* (Princeton, NJ: Princeton University Press, 2009); George Edwards, *On Deaf Ears: The Limits of the Bully Pulpit* (New Haven, CT: Yale University Press, 2006).

[c] Ibid.

14.1

14.2

14.3

14.4

14.5

mandate
the idea that the public provided clear policy guidance in the results of the prior election.

unified government
the presidency and both houses of Congress are controlled by the same party.

Sizable Election Victories Lead Presidents to Claim They Have a Mandate

Presidents elected to office with sizable victories, and who ran on a clear policy platform, are often in an advantageous position when dealing with Congress. These presidents can claim that they have received a **mandate** from the American people; that is, the public spoke clearly in the election about the direction in which it wanted the country to move. Of course, the more consistent the election results are nationally, the stronger the president's case. It is a matter of perception: Can the president convince the country or, more immediately, Congress that he has a mandate? Most will try.[41]

Barack Obama could make a compelling case for having received a popular mandate in 2008. Not only did he carry 28 states for a total of 365 electoral votes and 52.9 percent of the popular vote, he did so by winning states such as North Carolina and New Mexico that traditionally had gone to Republicans. Furthermore, on Obama's coattails, the Democratic Party in the 2008 elections strengthened its hold in both the House and Senate. When he assumed office, Obama's job-approval rating was 68 percent, second only to John F. Kennedy among newly elected presidents. Having campaigned expressly on the theme of change, Obama was poised to claim a mandate and tackle important elements of his policy agenda.[42] And so he would, as he quickly orchestrated the single largest stimulus package in the nation's history, a blend of infrastructure investments, tax cuts, and state funding that collectively carried a price tag of nearly $1 trillion. Later in the year, the president advanced a variety of education, stem cell research, and, most dramatically, health care initiatives.

Although presidents may successfully use mandates to push through their legislative agendas, their success is often short lived. Indeed, many presidents claiming a popular mandate have overreached, allowing their electoral victories to convince them they could tackle contentious political issues once in office. After winning 46 of the then 48 states in his 1936 reelection bid, President Franklin Roosevelt felt empowered to propose legislation that would have increased the number of justices on the Supreme Court. Roosevelt's hope was that by appointing additional members, he could ensure that a more sympathetic Court would not overturn his ambitious New Deal agenda. Despite the president's popular mandate, as well as their own repeated support of the New Deal, the Democratic majority in Congress viewed Roosevelt's so-called "court-packing" plan as a bridge too far. The Senate overwhelmingly rejected the proposed legislation. As a result, President Roosevelt squandered much of the political capital gained from his reelection mandate, and popular and congressional support for the New Deal as a whole began to decline. Whereas a large electoral victory grants presidents some political leverage, it often deludes them into attempting misguided political maneuvers that subsequently waste much of the advantage they have gained.

Presidents Rely on Fellow Partisans to Promote Their Policies

Normally, the president can count on the members of his party in Congress to help him enact his policy ideas. The more members of the president's party elected to Congress, the better his chances are for legislative victories. This is a valuable electoral resource. The president still needs to persuade his fellow partisans to go along with him, but that task will usually be simpler than convincing members of the other party.

UNIFIED AND DIVIDED CONTROL OF GOVERNMENT Presidents, of course, do not choose the partisan balance in Congress, so they need to figure out how to work with the situation they face. Because fellow partisans in Congress share many of their goals, presidents would prefer to have their party in control of both chambers of Congress. When Democrat Barack Obama became president, his party held a majority of seats in both the House and Senate, a situation known as **unified government**. The president thus was in a strong position to pass legislation to his liking. Success is not certain, however, because party members do not always fall in line. In most years since 1953, fellow party members in the House voted against the president's position more than 20 percent of the time; and in some years, particularly at the end of a president's second term in office, co-partisans in Congress voted against the president's position by considerably more.[43] Popular media accounts that criticize members of Congress for blindly supporting the president are therefore somewhat exaggerated. But why would fellow partisans defy their president?

divided government
the presidency is held by one party and at least one house of Congress is controlled by a different party.

Multiple factors affect whether or not legislators support the president on a vote. Constituency pressure, district economic interests, public opinion, personal philosophy, and other factors may cause a member of the president's party to vote against the president. In 2010, President Obama's comprehensive health care reform legislation passed Congress in spite of entrenched opposition from a significant minority of House Democrats. And in 2011, several Democratic senators joined with a unified Republican bloc to vote down President Obama's proposed jobs bill. In both of these instances, Democratic members of Congress concluded that challenging the president's position would enhance their electoral fortunes.

In **divided government**, the opposition party holds a majority of seats in one or both houses of Congress. If his party controls neither chamber, the president will typically face his most difficult challenges.[44] To succeed, the president needs to gain the support of a larger share of the opposition party by moving closer to its position, but without moving so far that he loses the support of his own partisans. The opposition party may want to deny the president victories, so it is likely to discourage its members from siding with the president. The president's success will be influenced by several factors, including how cohesive his party is, how cohesive the opposition party is, and the relative size of the two parties. The larger and more cohesive the opposition party is, the more difficult the president's legislative challenge will be.

Political scientists have found that party control of Congress complicates their analysis of presidential leadership. Politicians are strategic. In divided government, the president may have plans that he does not present to Congress because he believes they will have little chance at success. Or the president might offer a plan that he believes has as much or even more support in the opposition party than in his own. This was true for welfare reform during Bill Clinton's presidency and immigration reform during George W. Bush's. Similarly, with unified government, the president might offer bold legislative proposals that do not initially have strong support in the hope that he can coax fellow party members to support him. Neither of these strategic actions changes the overall pattern that presidents have more legislative success in unified than in divided government. But the net effect of these actions would be some additional wins when the opposition party controls Congress and some additional losses when the president's party controls Congress.

DIFFERENCES BETWEEN PRESIDENTIAL AND PARLIAMENTARY SYSTEMS These party dynamics make the president's relationship with Congress different from that of prime ministers' dealings with their legislatures in other countries. Whereas an American president is elected independently from members of Congress, and he can serve even if his own party is a minority in Congress, a prime minister will be in office only if his party is the majority party. A president is elected in a national election, but in a parliamentary system, constituents elect only legislators.[45] The prime minister is then selected by his or her party peers within the parliament.[46] If the party loses control of the legislature in the next election, someone from the new majority party will replace the prime minister. Should no single party secure a majority of the seats within Parliament, as occurred in the 2010 British elections, then a coalition government must be formed from at least two parties that constitute such a majority, and a prime minister is chosen from its ranks.

These differences make for significantly tighter ties between prime ministers and Parliament than between U.S. presidents and Congress. Prime ministers, as well as the heads of major government departments, emerge directly from the parliament.

There is little need for "getting to know you" time. Not only do members of the party majority know the prime minister, they have *chosen* him or her as the person they wish to lead the country. Typically, they are ready to work with that person from day one. Members of the prime minister's party in Parliament also know that if the prime minister is seen as a failure, their party is almost certain to be relegated to minority status in the next election. They, therefore, have an even stronger incentive than the U.S. president's partisans in Congress to support their chief executive. However, because parliamentary elections are not bound to a fixed schedule, the prime minister must make a determined effort to keep ties with members of the legislature strong, and members rarely cross party lines to support another party's position. U.S. presidents, by contrast, often need to forge ties across party lines to enact parts of their agenda.

☐ Presidents Have Advantages in Foreign Policy

The context of policy making differs between foreign and domestic policy. In foreign policy, fewer interest groups, journalists, voters, and members of Congress care deeply about these issues—a climate that gives the president a somewhat freer hand at advancing his agenda.[47] Because of this difference, some political scientists speculate that there are essentially two presidencies: a foreign policy president, who has wide range to act unilaterally and accrue support for his decisions after the fact, and a domestic policy president, who must rely on congressional support to achieve his objectives. The "two presidencies" theory thus argues that presidents exert significantly more influence over the writing and implementation of foreign policy than they do over domestic policy.[48]

Does the different nature of the foreign policy-making environment lead to greater presidential success? Systematic evidence supports the two presidencies theory in some aspects of public policy making but not in others. Presidential success on foreign policy votes in Congress has not been consistently better than in domestic policy votes. But one analysis found that presidents are able to secure funding that better matches their budget priorities in foreign policy than they are in domestic policy. And when going public, presidents can sway public opinion more easily in foreign affairs than domestic affairs.[49]

Both Obama's and Bush's tenures in office would appear to offer support for the two presidencies theory. In waging wars against governments in Afghanistan and Iraq and against terrorist networks worldwide, these president exerted their commander-in-chief authority, challenging the applicability of some U.S. laws and international treaties. But when these efforts had domestic implications, such as the trial and detention of terrorism suspects, Congress and the courts tended to resist these presidents' authority. And their stiffest legislative challenges were on domestic issues such as Social Security, immigration, and health care reform.

Institutional Resources for Presidential Leadership

14.4 Assess the role of the cabinet, the Executive Office of the President, and the White House staff in assisting the president.

To improve their chances at leading successfully, presidents rely on the established agencies and offices of the executive branch; they may also create an array of new supporting institutions. Think of these institutions as concentric circles, with the president in the center. The outer ring consists of the cabinet departments. Closer in to the president is the Executive Office of the President, established during the presidency of Franklin Roosevelt. Closest to the president is the White House staff. These institutions provide different kinds of resources for presidential leadership efforts. All have grown in size over time, especially since World War II.[50]

☐ The Cabinet Departments Implement Federal Programs

The outer ring of institutional resources, furthest away from the president, is the **cabinet**, which includes departments that implement nearly all government programs and provide the vast majority of government services (see Figure 14.1). The Senate must approve the president's appointments to leadership positions in the 15 cabinet departments. The heads of these departments are known as "secretaries" except for the Department of Justice, whose head is the attorney general. These individuals are appointed first to run the major departments of the government and second to provide advice to the president and help him implement his agenda. Although the president often meets with the cabinet as a group, he can also call on its members' individual expertise. Defense, Justice, State, and Treasury are generally considered the most important and powerful departments.

cabinet
a group of the top-ranking officials of every major federal department, plus other officials included by the president, who meet periodically with the president to discuss major administration priorities and policies.

All department secretaries are permanent members of the cabinet, but the president may also include other agencies that are not under the organizational control of any of the major departments. President Clinton, for example, included the Environmental Protection Agency. Presidents will add these agencies to the cabinet primarily because they genuinely want to hear their input at cabinet meetings or because they want to make a symbolic show of support for a particular issue; sometimes it's for both of these reasons.

From the president's point of view, there is always a risk that a department secretary will become so closely attached to the interests and perspectives of his or her department—become "captured"—that rather than communicating the president's viewpoint to the department, the secretary may push the department's views onto the president. When the president's ideas meet resistance from department personnel, will

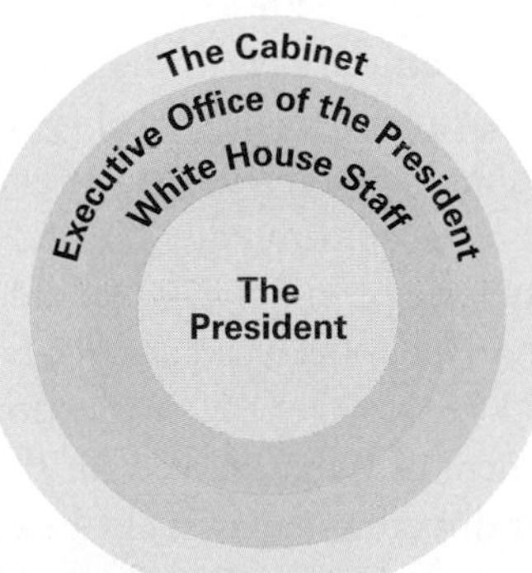

The Cabinet

Department Secretaries

State
Treasury
Defense
Justice
Health and Human Services
Labor
Commerce
Transportation
Energy
Housing and Urban Development
Veterans Affairs
Agriculture
Interior
Education
Homeland Security

Others Granted Cabinet Rank

White House Chief of Staff
Vice President
Administrator, Environmental Protection Agency
Director, Office of Management and Budget
U.S. Trade Representative
Director, Office of National Drug

White House Staff

Chief of Staff
Press Secretary
Legislative Affairs
Political Affairs
Public Liaison
Communications Director
White House Counsel
Intergovernmental Affairs
Policy Planning and Development
Cabinet Liaison
Domestic and Economic Affairs
Science and Technology Policy
National Security Affairs
Strategic Initiatives

Executive Office of the President

Council of Economic Advisors
Office of Management and Budget
Office of National AIDS Policy
Office of National Drug Control Policy
United States Trade Representative
Council on Environmental Quality
National Security Council
Domestic Policy Council
National Economic Council
Office of Administration
Office of Science and Technology Policy
President's Foreign Intelligence Advisory Board
Office of Faith-Based and Community Initiatives
Homeland Security Council
Privacy and Civil Liberties Oversight Board
USA Freedom Corps
White House Fellows Office
White House Military Office
Office of the First Lady
White House Office of Health Reform

FIGURE 14.1 THE INSTITUTIONAL PRESIDENCY, 2012.

The president relies on the cabinet departments to implement programs, the Executive Office of the President to provide policy advice, and the White House staff to provide political advice.

Source: www.whitehouse.gov.

the secretary support the president or will he or she obstruct the president's agenda? One notable case during the George W. Bush presidency concerned Christine Todd Whitman, the administrator of the Environmental Protection Agency (who had cabinet status). She resigned after a series of policy disagreements with the president and his closest advisers, including Vice President Dick Cheney, out of concern that the opinions of agency scientists were being overruled.

Because they are relatively high-profile figures, cabinet officials also have the potential to put the president in the awkward situation of either defending or repudiating them. For example, Attorney General Eric Holder came under intense criticism in 2011 after it emerged that the Justice Department's Bureau of Alcohol, Tobacco and Firearms (ATF) was permitting illegal gun purchases along the Mexican-American border. According to reports, federal agents sold more than 2,000 guns to unknown parties as part of a plan to track the guns back to Mexican drug cartels. Most of the guns, however, were lost, and two that were found had been used to kill a U.S. Border Patrol agent. Testifying before Congress, Attorney General Holder denied any prior knowledge of the gun-selling plan, but congressional Republicans released evidence to the contrary. Despite the controversy, President Obama came out publicly in support of his attorney general. In a strongly worded statement issued at a White House news conference, Obama said that he had, "complete confidence" in Holder and "complete confidence in the process [initiated by Holder] to figure out who, in fact, was responsible for that decision."[51] Holder later refused to hand over documents relating to the investigation. In the summer of 2012, the House responded by formally holding the Attorney General in contempt, setting off an inter-branch constitutional showdown, with neither side showing much of an inkling to back down.[52]

One sign of the strain between presidents and the cabinet is the high turnover of cabinet officials in presidents' second terms. Although a cabinet official sometimes simply wants to move on to a new challenge, obtain a more lucrative job in the private sector, or have a less hectic lifestyle, cabinet turnover often results from presidential displeasure with the official's performance. In the twentieth century, an average of about two cabinet department heads served for both terms of a two-term presidency.[53] After being reelected in 2004, President George W. Bush replaced 9 of 15 department secretaries. Of the 6 who continued, 4 had taken their positions at the start of the president's first term. One of these was Donald Rumsfeld, who, long under fire from both Democratic and Republican legislators, resigned shortly after the Republicans' loss of the House and Senate in the 2006 elections. Only one department head, Elaine Chao at the Department of Labor, served for Bush's entire presidency.

The problems of directing department heads are more severe for U.S. presidents than for prime ministers in European parliamentary systems. The U.S. president selects department heads from outside the legislature; the prime minister puts fellow legislators in charge of departments. The president cannot be sure that he or Congress will be able to work well with the heads of the cabinet departments. Although the president appoints these officials, they are often people the president does not know well and has not worked with. The prime minister, on the other hand, chooses members of his or her party in the Parliament to head the government departments. This would typically mean the prime minister has worked with these individuals and has confidence in them.

To avoid some of the challenges of working with cabinet secretaries, some recent presidents have turned to policy "czars" for advice. These czars report directly to the president, do not require Senate confirmation, and assist in the coordination of policies across different departments. The use of the term *czar* dates back to the Franklin Roosevelt administration, but Richard Nixon was the first president to actually appoint one—a drug czar. Every president since has appointed multiple special advisers. During his tenure in office, President George W. Bush had 36 czars. And depending on the source, President Obama has had anywhere from 18 to 32 czars charged with policy responsibilities ranging from oversight of the car industry to executive compensation, Afghanistan, and climate change.[54] But some members of Congress have expressed displeasure with the appointment of policy czars who do not face careful vetting from the Senate.[55]

The Executive Office of the President Provides Policy Advice to the President

Executive Office of the President
a group of agencies in the executive branch that primarily generate policy alternatives for the president's consideration.

The next concentric ring is the **Executive Office of the President** (EOP), which consists of a number of policy-related groups that aid the president. Officials in the EOP generate policy alternatives and suggestions that are especially faithful to the president's political agenda.[56] Their primary responsibility is to provide the president with trusted policy advice. Unlike cabinet departments, EOP agencies generally do not administer programs (except in the sense of coordinating and directing the efforts of other federal agencies), and they do not have large staffs of career civil servants.[57] Therefore, from the president's perspective, EOP officials do not have to wrestle with the pull of departmental loyalty that might cloud the judgment of cabinet secretaries. As Figure 14.1 indicates, the EOP provides advice and guidance across a number of policy areas, in some ways paralleling the areas covered by the cabinet departments.

The single most important EOP agency is the Office of Management and Budget (OMB). OMB serves as a gateway through which departments must pass in making their budgetary requests, and it approves proposed regulations and testimony that a department wants to bring before Congress. In effect, OMB serves as a filter to make sure that departments do not seek funds or regulations that are contrary to the president's program. Other especially important EOP agencies are the Central Intelligence Agency, the Council of Economic Advisers, and the National Security Council.

The vice president is officially part of the EOP. Historically, however, most vice presidents have been selected not only to offer policy expertise but also to provide the president with electoral advantages. A president with no Washington experience, for example, might select a vice president who has held office in the nation's capital. Or a vice president might be chosen because he or she increases the president's chances of winning a key state or region. The vice presidency is an often maligned institution,

VICE PRESIDENTS MAY PROVIDE ELECTORAL ADVANTAGES

Vice President Joe Biden has played a strong role advising President Obama on foreign policy. On July 4, 2010, he addressed troops in Baghdad, Iraq. Vice presidents are often selected not only to offer policy advice and expertise, but also to provide presidents with electoral advantages.

White House staff
a group of offices in the executive branch that provides the president with political advice, promotes the president's program with legislators and interest groups, and handles the president's public relations.

mostly because it has only two defined duties: to break tie votes in the Senate and to succeed the president in case of the death, incapacity, or removal of the president from office. Yet, more recent administrations have bucked this trend, with vice presidents playing a far greater role in policy making. In the Bush administration, for example, Vice President Dick Cheney often took the lead on security issues, overseeing the use of highly controversial "enhanced interrogation" techniques used to extract information from alleged enemy combatants. Although perhaps not as powerful as Cheney, Vice President Joe Biden has also enjoyed significant influence over military and foreign policy in the Obama administration. And after Republicans gained control of the House in the 2010 midterm elections, Biden also became the White House's lead negotiator with a divided Congress, in which he had served for 36 years.

The Offices of the White House Staff Provide Political Advice to the President

The institutional circle closest to the president is the **White House staff** (WHS), sometimes referred to as the White House Office. The WHS provides the president with political advice, promotes the president's program with legislators and interest groups, and handles the president's public relations. With only about 450 employees in the Obama administration, the WHS is relatively small compared to the EOP, which has more than 1,800 employees, and the cabinet departments, which total nearly 2 million civilian employees. The WHS consists of small units such as the offices of the press secretary, legislative affairs, public liaison, and intergovernmental affairs, to name a few. The primary concern of the WHS is the political well-being of the president. Whereas the EOP provides the president with policy advice and might be thought of as the president's policy filter, the White House staff is the political filter. Figure 14.2 provides examples of the issues raised by the WHS when it considers policy proposals that emerge either from executive departments or Congress.

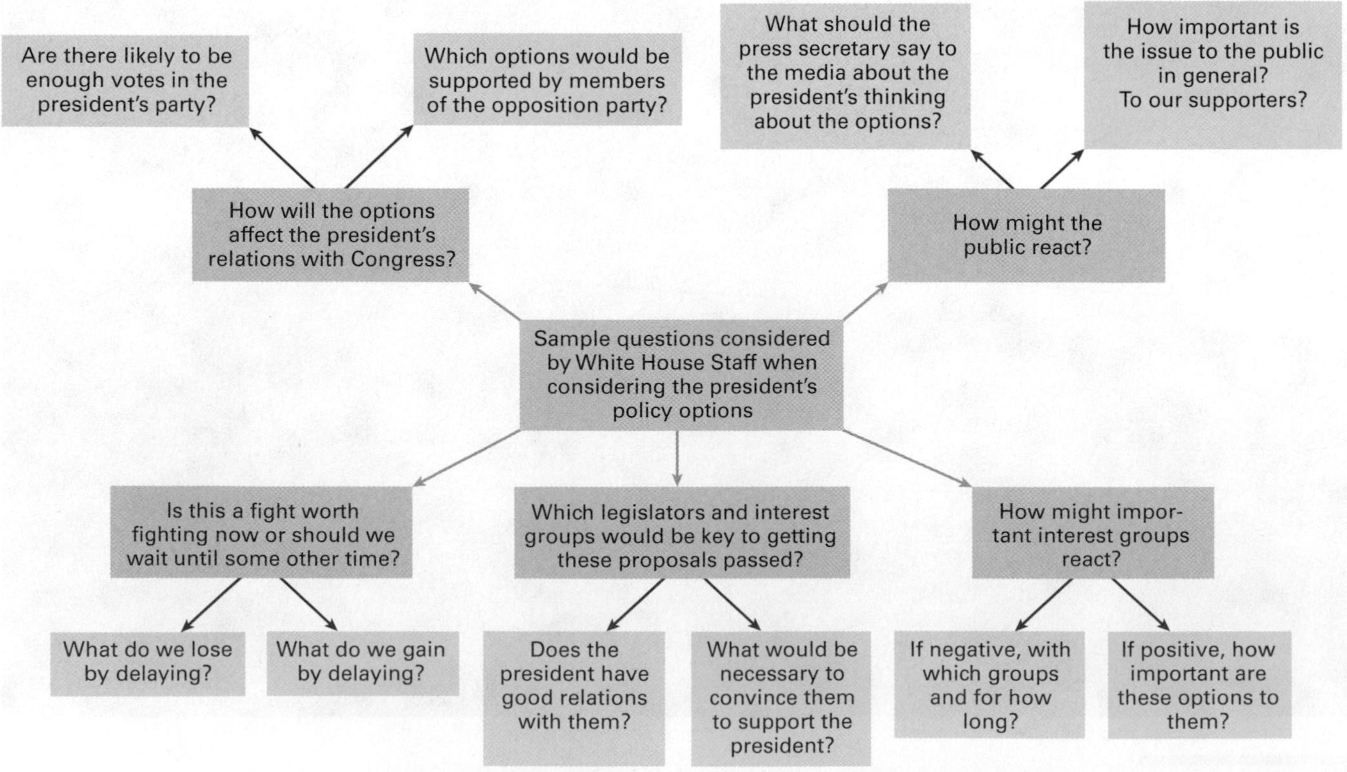

FIGURE 14.2 TYPES OF QUESTIONS ASKED BY THE WHITE HOUSE STAFF.
The White House staff provides the president with an analysis of the political environment.

For President George W. Bush, Karl Rove was the key political confidante. A senior adviser since Bush's Texas days, Rove headed three WHS offices. In his words, "my job is to pay attention to the things that affect his political future."[58] Rove was credited with fostering close ties between the president and evangelical Christians. He also, however, came under fierce criticism in Bush's second term for the administration's political missteps concerning Hurricane Katrina, the war in Iraq, and allegations of government corruption.

When President Obama named Illinois Congressman Rahm Emanuel as his chief of staff, he likewise tapped an accomplished political strategist for a leading WHS role. Emanuel was a senior adviser to President Clinton for seven years, led the Democratic Congressional Campaign Committee in 2006 when Democrats won a majority in the U.S. House, and as chair of the Democratic Congressional Caucus in 2007–2008 was instrumental in setting party strategy on policy positions and communications. Emanuel's time in the White House, however, would prove short lived, as he would leave the WHS in 2010 to run for (and win) the position of mayor of Chicago.

approval rating
the percentage of the public that approves of the job the president is doing overall.

Public Opinion of the President

14.5 Describe how party identification, the economy, and other factors shape how the president is perceived by the American public.

Since the late 1930s, assessments of the president's job performance have been measured by his public **approval rating**, the percentage of the public that approves of the job the president is doing overall. To collect this information, public opinion firms conduct surveys and ask respondents whether they approve or disapprove of the president's performance. Political scientists, meanwhile, have investigated the ways in which specific factors shape public perceptions of the president. And among individual-level factors, a person's party identification stands out as perhaps the single most important.

Presidents Depend on Support from Constituents of Their Own Political Party

Party identification is a key factor in approval ratings. Democrats will be more likely to approve of a Democratic president's job performance, Republicans less likely, and independents somewhere in between. This pattern does not mean that, for instance, Democrats will blindly approve of President Obama because of the party label, but rather that Democrats are more likely than Republicans to agree philosophically with actions taken by a Democratic president. In recent years, as the electorate has generally become more polarized along party lines, the support for presidents has increasingly become one-sided and partisan (see Figure 14.3).

Although presidents can always depend more on members of their own party for support, the level of that support—and of support more generally—varies widely over the course of their time in office. Presidents often enter office with a significant degree of bipartisan support: Expectations for a new president are high, and even members of the opposing party appear willing to give an incoming executive a chance to prove himself. At some point in their first term, however, presidents inevitably face strong tests of their ability to lead: a failing economy, a military crisis, or a major policy initiative that goes awry. These challenges also test the public's opinion of the president. The degree to which presidents are able to weather these crises and convince the public of their leadership abilities determines whether or not they get elected to a second term in office. For one-term presidents such as Johnson, Ford, Carter, and George H. W. Bush, bipartisan support had eroded to such an extent by the end of their terms that even some of their partisan backers began to jump ship. In contrast, two-term presidents such as Reagan and Clinton were able to bounce back from initial setbacks; they both maintained relatively high approval ratings even as they left office after eight years of tribulations (see Figure 14.4).

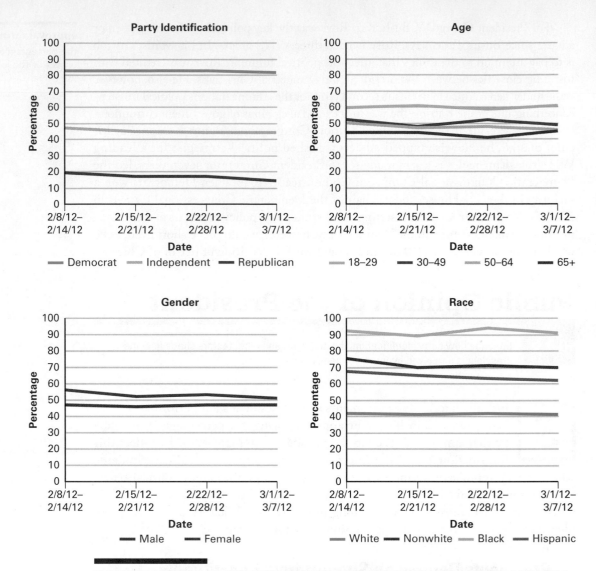

FIGURE 14.3 PARTISAN AND DEMOGRAPHIC DIFFERENCES IN PRESIDENTIAL APPROVAL RATINGS.

The panels in this figure show the results of job approval ratings for President Obama registered in a daily tracking poll conducted in 2012. Results are separated out by party identification, age, gender, and race. The largest and most consistent differences in presidential approval ratings register between Democrats and Republicans. Nonetheless, important differences exist among demographic groups as well. Obama's greatest support can be found among the young, women, blacks, Hispanics, and other nonwhite populations.

Source: Gallup Daily Tracking Poll, February 2012. http://www.gallup.com/poll/121199/Obama-Weekly-Job-Approval-Demographic-Groups.aspx

The Economy Is a Key Factor in Presidential Approval Ratings over Time

The state of the economy is significantly correlated with a president's job approval rating over time. Improvements in economic performance tend to improve people's assessments of the president. Although political scientists disagree about which economic indicator is paramount—unemployment, inflation, growth, or something else—virtually all concede that the economy's recent performance has a profound bearing on public assessments of the president.

These assessments, what is more, have important implications for people's vote choices on Election Day. When the national economy declines in the year before a presidential election, the incumbent president's vote share predictably declines. As the 2008 presidential election made clear, a flagging national economy also can have important implications for the electoral prospects of a presidential candidate from the

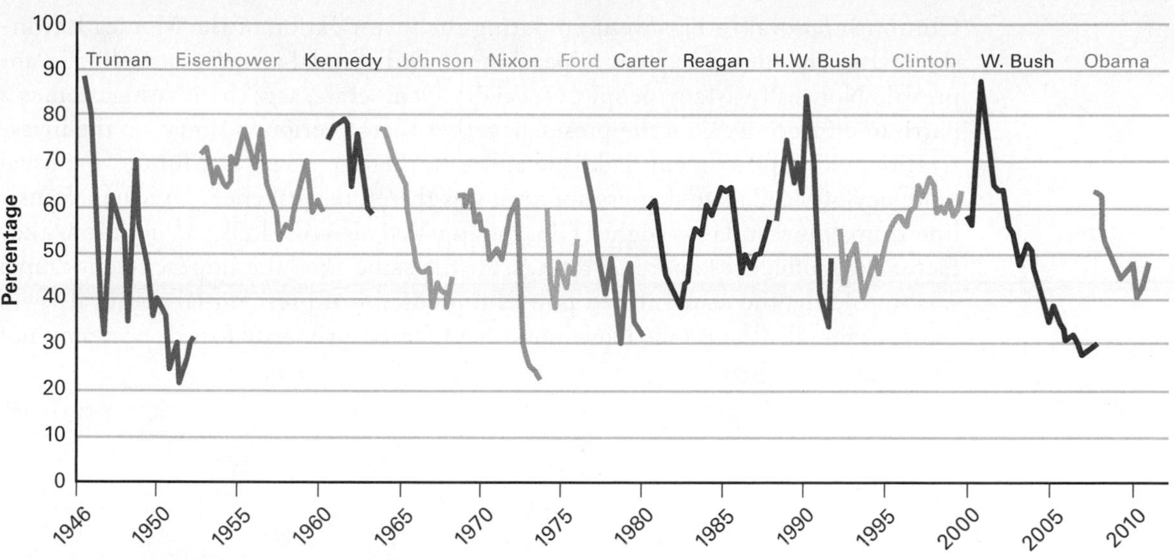

FIGURE 14.4 PRESIDENTIAL APPROVAL RATINGS.

During their time in office, most modern president experience rather rapid declines in their approval ratings. Indeed, with the exceptions of Reagan and Clinton, every president saw their approval ratings plummet in the later stages of their tenures.

Source: How the Presidents Stack Up, Presidential Approval Ratings: http://online.wsj.com/public/resources/documents/info-presapp0605-31.html.

same party as the incumbent. Already facing long odds, John McCain's chances of winning the presidency were all but dashed when the economy spiraled downward in early October 2008.

rally event
short-term international event or military action that boosts presidential approval ratings temporarily.

Honeymoon Periods, Rally Effects, and Scandals Can All Shift Public Perception in the Short Term

Approval ratings tend to start high and drift down over time. During the early "honeymoon" period of a president's term, when opposition to the president's plans has not yet solidified, the public is still likely to give him the benefit of the doubt. He will not likely be blamed for problems inherited from his predecessor. And, usually, he has not had time to make any major mistakes. As these mistakes happen, and as it gets harder to blame the predecessor, people find reasons to criticize the president's performance. When Obama first took office in January 2009, he enjoyed an approval rating of 68 percent, and just 15 percent of the American public actively disapproved of the president. By the end of his first term, the president's approval ratings registered at just 50 percent, and his disapproval numbers 48.[59]

Rally events are another factor in approval ratings. Rally events are short-term international events or military actions that boost approval ratings. John F. Kennedy's rating surged 13 points in 1962 when the United States set up a blockade around Cuba after it was revealed that Soviet bases were being installed there. President George W. Bush's approval rating started out in the upper 50s and low 60s, substantially higher than his percentage of the vote in the 2000 election. It began drifting downward as perceived economic conditions deteriorated. Then, his approval rating rose enormously after the terrorist attacks on September 11, 2001. A similar trend can be seen in President Obama's approval ratings after the killing of Osama bin Laden—an initial boost, followed by a decline in the face of continued fears surrounding the economy.

On the other end of the spectrum, scandals usually depress presidential approval ratings. During the Watergate investigation of the early 1970s, Richard Nixon's job approval plummeted. However, scandals do not always cause ratings to drop. Bill

14.1

14.2

14.3

14.4

14.5

Clinton's approval ratings went up during the investigation of the Monica Lewinsky matter and his subsequent impeachment. Did scandal actually cause higher approval? Not really. Many people, especially Democrats, saw the investigation as a partisan effort to weaken the president rather than a serious scandal, so the investigation and impeachment had little effect on their approval of Clinton. The usual tendency of scandals to depress approval was therefore weakened. Drawing a causal line from this scandal to higher Clinton approval also overlooks an additional key factor that influences approval ratings. At the same time the impeachment drama was unfolding, the economy—a powerful predictor of presidential approval—was growing rapidly. The public likely rewarded Clinton primarily for the economy, not for being impeached.

Review the Chapter

 **Listen** to **Chapter 14** on **MyPoliSciLab**

Presidential Authority and Leadership

14.1 Trace the constitutional origins and historical expansion of presidential power, p. 469.

The Constitution created the presidency, but the office subsequently underwent extraordinary changes. The American presidency was an attempt by the Framers to balance many competing ideas about executive power. As a compromise, it contains some inherent contradictions. It is the office that Americans demand the most from, but its constitutional list of specific duties is relatively meager. The very vagueness of the job description has accommodated a historical expansion of the meaning and impact of the presidency from the time of the early republic to the present.

Powers of the President

14.2 Distinguish between the formal and informal powers of contemporary presidents, p. 481.

Presidents have both formal and informal powers to reach their goals. Formal powers such as the veto, executive orders, and the role of commander in chief are specified in law or the Constitution or are realized through independent executive initiative. The origins of informal powers are less easily identified. These powers include the president's skill at persuading others to do what he wants and the ability to tap into and strategically exploit the reservoir of support for basic values in American political culture. The manner in which presidents use their powers can be checked by the courts, which can declare presidential actions unconstitutional or inconsistent with law, and by Congress, which can use its legislative, budgeting, and, in extreme cases, impeachment powers to thwart presidents.

Public, Electoral, and Contextual Resources for Presidential Leadership

14.3 Analyze how presidents use public support, electoral victories, and congressional allies to push through their policies, p. 488.

Presidents draw on a variety of public, electoral, and contextual resources to exercise leadership. The president's public approval rating receives substantial attention from politicians and political observers, and presidents devote significant amounts of time to appealing to the public to support their proposals. A president with a convincing election victory and his party in the majority in the House and Senate is in a strong position for successful leadership. Other factors that affect a president's success are the support for existing policies as well as differences between foreign and domestic policy.

Institutional Resources for Presidential Leadership

14.4 Assess the role of the cabinet, the Executive Office of the President, and the White House staff in assisting the president, p. 494.

Presidents also rely on institutional resources to advance their policy agenda. The cabinet departments implement nearly all federal programs and are therefore crucial to the president's agenda. The Executive Office of the President provides the president with policy advice. And the White House staff specializes in providing the president with political advice and services.

Public Opinion of the President

14.5 Describe how party identification, the economy, and other factors shape how the president is perceived by the American public, p. 499.

At the individual level, no predictor of presidential approval is greater than party identification. Numerous contextual factors, however, also affect the president's approval ratings. Typically, presidential approval ratings decline in a poor economy and the aftermath of scandal, and they surge during the honeymoon era and following rally events.

Learn the Terms

approval rating, p. 499
cabinet, p. 495
delegation, p. 477
divided government, p. 493
Electoral College, p. 471
executive agreement, p. 484
Executive Office of the President, p. 497
executive order, p. 484
executive privilege, p. 476
formal powers, p. 481
going public, p. 489
impeachment, p. 487
leadership, p. 481
line-item veto, p. 482
mandate, p. 492
necessary and expedient clause, p. 473
pocket veto, p. 482
take care clause, p. 473
rally event, p. 501
unified government, p. 492
veto, p. 482
White House staff, p. 498

Test Yourself

Study and **Review** the **Practice Tests**

14.1 Trace the constitutional origins and historical expansion of presidential power.

Which of the following was initially thought of as a way to insulate the selection of the president from direct public pressure?

a. a constitutional monarchy
b. the Virginia Plan
c. a constitutional convention
d. the Electoral College
e. a separation of powers

14.2 Distinguish between the formal and informal powers of contemporary presidents.

Which of the following is an informal power of contemporary presidents?

a. enacting legislation
b. persuading elected officials of the merits of policy positions
c. issuing executive agreements and executive orders
d. vetoing legislation
e. commanding the armed forces

14.3 Analyze how presidents use public support, electoral victories, and congressional allies to push through their policies.

What does it mean for a president to "go public"?

a. The president uses highly visible activities, such as speeches, interviews, and campaign trips, to galvanize support for his or her agenda.
b. The president establishes protocols for dealing with the press corps.
c. The president claims he has a mandate based on election results.
d. The president uses private meetings with legislators to demand action on policy priorities.
e. The president uses the vice president as a spokesperson with the media and the public.

14.4 Assess the role of the cabinet, the Executive Office of the President, and the White House staff in assisting the president.

Which agency or office could be considered institutionally closest to the president?

a. Executive Office of the President
b. cabinet
c. Office of Management and Budget
d. White House staff
e. National Security Agency

14.5 Describe how party identification, the economy, and other factors shape how the president is perceived by the American public.

Which of the following is NOT a vital factor in shaping presidential approval ratings over time?

a. the economy
b. rally events
c. party identification
d. scandals
e. the president's age

Explore Further

SUGGESTED READINGS BY TOP SCHOLARS

Charles Cameron. *Veto Bargaining: Presidents and the Politics of Negative Power*. New York: Cambridge University Press, 2000. Provides a formal analysis of the conditions under which presidents exercise their veto power and the consequences this has for the content of public policy.

Brandice Canes-Wrone. *Who Leads Whom?* Princeton, NJ: Princeton University Press, 2006. Identifies the conditions under which presidential appeals successfully alter public opinion and thereby change legislative behavior.

George Edwards. *The Strategic Presidency*. Princeton, NJ: Princeton University Press, 2009. Argues that rather than transform their political environment, successful presidents recognize and take advantage of opportunities not of their own making to effect policy change.

William Howell. *Power without Persuasion: The Politics of Direct Presidential Action*. Princeton, NJ: Princeton University Press, 2003. Examines the conditions under which presidents pursue policy change through unilateral directives rather than legislation.

Stephen Skowronek. *The Politics Presidents Make: Leadership from John Adams to Bill Clinton*. Cambridge, MA: Harvard University Press,2007. Provides a rich account of the various political environments that confront presidents when they assume office and the limits and opportunities for leadership in those environments.

SUGGESTED WEBSITES

White House: www.whitehouse.gov

This site provides an overview of the president's initiatives, text of presidential statements, and links to executive branch agencies and offices.

American President: An Online Reference Resource: www.millercenter.org/academic/americanpresident

This site provides detailed biographical information on each president and key administration officials, with links to audio files of major presidential speeches and interviews with major figures from the presidencies of Jimmy Carter through Bill Clinton.

American Presidency Project: www.presidency.ucsb.edu

This outstanding collection of resources contains nearly 80,000 documents related to the presidency, campaigns, and presidential activities in office.

National Archives: Presidential Libraries and Museums: www.archives.gov/presidential-libraries

This guide to the presidential library system includes links to online archival documents.

U.S. Presidency Links: http://cstl-cla.semo.edu/renka/presidencylinks.htm

This is a comprehensive and helpful A-to-Z guide to presidential information maintained by Russell Renka at Southeast Missouri State University.

Listen to Chapter 15 on MyPoliSciLab

15

The Federal Court System

THE COURTS RULE ON CAMPAIGN FINANCE

On January 21, 2009, a deeply divided Supreme Court struck down limits on campaign funding by corporations, nonprofits, and labor unions. The groundbreaking 5–4 decision allows businesses and unions to spend millions on political campaigns. The case, *Citizens United v. Federal Election Commission*, centered on a dispute over whether the Federal Election Commission could regulate the campaign usage of the documentary *Hillary: The Movie,* which attacked the 2008 presidential candidate Hillary Clinton and was produced by a conservative nonprofit organization. The Court ruled that regulating the documentary and the funds used to create and disseminate it constituted an infringement on free speech.[1]

Reaction to the ruling was split along ideological lines. Republicans praised the Court for upholding free speech.[2] Democrats, however, depicted the decision as a setback for fair elections. President Barack Obama weighed in with criticisms of his own, condemning the Supreme Court in his first State of the Union Address: "With all due deference to separation of powers, last week, the Supreme Court reversed a century of law that I believe will open the floodgates for special interests, including foreign corporations, to spend without limit in our elections."[3]

The Court's rationale for ruling as it did focused on free speech and opposition to regulation. Writing for the majority, Justice Anthony Kennedy explained that "when government seeks to use its full power, including the criminal law, to command where a person may get his or her information or what distrusted source he or she may not hear, it uses censorship to control thought." Referencing the First Amendment of the Constitution, the majority claimed that the regulation of corporate spending in elections inhibited political dialogue and debate.

Before President George W. Bush's two appointments, John Roberts and Samuel Alito, swung the Supreme Court in a conservative direction, the Court had ruled differently on similar cases on election spending. Former Justice John Paul Stevens cited this factor in his scathing

15.1
Determine the role of the judiciary as established by the Framers of the U.S. Constitution, p. 509.

15.2
Outline the structure of the U.S. judiciary, p. 511.

15.3
Distinguish between civil and criminal cases, and describe methods used to manage the judicial caseload, p. 516.

15.4
Explain how judges decide cases that involve public policy, p. 520.

15.5
Analyze the process of judicial appointments and selection, p. 529.

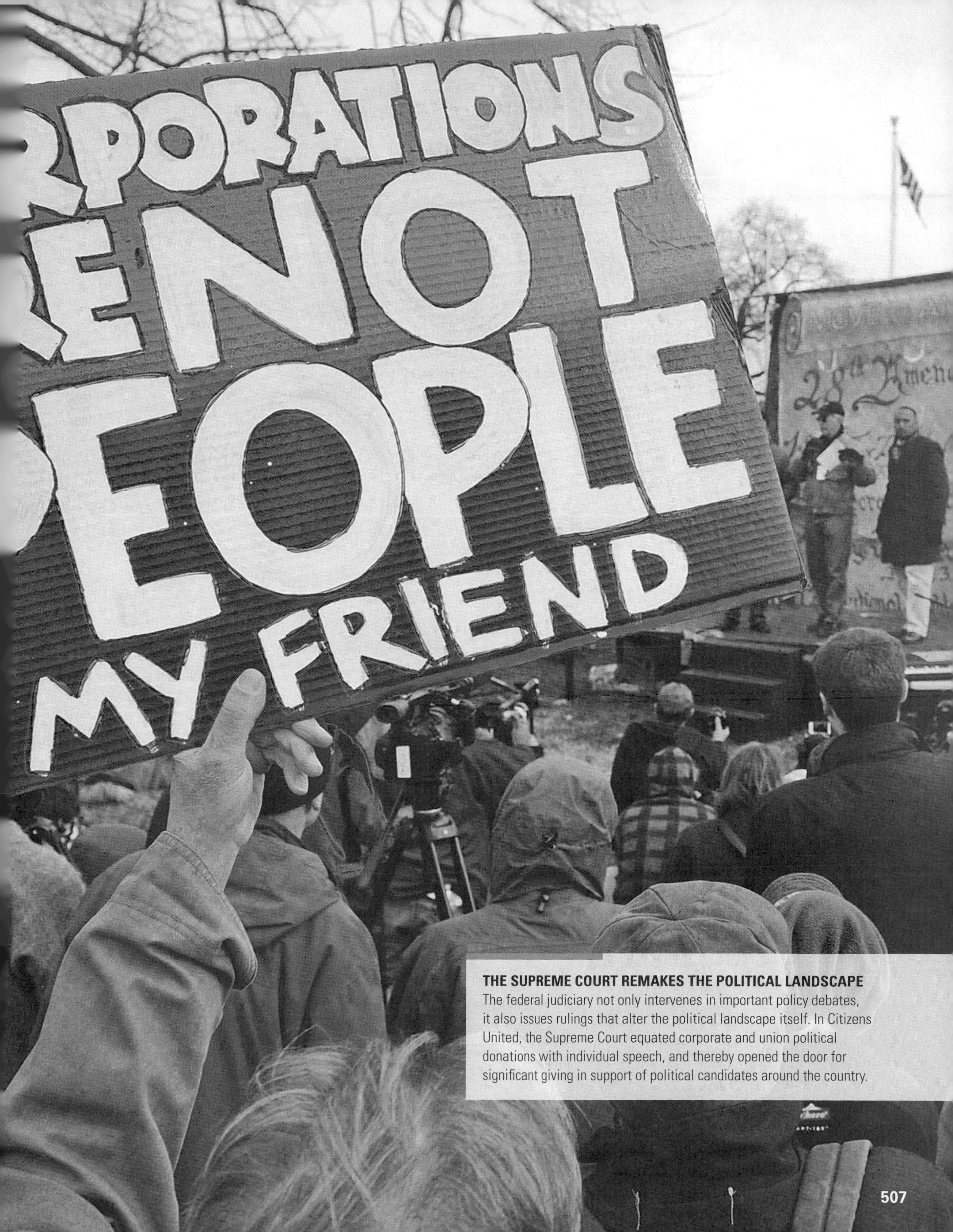

THE SUPREME COURT REMAKES THE POLITICAL LANDSCAPE
The federal judiciary not only intervenes in important policy debates, it also issues rulings that alter the political landscape itself. In Citizens United, the Supreme Court equated corporate and union political donations with individual speech, and thereby opened the door for significant giving in support of political candidates around the country.

The Big Picture At one point, Alexander Hamilton referred to the Supreme Court as government's weakest branch. Author William G. Howell argues why this is not the case by looking at Roe v. Wade and the impact that decision has on women's health and opinions about the rights of the unborn today.

The Basics Do you have confidence in the U.S. court system? Watch this video to discover what the founders did to make sure the federal judiciary would be independent of political influence. You'll also learn about an important check the Supreme Court has on the other two branches of U.S. government.

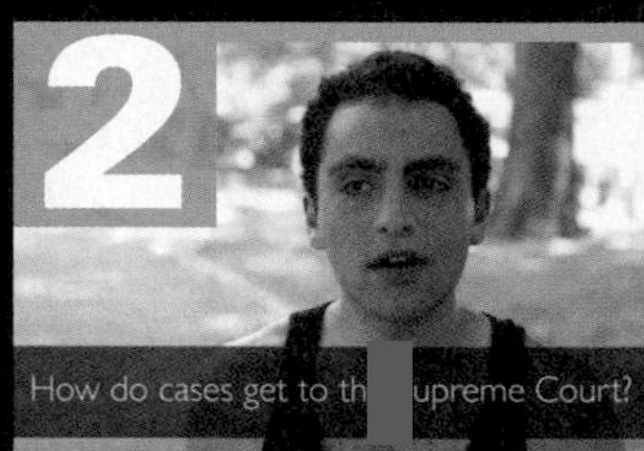

How do cases get to th upreme Court?

In Context Discover how the Supreme Court gained a check on the other two branches after the U.S. Constitution was written. East Central University political scientist Christine Pappas discusses Marbury v. Madison and analyzes how the power of judicial review has impacted campaign finance law.

Think Like a Political Scientist Why do legal scholars and political scientists disagree over how judges make decisions? East Central University political scientist Christine Pappas analyzes this and other questions scholars study. She explains how the other branches of government limit the role of the judiciary in public policy-making, and discusses research on how public opinion influences the courts.

In the Real World Should the Supreme Court have the power to knock down popular laws? This segment uses the Supreme Court's decision in U.S. v. Arizona (2012) to illustrate the tension between protecting the law and having a government that's run by the people.

So What? Are demonstrations on the steps of the Supreme Court Building worth it? Even though voters cannot choose who holds the gavel, author William G. Howell explains why the public has a bigger effect on Supreme Court decisions than we think.

dissenting opinion: "The only relevant thing that has changed since *Austin and McConnell* [past cases on election spending] is the composition of this Court."

The GOP was quick to embrace the Court's *Citizens United* ruling. Beginning in the 2010 congressional midterm elections, corporate supporters of Republican candidates began pouring money into special political action committees, known as "Super PACs." These groups, created as a direct result of the Court decision to overturn campaign finance limits, quickly ballooned in size. By the end of 2011, Super PACs had raised more than $180 million, mostly for GOP candidates. Super PACs also played a crucial role in the early months of the Republican presidential primary of 2012, as groups aligned with candidates Newt Gingrich, Mitt Romney, and Rick Santorum all spent millions of dollars on negative ads attacking opposing candidates.[4]

Democrats, for their part, initially sought legislation to curb the effects of corporate funding in elections. It quickly proved difficult, however, to craft new limits on election spending that would comport with the Court's ruling.[5] Early in 2012, therefore, Democrats reversed course. In fact, instead of continuing to rail against the *Citizens United* decision, President Obama's reelection campaign suddenly began urging supporters to donate money to Priorities Action USA, a Democratic Super PAC. As Obama's campaign manager Jim Messina put it, "This cycle, our campaign has to face the reality of the law as it currently stands."[6]

Meanwhile, opponents of the *Citizens United* decision mounted a renewed assault via the state court system. In December 2011, the Montana Supreme Court upheld the state's century-old ban on corporate donations. The Montana court judges argued that the decision "concerns Montana law" and was thus separate from the federal laws in question in *Citizens United*.[7] Pundits, however, saw the ruling as a refutation of the Supreme Court's decision. On June 25, 2012 the Supreme Court reversed the Montana court ruling and struck down the state's ban.[8]

Whether the Court's *Citizens United* ruling will stand remains to be seen. The case itself, though, reveals two important facts about the Supreme Court. First, and most obvious, the Court adjudicates disputes that have extremely important political and, by extension, policy consequences. Second, factors that cause justices to rule one way or another often go beyond the legal and constitutional arenas and into the ideological one. Rather than being shielded from politics, as the Framers had hoped, the judiciary directly engages and often fuels some of the deepest ideological controversies.

Constitutional Design of the Federal Judiciary

15.1 Determine the role of the judiciary as established by the Framers of the U.S. Constitution.

At the nation's founding, the Framers sought to build a federal judiciary that would serve the federal government in much the same way that state judiciaries had done in state governments for years. A federal judiciary was needed to perform the core functions of (1) interpreting the laws that Congress and the president enacted, (2) issuing rulings over disputes for which no guiding legislation previously existed, (3) ensuring that individuals who violated these laws and rulings were appropriately punished, and (4) compensating (when possible) the victims of these violations.

The first three articles of the Constitution lay out the powers, resources, and responsibilities of Congress (in Article I), then of the president (in Article II), and finally of the judiciary (in Article III). Last in order, Article III also is the shortest in length. It establishes a "supreme Court" and "inferior Courts" operating underneath its jurisdiction; it recognizes a "judicial power" that applies to laws, treaties, and other

15.1
15.2
15.3
15.4
15.5

formal acts of government; and it offers some brief guidelines about the prosecution of cases involving criminal behavior and treason. And that is all.

The Framers gave the judiciary a brief and rather vague mandate. A complete system of courts did not appear until 1789, when Congress enacted the Judiciary Act, which created a system of lower courts that would ease the workload of the one Supreme Court. It should not come as a surprise, then, that most of the Framers expected that the judiciary would be the weakest of the three branches of government. According to Alexander Hamilton, the judiciary would be the "least dangerous branch." Whereas Congress had the power of the purse (i.e., the power to levy taxes) and the president had the power of the sword (i.e., control over the military), the judiciary had only its judgment. Thus, the ability of judges to exert political power ultimately depended on the persuasive appeal of the substantive rulings that they handed down. Recognizing its original design, political scientist Robert Dahl concluded that the judiciary's "most important [base of power] is the unique legitimacy attributed to its interpretations of the Constitution."[9]

Consequentially, from the nation's beginning, judicial proceedings were structured to foster notions of respect and legitimacy. Deliberations in courts are different from those in any other political institution. When judges enter courtrooms, parties to a case must stand. Judges are referred to as "your honor." When serving on the bench, judges wear robes. All of this symbolic imagery is meant to increase the chances that citizens and other political actors will accept court rulings as binding—for again, lacking the powers of either the purse or the sword, the courts have little means by which to independently ensure that others heed their orders.

Perhaps most important, judges do everything possible to exude the qualities of trustworthy and independent arbiters of justice. Judges go out of their way to distinguish themselves from elected political actors, whose job it is to represent the interests of a diverse and often fickle public. In the tumult of daily political life, courts protect individual rights, constitutional principles, and time-tested legal doctrine against the "tyranny of the majority." Judges do their utmost to rise above politics, rather than engage in them.

For the most part, such efforts of successive generations of judges seem to have borne fruit. Citizens tend to hold the courts in higher regard than any other branch of government. According to national public opinion polls conducted in the summer of 2010, for example, 69 percent of Americans expressed favorable views of the Supreme Court. By comparison, roughly 45 percent of Americans approved of the job Barack Obama was doing as president, and only 21 percent had a favorable perception of Congress at that time.[10] Even when public approval of the Supreme Court dips, it usually remains at least as high as that of the other branches. For instance, by the end of 2011, the number of people who said they trusted the Supreme Court had fallen to 63 percent. Yet even then, public support for the Court remained 16 percentage points higher than the president's job approval rating and 32 percentage points higher than support for Congress.[11]

With such strong public support, the courts stand at the center of some of the most pressing national controversies—about freedom of speech, reproduction, civil rights, and the like. Failing to advance their preferred political reforms in the legislative and executive branches, interest groups often turn to the courts. Both state and federal law enforcement agencies prosecute criminal activities through the courts. And when individuals believe that their constitutional rights have been violated, they regularly seek redress in the judiciary.

This chapter examines how the federal court system is structured, and how federal judges make decisions about cases. When we analyze the latter issue, though, it will not do to simply take the supposed impartiality of the judiciary at face value. Simply because judges claim to operate outside the realm of politics does not mean, as a matter of practice, that they do. In fact, politics plays an integral role in both the selection of judges and in judicial decision making itself.

Organization of the Federal Judiciary

15.2 Outline the structure of the U.S. judiciary.

The core elements of the federal judiciary consist of district courts, appellate courts, and the Supreme Court. These courts accept three kinds of cases: those in which the federal government is a party; those that involve a question about the U.S. Constitution, a federal law, or a federal treaty; and those involving a large civil suit between two parties from different states. These courts also are responsible for adjudicating the vast preponderance of cases that come before the federal judiciary.

district court
the first tier of the federal judiciary that decides most cases.

magistrate judges
judges who support federal district judges by hearing and deciding minor cases at the district court level.

The Federal Judiciary Is Hierarchical

Figure 15.1 shows the primary three tiers of the federal judiciary; and just below are the various other entities that make up the federal judiciary. The bottom tier consists of 94 district or trial courts. Every state contains at least one **district court**, and the most populous (California, Texas, and New York) contain as many as four. Individual judges oversee district court proceedings. In 2010, a total of 678 full-time federal judges worked in district courts. These judges, appointed by the president, may hold office for life. They have the power to appoint **magistrate judges,** who serve either four- or eight-year terms. By hearing and deciding minor cases, and by overseeing the early stages of major cases, magistrate judges help reduce the caseload of district court judges. In 2010, a total of 527 magistrate judges worked in district courts around the nation.[12]

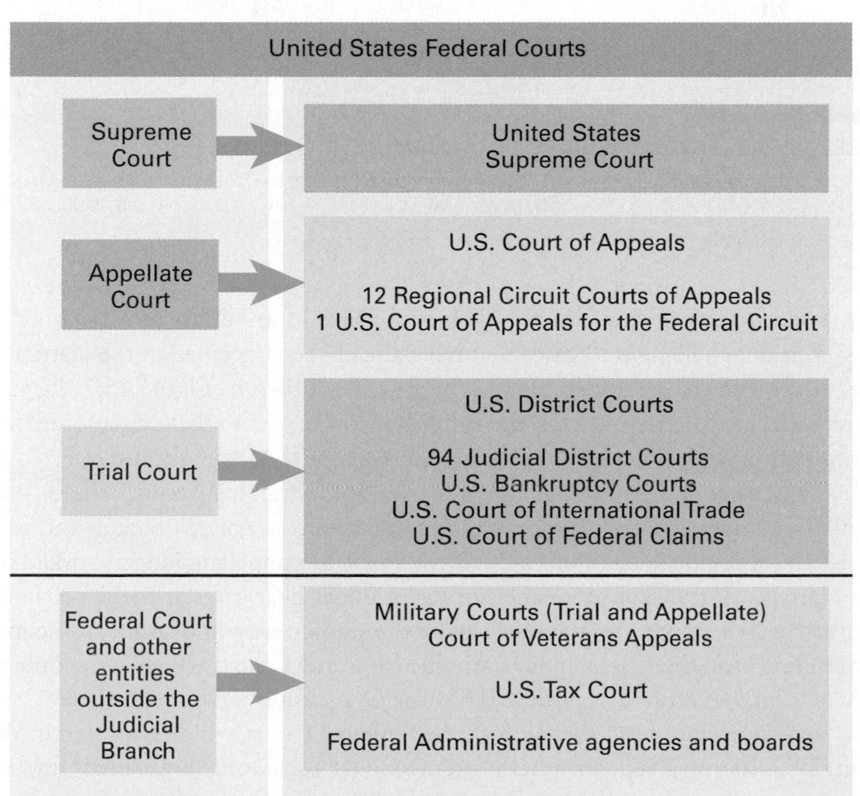

FIGURE 15.1 THE FEDERAL JUDICIARY IS HIERARCHICAL.
Most federal cases are decided in district courts. Some are then appealed to appellate courts. A tiny fraction of these make it to the Supreme Court, which has final say over the outcome.

Source: Administrative Office of the U.S. Courts, http://www.uscourts.gov/EducationalResources/FederalCourtBasics/CourtStructure/StructureOfFederalCourts.aspx.

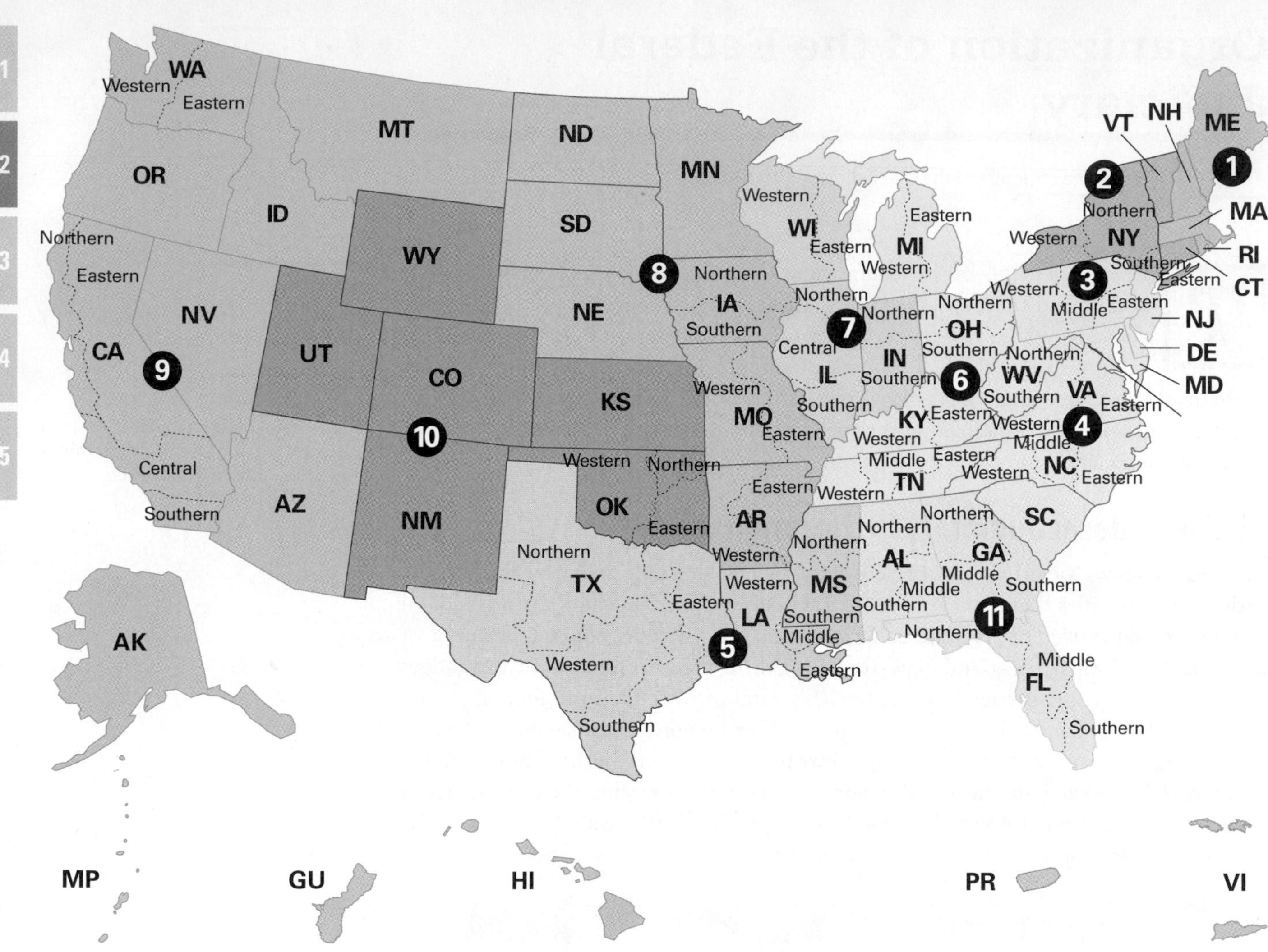

FIGURE 15.2 U.S. FEDERAL COURTS ARE DIVIDED INTO CIRCUITS.

Circuits serve different geographic regions, which vary dramatically in size. The first circuit includes only the northeastern portion of the country. The ninth, by contrast, includes the entire West, along with Alaska and Hawaii.

Source: Administrative Office of the U.S. Courts, http://www.uscourts.gov/courtlinks.

appellate courts
the second tier of the federal judiciary, primarily responsible for reviewing decisions rendered by the first tier of district courts.

Supreme Court
the highest court in the country, where all decisions are final.

The second tier of the federal judiciary consists of **appellate courts,** which primarily consider challenges to cases that have already been decided at the district level. Appellate courts are organized into 13 circuits. As shown in Figure 15.2, 12 circuits have regional jurisdictions; that is, the rulings of courts within these circuits are legally binding within a specified geographic area. Eleven of these circuits are referred to by number, and one is referred to as the "District of Columbia Circuit." There is also a federal circuit, which accepts cases within certain narrow policy domains rather than on the basis of regional location. In 2010, a total of 179 appellate judges worked in the federal circuit courts. Typically, panels of three judges hear cases at the appellate level. To win a case, therefore, a party must secure the support of two or three of the judges.

Standing atop the federal judiciary is the **Supreme Court,** which is the only court that is explicitly identified in Article III of the Constitution. Although there are many district and appellate courts, there is just one Supreme Court, which is located in Washington, D.C. In any given year, the Supreme Court considers only a small fraction of the cases that have proceeded through the district and appellate courts. Between 2004 and 2011, the Supreme Court heard no more than 92 cases per year, and it never offered a decision on more than 85.[13] Although the Supreme Court decides far fewer cases than the other courts, those that it does decide tend to have the biggest impact on society. Some of the most important have included *Brown v. Board of Education* (1954), which struck down state-mandated segregation in public schools; *Gideon v. Wainwright* (1963), which required the government to ensure that all individuals charged with criminal acts were granted adequate legal representation; *U.S. v. Nixon* (1974), which forced President Nixon to turn over White House audio recordings that would ultimately lead to his resignation from office; *Bush v. Gore* (2000), which put George W. Bush in the White House; and *National Federation of Independent Business v. Sebelius* (2012), which upheld the core elements of President Obama's signature health care law.

In the United States, the three tiers of state-level courts mirror (in name and function) the three tiers of federal-level courts. Other countries, however, have structured their systems rather differently. In Israel, for example, religious courts—which deal with disputes about Jewish dietary laws, the necessary qualifications to become a rabbi, and other matters relating to religious law and custom—coexist with secular magistrate, district, and supreme courts that focus on civil and criminal proceedings. Portugal's Supreme Court is at the top of a tiered system that handles civil and criminal cases, but a separate Constitutional Court is responsible for judging the constitutionality of legislative acts and international agreements. Finland has created special courts to handle certain types of civil cases, such as land, water, or labor disputes. Clearly, there is no single template for how a judicial system ought to be structured. Instead, countries tend to develop legal systems that reflect their political histories and cultural norms, and that best suit the particular kinds of local cases that require resolution.[14]

writ of certiorari
a formal acceptance by the Supreme Court to review a decision of a lower court.

original jurisdiction
the right of the Supreme Court to be the first to hear a case rather than simply review the decision of a lower court.

District and Appellate Rulings Can Be Appealed to the Next Level

Almost all federal court cases start at the district level. District judges, though, do not have the final say about a case's outcome. The losing side always has the option of appealing to the appellate court, which can affirm the district court's decision, reverse it, or refuse to take the case—thereby letting the district ruling stand. Whatever the outcome at the appellate level, the losing side has yet another opportunity to appeal—this time to the Supreme Court. The highest court to issue a ruling has the final say on the outcome of the case.

The vast majority of cases terminate at the district court, and therefore it is the district court's judgment that usually settles the matter. The high cost of litigation and the extraordinary amount of time it can take for a case to wind its way through the federal judiciary, combined with the fact that higher courts usually come to the same judgment as lower courts, generally convince the losing side to accept defeat.

The Supreme Court is especially choosy about which cases it will hear. Historically, the Supreme Court has accepted—or, to use the technical term, granted a **writ of certiorari** to—around 5 percent of petitions for appeals. As a result of the astronomical rise of cases filed with the Supreme Court in the past half-century, this number has dwindled to about 1 percent. In 1945, just over 1,000 cases were appealed to the Supreme Court. By 2000, the number surpassed 9,000 cases, but it declined to 7,857 in the 2010 term.[15]

The Supreme Court is the only judicial body that grants "cert," short for *writ of certiorari*. Doing so requires the support of four Supreme Court justices, the so-called "rule of four." The Court typically grants cert either when an important legal or constitutional issue is at stake or when lower courts in different circuits come to different conclusions about a particular issue.[16] Such was the case in 2005 when the Court chose to hear two cases dealing with the display of the Ten Commandments on government property. In *McCreary County v. ACLU of Kentucky*, the Sixth Circuit ruled that two Kentucky counties' displays of the Ten Commandments on the walls of their courthouses violated the establishment clause of the First Amendment. Around the same time, the Fifth Circuit in *Van Orden v. Perry* ruled that the display of the Ten Commandments on the grounds of the Texas State Capitol *was* constitutional. The Supreme Court intervened, clarifying that the intended purpose of such displays—whether purely religious or partially secular—must be taken into account in deciding matters of constitutionality with regard to the establishment clause.

Although most cases start at the district level, some go straight to the Supreme Court. Article III of the Constitution stipulates that "all Cases affecting Ambassadors, other public Ministers and Consuls, and those in which a State shall be Party" shall be decided by the Supreme Court. When the Supreme Court has **original jurisdiction,**

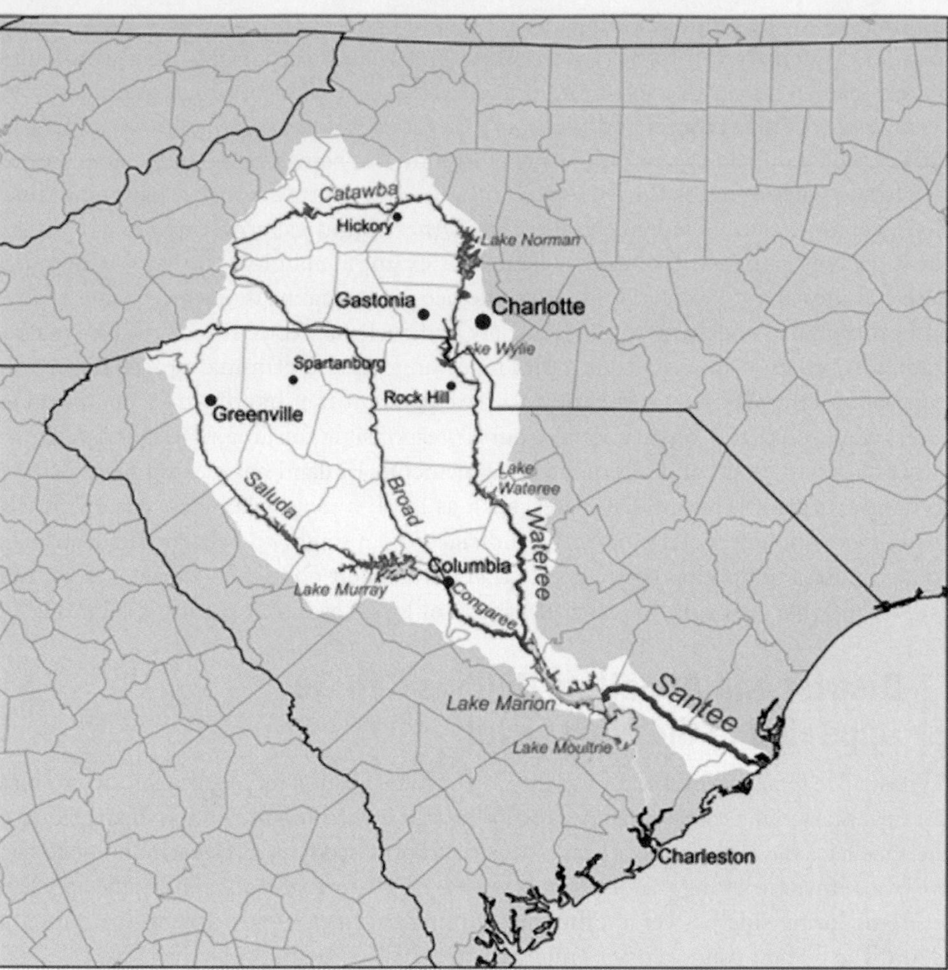

WHOSE WATER IS IT?

The Supreme Court often resolves disputes between states. As one example, North and South Carolina have been embroiled in a long-standing disagreement about rights to the water in the Catawba River. In your view, what right, if any, does South Carolina have to water from a river that originates in North Carolina?

briefs
documents that contain the legal arguments of a dispute.

oral argument
a lawyer's spoken presentation to the court of the legal reasons that his or her side should prevail.

it is the first and last court to hear a federal case. The most common instance of original jurisdiction occurs when two states are in conflict. North Carolina and South Carolina, for instance, spent years fighting over the water from the Catawba River. The river originates in the mountains of North Carolina but then flows into South Carolina through Lake Wylie. South Carolina complained that North Carolina's use of more than its fair share of water was threatening the state's power and agriculture. In *South Carolina v. North Carolina* (2010), the Supreme Court ruled that a third-party private entity would be responsible for the fair distribution of the Catawba's water.

Other cases bypass the federal district courts for other reasons. Challenges to actions taken by federal administrative agencies often begin in the D.C. Court of Appeals. In other instances, the U.S. Supreme Court directly receives appeals to state supreme court rulings.

□ Supreme Court Proceedings Are Highly Scripted

Whereas *judges* serve on district and appellate courts, *justices* serve on the Supreme Court. Once the nine justices who comprise the Supreme Court agree to hear a case, both sides to a dispute submit **briefs,** which contain legal arguments about the dispute at hand. These briefs discuss relevant case law, outline the case's key facts, and present additional research that might bear on a particular policy issue. After the justices and their clerks have reviewed these briefs, they meet to hear **oral arguments** directly from the lawyers. During these sessions, the lead lawyer for each side is granted a half-hour to make his or her argument. Typically, though, the justices interrupt the lawyers, long before their time is up, to ask pointed questions.

Following oral arguments, the justices gather for a **conference,** during which they discuss their current thinking on the case and cast preliminary votes. This meeting provides each justice with some sense of where the other justices stand on the case. Conferences are completely confidential, however, and no formal record is kept of what is said or done during them. Justices also are completely free to change their minds after the casting their preliminary votes in conference.

The **chief justice,** who currently is John Roberts, presides over the conference. If he is part of the majority, he then selects which justice will write the majority opinion of the Court.[17] As its name implies, the **majority opinion** reflects the collective judgment of those justices—typically five or more—who are on the majority side of the vote.[18] The majority opinion represents the final determination of the Court. Whoever has the job of writing this opinion will do so with great care. It is not uncommon for justices to compose multiple drafts of an opinion. They usually write these drafts in ways that intentionally curry the support of every individual member of the majority.

In addition to the majority opinion, some members of the majority may decide to write **concurring opinions,** which outline additional considerations that they think are important and provide alternative rationales for the majority opinion. Members of the minority typically write **dissenting opinions,** which outline their reasoning on the case and often identify the flaws that they perceive in the majority or concurring opinions. Concurring and dissenting opinions are elements of the final record of the Court, but only the majority opinion is officially binding. Lawyers and judges in subsequent court cases, nonetheless, may cite elements of concurring and dissenting opinions to justify their positions. In fact, the most influential element of a court case can sometimes be a passing reference or footnote found in a concurring or dissenting opinion, as was the case in *Youngstown v. Sawyer*, in which Justice Jackson's concurring opinion subsequently received a good deal more attention than the majority ruling. Having issued its decision, the Supreme Court typically sends a case back to a lower court for implementation. The justices tend to see their job as establishing broad principles that are meant to guide judicial decision making at the district and appellate levels. As a consequence, the justices tend not to become especially involved in the details of the cases that come before them. Instead, having resolved the largest points of contention in a dispute, the justices rely on district and appellate judges to implement their ruling appropriately.

conference
the confidential gathering of justices in which they discuss their thoughts about the case and cast preliminary votes.

chief justice
the presiding member of the Supreme Court who serves as chair of the conference and, if in the majority, selects the justice who will write the majority opinion.

majority opinion
the written document that reflects the collective judgment of the justices who are on the majority side of a ruling.

concurring opinion
a document written by a justice on the majority side of a ruling that outlines additional considerations he or she thinks are important.

dissenting opinion
a document written by a justice on the minority side of a ruling that outlines his or her own reasoning on the case and identifies perceived flaws in the majority opinion.

THE CURRENT SUPREME COURT
Current members of the Supreme Court are, beginning in the top row at left, Sonia Sotomayor, Stephen Breyer, Samuel Alito, and Elena Kagan. In the bottom row are Clarence Thomas, Antonin Scalia, John Roberts (the chief justice), Anthony Kennedy, and Ruth Bader Ginsburg.

15.1

15.2

15.3

15.4

15.5

Number and Types of Cases That Courts Process

15.3 Distinguish between civil and criminal cases, and describe methods used to manage the judicial caseload.

plaintiff
the party who initiates a lawsuit by filing a complaint.

defendant
the party being sued or accused of a crime.

jury
a group of private citizens selected to listen to a trial and issue a final verdict.

criminal case
a case that involves a violation of the statutes that are intended to protect the public's health, order, safety, and morality.

As should now be clear, the primary responsibility of judges is to resolve disputes. Judges play the role of referee both in society and, as we'll soon see, in politics as well. They identify when an individual, a group of individuals, or an organization has suffered because of actions that either are unlawful or violate established agreements; judges then determine the appropriate course of action. They take cases that determine whether one person stole money from another person, who was at fault in a car accident, and whether a business unlawfully fired an employee. In each instance, judges then decide the appropriate remedy—whether it be time spent in prison, financial compensation for automobile damages, or back pay for lost wages.

In an Adversarial System, Judges Decide Criminal and Civil Cases

U.S. courts have a rather peculiar way of resolving disputes. Rather than encouraging the two parties in the dispute to behave cooperatively, U.S. courts encourage the parties to behave adversarially. Legal counsels for each side independently decide what arguments and evidence to put forward. They do so, moreover, in an explicit effort to advance their own interests and undermine those of their adversary. This system sharply differs from the inquisitorial approach used in some European countries. In Germany and France, for example, judges lead the investigation, unearthing evidence and questioning witnesses. Lawyers, by contrast, play a relatively passive, supporting role.[19] The adversarial and inquisitorial systems derive from very different legal traditions. The U.S. adversarial system finds its historical roots in English common law, whereas the inquisitorial systems of Germany and France originate in Roman law.

In U.S. court cases, the **plaintiff** brings the case before the court and, usually, makes accusations of wrongdoing. The **defendant** is the person or institution against whom the complaint is made. In a trial, both sides offer arguments and evidence to support their positions. A judge presides over the deliberations, deciding what kinds of evidence and arguments can be presented. At the end of a trial, a court ruling is made about which side made the stronger case and what should happen as a consequence.

The power to issue a court ruling is given to judges and juries. In the sections that follow, we will have much more to say about the ways in which judges go about making their decisions on matters of law. **Juries,** meanwhile, render decisions on matters of fact. Hence, juries typically decide whether the facts best support one party or another, and judges then determine the appropriate outcome of the case. Juries consist of private citizens who are selected to listen to the trial and as a group offer a final verdict. In the lead-up to a trial, lawyers for both the plaintiff and defendant select members of the jury by questioning candidates to determine those who are most free from any bias or prejudice that may impair the jury's judgment. Lawyers tend to reject those who they think will rule against their side. Juries are meant to provide an impartial judgment about a defendant's actions by his or her peers. Whether the practice of jury trials reaches this objective, though, is the subject of considerable controversy.[20]

Judges issue rulings on two kinds of cases: criminal and civil. **Criminal cases,** as the name implies, involve violations of the criminal code—that is, those statutes that are intended to protect the public's health, order, safety, and morality. In criminal cases, the plaintiff (also called the prosecutor) is always the government, and the defendant is the individual accused of committing a crime—whether it involves using illegal drugs or robbing a store or conducting fraudulent business practices. If the evidence suggests "beyond a reasonable doubt" that the defendant is guilty of committing a crime, then he or she faces punishments ranging from fines or probation to imprisonment or even execution. The severity of the punishment, which is the purview of the judge, depends on the seriousness of the crime. If the jury decides that the evidence is not sufficiently strong, however, then the defendant may avoid punishment altogether.

civil case
a case that concerns a violation of the legal rights or obligations of one individual toward another.

class action suit
a lawsuit in which the plaintiff is a group of individuals who have suffered a common injury.

Civil cases concern violations of the civil code, which summarizes the legal rights and obligations that individuals have toward one another. When an individual slips and falls in a grocery store, he might sue the owner for negligence; when a husband and wife get divorced, they might fight over the fair division of belongings; or when a stockholder loses money from an investment, she might sue the corporation for bad business practices. In civil cases, the plaintiff is not the government, but instead a private individual, group of individuals, or institution. To win a case, the plaintiff in a civil trial need show only that most—or more technically, a "preponderance"—of the evidence supports his or her position. If a jury finds in favor of the plaintiff, the defendant does not confront many of the punishments that accompany criminal violations. Rather, the defendant has to pay damages (typically monetary in nature) to the plaintiff. Occasionally, the defendant must also take certain corrective actions that reduce the chances that other individuals or groups will suffer similar harm.

In some instances, multiple individuals come together to bring a civil case to trial. In these **class action suits,** the plaintiff typically consists of a group that suffered a common injury. Examples might include residents of a small town whose water is polluted, members of a minority group who have been discriminated against, or parents

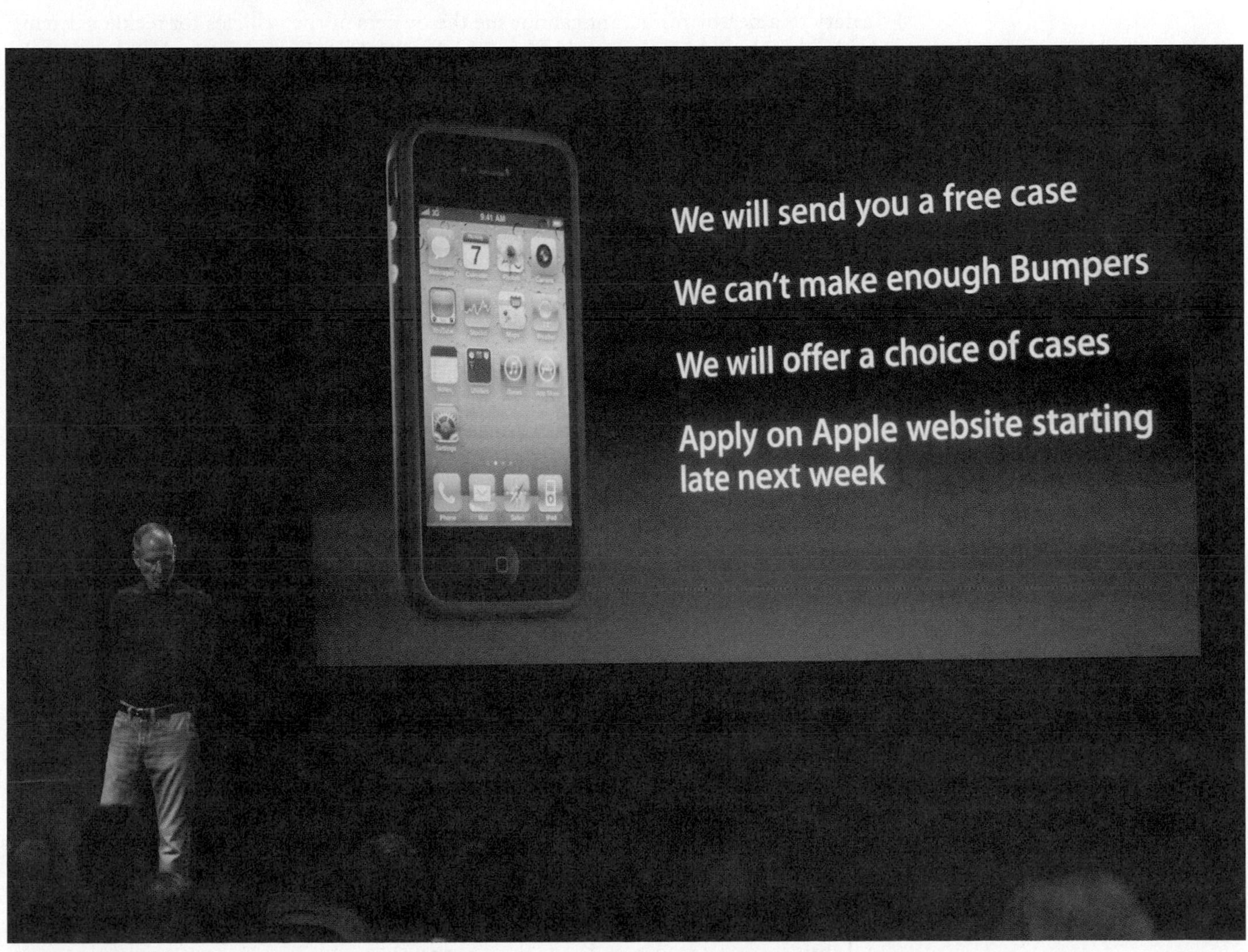

APPLE CLASS ACTION LAWSUIT WITH ANTENNAE ISSUES

When Apple's fabled iPhone 4 was released in 2010, a number of antennae problems were detected. In an effort to ward off a class action suit, then-CEO Steve Jobs held a news conference at which he promised to provide free cases to customers who purchased the new mobile phone.

15.1

15.2

15.3

15.4

15.5

standing
the requirement establishing that for a plaintiff to bring a case to court, he or she must have suffered a well-defined injury that is a result of violation of the civil code.

ripeness doctrine
principle by which the courts will accept cases only when the actual harm has already taken place.

plea bargain
an agreement between the prosecutor and the defendant in a criminal case through which the parties agree to a specified crime and punishment.

of children who have been injured by a dangerous toy. If successful, the financial rewards of a class action suit are divided among the members of the group.

The tech company Apple was recently involved in a class action lawsuit that gained national attention. In 2010, Apple released the iPhone 4, the newest model of its immensely popular smartphone. Although the new iPhone was touted for its slimmer frame, owners soon began to report problems with reception. Initially, the company denied any flaws in the phone's design. After investigating further, however, Apple CEO Steve Jobs held a rare public news conference, in which he admitted that the way the phone's antenna was wrapped around its outer edge was causing some calls to be dropped. Multiple people sued the company, claiming that Apple had dismissed their earlier complaints and failed to communicate the device's flaws. These various cases were eventually combined into a single class action suit. Rather than go to trial, Apple eventually agreed to settle the case out of court. In February 2012, the company agreed to compensate any customer who had bought the initial model of the phone, either by giving them a free iPhone case or by paying them $15. The settlement required Apple to e-mail more than 21 million customers eligible for the payout.[21]

Courts Do Not Resolve All Disputes

Not everyone can bring a civil case to trial. To do so, one must have **standing**—that is, one must personally have suffered a well-defined injury because of actions that violate the civil code. A pedestrian who watches two cars crash into each other from the safety of a nearby restaurant cannot sue the owners of the vehicles for reckless driving, and citizens who are outraged but personally unaffected by a business's hiring and firing decisions cannot sue for discrimination. To bring a case, the plaintiff must have experienced personal harm.

Even if an individual has standing, a judge may decide to dismiss a case on other grounds. A case, for instance, may not be "ripe" for consideration if an actual harm has not yet arisen. The **ripeness doctrine** is intended to "prevent the courts . . . from entangling themselves in abstract disagreements over administrative policies."[22] Before agreeing to accept a case, the ripeness doctrine says, judges must determine that a tangible harm has been inflicted upon an individual or group. So, for example, a citizen cannot sue a city for a poorly drafted law if that law has not been enforced, and a corporation cannot take another corporation to court for actions that it merely anticipates.

Many civil cases do not make it to trial because the two parties resolve their differences out of court. The plaintiff and defendant may decide that the costs of going to trial and the uncertainty of the outcome are too great, and they may negotiate a settlement. In these instances, the two parties are not required to disclose the terms of the settlement to either the court or the public.

Most criminal cases are also decided without going to trial because the prosecutor and the defendant's lawyer reach a deal outside the court. In such **plea bargains,** both parties agree to a specified crime and punishment. A judge must approve the terms of plea bargains, which are then put into the public record. The prosecutor benefits from plea bargains by locking in a conviction, the defendant benefits by typically receiving a lesser punishment, and the court system benefits by avoiding the considerable costs of holding a trial.

Today, the vast majority of criminal cases are resolved through plea bargains. In 1989, according to one report, 84 percent of federal criminal cases were settled via plea bargains. By 1995, the figure had risen to 90 percent, and by 2001, it had reached 94 percent. Today, fewer than 5 percent of all criminal cases go to trial.[23]

Federal Courts Process Hundreds of Thousands of Cases Each Year

Even though many cases do not make it to court, federal judges around the nation face massive caseloads. Each year from 1998 to 2004, about 65,000 criminal cases were filed in federal district courts.[24] In 2010, 78,482 criminal cases were filed.[25]

Meanwhile, litigants filed 282,895 civil cases that year in federal district courts.[26] In an average year, these cases came before just over 1,000 full-time and magistrate federal district judges. As a consequence, each judge processed an average of several hundred criminal and civil cases each year.

The total number of federal court cases was not always so large. In fact, caseloads have trended steadily upward in recent decades. From 1960 to 1995, federal district court filings more than tripled, and appeals to higher courts grew by more than 13 times over.[27] These trends have multiplied court costs and delayed the implementation of government policy. For example, the amount of money annually spent on legal services in the United States increased from $9 billion in 1960 to $54 billion in 1987.[28] Additionally, the budget of the Justice Department rose from $236 million in fiscal year 1962 to $27.5 billion in 2011.[29]

Federal appeals judges now must read 1,500 to 2,000 new opinions per year to remain up-to-date with legal developments.[30] Facing such a heavy workload, judges often have a difficult time keeping track of goings-on within their own courtrooms. Consider the experience of appellate judge Donald Lay: "A few months ago I was reading an opinion from our court; after reading several pages on a certain point, I wondered who wrote it. I was amazed to find that I had authored the opinion some 10 years before. The point is we read so much that we can no longer even recognize—let alone remember—our own opinions."[31]

The "litigation explosion" has led some observers to assert that "litigation has become the nation's secular religion."[32] Former Supreme Court Chief Justice Warren E. Burger warned in the late 1970s, "We may well be on our way to a society overrun by hordes of lawyers."[33] Similarly, President George W. Bush commented in 2004, "I'm deeply concerned about a legal system that is fraught with frivolous and junk lawsuits."[34]

Is the United States more litigious relative to other countries? The question has unleashed significant debate. Numerous studies conducted in the 1980s found that Americans were more likely than citizens of other democracies to bring disputes to court.[35] More recent scholarship, however, questions this view. One study concluded that the total volume of litigation in United States was actually comparable to that in Germany and Britain.[36] Like their counterparts in America, British government officials have expressed fears that Britain is developing a "compensation culture" in which "people with frivolous and unwarranted claims bring cases to court with a view of making easy money."[37] So although the United States is certainly more litigious now than it was 40 years ago, it remains unclear whether American legal culture is unusually litigious compared with that of other countries.

THE ANNALS OF LAW

The sheer volume of existing case law requires lawyers and judges to conduct a tremendous amount of research in preparation for trial. What challenges does this expansion of case law present for lawyers and litigants?

☐ States Have Their Own Judicial Systems

In addition to an active federal judiciary, each state also has its own court system. Whereas federal courts have jurisdiction over laws passed by Congress, state courts make rulings on all areas of law that are decided by state legislatures. For example, the Constitution gives the federal government the power to oversee bankruptcy, so all court cases on that issue are decided at the federal level. On the other hand, the Constitution is silent on issues pertaining to marriage. Because laws about marriage and divorce are made at the state level, legal disputes on these issues are generally resolved in state courts.

Like the federal judiciary, the state court system is hierarchical, although the exact structure varies from place to place. Most states haves a three-tiered judiciary that mirrors the federal system. The first tier consists of trial courts similar to federal district courts. Many of these courts have general jurisdiction over a variety of civil and criminal cases. Depending on the state, these general jurisdiction trial courts are called circuit courts, superior courts, or courts of common pleas. In addition to general courts, a slew of other first-tier state courts have limited jurisdiction on a particular issue. Most states, for example, have special family courts, which decide only cases about marriage and divorce, child custody, adoption, and other family issues. Additional

15.1

15.2

15.3

15.4

15.5

common law
law made by judges when no legislation currently exists.

public law
those laws enacted by presidents and Congress that define the relationship between individuals (and organizations) and the state.

judicial review
the power of the judiciary to interpret and overturn actions taken by the legislative and executive branches of government.

examples of limited jurisdiction state courts include probate court (handling wills and estates), traffic court, juvenile court, and municipal court (handling breaches of city ordinances).

If defendants or plaintiffs dispute the decision of a lower state court, they may appeal to a higher one. In some states, there are two additional tiers of the judiciary: appellate courts and the state supreme court, similar to the federal system. In other states, the appellate tier does not exist, and all lower court decisions must be appealed directly to the supreme court of the state. Following the federal example, the highest state court is usually called the supreme court, although that is not the case in every state. In New York, for example, the lower trial courts are called supreme courts, and the highest court is referred to as the court of appeals.

Occasionally, a case that is initially decided at the state level may make its way into the federal court system. Usually, this takes place when the party appealing the state decision argues that the issue involves the U.S. Constitution. In the case *Michigan Department of Police v. Sitz*, for instance, a civil class action suit was brought against the Michigan state police for instituting a policy of using random sobriety tests at highway checkpoints. The litigants accused the police of violating the Fourth Amendment of the Constitution, which prohibits "unreasonable searches and seizures." After both the trial court and the state supreme court ruled in the litigants' favor, the police department appealed to the U.S. Supreme Court. The Supreme Court ruled that it had jurisdiction, and it then sided with the defendants. However, the challenging litigants returned to the state court system and argued that the police department was also violating a specific section of the Michigan state constitution. The lower court and state supreme court again ruled in the litigants' favor. However this time, because the issue concerned a violation of state law, the police department could not appeal to the federal court system.[38]

Although there are many federal judges, even more judges work in the state judicial systems. Across all 50 states, roughly 360 judges work at the supreme court level, 970 judges at the intermediate appellate level, and more than 30,000 judges work in trial courts of either limited or general jurisdiction. Depending on the state, these judges are either appointed by the governor or elected by ballot along with holders of other political offices. Like federal judges, state judges carry massive caseloads. In 2009, for instance, state trial courts alone resolved more than 10 million civil cases and 12 million criminal cases across the country.[39]

Making and Interpreting the Law

15.4 Explain how judges decide cases that involve public policy.

Explore on MyPoliSciLab
Simulation: You Are a Supreme Court Clerk

Judges can influence public policy in two ways. The first is through actually making law. When no legislation exists, judges can develop rules that dictate how to resolve certain disputes. In these instances, judges create **common law** that becomes binding in future cases. For instance, most rulings in cases involving contracts, property, and personal injuries are based on common law.

Judges also resolve political disputes about **public law,** which deals with the statutes that presidents and Congress write and that bureaucrats implement. Sometimes judges help interpret the correct meaning of a statute; at other times, they determine whether statutes are consistent with basic constitutional provisions, step in when state or local laws conflict with national laws, or intervene because bureaucrats failed to implement congressional statutes. Collectively, these cases provide judges with considerable influence over the policy-making process.

Through the power of **judicial review,** judges interpret and, when necessary, overturn actions taken by the legislative and executive branches of government. Unlike many of the court's other powers, however, this one cannot be found in Article III of the Constitution. It is a power, instead, that the judiciary claimed for itself in the landmark 1803 court case *Marbury v. Madison*. The case is sufficiently important to warrant recounting in some detail. After losing his bid for reelection in 1800, President John Adams appointed 42 individuals to the federal judiciary before his term expired. In the confusion of changing presidential administrations, however, the official commissions were never delivered to the new appointees. When the newly elected president, Thomas Jefferson, took office, he refused to do so. As a consequence, these individuals could not assume their new posts in the judiciary.

What recourse was available to these appointees whose commissions were never delivered? According to the Judiciary Act of 1789, the appointees could request that the federal courts issue an order forcing Jefferson and his secretary of state, James Madison, to finalize the appointments. One of the appointees, William Marbury, did so, which put the newly formed federal judiciary in a difficult spot. On the one hand, the Supreme Court was being asked to take on a popularly elected president who might well ignore a court order that he opposed. On the other hand, if it did not force the president to deliver the commissions, the Court might appear weak and ineffectual.

In a brilliant move, the Supreme Court managed to assert its own power without offending the new presidential administration. Rather than demand that the president appoint Marbury to his office, as the Judiciary Act seemed to require, the Supreme Court ruled that portions of the act itself were unconstitutional. In so doing, the judiciary claimed the power of deciding which laws were constitutional and which were not—transforming it from the weakest of the three branches of government to, perhaps, one on equal footing with the other branches. As Chief Justice John Marshall stated in the Supreme Court's opinion, "it is emphatically the province and duty of the judicial department to say what the law is." And when judges determine that a law enacted by Congress conflicts with the Constitution, they are obligated to rule that the law either be amended or be stricken from the books.

With the power of judicial review, the judiciary established a place for itself in the policy debates that would preoccupy the national government over time—debates about such issues as slavery, labor-management relations, racial and gender discrimination, and federalism. With the power of judicial review, the courts claimed the authority to have the final say about which laws violated the Constitution and which did not. But how would it use this power? How, exactly, would judges determine when a law was unconstitutional and when it was not? Political scientists have identified three models of judicial decision making: legal, attitudinal, and strategic. As the discussion that follows makes plain, each model casts the courts in a very different light.

legal model
a theory of judicial decision making in which judges make decisions by deciphering the correct interpretation of the law and the relevant portion of the Constitution and determining whether there is a conflict between the two.

Judges Develop and Apply Legal Principles in the Legal Model

The Constitution is a notoriously vague document. As a consequence, it is not always obvious whether a particular law does or does not violate it. According to the **legal model** of judicial decision making, to which most constitutional law scholars adhere, judges rely on their judgment and expertise to decipher the correct interpretation of a law, the relevant portion of the Constitution, and whether there is any conflict between the two.

Different judges interpret the Constitution in different ways. Some pay careful attention to the intentions of those who wrote and ratified the document. For these judges, the Constitution can be understood only by reference to its historical record. Other judges think of the Constitution as a document that changes over time. For these judges, the Constitution has no fixed or final meaning. Rather, the correct meaning depends on the context in which it is applied. Still other judges prefer to concentrate on a literal reading of the Constitution's text. For them, neither the intentions of the Constitution's authors nor changing historical norms are relevant. Instead, they focus on the actual words of the Constitution and what implications they have for the dispute at hand.

Explore on MyPoliSciLab

Who Are the Activist Judges?

In practice, an activist judge—liberal or conservative—is one who overturns a law as unconstitutional. Even though the current Supreme Court hands down fewer decisions, 19 out of 408 decisions declared laws unconstitutional between 2005 and 2010. The data below shows which judges are most responsible for these controversial decisions.

Supreme Court Decisions

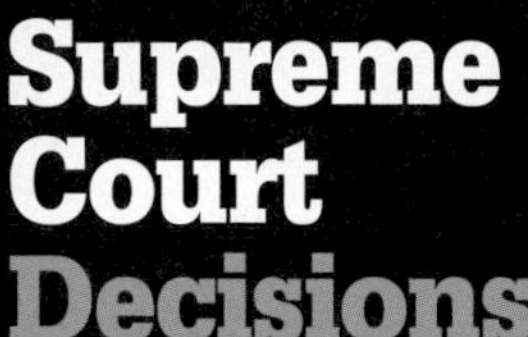

Supreme Court Approval Rating by Moderates

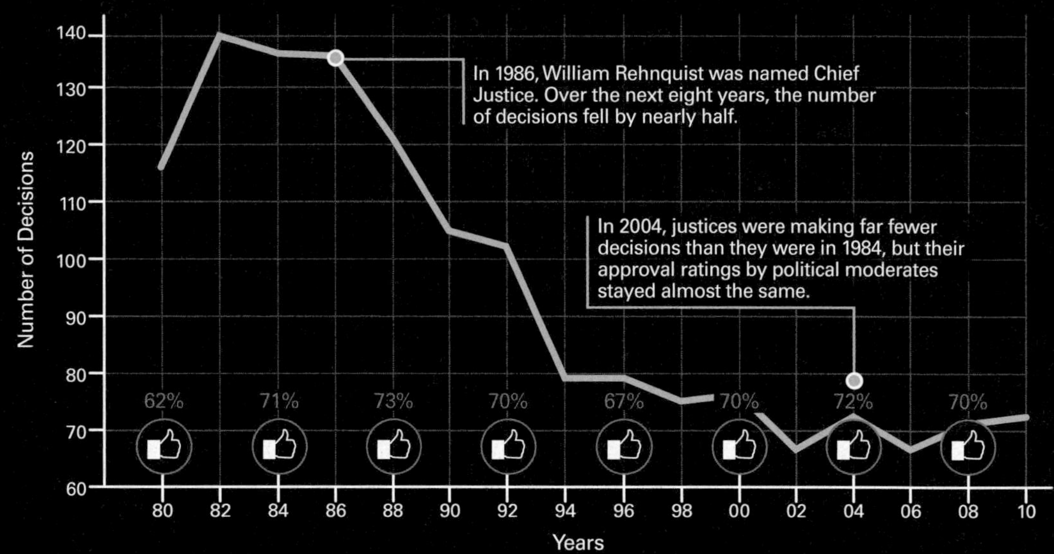

Number of Decisions
Years
In 1986, William Rehnquist was named Chief Justice. Over the next eight years, the number of decisions fell by nearly half.
In 2004, justices were making far fewer decisions than they were in 1984, but their approval ratings by political moderates stayed almost the same.
62%
71%
73%
70%
67%
70%
72%
70%

Judicial Activism on the Roberts Court

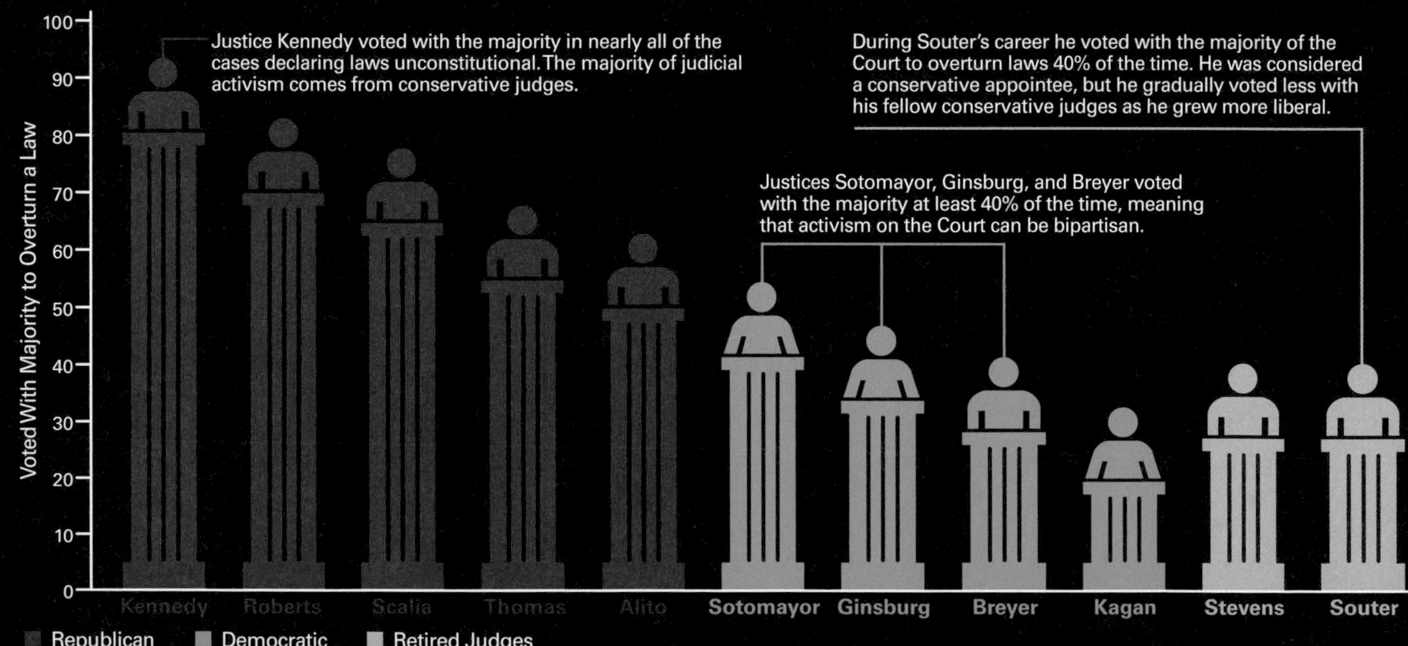

Voted With Majority to Overturn a Law
Justice Kennedy voted with the majority in nearly all of the cases declaring laws unconstitutional. The majority of judicial activism comes from conservative judges.
During Souter's career he voted with the majority of the Court to overturn laws 40% of the time. He was considered a conservative appointee, but he gradually voted less with his fellow conservative judges as he grew more liberal.
Justices Sotomayor, Ginsburg, and Breyer voted with the majority at least 40% of the time, meaning that activism on the Court can be bipartisan.
Kennedy
Roberts
Scalia
Thomas
Alito
Sotomayor
Ginsburg
Breyer
Kagan
Stevens
Souter
Republican
Democratic
Retired Judges

SOURCE: Data from the United States Supreme Court and the General Social Survey, 1980-2010.

Investigate Further

Concept Why is judicial activism controversial? By declaring a law unconstitutional, judicial activism overturns legislation that is a product of the democratic process. It sets precedents for controversial or divisive issues, and it limits future legislation.

Connection Does judicial activism affect public confidence? Over two-thirds of American moderates continued to express confidence in the Court, even as it became less active and more conservative in the 2000s.

Cause Is judicial activism conservative or liberal? On the Roberts Court, the decisions that overturn laws can be bipartisan, but they are usually decided by the conservative justices.

Although judges may rely on different ways of interpreting the Constitution, they all try to apply basic principles of jurisprudence. The most important of these is ***stare decisis***, which literally translates into "to stand by things already decided." According to this principle, judges deciding cases today must carefully weigh the decisions made by their predecessors in similar cases. And if the basic elements of the case are the same, they should come to the same decision about a law's constitutionality.

Of course, the principle of *stare decisis* is not a hard and fast rule. And different judges appear more or less willing to overturn established precedent. Advocates of **judicial restraint** insist that judges should almost never overturn past decisions; when they must, it should be on the narrowest possible grounds. Advocates of **judicial activism,** by contrast, suggest that judges have considerably more leeway when deciding whether or not to abide by past court decisions. They suggest that the principle of *stare decisis* should not force judges to repeat mistakes from the past or apply the Constitution in ways that plainly are at odds with the dominant political culture at the time. Advocates of judicial restraint argue that the Supreme Court should stand by its ruling in *Roe v. Wade* (1973), which affirmed a woman's right to obtain an abortion. Advocates of judicial activism, by contrast, encourage the Court to abandon its previous position, which they view as legally flawed, and allow more restrictions on a woman's right to have an abortion. Still others claim that *Roe v. Wade* itself was the product of judicial activism, and that legal restraint requires that the ruling be overturned to honor earlier precedent. For a further discussion of judicial activism, see *Unresolved Debate: Are Liberal Judges Really More Likely Than Conservative Judges to Be Activist?*

Evidence in support of the legal model would appear plentiful. Judges, after all, routinely cite legal principles and the relevant case law when making their arguments. Beyond *stare decisis*, judges apply many other principles to the cases that come before them. Some we have already discussed, such as standing and ripeness, which concern decisions about whether or not to hear a particular case. Others are developed to help guide judicial decision making in particular areas of the law, such as employment, contracts, or copyright. It is extremely difficult, though, to show that such principles and precedents alone cause judges to rule as they do. Judges, after all, have a tremendous amount of discretion to choose which cases they want to cite, and how they want to cite them. Perhaps judges first figure out how they want to rule on a case and then search existing case law for those that best support their position. If true, then the observed relationship between past and present rulings misleads proponents of the legal model into thinking that the principle of *stare decisis* causes judges to rule as they do.

stare decisis
the principle that judges deciding a case must carefully weigh the decisions of their predecessors in similar cases and come to the same decision if the basic elements of the case before them are the same.

judicial restraint
the practice judges engage in when they limit the exercise of their own power by overturning past decisions only when they are clearly unconstitutional.

judicial activism
the tendency of judges to give themselves leeway in deciding whether to abide by past court decisions, which allows them to consider possible outcomes, public opinion, and their own preferences before issuing a ruling.

attitudinal model
the theory of judicial decision making in which judges use their own policy preferences in deciding cases.

Judges Advance Their Own Policy Preferences in the Attitudinal Model

Many other political scientists argue that the legal principles that judges use to justify their rulings constitute nothing more than convenient fiction. Although judges try to project an image of neutrality and objectivity, they still use their powers to advance their policy preferences. According to the **attitudinal model** of judicial decision making, courts "are not importantly different than legislatures and judges are no different than elected politicians."[40]

To justify these claims, political scientists have developed a variety of ways to measure judges' policy preferences. The most common of these is the party identification of the president who appointed the judge. Judges appointed by Republicans tend to be conservative, and judges appointed by Democrats tend to be liberal. Moreover, the great majority of judicial appointees identify with the same political party as the president who nominated them. Over the past 30 years, roughly 90 percent of district and appellate court appointees were members of the president's party. This pattern held for Republican and Democratic administrations alike. These judicial nominees, moreover, were not passive party members. Most of them actively supported their political parties in the past. In fact, more than 66 percent of appellate court appointees

15.1

15.2

15.3

15.4

15.5

Unresolved Debate

Are Liberal Judges Really More Likely Than Conservative Judges to Be Activist?

In the 1980s, the Reagan administration made a concerted effort to shape public policy according to conservative values. However, it quickly identified what it saw as a roadblock to these efforts: liberal activist judges, who the administration believed were making policy through their decisions instead of ruling according to strict, limited interpretations of the Constitution.[a] In the decades since, the overreach of activist judges on the left has become a rallying cry for those wishing to promote conservative social values. But are liberal judges really more likely than conservative judges to be activist?

Judicial activism and fidelity to the Constitution are, so very often, merely in the eyes of the beholder.

YES

Despite recent efforts to characterize conservative justices as activists, a cohort of legal scholars argues that judicial activism is decidedly the product of left-wing ideology. Robert Bork, a notable legal scholar, has argued that judicial activism arose when a "new class" of liberal intellectuals, academics, and scholars developed a judicial philosophy that refuses to strictly interpret the Constitution, preferring instead to weight other more ambiguous factors.[b] *Bork undertook a comparative study of the legal procedures in the United States, Canada, and Israel, and used this comparative approach to emphasize what he sees as a liberal approach that empowers judges to make decisions over democratic majorities:*

- In the United States, courts have repeatedly made liberal decisions that protect pornography, abortion rights, homosexuality, and other issues that have not always enjoyed popular support.
- In Canada and Israel, liberal courts have asserted broad notions of what types of cases they have jurisdiction over, allowing them to rule on controversial social issues—a practice U.S. courts have mimicked.

NO

A recent spate of scholarly research has shown that the Supreme Court under Chief Justice William Rehnquist (1994–2005), which is generally acknowledged to have had a majority of conservative justices, was in fact "the most activist Supreme Court in history."[c] *Political scientist Thomas Keck claims that the anti-activism position of the Reagan administration really stemmed from the fact that the Supreme Court had long been considered too left leaning for conservatives' tastes. Keck bases this conclusion on a statistical assessment of the Rehnquist Court's decisions, specifically, the Court's willingness to strike down laws passed by Congress:*[d]

- The conservative-majority Supreme Court struck down 30 provisions of federal law from 1995 to 2001, which is more than any previous Court during a similar time span.
- The Court struck down provisions of laws such as the Gun Free School Zones Act and the Violence Against Women Act that had previously been considered uncontroversial.

CONTRIBUTING TO THE DEBATE

Disagreement over which judges tend to be the most activist fundamentally stems from disputes over how judicial activism is defined. For a conservative, a judge's sole concern must always be to interpret the law as it is written. Liberals, on the other hand, frequently argue that every judicial decision involves interpretation, which inevitably requires judges to place a particular law in its current context. Despite this philosophical disagreement, both conservative and liberal judges continue to reliably decide cases according to their policy preferences, even as they couch their decisions in legal justifications. Given this reality, *any* judicial decision can be seen as an activist decision. To make headway, then, scholars need to develop clear measures of activism upon which both liberals and conservatives can agree.

WHAT DO YOU THINK?

1. Explain two competing characterizations of judicial activism.
2. Is judicial activism inherently a consequence of liberalism? Why or why not?

[a] http://www.hoover.org/publications/hoover-digest/article/6238.
[b] Robert Bork, *Coercing Virtue: The Worldwide Rule of Judges* (Washington, DC: AEI Press, 2003).
[c] Thomas M. Keck, *The Most Activist Supreme Court in History: The Road to Modern Judicial Conservatism* (Chicago: University of Chicago Press, 2004).
[d] Ibid.

and 57 percent of district court appointees over this period had a record of party activism.[41]

Political scientists have also found an extremely strong relationship between judges' ideologies and the decisions they make—a fact that should not hold if judges are merely applying well-established legal principles to the cases that come before them. According to one study, judges rule on civil liberties cases in ways that are consistent with their ideological preferences roughly 80 percent of the time. Even after accounting for a wide range of other influences on judicial decision making, judges' personal ideologies appear to be far and away the most important determinant of case outcomes.[42] As one political scientist notes, "even critics of the attitudinal model have conceded [the] exceptional explanatory ability" of judges' policy preferences.[43] And as the "How Do We Know" feature explores in some detail later in this section, the ideological dispositions of individual justices appear to utterly dominate the opinions of some of the most consequential Supreme Court rulings.

Conservative and liberal critics of the court system regularly accuse judges of projecting their own policy preferences onto the cases that come before them. "We still see judges ruling far too often on the basis of their personal opinions or their view of the good society," wrote Edwin Meese and Todd Gaziano of the conservative Heritage Foundation.[44] Adam Cohen, assistant editor for the liberal leaning *New York Times* editorial board, expressed dismay that many of the Supreme Court's decisions in 2006 were driven by ideology: "The most basic charge against activist judges has always been that they substitute their own views for those of the elected branches. The [C]ourt's conservative majority did just that this term."[45]

The fact that judges' ideologies are such a powerful predictor of case outcomes does not mean that ideology is the only, or even the most important, causal factor in the outcome of every case. Political scientists generally concede, for instance, that ideology plays little role in determining the outcome of criminal cases. Even among civil cases, ideology may not be the only relevant factor. For instance, if public opinion strongly leans in one direction or another, or if the nation is at war, or if the president indicates that he will ignore an objectionable court ruling, then judges may be persuaded to set aside their own policy preferences when formulating their decision.

Just the same, it is worth underscoring how radical the attitudinal model really is. In law schools, students spend years learning about the principles that are supposed to guide judicial decision making; law journals are filled with articles about how the Constitution is appropriately interpreted; and when advancing arguments, both lawyers and judges constantly pay tribute to the relevant case law at hand. If the attitudinal model is correct, then all of these principles amount to little more than theater, merely dressing up what are, at their heart, political motivations and interests.

□ Judges Pay Attention to Politics in the Strategic Model

Most political scientists agree that judges issue rulings that are consistent with their policy preferences. Advocates of the **strategic model** of judicial decision making, however, argue that judges also keep an eye on the long-term integrity of their rulings. According to this view, justices are strategic actors who recognize that their own ability to advance their policy preferences depends on the larger political environment in which they work.[46] Justices see that their word is not final on any policy matter. And they understand that other political institutions (most notably Congress) may subsequently amend or overturn their rulings. When a reversal is imminent, therefore, justices may craft opinions that do not perfectly reflect their policy preferences in order to avoid a clash with either adjoining branch of government.

Judges must also think about how their rulings will be implemented. Different administrative units in federal, state, and local governments may choose to interpret court orders either narrowly or broadly, depending on their own views about a policy dispute. When the court rulings appear entirely out of step with public opinion, administrative agencies and state governments may actively resist a court order. For instance, when the Supreme Court in 1955 required school districts to desegregate their schools "with all

strategic model
the theory of judicial decision making in which judges consider their own policy preferences as well as the possible actions of the other branches of government when making decisions.

15.1

15.2

15.3

15.4

15.5

solicitor general
the individual who represents the federal government in the Supreme Court.

amicus curiae
a brief written by someone who is not a party to a case but who submits information or an argument related to the dispute at hand.

deliberate speed," responses varied widely across the country. Some districts promptly implemented the court edict, whereas others simply dragged their feet.

Not surprisingly, then, judges often monitor the political views of key political actors outside the judiciary. Consider, for instance, the impact of the **solicitor general**, who is appointed by the president and who represents the interests of the executive branch in the Supreme Court. The solicitor general's influence with the Supreme Court is so great that the position is sometimes referred to as "the tenth justice." The Court accepts only about 5 percent of all cases, but it accepts more than 75 percent of the cases in which the solicitor general's office is the petitioning party.[47] And among those accepted cases, the office maintains an impressive record. According to one study, the executive branch won more than 60 percent of its cases in the nineteenth century and almost 70 percent from 1953 to 1983.[48] Another study of all Supreme Court cases to which the U.S. government was a party between 1933 and 2007 also put the solicitor general win-rate at nearly 70 percent.[49] The government's success is notable even when it is not a party to the case. According to some estimates, the side of a case that receives the endorsement of the solicitor general wins upward of 87 percent of the time.[50]

Courts also pay attention to the arguments made by relevant interest groups. Individuals and organizations that are not party to a court case may nonetheless express their opinions through ***amicus curiae*** ("friend of the court") briefs. The practice of *amicus curiae* allows groups that may not have standing to be able to bring a case forward themselves to, nonetheless, present arguments to the court. One study of court challenges to executive orders found that courts were more likely to rule against the president when *amicus curiae* briefs were filed in opposition.[51]

THE SOLICITOR GENERAL

Solicitor General Donald Verrilli (right) speaks to Justice Antonin Scalia (left) during the 2012 oral arguments for the landmark Supreme Court case on Obama's signature health care reform law.

How Do We Know?

Was *Bush v. Gore* a Political Decision?

The Question

A full month after the 2000 presidential election, the United States still had not declared a new president. The race between George W. Bush and Al Gore had been so close that determination of a winner rested entirely on which candidate was to receive Florida's 25 electoral votes.[a] With the presidency hanging by a thread, Gore requested manual recounts of ballots in four Florida counties. Two of the four counties, however, did not complete the recounts by the deadline established under Florida state law. Moreover, each of the counties used different procedures to process ballots that the machines had failed to read. Despite the fact that the recounts turned up additional votes for Gore, Florida Secretary of State Katherine Harris declared Bush the winner on November 26, 2000.[b]

Gore next contested the election in the Florida state court system. The Florida Supreme Court ruled in his favor, but Bush immediately appealed this decision to the U.S. Supreme Court. Within days, a five-member majority of the Court ruled that the manual recounts were unconstitutional. The vote tallies announced by Harris on November 26, therefore, became final.[c] As a direct result of the Court's decision, George W. Bush became president of the United States. Unsurprisingly, Bush followers praised the Court, whereas Gore supporters were outraged. Was *Bush v. Gore* a political decision? How do we know?

Why It Matters

Judges' decisions can have extremely important consequences: In *Bush v. Gore*, justices decided who would be president for the next four years. Because of their immense importance to society, we expect judges to be neutral and open minded, free of all the influences of political bargaining and allegiance. But politics often seems to intrude. It is important, then, to understand how judges make decisions that give shape, meaning, and force to the nation's law and politics.

Investigating the Answer

The legal underpinnings of any Supreme Court decision can readily be found in the arguments made, the *amicus* briefs filed, and the opinions written in a case. A political scientist applying the legal model to a case would, therefore, want to determine whether the precedent the Court used was appropriate and whether the Court's interpretation of the law made sense. In deciding *Bush v. Gore*, the Supreme Court relied on the equal protection clause of the Fourteenth Amendment. Seven of the nine justices agreed that the use of different standards to recount votes violated Floridians' right to have their votes count equally. Two of these seven wanted to give the counties a chance to come up with a uniform method of recounting that would guarantee voters equal and fair treatment. The remaining five, however, opted to stop the recounting entirely. They cited the Florida Supreme Court's earlier decision that the state would abide by a federal law that required presidential election disputes to be settled by December 12, 2000. The U.S. Supreme Court decision was handed down that very day, leaving no time for additional recounts.

A political scientist applying the attitudinal model would argue that these legal explanations simply provided cover for the real reasons justices voted the way they did. Rather than analyzing the written opinions for a particular case, an attitudinalist typically uses data on many court decisions to show how often conservative judges make conservative choices, how often liberal judges make liberal choices, and how closely judges adhere to precedent. Jeffrey Segal and Harold Spaeth, for example, analyzed 40 years of Supreme Court justices' votes and found that justices who dissented in important cases rarely changed their stance when the same issue came up in later cases.[d] Segal and Spaeth later said of the *Bush v. Gore* decision, "Never in its history has a majority of the Court behaved in such a blatant politically partisan fashion."[e] The five most conservative justices, all appointed to the Court by

[a]Abner Greene, *Understanding the 2000 Election* (New York: New York University Press, 2001).
[b]Ibid.
[c]Ibid.
[d]Jeffrey A. Segal and Harold J. Spaeth, "The Influence of Stare Decisis on the Votes of United States Supreme Court Justices," *American Journal of Political Science* 40, 4 (1996): 971–1003.
[e]Jeffrey A. Segal and Harold J. Spaeth, *The Supreme Court and the Attitudinal Model Revisited* (New York: Cambridge University Press, 2002), 171.

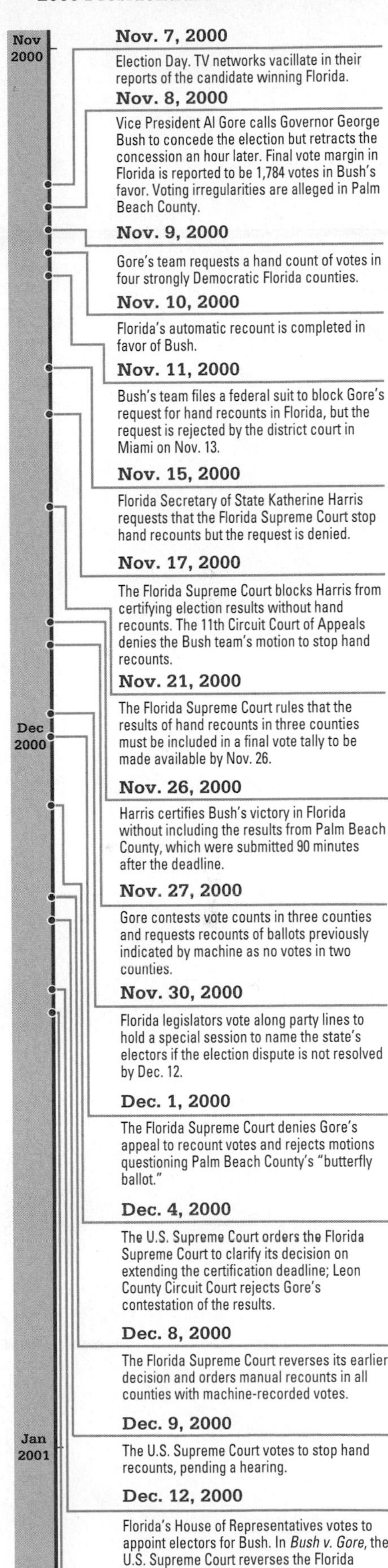

2000 Presidential Election Timeline
Nov 2000
Dec 2000
Jan 2001
Nov. 7, 2000
Election Day. TV networks vacillate in their reports of the candidate winning Florida.
Nov. 8, 2000
Vice President Al Gore calls Governor George Bush to concede the election but retracts the concession an hour later. Final vote margin in Florida is reported to be 1,784 votes in Bush's favor. Voting irregularities are alleged in Palm Beach County.
Nov. 9, 2000
Gore's team requests a hand count of votes in four strongly Democratic Florida counties.
Nov. 10, 2000
Florida's automatic recount is completed in favor of Bush.
Nov. 11, 2000
Bush's team files a federal suit to block Gore's request for hand recounts in Florida, but the request is rejected by the district court in Miami on Nov. 13.
Nov. 15, 2000
Florida Secretary of State Katherine Harris requests that the Florida Supreme Court stop hand recounts but the request is denied.
Nov. 17, 2000
The Florida Supreme Court blocks Harris from certifying election results without hand recounts. The 11th Circuit Court of Appeals denies the Bush team's motion to stop hand recounts.
Nov. 21, 2000
The Florida Supreme Court rules that the results of hand recounts in three counties must be included in a final vote tally to be made available by Nov. 26.
Nov. 26, 2000
Harris certifies Bush's victory in Florida without including the results from Palm Beach County, which were submitted 90 minutes after the deadline.
Nov. 27, 2000
Gore contests vote counts in three counties and requests recounts of ballots previously indicated by machine as no votes in two counties.
Nov. 30, 2000
Florida legislators vote along party lines to hold a special session to name the state's electors if the election dispute is not resolved by Dec. 12.
Dec. 1, 2000
The Florida Supreme Court denies Gore's appeal to recount votes and rejects motions questioning Palm Beach County's "butterfly ballot."
Dec. 4, 2000
The U.S. Supreme Court orders the Florida Supreme Court to clarify its decision on extending the certification deadline; Leon County Circuit Court rejects Gore's contestation of the results.
Dec. 8, 2000
The Florida Supreme Court reverses its earlier decision and orders manual recounts in all counties with machine-recorded votes.
Dec. 9, 2000
The U.S. Supreme Court votes to stop hand recounts, pending a hearing.
Dec. 12, 2000
Florida's House of Representatives votes to appoint electors for Bush. In Bush v. Gore, the U.S. Supreme Court reverses the Florida Supreme Court order to recount.
Dec. 13, 2000
Gore concedes the presidency to Bush.
Jan. 20, 2001
Bush is sworn in as president.

15.1

15.2

15.3

15.4

15.5

Republican presidents, joined together in a decision that handed the presidency to the Republican candidate, whereas the Court's most liberal members dissented.[f]

The strategic model highlights the political context in which justices consider a case. The Supreme Court was under a great deal of pressure to hear and decide the case of *Bush v. Gore*. Many Americans worried that the impasse would raise doubts about the legitimacy of American government.[g] At the time, outgoing President Clinton felt the need to assure world leaders that there was "nothing to worry about."[h] In deciding the case, did the Court respond to a nationwide desire to have the matter resolved? The issue was so politically charged that the majority decided to hand down a *per curiam* decision, one that is not signed by any justice, suggesting that no justice wanted to be associated with its authorship, perhaps for fear the author would be a target for intense personal criticism.

Which view of the courts is correct? In a researcher's ideal world, a political scientist would be able to interview the justices and ask them directly. She or he might even conduct a survey of federal judges to ask about their true motivations in deciding cases. In the American political system, however, judges tend to stay out of the public eye, and most judges would not admit to being influenced by politics.

Although conservative judges consistently vote conservatively and liberal judges vote liberally, this trend may not reveal political motivation. Perhaps conservative and liberal judges just use different methods of interpreting the Constitution. In other words, maybe judges divide not on political lines but on beliefs about interpreting the law. To test this proposition, one would ideally like to replay history and allow Gore to have a slight lead in Florida and Bush to call for a manual recount. If the attitudinal model is correct, this basic fact would cause the justices to rethink their positions. If the legal model is right, the underlying principles would stand and the votes would remain the same.

The Bottom Line

Although judges go to great lengths to justify their opinions, it is extremely difficult to identify their true motivations. Taken at face value, the written record that judges leave behind suggests that legal and constitutional issues are paramount. But the inescapable fact is that judges' partisan identifications are powerful predictors of the votes they cast. This is abundantly clear in *Bush v. Gore*, which had the selection of the next president at stake. The conservative justices sided with the Republican candidate, and the liberal justices sided with the Democratic candidate. On this case in particular, then, the justices' political views probably did influence the Court's ruling.

Thinking Critically

- Had Bush, rather than Gore, stood to benefit from a recount of the Florida votes, do you think the Supreme Court would have ruled the same way? Why or why not?
- Does carefully crafted legal reasoning in the Court opinions in *Bush v. Gore* rule out the possibility that the justices ultimately decided on the basis of political considerations? Why or why not?

---

[f]Ibid., 172–74.
[g]See, for example, Richard Z. Chesnoff, "Europe Worries as U.S. Re-Counts," *Daily News*, November 12, 2000; "The Nation's Mood: Get It Resolved, but Get It Right; Americans Express Faith in the Electoral System, but Many Say, 'We Need to Move On,'" *Grand Rapids Press*, November 12, 2000.
[h]Terrence Hunt, "Election Impasse 'Nothing to Worry About,' Clinton Tells Putin," *Star-Ledger*, November 15, 2000, 11.

Political scientists have generated a substantial body of evidence suggesting that judges are sensitive to public opinion. When the public overwhelmingly supports a particular policy, judges are less likely to overturn it; when the public opposes the policy, judges are more likely to do so as well. There probably is no starker example of the Supreme Court's setting aside legal and constitutional principles in order to cater to public opinion than the 1944 case *Korematsu v. United States*. During World War II, President Franklin Roosevelt unilaterally decided to place 120,000 Japanese Americans into internment camps. In the aftermath of the Japanese attack on Pearl Harbor, Roosevelt argued, Japanese Americans represented a latent security threat. The only cause of the president's action, however, was their national origin.

These individuals had done nothing at all to warrant their forced removal from their homes. The Supreme Court nonetheless ruled in favor of Roosevelt's policy. When the nation was at war, and the public stood squarely behind its president, the justices dared not intervene, even though the president's actions, most would agree, were unconstitutional.[52]

Studies of public opinion, in particular, require special sensitivity to issues of causation. It is not always clear, after all, whether the courts are following the public, or the public is following the courts. A number of scholars have shown that public opinion changed in the direction of court rulings in the aftermath of important desegregation and abortion cases.[53] It is possible, though, that judges sensed or anticipated these shifts in public opinion, in which case the public may have influenced the court ruling. For a further examination of the relationship between court rulings and public opinion, see *How Do We Know? Was Bush v. Gore a Political Decision?*

CHALLENGING THE JAPANESE INTERNMENT IN WORLD WAR II

Fred Korematsu, shown here in 1983, was the subject of one of the most important wartime cases ever decided by the Supreme Court. In a case that bore Korematsu's name, the Supreme Court upheld the internment of Japanese Americans during World War II.

Judicial Appointments

15.5 Analyze the process of judicial appointments and selection.

The Constitution gives the president the power to appoint judges and justices with "the advice and consent" of the Senate. Because judges hold office for life, these appointments enable presidents to have a lasting impact on the workings of government long after they have left office. And because of the stakes involved, presidents take great care when selecting individuals for federal judgeships.

Over the past half-century, each president has appointed scores of individuals to the federal judiciary. Recent presidents have had the opportunity to appoint even more. Every president since World War II has appointed more than 100 judges and justices (except Gerald Ford, who failed to do so only because he held office for just two years). Ronald Reagan and Bill Clinton, both of whom served two consecutive terms, appointed upward of 400 individuals to the bench. During his two terms in office, George W. Bush appointed 328. In his first three years in office, Barack Obama appointed 126.[54] The power to appoint so many federal judges gives presidents some control over the policy preferences and priorities of those individuals who wield the extraordinary power of judicial review.

In terms of race and gender, judges are beginning to look more and more like a cross section of America. Among Ronald Reagan's appointments, only 8 percent were women; 2 percent African American; and 4 percent Hispanic. Among Barack Obama's appointments during his first two and a half years in office, by contrast, 47 percent were women, 21 percent African American, and 11 percent Hispanic. In terms of other demographics, however, nominees to the federal judiciary continue to look very different from the rest of the population. Almost two-thirds of Obama's nominees, for instance, had a net worth of more than $1 million. The average age of a nominee has remained steady at about 50 years. And not surprisingly, almost all nominees worked in politics as either elected or appointed officials or as lawyers before being nominated to a judgeship.[55]

The process for making judicial appointments varies from country to country. In the United States, the president nominates federal judges and Congress votes to approve the appointments. In countries such as India and Israel, however, the heads of state have complete say over appointments to their highest courts. The president of Pakistan also appoints judges to the supreme court, but the Pakistani constitution stipulates that the president must at least first consult with the chief justice. The judges of Australia's highest court are officially appointed by the governor-general, who represents the British monarch—because Australia is still technically part of the British commonwealth—but it is more common in practice for the prime minister to

LOWER COURT CONTROVERSIES

Among the more controversial appointments made by President Obama to the appellate courts was Goodwin Liu, a constitutional law professor at U.C. Berkeley who espoused traditionally liberal views on a variety of policy issues. Here he is seen greeting Senator Dianne Feinstein just before testifying before the Senate Judiciary Committee. After a protracted battle, Republicans in the Senate derailed his appointment.

senatorial courtesy

the custom by which the senior senator from the state in which there is a district court vacancy assists the president in selecting a replacement for that seat.

nominate judges. Court systems of some other countries are undergoing changes. For instance, the appointment process for the supreme court of the United Kingdom was reformed in 2005 to weaken the executive branch's influence over the process; the office of lord chancellor was stripped of some of its judicial powers and a selection commission was formed to make judicial appointments.

Confirmation Hearings for District and Federal Courts Are Political

Presidents try to appoint individuals who are competent at what they do, have legal expertise, and have a strong record of accomplishment. But politics also looms large in judicial appointments. Presidents regularly appoint judges who share their partisan affiliation. In the time since President Nixon held office, upward of 90 percent of judicial appointments to district and appellate courts have come from the president's own party. Most recently, no less than 93 percent of Obama's appointments during his first three years in office were Democrats.

Despite this political favoritism, most lower court nominees are confirmed. In the 1980s and early 1990s, Congress confirmed the appointments of roughly four in five district and appellate nominees. With the Republican takeover of the 104th Congress (1995–1996), however, and the advent of divided government, nominees for appellate courts were significantly less likely than nominees for district courts to be confirmed. Indeed, in every subsequent Congress, confirmation rates among appellate court nominees have been significantly lower than those among district court nominees.

Part of the reason most district nominees are confirmed is that senators play an important role in their selection. When choosing a judicial nominee for a district court, the president will often seek the approval of the senior senator who represents the state where the court is located. This norm, known as **senatorial courtesy,** tends to hasten the process of selecting and confirming district court judges around the nation.

The situation gets more complicated at the appellate levels, however. For starters, senatorial courtesy applies only to district court appointments. Moreover, appellate court judges tend to be subjected to greater scrutiny by both the president and the Senate. As a consequence, some individuals are easily confirmed at the district level but are denied assignment to an appellate judgeship.

The saga of Judge Charles Pickering is a case in point. In 1990, George H. W. Bush appointed Pickering to a federal district court in southern Mississippi. Twelve years later, George W. Bush nominated Pickering for a position on the Fifth Circuit Court of Appeals. At the time, the Democrats controlled the Senate, and they refused to confirm Pickering's nomination. Democrats levied a variety of charges against Pickering, including racial insensitivity and political views that were "out of step" with mainstream America. The next year, when the Republicans regained control of the Senate, Bush renominated Pickering for the position. This time Democrats filibustered the nomination, and the Republicans lacked the needed votes to cut off debate. Not to be outdone, when the Senate was not in session in early 2004, Bush granted Pickering a recess appointment. This allowed him to hold the position until the end of the Congress's next session. When Congress began to formally consider Pickering's case, concerns about his political positions resurfaced. Rather than drag the confirmation out any longer, Pickering withdrew his name from consideration and retired from the federal judiciary.

In this confirmation process, it is difficult to figure out just how much influence the president and the Senate wield. On the one hand, the fact that most presidential nominees are appointed would appear to be a clear testament to the president's influence. If the president were weak, the Senate might decide to block a greater number of his nominees. On the other hand, the fact that most nominees are confirmed might instead indicate congressional influence. Fearing that the Senate will refuse to confirm them, the president might not even nominate certain individuals—even though he would like them to serve on the bench. Instead, the president might nominate only those individuals who he thinks stand a good chance of being confirmed. As a consequence, senators may approve nominees not because the president is strong, but because the president has chosen candidates that are to the senators' liking.

CONFIRMING THOMAS

Among Supreme Court confirmation hearings, Clarence Thomas's in 1991 was one of the most politically charged in recent memory.

Confirmation Hearings for the Supreme Court Are Especially Political

If the stakes involved in district and appellate court nominations are high, those in Supreme Court nominations are off the charts. Norms of senatorial courtesy play no role in Supreme Court appointments. Instead, presidents consult directly with their closest advisers and heed the demands of different political constituencies. The goal is to find an individual with just the right mix of judicial experience, expertise, and policy preferences. Occasionally, presidents also find it advantageous to select a candidate with a particular demographic background. For example, George H. W. Bush in 1991 nominated Clarence Thomas to the Court. Thomas was a strong conservative who did not have a wealth of judicial experience.[56] Some political observers argued, however, that by selecting an African American, Bush managed to mute some liberals' criticisms of the nomination.

Once he comes up with a potential Supreme Court nominee, the president asks the Federal Bureau of Investigation to conduct a full background check on the individual. This check is intended to identify any evidence of unlawful behavior that a nominee might have engaged in. Some recent presidents have also sent the names of prospective nominees to the American Bar Association (ABA), an interest group that represents the legal profession and that provides ratings of the qualifications of candidates. The ABA's Standing Committee on the Federal Judiciary typically rates nominees as either "well qualified," "qualified," or "not qualified." If a presidential nominee survives these background checks, he or she then must face the public. From the moment the president announces a name, a torrent of media scrutiny follows. Interest groups take out radio and television advertisements to highlight the candidate's strengths and foibles. Legal scholars write opinion pieces about the candidate's qualifications and judicial philosophies. Journalists investigate the candidate's personal and professional histories. When an individual is being considered for appointment to the Supreme Court, no element of his or her past is considered off limits.

During the 2009 Senate confirmation hearings for Supreme Court Justice Sonia Sotomayor, for instance, the media and politicians fixated on comments she had made in a 2001 speech, in which she said, "I would hope that a wise Latina woman with the richness of her experiences would more often than not reach a better conclusion than a white male who hasn't lived that life."[57] The quote was repeated many times by the press, and some Republican members of Congress expressed concern that she believed that race and gender figured prominently in the capacity of justices to perform their duties in office. Like most Supreme Court nominees, however, Sotomayor deflected accusations made about her ideological views. Her record as a district and appellate judge, she claimed, reflected her impartiality.

The real action of the judicial appointment process occurs during the confirmation hearings, which are open to the public. Members of the Senate Judiciary Committee have the opportunity to directly interrogate a nominee about decisions he or she made as a lawyer or lower court judge. They may ask about his or her views on issues ranging from abortion to campaign finance. Given that they may eventually issue rulings that fundamentally alter these public policies, it is perfectly appropriate that these nominees be interrogated on their views. Whether the nominees are completely forthcoming in their answers, however, is another matter.

In general, the Senate is less likely to confirm Supreme Court nominees than appellate or district court nominees. Since the nation's founding in 1789, presidents have formally submitted 158 nominations to the Court, including those for chief justice. Of these, the Senate confirmed 122, and 115 actually took office.[58] Indeed, dissenters

15.1

15.2

15.3

15.4

15.5

can be found in all of the recent Supreme Court confirmation hearings. In some cases, such as Clarence Thomas's, full-blown controversies can erupt. Of late, however, nothing compares to the confirmation hearings of Robert Bork, whom Reagan nominated to the Supreme Court in 1987. No fewer than 86 interest groups testified at his confirmation hearings.[59] Critics focused not on Bork's knowledge of the law—the ABA rated him "well qualified"—but on his political views on abortion, civil rights, and civil liberties. Less than an hour after Reagan announced Bork's nomination, Senator Edward Kennedy declared, "Robert Bork's America is a land in which women would be forced into back alley abortions, blacks would sit in segregated lunch counters," and "rogue police could break down citizens' doors in midnight raids."[60] For the next three and a half months, an avalanche of criticism fell upon the nominee. On October 23, 1987, the Senate rejected Bork's confirmation by a vote of 58 to 42.

In 2010, President Obama named his second nominee to the Supreme Court: Elena Kagan, the solicitor general. Kagan would become the third woman serving on the Roberts Court and its youngest justice. A former law school professor and aide to President Clinton, Kagan had never served on the bench. Moreover, throughout her legal career, she left a thin paper trail. Because her views on the Constitution were not well known, the White House released more than 150,000 pages of correspondence dating back to Kagan's time on President Clinton's staff. Despite the usual partisan wrangling in the media and the scoring of political points by the senators at her confirmation hearing, it seemed certain, even before the hearings began, that Kagan would soon follow Sonia Sotomayor to the Supreme Court. And so she did. In early August, the Senate confirmed her nomination by a vote of 63 to 37.

Review the Chapter

 Listen to Chapter 15 on MyPoliSciLab

Constitutional Design of the Federal Judiciary

15.1 Determine the role of the judiciary as established by the Framers of the U.S. Constitution, p. 509.

Many of the original framers of the Constitution anticipated that the federal judiciary would be the weakest of the three branches. Lacking the powers of both the sword and the purse, judges were left merely with the persuasive appeal of their judgment. From the nation's beginning, therefore, judges worked hard to promote the legitimacy of their institution. Over time, the public learned to hold the courts in high regard.

Organization of the Federal Judiciary

15.2 Outline the structure of the U.S. judiciary, p. 511.

The federal judiciary is organized hierarchically, with district courts at the bottom, appellate courts in the middle, and the Supreme Court on top. Most decisions are decided at the district court level. The losing party to a case, however, has the option of appealing the decision to appellate courts and the Supreme Court. Decisions made by higher courts are binding for lower courts.

Number and Types of Cases That Courts Process

15.3 Distinguish between civil and criminal cases, and describe methods used to manage the judicial caseload, p. 516.

In civil and criminal cases, the judiciary resolves disputes among individuals, organizations, and the government. Criminal cases involve violations of the criminal code, and the plaintiff is always the government. Civil cases concern violations of the civil code, and the plaintiff is a private individual, group of individuals, or institution. Although many cases are settled before ever going to trial, federal courts nonetheless process hundreds of thousands of cases each year.

Making and Interpreting the Law

15.4 Explain how judges decide cases that involve public policy, p. 520.

With the power of judicial review, judges exert considerable influence over the interpretation and implementation of laws. When deciding a case, judges rely on a variety of considerations. They attempt to correctly interpret the Constitution and apply legal principles to the case at hand. They turn to their own political preferences and ideas about what constitutes good public policy. And they pay attention to politics more generally, trying to steer clear of certain decisions that are likely to evoke widespread opposition.

Judicial Appointments

15.5 Analyze the process of judicial appointments and selection, p. 529.

Politics, in varying degrees, intrudes on the process of appointing judges to the federal judiciary. Presidents have strong incentives to select individuals who share their views and will advocate on behalf of these views long after the president has left office. As a consequence, the Senate confirmation process can be highly contentious. Nominees to the Supreme Court, in particular, face an extraordinary amount of public scrutiny. Occasionally, these nominees fail to be confirmed, either because the Senate votes against them or because the president withdraws the nomination.

Learn the Terms

amicus curiae, p. 526
appellate courts, p. 512
attitudinal model, p. 523
briefs, p. 514
chief justice, p. 515
civil case, p. 517
class action suit, p. 517
common law, p. 520
concurring opinion, p. 515
conference, p. 515
criminal case, p. 516
defendant, p. 516
dissenting opinion, p. 515
district court, p. 511
judicial activism, p. 523
judicial restraint, p. 523
judicial review, p. 520
jury, p. 516
legal model, p. 521
magistrate judges, p. 511
majority opinion, p. 515
oral argument, p. 514
original jurisdiction, p. 513
plaintiff, p. 516
plea bargain, p. 518
public law, p. 520
ripeness doctrine, p. 518
senatorial courtesy, p. 530
solicitor general, p. 526
standing, p. 518
stare decisis, p. 523
strategic model, p. 525
Supreme Court, p. 512
writ of certiorari, p. 513

Test Yourself

Study and **Review** the **Practice Tests**

15.1 Determine the role of the judiciary as established by the Framers of the U.S. Constitution.

The Framers established a judiciary

a. that they intended to be the strongest of the three branches of government.
b. with a brief and vague mandate.
c. with a long and detailed mandate.
d. that included a complete system of courts.
e. that Alexander Hamilton would later refer to as the "most dangerous branch."

15.2 Outline the structure of the U.S. judiciary.

Which of the following is NOT a type of U.S. federal court?

a. U.S. County Court
b. U.S. Supreme Court
c. U.S. Court of Appeals
d. U.S. Tax Court
e. U.S. District Court

15.3 Distinguish between civil and criminal cases, and describe methods used to manage the judicial caseload.

Which of the following is TRUE about civil and criminal cases in the United States?

a. In a civil case, the government brings a suit against a defendant; in a criminal case, an individual brings a suit against a defendant.
b. In a civil case, the plaintiff is always the government; in a criminal case, the plaintiff is always a private individual.
c. In a civil case, an individual, group of individuals, or institution brings a suit against a defendant; in a criminal case, the government brings a suit against a defendant.
d. In both civil and criminal cases, a defendant is accused of violations of the criminal code.
e. In both civil and criminal cases, a defendant is accused of violations of the civil code.

15.4 Explain how judges decide cases that involve public policy.

In which model of judicial decision making do judges rely on their judgment and expertise to decipher the correct interpretation of a law, the relevant portion of the Constitution, and whether there is any conflict between the two?

a. attitudinal model
b. strategic model
c. judicial activist model
d. judicial review model
e. legal model

15.5 Analyze the process of judicial appointments and selection.

What is the custom by which the senior senator from the state in which there is a district court vacancy assists the president in selecting a replacement for that seat?

a. senatorial courtesy
b. *writ of certiorari*
c. original jurisdiction
d. standing
e. *amicus curiae*

Explore Further

SUGGESTED READINGS BY TOP SCHOLARS

Michael Bailey and Forrest Maltzman. *The Constrained Court: How the Law and Politics Shape the Decisions Justices Make.* Princeton, NJ: Princeton University Press, 2011. Studies the interactions between politics and the law on judicial decision making.

Tom Clark. *The Limits of Judicial Independence.* New York: Cambridge University Press, 2010. Examines congressional responses to judicial rulings, and the impacts these responses have on court behavior.

Lee Epstein and Jeffrey Segal. *Advice and Consent: The Politics of Judicial Appointments.* New York: Oxford University Press, 2005. Provides a contemporary look at the politics of judicial appointments.

Gregory A. Huber and Sanford C. Gordon. "Accountability and Coercion: Is Justice Blind When It Runs for Office?" *The American Journal of Political Science* 48 (2004): 247–63. Investigates the relevance of judicial elections for sentencing in criminal cases.

Jeffrey Segal and Harold Spaeth. *The Supreme Court and the Attitudinal Model Revisited.* New York: Cambridge University Press, 2002. Examines, thoroughly, the attitudinal model of judicial decision making.

SUGGESTED WEBSITES

Official website of the federal judiciary: www.uscourts.gov

At this site, it is possible to track information about all courts and look up case rulings throughout the federal judiciary.

Federal Judicial Center: www.fjc.gov

This site houses research reports on a wide range of issues involving the federal judiciary and the law.

American Bar Association: www.abanet.org

This is the oldest and most prominent organization representing the interests of the legal profession.

Federalist Society: www.fed-soc.org

A conservative organization that professes to fight the "liberal orthodoxy" that pervades law schools and the legal profession.

16

Listen to Chapter 16 on MyPoliSciLab

The Bureaucracy

A BUREAUCRACY TO PROTECT OUR ENVIRONMENT

Upon signing the first act of Congress of his administration, Republican President Richard Nixon in 1969 declared that the 1970s would be the "environmental decade." The new law, the National Environmental Policy Act, was the first of several to dramatically expand the role of the federal government in protecting the environment. At the time, the president and Congress were eager to respond to a widely publicized environmental movement and a growing number of powerful environmental interest groups.[1]

In 1970, Congress established the Environmental Protection Agency (EPA), whose most important responsibility was implementing the Clean Air Act. Under the act, EPA officials were charged with setting limits for the amount of pollution that could be emitted by steel mills, chemical plants, motor vehicles, and other sources. As Congress passed more and more environmental legislation, the EPA saw its budget grow from $500 million in 1973 to $1.3 billion in 1980. Bureaucrats within the agency worked hard to implement and enforce the new environmental policies. During the first 10 years of its existence, emissions of major air pollutants decreased by 21 percent. By 1980, the EPA had 10,600 full-time employees who were committed to strict enforcement of the nation's clean air laws.[2]

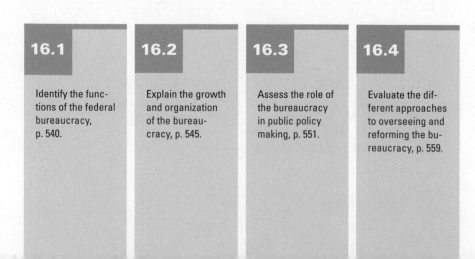

However, when Ronald Reagan won the presidential election in 1980, he made the EPA one of his first targets. During his campaign, Reagan had promised to address the nation's economic problems and drastically reduce the size of the federal government. He interpreted his victory

HAMSTRINGING THE REGULATORS Sometimes, political principals seek to restrict the industrious work of bureaucratic agencies. During their time in office, Presidents Ronald Reagan and George W. Bush attempted to curtail the efforts of the Environmental Protection Agency to enforce federal clean air standards.

The Big Picture Fighting fires, teaching classrooms, collecting information about national security threats—maybe studying the bureaucracy isn't so boring after all. Author William G. Howell defines bureaucracy as the body of the American government as it is the political system behind most policy implementation.

The Basics What does the bureaucracy do? What is its role in our democracy? In this video, you will listen to what people think about bureaucrats and the job they do. You will also learn why the bureaucracy can have such a big impact on your life.

2
Vhat does the bureacracy do? Is it effective?

3

In Context Why is the bureaucracy important in the policymaking process? In this video, University of North Texas political scientist Matthew Eshbaugh-Soha talks about not only the bureaucracy and its importance at the federal level, but also the role the federal bureaucracy plays in cooperation with state and local bureaucracies.

Think Like a Political Scientist Are bureaucracies democratic? And if so, how are they democratic? University of North Texas political scientist Matthew Eshbaugh-Soha tackles this question and also looks at political appointments and other important research topics associated with bureaucracies.

In the Real World Is the federal bureaucracy too big and too powerful? Real people weigh in on this question and discuss whether they feel reducing the size of the bureaucracy is worth losing the protections that those agencies provide.

So What? What does visiting the post office and picnicking in the park have in common? Both are made possible by the big, bad bureaucracy In this video, William G. Howell humanizes government agencies and reveals how bureaucracy works in our daily lives.

against Democrat Jimmy Carter as a mandate to cut domestic program budgets and push business-friendly policies, and the EPA was not well liked by business and industry leaders.[3]

Reagan started by filling EPA leadership positions with lobbyists, lawyers, and scientists who were closely tied to the very business interests the EPA was supposed to regulate.[4] In May 1981, he appointed Anne Gorsuch to run the EPA. Gorsuch did not try to conceal her plan to ease enforcement of the Clean Air Act.[5] She disbanded the agency's Office of Enforcement and then recreated it with a smaller staff.[6] The decisions she made in the name of "administrative efficiency" outraged environmentalists, who accused her and Reagan of intentionally sabotaging the EPA.

Reagan also pursued an aggressive legislative strategy through proposed budget cuts. During his first year in office, Republicans controlled the Senate, and few of the Democrats who held the majority in the House were willing to stand up against a president who had just won office with such a large victory margin.[7] As a consequence, the EPA saw its operating budget reduced by 24 percent in 1982. Funding for air pollution enforcement alone dropped by 42 percent between 1980 and 1983, and the number of EPA employees assigned to clean air responsibilities fell by 31 percent.[8]

Many analysts believed that the combination of drastic budget and staff cuts and Gorsuch's leadership would be the EPA's undoing. In the short run, Reagan's budget cuts produced the desired result—a weaker, less effective organization. The EPA conducted 41 percent fewer inspections and compliance tests of air pollution sources in 1982 than it had in 1981, and it took 69 percent fewer enforcement actions to rein in over-polluters. His initial personnel changes, however, did not appear to affect the enforcement activity of the EPA. The agency's employees continued to do their jobs as they had before Reagan came into office. If anything, they increased the intensity of their enforcement activity, remaining committed to faithful implementation of the clean air policies of the 1970s.[9]

Reagan's attempts to curtail EPA enforcement ultimately failed. By the end of 1982, it had become clear that the public did not want federal clean air regulations to be relaxed: 48 percent of Americans thought the EPA's old air pollution policies were fine as they were, and 38 percent wanted the Clean Air Act to be made stricter.[10] In another blow to Reagan's agenda, the 1982 congressional elections brought more pro-environment Democrats to the House. They cited Gorsuch for contempt of Congress for her mismanagement of the EPA hazardous waste program, and she later resigned in March 1983.[11]

Reagan was not the last president to attempt to curb the EPA. President George W. Bush attempted to ease air pollution restrictions, relax enforcement of emissions standards, reduce requirements for industries' capital maintenance and upgrades, and roll back wilderness and wildlife regulations. His proposed policies led to clashes with EPA leaders—even with his own appointee, EPA administrator Christine Todd Whitman.[12]

The election of Barack Obama revitalized the federal government's efforts to protect the environment. Soon after he took office, Obama proposed a $10.5 billion budget for the EPA—the largest in the agency's history—signaling that environmental protection and enforcement would be a priority for the new president. During the president's first year in office, the EPA reversed numerous pro-industry rules from the prior Bush administration.[13] And, in the aftermath of one of the nation's greatest environmental disasters—the oil spill in the Gulf of Mexico in 2010—Obama imposed a six-month moratorium on deep-well offshore drilling and pressured the company responsible to set aside $20 billion to begin compensating U.S. citizens whose livelihoods were affected by the spill. Obama also renamed the Minerals Management Service (the federal agency charged with overseeing offshore drilling) the Bureau of Ocean Energy Management, Regulation, and Enforcement, an act that many viewed as a precursor to an even more vigorous regulation of the oil industry.

Contestations over an agency's policy objectives and behavior are the stuff of bureaucratic politics. In spite of Progressive Era efforts to embed principles of expertise and merit into the federal bureaucracy, politics greatly affects the daily lives of bureaucratic agencies. To make sense of a bureaucratic agency's effectiveness at solving social problems, then, we must critically assess the various efforts of presidents and Congress to control them. The root causes of administrative success and failure, as we shall see, trace back to much more than civil servants faithfully trying to serve the public good.

What Bureaucrats Do

16.1 Identify the functions of the federal bureaucracy.

bureaucracy
a group of departments, agencies, and other institutions that for the most part are located in the executive branch of government and that develop and implement public policy.

Explore on MyPoliSciLab
Simulation: You Are Head of FEMA

What do bureaucrats do? The staggering number of functions that government bureaucracies perform might instead raise the question: What *don't* bureaucrats do? Bureaucrats, the individuals who work within a **bureaucracy**, run the nation's prisons and schools, collect garbage, maintain job training programs, write Social Security checks, monitor the pollution of our rivers, pave highways, patrol streets, regulate industries, put out fires, issue drivers' licenses, and so much more. When we experience government in our daily lives, we typically interact with employees of one or another local, state, or federal bureaucracy—teachers, police and parole officers, prison guards, firefighters, garbage collectors, auditors, inspectors, customer service representatives, and more. Such interactions, however, reflect just a small portion of the things that bureaucrats actually do.

Bureaucrats Interpret and Implement Laws

When Congress enacts a law, when the president issues a unilateral directive, or when a court issues a decree of one sort or another, somebody must figure out what exactly these policies require in practice, and then they must ensure that the government actually takes the steps needed to realize them. Both of these tasks fall to bureaucrats. And both are remarkably difficult.

Laws, after all, are often quite vague. Take, for example, the Full Employment Act, which Congress enacted after World War II. Facing the transition from a wartime to a peacetime economy, and anticipating the return of hundreds of thousands of discharged veterans, Congress sought to encourage the development of broad economic policies for the country. With the Full Employment Act, Congress mandated certain actions. It required the president to submit an annual economic report along with his proposed budget. It created the Council of Economic Advisors, an appointed board to advise and assist the president in formulating economic policy. And it established the Joint Economic Committee, composed of members of Congress and charged with reviewing the government's economic policy at least annually. The overriding purpose of the law, meanwhile, was to ensure that federal policies "promote maximum employment, production, and purchasing power."

What do all these legislative provisions mean? Consider the beginning of the first clause: "promote maximum employment." What is maximum employment? Is 95 percent enough? Or does it require the employment of every single healthy adult who would like to work? Whatever the amount, is the specified goal of maximum employment fixed for all times? Or does the law allow for different objectives depending, for example, on whether the nation is at war or whether the economy is experiencing a downturn? And what does it mean to "promote" maximum employment? Are any means justified? Or should the government weigh the objective of maximizing employment against other objectives, such as reducing deficits or encouraging private enterprise?

It falls upon bureaucrats to formulate answers to these difficult questions, and they must do so in many other policy domains as well. Either when the language of a statute is vague or when Congress expressly delegates the responsibility to them, bureaucrats must decipher the exact meaning of broad legislative pronouncements. They must determine the exact amount of various pollutants that an industry can release into the air, the precise number of questions that students must answer correctly on standardized tests in order to graduate from high school, the particular design of highway exit signs, and the regularity with which such signs must be replaced. In the summer of 2010, bureaucrats were charged with making sense of the extraordinarily complex overhaul of the financial industries. Earlier in the year, Congress enacted legislation that increased regulation of various financial services in an attempt to guard against the economic meltdown associated with the housing crash of 2008. The law, however, is short on details. The legislation, for instance, requires banks to set aside funds in case of investment losses, but it leaves it up to bureaucrats to decide how much must be held in reserve. The legislation calls for caps on the amount of fees that banks can charge for ATM transactions, but it leaves it up to bureaucrats to set the exact level. As the *New York Times* reported, the law "is basically a 2,000-page missive to federal agencies, instructing regulators to address subjects ranging from derivatives trading to document retention. But it is notably short on specifics, giving regulators significant power to determine its impact."[14]

Having deciphered the meaning of laws, bureaucrats then are charged with putting them into practice—that is, with implementing them. The **implementation** of public policy constitutes the single biggest task assigned to bureaucrats. Laws, after all, constitute nothing more than words on paper until bureaucrats put them into practice. The implementation of public policy is where the "rubber hits the road."

implementation
the process by which policy is executed.

DEA AGENTS MUST EXERCISE DISCRETION

Combating the drug trade requires bureaucrats, which include DEA agents, to exercise all kinds of independent judgment about who to arrest, who to cultivate as informants, when to bring charges, how to collect information, and so much more besides. Here, we see drug kingpin Francisco Javier Arellano Felix in DEA custody as he arrives in San Diego in 2006. Arellano Felix pleaded not guilty to federal charges of transporting tons of cocaine and marijuana across the California-Mexico border.

16.1

16.2

16.3

16.4

rules
administrative determinations about how laws will be interpreted and implemented.

Just as bureaucrats have considerable discretion to interpret laws, they also have considerable discretion when implementing them. Imagine, for example, a hypothetical agent working for the U.S. Drug Enforcement Administration (DEA) whose job is to enforce the nation's drug laws. This agent receives a tip that drugs are being sold out of an abandoned house on the outskirts of town. When he goes to investigate, he finds a teenage girl selling small amounts of cocaine. After arresting her, though, he learns that this teenager works for a well-known drug dealer in the region. To capture this dealer, the DEA agent will need the teenager's cooperation. To secure that, can the DEA promise not to prosecute her? Or must he enforce the law every time that he observes a violation? The laws that DEA agents are sworn to uphold provide little guidance on the matter. Instead, DEA agents—and bureaucrats everywhere—must draw on their expertise, their common sense, and whatever recommendations their superiors provide in order to determine the best way to enforce the laws.

In the United States, bureaucrats are responsible for interpreting the meaning of statutes. That is not the case in some countries with more centralized governments. In Venezuela, for example, most policy decisions are made at the top, by the president and his closet advisers. The president may then issue legislation in the form of presidential decrees or have his allies in the legislature pass his proposed policies into law legislatively. In this system, bureaucrats are responsible for carrying out specific policy tasks assigned to them that are usually not subject to interpretation. Quite the contrary, if bureaucrats fail to carry out their superiors' orders exactly as stated, or if they deviate from the party line, they may be summarily fired from their positions.

☐ Bureaucrats Make Rules

One of the principal ways in which bureaucrats flesh out the meaning of congressional statutes, presidential directives, and court orders is by issuing **rules.** Rules typically provide more specific directions about how policy is to be interpreted and implemented. Moreover, once rules are issued, they take on the weight of law. For this reason, political scientists refer to bureaucratic rules as "quasi-legislation."[15]

Rules have a dramatic effect on a vast array of policies—environmental, worker safety, food safety, to name only a few. They also influence what we watch on television almost every day. Consider, for example, the efforts of the Federal Communications Commission (FCC) to regulate television and radio under the Communications Acts of 1934, the Communications Satellite Act of 1962, and the Telecommunications Act of 1996. Under these laws, the FCC is charged with "promoting safety of life and property and for strengthening the national defense." Part of this duty is the oversight of "obscene" and "indecent" programming. But what kind of programming qualifies as obscene or indecent? Does it matter whether the programming is aired when children are likely to be watching television? What, exactly, is to be done about violations? None of the three acts just listed provides clear answers to these questions. The FCC, therefore, has had to issue rules that clarify the original laws enacted by Congress.

Through such rules, the FCC has decided to forbid the airing of "obscene" programming at any time and the airing of "indecent programming" or "profane language" during certain hours. The FCC defines "obscene" material according to a three-pronged standard: (1) an average person, applying contemporary community standards, must find that the material, as a whole, appeals to prurient interests; (2) the material must depict or describe, in a patently offensive way, sexual conduct specifically defined by applicable law; and (3) the material, taken as a whole, must lack serious literary, artistic, political, or scientific value.[16] The FCC defines "indecent programming" as "language or material that, in context, depicts or describes, in terms patently offensive as measured by contemporary community standards for the broadcast medium, sexual or excretory organs or activities." It defines "profanity" as "language so grossly offensive to members of the public who actually hear it as to amount to a nuisance."[17] The FCC has further decided that neither indecent programming nor profanity can be aired between 6 a.m. and 10 p.m., when there is a reasonable risk that children may be in the audience.

After the FCC develops guidelines, however, its work is still not complete. It must then ensure that media outlets abide by the rules. The FCC does so by monitoring the content of programming and then punishing infractions by issuing warnings, imposing fines, or revoking station licenses. As one example, comments made by Bono at the 2003 Golden Globe awards caught the attention of the FCC. During his televised acceptance speech, U2's lead singer used a well-known expletive to convey how excited he was to have won an award. Prior to the incident, the FCC had tolerated fleeting expletives in broadcasts. Prompted by complaints about Bono's language, however, the FCC declared that it would begin to fine networks that broadcast fleeting expletives. The FCC explained that the particular word used by Bono "invariably invokes a coarse sexual image and that its isolated and gratuitous utterance could be punished to safeguard the well-being of the nation's children from the most objectionable, most offensive language."[18] Fox Televisions Inc. challenged the new rule in court, claiming that it was arbitrary and contradicted the First Amendment of the Constitution.[19] In 2009, in a 5–4 decision, the Supreme Court upheld the FCC's new rule. Yet in a related case in 2010, the Court of Appeals for the Second District in New York sided with broadcasters in their assessment that the FCC had overstepped its authority, arguing that the agency's powers as a watchdog of public decency were vague. In October of 2011, the Supreme Court upheld the appellate ruling, and the charges against the broadcasters were vacated.[20]

The specific rules that the FCC developed are intended to guide bureaucrats who do the everyday work of implementing public policy. Obviously, though, these rules alone do not resolve the matter entirely. Considerable judgment is required to figure out whether a specific word or image on a television show meets the FCC's definitions of obscene, indecent, and profane and if so, to decide what kind of punishment, if any, should apply. Such judgments involve **norms,** which are especially important when an agency's stated goals are vague. Norms come from an organization's culture and sense of mission. They are informal expressions of the customs, attitudes, and expectations

norms
informal expressions of the customs, attitudes, and expectations put before people who work within a bureaucratic agency.

STERN VERSUS THE FCC

After receiving numerous fines from the FCC, popular shock-jock Howard Stern announced in 2004 that he would begin airing his show via satellite radio. So doing, he has avoided many of the rules and regulations that the FCC enforces. In your opinion, should the FCC also regulate the content of satellite radio?

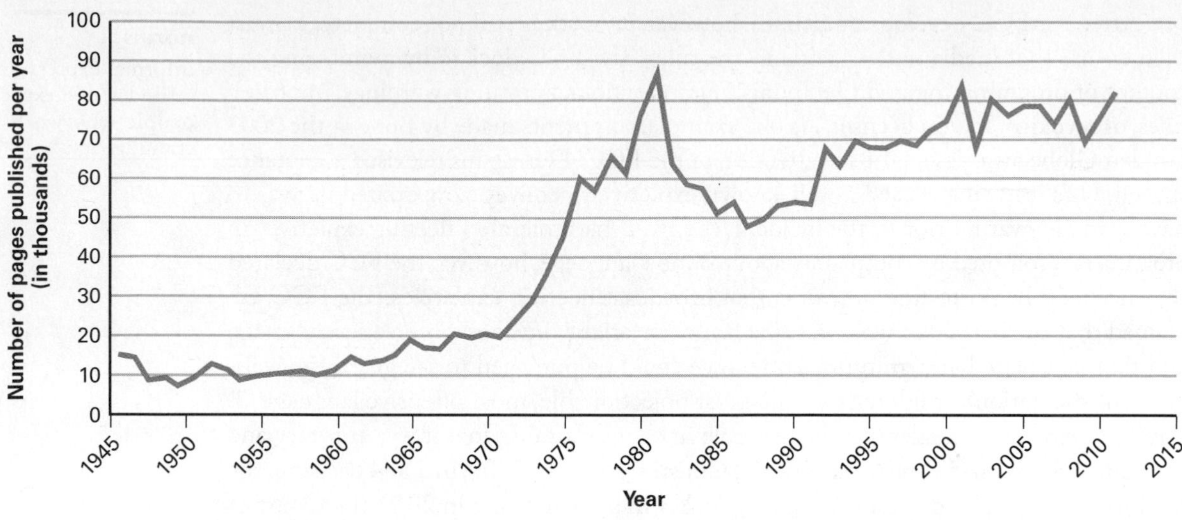

FIGURE 16.1 THE SIZE OF THE FEDERAL REGISTER.

During the past half-century, the federal bureaucracy has issued more and more rules.

Source: Office of the Federal Register, National Archives and Records Administration, *The Federal Register*, Vols. 1–76, Washington, DC. Available online at http://www.heinonline.org.

put before people who work within a bureaucratic agency. Within the FCC, for example, norms help employees determine which specific words ought to be deemed indecent. They also play an important role in deciding how aggressively to prosecute violations.

In contrast to norms, rules emerge from a well-defined process. The 1946 Administrative Procedures Act lays out the specific steps that agencies must follow when they issue rules. To begin, rules are offered as proposals, allowing interested parties an opportunity to express their opinions. Agencies then must respond to each of the issues raised during the public comment period, which varies in length depending on the complexity of the rule. Further, the agency may be required to issue formal reports to Congress and the president to identify how, for instance, a rule will impact the economy. Finalized rules are then published in the *Federal Register*, a compendium of government rules, proposed rules, and notices. As agencies have issued increasing numbers of rules over the past 60 years, the *Federal Register* has grown longer and longer. To provide some indication of the volume of rules that the federal bureaucracy produces each year, Figure 16.1 shows the number of pages included in the *Federal Register* each year from 1945 to 2011. Note that whereas rules, notices of rules, and other executive branch policies required fewer than 8,000 pages in 1949, they now take up about 80,000 pages each year.[21]

□ Bureaucrats Provide Expert Advice

Bureaucrats in a particular area typically know a great deal more about the specifics of public policy than do members of Congress or the president. This know-how should come as no surprise, for bureaucrats usually are experts who have devoted their professional lives to a specific policy issue, while paying considerably less attention to most other issues. By contrast, members of Congress and presidents are policy generalists who have collected relatively small amounts of information on many different issues.

When determining which public policies are most in need of change, and then figuring out how best to change them, members of Congress and presidents regularly consult bureaucrats. The main responsibility of the Government Accountability Office (GAO), for example, is to provide formal reports to members of Congress about specific policy issues. When a lawmaker wants to learn more about the test score achievement gap between African Americans and whites or the threat of terrorism to our nation's seaports, she can request that the GAO investigate the issue. The GAO, then, consults with nongovernment experts, reads the relevant scholarship, and communicates with bureaucratic agencies that deal with the particular policy domain. Having completed its investigation, the GAO reports back to the lawmaker who is now better equipped to address the issue at hand.

Often, though, members of Congress and presidents consult with bureaucrats through less formal means. Through testimony in congressional hearings, advisory meetings, or simple conversations, bureaucrats provide lawmakers with vital information about how policies are affecting citizens, which policies seem to be working, which are not, and what should be done about them. Indeed, it is their expertise that makes bureaucrats so useful to lawmakers trying to figure out how best to solve the problems of the day.

☐ Bureaucrats Resolve Disputes

Just as bureaucrats serve core executive functions by implementing laws and core legislative functions by issuing rules and providing expertise, so too do they serve core judicial functions by resolving disputes. The National Labor Relations Board (NLRB), for instance, is an independent government agency that regularly settles disputes between private corporations and employees who believe that their rights have been infringed upon.

Employees, often organized into unions, may file complaints of unfair labor practices with the NLRB. If these complaints are found to have merit, a case may then come before one of the 40 NLRB judges. The assigned judge will conduct a hearing, much like a regular court hearing, in which both the corporation and the employees present arguments, evidence, and witnesses to make their case. Once the judge decides the case, either side can appeal directly to the board, which is composed of five members appointed by the president and confirmed by the Senate. Each year, the board decides several hundred cases in this manner. If the losing party is still not satisfied, it can appeal the board's decision to a U.S. court of appeals or even to the Supreme Court itself.[22]

Growth and Organization of the Bureaucracy

16.2 Explain the growth and organization of the bureaucracy.

ost of the federal bureaucracy is located within the executive branch of government. But the bureaucracy is not a unitary body operating in a single building down the street from Congress and the president. Rather, it is spread out all over the country and consists of many different units, some more independent than others. The type and number of those units, as well as the kinds of people who work within them, have evolved over time.

☐ The Bureaucracy Has Changed Dramatically over the Nation's History

In most of Western Europe, national political systems were bureaucratized long before they were democratized. Particularly in France and Germany, bureaucracies served kings and emperors before they did presidents and prime ministers. With bureaucratic organizations already in place when these countries became democracies, elected officials merely had to redirect administrative activities to serve popular ends. Today, civil servants hold much more prominent positions in European governments, regularly serving in the British prime minister's office and cabinet office, the French president's Secretariat and prime minister's cabinet office, and the office of the German chancellor.[23]

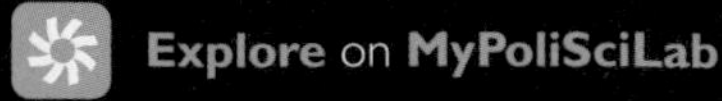

What Puts the "Big" in Big Government?

The national government is actually not as big as it once was. Since 1962, the total number of government employees has fallen due to a reduction in the number of military personnel after Vietnam and the Cold War. The number of civilians employed by the government has also declined since the 1980s. However, even as the size of government has grown smaller, its spending has increased to the point that one-fourth of the U.S. economy comes from government funded programs, contracts, and benefits.

Size of the Government Workforce*

* In Thousands

	EXECUTIVE	MILITARY	LEGISLATIVE AND JUDICIAL	TOTAL
1962	2,485	2,840	30	5,354
1972	2,823	2,360	42	5,225
1982	2,770	2,147	55	4,972
1992	3,017	1,848	66	4,931
2002	2,630	1,456	66	4,152
2012	2,500	1,602	64	4,170

Government as Percent of GDP

Government consumed just under one-fifth of the total economy and paid for that consumption with income such as taxes.

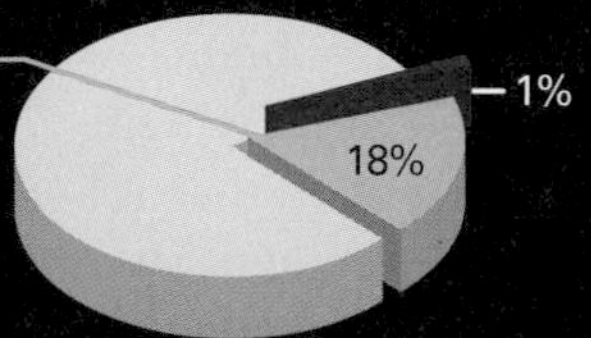

2012

Government consumed one-fourth of the total economy and paid a larger portion of it by taxing than borrowing.

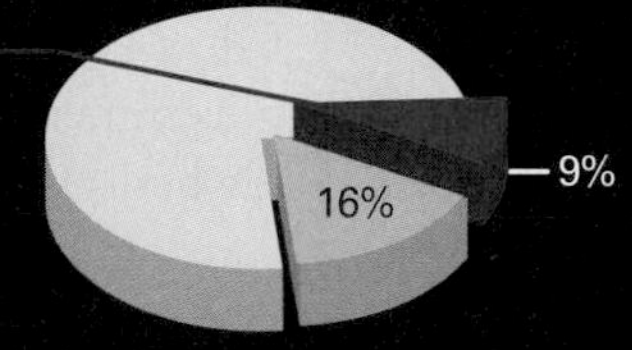

■ Government Spending Through Taxing
■ Government Spending Through Borrowing

SOURCE: Data from Voteview and U.S. Office of Management and Budget.

Investigate Further

Concept Is the federal government growing larger? The number of federal employees has actually decreased by over one million in a half-century. Since the late 1960s, the main difference in the size of its workforce is due to a smaller military.

Connection Do fewer federal employees mean smaller government? While the number of employees may be smaller, the federal government's share of the country's gross domestic product has grown every decade since the 1960s.

Cause If the government employs fewer people, how is it "bigger" than it was in 1962? Even with fewer people, the government implements more expensive programs that contribute to the total U.S. economy. Higher salaries, more expensive defense programs, larger entitlement programs, and increased spending to pay for past debt drive up costs.

The evolution of the U.S. bureaucracy looks quite different from that in Western Europe. In the United States, democratic political institutions existed prior to the development of a fully fledged bureaucracy. In fact, America's founders, disgusted by the British government's abuse of the colonies, intentionally restricted the size and powers of the bureaucracy. In the early years of the Republic, Congress assumed responsibility for most administrative decisions in the new nation. Although the legislature later recognized the need for a fully functional bureaucracy, members of Congress outnumbered civil servants in Washington until the 1820s.[24]

The modest beginnings of the U.S. bureaucracy should not come as a great surprise. The federal government in the nineteenth century, after all, was dramatically smaller than it is today. Its involvement in the daily lives of citizens was minimal by twenty-first–century standards. It produced and implemented far fewer policies than today, provided little or no regulation of business practices, and also assumed little responsibility for the welfare of average citizens.

Nineteenth-century federal bureaucrats, therefore, had relatively little to do. Furthermore, they tended to be hired not for their expertise, but for their political allegiance to the party in power. The **spoils system,** as it came to be known, defined the common practice of handing out government jobs, contracts, and other favors not on the basis of merit, but on the basis of political friendships and alliances. When a new president was elected and a different political party assumed control of the executive branch, they would promptly fire most bureaucrats then in office and replace them with their own loyalists.

The spoils system served the political needs of people in power. Most obviously, it provided a basis on which to reward individuals for their political support. And with a growing number of citizens gaining the right to vote, it became more and more important to reward political activists who got people to the polls. Politicians could also raise money for their campaigns by promising jobs. By delivering jobs to key political allies, and thereby shoring up their own electoral fortunes, politicians often secured the passage of a favorite law.

The spoils system had disadvantages as well. Because bureaucrats tended to be employed only as long as their party remained in office, turnover tended to be quite high. Rather than devoting their lives to a particular policy, bureaucrats often worked for just a few short years. This turnover, in combination with the fact that bureaucrats were selected on the basis of their party support rather than their skills, education, or experience, meant that agencies were less professional and often less capable of furnishing much-needed expertise about public policy.

During the latter half of the nineteenth century, increasing pressure emerged to replace the spoils system with a **civil service system,** which awarded jobs primarily on the basis of merit. Decrying the abuses and waste of a bureaucracy filled with partisan hacks, a diverse group of professional elites pushed for reform. When President James Garfield was assassinated by a disgruntled (and mentally ill) office seeker in 1881, Congress finally saw fit to address their concerns. In 1883, Congress enacted the Pendleton Act, which established the Civil Service Commission (later the Office of Personnel Management). The Civil Service Commission oversaw the hiring and firing of federal bureaucrats on the basis of new procedures, examinations, and qualifications. Merit, rather than party allegiances, constituted the employment qualification that mattered most.

For the most part, though, the transition from the spoils system to a fully developed civil service occurred gradually. Because politicians still had incentives to reward their partisan backers with jobs, the spoils system did not disappear overnight. Indeed, its final death knell was not heard until 1939, when the vast majority of bureaucrats could truly be called civil servants, and when Congress enacted the Hatch Act after concerns that the president might become the boss of a vast political machine, thereby enabling him not only to reward top political loyalists with spoils but also to use whole government agencies for political purposes. This type of machine politics had become popular in major cities such as Chicago at the time. Following a scandal in which

spoils system
a system of government in which a presidential administration awards jobs to party loyalists.

civil service system
a system of government in which decisions about hiring, promotion, and firing are based on individuals' work experience, skills, and expertise.

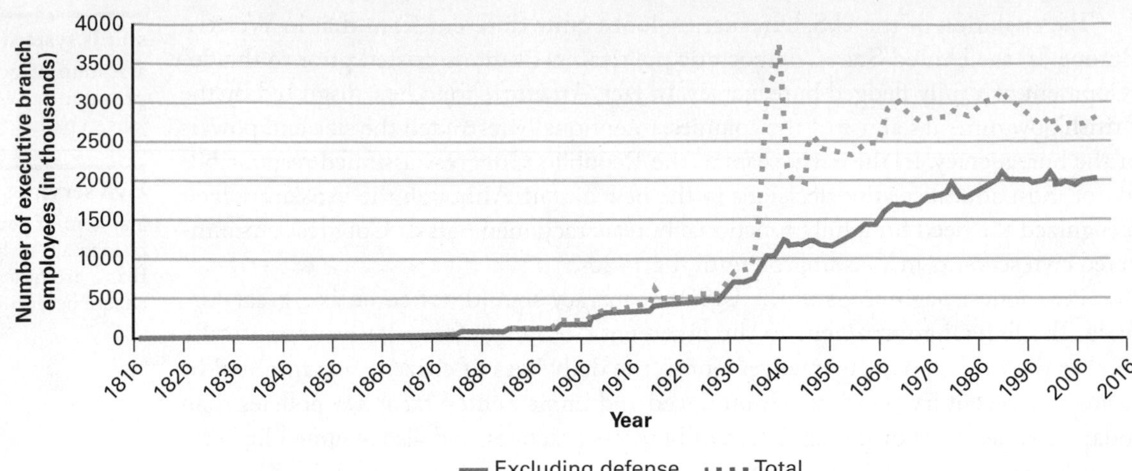

FIGURE 16.2 THE SIZE OF THE FEDERAL BUREAUCRACY.

During the past century, the number of employees in the federal bureaucracy has increased dramatically. The dotted line includes all civilian executive branch employees. The solid line represents that total minus the number of civilian defense employees.

Source: U.S. Bureau of Census, *Historical Statistics of the United States: Colonial Times to 1970* (Washington, DC: Government Printing Office, 1975), 1102–1103, series 312–314. U.S. Bureau of the Census, *Statistical Abstract of the United States: 2012,* (Washington, DC: Government Printing Office, 2011),

department
a major administrative unit that is composed of many agencies serving many policy functions, and that is headed by a secretary, who serves in the president's Cabinet.

members of the bureaucracy were shown to have used their authority to swing votes in favor of the Democratic Party, Democratic Senator Carl Hatch sponsored legislation to put an end to this practice. The Hatch Act prevented the federal government from becoming a large political tool of the party in power. It forbade all federal employees outside the Executive Office of the President from engaging in any political activities such as campaigning, fund-raising, or even contributing money to partisan causes. The Hatch Act was later amended to include all local government employees who received any federal funds as part of their salaries.

During the same time period that the management of federal bureaucracy personnel experienced dramatic reform, the size of the federal bureaucracy began to grow rapidly. Figure 16.2 tracks the growth in the number of executive branch employees from 1816 to 2011. As the government took on greater and greater responsibility, it needed more agencies and employees to administer public policy. In the late nineteenth and early twentieth centuries, the federal government created agencies to establish and enforce rules on industry, trade, commerce, and transportation so that it could keep pace with the expanding American economy.[25] In 1871, the entire executive branch had only about 50,000 employees. Fifty years later, it had more than 400,000.

In the 1930s, Franklin D. Roosevelt created several new agencies through his "New Deal" program in an effort to lift the nation out of the Great Depression. The size of the bureaucracy skyrocketed when the United States became involved in World War II. Since 1946, the total number of executive branch employees has remained fairly stable. However, the number of nondefense employees has continued to grow throughout the past 60 years.

☐ The Bureaucracy Today Consists of Many Different Units

Since the end of World War II, the size of the federal bureaucracy has leveled off. In 1946, roughly the same number of bureaucrats worked for the federal government as today—slightly over 2 million.[26] These bureaucrats work within very different kinds of governing structures: departments, independent agencies and regulatory commissions, and government corporations.

DEPARTMENTS Most bureaucratic agencies are housed in a **department,** which is the largest organizational unit in the federal bureaucracy. Departments address broad areas of government responsibility, and the head of each department is appointed by the president to serve in his cabinet.

Today, there are 15 departments. The Department of Homeland Security is the latest addition to the list. As Table 16.1 shows, at the nation's founding, George Washington oversaw only four departments: Treasury, War (now Defense), Post Office (now the Postal Service as an independent agency), and State. During the nineteenth century, three more departments were added: Interior, Justice, and Agriculture. But during the twentieth century, especially during the latter half, the number of departments really expanded. As citizens expected the federal government to do more and more on their behalf, departments were created to help write and implement policy. Health and Human Services, Housing and Urban Development, Transportation, Energy, Education, Veterans Affairs, and finally Homeland Security were all created to confront concerns ranging from the mental and physical health of citizens to the looming threat of terrorism.

Now take a look at Figure 16.3, which shows the amount of money spent by each of the departments in fiscal year 2010. The department that spent the most annually is Health and Human Services, whose budget surpassed $900 billion in 2011. Many of these funds covered the costs of expanded support services for patients, as well as larger outlays to health insurance providers and hospitals. In close second to Department of Health and Human Services was Defense, which spent nearly $850 billion. These costs covered such massive entitlement programs as Medicaid and Medicare, as well as such prominent agencies as the Food and Drug Administration, the National Institutes of Health, and the Centers for Disease Control and Prevention. Education, Housing and Urban Development, and Energy, by contrast, are the three smallest agencies in terms of the number of people they employ. Combined, they spend roughly $180 billion each year and have fewer than 35,000 employees.

TABLE 16.1 FOUNDING DATE AND PURPOSE OF FEDERAL DEPARTMENTS

Department	Year founded	Responsibilities
War Department, renamed Department of Defense in 1949	1789	Coordinates and oversees the U.S. Army, Navy, and Air Force, as well as smaller agencies that are responsible for national security.
Department of the Treasury	1789	Manages the government's money; prints paper currency, mints coins, and collects taxes through the Internal Revenue Service.
Department of State	1789	Develops and executes the president's foreign policy agenda. The department head, the secretary of state, is the chief foreign policy adviser to the president.
Department of the Interior	1849	Conserves land owned by the federal government; manages cultural and natural resources including national parks, dams, wildlife refuges, and monuments.
Department of Justice	1870	The U.S. legal department that houses several law enforcement agencies, including the Federal Bureau of Investigation, Drug Enforcement Administration, and Federal Bureau of Prisons. Its lawyers represent the government in court. The chief lawyer of the federal government is the attorney general.
Department of Agriculture	1889	Develops policy to protect farmers, promote agricultural trade, and alleviate hunger in the United States and abroad. It also inspects food to ensure that it is safe to consume.
Department of Labor	1903	Oversees labor practices in the United States; makes sure that workplaces are safe, enforces a minimum wage, and provides unemployment insurance.
Department of Commerce	1903	Works to maintain the health of the U.S. economy; supports businesses, promotes the creation of jobs, gathers and provides economic data, and issues patents and trademarks.
Department of Health and Human Services	1953	Administers more than 300 federal programs to protect the health and safety of Americans; provides health insurance to the elderly and disabled, offers immunization services and treatment for substance abuse, and inspects drugs to ensure their safety.
Department of Housing and Urban Development	1965	Works to increase home ownership in the United States. It also helps low-income individuals secure affordable housing.
Department of Transportation	1966	Ensures the safety, accessibility, and efficiency of air travel, the national highway network, railroads, and public transportation systems.
Department of Energy	1977	Oversees domestic energy production and conservation. It also manages the nation's nuclear weapons and reactors as well as the disposal of radioactive waste.
Department of Education	1980	Provides funding to education programs and enforces federal education laws such as No Child Left Behind.
Department of Veterans Affairs	1988	Provides a wide array of benefits to war veterans, including general compensation, health care, education, life insurance, and home loans.
Department of Homeland Security	2002	Responsible for protecting the United States from terrorist attacks and responding to natural disasters.

A PRESIDENT'S CABINET

Cabinet members applaud President Barack Obama's 2012 State of the Union address on Capitol Hill. From left are: Interior Secretary Ken Salazar, White House Chief of Staff William Daley, Attorney General Eric Holder, Veterans Affairs Secretary Eric Shinseki, Defense Secretary Leon Panetta, Treasury Secretary Timothy Geithner, Commerce Secretary Gary Locke, Secretary of State Hillary Rodham Clinton and Transportation Secretary Ray LaHood.

independent agencies and commissions
bureaucratic organizations that operate outside of Cabinet-level departments and are less subject to congressional or presidential influence.

INDEPENDENT AGENCIES AND REGULATORY COMMISSIONS Not all agencies operate within a department. Many **independent agencies and commissions** operate outside departments. These agencies and commissions are directed by administrators or boards that are appointed by the president, subject to Senate confirmation. The

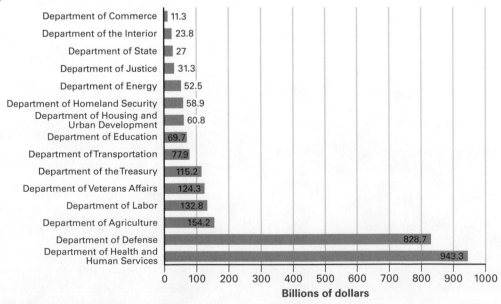

Department	Billions of dollars
Department of Commerce	11.3
Department of the Interior	23.8
Department of State	27
Department of Justice	31.3
Department of Energy	52.5
Department of Homeland Security	58.9
Department of Housing and Urban Development	60.8
Department of Education	69.7
Department of Transportation	77.9
Department of the Treasury	115.2
Department of Veterans Affairs	124.3
Department of Labor	132.8
Department of Agriculture	154.2
Department of Defense	828.7
Department of Health and Human Services	943.3

0 100 200 300 400 500 600 700 800 900 1000
Billions of dollars

FIGURE 16.3 DEPARTMENT SPENDING IN 2011.

The amount of money spent by departments that make up the federal bureaucracy varies dramatically. Those departments that oversee the provision of the nation's security and entitlement programs are vastly larger than those that attend to discretionary activities.

Source: U.S. Government Accountability Office, *Financial Statements of the United States Government for the Years Ended September 30, 2011, and 2010.* Available online at www.gao.gov/financial/fy2011/11stmt.pdf.

heads of these organizations, however, do not usually serve in the president's cabinet. Unlike department heads, whom the president can select freely and who can be fired at any time, heads of independent agencies and regulatory commissions must meet well-defined qualifications, and they hold office for fixed periods. These restrictions on the hiring and firing of agency leaders tend to protect them from the efforts of presidents and members of Congress to meddle in their affairs—a topic we discuss further later in the chapter.

Independent agencies, like those listed in Table 16.2, perform all sorts of functions. They manage national museums such as the Smithsonian Institution. Through the Peace Corps, they send college graduates to volunteer in countries all over the globe. The National Aeronautics and Space Administration launches men and women into space, the Social Security Administration writes millions of checks each year, and the United States Postal Service delivers the mail. Recently, still more agencies have been created, which, as their names imply, undertake an equally diverse array of responsibilities. Standouts include the U.S. Election Assistance Commission, the Office of the National Counterintelligence Executive, and most recently the Bureau of Consumer Financial Protection, which was created in 2010.

The first regulatory commission was the Interstate Commerce Commission, created in 1887 to regulate railroads. The nation subsequently experienced a rapid rise of commissions with the Administrative Procedures Act, which, as previously noted, established the governing framework for administrative agencies in the modern era. These commissions regulate all kinds of industries and organizations, ranging from toy manufacturers to stock markets to television stations. Among the especially significant regulatory commissions are the Consumer Product Safety Commission, the Securities and Exchange Commission, the Federal Trade Commission, and the Federal Communications Commission.

government corporation
a corporation created and funded by the government to provide some public service that would be insufficiently provided by the private sector.

GOVERNMENT CORPORATIONS Even more removed from presidential and congressional control are **government corporations**.[27] These organizations most closely resemble private companies. Unlike private companies, however, government corporations receive steady streams of government funding and are subject to modest oversight. In most cases, Congress or the president has decided that the private marketplace does not provide sufficient monetary incentives to provide these services (especially to low-income individuals). As shown in Table 16.2, prominent examples of government corporations include the National Railroad Passenger Corporation (Amtrak), which takes citizens to work, and the Federal Deposit Insurance Corporation, which ensures the safety of bank deposits. Although these organizations are essentially run like companies, their boards of directors are appointed by the president and confirmed by the Senate.

Challenges of Bureaucracy

16.3 Assess the role of the bureaucracy in public policy making.

Bureaucrats provide vital services in an increasing number of policy areas. Indeed, hardly a day passes when we fail to interact with a bureaucrat of one type or another. But the bureaucracy is not without its problems, which partially explains why so many politicians call for its reform. Sometimes bureaucrats attend to their own private interests or those of a narrow band of citizens rather than to the interests of the broader public. Sometimes the organizations in which bureaucrats work are extraordinarily inefficient. As a result, the services

TABLE 16.2 FOUNDING DATE AND PURPOSE OF SELECT INDEPENDENT AGENCIES, REGULATORY COMMISSIONS, AND GOVERNMENT CORPORATIONS

The federal bureaucracy contains more than 100 independent agencies, regulatory commissions, and government corporations. The lists here contain some highlights.

Independent Agencies and Regulatory Commissions	Year founded	Responsibilities
United States Postal Service (USPS); became an independent agency in 1971	1775	Delivers all first- and third-class mail; was a department for almost 200 years before it was reorganized as an independent agency. It is the only organization that can deliver mail to private mailboxes.
Board of Governors of the Federal Reserve System	1913	Governing body of the Federal Reserve System, which is the central bank of the United States; manages the nation's money supply, working to control inflation and maintain economic growth.
Federal Trade Commission (FTC)	1914	Created to protect consumers from deceptive and anti-competitive business practices; ensures that businesses advertise truthfully and provide buyers with adequate information about their products and services.
Securities and Exchange Commission (SEC)	1934	Enforces laws against insider trading and accounting fraud; created to regulate the stock market after the stock market crash of 1929 that led to the Great Depression.
Federal Communications Commission (FCC)	1934	Regulates radio and television broadcasting as well as interstate wire, satellite, and cable telecommunications; governed by five commissioners who are appointed by the president and confirmed by the Senate.
Social Security Administration	1935	Manages Social Security, the nation's social insurance program that delivers benefits to the elderly and disabled.
Central Intelligence Agency (CIA)	1947	Provides national security information on foreign governments, people, and corporations to senior officials in the federal government. Its secret operations are directed by the president and overseen by Congress.
National Aeronautics and Space Administration (NASA)	1958	Responsible for the nation's space program, including space exploration and scientific research.
Environmental Protection Agency (EPA)	1970	Protects Americans from the harmful health effects of air, water, and land pollution. Safeguards the natural environment by establishing and enforcing emissions standards for various types of pollutants.
Privacy and Civil Liberties Oversight Board	2007	Previously housed in the Executive Office of the President, this board was reconstituted in 2007 as an independent commission; it offers advice regarding civil liberties and privacy concerns in all matters involving antiterrorism policies.
Bureau of Consumer Financial Protection	2010	Through oversight and education, this agency advances the interests of consumers in housing and financial markets.
Government Corporations		
Tennessee Valley Authority (TVA)	1933	A federally owned power company that provides electricity to the Tennessee Valley, an area that includes most of Tennessee and parts of six other states in the region.
Federal Deposit Insurance Corporation (FDIC)	1933	Created during the Great Depression to promote confidence in the U.S. banking system; insures the money people deposit into checking and savings accounts in banks.
Corporation for Public Broadcasting (PBS)	1967	Private, nonprofit corporation that distributes funding for public television and radio programming, including programming made available through the Public Broadcasting Service and National Public Radio (NPR); funded almost entirely by the federal government.
Amtrak (National Railroad Passenger Corporation)	1971	Provides passenger train service between U.S. cities; receives funding from both the federal government and ticket sales. Members of its board of directors are appointed by the president and confirmed by the Senate.
Overseas Private Investment Corporation (OPIC)	1971	Assists American businesses when they make investments abroad; helps companies manage the risk involved in overseas investments and promotes economic development in emerging markets. It gets most of its revenue from fees for its products.
Millennium Challenge Corporation (MCC)	2004	Provides funding to poverty-stricken countries in order to promote economic growth, infrastructure investment, and good government.

that the government bureaucracy provides are often more expensive and less effective than we might like. In addition, it often is incredibly difficult to know just how effective our bureaucracy really is. (See *How Do We Know? Does the Federal Bureaucracy Deserve Credit for Preventing Another 9/11?*)

How Do We Know?

Does the Federal Bureaucracy Deserve Credit for Preventing Another 9/11?

The Question

Less than a month after the terrorist attacks of September 11, 2001, newly appointed presidential adviser Tom Ridge reminded fellow Homeland Security Council members about the dangers of bureaucratic infighting. "The only turf we should be worried about protecting is the turf we stand on," he warned.[a] A report prepared for the 9/11 Commission partially blamed the national security failure on a bureaucratic culture that discouraged intelligence information sharing.[b] In the wake of this failure, Congress and the president worked to reorganize the federal bureaucracy so that various intelligence and law enforcement agencies would be coordinated under a single homeland security umbrella. Since that time, America has not suffered another major terrorist attack on its soil.

In the years since the 9/11 attacks, bureaucrats working under two presidential administrations and three Homeland Security secretaries have seen the U.S. successfully thwart several high-profile terrorist plots. Yet, a variety of crucial factors go into preventing such attacks: military operations targeting terrorist cells abroad, economic sanctions of countries suspected of funding terrorist operations, and even the capabilities (or lack thereof) of terrorists themselves. Some pundits assert that it is futile to credit the national security bureaucracy with keeping the country safe, because "there are too many current and future contingencies" that cannot be accounted for.[c] Does the federal bureaucracy deserve credit for preventing another 9/11? How do we know?

Why It Matters

By analyzing the effectiveness of the federal bureaucracy, we may contribute to policy discussions about what could be done better. These discussions shape decisions that affect us every time we take a prescription drug approved by the FDA, eat chicken inspected by the Department of Agriculture, or send a piece of mail through the U.S. Postal Service. Because we both consume those services and pay for them through taxes, we must think critically about whether our money is being spent well and whether the services provided by the bureaucracy meet our expectations. The national security bureaucracy directly affects all Americans, because its primary responsibility is to keep the country safe from attacks.

Investigating the Answer

In the aftermath of September 11th, many high-level government officials warned that another terrorist attack on America was not just likely, but inevitable. On October 2, 2001, an unnamed intelligence official briefing the Senate Intelligence Committee said there was a "100 percent" chance terrorists would strike again soon.[d] And, as recently as 2011, Defense Secretary Leon Panetta asserted that the threat of another terrorist attack "remains very real."[e] The fact that such a terrible event has not reoccurred would therefore seem to be a remarkable accomplishment in the face of overwhelming odds. It remains unclear, however, who is responsible for such success.

Some observers have argued that it was President Bush and his advisers who deserve the credit. Indeed, former Vice President Cheney claimed as much in a 2009 interview: "If it hadn't been for what we did—with respect to the terrorist surveillance program, or enhanced interrogation techniques for high-value detainees,

TIMELINE OF FOILED TERRORIST PLOTS SINCE 9/11

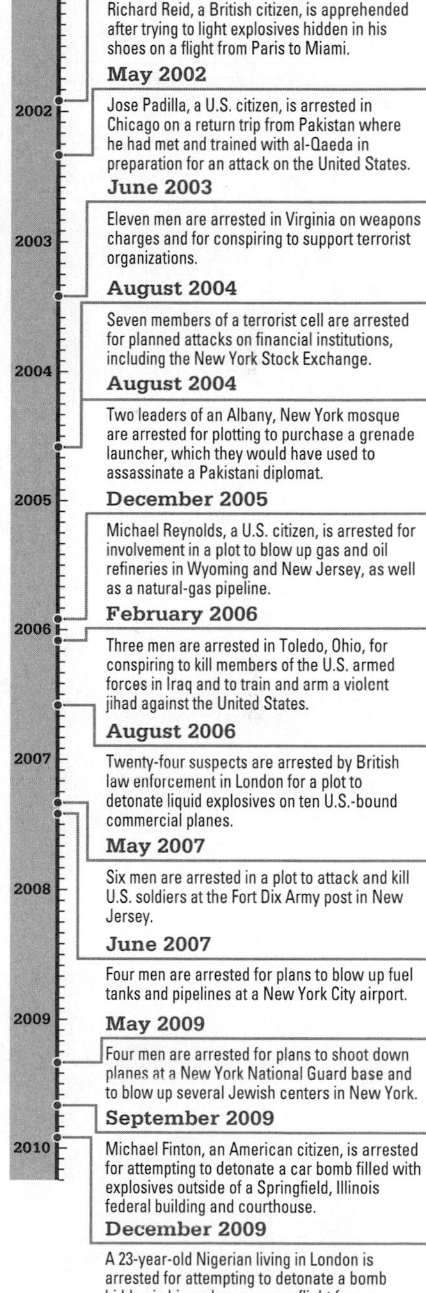

2001
2002
2003
2004
2005
2006
2007
2008
2009
2010
December 2001
Richard Reid, a British citizen, is apprehended after trying to light explosives hidden in his shoes on a flight from Paris to Miami.
May 2002
Jose Padilla, a U.S. citizen, is arrested in Chicago on a return trip from Pakistan where he had met and trained with al-Qaeda in preparation for an attack on the United States.
June 2003
Eleven men are arrested in Virginia on weapons charges and for conspiring to support terrorist organizations.
August 2004
Seven members of a terrorist cell are arrested for planned attacks on financial institutions, including the New York Stock Exchange.
August 2004
Two leaders of an Albany, New York mosque are arrested for plotting to purchase a grenade launcher, which they would have used to assassinate a Pakistani diplomat.
December 2005
Michael Reynolds, a U.S. citizen, is arrested for involvement in a plot to blow up gas and oil refineries in Wyoming and New Jersey, as well as a natural-gas pipeline.
February 2006
Three men are arrested in Toledo, Ohio, for conspiring to kill members of the U.S. armed forces in Iraq and to train and arm a violent jihad against the United States.
August 2006
Twenty-four suspects are arrested by British law enforcement in London for a plot to detonate liquid explosives on ten U.S.-bound commercial planes.
May 2007
Six men are arrested in a plot to attack and kill U.S. soldiers at the Fort Dix Army post in New Jersey.
June 2007
Four men are arrested for plans to blow up fuel tanks and pipelines at a New York City airport.
May 2009
Four men are arrested for plans to shoot down planes at a New York National Guard base and to blow up several Jewish centers in New York.
September 2009
Michael Finton, an American citizen, is arrested for attempting to detonate a car bomb filled with explosives outside of a Springfield, Illinois federal building and courthouse.
December 2009
A 23-year-old Nigerian living in London is arrested for attempting to detonate a bomb hidden in his underwear on a flight from Amsterdam to Detroit on Christmas Day.

This is a sampling from 40 identified foiled plots since 9/11.

---

[a] Elizabeth Becker and Elaine Sciolino, "A Nation Challenged: Homeland Security; A New Federal Office Opens Amid Concern That Its Head Won't Have Enough Power," *New York Times*, October 9, 2001, B11.

[b] "Legal Barriers to Information Sharing: The Erection of a Wall Between Intelligence and Law Enforcement Investigations," Commission on Terrorist Attacks Upon the United States, Staff Monograph, August 20, 2004, available online at http://www.fas.org/irp/eprint/wall.pdf.

[c] Timothy Noah, "Why No More 9/11s?" *Slate*, March 5, 2009, http://www.slate.com/articles/news_and_politics/chatterbox/2009/03/why_no_more_911s.single.html.

[d] Susan Schmidt and Bob Woodward, "FBI, CIA Warn Congress of More Attacks as Blair Details Case Against Bin Ladin," *Washington Post*, October 5, 2001.

[e] Robert Burns, "Panetta: Threat of Another 9/11 Is Real," *The Washington Times*, September 6, 2011, http://www.washingtontimes.com/news/2011/sep/6/panetta-threat-another-911-real/?page=all.

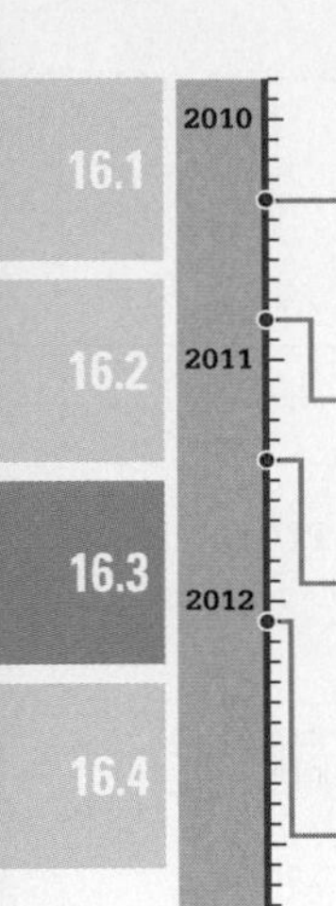

May 2010

A naturalized citizen from Pakistan is arrested for attempting to detonate explosives in an SUV parked in Times Square, New York.

November 2010

A 19-year-old Somali-American is arrested after an attempted car bombing at a Portland, Oregon tree lighting ceremony.

June 2011

Two men are arrested for attempting to purchase automatic machine guns and grenades that would later be used in an attack on a Seattle, Washington military recruiting station.

February 2012

Federal law enforcement officials arrest a Moroccan man who planned a suicide attack on the U.S. Capitol.

the Patriot Act, and so forth—then we would have been attacked again."[f] Others, meanwhile, offered plaudits to the Obama administration. Many Democrats and Republicans agreed that U.S. attacks in Afghanistan, which Congress approved and the president oversaw, killed a significant portion of al-Qaeda's leadership, thereby weakening the terrorist organization's ability to carry out expensive, highly coordinated attacks. More recently, both parties praised President Obama's decision to initiate the secret raid on a compound in Pakistan that led to the killing of al-Qaeda leader Osama bin Laden.

These various assessments, however, present two basic challenges to assessing bureaucratic performance. First, it is difficult to evaluate the bureaucracy's role in successfully keeping America safe without assessing the policies assigned to it by leaders in the White House and Congress. Government agencies do not work in isolation. Rather, they work diligently on behalf of policies prescribed by their political superiors, making it nearly impossible to distinguish the quality of the policy from the adequacy of its implementation when evaluating outcomes. Second, it is difficult to assess an antiterrorism agency's competence without knowing the size of the material threat it confronts. According to one think tank, the U.S. successfully foiled 40 terrorist attacks between September 11, 2001, and September 11, 2011.[g] And those are just the ones that have been made public. But most of the counterterrorism work done by agency and department bureaucrats has gone on behind closed doors and behind enemy lines, at home and abroad—leaving us to wonder whether they are remarkably adept at thwarting terrorism or whether their assessments of terrorist threats are merely inflated.

The Bottom Line

In the end, it remains an open question how much credit bureaucrats deserve for successfully preventing terrorist attacks on America. To some degree, the bureaucracy is merely responsible for implementing the policies of a given administration, and it is the policies themselves that help determine success or failure. At the same time, it is people who put policies into action. The fact that there has yet to be another major attack can be attributed to a variety of sources, and bureaucrats may deserve more credit than they are accustomed to getting. Politicians are quick to claim credit for positive outcomes. In the case of failure, however, those same politicians are liable to pin blame on nameless and faceless "bureaucrats." If the intelligence and national security bureaucracy was partially responsible for failing to thwart the September 11th attacks, then they should be given at least some plaudits for the success of counterterrorism operations since.

Thinking Critically

- If another major terrorist attack had occurred in the years immediately following September 11th, would the bureaucracy have been to blame? Why or why not?
- What other administrative agencies are charged with preventing events that, similar to a terrorist attack, rarely occur? Are the challenges associated with assessing these agencies' competence similar? Why or why not?

[f] John F. Harris, Mike Allen, and Jim Vandehei, "Cheney Warns of New Attacks," *Politico*, February 4, 2009, http://www.politico.com/news/stories/0209/18390.html.

[g] James Jay Carafano and Jessica Zuckerman, "40 Terrorist Plots Foiled Since 9/11: Combating Complacency in the Long War on Terror," Heritage Foundation, http://www.heritage.org/research/reports/2011/09/40-terror-plots-foiled-since-9-11-combating-complacency-in-the-long-war-on-terror.

□ Bureaucrats Have Their Own Interests

In principle, bureaucrats are supposed to implement the policies written by their political superiors. When needed, bureaucrats are also supposed to clarify the meaning of laws, either through rules or through norms. In practice, though, bureaucrats have their own interests, which may or may not align with those of the president or Congress. Because bureaucrats tend to have more expertise than the latter, they enjoy considerable discretion to pursue these ends, sometimes at a cost to the larger public.

To understand the problem of different interests, imagine that while you are driving home one day, your car suddenly breaks down. What do you do? If you are like most Americans, you do not have a clue how to fix the car yourself. So you have the car towed to the local mechanic to have it fixed. At this point, the interests of two people become involved. You need the mechanic for her expertise; the mechanic needs you for your money. The subsequent exchange, then, would appear perfectly straightforward. The mechanic fixes your car in exchange for a mutually agreed-upon price.

But therein lies the rub. Precisely because you do not understand what is wrong with your car, you have little ability to determine how much it ought to cost to fix it. This would not ordinarily be a problem, at least not if the mechanic were honest and forthcoming. The trouble is that the mechanic's interests are different from yours. You want to pay the least amount of money for the most amount of work using the best possible parts. The mechanic, by contrast, wants to receive the most amount of money for the least amount of work using the least expensive parts. And because the mechanic knows more than you about what is wrong with your car and what is needed to fix it, the mechanic often wins out in this exchange.

The resulting inefficiencies are an example of what is commonly referred to as a **principal-agent problem.** In this example, you are the principal, and the mechanic is the agent. Both individuals are made better off by having the work done to the car at a fair price. But because the mechanic, as the agent, has private information that you, as the principal, cannot know, the mechanic is made even better off, and you worse off—either because the mechanic charges you for services that your car does not really need, or because the mechanic does not do as good a job as promised on the work order.

This principal-agent problem fundamentally defines the relationship between Congress and the president (the principals), on the one hand, and the bureaucracy (the agent), on the other. Congress and the president, as policy generalists, need bureaucrats for their expertise. Bureaucrats, however, do not necessarily share the same interests as Congress and the president.[28] Bureaucrats may not want to work as hard as Congress and the president would like them to—generating what political scientists refer to as **slack.** Anyone who has stood for hours at the local post office can attest to its frustrations. Alternatively, bureaucrats may be perfectly willing to work hard, but they choose to do so in the service of objectives that Congress and the president oppose—generating what political scientists refer to as **drift.** Examples of drift include the district attorney who aggressively pursues white-collar criminals but prefers not to prosecute minor drug offenses, or the park ranger who uses funds to purchase new computers for his staff rather than equipment to clean campgrounds, or the teacher who decides to stick with her tried-and-true lesson plans rather than teach a new state-mandated curriculum.

An essential element of what makes slack and drift possible is the principal's difficulty in monitoring the agent. Congress and the president cannot personally watch the decisions of every district attorney, park ranger, or teacher. Moreover, outcomes are often hard to measure. Because all of the available measures of criminal activity, park cleanliness, and student learning are imperfect, it is difficult for Congress and the president to know for sure whether bureaucrats are working as effectively as they can in the service of their formal goals and responsibilities. Moreover, because there are so many contributors to each of these outcomes—what bureaucrats do, or do not do, is only part of the equation—bureaucrats can often explain away any observed failures to achieve stated objectives as being beyond their control. After all, as agents, they are the ones who are experts, whereas Congress and the president, as principals, are not.

The troubles, though, do not end there. In the example of the broken car, there is but one agent and one principal. In government, by contrast, at any given moment there are many principals and many agents. And the interests of each do not perfectly overlap. When Congress and the president disagree about a policy issue, as they typically do during periods of divided government, agents may be able to play off one principal against the other. And when multiple agents are responsible for a particular policy issue, each can attempt to blame the others when failures are observed.

principal-agent problem
the problem that occurs when one person (the principal) contracts with another person (the agent) to provide a service and yet cannot directly observe what the agent is actually doing; the agent, meanwhile, is motivated to take advantage of the principal.

slack
a situation in which bureaucrats do not work as hard as Congress or the president would like.

drift
a situation in which bureaucrats create policy that does not match the policy preferences of Congress or the president.

16.1

16.2

16.3

16.4

agency capture
an agency primarily serves the interests of a nongovernmental group rather than those of elected officials.

Consider the extraordinary efforts of the federal government to monitor and improve student learning in public schools. Under the No Child Left Behind Act, students are regularly evaluated on newly developed state tests; depending on student performance, schools may face consequences ranging from funding cuts to restructurings. Bureaucrats in local school districts, state education departments, and the federal government all work hard to implement the law. But given the stakes involved, and the controversies that surround standardized tests, these bureaucrats occasionally work at cross purposes. Federal bureaucrats may blame state and local officials for refusing to fully incorporate the provisions of No Child Left Behind; local and state officials, meanwhile, blame the federal government for imposing undue burdens on schools without providing sufficient funding.

Compounding the principal-agent problem is the fact that in government, the preferences of the principals change every two or four years. A coalition within Congress may set a bureaucratic agency's official mandate one year, but following an election, the individuals who comprised this coalition may no longer be in power. Those individuals who replaced them, meanwhile, may have very different ideas about what bureaucrats ought to be doing. In addition, the principals—Congress and the president—frequently try to set different agendas for the bureaucrats to follow. Thus, bureaucratic agents not only must contend with shifting priorities, but often, they must also parse out which current priorities they are supposed to follow.

In 2001, for example, President Bush and a bipartisan group of members of Congress worked together to pass No Child Left Behind. The new law completely overhauled and expanded the federal government's role in education by mandating the development of new state tests, new standards for evaluating student development, and a new array of punishments for school failure. For obvious reasons, such changes placed an incredible burden on bureaucrats at the federal and state levels charged with interpreting and implementing the new legislative mandate. Upon taking office in 2009, however, President Obama actively sought to revise the standards set by No Child Left Behind. In 2011, he announced he would unilaterally give states the ability to waive certain constraints imposed by the original legislation. In exchange, the president said he expected state officials to adopt the administration's education agenda. Leading Republican members of Congress, however, argued that Obama was overstepping his executive authority and that Congress was in the process of rewriting No Child Left Behind, which would create an entirely new set of policies and priorities. Clearly, this disagreement posed a difficult problem for bureaucrats. Even as they worked to implement the current law, they simultaneously had to respond to the president's new directives, all the while planning for the possibility of new congressional legislation.

Bureaucrats Sometimes Serve the Interests of Unelected Groups

Bureaucrats occasionally stray from their mandate not in the pursuit of their own interests, but rather in the pursuit of someone else's. Sometimes it is a well-funded special interest group. At other times, it is a highly mobilized segment of the population, or it might be the industry that a bureaucratic agency is supposed to be regulating. In any one of these instances, bureaucrats would appear to be taking their cues not from their political superiors, but instead from individuals and organizations that operate outside of government entirely.

Political scientists use the term **agency capture** to describe the situation when an agency primarily serves the interests of a nongovernmental group rather than those of elected officials. The possibility of agency capture is especially high under two conditions.[29] The first is when the benefits of agency actions are concentrated on a few individuals or organizations, but the costs are spread more or less evenly throughout society. Consider, for example, bureaucratic agencies that direct financial subsidies to farmers. These subsidies are not especially large. For the farmers who benefit from them, however, they mean a great deal. Thus, organizations such as the American Farm Bureau Federation work hard to ensure that the federal government continues to dole out these benefits year in and year out, regardless of whether they serve a larger public purpose.

Agency capture also occurs when the costs of policy implementation fall on a small group of individuals or organizations, but the social benefits are more diffuse. Consider, for example, an agency that is charged with monitoring the air pollutants produced by an industry on the edge of a large city. If the agency vigorously enforces rules that limit pollution, the industry will incur the high costs of compliance. These costs include both the fines it may have to pay for violating clean air rules and the new machinery it may need to purchase in order to comply with the law. From the perspective of each city resident, though, the benefits of the agency's actions are relatively small. They certainly prefer that the industry produce less waste, but their daily lives are probably not deeply affected by the agency's efforts to reduce industrial pollutants. Consequently, the regulated industries have strong incentives to influence agency behavior, whereas the general public does not. The resulting mismatch between highly mobilized and organized interest groups and a less attentive public invites agency capture.

Some critics have argued that the Food and Drug Administration (FDA) has been captured by pharmaceutical companies, which help fund FDA activities, lobby members of Congress, and launch major public relations campaigns.[30] Pharmaceutical companies stand to make massive amounts of money when a drug is approved for public consumption. As a result, companies with existing drugs sometimes encourage raising the standards of evaluations, thereby reducing the opportunities for new treatments to enter the market. At other times, companies pressure the FDA to approve drugs before the safety of those drugs has been conclusively established.

It is worth noting, though, that the FDA is often placed in an impossible position. If it does not approve drugs fast enough, it appears to be ignoring citizens in need of new treatments. But if it approves drugs hastily, it risks exposing the public to unsafe drugs. It is often difficult, therefore, to know whether the actions that the FDA takes are an attempt to balance these competing considerations, or whether the agency is ultimately guided by the very drug companies it is supposed to regulate.

□ Bureaucrats Can Be Inefficient

The most common complaint about bureaucrats is not that they serve their own interests or those of a narrow band of the U.S. public. Rather, it is that they do not do a good job of serving anyone's interest. For some, the very word *bureaucracy* has come to imply inefficiency, waste, and **red tape.**

red tape
the inefficiency and waste that result from excessive regulation and overly formal procedures.

Every few months, it seems, a story breaks in the news about a \$1,000 hammer purchased by the federal government, a half-built bridge that never seems to be completed, a dozen agencies that are all supposed to be doing the same thing, piles of mail that sit for weeks in warehouses, or bureaucrats paid large amounts of money to do little but sit. A predictable set of charges follows: bureaucrats waste public funds, fail to complete their tasks, ignore pressing public needs, and live off the public's dole without any apparent justification.

Boston's "Big Dig" project stands out as one of the more recent and alarming examples of bureaucratic waste and mismanagement. Intended to reduce traffic in the downtown area and to clear space for parks, the public works project was officially launched in 1991, when Congress appropriated funds for the project over a presidential veto. Early plans for the project suggested an official price of \$2.5 billion. In less than a decade, though, costs rose to \$7.5 billion, and by 2006 costs reached an astronomical \$14.6 billion. For all the money spent, the project was awash (literally) in scandal. After the tunnels opened in January 2006, hundreds of water leaks sprung; multiple investigations uncovered the use of faulty materials; falling ceiling tiles killed a commuter; and charges of corruption and waste were leveled against both the companies that undertook the work and the government agencies charged with overseeing them.[31] In 2008, three of the private contractors involved in the Big Dig collectively

GOVERNMENT WASTE

Boston's Big Dig was hardly a paragon of government efficiency. In addition to high costs and delays, the public works project had numerous design setbacks. In 2006, a 12-ton portion of the tunnel collapsed and killed a driver.

paid almost half a billion dollars to the city of Boston and the state of Massachusetts for these various blunders and catastrophes.

Some critics blame these kinds of problems on a culture of inertia that exists within the government's bureaucracy. Culture, in this instance, emerges from worker incentives. Bureaucrats have strong job protections—a product of the civil service reforms previously discussed. And they are not driven by the profit motive. Quite the contrary. The culture of bureaucracy sometimes rewards individuals not for the impact that their labor has on the lives of citizens, but rather for their faithful adherence to a stated process for how things ought to be done. Indeed, it was not until Massachusetts's governor and attorney general stepped in that the head of the Massachusetts Turnpike Authority was fired, companies were sued for "shoddy work," and responsibility for the Big Dig project shifted to the state government.

Although the waste and mismanagement of the Big Dig were extreme, smaller versions of such failures are common. Moreover, they are entirely predictable. The bureaucracy, after all, is not designed merely for the sake of efficiency. It is also supposed to promote notions of fairness and equity. To ensure that individual bureaucrats follow these directives, politicians have insisted that bureaucrats follow painstaking procedures for even the simplest of tasks.

Take, for example, the job of purchasing a new computer. An individual working in private industry need only find the company that will provide the best possible machine that suits his or her individual needs for the lowest price. In a government agency, by contrast, bureaucrats must solicit bids from government-approved vendors, choose from a select group of machines, and maintain careful documentation of all transactions. In this way, the public can rest assured that the companies that supply computers to the federal government do not discriminate against their workers, that bureaucrats are not spending lavish amounts of money, and that all monies are accounted for. The process is long and costly, but it exists to promote the important goals of fairness and equality.

Moreover, there are political explanations for certain bureaucratic failures or inefficiencies. Congress and the president often oversee agencies whose activities they would just as soon reduce, or even eliminate. So rather than appoint individuals who will vigorously pursue an agency's mission, they choose people who will take a more lax approach to regulatory enforcement. James Watt's tenure as secretary of the interior under President Ronald Reagan and Gale Norton's under President George W. Bush were both marked by such charges. Critics claimed that both Reagan and Bush were less interested in protecting federal lands and more interested in developing housing and increasing energy production. Accordingly, these presidents deliberately chose secretaries they knew would take a restricted (some supporters would argue, balanced) view of their duties to secure the well-being of the nation's parks and lands. Thus, their choices for interior secretary were two former attorneys for the Mountain States Legal Foundation, an organization whose mission is to provide a "strong and effective voice for freedom of enterprise, the rights of private property ownership, and the multiple use of federal and state resources."[32]

Some political scientists argue that the very design of our system of governance undermines opportunities for effective bureaucracy. They claim that regular elections, multiple principals, and political compromise lend themselves to inefficiencies and mismanagement, even in domains that everyone agrees are essential to the nation's well-being. One political scientist, for instance, argues that the core agencies charged with intelligence gathering—the Central Intelligence Agency, the Joint Chiefs of Staff, and the National Security Council—are "flawed by design."[33] The Joint Chiefs of Staff (JCS) emerged from "a brass-knuckle fight to the finish" pitting President Truman and the War Department (now the Department of Defense), who sought to bring the military services under one umbrella, against the Department of the Navy, which fiercely guarded its independence.[34] The resulting structure of the JCS pleased few and did little to quell interservice rivalry. Bureaucratic infighting during the Korean War was bitter enough that it "extended to conflicts over which service would operate a laundry in Alaska."[35]

Even the redundancy that pervades so much of the federal bureaucracy has a certain inherent political logic. Imagine the challenge faced by a president who assumes office after a long stretch of control by the opposition party. Should the newly elected president rely on individuals appointed under the former administrations to formulate his policy agenda? Or, after recognizing the awesome challenges of dismantling existing agencies, might he instead construct altogether new ones? Both options have advantages and disadvantages. Therefore, when advancing a new policy initiative, presidents often spread responsibilities across multiple agencies while also creating new ones. This is the tactic President Barack Obama used when launching his plan to increase financial regulations in the wake of the 2008 financial crisis. In an effort to fortify government oversight and limit certain types of corporate trading, Obama proposed legislation that would strengthen existing Cabinet departments (Treasury) and government organizations (FDIC), as well as create a new Consumer Financial Protection Bureau. This plan became the basis for the Dodd-Frank Wall Street Reform and Consumer Protection Act, which Congress passed in the summer of 2010.[36]

Controlling and Reforming the Bureaucracy

16.4 Evaluate the different approaches to overseeing and reforming the bureaucracy.

Reformers have long sought solutions to the various problems of bureaucratic drift, slack, agency capture, and inefficiency. None works perfectly. But each manages to give the president, Congress, and the larger public somewhat more influence over the

16.1

16.2

16.3

16.4

politicization
a phenomenon that occurs when Congress and the president select bureaucracy leaders who share their political views.

recess appointment
the means by which the president fills a vacant position in the bureaucracy when Congress is not in session, thus avoiding the need for prior congressional approval.

bureaucracy than would otherwise occur. These reforms generally fit into one of three categories: those that focus on the bureaucrats who work within agencies, those that focus on the structural relationship between agencies and their political superiors, and those that attempt to promote market forces of competition.

Presidents and Congress Exercise Control Through Appointments

The president appoints the secretaries of all Cabinet-level departments, subject to Senate confirmation. The president is free to choose whomever he likes to fill these positions. The president can also select the individuals and boards that govern independent agencies, regulatory commissions, and government corporations, although these appointees often must satisfy various rules and restrictions. Moreover, all appointments can take a long time to complete. As late as December 2011, 80 appointed positions in President Obama's administration remained open.[37]

When making their selections, what criteria might Congress and the president consider? Both want to appoint individuals who are well qualified, who have expertise and experience in the given policy arena, and who are likely to inspire their workforce. All of these characteristics reflect the civil service reforms of the early twentieth century. The appointment process, however, remains deeply political. Precisely because bureaucrats have a tendency to drift away from their given mandate, Congress and the president have strong incentives to choose leaders on the basis of their expressed ideological views and policy commitments. In other words, Congress and the president try to solve the principal-agent problem by selecting agents who share their worldview, and who appear committed to seeing it realized by the department or agency that they will eventually run.

Political scientists call this phenomenon the **politicization** of the bureaucracy.[38] Presidents and Congress select individuals they can trust to implement their wishes and ensure that their staff will follow suit. And they do so for good reason. What is the point, after all, of appointing someone who is highly skilled and experienced but has no interest in following your wishes? Competence is important, but in politics it is not enough. Presidents and Congress also need to know that those under their command will work hard on behalf of their interests, even when these individuals are not being watched.

Politicization, though, can come at a cost. By emphasizing loyalty, presidents may erode an agency's institutional memory—that is, employees' accumulated knowledge about an agency's internal operations. When political appointees replace policy experts, and when agency turnover increases, bureaucratic operations may founder. According to one study, agencies with larger proportions of political appointees were systematically less effective than agencies with fewer political appointees.[39]

Of course, presidents and members of Congress themselves may disagree about the kinds of policies that bureaucratic agencies ought to implement. In these instances, the appointment process can be highly controversial. Take, for example, President Obama's decision to appoint Dr. Donald Berwick head of the Centers for Medicare and Medicaid Services, which oversee the government's two biggest health care programs. When Obama first nominated Berwick for the position in April 2011, Republicans in the Senate argued that the co-founder of the Institute for Health Improvement was a liberal extremist who would advocate for unpopular reforms such as health care rationing.[40] They vowed to use the nomination as a forum to debate the Patient Protection and Affordable Care Act, a major overhaul of the health care system that President Obama and Democratic congressional leaders had passed over Republican objections. Rather than tie this appointment to a larger debate over health care reform, however, Obama went ahead with the appointment.

When the Senate will not confirm a president's appointment, the president has two choices. He can withdraw the nomination and offer up an entirely new candidate. Or he can issue what is known as a **recess appointment.** Historically, presidents relied on recess appointments to ensure that the government continued to function when the Senate adjourned for long periods of time. Increasingly, though, presidents have relied on recess appointments to circumvent political opposition within Congress, as Obama did in the case of Berwick. Recess appointments can be used only under very specific conditions. Each year after the Senate term ends, the president may appoint individuals who immediately assume their positions of leadership in the federal bureaucracy. When Congress reconvenes, the Senate may choose whether to formally confirm these candidates. If a confirmation vote is not held, the candidate can remain in office at least until the end of Congress's session. Presidents can repeatedly appoint the same individuals during subsequent congressional recesses. In practice, though, they tend not to do so.

Whether the result of presidents acting on their own or with Congress, the politicization of the bureaucracy has invited much criticism. Grumblings turned to heated condemnations when President George W. Bush selected Michael Brown to help run the Federal Emergency Management Agency. Brown, a former commissioner for the International Arabian Horse Association, had no prior experience running a major disaster relief organization. Many argued that Brown was selected because of his political allegiance to the president rather than on the basis of merit. When he failed to demonstrate clear leadership during the lead-up to and aftermath of Hurricane Katrina, many called for his resignation and attacked the Bush administration for having placed a purely political appointee in a position of such responsibility.

The politicization of the bureaucracy, however, concerns more than just the decision to hire individuals. It also relates to the decision to fire them. In 2009, President Obama fired Gerald Walpin, the inspector general for the Corporation for National and Community Service. As inspector general, Walpin was responsible for looking into charges of waste or fraud made against organizations that received government money through programs such as AmeriCorps. Walpin investigated a community group called St. HOPE Academy that received nearly $1 million in federal funding through the AmeriCorps program. St. HOPE's founder Kevin Johnson—a former basketball player for the Phoenix Suns and a strong political ally of President Obama—was in the process of running for mayor of Sacramento. Johnson's campaign argued that Walpin's timing was politically motivated, noting that Walpin had once introduced Republican Mitt Romney at an event in Washington D.C. Although Walpin vehemently denied these charges, the Obama administration fired him with little public fanfare, citing his lack of independence as a reason. Obama asserted that he was just "exercising my powers as president." Republican Senator Charles Grassley, however, criticized the president, saying that Obama had fired Walpin for "doing his job," insinuating that the president himself was politically motivated. In this instance, the firing of a lower-level bureaucrat in a small government agency led to a much larger debate about the further politicization of the bureaucracy under President Obama.[41]

Note, though, that the threat of firing individuals who do not share the president's mission helps address the basic problems of drift, slack, and agency capture. One could argue that if presidents discover that bureaucrats are not working hard or are implementing their own policies or those of an unelected subset of the population, the administration has cause to fire them. One might go so far as to argue that President Obama had every right, and even the responsibility, to ensure that those individuals working within the Corporation for National and Community Service were performing their duties according to the standards set by Congress and the executive branch.

Of course, the high levels of turnover that result from all of these hirings and firings can create problems of their own. The election of each new president brings an entirely new set of appointments. Although the vast majority of workers within the bureaucracy enjoy strong job protection—the core result of the switch from the spoils system to the civil service system—many agency heads leave office at the end of a presidential term.[42] Such short tenures can diminish their ability to learn the culture of their agencies, secure the trust of their subordinates, and implement lasting policy changes. And sometimes, a change in culture at the top can cause even lower-level administrators to leave their posts and seek out other employment in the public or private sector.

In other countries, by contrast, a much more stable supply of policy experts runs the administrative apparatus. Take, for example, Canada. Whereas about 20 percent of American public servants leave their jobs in a typical year, only 4 percent of Canadian civil service employees do so.[43] One reason for this difference may be that the Canadian bureaucracy is composed almost entirely of career civil servants (who serve for decades) rather than political appointees (who tend to serve shorter terms). In Canada, nonpartisan career civil servants occupy all Canadian bureaucratic positions from the rank of deputy minister down the chain. Indeed, only the Cabinet-level ministers, of which there are about 30, can be appointed by the prime minister based on their partisan affiliation.[44] By contrast, in the United States, the president chooses roughly 3,000 political appointees to serve in the bureaucracy.[45] Although comprising less than 1 percent of the total civilian workforce, these partisan appointees dominate the highest echelons of agency management. Moreover, more than half of the 2.5 million American civil servants are "excepted" from the traditional merit-based guidelines, serving instead under agency-specific personnel systems.[46] Although these systems officially operate under the merit scheme, the flexibility they give to managers makes it easier to circumvent merit rules in hiring and promotion.[47] As a result, agency-based personnel systems "blur the line between appointees and careerists."[48] For all of these reasons, the U.S. civil service may not possess the same level of stability, independence, and expertise found in Canada and elsewhere.

Presidents and Congress Use Money, Rules, and Structure to Control Bureaucracies

In addition to the hiring and firing of individuals who run the federal government's agencies, the president, Congress, and the courts have additional opportunities to influence bureaucratic behavior. Agencies do not run on their own. They require money to pay their employees; they must regularly report to their political superiors; they are situated within a larger bureaucratic structure; and their very survival often depends on continued political support. Each of these facts allows for even further control over the federal bureaucracy.

BUDGETS Every year, the president must propose a budget, and Congress must enact it. The budget process affords opportunities to reflect on the performance of each bureaucratic agency, and to punish or reward it accordingly. When agencies are doing well, Congress can reward them with higher budgets; when agencies are not performing effectively, Congress may decide to slash their budgets. With control of the purse strings, Congress can create strong incentives for agencies to abide by their interests.

Beyond adjusting the amount of money granted to different agencies, Congress can attach any number of stipulations on how these monies are to be spent. Rather than give each agency a lump-sum payment, which its employees then decide how to spend, Congress may write detailed instructions about which projects an agency should pursue and which it should abandon. These instructions often come in the form of "suggestions" that legislators expect agency bureaucrats to follow. In 2008, for instance, Congress instructed USAID to allocate $2.5 million of its budget for a short-wave radio program in Madagascar sponsored by a Christian broadcasting organization. The program was sponsored by Texas Republican Congressman Pete Sessions. These allocations to federal agencies are sometimes called "soft earmarks," because they allow members of Congress to divert spending to specific programs they like and still bypass rules regulating earmark spending.[49]

OVERSIGHT In a principal-agent relationship, you will recall, the agent's great advantages are information and expertise. So it is with the bureaucracy. Agencies are great reservoirs of expertise about a vast array of public policies. They know what should be done, what is being done, and what plans are in place for the future. As policy generalists, the principals (Congress and the president) to some extent must rely on that knowledge for their decisions and directives. To make sure that bureaucratic agencies use this information and expertise in ways that conform to the wishes of their political superiors, **oversight** is crucial. Through oversight, presidents and members of Congress monitor and supervise goings-on within the federal bureaucracy.

oversight
congressional and presidential efforts to monitor and supervise the actions of bureaucratic agencies.

One of the best oversight mechanisms is **hearings.** Should an issue or a problem come to light, committees and subcommittees can call upon bureaucrats to testify in formal settings. Although members of Congress often use these opportunities to show off before the television cameras, they also direct pointed questions about agency actions, policies, and procedures. Members of Congress may also choose to bring in outside experts and former agency employees to verify or dispute the claims made by current bureaucrats. With the information they gather, members of Congress are in a better position to decide whether agency budgets need to be adjusted, whether their legislative mandates need to be revised, and sometimes whether criminal charges need to be brought forward.

hearing
a formal process in which committees in Congress call upon bureaucrats and other experts to help them understand and oversee a particular agency.

In addition to hearings, members of Congress can choose to launch their own investigations into perceived abuses of power. A number of agencies have the specific responsibility of monitoring other agencies and reporting their findings back to Congress. The Government Accountability Office, the Congressional Research Service, and the Congressional Budget Office all provide independent sources of information about public policy and agency behavior. Often, this information comes in the form of reports about specific issues that individual members request. With this information, members of Congress can further influence agency behavior and reduce problems that might arise from principal-agent relations.

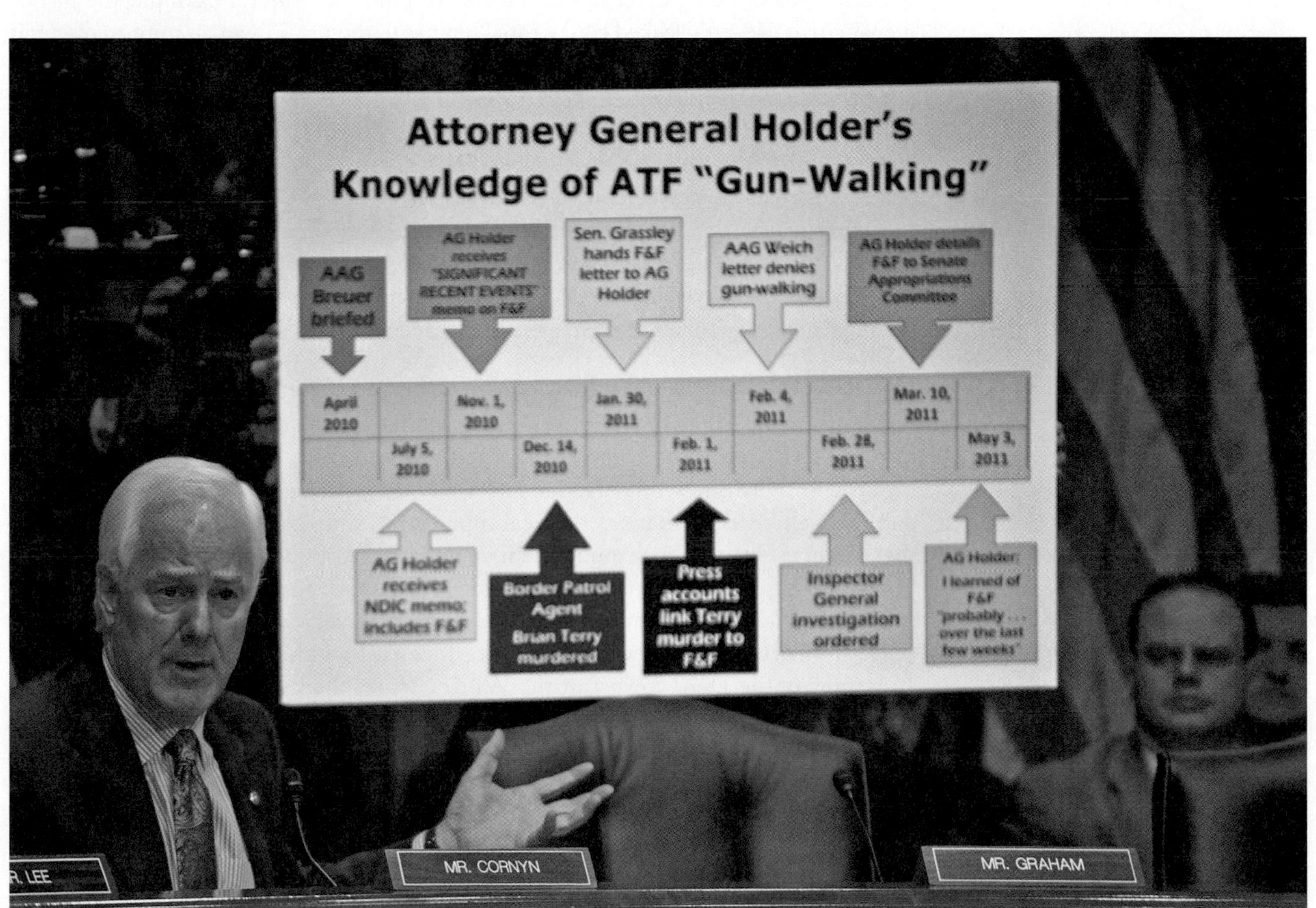

MONITORING THE BUREAUCRACY

Through hearings, members of Congress can monitor what is happening within the federal bureaucracy. Here, Senator John Cornyn (R-TX) grilled Attorney General Eric Holder about his knowledge of Fast and Furious, a highly controversial undercover investigation of the gun trade led by the Bureau of Alcohol, Tobacco, Firearms and Explosives.

16.1

16.2

16.3

16.4

whistle-blower
a bureaucrat who witnesses and publicly exposes wrongdoing by either contacting his or her political superiors or tipping off the press.

centralization
the method of increasing the president's power by moving key administrative functions from the departments to the Executive Office of the President.

Congress has also enacted a number of laws intended to make bureaucratic behavior more transparent. The 1967 Freedom of Information Act, for instance, enables members of Congress (as well as all citizens) to inspect a wide variety of government documents. If agencies raise concerns about releasing these documents to the public, they must state their case before a federal judge. Similarly, the 1976 Sunshine Law requires that agency meetings be held in public, unless classified information is being discussed. Both of these laws are designed to open to public scrutiny the federal government in general and the bureaucracy in particular.

Finally, members of Congress depend on **whistle-blowers** to expose bureaucratic waste, mismanagement, and illegal behavior. The term refers to the bureaucrats who witness and publicly expose wrongdoing by either contacting their political superiors or tipping off the press. To encourage these individuals to come forward, Congress passed a number of laws (such as the 1989 Whistle-Blower Protection Act) making it illegal to demote, fire, or otherwise punish whistle-blowing bureaucrats.[50] In 2011, Agent John Dodson relied on the Whistle-Blower Protection Act when he came forward to publicly expose a program run by the Federal Bureau of Alcohol, Tobacco, and Firearms (ATF), which had allowed guns to be sold illegally across the Mexican border in the hope of tracking them back to drug cartels.[51] In addition, Congress supports toll-free lines for bureaucrats working in different agencies to call and report problems that they witness. Congress has created an independent agency, the Office of Special Counsel, which is also charged with investigating complaints by whistle-blowers who have been punished by their immediate superiors. These efforts to protect whistle-blowers, however, are not foolproof. Bosses can find any number of ways of sanctioning whistle-blowers without being detected. In the case of John Dodson, for example, the Justice Department allegedly leaked confidential reports to the press in an attempt to discredit Dodson's testimony.[52] In addition, the Supreme Court has often been unwilling to interfere with the operations of other government agencies in order to protect whistle-blowers. In 2006, in *Garcetti v. Ceballos*, the Court ruled that administrative agencies have a right to discipline at least some whistle-blowers. The case concerned a former deputy district attorney who claimed he was reassigned and denied a promotion after testifying against the government regarding the legality of a specific search warrant. In its decision, the Supreme Court ruled that whereas private citizens are protected if they publicly criticize a government action, government employees are still accountable to the management policies of their specific bureaucratic agency.

CENTRALIZATION Left to their own devices, bureaucrats may wander from their policy mandate. This behavior takes place especially when their agencies are shielded from media scrutiny, and when Washington elites have few ways of directly monitoring their activity. These bureaucrats may well be advancing policies that improve the public's welfare. But what are political superiors to do when these bureaucrats resist their orders? One solution: round them up and bring them closer to home.

Political scientists have made much of presidents' use of **centralization**—that is, moving key functions from the departments to the Executive Office of the President (EOP), sometimes referred to as the "presidential branch." The core administrative structures in the EOP consist of the White House, the Office of Management and Budget, and the Council of Economic Advisors. It also contains the Office of National Drug Control Policy, the Office of Science and Technology Policy, the United States Trade Representative, the President's Foreign Intelligence Advisory Board, and many other units. In fact, throughout the EOP are people working on every imaginable policy. By relying on these individuals, the president can more easily monitor their behavior and ensure that they are advancing his core interests.[53]

When do presidents rely on individuals within the EOP for policy advice, and when do they turn to bureaucrats employed in the departments? The choice, some analysts argue, comes down to the perceived costs and benefits of loyalty and expertise. Individuals within the EOP are more likely to follow the president's lead, but they tend to know less about policy issues. By contrast, employees in the departments typically have extensive expertise about policy, but they cannot so easily be trusted to promote the president's interests. According to one study, presidents tend to worry more about the importance of expertise when an issue is either new or very complex; in these instances, the president turns to department bureaucrats when developing his policy agenda.[54] When large numbers of people from the opposition party hold seats in Congress, however, presidents worry more about loyalty; under these conditions, presidents are more likely to depend on EOP staffers.

This same study finds that the president's legislative initiatives are less likely to be enacted when the president centralizes authority. It is not clear why this is the case. Perhaps members of Congress are less likely to trust the president when he forsakes the expertise located in the departments in favor of the judgments of loyalists in the EOP. Alternatively, presidents may choose to centralize when they anticipate a difficult legislative road ahead. If so, then causality would appear to be reversed—expectations about legislative failure promote centralization, rather than centralization leading to legislative breakdown.

Beyond its impact on the likelihood of enacting presidential initiatives, centralization creates other problems. With increasing numbers of individuals and organizations working on any particular policy issue, lines of responsibility begin to blur. As the EOP grows, critics argue that there emerges "an unwieldy, tower hierarchy in which accountability is diffuse at best and the president is sometimes the last to know."[55] With the passage of time, one can well imagine presidents opting to centralize authority still further within the EOP—with loyalists working close by, and experts toiling away in the outer reaches of the presidential branch.

AGENCY ELIMINATIONS If all else fails, Congress and the president can eliminate an agency outright. Contrary to conventional wisdom, agencies are not immortal. In fact, agencies are eliminated with a fair amount of frequency. According to one analysis, fully 60 percent of all agencies created between 1946 and 1997 had been eliminated by 2000.[56] When President Nixon assumed office after eight years of Democratic control, for instance, he eliminated the Office of Economic Opportunity, which was then responsible for administering many of the social welfare programs created under President Johnson. In an effort to reduce the ability of the Environmental Protection Agency to regulate industries, President Reagan eliminated the Office of Enforcement.

Different kinds of agencies tend to survive for different amounts of time. Government corporations and independent agencies and commissions, which are intentionally given more autonomy, tend to live longer than do agencies located within the EOP, which are subject to more presidential control. Congress and the president also have a more difficult time eliminating an agency when they are more constrained in their ability to hire and fire agency heads, either because these heads must be from a specific party or because they serve for fixed terms.

Politics also appears to contribute to the lifespan of different agencies. Agencies are more likely to be eliminated when the current president is of the opposite party of the president who was in power when the agency was created. It is unclear, though, what exactly to make of this finding. Perhaps presidents tend to kill programs that they oppose, and these programs tend to be created by predecessors from the opposition party. On the other hand, a switch from one party to another in the presidency may reflect broader changes in the public's spending priorities. If true, then the fact that agencies tend to die when a new party takes control of the White House has less to do with the independent policy agenda of the president and more to do with the efforts of elected officials to keep pace with public opinion.

☐ Reformers Seek to Introduce Market Forces

All of the methods that presidents and Congress use to control the bureaucracy represent efforts to reform the existing system of bureaucratic governance. Increasingly, though, reformers are suggesting that the problems of bureaucracy, especially those that involve inefficiencies, are best solved by looking beyond the individuals

Unresolved Debate

Should Businesses Be Required to Privately Fund Public Services?

Glitzy shopping districts in Manhattan and Chicago owe their cleaner and safer streets, in no small part, to their status as Business Improvement Districts (BIDs). In the nearly 1,000 BIDs that exist in major cities across the United States, business owners are legally obligated to pay a fee that goes toward enhancing public services in those districts. This fee is in addition to the standard taxes that they must pay to the national, state, and local governments. Examples of public services paid for by these fees include policing and street cleaning. However, private vendors provide some of these public services. Who benefits from district-financed public services? Should businesses be required to privately fund public services?

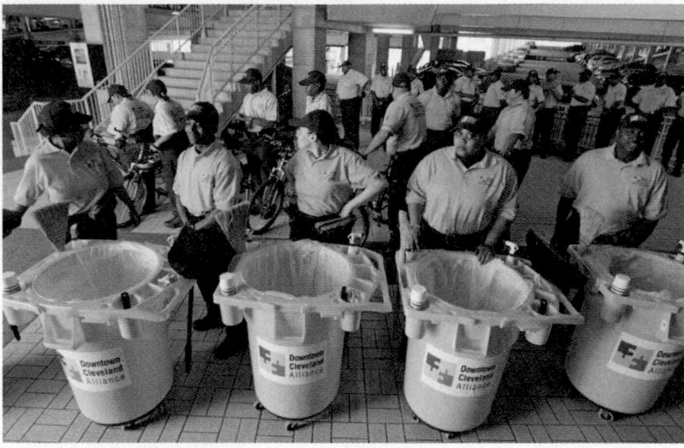

BUSINESSES IMPROVING NEIGHBORHOODS

In 2006, organizers of downtown Cleveland's Business Improvement District unveiled the uniforms and equipment that will be used by their employees. The workers are responsible for patrolling downtown streets, cleaning the sidewalks, and offering directions and other assistance to visitors.

YES

John MacDonald, a criminology expert, finds that in terms of crime there is every reason to encourage private-sector investment in BIDs. Relying on a variety of statistical tools, MacDonald produces empirical evidence demonstrating the effectiveness of private actions in crime control[a]:

- Significant declines in crime rates accompany the implementation of BIDs.
- Rising security expenditures by BIDs contribute to further reductions in crime rates and increases in police arrests.
- BIDs do not meaningfully affect crime rates in neighboring areas, suggesting that criminal activity, which previously took place in BIDs, is not simply moving to surrounding areas.

NO

Although they are financed by private investment, BIDs also have a public character. Richard Briffault, a prominent legal scholar, emphasizes that local governments have a duty to ensure that public services are distributed in a way that promotes the public interest. Briffault draws on legal doctrines and analyzes Supreme Court judgments to warn against the perils of taxing specific districts[b]:

- BIDs undermine the government's responsibility of providing services according to an overall determination of welfare.
- Mandatory BID assessments resemble taxes and may violate state taxation limits.
- Businesses may reduce their support for general taxation levels, thus compromising the government's ability to provide public services for poorer areas.

CONTRIBUTING TO THE DEBATE

The studies point to different ways in which BIDs might either hurt or help the public welfare. On the one hand, we have some evidence of lower crime rates within BIDs, but on the other, we have reasons to believe that BIDs may reduce public support for general taxation levels. To make headway on this issue, then, we need to investigate the economic consequences of BIDs. Future studies, therefore, should compare the types and profits of businesses before and after BID legislation. In addition, studies should track similar trends in adjoining districts that do not receive the added services enjoyed by the BID.

WHAT DO YOU THINK?

1. If it turns out that BIDs lead to lower revenue shares for local governments, should the districts be restricted?
2. What other kinds of private initiatives offer specialized services that were previously the province of government activity?

[a]Philip Cook and John MacDonald, "Public Safety Through Private Action: An Economic Assessment of BIDs," *The Economic Journal* 121, 552 (2011), pp. 445–462
[b]Richard Briffault "A Government for Our Time? Business Improvement Districts and Urban Governance," *Columbia Law Review* 99, 2 (1999), pp. 365–477.

and agencies that work within the federal government. These reformers suggest that increased effectiveness and efficiency can come about only through deregulation or privatization.

DEREGULATION Some people argue that the best way to deal with the bureaucracy is to temper its impulse to regulate more and more areas of business activity. Claiming that government regulations cripple the entrepreneurial spirit of private industries, reformers argue that rather than restructuring these agencies or introducing better oversight mechanisms, political leaders ought to scale back their activities altogether.

Through **deregulation,** the government reduces the workload of bureaucrats. It cordons off certain areas of business activity, insisting that bureaucrats not interfere with market forces of supply and demand. During the 1970s and 1980s, substantial efforts were made to deregulate the airline, trucking, telecommunications, and financial services industries. Through these efforts, the government encouraged new companies to form, providing more choices and cheaper services to consumers. For example, the deregulation of the telecommunications industry made possible the emergence of companies such as Sprint and MCI (and later, Verizon, T-Mobile, and others).

Occasionally, though, deregulation can backfire. When the government deregulated the financial services industry in the early 1980s, savings and loan companies suddenly had many of the powers of traditional banks—such as the ability to issue credit cards, borrow money from the Federal Reserve, and make commercial loans—without the regulations of traditional banks. With their new powers, savings and loan companies began to invest large amounts of money in highly risky ventures. Not surprisingly, many of these ventures failed, and savings and loan companies were left without the money needed to pay back their investors. In total, these defaults cost the federal government (and taxpayers) more than $100 billion. Congress responded in 1989 by enacting the Financial Institutions Reform Recovery and Enforcement Act, which reintroduced many of the regulations that had been eliminated earlier in the decade.

PRIVATIZATION Whereas deregulation concerns the relaxation of bureaucratic oversight of different industries, **privatization** concerns the transfer of government functions from the federal government to private companies. Rather than government bureaucrats providing certain services, private companies do so. In communities around the country, private contractors have replaced government agencies to run prisons, provide security services, and manage hospitals. (See *Unresolved Debate: Should Businesses Be Required to Privately Fund Public Services?*)

Note that privatization is not an all-or-nothing arrangement. Many bureaucratic agencies turn to private companies to perform selected tasks. The military, for instance, pays billions of dollars each year to private contractors that build parts, conduct research, and provide strategic advice. Even when it decides to hand over complete responsibility for a certain public service to private companies, the government may continue to fund their work. When writing contracts with these companies, moreover, the government may introduce any number of requirements about how they conduct their business. The key question, then, is not whether a government service has been privatized, but how much it has been privatized.

deregulation
the process of decreasing the number of agency rules that apply to a particular industry or group of industries so as to introduce market forces to their operations.

privatization
the transfer of government functions from the federal government to private companies.

On MyPoliSciLab

Review the Chapter

Listen to **Chapter 16** on **MyPoliSciLab**

What Bureaucrats Do

16.1 Identify the functions of the federal bureaucracy, p. 540.

Bureaucrats serve a wide variety of vital functions for the American public. They implement the policies that Congress and the president write; they write rules that clarify these policies; they provide expert advice to their political superiors; and they help resolve disputes. Thus, the bureaucracy serves quasi-legislative, executive, and judicial functions.

Growth and Organization of the Bureaucracy

16.2 Explain the growth and organization of the bureaucracy, p. 545.

During much of the nineteenth century, the bureaucracy was quite small and tended to employ individuals better known for their political ties than for their experience or expertise. At the turn of the twentieth century, however, the nation witnessed the transformation of the spoils system into a merit-based system. During this period, the federal bureaucracy also expanded dramatically. Today, the bureaucracy consists of Cabinet departments, independent agencies, regulatory commissions, and government corporations.

Challenges of Bureaucracy

16.3 Assess the role of the bureaucracy in public policy making, p. 551.

Although the bureaucracy serves important functions, it also presents serious challenges. Because bureaucrats know more about the policy issues that they oversee, they can act in ways that do not always represent the interests of Congress, the president, the courts, or the American public. Sometimes bureaucrats act on behalf of their own policy interests, sometimes they serve the interests of other unelected officials, sometimes they do not work especially hard, and often they are less efficient than the public would like.

Controlling and Reforming the Bureaucracy

16.4 Evaluate the different approaches to overseeing and reforming the bureaucracy, p. 559.

Congress and the president have devised a number of ways to address the problems of bureaucracy. Through appointments, they put like-minded individuals in charge of federal agencies. Through budgets, oversight hearings, and centralization efforts, Congress and the president reshape the incentives of bureaucrats and monitor their actions. When all else fails, Congress and the president can eliminate agencies, substantially reduce their regulatory powers, or turn to the private marketplace for help in providing public services.

Learn the Terms

Study and **Review** the **Flashcards**

agency capture, p. 556
bureaucracy, p. 540
centralization, p. 564
civil service system, p. 547
department, p. 548
deregulation, p. 567
drift, p. 555
government corporation, p. 551
hearing, p. 563
implementation, p. 541
independent agencies and commissions, p. 550
norms, p. 543
oversight, p. 563
politicization, p. 560
principal-agent problem, p. 555
privatization, p. 567
recess appointment, p. 560
red tape, p. 557
rules, p. 542
slack, p. 555
spoils system, p. 547
whistle-blower, p. 564

Test Yourself

16.1 Identify the functions of the federal bureaucracy.

Which of the following is NOT a function of the federal bureaucracy?

- **a.** making laws
- **b.** interpreting laws
- **c.** providing expert advice
- **d.** making rules
- **e.** implementing laws

16.2 Explain the growth and organization of the bureaucracy.

What was one ramification of the Pendleton Act passed by Congress in 1883?

- **a.** Party allegiance became the employment qualification that mattered most.
- **b.** Personal relationships with the president became the determining factor in political appointments.
- **c.** Merit became the most important employment qualification.
- **d.** President James Garfield was assassinated by a disgruntled office seeker.
- **e.** Both party allegiance and merit became equally important employment qualifications.

16.3 Assess the role of the bureaucracy in public policy making.

Which of the following exemplifies the principal-agent problem?

- **a.** The president and Congress need federal bureaucrats for their expertise, but federal bureaucrats do not share the same interests as the president and Congress.
- **b.** A district attorney aggressively pursues white-collar criminals but prefers not to prosecute minor drug offenses.
- **c.** The president and Congress disagree over the action a federal agency should take.
- **d.** Bureaucrats do not want to work as hard as Congress and the president would like them to.
- **e.** Congress captures a federal agency.

16.4 Evaluate the different approaches to overseeing and reforming the bureaucracy.

All of the following are methods that presidents and Congress routinely use to directly control the bureaucracy EXCEPT

- **a.** oversight.
- **b.** money.
- **c.** centralization.
- **d.** privatization.
- **e.** agency elimination.

Explore Further

SUGGESTED READINGS BY TOP SCHOLARS

D. P. Carpenter. *The Forging of Bureaucratic Autonomy: Reputations, Networks, and Policy Innovation in Executive Agencies 1862–1928.* Princeton, NJ: Princeton University Press, 2001. Demonstrates how bureaucratic agencies, through reputation building, can exercise influence over public policy that neither Congress nor the president would prefer to grant.

Sean Gailmard and John W. Patty. "Slackers and Zealots: Civil Service, Policy Discretion, and Bureaucratic Expertise." *American Journal of Political Science* 51, 4 (2007): 873–89. Presents a formal model that demonstrates why members of Congress might want to appoint individuals with more extreme political views to positions in the federal bureaucracy.

John D. Huber and Charles R. Shipan. *Deliberate Discretion?* New York: Cambridge University Press, 2002. Examines the conditions under which members of Congress will delegate more or less authority to administrative agencies to create public policy.

David Lewis. *The Politics of Presidential Appointments: Political Control and Bureaucratic Performance.* Princeton, NJ: Princeton University Press, 2008. Provides a detailed empirical account of the politicization of the bureaucracy.

Terry M. Moe. "Political Control and the Power of the Agent." *Journal of Law, Economics, and Organization* 22, 1 (2006): 1–29. Challenging standard accounts of principal-agent relations, this article demonstrates how teachers, through elections, can alter the composition of the school boards with which they must negotiate.

SUGGESTED WEBSITES

Federal Emergency Management Agency: www.fema.gov
This is the primary federal agency that assumes responsibility for overseeing disaster relief.

Environmental Protection Agency: www.epa.gov
This organization oversees the implementation of environmental and energy legislation.

Government Accountability Office: www.gao.gov
This agency monitors goings-on throughout the federal bureaucracy.

Executive Office of the Presidency: www.whitehouse.gov/administration/eop
This bureaucracy houses, among other units, the Council of Economic Advisors, the Domestic Policy Council, and the National Security Council.

OMB Watch: www.ombwatch.org
This is a nonpartisan watchdog organization that pays particular attention to regulatory and budgetary processes in the federal bureaucracy.

USA.gov: http://www.usa.gov/Agencies/Federal/Executive.shtml
This is a listing of all the major departments, agencies, and commissions in the federal bureaucracy.

17

Listen to Chapter 17 on MyPoliSciLab

Economic and Social Policy

AN ECONOMY STRUGGLING TO RECOVER

Over the course of 2008, the U.S. economy collapsed. In March, Bear Stearns, one of the nation's most important investment banks, announced that it needed to turn to the federal government and rival JP Morgan Chase for emergency bailout funds. In September, the government assumed control of two of the nation's largest mortgage finance companies, Fannie Mae and Freddie Mac. Lehman Brothers filed for bankruptcy shortly thereafter, marking the largest bankruptcy filing in U.S. history. Washington Mutual then went under, the biggest bank failure in history. In October, the stock market fell 22 percent in just eight days.[1]

The effects of the financial meltdown rippled across the country. Housing foreclosures skyrocketed, and millions of Americans lost their jobs. Those banks that did not shut down nonetheless cut way back on their credit, making it extraordinarily difficult for students to secure education loans and entrepreneurs to acquire business loans. In October 2008, the unemployment rate was 6.2 percent. A year later, unemployment shot up to 10 percent, the highest in 26 years. In spite of government spending and private-sector growth, the employment rate remained persistently high, sitting at just over 8 percent in the summer of 2012.[2]

Across the nation, state and local governments were forced to cut basic services. Philadelphia, for example, slashed its sanitation costs by limiting residential street cleaning and eliminating leaf, bulk, and tire collections. The state of New York reduced the aid given to schools by $686 million for the 2009–2010 academic year. And Los Angeles drastically reduced its public transportation sector, eliminating 10 Metrolink train lines and curtailing bus traffic.[3] By the end of 2011, local governments across the United States had cut a total of 535,000 government jobs.[4]

17.1 Identify the conditions under which policy innovations are created, p. 574.

17.2 Assess efforts by the federal government to manage the domestic economy, p. 577.

17.3 Trace the development of the largest federal social program, which assists the elderly, p. 581.

17.4 Analyze changes in welfare policy within the United States, p. 585.

17.5 Outline the federal government's expanding involvement in education, p. 588.

17.6 Evaluate the government's efforts to provide health care to the poor and aged, p. 596.

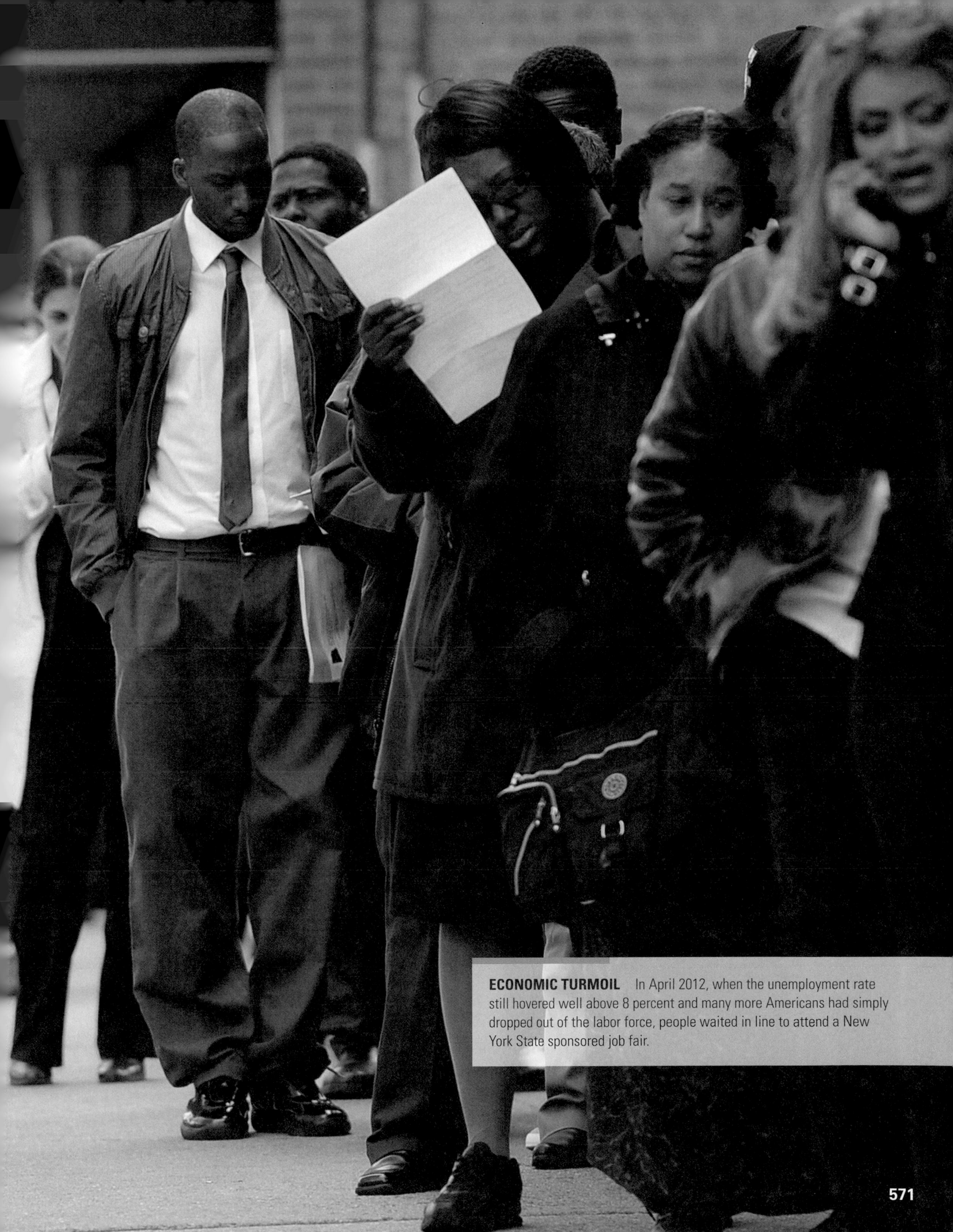

ECONOMIC TURMOIL In April 2012, when the unemployment rate still hovered well above 8 percent and many more Americans had simply dropped out of the labor force, people waited in line to attend a New York State sponsored job fair.

The Big Picture How should the government fix our struggling economy? Are things even as bad as we think? Author William G. Howell illustrates the biggest challenges that government employees face when addressing and quantifying social and economic issues.

The Basics Find out what public policy is, who makes public policy, and how they make it. In this video, you will also explore the major social policy issues we face and consider the role of the federal and state governments in specific areas such as education.

Should the federal government have a say in education policy?

In Context Discover the history of social policy in the United States. In this video, Columbia University political scientist Ester Fuchs discusses why social policy emerged and how the focus of social policy had changed over time.

Think Like a Political Scientist What role do political scientists play in policy-making? Columbia University political scientist Ester Fuchs examines not only the research of political scientist on public policy, but the impact of this research on the policy-making process.

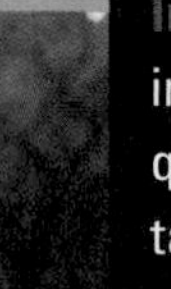

In the Real World Should the wealthy pay a larger percentage of their income in taxes than people with lower incomes? Real people tackle this central question, and they weigh in on what they believe is the fairest system of taxation and what tax reforms need to be made in the United States.

So What? What do the Occupy movement and the Tea Party have in common? Using these two groups, author William G. Howell describes different strategies and questions that need to be considered when trying to make some social or economic change.

According to many economists, the downturn began with a housing crisis. As a result of large inflows of foreign investment and government regulations that were designed to increase home ownership rates among the poor, the housing market in the early 2000s experienced rapid and widespread growth. Banks went out of their way to extend loans to an ever-increasing proportion of the American public, some of whom were ill-equipped to make the mortgage payments. The lenders then sold these mortgage loans to investors such as Fannie Mae and Freddie Mac for huge profits. Still more investment firms sold complex insurance packages, tying vast swaths of the domestic and international economy to the U.S. housing market.

The housing growth proved to be unsustainable. Beginning in 2006, housing prices nationwide began to fall as people defaulted on loans that they could no longer afford. Then the "housing bubble" popped. In one year, housing prices dropped by 11.8 percent in Tampa and 12.4 percent in Miami. Los Angeles, one of the nation's largest metropolitan areas, suffered an 8.8 percent drop over the same time span.[5]

The domino effect continued as banks and their investors experienced huge losses and stopped lending money, throwing the entire economy into chaos. In 2008, 25 banks failed; in 2009, nearly 100 additional banks failed and in the following year, well over 100 more did so.[6]

In a major national address in the fall of 2008, President George W. Bush proposed a $700 billion bailout to prevent an economic collapse, and Congress approved the bailout, which purchased unwanted assets that were clogging the financial system. The bailout, the president argued, would reduce the financial burden on banks and encourage them to resume lending.

Government efforts to curtail the economic meltdown did not end there. Soon after he became president in 2009, Barack Obama proposed the American Recovery and Reinvestment Plan, which aimed to create jobs and encourage long-term growth. Approved by Congress, the plan included a $787 billion stimulus to the economy and tax cuts for working families. In addition, Obama sought to jumpstart the economy by repairing schools, creating a clean energy program, and improving the quality of health care; he also underscored the need to rebuild the nation's financial regulatory framework.[7] In the summer of 2010, public pressure led Congress to enact regulatory reform for the nation's financial institutions.

Although the financial crisis initially sparked a bold legislative response, Congress and the public's appetite for government intervention dwindled over time. In September 2011, with high unemployment and slow economic growth persisting, President Obama proposed a $447 billion American Jobs Act. The bill called for creating new jobs and providing tax relief to small businesses by raising taxes on wealthy Americans. Despite vigorously campaigning for the legislation, the president was unable to convince members of Congress to pass the bill. Republican Senator Jon Kyl said Obama's plan was based on "flawed economic theories" that relied on government spending to spur economic growth and job creation.[8] By the end of 2011, it was clear that Congress's willingness to spend money on major economic legislation had disappeared as quickly as it had arisen.

The hubbub over the financial meltdown and the government's response reveals a basic fact about domestic policy making: the wheels of policy making whirl fastest during periods of crisis. Spurred by pressing social needs, politicians entertain all sorts of economic and social reforms. In this instance, the financial crisis introduced new political pressure for economic reforms. As we saw in Obama's economic recovery plan, reforms in education, energy, and health care can follow at the heels of a crisis. And as we shall soon see, these kinds of social programs almost always live longer than the crises that created them.

This chapter examines domestic policies supported by the federal government. Although domestic policy covers issues ranging from environmental protection to patent law, here we focus on economic policy and social programs—programs purposefully designed to enhance the well-being of U.S. citizens.

Enacting Economic and Social Policies

17.1 Identify the conditions under which policy innovations are created.

Great Society
a set of large-scale social initiatives proposed by President Lyndon Johnson in the 1960s to reduce poverty, racial discrimination, environmental degradation, and urban decay.

hat prompts the federal government to create new public policies? Detailed histories of individual policy interventions often highlight the idiosyncrasies that lead to public policy making. In retrospect, major policy innovations often appear to arise from chance meetings between key politicos or a particularly well-timed protest in Washington, D.C. For such seemingly random occurrences to bear fruit, however, at least three factors must converge: a problem warranting a governmental response must be identified, a solution to the problem must be articulated, and some kind of focusing event must prod politicians into action. In this section, we reflect on each of these ingredients of domestic policy making.[9]

Identifying a Problem Is the First Step in Developing a Policy

There are many things about the world that we may wish were not true. Apple iPads may be more expensive than we would like. Our friends may not always act like friends. Our grandparents might have a difficult time paying for their medication. When the economy hits a rough spot, some relatives may lose their jobs. It is difficult to imagine the federal government passing a law that requires Apple to lower its prices or that requires friends to be more responsive to one another's needs. But what of the other problems? Which of them warrant government action? Much depends on public opinion, which varies over time and across the country. Historically, though, those problems that appear to violate basic elements of the American creed or that threaten the nation's security have stood the best chance of attracting the attention of politicians in Washington, D.C.

THE AMERICAN CREED Problems are especially likely to attract the attention of the federal government when they violate elements of the American creed. Concerns about equity stand out in this regard. Many social programs funded by the government aim to reduce long-standing inequalities—whether they involve access to sports programs among men and women, the relative incomes of the rich and poor, or the test scores of white and black schoolchildren. Of course, certain inequalities are inevitable. Some are even desirable. But the federal government is especially likely to enact social programs designed to reduce gross and persistent inequalities that systematically limit the life chances of certain citizens. Although the federal government may accept some inequality of outcomes, it often intervenes in the lives of citizens in order to promote a base level of equality of opportunities.

In the past half-century, concerns about equality were never more prominent than during Lyndon Johnson's presidency in the 1960s. Johnson sought to create a **Great Society** "where the demands of morality, and the needs of the spirit, can be realized in the life of the Nation."[10] He called upon the nation to tackle the problems of poverty, racial discrimination, environmental degradation, and urban decay. Only by doing so, Johnson argued, could the ideals of the Founders enshrined in the Declaration of Independence and the U.S. Constitution, be realized. With strong Democratic support within Congress, Johnson managed to enact more large-scale social programs than any other president since Franklin Roosevelt. Many of these programs are described in this chapter.

NATIONAL SECURITY Above all else, the federal government's fundamental objective is to protect its citizens from foreign harm. Military threats, terrorist activity, and the proliferation of nuclear weapons, among others, rise to the top of governmental concerns. Domestic problems that could impact U.S. security interests, either directly or indirectly, gain an important advantage in the contest to attract the attention of federal politicians.

To understand these priorities, recall the discussion of energy in primaries to the 2012 presidential election. Both Democratic candidate Barack Obama and the field of Republican candidates claimed it was risky for the nation to depend on imported oil from the Middle East. They proposed various means to increase American energy production, either through untapped domestic oil reserves or alternate sources of energy. "We send over $300 billion a year to countries . . . that are frankly in some cases hostile to who America is," declared Republican candidate Rick Perry during a presidential debate, "What a great day it would be to just say no thank you Mr. Chavez, we don't need your oil." Rick Perry referenced Hugo Chavez, president of oil-rich Venezuela, who has been sharply critical of capitalism and the United States in general.[11] Linking energy independence to national security concerns increased the pressure on the federal government to solve the nation's energy issues.

Energy interests, of course, are not unique among security issues. Immigration activists regularly argue that stemming the flow of undocumented workers across U.S. borders is an important element of national security. Presidents Lyndon Johnson and Ronald Reagan did not merely support antipoverty and anti-drug programs—they waged self-declared "wars" against these looming threats.[12] National security interests spurred the federal government's initial foray into public education as well. At every step, advocates for policy change justified the importance of deploying significant resources to combat a perceived security problem.

policy entrepreneurs
professionals working in think tanks, universities, lobby groups, unions, and interest groups who propose solutions to policy problems and persuade politicians to adopt them.

Identifying a Government Solution Is the Next Step in Developing Policy

For social legislation to emerge, problems must have solutions. Lacking solutions, politicians can offer little more than their sympathies for those who suffer from society's ailments and injustices.

Policy entrepreneurs play an important role in identifying solutions and linking them to observed problems.[13] These individuals work in think tanks, universities, lobbying organizations, unions, and interest groups. Backed by data, conviction, and persuasive skills, they design solutions for the many problems facing the federal government. Often, like-minded entrepreneurs form networks that operate at the local, state, and federal levels of government. These entrepreneurs coordinate with one another, with the intention of convincing politicians to adopt one policy reform or another.

Take, for example, the activities of the American Federation of Teachers (AFT) and the National Education Association (NEA), the two largest teachers unions in the nation. Both advocate policies to support teachers, such as higher pay and fewer restrictions on how they perform in the classroom. Lobbyists for both unions work at all levels of government to convince politicians about the merits of their preferred policies, emphasizing the ways they will solve problems in education.

In most areas of life, there is a logical ordering of problems and solutions. We devise solutions for problems, not the other way around. When the problems disappear, the solutions usually are discarded. In politics, though, things do not always work this way. If one day the nation no longer suffered from a shortage of public school teachers, the NEA and AFT, like all policy entrepreneurs, would look for other problems to attach their solutions to. In this sense, solutions in politics can arise independently of problems and often outlive the problems they were intended to solve.

17.1

17.2

17.3

17.4

17.5

17.6

focusing event
a visible and dramatic event that focuses the domestic polity on a specific problem and accompanying course of action.

Great Depression
a period of severe economic recession in the United States precipitated by the stock market crash in October 1929.

Focusing Events Spark Government Action

At any given moment, many domestic problems demand government action. Many solutions also float about the corridors of Congress. Bringing problems and solutions together often requires some kind of **focusing event**—a visible and dramatic event that focuses the domestic polity on a specific problem and accompanying course of action. As we have already seen, the failure of the nation's largest banking institutions and the collapse of housing markets in 2008 put the topic of financial regulatory reform front and center. These events infused the issue with a new urgency, to which politicians felt compelled to respond.

Focusing events can take many forms. Human tragedies, foreign crises, and even the weather can serve this role. The devastation wrought by Hurricane Katrina in 2005 exposed deep problems of poverty, crime, and corruption in New Orleans. Policy entrepreneurs descended upon the region, insisting that they could assist the government's efforts to solve these problems. The images of families stuck on rooftops days after the levees broke infused the ensuing deliberations with a genuine sense of urgency. Among twentieth-century focusing events, nothing had more impact than the **Great Depression**, which was a period of unprecedented economic hardship for the nation. The stock market collapse in 1929 led to the utter devastation of the domestic economy. When Franklin Roosevelt became president four years later, the banks in

THE GREAT DEPRESSION SERVES AS A FOCUSING EVENT

The most severe economic downturn of the 20th century and perhaps the nation's history, occurred in the late 1920s and early 1930s. Just as unemployment rates skyrocketed, so did poverty rates. Here, Sharecropper Bud Fields and his family are shown in their home in Hale County, Alabama.

32 states had been closed by state government edict, and bank operations in the remaining 16 states remained severely curtailed. No fewer than 15 million Americans—roughly 25 percent of the total workforce at the time—were unemployed. The gravity of the nation's problems spurred the federal government into action never before experienced. As many of the social policies described in this chapter attest, federal government agencies assumed altogether new responsibilities for the management of the economy and the welfare of the nation's citizens.

gross domestic product (GDP)
a statistic that measures all goods and services produced by a nation's economy.

Economic Policy

17.2 Assess efforts by the federal government to manage the domestic economy.

One of the government's greatest responsibilities involves regulating the domestic economy. After all, the domestic economy fundamentally determines the well-being of a citizenry. The ability of manufacturers to sell their goods at a profit, the ability of consumers to purchase them, and the willingness of intermediaries to facilitate the exchange critically depend on a healthy domestic economy.

Explore on MyPoliSciLab
Simulation: You Are a Federal Reserve Chair

Economists Monitor Different Aspects of the Domestic Economy

When gauging the health of the economy, economists tend to monitor three main indicators. First, they focus on unemployment trends, which reveal the percentage of people who would like to work but do not have a job. The unemployment rate typically has been 4 percent to 6 percent. In the early 1990s, though, it reached as high as 8 percent, and in both the early 1980s and late 2009, it reached double digits. By the summer of 2012, the U.S. unemployment rate had fallen as low as 8.1 percent, an indication that perhaps the economy was, if not rebounding, perhaps stabilizing.[14]

Second, economists also monitor inflationary trends, which concern how the costs of basic goods and services change over time. When inflation is high, costs increase at a rapid rate; when inflation is low, costs increase at a more moderate pace. The government tends to measure inflation through the consumer price index (CPI), which tracks the costs of food, clothing, medical services, and other essential items from year to year. For all goods and services, the annual CPI in November 2011 was 3.4 percent, which is somewhat higher than the annual average of 2.8 percent recorded between 1913 and 2007.[15]

Third, analysts monitor the overall growth of the economy. A prime indicator is the **gross domestic product (GDP)**, a statistic that measures all goods and services produced by individuals and businesses within the United States.[16] Currently, the U.S. GDP is between $14.5 and $15 trillion, which is nearly three times as large as the second highest country, China. Indeed, the U.S. GDP alone constitutes almost 20 percent of all spending worldwide. Economists, though, tend to focus on annual changes in GDP, which in recent U.S. history have ranged between 2 percent and 4 percent. In the past few years, however, growth has slowed significantly on average. As of the third quarter of 2012 the growth rate was 1.5 percent.

Economists Have Different Ideas About How to Improve the Economy

How might the government respond to fluctuations in the economy, as reflected in changes in unemployment, inflation, or GDP? Economists, like all social scientists, regularly disagree about the best course of action. (For a discussion of the efficacy of recent government interventions into the economy, see *Unresolved Debate: Did the 2009 Economic Stimulus Package Work?*) The first option is to do nothing—or at

Unresolved Debate

Did the 2009 Economic Stimulus Package Work?

Less than one month after entering office in January 2009, President Barack Obama successfully lobbied Congress to pass a large economic stimulus package. The bill, known as the American Recovery and Reinvestment Act (ARRA), cost nearly $800 billion dollars. The ARRA featured a variety of programs aimed at immediately creating jobs and encouraging spending in both the public and private sectors. By the end of 2011, the economy appeared to be slowly improving, with GDP expanding and unemployment gradually in decline. In the wake of this apparent turnaround, President Obama and his economy team proclaimed the ARRA to have been a success. At a press conference, the president told Americans that he was "absolutely convinced, and the vast majority of economists are convinced, that the steps we took in the Recovery Act saved millions of people their jobs or created a whole bunch of jobs."[a] In fact, however, economists remain divided over the Recovery Act's impact. Did the 2009 economic stimulus package work?

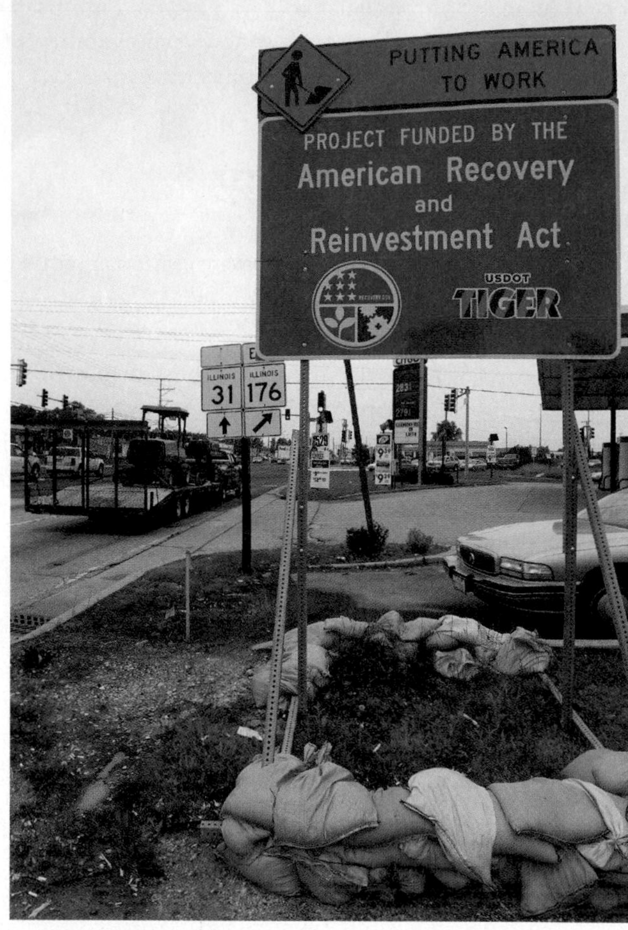

AN INFUSION OF GOVERNMENT SPENDING

The ARRA provided block grants to states, reduced taxes, and supported public works projects around the country, like these road repairs along Route 120 in Crystal Lake, Illinois.

YES

Although the ARRA may not have prompted state and local governments to spend more, there are still other ways of measuring its effect upon the economy. Economists Mark Zandi and Alan Blinder, for example, argue that government spending should not be taken into account when assessing the Recovery Act's success, because "legislative and administrative decisions do not respond predictably to economic conditions."[b] Instead, they consider three hypothetical situations: The federal government passed the Troubled Asset Relief Program (TARP) and other financial measures but not a stimulus bill, the government passed the ARRA stimulus but did not pass TARP or take other financial actions, or the government did not take any action to combat the recession. Zandi and Blinder compare these three hypotheticals to the reality (the government passed both TARP and the ARRA stimulus) and find that the stimulus did significantly affect the way the economy performed.

Unlike Taylor's empirical approach, which examines actual outcomes, Zandi and Blinder rely on a theoretical macroeconomic model that predicts how the economy as a whole will respond to certain events:

NO

According to research conducted by Stanford University economist John Taylor, the ARRA had "little if any direct impact" on the economy.[c] Taylor assesses two main aspects of the Recovery Act: tax transfers to individuals and families and aid to state and local governments. He finds that in both cases, stimulus dollars failed to have their intended effect of increasing spending by the parties in question. As a result, Taylor asserts that the economy would have performed more or less the same way it did with or without the ARRA and other federal stimulus packages.

Taylor uses econometric tools to analyze real-world empirical evidence in order to gauge the impact of stimulus spending on the behavior of those who benefited from it:

- The timing of the increase in disposable income individuals gained from ARRA tax breaks did not correspond with those individuals consuming more goods and services.
- The timing of the increase in state and local purchasing power gained from federal stimulus aid did not correspond with more purchasing by those governments.

- If the government had taken no action to combat the recession, GDP in 2010 would have been 11.5 percent lower, there would have been 8.5 million fewer jobs, and the economy would have experienced deflation.
- Separating out different government actions, the effects of the stimulus alone raised real GDP by 3.4 percent, lowered the unemployment rate by 1.5 percent, and added 2.7 million jobs to the U.S. economy.
- Although TARP and other financial-market policies played a big role in the recovery, the stimulus helped the government's larger effort to prevent a deepening economic crisis, successfully averting what could have become a second Great Depression.

- As a result, the stimulus did not achieve its primary purpose—to stimulate spending and jumpstart the economy.

CONTRIBUTING TO THE DEBATE

Economists continue to clash over the best way to assess the impact of government intervention on the economy. Critics of Taylor's research, for example, argue that he does not do a good enough job of accounting for all of the other variables that might affect government spending. On the opposite end of the spectrum, some analysts take issue with Zandi and Blinder's approach. These critics claim that the two economists use a theoretical model disconnected from reality, which allows them to set up their model however they want in order to achieve a specific preordained outcome. It may be years, though, before the debate is settled. As more data are collected, and as the economic recovery progresses (or not), debates about the efficacy of the ARRA will be clarified.

WHAT DO YOU THINK?

1. What are two methods for looking at the impact of the ARRA stimulus package on the domestic economy?
2. Suppose the stimulus were proven conclusively to have had no effect on the economy. What other reasons might account for the gradual economic turnaround in the years since?

[a]President Barack Obama, White House Press Conference, July 11, 2011, http://www.whitehouse.gov/the-press-office/2011/07/11/press-conference-president.
[b]Mark Zandi and Alan Blinder, "How the Great Recession was Brought to an End," Working paper, July 27, 2010, http://www.economy.com/mark-zandi/documents/End-of-Great-Recession.pdf.
[c]John B. Taylor, "An Empirical Analysis of the Revival of Fiscal Activism in the 2000s," *Journal of Economic Literature*, 49, 3 (2011): 686–702.

---

least very little. This is the governing philosophy of **laissez-faire economics**. According to this theory, the private marketplace experiences natural periods of expansion and decline, and the best thing for the government to do, by and large, is to stay out of the way. When the government tries to regulate the otherwise free exchange of goods and services between private parties, this theory suggests, it introduces fundamental distortions and inefficiencies. In the long run, the public benefits most by minimal government involvement in the economy.[17]

Most economists, however, admit that a vibrant economy requires at least some government intervention. The government, for instance, might alter the supply of money in the marketplace, which is the central objective of **monetary policy**. The nation's central bank system, called the **Federal Reserve**, retains the power to set interest rates, which affect the flow of money in the domestic economy. By increasing interest rates, the Federal Reserve can restrain economic growth and inflationary pressures. By decreasing interest rates, the Federal Reserve can stimulate economic activity, although at the risk of increasing inflation rates. The president has the power to appoint the chair of the Federal Reserve. For the most part, though, the Federal Reserve is kept independent from political pressures.

Finally, the government can directly intervene in the economy through taxing and spending, the central elements of **fiscal policy**. The government can attempt to

laissez-faire economics
a theory that discourages the government from becoming involved in the economy.

monetary policy
policy designed to improve the economy by controlling the supply of available money.

Federal Reserve
the federal agency that controls the supply of money in the domestic economy.

fiscal policy
policy designed to improve the economy through spending and taxation.

17.1
17.2
17.3
17.4
17.5
17.6

deficit
the amount of money a government spends in a year above and beyond what it brings in through taxation and other means.

public debt
the total amount of money that the federal government owes.

stimulate economic activity either by spending in the marketplace (as Obama did in 2009) or by decreasing taxes (as both Bush and Obama did during their presidencies). Conversely, in more prosperous times, when inflationary trends may need to be curbed, the government may opt to cut spending or increase taxes.

Historically, the Treasury Department and Congress have overseen fiscal policy, and the Federal Reserve has overseen monetary policy. Of late, though, the Federal Reserve has become involved in both ventures. In January 2012, a minor controversy erupted when the "Fed," as the Federal Reserve is sometimes called, published a policy memo advising Congress about how to fix the country's persistent housing crisis: namely, to become involved in fiscal policy issues. Orrin Hatch, a ranking Republican member of the Senate Finance Committee, wrote Federal Reserve Chair Ben Bernanke a letter taking the Fed to task for repeatedly overstepping its bounds. "The Fed often blurred the distinction between monetary policy and fiscal policy during the financial crisis," Hatch wrote, "and it is time to move back toward a clearer distinction between the two."[18] Some libertarian politicians would go a step further and abolish the Federal Reserve altogether. Ron Paul, a presidential candidate in the 2008 and 2012 Republican primaries, has argued that the government, through the Fed, has no authority to interfere in interest rates, which he believes should be determined by the free market.

When the government spends less than it recovers through taxes, it incurs a surplus. More commonly, though, the government spends more than it recovers through taxes. In so doing, it contributes to the annual **deficit**, which represents the total amount of money that the federal government had to borrow from U.S. citizens and foreign governments in order to meet its spending obligations. For most of the past century, the United States has run a deficit. After an economic boom in the 1990s, the country reached a surplus for the first time in decades. However, this surplus quickly disappeared in the wake of repeated tax cuts, a declining economy, foreign wars, and economic stimulus packages. At the end of 2011, the federal government was running a deficit of about $1.3 trillion.

Over time, of course, these deficits mount. The **public debt** refers to the total amount of money that the federal government owes. As of 2011, the public debt surpassed the GDP, meaning that the United States owed more money than then existed in the economy as a whole. The debt now stands at just over $15 trillion, which amounts

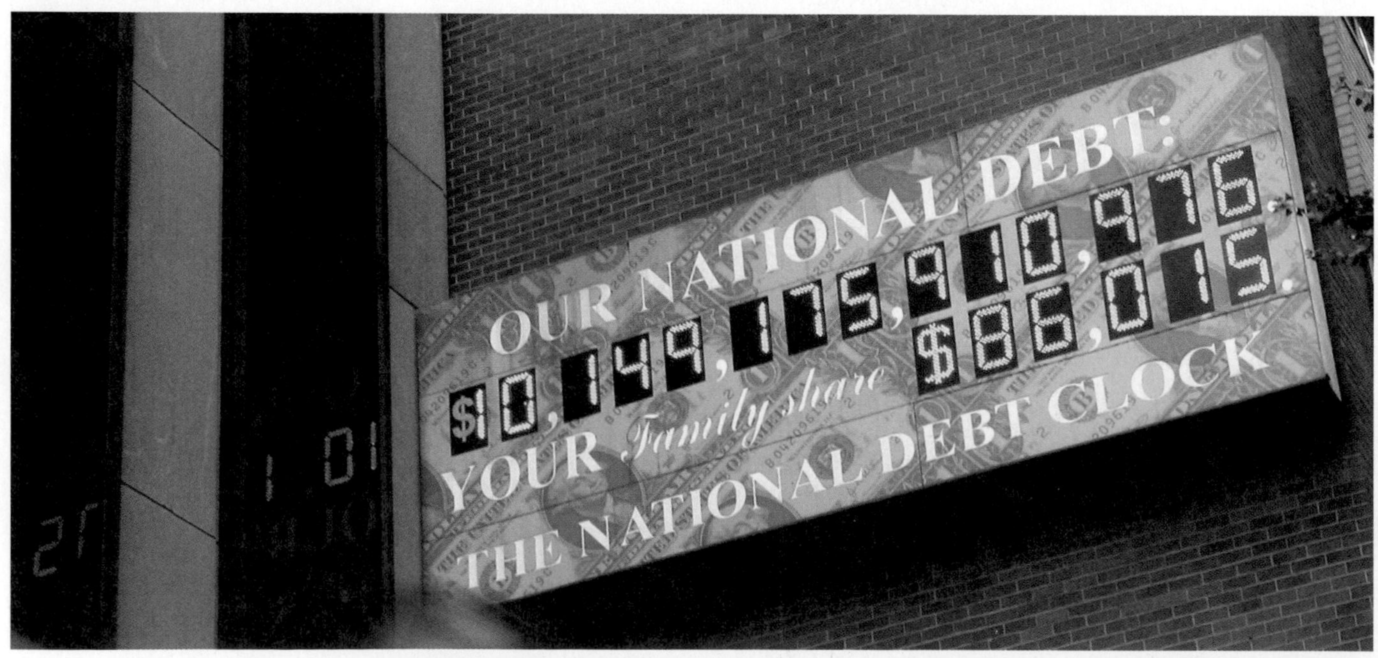

THE GROWTH OF THE PUBLIC DEBT

With government spending vastly exceeding revenues, "national debt clocks" have popped up around the country, with the intention of raising citizen awareness of the issue.

to approximately $50,000 per person living in the United States. Just to finance the interest on the debt, the federal government must pay hundreds of billions of dollars each year.[19] With more recent efforts to stimulate the economy, the debt has only increased in magnitude, a path Fed Chair Bernanke has repeatedly called "unsustainable."[20]

With the U.S. economy increasingly dependent on foreign sources of revenues, particularly from China, some scholars have raised concerns about the impact of the rising national debt on U.S. foreign policy. China holds more than $1 trillion in U.S. Treasury securities, making it the largest foreign investor in the United States. As long as the United States remains beholden to Chinese debtors, some worry the U.S. government lacks the necessary leverage to press for a variety of human rights reforms or to confront China on its efforts to artificially depress the value of its currency, which contributes to its widening trade gap with the United States.[21] Others, however, insist that such fears are ungrounded. Just as the United States needs China, so too does China need the United States. And, should it divest from the United States, China would suffer substantial economic losses.[22]

The U.S. debt is higher now than it has ever been, both as a total amount and as a percentage of the GDP. By international standards, however, the U.S. debt appears more moderate. Although some countries such as South Korea and Luxemburg have much lower debt levels, others such as Switzerland, Japan, Belgium, France, and Italy hold debt levels that, as a percentage of their GDP, are similar to or surpass that of the United States. Beginning in 2010, alarmingly high levels of debt in Italy (120 percent of GDP) and Greece (140 percent of GDP) led the European Union to pass several financial stability packages worth more than 1 trillion euros. In 2012, Standard and Poor's (S&P) downgraded the credit status of nine European nations, including Portugal, whose debits were officially deemed to have "junk" status. In addition, 14 other countries were said to have a "negative" outlook, meaning that S&P believes there is a chance their bond ratings will also be lowered in the coming year.[23] These developments have raised concerns about the soundness of the European Union's financial structure.

Economists have long debated the relative benefits of fiscal and monetary policy.[24] As a matter of course, though, the federal government does not have to choose between the two. It regularly implements both. In early 2008, economists worried about the onset of a **recession**, which exists when the GDP declines for two successive quarters. To encourage economic growth, the Federal Reserve decreased interest rates by 0.75 points. Shortly thereafter, Congress enacted an economic stimulus package that disbursed funds to individuals and families around the country in the hopes of jump-starting the economy.[25] In 2009, a newly elected President Obama enacted a massive stimulus package, the American Recovery and Reinvestment Act. Concurrently, the Federal Reserve kept interest rates at historic lows to combat the declining GDP. Whereas economists worried about a second recession in 2011, although the economy was relatively stagnant, economic growth never actually became negative.

Different people are affected by the economy in different ways. In the sections that follow, we examine a variety of social programs that are designed to address the specific challenges facing different populations within the United States.

recession
a period when the nation's GDP declines in two successive quarters.

Social Security

17.3 Trace the development of the largest federal social program, which assists the elderly.

Think what it must have been like for the elderly during the Great Depression. After working for decades and putting money aside for their eventual retirement, they watched as their savings vanished overnight. The collapse of the banking system drained the money they expected to live on during

17.1

17.2

17.3

17.4

17.5

17.6

Social Security Act
a 1935 law that established Social Security, an entitlement program providing retirees with a monthly income in order to reduce poverty among the elderly.

entitlements
benefits that all qualifying individuals have a legal right to obtain.

their golden years. Unlike younger people, the elderly could not readily start over again and recover what they had lost, and many spent their last years in poverty.

The **Social Security Act**, enacted in 1935, attempted to correct this state of affairs. The act established the framework for the Social Security Administration (SSA), charged with providing a reliable income stream for the elderly.[26] Social Security is perhaps best thought of as an antipoverty program for the elderly. Today, most individuals qualify for Social Security benefits either when they turn 67 or when they become disabled and cannot work.[27] The benefits come in the form of a monthly check, the size of which varies according to the amount of money that the individual paid into the Social Security fund during years of employment.

Funding for Social Security is different from that for other social programs that we will review later in the chapter. During the course of their working lives, employees pay a portion of their income into a fund, which the SSA maintains. These payments, however, are not like deposits in a bank. A worker's contributions do not sit in the fund until he or she wishes to withdraw them. Rather, most of the contributions made today are promptly paid out to today's beneficiaries. This "pay as you go" system means that funds flow into and out of the Social Security fund at a continual rate.

Social Security benefits are **entitlements**—benefits that all qualifying individuals have a legal right to obtain. Social Security beneficiaries include people as young as 62

THE BIRTH OF SOCIAL SECURITY

Several members of the House and Senate look on as President Franklin Roosevelt signs the Social Security Act in August 1935.

who have paid into the system (or, if they are deceased, their survivors). Thus, to receive Social Security benefits, one does not need to demonstrate financial need. Indeed, the size of the payments is unrelated to the amount of private savings an individual has. With this design, Social Security checks are an essential form of income for some people, and a welcome supplementary income for others.

☐ Social Security Benefits Have Steadily Expanded

Since its enactment in 1935, Social Security has grown from a modestly sized government program to a massive one. Originally, the Social Security Act excluded many types of workers, including farm workers, government employees, the self-employed, and individuals working for small businesses. Indeed, roughly one-half of the civilian labor force was excluded from the Social Security system. In 1950, farmers qualified for Social Security. Since then, virtually all industry restrictions have been lifted. In 2011, almost 55 million individuals received Social Security benefits in the United States.[28]

The size of the benefits has also increased. In part, this reflects the natural maturation of the program. During the program's early years, retired workers had paid into the system for relatively short periods of time. Upon retirement, therefore, these individuals qualified for relatively small payments. As their total contributions increased, however, workers stood to receive larger benefits when they retired. And workers who have contributed into the system over their entire working lives can expect to receive, on average, around $1,180 each month.[29]

The government itself also contributed to increases in Social Security benefits. The most important action occurred in 1975, when Congress revised the act to account for changes in the cost of living. Automatic increases in the size of benefits—COLAs, short for "cost of living adjustments"—were mandated. However, the COLAs eventually exceeded inflation, so that average benefits in 2010 were roughly 41 percent larger than they were in 1975, even after accounting for inflation.[30]

Obviously, total Social Security outlays have increased dramatically since 1935. In that year, Social Security expenditures hovered at around $1 million. They broke the $1 billion mark in 1950, and the $100 billion mark in 1980. In 2011, the Social Security system paid out around $727 billion in benefits.[31]

☐ The Future of Social Security Is Uncertain

Changing demographics in the United States have introduced new challenges to the Social Security system. Recall that the program critically depends on the ability of today's workers to fund the payments to today's elderly. The balance of workers to beneficiaries, however, has changed markedly over time. When the Social Security Act went into effect, roughly nine workers supported each elderly beneficiary. Today, just fewer than three workers support each beneficiary. By some projections, this number will drop to only two workers per beneficiary by 2036.[32]

Because workers dramatically outnumbered the elderly for so long, Social Security managed to build up substantial reserves, known as Old-Age, Survivors, and Disability Insurance (OASDI) trust funds. As Figure 17.1 shows, though, these reserves will begin to fall in the not-too-distant future. By some economists' projections, Social Security expenditures will exceed both receipts and available reserves by as soon as 2037. The effects of a large Baby Boom generation entering retirement, COLAs that mandate higher payments each year, and longer life expectancies are straining the Social Security system. In his second term in office, President George W. Bush tried unsuccessfully to get Congress to pass Social Security reform by appealing to young voters: "If you're 20 years old, in your mid-twenties, and you're beginning to work, I want you to think about a Social Security system that will be flat bust, bankrupt, unless the United States Congress has got the willingness to act now."[33] In 2011, President Obama also proposed that Congress make cuts to Social Security entitlements.[34] However, he rescinded his proposal after strong negative reactions from liberal organizations and lobbying groups for the elderly.[35]

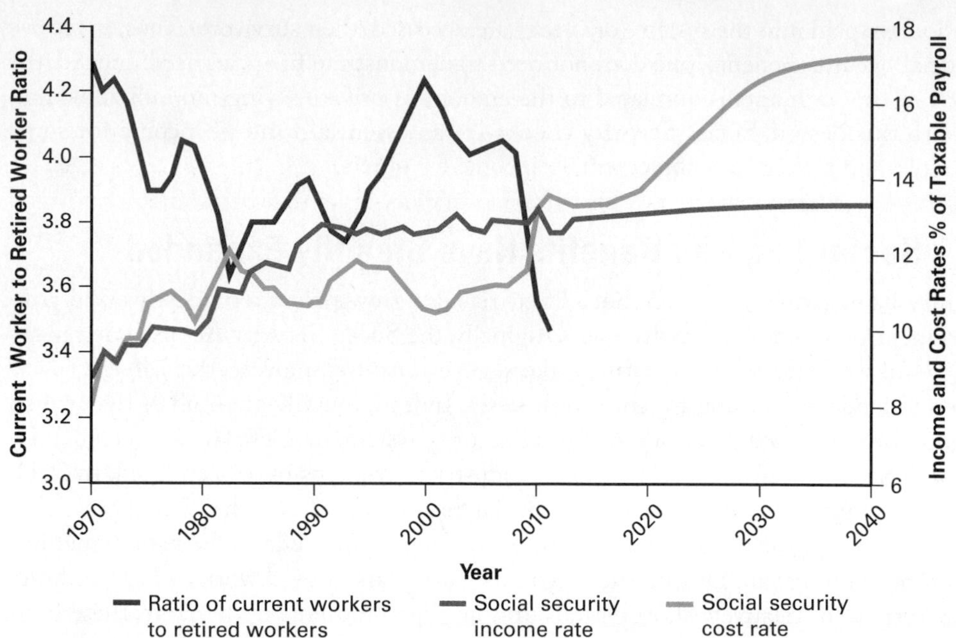

FIGURE 17.1 SOCIAL SECURITY TAXES ARE NOT EXPECTED TO COVER FUTURE OUTLAYS.

Based on the current policy and the best available information about the size of the contributing workforce and the number of retired individuals, Social Security reserves are expected to rapidly decline. Future cost and income rates refer to experts' predictions about the amount of money that Social Security programs will bring in as revenues and disburse as payments. Changes in demographics and the economic downturn have contributed to the recent decline in the ratio of current workers (who pay into Social Security) and retired workers (who draw from Social Security).

Source: Bloomberg.com, "Social Security's Finances, Past and Future: Echoes. Available at http://www.bloomberg.com/news/2011-06-03/social-security-s-finances-past-and-future-echoes.html.

What can the government do about these dwindling reserves? For starters, it can reduce the size of Social Security benefits doled out each year. To do this, it could raise the age at which individuals qualify for benefits—thereby reducing the number of beneficiaries. Alternatively, the government could decrease the benefits that it gives to each individual. Neither option, though, is especially attractive. Having paid into the Social Security system throughout their working lives, the elderly rightly expect to receive their due. And should they feel slighted, they will likely punish the offending politicians at the next election. So charged is the issue of Social Security reform, in fact, that it is referred to as the "third rail" of American politics: you touch it, you can expect to be toast!

Although cutting Social Security benefits is difficult, it is not impossible. In 1983, after several years of stagflation—periods of high unemployment and high inflation—the federal government decided to reduce Social Security outlays. Such periods take an especially heavy toll on Social Security because high inflation triggers larger COLAs than normal, and high unemployment means that fewer workers are paying into the Social Security system. To ensure the program's solvency, the government for the first time began to tax Social Security benefits, increased the eligible age for full benefits from 65 to 67, and added federal civil employees to the workers who could contribute to Social Security. However, these amendments will not solve the longer-term challenges facing the program.

Another way to protect Social Security would be to increase taxes. Historically, this has been the approach most commonly adopted. When the Social Security Act was enacted in 1935, the Social Security tax was set at 1 percent of the first $3,000 earned. Over the next 65 years, both the tax rate and the maximum taxable earning were increased 20 times. In 2011, the rate for individuals who were not self-employed was 6.2 percent of the first $106,800 earned.[36] Of course, political costs are associated with increasing taxes, and these explain why both political parties at the national level tout their records at cutting taxes, not raising them.

Finally, a number of politicians have recommended the adoption of private investment accounts. Rather than depositing funds into a general reserve account, which typically receives a low yield, workers under this scheme could invest a portion of their Social Security contributions into government-approved stocks and bonds. This reform represented the core innovation in President George W. Bush's 2005 effort to shore up Social Security. Under Bush's plan, workers could direct up to 5 percent of their Social Security taxes into private accounts. Ultimately, however, Bush's plan flopped. Worried about the risks of private investments, members of Congress proved unwilling to fundamentally restructure the largest and most popular domestic social program.

Earlier in this chapter, we suggested that a focusing event is often needed to propel government action. We now see that this event often needs to underscore a problem that the American public faces in the here and now. From the vantage point of most politicians, several decades—the time when Social Security reserves are expected to run out—is a virtual eternity. Consequently, and perhaps unfortunately, these politicians are likely to shift their attention to other, more immediate problems.

means-tested program
any program that targets the poor and for which eligibility is based on financial need.

Welfare

17.4 Analyze changes in welfare policy within the United States.

The federal government supports a wide range of programs designed to assist the poor. Collectively, these public assistance programs are often referred to as "welfare." Some of these programs involve direct cash transfers to the poor, others provide the equivalent of food vouchers, and others supply modest income subsidies. In one way or another, though, all attempt to alleviate the hardships experienced by the poor.

Who Are the Poor?

All of the programs described in this section are **means tested**—that is, they target those who demonstrate a lack of financial resources. To qualify for benefits, individuals must prove either that they are unemployed or that their income falls below a certain level. Means-tested programs are quite different from Social Security, which distributes benefits to all who have paid into the fund, no matter how well off they might be.

To ascertain eligibility for welfare programs, the federal government has developed a standard measure for identifying the poor: the poverty level. The poverty level varies according to a family's size: the larger the family, the higher the threshold. The precise level is calculated according to the cost of a family's basic needs. Specifically, it equals three times the cost of a minimally nutritious diet for a family of a given size. In 2011, the federal government calculated that a family of four would need to pay a minimum of $7,450 for food. For such a family, therefore, the pretax poverty threshold was set at $22,350.[37] This way of calculating poverty does not do a good job of accounting for unreported incomes, which often include earnings from tips or domestic work.[38]

Figure 17.2 shows the percentage of the U.S. population living in poverty since 1960. The number peaks early and then steadily declines. Indeed, poverty rates continued to drop until the early 1970s, when they leveled off at roughly 12 percent. As the U.S. population has increased in size, however, the number of people living in poverty has steadily increased since the early 1970s.

The poor do not represent a random sample of U.S. adults. Young people, nonwhite adults, and single parents are disproportionately represented among the poor. No less than 22 percent of those younger than age 18 live in poverty, as compared to 9 percent of adults older than age 65. More than one in four blacks and Hispanics are poor, as compared to roughly one in eight whites. Six percent of married couples live in poverty, as compared to 16 percent of male single parents and 32 percent of female single parents.[39]

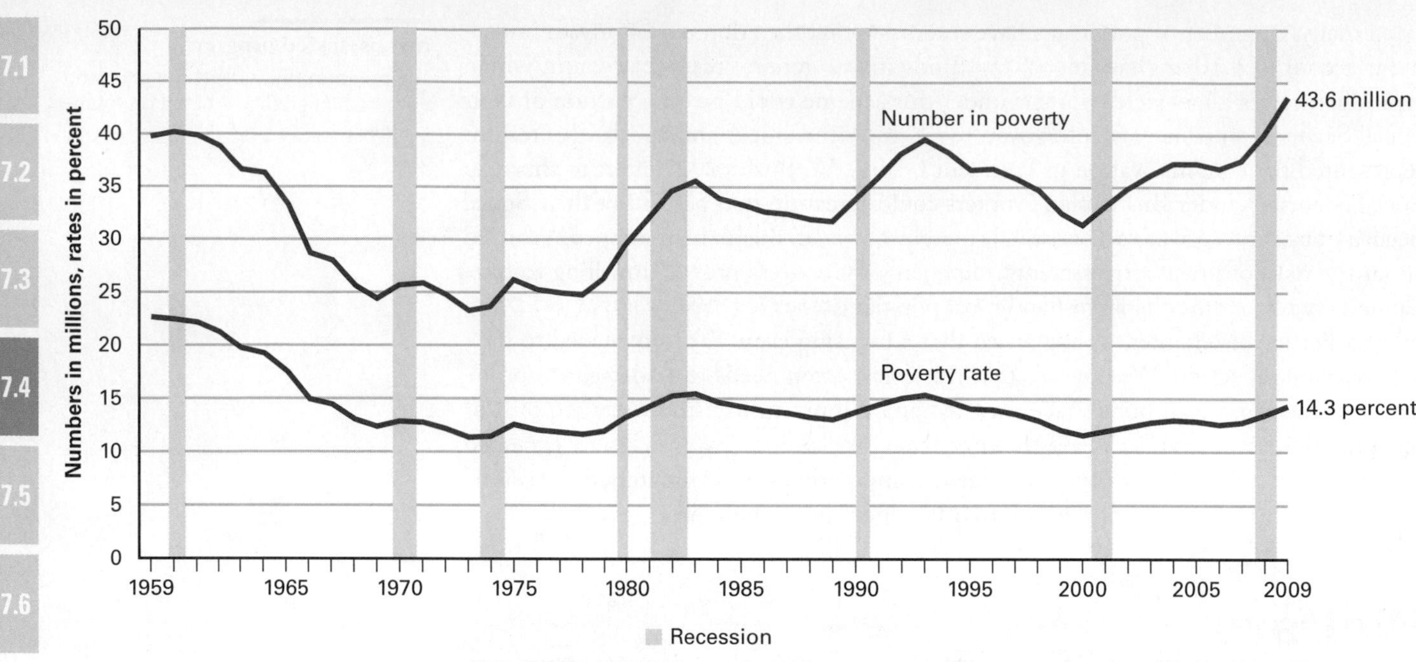

FIGURE 17.2 NUMBER AND PERCENTAGE OF U.S. POPULATION IN POVERTY.

Although the percentage of Americans living in poverty declined during the 1960s, it has remained steady ever since. Because of population increases, meanwhile, the number of individuals living in poverty since 1970 has increased by more than 10 million.

Note: The data points are placed at the midpoints of the respective years.

Source: U.S. Census Bureau, Current Population Survey, 1960–2010 Annual Social and Economic Supplements.

Aid to Families with Dependent Children (AFDC)
a federal program in effect from 1935 to 1996 that provided assistance to households with needy children.

Temporary Assistance for Needy Families (TANF)
a program replacing AFDC in 1996 that established new work requirements for welfare recipients and limits on the number of years an individual can receive assistance.

The Federal Government Supports a Variety of Welfare Programs

The federal government has devised a variety of ways to help the poor. Historically, the most significant effort was **Aid to Families with Dependent Children (AFDC)**. Enacted in 1935 as part of the Social Security Act, this program provided assistance to needy children whose mother or father was missing from the home, physically handicapped, deceased, or unemployed. In 1950, the program expanded to distribute benefits to the parents of children in need as well. Not surprisingly, this reform led to a marked rise in expenditures. By 1962, AFDC distributed upward of half a billion dollars in benefits nationwide. Expenditures rose steadily through the 1970s. The Reagan administration cut AFDC benefits slightly, but by the mid-1990s, the program distributed more than $16 billion to citizens living in poverty around the nation.[40]

Throughout its history, AFDC attracted considerable controversy. Critics charged that it discouraged parents from working and staying together.[41] In 1996, therefore, the federal government replaced AFDC with a new program entitled **Temporary Assistance for Needy Families (TANF)**. This program imposed many more restrictions on benefits than did its predecessor. In particular, TANF established new work requirements and firm limits on the time that any individual could receive welfare benefits. As a consequence, the number of citizens receiving this form of welfare benefit has dropped by more than 60 percent.[42]

With the downturn of the U.S. economy, the federal government has substantially increased its assistance to the unemployed. Since 2008, Congress has voted nine times to extend unemployment benefits. These extensions, however, are beginning to put Democrats and Republicans at odds. Democrats tend to emphasize the need to help out those most in need. As Sander Levin, the Democratic chair of the House Ways and Means Committee, put it, "We are a community of people. When people lose their jobs and can't find them, we don't simply stand idly by."[43] Republicans, by contrast, cite the growing federal deficit as their biggest concern. Dave Camp, the ranking Republican on the House Ways and Means Committee, explained, "This issue isn't should we extend benefits to the unemployed, the issue is should they be paid for."[44] Given the continuing economic difficulties, these partisan disputes are likely to persist.

Other programs, such as Supplemental Security Income (SSI), focus on those who are having an especially difficult time. The program's origins lay in a section of the 1935 Social Security Act that provided for cash payments to the poor, the elderly, and the blind. In 1950, however, the program was expanded to include individuals who suffered from severe and permanent disabilities. The SSA runs the program, but aid comes from general tax revenues rather than from Social Security contributions. To qualify for SSI support, individuals must demonstrate not only that they are poor, but also that they have few possessions. To qualify in 2011, a single individual or child usually could not own in excess of $2,000 worth of goods, and married couples could not own more than $3,000.[45] SSI is directed toward reaching the destitute. In 2010, SSI disbursed a total of $47 billion in aid.[46]

Other federal programs assist the poor in obtaining specific necessities. The federal government supports a variety of food programs for the needy, including a nutritional program for women, infants, and children (WIC) and a school breakfast and lunch program. The largest, though, is the Supplemental Nutrition Assistance Program (SNAP), formerly the Food Stamp Program. After operating briefly in the late 1930s and early 1940s, the program became a permanent component of the welfare landscape in 1964. Administered by the Department of Agriculture, it provides the poor with coupons that can be redeemed at local grocery stores to purchase approved food items. The income restrictions for SNAP are not quite as strict as those for AFDC, TANF, or SSI. Consequently, the program benefits more U.S. residents. Over the past 40 years, the program has grown dramatically. In 1969, 3 million individuals received food stamps whose costs totaled $250 million. By 2011, more than 44 million people received them at a total cost of more than $70 billion.[47]

Other programs are designed expressly to support the working poor. The Earned Income Tax Credit (EITC), created in 1974, subsidizes the wages of low-income individuals. Specifically, it reduces the amount of income taxes they must pay; for some individuals, the EITC results in a government refund. Throughout its history, the EITC has received bipartisan support, largely because it encourages work, unlike

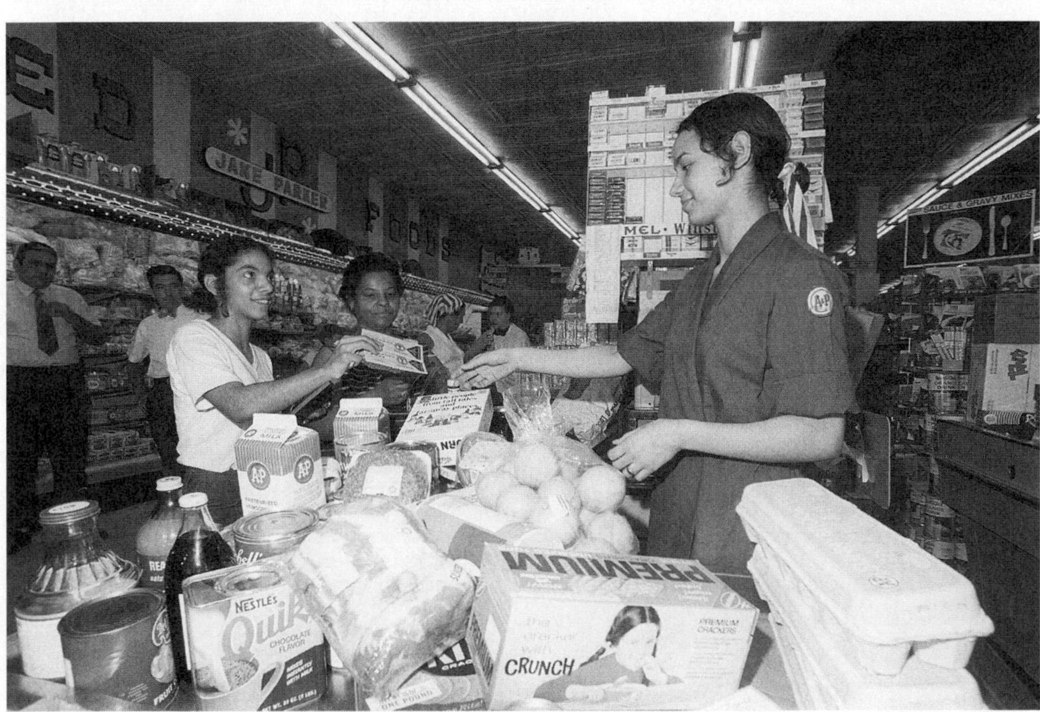

SNAP IS THE LARGEST FEDERAL FOOD PROGRM FOR THE NEEDY

In 1970, when this photo was taken, the federal government launched the federal food stamp program. This customer used the stamps to purchase a supply of groceries.

17.1

17.2

17.3

17.4

17.5

17.6

other welfare programs (notably AFDC). EITC eligibility requirements have both an income ceiling and a floor. Although the ceiling is as much as twice the poverty threshold for a household, the floor requires that families have a nonzero income. Consequentially, individuals who are unemployed for the entirety of a year cannot receive EITC benefits. Estimates suggest that more than 27 million individuals will claim EITC benefits totaling $54 billion in 2012.[48]

U.S. Welfare Programs Are Small by International Standards

By European standards, the U.S. welfare system is quite young. Whereas most U.S. welfare programs were created in the 1930s and 1960s, many European programs trace back to the nineteenth century. Germany pioneered early welfare efforts, enacting laws in the 1880s to aid poor people who could not work because of industrial accidents, illness, or old age. Other countries soon followed. These programs mainly resulted from the dramatic socioeconomic changes going on in Europe at the time. The emergence of factories, the rise of the working classes, and massive migration from rural areas into cities brought new social problems to the fore and exacerbated the hard conditions facing workers. Welfare assistance served as a way of quelling discontent among the working classes, who many feared might rise up against their governments. By the eve of World War I in 1914, Austria, Belgium, Britain, Denmark, Finland, France, Germany, Italy, the Netherlands, Norway, Sweden, and Switzerland all had some form of welfare in place. These programs expanded greatly in the years between the world wars, and then again after World War II.[49]

The American welfare system is also smaller than those found in other countries. The amount of money the U.S. government devotes to social programs lags far behind the sums spent in Western Europe, Australia, and Canada. According to the most recent analysis on the topic, the United States ranked last out of 10 Western democracies in public welfare expenditures, spending little more than half of the average expenditure of the other Western democracies.[50] In 2010, the United States contributed 15 percent of its national income to government welfare programs.[51] According to two Harvard University economists, as a percentage of its national income, France spends almost double what the United States spends on social programs, and Nordic countries spend even more.[52]

Scholars continue to debate the causes of the differences between U.S. and European welfare systems. Some have argued that American political culture, which prizes individualism and personal responsibility, is less amenable to social welfare programs than European cultures, which stress collective values. Others contend that the American system of checks and balances makes it harder to enact major social legislation. Both of these explanations, however, have obvious limitations. Programs such as Social Security, which provides government support for all older Americans, remain wildly popular despite the individualistic culture of the United States. And sweeping antipoverty measures such as Lyndon Johnson's Great Society initiative managed to overcome both cultural and institutional hurdles.[53]

Education

17.5 Outline the federal government's expanding involvement in education.

The U.S. Constitution does not discuss the education of children. The obligation to educate, therefore, fell upon state and local governments. Since the nation's founding, public schools in this country have been locally controlled. As public education took hold in the nineteenth century, school boards contended with a loosely knit assembly of schools whose principals and teachers retained considerable freedom to do as they pleased. As the education historian David Tyack notes, public education constituted "more a miscellaneous collection of village schools than a coherent system."[54] Metaphorically, public schools around the nation looked less like peach trees in an orchard and more like brightly colored and misshapen stones in a mosaic.

During the nineteenth century, the federal government granted public lands to states for educational use, but it had little say over what happened within the newly constructed schoolhouses. The Office of Education, established in 1870, collected descriptive statistics on public schools but otherwise rarely interfered. More than half a century later, though, the federal government would burst onto the education scene.

The needed focusing event occurred on October 4, 1957, when the Soviet Union stunned the world with its successful launch of *Sputnik I*, the first satellite to circle the globe. The feat left many Americans deeply concerned about their ability to compete with the communist regime. Within a few months, President Dwight Eisenhower responded by outlining education reforms designed to improve U.S. schools. "As never before," he warned, "the security and continued well-being of the United States depend on extension of scientific knowledge."[55] Concerns about national security spurred the federal government's entry into the business of education.

On September 2, 1958, Eisenhower signed into law the National Defense Education Act. The act, the president declared, would "do much to strengthen our American system of education so that it can meet the broad and increasing demands imposed upon it by considerations of basic national security."[56] Most of the aid went to science, math, and foreign language training, although smaller amounts went to school construction and low-interest loans. Even though the act did not change the curriculum or method of instruction of any public school, it opened the door for increased federal involvement in public education.

Elementary and Secondary Education Act (ESEA)
a federal law passed in 1965 designed to reduce educational inequities by directly aiding school districts with large numbers of poor citizens.

unfunded mandate
a law requiring certain actions without appropriating the necessary funds to carry them out.

The Federal Government Seeks to Equalize Education Funding

In principle, states and municipalities are supposed to provide a basic education to all children. For much of U.S. history, however, they did not. Boys had greater opportunities than girls to join sports teams. The amount of money spent on schools varied dramatically across school districts and states. And the educational options granted to white citizens were usually superior to those of blacks, Hispanics, and other ethnic minorities. Testifying before a Senate subcommittee in 1963, Commissioner of Education Frances Koppel cited a troubling statistic: Whereas nearly 75 percent of the young white population had completed high school, only 40 percent of nonwhites had done so. Such inequalities in education, moreover, perpetuated inequalities in the workplace. For example, although blacks then comprised 11 percent of the total population, they made up only 3.5 percent of all professional workers.[57]

During the 1960s and 1970s, the federal government sought to redress such inequalities. Most importantly, in 1965 it enacted the **Elementary and Secondary Education Act (ESEA)**, which provided direct aid to local school districts with large concentrations of poor residents. The original law and its subsequent amendments funneled additional assistance to Native Americans and to students whose primary language was not English.

In the 1970s, the federal government turned its attention to the educational needs of the physically handicapped. In 1975, Congress enacted what is now called the Individuals with Disabilities Education Act (IDEA). The act proclaimed that all citizens are entitled to a "free appropriate public education." It then mandated public schools to make the accommodations needed to ensure that students with disabilities received this. As a consequence, public schools needed to change their buildings, alter their curricula, and introduce classes that would suit the needs of disabled students. However, the federal government covers just a fraction of these costs. As a consequence, the IDEA is often referred to as an **unfunded mandate**.

THE VANGUARD OF INTEGRATION

Pictured are eight of the nine African American students who helped integrate Central High School in Little Rock, Arkansas, in 1957.

Educational inequities persist. For example, in 2009 the federal government found that the high school dropout rate for whites was around 5 percent; for blacks, it was closer to 9.5 percent. For Hispanics, the dropout rate was a whopping 17.6 percent.[58] In addition, disparities remain between the genders as well. Among college graduates who obtained bachelor's degrees in physics, computer science, and engineering in 2010, men outnumbered women 4 to 1.[59]

Other historical inequalities, meanwhile, have actually flipped. Women today outnumber men at colleges and universities across the country. In 2009, women represented no less than 57 percent of the nation's college students.[60] Women also, on average, perform better and have higher graduation rates than their male counterparts. If current trends persist, by 2020 women will earn 156 bachelor of arts degrees to men's 100.[61] Educators say that the top male students are just as competent as the top female students, but that struggling males crowd the other end of the spectrum.[62]

□ The Federal Government Attempts to Impose Standards

In the early 1980s, concerns about the ability of U.S. citizens to compete with others around the globe again intensified. In *A Nation at Risk*, a report that was sufficiently influential to be considered a focusing event, a panel of education experts complained about the "rising tide of mediocrity" infecting U.S. schools. International comparisons of student achievement, which had been completed a decade earlier, revealed that "on 19 academic tests American students were never first or second and, in comparison with other industrialized nations, were last seven times."[63] At the turn of the millennium, lackluster performance remained an issue. In a test administered in 2006 to 15-year-olds in 31 countries, the United States ranked 21 in science, and 25 in mathematics. As Table 17.1 shows, when averaging across the two subjects, the United States ranked 24. Increasingly, it seemed, states and local districts could not be counted on to provide the level of excellence required to keep pace with students abroad.

The precise reasons why U.S. students fail to keep pace with their peers abroad remain something of a mystery. (See *How Do We Know? Why Are U.S. Students Falling*

TABLE 17.1 U.S. STUDENTS LAG BEHIND THEIR INTERNATIONAL COUNTERPARTS ON STANDARDIZED TESTS

Rank	Country	Average math and science scores on the program for International Student Assessment for 15-years-olds in OECD countries
1	Finland	552.85
2	Korea, Republic of	541.88
3	Canada	529.50
4	New Zealand	524.47
5	Netherlands	520.75
6	Australia	519.89
7	Japan	517.48
8	Switzerland	513.49
9	Belgium	510.54
10	Ireland	509.04
11	Germany	504.79
12	Sweden	504.33
13	Austria	502.17
14	Czech Republic	501.81
15	United Kingdom	501.77
16	Denmark	501.13
17	Poland	500.29
18	Iceland	493.59
19	France	492.82
20	Hungary	492.41
21	Norway	486.89
22	Luxembourg	485.23
23	Slovak Republic	482.30
24	**United States**	481.63
25	Spain	476.40
26	Portugal	470.92
27	Italy	468.54
29	Greece	464.10
30	Turkey	431.64
31	Mexico	408.60

Source: Digest of Education Statistics, 2009, Table 402, http://nces.ed.gov/programs/digest/d09/tables/dt09_402.asp.

Behind?) Some plausible reasons can be readily eliminated. For instance, a lack of public school funding is probably not the cause, as per-pupil expenditures in the United States are higher than in the vast majority of other industrialized nations, including those such as Japan and South Korea that regularly rank near the top on international tests.[64] And within the United States, some of the highest-performing students come from states such as Utah, which spend relatively little on their public schools. What, then, explains the gap? Some people emphasize the lack of discipline in U.S. public schools. Others fault poor teacher recruitment and training. For many, though, the primary culprit is the lack of strict standards to which students are held accountable.

The demand for standards and accountability came to a head in 2001, when Congress enacted the **No Child Left Behind Act (NCLB)**.[65] For the first time, the federal government assumed the responsibility of monitoring individual schools and doling out punishments and rewards on the basis of their performance. Specifically, NCLB requires states to establish a testing regime that evaluates student learning trends from

No Child Left Behind Act (NCLB)
a 2001 federal law that rewards public schools for meeting certain educational benchmarks and punishes schools that fail to do so.

How Do We Know?

Why Are U.S. Students Falling Behind?

The Question

On international tests that measure aptitude for critical and analytical thinking and substantive knowledge, U.S. students routinely perform poorly compared to students from other countries.[a] Why are U.S. students falling behind? How do we know?

Why It Matters

In an era of rising globalization, businesses face more options than ever before when determining where to locate their operations. Many of these decisions depend upon the availability of skilled labor. Recent studies showing that students from the United States lag behind their peers in other countries therefore portend serious danger.[b] Rather than rely upon the U.S. labor force, multinational corporations may find it more advantageous to move their operations abroad. To keep existing businesses and attract new ones, then, the United States must improve its education system. And the first step in doing so is to diagnose the reasons why U.S. students are not keeping pace with their European and Asian counterparts.

Investigating the Answer

A reasonable place to start an investigation of why American students do comparatively worse in school is in the allocation of resources to educational systems around the globe. Are U.S. students struggling simply because less is being spent on their behalf? The data suggest otherwise. At an annual average of over $14,000 per year, the United States spend much more per student on education than higher-ranking countries. For instance, Finland, Japan, and Korea spend roughly a third to two-fifths less than the United States.

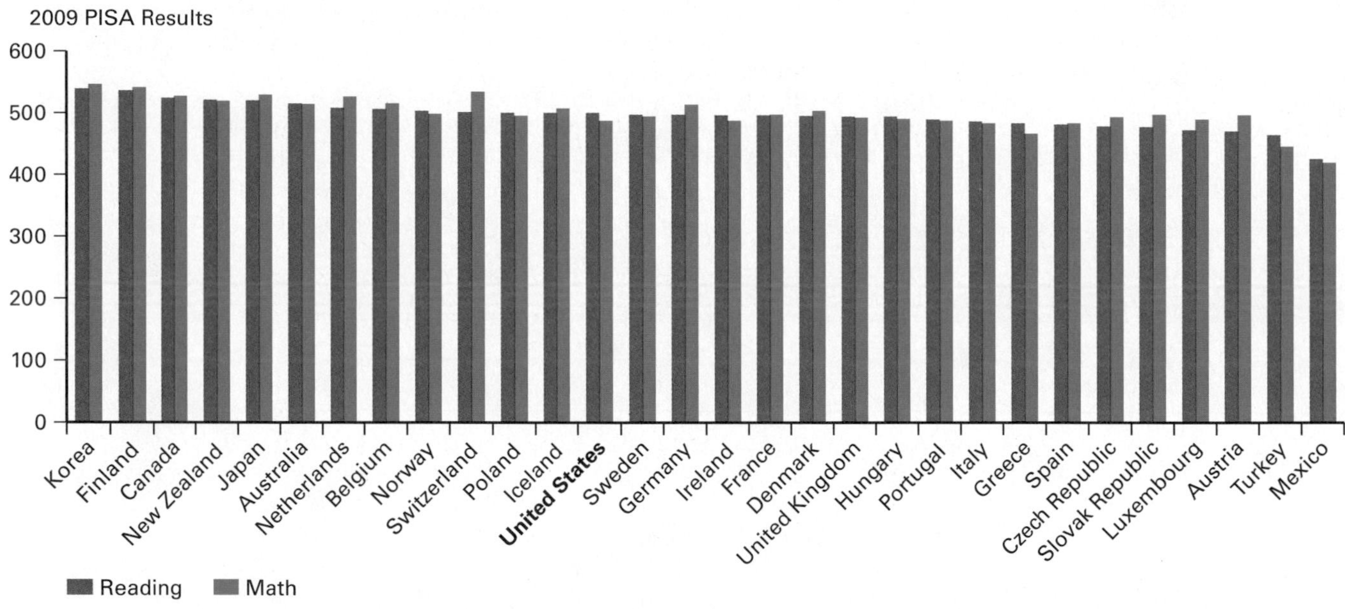

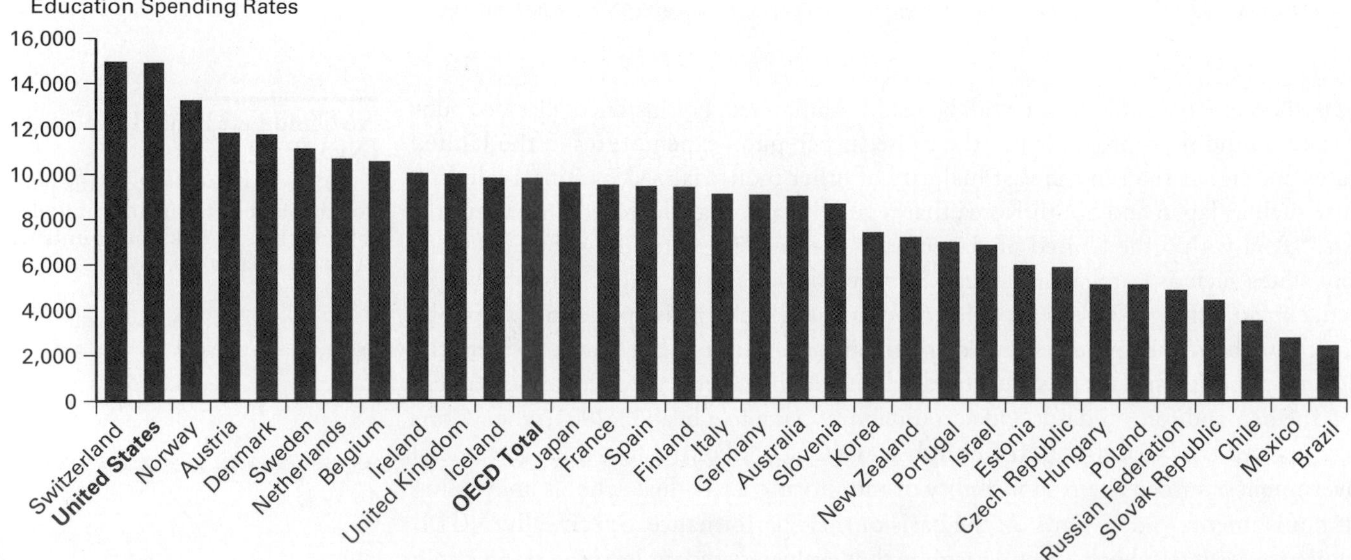

If not in the average per pupil expenditures, evidence of the importance of money in student outcomes may be found in its distribution. Researchers have found significant differences in education spending both between and within states. Whereas New York spends, on average, more than $18,000 per child, Utah spends just over $6,000. Here again, though, it is difficult to know what to make of these disparities, as Utah students regularly outperform New York students on standardized tests.[c]

The Program for International Student Assessment (PISA) is an international study that seeks to evaluate participating countries' educational systems by testing students' skills and knowledge. According to one evaluation of the tests administered by PISA, whites and Asians living in the United States scored between 5 and 30 points above the Organisation for Economic Co-operation and Development (OECD) average in all categories tested: reading, science, mathematics, and problem solving. Hispanics, by contrast, lagged behind the OECD average by between 40 and 65 points for each category, whereas the corresponding figures for blacks were between 65 and 90 points behind.[d]

Of course, money itself does not have any educational value. Rather, what matters is how money is spent on educational services. Pursuing this line, scholars have examined the policies of successful education systems and have noticed several shared priorities. For instance, although few countries require teachers to have obtained master's degrees, high-performing education systems generally make substantial investments in educators. Teachers are not only paid competitively to attract well-qualified candidates, they also participate in activities to improve their teaching. Highly ranked countries, such as Finland, South Korea, and Singapore all expend substantial proportions of their education resources on behalf of teachers.

Might investments in higher teacher salaries improve student performance here in the United States? Perhaps it may, particularly if higher salaries attract higher-quality teachers. In one recent inquiry, economists collected 20 years of data from 2.5 million American students to determine the impact of teacher quality on students in the United States. They concluded that, everything else being equal, replacing a weak teacher with an average one had the effect of increasing the lifetime earnings of a single classroom of students by more than a quarter million dollars.[e]

Whereas the success of an educational system would appear to depend a great deal on the quality of teachers working within it, scholars note that we do in fact have schools that employ well-trained teachers who are paid well for their services. The problem, then, may be in how these teachers are distributed across schools. Scholars note that in districts across the nation, the least-qualified teachers are regularly assigned to students with the greatest challenges, whereas the best teachers are often assigned to students who already are performing quite well.[f] As a consequence, there is a basic mismatch between teacher quality and student needs.

Nearly all of these studies, it bears emphasizing, rely upon observational data—that is, data taken from existing educational systems in the real world. These investigations study the effects of individual factors on student performance while holding other observable characteristics of schools, students, and neighborhoods constant by using advanced statistical tools. It is always possible, however, that an unobserved factor (such as parental involvement) affects both the explanatory factor (in this case, money or teachers) and outcome (test scores). In order to more definitively establish a genuine causal relationship, then, scholars typically prefer to conduct randomized field trials at the local level. Although they are almost never conducted on a scale that permits international comparison, they are designed in ways that allow scholars to better assess the relative influence of different contributors to education outcomes.

The Bottom Line

The amount of money spent on students and teachers, of course, does not exhaust the possible explanations for U.S. students' poor performance on international tests. Cultural and family norms, high-stakes accountability systems, the federal nature of the U.S. educational system, and plenty of other factors may also play a role. Still, scholars have assembled some evidence that at least suggests the underlying importance of financial and human resources in student outcomes. Moving forward, scholars would do well to employ studies that permit even more careful assessments of the causal relationships between money and teachers and a richer variety of student outcomes, such as college attendance rates, incarceration rates, and long-term earnings.

Thinking Critically

- Based on the findings about money and teachers, how might the federal government help U.S. students compete in an increasingly globalized economy?
- How can we explain the poor results of U.S. students on international tests when other aspects of national influence and power (military, economic, and social) suggest America remains strong?

---

[a] *PISA 2009 Results: What Students Know and Can Do—Student Performance in Reading, Mathematics and Science (Volume I)* (Organisation for Economic Co-operation and Development [OECD], 2010).

[b] *Digest of Education Statistics*, 2009, Table 402, http://nces.ed.gov/programs/digest/d09/tables/dt09_402.asp.

[c] The most recent state spending comparisons can be found at http://www2.census.gov/govs/school/09f33pub.pdf.

[d] Elizabeth Stage, "Why Do We Need These Assessments?" *The Natural Selection*, pp. 11–13 (Biological Sciences Curriculum Study, Winter 2005).

[e] Raj Chetty, John Friedman, and Jonah Rockoff, "The Long-Term Impacts of Teachers: Teacher Value-Added and Student Outcomes in Adulthood," National Bureau of Economic Research Working Paper No. 17699, December 2011, http://obs.rc.fas.harvard.edu/chetty/value_added.pdf.

[f] Linda Darling-Hammond, *The Flat World and Education: How America's Commitment to Equity Will Determine Our Future* (New York: Teachers College Press, 2010).

THE FEDERAL GOVERNMENT GETS INTO THE EDUCATION BUSINESS

Student journalist Gopa Praturi, age 10, interviews U.S. Secretary of Education Arne Duncan on the first day of classes at Wakefield High School in Arlington, Virginia, September 8, 2009. In your view, how much influence should the federal Department of Education have over public schools?

year to year. Furthermore, states must identify the percentage of students who perform at a certain level each year. Schools that fail to meet designated benchmarks are deemed "in need of improvement." If a public school fails to attain testing standards for two years, its attendees may transfer to higher-performing schools within their district. After three years, students qualify for supplemental tutoring services. Schools that fail for longer periods of time face harsher sanctions still, including loss of funding or in some cases even closure.

No Child Left Behind has yet to produce dramatic improvements in the educational performance of U.S. students. According to some research, math scores of U.S. fourth graders have increased, but reading scores have remained stagnant.[66] Nonetheless, NCLB has had a dramatic effect on the U.S. education system. Two consequences are especially noteworthy. First, the federal government has become an important agenda setter in public education. Rather than merely providing support services and ensuring a roughly even playing field, the federal government now plays an important role in determining the curricula of schools around the nation. Second, NCLB has raised the stakes of standardized testing dramatically. Never before has so much ridden on children's performance on state-mandated standardized tests.

In 2011, claiming that legislators were dragging their feet in efforts to revise No Child Left Behind, President Obama unilaterally decided to relax some of the strict NCLB standards and empowered states to come up with their own standards for measuring schools.[67] At the same time, Obama also delegated broad authority to his secretary of education, Arne Duncan, to determine whether or not states were implementing sufficiently tough standards to warrant federal funding. In this way, the federal government's authority over education policy continues to grow.

charter schools
public schools, administered by chartering boards, that are exempt from many rules and regulations applicable to traditional public schools.

vouchers
tuition subsidies that reduce the costs of sending children to private schools.

□ Reformers Challenge the "Public School Monopoly"

During the past two decades, reformers have issued a series of challenges against public schools. According to these reformers, public schools fail to perform well because they are not subject to competition. For the most part, government-run schools can count on a steady supply of students, even when these schools perform poorly. As a result, public schools lack the competitive incentive to improve that drives most industries in the private marketplace. These reformers have proposed two policy innovations to increase the schooling options available to parents, especially those in urban settings. The first concerns **charter schools**, which are public schools that are exempted from many rules and regulations faced by traditional public schools. For instance, when hiring teachers and choosing their curriculum, charter schools tend to have greater freedom than do traditional public schools. Charter schools are directly responsible to a chartering board, which oversees their operations. Although their character varies, most charter schools focus on a particular population of students (such as those with special needs) or offer a distinctive curriculum (such as one that emphasizes science).

In 1991, the first charter school opened in Minnesota. Since then, more than 40 states have enacted charter school legislation. The highest concentration of such schools is in Washington, D.C., where almost 20 percent of children attend a charter school. The devastation wrought by Hurricane Katrina in southern states along the Gulf of Mexico created new opportunities to replace many of the affected region's traditional public schools with charter schools. Since 2005, roughly half of the schools reopening in New Orleans have been charter schools.[68] As Figure 17.3 shows, more than 5,000 charter schools now serve upward of 1.5 million students around the country.[69]

The second innovation is school **vouchers**, which are tuition subsidies that reduce the costs of sending a child to a private school. The first voucher experiment in the United States began in 1990 in Milwaukee, which offered tuition subsidies of (initially) up to $2,500 to low-income families. For the first eight years, the program could legally serve no more than 1.5 percent of the city's public school population

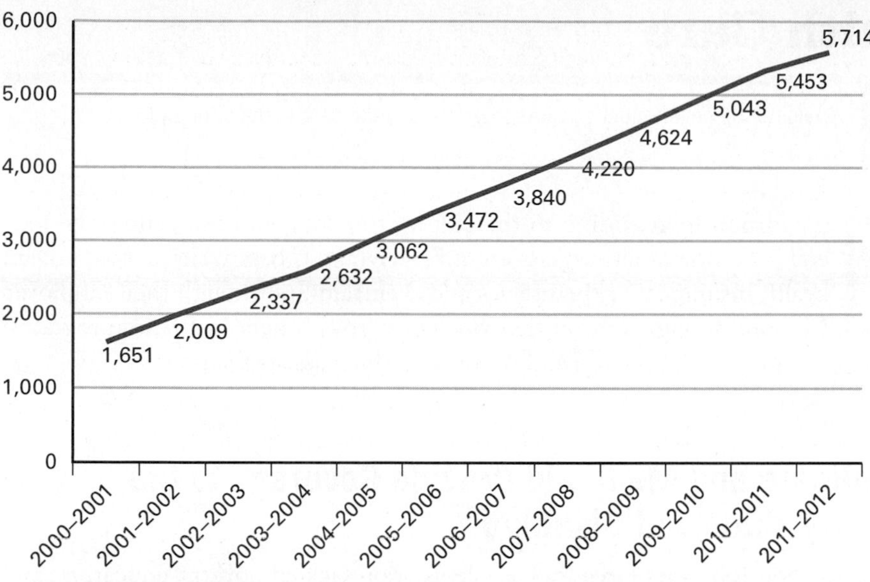

FIGURE 17.3 THOUSANDS OF CHARTER SCHOOLS OPERATE AROUND THE NATION.

Since the early 1990s, the number of charter schools has steadily risen.

Source: Reprinted with the permission of The Center for Education Reform, www.edreform.com.

(approximately 1,700 students), and only secular schools were allowed to participate. In 1996, the state of Wisconsin permitted up to 15 percent of the public school population to participate in the program, expanded the menu of private schooling options to include religious institutions, and increased the monetary value of the vouchers.

Other publicly funded voucher programs now operate in Ohio, Florida, and Washington D.C.; Vermont and Maine have voucher-like programs that assist children in rural districts to attend either a secular private school or a public school in another district. Currently, thousands of non-special education students make use of voucher programs, and tens of thousands more receive scholarships, roughly equivalent to vouchers, through tax credit programs. In addition, thousands of students have enrolled in privately funded voucher programs. Such efforts include a national program operated by the Children's Scholarship Fund, as well as local initiatives in several cities.

Although controversial within the United States, vouchers have attracted widespread support in other nations. In 1980, Chile enacted the equivalent of a national voucher program. Private schools in Chile are fully subsidized, and public schools face significantly fewer regulations than their U.S. counterparts. As a result, almost 40 percent of students in Chile attend private schools, as compared to just 10 percent in the United States. Whether Chilean students have benefited from these new educational opportunities, however, remains a subject of continued academic debate. Some scholars have found that the private school students outperform their public school peers, whereas others argue that the differences are negligible.[70]

Although they are all prominent education reforms, NCLB, vouchers, and charters have important differences. NCLB increases the government's involvement in schools. Because of NCLB, schools must regularly test children, report their results, and then be graded accordingly. Moreover, a central premise of NCLB is that principals and teachers in failing schools will change their behavior because of the law's direct intervention in their schools. Vouchers and charters, on the other hand, are intended to reduce the role of the government in the administration of schools. In both instances, participating students attend schools with considerably less oversight than that imposed on traditional public schools.

Health Care

17.6 Evaluate the government's efforts to provide health care to the poor and aged.

Medicare
a federally funded entitlement program that offers health insurance to the elderly.

Medicaid
a means-tested program, funded by federal and state governments, that extends health insurance to the poor and disabled.

In addition to attending to the elderly, the poor, and the young, the federal government also assists the infirm. Many U.S. citizens receive private health insurance for themselves and their families through their employer. Millions, though, rely on the two largest government insurance programs: Medicare, which assists the elderly; and Medicaid, which assists the poor.

Medicare and Medicaid Provide Coverage to the Elderly, Poor, and Disabled

Although Lyndon Johnson's Great Society legislation tackled poverty, education, and discrimination, its most sweeping achievements were reserved for the infirm. Through two programs enacted in 1965, Johnson put the government firmly into the health care business. **Medicare** provided government health insurance to the elderly, and **Medicaid** did so for the poor and disabled.[71]

When originally enacted, Medicare covered physicians' fees and the costs of compulsory hospitalization for citizens older than age 65. Over time, though, the program has expanded dramatically. Today, it allows the elderly to secure a wide range of services, including inpatient hospital care, certain kinds of home health care, hospice assistance, and outpatient hospital care. In 2003, the government added prescription drug benefits to Medicare. These benefits constitute the single largest expansion of Medicare in decades.

By any calculation, Medicare is a massive government program. In 2010, Medicare assisted 47.5 million citizens at a total cost of $516 billion—almost as much as all Social Security outlays, and far more than any other federal education or welfare program.[72] Medicare is financed through a variety of means. As with Social Security, workers must pay a Medicare-specific tax. Additionally, for those receiving such medical services as x-rays, laboratory and diagnostic tests, and influenza and pneumonia vaccinations, the federal government deducts a portion of their Social Security payments and then covers the remaining costs with general revenues.

In many ways, though, Medicaid is even bigger than Medicare. In 2010, Medicaid provided health insurance to 48.6 million low-income and disabled citizens. It also assumed responsibility for providing a larger proportion of health care services. For instance, Medicaid now covers one-third of the nation's childbirths, nearly 40 percent of long-term care expenses, and more services for AIDS patients than any other provider in the country.[73]

Medicaid expenditures, however, are quite a bit lower than those of Medicare. In 2009, Medicaid cost federal and state governments a total of $277 billion, just over half that of Medicare.[74] Two primary reasons explain why Medicaid today is less expensive than Medicare, even though it provides more services to more people. First, Medicaid does not offer as generous a prescription drug benefit program. Indeed, before Medicare's 2003 drug benefit enhancement, the costs of the two programs tracked one another quite closely. Second, the costs of caring for the elderly have steadily increased over time. Today, the elderly are living eight years longer, on average, than they did when Medicare began. The elderly, moreover, typically require more expensive medical procedures than other citizens. And Medicare is picking up most of these extra costs.

Certain populations—such as the disabled and poor seniors—qualify for both Medicare and Medicaid. And because the two programs cover different kinds of medical services, these individuals draw benefits from both. In important respects, though, the two programs operate very differently. Whereas Medicare is an entitlement

Is Health Care a Public Good?

Explore on MyPoliSciLab

A public good is a material item or service provided by the government to all members of society without competition or exclusion. Before Obama's presidency, most Americans believed the government should guarantee healthcare coverage to all citizens, but after 2009, the debate on healthcare reform divided public opinion. After the signing of The Patient Protection and Affordable Care Act (PPACA), Americans remained dissatisfied with the cost of healthcare and the number of of people who disagree with government provided healthcare increased.

Should the Government Provide Americans with Healthcare Coverage?

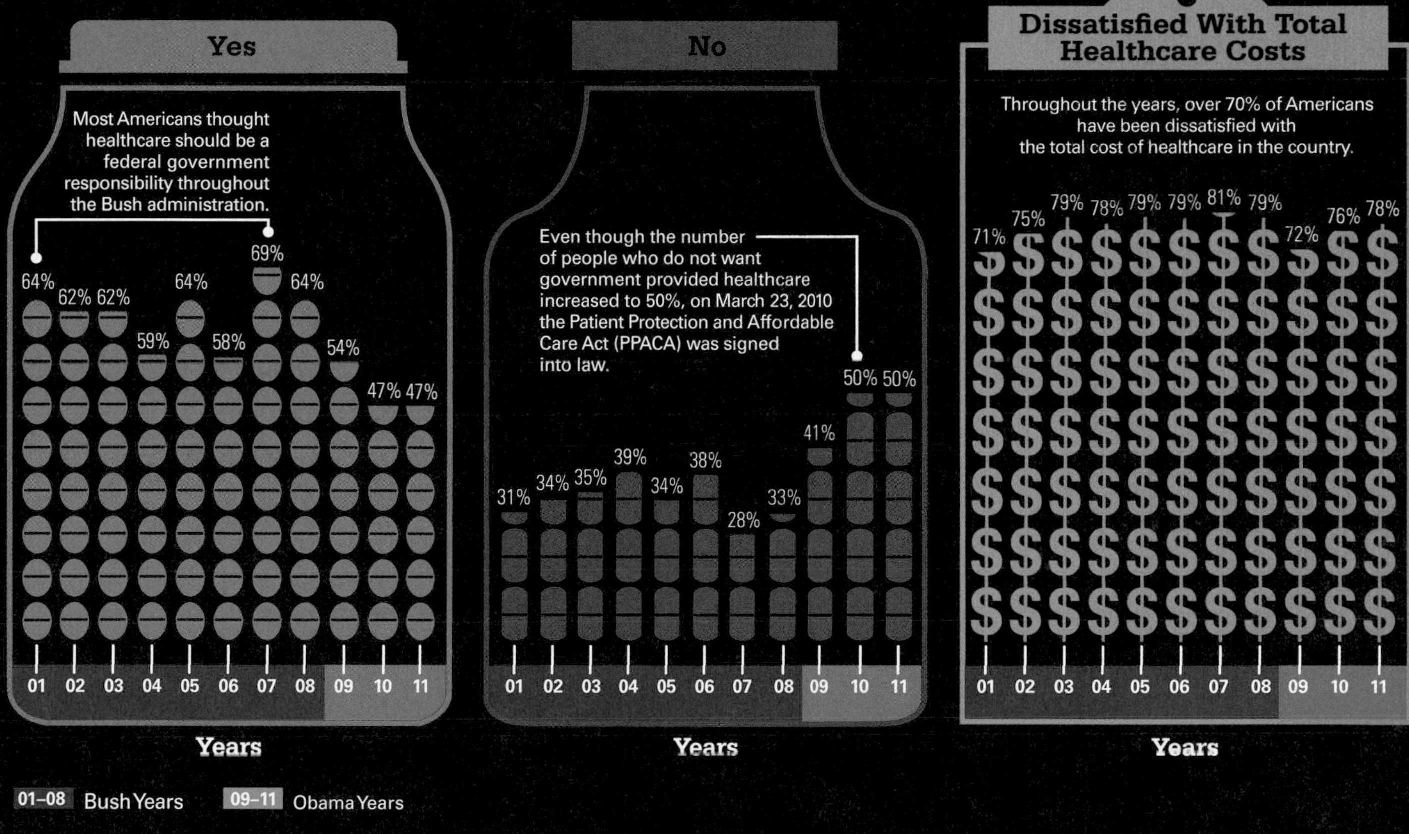

SOURCE: Data from Gallup

Investigate Further

Concept Do Americans think health care is a public good? During Bush's presidency, most Americans wanted government provided healthcare. However, in recent years, support has declined and more people believe private insurers should provide healthcare.

Connection Is the public unhappy with their healthcare costs? Yes, most Americans are dissatisfied with healthcare costs. Concern about healthcare is driven more by the perception that healthcare costs are too high, than by personal dissatisfaction. People are upset with healthcare because of broad circumstances, rather than individual circumstances.

Cause Why did public support for guaranteed government healthcare decline? After Obama took office, support and opposition for reform became a party issue. In a heavily polarized political environment, support for government funded healthcare declined and the public split evenly on the issue. After the Obama administration passed the Patient Protection and Affordable Care Act, a majority of the public remained dissatisfied with the costs of healthcare.

program for the elderly, Medicaid is a means-tested program for the needy. And whereas Medicare is run exclusively by the federal government, Medicaid also receives funding from the states. Consequently, whereas Medicare looks exactly the same across the country, Medicaid programs differ markedly from state to state.[75]

U.S. Health and Health Care Are Poor by International Standards

Despite massive government programs such as Medicare and Medicaid, as well as the patchwork of private insurance plans, many Americans lack health insurance. In 2010, more than 16 percent of U.S. citizens lacked any health insurance. Every other major industrialized nation in the world, by comparison, has some form of universal health care. The United Kingdom was the first nation to offer universal medical coverage. In 1948, it established the National Health Service, which uses general tax revenue to support hospitals that serve all citizens. Thus far, more than 30 other European countries have followed suit with universal programs of their own, as have many other countries, including India, Israel, Japan, and Uruguay.

Coverage rates in the United States are all the more troubling given the extraordinary costs of health care. In 2010, the United States spent more than 17 percent of its gross national product (GNP) on health costs. As a percentage of their economies, this proportion is higher than that of any other advanced industrialized nation. Indeed, U.S. costs are 50 percent to 80 percent higher than those in Canada, France, Germany, and the United Kingdom, all of which provide universal health care to their citizens.

Although they pay a great deal for health care, U.S. citizens remain comparatively unhealthy. Consider, for example, the number of years that people in different nations can expect to live. In 2009, the life expectancy of U.S. citizens trailed that of 26 other major industrialized nations. Ranking just above citizens of the Czech Republic, Mexico, and Poland, U.S. men live an average of 75 years, and U.S. women, 80. Both figures trailed those of every nation in Western Europe.[76] American citizens also have unhealthier lifestyles than their international counterparts. In 2009, for instance, U.S. obesity rates eclipsed those of every other industrialized nation in the world. Fully 34 percent of U.S. citizens were deemed obese, as compared to just 4 percent of the Japanese, 8 percent of the Swiss, 11 percent of the French, and 23 percent of the English.[77]

Given international differences in coverage rates and lifestyles, it is difficult to assess the overall quality of different health care systems. Those who have tried to do so, however, have not given the United States high marks. In the most recent comprehensive ranking of health care systems by the World Health Organization (WHO), the United States was 37th out of 50 countries. This places the American system behind those of all Western European countries as well as Australia, Canada, and Japan. A number of South and Central American countries, including Colombia, Chile, and Costa Rica, also outperform the United States by this measure. And as Figure 17.4 shows, on indicators such as infant mortality rates, the United States continues to lag other countries.

By international standards, the United States health care system appears mediocre. Nevertheless, overall system performance is just one of many ways to evaluate national health care quality. The WHO report, for instance, bases its rankings on a composite measure that includes factors such as the health of a nation's citizens, the responsiveness of a health care system to patients' non-health concerns, and the extent to which health care systems accommodate patients' financial limitations. Although the United States performs poorly on financing, ranking 54, it comes in 24th in health attainment and 1st in system responsiveness.[78]

Moreover, ranking a nation's health care system based partly on the wellness of its population, as the WHO does, can be tricky. On the one hand, a healthy citizenry could indicate that the system is working effectively. Residents may be living longer and healthier lives because of good preventive medicine or access to excellent doctors and facilities. On the other hand, it could reflect considerations that have little to do

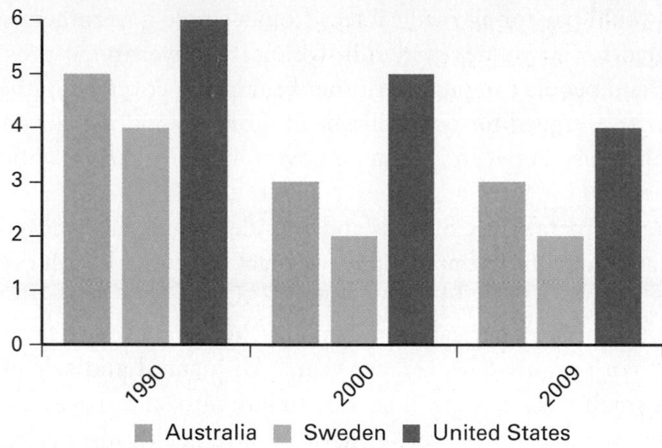

FIGURE 17.4 INFANT MORTALITY RATES.

In absolute terms, infant mortality rates are dropping in the United States. Relative to other countries, however, the United States retains high rates.

Source: http://www.nejm.org/doi/full/10.1056/NEJMp0910064.

with the health care system, such as culture, the environment, or economic development. For instance, people may live longer in a nation where the traditional diet consists of low-fat foods such as fish, fruits, and vegetables. Conversely, populations of developing countries may be exposed to higher levels of pollution, which can trigger a variety of ailments.

Comprehensive Health Care Reform Was Eventually Achieved in 2010

Almost everyone agrees that something needs to be done about the state of U.S. health care. It is too costly. Too many people are uninsured. For many, the quality of care is unacceptable. What people cannot agree about is the right way to go about improving this state of affairs. Some suggest that allowing U.S. citizens to purchase prescription drugs from foreign countries might drastically reduce costs. Others push for closer regulation of the pharmaceutical industry. The most ambitious, however, advocate government-provided health insurance that covers every U.S. citizen.

Advocates of universal health care are generally liberals. They couch their arguments in terms of traditional American values about fairness and equity, asking, "Isn't health the most basic right?" Indeed, doesn't the exercise of all other rights depend on citizens being healthy? And if so, how can we deny health insurance to millions of U.S. citizens?[79] Advocates also note that the United States is the only major industrialized nation in the world not to offer health care to all of its citizens.

There are powerful opponents, however, to universal health care. Most conservatives are deeply suspicious of what they call "socialized medicine."[80] Libertarian organizations, such as the Cato Institute, oppose reforms that would increase federal regulations of hospitals. And the American Medical Association is wary of any plan that would reduce the role of private insurance. Moreover, critics insist, government-provided health insurance threatens to reduce the number of hospital and doctor options available to the public. In this sense, universal health care violates other basic tenets of the American creed, notably individualism and freedom of choice. These individuals do not dispute the importance of decreasing the number of uninsured individuals around the country. But they insist that private insurers, rather than the federal government, should assume primary responsibility for achieving this important goal.

These forces set the stage for an epic showdown on health care reform during the fall of 2009 and spring of 2010. The national debate evoked long-standing disputes about the effect of government-provided health insurance on private insurance markets. According to proponents of a vigorous government intervention, a single-payer system, which would pay for all medical fees from a single government source, is best. Others advocated for a two-tier system in which the government provides for basic health services, and people can purchase other health care coverage in the private marketplace. Still others argued for nonprofit, health care co-ops, which constitute something of a compromise between a genuine government insurance option and purely private providers.

Ultimately, Democrats in Congress and President Obama managed to overcome nearly unanimous Republican opposition and enact sweeping health care reform. The Patient Protection and Affordable Care Act (PPACA) extends health care coverage to 32 million uninsured Americans and expands Medicaid to cover families of four that earn less than roughly $29,327 per year.[81] Uninsured and self-employed citizens, as well as small businesses, will be able to buy into state-based insurance plans. By 2014, the act mandates that every American have health insurance, or they pay a yearly fine of $695. Similarly, employers with more than 50 workers will have to provide insurance or pay a yearly fine of $2,000 per worker. The legislation also regulates the practices of insurance companies. Under the PPACA, starting in 2014, insurance companies can no longer deny patients coverage because of preexisting conditions. Moreover, insurance companies are obligated to allow children to stay under their parent's plan until the age of 26.

Just after the president signed the bill into law on March 23, 2010, Senate Majority Leader Harry Reid proclaimed, "We have worked and waited for this moment for over a century. This, of course, was a health bill. But it was also a jobs bill. It was also an economic recovery bill. It was a deficit reduction bill. It was truly a bill of rights. And now it is the law of the land."[82] Others, though, were not nearly so effusive. Raising concerns about its costs and the expansion of government involvement in health care, some Republican opponents of the PPACA began calling for the legislation's repeal just hours after its enactment. Four federal appeals courts heard cases questioning PPACA's legality in the two years after President Obama signed the bill into law. Three of those circuit courts ruled that the legislation was constitutional; a fourth ruled it was not, calling the law "breathtaking in its expansive scope."[83] In 2011, the Supreme Court agreed to decide a case on the constitutionality of PPACA. And a year later, in a landmark Supreme Court ruling, the constitutionality of the PPACA was affirmed.

Review the Chapter

 **Listen** to **Chapter 17** on **MyPoliSciLab**

Enacting Economic and Social Policies

17.1 Identify the conditions under which policy innovations are created, p. 574.

For social policies to be enacted, problems must be identified, solutions must be suggested, and a focusing event must propel action. Problems are most likely to attract government attention when they raise concerns about national security or equity. Politically viable solutions typically require the backing of organized interest groups. And focusing events can take a wide range of forms, ranging from environmental disasters to high-profile government reports.

Economic Policy

17.2 Assess efforts by the federal government to manage the domestic economy, p. 577.

The government regularly monitors the health of the economy, paying particular attention to unemployment rates, inflation trends, and the gross domestic product. Depending on how well the economy is performing, the government may alter fiscal or monetary policy. Some economists recommend that the government intervene in the economy as little as possible, so as to allow markets to adjust to new economic realities.

Social Security

17.3 Trace the development of the largest federal social program, which assists the elderly, p. 581.

As the backbone of the modern welfare state, Social Security provides a steady income stream to the nation's elderly. During their working lives, individuals pay into the system with the expectation that they can draw from it when they retire. Over the past 70 years, the number of people paying into the system has increased markedly, but so has the amount of the benefits paid out. This, in combination with recent demographic changes, has raised deep concerns about the program's long-term sustainability.

Welfare

17.4 Analyze changes in welfare policy within the United States, p. 585.

The U.S. welfare system consists of a patchwork of programs, each of which directs benefits to a different segment of the U.S. population. These programs provide varying levels and types of support, including direct cash transfers and subsidies for life necessities. Whereas most social programs expand over time, welfare has experienced some cutbacks, particularly since President Clinton fulfilled his campaign promise to "end welfare as we know it" by replacing AFDC with the more restrictive TANF.

Education

17.5 Outline the federal government's expanding involvement in education, p. 588.

Historically, state and local governments assumed primary responsibility for the education of their residents. Although these governments continue to cover the vast majority of education expenses, over the past half-century, the federal government has increased its aid to public schools and its regulatory demands on them. Contemporary efforts to reform public schools focus on raising standards and increasing accountability (which further augment the federal government's involvement in public education) and expanding choice and competition (which reduces government regulations over where children attend school).

Health Care

17.6 Evaluate the government's efforts to provide health care to the poor and aged, p. 596.

More money is spent on health care than any other social program. Total expenditures of the two largest programs, Medicare and Medicaid, run in the hundreds of billions of dollars. Overseen exclusively by the federal government, Medicare provides medical insurance to the elderly. A joint venture of federal and state governments, Medicaid assists the poor and disabled. In 2010, the federal government enacted the most sweeping changes to U.S. health care since the original enactment of Medicare and Medicaid. The subject of great political controversy, the Patient Protection and Affordable Care Act (PPACA) expanded health care coverage through both mandates and new support systems.

Learn the Terms

Aid to Families with Dependent Children (AFDC), p. 586
charter schools, p. 594
deficit, p. 580
Elementary and Secondary Education Act (ESEA), p. 589
entitlements, p. 582
Federal Reserve, p. 579
fiscal policy, p. 579
focusing event, p. 576
Great Depression, p. 576
Great Society, p. 574
gross domestic product (GDP), p. 577
laissez-faire economics, p. 579
means-tested program, p. 585
Medicaid, p. 596
Medicare, p. 596
monetary policy, p. 579
No Child Left Behind Act (NCLB), p. 591
policy entrepreneurs, p. 575
public debt, p. 580
recession, p. 581
Social Security Act, p. 582
Temporary Assistance for Needy Families (TANF), p. 586
unfunded mandate, p. 589
vouchers, p. 594

Test Yourself

17.1 Identify the conditions under which policy innovations are created.

A focusing event is

a. any dramatic event that the media covers.
b. a staged media event to highlight a public policy problem.
c. a press conference held by a politician to focus the media's attention on an issue.
d. a small event that has little initial impact on a specific policy problem.
e. a visible and dramatic event that focuses the public on a specific problem and accompanying course of action.

17.2 Assess efforts by the federal government to manage the domestic economy.

According to laissez-faire economics, the best thing the government can do for the economy is to

a. regulate the exchange of goods.
b. stay out of the way.
c. heavily regulate interest rates.
d. increase spending.
e. increase taxes.

17.3 Trace the development of the largest federal social program, which assists the elderly.

Which of the following is NOT true of Social Security benefits?

a. Social Security benefits are entitlements.
b. One does not need to demonstrate financial need in order to receive Social Security benefits.
c. The size of payments one receives from Social Security is unrelated to the amount of an individual's private savings.
d. Social Security benefits are means tested.
e. Social Security benefits have steadily expanded.

17.4 Analyze changes in welfare policy within the United States.

Which of the following is a means-tested program?

a. Temporary Assistance for Needy Families (TANF)
b. Social Security
c. Medicare
d. universal health insurance
e. short-term disability insurance

17.5 Outline the federal government's expanding involvement in education.

The No Child Left Behind Act represented

a. a reauthorization of the policies established under the Elementary and Secondary Education Act.
b. a wholesale repudiation of the policies established under the Elementary and Secondary Education Act.
c. the first time local school districts assumed responsibility for monitoring student test scores in individual schools.
d. the first time the federal government assumed responsibility for monitoring student test scores in individual schools.
e. the first time state governments assumed responsibility for monitoring student test scores in individual schools.

17.6 Evaluate the government's efforts to provide health care to the poor and aged.

How does U.S. health care compare to the health care provided by other major industrialized nations in the world?

a. U.S. health care is far above average by international standards.
b. U.S. health care is far below average by international standards.
c. U.S. health care is mediocre by international standards.
d. U.S. health care is poor by international standards, but it is not as costly as the health care provided by other advanced industrialized nations.
e. U.S. health care is above average by international standards, but it is more costly than the health care provided by other advanced industrialized nations.

Explore Further

SUGGESTED READINGS BY TOP SCHOLARS

Christopher Berry. *Imperfect Union*. New York: Cambridge University Press, 2009. Demonstrates how the proliferation of overlapping single-function governments leads to systematically higher tax burdens on average Americans.

Martin Gilens. *Why Americans Hate Welfare: Race, Media, and the Politics of Antipoverty Policy*. Chicago: University of Chicago Press, 2001. Examines the foundations of public attitudes toward welfare policy and welfare recipients.

Jacob Hacker and Paul Pierson. *Winner-Take-All Politics: How Washington Made the Rich Richer—and Turned Its Back on the Middle Class.* New York: Simon & Schuster, 2010. Examines how changes in the tax and regulatory structures of American politics have contributed to rising income inequalities in the United States.

Terry Moe. *Special Interest*. Washington, DC: Brookings, 2011. Takes a comprehensive, uncompromising look at the influence of teachers' unions on public education.

Eric Patashnik. *Reforms at Risk*. Princeton, NJ: Princeton University Press, 2010. Characterizes the lifespans of major policy initiatives, which are replete with political struggle, after their enactment.

SUGGESTED WEBSITES

Social Security Administration: www.ssa.gov

This organization governs the single largest entitlement program run by the federal government.

World Health Organization: www.who.int

This organization oversees global trends in different health indicators.

U.S. Department of Education: www.ed.gov

This department monitors, among other laws, the recently enacted No Child Left Behind Act.

Board of Governors of the Federal Reserve System: www.federalreserve.gov

This agency oversees U.S. monctary policy.

Economics and Statistics Administration: www.economicindicators.gov

A vast array of statistics on the state of the U.S. economy is available at this site.

Listen to Chapter 18 on MyPoliSciLab

18

Foreign Policy

MEXICO AND THE WAR ON DRUGS

In 2010, a total of 15,273 people were killed in activities related to Mexico's drug trade, marking the deadliest year in the history of Mexico's ongoing drug wars.[1] By contrast, Iraq suffered slightly more than 4,000 civilian casualties that year.[2] Large criminal organizations known as cartels continue to dominate Mexico's illegal drug-trafficking business, fighting each other and the Mexican government for the ability to smuggle drugs across the border into the United States. Cartels frequently bribe local law enforcement and government officials. In addition, the organizations intimidate officials and one another with threats of violence. Recent years have seen that violence escalate to unprecedented heights.

The violence in Mexico affects the United States in a number of significant ways. Since President Richard Nixon first declared a War on Drugs in 1971, the United States has taken a hard-line approach to preventing illegal drugs from entering its borders. Over four decades, the United States has spent more than $1 trillion in its efforts to fight the drug trade.[3] The majority of this money goes toward domestic costs, particularly law enforcement in American cities and along the nation's border with Mexico. Yet, the United States also gives a significant amount of federal dollars to the Mexican government to aid its ongoing war against the drug cartels. Since 2008, Congress has appropriated $1.5 billion in aid to Mexico as part of the Merida Initiative, which the State Department calls a "partnership between the United States and Mexico to fight organized crime and associated violence."[4]

18.1 Outline the history of U.S. foreign policy, p. 608.

18.2 Identify the powers of the president to direct foreign policy and the executive agencies that support the president, p. 615.

18.3 Describe the power of Congress to shape foreign policy, p. 624.

18.4 Analyze the role of interest groups in foreign policy making, p. 628.

18.5 Assess three of the foreign policy challenges that the United States faces today, p. 630.

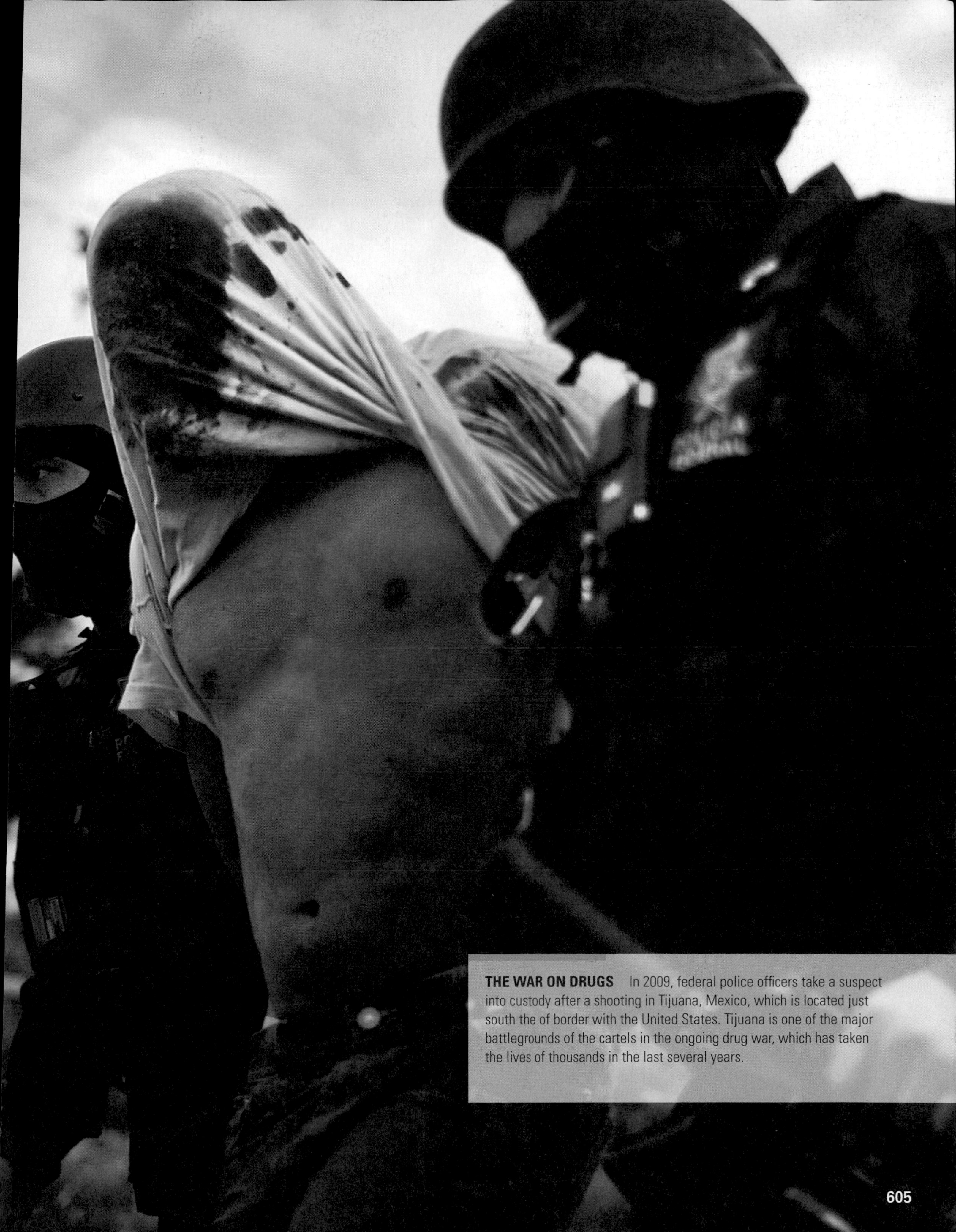

THE WAR ON DRUGS In 2009, federal police officers take a suspect into custody after a shooting in Tijuana, Mexico, which is located just south the of border with the United States. Tijuana is one of the major battlegrounds of the cartels in the ongoing drug war, which has taken the lives of thousands in the last several years.

The Big Picture Is America too involved in foreign affairs? In order to fully understand the U.S.'s role abroad, author William G. Howell stresses the importance of knowing the historical trends in U.S. foreign policy and the three key challenges faced by government employees making these decisions.

The Basics Who develops America's foreign policy? How has America emerged as a world leader and what challenges does this present? In this video, you will learn about the actors in the foreign policy arena and consider the United States' role in international affairs.

Why is the United States
considered a "superpower"?

In Context Explore the history of American foreign policy. In this video, Boston University political scientist Neta C. Crawford explains the international challenges the Unites States has faced during three stages of development. She also reveals who is chiefly responsible for deciding foreign policy.

Think Like a Political Scientist Learn what foreign policy scholars are researching. Boston University political scientist Neta C. Crawford reveals how scholars use levels of analysis and advances in cognitive psychology to assess decision-making.

In the Real World The United States has intervened in many countries in order to promote democracy, including Iraq, Germany, Japan, and most recently, Libya. Is this the right thing to do? Learn what real people have to say about this divisive issue, and about the consequences brought on by U.S. involvement abroad.

So What? Remember when the majority of Americans could not find Iraq or Afghanistan on a map? Author William G. Howell describes how the public has become increasingly interested and involved in U.S. foreign policy over the last decade.

With the increase in violence in 2010, the Obama administration saw fit to increase the assistance it gave Mexican authorities. In addition to money, the American military sent its Mexican counterpart state-of-the-art helicopters and trained Mexican officers in new combat techniques. As concerns over corruption in Mexico's military and government institutions increased, however, many working in the foreign policy bureaucracy worried that this assistance was being squandered. The Obama administration, therefore, began sending CIA operatives and former military personnel to work side-by-side with Mexican law enforcement to ensure the proper conduct of operations against the drug cartels.[5]

American officials openly worry that the violence will spill over the border into Texas, Arizona, and California. The Mexican government, for its part, claims that the United States is not doing enough to prevent handguns from being smuggled into Mexico, thereby facilitating warfare between the cartels. Diplomatic tensions between the two countries reached their peak in December 2010, when the controversial website Wikileaks published a series of classified cables in which U.S. officials painted a bleak portrait of their Mexican counterparts. One cable, addressed from the U.S. embassy in Mexico to the State Department in Washington, noted that throughout the Mexican government, "official corruption is widespread." Another claimed that Mexico was losing the ability to control significant parts of its own national territory, in part because of a "risk averse" military that did not actively seek to destroy cartel organizations.[6] Newspapers in both countries covered the story extensively. And the diplomatic crisis only deepened weeks later, when U.S. Immigration and Customs Enforcement special agent Jaime Zapata was shot on a highway in Northern Mexico, with a gun purchased by a cartel member in Dallas.

In response to the leaked cables and the murder of Zapata, Mexican president Felipe Calderon publicly defended his administration and blamed the United States for failing to take responsibility for its own role in the drug-related violence. He said that U.S. officials' "ignorance has translated into a distortion of what is happening in Mexico." He also accused American agencies of dragging their feet in supplying Mexico with promised assistance to fight against cartels: "The institutional cooperation ends up being notoriously insufficient." More specifically, Calderon pointed out that Mexico's drug problem was largely America's drug problem, as Zapata's death made clear. He asserted that until the United States curbed its own population's demand for drugs and guns, drugs would continue to be smuggled into America, and guns would continue to find their way into the hands of Mexican cartels.

The Obama administration responded to the escalating tensions by immediately seeking to assuage any apparent diplomatic rift between the two countries. "This bilateral relation has matured to a level in which a simple statement or a given event does not have the power to wreck the relation entirely," said a State Department spokesperson.[7] By the time President Obama met with President Calderon at the White House in March 2011, both sides downplayed any appearance of ill will. Calderon praised America for continuing to support Mexico in the War on Drugs, and Obama made sure to acknowledge his commitment to fighting Mexican cartels. "We are very mindful that the battle President Calderon is fighting inside of Mexico is not just his battle. It's also ours. We have to take responsibility, just as he's taking responsibility," said President Obama.[8] Later that day, Calderon also met with John Boehner, Republican Speaker of the House, to ensure that Congress would continue to funnel aid to Mexico as part of the Merida Initiative. And, several months later, America's ambassador to Mexico, who Calderon largely blamed for the leaked cables, was forced to resign.

The U.S. decision to immediately smooth over its relationship with Mexico can be traced to several causes. In part, the United States needs the cooperation of Mexican authorities in order to wage a successful war on drugs within its own borders, because most of the drugs in the United States come from Mexico. In addition to concerns over drug trafficking, however, Mexico is also one of America's primary trading partners. In 2011, for example, the two countries exchanged roughly $450 billion in goods. Indeed, the United States trades more with Mexico than with any other country except Canada and China.[9]

Given the close political and economic ties between the two countries, American politicians in the White House and in Congress must walk a fine line. On the one hand, they must take an aggressive stance toward securing the border with Mexico and fighting

18.1
18.2
18.3
18.4
18.5

foreign policy
the mix of military, diplomatic, and economic policies that define U.S. relations with other nations around the world.

grand strategy
a plan that determines American national security interests, outlines possible threats to those interests, and recommends military and diplomatic policies to attain them.

isolationism
the grand strategy of minimizing a nation's involvement in world affairs.

internationalism
the grand strategy of actively engaging in world affairs.

Explore on MyPoliSciLab
Simulation: You Are a President During a Foreign Policy Crisis

Mexican drug cartels to prevent illegal drugs from entering the country. At the same time, they must continue to support the Mexican government, both in its efforts to curb violence and in its efforts to trade with the United States. Finally, politicians must make decisions about America's policy toward Mexico in the context of the domestic political climate, in which concerns such as gun control and immigration are hot-button issues. In this chapter, we examine key players in U.S. foreign policy making, offering examples of some of the policies they create and the domestic political struggles they engender.

A Brief History of U.S. Foreign Policy

18.1 Outline the history of U.S. foreign policy.

Since its founding, the United States has formulated **foreign policies** that define its political and economic relationships with other nations. At the heart of foreign policy debates lies concern about the nation's **grand strategy**, the larger, organizing principles that define national interests, outline possible threats to those interests, and recommend military and diplomatic policies to protect those interests.

Until the twentieth century, the United States followed a grand strategy of **isolationism**, a policy of minimizing the nation's involvement in world affairs. The alternative policy, **internationalism**, is based on the belief that intervention in the affairs of other nations is sometimes necessary to protect one's own interests. The nation's founders, however, feared that alliances with European countries could entangle the nation in overseas wars—or even worse, draw European wars to the North American continent. As a result, early American leaders sought to distance the country from European politics and conflicts. In his farewell address, President George Washington set the tone for this policy, famously urging the country to avoid the mischiefs of foreign intrigue.[10]

Although subsequent presidents stayed out of European affairs, they actively intervened in the Western Hemisphere throughout the nineteenth century. "Manifest Destiny," the belief that the United States should expand across North America, took hold of the nation. In pursuit of this goal, the United States purchased large portions of land from Spain, France, and Britain. The largest such acquisition, the 1803 Louisiana Purchase, more than doubled the size of U.S. territory. The United States also tried to seize Canada from Britain in the War of 1812, although this attempt failed. In December 1823, American leaders issued the Monroe Doctrine, a policy statement that warned European countries not to meddle in the Western Hemisphere. The United States fought a war with Mexico from 1846 to 1848, which resulted in the gain of California and other territory in the Southwest. By 1900, the United States had become the most powerful country west of the Atlantic Ocean.[11]

In the Early Twentieth Century, U.S. Involvement in World Politics Was Sporadic

At the dawn of the twentieth century, internal and external pressures forced American leaders to reconsider their grand strategy of isolationism. Industrialization and the expansion of the financial sector led to increased trade and investment abroad.[12] Economic ties to Europe then grew exponentially with the onset of World War I in 1914. The United States lent money and supplies to Britain and France as they fought Germany in one of the bloodiest wars in modern times. As a result, exports as a share of American national income doubled from 6 percent in 1914 to 12 percent in 1916. In 1916, fully 83 percent of those exports were bound for Britain, France, Italy, and the Russian Empire.[13]

Ultimately, concerns about trade with European allies convinced the United States to enter World War I. The German decision to launch unrestricted submarine warfare in January 1917 jeopardized American shipments to Britain and France. In April, the United States declared war on Germany.[14] The vast resources the United States brought to the war effort sealed the victory over Germany, Austria-Hungary, and the Ottoman Empire in 1918.

World War I officially concluded with the Treaty of Versailles in 1919. Believing that the United States and its allies should use the historic occasion to reshape the world political order, President Woodrow Wilson urged acceptance of his "Fourteen Points" proposal for peace. Wilson called for a new international system based on the principles of democracy, self-determination, and the rule of law. He also championed the establishment of the League of Nations, a collective security institution designed to uphold European peace.

This brief turn toward internationalism in American foreign policy, however, did not last. Although Wilson's ideas received support in Europe, they foundered back home. The American public and many members of Congress were unwilling to give up their vision of a United States that remained apart from European power struggles. In the biggest defeat of his presidency, Wilson failed to secure Senate approval to join the League of Nations, and a spirit of isolationism once again infused U.S. foreign policy.[15]

The next 25 years saw great political and economic instability in Europe. The Great Depression devastated European economies. Hyperinflation, massive unemployment, and mandatory reparations established under the Treaty of Versailles brought ruin to the Weimar Republic, the weak democratic government established in Germany after the war. Ultimately, the Weimar government could not survive the turmoil unleashed by the depression, and the ultranationalist Nazi party under Adolf Hitler came to power in 1933. Around the same time, Italy descended into fascism under Benito Mussolini, and Spain became engulfed in civil war. The United States remained largely distant from these developments as it dealt with its own economic difficulties.

As the 1930s wore on, an increasingly aggressive Japan, Germany, and Italy brought Europe and Asia to the brink of war. Japan's invasion of China, Italy's invasion of Ethiopia and Albania, and German expansion into Austria and Czechoslovakia raised serious concerns in the United States. Yet, optimists hoped that the strong coalition of Russia, France, and Great Britain could contain Germany, Italy, and Japan.

This hope, however, did not materialize. World War II officially began on September 1, 1939, when Germany invaded Poland, provoking a declaration of war from Britain and France. In 1940, Hitler's forces quickly overran France, "divert[ing] the flow of history into darker channels."[16] British forces then departed from the continent at Dunkirk, leaving Western Europe to Hitler's devices. To humiliate the French, who had lost to the Nazis despite superior human resources and materiel, Hitler forced the country's leaders to formally capitulate in the same railcar in which the Germans had surrendered in 1918.[17] The following year, Nazi armies invaded deep into the Soviet Union.

The U.S. president, Franklin Roosevelt, was highly sympathetic to the plight of the British, French, and Soviets.[18] He recognized that a Europe dominated by Hitler posed a great threat to American national security. If Hitler conquered all of Europe, he could readily secure the resources needed to challenge U.S. supremacy in North America. Still, the American public had little appetite for war. Roosevelt was able to assist the allies through his lend-lease program, which provided war material to the British and, eventually, to the Soviets and Chinese. But even this aid faced resistance in Congress.

Any such hesitancy changed with Japan's surprise attack on Pearl Harbor in the early morning hours of December 7, 1941—a day that President Roosevelt said would "live in infamy." During the battle, Japanese planes damaged or destroyed 347 of the roughly 400 American aircraft stationed on Oahu, Hawaii. In all, 2,400 American service members were killed and 1,200 were injured. Most of the destruction occurred within a scant 30 minutes.[19]

18.1
18.2
18.3
18.4
18.5

Marshall Plan
a program that provided aid to rebuild Western European economies after World War II.

United Nations
an international organization founded in 1945 dedicated to the advancement of world peace, economic prosperity, and the protection of human rights.

The attack on Pearl Harbor catapulted the United States into World War II. The United States spent the next four years fighting Germany, Italy, and Japan. Yet, the impact of Pearl Harbor reached far beyond American entry into the war. It ushered in a new era of American leadership in world affairs.

After World War II, the United States Entered the World Stage for Good

In 1945, the United States and its allies emerged victorious after years of war in Europe and Asia. The war transformed American foreign policy. Politically, isolationism was no longer generally viewed as a viable option. Even though the United States and the Soviet Union had collaborated to defeat Hitler, good will between the countries quickly evaporated after the war. The looming presence of the Soviet army in Europe raised fears that an American departure from the continent would lead to Soviet domination. Economically, the United States was the only country to survive the war with its major industries intact. World War II had reduced Europe to shambles. Through the **Marshall Plan,** the United States supported vast reconstruction efforts in Western Europe, helping its war-torn allies rebuild their economies, with an eye toward bolstering their security against the Soviet communist threat. At the same time, the United States also played a key role in establishing the **United Nations (UN),** an

A DAY THAT WOULD LIVE IN INFAMY

The Japanese bombing of the U.S. naval fleet stationed in Pearl Harbor, Hawaii launched United States headlong into the most catastrophic war of the 20th century.

international organization dedicated to the reduction of inter-state violence and protection of human rights. With its headquarters located in New York City, the UN grants the United States disproportionate influence over its now more than 75 member states.

Over time, there emerged a new type of conflict that divided Europe along ideological lines. In the east, the Soviet Union established communist satellite governments in Bulgaria, Romania, Yugoslavia, Hungary, Poland, East Germany, and Czechoslovakia.[20] The Warsaw Pact formalized this alliance. In Western Europe, the United States constructed a web of democratic allies, including Great Britain, France, the Netherlands, Italy, and West Germany. In 1949, the United States and its allies created the **North Atlantic Treaty Organization (NATO)** to solidify their common defense. Signatories to the NATO treaty pledged to come to one another's aid if attacked by the Soviet Union. Through NATO, the United States maintained a strong combat presence in Europe for more than 40 years.

In the late 1940s, the United States adopted a grand strategy of **containment,** a particular type of internationalism meant to counter the threat the Soviet Union posed to Europe and America. Hitler's near takeover of Europe convinced America's leaders that the United States could not afford the rise of a hostile power that spanned the Eurasian continent. Such a country would possess vast economic resources and could threaten the American homeland. Advocated by State Department diplomat George F. Kennan, containment sought to guard against Soviet expansion by adopting policies that checked Soviet power. Kennan thought that the Soviets could not be negotiated with, but that the Soviet economic system bore within itself "the seeds of its own decay, and . . . the sprouting of these seeds is well advanced." The United States needed only to bide its time until the Soviet system of government inevitably faltered. So although the United States would not directly confront the Soviets or their allies, American foreign policy would meet Soviet challenges at every turn.[21]

Tensions ran high between America and the Soviet Union for the better part of 40 years, from the end of World War II until the revolutionary year of 1989. This period has been dubbed the **Cold War**—a state of diplomatic and economic hostility between the superpowers but not open, "hot" warfare. Each side consistently accused the other of unprovoked aggression as they competed for allies and influence throughout the world. This competition, however, never erupted into direct military confrontation.[22] Despite resulting in a state of constant military tension, the Cold War actually coincided with a time of relative global peace. Indeed, after nearly 50 years of political upheaval, Europe returned to an era of stability not seen since the early nineteenth century.[23]

While Europe remained in a state of fragile peace, the rest of the world was not so fortunate. Indeed, the first major conflict between the East and West arose in Korea in 1950, when the Soviet-backed government of North Korea invaded South Korea, an American ally. The Korean War, which lasted from 1950 to 1953, confirmed the fears of many Americans that the Soviet Union was determined to spread its power and ideology across the globe. From the standpoint of American foreign policy, the Korean War was the final nail in the coffin of isolationism. Containment was widely viewed as a necessary policy that would require an extensive investment of American blood and treasure.

The United States vastly expanded its involvement in international affairs over the next several decades. The government sponsored coups in Iran (1953), Guatemala (1954), and the Dominican Republic (1956). It aided governments fighting communist insurgencies in the Philippines (1954), Chile (1964), and El Salvador (1980s). And it funded anticommunist insurgencies in Chile (1973), Ghana (1961), Cuba (1960s), and Nicaragua (1980s). American policy makers viewed nearly every problem through the lens of the Cold War. International politics became a **zero-sum game** (i.e., a contest in which gains achieved by one side necessarily involved equivalent losses by the other) between Soviet interests and American ones.

The largest and most extensive conflict in the developing world would unfold in Vietnam, a former French colony. Throughout the late 1950s and early 1960s, the

North Atlantic Treaty Organization (NATO)
established in 1949, a military alliance of the United States and a number of European nations that pledged to join forces against an attack by the Soviet Union, or any other external threat.

containment
the strategy of guarding against Soviet power by adopting policies that limited the geographic expansion of Soviet power.

Cold War
the period from the late 1940s to the late 1980s in which the United States and the Soviet Union engaged in diplomatic and economic hostility but not full-fledged war.

zero-sum game
a situation, for example in foreign policy, in which one side's gains are always at the expense of the other side.

18.1
18.2
18.3
18.4
18.5

STORMING THE BEACH HEAD

While under enemy fire in November 1965, American soldiers of the 7th Marines waded ashore at Cape Batangan, Vietnam. Although the United States had sent thousands of "military advisers" to Vietnam in the early 1960s, the Vietnam War began in earnest in the middle of the decade. How did the nation's experience in Vietnam inform the nation's conduct of subsequent wars in Iraq and Afghanistan?

United States sent military aid to South Vietnam in an effort to curb the influence of Soviet-backed North Vietnam and an insurgency group called the National Front for the Liberation of South Vietnam. South Vietnam's leaders became completely dependent on American military support for their power. This reliance turned much of the population of South Vietnam against its own government. In 1964, after a purported attack by the North on American military personnel, known as the Gulf of Tonkin incident, President Lyndon Johnson asked Congress for the authority needed to conduct "all necessary action to protect our Armed Forces."[24] Congress granted Johnson's request and the Vietnam War began in earnest. At its height, the war involved more than half a million American troops. The war lasted until 1973 and resulted in nearly 60,000 Americans and 3 million South and North Vietnamese dead.[25]

The Vietnam War was a watershed event for American foreign policy. It was the first major foreign war that the United States is perceived to have lost. Many Americans questioned the strategic interests in sending young men and women to fight and die in a distant land. And with television crews for the first time showing the carnage wrought by the war, protests mounted against the emergence of an "imperial presidency" in foreign affairs.[26] Congress, the media, and the public sought ways to restrict the president's foreign policy powers, lest America find itself mired in another unpopular, seemingly unwinnable war.[27]

In the aftermath of Vietnam, both the Soviet Union and the United States started to rethink whether fighting wars in far-off lands was worth the steep costs in lives and money. Many in the United States began to question whether the Soviets presented such a large threat. Meanwhile, the financial costs of the Cold War were taking their toll on the Soviet economy. In response to these changes in both states, a move toward more peaceful relations took place. This period of easing of tensions, known as **détente,** fostered Soviet-American cooperation on issues ranging from agricultural trade to space exploration.

détente
a period of reduced Cold War tensions in the 1970s.

Although the 1970s saw declining tensions between the Soviet Union and the United States, the era of cooperation did not last. The 1979 Soviet invasion of Afghanistan soured relations between the two superpowers. American leaders, especially President Ronald Reagan, viewed the Soviets as aggressively pursuing expansion at the expense of the United States and its allies. Referring to the Soviet Union as the "evil empire," Reagan's administration launched a military buildup that nearly doubled Pentagon spending from 1980 to 1985.[28] This resurgence of Cold War hostilities, however, did not last long.

☐ With the End of the Cold War, New Conflicts Surfaced

Nearly as quickly as détente faded, the Cold War came to a close. In 1985, reform-minded Mikhail Gorbachev took over as Soviet premier. Over the next four years, Gorbachev passed numerous political and economic reforms intended to shore up the flagging Soviet economy. He withdrew Soviet troops from Afghanistan, agreed to arms control with the United States, and permitted democratic reform in the member states of the Warsaw Pact. By the end of 1989, the Berlin Wall, which had long divided communist East Berlin from capitalist West Berlin, had fallen. And by the end of 1991, East and West Germany had reunited and the Soviet Union had dissolved.

Scholars continue to argue about why the Cold War ended in the way that it did. Some, echoing Kennan, claim that the demise of the Soviet Union was inevitable. A system of centralized government and tight economic controls simply was not sustainable. Others argue that the inability of the Soviet Union to keep pace with American ingenuity proved decisive. According to this line of argumentation, left to its own devices, the Soviet Union might have persisted indefinitely. Competition from the West, however, provided the needed pressure to topple the communist regime. Whatever the precise cause, the peaceful revolutions of 1989–1991 were the most important international events since Pearl Harbor. For four decades, American foreign policy had focused almost exclusively on the Soviet threat. Now, the United States was suddenly the world's lone superpower.

The dramatic end of the Cold War spurred a vigorous debate among scholars and policy makers over what America's new grand strategy should be. Four main options arose from this debate. Some proposed a return to isolationism, arguing that geography and the U.S. nuclear arsenal made America secure enough to disengage from Europe. Others advocated a strategy of *selective engagement*, whereby the United States would monitor Europe and the Middle East and intervene only if a clear threat emerged. A third option was *cooperative security*, which envisioned the United States as the leader of a "new world order" that would check aggression anywhere in the world. Finally, some recommended a strategy of American *primacy*, designed to maintain America's overwhelming military and economic power advantage.[29]

In practice, the American grand strategy during the 1990s consisted of a mix of all these policies. The 1991 Persian Gulf War, for instance, combined elements of selective engagement and cooperative security. In 1990, Iraq, then led by President Saddam Hussein, invaded and occupied oil-rich Kuwait. The invasion surprised the international community and drew criticism from nearly every country in the world. By conquering Kuwait, Hussein controlled 20 percent of the world's oil reserves. If he conquered Saudi Arabia next, that number would jump to 40 percent—allowing Hussein to manipulate world oil prices and threaten American interests.[30] The invasion also constituted an act of naked aggression, setting a troubling precedent for the post–Cold War world.

In response to the invasion, the United States led a United Nations–sponsored military force to liberate Kuwait and drive back Hussein's Iraqi forces. For many, this

Bush Doctrine
a grand strategy pursued after September 11, 2001, that emphasized an aggressive posture toward nations that provide safe haven for terrorists, preemptive action, and a willingness to unilaterally launch military actions.

successful military campaign signaled the beginning of a new collective security system led by the United States and the United Nations. Japan, Russia, and European Union members all participated in some fashion. Many analysts hoped that a newly empowered United Nations could put a stop to territorial aggression, civil wars, and humanitarian disasters. This had been the organization's founding purpose, and in the Persian Gulf War it succeeded.

Unfortunately, cooperative security proved to be short lived. For decades, tensions between the Soviet Union and the United States had kept regional conflicts in check. Local populations dared not provoke either superpower in their desire for independence or domination over other populations. With the Cold War's demise, however, these tensions quickly flared, and the United States found itself involved in regional wars in Somalia, Bosnia, Serbia, Croatia, and Kosovo.

It was not until September 11, 2001, that U.S. foreign policy makers would fundamentally redefine the grand strategy. The simultaneous attacks that day on the Pentagon and New York's World Trade Center changed the course of American foreign policy—focusing attention on terrorist groups and non-state actors as never before. Turning away from the previous strategy of collective security, in which the United States and its allies shared responsibility for each country's safety, President George W. Bush announced a series of go-it-alone principles that collectively would become known as the **Bush Doctrine.** When formulating foreign policy, the president said, the United States would treat nations that harbored terrorists the same as it treated the terrorists themselves. The United States would no longer wait for terrorist activities to occur; it would instead launch preemptive strikes (military and otherwise) against emergent threats. And finally, the United States would not allow the United Nations or any other international organization to dictate when the United States could flex its military muscle. If need be, the United States would wage unilateral wars to protect its interests at home and abroad.

In the immediate aftermath of the attacks, the United States began a war to evict al-Qaeda, the terrorist organization responsible for the September 11 attacks, from its safe haven in Afghanistan. Osama bin Laden and his followers had benefited from ties to the Taliban government, which sympathized with their cause. The Taliban allowed the terrorist group to recruit and train members, as well as plan attacks, from its bases in the country. America's allies and the U.S. public strongly supported the war in Afghanistan, which they saw as a necessary response to September 11.

America's next choice of target, however, stirred controversy. In the spring of 2003, President Bush launched a war against the Saddam Hussein regime in Iraq. The Bush administration based its case for war on intelligence suggesting that Hussein had weapons of mass destruction (WMDs) and ties to al-Qaeda operatives. Bush warned that a preventive war against Iraq was necessary, claiming, "we cannot wait for the final proof—the smoking gun—that could come in the form of a mushroom cloud."[31] Critics argued that the administration was manipulating intelligence, that Hussein had no relationship with al-Qaeda, and that he could be contained through diplomacy.[32]

The initial invasion of Iraq went quite well for the Americans. However, the process of rebuilding the country and achieving political stability there proved far more difficult. Over the first four years of occupation, American forces suffered nearly 4,000 casualties—this after losing only 138 during the initial invasion. Moreover, extensive investigations found no evidence of WMDs in Iraq, suggesting that the rationale for the invasion was misguided. The lack of WMDs and the struggle to stabilize Iraq led to dissatisfaction with the Bush administration over the war. In January 2008, polls showed that only 30 percent of the American public approved of Bush's handling of Iraq.[33] In the 2008 presidential campaign, Barack Obama repeatedly vowed to withdraw all American troops from Iraq. A few years after entering office, he followed through on his promise: By the end of 2011, the United States had officially withdrawn its fighting troops from Iraq, even as skeptics worried that the country had not yet been stabilized.

While America struggled to deal with Iraq, new threats and challenges emerged. These included the rising distrust of America in Pakistan, a nuclear nation and former American ally in the "war on terror", concerns over the rising power of a nondemocratic

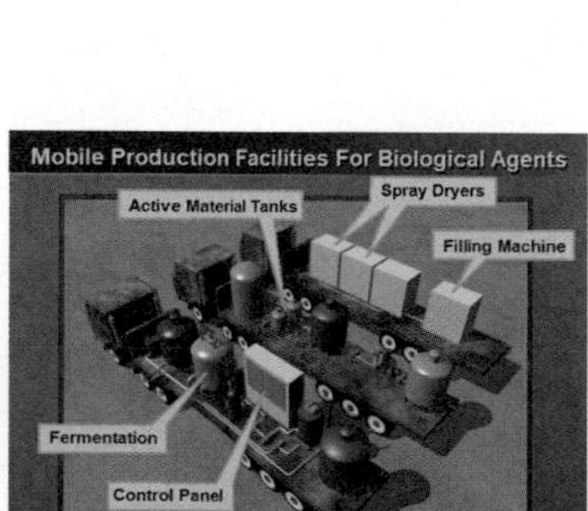

MAKING THE CASE FOR WEAPONS OF MASS DESTRUCTION

In February 2003, Secretary of State Colin Powell came before the United Nations Security Council to make the case for war against Iraq. Just over a year later, Powell acknowledged that the "most dramatic" part of his presentation, which focused on mobile chemical weapons laboratories, was based on flawed intelligence. Shown here is a slide from Powell's presentation. Knowing now that Iraq did not possess WMDs, should the United States nonetheless have invaded the country in 2003?

China, the persistence of the Taliban in Afghanistan, Russia's backsliding toward totalitarianism, and continued violence between Israelis and Palestinians. At the end of this chapter, we further examine a handful of the many daunting challenges that now face the United States.

National Security Council (NSC)
an advisory body, formed in 1947 by the National Security Act, that assists the president in gathering information from military services and other security-related executive agencies.

diplomacy
the peaceful negotiation of economic and political relationships between different countries.

State Department
the agency home of diplomats, embassies, treaty negotiators, and most foreign aid programs run by the U.S. government.

The Role of the Foreign Policy Bureaucracy

18.2 Identify the powers of the president to direct foreign policy and the executive agencies that support the president.

No other individual dominates U.S. foreign policy making as much as the president. Presidents exercise extraordinary power in foreign affairs. As commander in chief, the president regularly decides when troops will be deployed, for how long, and what their mission will be. As chief diplomat, the president often holds summits with foreign heads of state about the major issues of the day. As chief administrator, the president appoints many of the individuals who are charged with developing and implementing foreign policy. Serving the president in these various roles is a massive foreign policy bureaucracy.

The National Security Council Advises the President

Thousands of individuals within the executive branch oversee foreign affairs, as discussed in the chapters on the presidency and the bureaucracy. In many ways, the executive agency closest to the president on issues of foreign policy is the **National Security Council (NSC)**. Formed in 1947, the NSC coordinates the activities of the armed forces and other executive agencies (e.g., the State and Defense Departments and the CIA) to increase national security cooperation. The NSC assists the president in gathering advice from agencies and departments.

By law, the NSC must include the vice president, the national security adviser, the secretaries of state and defense, and the chair of the Joint Chiefs of Staff. In practice, most presidents have chosen to include more individuals than these. In addition to the formal council, the NSC also includes staff assistants, whose roles have grown in size and importance over the years. Over time, the formal decision-making council of the NSC has declined in importance.

The State Department Oversees U.S. Diplomacy

At its core, foreign policy is about **diplomacy**—the ongoing negotiation of economic and political relationships between different countries. Historically, the State Department has held primary responsibility for U.S. diplomacy. The **State Department** is the agency home of diplomats, embassies, and most foreign aid programs run by the U.S. government. The primary job of the State Department is to represent U.S. interests overseas and in various international organizations. In so doing, it communicates with foreign governments and publics, and it provides analysis on events abroad and their implications for American foreign policy. The State Department also negotiates treaties and agreements, makes policy recommendations, and takes steps to implement them. The department coordinates with the Agency for International Development (USAID) to oversee American foreign aid. And finally, the department provides crucial information about how the United States should deal with emergent problems abroad, whether by military force, diplomacy, or the imposition of sanctions. (See *How Do We Know? Do Economic Sanctions Work?*)

As Figure 18.1 highlights, the State Department operates hundreds of foreign embassies and consulates all over the globe. Roughly 30,000 employees, of whom

How Do We Know?

Do Economic Sanctions Work?

The Question

Effective diplomacy includes the right blend of carrots and sticks. Carrots typically include foreign aid, preferential trade agreements, and promises of military assistance that are meant to reward other governments for doing things that the United States supports. Sticks, by contrast, consist of various forms of punishment that are meant to discourage certain behaviors and policies.

In foreign affairs, economic sanctions are some of the sticks most frequently employed by the U.S. government against either single countries or groups of countries. Through sanctions, the State Department can pursue objectives ranging from signaling its displeasure toward other countries to undermining domestic support for another government. Although they have a long history, do economic sanctions work? How do we know?

Why It Matters

During the 1990s and 2000s, the United States levied sanctions against countries ranging from Iran to Cuba to Iraq to India. In 2002 the George W. Bush administration temporarily imposed tariffs on imported goods from China and India, leading the World Trade Organization to organize sanctions of its own against the United States. And more recently, President Obama unveiled new sanctions against Syria and Iran. If sanctions are ineffective, then other more aggressive tactics might be called for, at the possible expense of U.S. lives and treasure. However, a primary goal of sanctions is to avoid military action.

Investigating the Answer

How might we determine whether sanctions are effective tools of foreign policy? Scholars began to assess the effectiveness of sanctions by building a large data set that cataloged incidents of sanctions, their goals, and their effects. This initial work, by Gary Hufbauer, Jeffrey Schott, and Kimberly Elliot, found 116 episodes of economic sanctions placed by all states in the world from World War I to 1990.[a]

These scholars concluded that sanctions could be effective as long as the goals were modest. Sanctions that were designed to change aspects of a foreign government's trade policies, for instance, stood some chance of success. But sanctions put in place to achieve more difficult goals, such as unseating powerful and entrenched regimes, have not performed as well. Moreover, Hufbauer and his colleagues argued that more recent sanctions have been less successful overall—likely owing to increasing globalization and the ease with which states can find new trade partners to replace those cut off by sanctions.

Numerous scholars, however, have questioned these conclusions. Daniel Drezner has argued that the key to success is the threat of future conflict between the sanctioner and the sanctioned.[b] If sanctions are part of a larger pattern of conflict between states (i.e., they are placed after a war or years of disagreement), they are unlikely to work.

Later, Dean Lacy and Emerson Niou challenged the earlier scholars, claiming the sanctions data were incomplete.[c] They argued that potential targets of sanctions, hoping to prevent damage to their economies, may give in to international pressure prior to sanctions' taking effect. If the sanctions are never levied, they are not cataloged in the sanctions data set; therefore, scholars did not account for those instances when the threat of sanctions was sufficient to cause change.

Even if a complete data set of sanctions were assembled, it would remain difficult to systematically evaluate their success. How, after all, should analysts go about determining whether sanctions achieved their stated goals? On the one hand, assessment seems straightforward—states adopt sanctions to force other states to change their behavior in reasonably clear ways, and scholars observe whether or not target states change their behavior. On the other hand, assessment is more complicated.

Sanctions, it bears emphasizing, are often multilateral—that is, they are levied by multiple states, frequently with different goals. This fact makes it all the more difficult to assess whether sanctions have succeeded. For example, were the sanctions placed on Iraq after its 1990 invasion of Kuwait successful? They did not bring about a withdrawal from Kuwait—that took a war in 1991 led by the United States and a large coalition of other states. After the war, many states continued the sanctions in order to pressure Saddam Hussein not to attack Kurds and Shiites, to undermine his ability to rebuild his army, and ultimately to unseat him. Not only did states have different justifications for the sanctions, but they also had different assessments of whether the sanctions worked, leading some to lift sanctions against Iraq long before others were willing to do so. Much of the existing scholarship on sanctions has not dealt with this complication. Rather, most scholars continue to use the Hufbauer data, which treat each sanction episode as one unified sender and target, even if multiple states are senders or targets.

The Bottom Line

The debate over the effectiveness of economic sanctions is complex. Given the frequent use of sanctions by foreign policy makers, it is crucial to be able to evaluate their effectiveness. The general conclusion is that under certain circumstances, sanctions can be effective: namely, when the goals are modest, when the sanctions are against an ally, and when the costs to the sanctioned state are very high. Research continues in this area, and future studies will no doubt further refine our knowledge of the conditions under which economic sanctions are likely to be successful.[d]

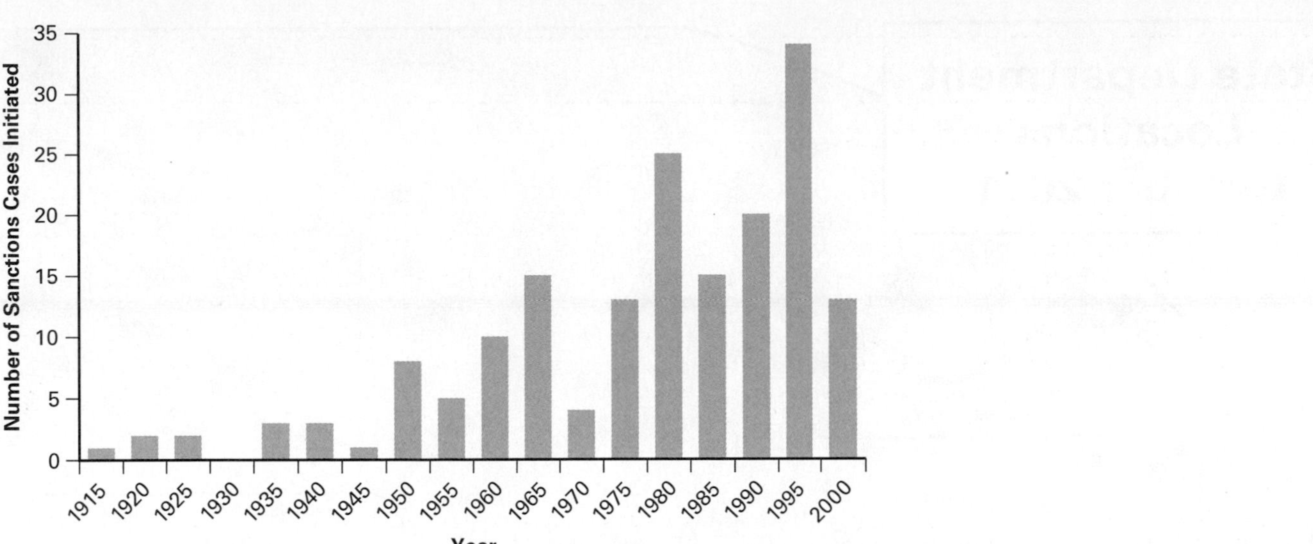

HISTORICAL TRENDS IN ECONOMIC SANCTIONS

Thinking Critically

- When trying to assess whether sanctions work, how should we compare cases when sanctions were merely threatened with cases when they were actually imposed?
- Other than sanctions, what foreign policy options are available to the United States when another country behaves in ways that are objectionable? How might we go about evaluating the effectiveness of sanctions vis-à-vis these other options?

---

[a]Gary Hufbauer, Jeffrey Schott, and Kimberly Elliot, *Economic Sanctions Reconsidered: History and Current Policy* (Washington, DC: Peterson Institute, 1990).
[b]Daniel Drezner, *The Sanctions Paradox: Economic Statecraft and International Relations* (New York: Cambridge University Press, 1999).
[c]Dean Lacy and Emerson M. S. Niou, "Theory of Economic Sanctions and Issue Linkage: The Roles of Preferences, Information, and Threats," *Journal of Politics* 66, 1 (2004): 25–42.
[d]For additional reading, see David Baldwin, *Economic Statecraft* (Princeton, NJ: Princeton University Press, 1985); Robert Pape, "Why Economic Sanctions Do Not Work," *International Security* 22, 2 (1997): 90–136; A. Cooper Drury, "Sanctions as Coercive Diplomacy: The U.S. President's Decision to Initiate Economic Sanctions," *Political Research Quarterly* 54, 3 (2001): 485–508.

3,500 are foreign service officers (FSOs), work in these outposts. These FSOs work alongside personnel from other federal departments and agencies, including Defense, Commerce, Agriculture, Homeland Security, USAID, and the Peace Corps.[34]

Occasionally, the State Department must close an embassy abroad and remove its FSOs from the country. This usually occurs when the country is in turmoil or when diplomatic relations between the country and the United States sour, to the point that the U.S. government fears for its officers' safety. In February 2011, for example, a fresh wave of violence broke out in Syria after the Bashar al-Assad regime cracked down on protestors. After one assault left more than 200 people dead, the State Department decided to shut down its embassy in the Syrian capital of Damascus. U.S. Ambassador to Syria Robert Ford left the country, along with all U.S. citizens working at the embassy, and the State Department issued a travel warning urging all additional Americans to "depart immediately."[35]

The State Department is hierarchical. The secretary of state leads the department and is the most visible and notable figure of American diplomacy. Beneath the secretary is the deputy secretary and then several undersecretaries in charge of planning and coordination. State Department bureaus are organized in two ways: by issue and by region. Some bureaus focus on particular regions, whereas others are tasked with particular issues cutting across regions (such as AIDS policy or counterterrorism). Bureaus charged with regions then coordinate desk officers and personnel who focus on particular countries.

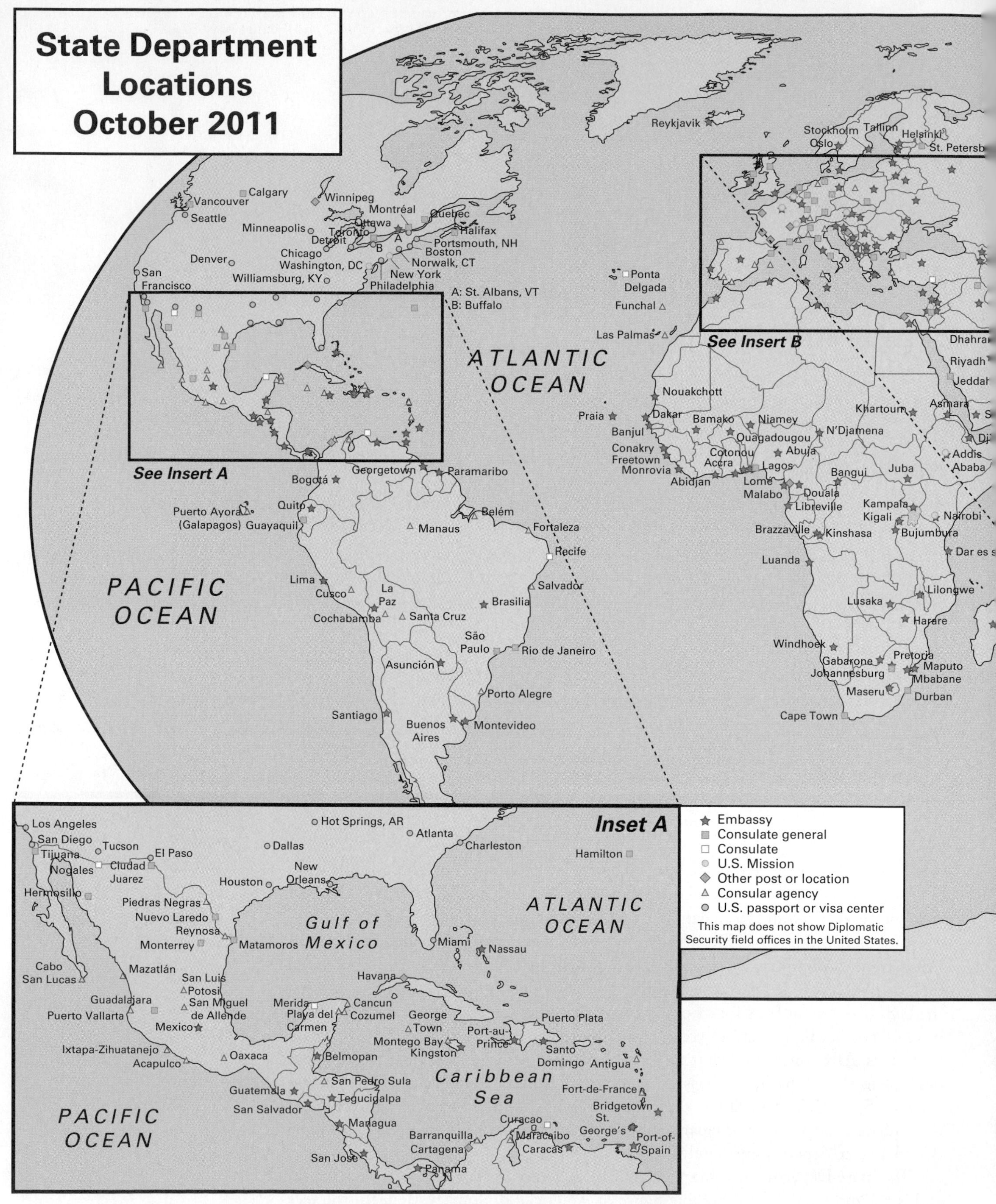

FIGURE 18.1 STATE DEPARTMENT EMBASSIES, CONSULATES, AND OTHER ADMINISTRATIVE OUTPOSTS.

In order to assert its global presence, the United States posts foreign service officers to virtually every nation around the globe.

Source: US State Department, available online at http://www.state.gov/documents/organization/177397.pdf .

18.1
18.2
18.3
18.4
18.5

18.1

18.2

18.3

18.4

18.5

Defense Department
the agency created by the National Security Act in 1947 that replaced the Departments of War and the Navy.

The State Department's structure is also fairly stable over time. The majority of department officials are career civil servants, not political appointments. As a result, the bureaucracy largely remains in place, even as presidential administrations change. This bureaucratic stability gives American foreign policy a degree of permanence as well. Civil servants who are lifetime government employees feel less beholden to any given president or administration than they do to maintaining the status quo. At times, this puts the State Department bureaucracy at odds with the current president, who may want to push for a significant new direction in U.S. policy abroad. These divergent interests sometimes lead to friction between department officials and their superiors inside the White House.

The Defense Department Oversees the Military

The primary responsibility of the **Defense Department** is to defend the nation from external attack. Increasingly, though, the United States also has relied on the Defense Department to pursue a wide variety of other objectives. In just the past two decades, the military has conducted counterterrorism efforts in the Middle East, provided assistance to war-torn areas in Africa, trained other militaries for antidrug operations in South America, and struggled to maintain stability in Afghanistan. This expansive set of missions has raised conflicts between the military and its civilian leaders over the appropriate uses of American military personnel.

As shown in Figure 18.2, expenditures by the Defense Department far eclipse expenditures by the State Department. Although defense spending has varied with historical events—such as the escalation of the Vietnam War in the mid-1960s and the Reagan buildup of the 1980s—it trends clearly upward. State Department spending has also grown over time, but at a much slower rate.

At the end of the Cold War, military spending fell significantly, creating a small "peace dividend" brought by declining superpower tensions. This trend, however, quickly reversed with the terrorist attacks of 2001. Between 2001 and 2010, American military spending increased by 81 percent, compared to an average increase of 32 percent in other countries during that time period. U.S. military expenditures

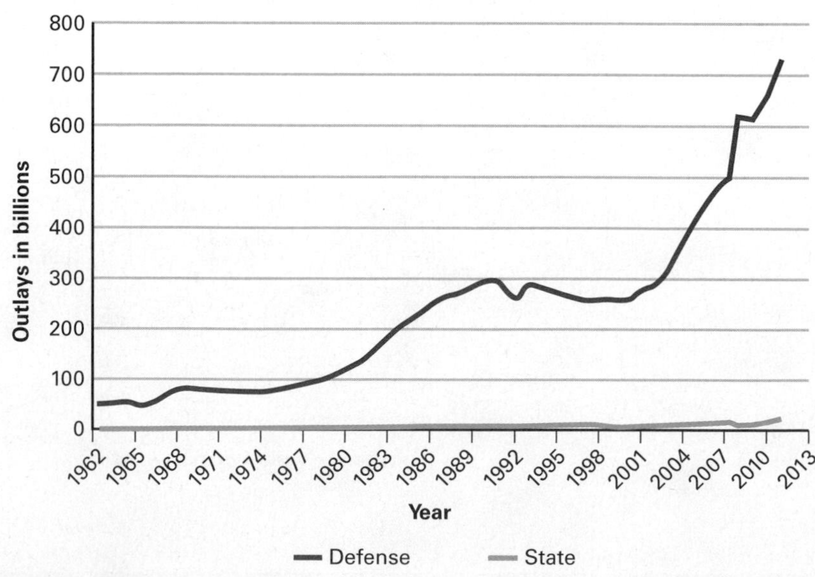

FIGURE 18.2 DEFENSE DEPARTMENT BUDGET VS. STATE DEPARTMENT BUDGET.
Shown here are the annual Defense and State Departments' outlays between 1962 and 2011. The Defense Department has always had a larger budget than the State Department, but the discrepancy between the two increased substantially beginning in the Reagan administration.

Source: http://www.gpo.gov/fdsys/browse/collectionGPO.action?collectionCode=BUDGET

Explore on MyPoliSciLab

How Much Does America Spend on Defense?

The United States has the largest defense budget in the world, but many observers still ask "Do we spend enough?" At the end of the Vietnam War, Americans all agreed that defense spending should be increased. Since then, Democrats and Independents became more "dovish" (anti-defense spending), while Republicans became far more "hawkish" (pro-defense spending). These differences became most pronounced in the years following the Iraq War and after George W. Bush's reelection in 2004.

Partisan Differences over Defense Spending

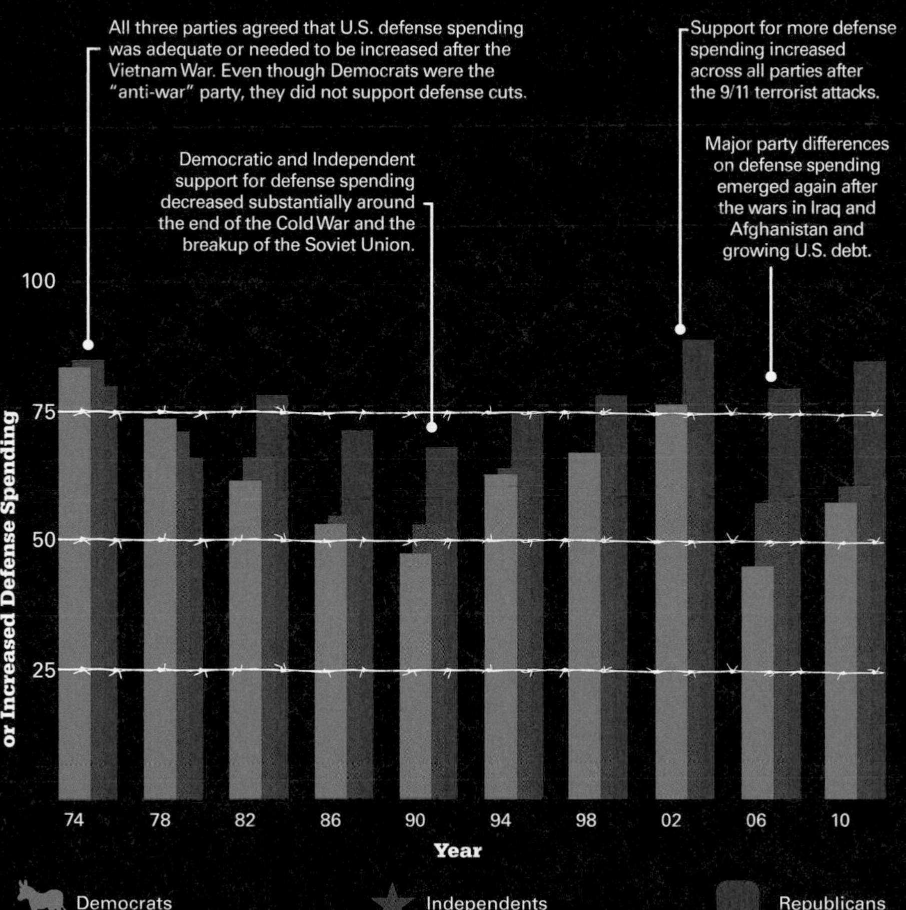

All three parties agreed that U.S. defense spending was adequate or needed to be increased after the Vietnam War. Even though Democrats were the "anti-war" party, they did not support defense cuts.
Democratic and Independent support for defense spending decreased substantially around the end of the Cold War and the breakup of the Soviet Union.
Support for more defense spending increased across all parties after the 9/11 terrorist attacks.
Major party differences on defense spending emerged again after the wars in Iraq and Afghanistan and growing U.S. debt.
100
75
50
25
% of Respondents who Support Existing or Increased Defense Spending
74
78
82
86
90
94
98
02
06
10
Year
Democrats
Independents
Republicans

The United States Spends the Most on Defense

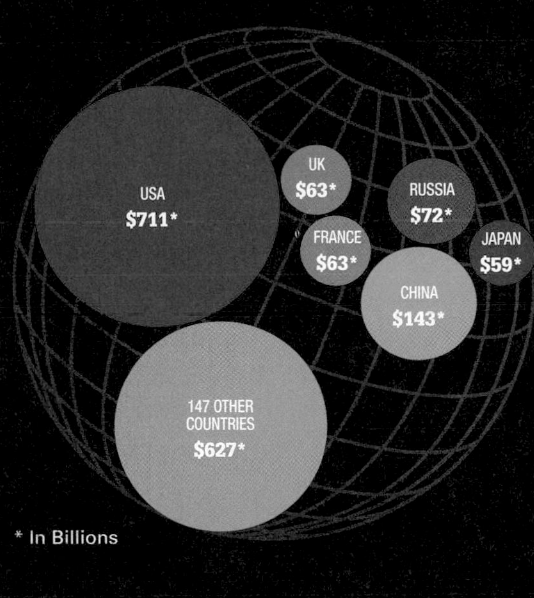

* In Billions

SOURCE: Data from Stockholm International Peace Research Institute (SIPRI) Yearbook, www.sipri.org; and the General Social Survey, 1982-2010.

Investigate Further

Concept Do Americans view defense spending as excessive? The United States currently has the largest defense budget in the world—twice the amount of China, the U.K., France, Japan, and Russia combined. But most Americans think the U.S. spends enough or should spend even more on defense.

Connection How do events relate to changes in support for defense spending? Wars, terrorist attacks, and recessions all influence public opinion of government spending. After the Cold War, both parties agreed not to maintain or increase the defense budget. After the 9/11 attacks, both parties supported increased spending.

Cause How does partisanship shape perceptions of defense spending? Democrats and Independents are more likely than Republicans to say that we spend too much on defense. These differences have become more pronounced in the last decade as the global war on terrorism became increasingly politicized.

now outstrip even those observed during the Cold War, surpassing $700 billion annually. In 2010, the United States accounted for 43 percent of the world's total military expenditures. America now spends more on its military than the next 14 nations combined.[36] By comparison, the country with the second largest military, China, spends less than a fifth of what the United States spends. In part, this is due to the sheer size of America's economy. Yet, it is also a consequence of spending priorities: In the United States, military expenditures make up almost 5 percent of GDP. In contrast, the average spending amount for the nations with the 14 biggest militaries is 2.6 percent of GDP. Out of these countries, only oil-rich Saudi Arabia devotes more of its economy to military spending (10.4 percent of GDP) than the United States does.

Although the U.S. military is unquestionably powerful, there is some debate among policy experts over whether its vast size actually makes America safer. Some analysts argue that America's insistence on having such a large military is antiquated, more fitting of a time when the country feared attacks from other countries, such as the Soviet Union. In today's global climate, these analysts say, the greatest threat to American security comes from non-state actors, such as al-Qaeda and other terrorist groups. They argue that maintaining an incredibly powerful army forces other countries to depend on the United States for their own defense, thereby making America a global police force. This role, in turn, makes the United States a greater target for terrorist groups.[37] Other policy experts dispute this assessment. They claim that America's overwhelming military advantage acts as a deterrent that prevents state and even non-state actors from attacking the United States (and each other) for fear of a powerful reprisal by U.S. forces.

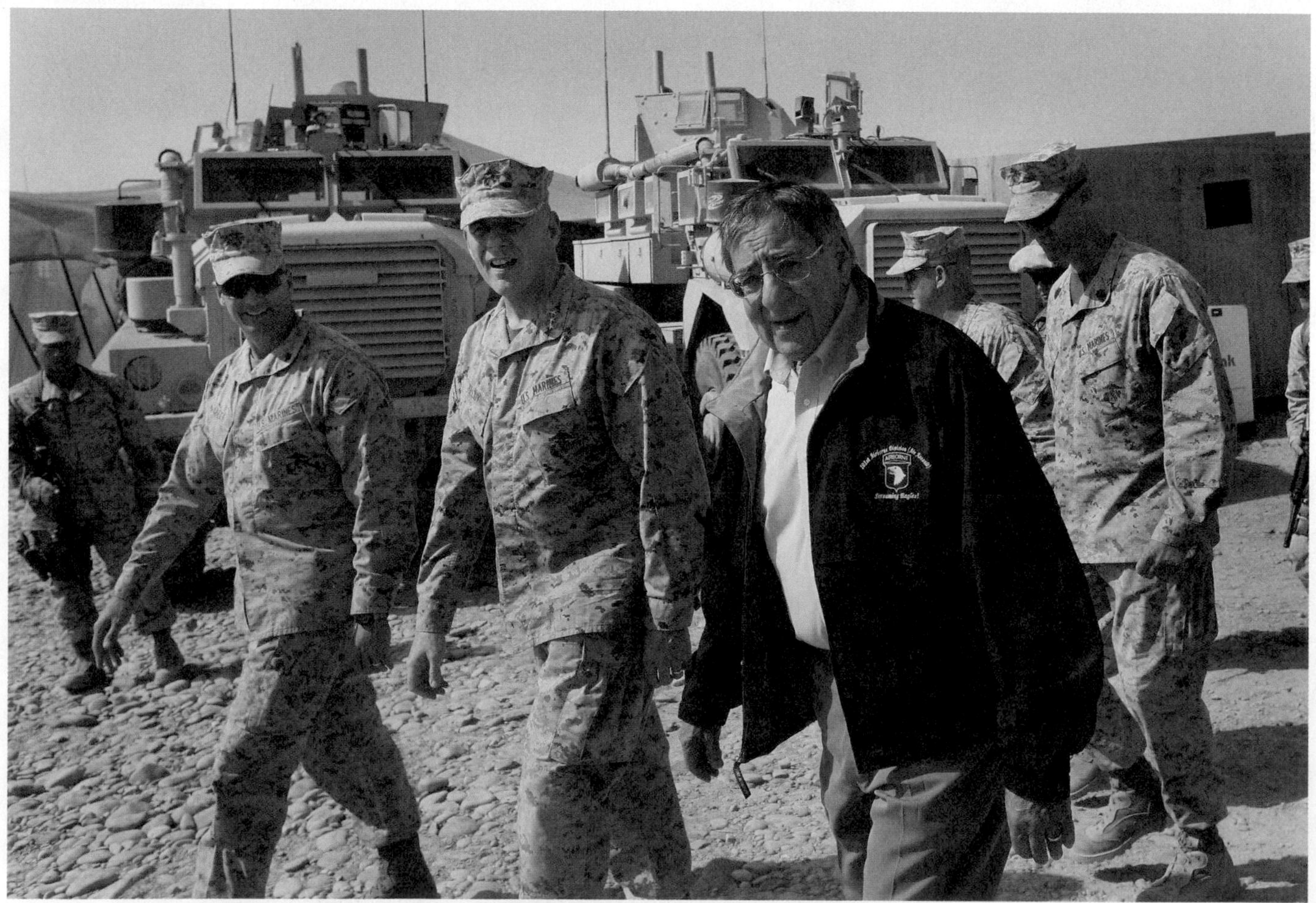

A CIVILIAN LEADER OF THE U.S. MILITARY

Secretary of Defense Leon Panetta takes time to meet with U.S. soldiers serving in military bases in Afghanistan.

Despite its size, the Defense Department is relatively young. It was created in 1947 to replace the Department of War, a weak institution that did not include the U.S. Navy and usually lay dormant until a major conflict arose. In the Cold War era, when the United States sought to meet any threat presented by the Soviet Union, a more permanent military establishment was needed. Thus began the growth of the Defense Department into the largest executive branch agency—an agency that employed over 34 percent of all federal government workers in 2008.[38]

Leon Panetta assumed the office of secretary of defense in July 2011. Like his predecessor Robert Gates, Panetta came into the position after serving as director of the Central Intelligence Agency (CIA). While heading the CIA, Panetta oversaw the covert operation in Pakistan that led to the death of al-Qaeda leader Osama bin Laden. The move from Gates to Panetta was seen in large part as an attempt by the Obama administration to project an image of continuity in the Defense Department. The two men are good friends and have repeatedly recommended each other for top government positions.[39] To date, Panetta has largely continued to implement the same policies as his predecessor.

Central Intelligence Agency (CIA)
the cornerstone of U.S. efforts to gather and analyze data in order to confront America's actual and potential enemies.

Numerous Executive Agencies Provide Intelligence Services

To formulate U.S. foreign policy, the government needs reliable information about goings-on around the globe—about the activities and objectives of other states, the creation of new alliances between states and the dissolution of old ones, possible threats to U.S. economic and political interests, and many other things. This intelligence crucially facilitates the State Department's diplomatic efforts and the Defense Department's war planning.

Since World War II, the **Central Intelligence Agency (CIA)** has had primary responsibility for collecting and analyzing foreign intelligence. The CIA is a fairly large organization, although the exact size of its budget and staff is classified. The popular conception of the CIA depicts the agency's employees as shadowy figures staging cloak-and-dagger operations to overthrow foreign governments. This reputation is not altogether undeserved. In the immediate aftermath of World War II, for instance, the CIA engaged in activities as diverse as influencing election outcomes, sponsoring coups, and assassinating foreign leaders. The CIA's success in these endeavors led to its increased use as an operational foreign policy tool, sometimes replacing traditional military forces.

For the most part, though, CIA employees undertake far more mundane operations: monitoring overseas news for signs of crises, reading and analyzing reports from field offices abroad, briefing executive branch members or Congress of looming threats to American interests, or simply distilling the massive amounts of information it gathers. Historically, the CIA has enjoyed tremendous power and latitude to conduct such operations, yet it is subject to considerable scrutiny and occupies a challenging role. When a surprise event occurs, Congress often holds the CIA accountable for neglecting to anticipate it. If the CIA fails, all Americans see the outcome—a revolution, bombing, or other incident that harms American interests. Yet when the agency succeeds in thwarting secret threats, it receives no public accolades. The CIA must walk a fine line between "crying wolf" and keeping the White House prepared for potential problems.

It is not surprising, then, that the agency received substantial blame for failing to foresee the September 11 terrorist attacks. Some criticisms, though, were perhaps unwarranted. After all, the CIA had been taking steps since the late 1990s to capture al-Qaeda ringleader Osama bin Laden, who justified terrorist methods on the basis of perceived Western imperial designs and Islamic doctrine. During the summer of 2001, American intelligence had intercepted 34 al-Qaeda messages referencing an upcoming event. This "chatter" indicated something was brewing, but it did not provide the date or location of the attack.[40]

18.1

18.2

18.3

18.4

18.5

Department of Homeland Security (DHS)
the agency created in the aftermath of September 11 to coordinate the work of agencies involved in preventing and responding to attacks on the United States.

The CIA, however, is not the only agency charged with collecting and analyzing national security intelligence. In fact, a veritable alphabet soup of agencies has such responsibilities. The National Security Agency (NSA) is one of the more prominent ones. Formed in 1952, the NSA monitors communications coming into and out of the United States. The NSA also specializes in cryptography—the making and breaking of secret codes.[41] For decades, denial of the agency's existence by the U.S. government led many to quip that NSA stood for "No Such Agency."

The State and Defense Departments also include their own intelligence arms. The Defense Department operates the Defense Intelligence Agency (DIA). Founded in 1961, the DIA is supposed to supply intelligence and analysis to the secretary of defense and the Joint Chiefs. Similarly, each military service branch conducts its own intelligence activities. The U.S. Army, Navy, Air Force, and Marines regularly contribute to the development of foreign policy strategies. In the State Department, the Bureau of Intelligence and Research (INR) does not gather intelligence directly, but it creates intelligence reports for the secretary of state based on the knowledge of its area experts. Even the Federal Bureau of Investigation (FBI), which is supposed to focus on domestic security issues, is involved in intelligence. The FBI tracks international terrorism suspects who travel to the United States and keeps tabs on any terrorist group that may attempt to find resources in America.

With so many different agencies pursuing overlapping mandates, the foreign policy bureaucracy is neither as efficient nor as effective as many critics would like. In the aftermath of September 11, therefore, the Office of the Director of National Intelligence (ODNI) was created to oversee the many intelligence agencies in the federal government. In theory, the ODNI coordinates the analysis of intelligence from *all* sectors of the intelligence community, including the CIA, FBI, INR, and all Defense Department agencies. In practice, this goal is difficult, because each agency attempts to protect its turf (and thereby its budget). Although the ODNI has worked hard to coordinate the activities of all these executive branch agencies, it continues to encounter significant resistance.[42]

The **Department of Homeland Security (DHS)** was also created in the aftermath of September 11. Like the ODNI, the DHS coordinates the work of agencies involved in preventing and responding to attacks on the United States. The director of homeland security is a Cabinet-level official who, in theory, has the power to coordinate intelligence, analysis, and response to strikes against the United States. Creation of the DHS merged 22 agencies with more than 177,000 employees. It combined agencies as varied as the Secret Service, U.S. Customs, the Immigration and Naturalization Service (INS), the Federal Emergency Management Agency (FEMA), and the Coast Guard. It has yet to be seen whether the ODNI and the DHS, in combination, can effectively coordinate the efforts of their respective agencies charged with collecting the information needed to protect the country.

The Role of Congress

18.3 Describe the power of Congress to shape foreign policy.

Presidents stand front and center in debates about foreign policy. Congress, nonetheless, often appears as a worthy adversary. True, legislators may be less involved in foreign policy than in domestic policy, but it would be incorrect to claim, even during the Cold War, that Congress sat silently by, ceding all authority to the president. As we survey the various foreign policy powers of Congress, we will highlight historical examples in which Congress attempted to check presidential influence over foreign policy.

Congress Enacts Foreign Policy Statutes

Congress legislates on a variety of foreign policy topics: weapons programs, foreign aid, environmental standards, and numerous other issues. Sometimes Congress wields influence by crafting legislation. In October 2011, for instance, a law that had previously been passed by Congress automatically cut off all funding for the United Nations Educational, Scientific and Cultural Organization (UNESCO), after that body voted to admit Palestine as a member. At other times, Congress uses appropriations bills to provide more or less funding than the president has requested for specific projects, ranging from military operations in the Middle East to humanitarian ventures in Southeast Asia.

Members of Congress tend to pay special attention to foreign trade, for it has immediate implications for the nation's economic growth, unemployment rate, and the cost of goods to the average citizen. The key issue in trade policy concerns **tariffs,** which are taxes on goods exchanged between nations. High tariffs tend to discourage trade, whereas lower tariffs tend to promote it.

The most significant trade agreement in recent history is the **North American Free Trade Agreement (NAFTA).** NAFTA's roots lie in the 1988 Canada–U.S. Free Trade Agreement, which aimed to steadily decrease tariffs and other barriers to trade and investment between the two countries. In the early 1990s, Mexican President Carlos Salinas expressed strong interest in extending the agreement to his own country. Salinas, U.S. President George H. W. Bush, and Canadian Prime Minister Brian Mulroney worked to build domestic support for the trilateral measure, and the three executives signed NAFTA in December 1992. Bush's failed reelection bid that year could have derailed congressional ratification, but instead the incoming president, Bill Clinton, took up the cause in 1993. In November 1993, NAFTA passed in both the House and the Senate.[43]

How has NAFTA affected the U.S. economy? Some areas of the country benefit from freer trade because their industries produce goods that are export oriented—that is, most of the goods made are sold overseas. Given that free trade agreements also mean that the other countries in the agreement will cut their own tariffs, this step decreases the price of American goods overseas and leads to more sales. These can increase revenue, create jobs, and cut the cost of goods to consumers. Other industries,

tariff
a tax on goods exchanged between nations.

North American Free Trade Agreement (NAFTA)
an agreement, signed in 1992, to reduce tariff and nontariff barriers to trade and investment among Canada, Mexico, and the United States.

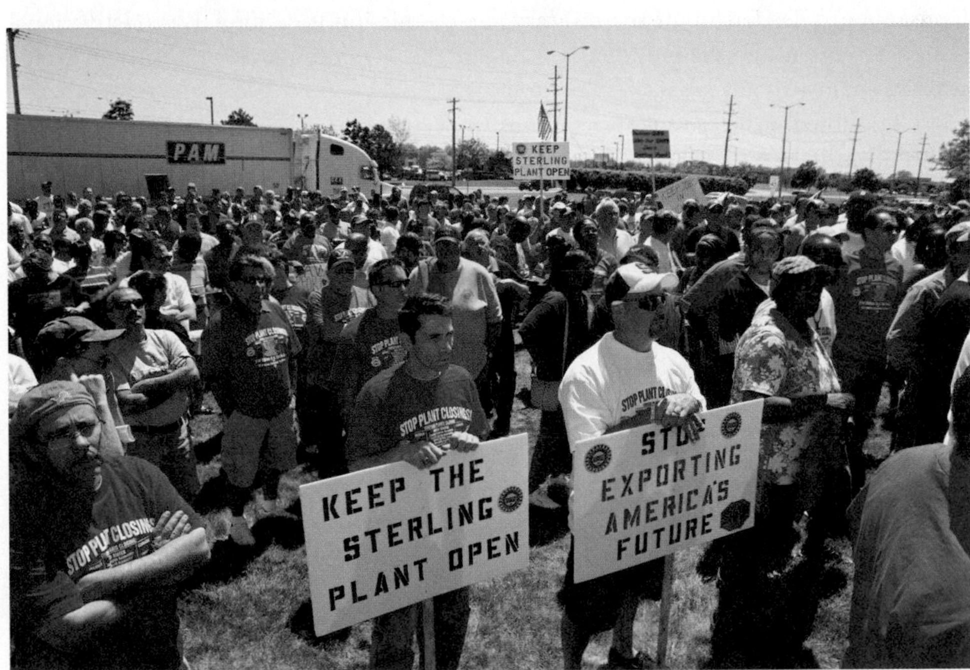

THE COSTS OF FREE TRADE

With the reduction of tariff barriers and the rise of globalization, numerous U.S. manufacturing plants have relocated abroad. Here, autoworkers rally to keep a domestic Chrysler assembly plant open. How should policy makers weigh the relative costs and benefits of free trade?

though, may suffer from free trade. The increased competition inspired by NAFTA means that domestic factories that are less efficient may close, jobs may be lost, and economic growth may falter. Further, different countries and districts have different specializations, which NAFTA also stands to disrupt. Thus, free trade can be seen as good or as bad, depending on the particular district in question and the country with which the United States is signing the agreement.

Congress also influences the foreign policy-making process through procedural legislation—legislation that changes how institutions in the executive branch are structured or operate on a day-to-day basis. For example, after a number of high-profile military operations were carried out in a haphazard manner, Congress passed the Goldwater-Nichols Act of 1986, which mandated that the chair of the Joint Chiefs of Staff be the primary military adviser to the president and be in charge of long-term military planning and budget coordination. It also required that the staff of the Joint Chiefs serve only the chair, rather than the commanders of the individual service branches. With this act, members of Congress hoped to give the chair more institutional powers, thereby reducing interbranch competition for budget and operations and leading to better military advice and performance.

Finally, Congress occasionally enacts symbolic resolutions that have implications for foreign policy. On March 4, 2010, for instance, the House Foreign Affairs Committee passed a resolution labeling the mass killings of Armenians in Turkey in 1915 a "genocide." Despite last-minute pressure by the Obama administration, the nonbinding resolution passed the committee by a vote of 23–22. Turkey reacted negatively to the vote, temporarily endangering the relationship between the two countries.[44]

☐ Congress Retains the Power to Declare War

Congress's constitutional authority to declare war places it in the middle of debates over proposed uses of force by the American military. Perhaps no area of congressional-presidential politics has received more attention than the question of who has the ultimate authority to initiate and oversee the conduct of war.[45] One reason for the pitched debate is that the Constitution is vague by design: whereas Congress is given the power to declare war, the president is the commander in chief of the military. Consequently, leadership of the military and its mission is divided. By constitutional design, Congress and the president must share the power to initiate and sustain armed conflict against an adversary.

Undoubtedly, the president maintains important advantages over Congress in the realm of military policy. For example, Congress can call hearings to gather information about a potential or actual military conflict; however, a president has the NSC, including all the major military and civilian figures, at his beck and call at a moment's notice. As a result, the president is able to respond to foreign crises more quickly—and with more information—than is Congress.

Congress, however, occasionally challenges the president's war powers. In response to what many critics argued was a failed deployment in Vietnam, Congress passed the War Powers Act in 1973. The law, passed over President Nixon's veto, placed several legal constraints on the executive's ability to initiate international conflict. First, the president must consult with Congress *before* committing armed forces into hostile situations. Second, the president must report to Congress within 48 hours after troops are introduced into an area where hostilities exist or are imminent. Third, and most important, the troops must be withdrawn within 60 days unless Congress authorizes them to stay longer.[46]

On paper, the War Powers Act would appear to be a significant constraint on executive authority. In practice, though, the act has constrained presidents less than its designers had hoped. Never has the act been used to end a military venture. Indeed, the 60-day clock has been started only twice. The first time, after the 1983 invasion of Lebanon, Congress immediately approved an 18-month extension. More recently, in March 2011, President Obama sent U.S. planes to assist NATO forces in bombing

Libya, without prior approval from Congress. The Obama administration argued that the 60-day clock had not started, because the move did not constitute military action under the definition of the War Powers Act. Congress responded by passing two bills. In the first bill, legislators voted not to extend the operations in Libya, issuing a strong rebuke to President Obama. Yet, in the second bill, the body voted to approve funding for the Libyan military operation. As a result, Obama continued to support the NATO efforts, despite apparently having failed to abide by the War Powers Act.

The infrequency and inefficacy of its use has led some scholars to condemn the War Powers Act as "a sellout, a surrender."[47] Other scholars, however, argue that the act has caused at least some presidents to limit military actions to shorter, smaller campaigns.[48]

treaty
an international agreement in which the United States becomes a party once the president has signed and two-thirds of the Senate has ratified it.

executive agreement
an international agreement in which the United States becomes a party once the president has signed it, without requiring approval from two-thirds of the Senate.

Congress Confirms Nominees for Foreign Policy Positions

The Senate has the power to confirm individuals nominated to various Cabinet-level and ambassadorial posts. Although the vast majority of appointees are confirmed, the hearings often reveal pointed disagreements over aspects of foreign policy. Controversy is especially likely when a nominee seems underqualified or espouses views that substantially diverge from the policy positions held by members of the Senate Committee on Foreign Relations, which must first approve the nomination.

Occasionally, a high-profile nominee is rejected or held up to such scrutiny that a president opts to withdraw the nomination. In September 2010, President Barack Obama took advantage of a congressional recess to appoint Mari Carmen Aponte as ambassador to El Salvador. When her temporary appointment expired at the end of 2011, Obama nominated her to continue serving in the post. Senate Republicans opposed the selection, based on unsubstantiated rumors that Aponte's former boyfriend had been a Cuban spy. Despite holding a minority of seats in the Senate, Republicans successfully filibustered Aponte's confirmation vote.[49] For the most part, though, controversial appointments for high-level diplomatic positions have been rare. Foreign states and international organizations, after all, want to have assurances that the U.S. officials with whom they negotiate have the full backing of the U.S. government.

Congress Provides Advice and Consent on International Treaties

The Senate also has the power to ratify **treaties** signed by the president. There have been several high-profile instances of the Senate's rejecting treaties signed by a president, thus dealing a blow to the ongoing conduct of foreign policy. In the most famous instance, as mentioned earlier, the Senate rejection of American involvement in the League of Nations after World War I returned the United States to a course of isolationism for another two decades. In 1999, the U.S. Senate rejected the Comprehensive Test Ban Treaty (CTBT) after Republicans objected to several provisions.

Rejection is rare, however. In fact, the Senate itself reports that it rejected only 21 of the approximately 1,500 treaties it has considered since 1789.[50] Still, if they are worried about Congress's reaction, presidents can bypass the treaty ratification process by signing an **executive agreement,** which is automatically binding on state signatories. Between 1939 and 2009, the United States has entered into roughly 1,100 treaties compared with approximately 16,500 executive agreements.[51] The ratio of executive agreements to treaties has steadily increased during the past half-century. Presidents have made executive agreements involving security alliances, trade, finance, and a variety of other areas. Executive agreements, however, do not allow presidents to do exactly as they please. Congress may pass a law that rescinds an executive agreement, or it may refuse to appropriate the funds needed for implementation. In addition, executive agreements tend to survive for shorter periods of time, as future presidents are free to overturn them unilaterally.

18.1

18.2

18.3

18.4

18.5

ethnic lobby
an interest group that advocates policies focusing on specific foreign states.

Congress Oversees Foreign Policy Bureaucracies

Congress also influences foreign policy through oversight. At any point, either chamber can convene hearings on topics related to the conduct of foreign policy. Although legislation may or may not result from these fact-finding exercises, the hearings themselves sometimes generate tremendous publicity about issues. This power of investigation can be highly influential in setting the stage for new laws or in simply bringing the public's attention to a particular issue.

In September 2007, for example, General David Petraeus and Ambassador Ryan Crocker provided much-anticipated testimony concerning the ongoing war in Iraq. Democrats and Republicans alike used the hearings to trumpet their positions.[52] Through the hearings, the American public also learned of some nagging uncertainties. Asked whether ethnic reconciliation in Iraq appeared likely, Ambassador Crocker pointed to encouraging signs but admitted, "How long that is going to take and . . . whether it will succeed, I can't predict." When Senator John Warner (R-VA) inquired whether Petraeus's proposed troop surge would make the U.S. safer, the general replied, "Sir, I don't know, actually."[53]

In April 2008, General Petraeus and Ambassador Crocker returned to the Hill to brief Congress on the developing situation in Iraq. In the midst of a contested presidential election, Petraeus pleaded his case for maintaining substantial troops on the ground, claiming that "withdrawing too many forces too quickly could jeopardize the progress of the past year."[54] Senators on both sides of the aisle used the testimony as an opportunity to elaborate their own foreign policy positions. Senator McCain, who would become the Republican nominee for president, called the withdrawal "reckless and irresponsible," whereas Democratic presidential candidate Senator Hillary Clinton warned about perpetuating the "same failed policy." George Voinovich (R-OH) claimed that "the American people have had it up to here" with the war and demanded a more precise timeline for withdrawal.[55] Petraeus counseled continued patience, insisting that progress remained possible but that it would require continued military and diplomatic investments.

The Role of Interest Groups

18.4 Analyze the role of interest groups in foreign policy making.

The federal government does not create foreign policy in a vacuum. Indeed, numerous interest groups weigh in with advice of their own. And given their organization and funding, foreign policy interest groups often exert a tremendous amount of influence. They include three major types: ethnic lobbies, business groups, and think tanks.

Ethnic Lobbies Advocate Foreign Policies That Concern Specific Countries

Some of the most prominent foreign policy interest groups are **ethnic lobbies.** These groups advocate policies that focus on specific foreign states. In some instances, ethnic lobbies encourage U.S. assistance to a foreign state. In other instances, they pressure the federal government to take a hard line against the foreign state's governing regime.

One of the more controversial interest groups in American foreign affairs is the American-Israeli Public Affairs Committee (AIPAC). Founded in 1953, AIPAC promotes close ties between Israel and the United States. Detractors have long criticized it for pressuring American decision makers to support and aid Israel even when its policies disrupt American relations with other Middle Eastern countries. However, the close relationship between the United States and Israel would likely have developed and prospered without AIPAC. After all, the United States began sending large quantities of weapons to Israel in the mid-1960s, well before AIPAC was a major player in U.S. politics. Even then, U.S. decision makers saw Israel as one of the few stable, pro-Western allies in a hostile region. The Soviet Union had garnered staunch allies such as Syria and Egypt, and other pro-Western states such as Lebanon and Jordan faced consistent internal threats.[56]

Cuban Americans make up another powerful ethnic lobby. Following Fidel Castro's 1959 communist revolution, many Cubans fled to the United States, particularly to Florida. Initially, the exiles hoped to return to their homeland once democracy had been restored. As Castro solidified one-party communist rule, however, the focus turned to isolating Cuba in the international arena. By 1962, the United States had enacted an economic embargo against its neighbor to the south, and in 1996 the Helms-Burton Act, which placed even more stringent restrictions on U.S. relations with Cuba, bolstered the embargo. Only recently, following Castro's retirement after 50 years of rule, has communication between the two countries shown some initial signs of reviving.

To be sure, the Cuban American ethnic lobby exhibits a number of characteristics that could contribute to foreign policy influence: it is well organized, geographically concentrated, well funded, and motivated by involuntary exile.[57] However, in light of the anticommunism atmosphere of the Cold War, one could question whether the lobby was decisive in U.S. efforts to isolate Cuba. Just because American foreign policy choices support the interests of a pressure group does not mean the pressure group is instrumental in the outcome. Consider the classic political science definition of power paraphrased from the political scientist Robert Dahl: power is the ability to convince others to do things they would otherwise not do.[58] To show that an interest group has power or influence, one must show that a policy would have been different without the group's pressure. This is difficult to determine, for it requires us to intuit how the world would differ in the absence of a particular interest group.

Business Groups Increasingly Attempt to Influence Foreign Policy

Perhaps the most powerful set of foreign policy pressures arises from multinational business and defense firms. Traditionally, some of the more powerful lobbying groups in America have been those involved in the production and sale of military goods. In his farewell address, President Eisenhower warned against "the acquisition of unwanted influence, whether sought or unsought, by the military-industrial complex."[59] The "military-industrial complex" has become a pejorative catchphrase used by those who oppose the political influence of big business, especially in the realm of national security policy.

The phrase suggests a handful of business and military elites conspiring to drive up (possibly unnecessary) defense spending. The fact is, though, that numerous segments of American society—including Congress, academia, business, and the military establishment—have aligned interests concerning defense spending. Various interests clearly benefit from defense spending: The military can be ready to defend the national interest, businesses can make money and spur economic growth, individuals can find and keep jobs, and each of these benefits helps members of Congress get reelected. One analysis of defense spending during the Cold War concluded that 1 in 10 jobs in the United States relied, either directly or indirectly, on federal defense spending.[60] At a time when defense budgets are hovering close to $700 billion, the dependence of many businesses on defense spending is clearly enormous.

Other businesses lobby the government on a host of foreign policy issues, but perhaps no issue is more common than trade. As previously discussed, because so many individuals benefit *and* suffer from trade, thousands of industry-based groups have formed to lobby Congress and the president for more or less protection. Each time free trade discussions begin with a new country, lobbying groups support or oppose the proposals, based on whether their industries will be helped or harmed.[61]

Think Tanks Offer Foreign Policy Advice

Think tanks support and publicize the work of scholars, many of whom have significant foreign policy expertise. Drawing on their government experience or academic research, these scholars contribute to newsletters, magazines, journals, and opinion pieces advocating particular policies. Under certain circumstances, their opinions resonate widely.

One of America's most prominent think tanks is the New York–based Council on Foreign Relations (CFR), which publishes the influential journal *Foreign Affairs*. Founded in 1921, the CFR grew out of an informal band of foreign policy experts who advised President Woodrow Wilson toward the end of World War I. In planning for a postwar world, this group helped formulate Wilson's Fourteen Points initiative, planting the seed for the United Nations and other innovations in international relations. Following World War II, the CFR again demonstrated its influence. In an anonymous *Foreign Affairs* article, George Kennan—a council member and State Department official—made the case that the United States should limit the Soviet Union's expansionist tendencies.[62] Containment, as discussed earlier, became the key American grand strategy during the Cold War.

The Council on Foreign Relations is not alone in offering foreign policy insights. In July 2007, two members of the Brookings Institution, a left-of-center think tank based in Washington, D.C., published a striking op-ed in the *New York Times*. Following an eight-day visit to Iraq, Michael O'Hanlan and Kenneth Pollack praised the "surge" in U.S. troop levels and chided opponents for ignoring encouraging changes. "We are finally getting somewhere in Iraq, at least in military terms," they declared.[63] The opinion piece drew attention to improvements that numerous observers had overlooked. Because it was written by critics of George W. Bush's prior handling of the Iraq War, the opinion piece had a dramatic influence on Washington debates about the war.

Contemporary Foreign Policy Challenges

18.5 Assess three of the foreign policy challenges that the United States faces today.

The United States continues to face extraordinary foreign policy challenges. It oversees a remarkably complex and dangerous international environment. And, because of its status as a world superpower, foreign nations regularly look to the United States to formulate solutions to both global and regional problems. This section highlights recent efforts of presidents, the foreign policy bureaucracy, Congress, interest groups, and other domestic political actors to confront three of the many critical foreign policy challenges faced by the United States today: how to reduce the threats of a North Korean nuclear program, how to respond to political upheaval in the Middle East, and how to manage China's rapid economic growth.

Diplomatic Efforts to Halt North Korea's Nuclear Program Have Proceeded Haltingly

On August 6, 1945, during World War II, a U.S. military plane dropped an atomic bomb code-named "Little Boy" that leveled the Japanese city of Hiroshima, killing tens of thousands almost immediately. Three days later, another U.S. plane dropped the atomic bomb code-named "Fat Man" on the Japanese city of Nagasaki. The United States, thereby, became the first—and to date the only—country to use a nuclear weapon against another country. The demonstration of such weapons' devastating strength, coupled with the crystallizing Cold War, fueled an international race for nuclear weapons. In 1949, the Soviet Union tested bombs of its own. By 1964, the United Kingdom, France, and China had acquired nuclear capabilities. Developments in rocket science made the specter of nuclear-armed states, able to project their power to far corners of the globe, much more real. And U.S. foreign policy needed to contend not only with the ramifications of America's own nuclear capability, but also with that of its allies and rivals.

Some observers saw this dilemma as a benefit for U.S. foreign policy. Perhaps the overwhelming might of nuclear weapons actually made them integral for *deterring* open hostilities between the East and West. By pursuing certain tactics—such as dividing up arsenals and placing warheads in underground facilities—nuclear powers could maintain second-strike capabilities. Thus, states would think hard about offensive moves, for even though the instigator might wreak havoc on its enemy, it would bring similarly devastating retaliation upon itself. This notion of "mutually assured destruction" may be one of the key reasons why the Cold War remained cold.

Diplomatic efforts to stem the proliferation of nuclear weapons were codified in the Nuclear Non-Proliferation Treaty, which opened for signature in 1968. The United States, the United Kingdom, and the Soviet Union signed almost immediately. The treaty stipulates that nonnuclear countries will not seek nuclear capabilities, preexisting nuclear states will not facilitate proliferation to more states, countries can acquire nuclear technology for peaceful uses such as energy, and all will work toward a somewhat vague disarmament goal. Currently, 190 countries are signatories.[64]

Still, considerable uncertainties persisted. Miscalculations, laxity, or accidents in *any* of the nuclear-capable states promised dire consequences. Moreover, nonnuclear countries reacted strongly. Although some called for total disarmament, others were eager to obtain nuclear power for themselves. During the 1970s, 1980s, and 1990s, countries such as South Africa, Libya, and Iraq launched, and then subsequently abandoned, efforts to acquire nuclear weapons. More recently, other countries, such as Iran and North Korea, have been accused of concealing weapons development behind civilian energy programs.

Since the end of the Cold War, concerns about nuclear proliferation have only intensified. The breakup of the Soviet Union scattered a massive stockpile among the newly independent countries. Even though much of the arsenal has been returned to Russia, part remains missing. And ensuring the stability of nuclear states such as Pakistan and ascertaining the motivations of "rogue states" are key priorities in U.S. foreign policy.

North Korea represents a key challenge for U.S. efforts to hinder the proliferation of nuclear weapons. Since the Korean War, relations between the United States and North Korea have fluctuated between strained and nonexistent. In 1990, satellite photos revealed a facility that appeared capable of producing weapons-grade plutonium from fuel rods. Deeply concerned, the United States, South Korea, and a number of other countries pushed for United Nations sanctions. The Clinton administration also engaged North Korean president Kim Il-Sung diplomatically, reaching a pact called the "Agreed Framework" in late 1994.[65]

Neither side, however, fulfilled all of its obligations. In the aftermath of the terrorist attacks of September 11, 2001, new intelligence indicated that North Korea was still pursuing a nuclear weapons program. In his 2002 State of the Union Address, President Bush denounced the developments and designated North Korea (as well as Iraq and Iran, which also were suspected of developing nuclear weapons) as a lynchpin of the "Axis of Evil."[66] A year later, North Korea announced its withdrawal from the Nuclear Non-Proliferation Treaty, declaring that it absolutely needed nuclear weapons to protect itself from U.S. "hostility."[67]

In 2007, North Korea detonated a nuclear bomb in an underground test. The following year, in return for fuel oil, North Korea agreed to dismantle its facilities and disclose its nuclear programs, and President Bush held out the prospect of open trade and political engagement if North Korea upheld its obligations under the agreement.

Further signs of progress surfaced in June 2008, as the cooling tower at the country's main nuclear weapons plant was destroyed—a visible indication that Kim Jong-Il was willing to back off from his nuclear program. President Bush called the event "a moment of opportunity for North Korea," and presumably the United States as well.

Tensions between North Korea and the United States resurfaced in April 2009, however, when North Korea test-launched a long-range ballistic missile. As an early challenge for President Obama, all eyes were on Washington to see how the new administration would respond. Obama criticized Kim's violations of international law and declared that "now is the time for a strong international response."[68] It proved difficult to turn words into actions, however, as the United States failed to rally the United Nations to punish North Korea for its actions.

Secretary of State Hillary Clinton subsequently offered to reconvene talks, but North Korea rejected the invitation, further isolating itself from the United States. In May 2009, news broke that North Korea successfully tested its second nuclear weapon. This time, the international response was much stronger as many nations condemned the test. Obama used the event to strengthen ties with South Korea and other international allies. The United Nations Security Council tightened sanctions on North Korea, and Japan enacted additional economic sanctions on exports to the country.[69]

Although U.S. attempts to curb North Korea's nuclear ambitions have failed more often than they have succeeded, recent developments have given American policy makers some cause for optimism. Following the death of North Korean leader Kim Jong-Il in December 2011, his son Kim Jong-Un assumed power. In a surprise move, the younger Kim soon announced that North Korea would suspend all nuclear weapons testing and uranium enrichment in exchange for substantial food aid from the United States. Further, the North Korean leader pledged to once again allow international inspectors to monitor the country's nuclear facilities. Although a positive development, U.S. officials greeted the move with mistrust, all too aware of North Korea's history of backing out of such agreements. After expressing hope that Kim Jong-Un was finally ready to seriously engage in disarmament, Secretary of State Clinton quickly added that the Obama administration still had "profound concerns."[70]

An Arab Spring Forces the United States to Reconsider Its Policies in the Middle East

In 1938, two American companies—Texaco and Standard Oil of California—discovered vast, untapped oil reserves lying under the ground in the deserts of Saudi Arabia. More discoveries of oil followed in neighboring areas such as Kuwait, Iraq, Iran, and Bahrain. Soon, it became apparent that a small portion of the world's landmass in the Middle East contained much of the world's most valuable reserves of oil. By the end of World War II, government policy makers suddenly described a region that had previously received little attention from the United States as "one of the greatest material prizes in world history."[71] The discoveries by Texaco and Standard Oil began a long and tumultuous history of U.S. involvement in the Middle East.

In an effort to advance its own interests in the region, the United States repeatedly intervened in Middle Eastern politics. At first, a desire to guard America's stake in oil, which grew steadily over time, motivated these interventions. In 1953, for example, the Eisenhower administration worked with Britain to help organize a coup overthrowing the Iranian government, which they saw as a threat to Iran's substantial oil supply. But as the United States continued to maintain a strong presence in the region, its strategic interests became more complex. During the Cold War, for instance, America solidified a strong alliance with Israel after its rival, Egypt, bought arms from the Soviet Union. At other times, the United States worked to secure stability in the region, helping to broker a series of peace agreements between Israel and Arab countries during the Carter and Clinton administrations.

By the time of the September 11 attacks on the World Trade Center and the Pentagon, America's economic and security interests in the Middle East were inseparable. Thus, when the Bush administration ordered the military to invade Iraq in 2003,

TENSIONS RISE AGAIN

In April 2012, South Koreans watched a television report on the launch of an earth observation satellite by the autocratic regime in North Korea. The satellite failed to enter orbit, which proved to be a mild embarrassment to the newly installed North Korean regime.

Unresolved Debate

Is There Such a Thing as the Democratic Peace?

In 1795, philosopher Immanuel Kant asserted that if every government were a democracy, then the world would exist in a state of "perpetual peace," because peoples from different countries would never vote to go to war with each other. Since the 1980s, this notion, now termed a "democratic peace," has gained traction, as few instances of armed conflict have occurred between democratic countries since the nineteenth century. If recent experience bears on the future, then Kant's observations have significant consequences for America foreign policy, primarily because they imply that the United States should promote international stability by actively encouraging other countries to become democracies. But can democracies really be counted on to refrain from going to war with one another? Is there such a thing as the democratic peace?

A DEMOCRATIC PEACE?

In 2012, President Barack Obama talks with British Prime Minister David Cameron while attending the NCAA Division I Men's Basketball Championship tournament. No ally is closer to the United States than Britain. Do the fact that they are both democracies contribute at all to their mutual cooperation?

YES

Although the mere existence of a correlation is not enough to say that democracy prevents countries from waging war on other democracies, democratic countries do appear to repeatedly avoid war by bargaining with one another in specific cases. Charles Lipson, another international relations scholar, argues that evidence shows that democracies have a "contracting advantage" when it comes to settling disputes with one another, which they do not enjoy with nondemocracies.[a]

- Four factors are common to all established democratic governments—a high level of transparency, continuity from one administration to the next, leaders' accountability to the citizenry, and constitutional laws that leaders must abide by.
- These factors make democracies reliable bargaining partners, because their foreign policy decisions are made fairly openly and, once made, usually remain stable over long periods of time.

NO

According to international relations scholar Christopher Layne, the idea that democracies always maintain peace with one another is a "myth."[b] *Layne takes a classic "realist" perspective, arguing that international politics always takes place in a state of anarchy, in which countries must compete with one another for a limited amount of resources. As a result, he concludes, the fact that democracies have rarely fought is merely a coincidence: given the right circumstances, countries will always enter into conflict with one another if they believe they can win a strategic advantage by doing so.*

- If populations really prevent democracies from waging war, then we should never see democracies waging war against nondemocratic countries either.
- Whatever correlation there is between democracy and peace does not prove causation, because other factors such as military capability play a crucial role in whether or not countries decide to go to war.

CONTRIBUTING TO THE DEBATE

Efforts to assess the existence and causes of the democratic peace run into two major roadblocks. First, it is not always clear how to define the terms of the debate: what constitutes a "democracy," for example, and what constitutes a war. And a second problem, related to the first, lies in the difficulty of proving causation. So long as it is unclear what examples are being studied, scholars will never be able to reach any sort of consensus on why democracies act the way they do.

These problems within the debate remain deep seated. As time passes, however, the sample size of total wars—and, potentially, total democracies—will continue to grow. This new evidence may help clarify for certain whether or not democracies are less likely to go to war. Once the general terms of the debate can be agreed upon, then the various causal arguments for why the peace might exist can be debated more fully.

WHAT DO YOU THINK?

1. What sort of evidence might be necessary to make a causal argument that democracy allows countries to coexist peacefully?
2. How might the existence of a democratic peace dictate the way the United States makes foreign policy decisions?

[a]Charles Lipson, *Reliable Partners: How Democracies Have Made a Separate Peace* (Princeton, NJ: Princeton University Press, 2003).
[b]Chrisopher Layne, "Kant or Cant: The Myth of the Democratic Peace," in Michael Brown, Sean M. Lynn-Jones, and Steven E. Miller, eds., *Debating the Democratic Peace* (Cambridge, MA: MIT Press, 1996).
[c]Layne, "Kant or Cant," 194.

18.1

18.2

18.3

18.4

18.5

Arab Spring
the popular uprisings that occurred in rapid succession throughout the Middle East beginning in 2010.

critics hotly disputed his motives. President Bush pointed to links between Iraq and al-Qaeda, as well as to suspicions about an Iraqi nuclear weapons program, as evidence that Saddam Hussein represented a security threat to the United States. Moreover, some argued, the transition of Iraq to a democracy would reduce tensions with the United States (see *Unresolved Debate: Is There Such a Thing as the Democratic Peace?*). However, critics maintained that Bush was interfering only to protect the interests of American oil companies, which had supported Bush politically since his time as governor of Texas. Still other political observers, such as Christopher Hitchens, made the case for American intervention in humanitarian terms, arguing that Hussein was a murderous dictator who had to be stopped from killing his own people.[72]

Although humanitarian arguments for intervening in the Middle East may have had merits, until recently the United States has rarely justified its foreign policy in the region on humanitarian reasons. Indeed, America has long supported regimes in countries such as Saudi Arabia and even Iraq that repressed their people but maintained positive diplomatic relations with the United States. And, since September 11, the American military has only increased its reliance on these regimes, whose assistance it needs in fighting the War on Terror.

For example, intelligence information from Pakistan—a country whose military helped harbor Osama bin Laden and other al-Qaeda operatives—also made the covert action that led to the death of Osama bin Laden in May 2011 possible.[73] At the same time as they worked with monarchical and dictatorial regimes, however, U.S. leaders proclaimed their support for the right of peoples around the world to democratically elect their own leadership. "We stand with democracies," President Bush asserted in 2006.[74] His successor, Barack Obama, echoed this statement in his 2009 inaugural address: "To those who cling to power through corruption and deceit and the silencing of dissent, know that you are on the wrong side of history."[75]

The tension between America's reliance on repressive regimes friendly to U.S. interests and its support of democratic governance came to a head during the early months of 2011. Just as America was drawing down its 200,000 troops from Iraq and Afghanistan, a tide of popular uprisings swept through the Middle East. On December 17, 2010, a young man in Tunisia named Mohamed Bouzid set himself on fire in protest against police interference with his business. This dramatic action ignited widespread protests that ultimately gave rise to the **Arab Spring.**

Bouzid's plight struck a chord among fellow Tunisians, who inhabit a country with one of the region's highest per capita GDPs, but who were governed by a repressive and corrupt political regime that failed to address unemployment and inflation. After Bouzid's suicide, other young Tunisians began organizing peaceful protests that spread rapidly with the aid of online social networking tools such as Twitter and Facebook. The Tunisian government responded rapidly and forcefully. First, it attempted to curtail access to media and the Internet. When protests continued, government leaders alternated between offering political concessions and cracking down on protests with brute force. Despite their best efforts, however, protests continued to grow, spurred on by local anger and substantial coverage from international media outlets. Finally, after 23 years of rule, Tunisian President Zine al-Abidine Ben Ali fled the country on January 14, 2011.

The success of Tunisia's protest spurred opposition forces throughout the Arab world into action. In the months that followed, Algeria, Egypt, Yemen, Bahrain, Libya, and Syria all experienced massive protests in quick succession. These Middle Eastern countries all shared a youthful demographic unable to find adequate employment. Their economic hardship meshed with simmering anger toward the repressive authoritarian regimes, which frequently squandered money through government corruption and inefficiency. The resulting tide of protests, which began peacefully, quickly escalated into violence, as those in power repeatedly resorted to using their country's security forces to physically stop public rallies and meetings. Each day, media outlets in the United States led with the latest news of widespread revolt and protestor casualties. While the West watched, the turmoil in the Arab world grew.

THE ARAB SPRING

What would eventually be known as the Arab Spring began with protests in Tunisia in late 2010. Here, a Tunis resident throws a stone while a police officer shoots tear gas canisters in front of Prime Minister Mohammed Ghannouchi's office.

This upheaval placed the Obama administration in a difficult position. As we discussed earlier in the chapter, policy making within the State Department tends to occur at an incremental pace. The Arab Spring, however, jeopardized several previous U.S. commitments in the region. As a result, the president, the State Department, and other officials were forced to adapt long-standing American foreign policies on the fly to fit the changing realities of power and interest in the Middle East.

This process did not always proceed smoothly. In Egypt, for instance, the United States had long considered authoritarian dictator Hosni Mubarak to be an important ally. When his regime began to lose its grip on power in the wake of massive protests, the initial response from the White House appeared confused, at times even contradictory. Some officials publicly stated that the United States continued to support the Mubarak regime; yet, just days later, a member of the National Security Council told reporters, "transition must begin without delay and produce immediate, irreversible progress that the people of Egypt can see and are demanding."[76] This difference in opinion reflected the complicated interests America has in the country. On the one hand, the United States did not want to alienate an important ally. On the other hand, American officials feared that if they supported the regime, only to see it fail, whoever eventually gained control of Egypt's government would then be hostile to the United States. Additionally, America, which had long supported the idea that people have a right to decide who controls their own country, knew it would appear hypocritical to support a dictator intent on repressing his citizens' freedom of expression. Ultimately, U.S. policy makers settled on cautiously supporting a safe and stable transition

18.1

18.2

18.3

18.4

18.5

to power. And, on February 11, 2011, Mubarak acquiesced, resigning unceremoniously to allow Egypt to eventually hold free elections.

As the Arab Spring continues to play out, American foreign policy makers will face further challenges in the Middle East. Already, President Obama has had to send U.S. planes to aid NATO airstrikes against the repressive regime in Libya—which, like Egypt, was finally overthrown by a popular revolution. There is also a possibility that airstrikes may eventually be seen as necessary in Syria as well, where the Assad regime has turned tanks on its protesting citizens. Meanwhile, the transition from authoritarianism to democracy is not easy for any of these nations. In Egypt and Libya, for example, no strong central government yet exists. Recent developments also indicate that Islamic political groups, such as the Muslim Brotherhood, may soon gain power in these countries. The rise of the Brotherhood, which Israel considers a threat and which opposed the 1979 peace treaty between Egypt and Israel, may become a difficult test of America's interests in the region.[77] The United States must continue to balance its ideological interests in democracy with its realist interests in stability and access to foreign oil. Whatever decisions are made, it is clear that the United States will remain an active player in Middle East politics for years to come.

The U.S. Reaction to the Rise of China as a Global Superpower Has Been Decidedly Mixed

China's unique presence as one of the largest and most populous countries in the world has presented U.S. foreign policy with a unique set of challenges. Since as far back as the eighteenth century, Sino-American relations have remained stuck in a relatively complex cycle. According to this cycle, U.S. officials first encourage an isolationist Chinese government to embrace openness. The resulting Chinese openness, however, inevitably threatens U.S. interests at home and abroad, leading the United States to scale back its enthusiasm for Chinese expansion. At times, these two countervailing and contradictory forces in U.S. foreign policy toward China occur simultaneously.

The first American trade ship reached China just after the American Revolution ended, in 1784. It was a natural partnership for both sides. In the United States, a growing wealthy class of people was hungry to buy exotic-seeming furniture, textiles, and other crafts. China, for its part, had a strong demand for raw materials such as ginseng and furs, which were abundant in the New World at the time. Trade between the two countries expanded during the 1800s, leading to the beginnings of a cultural exchange as well. During the 1860s, large numbers of Chinese immigrants flooded to the United States to work low-paying jobs, many of which involved the building of America's first transcontinental railroad.

This sudden influx of Chinese workers put American policy makers in a difficult position. In the foreign arena, America began actively pushing the Open Door Policy, which encouraged China to keep all of its ports open and free from exclusionary trade deals with specific European powers. At home, however, rising unemployment led American workers to resent Chinese immigrants, who they believed were stealing their jobs and driving wages down by being willing to work for less pay. This resentment led Congress to pass a series of restrictions barring prospective Chinese immigrants from entering the country. Despite the apparent contradiction, the United States pursued both a foreign policy that promoted opening China's borders and a domestic policy that closed off America's own borders to the Chinese.

In the first half of the twentieth century, this cycle of push and pull continued. Over the first few decades, American interests in the Far East region regularly clashed with Japan's, China's neighbor and longtime adversary. As a result, successive U.S. governments poured aid into China, which came to be seen as an important military ally in the region. This aid increased after 1937, when Japan attacked China and increased further still after 1941, when Japan attacked the United States at Pearl Harbor. After World War II, however, American support for a more pro-Western Chinese government quickly backfired.

In 1949, the Communist Party came to power in China with the charismatic leader Mao Zedong at its head. The American-supported Chinese regime fled to the nearby island of Taiwan, where it set up a parallel government that claimed to be the rightful Chinese government. The United States continued to ally itself with the deposed government, refusing to diplomatically recognize the Communist Party government on Mainland China. The Mao regime quickly became a primary front of the United States' larger ideological war on communism. Along with the Soviet Union, military and diplomatic officials saw China as part of a larger communist Eastern Bloc. Throughout the 1950s and 1960s, the ideological divide between America and the new Chinese government spilled over into military confrontation, as Mao supported communist insurgencies in Korea and Vietnam that the United States committed forces to opposing.

Beginning with the Nixon administration in the 1970s, however, America's relationship with China showed signs of improvement. Initially, the United States profited from a sudden split between China and the Soviet Union over disputed borders between the two countries. After the split, both America and China saw strategic value in allying, at least tenuously, as mutual opponents of Soviet interests in the Eastern Hemisphere. Over time, however, the Sino-American relationship became progressively more predicated on shared economic interests. As the Soviet Union declined and the Cold War slowly drew to a close, China began to emerge as first a regional and later a global economic power. By the end of the twentieth century, the United States found itself in a familiar place: once again encouraging China to open its borders to foreign trade and investment. And once again, China complied. Although the communist regime remained in place, the government began relaxing many of its financial restrictions over the flow of capital. Finally, in 2001, after 15 years of negotiations, China joined the World Trade Organization (WTO), thereby officially opening itself up to international markets and entering into the global economic order.

As per the pattern, however, U.S. officials have met the past 10 years of increased Chinese openness and expansion, which many U.S. officials had long pushed for, with lukewarm enthusiasm. Since it joined the WTO in 2001, China's economy has performed spectacularly. The country's per capita real GDP tripled in its first decade as a WTO member, and its external trade ballooned to $2.9 trillion in 2010. That same year, China surpassed Japan to become the world's second largest economy. Chinese success has had substantial implications for the U.S. economy. For instance, the U.S. trade deficit with China has grown from $84 billion in 2000 to $273 billion in 2010. In part, this is the result of the Chinese government's insistence on undervaluing its currency, the Yuan. By most estimates, until 2009, the Yuan was undervalued from 25 percent to 40 percent against the dollar. Even after recent currency appreciation, the Yuan remains undervalued by 5 percent to 20 percent.[78] By artificially suppressing the Yuan and allowing foreigners to purchase the currency using fewer dollars, Chinese products become particularly affordable on the global market, boosting the demand for Chinese exports. In addition, China has increasingly invested more and more money into the United States. Today, the Chinese government is the largest foreign holder of U.S. debt.[79]

The expansion of China's economy has forced American officials to once again walk a careful tightrope. On the one hand, the United States must continue to encourage Chinese growth, if for no other reason than a stumbling Chinese economy would have dangerous implications for U.S. economic stability. At the same time, policy makers face substantial pressure to curb patent violations in the Chinese economy.

For corporations, the concerns revolve around the rampant piracy and counterfeiting that have accompanied increased economic openness. In 2008, Apple opened its first Chinese retail store in Beijing and later expanded into Shanghai. Shortly before its first Hong Kong branch opened in September 2011, an American blogger alerted the company to a new Apple store in Kunming that the company had neither planned for nor known about.[80] The counterfeit store came complete with a winding staircase, a Genius Bar, and employees donned in blue Apple t-shirts.[81] As Treasury

THE RISE OF CHINA

Over the last decade, growth rates in China have ranged between 6 and 11 percent. Construction has been a primary driver of much of this growth. Here we see an aerial view of Expo Village in Shanghai, where China hosted the 2010 World Expo.

Secretary Timothy Geithner complained, "They [the Chinese] have made possible systematic stealing of intellectual property of American companies and have not been very aggressive to put in place the basic protections for property rights that every serious economy needs over time."[82] Indeed, the U.S. International Trade Commission estimates that the infringement of intellectual property rights of U.S. companies in China has resulted in losses of $48 billion in sales, royalties, and license fees.[83]

Aside from economic concerns, U.S. policy toward China remains fraught with competing ideological interests. Since 1989, when China violently repressed revolts in Tiananmen Square, American human rights groups have urged foreign policy makers to pressure China into improving its dismal record on human rights. Additionally, China's economic openness has made it willing to trade with and economically support authoritarian regimes in North Korea and Iran, to which the United States is ideologically opposed. Indeed, multiple attempts by the United States to impose sanctions on these countries have failed as a result of China's veto power on the United Nations Security Council.

In Sino-American relations, history has frequently repeated itself. But China's rise as a dominant economic power may upend the usual pattern. Much as it may want to, America may no longer have the ability to push back on China's economic openness and growth. Moving forward, the United States and China must find ways to put aside ideological and economic differences in order to sustain mutually stable economic growth.

Review the Chapter

 **Listen** to **Chapter 18** on **MyPoliSciLab**

A Brief History of U.S. Foreign Policy

18.1 Outline the history of U.S. foreign policy, p. 608.

Throughout the nineteenth century, U.S. foreign policy was guided by a grand strategy of isolationism. After fighting two world wars in the first half of the twentieth century, a new spirit of internationalism gripped the country. During the Cold War, the United States sought to contain the spread of communism, but it never fought directly against the Soviet Union. Since the Cold War ended in 1989, the United States has been the world's primary superpower, with economic and military interests that span the globe.

The Role of the Foreign Policy Bureaucracy

18.2 Identify the powers of the president to direct foreign policy and the executive agencies that support the president, p. 615.

As commander in chief, chief diplomat, and chief administrator, the president has extraordinary powers and responsibilities in foreign policy. Moreover, a vast network of administrative units, most importantly the State and Defense Departments, assists the president in formulating and implementing his foreign policy agenda.

The Role of Congress

18.3 Describe the power of Congress to shape foreign policy, p. 624.

Congress has a variety of means at its disposal to influence U.S. foreign policy making. By enacting statutes, retaining the power to declare war, confirming bureaucratic nominees, ratifying treaties, and exercising its oversight responsibilities, Congress can influence U.S. foreign policy in important ways.

The Role of Interest Groups

18.4 Analyze the role of interest groups in foreign policy making, p. 628.

Interest groups also contribute to foreign policy. Business groups, ethnic lobbies, and think tanks, in particular, can provide important insights. They can also shape national conversations about particularly pressing foreign policy issues; in so doing, they occasionally put pressure on Congress to challenge presidential powers in foreign policy.

Contemporary Foreign Policy Challenges

18.5 Assess three of the foreign policy challenges that the United States faces today, p. 630.

Presidents, officials in the State and Defense Departments, Congress, and a wide variety of interest groups and organizations all participate in ongoing foreign policy debates. Some of the most important issues concern the spread of nuclear weapons, the expansion of democracy within the Middle East, and the rapid growth of China's economy.

Learn the Terms

 **Study** and **Review** the **Flashcards**

Test Yourself

18.1 Outline the history of U.S. foreign policy.

Which event ushered in a new era of American leadership in world affairs?

a. Germany's launch of unrestricted submarine warfare jeopardizing American shipments in 1917
b. President Woodrow Wilson's issuance of his Fourteen Points proposal for peace in 1919
c. Germany's invasion of Poland in 1939
d. Germany's invasion of the Soviet Union in 1941
e. Japan's attack on Pearl Harbor in 1941

18.2 Identify the powers of the president to direct foreign policy and the executive agencies that support the president.

All of the following departments and agencies support the president in foreign policy making EXCEPT the

a. National Security Council.
b. Defense Department.
c. State Department.
d. Department of Justice.
e. Central Intelligence Agency.

18.3 Describe the power of Congress to shape foreign policy.

Which of the following is NOT one of Congress's powers when it comes to shaping foreign policy?

a. commanding the military
b. declaring war
c. overseeing foreign policy bureaucracies
d. providing advice and consent on international treaties
e. confirming nominees for foreign policy positions

18.4 Analyze the role of interest groups in foreign policy making.

Which of the following statements is true of AIPAC?

a. AIPAC is a think tank that publicizes and supports the work of scholars but has no practical influence on foreign policy.
b. AIPAC is an ethnic lobby that promotes close ties between Israel and the United States.
c. AIPAC is an ethnic lobby that promotes close ties between Cuba and the United States.
d. AIPAC is a business that promotes close ties between Israel and the United States.
e. AIPAC is a multinational defense firm that promotes close ties between Israel and the United States.

18.5 Assess three of the foreign policy challenges that the United States faces today.

What has been the U.S. reaction to China's rise as a global superpower?

a. U.S. reaction has been universally positive.
b. U.S. reaction has been universally negative.
c. U.S. reaction has been decidedly mixed, at times both positive and negative.
d. U.S. reaction has been neither positive nor negative.
e. The United States, as a whole, does not consider China to be a rising global superpower.

Explore Further

SUGGESTED READINGS BY TOP SCHOLARS

Bruce Bueno de Mesquita and Alastair Smith. *The Dictator's Handbook.* New York: PublicAffairs, 2011. Examines how leaders' concern for maintaining power explains their behavior in both democratic and autocratic regimes.

Stephen Hook and John Spanier. *American Foreign Policy Since World War II*, 17th ed. Washington, DC: CQ Press, 2007. Traces the major phases of American foreign policy since World War II through September 11, with special attention to the political process and context in which decisions were made.

Steven Pinker. *The Better Angels of Our Nature: Why Violence Has Declined.* New York: Viking, 2011. Draws upon insights from psychology to explain the dramatic reduction in human violence over broad stretches of human history.

Bruce Russett and John Oneal. *Triangulating Peace: Democracy, Interdependence, and International Organizations.* New York: Norton, 2001. Examines different explanations for the empirical observation that democracies rarely fight one another.

David A. Welch. *Painful Choices: A Theory of Foreign Policy Change.* Princeton, NJ: Princeton University Press, 2005. Outlines organizational and psychological theories about when foreign policy decision makers attempt to make major changes in policy, and uses historical case studies to examine each theory.

SUGGESTED WEBSITES

Department of Defense: www.defenselink.mil
Assumes primary responsibility for the U.S. military.

State Department: www.state.gov
Assumes primary responsibility for U.S. diplomatic relations with foreign countries.

Council on Foreign Relations: www.cfr.org
Provides substantial research and commentary on foreign policy issues.

United Nations: www.un.org
The most prominent international organization to facilitate diplomatic relations between nations.

Senate Foreign Relations Committee: www.foreign.senate.gov
Primarily responsible for overseeing the foreign policy apparatus within the executive branch.

GLOSSARY

527 committee an independent, nonparty group that raises and spends money on political activities.

A

advocacy journalism news outlets that present news with either an explicit or implicit point of view favoring certain political positions.

affirmative action efforts to reach and attract applicants for jobs, college admissions, and business contracts from traditionally underrepresented groups, ranging from extensive publicity and outreach to quota plans.

agency capture an agency primarily serves the interests of a nongovernmental group rather than those of elected officials.

agenda setting the media's role in determining which issues the public considers important, by covering some issues and ignoring others.

Aid to Families with Dependent Children (AFDC) a federal program in effect from 1935 to 1996 that provided assistance to households with needy children.

American creed the dominant political culture in the United States, marked by a set of beliefs in individualism, democracy, liberty, property, and religion, tied together by the value of equality.

amicus curiae a brief written by someone who is not a party to a case but who submits information or an argument related to the dispute at hand.

Anti-Federalists individuals opposed to the proposed Constitution, fearing it concentrated too much power in the national government.

appellate courts the second tier of the federal judiciary, primarily responsible for reviewing decisions rendered by the first tier of district courts.

appropriations the granting of funds to operate authorized federal programs and agencies.

approval rating the percentage of the public that approves of the job the president is doing overall.

Arab Spring the popular uprisings that occurred in rapid succession throughout the Middle East in 2010.

Articles of Confederation the first constitution of the United States, which based most power in the states.

attitudinal model the theory of judicial decision making in which judges use their own policy preferences in deciding cases.

Australian ballot an official government-produced ballot for elections that lists all offices and all the candidates and parties that have qualified to be on the ballot.

authoritarian (or totalitarian) system a political system in which one person or group has absolute control over the apparatus of government, and in which popular input in government is minimal or nonexistent.

authorization the granting of legal authority to operate federal programs and agencies.

autocracy a form of government in which a single person rules with effectively unlimited power.

B

bad tendency standard a free speech standard that took as its starting point a presumption that government restrictions on speech were reasonable and constitutional, thus leaving the burden of proof to those who objected to the restriction.

balancing test used by the Supreme Court in free exercise of religion cases, this two-part test first determined whether a government action or law was a burden on religious practice and, if it was, whether a compelling government interest was at stake that would make the burden constitutionally acceptable.

battleground states competitive states in which no candidate has an overwhelming advantage, and therefore Electoral College votes are in play.

bias favorable treatment to certain politicians, policy positions, groups, and political outcomes.

bicameral an institution consisting of two chambers.

Bill of Rights the first 10 amendments to the U.S. Constitution, intended to protect individual liberties from federal government intrusion.

block grant funds provided by the federal government to a state or local government in general support of a broad government function such as education or transportation.

blue states largely uncontested states in which the Democratic candidate for president is very likely to win.

briefs documents that contain the legal arguments of a dispute.

Brown v. Board of Education Supreme Court ruling in 1954 that in public education, mandatory separation of children by race leads to inherently unequal education. The decision overturned the separate but equal doctrine.

bundling the practice of collecting individual checks and presenting them to a candidate at one time.

bureaucracy a group of departments, agencies, and other institutions that for the most part are located in the executive branch of government and that develop and implement public policy.

Bush Doctrine a grand strategy pursued after September 11, 2001, that emphasized an aggressive posture toward nations that provide safe haven for terrorists, preemptive action, and a willingness to unilaterally launch military actions.

C

cabinet a group of the top-ranking officials of every major federal department, plus other officials included by the president, who meet periodically with the president to discuss major administration priorities and policies.

casework the direct assistance that members of Congress give to individuals and groups within a district or state.

categorical grant funds provided by the federal government to a state or local government for a specific, defined purpose.

caucus a small meeting at which registered political party members select delegates to attend the national party convention and nominate a presidential candidate.

causal question a question regarding the factors responsible for a particular outcome.

causation a relationship between variables such that change in the value of one is directly responsible for change in the value of the other.

Central Intelligence Agency (CIA) the cornerstone of U.S. efforts to gather and analyze data in order to confront America's real and potential enemies.

centralization the method of increasing the president's power by moving key administrative functions from the departments to the Executive Office of the President.

charter a document that, like a constitution, specifies the basic policies, procedures, and institutions of a local government.

charter schools public schools, administered by chartering boards, that are exempt from many rules and regulations applicable to traditional public schools.

checks and balances the principle that each branch of the federal government has the means to thwart or influence actions by other branches of government.

chief justice the presiding member of the Supreme Court who serves as chair of the conference and, if in the majority, selects the justice who will write the majority opinion.

civic skills the skills of writing, speaking, analyzing, and organizing that reduce the cost of political participation.

civil case a case that concerns a violation of the legal rights or obligations of one individual toward another.

civil disobedience strategy of breaking law nonviolently in order to protest a law one considers unjust and draw attention to one's cause.

civil liberties individual rights and freedoms that government is obliged to protect, normally by not interfering in the exercise of these rights and freedoms.

civil rights guarantees of equal opportunities, privileges, and treatment under the law that allow individuals to participate fully and equally in American society.

civil service system a system of government in which decisions about hiring, promotion, and firing are based on individuals' work experience, skills, and expertise.

class action suit a lawsuit in which the plaintiff is a group of individuals who have suffered a common injury.

clear and present danger standard used in free speech cases, this standard permitted government restrictions on speech if public officials believed that allowing the speech created a risk that some prohibited action would result.

closed primary an election in which only registered members of a political party can participate in the party's primary election.

closed rule the terms and conditions applied to a particular bill that restrict the types of amendments that can be made to it.

cloture a mechanism by which 60 or more senators can end a filibuster and cut off debate.

cognitive dissonance a state in which some of one's attitudes, beliefs, or understandings are inconsistent with others.

Cold War the period from the late 1940s to the late 1980s in which the United States and the Soviet Union engaged in diplomatic and economic hostility but not full-fledged war.

collective action problem a problem that arises when individuals' incentives lead them to avoid taking actions that are best for the group as a whole, and that they themselves would like to see accomplished.

collective action problem This situation arises when many or all members of a population would benefit from some sort of activity or a policy that activity is trying to influence, even if they did not not actively participate in the effort.

collective benefit a benefit all people enjoy, regardless of whether or not they contributed to its attainment.

commerce clause a provision in the U.S. Constitution that gives Congress the power to regulate commerce with other countries, among the states, and with Indian tribes.

common law law made by judges when no legislation currently exists.

communitarianism the view that the needs of the community are of higher priority in government than the needs of the individual, even if the result is a restriction of individual liberties.

compact theory a theory of the founding of the American government that argues states were sovereign units that joined together in the new national government but did not give up their status as sovereign, independent governments.

concurring opinion a document written by a justice on the majority side of a ruling that outlines additional considerations he or she thinks are important.

confederation a loose grouping of independent political units, such as states or countries, whose main purpose is to govern the relationship between those units.

conference committee a committee made up of members of both chambers that is responsible for ironing out the differences between House and Senate versions of a bill.

conference the confidential gathering of justices in which they discuss their thoughts about the case and cast preliminary votes.

constituents the people who reside within an elected official's political jurisdiction.

constitutional democracy a form of democracy in which there is a foundational document (such as the U.S. Constitution) that describes the structure, powers, and limits of government.

containment the strategy of guarding against Soviet power by adopting policies that limited the geographic expansion of Soviet power.

continuing resolution funds used to keep programs up and running when regular appropriations have not been approved by the end of the fiscal year.

cooperative federalism a form of federalism in which the national and state governments share many functions and areas of authority.

coordinated expenditures legally limited purchases or payments made by a political party on behalf of, and in coordination with, a specific campaign.

correlation a relationship between factors such that change in one is accompanied by change in the other.

county a district created by state government for establishing a local government responsible for implementing a variety of state laws and for providing general governmental services.

criminal case a case that involves a violation of the statutes that are intended to protect the public's health, order, safety, and morality.

cycling a phenomenon that occurs when multiple decision makers must decide among multiple options and cannot agree on a single course of action.

D

data mining a catch-all term that refers to analysts using increasingly powerful computers and statistical tools to extract useable information or insights from extremely large data sets.

de facto segregation racial segregation that results not because of explicit law, policy, or procedures, but from patterns of behavior that have the effect of segregating the races.

de jure segregation racial segregation that occurs because it is written into law, policy, or government procedures.

dealignment a substantial reduction in the proportion of the voting population consistently voting for and identifying with one party.

Declaration of Independence document announcing the intention of the colonies to separate from Great Britain based on shared grievances about the treatment of the colonists by the British government.

defendant the party being sued or accused of a crime.

Defense Department the agency created by the National Security Act in 1947 that replaced the Departments of War and the Navy.

deficit the amount of money a government spends in a year, above and beyond what it brings in through taxation and other means.

delegate model of representation the type of representation by which representatives are elected to do the bidding of the people who elected them; representatives are "delegates" in that they share the same policy positions as the voters and promise to act upon them.

delegates individuals who represent a state's voters in the selection of a political party's presidential candidate.

delegation the granting of authority by Congress to the president to be the first or main actor in a policy area, usually with implicit or explicit limits on actions that Congress would find acceptable.

democracy a form of government in which the people rule; this can take place directly, through participation by the people in actual lawmaking, or indirectly, through free elections in which the people choose representatives to make laws on their behalf.

department a major administrative unit that is composed of many agencies serving many policy functions, and that is headed by a secretary, who serves in the president's Cabinet.

Department of Homeland Security (DHS) the agency created in the aftermath of September 11 to coordinate the work of agencies involved in preventing and responding to attacks on the United States.

deregulation the process of decreasing the number of agency rules that apply to a particular industry or group of industries so as to introduce market forces to their operations.

détente a period of reduced Cold War tensions in the 1970s.

devolution a process in which the authority over a government program's rules and implementation is largely transferred from a higher-level government to a lower-level government.

diplomacy the peaceful negotiation of economic and political relationships between different countries.

direct democracy a form of democracy in which the people themselves make the laws and set the policies adopted by the government.

direct mail political advertising in which messages are sent directly to potential voters in the form of mail or e-mail, rather than using a third-party medium.

direction in public opinion, the tendency for or against some phenomenon.

discrimination the view that not all groups in society are deserving of equal rights and opportunities.

dissenting opinion a document written by a justice on the minority side of a ruling that outlines his or her own reasoning on the case and identifies perceived flaws in the majority opinion.

district court the first tier of the federal judiciary that decides most cases.

disturbance theory the theory that when social, political, and economic relationships change, individuals form groups in response.

divided government the presidency is held by one party and at least one house of Congress is controlled by a different party.

Dred Scott v. Sandford Supreme Court decision in 1857 declaring that neither slaves nor the descendants of slaves could be U.S. citizens.

drift a situation in which bureaucrats create policy that does not match the policy preferences of Congress or the president.

dual citizenship the idea that an individual is a citizen of both his or her state and the United States. Rights and responsibilities can vary from state to state and can be different on the state and national levels.

dual federalism a form of federalism in which the national and state governments have distinct areas of authority and power, and individuals have rights as both citizens of states and citizens of the United States.

dual sovereignty the idea that both the national and state governments have sovereignty, but over different policy areas and functions.

due process procedural safeguards that government officials are obligated to follow prior to restricting rights of life, liberty, and property.

E

earmarks federal funds that support specific local projects.

earned media news coverage that is determined to be important to a news outlet's audience, solely by virtue of the news story's content.

Electoral College the meeting, in each state and the District of Columbia, of electors who cast votes to elect the president.

electoral realignment a shift in the composition of party coalitions that produces a new, relatively durable pattern of party competition.

Elementary and Secondary Education Act (ESEA) a federal law passed in 1965 designed to reduce educational inequities by directly aiding school districts with large numbers of poor citizens.

entitlements benefits that all qualifying individuals have a legal right to obtain.

enumerated powers the specifically listed duties that the U.S. Constitution assigns to Congress.

equal privileges and immunities clause a clause in the Constitution stating that states are to treat their citizens and the citizens of other states equally.

equal protection clause clause in the Fourteenth Amendment stating that states are not to deny any person equal treatment under the law.

equality the value that all Americans should be treated the same under the law, be able to influence government, and have equal opportunity to succeed in life.

establishment clause a clause in the First Amendment that prevents government from establishing an official religion, treating one religion preferably to another, proselytizing, or promoting religion over non-religion.

ethnic lobby an interest group that advocates policies focusing on specific foreign states.

exclusionary rule principle established by the Supreme Court, according to which evidence gathered illegally cannot be introduced into trial, and convictions cannot be based on this evidence.

executive agreement an international agreement in which the United States becomes a party once the president has signed it, without requiring approval from two-thirds of the Senate.

Executive Office of the President a group of agencies in the executive branch that primarily generate policy alternatives for the president's consideration.

executive order a presidential directive or proclamation that has the force of law.

executive privilege the idea that executive branch officials need to be able to advise the president in confidence, and that the president has a right to prevent that advice from becoming public.

F

Federal Reserve the federal agency that controls supply of money in the domestic economy.

federalism a form of government that distributes power across a national government and subnational governments and ensures the existence of the subnational governments.

federalism a form of government that distributes power across a national government and subnational governments and ensures the existence of the subnational governments.

Federalists individuals who supported the proposed Constitution and favored its ratification.

field operations the "ground war" intended to produce high turnout among party loyalists, particularly in battleground states.

filibuster a procedure by which senators delay or prevent action on a bill by making long speeches and engaging in unlimited debate.

fiscal federalism a technique of persuasion in which the federal government offers resources to states that agree to take certain actions.

fiscal policy policy designed to improve the economy through spending and taxation.

focus group in-depth interview with a small number of people representing important voter constituencies.

focusing event a visible and dramatic event that focuses the domestic polity on a specific problem and accompanying course of action.

foreign policy the mix of military, diplomatic, and economic policies that define U.S. relations with other nations around the world.

formal powers specific grants of authority defined in the Constitution or in law.

framing a media effect in which a journalist simplifies and condenses information in a story in order to put the issue into clear focus for the audience.

free exercise clause a clause in the First Amendment that prohibits government from interfering with individuals' practice of their religion.

free-rider problem a barrier to collective action because people can reap the benefits of group efforts without participating.

full faith and credit clause a clause in the Constitution stating that states are to honor the official acts of other states.

fusion a strategy in which third parties endorse a major party candidate but list that candidate separately on the ballot so that voters can vote for the candidate under the third-party label.

G

gate-keeping authority the power to decide whether a particular proposal or policy change will be considered.

generational effect the situation in which younger citizens are influenced by events in such a fashion that their attitudes and beliefs are forever rendered distinct from those of older generations.

gerrymandering the majority party in Congress draws lines around districts in such a way as to maximize the number of seats that party will win; this process often produces districts with contorted boundaries.

going public activities of presidents such as highly visible trips, press conferences, interviews, speeches, and public appearances in an attempt to raise public support for a policy agenda.

GOTV (get-out-the-vote) term used by campaign professionals to describe the various activities candidates, political parties, activists, and interest groups use to make sure their likely supporters go to the polls on Election Day.

government corporation a corporation created and funded by the government to provide some public service that would be insufficiently provided by the private sector.

government the institutions that have the authority and capacity to create and enforce public policies (rules) for a specific territory and people.

grand strategy a plan that determines American national security interests, outlines possible threats to those interests, and recommends military and diplomatic policies to attain them.

grassroots lobbying efforts to persuade citizens to contact their elected officials regarding a particular issue or piece of legislation.

gravity of the danger standard a free speech standard in which the Supreme Court allowed restrictions on speech if the danger espoused by the speech was sufficiently evil, even if that evil was unlikely to occur.

Great Compromise the agreement between small states and large states that representation in the Senate would be equal for each state, as small states preferred, and representation in the House would be based on population, as large states preferred.

Great Depression a period of severe economic recession in the United States precipitated by the stock market crash in October 1929.

Great Society a set of large-scale social initiatives proposed by President Lyndon Johnson in the 1960s to reduce poverty, racial discrimination, environmental degradation, and urban decay.

gross domestic product (GDP) a statistic that measures all goods and services produced by a nation's economy.

H

hard money funds to be used by candidates or parties for the express purpose of running an election campaign, or by PACs for contributing to candidates.

hearing a formal process in which committees in Congress call upon bureaucrats and other experts to help them understand and oversee a particular agency.

home rule a local government with authority to pass laws and provide services as long as those laws or services are not provided by a special district or otherwise prohibited under state law.

horse race a focus in election coverage on who and what are up or down in the latest poll numbers.

I

ideology a consistent set of ideas about a given set of issues.

impeachment performed by the House of Representatives, the act of charging government officials with "treason, bribery, or other high crimes and misdemeanors"; the Senate then decides whether to convict and remove the official from office.

implementation the process by which policy is executed.

implied powers functions and actions that Congress could perform in order to implement and exercise its enumerated powers.

incorporation process the application, through the Fourteenth Amendment, of the civil liberties protections in the Bill of Rights to state governments.

incumbent the individual in an election who currently holds the contested office; as distinct from the challenger, who seeks to remove the incumbent from power.

independent agencies and commissions bureaucratic organizations that operate outside of Cabinet-level departments and are less subject to congressional or presidential influence.

independent expenditures funds spent to elect or defeat candidates but not coordinated with any candidate's campaign.

indirect election an election in which voters select other individuals who directly vote for candidates for a particular office; U.S. Senate and presidential elections were of this type in the Constitution, but Senate elections are now direct elections.

individualism a belief that all individuals should be able to succeed to the maximum extent possible given their talents and abilities, regardless of race, religion, or other group characteristics.

initiative a process in which a proposal for legislation is placed on the ballot and voters can either enact or reject the proposal without further action by the governor or legislature.

inside lobbying meeting directly with public officials to influence political decisions.

intensity the strength of the direction of public opinion.

interest group entrepreneur one who overcomes the costs of collective action by launching and managing an interest group.

interest groups organizations that seek to influence government decisions.

internationalism the grand strategy of actively engaging in world affairs.

invisible primary the race to raise the most money and achieve front-runner status before the primary season begins.

isolationism the grand strategy of minimizing a nation's involvement in world affairs.

issue evolution a change in the partisan base of support for an issue over time, such that the positions of Democrats and Republicans switch.

issue voting voting style in which the voter judges candidates based on the voter's and the candidates' opinions on specific issues and preferences for certain policies.

J

Jim Crow system of laws that separated the races in schools, public accommodations, and other aspects of daily life.

joint committee a committee made up of members of both chambers of Congress to conduct a special investigation or study.

judicial activism the tendency of judges to give themselves leeway in deciding whether to abide by past court decisions, which allows them to consider possible outcomes, public opinion, and their own preferences before issuing a ruling.

judicial restraint the practice judges engage in when they limit the exercise of their own power by overturning past decisions only when they are clearly unconstitutional.

judicial review the power of the judiciary to interpret and overturn actions taken by the legislative and executive branches of government.

jury a group of private citizens selected to listen to a trial and issue a final verdict.

L

laissez-faire economics a theory that discourages the government from becoming involved in the economy.

leadership the ability to influence and guide others to achieve some desired policy or action.

legal model a theory of judicial decision making in which judges make decisions by deciphering the correct interpretation of the law and the relevant portion of the Constitution and determining whether there is a conflict between the two.

***Lemon* test** a three-part establishment clause test used by the Supreme Court that states that to be constitutional, a governmental action must have a plausible nonreligious purpose; its primary or principal effect must be to neither advance nor inhibit religion; and it must not foster excessive government entanglement with religion.

libertarianism a view that emphasizes the importance of individual choice and responsibility, the private sector, and the free market, in which government's primary obligations are to defend the country militarily, protect individuals from crime, and ensure that people fulfill contracts entered into freely.

liberty the belief that government should leave people free to do as they please and exercise their natural rights to the maximum extent possible.

life-cycle effect attitudes or physical characteristics that change as one ages, no matter the time period or generation. The graying of one's hair is a life-cycle effect.

limited government the idea that the scope of government activities should be narrow and that government should act only when the need is great and other sectors of society are unable to meet the need.

line-item veto the authority of a chief executive to reject part of a bill passed by the legislature.

lobbying communicating with government officials to persuade them toward a particular policy decision.

M

magistrate judges judges who support federal district judges by hearing and deciding minor cases at the district court level.

majority leader the individual in each chamber who manages the floor; in the Senate, he or she is the most powerful member in the chamber; in the House, he or she is the chief lieutenant of the Speaker.

majority opinion the written document that reflects the collective judgment of the justices who are on the majority side of a ruling.

majority-minority districts legislative districts in which district boundaries are drawn in a manner to ensure that a majority of the district residents are members of minority groups, intended to increase the probability of minorities being elected.

majority-minority voting districts legislative districts in which district boundaries are drawn in a manner to ensure that a majority of the district residents are members of minority groups, intended to increase the probability of minorities being elected.

mandate an order from the federal government that requires state governments to take a certain action.

mandate the idea that the public provided clear policy guidance in the results of the prior election.

margin of error the range surrounding a sample's response within which researchers are confident the larger population's true response would fall.

markup the process by which the members of a committee or subcommittee rewrite, delete, and add portions of a bill.

Marshall Plan a program that provided aid to rebuild Western European economies after World War II.

mass media various modes of communication intended to reach a mass audience—including television, radio, newspapers, newsmagazines, and the Internet.

matching funds public monies given to qualifying candidates to match a certain percentage of the funds they have raised from private donors.

material benefit a good or service offered to encourage participation in group activity.

means-tested program any program that targets the poor and for which eligibility is based on financial need.

Medicaid a means-tested program, funded by federal and state governments, that extends health insurance to the poor and disabled.

Medicare a federally funded entitlement program that offers health insurance to the elderly.

microtargeting campaign efforts that aim to hit particular voters with very specific messages tied to their individual demographics and attitudes.

minimal effect the theory that change in voting intent as a result of mass media exposure was relatively rare.

minority leader the individual who speaks on behalf of the party that controls the smaller number of seats in each chamber.

miracle of aggregation the phenomenon that occurs when a group consists of individuals who are largely ignorant of a particular issue, but their collective opinion tends to makes sense.

***Miranda* warning** ruling that requires police, when arresting suspects, to inform them of their rights, including the right to remain silent and have an attorney present during questioning.

modified open primary an election in which registered voters who are not affiliated with either party can vote in either party's primary.

momentum the boost in media coverage, name recognition, fund-raising, and perceptions of electability that accompanies unexpected and repeated primary success.

monetary policy policy designed to improve the economy by controlling the supply of available money.

multiculturalism the view that group identity influences political beliefs and that because groups are naturally diverse in their beliefs, the idea of a shared or dominant political culture merely reflects the imposition of a dominant group's beliefs on subordinate groups.

N

nation a shared sense of understanding and belonging among a people that they are different and separate from other peoples with particular characteristics and that they have a right to self-government over a defined territory.

national party convention a meeting held over several days at which delegates select the party's presidential nominee, approve the party platform, and consider changes in party rules and policies.

National Security Council (NSC) an advisory body, formed in 1947 by the National Security Act, that assists the president in gathering information from military services and other security-related executive agencies.

nationalist theory a theory of the founding of the American government that sees the Constitution more as the joining together of the people than the joining together of the states.

natural rights rights inherent in the essence of people as human beings; government does not provide these rights but can restrict the exercise of them.

necessary and expedient clause a clause in Article II, Section 3, of the Constitution that authorizes the president to recommend legislation to Congress.

necessary and proper clause a provision in the U.S. Constitution that gives Congress the authority to make the laws needed to carry out the specific duties assigned to Congress by the Constitution.

neutrality test the Supreme Court's most recent approach to deciding free exercise of religion cases, this test declares that a government law or action with a neutral intent and application is constitutional, even if it burdens religion and there is no compelling government interest at stake.

New Jersey Plan one of the rival plans at the Constitutional Convention, it called for, among other things, equal representation of the states in a single-house legislature.

No Child Left Behind Act (NCLB) a 2001 federal law that rewards public schools for meeting certain educational benchmarks and punishes schools that fail to do so.

nondecisions decisions not to consider particular issues or incorporate them into the policy agenda.

nonresponse bias a nonrandom error that occurs when people who choose to participate in a survey have different attitudes from those of people who decline to participate.

norms informal expressions of the customs, attitudes, and expectations put before people who work within a bureaucratic agency.

North American Free Trade Agreement (NAFTA) an agreement, signed in 1992, to reduce tariff and nontariff barriers to trade and investment among Canada, Mexico, and the United States.

North Atlantic Treaty Organization (NATO) established in 1949, a military alliance of the United States and a number of European nations that pledged to join forces against an attack by the Soviet Union, or any other external threat.

nullification the theory that states have the right to nullify national laws to which they object and believe violate the U.S. Constitution.

O

open primary an election in which a voter can participate in either party's primary (but not both), regardless of party registration.

open rule the terms and conditions applied to a particular bill that allow members of Congress to make a wide range of amendments to it.

opinion leaders individuals with high levels of interest and expertise in politics who seek to communicate their political beliefs to others.

oral argument a lawyer's spoken presentation to the court of the legal reasons that his or her side should prevail.

original jurisdiction the right of the Supreme Court to be the first to hear a case rather than simply review the decision of a lower court.

outside lobbying lobbyng that takes place outside Washington DC.

oversight congressional and presidential efforts to monitor and supervise the actions of bureaucratic agencies.

P

paid media advertising.

paradox of participation The fact that people participate in politics, even though the impact of their individual participation would seem far too small to matter.

parliamentary system a political system in which the head of the executive branch is selected by members of the legislature rather than by popular vote.

party caucus the gathering of all Democratic members of the House or Senate.

party conference the gathering of all Republican members of the House or Senate.

party machine disciplined local party organizations that selected candidates; got out the vote; provided benefits to supporters including government workers, local constituents, and businesses; and served as social service agencies for their followers.

party platform a document expressing the principles, beliefs, and policy positions of the party, as endorsed by delegates at the national party convention.

patron an individual who supports an interest group by providing the resources needed for it to organize and flourish.

patronage awarding jobs in government on the basis of party support and loyalty rather than expertise or experience.

period effect an event that influences the attitudes and beliefs of people of all ages.

persistence the principle that political lessons, values, and attitudes learned early in life tend to structure political learning later on in life.

plaintiff the party who initiates a lawsuit by filing a complaint.

plea bargain an agreement between the prosecutor and the defendant in a criminal case through which the parties agree to a specified crime and punishment.

Plessy v. Ferguson Supreme Court decision in 1896 upholding the constitutionality of laws and government policies that required segregated facilities for blacks and whites.

pluralism the theory that all groups are well represented and no single interest controls government decisions.

plurality elections elections in which the candidate with the most votes, not necessarily a majority, wins.

plurality rule a candidate wins office by getting more votes than his or her opponent, even if that candidate does not receive an absolute majority of the votes.

pocket veto the president's veto of a bill without the opportunity for Congress to override the veto; it occurs if the president does not act on a bill within 10 days after passage by Congress and Congress adjourns during that time.

police power the protection of public safety, health, welfare, and morality by a government.

policy agenda the set of issues under consideration by policy makers.

policy entrepreneurs professionals working in think tanks, universities, lobby groups, unions, and interest groups who propose solutions to policy problems and persuade politicians to adopt them.

political action committee (PAC) a group that collects money from individuals and makes donations to political parties and candidates.

political attentiveness an individual's general attention to and knowledge of politics.

political culture the values and beliefs of citizens toward the political system and toward themselves as actors in it.

political efficacy an individual's belief that he or she can influence what happens in the political world.

political parties organized groups with public followings that seek to elect officeholders who identify themselves by the group's common label, for the purpose of exercising political power.

political predisposition the interests, values, and experiences that help organize one's thinking about politics.

political socialization the learning process in which individuals absorb information and selectively add it to their knowledge and understanding of politics and government.

politicization a phenomenon that occurs when Congress and the president select bureaucracy leaders who share their political views.

politics individual and collective efforts to influence the workings of government.

poll tax fee assessed on each person who wishes to vote; prohibited by the Twenty-fourth Amendment in 1964.

preemption legislation legislation that declares, or mandates, certain actions off-limits for state governments.

preferred position the idea, endorsed by the Supreme Court, that protections of First Amendment rights predominates over other rights.

presidential system a political system in which the head of the executive branch is selected by some form of popular vote and serves a fixed term of office; the United States has a presidential system.

primacy the principle that what is learned first is learned best and lodged most firmly in one's mind.

primary election in which voters choose the candidate who will represent their political party in the general election.

priming a media effect in which the public assesses the performance of politicians and candidates in terms of the issues that the media have emphasized.

principal-agent problem the problem that occurs when one person (the principal) contracts with another person (the agent) to provide a service and yet cannot directly observe what the agent is actually doing; the agent, meanwhile, is motivated to take advantage of the principal.

prior restraint government intervention to prevent the publication of material it finds objectionable.

privatization the transfer of government functions from the federal government to private companies.

Progressive movement movement advocating measures to destroy political machines and instead have direct participation by voters in the nomination of candidates and the establishment of public policy.

Progressive reforms a set of political and electoral reforms in the early twentieth century that had the combined effect of weakening political parties.

property rights the belief that people should be able to acquire, own, and use goods and assets free from government constraints, as long as their acquisition and use does not interfere with the rights of other individuals.

proportional representation an election system in which candidates are elected from multimember districts, with a party's share of seats from a district being roughly proportional to their share of the popular vote.

prospective voting voting style in which voters judge a candidate based on their assessment of what the candidate will do in office if elected.

public debt the total amount of money that the federal government owes.

public goods goods (and services) that are enjoyed by all citizens and unlikely to be provided by any organization other than government.

public law those laws enacted by presidents and Congress that define the relationship between individuals (and organizations) and the state.

public money taxpayer funds used to help finance presidential campaigns.

public opinion the collective political beliefs and attitudes of the public, or groups within the public, on matters of relevance to government.

purposive benefit benefit that encourages group participation by connecting individuals to an organization's political purpose.

R

Racial profiling law enforcement investigation of individuals at least in part because of their race or ethnicity rather than direct evidence of wrongdoing.

rally event short-term international event or military action that boosts presidential approval ratings temporarily.

random sample a population sample in which it is equally likely that each member of the population will be included in the sample.

recall a process in which voters can petition for a vote to remove officials between elections.

recess appointment the means by which the president fills a vacant position in the bureaucracy when Congress is not in session, thus avoiding the need for prior congressional approval.

recession a period when the nation's GDP declines in two successive quarters.

red states largely uncontested states in which the Republican candidate for president is very likely to win.

red tape the inefficiency and waste that result from excessive regulation and overly formal procedures.

redistricting the drawing of boundaries around legislative districts, generally every 10 years after the U.S. Census; each district elects one legislator.

Regents of the University of California v. Bakke Supreme Court decision in 1978 that a rigid quota plan for admissions violates the Constitution's equal protection guarantee, but race could be considered a "plus factor" in college admissions to increase student body diversity.

regular appropriations the standard mode by which federal moneys are allotted to programs.

religious freedom a belief that individuals should be free to choose and practice their religious faith and that government should not establish any particular religion as the official or preferred religion.

representative democracy a form of democracy in which the people, through free elections, select representatives to make laws on their behalf and set policies adopted by the government.

republic a system in which people elect representatives to make policy and write laws, in contrast to direct democracy in which the people do these activities themselves.

reserved powers Tenth Amendment guarantee to state governments of any powers other than those granted to the national government or those specifically prohibited for the states.

responsible party model the idea that political parties should run as unified teams, present a clear policy platform, implement that platform when in office, and run on their record in the subsequent election.

retrospective voting voters judge candidates based on the performance of the candidates or their parties rather than issue stands and assessments of what each candidate would do if elected.

retrospective voting voting style in which voters judge candidates based on the performance of the candidates or their parties rather than issue stands and assessments of what each candidate would do if elected.

ripeness doctrine principle by which the courts will accept cases only when the actual harm has already taken place.

rules administrative determinations about how laws will be interpreted and implemented.

S

salience an issue's importance to a person or to the public in general.

sampling error the difference between the reported characteristics of the sample and the characteristics of the larger population that result from imperfect sampling.

sampling taking a small fraction of something that is meant to represent a larger whole, for example, a group of people who represent a larger population.

select committee a temporary committee created to serve a specific purpose.

selective benefit benefit that can be accessed only by those who participate in or contribute to group activity.

selective benefit benefit that only those who contributed to its attainment get to enjoy (compare to collective benefit).

selective exposure the tendency of people to expose themselves to information that is in accord with their beliefs.

selective incorporation the process by which protections in the Bill of Rights were gradually applied to the states, as the Supreme Court issued decisions on specific aspects of the Bill of Rights.

selective perception the tendency of individuals to interpret information in ways consistent with their beliefs.

selective retention the tendency of individuals to recall information that is consistent with existing beliefs and to discard information that runs counter to them.

senatorial courtesy the custom by which the senior senator from the state in which there is a district court vacancy assists the president in selecting a replacement for that seat.

seniority the length of time a legislator has served in office.

separate but equal doctrine Supreme Court doctrine that laws or policies requiring segregated facilities for the races are constitutionally acceptable as long as the facilities are of equal quality.

separation of powers the principle that the executive, legislative, and judicial functions of government should be primarily performed by different institutions in government.

Shays's Rebellion a protest by farmers in western Massachusetts in 1786–1787 to stop foreclosures on property by state courts; it convinced many political leaders that the Articles of Confederation were insufficient to govern the United States.

single-member districts electoral districts in which only one person is elected to represent the district in a representative body.

slack a situation in which bureaucrats do not work as hard as Congress or the president would like.

social benefit benefit that encourages individuals to join a group in order to enjoy the company of those who share similar opinions and interests.

social contract an agreement among members of a society to form and recognize the authority of a centralized government that is empowered to make and enforce laws governing the members of that society.

Social movement an informal alliance of groups or individuals who join together for the purpose of enacting or resisting social change.

Social Security Act a 1935 law that established Social Security, an entitlement program providing retirees with a monthly income in order to reduce poverty among the elderly.

socioeconomic status (SES) a combination of an individual's occupation, income, and education levels.

soft money funds to be used for political purposes other than running a campaign, for example, get-out-the-vote efforts; or by some interest groups for political ads praising or attacking candidates.

solicitor general the individual who represents the federal government in the Supreme Court.

sovereign immunity the principle that state governments cannot be sued by private parties in federal court unless they consent to the suits or Congress has constitutionally provided an exemption that allows suits to be filed.

sovereign power the individual or institution in a political system whose decisions are binding and cannot be overturned by other individuals or institutions.

sovereignty having the ultimate authority to make decisions within one's borders, without interference by other governments.

Speaker of the House the person who presides over the House and serves as the chamber's official spokesperson.

special district local governments created for a narrowly defined purpose and with a restricted source of revenue.

spoils system a system of government in which a presidential administration awards jobs to party loyalists.

sponsor a member of Congress who introduces a bill.

spurious relationship a relationship between variables that reflects correlation but not causation.

stability the speed with which the change will occur, and the likelihood that the new opinion will endure.

standing committee a permanent committee with a well-defined, relatively fixed policy jurisdiction that develops, writes, and updates important legislation.

standing the requirement establishing that for a plaintiff to bring a case to court, he or she must have suffered a well-defined injury that is a result of violation of the civil code.

stare decisis the principle that judges deciding a case must carefully weigh the decisions of their predecessors in similar cases and come to the same decision if the basic elements of the case before them are the same.

state action Supreme Court interpretation of the equal protection clause holding that the clause prohibited unfair discriminatory actions by government, not by private individuals.

State Department the agency home of diplomats, embassies, treaty negotiators, and most foreign aid programs run by the U.S. government.

strategic model the theory of judicial decision making in which judges consider their own policy preferences as well as the possible actions of the other branches of government when making decisions.

subcommittee a smaller organizational unit within a committee that specializes in a particular segment of the committee's responsibilities.

substantive due process an interpretation of the due process clause in the Fourteenth Amendment that says the clause's guarantee of "life, liberty, and property" provides a means to discover new rights not mentioned elsewhere in the Constitution, and that these rights would exist at both the national and state levels of government.

suffrage the right to vote.

sunset provision a condition of a law that requires it to be reauthorized after a certain number of years.

supplemental appropriations the process by which Congress and the president can provide temporary funding for government activities and programs when funds fall short because of unforeseen circumstances.

supremacy clause a clause in the Constitution that declares that national laws and treaties have supremacy over state laws and treaties.

Supreme Court the highest court in the country, where all decisions are final.

T

take care clause the constitutional clause that grants the president the authority and leeway to determine if laws are being "faithfully executed" and to take action if in his judgment they are not.

tariff a tax on goods exchanged between nations.

Temporary Assistance for Needy Families (TANF) a program replacing AFDC in 1996 that established new work requirements for welfare recipients and limits on the number of years an individual can receive assistance.

Three-fifths Compromise an agreement between slave states and free states that a state's slave population would be counted at 60 percent for purposes of determining a state's representation in the House of Representatives.

treaty an international agreement in which the United States becomes a party once the president has signed and two-thirds of the Senate has ratified it.

trustee model of representation the type of representation by which representatives are elected to do what they think is best for their constituents.

two-party system a system of electoral competition in which two parties are consistently the most likely to win office and gain power.

unfunded mandate a law requiring certain actions without appropriating the necessary funds to carry them out.

unified government the presidency and both houses of Congress are controlled by the same party.

unitary system a form of government in which government at the highest level has the power to create, combine, or disband lower-level governments and determine what powers will be allowed at the lower levels.

United Nations an international organization founded in 1945 dedicated to the advancement of world peace, economic prosperity, and the protection of human rights.

valence issues issues on which virtually everyone agrees.

veto the president's power to reject legislation passed by Congress; Congress can override a veto with a two-thirds vote in both the House and Senate.

veto the president's rejection of a bill passed by both chambers of Congress, which prevents the bill from becoming law.

Virginia Plan one of the rival plans at the Constitutional Convention, it argued for a two-house legislature, with representation based on a state's population; the lower house would be elected directly by the people, and that house would then select the members of the upper house.

Voting Rights Act of 1965 legislation that abolished literacy tests as a requirement to register to vote.

vouchers tuition subsidies that reduce the costs of sending children to private schools.

watchdog the media's role in keeping a close eye on politicians and presenting stories and information that politicians might not willingly reveal to the media on their own.

whips designated members of Congress who deliver messages from the party leaders, keep track of members' votes, and encourage members to stand together on key issues.

whistle-blower a bureaucrat who witnesses and publicly exposes wrongdoing by either contacting his or her political superiors or tipping off the press.

White House staff a group of offices in the executive branch that provides the president with political advice, promotes the president's program with legislators and interest groups, and handles the president's public relations.

white primary primary elections in southern states in which only white voters were allowed to participate.

winner-take-all election in which the candidate who gets the most votes wins; any other candidate loses and receives nothing.

writ of certiorari a formal acceptance by the Supreme Court to review a decision of a lower court.

Z

zero-sum game a situation, for example in foreign policy, in which one side's gains are always at the expense of the other side.

NOTES

1

1. Thomas Hobbes, *Leviathan*, ed. Richard Tuck (New York: Cambridge University Press, 1996).
2. See Hobbes, *Leviathan*; John Locke, *Second Treatise on Government*, ed. C. B. Macpherson (Indianapolis: Hackett, 1980); and Jean-Jacques Rousseau, *Basic Political Writings*, ed. Donald A. Cress (Indianapolis: Hackett, 1987).
3. Free, Fair, and Regular Elections: Venezuela, from Democracy Web: Comparative Studies in Freedom http://www.democracyweb.org/elections/venezuela.php
4. Judge Learned Hand, "We Seek Liberty," address in Central Park, New York, May 21, 1944.
5. Foreign Affairs Big Mac I, http://www.nytimes.com/1996/12/08/opinion/foreign-affairs-big-mac-i.html
6. FBI reports 5% drop in crime rates, http://articles.latimes.com/2010/sep/14/nation/la-na-crime-rate-20100914

2

1. http://www.commonwealthfund.org/Publications/Fund-Reports/2010/Sep/Health-Insurance-Exchanges-and-the-Affordable-Care-Act.aspx.
2. http://www.hhs.gov/news/press/2012pres/01/20120120a.html
3. See, for example, the comments of House Democratic Minority Leader and former Speaker of the House Nancy Pelosi, http://thehill.com/homenews/house/217319-pelosi-fundraising-for-democrats-accuses-gop-of-waging-war-on-women.
4. http://www.usccb.org/issues-and-action/religious-liberty/our-first-most-cherished-liberty.cfm
5. Steven Erlanger, "France Debates Its Identity, but Some Question Why," *New York Times*, November 29, 2009, p. A16.
6. Hazel Erskine, "The Polls: Freedom of Speech," *Public Opinion Quarterly* 34, 3 (1970): 483-96.
7. The creed is grounded in the "classical liberal" political theory of the seventeenth and eighteenth centuries. See Louis Hartz, *The Liberal Tradition in America: An Interpretation of American Political Thought Since the Revolution* (New York: Harcourt Brace, 1955); David F. Ericson and Louisa Bertch Green, eds., *The Liberal Tradition in American Politics: Reassessing the Legacy of American Liberalism* (New York: Routledge, 1999); Seymour Martin Lipset. *American Exceptionalism: A Double-Edged Sword* (New York: W. W. Norton, 1997).
8. Peter A. Morrison, "A Demographic Perspective on Our Nation's Future," RAND Report, 2001, http://www.rand.org/publications/DB/DB320/. See also Laura B. Shrestha, "The Changing Demographic Profile of the United States," Congressional Research Service, May 5, 2006, http://www.fas.org/sgp/crs/misc/RL32701.pdf; and Jeffrey S. Passel and D'Vera Cohn, "U.S. Population Projections: 2005–2050," Pew Research Center, February 11, 2008 (http://pewhispanic.org/files/reports/85.pdf).
9. See the discussion of conflicts over language policy in Melissa J. Marschall, Elizabeth Rigby, and Jasmine Jenkins, "Do State Policies Constrain Local Actors? The Impact of English Only Laws on Language Instruction in Public Schools," Publius 41, 4 (2011): 586-609; and Sarah Song, "What Does It Mean to Be an American?" *Daedalus* 138, 2 (2009): 31-40.
10. Daniel J. Hopkins, "Politicized Places: Explaining Where and When Immigrants Provoke Local Opposition," *American Political Science Review* 104, 1 (2010): 40–60; Jens Hainmueller and Michael J. Hiscox, "Attitudes toward Highly Skilled and Low-skilled Immigration: Evidence from a Survey Experiment," *American Political Science Review* 104, 1 (2010): 61–84.
11. Werner Sombart's argument was published in German in 1905. It appears in English as *Why Is There No Socialism in the United States?* trans. Patricia M. Hocking (Armonk, NY: M. E. Sharpe, 1976).
12. See Theda Skocpol, "The Origins of Social Policy in the United States: A Polity-Centered Analysis," in Lawrence C. Dodd and Calvin Jillson, eds., *The Dynamics of American Politics: Approaches and Interpretations* (Boulder, CO: Westview Press, 1994); Adam Przeworski, "The Material Bases of Consent," in Adam Przeworski, ed., *Capitalism and Social Democracy* (New York: Cambridge University Press, 1985).
13. Edward S. Herman and Noam Chomsky, *Manufacturing Consent: The Political Economy of the Mass Media* (New York: Pantheon, 2002); Robert Justin Goldstein, *Political Repression in Modern America: From 1870 to 1976* (Champaign: University of Illinois Press, 2001); Victoria Hattam, *Labor Visions and State Power: The Origins of Business Unionism in the United States* (Princeton, NJ: Princeton University Press, 1992).
14. See Michael Lind, "The American Creed: Does It Matter? Should It Change?" *Foreign Affairs*, March/April 1996; and Forrest Church, "The American Creed," *The Nation*, September 16, 2002.
15. Pew Values Survey, 2012, http://www.people-press.org/files/legacy-questionnaires/Values%20topline%20for%20release.pdf; Pew Forum on Religion and Public Life, Religion and Public Life Survey, 2002, http://people-press.org/reports/display.php3?PageID=388.
16. New Zealand scored lower, by less than one percentage point.
17. Survey data from International Social Science Programme, 2006, http://zacat.gesis.org. Question wording: "On the whole, do you think it should or should not be the government's responsibility to reduce income differences between the rich and the poor?"
18. Data collected in 2007 survey for Benjamin I. Page and Lawrence R. Jacobs, *Class War? What Americans Really Think about Economic Inequality* (Chicago: University of Chicago Press, 2009), question QWAG3. http://www.press.uchicago.edu/books/page/Class_War_Marginal_Frequencies.pdf.
19. Lars Osberg and Timothy Smeeding, "An International Comparison of Preferences for Leveling," October 3, 2003, http://www-cpr.maxwell.syr.edu/seminar/fall03/osberg.pdf; Lars Osberg and Timothy Smeeding, "'Fair' Inequality? An International Comparison of Attitudes to Pay Differentials,"*American Sociological Review* 71, 3 (2006): 450-73. ,Pew Research Center, Global Attitudes Project 2011, http://www.pewglobal.org/2011/11/17/the-american-western-european-values-gap/.
20. See James Morone, *The Democratic Wish: Popular Participation and the Limits of American Government,* rev. ed. (New Haven, CT: Yale University Press, 1998).
21. John Locke, *Two Treatises of Government*, originally published in 1689.

22. See Jeffrey A. Winters and Benjamin I. Page, "Oligarchy in the United States?" *Perspectives on Politics* 7, 4 (2009): 731–52, and Martin Gilens, "Preference Gaps and Inequality in Representation," *PS* 42, 2 (2009): 335–42.
23. Pew Values Survey 2012, http://www.people-press.org/files/legacy-questionnaires/Values%20topline%20for%20release.pdf.
24. That people had natural rights, and the idea that government exists to protect these rights, not grant them, was central to the thinking of philosopher John Locke, who had a strong influence on the founders. And for political theorist Thomas Hobbes, the idea that government had a role in protecting individuals from the threatening actions of other individuals was central.
25. Surveys in late 2009 frequently showed support in the range of two-thirds to three-quarters of Americans supporting restrictions on pay if a company had received federal bailout funds. When funds had been paid back, or the question did not mention bailouts, the public was evenly split on whether any pay limitations were appropriate. A CBS News Poll in August 2009 found a 46%–46% split. A Time/Abt SRBI Poll in October 2009 found a 49%–45% split.
26. A classic articulation of this view is by Milton Friedman, *Capitalism and Freedom* (Chicago: University of Chicago Press, 1962).
27. Anne Norton, *Republic of Signs: Liberal Theory and American Popular Culture* (Chicago: University of Chicago Press, 1993).
28. James T. Kloppenberg, "The Virtues of Liberalism: Christianity, Republicanism, and Ethics in Early American Political Discourse,"*Journal of American History* 74 (1987): 9–33.
29. Pew Center for the People and the Press, 2009 Values Survey, http://peoplepress.org/reports/questionnaires/517.pdf.
30. Pew Values Survey 2012, http://www.people-press.org/files/legacy-questionnaires/Valuestoplineforrelease.pdf; andPew Forum on Religion and Public Life, Religion and Public Life Survey, August 2008, http://people-press.org/reports/questionnaires/445.pdf.
31. Rachel M. McCleary, "Religion and Economic Development," *Policy Review* 148 (March 28, 2008), http://www.hoover.org/publications/policy-review/article/5729.
32. Pew Research Center, Global Attitudes Project 2011, http://www.pewglobal.org/2011/11/17/the-american-western-european-values-gap/; William Roberts Clark, "Toward a Political Economy of Religion?" *The Political Economist* 12, 1, Spring 2010.
33. Critics argue that individualist beliefs obscure perceptions of structural problems in the economy and society. See Jack Turner, "American Individualism and Structural Injustice: Tocqueville, Gender, and Race," *Polity* 40, 2 (2008): 197–215.
34. Paul C. Light, *The True Size of Government* (Washington, DC: Brookings Institution Press, 1999).
35. See Benjamin I. Page and Lawrence R. Jacobs, *Class War? What Americans Really Think About Economic Inequality* (Chicago: University of Chicago Press, 2009).
36. http://www.people-press.org/files/legacy-questionnaires/Feb11%20topline.pdf; http://www.people-press.org/files/legacy-questionnaires/toplines%20for%20release.pdf; http://www.people-press.org/2012/02/23/auto-bailout-now-backed-stimulus-divisive/.
37. See Steven Rathgeb Smith and Michael Lipsky, *Nonprofits for Hire: The Welfare State in the Age of Contracting* (Cambridge, MA: Harvard University Press, 1995); Irwin Garfinkel, Lee Rainwater, and Timothy Smeeding, *Wealth and Welfare States: Is America a Laggard or Leader?* (New York: Oxford University Press, 2010).
38. The ANES (American National Election Studies) Guide to Public Opinion and Electoral Behavior provides a handful of measures of political trust over time: http://www.electionstudies.org/nesguide/gd-index.htm#5.
39. CNN/Opinion Research Corporation Poll, February 2010; Quinnipiac University Poll, March 2010.
40. Joseph S. Nye Jr., Philip D. Zelikow, and David C. King, eds., *Why People Don't Trust Government* (Cambridge, MA: Harvard University Press, 1997); Pew Research Center for the People and the Press, "How Americans View Government: Deconstructing Distrust," March 10, 1998, http://people-press.org/reports/print.php3?ReportID=95; Russell J. Dalton, "The Social Transformation of Trust in Government," *International Review of Sociology* 51, 1 (2005): 133-54.
41. Marc J. Hetherington, "The Political Relevance of Political Trust," *American Political Science Review* 92, 4 (December 1998): 791–808.
42. Richard J. Ellis, *American Political Cultures* (New York: Oxford University Press, 1993).
43. Daniel J. Elazar, *American Federalism: A View from the States*, 3rd ed. (New York: HarperCollins, 1984). A map is available at http://www.valpo.edu/geomet/pics/geo200/politics/elazar.gif.
44. Daniel T. Rodgers, *Contested Truths: Keywords in American Politics Since Independence* (Cambridge, MA: Harvard University Press, 1998).
45. *Wesberry v. Sanders* and *Reynolds v. Sims*
46. Matthew Hayes, Matthew V. Hibbing, and Tracy Sulkin, "Redistricting, Responsiveness, and Issue Attention," *Legislative Studies Quarterly* 35, 1 (2010): 91–116.
47. Communitarianism is a modern version of a political philosophy known as classical republicanism. Although there are some distinctions between communitarianism and classical republicanism, they are similar enough for us to use the single label in this discussion.
48. Cited in Gordon S. Wood, *The Creation of the American Republic, 1776–1787* (New York: W. W. Norton, 1969), 61.
49. Wood, *The Creation of the American Republic, 1776–1787;* Bernard Bailyn, *The Ideological Origins of the American Revolution* (Cambridge, MA: Harvard University Press, 1992).
50. In the words of a colonist in 1776, "No man is a true republican that will not give up his single voice to that of the public." Cited in Wood, *The Creation of the American Republic, 1776–1787*, 61.
51. One of the best-known popularizers of communitarian ideas is Amitai Etzioni. See, for example, his *The Spirit of Community: The Reinvention of American Society* (New York: Touchstone, 1993).
52. Karl Polanyi, *The Great Transformation: The Political and Economic Origins of Our Times*, 2nd ed. (Boston: Beacon Press, 2001); Andrew Stark, "The Consensus School, Its Critics, and Welfare Policy: A Study of American Political Discourse," *Journal of Politics* 71, 2 (2009): 627–43.
53. Pew Values Survey 2010, http://www.people-press.org/files/legacy-questionnaires/Values%20topline%20for%20release.pdf.
54. Paul A. Lombardo, ed., *A Century of Eugenics in America: From the Indiana Experiment to the Human Genome Era* (Bloomington: Indiana University Press, 2011).
55. Rogers M. Smith, "Beyond Tocqueville, Myrdal, and Hartz: The Multiple Traditions in America," *American Political Science Review* 87, 3 (1993): 549–66. Survey data in this paragraph are from the General Social Survey.
56. See the 2009 survey data in "A Place to Call Home: What Immigrants Say Now About Life in America," Public Agenda, http://www.publicagenda.org/pages/immigrants; Maria Hsia Chang, "Multiculturalism, Immigration and Aztlan," paper presented at the Second Alliance for Stabilizing America's Population Action Conference, Breckenridge, Colorado, August 6, 1999, http://www.diversityalliance.org/docs/Chang-aztlan.html.
57. Doriane Lambelet Coleman, "Individualizing Justice Through Multiculturalism: The Liberals' Dilemma," *Columbia Law Review* 96, 5 (1996): 1093–1167.

58. Susan Moller Okin, "Is Multiculturalism Bad for Women?" in Joshua Cohen and Matthew Howard, eds., *Is Multiculturalism Bad for Women?* (Princeton, NJ: Princeton University Press, 1999). See also Cynthia Lee, "Cultural Convergence: Interest Convergence Theory Meets the Cultural Defense?" *Arizona Law Review* 49, 4 (2007).
59. http://www.kaiserhealthnews.org/stories/2010/september/16/census-uninsured-rate-soars.aspx.

3

1. This discussion draws extensively on Alexander Keyssar, *The Right to Vote: The Contested History of Democracy in the United States* (New York: Basic Books, 2000).
2. Gregory A. Caldeira, "Constitutional Change in America: Dynamics of Ratification under Article V," *Publius* 15, 4 (1985): 29–49.
3. Bernard Bailyn, *The Ideological Origins of the American Revolution* (Cambridge, MA: Harvard University Press, 1967), 160.
4. See Gordon S. Wood, *The Creation of the American Republic, 1776–1787* (New York: W. W. Norton, 1969), 7–8.
5. Edmund S. Morgan, *Inventing the People: The Rise of Popular Sovereignty in England and America* (New York: W. W. Norton, 1989).
6. Bailyn, *Ideological Origins*, 173.
7. All colonies except Georgia sent representatives to the Congress.
8. See Stephen Howard Browne, "Jefferson's First Declaration of Independence: A Summary View of the Rights of British America Revisited," *Quarterly Journal of Speech* 89, 3 (2003): 235–52.
9. Social scientists label this the *state*," but that terminology is complicated by the fact that in the United States the word *state* is most often used in reference to state governments.
10. See Merrill Jensen, *The Articles of Confederation* (Madison: University of Wisconsin Press, 1970).
11. On the despair of the 1780s, see Wood, *Creation of the American Republic*, chap. 10.
12. He is also famously, or infamously, known for losing his life in a duel with Aaron Burr.
13. Michael Kammen, *The Origins of the American Constitution: A Documentary History* (New York: Penguin Books, 1986); Catherine Bowen, *Miracle at Philadelphia: The Story of the Constitutional Convention, May–September 1787* (Boston: Little, Brown, 1966); Jack Rakove, *Original Meanings: Politics and Ideas in the Making of the Constitution* (New York: Alfred A. Knopf, 1996).
14. Some historians believe that the Framers were influenced by the governing practices of the Six Nations, known more commonly as the Iroquois Confederacy, which included the Cayuga, Mohawk, Oneida, Onondaga, Seneca, and Tuscarora tribes. Certainly many of the features of U.S. government were present in the confederacy: checks and balances, federalism, participation, and civil liberties protections. The preamble to the Constitution echoes the language in a 1520 Iroquois treaty: "We the people, to form a union, to establish peace, equity, and order." The Iroquois occupied territory now in New York State. Members of the Iroquois visited the Continental Congress in June 1776. See Bruce E. Johansen, *Forgotten Founders: Benjamin Franklin, the Iroquois and the Rationale for the American Revolution* (Ipswich, MA: Gambit, 1982).
15. Randolph presented a resolution at the outset of the convention that served, in effect, as a draft for a new system of government.
16. The New Jersey Plan was geared more toward revising the Articles rather than discarding them, but delegates had already gravitated toward the idea that a new system was needed.
17. The three-fifths calculation would also apply for federal taxation purposes.
18. Discussions of slavery as an issue for the Framers can be found in Jeremy C. Pope and Shawn Treier, "Reconsidering the Great Compromise at the Federal Convention of 1787: Deliberation and Agenda Effects on the Senate and Slavery," *American Journal of Political Science* 55, 2 (2011): 289–306; and Keith L. Dougherty and Jac C. Heckelman, "Voting on Slavery at the Constitutional Convention," *Public Choice* 136 (2008): 293–313.
19. See Mark A. Graber, *Dred Scott and the Problem of Constitutional Evil* (New York: Cambridge University Press, 2008), and Justin Buckley Dyer, "After the Revolution: *Somerset* and the Antislavery Tradition in Anglo-American Constitutional Development," *Journal of Politics* 71, 4 (2009): 1422–34.
20. See Bryan D. Jones, Heather Larsen-Price, and John Wilkerson, "Representation and American Governing Institutions," *Journal of Politics* 71, 1 (2009): 277–90.
21. In everyday language, when people think "democracy" they are thinking along the lines of republican government. "Direct democracy" is often used to describe democracy in which the people themselves make law.
22. This phrase was first used in Richard E. Neustadt, *Presidential Power and the Modern Presidents: The Politics of Leadership from Roosevelt to Reagan* (New York: Free Press, 1991).
23. Nolan McCarty, "Presidential Vetoes in the Early Republic: Changing Constitutional Norms or Electoral Reform?" *Journal of Politics* 71, 2 (2009): 369–84.
24. Mark A. Graber, "Establishing Judicial Review? *Schooner Peggy* and the Early Marshall Court," *Political Research Quarterly* 51, 1 (1998): 221–39. For judicial review and its relationship to democracy, see J. Mitchell Pickerill, *Constitutional Deliberation in Congress: The Impact of Judicial Review in a Separated System* (Durham, NC: Duke University Press, 2004); Annabelle Lever, "Democracy and Judicial Review: Are They Really Incompatible?" *Perspectives on Politics* 7, 4 (2009): 805–22.
25. In *Federalist 51*, Madison notes that the legislature predominates, but creating two houses with different modes of election can moderate its power.
26. Ibid.
27. Ibid.
28. The Supreme Court verified national supremacy on this issue in its decision in *Lorillard Tobacco Company v. Reilly* (2001).
29. See David J. Siemers, *Ratifying the Republic: Antifederalists and Federalists in Constitutional Time* (Stanford, CA: Stanford University Press, 2002).
30. William Riker, *Federalism: Origin, Operation, Significance* (Boston: Little, Brown, 1964).
31. Iain McLean, "William H. Riker and the Invention of Heresthetic(s)," *British Journal of Political Science* 32 (2002): 535–58.
32. These names are misnomers. Federalism connotes a sharing of power across the national and state governments, and the Anti-Federalists ardently advocated this position.
33. Herbert Storing, *What the Anti-Federalists Were For: The Political Thought of the Opponents of the Constitution* (Chicago: University of Chicago Press, 1981).
34. See Robert W. T. Martin, "James Madison and Popular Government: The Neglected Case of the 'Memorial.'" *Polity* 42, 2 (2010): 185-209; Tiffany Jones Miller, "James Madison's Republic of 'Mean Extent' Theory: Avoiding the Scylla and Charybdis of Republican Government," *Polity* 39, 4 (2007): 545–69.

35. Nathalie Behnke and Arthur Benz, "The Politics of Constitutional Change between Reform and Evolution," *Publius* 39, 2 (2009): 213–40.
36. John R. Vile, "The Long Legacy of Proposals to Rewrite the U.S. Constitution," *PS: Political Science and Politics*, June 1993, 208–11.
37. Michael B. Rappoport, "Renewing Federalism by Reforming Article V: Defects in the Constitutional Amendment Process and a Reform Proposal," *Policy Analysis* 691 (January 18, 2012); Michael L. Stern, "Reopening the Constitutional Road to Reform: Toward a Safeguarded Article V Convention," *Tennessee Law Review* 78, 3 (2011): 765-87.
38. Christopher P. Manfredi, "Institutional Design and the Politics of Constitutional Modification: Understanding Amendment Failure in the United States and Canada," *Law & Society Review* 31, 1 (1997): 111–36.
39. See Caldeira, "Constitutional Change in America."
40. The average length of state constitutions is about three times that of the federal document, and the average number of amendments is more than four times that of the U.S. Constitution.
41. See Bruce Ackerman, *We the People, Volume One: Foundations* and *We the People, Volume Two: Transformations* (Cambridge, MA: Harvard University Press, 1993 and 2000, respectively).

4

1. They charge that same-sex marriage is not consistent with the traditional conceptual understanding of marriage.
2. See National Conference of State Legislatures, http://www.ncsl.org/IssuesResearch/HumanServices/SameSexMarriage/tabid/16430/Default.aspx#DOMA; and the Pew Forum on Religion and Public Life, http://pewforum.org/Gay-Marriage-and-Homosexuality/Gay-Marriage-Around-the-World.aspx.
3. Nullification made its first appearance in 1798 when Virginia and Kentucky nullified the Alien and Sedition Acts.
4. http://www.ncsl.org/issues-research/health/state-laws-and-actions-challenging-aca.aspx
5. The president indicated his support for a new public insurance plan that would compete with private insurance companies. Some of the president's more liberal supporters wanted him to push for a single-payer system, in which all payment for health care would be routed through government.
6. See Virginia Gray, David Lowery, James Monogan, and Erik K. Godwin, "Incrementing Toward Nowhere: Universal Health Care Coverage in the States," *Publius* 40 (2010): 82–113, for a review of state efforts to achieve universal coverage. See also http://www.ncsl.org/issues-research/health/state-laws-and-actions-challenging-aca.aspx.
7. G. Alan Tarr, *Understanding State Constitutions* (Princeton, NJ: Princeton University Press, 1999).
8. Albert L. Sturm, "The Development of State Constitutions," *Publius* 12 (Winter 1982): 60–67.
9. Albert L. Sturm, *Thirty Years of State Constitutions-Making 1938–1968* (New York: National Municipal League, 1970).
10. Stefan Voigt, "Explaining Constitutional Garrulity," *International Review of Law and Economics* 29 (2009): 290–303.
11. David C. Nice, "Interest Groups and State Constitutions—Another Look," *State and Local Government Review* 20 (Winter 1988): 21–29.
12. *United States v. Mazurie* (1975).
13. See U.S. Department of Energy, Office of Environmental Management, "American Indian Executive Orders (1994 to Present)," http://www.em.doe.gov/tribalpages/orders.aspx U.S. Department of Justice, Office of Tribal Justice, "Department of Justice Policy on Indian Sovereignty and Government-to-Government Relations with Indian Tribes," http://www.justice.gov/ag/readingroom/sovereignty.htm.
14. See http://www.bia.gov for information and statistics on Indian tribes.
15. See Steven Andrew Light and Kathryn R. L. Rand, *Indian Gaming and Tribal Sovereignty: The Casino Compromise* (Lawrence: University Press of Kansas, 2007).
16. Kathryn A. Foster, *The Political Economy of Special Purpose Government* (Washington, DC: Georgetown University Press, 1997); and Nancy Burns, *The Formation of American Local Governments: Private Values in Public Institutions* (New York: Oxford University Press, 1994).
17. Dale Krane, Platon N. Rigos, and Melvin B. Hill Jr., *Home Rule in America: A Fifty State Handbook* (Washington, DC: Congressional Quarterly Press, 2001).
18. The District has been given some statelike features, such as votes in the Electoral College, but it does not have formal voting representation in the House and Senate.
19. http://www.ncsl.org/issues-research/env-res/state-constitutional-right-to-hunt-and-fish.aspx
20. http://www.ghsa.org/html/stateinfo/laws/cellphone_laws.html
21. *United States v. E. C. Knight Co. et al.* (1895).
22. The Court's language is clearly that of dual federalism: "The relief of the citizens of each state from the burden of monopoly and the evils resulting from the restraint of trade among such citizens was left with the states to deal with, and this court has recognized their possession of that power . . . . On the other hand, the power of Congress to regulate commerce among the several states is also exclusive."
23. Specifically, the law forbade the interstate transport of a product from a factory that within the previous 30 days had employed children under the age of 14 or permitted children ages 14 through 16 to work more than eight hours in a day, more than six days a week, after 7 P.M., or before 6 A.M.
24. *Hammer v. Dagenhart* (1918).
25. See also the Marshall Court decisions in *Martin v. Hunter's Lessee* (1816) and *Cohens v. Virginia* (1821).
26. *United States v. Darby* (1941). See also Donald F. Kettl, "Real-Life Federalism," *Governing Magazine*, August 2001.
27. Ira Katznelson and Quinn Mulroy, "Was the South Pivotal? Situated Partisanship and Policy Coalitions during the New Deal and Fair Deal," *Journal of Politics* 74, 2 (2012): 604–20.
28. Any employee working for a business involved in interstate commerce is covered, as is any employee working for a business with sales volume exceeding $500,000.
29. See Suzanne Mettler, *Dividing Citizens: Gender and Federalism in New Deal Public Policy* (Ithaca, NY: Cornell University Press, 1998).
30. Paul Rogers, "Increase in National Gas Mileage Standards Announced; California Drove Obama Policy," *Silicon Valley Mercury News*, April 1, 2010.
31. Robert L. Fischman, "Cooperative Federalism and Natural Resources Law," *NYU Environmental Law Journal* 14 (2005): 179–231.
32. The National Conference of State Legislatures tracks immigration law, http://www.ncsl.org; http://www.ncsl.org/issues-research/educ/undocumented-student-tuition-overview.aspx. The Supreme Court decision is *Plyler v. Doe* (1982). See also Lina Newton and Brian E. Adams, "State Immigration Policies: Innovation, Cooperation or Conflict?" *Publius* 39 (2009): 408–31.
33. See, for example, Timothy J. Conlan and Paul L. Posner, "Inflection Point? Federalism and the Obama Administration," *Publius* 41, 3 (2011): 421-46.
34. Douglas Elmendorf, "A Review of CBO's Activities in 2011 Under the Unfunded Mandates Reform Act,"

http://www.cbo.gov/sites/default/files/cbofiles/attachments/03-30-UMRA.pdf.

35. http://www.cbo.gov/sites/default/files/cbofiles/attachments/03-30-UMRA.pdf, table 1.
36. Angela Antonelli, "Promises Unfulfilled: Unfunded Mandates Reform Act of 1995," *Regulation* 19, 2 (1996); David S. Broder, "Those Unfunded Mandates," *Washington Post*, March 17, 2005, A25.
37. U.S. Government Accountability Office, *Unfunded Mandates: Views Vary About Reform Act's Strengths, Weaknesses, and Options for Improvement*, GAO-05-454, March 31, 2005, http://www.gao.gov/products/GAO-05-454. See also U.S. Government Accountability Office, *Unfunded Mandates: Analysis of Reform Act Coverage*, GAO-04-637, May 2004, http://www.gao.gov/new.items/d04637.pdf.
38. James Dao, "Rebellion of the States: Red, Blue, and Angry All Over," *New York Times*, January 16, 2005. See also http://www.ncsl.org/standcomm/scbudg/manmon.htm.
39. U.S. House of Representatives, Committee on Government Reform, Minority Staff Special Investigations Division, "Congressional Preemption of State Laws and Regulations," June 2006. See also the Preemption Monitor published regularly by the National Conference of State Legislatures, http://www.ncsl.org.
40. U.S. Government Accountability Office, *Formula Grants: Funding for the Largest Federal Assistance Programs Is Based on Census-Related Data and Other Factors*, December 2009, GAO-10-263, http://www.gao.gov/new.items/d10263.pdf.
41. U.S. Census Bureau, *Statistical Abstract of the United States 2012*, tables 430 and 431, http://www.census.gov/compendia/statab/cats/state_local_govt_finances_employment/receipts_expenditures_investment.html
42. Budget of the United States Government: Historical Tables Fiscal Year 2013, Table 12-2, http://www.whitehouse.gov/omb/budget/Historicals.
43. Daniel B. Wood, "California's Education Reforms Hand More Power to Parents," *Christian Science Monitor*, January 7, 2010.
44. Within each region, states vary in whether they receive more than they pay or pay more than they receive.
45. Under revenue sharing, the federal government provided funds to the states based on a formula that considered population, per capita income, and the property tax base. States were dropped from the program in 1981, and revenue sharing was completely eliminated in 1987.
46. Nathan J. Kelly and Christopher Witko, "Federalism and American Inequality," *Journal of Politics* 74, 2 (2012): 414–26.
47. http://www.politico.com/news/stories/1111/68441.html.
48. Paul Peterson, *The Price of Federalism* (Washington, DC: Brookings Institution Press, 1998); Kevin M. Esterling, "Does the Federal Government Learn from the States? Medicaid and the Limits of Expertise in the Intergovernmental Lobby," *Publius* 39 (2009): 1–21.
49. Richard Simeon, "Constitutional Design and Change in Federal Systems: Issues and Questions," *Publius* 39, 2 (2009): 241–61.
50. Nancy Bermeo, "Conclusion: The Merits of Federalism," in Ugo M. Amoretti and Nancy Bermeo, eds., *Federalism and Territorial Cleavages* (Baltimore: Johns Hopkins University Press, 2004); Nicholas Charron, "Government Quality and Vertical Power-Sharing in Fractionalized States," *Publius* 39 (2009): 585–605.
51. Dean E. McHenry Jr., "Federalism in Africa: Is It a Solution to, or a Cause of, Ethnic Problems?" Paper presented at the annual meeting of the African Studies Association, Columbus, Ohio, November 1997.
52. The *Federal Register* lists pending regulations and also the period for public comment on them.
53. The case concerned Alfonso Lopez Jr., a grade 12 student at Edison High School in San Antonio who brought a concealed handgun and ammunition to school and was charged with violating the Gun-Free School Zone Act.
54. Section 5 of the Fourteenth Amendment provides the authority to override this immunity.
55. *Alden v. Maine* (1999); *Gregory v. Ashcroft* (1991); *Kimel v. Florida Board of Regents* (2000); *Board of Trustees of the University of Alabama v. Garrett* (2001); and *Seminole Tribe v. Florida* (1996).
56. William Van Allstyne, "When *Can* A State Be Sued?" *Popular Government* (Spring 2001): 44-46.
57. Keith E. Whittington, "Taking What They Give Us: Explaining the Court's Federalism Offensive," *Duke Law Journal* 51, 1 (2001): 477–520.
58. See http://www.ncsl.org/realid/.
59. Priscilla M. Regan and Christopher J. Deering, "State Opposition to REAL ID," *Publius* 39, 3 (2009): 476–505.
60. Updates from 2011 and 2012 by the American Civil Liberties Union: http://www.aclu.org/blog/national-security-technology-and-liberty/slow-quiet-death-real-id; http://www.aclu.org/blog/technology-and-liberty/reading-tea-leaves-real-id; http://www.aclu.org/blog/technology-and-liberty/yes-states-really-reject-real-id.
61. See, for example, Barry Rabe, "Environmental Policy and the Bush Era: The Collision Between the Administrative Presidency and State Experimentation," *Publius* 37, 3 (2007): 413–31; Paul Posner, "The Politics of Coercive Federalism in the Bush Era," *Publius* 37, 3 (2007): 390–412.
62. Posner, "The Politics of Coercive Federalism in the Bush Era"; and see Universal Right to Vote by Mail Act, H.R. 1604.
63. http://www2.ed.gov/programs/racetothetop/index.html.
64. In *Nevada Department of Human Resources v. Hibbs* (2003).
65. Marci Hamilton, "The Supreme Court's Federalism Cases This Term: A String of Decisions Upholding Federal Power Show the Portrayal of the Court as Extreme Is a Caricature," *FindLaw*, June 3, 2004, http://writ.news.findlaw.com/hamilton/20040603.html.
66. *American Insurance Association v. Garamendi* (2004).
67. In October 2009, U.S. Attorney General Eric Holder announced that the Justice Department would no longer prosecute individuals who were using marijuana strictly for medical purposes in states where such use was allowed. See http://medicalmarijuana.procon.org/view.resource.php?resourceID=000881.

5

1. Campaign Media Analysis Group, Kantar Media.
2. http://www.opensecrets.org/outsidespending/summ.php?disp=O.
3. Ronald Dworkin, "The 'Devastating' Decision," *New York Review of Books*, January 25, 2010. See also his "The Decision That Threatens Democracy," *New York Review of Books*, May 13, 2010.
4. Bradley Smith, "Newsflash: First Amendment Upheld," *Wall Street Journal*, January 22, 2010. See also his "*Citizens United* We Stand," *American Spectator*, May 2010.
5. DISCLOSE stood for "Democracy Is Strengthened by Casting Light on Spending in Elections."
6. We discuss freedom of the press in Chapter 10.
7. Where rights come from is a matter of philosophical dispute.
8. Freedom House's 2012 report can be found at http://www.freedomhouse.org/sites/default/files/inline_images/FIW%202012%20Booklet—Final.pdf. For civil liberties, Freedom House assesses a country's freedom of expression and belief, association and organization rights, rule of law and human rights, and personal autonomy and economic rights.

9. See also the twin studies by Robert Barro, "Determinants of Democracy," *Journal of Political Economy* 107, 6 (1999); and *Determinants of Economic Growth: A Cross-Country Empirical Study* (Cambridge, MA: MIT Press, 1997).
10. See Akhil Reed Amar, *The Bill of Rights: Creation and Reconstruction* (New Haven, CT: Yale University Press, 2000) for an overview.
11. Seventeen amendments had been adopted in the House of Representatives; the Senate accepted 12 of these. Ten were ratified by the states in December 1791.
12. Two cases kicked off the incorporation process: *Chicago, Burlington, and Quincy Railroad Company v. Chicago* (1897) and *Gitlow v. New York* (1925).
13. The language of the due process clause in the Fourteenth Amendment is based on a nearly identically worded clause in the Fifth Amendment.
14. See Lawrence Baum, "Membership Change and Collective Voting Change in the United States Supreme Court," *Journal of Politics* 54, 1 (1992): 3–24.
15. See Shawn Francis Peters, *Judging Jehovah's Witnesses: Religious Persecution and the Dawn of the Rights Revolution* (Lawrence: University Press of Kansas, 2000); Ken I. Kirsch, *Constructing Civil Liberties: Discontinuities in the Development of American Constitutional Law* (New York: Cambridge University Press, 2004).
16. *McDonald v. Chicago* (2010).
17. Arati Korwar, *War of Words: Speech Codes at Public Colleges and Universities* (Nashville, TN: Freedom Forum First Amendment Center, 1994).
18. *R.A.V. v. City of St. Paul* (1992).
19. A government can regulate the nature of these activities by requiring permits, but it must be content neutral toward what it allows.
20. See Jon B. Gould, *Speak No Evil: The Triumph of Hate Speech Regulation* (Chicago: University of Chicago Press, 2005); Martin P. Golding, *Free Speech on Campus* (Lanham, MD: Rowman and Littlefield, 2000).
21. Geoffrey R. Stone, "The Origins of the 'Bad Tendency' Test: Free Speech in Wartime," *Supreme Court Review* (2002): 411–53.
22. In *Terminiello v. Chicago* (1949), the Court declared that speech should be punished only when it creates a clear and present danger of a "serious substantive evil that rises far above public inconvenience, annoyance, or unrest."
23. *American Communications Association v. Douds* (1950); *Dennis v. United States* (1951). See Ken I. Kersch, "'Guilt by Association' and the Post War Civil Libertarians," *Social Philosophy and Policy* 25, 2 (2008).
24. *Martin v. City of Struthers* (1943).
25. See *Konigsberg v. State Bar of California* (1961).
26. *Murdock v. Pennsylvania* (1943).
27. *Chaplinsky v. New Hampshire* (1942).
28. *Beauharnais v. Illinois* (1952).
29. *New York Times Co. v. Sullivan* (1964); *Gertz v. Robert Welch, Inc.* (1974); *Milkovich v. Lorain Journal Co.* (1990).
30. *Valentine v. Chrestensen* (1942); *Greater New Orleans Broadcasting Association v. United States* (1999); *Lorillard Tobacco v. Reilly* (2001); *Sorrell v. IMS Health* (2011).
31. *U.S. v. Stevens* (2010). The decision struck down a federal law that prohibited the distribution or possession of videos that depicted animal cruelty. Regarding child pornography, the Court issued a unanimous decision in *New York v. Ferber* (1982) upholding a state statute prohibiting the distribution of child pornography. In 2008 (*U.S. v. Williams*), the Court upheld the national Protect Act of 2003. The law prohibited the offering or soliciting of any form of child pornography, including computer-generated pornography.
32. In *Jacobellis v. Ohio* (1964), which concerned the French film *Les Amants*.
33. Federal law and court rulings have established that any sexually explicit depictions of children or depictions of children in sexual acts inherently violate these guidelines and are not constitutionally protected.
34. *Reno v. American Civil Liberties Union* (1997).
35. *United States et al. v. American Library Association, Inc., et al.* (2003).
36. David M. O'Brien, *Constitutional Law and Politics: Civil Rights and Civil Liberties*, 5th ed. (New York: W. W. Norton, 2003), 506.
37. As noted earlier, Article VI of the Constitution prohibits religious tests or oaths for public office.
38. Frank Lambert, *The Founding Fathers and the Place of Religion in America* (Princeton, NJ: Princeton University Press, 2003).
39. Article 11 of the 1797 Treaty with Tripoli states that "the government of the United States of America is not in any sense founded on the Christian Religion." Although there is substantial dispute about precisely how and when this article was inserted into the treaty, this text was approved unanimously by the Senate and signed into law by President John Adams.
40. The United Nations has a list of constitutions and their religious references at http://www.unesco.org/most/rr2nat.htm.
41. *Aguilar v. Felton* (1985).
42. *Engale v. Vitale* (1962); *Abington School District v. Schempp* (1963); *Lee v. Weisman* (1992); *Wallace v. Jaffrie* (1985); *Santa Fe Independent School District v. Doe* (2000).
43. *County of Allegheny v. ACLU Greater Pittsburgh Chapter* (1989). The Texas case is *Van Orden v. Perry* (2005); the Kentucky case is *McCreary County v. A.C.L.U. of Kentucky* (2005).
44. http://www.upi.com/Top_News/US/2011/11/06/Under-the-US-Supreme-Court-Thomas-spanks-court-on-religious-displays/UPI-80331320575400/.
45. O'Brien, *Constitutional Law and Politics*, 782–85.
46. BBC News, "The Islamic Veil Across Europe," April 22, 2010, http://news.bbc.co.uk/2/hi/5414098.stm; http://www.nytimes.com/2011/04/12/world/europe/12france.html.
47. In *Wisconsin v. Yoder* (1971), the Supreme Court determined that Amish religious exercise was burdened by Wisconsin's requirement that students remain in school until age 16, and that the states' interest was not compelling enough to justify the burden.
48. The Court's decision noted that the laws did not make clear why the Santeria practice should be treated differently from a number of similar practices.
49. *Christian Legal Society v. Martinez* (2010). See Jonathan Turley, "Inequality, in the Name of Equality," *Washington Post*, April 18, 2010, for a discussion of the issues in the case. See also Stanley Fish, "Being Neutral Is Oh So Hard to Do," *New York Times*, July 29, 2010, http://opinionator.blogs.nytimes.com/2010/07/19/being-neutral-is-oh-so-hard-to-do/.
50. *Gonzales v. O Centro Espírita Beneficente União do Vegetal* (2006).
51. The law also granted churches great leeway in building projects, which had been the subject matter in the case that overturned RFRA.
52. *California v. Greenwood* (1988).
53. *Michigan Department of State Police v. Sitz* (1990).
54. *Illinois v. Caballes* (2005); *Kyllo v. United States* (2001).
55. http://www.nytimes.com/2008/07/19/us/19exclude.html?_r=1.
56. *United States v. Leon* (1984), *Arizona v. Evans* (1995), *Hudson v. Michigan* (2006), and *Herring v. United States* (2009) are key rulings in this area. They allowed evidence to be introduced—"good faith exceptions"—despite faulty search warrants, inadvertent police error due to faulty arrest warrants, a violation of the police following a normal "knock and

announce" before conducting a search, and an error in paperwork from another jurisdiction, respectively.

57. *Davis v. United States* (1994). See also *Arizona v. Fulminante* (1991) and *Dickerson v. United States* (2000).
58. *Coker v. Georgia* (1977); *Kennedy v. Louisiana* (2008).
59. *Atkins v. Virginia* (2002) concerns the mentally retarded. *Roper v. Simmons* (2005) overturned the Court's *Stanford v. Kentucky* (1989) decision on capital punishment for minors.
60. *Graham v. Florida* (2010); *Miller v. Alabama* (2012).
61. *Rompilla v. Beard* (2005).
62. When Timothy McVeigh, one of the bombers of an Oklahoma City federal building in 1995, was executed in 2001, it was the first execution by the federal government in nearly 40 years.
63. http://www.deathpenaltyinfo.org/executions-united-states.
64. http://articles.chicagotribune.com/2011-03-10/news/ct-met-illinois-death-penalty-history20110309_1_death-penalty-death-row-death-sentences; http://www.nytimes.com/2011/03/10/us/10illinois.html; Rob Warden, "Illinois Death Penalty Reform: How It Happened, What It Promises," *Journal of Criminal Law and Criminology* 95, 2 (2005): 381–426.
65. Death Penalty Statistics, Amnesty International, http://www.amnesty.org/en/death-penalty/abolitionist-and-retentionist-countries.
66. See Philippa Strum, *Privacy: The Debate in the United States Since 1945* (New York: Harcourt Brace, 1998); Ken I. Kersch, "The Right to Privacy," in James W. Ely Jr. and David Bodenhamer, eds., *The Bill of Rights in Modern America*, 2nd ed. (Bloomington: Indiana University Press, 2008).
67. The anti-obscenity law was known as the Comstock Act.
68. *Eisenstadt v. Baird* (1972).
69. The Court's opinion famously stated that "specific guarantees in the Bill of Rights have penumbras, formed by emanations from those guarantees that help give them life and substance." Penumbras are partial shadings or shadows that are cast on outlying regions or peripheries.
70. The Court did not rule whether a fetus is a person but stated that throughout the early nineteenth century, "prevailing legal abortion practices were far freer than they are today, persuad[ing] us that the word 'person,' as used in the Fourteenth Amendment, does not include the unborn."
71. In *Webster v. Reproductive Health Services* (1989), the Court declared constitutional a Missouri law outlawing abortions in public hospitals and prohibiting public employees from being involved in abortion services.
72. Guttmacher Institute, http://www.guttmacher.org/statecenter/spibs/spib_RFU.pdf; http://www.guttmacher.org/statecenter/spibs/spib_MWPA.pdf.
73. Lance Whitney, "Consumer Groups: Online Tracking at 'Alarming Levels,'" CNet, May 4, 2010, http://news.cnet.com/8301-1009_3-20004071-83.html?tag=mncol;1n; Julia Angwin and Tom McGinty, "Sites Feed Personal Details to New Tracking Industry," *Wall Street Journal*, July 30, 2010, http://online.wsj.com/article/SB10001424052748703977004575393173432219064.html.
74. *City of Ontario v. Quon* (2010).
75. *Washington v. Glucksberg* (1997); *Vacco v. Quill* (1997); *Gonzales v. Oregon* (2006).
76. The relevant cases are, respectively, *NAACP v. Alabama* (1958); *Boy Scouts of America v. Dale* (2000); *West Virginia v. Barnette* (1943); *Pierce v. Society of Sisters* (1925); *Miranda v. Arizona* (1966); and *Skinner v. Oklahoma* (1942). The Court's opinion in *Washington v. Glucksberg* (1997) provides a good discussion of substantive due process.
77. *Palko v. Connecticut* (1937) and *Moore v. East Cleveland* (1977), respectively.
78. Note the Court's comment in *Roe*: "This right of privacy, whether it be founded in the Fourteenth Amendment's concept of personal liberty and restrictions upon state action, as we feel it is, or, as [others have] determined, in the Ninth Amendment's reservation of rights to the people."
79. *Collins v. Harker Heights* (1992); *Sacramento County v. Lewis* (1998); *Kansas v. Hendricks, 1997.*
80. For example, the Court concluded in *Troxel v. Granville* (2000) that a law in the state of Washington that allowed "any person" "at any time" to petition for visitation rights with children violated the parents' "fundamental right to rear children," a right previously established by substantive due process.

6

1. *Korematsu v. United States* (1944).
2. This discussion is based on Steven Kelman et al., "Against All Odds: The Campaign in Congress for Japanese-American Redress," Case Program, Kennedy School of Government, C16-90-1006.0.
3. See Janice Fine and Daniel J. Tichenor, "A Movement Wrestling: American Labor's Enduring Struggle with Immigration, 1866–2007," *Studies in American Political Development* 23, 2 (2009): 218–48.
4. Abraham Hoffman, *Unwanted Mexican Americans in the Great Depression: Repatriation Pressures 1929–1939* (Tucson: University of Arizona Press, 1974); Camille Guerin-Gonzales, *Mexican Workers and American Dreams: Immigration, Repatriation, and California Farm Labor, 1900–1939* (New Brunswick, NJ: Rutgers University Press, 1994); Francisco E. Balderama and Raymond Rodriguez, *Decade of Betrayal: Mexican Repatriation in the 1930s*, rev. ed. (Albuquerque: University of New Mexico Press, 2006); Wendy Koch, "U.S. Urged to Apologize for 1930s Deportations," *USA Today*, April 5, 2006.
5. The question of public apologies or reparations for past actions is one facing governments outside the United States as well.
6. Article I, Section 2; I, 9; and IV, 2, respectively.
7. This position was consistent with the stance of the northern states that considered slaves to become free when they traveled in free states.
8. The act was a response to so-called Black Codes passed by southern states in 1865 and 1866.
9. Fearing that the act might be declared unconstitutional, supporters moved quickly to include its major provisions in the Fourteenth Amendment.
10. Eric Foner, *A Short History of Reconstruction, 1863–1877* (New York: Harper and Row, 1990).
11. The Thirteenth Amendment was particular to slavery, not private racial discrimination in general, the Court ruled, so it could not be pointed to as justification for the act.
12. To free blacks prior to the Thirteenth Amendment, the Court argued, "[m]ere discriminations on account of race or color were not regarded as badges of slavery."
13. Plessy was one-eighth black, so one issue in the case was whether he should be considered white or black. The Supreme Court concluded that what constitutes "black" or "white" should be determined by the laws of each state, so on those grounds Louisiana could consider Plessy to be black.
14. See Jeffery A. Jenkins, Justin Peck, and Vesla M. Weaver, "Between Reconstructions: Congressional Action on Civil Rights, 1891–1940," *Studies in American Political Development* 24, 1 (2010): 57–89.
15. Executive Order 8802. Executive Order 9346 expanded the FEPC's budget and enforcement power. See Kevin J. McMahon, *Reconsidering Roosevelt on Race: How the Presidency Paved*

the Road to Brown (Chicago: University of Chicago Press, 2004).

16. *State of Missouri ex rel. Gaines v. Canada* (1938).
17. The Texas decision is *Sweatt v. Painter.* The Oklahoma decision is *McLaurin v. Oklahoma State Regents for Higher Education*.
18. Seventeen states required segregation; another four allowed it as a local option.
19. The timetable applied to the District of Columbia also. On the same day as *Brown I*, the Court ruled in *Bolling v. Sharpe* (1954) that segregated schools in the district, a federal entity, violated the Fifth Amendment's guarantee of due process.
20. Gary Orfield and Chungmei Lee, "Racial Transformation and the Changing Nature of Segregation," The Civil Rights Project at Harvard University, January 2006, http://www.civilrightsproject.ucla.edu/research/deseg/Racial_Transformation.pdf.
21. *Green v. County School Board of New Kent County* (1968).
22. *Milliken v. Bradley* (1974).
23. The two cases were consolidated as *Parents Involved in Community Schools v. Seattle School District No. 1* (2007).
24. Erica Frankenberg and Chungmei Lee, "Race in American Public Schools: Rapidly Resegregating School Districts," The Civil Rights Project at Harvard University, August 2002. See also the document submitted to the Supreme Court in the Seattle and Louisville case by a group of social scientists: "Brief of 553 Social Scientists as Amici Curiae in Support of Respondents," October 2006.
25. http://civilrightsproject.ucla.edu/research/k-12-education/integration-and-diversity/reviving-the-goal-of-an-integrated-society-a-21st-century-challenge/orfield-reviving-the-goal-mlk-2009.pdf.
26. Adam J. Berinsky, "The Two Faces of Public Opinion," *American Journal of Political Science* 43, 4 (1999): 1209–30; Erica Frankenberg and Rebecca Jocobsen, "Trends: School Integration Polls," *Public Opinion Quarterly* 75, 4 (2011): 788–811. For an analysis arguing that desegregated schools produced long-term positive results for black students, see Rucker C. Johnson, "Long-run Impacts of School Desegregation and School Quality on Adult Attainments," National Bureau of Economic Research Working Paper no. 16664 (2011), http://www.nber.org/papers/w16664.
27. The uhttp:se of Congress's commerce clause and spending powers in the Civil Rights Act of 1964 was upheld by the Supreme Court in *Heart of Atlanta Motel v. United States* (1964) and *Katzenbach v. McClung* (1964).
28. The Voting Rights Act of 1965 was upheld by the Supreme Court in *South Carolina v. Katzenbach* (1965).
29. *Harper v. Virginia Board of Elections* (1966).
30. http://www.foxnews.com/projects/pdf/061209_poll.pdf; http://people-press.org/reports/display.php3?ReportID=293; NBC News/*Wall Street Journal* Poll, April 2006.
31. http://www.ncsl.org/legislatures-elections/elections/voter-id.aspx.
32. Executive Orders 10925 (Kennedy), 11246 and 11375 (Johnson), 12106 (Carter), 13087 and 13152 (Clinton).
33. Executive Orders 10925 (Kennedy), 11246 and 11375 (Johnson), and 11478 (Nixon).
34. John David Skrentny, *The Ironies of Affirmative Action: Politics, Culture, and Justice in America* (Chicago: University of Chicago Press, 1996).
35. Robert C. Lieberman, *Shaping Race Policy: The United States in Comparative Perspective* (Princeton, NJ: Princeton University Press, 2005); Erik Bleich, *Race Politics in Britain and France: Ideas and Policymaking Since the 1960s* (New York: Cambridge University Press, 2003); Martin A. Schain, "Managing Difference: Immigrant Integration Policy in France, Britain, and the United States," *Social Research* 77, 1 (2010): 205–36.
36. See Richard M. Valelly, *The Two Reconstructions: The Struggle for Black Enfranchisement* (Chicago: University of Chicago Press, 2004).
37. King was arrested at the protest, and it was at this time that he penned his famous essay, "Letter from Birmingham Jail, 1963." He included it in his book *Why We Can't Wait* (New York: HarperCollins, 1964).
38. See Dennis Chong, *Collective Action and the Civil Rights Movement* (Chicago: University of Chicago Press, 1991); and Taeku Lee, *Mobilizing Public Opinion: Black Insurgency and Racial Attitudes in the Civil Rights Era* (Chicago: University of Chicago Press, 2002) as examples of these two research styles.
39. Mark I. Lichbach, "Where Have All the Foils Gone? Competing Theories of Contentious Politics and the Civil Rights Movement," in Anne N. Costain and Andrew S. McFarland, eds., *Social Movements and American Political Institutions* (Lanham, MD: Rowman and Littlefield, 1998).
40. *Smith v. Allright* (1944).
41. Alan Ware, *The Democratic Party Heads North, 1877–1962* (New York: Cambridge University Press, 2006).
42. Edward G. Carmines and James A. Stimson, *Issue Evolution: Race and the Transformation of American Politics* (Princeton, NJ: Princeton University Press, 1990).
43. Lieberman, *Shaping Race Policy*.
44. Bruce J. Dierenfield, *The Civil Rights Movement* (Harlow, Eng.: Pearson, 2004), 104.
45. The argument is most forcefully made in Paul Frymer, *Uneasy Alliances: Race and Party Competition in America* (Princeton, NJ: Princeton University Press, 1999).
46. See Claudine Gay, "Spirals of Trust? The Effect of Descriptive Representation on the Relationship between Citizens and Their Government," *American Journal of Political Science* 46, 4 (2002): 717-32; Gabriel R. Sanchez and Jason L. Morin, "The Effect of Descriptive Representation on Latinos' Views of Government and of Themselves," *Social Science Quarterly* 92, 2 (2011): 483–508.
47. *Shaw v. Reno* (1993); *Miller v. Johnson* (1995); *Hunt v. Cromartie* (2001).
48. Vincent L. Hutchings and Nicholas A. Valentino, "The Centrality of Race in American Politics," *Annual Review of Political Science* 7 (2004): 383–408.
49. David Epstein and Sharyn O'Halloran, "Measuring the Electoral and Policy Impact of Majority-Minority Voting Districts," *American Journal of Political Science* 43, 2 (1999): 367-95; Epstein and O'Halloran, "Introduction," in David L. Epstein, Richard H. Pildes, Rodolfo O. de la Garza, and Sharyn O'Halloran, eds., *The Future of the Voting Rights Act* (New York: Russell Sage, 2006).
50. See John D. Griffin and Brian Newman, *Minority Report: Evaluating Political Equality in America* (Chicago: University of Chicago Press, 2008).
51. *Bartlett v. Strickland* (2009).
52. This system had its origin in *United States v. Carolene Products* (1938). In its decision, most notably in footnote 4, the Court determined that economic regulation would normally be assumed to be constitutional so long as there was some rational basis for the regulation. However, laws affecting "discrete and insular minorities," especially when political processes were not likely to be open to their concerns, were deserving of higher levels of judicial scrutiny.
53. *Reed v. Reed* (1971) was the Court's first decision applying the Equal Protection Clause to discrimination by sex, but it did not require an intermediate level of scrutiny.
54. See *Nordinger v. Hahn* (1992).
55. http://quickfacts.census.gov/qfd/states/00000.html.

56. http://www.dhs.gov/xlibrary/assets/statistics/publications/lpr_fr_2011.pdf.
57. http://www.pewhispanic.org/2012/04/23/net-migration-from-mexico-falls-to-zero-and-perhaps-less/.
58. The 2012 *Statistical Abstract of the United States* reports that 39 percent of blacks had household incomes less than $25,000, Hispanics 32%, whites 23%, and Asians 20% (http://www.census.gov/compendia/statab/2012/tables/12s0690.pdf). See also Gary M. Segura and Helena Alves Rodrigues, "Comparative Ethnic Politics in the United States: Beyond Black and White," *Annual Review of Political Science* 9 (2006): 375–95; Rodney E. Hero and Robert R. Preuhs, "Beyond (the Scope of) Conflict: National Black and Latino Advocacy Group Relations in the Congressional and Legal Arenas," *Perspectives on Politics* 7, 3 (2009): 501–18.
59. *Yick Wo v. Hopkins* (1886).
60. *Elks v. Wilkins* (1884).
61. Diane Kravetz, "Consciousness-Raising Groups in the 1970's," *Psychology of Women Quarterly* 3, 2 (1979): 168–86; Barbara Epstein, "What Happened to the Women's Movement?" *Monthly Review* 53, 1 (2001).
62. In 1961, the Supreme Court ruled in *Hoyt v. Florida* that Florida could exclude women from jury service.
63. *Meritor Savings Bank FBD v. Vinson* (1986).
64. http://www.eeoc.gov/policy/docs/veterans_preference.html; http://www.nytimes.com/2012/02/10/us/pentagon-to-loosen-restrictions-on-women-in-combat.html?_r=1.
65. http://www.npr.org/2012/02/13/146802589/foreign-policy-women-on-the-front-lines.
66. Gohar Grigorian, "Women and the Law in Comparative Perspective," UCLA International Institute, July 4, 2004, http://www.international.ucla.edu/article.asp?parentid=13036.
67. Mark R. Daniels and Robert E. Darcy, "As Time Goes By: The Arrested Diffusion of the Equal Rights Amendment," *Publius* 15, 4, (1985): 51–60.
68. Jane J. Mansbridge, *Why We Lost the ERA* (Chicago: University of Chicago Press, 1986) is the classic account of the conflict over the ERA.
69. A Supreme Court decision in 2000 (*Kimel v. Florida Board of Regents*) narrowed the law by stating that it did not apply to state government employees.
70. Samuel R. Bagenstos, "Comparative Disability Employment Law from an American Perspective," *Comparative Labor Law and Policy Journal* 24 (2003): 650.
71. This discussion relies heavily on Bagenstos, "Comparative Disability Employment Law from an American Perspective."
72. *Oncale v. Sundowner Offshore Services* (1998).
73. *Boy Scouts of America v. Dale* (2000).
74. See Section 8 of Department of Defense Instruction 1332.14, March 29, 2010, http://www.dtic.mil/whs/directives/corres/pdf/133214p.pdf
75. *Wong Wing v. U.S.* (1896); *Yick Wo v. Hopkins* (1886).
76. Some of the key cases are cited by Eugene Volokh, "Free Speech and Non-Citizens," August 8, 2005, http://volokh.com/posts/1123520953.shtml.
77. For an overview of research, see Michael A. Zarate and Stephanie Quezada, "Future Directions in Research Regarding Attitudes Toward Immigrants," *Analyses of Social Issues and Public Policy* 12, 1 (2012).
78. Jason A. Nier, Samuel L. Gaetner, Charles L. Nier, John F. Dovidio, "Can Racial Profiling Be Avoided Under Arizona Immigration Law? Lessons Learned From Subtle Bias Research and Anti-Discrimination Law," *Analyses of Social Issues and Public Policy* 12, 1 (2012). For an overview of the research, particularly regarding traffic stops, see Rob Tillyer and Robin S. Engel, "Racial Differences in Speeding Patterns: Exploring the Differential Offending Hypothesis," *Journal of Criminal Justice* 40, 4 (2012): 285-95.
79. *Plyler v. Doe* (1982).
80. *St. Mary's Honor Center v. Hicks* (1993).
81. Paul M. Sniderman and Edward G. Carmines, *Reaching Beyond Race* (Cambridge, MA: Harvard University Press, 1997), pp. 25-27.
82. Sniderman and Carmines, *Reaching Beyond Race*, pp. 126-29.

7

1. Excerpted, with edits, from James Surowiecki, *The Wisdom of Crowds* (New York: Random House, 2004).
2. Lynne Perry, "Mood of the Country: 'Anxiety-Ridden,'" http://americawhatwentwrong.org/story/mood-country/.
3. Robert S. Erikson and Kent L. Tedin, *American Public Opinion* (New York: Pearson Education, 2005), 6.
4. "Changing Faiths: Latinos and the Transformation of American Religion," http://pewhispanic.org/files/reports/75.7.pdf.
5. Pew Charitable Trusts, "As Deportations Rise to Record Levels, Most Hispanics Oppose Obama's Policy," http://www.pewtrusts.org/our_work_report_detail.aspx?id=85899368155.
6. Pew Research Center for People and the Press, "Unabated Economic Gloom, Divides on Afghanistan and Health Care," December 16, 2009, http://people-press.org./reports/pdf/572.pdf.
7. David Easton and Jack Dennis, *Children in the Political System* (Chicago: University of Chicago Press, 1969), 236.
8. Edward Greenberg, "Black Children in the Political System," *Public Opinion Quarterly* 34 (1970): 335–48; Chris F. Garcia, *Political Socialization of Chicano Children* (New York: Praeger, 1973); Dean Jaros, Herbert Hirsch, and Frederick Fleron, "The Malevolent Leader: Political Socialization in an American Sub-Culture," *American Political Science Review* 62 (June 1968): 564–75; and Erikson and Tedin, *American Public Opinion*, 121, but see also 122.
9. Easton and Dennis, *Children in the Political System*, 115.
10. Erikson and Tedin, *American Public Opinion*, 146; and Fred Greenstein, *Children and Politics* (New Haven, CT: Yale University Press, 1965), 58–59.
11. Greenstein, *Children and Politics*, 58–59; and Easton and Dennis, *Children in the Political System*, 138.
12. Easton and Dennis, *Children in the Political System*, 256.
13. M. Kent Jennings and Richard G. Niemi, *The Political Character of Adolescence* (Princeton, NJ: Princeton University Press, 1974), 274; and Greenstein, *Children and Politics*, 55.
14. Robert W. Connell, *The Child's Construction of Politics* (Melbourne: Melbourne University Press, 1971), 46–49, 59, 62.
15. Robert D. Hess and Judith V. Torney, *The Development of Political Attitudes in Children* (Chicago: Aldine, 1967), 215.
16. Connell, *The Child's Construction of Politics*, 58.
17. Greenstein, *Children and Politics*, 68, 73.
18. Jennings and Niemi, *The Political Character of Adolescence*, 266.
19. Connell, *The Child's Construction of Politics*, 50.
20. Jennings and Niemi, *The Political Character of Adolescence*, 275–76.
21. Roberta S. Sigel, *Learning About Politics* (New York: Random House, 1970), 103.
22. Kenneth P. Langton, *Political Socialization* (New York: Oxford University Press, 1969), 53.
23. M. Kent Jennings and Richard Niemi, *Generations and Politics* (Princeton, NJ: Princeton University Press, 1981), 90.
24. Hess and Torney, *The Development of Political Attitudes in Children*, 134–37; Frank J. Sorauf and Paul Allen Beck, *Party Politics in America* (New York: HarperCollins Publishers, 1988), 180–82.
25. Sigel, *Learning About Politics*, 412.

26. Hess and Torney, *The Development of Political Attitudes in Children*, 137–43; Erikson and Tedin, *American Public Opinion*, 127–28.
27. For an overview of the role of school and education in the socialization process, see Hess and Torney, *The Development of Political Attitudes in Children*, 120–32.
28. M. Kent Jennings, "Residuals of a Movement: The Aging of the American Protest Generation," *American Political Science Review* 81 (June 1987): 365–81.
29. Gallup Poll, "Americans Remain Divided on Defense Spending" February 15, 2011, http://www.gallup.com/poll/146114/Americans-Remain-Divided-Defense-Spending.aspx.
30. William G. Mayer, *The Changing American Mind* (Ann Arbor: University of Michigan Press, 1992), 252–54.
31. Erikson and Tedin, *American Public Opinion*, 142.
32. Ibid., 140.
33. John Zaller and Stanley Feldman, "A Simple Theory of the Survey Response: Answering Questions Versus Revealing Preferences," *American Journal of Political Science* 36, 3 (1992): 379.
34. Gallup Poll, "Most Important Problem," http://www.gallup.com/poll/1675/most-important-problem.aspx.
35. Benjamin I. Page and Robert Y. Shapiro, *The Rational Public* (Chicago: University of Chicago Press, 1992), 341–48.
36. One of the most important and influential discussions of the role of party identification in shaping Americans' thinking about politics appears in Angus Campbell, Philip E. Converse, et al., *The American Voter* (New York: Wiley, 1960). See especially chap. 6.
37. Campbell et al., *The American Voter*, 201. Reference is to 1980 reprint.
38. For a discussion of this phenomenon as applied to presidential economic performance, see Ibid., chap. 14.
39. James A. Stimson, *Tides of Consent: How Public Opinion Shapes American Politics* (Cambridge, Eng.: Cambridge University Press, 2004), 163.

8

1. Steven F. Lawson, *Black Ballots: Voting Rights in the South, 1944–1969* (New York: Columbia University Press, 1976).
2. Sidney Verba, Kay Shlozman, and Henry Brady, *Voice and Equality* (Boston: Harvard University Press, 2006), 127.
3. Anthony Downs, *An Economic Theory of Democracy* (New York: Harper, 1957), 267–68.
4. It was political scientist Mancur Olson who introduced the idea of selective benefits, which he called "selective incentives," in a classic work: *The Logic of Collective Action.* We have much more to say about this book in Chapter 12 on interest groups.
5. Riker and Ordeshook elaborated on this article in a 1973 book entitled *Introduction to Positive Political Theory.* Their logic does not apply as well to other forms of political behavior—writing a letter to a member of Congress, for example, or gathering signatures on a petition. The concept of *civic duty* does not apply as well to such activities. To cover these other kinds of participation, therefore, political scientists have tended to talk about their "psychic benefits." Psychic benefits is just another way of saying that people derive satisfaction from participating in politics, regardless of whether or not their participation has any effect on relevant political outcomes.
6. Verba et al., *Voice and Equality,* 115, 550.
7. Ibid., 349.
8. Some states allowed women and those ages 18 to 20 to vote prior to these amendments.
9. Roger Clegg, "Felon Disenfranchisement Is Constitutional, and Justified," National Constitution Center, http://www.constitutioncenter.org/education/ForEducators/Viewpoints/FelonDisenfranchisementIsConstitutional,AndJustified.shtml.
10. United States Election Project, "2008 Current Population Survey Voting and Registration Supplement," November 20, 2009, http://elections.gmu.edu/CPS_2008.html.
11. Robert A. Jackson, "The Mobilization of State Electorates in the 1988 and 1990 Elections," *Journal of Politics* 59 (1999): 520–37; Richard W. Boyd, "The Effects of Primaries and Statewide Races on Voter Turnout," *Journal of Politics* 51 (1989): 730–39.
12. Priscilla L. Southwell, "Voter Turnout in the 1986 Congressional Elections: The Media as a Demobilizer?" *American Politics Quarterly* 19 (1991): 96–108; and Dean Lacy and Barry C. Burden, "The Vote-Stealing and Turnout Effects of Ross Perot in the 1992 U.S. Presidential Election," *American Journal of Political Science* 43 (1999): 233–55.
13. Gary W. Cox and Michael C. Munger, "Closeness, Expenditures, and Turnout in the 1982 U.S. House Elections," *American Political Science Review* 83 (1989): 217–31; Mark N. Franklin and Wolfgang P. Hirczy de Mino, "Separated Powers, Divided Government, and Turnout in U.S. Presidential Elections," *American Journal of Political Science* 42 (January 1998): 316–26; and Gregory A. Caldeira and Samuel C. Patterson, "Getting Out the Vote: Participation in Gubernatorial Elections," *American Political Science Review* 77 (1982): 675–89.
14. Steven J. Rosenstone and John M. Hansen, *Mobilization, Participation, and Democracy in America* (New York: Macmillan, 1993), 29.
15. "Phone Booking for the Modern Political Campaign," What Are You Looking At? http://whatareyoulookingatpolitics.blogspot.com/2009/07/phone-banking-for-modern-political.html.
16. Rosenstone and Hansen, *Mobilization, Participation, and Democracy in America*, 44.
17. "Voter Turnout: An International Comparison," *Public Opinion Quarterly* (1984).
18. Robert Stein and Greg Vonnahme, "Early, Absentee, and Mail in Voting," in Jan E. Leighley, ed., *The Oxford Handbook of American Elections and Political Behavior* (Oxford: Oxford University Press, 2010), 185.
19. Mark Mellman, "Bipartisan, Post-Partisan, Just Partisan" *The Hill*, http://thehill.com/opinion/columnists/mark-mellman/8659-bipartisan-post-partisan-just-partisan
20. Campbell, Converse, Miller, and Stokes. 1960. *The American voter*. New York: John Wiley & Sons, Inc..
21. Ken Jennings and Gregory Markus. "Partisan Orientations Over the Long Haul: Results from the Three-Wave Political Socialization Panel Study," *The American Political Science Review* 78 (1984).
22. Fiorina, Morris. 1981. Retrospective Voting in American Elections. New Haven: Yale University Press.
23. "The Life of Ronald Wilson Reagan: 1911–2004," *The Washington Times*, 7 June 2004, A12, referenced in http://archive.frontpagemag.com/readArticle.aspx?ARTID=11100
24. William H. Flanigan and Nancy H. Zingale, *Political Behavior of the American Electorate* (Washington, DC: Congressional Quarterly Press, 2002), 93.
25. Michael Gant and Norman Luttbeg, "The Cognitive Utility of Partisanship," *Western Political Quarterly* 40 (1987): 499–517.
26. Flanigan and Zingale, *Political Behavior of the American Electorate*, 78.
27. Quoted in Michael R. Alvarez, *Information and Elections* (Ann Arbor: University of Michigan Press, 1998), 8.

28. V. O. Key, *The Responsible Electorate, Rationality in Presidential Voting, 1936–1960* (Cambridge, MA: Belknap Press, 1966); Gregory B. Markus and Philip Converse, "A Dynamic Simultaneous Equation Model of Electoral Choice," *American Political Science Review* 73 (1979).
29. Edward G. Carmines and James A. Stimson, *Issue Evolution: Race and the Transformation of American Politics* (Princeton, NJ: Princeton University Press, 1989).
30. Larry M. Bartels, "Impact of Candidate Traits in American Presidential Elections," in Anthony King, ed., *Leaders' Personalities and the Outcomes of Democratic Elections* (New York: Oxford University Press, 2002), 46.
31. Angus Campbell et al., *The American Voter* (Chicago: University of Chicago Press, 1980), 44–45.
32. Markus and Converse, "A Dynamic Simultaneous Equation Model of Electoral Choice."
33. Campbell et al., *The American Voter*; Stanley Kelley Jr. and Thad W. Mirer, "The Simple Act of Voting," *American Political Science Review* 68 (1974): 572–91; Markus and Converse, "A Dynamic Simultaneous Equation Model of Electoral Choice"; Warren E. Miller and J. Merrill Shanks, *The New American Voter* (Cambridge, MA: Harvard University Press, 1996), chap. 17.
34. Kelley and Mirer, "The Simple Act of Voting"; Markus and Converse, "A Dynamic Simultaneous Equation Model of Electoral Choice."
35. Rosenstone and Hansen, *Mobilization, Participation, and Democracy in America*, 156.
36. As noted in Kenneth M. Goldstein, *Interest Groups, Lobbying, and Participation in America* (New York: Cambridge University Press, 1999).
37. Teixeira, Ruy. 1992. The Disappearing American Voter. Washington, DC: Brookings Institution

9

1. Jim Rutenberg and Marjorie Connelly, "Obama's Rating Falls as Poll Reflects Volatility," *New York Times*, March 12, 2012.
2. Jimmy Carter, "Remarks Accepting the Presidential Nomination at the 1980 Democratic National Convention," August 14, 1980, Public Papers of the Presidents of the United States: Jimmy Carter: 1977–1981, 9 vols. (Washington, DC: Government Printing Office, 1977–1982), http://www.4president.org/speeches/carter1980convention.htm.
3. Finkel, Steven E. 1993. "Reexamining the 'Minimal Effects' Model in Recent Presidential Campaigns." Journal of Politics 55: 1-21.
4. Gelman, Andrew, and Gary King. 1993. "Why Are Presidential Election Campaign Polls so Variable When Votes Are so Predictable?" *British Journal of Political Science* 23(4): 409-51.
5. D. W. Miller, "Election Results Leave Political Scientists Red-Faced over Their Forecasting Models," *Chronicle of Higher Education*, November 8, 2000.
6. This isn't so in two states: Louisiana and Washington both use a "top two" system in which the two final candidates (if no candidate receives more than 50 percent in the first round) could both be Democrats or both be Republicans.
7. "New Hampshire Primary," Wikipedia, http://en.wikipedia.org/wiki/New_Hampshire_primary#Democrats.
8. http://www.washingtonpost.com/blogs/right-turn/post/santorum-messes-up-again/2012/03/14/gIQA16uDCS_blog.html
9. Michael Tomasky, "A Possibly Super Problem," *New York Review of Books*, March 20, 2008, http://www.nybooks.com/articles/archives/2008/mar/20/a-possibly-super-problem/.
10. Michael Cooper, "Delegate System Gives Small States Outsize Clout at Convention," *New York Times*, March 13, 2012, http://www.nytimes.com/2012/03/14/us/politics/delegate-system-gives-small-states-clout-at-convention.html
11. Lawrence D. Longley and Neal R. Peirce, *The Electoral College Primer 2000* (New Haven: Yale University Press, 1999), 18–19.
12. Gary L. Gregg II, *Securing Democracy: Why We Have an Electoral College* (Wilmington, DE: ISI Books, 2001), 6.
13. Ibid., 7, 8.
14. Ibid., 27–29. Originally the second-place finisher became the vice president. This was changed by constitutional amendment in 1804 so that electors cast votes separately for president and vice president. By awarding the vice presidency to the second-place finisher, the previous system set up the possibility for severe disharmony in the executive branch.
15. Markus, Gregory B., and Philip E. Converse. 1979. A dynamic simultaneous equation model of electoral choice. APSR, 73: 1055-1070.
16. Larry M. Bartels, *Presidential Primaries and the Dynamics of Public Choice* (Princeton, NJ: Princeton University Press, 1998).
17. American Political Science Association, "6 of 9 Presidential Election Forecasts Predict Obama Will Win 2008 Popular Vote," October 16, 2008, http://www.apsanet.org/content_58969.cfm.
18. James E. Campbell, "Forecasting the Presidential Vote in the States," *American Journal of Political Science* 36 (1992): 386–407.
19. Randall J. Jones Jr., *Who Will Be in the White House: Predicting Presidential Elections* (New York: Longman, 2002), 31.

10

1. http://www.law.ou.edu/hist/sedact.html.
2. Margaret A. Blanchard, "Freedom of the Press," in W. David Sloan and Lisa Mullikin Parcell, eds., *American Journalism: History, Principles, Practices* (Jefferson, NC: McFarland, 2002), 127.
3. Richard W. T. Martin, *The Free and Open Press* (New York: New York University Press, 2001), 132.
4. W. D. Sloan and L. M. Parcell, eds., *American Journalism: History, Principles, Practices* (Jefferson, NC: McFarland, 2002); Martin, *The Free and Open Press.*
5. Samuel D. Warren and Louis D. Brandeis, "The Right to Privacy," *Harvard Law Review* 4, 5 (1890): 195.
6. W. Overbeck, *Major Principles of Media Law* (Belmont, CA: Wadsworth, 2007).
7. D. C. Hallin and R. Giles, "Presses and Democracies," in G. Overholser and K. Hall Jamieson, eds., *The Press* (New York: Oxford University Press, 2005), 7.
8. S. Djankov et al., Who Owns the Media? 2001, http://papers.ssrn.com/sol3/papers.cfm?abstract_id=267386.
9. Hallin and Giles, "Presses and Democracies."
10. New York Times Co. v. United States, 403 U.S. 713 (1971).
11. Dimitri Kelly, "Unbiased, Credible, and Useful: Motivating Partisan News Choice," http://users.polisci.wisc.edu/behavior/Papers/Kelly2012.pdf.
12. http://www.journalism.org/analysis_report/obamas_first_100_days, http://abcnews.go.com/blogs/politics/2008/11/halperin-decrie/.
13. http://www.freedomhouse.org/report/freedom-press/freedom-press-2012
14. Stephanie Guttmann, *The Other War, Israelis Palestinians and the Struggle for Media Supremacy* (San Francisco: Encounter Books, 2005), 7.
15. T. Patterson and P. Seib, "Informing the Public," in Overholser and Jamison, eds., *The Press*, 194.

16. Patterson and Seib, "Informing the Public," 195; T. E. Patterson, *Out of Order* (New York: Knopf, 1993).
17. http://www.people-press.org/2011/01/04/internet-gains-on-television-as-publics-main-news-source.
18. Paul Farhi, "Limbaugh's Audience Size? It's Largely Up in the Air," *Washington Post*, March 7, 2009, http://www.washingtonpost.com/wp-dyn/content/article/2009/03/06/AR2009030603435.html.
19. Schudson, M. and S. Tifft (2005) '*American Journalism in Historical Perspective*', pp. 17-46 in G. Overholser and K.H. Jamieson (eds) The Press. New York.
20. http://www.people-press.org/2011/01/04/internet-gains-on-television-as-publics-main-news-source/.
21. Travis N. Ridout, Michael Franz, Kenneth M. Goldstein, and William J. Feltus, "Separation by Television Program: Understanding the Targeting of Political Advertising in Presidential Elections," *Political Communication* 29 1 (2012): 1–23.
22. Ibid., 3
23. Ibid.
24. Ibid., 5
25. Ibid., 3–4
26. Ibid., 17
27. R. Coen, "New Study: Center/Right Think Tanks Dominate News," 2000, FAIR Press Release, www.fair.org/index.php?page=1888.
28. The Center for Media and Public Affairs, "Election Watch: Campaign 2008 Final: How TV News Covered the General Election Campaign," *Media Monitor* 23, 1 (2009), www.cmpa.com/pdf/media_monitor_jan_2009.pdf.
29. S. Tiner, "Why Editors Are Dumber than Mules," 1999, http://asne.org/kiosk/editor/97.jan-feb/tiner1.htm.
30. R. Parry, "Media Mythology: Is the Press Liberal?" 1997, http://www.consortiumnews.com/archive/story21.html.
31. http://www.stateofthemedia.org/files/2011/02/Journalists-topline.pdf.
32. D. D'Alessio and M. Allen, "Media Bias in Presidential Elections: A Meta-Analysis," *Journal of Communication* 50, 4 (2000): 148.
33. D'Alessio and Allen, "Media Bias in Presidential Elections," 145.
34. J. Bryant and D. Zillman, eds., *Media Effects: Advances in Theory and Research*, Lea's Communication Series (Mahwah, NJ: Lawrence Erlbaum, 2002).
35. Bryant and Zillman, eds., *Media Effects.*
36. Angus Campbell, Philip E. Converse, Warren E. Miller, and Donald Stokes, *The American Voter* (New York: Wiley, 1960).
37. John Zaller, "The Myth of Massive Media Impact Revived: New Support for a Discredited Idea," in Diana C. Mutz, Paul M. Sniderman, and Richard A. Brody, eds., *Political Persuasion and Attitude Change* (Ann Arbor: University of Michigan Press, 1996), 17.
38. http://www.scienzepolitiche.unimi.it/files/_ITA_/COM/3-Framing-AgendaSetting.pdf .
39. C. Trumbo, "Longitudinal Modeling of Public Issues: An Application of the Agenda-Setting Process to the Issue of Global Warming," *Journalism and Communications Monographs*, 1995, 152; Larry Bartels, "Politicians and the Press: Who Leads, Who Follows?" Annual meeting of the American Political Science Association, San Francisco, 1996.
40. Time of Presidential Election Vote Decision 1948–2004, 2005, http://electionstudies.org/nesguide/toptable/tab9a_3.htm.
41. L. Festinger, *Theory of Cognitive Dissonance* (Stanford, CA: Stanford University Press, 1957).
42. John Zaller, *The Nature and Origins of Mass Opinion* (New York: Cambridge University Press, 1992). Zaller's work forms the basis for much of the discussion in this section.
43. Bartels, "Politicians and the Press"; T. Patterson, *Mass Media Election* (New York: Praeger, 1980); S. J. Farnsworth and S. R. Lichter, "No Small Town Poll: Network Coverage of the 1992 New Hampshire Primary," *Harvard International Journal of Press/Politics* 4 (1999): 51–61.
44. Bartels, "Politicians and the Press"; Zaller, *The Nature and Origins of Mass Opinion*, 23, 37, 48.
45. Patterson, *Out of Order.*

11

1. Marjorie Randon Hershey, *Party Politics in America,* 13th ed. (New York: Longman, 2009), 205; Peter Wallsten and Tom Hamburger, "The GOP Knows You Don't Like Anchovies," *Los Angeles Times*, June 25, 2006, http://www.latimes.com/news/opinion/commentary/la-op-hamburger-25jun25,0,906381.story.
2. Matthew J. Burbank, Ronald J. Hrebenar, and Robert C. Benedict, *Parties, Interest Groups, and Political Campaigns* (Boulder, CO: Westview Press, 1999), 149.
3. Evan Wyloge, "Microtargeting: Election Profiteering or Political Precision?" Arizona Capitol Times, January 9, 2012, http://azcapitoltimes.com/news/2012/01/09/microtargeting-election-profiteering-or-political-precision/; Terrence McCoy, "The Creepiness Factor: How Obama and Romney Are Getting to Know You," *The Atlantic*, April 10, 2012, http://www.theatlantic.com/politics/archive/2012/04/the-creepiness-factor-how-obama-and-romney-are-getting-to-know-you/255499/.
4. David Talbot, "The Democrats' New Weapon," *Technology Review*, December 18, 2008; Jim Rutenberg and Christopher Drew, "National Push by Obama on Ads and Turnout," *New York Times*, June 22, 2008, http://www.nytimes.com/2008/06/22/us/politics/22obama.html.
5. The discussion in this case study relies extensively on Hershey, *Party Politics in America*, 205–06; and Burbank et al., *Parties, Interest Groups, and Political Campaigns*, 148–50
6. Travis N. Ridout, Michael Franz, Kenneth M. Goldstein, and William J. Feltus, "Separation by Television Program: Understanding the Targeting of Political Advertising in Presidential Elections," *Political Communicatio* 29 (2012): 1–23.
7. Tanzina Vega, "Online Data Helping Campaigns Customize Ads," *New York Times*, February 20, 2012, http://www.nytimes.com/2012/02/21/us/politics/campaigns-use-microtargeting-to-attract-supporters.html.
8. David Paul Kuhn, "DNC Blunts GOP Microtargeting Lead," May 23, 2008, www.politico.com http://www.politico.com/news/stories/0508/10573.html.
9. Eitan D. Hersh and Brian F. Schaffner, "When Is Pandering Persuasive? The Effects of Targeted Group-Based Appeals." Manuscript, August 2011, http://papers.ssrn.com/sol3/papers.cfm?abstract_id=1901820.
10. The definition here is based on William N. Chambers, "Party Development and the American Mainstream," in William N. Chambers and Walter Dean Burnham, eds., *The American Party Systems: Stages of Political Development*, 2nd ed. (New York: Oxford University Press, 1975), 5; and Leon D. Epstein, *Political Parties in the American Mold* (Madison: University of Wisconsin Press, 1986), 18–19.
11. See Gregory Koger, Seth Masket, and Hans Noel, "Partisan Webs: Information Exchange and Party Networks," *British Journal of Political Science* 39 (2009): 633–53; Paul S. Herrnson, "The Roles of Party Organizations, Party-Connected Committees, and Party Allies in Elections," *Journal of Politics* 71, 4 (2009): 1207–24.
12. John H. Aldrich, *Why Parties? A Second Look* (Chicago: University of Chicago Press, 2011). See also Seth E. Masket, "It

Takes an Outsider: Extra Legislative Organization and Partisanship in the California Assembly, 1849–2006," *American Journal of Political Science* 51, 3 (2007): 482–97.

13. John J. Coleman, "Unified Government, Divided Government, and Party Responsiveness," *American Political Science Review* 93, 4 (1999): 821–35; Sarah A. Binder, "The Dynamics of Legislative Gridlock, 1947–96," *American Political Science Review* 93, 3 (1999): 519–33; William G. Howell, E. Scott Adler, Charles Cameron, and Charles Riemann, "Divided Government and the Legislative Productivity of Congress, 1945–1994," *Legislative Studies Quarterly* 25, 2 (2000): 285–312; Jeffrey E. Cohen, "Presidents, Polarization, and Divided Government," *Presidential Studies Quarterly* 41, 3 (2011): 504–20. See David R. Mayhew, *Divided We Govern: Party Control, Lawmaking, and Investigations, 1946–2002,* 2nd ed. (New Haven, CT: Yale University Press, 2005), for a contrary view.
14. Seth E. Masket, "Did Obama's Ground Game Matter? The Influence of Local Field Offices During the 2008 Presidential Election," *Public Opinion Quarterly* 73, 5 (2009): 1023–39.
15. Kenneth M. Goldstein and Travis Ridout, "The Politics of Participation: Mobilization and Turnout over Time," *Political Behavior* 24, 1 (2002): 3–29; R. Michael Alvarez, Asa Hopkins, and Betsy Sinclair, "Mobilizing Pasadena Democrats: Measuring the Effects of Partisan Campaign Contacts," *Journal of Politics* 72, 1 (2010): 31–44.
16. Anna Harvey, *Votes Without Leverage: Women in American Electoral Politics, 1920–1970* (New York: Cambridge University Press, 1998).
17. See, for example, Richard Jensen, *The Winning of the Midwest, 1888–1896* (Chicago: University of Chicago Press, 1971); Paul J. Kleppner, *The Cross of Culture: A Social Analysis of Midwestern Politics, 1850–1900* (New York: Free Press, 1970).
18. Zoltan L. Hajnal and Taeku Lee, *Why Americans Don't Join the Party: Race, Immigration, and the Failure (of Political Parties) to Engage the Electorate* (Princeton, NJ: Princeton University Press, 2011); http://www.nytimes.com/2012/06/10/us/politics/latino-growth-not-fully-felt-at-voting-booth.html?pagewanted=all.
19. Michael E. McGerr, *The Decline of Popular Politics: The American North, 1865–1928* (New York: Oxford University Press, 1986).
20. Hans von Spakovsky, "Requiring Identification by Voters," in David T. Canon, John J. Coleman, and Kenneth R. Mayer, eds., *Faultlines: Debating the Issus in American Politics*, 3rd ed. (New York: W. W. Norton); Chandler Davidson, "The Historical Context of Voter Photo-ID Laws," *PS: Political Science and Politics* 42, 1 (2009): 93–96 (reprinted in Canon et al., *Faultlines*).
21. Alan S. Gerber and Gregory A. Huber, "Partisanship, Political Control, and Economic Assessments," *American Journal of Political Science* 54, 1 (2010): 153–73.
22. On voting systems, see the list at www.idea.int/esd/world.cfm and the analysis by Gary W. Cox, *Making Votes Count: Strategic Coordination in the World's Electoral Systems* (New York: Cambridge University Press, 1997).
23. For overviews, see Alan Ware, *Political Parties and Party Systems* (New York: Oxford University Press, 1996); and Steven J. Rosenstone, Roy L. Behr, and Edward H. Lazarus, *Third Parties in America: Citizen Response to Major Party Failure*, 2nd ed. (Princeton, NJ: Princeton University Press, 1996).
24. Harold W. Stanley and Richard G. Niemi, *Vital Statistics on American Politics, 2007–08* (Washington, DC: Congressional Quarterly Press, 2008), 43; Clerk of the U.S. House of Representatives, http://artandhistory.house.gov/house_history/partyDiv.aspx
25. Candidates of third parties that are relatively large, such as the People's Party of the 1890s or the Progressive Party of the early twentieth century, may eventually absorb back into the major parties and can work to change the major parties' positions from within.
26. Barry C. Burden: "Minor Parties and Strategic Voting in Recent U.S. Presidential Elections," *Electoral Studies* 24, 4 (2005): 603–18; and "Ralph Nader's Campaign Strategy in the 2000 U.S. Presidential Election," *American Politics Research* 33, 5 (2005): 672–99.
27. ABC News/*Washington Post* Poll. Jan. 12–15, 2012. N=1,000 adults nationwide. Margin of error ± 3.5; 48 percent said the United States needed a third major party, 49 percent said it did not. Over time, support ranges from the high 40s to the high 50s.
28. William H. Riker, "The Two-Party System and Duverger's Law: An Essay on the History of Political Science," *American Political Science Review* 76 (1982): 753–66; and William Roberts Clark and Matt Golder, "Rehabilitating Duverger's Theory: Testing the Mechanical and Strategic Modifying Effects of Electoral Laws," *Comparative Political Studies* 39, 6 (2006): 679–708.
29. Most systems employ a threshold and deny seats to very small parties.
30. Josep M. Colomer, "It's Parties That Choose Electoral Systems (Or, Duverger's Laws Upside Down)," *Political Studies* 53, 1 (2005): 1–21. See also Kenneth Benoit, "Electoral Laws as Political Consequences: Explaining the Origins and Change of Electoral Institutions," *Annual Review of Political Science* 10 (2007): 363–90.
31. Aldrich, *Why Parties?* See also Anthony Downs, *An Economic Theory of Democracy* (New York: Harper, 1957).
32. Maine and Nebraska award two electoral votes to the presidential candidate who wins the state, and one electoral vote for winning a congressional district.
33. Pradeep Chhibber and Ken Kollman, "Party Aggregation and the Number of Parties in India and the United States," *American Political Science Review* 92, 2 (1998): 329–42.
34. Lisa Disch, *The Tyranny of the Two-Party System* (New York: Columbia University Press, 2002).
35. See Rosenstone et al., *Third Parties in America: Citizen Response to Major Party Failure*, 254–56.
36. John Zaller and Mark Hunt, "The Rise and Fall of Candidate Perot: Unmediated Versus Mediated Politics—Part I," *Political Communication* 11, 4 (1994): 357–90; Paul R. Abramson, John H. Aldrich, Philip Paolino, and David W. Rohde, "Challenges to the American Two-Party System: Evidence from the 1968, 1980, 1992, and 1996 Presidential Elections," *Political Research Quarterly* 53, 3 (2000): 495–522.
37. Rosenstone et al., *Third Parties in America.*
38. See www.fairvote.org for discussion of a number of alternative voting systems.
39. Designed for use in multimember districts such as school board elections, especially to increase minority representation, cumulative voting could potentially be modified for single-member district use.
40. Ronald P. Formisano, "The 'Party Period' Revisited," *Journal of American History* 86, 1 (1999): 93–120.
41. Jessica Trounstine, *Political Monopolies in American Cities: The Rise and Fall of Bosses and Reformers* (Chicago: University of Chicago Press, 2008).
42. Alan Ware, *The American Direct Primary: Party Institutionalization and Transformation in the North* (New York: Cambridge University Press, 2002); and "Anti-partism and Party Control of Political Reform in the United States: The Case of the Australian Ballot," *British Journal of Political Science* 30, 1 (2000): 1–29.
43. Epstein, *Political Parties in the American Mold*; Amy Bridges, *Morning Glories: Municipal Reform in the Southwest* (Princeton, NJ: Princeton University Press, 1997); and Byron E. Shafer, *Quiet Revolution: The Struggle for the Democratic Party*

and the Shaping of Post-Reform Politics (New York: Russell Sage Foundation, 1983).

44. See Cornelius P. Cotter, James L. Gibson, John F. Bibby, and Robert J. Huckshorn, *Party Organizations in American Politics* (New York: Praeger, 1984); and Paul S. Herrnson, "The Revitalization of National Party Organizations," in L. Sandy Maisel, ed., *The Parties Respond* (Boulder, CO: Westview Press, 1994).
45. Paul S. Herrnson, *Party Campaigning in the 1980s* (Cambridge, MA: Harvard University Press, 1988); John J. Coleman, "Party Organizational Strength and Public Support for Parties," *American Journal of Political Science* 40, 3 (1996): 805–24.
46. Hershey, *Party Politics in America*, 76.
47. Campaign Finance Institute, www.cfinst.org/data/pdf/VitalStats_t12.pdf.
48. See Ben Clift and Justin Fisher, "Comparative Party Finance Reform: The Cases of France and Britain," *Party Politics* 10, 6 (2004): 677–99; Susan E. Scarrow, "Explaining Political Finance Reforms: Competition and Context," *Party Politics* 10, 6 (2004): 653–75.
49. Ruth Marcus, "President Obama Is Making Nobody Happy," *Washington Post*, April 3, 2010, http://www.washingtonpost.com/wp-dyn/content/article/2010/04/02/AR2010040201758.html.
50. The scholarship is reviewed in John J. Coleman, "Responsible, Functional, or Both? American Political Parties Fifty Years After the APSA Report," in John C. Green and Rick Farmer, eds., *The State of the Parties*, 4th ed. (Lanham, MD: Rowman and Littlefield, 2003); and Nicol C. Rae, "Be Careful What You Wish For: The Rise of Responsible Parties in American National Politics," *Annual Review of Political Science* 10 (2007): 169–91.
51. Paul Frymer, *Uneasy Alliances: Race and Party Competition in America* (Princeton, NJ: Princeton University Press, 1999).
52. Philip A. Klinkner, *The Losing Parties: Out-Party National Committees, 1956–1993* (New Haven, CT: Yale University Press, 1994); Zeynep Somer-Topcu, "Timely Decisions: The Effects of Past National Elections on Party Policy Change," *Journal of Politics* 71, 1 (2009): 238–48.
53. Theda Skocpol and Vanessa Williamson, *The Tea Party and the Remaking of Republican Conservatism* (New York: Oxford University Press, 2012).
54. Edward G. Carmines and Michael W. Wagner, "Political Issues and Party Alignments: Assessing the Issue Evolution Perspective," *Annual Review of Political Science* 9 (2006): 67–81; David Karol, *Partisan Position Change in American Politics: Coalition Maintenance* (New York: Cambridge University Press, 2009).
55. For an overview and critique, see David R. Mayhew, *Electoral Realignments: A Critique of an American Genre* (New Haven, CT: Yale University Press, 2002).
56. See James L. Sundquist, *Politics and Policy: The Eisenhower, Kennedy, and Johnson Years* (Washington, DC: Brookings Institution Press, 1968); and Donald Green, Bradley Palmquist, and Eric Schickler, *Partisan Hearts and Minds: Political Parties and the Social Identities of Voters* (New Haven, CT: Yale University Press, 2002).
57. William G. Mayer, *The Divided Democrats: Ideological Unity, Party Reform, and Presidential Elections* (Boulder, CO: Westview Press, 1996), chap. 5; Paul R. Abramson, John H. Aldrich, and David W. Rohde, *Change and Continuity in the 2004 Elections* (Washington, DC: Congressional Quarterly Press, 2006), chap. 5.
58. Larry M. Bartels, "Where the Ducks Are: Voting Power in a Party System," in John G. Geer, ed., *Politicians and Party Politics* (Baltimore, MD: Johns Hopkins University Press, 1998); Alan I. Abramowitz and Kyle L. Saunders, "Ideological Realignment in the U.S. Electorate," *Journal of Politics* 60, 3 (1998): 634–52; and Abramson et al., *Change and Continuity in the 2004 Elections*.
59. Walter Dean Burnham, "The 1980 Election: Realignment, Reaction, or What?" in Thomas Ferguson and Joel Rogers, eds., *The Hidden Election: Politics and Economics in the 1980 Presidential Campaign* (New York: Pantheon, 1981). See also Brett M. Clifton, "Romancing the GOP: Assessing the Strategies Used by the Christian Coalition to Influence the Republican Party," *Party Politics* 10, 5 (2004): 475–98.
60. Democrats controlled the Senate from mid-2001 until the end of 2002 after James Jeffords, a Republican senator from Vermont, declared himself an independent and aligned with the Democrats.
61. Larry M. Bartels, "Partisanship and Voting Behavior, 1952–1996," *American Journal of Political Science* 44, 1 (2000): 35–50; Joseph Barfumi and Robert Y. Shapiro, "A New Partisan Voter," *Journal of Politics* 71, 1 (2009): 1–24; and David A. Hopkins, "The 2008 Election and the Political Geography of the New Democratic Majority," *Polity* 41, 3 (2009): 368–87.
62. This argument is made most prominently by Thomas Frank, *What's the Matter with Kansas: How Conservatives Won the Heart of America* (New York: Macmillan, 2005).
63. Andrew Gelman, *Red State, Blue State, Rich State, Poor State: Why Americans Vote the Way They Do* (Princeton, NJ: Princeton University Press, 2008).
64. Robert S. Erikson, Michael B. MacKuen, and James A. Stimson argue that public opinion tends to push against the ideological grain of current policy. See *The Macro Polity* (New York: Cambridge University Press, 2002).
65. See John Gerring, *Party Ideologies in America, 1828–1996* (New York: Cambridge University Press, 1998); Edward G. Carmines and Geoffrey Layman, "Issue Evolution in Postwar American Politics: Old Certainties and Fresh Tensions," in Byron E. Shafer, ed., *Present Discontents: American Politics in the Very Late Twentieth Century* (Chatham, NJ: Chatham House, 1997).
66. Pew Research Center survey, January 23, 2012, http://www.people-press.org/2012/01/23/section-1-the-publics-policy-priorities/.
67. John R. Petrocik, William L. Benoit, and Glenn J. Hansen, "Issue Ownership and Presidential Campaigning, 1952–2000," *Political Science Quarterly* 118, 4 (2003–04): 599–626; David R. Jones, "Partisan Polarization and Congressional Accountability in House Elections," *American Journal of Political Science* 54, 2 (2010): 323–37.

12

1. Johnson, Haynes; Broder, David S. (May 1996). *The System: the American way of politics at the breaking point.* Boston: Little, Brown and Company. ISBN 0-316-46969-6.
2. Bob Cusack, "After Obama Rips Lobbyists, K Street Insiders Get Private Policy Briefings," *The Hill*, January 28, 2010, http://thehill.com./homenews/administration/78509-after-obama-rips-k-street-administration-invites-lobbyists-to-private-briefings.
3. Earl Latham, *The Group Basis of Politics: A Study in Basing-Point Legislation* (New York: Octagon, 1965), 221.
4. David B. Truman, *The Governmental Process: Political Interests and Public Opinion* (New York: Knopf 1951), 507.
5. Ibid., 289.
6. U.S. Census Bureau About Poverty Highlights, http://www.census.gov/hhes/www/poverty/about/overview/index.html
7. Quoted in Nelson W. Polsby, "How to Study Community Power: The Pluralist Alternative," in Roderick Bell, David V. Edwards, and R. Harrison Wagner, eds., *Political Power: A Reader in Theory and Research* (New York: Free Press, 1969),

33. Excerpted from *Journal of Politics* 22 (1960): 474–84; and Nelson W. Polsby, *Community Power and Political Theory* (New Haven: Yale University Press, 1980), 116.

8. Jack Walker. 1991. *Mobilizing Interest Groups in America.* University of Michigan Press.
9. Peter Bachrach and Morton S. Baratz, "Two Faces of Power," *American Political Science Review* 56, 4 (1962): 947–52.
10. Peter Bachrach and Morton S. Baratz, "Decisions and Nondecisions: An Analytical Framework," *American Political Science Review* 57, 3 (1963): 632–42.
11. Polsby, "How to Study Community Power," 71.
12. Truman, *The Governmental Process.*
13. Mancur Olson, *The Logic of Collective Action: Public Goods and the Theory of Groups* (Cambridge, MA: Harvard University Press, 1965), 2.
14. Ibid., 16.
15. Ibid., 51. Olson coined the term *selective incentives.*
16. Paul C. Light, *Artful Work: The Politics of Social Security Reform* (New York: Random House, 1985), 76.
17. Compassionate Action for Animals, "Volunteer Testimonials," http://www.exploreveg.org/help/volunteer-testimonials.
18. Robert H. Salisbury, "An Exchange Theory of Interest Groups," *Midwest Journal of Political Science* 13, 1 (1969): 1–32.
19. Violence Policy Center, "National Rifle Association Information," http://www.vpc.org/nrainfo/chapter1.html.
20. Hoover Institute Public Policy Inquiry, "Campaign Finance: Current Structure," March 8, 2004, http://www.campaignfinancesite.org/structure/opinions16.html; Jerry Seper, "Soros-Supported Voter-Registration Drive Probed," *Washington Times*, October 18, 2004, http://www.mdfva.org/2004News/Washtimes041018_041024.html#M041020%20%20%20Soros-supported%20voter-registration%20drive.
21. National Association of Counties, "About NACO," http://www.naco.org/Content/NavigationMenu/About_NACo/Membership/Membership.htm; http://congressional.energy.gov/state_local.htm.
22. Richard Hume Werking, "Bureaucrats, Businessmen, and Foreign Trade: The Origins of the United States Chamber of Commerce," *Business History Review* 52, 3, *Corporate Liberalism* (Autumn 1978): 321–41.
23. Opensecrets.org, Center for Responsible Politics, "Stats at a Glance," http://www.opensecrets.org/overview/index.php.
24. Opensecrets.org, Center for Responsible Politics, "Most Expensive Races," http://www.opensecrets.org/overview/topraces.php.
25. BarackObama.com, "Ethics," November 10, 2007, http://www.barackobama.com/issues/ethics/.
26. LEAnet alert, December 11, 2007, www.theleanet.com.
27. American Veterinary Medical Association, "News," March 1, 2004, http://www.avma.org/onlnews/javma/mar04/040301j.asp.
28. Glen Justice and Aron Pilhofer, "Unwavering Bush Ally Acts Quickly on Court Choices," *New York Times*, November 14, 2005, http://www.nytimes.com/2005/11/14/politics/politicsspecial1/14progress.html?pagewanted=print.
29. Quoted in Jeffrey Birnbaum, "Returning to the Game He Started," *Washington Post*, November 28, 2004, http://www.washingtonpost.com/wp-dyn/articles/A18417-2004Nov28.html.
30. Matthew A. Crenson, The Un-Politics of Air Pollution: a Study of Non-Decisionmaking in the Cities. Baltimore and London: The Johns Hopkins Press [Toronto: Copp Clark], 1971, pp. viii, 227.
31. John Gaventa, 1982. *Power and Powerlessness Quiescence and Rebellion in an Appalachian Valley.* University of Illinois Press.

13

1. Shawn Reese, Congressional Research Service Report for Congress, *Fiscal Year2005 Homeland Security Grant Program: State Allocations and Issues for Congressional Oversight* (Washington, DC: Congressional Research Service, 2004). See also "FY 2010 Homeland Security Grant Program," Federal Emergency Management Agency, www.fas.org/sgp/crs/homesec/RL32696.pdf.
2. These figures are based on spending figures found in "Homeland Security and Grant Program, Guidance and Application Kit," Department of Homeland Security, 27; and population figures found in "Annual Estimates of the Resident Population for the United States, Regions, and Puerto Rico," U.S. Census Bureau, January 26, 2009. See also Kathleen Hunter, "Per Capita, New Anti-terror Funds Still Favor Wyoming," Pew Research Center, December 16, 2004, http://www.pewstates.org/projects/stateline/headlines/per-capita-new-anti-terror-funds-still-favor-wyoming-85899393484.
3. The remaining 60 percent of the funds are distributed by formula according to population.
4. "U.S. Not 'Well-prepared' for Terrorism," December 5, 2005, http://articles.cnn.com/2005-12-04/us/911.commission_1_first-responders-recommendations-issue-report?_s=PM:US.
5. Judy Holland, "Anti-terror Funding open to 'Pork Barrel' Politics," *Milwaukee Journal Sentinel*, August 22, 2004, 18A.
6. Kathleen Hunter, "Budget Would Revise Anti-terrorism Funding," Pew Research Center, February 8, 2005 httphttp://www.pewstates.org/projects/stateline/headlines/budget-would-revise-anti-terrorism-funding-85899389932.
7. Veronique de Rugy, "Homeland-Security Scuffle," *National Review*, October 15, 2004, http://www.nationalreview.com/comment/rugy200410150840.asp.
8. Veronique de Rugy, AEI working paper available online at http://www.aei.org/paper/21483.
9. John Mueller, *Overblown: How Politicians and the Terrorism Industry Inflate National Security Threats, and Why We Believe Them* (New York: Free Press, 2009), 37.
10. The Homeland Security Grant Program, however, has gradually reduced the total amount of money distributed through State Homeland Security Program and has increased the amount of anti-terrorism funding awarded through another of its programs, the Urban Areas Security Initiative, which is relatively free to distribute federal funding to the cities that need it most. U.S. Department of Homeland Security, Office of Grants and Training, *Overview: FY 2007 Homeland Security Grant Program*, January 5, 2007.
11. Nonvoting members come from the District of Columbia, American Samoa, Guam, Puerto Rico, and the Virgin Islands.
12. At the nation's founding, state legislatures appointed senators to office. In 1913, however, the states ratified the Seventeenth Amendment, which required the direct election of senators. Representatives in the House have always been popularly elected.
13. Max Farrand, ed., *The Records of the Federal Convention of 1787* (New Haven: Yale University Press, 1966), 151.
14. David Mayhew, *The Electoral Connection* (New Haven: Yale University Press, 1974).
15. "Lobbying: Top Spenders," Open Secrets: Center for Responsive Politics, http://www.opensecrets.org/lobby/top.php?showYear=2010&indexType=s.
16. Mayhew, *The Electoral Connection*, 16.
17. Brandice Canes-Wrone, David Brady, and John Cogan, "Out of Step, Out of Office: Electoral Accountability and House

Members' Voting," *American Political Science Review* 96, 1 (2002): 127–40.

18. Edmund Burke, "Speech to the Electors of England" in *The Works of the Right Honorable Edmund Burke*, vol. 2. (New York: Oxford University Press, 1774 [1907]).
19. Based on figures from fiscal year 2000. Congressional Budget Office, "Federal Spending on the Elderly and Children," July 2000, http://cbo.gov/ftpdocs/23xx/doc2300/fsec.pdf.
20. Gary Jacobson, *The Politics of Congressional Elections*, 6th ed. (New York: Longman, 2003).
21. Brody Mullins, "Growing Role for Lobbyists: Raising Funds for Lawmakers," *Wall Street Journal*, January 27, 2006, 1.
22. Kenneth Goldstein, *Interest Groups, Lobbying, and Participating in America* (New York: Cambridge University Press, 1999); John Mark Hansen, *Gaining Access: Congress and the Farm Lobby, 1919–1981* (Chicago: University of Chicago Press, 1991).
23. Keith T. Poole and Thomas Romer, "Ideology, 'Shirking,' and Representation," *Public Choice* 77 (1993): 185–96.
24. Kenneth N. Bickers and Robert M. Stein, "The Congressional Pork Barrel in a Republican Era," *Journal of Politics* 62, 4 (2000): 1070–86.
25. For more on descriptive or numerical representation, see Jane Mansbridge, "Should Blacks Represent Blacks and Women Represent Women? A Contingent 'Yes,'" *Journal of Politics* 61, 3 (1999): 628–57.
26. Michele Swers, *The Difference Women Make* (Chicago: University of Chicago Press, 2002).
27. There have been multi-legislator districts in some states at some times, but they have been a very small share of the total.
28. *Wesberry v. Sanders* and *Reynolds v. Sims*.
29. *Vieth v. Jubilerer*.
30. Four cases were consolidated as *League of United Latin American Citizens v. Perry*.
31. Because of its small population, Alaska has just one House representative.
32. Daniel Gitterman, *Boosting Paychecks: The Politics of Supporting America's Working Poor* (Washington, DC: Brookings Institution, 2009).
33. For one study of the role of information in Congress, see Keith Krehbiel, *Information and Legislative Organization* (Ann Arbor: University of Michigan Press, 1992).
34. As discussed in Chapter 12, the same kinds of problems plague the organization of citizens into interest groups.
35. Kenneth Shepsle, *The Giant Jigsaw Puzzle: Democratic Committee Assignments in the Modern House* (Chicago: University of Chicago Press, 1978).
36. Robert C. Albright, "Two-Stage Battle, If Necessary, Planned for Urban Affairs Unit," *Washington Post, Times Herald*, January 24, 1962, A2; Russell Baker, "Kennedy Accused on Urban Moves: G.O.P Sees Racism in Plan to Create Cabinet Post," *New York Times*, January 26, 1962, 14; Richard L. Lyons, "House Kills Urban Plan by 262-150" *Washington Post, Times Herald*, February 22, 1962, A1; Chalmers M. Roberts, "Anguish in Urban Affairs: Kennedy Nudges GOP into Own Booby Trap," *Washington Post, Times Herald*, January 26, 1962, A2; and House of Representatives Committee on Rules, "Committee on Rules: A History," http://democrats.rules.house.gov/archives/rules_history.htm.
37. Gary Cox and Mathew McCubbins, *Setting the Agenda: Responsible Party Government in the U.S. House of Representatives* (New York: Cambridge University Press, 2005).
38. See, for example, Keith Krehbiel, "Where's the Party?" *British Journal of Political Science* 23 (1993): 235–66.
39. Since the Civil War, southern politicians retained strong loyalties to the Democratic Party. Ideologically, however, they had more in common with northern Republicans. Beginning in the 1970s, a century after the Civil War's end, southern Democrats began to abandon their former partisan commitments in order to join the ranks of the Republican Party.
40. Nolan McCarty, Keith Poole, and Howard Rosenthal, *Polarized America: The Dance of Ideology and Unequal Riches* (Cambridge, MA: MIT Press, 2005).
41. William A. Galston, "The GOP's Grassroots Obstructionists," *Washington Post*, May 16, 2010.
42. Figures are available at http://people-press.org/party-identification-trend/ and http://people-press.org/2011/05/04/section-1-the-political-typology-2/.
43. For a profile of congressional staffers in 2007, see "The Hill People 2007: A Special Report," National Journal, June 23, 2007.
44. Barbara Sinclair, *Unorthodox Lawmaking: New Legislative Processes in the U.S. Congress* (Washington, CQ Press, 1997).
45. It is possible to bypass the Rules Committee. With a two-thirds vote, members can send a bill directly to the floor, where only 40 minutes of debate are allowed and all amendments are forbidden. To enact the bill under this fast-track procedure, though, supporters must garner the support of two-thirds of the House. Typically, only those bills that are either trivial in importance or that enjoy widespread support are thus considered.
46. The Senate also offers its members several other ways of prolonging the legislative process. For instance, senators can place anonymous holds on bills, which prevent them from moving forward. Additionally, senators have more opportunities to introduce amendments to bills than do representatives in the House, where the party leadership exercises more control over deliberations.
47. It is worth noting, though, that floors have some powers to check such tendencies—for example, the discharge petition allows a majority of floor members to force a committee to release a bill for a floor vote.
48. Norman Ornstein, Thomas Mann, and Michael Malbin, *Vital Statistics on Congress, 1995–1996* (Washington, DC: CQ Press, 1996), 169. For more on the filibuster, see Gregory Wawro and Eric Schickler, *Filibuster: Obstruction and Lawmaking in the U.S. Senate* (Princeton, NJ: Princeton University Press, 2006).
49. The two exceptions: Franklin Pierce, who ranks near the bottom of most ratings of presidential greatness; and Andrew Johnson, who ranks no higher and whom the House went on to impeach. See Lyn Ragsdale, *Vital Statistics on the Presidency* (Washington, DC: CQ Press, 1998), 27–28.
50. Barbara Sinclair, *Unorthodox Lawmaking: New Legislative Processes in the U.S. Congress,* (Washington, DC: CQ Press, 2011).
51. "Self-Executing Rules Reported by the House Committee on Rules," Walter J. Oleszek, December 21, 2006, http://usgovinfo.about.com/library/PDF/self_executing.pdf.
52. Don Wolfensberger, "Bimonthly Column on Procedural Politics," June 19, 2006, http://www.wilsoncenter.org/publication/house-executes-deliberation-special-rules.
53. Adam Nagourney, "Political Maneuvering and Public Opinion," *New York Times*, March 19, 2010.
54. William Howell et al. 2000. "Divided Government and the Legislative Productivity of Congress, 1945–1994." Legislative Studies Quarterly. 25(2): 285–312.
55. Sandy Streeter, CRS Report 97-684, *The Congressional Appropriations Process: An Introduction* (Washington, DC: Congressional Research Service, 2006), 4.
56. Allen Schick and Felix LoStracco, *The Federal Budget: Politics, Policy, and Progress* (Washington, DC: Brookings Institution, 2000), 235, 236, 238.

57. Streeter, *The Congressional Appropriations Process*, 17; http://nationalpriorities.org/resources/federal-budget-101/budget-briefs/federal-discretionary-and-mandatory-spending/.
58. See Taxpayer's for Common Sense, http://www.taxpayer.net.
59. Katie Brandenburg, "Texas Rakes in $1.6 Billion for Federal Pet Projects," *Houston Chronicle*,April 26, 2010, http://www.chron.com/news/houston-texas/article/Texas-rakes-in-1-6-billion-for-federal-pet-1605716.php.
60. This database is available at http://earmarks.omb.gov.
61. See http://appropriations.house.gov.
62. Leslie Paige of Citizens Against Government Waste, quoted in Cole Deiner, CNN website, online at http://articles.cnn.com/2011-05-28/politics/mysterious.fund_1_pet-projects-defense-bill-corrosion?_s=PM:POLITICS.
63. Streeter, *The Congressional Appropriations Process*, 14.
64. Linda Bilmes and Joseph E. Stiglitz "The Iraq War Will Cost Us $3 Trillion, and Much More," *Washington Post*, March 9, 2008.
65. Joseph Stiglitz and Linda Bilmes, *The Three Trillion Dollar War: The True Cost of the Iraq Conflict* (New York: Norton, 2008).
66. http://boehner.house.gov/news/documentsingle.aspx?DocumentID=234963.

14

1. "Obama: Victory Speech," *New York Times*, November 5, 2008. http://elections.nytimes.com/2008/results/president/speeches/obama-victory-speech.html.
2. Interview with Oprah Winfrey, CNN, December 13, 2009.
3. President Obama's Inaugural Address, January 20, 2009, http://www.whitehouse.gov/blog/inaugural-address.
4. Dan Merica, "Poll: Americans Trust Local Government More Than Federal Government," CNN Politics, http://politicalticker.blogs.cnn.com/2011/10/03/poll-americans-trust-local-government-more-than-federal.
5. See Richard Pious, *The Presidency* (New York: Longman, 1995).
6. For an analysis of the president's place in the American political system, see Charles O. Jones, *The Presidency in a Separated System* (Washington, DC: Brookings Institution, 1994).
7. See, for example, John Yoo, *Crisis and Command: A History of Executive Power from George Washington to George W. Bush* (New York: Kaplan, 2009); Steven Calabresi and Christopher Yoo, *The Unitary Executive: Presidential Power from Washington to Bush* (New Haven: Yale University Press, 2008).
8. See, for example, James Pfiffner, *Power Play: The Bush Presidency and the Constitution*. (Washington, DC: Brookings Institution, 2009).
9. William Stinchcombe, "Review of the Papers of George Washington: Revolutionary War Series," Volume 10; Presidential Series, Volume 9, http://gwpapers.virginia.edu/project/reviews/stinchcombe.html.
10. The Twenty-second Amendment, a reaction to Franklin Roosevelt's four-term presidency, limited the president to two terms in office.
11. Technically, Lincoln suspended the writ of habeas corpus. A defendant can request a writ of habeas corpus, which is a court order that requires a government official to explain to a judge why an individual is incarcerated.
12. Roosevelt proposed that for every justice older than age 70, the president could nominate one additional justice until the Supreme Court reached a maximum size of 15. The plan would have allowed Roosevelt to offset older, more conservative justices with those more likely to accommodate his proposals. For more on this court-packing plan, see Jeff Shesol, *Supreme Power: Franklin Roosevelt vs. the Supreme Court* (New York: Norton, 2010).
13. The scandal was so named because of the break-in at the Democratic National Committee's headquarters at the Watergate Hotel in Washington, D.C., on June 17, 1972. The president's aides were responsible for arranging the break-in, and the president engineered a cover-up designed to keep the truth from coming out. The discovery of that break-in prompted investigations that revealed a wide range of White House abuses of power, ultimately leading to Nixon's resignation in August 1974.
14. Yoo and Calabresi, *The Unitary Executive*.
15. Jeffrey Rosen, "Bush's Leviathan State," *The New Republic*, July 24, 2006.
16. Cass Sunstein, "What the 'Unitary Executive' Debate Is and Is Not About," University of Chicago Law School Faculty Blog, 6 August 2007, http://uchicagolaw.typepad.com/faculty/2007/08/what-the-unitar.html.
17. "Statement by the President on H.R. 1473," Office of the Press Secretary, the White House, April 15, 2011, http://www.whitehouse.gov/the-press-office/2011/04/15/statement-president-hr-1473.
18. Charlie Savage, "House Panel's Vote Steps Up Partisan Fight on Gun Inquiry." *New York Times*. June 21, 2012, p. A1.
19. Robert Byrd, Daniel Inouye, Strom Thurmond, Edward Kennedy. See Senate website for full list: http://www.senate.gov/senators/Biographical/longest_serving.htm.
20. Ron Kirk, "A New Era for U.S. Trade Policy," *Politico*, October 20, 2011, http://dyn.politico.com/printstory.cfm?uuid=82689CA1-28C8-409C-B202-B40D619AC8C5.
21. Isaiah J. Poole, "Two Steps Up, One Step Down," *CQ Weekly*, January 9, 2006, 80.
22. See two Gallup polls: http://www.gallup.com/poll/150497/Three-Four-Americans-Back-Obama-Iraq-Withdrawal.aspx and http://www.gallup.com/poll/142667/Americans-Oppose-Renewing-Combat-Operations-Iraq.aspx.
23. Whether or not the bill was originally one of interest to the president, to become law both the Congress and the president must approve of the legislation.
24. Charles M. Cameron, *Veto Bargaining: Presidents and the Politics of Negative Power* (New York: Cambridge University Press, 2000).
25. Eric Ostermeier, "Obama the Most Veto-Shy President Since James Garfield," *Smart Politics* Blog, June 9, 2011, http://blog.lib.umn.edu/cspg/smartpolitics/2011/06/obama_the_most_veto-shy_presid.php.
26. For instance, Obama threatened to veto bills requiring excessive military spending for fighter jets and military helicopters, forcing Senate Republicans to strip the initial bill of its multi-billion-dollar line item. "Senate Blocks Financing for F-22s,"*New York Times*, July 21, 2009, http://thecaucus.blogs.nytimes.com/2009/07/21/senate-blocks-financing-for-f-22s/?scp=7&sq=F-22&st=Search.
27. William G. Howell, *Power Without Persuasion: The Politics of Direct Presidential Action* (Princeton, NJ: Princeton University Press, 2003).
28. For a summary of Bush's early faith-based initiatives, see Anne Farris, Richard Nathan, and David Wright, "The Expanding Administrative Presidency: George W. Bush and the Faith-Based Initiative." Albany, NY: Rockefeller Institute of Government, 2004.
29. Craig Crawford, "Stubborner than a Donkey," *CQ Weekly*, May 28, 2007, 1638.
30. See Richard Neustadt, *Presidential Power and the Modern Presidents: The Politics of Leadership from Roosevelt to Reagan* (New York: Free Press, 1991).
31. "Statement by the President on H.R. 1473," *White House Office of the Press Secretary*, April 15, 2011.

32. U.S. Government Accountability Office, "Presidential Signing Statements Accompanying the Fiscal Year 2006 Appropriations Acts," June 18, 2007, http://www.gao.gov/decisions/appro/308603.pdf. The investigation looked at appropriations bills only. Of the 12 bills, the president questioned a total of 160 provisions in 11 of the bills. The investigation tracked 19 of these and found noncompliance on 6 of those 19.
33. Congress can also impeach other executive branch officials or members of the judiciary.
34. Tyler was the first vice president to assume the office of president, and his tenure was uncertain: The Constitution did not make it clear whether he should be an acting president until another was chosen or whether he was in fact president. A former Democrat, he was elected to the vice presidency as a member of the Whig party, but he soon antagonized the Whigs, leading to the resignation of his entire cabinet and heated battles with Congress. After a series of controversial vetoes, an attempt was made to impeach him for misusing his power and not taking care to pass legislation fundamental to the government's operation. The failure of this attempt led to his censure by the Senate.
35. See, for example, Mark Peterson, *Legislating Together: The White House and Capitol Hill from Eisenhower to Reagan* (Cambridge, MA: Harvard University Press, 1990).
36. George Edwards, *At the Margins: Presidential Leadership of Congress* (New Haven, CT: Yale University Press, 1990).
37. Samuel Kernell, *Going Public: New Strategies of Presidential Leadership*, 3rd ed. (Washington, DC: CQ Press, 1997).
38. "House Passes Health Care Reform Bill," CNN, November 8, 2009, http://www.cnn.com/2009/POLITICS/11/07/health.care/index.html.
39. "Obama Calls on Bloggers to Keep Health Care Pressure on Congress," Huffington Post, July 20, 2009, http://www.huffingtonpost.com/2009/07/20/obama-calls-on-bloggers-t_n_241570.html.
40. Patricia Heidotting Conley, *Presidential Mandates: How Elections Shape the National Agenda* (Chicago: University of Chicago Press, 2001).
41. Chris Cillizza, "The White House Cheat Sheet: The Obama Mandate," *Washington Post*, January 27, 2009, http://voices.washingtonpost.com/thefix/cheat-sheet/white-house-cheat-sheet-pollin.html.
42. See John J. Coleman, "Unified Government, Divided Government, and Party Responsiveness," *American Political Science Review* 93, 4 (1999): 821–35, for an overview of literature on lawmaking during unified and divided government.
43. As was demonstrated in 2000, the presidential election is not technically a national election in which the candidate receiving the most popular votes nationally wins. Instead, it is 51 separate elections—with each state and the District of Columbia selecting electors to the Electoral College, and the candidate amassing a majority of electoral votes might not be the one who received a majority of the popular vote. The election is national in the sense that voters from around the country will be voting for president.
44. Although still distinctive from the presidential system, recent elections in Great Britain have had the appearance of presidential races, with the faces and words of the leading contenders for prime minister plastered around the country, even though the population at large is unable to vote for these candidates.
45. Representative Tammy Baldwin of Wisconsin expresses this sentiment in these remarks: "I think one of the challenges I've had as I've moved from working on domestic issues to now having a vote and a say on international issues is, I would say, a frustration with the limits to your information sources. If I look at almost any domestic issues imaginable, I can easily obtain information from a variety of perspectives and weigh the pros and cons of most policy decisions. It's much more difficult on a wide range of international issues, be they trade issues, global environmental issues, issues of war and peace. The information that's easiest to obtain is usually through the filter of the State Department, the military, or an agency of the United States government. It has been a real challenge for me to try to get information from a broader array of resources." *Badger Herald*, July 8, 1999, University of Wisconsin.
46. See Aaron Wildavsky. "The Two Presidencies." *Trans-Action* 4(1966): 7-14.
47. B. Canes-Wrone, W. Howell, and D. Lewis, "Executive Influence in Foreign versus Domestic Policy Making: Toward a Broader Understanding of Presidential Power." *Journal of Politics* 70, 1 (2008): 1–16.
48. John P. Burke, *The Institutional Presidency: Organizing and Managing the White House from FDR to Clinton* (Baltimore: Johns Hopkins University Press, 2000).
49. Richard A. Serrano, "President Obama Defends Attorney General Regarding ATF Tactics," *Los Angeles Times*, October 6 2011. http://articles.latimes.com/2011/oct/06/nation/la-na-atf-guns-20111007.
50. Tim Mak, "Eric Holder Contempt Vote Supported by Most Americans, poll says." *Politico*, July 9, 2012. http://www.politico.com/news/stories/0712/78235.html.
51. Charles O. Jones, "Clinton's Cabinet: Stability in Disorder," *PRG Report* 24, 1 (2001): 13–16.
52. One such list is available at http://www.glennbeck.com/content/articles/article/198/29391/.
53. Fletcher and Dennis, "Obama's Many Policy 'Czars' Draw Ire from Conservatives," , *Washington Post,* September 16, 2009. http://www.washingtonpost.com/wp-dyn/content/article/2009/09/15/AR2009091501424.html. See also Mimi Hall, "Number, Role of Obama's Policy 'Czars' Spark Debate," *USA Today*, September 30, 2009. http://www.usatoday.com/news/washington/2009-09-29-obama-czars_N.htm.
54. Like the secretaries of cabinet departments, the president's appointments of the heads of the various EOP offices must be confirmed by the Senate.
55. David Lewis, *The Politics of Presidential Appointments: Political Control and Bureaucratic Performance.* (Princeton, NJ: Princeton University Press, 2008).
56. James Carney and John F. Dickerson, "The Busiest Man in the White House," *Time*, April 22, 2001, Time Online Edition, http://www.time.com/time/nation/article/0,8599,107219,00.html.
57. The exact figures are available at http://www.gallup.com/poll/113980/Gallup-Daily-Obama-Job-Approval.aspx.

15

1. *Citizens United v. Federal Election Commission*, 558 U.S. —(2010).
2. Jess Bravin, "Court Kills Limits on Corporate Politicking," *Wall Street Journal*, January 22, 2010,, http://online.wsj.com/article/SB10001424052748703699204575016942930090152.html.
3. Barack Obama, "Remarks of President Barack Obama—As Prepared for Delivery," Address to Joint Session of Congress, February 24, 2009.
4. Figures for Super PAC spending available at http://www.illinoispirg.org/sites/pirg/files/reports/AuctioningDemocracy.pdf.
5. Keith Perine and Alex Knott, "Court Loosens Campaign Spending Law," *CQ Weekly* (2010): 238–239. *CQ Weekly*. Web. 7 Feb. 2010, http://library.cqpress.com/cqweekly/weeklyreport111-000003283407
6. Shira Schoenberg, "Barack Obama Embraces Super PAC Funding, Despite Past Criticisms," *Boston Globe*,

Feb. 18, 2012, http://articles.boston.com/2012-02-08/politics/31032826_1_super-pacs-super-pacs-obama-campaign.

7. Full text of decision available online at http://electionlawblog.org/wp-content/uploads/MT-expenditures-decision.pdf.
8. Ariane de Vogue, "Will the Supreme Court Reconsider Citizens United? Two Justices Hope So," *ABC News*, Legal Blog, February 23, 2012, http://abcnews.go.com/blogs/politics/2012/02/will-supreme-court-reconsider-citizens-united-two-justices-hope-so/.
9. Robert A. Dahl, "Decision-Making in a Democracy: The Supreme Court as a National Policy-Maker," *Journal of Public Law* 6, 2 (1957): 279–95. Quote on p. 293.
10. See http://www.realclearpolitics.com/polls/.
11. Numbers from two Gallup polls (the last available date for numbers on the judiciary): http://www.gallup.com/poll/149906/supreme-court-approval-rating-dips.aspx; http://www.gallup.com/poll/149888/local-state-governments-retain-positive-ratings.aspx (includes figures for legislative and executive branches).
12. See Judicial Facts and Figures, http://www.uscourts.gov/uscourts/Statistics/JudicialFactsAndFigures/2010/Table101.pdf.
13. Data available at http://www.supremecourt.gov/publicinfo/year-end/year-endreports.aspx.
14. U.S. Library of Congress, Federal Research Division, "Country Studies," http://lcweb2.loc.gov/frd/cs/.
15. Most recent data available at http://www.supremecourt.gov/publicinfo/year-end/2011year-endreport.pdf.
16. Strictly speaking, appellate court rulings in one circuit are not binding for appellate courts in other circuits. As a result, different circuits can produce different appellate rulings on similar cases.
17. If the chief justice is part of the minority, then the justice in the majority who has the most seniority makes the assignment.
18. If a justice recuses himself or herself from a case, a majority can be achieved with fewer than five supporters.
19. Timothy L. Hall, ed., *The U.S. Legal System* (Pasadena, CA: Salem, 2004).
20. For a sampling of the arguments made for and against jury trials, see Jeffrey Abramson, *We, the Jury: The Jury System and the Ideal of Democracy* (Cambridge, MA: Harvard University Press, 2000); William Dwyer, *In the Hands of the People: The Trial Jury's Origins, Triumphs, Troubles, and Future in American Democracy* (New York: St. Martin's Griffin, 2004); Stephen Adler, *The Jury: Trial and Error in the American Courtroom* (New York: Times Books, 1994).
21. Doug Gross, "Apple Settles Class-Action Suit Over iPhone 4 Antenna Problem," *CNN*, Tech Blog, February 20, 2012, http://articles.cnn.com/2012-02-20/tech/tech_mobile_iphone-4-antenna-settlement_1_antenna-problem-iphone-protective-case?_s=PM:TECH.
22. *Abbott Laboratories v. Gardner*, 387 U.S. 136 (1967), at 148.
23. George Fisher, *Plea Bargaining's Triumph: A History of Plea Bargaining in America*. (Stanford, CA: Stanford University Press, 2003), 222. See also Robert Burns, *The Death of the American Trial* (Chicago: University of Chicago Press, 2009).
24. See Judicial Facts and Figures, http://www.uscourts.gov/Statistics/JudicialFactsAndFigures/JudicialFactsAndFigures2006.aspx. During the same period, fully 7.7 million criminal cases were filed in state trial courts.
25. See Judicial Facts and Figures, http://www.uscourts.gov/uscourts/Statistics/JudicialFactsAndFigures/2010/Table501.pdf.
26. See Judicial Facts and Figures, http://www.uscourts.gov/uscourts/Statistics/JudicialFactsAndFigures/2010/Table401.pdf. For data between 1998 and 2004, see table 6.1 at http://www.uscourts.gov/Statistics/JudicialFactsAndFigures/JudicialFactsAndFigures2006.aspx. During the same period, nearly 11 million civil cases were filed per year in state trial courts. State trial court data include limited and general jurisdiction courts. Sources: *Judicial Business of the United States Courts*, vols. 2001–2005 (Washington, DC: Administration of the United States Courts); *Examining the Work of State Courts: A National Perspective from the Court Statistics Project*, vols. 1999–2006 (Washington, DC: Administration of the United States Courts), http://www.ncsconline.org/D_Research/csp/CSP_Main_Page.html.
27. Richard A. Posner, *The Federal Courts: Challenge and Reform* (Cambridge, MA: Harvard University Press, 1996), 59–61.
28. Figures are in constant 1983 dollars. Source: Robert A. Kagan, "American Lawyers, Legal Cultures, and Adversarial Legalism," in Lawrence M. Friedman and Harry N. Scheiber, *Legal Culture and the Legal Profession* (Boulder, CO: Westview, 1996), 13–14.
29. These figures are in current dollars. Office of Management and Budget, "Historical Tables, Budget of the United States Government, FY 2011," 77, 83, available online at http://www.gpoaccess.gov/usbudget/fy11/pdf/hist.pdf. 2011 FY final expenditures available at http://www.justice.gov/ag/annualreports/pr2011/section1.pdf#nameddest=part4.
30. David M. O'Brien, "The Dynamics of the Judicial Process," in David M. O'Brien, ed., *Judges on Judging: Views from the Bench* (Chatham, NJ: Chatham House, 1997), 34.
31. Quoted in ibid., 34.
32. Quoted in Jethro K. Lieberman, *The Litigious Society* (New York: Basic Books, 1981), xi.
33. Quoted in ibid., 8.
34. "President Outlines Path for Lasting Prosperity in Wednesday Speech," White House Press Release, April 21, 2004, http://www.whitehouse.gov/news/releases/2004/04/20040421-5.html.
35. Kagan, "American Lawyers, Legal Cultures, and Adversarial Legalism," 8–10.
36. The only notable difference was the rate of tort filings, which was much lower in Britain. The British filed 1,200 tort claims—which concern personal injuries to one's property, body, or rights—for every million of the British population, whereas Americans filed 3,750 suits per million and Germany, 3,278. See Basil S. Markensinis, *Foreign Law and Comparative Methodology: A Subject and a Thesis* (Oxford, UK: Hart, 1997), 452. Herbert M. Kritzer similarly shows that the British are no less likely to litigate than Americans, except in cases of personal injury torts. Herbert M. Kritzer, "Courts, Justice, and Politics in England," in Herbert Jacob et al., eds., *Courts, Law, and Politics in Comparative Perspective* (New Haven, CT: Yale University Press, 1996), 125–35.
37. Catherine Elliot and Frances Quinn, *English Legal System*, 7th ed. (Harlow, UK: Pearson Education, 2006), 474. See also Martin Partington, *Introduction to the English Legal System*, 3rd ed. (Oxford, UK: Oxford University Press, 2006), 206–7.
38. For more on this case and the parallel structures of state and federal courts, visit the U.S. court system's educational resources page, online at http://www.uscourts.gov/Educational-Resources.aspx.
39. Statistics on number of state judges, number of cases, and other figures available online at http://www.courtstatistics.org/Other-Pages/StateCourtCaseloadStatistics.aspx.
40. John Ferejohn and Barry Weingast, "A Positive Theory of Statutory Interpretation," *International Review of Law and Economics* 12 (1992): 265.
41. Averages calculated from data found in Sheldon Goldman, Elliot Slotnick, Gerard Gryski, and Sara Schiavoni, "W. Bush's Judiciary: The First Term Record," *Judicature* 88, 6 (May–June 2005): 269, 274.
42. Jeffrey Segal, Lee Epstein, Charles Cameron, and Harold Spaeth, "Ideological Values and the Votes of U.S. Supreme Court Justices Revisited," *Journal of Politics* 57, 3 (1995): 812–23. See also Jeffrey Segal and Harold Spaeth,, *The Su-*

preme Court and the Attitudinal Model Revisited (New York: Cambridge University Press, 2002).

43. Jeffrey Segal, "Separation-of-Powers Games in the Positive Theory of Congress and Courts," *American Political Science Review* 91 (1997): 33.
44. Edwin Meese III and Todd Gaziano, "Restoring the Proper Role of the Courts," in Heritage Foundation (ed), *Mandate For Leadership: Principles to Limit Government, Expand Freedom, and Strengthen America* (Washington, D.C.: Heritage Foundation Press, 2005).
45. Adam Cohen, "Last Term's Winner at the Supreme Court: Judicial Activism," *New York Times*, July 9, 2007. http://www.nytimes.com/2007/07/09/opinion/09mon4.html.
46. See Lee Epstein and Jack Knight, *The Choices Justices Make* (Washington, DC: CQ Press, 1998); Forrest Maltzman, James Spriggs, and Paul Wahlbeck, "Strategy and Judicial Choice: New Institutionalist Approaches to Supreme Court Decision Making," in Cornell W. Clayton and Howard Gillman, eds., *Supreme Court Decision-Making: New Institutional Approaches* (Chicago: University of Chicago Press, 1999).
47. For more on the solicitor general, see Rebecca Mae Salokar, *The Solicitor General: The Politics of Law* (Philadelphia, PA: Temple University Press, 1992), and more recently, Margaret Meriwether Cordray and Richard Cordray, "The Solicitor General's Changing Role in Supreme Court Legislation," *Boston College Law Review*, 51, 1323–82.
48. Lincoln Caplan, *The Tenth Justice: The Solicitor General and the Rule of Law* (New York: Knopf, 1987), 295.
49. William Howell and Faisal Ahmed, 2010. "Voting for the President: The Supreme Court during War," University of Chicago Typescript.
50. David G. Savage, *Guide to the U.S. Supreme Court*, 4th ed., vol. 2 (Washington, DC: CQ Press, 2004), 809.
51. See Chapter 6 of William Howell, *Power Without Persuasion: The Politics of Direct Presidential Action* (Princeton, NJ: Princeton University Press, 2003).
52. Decades later, the U.S. government would officially apologize for the internment of Japanese Americans and pay upward of $1 billion in reparations to their families. In 1998, President Bill Clinton selected Fred Korematsu as a recipient of the Presidential Medal of Freedom.
53. Timothy Johnson and Andrew Martin, "The Public's Conditional Response to Supreme Court Decisions," *American Political Science Review* 92 (1998): 299–309; Jennifer Hochschild, *The New American Dilemma: Liberal Democracy and School Desegregation* (New Haven, CT: Yale University Press, 1984).
54. Data available at Judges and Judgeships, http://www.uscourts.gov/JudgesAndJudgeships/Viewer.aspx?doc=/uscourts/JudgesJudgeships/docs/apptsbypres.pdf.
55. Goldman et al., "W. Bush's Judiciary," 269; figures for Obama and minorities cited online at http://www.huffingtonpost.com/2011/09/13/obama-judicial-nominees-women-minorities_n_959745.html; figures for Obama's appointees found at: http://www.uvm.edu/~polisci/Lehrer%20Thesis%202011.pdf.
56. The ABA refused to give Thomas a "well-qualified" rating.
57. Sonia Sotomayor, "A Latina Judge's Voice," University of California, Berkeley, School of Law, 26 Oct. 2001. Available online at http://www.nytimes.com/2009/05/15/us/politics/15judge.text.html?pagewanted=all http://berkeley.edu/news/media/releases/2009/05/26_sotomayor.shtml.
58. Seven justices who were confirmed nonetheless declined to serve, the most recent being Roscoe Conkling in 1882. Data available online at http://www.senate.gov/pagelayout/reference/nominations/Nominations.htm.
59. Karen O'Connor, Alixandra Yanus, and Linda Mancillas Patterson, "Where Have All the Interest Groups Gone? An Analysis of Interest Group Participation in Presidential Nominations to the Supreme Court of the United States," in Allan Cigler and Burdett Loomis, eds., *Interest Group Politics*, 7th ed. (Washington, DC: CQ Press, 2007).
60. Manuel Miranda, "The Original Borking: Lessons from a Supreme Court Nominee's Defeat," *Wall Street Journal*, August 24, 2005, http://www.mirandafund.com/The%20Next%20Justice.PDF.

16

1. Norman J. Vig and Michael E. Kraft, "Environmental Policy from the Seventies to the Eighties," in Norman J. Vig and Michael E. Kraft, eds., *Environmental Policy in the 1980s: Reagan's New Agenda* (Washington, DC: CQ Press, 1984), 3–26.
2. Ibid.
3. Michael E. Kraft, "A New Environmental Policy Agenda: The 1980 Presidential Campaign and Its Aftermath," in Vig and Kraft, *Environmental Policy in the 1980s*, 29–50.
4. Norman J. Vig, "The President or the Environment: Revolution or Retreat?" in Vig and Kraft, *Environmental Policy in the 1980s*, 77–95.
5. J. Clarence Davies, "Environmental Institutions and the Reagan Administration," in Vig and Kraft, *Environmental Policy in the 1980s*, 143–60.
6. Ibid.
7. Kraft, "A New Environmental Policy Agenda"; Henry C. Kenski and Margaret Corgan Kenski, "Congress Against the President: The Struggle over the Environment," in Vig and Kraft, *Environmental Policy in the 1980s*, 97–120.
8. B. Dan Wood, "Principals, Bureaucrats, and Responsiveness in Clean Air Enforcements," *American Political Science Review* 82, 1 (1988): 213–34; Kenski and Kenski, "Congress Against the President."
9. Wood, "Principals, Bureaucrats, and Responsiveness in Clean Air Enforcements."
10. Richard Tobin, "Revising the Clean Air Act: Legislative Failure and Administrative Success." In Norman Vig and Michael Kraft (eds), *Environmental Policy in the 1980s,* (Washington, D.C.: Congressional Quarterly Press, 1984).
11. Davies, "Environmental Institutions and the Reagan Administration."
12. See Joel A. Mintz, "'Treading Water': A Preliminary Assessment of EPA Enforcement During the Bush II Administration," *Environmental Law Institute* 2004, http://www.environmentalintegrity.org/pdf/publications/ERL_Article.pdf.
13. See, for example, Edward Felker, "EPA Rapidly Reversing Bush Policies," *Washington Times*, May 1, 2009, http://www.washingtontimes.com/news/2009/may/01/epa-reviewing-bush-policies/?page=all.
14. Binyamin Appelbaum, "On Finance Reform Bill, Lobbying Shifts to Regulations," *New York Times*, June 26, 2010, http://www.nytimes.com/2010/06/27/business/27regulate.html?pagewanted=all.
15. Cornelius Kerwin, *Rulemaking: How Government Agencies Write Law and Make Policy* (Washington, DC: CQ Press, 2003).
16. The FCC adopted its three-prong definition of obscenity from a 1973 U.S. Supreme Court case, *Miller v. California*.
17. FCC rules can be found at http://ecfr.gpoaccess.gov/cgi/t/text/text-idx?c=ecfr&tpl=/ecfrbrowse/Title47/47tab_02.tpl.
18. Jess Bravin, "Court Backs Fines for On-Air Expletives," *Wall Street Journal*, April 29, 2009, http://online.wsj.com/article/SB124091903135863347.html.
19. Joan Biskupic, "High Court Hears FCC Obscenity Case," *USA Today*, November 4, 2008.

20. The Supreme Court opinion is available at: http://www.supremecourt.gov/opinions/11pdf/10-1293f3e5.pdf.
21. Some of the increase in the length of the *Federal Register* can be explained by the introduction of stricter requirements for publication of final rules. In 1973, the Administrative Committee of the Federal Register decided that every rule must include a summary of its subject matter in its preamble. As of 1977, the preamble of a rule must also include a summary of public comments about the rule as well as the agency's answers to questions raised by the public.
22. In June 2010, for example, the Supreme Court ruled that the NLRB had made decisions unconstitutionally during a period when it was had three vacancies and was made up of only two members. The Court said that parties were entitled to have their cases reviewed by a more complete board. Hundreds of cases decided by the two-person board were sent back to the full board to be rereviewed. Like the NLRB, other bureaucratic agencies have similar judicial responsibilities.
23. James Fesler, "The Higher Public Service in Western Europe," in Ralph Clark Chandler, ed., *A Centennial History of the American Administrative State* (New York: Free Press, 1987).
24. Michael Nelson, "A Short, Ironic History of American National Bureaucracy," *Journal of Politics* 44, 3 (1982): 747–78. See also William Nelson, *The Roots of American Bureaucracy, 1830–1900* (Cambridge, MA: Harvard University Press, 1982).
25. Stephen Skowronek, *Building a New American State: The Expansion of National Administrative Capabilities, 1877–1920* (New York: Cambridge University Press, 1982).
26. The number of bureaucrats working for state and local government, however, has increased dramatically. At the local level, there were approximately 3 million bureaucrats in 1946. By 2003, that number climbed to upward of 14 million. During the same period, state bureaucrats grew from less than 1 million to more than 5 million. Source: U.S. Bureau of the Census, *Historical Statistics of the United States: Colonial Times to 1970* (Washington, DC: Government Printing Office, 1975); *Statistical Abstract of the United States, 2006* (Washington, DC: GPO, 2006).
27. All in all, the 2006–2007 edition of the *U.S. Government Manual* lists 110 independent agencies and government corporations. However, the actual number may be larger than 110. It is particularly difficult to determine the number of government corporations in operation; actual counts vary significantly. National Archives and Records Administration, Office of the Federal Register, *U.S. Government Manual 2006–2007* (Washington, DC: Government Printing Office, 2006), 361–554, http://www.gpoaccess.gov/gmanual/browse-gm-06.html. See also General Accountability Office, *Government Corporations: Profiles of Existing Government Corporations*, GAO/GGD-96-14 (Washington, DC: General Accounting Office, 1995), http://www.gao.gov/archive/1996/gg96014.pdf.
28. For a classic treatment of this topic, see Max Weber, "Bureaucracy," in H. H. Gerth and C. Wright Mills, eds., *From Max Weber: Essays in Sociology* (New York: Oxford University Press, 1946).
29. This idea was developed most fully by the Nobel Prize–winning economist George Stigler. See, for example, *Citizen and the State: Essays on Regulation* (Chicago: University of Chicago Press, 1975).
30. John Carey, "A Shot at Making Drugs Safer: Congress Could Revamp the Cozy Ties Between Drug Makers and the FDA. Will It?" *Business Week*, May 21, 2007, 71.
31. Michael Powell, "Boston's Big Dig Awash in Troubles: Leaks, Cost Overruns Plague Project," *Washington Post*, November 19, 2004, A3; Elizabeth Taurasi, "Boston's Big Dig: One of Engineering's Biggest Mistakes?" *Design News*, July 28, 2006, http://www.washingtonpost.com/wp-dyn/articles/A61112-2004Nov18.html.
32. See http://www.mountainstateslegal.org/mission.cfm.
33. Amy Zegart, *Flawed by Design: The Evolution of the CIA, JCS, and NSC* (Stanford, CA: Stanford University Press, 1999).
34. Ibid., 57.
35. Ibid., 159–60.
36. "Brief Summary of the Dodd-Frank Wall Street Reform and Consumer Protection Act," Senate Banking Committee, banking.senate.gov/public/_files/070110_Dodd_Frank_Wall_Street_Reform_comprehensive_summary_Final.pdf/.
37. Appointment trends during Obama's presidency are available at http://projects.washingtonpost.com/2009/federal-appointments/.
38. Thomas Weko, *The Politicizing Presidency: The White House Personnel Office, 1948–1994* (Lawrence: University Press of Kansas, 1995); Terry Moe, "The Politicized Presidency," in John Chubb and Paul Peterson, eds.,*New Directions in American Politics* (Washington, DC: Brookings Institution, 1985); David Lewis, *The Politics of Presidential Appointments: Political Control and Bureaucratic Performance* (Princeton, NJ: Princeton University Press, 2008).
39. Lewis, *The Politics of Presidential Appointments*.
40. Robert Pear, "Obama to Bypass Senate to Name Health Official," *New York Times*, July 7, 2010, A11.
41. Huma Kahn, "President Obama Fires Controversial Inspector General," http://abcnews.go.com/blogs/politics/2009/06/president-obama-fires-controversial-inspector-general/.
42. See Lewis, *The Politics of Presidential Appointments*.
43. U.S. Office of Personnel Management, *Federal Civilian Workforce Statistics: The Fact Book, 2005 Edition*, http://www.opm.gov/FedData/factbook/index.asp; Government of Canada Privy Council Office, *Fifteenth Annual Report to the Prime Minister on the Public Service of Canada*, March 31, 2008, http://www.clerk.gc.ca/eng/feature.asp?featureId=19&pageId=216.
44. See Donald J. Savoie, *Breaking the Bargain: Public Servants, Ministers, and Parliament* (Toronto: University of Toronto Press, 2003), 28, 136.
45. Lewis, *The Politics of Presidential Appointments*, 98.
46. Ibid., 20–21.
47. Ibid., 25.
48. Ibid., 218.
49. Ron Nixon, "Pork Barrel Remains Hidden in U.S. Budget," *New York Times*, April 7, 2008, http://www.nytimes.com/2008/04/07/washington/07earmarks.html?pagewanted=all.
50. In 2007, the House passed the Whistleblower Protection Enhancement Act of 2007. It would have amended the original Whistleblower Protection Act by providing protections for national security, government contractor, and science-based agency whistle-blowers and by enhancing the existing whistleblower protections for all federal employees. The bill, however, never passed the Senate. For more on the legislative history of this bill, see L. Paige Whitaker, "The Whistleblower Protection Act: An Overview," *Congressional Research Service*, March 12, 2007.
51. For more on this story, see http://www.cbsnews.com/stories/2011/03/03/eveningnews/main20039031.shtml.
52. Frank Miniter, "Inside President Obama's War on the Fast & Furious Whistleblowers," http://www.forbes.com/sites/frankminiter/2011/12/07/inside-president-obamas-war-on-the-fast-furious-whistleblowers/.
53. John Hart, *The Presidential Branch: Executive Office of the President from Washington to Clinton*, 2nd ed. (Chatham, NJ: Chatham House, 1995); Matthew Dickinson, *Bitter Harvest: FDR,*

Presidential Power, and the Growth of the Presidential Branch (New York: Cambridge University Press, 1997).

54. Andrew Rudalevige, *Managing the President's Program: Presidential Leadership and Legislative Policy Formation* (Princeton, NJ: Princeton University Press, 2002).
55. Paul Light, *Thickening Government: Federal Hierarchy and the Diffusion of Accountability* (Washington, DC: Brookings Institution, 1995), 1.
56. David Lewis, *Presidents and the Politics of Agency Design: Political Insulation in the United States Government Bureaucracy, 1946–1997* (Stanford, CA: Stanford University Press, 2003); David Lewis, "The Adverse Consequences of the Politics of Agency Design for Presidential Management in the United States: The Relative Durability of Insulated Agencies," *British Journal of Political Science* 34 (2004): 377–404.

17

1. Statement by Secretary Henry M. Paulson Jr. on Treasury and Federal Housing Finance Agency Action to Protect Financial Markets and Taxpayers. Department of the Treasury, September 7, 2008, http://www.treasury.gov/press-center/press-releases/Pages/hp1129.aspx . See also "Lehman Folds with Record $613 Billion Debt," Market Watch, September 15, 2008, http://www.marketwatch.com/story/lehman-folds-with-record-613-billion-debt?siteid=rss; "WaMu Is Seized, Sold Off to J.P. Morgan, in Largest Failure in U.S. Banking History," *Wall Street Journal*, September 26, 2008. p. A1; "Misery Math: Great Recession by the Numbers," *MSNBC*. Associated Press, October 11, 2009, http://www.msnbc.msn.com/id/33266915.
2. Figures available at http://data.bls.gov/timeseries/lns14000000.
3. City of Philadelphia, City of Philadelphia's Response to the Financial Crisis. November 6, 2008, http://www.phila.gov/pdfs/Rebalancing_Plan_FY09_FY13_Five_Yr_Plan.pdf. New York State Governor's Office, "Governor Paterson Proposes Two-Year, $5.0 Billion Deficit Reduction Plan to Address Current-Year Budget Gap, Improve New York's Long-Term Fiscal Stability," October 15, 2009, http://www.budget.ny.gov/pubs/press/2009/press_release09_deficitReductionPlan101509.html Rich Connell, "Metrolink Cuts 10 Trains but Fares Stay Put," *Los Angeles Times*, January 9, 2010. http://articles.latimes.com/2010/jan/09/local/la-me-metrolink9-2010jan09
4. Paul Davidson, "Budget Cuts Claim Hundreds of Thousands of County, City Jobs," *USA Today*, October 18, 2011, http://www.usatoday.com/money/economy/story/2011-10-17/local-government-job-losses/50807360/1.
5. Vikas Bajaj, "Home Prices Fall for 10th Straight Month." *New York Times*, December 26, 2007, http://www.nytimes.com/2007/12/26/business/27home-web.html.
6. The list of 2010 bank failures is available online at http://www.fdic.gov/bank/individual/failed/banklist.html.
7. Obama's Speech on the Economy, as recorded by Federal News Service, January 8, 2009, http://www.nytimes.com/2009/01/08/us/politics/08text-obama.html?pagewanted=1.
8. Quoted in Rosalind S. Helderman and David Nakamura, "Obama Proposes Higher Taxes for Wealthy to Fund Jobs Bill," *Washington Post*, September 12, 2011, http://www.washingtonpost.com/politics/obama-proposes-higher-taxes-for-wealthy-to-fund-jobs-bill/2011/09/12/gIQADrU3NK_story_1.html.
9. For further reading on this topic, see John Kingdon, *Agendas, Alternatives, and Public Policies*, 2nd ed. (New York: HarperCollins, 1995).
10. The full text of Johnson's University of Michigan speech on the Great Society is available in *Public Papers of the Presidents of the United States: Lyndon B. Johnson, 1963–64*, vol. 1, entry 357, 704–7 (Washington, DC: Government Printing Office, 1965).
11. Robert Farley, "Fact Check: Friends Lumped with Foes in Foreign Oil Debate," *USA Today*, November 4, 2011, http://www.usatoday.com/news/politics/story/2011-11-04/fact-check-foreign-oil-huntsman-perry/51074360/1.
12. In a 1988 ceremony honoring slain drug-enforcement officers, President Reagan drew vivid parallels between the War on Drugs and the American Revolution: "America's liberty was purchased with the blood of heroes [and] our release from the bondage of illegal drug use is being won at the same dear price. The battle is ultimately over what America is and what America will be. At our founding, we were promised the pursuit of happiness, not the myth of endless ecstasy from a vial of white poison." Public Papers of the President, "Remarks at a White House Ceremony Honoring Law Enforcement Officers Slain in the War on Drugs, April 19, 1988," http://www.presidency.ucsb.edu/ws/index.php?pid=35698&st=war+on+drugs&st1=.
13. In our own lives, we typically devise solutions after having recognized the existence of a specific problem. In politics, though, policy entrepreneurs often advocate on behalf of specific policies that they deem solutions to a wide variety of problems.
14. These figures come from the U.S. Department of Labor, http://www.bls.gov/fls/intl_unemployment_rates_monthly.pdf.
15. Figures available at http://www.bls.gov/cpi/cpid1111.pdf.
16. More specifically, GDP is the sum of all domestic consumption spending, investment spending, government spending, and the differences between export and import spending.
17. See, for example, Ron Paul, *Freedom Under Siege: The U.S. Constitution After 200-Plus Years* (Auburn, AL: Ludwig von Mises Institute, 2007).
18. Hatch's letter available in full at his government web page, http://hatch.senate.gov/public/index.cfm/releases?ID=eb82f537-a13d-42dd-ad5a-5f8d5d23e62d.
19. For the latest figures, see http://www.treasurydirect.gov/govt/reports/pd/feddebt/feddebt_ann2011.pdf.
20. The latest government figures are available at http://www.whitehouse.gov/omb/budget/Historicals/. For Bernanke quote, see Sewell Chan, "Bernanke Warns of 'Unsustainable' Debt," *New York Times*, June 9, 2010, http://www.nytimes.com/2010/06/10/business/economy/10fed.html.
21. For a longer discussion of these latter issues, see http://www.cfr.org/publication/20758/confronting_the_chinaus_economic_imbalance.html.
22. For more on this debate, see http://ricks.foreignpolicy.com/posts/2010/03/02/debt_s_life_debt_s_what_all_the_people_say_big_squeeze_coming_from_china.
23. Arnold Ahlert, "Back with a Vengeance: The EU Debt Crisis," *Front Page Mag*, January 16, 2012, http://frontpagemag.com/2012/01/16/back-with-a-vengeance-the-eu-debt-crisis/.
24. In the 1940s and 1950s, a lively debate persisted among two of the century's greatest economists, Milton Friedman and John Maynard Keynes, about the relative benefits of fiscal and monetary policy.
25. Associated Press, "Bush Calls for $145 Billion Stimulus Package," January 18, 2008, http://www.msnbc.msn.com/id/22725498/.
26. The Social Security Act also provided grants-in-aid and health and welfare services to states. The most important elements of the act, though, concern the establishment of a retirement account, which we focus on here.
27. Individuals born after 1938 qualify for full benefits at the age of 67.
28. Figures available at http://www.ssa.gov/pressoffice/factsheets/basicfact-alt.pdf.

29. Ibid.
30. Figures available at http://ssa.gov/cgi-bin/awards.cgi.
31. Figures available at http://www.ssa.gov/pressoffice/factsheets/basicfact-alt.pdf.
32. Ibid.
33. Michael A. Fletcher, "Bush Promotes Plan for Social Security," *Washington Post*, January 12, 2005, A4.
34. Lori Montgomery, "In Debt Talks, Obama Offers Social Security Cuts," *Washington Post*, July 6, 2011, http://www.washingtonpost.com/business/economy/in-debt-talks-obama-offers-social-security-cuts/2011/07/06/gIQA2sFO1H_story.html.
35. Ibid.
36. Tax rates available at http://www.ssa.gov/OACT/ProgData/taxRates.html. Maximum taxable earning available at http://www.ssa.gov/OACT/COLA/cbb.html#Series.
37. Figures available at http://aspe.hhs.gov/poverty/11fedreg.shtml.
38. These problems have led some scholars to conclude that poverty rates should be calculated on the basis of consumption patterns rather than reported income. See, for example, Bruce Meyer and James Sullivan, "Measuring the Well-Being of the Poor Using Income and Consumption," *Journal of Human Resources* 38 (2004): 1180–1220.
39. Figures available at http://www.census.gov/hhes/www/poverty/data/incpovhlth/2010/table4.pdf.
40. Figures available at http://aspe.hhs.gov/hsp/AFDC/baseline/4spending.pdf.
41. For an especially influential critique, see Charles Murray, *Losing Ground: American Social Policy, 1950–1980* (New York: Basic Books, 1984).
42. Figures available at http://www.acf.hhs.gov/programs/ofa/character/FY2007/indexfy07.htm .
43. Quoted in Stephen Ohlemacher, "House Rejects Extension of Unemployment Benefits," Associated Press, June 29, 2010, http://www.huffingtonpost.com/2010/06/29/house-rejects-extension-o_n_629716.html.
44. Quoted in Stephen Dinan, "Extension of Unemployment Benefits Rejected," *Washington Times*, June 29, 2010, http://www.washingtontimes.com/multimedia/collection/extension-of-unemployment-benefits-rejected/.
45. Figures available at http://socialsecurity.gov/ssi/text-eligibility-ussi.htm.
46. Figures available at http://www.whitehouse.gov/sites/default/files/omb/budget/fy2011/assets/socsec.pdf .
47. Figures available at http://www.fns.usda.gov/pd/SNAPsummary.htm.
48. Figures available at http://www.cbpp.org/cms/index.cfm?fa=view&id=2992.
49. For the origins of European welfare programs, see Peter Flora and Jens Alber, "Modernization, Democratization, and the Development of Welfare States in Western Europe," in Peter Flora and Arnold J. Heidenheimer, eds., *Development of Welfare State in Europe and America* (New Brunswick: Transaction Books, 1981); and Philip Manow, "Germany: Co-operative Federalism and the Overgrazing of the Fiscal Commons," in Herbert Obinger, Stephan Leibfried, and Francis G. Castles, eds., *Federalism and the Welfare State: New World and European Experiences* (Cambridge, UK: Cambridge University Press, 2005).
50. See Figure 1 of Irwin Garfinkel, Lee Rainwater, and Timothy M. Smeeding, "Equal Opportunities for Children: Social Welfare Expenditures in the English-Speaking Countries and Western Europe," *Focus* 23, 3 (2005); and Jacob S. Hacker, *The Divided Welfare State: The Battle over Public and Private Social Benefits in the United States* (Cambridge, UK: Cambridge University Press, 2002), 13–15.
51. Figure available at http://www.usgovernmentspending.com/us_welfare_spending_40.html.
52. Alberto Alesina and Edward Glaeser, "Why Are Welfare States in the U.S. and Europe So Different?" *Horizons Stratégiques* 2, 2 (2006): 51–61, http://www.cairn.info/article.php?ID_ARTICLE=HORI_002_0051.
53. Hacker, *The Divided Welfare State*.
54. David Tyack, *The One Best System: A History of American Urban Education* (Cambridge, MA: Harvard University Press, 1974).
55. Bess Furman, "President to Give Education Plans: Will Forward His Message to Congress Tomorrow on Spurring Science Study," *New York Times*, January 26, 1958, 60.
56. Public Papers of the President, American Presidency Project, "President Eisenhower's Statement upon Signing the National Defense Education Act," September 2, 1958, http://www.presidency.ucsb.edu/ws/index.php?pid=11211&st=eisenhower&st1=.
57. Marjorie Hunter, "More School Aid for Negro Urged," *New York Times*, June 26, 1963, 21.
58. Figures available at http://nces.ed.gov/fastfacts/display.asp?id=16.
59. Catherine Hill, Christianne Corbett, and Andresse St. Rose, "Why So Few?: Women in Science, Technology, Engineering, and Mathematics," published by AAUW, 2010, http://www.aauw.org/learn/research/upload/whysofew.pdf.
60. Tamar Lewin, "At Colleges Women Are Leaving Men in the Dust," *New York Times*, July 9, 2006, http://www.nytimes.com/2006/07/09/education/09college.html?pagewanted=all.
61. "Leaving Men Behind: Women Go to College in Ever-Greater Numbers," *Education Portal*, November 13, 2007, http://education-portal.com/articles/Leaving_Men_Behind:_Women_Go_to_College_in_Ever-Greater_Numbers.html.
62. Data on enrollment and degrees come from the U.S. Department of Education and are available at http://nces.ed.gov/fastfacts/display.asp?id=98 and http://nces.ed.gov/fastfacts/display.asp?id=72.
63. National Commission on Excellence in Education, A Nation at Risk: The Imperative for Educational Reform (Washington, D.C.: U.S. Department of Education, *1983*.
64. National Center for Education Statistics, http://nces.ed.gov/programs/digest/d07/tables/dt07_404.asp.
65. Frederick Hess and Michael Petrilli, *No Child Left Behind: A Primer* (New York: Peter Lang, 2006).
66. OECD Program for International Student Assessment, *PISA 2006 Science Competencies for Tomorrow's World*, December 2007, http://www.oecd.org/unitedstates/39722597.pdf.
67. Sam Dillon, "Obama to Waive Parts of No Child Left Behind," *New York Times*, September 22, 2011, http://www.nytimes.com/2011/09/23/education/23educ.html.
68. Joseph Berger, "A Post-Katrina Charter School in New Orleans Gets a Second Chance," *New York Times*, October 17, 2007, http://www.nytimes.com/2007/10/17/education/17education.html?pagewanted=all.
69. For more figures, see http://www.edreform.com/issues/choice-charter-schools/facts/.
70. See Patrick McEwan and Martin Carnoy, "The Effectiveness and Efficiency of Private Schools in Chile's Voucher System," *Education Evaluation and Policy Analysis* 22, 3 (2000): 213–39; Gregory Elacqua, Dante Contreras, and Felipe Salazar, "The Effectiveness of Private School Franchises in Chile's National Voucher Program," Princeton University Typescript, 2007.
71. In addition to the elderly, Medicare also provides some assistance to the disabled.
72. Figures available at https://www.cms.gov/ReportsTrustFunds/downloads/tr2011.pdf.
73. Alan Weil, "There's Something About Medicaid," *Health Affairs* 22, 1 (2003), http://content.healthaffairs.org/cgi/reprint/22/1/13.pdf.

74. Figures available at http://dhhs.gov/asfr/ob/docbudget/2010budgetinbriefm.html.
75. Figures available at http://www.oecd.org/dataoecd/24/8/49084488.pdf.
76. Figures available at http://www.oecd-ilibrary.org/economics/oecd-factbook-2011-2012/life-expectancy_factbook-2011-104-en.
77. Figures available at http://www.oecd.org/dataoecd/24/8/49084488.pdf.
78. World Health Organization, "The World Health Report 2000: Health Systems: Improving Performance," 176–84, 189, http://www.who.int/whr/2000/en/whr00_en.pdf.
79. See, for example, Center for Economic and Social Rights, "The Right to Health in the United States of America: What Does It Mean?" October 29, 2004, http://www.cesr.org/downloads/Right%20to%20Health%20in%20USA%202004.pdf.
80. See, for example, John Goodman, "Five Myths of Socialized Medicine," Cato Institute, *Cato's Letter*, Winter 2005, http://www.cato.org/pubs/catoslcttcr/catosletterv3n1.pdf.
81. Longer descriptions of the legislation's main provisions can be found at http://dpc.senate.gov/healthreformbill/healthbill04.pdf and http://www.cbsnews.com/8301-503544_162-20000846-503544.html. The legislation itself is available at http://democrats.senate.gov/reform/patient-protection-affordable-care-act-as-passed.pdf.
82. Quoted in Shailagh Murray, "Congress Approves Fixes to Health Care Bill," *Washington Post*, March 26, 2010, http://www.washingtonpost.com/wp-dyn/content/article/2010/03/25/AR2010032500006.html.
83. Bill Mears, "Supreme Court Takes Up Challenge to Health Care Reform Law," *CNN Politics*, November 2011, http://articles.cnn.com/2011-11-14/politics/politics_health-care_1_oral-arguments-health-care-reform-law-affordable-care-act?_s=PM:POLITICS.

18

1. "Polarization and Sustained Violence in Mexico's Cartel War," Stratfor Global Intelligence, January 24, 2012, http://www.stratfor.com/analysis/polarization-and-sustained-violence-mexicos-cartel-war.
2. Casualty figures available at http://www.iraqbodycount.org/database/ and http://www.globalsecurity.org/military/ops/iraq_casualties.htm.
3. "AP Impact: After 40 Years, $1 Trillion, US War on Drugs Has Failed to Meet Any of its Goals," *Associated Press*, May 13, 2010.
4. See http://www.state.gov/p/wha/rls/fs/2012/187119.htm.
5. Ginger Thompson, "U.S. Widens Role in Battle Against Mexican Drug Cartels," *New York Times*, August 6, 2011, http://www.nytimes.com/2011/08/07/world/07drugs.html?pagewanted=all.
6. Tracy Wilkinson, "Wikileaks Cables Reveal Unease Over Mexican Drug War," *Los Angeles Times*, December 2, 2010, http://articles.latimes.com/2010/dec/02/world/la-fg-wikileaks-mexico-20101203.
7. Jose de Cordoba, "Heads of U.S., Mexico to Meet as Tensions Rise," *Wall Street Journal*, March 3, 2011, http://online.wsj.com/article/SB1000142405274870355960457617658194164 5712.html.
8. Quotes from press conference available online at http://www.pbs.org/newshour/bb/world/jan-june11/mexico1_03-03.html.
9. Figures available at http://www.census.gov/foreign-trade/top/dst/current/balance.html.
10. Washington's Farewell Address, 1796; http://avalon.law.yale.edu/18th_century/washing.asp.
11. John J. Mearsheimer, *The Tragedy of Great Power Politics* (New York: Norton, 1999), 236–49.
12. Jeff Frieden, "Sectoral Conflict and Foreign Economic Policy: 1914–1940," *International Organization* 41, 2 (1988): 63.
13. Benjamin O. Fordham, "Revisionism Reconsidered: Exports and American Intervention in World War I," *International Organization* 61 (Spring 2007): 286.
14. Ibid.
15. For more on World War I, see Donald Kagan, *On the Origins of War and the Preservation of Peace* (New York: Anchor, 1996).
16. Williamson Murray and Allan R. Millet, *A War to Be Won: Fighting the Second World War* (Cambridge, MA: Harvard/Belknap Press, 2000), 75.
17. Ibid., 82.
18. For World War II, the Allied nations were Great Britain, France, the Soviet Union, and eventually the United States. The Axis nations were Germany, Italy, and Japan.
19. Murray and Millet, *A War to Be Won*, 177–8.
20. Ibid., 82.
21. George F. Kennan, "The Sources of Soviet Conduct," in *American Diplomacy*, expanded ed. (Chicago: University of Chicago Press, 1984), 115–20, 125.
22. The Cold War has also been called the "Long Peace." Coined by Yale historian John Lewis Gaddis, the Long Peace referred to the prolonged lack of war in Europe. John Lewis Gaddis, "The Long Peace: Elements of Stability in the Postwar International System," *International Security* 10, 4 (1986): 99–142.
23. For an overview of Cold War history, see John Lewis Gaddis, *The Cold War: A New History* (New York: Penguin, 2005).
24. President Johnson's message to Congress, August 5, 1964, http://www.mtholyoke.edu/acad/intrel/tonkinsp.htm.
25. Casualty data available online at http://www.archives.gov/research/militrary/vietnam-war/casualty-statistics.html.
26. Arthur Schlesinger Jr., *The Imperial Presidency* (New York: Mariner, 2004).
27. For more on the war in Vietnam, see George C. Herring, *America's Longest War: The United States and Vietnam, 1950–1975*, 3rd ed. (New York: McGraw-Hill, 1996); and Leslie H. Gelb and Richard K. Betts, *The Irony of Vietnam: The System Worked* (Washington, DC: Brookings Institution, 1979).
28. Gaddis, *The Cold War*, 225.
29. For the post–Cold War grand strategy debate, see Michael E. Brown et al., eds., *America's Strategic Choices*, rev. ed. (Cambridge, MA: MIT Press, 2000).
30. Robert Pape, *Bombing to Win: Air Power and Coercion in War* (Ithaca, NY: Cornell University Press, 1996), 214.
31. "President Bush Outlines Iraqi Threat," White House Press Release, October 7, 2002, http://georgewbush-whitehouse.archives.gov/news/releases/2002/10/20021007-8.html.
32. John J. Mearsheimer and Stephen M. Walt, "An Unnecessary War," *Foreign Policy* 134 (January/February 2003): 51–59.
33. Michael Abramowitz, "Economy, War to Dominate State of the Union; Bush's Challenge May Be Getting People to Listen," *Washington Post*, January 28, 2008, A1.
34. Consulates can be thought of as "subembassies," usually located in large noncapital cities abroad to help American citizens or to support the main embassy. Many employees of foreign embassies and consulates are foreign nationals providing support for American personnel.
35. "U.S. Closes Syria Embassy after U.N. Fails to Act, Crackdown Continues," *Washington Post*, February 6, 2012, http://www.washingtonpost.com/world/us-closes-syria-embassy-after-un-fails-to-act-crackdown-continues/2012/02/06/gIQAR5hpuQ_story.html.
36. Figures available at http://www.sipri.org/yearbook/2011/files/SIPRIYB1104-04A-04B.pdf.

37. Christopher Preble, "Does Military Power Keep Us Safe?" online at the Cato Institute, http://www.cato.org/pub_display.php?pub_id=10228.
38. This number excludes U.S. Postal Service employees, as well as those working for the CIA, NSA, Defense Intelligence Agency, and National Imagery and Mapping Agency. These latter four agencies do not make their employment figures public for national security reasons. See U.S. Department of Labor, Bureau of Labor Statistics, *Career Guide to Industries: Federal Government, Excluding the Postal Service*, http://www.bls.gov/oco/cg/cgs041.htm.
39. Elisabeth Bumiller, "Change (But Not Too Much) at the Top of the Pentagon," *New York Times*, July 1, 2011, http://www.nytimes.com/2011/07/02/us/politics/02pentagon.html.
40. Bob Woodward, *Bush at War* (New York: Simon and Schuster, 2002), 3–4.
41. The National Reconnaissance Office (NRO) is also in charge of data monitoring, but its tools are spy aircraft and reconnaissance satellites. Also unacknowledged for many years, the NRO operates under the cover of the U.S. Air Force.
42. Dana Priest and William M. Arkin, "A Hidden World, Growing Beyond Control," *Washington Post*, published as part of its "Top Secret America" project, http://projects.washingtonpost.com/top-secret-america/articles/a-hidden-world-growing-beyond-control/.
43. I. M. Destler, *American Trade Politics*, 3rd ed. (Washington, DC: Institute for International Economics, 1995).
44. Brian Knowlton, "House Panel Says Armenian Deaths Were Genocide," *New York Times*, March 4, 2010, http://www.nytimes.com/2010/03/05/world/europe/05armenia.html?_r=1&scp=2&sq=armenian%20genocide&st=cse.
45. See, for example, Louis Fisher, *Presidential War Power*, 2nd ed. (Lawrence: University Press of Kansas, 2004).
46. This 60-day clock can be extended for another 30 days if the president certifies that the time is necessary for the troops' safety.
47. Louis Fisher, *Congressional Abdication on War and Spending* (College Station: Texas A&M University Press, 2000), 65.
48. David Auerswald and Peter Cowhey, "Ballotbox Diplomacy: The War Powers Resolution and the Use of Force," *International Studies Quarterly* 41, 3 (1997): 505–28.
49. "Senate Blocks Obama Nominee for Ambassador to El Salvador," *Associated Press*, December 12, 2011.
50. Figures available online at http://www.senate.gov/artandhistory/history/common/briefing/Treaties.htm.
51. Michael John Garcia and R. Chuck Mason, "Congressional Oversight and Related Issues Concerning International Security Agreements Concluded by the United States," Congressional Research Service, June 2, 2009.
52. Previous two quotes can be found in Carl Hulse, "Political Fault Line Emphasized by Timing of Hearings," *New York Times*, September 11, 2007, A18.
53. Two quotes can be found in Warren P. Strobel, "Two Days of Iraq Testimony, but No Answer to 'How This Ends,'" Knight Ridder Tribune News Service, September 11, 2007, 1.
54. Quoted in Peter Baker and Jonathan Weisman, "A Plea from Petraeus," *Washington Post*, April 9, 2008, http://www.washingtonpost.com/wp-dyn/content/story/2008/04/08/ST2008040803715.html.
55. Quotes from Guy Raz, "Petraeus, Crocker Continue Testimony on Iraq," NPR, April 9, 2008.
56. For a more critical assessment, see John Mearsheimer and Stephen Walt, *The Israeli Lobby and U.S. Foreign Policy* (New York: Farrar, Straus and Giroux, 2008).
57. James M Lindsay, "Getting Uncle Sam's Ear: Will Ethnic Lobbies Cramp America's Foreign Policy Style?" Brookings Institution, 2002, http://www.brookings.edu/research/articles/2002/12/winter-diplomacy-lindsay.
58. Robert Dahl, *Who Governs? Power and Democracy in an American City* (New Haven, CT: Yale University Press, 1961).
59. As quoted in Alan Curtis, ed., *Patriotism, Democracy, and Common Sense* (New York: Rowman and Littlefield, 2005), xii.
60. Rone Tempest, "Servants or Masters? Revisiting the Military-Industrial Complex," *Los Angeles Times*, July 10, 1983, H1.
61. Elizabeth Becker and Larry Rohter, "U.S. and Chile Reach Free Trade Accord," *New York Times*, December 12, 2002, C1.
62. Council on Foreign Relations, "History," http://www.cfr.org/about/history/cfr/index.html.
63. Michael E. O'Hanlon and Kenneth M. Pollack, "A War We Just Might Win," *New York Times*, July 30, 2007, A17.
64. United Nations, "NPT Treaty Status," http://disarmament.un.org/treaties/t/npt.
65. http://www.iaea.org/Publications/Documents/Infcircs/Others/infcirc457.pdf.
66. American Presidency Project, "George W. Bush: Address Before a Joint Session of the Congress on the State of the Union, January 29, 2002," http://www.presidency.ucsb.edu/ws/index.php?pid=29644&st=state+of+the+union&st1=.
67. CNN, "Timeline: North Korea's Nuclear Weapons Development," January 6, 2004, http://www.cnn.com/2003/WORLD/asiapcf/east/08/20/nkorea.timeline.nuclear/.
68. "Korea's Obama Test." *Wall Street Journal*. May 26, 2009, p. A18, http://online.wsj.com/article/SB124329265169452457.html.
69. "Path of Peace Available to North Korea, Obama Says." *CNN*, June 16, 2009, http://www.cnn.com/2009/POLITICS/06/16/south.korea.meeting/index.html.
70. Steven Lee Myers and Choe Sang-Hun, "North Korea Agrees to Suspend Its Nuclear Program," *New York Times*, March 1, 2012, http://www.nytimes.com/2012/03/01/world/asia/us-says-north-korea-agrees-to-curb-nuclear-work.html?pagewanted=all.
71. Foreign Relations of the United States (Washington, DC: Government Printing Office, 1945), vol. 8, p. 4.
72. See, for example, Christopher Hitchens, "A War to Be Proud Of," *Weekly Standard*, 10, 47 (September 5, 2005).
73. Peter Baker, Helene Cooper, and Mark Mazzetti, "Bin Laden Is Dead, Obama Says," *New York Times*, May 1, 2011, http://www.nytimes.com/2011/05/02/world/asia/osama-bin-laden-is-killed.html?pagewanted=all.
74. Daniel Schorn, "Bush: 'We Stand With Democracies,'" CBSNEWS, http://www.cbsnews.com/stories/2006/09/06/five_years/main1979521.shtml.
75. Barack Obama, "Inaugural Address," January 20, 2009, http://www.whitehouse.gov/blog/inaugural-address.
76. Peter Nicholas and Cristi Parsons, "Obama's Advisors Split on When and How Mubarak Should Go," *Los Angeles Times*, February 10, 2011, http://articles.latimes.com/2011/feb/10/world/la-fg-obama-team-20110210.
77. Eli Lake, "Muslim Brotherhood Seeks End to Israel Treaty," *The Washington Times*, February 3, 2011, http://www.washingtontimes.com/news/2011/feb/3/muslim-brotherhood-seeks-end-to-israel-treaty/?page=all.
78. "Renminbi (Yuan)," *New York Times*, February 16, 2012, http://topics.nytimes.com/top/reference/timestopics/subjects/c/currency/yuan/index.html.
79. "Major Foreign Holders of Treasury Securities," U.S. Treasury Department, http://www.treasury.gov/resource-center/data-chart-center/tic/Documents/mfh.txt.

80. Melanie Lee, "Customers Angry, Staff Defiant at China's Fake Apple Store," *Reuters,* July 22, 2011, http://www.reuters.com/article/2011/07/22/us-china-apple-fakestore-idUSTRE76L20U20110722.
81. Uri Friedman, "Welcome to China's Fake Apple Store," *The Atlantic Wire,* July 20, 2011, http://www.theatlanticwire.com/global/2011/07/welcome-chinas-fake-apple-store/40191/.
82. Michael Martina, "Geithner Slams China's Intellectual Property Policies," *Reuters,* September23, 2011, http://www.reuters.com/article/2011/09/23/us-china-geithner-idUSTRE78M15G20110923.
83. United States International Trade Commission, *China: Effects of Intellectual Property Infringement and Indigenous Innovation Policies on the U.S. Economy,* Publication 4226 (Washington, DC: Author, 2011), http://www.usitc.gov/publications/332/pub4226.pdf.

PHOTO CREDITS

CHAPTER 1 p.11: Heather Ainsworth/AP Images; p.14: inset David Madison/Photodisc/Getty Images; p.14: Robert Michael/Flame/Corbis; p.18: Alexander Nemenov/AFP/Getty Images/Newscom; p.3: AP Photo/Carolyn Kaster; p.7: Mansell/Time Life Pictures/Getty Images; p.8: AP Photo/Claude Paris; p.9: JEWEL SAMAD/AFP/Getty Images

CHAPTER 2 p.23: AP Photo/Jake Danna Stevens/Scranton Times & Tribune; p.26: REUTERS/Shannon Stapleton; p.30: Tannen Maury/epa/Corbis; p.31: AP Photo/Virginian-Pilot Brian J. Clark File; p.37: Whitney Curtis/Getty Images News/Getty Images; p.38: Scott Speakes/Corbis RF/Alamy; p.40: Bettmann/Corbis; p.45: Jeff Malet Photography/Newscom; p.53: AP Photo/Paul Sakuma; p.54: AP Photo; p.55: Karl Merton Ferron/Baltimore Sun/MCT/Landov Media

CHAPTER 3 p.63: Larry Burrows/Time & Life Pictures/Getty Images; p.66: The Granger Collection NYC; p.69: The Granger Collection NYC; p.71: The Granger CollectionNYC; p.76: The Granger Collection NYC; p.80: REUTERS/Handout; p.81: Yale University Art Gallery/Art Resource NY; p.82: Jim Lo Scalzo/EPA/Newscom; p.83: AP Photo/Damian Dovarganes; p.89: AP Photo/Alex Menendez; p.95: AP Photo/Ken Heinen

CHAPTER 4 p.101: REUTERS/Andrew Burton; p.110: MCT/Contributor/McClatchy-Tribune/Getty Images; p.114: Tetra Images/Newscom; p.116: Saul Loeb/AFP/Getty Images; p.118: Jeff Kowalsky/Bloomberg via Getty Images; p.121: Bob Daemmrich/PhotoEdit Inc.; p.124: Antony Souter/Alamy; p.128: Kristoffer Tripplaar-Pool/Getty Images; p.134: AP Photo/Matt York; p.138: Erich Schlegel/Corbis

CHAPTER 5 p.143: AP Photo/Steven Senne; p.147: Mosefros/Redux Pictures; p.151: AP Photo/Anonymous; p.156: AP Photo/Seth Wenig; p.157: AP Photo/Michael A. Curlett/Tribune-Star; p.158: Scott Olson/Getty Images; p.161: Bettmann/Corbis; p.169: Jessica Mann/KRT/Newscom; p.172: Chang W. Lee/Redux Pictures; p.176: REUTERS/Handout/California Department of Corrections; p.182: Katherine Frey/The Washington Post via Getty Images

CHAPTER 6 p.187: AP PhotoFile; p.192: North Wind Picture Archives via AP Images; p.193: Library of Congress; p.196: Bettmann/CORBIS; p.204: Abbas/Magnum Photos; p.210: AP Photo; p.214: AP Photo/Robert Sutton, Tuscaloosa News; p.217: Paula Bronstein/Getty Images; p.220: AP Photo/Sal Veder

CHAPTER 7 p.229: Library of Congress; p.232: Mario Tama/Getty Images; p.237: Nancy G Fire Photography Nancy Greifenhagen/Alamy; p.240: Kevork Djansezian/Getty Images; p.241: Roger Malloch/Magnum Photos; p.243: Stephen Jaffe/AFP/Getty Images; p.244: Ralph Morse//Time Life Pictures/Getty Images; p.246: Jessica McGowan/Getty Images; p.246: Aric Crabb/MCT/Landov Media; p.246b: Robert Mankoff/The New Yorker Collection/www.cartoonbank.com; p.248: William B. Plowman/NBC/NBC NewsWire/Getty Images

CHAPTER 8 p.253: AP Photo/Horace Cort; p.256: AP Photo/The Joplin Globe T. Rob Brown; p.256b: Linda Davidson/The Washington Post via Getty Images; p.259: Natalie Behring/Getty Images; p.268: REUTERS/Brian Snyder; p.272: AP Photo/Paul White; p.273: Michal Czerwonka/EPA/Newscom; p.278: Ronald Reagan Presidential Library; p.285: Museum of History and Industry/Corbis; p.287: The Granger CollectionNYC; p.288: REUTERS/Mike Theiler

CHAPTER 9 p.293: Tim Boyle/Newsmakers/Getty Images; p.296: AP Photo/The Hawk Eye Brenna Norman; p.298: Rolls Press/Popperfoto/Getty Images; p.299: Michael Crawford/The New Yorker Collection/www.cartoonbank.com; p.302: REUTERS/Joshua Roberts; p.307: Ethan Miller/Getty Images; p.310: AP Photo/Jay LaPrete; p.313: JEWEL SAMAD/AFP/Getty Images; p.318: REUTERS/Yuri Gripas

CHAPTER 10 p.323: REUTERS/Mike Segar; p.329: AP Photo/Richard Drew; p.330: David Grunfeld/MCT/Getty Images; p.332: Bettmann/CORBIS; p.334: Alex Wong/Getty Images; p.336: AP Photo/Anjum Naveed; p.344: Hulton Archive/Getty Images; p.348: JIM WATSON/AFP/Getty Images

CHAPTER 11 p.357: Emmanuel Dunand/Staff/AFP/Getty Images; p.362: AP Photo/Erik S. Lesser; p.364: AP Photo/Toby Talbot; p.364: AP Photo/Damian Dovarganes; p.367: John Moore/Getty Images; p.374: Lucas Jackcon/Reuters/Landov Media; p.378: Bettmann/Corbis; p.381: Alex Wong/Getty Images; p.381r: REUTERS/Jonathan Ernst; p.385: Kevin Lamarque/CORBIS; p.390: AP Photo/Charles Dharapak

CHAPTER 12 p.401: STEPHEN BOITANO/Barcroft Media/Landov Media; p.409: Chuck Savage/CORBIS; p.410: JEWEL SAMAD/AFP/Getty Images; p.411: Scott Houston/Sygma/Corbis; p.412: Paul J. Richards/AFP/Getty Images; p.415: Bill Clark/CQ Roll Call/Getty Images; p.416: Stan Honda/AFP/Getty Images

CHAPTER 13 p.429: REUTERS/Handout; p.436: AP Photo/Saul Loeb; p.438: Michael Ainsworth/Dallas Morning News/Corbis; p.441: Ryan Kelly/Congressional Quarterly/Newscom; p.444: Rachel Epstein/PhotoEditInc.; p.449: REUTERS/Baz Ratner; p.451: AP Photo/Alex Brandon; p.456: Benjamin J. Myers/Corbis; p.457: Jim Ruymen/UPI /Landov Media; p.462: Chuck Kennedy/MCT/Getty Images

CHAPTER 14 p.467: Saul Loeb/AFP/Getty Images; p.470: REUTERS/Jim Young; p.471: Mark Wilson/Newsmakers/Getty Images; p.474: Jerry Morrison/UPI/Newscom; p.476: Bettmann/CORBIS; p.483: Diana Walker/Time Life Pictures/Getty Images; p.488: Luke Frazza/AFP/Getty Images; p.490: GL Archive/Alamy; p.490r: Bob Daemmrich/Alamy; p.491: Louis Van Oeyen/Western Reserve Historical Society/Getty Images; p.497: Ali Al-Saadi/AFP/Getty Images

CHAPTER 15 p.507: REUTERS/Jonathan Ernst; p.515: Chip Somodevilla/Getty Images; p.517: REUTERS/Kimberly White; p.519: Tetra Images Tetra Images/Newscom; p.524: Jesse Springer/Reproduction rights obtainable from www.CartoonStock.com; p.526: ART LIEN/AFP/Getty Images; p.529: Bettmann/CORBIS; p.530: AP Photo; p.531: AFP/Getty Images

CHAPTER 16 p.537: Paul Souders/Danita Delimont Photography/Newscom; p.541: AP Photo/Department of Justice; p.543: Brian Prahl/Splash News/Newscom; p.550: AP Photo/Evan Vucci; p.558: Darren McCollester/Getty Images News/Getty Images; p.563: Mary F. Calvert/ZUMA Press/Newscom; p.566: AP Photo/The Plain Dealer Roadell Hickman

CHAPTER 17 p.571: Justin Lane/EPA/Newscom; p.576: Everett Collection/SuperStock; p.578: AP Photo/Jim Prisching; p.580: REUTERS/Shannon Stapleton; p.582: AP Photo; p.587: Bettmann/Corbis; p.590: AP Photo/Ferd Kaufman; p.594: JONATHAN ERNST/Reuters/Corbis

CHAPTER 18 p.605: Shaul Schwarz/Edit/Getty Images; p.610: AP Photo; p.612: Paul Schutzer/Time & Life Pictures/Getty Images; p.614: Reuters/Landov Media; p.622: Scott Olson/Getty Images; p.632: PARK JIN HEE/Xinhua /Landov Media; p.633: Jim Watson/AFP/Getty Images; p.635: FETHI BELAID/AFP/Getty Images; p.638: ChinaFotoPress/Getty Images

TEXT CREDITS

CHAPTER 1 p.7: Mansell/Time Life Pictures/Getty Images; p.8: Claude Paris/Associated Press; p.9: CORBIS ; p.13: Judge Learned Hand, "We Seek Liberty," address in Central Park, New York, May 21, 1944; p.14: Robert Michael/Flame/Corbis

CHAPTER 2 p.30: Tannen Maury/epa/Corbis p.34: Bartels, Larry M, Unequal Democracy © 2008 by Russell Sage Foundation. Published by Princeton University Press. Reprinted by permission of Princeton University Press; p.38: Source: Survey data: Pew Center for the People and the Press, http://people-press.org/reports/display.php3?ReportID=167. Income data (Gross national income per capita, 2003): World Bank, http://siteresources.worldbank.org/DATASTATISTICS/Resources/GNIPC.pdf; p.39: Source: The American National Election Studies (www.electionstudies.org). THE 1948-2004 ANES CUMULATIVE FILE [dataset]. Stanford University and the University of Michigan [producers and distributors], 2008; p.38: Scott Speakes/Corbis RF/Alamy; p.40: Bettmann/Corbis; p.41: Public Wants Changes in Entitlements, Not Changes in Benefits: GOP Divided Over Benefit Reductions," July 7, 2011, the Pew Research Center for the People & the Press, a project of the Pew Research Center; p.42: "Public Trust in Government: 1958–2010," April 18, 2010, interactive created by the Pew Research Center, with the assistance of the iPOLL Databank provided by the Roper Center for Public Opinion Research, University of Connecticut; p.52: OECD (2010), "OECD Health Data: Health Status," OECD Health Statistics (database). http://dx.doi.org/10.1787/data-00540-en; p.53: Paul Sakuma/AP Images; p.54: Associated Press; p.55: Karl Merton Ferron/Baltimore Sun/MCT/Landov LLC

CHAPTER 3 p.66: The Granger Collection; p.69: The Granger Collection, NYC; p.76: The Granger Collection; p.81: Yale University Art Gallery/Art Resource; p.88: Forrest McDonald, We the People: The Economic Origins of the Constitution, Chicago: University of Chicago Press, 1958, pp. 86-110.

CHAPTER 4 p.114: Tetra Images/Newscom; p.121: Bob Daemmrich/PhotoEdit; p.124: Antony Souter/Alamy; p.134: Erich Schlegel/Corbis; p.134: Matt York/Associated Press; p.111: Source: U.S. Bureau of the Census, "Local Governments and Public School Systems by Type and State: 2007," April 27, 2010, http://www.census.gov; p.123: Copyright 1998 by Georgetown University Press. "Tools of Federal Influence over State Governments." From The Politics of Unfunded Mandates: Whither Federalism?, Paul L. Posner, p. 59. Reprinted with permission. www.press.georgetown.edu; p.126: Source: Budget of the United States Government: Historical Tables Fiscal Year 2013, Table 12-2, http://www.gpoaccess.gov/usbudget/fy13/hist.html; p.127: Source: Consolidated Federal Funds Report for Fiscal Year 2010: http://www.census.gov/prod/2011pubs/cffr-10.pdf; and Internal Revenue Service Tax Statistics: http://www.irs.gov/taxstats/article/0,,id=206488,00.html

CHAPTER 5 p.71: The Granger Collection; p.147: Mosefros/Redux Pictures; p.157: Michael A. Curlett/Tribune-Star/Associated Press; p.161: Bettmann / Bettmann Premium /Corbis; p.169: JESSICA MANN/KRT/Newscom; p.172: Chang W. Lee/Redux Pictures; p.176: Handout/California Department of Corrections/Reuters America; p.182: David Radlubowski/Redux Pictures; p.149: Source: Freedom House. http://www.freedomhouse.org/sites/default/files/inline_images/FIW%202012%20Booklet—Final.pdf; p.179: Guttmacher Institute, Counseling and waiting periods for abortion, State Policies in Brief (as of June 2012), New York: Guttmacher Institute, 2012, http://www.guttmacher.org/statecenter/spibs/spib_MWPA.pdf

CHAPTER 6 p.193: Library of Congress; p.196: Bettmann/CORBIS; p.199: Source: Gary Orfield, Reviving the Goal of an Integrated Society: A 21st Century Challenge (Los Angeles: University of California Civil Rights Project, 2009); p.207: Source: Doug McAdam, Political Process and the Development of Black Insurgency 1930–1970 (Chicago: University of Chicago Press, 1982), p. 121. Copyright © 1982 by the University of Chicago. Reprinted by permission; p.204: Abbas /Magnum Photos; p.210: Associated Press

CHAPTER 7 p.229: Library of Congress; p.233: "Mixed Views of Obama at Year's End: Unabated Economic Gloom, Divides on Afghanistan and Health Care," December 16, 2009, the Pew Research Center for the People & the Press, a project of the Pew Research Center; p.233: http://www.gallup.com/poll/146114/Americans-Remain-Divided-Defense-Spending.aspx Copyright © 2011 Gallup, Inc. All rights reserved. This content is used with permission; however Gallup retains all rights of republication; p.237: Nancy Greifenhagen / Nancy G Fire Photography/Alamy; p.241: Roger Malloch/Magnum Photos, Inc; p.244: Ralph Morse//Time Life Pictures/Getty Images; p.246: Aric Crabb/MCT /Landov LLC

CHAPTER 8 p.272: Paul White/Associated Press; p.278: Ronald Reagan Presidential Library; p.285: Museum of History and Industry/Historical/Corbis; p.287: The Granger Collection; p.257: Source: Authors' analysis of 2008 National Election Study, http://electionstudies.org; p.265: Source: Authors' analysis of 2008 American National Election Study, http:www.electionstudies.org; p.271: Source: Social Science Research Council, http://election04.ssrc.org/research/csae_2004_final_report.pdf. Reprinted with permission; p.271: Source: Center for the Study of the American Electorate; p.276: Source: American National Election Studies (www.electionstudies.org); p.277: Source: American National Election Studies (www.election-studies.org); p.283: Erikson, Robert S. Tedin, Kent L., American Public Opinion: Its Origin, Contents, and Impact, 7th Ed., © 2005). Reprinted and electronically reproduced by permission of Pearson Education, Inc., Upper Saddle River, New Jersey pages 201–3; p.283: Source: Authors' analysis of 2008 American National Election Study, http:www.electionstudies.org.

CHAPTER 9 p.298: Rolls Press/Popperfoto/Getty Images; p.310: Jay LaPrete/Associated Press; p.305: The Campaign Finance Institute: www.cfinst.org; p.309: © Kantar Media; p.314: © Kantar Media; p.317: Source: http://www.fec.gov/pages/brochures/contriblimits.shtml

CHAPTER 10 p.342: Pew Research Center's Project for Excellence in Journalism. Newspaper Journalists' Self-assessments 2011. http://www.stateofthemedia.org/files/2011/02/Journalists-topline.pd

CHAPTER 11 p.363: "Strategically Unambitious" by Christian Collet and Martin P. Wattenberg as found in The State of the Parties (3rd ed.) edited by John C. Green and Daniel M. Shea (Lanham, MD: Rowman and Littlefield, 1999). Reprinted with permission; p.368: National Conference of State Legislatures, Voter Identification Requirements. http://www.ncsl.org/?tabid=16602; p.375: Source: Dave Leip's Atlas of U.S. Presidential Elections, www.uselectionatlas.org; p.387: Source: Marjorie Randon Hershey, Party Politics in America, 13/e (New York: Pearson Longman, 2009), p.119. Reprinted with permission.

CHAPTER 12 p.414: Data provided by the Center for Responsive Politics: www.opensecrets.org; p.414: Source: Federal Election Commission: http://www.fec.gov/pages/brochures/contrib.shtml

CHAPTER 13 p.436: Saul Loeb/Associated Press; p.438: Michael Ainsworth/Dallas Morning News/Corbis; p.439: Data provided by the Center for Responsive Politics: www.opensecrets.org; p.440: Sources: Mildred L. Amer, Congressional Research Service Report for Congress, Membership of the 109th Congress: A Profile, May 31, 2006. Mildred L. Amer. CRS Report for Congress: Black Members of the United States Congress, 1870–2007. Washington, DC: Congressional Research Service; Carmen E. Enciso, 1995. Hispanic Americans in Congress, 1822–1995. Washington, DC: Library of Congress. Updated information, through 2011, is available at: http://www.loc.gov/rr/hispanic/congress/chron.html. Accessed April 12, 2012; p.441: Ryan Kelly/Congressional Quarterly/Newscom; p.444: Rachel Epstein / PhotoEdit; p.449: Baz Ratner/Reuters; p.451: Alex Brandon/Associated Press; p.455: Reproduced by permission of voteview.com, based on data from Polarized America: The Dance of Ideology and Unequal Riches. Cambridge, MA: MIT Press, 2006 (Keith T. Poole, Nolan M. McCarty and Howard Rosenthal) and Congress: A Political-Economic History of Roll Call Voting. New York: Oxford University Press, 1997 (Keith T. Poole and Howard Rosenthal); p.456: Benjamin J. Myers/Corbis News/Corbis; p.457: Jim Ruymen/UPI /Landov LLC; p.458: 1789–1968: U.S. Bureau of the Census, Historical Statistics of the United States, Series Y 189–198 (Washington, D.C.: Government Printing Office, 1975), 1081–1082; 1969–2011: Table 5-7; p.462: Chuck Kennedy/MCT/Getty Images.

CHAPTER 14 p.470: Jim Young/Reuters; p.471: Mark Wilson/Newsmakers/Getty Images; p.474: Jerry Morrison/UPI/Newscom; p.476: Bettmann/CORBIS; p.483: Diana Walker/Time Life Pictures/Getty Images; p.495: Source: www.whitehouse.gov; p.497: Ali Al-Saadi/AFP/Getty Images; p.500: Source: Gallup Daily Tracking Poll, February 2012. http://www.gallup.com/poll/121199/Obama-Weekly-Job-Approval-Demographic-Groups.aspx. Copyright © 2012 Gallup, Inc. All rights reserved. The content is used with permission; however, Gallup retains all rights of republication; p.514: Source: How the Presidents Stack Up, Presidential Approval Ratings. Reprinted with permission of The Wall Street Journal. Copyright © 2010. Dow Jones & Company, Inc. All Rights Reserved Worldwide. License number 2957840848205; 14-40: Source: How the Presidents Stack Up, Presidential Approval Ratings. Reprinted by permission of The Wall Street Journal Copyright © 2010. Dow Jones & Company, Inc. All Rights Reserved Worldwide. License number 2957840983693.

CHAPTER 15 p.511: Source: Administrative Office of the U.S. Courts, http://www.uscourts.gov/EducationalResources/FederalCourtBasics/CourtStructure/StructureOfFederalCourts.aspx; p.512: Administrative Office of the U.S. Courts, http://www.uscourts.gov/courtlinks

CHAPTER 16 p.543: Brian Prahl/Splash News/Newscom; p.544: Source: Office of the Federal Register, National Archives and Records Administration, The Federal Register, Vols. 1-76, Washington, DC. Available online at: http://www.heinonline.org; p.550: Source: US Government Accountability Office, Financial Statements of the United States Government for the Years Ended September 30, 2011, and 2010: http://www.gao.gov/financial/fy2011/11stmt.pdf

CHAPTER 17 p.582: Associated Press; p.584: Source: http://www.bloomberg.com/news/2011-06-03/social-security-s-finances-past-and-future-echoes.html ; p.586: Source: US Census Bureau, Current Population Survey, 1960-2010 Annual Social and Economic Supplements; p.587: Bettmann/Corbis; p.590: Ferd Kaufman/Associated Press; p.591: Source: Digest of Education Statistics, 2009, Table 402, http://nces.ed.gov/programs/digest/d09/tables/dt09_402.asp; p.594: Jonathan Ernst/Reuters/Corbis; p.595: Reprinted with the permission of The Center for Education Reform, www.edreform.com; p.599: Source: World Health Organization.

CHAPTER 18 p.618: Source: US Department of State, available online at: http://www.state.gov/documents/organization/177397.pdf ; p.620: Source: Historical Tables: Budget of the United States Government: Fiscal Year 2008, pp. 73–78. Available online from: http://www.gpoaccess.gov/usbudget/fy08/browse.html

INDEX

Page numbers followed by *f* or *t* indicate material in figures or tables, respectively.

A

B

C

D

E

F

H

I

J

K

L

M

N

O

P

Q

R

S

T

U

V

W